Nineteenth-Century
Literature Criticism

Guide to Gale Literary Criticism Series

When you need to review criticism of literary works, these are the Gale series to use:

If the author's death date is:	You should turn to:
After Dec. 31, 1959 (or author is still living)	**CONTEMPORARY LITERARY CRITICISM** for example: Jorge Luis Borges, Anthony Burgess, William Faulkner, Mary Gordon, Ernest Hemingway, Iris Murdoch
1900 through 1959	**TWENTIETH-CENTURY LITERARY CRITICISM** for example: Willa Cather, F. Scott Fitzgerald, Henry James, Mark Twain, Virginia Woolf
1800 through 1899	**NINETEENTH-CENTURY LITERATURE CRITICISM** for example: Fedor Dostoevski, Nathaniel Hawthorne, George Sand, William Wordsworth
1400 through 1799	**LITERATURE CRITICISM FROM 1400 TO 1800** **(excluding Shakespeare)** for example: Anne Bradstreet, Daniel Defoe, Alexander Pope, François Rabelais, Jonathan Swift, Phillis Wheatley **SHAKESPEAREAN CRITICISM** Shakespeare's plays and poetry
Antiquity through 1399	**CLASSICAL AND MEDIEVAL LITERATURE CRITICISM** for example: Dante, Homer, Plato, Sophocles, Vergil, the Beowulf poet *(Volume 1 forthcoming)*

Gale also publishes related criticism series:

CHILDREN'S LITERATURE REVIEW

This ongoing series covers authors of all eras. Presents criticism on authors and author/illustrators who write for the preschool through high school audience.

CONTEMPORARY ISSUES CRITICISM

This two volume set presents criticism on contemporary authors writing on current issues. Topics covered include the social sciences, philosophy, economics, natural science, law, and related areas.

ISSN 0732-1864

Volume 15

Nineteenth-Century Literature Criticism

Excerpts from Criticism of the
Works of Novelists, Poets, Playwrights,
Short Story Writers, Philosophers, and Other
Creative Writers Who Died between 1800
and 1900, from the First Published Critical
Appraisals to Current Evaluations

Cherie D. Abbey
Janet Mullane
Editors

Jelena Obradovic Kronick
Robert Thomas Wilson
Associate Editors

Gale Research Company
Book Tower
Detroit, Michigan 48226

STAFF

Cherie D. Abbey, Janet Mullane, *Editors*

Jelena Obradovic Kronick, Robert Thomas Wilson, *Associate Editors*

Gail Ann Schulte, *Senior Assistant Editor*

Rachel Carlson, Vivian L. Metcalf, Mary Nelson-Pulice, *Assistant Editors*

Phyllis Carmel Mendelson, Emily B. Tennyson, *Contributing Editors*
Denise Michlewicz Broderick, Melissa Reiff Hug, Paula Kepos,
Claudia Loomis, Debra A. Wells, *Contributing Assistant Editors*

Jeanne A. Gough, *Permissions & Production Manager*
Lizbeth A. Purdy, *Production Supervisor*
Denise Michlewicz Broderick, *Production Coordinator*
Kathleen M. Cook, *Assistant Production Coordinator*
Suzanne Powers, Jani Prescott, *Editorial Assistants*
Linda Marcella Pugliese, *Manuscript Coordinator*
Donna Craft, *Assistant Manuscript Coordinator*
Jennifer E. Gale, Maureen A. Puhl, Rosetta Irene Simms, *Manuscript Assistants*

Victoria B. Cariappa, *Research Supervisor*
Maureen R. Richards, *Assistant Research Coordinator*
Daniel Kurt Gilbert, Kent Graham, Michele R. O'Connell,
Filomena Sgambati, Mary D. Wise, *Research Assistants*

Janice M. Mach, *Text Permissions Supervisor*
Susan D. Battista, Kathy Grell, *Assistant Permissions Coordinators*
Mabel C. Gurney, Josephine M. Keene, Mary M. Matuz, *Senior Permissions Assistants*
H. Diane Cooper, *Permissions Assistant*
Eileen H. Baehr, Anita L. Ransom, Kimberly F. Smilay, *Permissions Clerks*

Patricia A. Seefelt, *Picture Permissions Supervisor*
Margaret A. Chamberlain, *Assistant Permissions Coordinator*
Colleen M. Crane, *Permissions Assistant*
Lillian Tyus, *Permissions Clerk*

Frederick G. Ruffner, *Chairman*
J. Kevin Reger, *President*
Dedria Bryfonski, *Publisher*
Ellen Crowley, *Associate Editorial Director*
Laurie Lanzen Harris, *Director, Literary Criticism Division*
Dennis Poupard, *Senior Editor, Literary Criticism Series*

Library of Congress Catalog Card Number 81-6943
ISBN 0-8103-5815-8
ISSN 0732-1864

Computerized photocomposition by
Typographics, Incorporated
Kansas City, Missouri

Printed in the United States

Contents

Preface

The nineteenth century was a time of tremendous growth in human endeavor: in science, in social history, and particularly in literature. The era saw the development of the novel, witnessed radical changes from classicism to romanticism to realism, and contained intellectual and artistic ideas that continue to inspire authors of our own century. The importance of the writers of the nineteenth century is twofold, for they provide insight into their own time as well as into the universal nature of human experience.

The literary criticism of an era can also give us insight into the moral and intellectual atmosphere of the past because the criteria by which a work of art is judged reflect current philosophical and social attitudes. Literary criticism takes many forms: the traditional essay, the book or play review, even the parodic poem. Criticism can also be of several types: normative, descriptive, interpretive, textual, appreciative, generic. Collectively, the range of critical response helps us to understand a work of art, an author, an era.

The Scope of the Work

The success of two of Gale's current literary series, *Contemporary Literary Criticism (CLC)* and *Twentieth-Century Literary Criticism (TCLC),* which excerpt criticism of creative writing from the twentieth century, suggested an equivalent need among students and teachers of literature of the nineteenth century. Moreover, since the analysis of this literature spans almost two hundred years, a vast amount of critical material confronts the student.

Nineteenth-Century Literature Criticism (NCLC) presents significant passages from published criticism on authors who died between 1800 and 1900. The author list for each volume of *NCLC* is carefully compiled to represent a variety of genres and nationalities and to cover authors who are currently regarded as the most important writers of their era as well as those whose contribution to literature and literary history is significant. The truly great writers are rare, and in the intervals between them lesser but genuine artists, as well as writers who enjoyed immense popularity in their own time and in their own countries, are important to the study of nineteenth-century literature. The length of each author entry is intended to reflect the amount of attention the author has received from critics writing in English and from foreign critics in translation. Articles and books that have not been translated into English are excluded. However, since many of the major foreign studies have been translated into English and are excerpted in *NCLC,* author entries reflect the viewpoints of many nationalities. Each author entry represents a historical overview of critical reaction to the author's work: early criticism is presented to indicate initial responses and later selections represent any rise or decline in the author's literary reputation. We have also attempted to identify and include excerpts from the seminal essays on each author as well as modern perspectives. Thus, *NCLC* is designed to serve as an introduction for the student of nineteenth-century literature to the authors of that period and to the most significant commentators on these authors.

NCLC entries are intended to be definitive overviews. In order to devote more attention to each writer, approximately fifteen authors are included in each 600-page volume, compared with about fifty authors in a *CLC* volume of similar size. Because of the great quantity of critical material available on many authors and because of the resurgence of criticism generated by such events as an author's centennial or anniversary celebration, the republication of an author's works, or publication of a newly translated work or volume of letters, an author may appear more than once. Usually, one or more author entries in each volume of *NCLC* are devoted to single works by major authors who have appeared previously in the series. Only those individual works that have been the subject of extensive criticism and are widely studied in literature courses are selected for this in-depth treatment. Nikolai Gogol's *Revizor (The Inspector General)* is the subject of such an entry in *NCLC,* Volume 15.

The Organization of the Book

An author section consists of the following elements: author heading, biographical and critical introduction, principal works, excerpts of criticism (each preceded by explanatory notes and followed by a bibliographical citation), and an additional bibliography.

7

- The *author heading* consists of the author's full name, followed by birth and death dates. The unbracketed portion of the name denotes the form under which the author most commonly wrote. If an author wrote consistently under a pseudonym, the pseudonym will be listed in the author heading and the real name given in parentheses on the first line of the biographical and critical introduction. Also located at the beginning of the introduction are any name variations under which an author wrote, including transliterated forms for authors whose languages use nonroman alphabets. Uncertainty as to a birth or death date is indicated by a question mark.

- A *portrait* of the author is included when available. Many entries also feature illustrations of materials pertinent to an author's career, including manuscript pages, letters, book illustrations, and representations of important people, places, and events in an author's life.

- The *biographical and critical introduction* contains background information that elucidates the author's creative output. When applicable, biographical and critical introductions are followed by references to additional entries on the author in past volumes of *NCLC* and in other literary reference series published by Gale Research Company. These include *Dictionary of Literary Biography*, *Children's Literature Review*, and *Something about the Author*.

- The list of *principal works* is chronological by date of first book publication and identifies genres. In those instances where the first publication was in other than the English language, the title and date of the first English-language edition are given in brackets. Unless otherwise indicated, dramas are dated by the first performance, rather than first publication.

- *Criticism* is arranged chronologically in each author section to provide a perspective on any changes in critical evaluation over the years. In the text of each author entry, titles by the author are printed in boldface type. This allows the reader to ascertain without difficulty the works being discussed. For purposes of easier identification, the critic's name and the publication date of the essay are given at the beginning of each piece of criticism. Unsigned criticism is preceded by the title of the journal in which it appeared. For an anonymous essay later attributed to a critic, the critic's name appears in brackets at the beginning of the excerpt and in the bibliographical citation.

- Essays are prefaced with *explanatory notes* as an additional aid to students using *NCLC*. The explanatory notes provide several types of useful information, including the reputation of the critic, the importance of a work of criticism, a synopsis of the essay, the specific approach of the critic (biographical, psychoanalytic, structuralist, etc.), and the growth of critical controversy or changes in critical trends regarding an author's work. In some cases, these notes include cross-references to related criticism in the author's entry or in the additional bibliography. Dates in parentheses within the explanatory notes refer to other essays in the author entry.

- A complete *bibliographical citation* designed to facilitate the location of the original essay or book follows each piece of criticism.

- The *additional bibliography* appearing at the end of each author entry suggests further reading on the author. In some cases it includes essays for which the editors could not obtain reprint rights.

An appendix lists the sources from which material in the volume is reprinted. It does not, however, list every book or periodical consulted for the volume.

Cumulative Indexes

Each volume of *NCLC* includes a cumulative index listing all the authors who have appeared in *Contemporary Literary Criticism*, *Twentieth-Century Literary Criticism*, *Nineteenth-Century Literature Criticism*, and *Literature Criticism from 1400 to 1800*, along with cross-references to the Gale series *Children's Literature Review*, *Authors in the News*, *Contemporary Authors*, *Contemporary Authors Autobiography Series*, *Dictionary of Literary Biography*, *Something about the Author*, and *Yesterday's Authors of Books for Children*. Users will welcome this cumulated author index as a useful tool for locating an author within the various series. The index, which lists birth and death dates when available, will be particularly valuable for those authors who are identified with a certain period but whose death dates cause them to be placed in another, or for those authors whose careers span two periods. For example, Fedor Dostoevski is found in *NCLC*, yet Leo Tolstoy, another major nineteenth-century Russian novelist, is found in *TCLC*.

NCLC also includes a cumulative nationality index to authors. Authors are listed alphabetically by nationality, followed by the volume numbers in which they appear.

A cumulative index to critics is another useful feature of *NCLC*. Under each critic's name are listed the authors on whom the critic has written and the volume and page where the criticism appears.

Acknowledgments

No work of this scope can be accomplished without the cooperation of many people. The editors especially wish to thank the copyright holders of the excerpts included in this volume, the permissions managers of the book and magazine publishing companies for assisting us in securing reprint rights, and the staffs of the Detroit Public Library, the Library of Congress, the University of Michigan Library, and Wayne State University Library for making their resources available to us. We are also grateful to Anthony J. Bogucki for his assistance with copyright research. The editors also wish to acknowledge The Granger Collection, New York, for the endpaper illustration of Henry Wheeler Shaw, and Mary Evans Picture Library for the endpaper illustration of Hippolyte Adolphe Taine.

Suggestions Are Welcome

The editors welcome the comments and suggestions of readers to expand the coverage and enhance the usefulness of the series.

Authors to Appear in Future Volumes

About, Edmond François 1828-1885
Aguilo I. Fuster, Maria 1825-1897
Aksakov, Konstantin 1817-1860
Aleardi, Aleardo 1812-1878
Alecsandri, Vasile 1821-1890
Alencar, José 1829-1877
Alfieri, Vittorio 1749-1803
Allingham, William 1824-1889
Almquist, Carl Jonas Love 1793-1866
Alorne, Leonor de Almeida 1750-1839
Alsop, Richard 1761-1815
Altimirano, Ignacio Manuel 1834-1893
Alvarenga, Manuel Inacio da Silva
1749-1814
Alvares de Azevedo, Manuel Antonio
1831-1852
Anzengruber, Ludwig 1839-1889
Arany, Janos 1817-1882
Arène, Paul 1843-1896
Aribau, Bonaventura Carlos 1798-1862
Arjona de Cubas, Manuel Maria de
1771-1820
Arnault, Antoine Vincent 1766-1834
Arneth, Alfred von 1819-1897
Arnim, Bettina von 1785-1859
Arnold, Thomas 1795-1842
Arriaza y Superviela, Juan Bautista
1770-1837
Asbjörnsen, Peter Christen 1812-1885
Ascasubi, Hilario 1807-1875
Atterbom, Per Daniel Amadeus
1790-1855
Aubanel, Theodore 1829-1886
Auerbach, Berthold 1812-1882
Augier, Guillaume V.E. 1820-1889
Azeglio, Massimo D' 1798-1866
Azevedo, Guilherme de 1839-1882
Bakin (pseud. of Takizawa Okikani)
1767-1848
Bakunin, Mikhail Aleksandrovich
1814-1876
Baratynski, Jewgenij Abramovich
1800-1844
Barnes, William 1801-1886
Batyushkov, Konstantin 1778-1855
Beattie, James 1735-1803
Beckford, William 1760-1844
Becquer, Gustavo Adolfo 1836-1870
Bentham, Jeremy 1748-1832
Béranger, Jean-Pierre de 1780-1857
Berchet, Giovanni 1783-1851
Berzsenyi, Daniel 1776-1836
Black, William 1841-1898
Blair, Hugh 1718-1800
Blicher, Steen Steensen 1782-1848
Bocage, Manuel Maria Barbosa du
1765-1805

Boratynsky, Yevgeny 1800-1844
Borel, Petrus 1809-1859
Boreman, Yokutiel 1825-1890
Borne, Ludwig 1786-1837
Botev, Hristo 1778-1842
Brinckman, John 1814-1870
Brontë, Emily 1818-1848
Brown, Charles Brockden 1777-1810
Browning, Robert 1812-1889
Büchner, Georg 1813-1837
Campbell, James Edwin 1867-1895
Campbell, Thomas 1777-1844
Carlyle, Thomas 1795-1881
Castelo Branco, Camilo 1825-1890
Castro Alves, Antonio de 1847-1871
Channing, William Ellery 1780-1842
Chatterje, Bankin Chanda 1838-1894
Chivers, Thomas Holly 1807?-1858
Claudius, Matthias 1740-1815
Clough, Arthur Hugh 1819-1861
Cobbett, William 1762-1835
Colenso, John William 1814-1883
Coleridge, Hartley 1796-1849
Collett, Camilla 1813-1895
Comte, Auguste 1798-1857
Conrad, Robert T. 1810-1858
Conscience, Hendrik 1812-1883
Cooke, Philip Pendleton 1816-1850
Corbière, Edouard 1845-1875
Crabbe, George 1754-1832
Cruz E Sousa, Joao da 1861-1898
Desbordes-Valmore, Marceline
1786-1859
Deschamps, Emile 1791-1871
Deus, João de 1830-1896
Dickinson, Emily 1830-1886
Dinis, Julio 1839-1871
Dinsmoor, Robert 1757-1836
Du Maurier, George 1834-1896
Echeverria, Esteban 1805-1851
Eminescy, Mihai 1850-1889
Engels, Friedrich 1820-1895
Espronceda, José 1808-1842
Ettinger, Solomon 1799-1855
Euchel, Issac 1756-1804
Ferguson, Samuel 1810-1886
Fernández de Lizardi, José Joaquín
1776-1827
Fernández de Moratín, Leandro
1760-1828
Fet, Afanasy 1820-1892
Feuillet, Octave 1821-1890
Fontane, Theodor 1819-1898
Freiligrath, Hermann Ferdinand
1810-1876
Freytag, Gustav 1816-1895
Ganivet, Angel 1865-1898

Garrett, Almeida 1799-1854
Garshin, Vsevolod Mikhaylovich
1855-1888
Gezelle, Guido 1830-1899
Ghalib, Asadullah Khan 1797-1869
Goldschmidt, Meir Aaron 1819-1887
Goncalves Dias, Antonio 1823-1864
Griboyedov, Aleksander Sergeyevich
1795-1829
Grigor'yev, Appolon Aleksandrovich
1822-1864
Groth, Klaus 1819-1899
Grun, Anastasius (pseud. of Anton
Alexander Graf von Auersperg)
1806-1876
Guerrazzi, Francesco Domenico
1804-1873
Gutierrez Najera, Manuel 1859-1895
Gutzkow, Karl Ferdinand 1811-1878
Ha-Kohen, Shalom 1772-1845
Halleck, Fitz-Greene 1790-1867
Harris, George Washington 1814-1869
Hayne, Paul Hamilton 1830-1886
Hazlitt, William 1778-1830
Hebbel, Christian Friedrich 1813-1863
Hebel, Johann Peter 1760-1826
Hegel, Georg Wilhelm Friedrich
1770-1831
Heiberg, Johann Ludvig 1813-1863
Herculano, Alexandre 1810-1866
Hernández, José 1834-1886
Hertz, Henrik 1798-1870
Herwegh, Georg 1817-1875
Hoffman, Charles Fenno 1806-1884
Hölderlin, Friedrich 1770-1843
Hood, Thomas 1799-1845
Hooper, Johnson Jones 1815-1863
Hopkins, Gerard Manley 1844-1889
Horton, George Moses 1798-1880
Howitt, William 1792-1879
Hughes, Thomas 1822-1896
Imlay, Gilbert 1754?-1828?
Irwin, Thomas Caulfield 1823-1892
Isaacs, Jorge 1837-1895
Jacobsen, Jens Peter 1847-1885
Jippensha, Ikku 1765-1831
Kant, Immanuel 1724-1804
Karr, Jean Baptiste Alphonse 1808-1890
Keble, John 1792-1866
Khomyakov, Alexey S. 1804-1860
Kierkegaard, Søren 1813-1855
Kinglake, Alexander W. 1809-1891
Kingsley, Charles 1819-1875
Kivi, Alexis 1834-1872
Koltsov, Alexey Vasilyevich 1809-1842
Kotzebue, August von 1761-1819
Kraszewski, Josef Ignacy 1812-1887

Kreutzwald, Friedrich Reinhold 1803-1882
Krochmal, Nahman 1785-1840
Krudener, Valeria Barbara Julia de Wietinghoff 1766-1824
Lampman, Archibald 1861-1899
Larra y Sánchez de Castro, Mariano 1809-1837
Lebensohn, Micah Joseph 1828-1852
Leconte de Lisle, Charles-Marie-René 1818-1894
Lenau, Nikolaus 1802-1850
Leontyev, Konstantin 1831-1891
Leopardi, Giacoma 1798-1837
Leskov, Nikolai 1831-1895
Lever, Charles James 1806-1872
Levisohn, Solomon 1789-1822
Lewes, George Henry 1817-1878
Leyden, John 1775-1811
Lobensohn, Micah Gregory 1775-1810
Longstreet, Augustus Baldwin 1790-1870
López de Ayola y Herrera, Adelardo 1819-1871
Lover, Samuel 1797-1868
Luzzato, Samuel David 1800-1865
Macedo, Joaquim Manuel de 1820-1882
Macha, Karel Hynek 1810-1836
Mackenzie, Henry 1745-1831
Malmon, Solomon 1754-1800
Mangan, James Clarence 1803-1849
Manzoni, Alessandro 1785-1873
Mapu, Abraham 1808-1868
Marii, Jose 1853-1895
Markovic, Svetozar 1846-1875
Martínez de La Rosa, Francisco 1787-1862
Mathews, Cornelius 1817-1889
McCulloch, Thomas 1776-1843
Merriman, Brian 1747-1805
Meyer, Conrad Ferdinand 1825-1898
Montgomery, James 1771-1854
Morton, Sarah Wentworth 1759-1846
Müller, Friedrich 1749-1825
Murger, Henri 1822-1861
Neruda, Jan 1834-1891
Nestroy, Johann 1801-1862
Newman, John Henry 1801-1890

Niccolini, Giambattista 1782-1861
Nievo, Ippolito 1831-1861
Nodier, Charles 1780-1844
Obradovic, Dositej 1742-1811
Oehlenschlager, Adam 1779-1850
O'Neddy, Philothee (pseud. of Theophile Dondey) 1811-1875
O'Shaughnessy, Arthur William Edgar 1844-1881
Ostrovsky, Alexander 1823-1886
Paine, Thomas 1737-1809
Peacock, Thomas Love 1785-1866
Perk, Jacques 1859-1881
Pisemsky, Alexey F. 1820-1881
Pompeia, Raul D'Avila 1863-1895
Popovic, Jovan Sterija 1806-1856
Praed, Winthrop Mackworth 1802-1839
Prati, Giovanni 1814-1884
Preseren, France 1800-1849
Pringle, Thomas 1789-1834
Procter, Adelaide Ann 1825-1864
Procter, Bryan Waller 1787-1874
Pye, Henry James 1745-1813
Quental, Antero Tarquinio de 1842-1891
Quinet, Edgar 1803-1875
Quintana, Manuel José 1772-1857
Radishchev, Aleksander 1749-1802
Raftery, Anthony 1784-1835
Raimund, Ferdinand 1790-1836
Reid, Mayne 1818-1883
Renan, Ernest 1823-1892
Reuter, Fritz 1810-1874
Rogers, Samuel 1763-1855
Ruckert, Friedrich 1788-1866
Runeberg, Johan 1804-1877
Rydberg, Viktor 1828-1895
Saavedra y Ramírez de Boquedano, Angel de 1791-1865
Sacher-Mosoch, Leopold von 1836-1895
Saltykov-Shchedrin, Mikhail 1826-1892
Satanov, Isaac 1732-1805
Schiller, Johann Friedrich von 1759-1805
Schlegel, Karl 1772-1829
Scribe, Augustin Eugène 1791-1861
Sedgwick, Catherine Maria 1789-1867
Senoa, August 1838-1881

Shelley, Percy Bysshe 1792-1822
Shulman, Kalman 1819-1899
Sigourney, Lydia Howard Huntley 1791-1856
Silva, Jose Asuncion 1865-1896
Slaveykov, Petko 1828-1895
Smith, Richard Penn 1799-1854
Smolenskin, Peretz 1842-1885
Stagnelius, Erik Johan 1793-1823
Staring, Antonie Christiaan Wynand 1767-1840
Stendhal (pseud. of Henri Beyle) 1783-1842
Stifter, Adalbert 1805-1868
Stone, John Augustus 1801-1834
Taunay, Alfredo d'Ecragnole 1843-1899
Taylor, Bayard 1825-1878
Tennyson, Alfred, Lord 1809-1892
Terry, Lucy (Lucy Terry Prince) 1730-1821
Thompson, Daniel Pierce 1795-1868
Thompson, Samuel 1766-1816
Thomson, James 1834-1882
Tiedge, Christoph August 1752-1841
Timrod, Henry 1828-1867
Tommaseo, Nicolo 1802-1874
Tompa, Mihaly 1817-1888
Topelius, Zachris 1818-1898
Turgenev, Ivan 1818-1883
Tyutchev, Fedor I. 1803-1873
Uhland, Ludvig 1787-1862
Valaoritis, Aristotelis 1824-1879
Valles, Jules 1832-1885
Verde, Cesario 1855-1886
Villaverde, Cirilio 1812-1894
Vinje, Aasmund Olavsson 1818-1870
Vorosmarty, Mihaly 1800-1855
Weisse, Christian Felix 1726-1804
Welhaven, Johan S. 1807-1873
Werner, Zacharius 1768-1823
Wescott, Edward Noyes 1846-1898
Wessely, Nattali Herz 1725-1805
Whitman, Sarah Helen 1803-1878
Wieland, Christoph Martin 1733-1813
Woolson, Constance Fenimore 1840-1894
Zhukovsky, Vasily 1783-1852

John Caldwell Calhoun

1782-1850

American statesman, philosopher, and orator.

A statesman, philosopher, and orator, Calhoun was a prominent figure in American politics during the first half of the ninteeenth century. He served in many capacities: as congressman, secretary of war, vice-president, senator, and secretary of state. During much of his career Calhoun, a native South Carolinian, was the leading spokesman in Congress for the interests of the southern United States. His influence was largely confined to that section of the country, but he was nationally recognized as an astute political thinker, and his ideas commanded the attention of both his colleagues and the public. Following the Civil War, Calhoun's reputation declined: primarily remembered as the foremost apologist for slavery, he came to symbolize a lost cause. His political ideas, in the minds of many historians, had been tested and had failed. In the twentieth century, scholars have shown a renewed interest in Calhoun's political theories, which are contained in his two posthumously published treatises, *A Disquisition on Government* and *A Discourse on the Constitution and Government of the United States,* and in his speeches, letters, congressional papers, and administrative documents. Of these works, the *Disquisition* and the *Discourse* have received the most critical attention. Together, they are today regarded as one of America's most original and significant contributions to political thought.

Born near Abbeville in northwestern South Carolina, Calhoun was the son of Martha Caldwell and Patrick Calhoun, a slaveholding farmer and member of the state legislature. Because few schools existed in the up-country of South Carolina during his boyhood, Calhoun's early education was largely self-directed. He began his formal schooling at the age of eighteen, when he was sent to a "log-college" operated by his brother-in-law, the Reverend Moses Waddel. After two years at Waddel's academy, Calhoun entered Yale University, graduating with honors in 1804. He then studied law and in 1807 opened a practice in Abbeville. The same year, he was elected to the South Carolina legislature. During his term there, Calhoun helped to revise the state's representation system according to a plan that recognized the up-country and the coastal district as two separate interests that required a veto power over one another. He later described this plan as an example of his famous "rule of the concurrent majority," the federal program of mutual checks that he devised as a solution to the sectional controversies between the northern and southern United States.

Many critics divide Calhoun's subsequent political career into nationalist and sectionalist phases, the first period extending until the mid-1820s and the second dating from that time until his death. Shortly after entering the United States House of Representatives in 1811, Calhoun gained prominence as one of the "War Hawks" who advocated war with Great Britain. When the War of 1812 was over, he emerged a zealous nationalist, using his considerable influence in the House to promote measures that would advance national unity and prosperity. Declaring that he spoke "not for South Carolina, but the nation," he sponsored such policies as moderate protective tariffs to encourage infant American industries and federal expenditures to strengthen the army and navy. In 1817, Calhoun

resigned his seat in the House to become secretary of war in James Monroe's cabinet. His eight years in this post increased his national following and in 1824, he joined the five-man race for the presidency. When it became apparent that he could not win, however, he withdrew and instead launched a successful campaign for the vice-presidency.

Scholars generally agree that Calhoun's shift from a nationalist to a sectionalist position occurred during his tenure as John Quincy Adams's vice-president. Foremost among the reasons cited for this conversion is Calhoun's belief that increasingly high tariff levels were enriching Northern industrialists at the expense of Southern planters. Calhoun, whose marriage in 1811 to his cousin Floride Bonneau Calhoun had brought him a considerable fortune, was now himself the owner of a plantation and, like other Southern farmers, he resented the tariffs, which had lowered the price of cotton. When the tariff rate on imported goods was raised again in 1828, Calhoun responded with the *South Carolina Exposition and Protest.* A report anonymously drafted for the South Carolina legislature, the *Exposition* denounced the so-called "Tariff of Abominations" as unconstitutional and further declared the right of a state to nullify within its boundaries federal laws that it deemed unconstitutional. The *Exposition* is considered not only the first significant indication of Calhoun's change from a nationalist to a sectionalist position but also the first expression of the political theory that he was later to develop in a more refined form in his masterpieces, the *Disquisition* and the *Discourse*. Stating that there was a "recognized diversity of geographical interests" between the North and the South, Calhoun maintained in the *Exposition* that the majority in the North had no right to impose its will on the minority in the South. To justify the doctrine of nullification, Calhoun constructed an argument in favor of states' rights. Starting with the premise that the constitution was a compact created by sovereign states, Calhoun contended that the states had the right to challenge the federal government when they believed it had exceeded its powers. The purpose of nullification as outlined by Calhoun in the *Exposition* was to bring about a settlement of a contested issue: the federal government could only enforce the disputed law if three-quarters of the states found that it was constitutional. In the event of such a situation, the "aggrieved" state had two alternatives—it could comply with the law or it could secede from the Union. The South Carolina legislature ordered the *Exposition* printed, and it was widely circulated. However, at Calhoun's urging, the state decided against adopting an ordinance of nullification immediately. It was Calhoun's hope that the new president, Andrew Jackson, would insist upon a reduction of the tariff levels, thereby making it unnecessary for South Carolina to execute its threat.

Reelected vice-president in 1828, Calhoun soon became aware that President Jackson was unsympathetic to the theory of states' rights. Jackson, who had learned of Calhoun's authorship of the *Exposition*, challenged the vice-president at a birthday dinner for Thomas Jefferson in 1830, declaring, "Our Federal Union—it must be preserved." Taking up the challenge, Calhoun retorted, "The Union—next to our liberty, the most dear." In 1831, Calhoun openly proclaimed his nullification doctrine in his "Address to the People of South Carolina." Written from his plantation at Fort Hill, South Carolina, this public letter is commonly referred to as the "Fort Hill Address." Calhoun further elaborated upon his idea of state sovereignty in a public letter to the governor of South Carolina, *Letter to Governor Hamilton on the Subject of State Interposition,* which was published in September 1832. The following November, the South Carolina legislature called a state convention in response to the tariff of 1832, which had not significantly reduced the duties on imported goods. The convention promptly nullified both the tariffs of 1828 and 1832 and forbade federal officials from collecting customs duties in the state after February 1, 1833. South Carolina's adoption of the nullification ordinance was the last of a series of controversies that destroyed friendly relations between Jackson and Calhoun. Seeing that he had no chance of succeeding Jackson as president, Calhoun resigned the vice-presidency and was elected by South Carolina voters to the United States Senate, where the battle over nullification was fought. Jackson soon denounced South Carolina's ordinance as "treason" and asked Congress to authorize a "Force Bill" that would enable him to use armed forces to execute the tariff laws in the state. Calhoun, in what are considered some of his best speeches, entered into a Senate debate with Daniel Webster on the "Force Bill" ("Speech on the Revenue Collection (Force) Bill") and on the theory of states' rights ("Speech on His Resolutions in Support of State Rights"). The crisis over nullification eventually ended during the winter of 1833, when Congress passed a compromise tariff act and South Carolina repealed its ordinance.

Calhoun spent the greater part of the remainder of his public career in the Senate, primarily defending the institution of slavery against the mounting abolitionist movement. In a speech in 1836 entitled "Speech on Abolition Petitions," he offered the theory of states' rights as a constitutional justification for slavery, arguing that it was "under the sole and exclusive control of the states" where it existed. When objections based on constitutional interpretation failed to stop the anti-slavery agitation, Calhoun attempted to vindicate the South's "peculiar institution" on moral and economic grounds. In 1837, in his "Speech on the Reception of Abolition Petitions," Calhoun declared that slavery was "a good—a positive good." In his opinion, slavery was the best possible relation between whites and blacks: not only was it more humane than the Northern system of wage and labor, but it freed the South from the conflicts between labor and capital that plagued the North. Underlying these pronouncements was Calhoun's belief that blacks were naturally inferior to whites. "There is no instance whatever," he asserted, "of any civilized colored race, of any shade, being found equal to the establishment and maintenance of free government."

Calhoun retired from the Senate in 1843 to launch his last presidential campaign. To promote his candidacy, a collection of his speeches and an anonymous *Life of John C. Calhoun* were published. The authorship of the *Life* has been disputed since its appearance. Some critics contend that it is an autobiography, but others attribute it to R.M.T. Hunter, a Virginia representative and friend of Calhoun. Both the *Speeches* and the *Life* sold poorly and in 1844, Calhoun withdrew from the race. In 1845, after serving as President John Tyler's secretary of state for one year, Calhoun returned to the Senate. There, suffering from a chronic respiratory ailment that caused his death five years later, he resumed his attack on the abolitionists. When the war with Mexico began, he vehemently opposed the Wilmot Proviso, which would have barred slavery from all lands that the United States might win in the conflict. Calhoun's last important speech, "Speech on the Slavery Question," was a response to the Compromise of 1850, which Henry Clay had proposed as a means of settling the controversy over permitting slavery in newly acquired territories. In this speech, Calhoun outlined his objections to the compromise, charging that it would render the slave states a permanent minority in Congress. As in all of his earlier pronouncements on the slavery issue, Calhoun insisted that his aim was to preserve the Union. "If I am judged by my acts," he once stated, "I trust I shall be found as firm a friend of the Union as any man in it. . . . If I shall have any place in the memory of posterity it will be in consequence of my deep attachment to it."

During the 1840s, Calhoun had begun restating his political ideas in definitive form in the *Disquisition* and the *Discourse,* both of which were published after his death. In the first work, he hoped to "lay a solid foundation for political science" by delineating the principles of government. In the second, unfinished work, he applied these principles to American democracy. The *Disquisition,* considered the more thoughtful of the two treatises, is primarily noted for its proposed solution to the problem of safeguarding the rights of minorities. This solution, which Calhoun called the "rule of the concurrent majority," rests on the premise that governments by majority rule tend toward absolutism. To prevent tyranny by the "numerical majority," Calhoun advocated a system of government in which both majorities and minorities are represented. Since, according to Calhoun, the right of suffrage cannot sufficiently prevent the abuse of power, governments should be constructed to give "to each division or interest, through its appropriate organ, either a concurrent voice in making and executing the laws, or a veto on their execution." In the *Discourse,* Calhoun showed how this system of mutual checks could provide the Southern minority with a permanent constitutional defense of its interests. Also in the *Discourse,* Calhoun proposed that the rights of minorities in America could be further protected by means of a dual executive, one elected by the North and one by the South.

Contemporary commentary on Calhoun focused as much on his personality as on the style and content of his political pronouncements. Austerely and unrelentingly intellectual, Calhoun was considered a "thinking machine" by many of his friends, acquaintances, and colleagues. Commentators noted that in his writings, as well as in conversation, he relied heavily on reasoning and displayed remarkable analytic skills. Even some of his most hostile critics were forced to admit that his logic was infallible. Calhoun's contemporaries were also favorably impressed by the lucidity of his prose; many preferred his simple language to the florid style that characterized the speeches of his two greatest rivals in the Senate, Webster and Clay. Reactions to Calhoun's political ideas varied widely during his lifetime. While Southern reviewers often praised him as a political prophet and patriot, Northern reviewers frequently labeled him an anarchist and traitor to the Union. Following the Civil War, a number of scholars accepted the Northern opinion, and Calhoun came to be regarded by many as a reactionary who instigated the Civil War by provoking controversy on the slavery question. In addition to dismissing Calhoun's political theories as nonsense, several late nineteenth-century critics faulted the inconsistency of his beliefs, maintaining that his conversion from a nationalist to a sectionalist position was the outgrowth of thwarted presidential aspirations.

During the early twentieth century, scholars began to reassess Calhoun's political ideas. In a 1927 essay that the critic Margaret L. Coit termed "a landmark in Calhoun historiography," Vernon Louis Parrington rejected the traditional view of the statesman as a doomed symbol of the slavery cause and proposed that his doctrine of the concurrent majority was a valid defense of minority rights that was applicable in the twentieth century. Since the appearance of Parrington's essay, biographical and critical studies on Calhoun have proliferated, the *Disquisition* and the *Discourse* have been reissued several times, and a plan for publishing a comprehensive collection of his writings, *The Papers of John C. Calhoun,* has neared completion. Modern commentary on Calhoun's political philosophy has centered on his concept of the concurrent majority. Numerous critics have expanded on Parrington's remarks, contending that the concurrent majority theory is the foundation of America's pluralistic political system; thus, the concurrent veto suggested by Calhoun is the blueprint by which the various interest and pressure groups in America operate today. The arguments of these "neo-Calhounites" have been disputed by the statesman's detractors, many of whom insist that Calhoun was not interested in defending the rights of all minorities; rather, he was solely concerned about protecting the rights of a single minority, the slaveholders of the South. Another aspect of Calhoun's political philosophy that is frequently discussed in the twentieth century is his theory of class conflict, which underlay his interpretation of the sectional controversy between the North and the South. In the opinion of some scholars, this theory prefigured many of the ideas of Karl Marx.

The recent revival of interest in Calhoun's political philosophy suggests that he will continue to be remembered more for his theories than for his accomplishments as a statesman. Although his life has often been described as a Greek tragedy because

he was the leader of the South's losing struggle, his writings have provided twentieth-century scholars with a better understanding of the political problems of both his own era and of modern times. For his original ideas and insight into the workings of government, particularly as expressed in the *Disquisition* and the *Discourse,* Calhoun is hailed as a major nineteenth-century American political philosopher.

(See also *Dictionary of Literary Biography,* Vol. 3: *Antebellum Writers in New York and the South.*)

*PRINCIPAL WORKS

South Carolina Exposition and Protest (congressional paper) 1828
"Address to the People of South Carolina" (letter) 1831; published in journal *Pendleton Messenger*
Letter to Governor Hamilton on the Subject of State Interposition (letter) 1832
"Speech on His Resolutions in Support of State Rights" (speech) 1833
"Speech on the Revenue Collection (Force) Bill" (speech) 1833
"Speech on Abolition Petitions" (speech) 1836
"Speech on the Circulation of Incendiary Papers" (speech) 1836
"Speech on the Reception of Abolition Petitions" (speech) 1837
Speeches of John C. Calhoun (speeches) 1843
"Speech on the Slavery Question" (speech) 1850
A Discourse on the Constitution and Government of the United States (unfinished treatise) 1851; published in *The Works of John C. Calhoun*
A Disquisition on Government (treatise) 1851; published in *The Works of John C. Calhoun*
The Works of John C. Calhoun. 6 vols. (treatises, speeches, congressional papers, and letters) 1851-56
Correspondence of John C. Calhoun (letters) 1900
The Papers of John C. Calhoun. 16 vols. to date. (congressional papers, speeches, letters, and administrative documents) 1959-

*Calhoun's individual speeches are chronologized by the date of delivery; all of these speeches are available in *The Works of John C. Calhoun.*

THE UNITED STATES MAGAZINE AND DEMOCRATIC REVIEW
(essay date 1837-38)

[*In the following excerpt from an essay written in 1837-38, the critic comments on the style and structure of Calhoun's speeches, his analytic skills, and his patriotism.*]

Mr. Calhoun has evidently taken Demosthenes for his model as a speaker—or rather, I suppose, he has studied, while young, his orations with great admiration, until they produced a decided impression upon his mind. His recent speech in defence of himself against the attacks of Mr. Clay, is precisely on the plan of the famous oration *De Corona,* delivered by the great Athenian, in vindication of himself from the elaborate and artful attacks of Aeschines. While the one says: "Athenians! to you I appeal, my judges and my witnesses!"—the other says: "In proof of this, I appeal to you, Senators, my witnesses and my judges on this occasion!'' Aeschines accused Demosthenes of having received a bribe from Philip, and the latter retorted by saying that the other had accused him of doing what he himself had notoriously done. Mr. Clay says, that Mr. Calhoun had gone over [to the Democratic Party], and he left to time to disclose his motives. Mr. Calhoun retorts: ''Leave it to time to disclose my motives for going over! I, who have changed no opinion, abandoned no principle, and deserted no party—I, who have stood still and maintained my ground against every difficulty, to be told that it is left to time to disclose my motive! The imputation sinks to the earth with the groundless charge on which it rests. I stamp it down in the dust. I pick up the dart which fell harmless at my feet. I hurl it back. What the Senator charges on me unjustly, he *has actually done*. He went over on a memorable occasion, and *did not* leave it to time to disclose his motive.'' In the conception and arrangement of the whole speech, in fact, there is a remarkable similarity to the speech of the great Athenian. And where could any man find a nobler model? For withering sarcasm—burning invective—lofty declamation—for all that is spirit-stirring and glorious in eloquence, there is not on record, in any language, as noble and perfect a specimen as this Oration for the Crown. (pp. 82-3)

In one faculty of the mind he surpasses any public man of the age, and that is in analysis. His power to examine a complex idea, and exhibit to you the simple ideas of which it is composed, is wonderful. Hence it is that he generalizes with such great rapidity, that ordinary minds suppose, at first, he is theoretical; whereas he has only reached a point at a single bound, to which it would require long hours of sober reflection for them to attain. It is a mistake to suppose that he jumps at his conclusions without due care and consideration. No man examines with more care, or with more intense labor, every question upon which his mind is called to act. The difference between him and others is, that he thinks constantly with little or no relaxation. Hence the restless activity and energy of his mind always place him far in advance of those around him. He has reached the summit, while they have just commenced to ascend, and cannot readily discover the path which has led him to his lofty and extensive view.

Mr. Calhoun evidently has studied our system of government very profoundly and philosophically, on the leading ideas of the school of Jefferson. His great speech in reply to Mr. Webster, on the federative principle of the Constitution, and the sovereignty of the States, is one of the most profound and finished commentaries upon that noble instrument and its formation, that has ever been produced by the genius of man. On that remarkable occasion, he simplified the points of controversy with his distinguished antagonist to such a degree, that he compelled him to deny that our system of Government was a *constitutional compact;* and finally forced him to the position, that the Government itself had substantive and independent rights, as if the Government was not made by the Constitution, and had no existence, in a single attribute, without it. This debate was managed with great power and ability on both sides. Both speakers saw that the whole argument turned upon the point whether the Constitution was a *compact* or not. If it was admitted, the wit of man could not avoid the conclusion, that each party to the compact must of necessity judge of its provisions and infractions, or surrender up their original character as sovereign contracting parties, to a government with power *to define its own limitations,* and, of necessity, to make and unmake the compact at the will and pleasure of those who might chance to give it impulse and vitality. This subject em-

inently suited Mr. Calhoun's mind and habits of thought, and he consequently exhibited a power of argument—a distinctness of analysis—and a luminous investigation of the attributes and nature of government—which will stand a monument to his fame, as long as the American eagle shall present to the world that bright constellation of independent States which now glitter and blaze around its brow. No human being can read that speech without feeling that it contains the same doctrines which were proclaimed in the Kentucky and Virginia resolutions of '98, and in the immortal report of Mr. Madison, around which the Republican party rallied with the devotion of those who felt the liberties of their country to be involved.

As a public speaker and debater, Mr. Calhoun is energetic and impressive to the highest degree. Without having much of the action of an orator, yet his compressed lip—his erect and stern attitudes—his iron countenance, compressed lip, and flashing eye—all make him at times eloquent in the full sense of the word. No man can hear him without feeling. His power is in *clear analysis—suppressed passion,* and *lofty earnestness*. As to the great questions connected with the currency of the present day, it is vain and idle to contend with him. It has been the subject of his daily thought for more than twenty years. He is before his age, but he will triumph, and posterity will be astonished at the profoundness and the sagacity of his views. Many suppose that he has an absorbing ambition; but this is a mistake, and it arises from the natural activity of his mind on all questions of much interest, and his constant and ardent patriotism. Devotion to the honor and liberties of his country is his consuming passion, and his ardent pursuit of what he conceives to be her interests is mistaken by the superficial observer for overweening ambition. Ambition he has, but it is high and noble, and like the Roman's, identified with love for Rome. His nullification, so much misunderstood and misrepresented, was with him a pure and enthusiastic devotion to the true spirit of the Constitution and the permanent interest of the whole Union, according to his understanding of them. His greatest weakness, if weakness it can be called, is his free and unreserved confidence in those who are not his friends. This arises from the natural integrity and unsuspecting character of his heart. Another weakness perhaps is, that he talks too much, forgetting that there is often dignity and power in impressive silence, particularly after a man has acquired fame. This arises, however, from the simplicity of character and great love of truth, which makes him eager to present her to others that they may receive and love her too, with veneration equal to his own. (pp. 83-4)

''John Caldwell Calhoun,'' in The United States Magazine and Democratic Review, *Vol. II. No. V, April, 1838, pp. 65-84.*

HARRIET MARTINEAU (essay date 1838)

[*A British novelist, journalist, and economist, Martineau was a passionate social reformer. From 1834 to 1836, she traveled throughout the United States, giving support to the abolitionist crusade. In her* Retrospect of Western Travel, *first published in 1838 and excerpted below, Martineau recorded her impressions of Calhoun, whom she met while touring America. Her remarks are famous for her often-quoted description of Calhoun as ''the cast-iron man, who looks as if he had never been born and never could be extinguished.''*]

Our pleasantest evenings [in Washington, D.C.] were some spent at home in a society of the highest order. Ladies, literary, fashionable, or domestic, would spend an hour with us on their way from a dinner or to a ball. Members of Congress would repose themselves by our fireside. Mr. Clay, sitting upright on the sofa, with his snuffbox ever in his hand, would discourse for many an hour in his even, soft, deliberate tone on any one of the great subjects of American policy which we might happen to start, always amazing us with the moderation of estimate and speech which so impetuous a nature has been able to attain. Mr. Webster, leaning back at his ease, telling stories, cracking jokes, shaking the sofa with burst after burst of laughter, or smoothly discoursing to the perfect felicity of the logical part of one's constitution, would illuminate an evening now and then. Mr. Calhoun, the cast-iron man, who looks as if he had never been born and never could be extinguished, would come in sometimes to keep our understandings upon a painful stretch for a short while, and leave us to take to pieces his close, rapid, theoretical, illustrated talk, and see what we could make of it. We found it usually more worth retaining as a curiosity than as either very just or useful. His speech abounds in figures, truly illustrative, if that which they illustrate were but true also. But his theories of government (almost the only subject on which his thoughts are employed), the squarest and compactest that ever were made, are composed out of limited elements, and are not, therefore, likely to stand service very well. It is at first extremely interesting to hear Mr. Calhoun talk; and there is a never-failing evidence of power in all he says and does which commands intellectual reverence; but the admiration is too soon turned into regret, into absolute melancholy. It is impossible to resist the conviction that all this force can be at best but useless, and is but too likely to be very mischievous. His mind has long lost all power of communicating with any other. I know of no man who lives in such utter intellectual solitude. He meets men, and haranges them by the fireside as in the Senate; he is wrought like a piece of machinery, set agoing vehemently by a weight, and stops while you answer; he either passes by what you say or twists it into a suitability with what is in his head, and begins to lecture again. Of course, a mind like this can have little influence in the Senate, except by virtue, perpetually wearing out, of what it did in its less eccentric days; but its influence at home is to be dreaded. There is no hope that an intellect so cast in narrow theories will accommodate itself to varying circumstances; and there is every danger that it will break up all that it can, in order to remould the materials in its own way. Mr. Calhoun is as full as ever of his nullification doctrines; and those who know the force that is in him, and his utter incapacity of modification by other minds (after having gone through as remarkable a revolution of political opinions as perhaps any man ever experienced), will no more expect repose and self-retention from him than from a volcano in full force. Relaxation is no longer in the power of his will. I never saw anyone who so completely gave me the idea of possession. Half an hour's conversation with him is enough to make a necessarian of anybody. Accordingly, he is more complained of than blamed by his enemies. His moments of softness in his family, and when recurring to old college days, are hailed by all as a relief to the vehement working of the intellectual machine; a relief equally to himself and others. Those moments are as touching to the observer as tears on the face of a soldier. (pp. 143-44)

> *Harriet Martineau, "Washington in Jackson's Day: Southern Slavery," in* America through British Eyes, *edited by Allan Nevins, revised edition, Oxford University Press, 1948, pp. 139-65.*

JAMES RUSSELL LOWELL (poem date 1848)

[*Lowell was a celebrated nineteenth-century American poet, critic, essayist, and editor of two leading journals, the* Atlantic Monthly *and the* North American Review. *He is noted for his satirical and critical writings, including* A Fable for Critics, *a book-length poem featuring witty critical portraits of his contemporaries. Commentators generally agree that Lowell displayed a judicious critical sense, despite the fact that he sometimes relied upon mere impressions rather than critical precepts in his writings. Most literary historians rank him with the major nineteenth-century American critics. In the poem below, in which Lowell parodies a Senate debate on the slavery question, he primarily directs his satire at Calhoun.*]

"Here we stan' on the Constitution, by thunder!
    It's a fact o' wich ther 's bushils o' proofs;
Fer how could we trample on 't so, I wonder,
    Ef 't worn't thet it 's ollers under our hoofs?"
        Sez John C. Calhoun, sez he;
            "Human rights haint no more
            Right to come on this floor,
        No more 'n the man in the moon," sez he.

"The North haint no kind o' bisness with nothin;
    An' you've no idee how much bother it saves;
We aint none riled by their frettin' an' frothin',
    We 're *used* to layin' the string on our slaves,"
        Sez John C. Calhoun, sez he;—
            Sez Mister Foote,
            "I should like to shoot
        The holl gang, by the gret horn spoon!" sez he.

"Freedom's Keystone is Slavery, thet ther 's no
        doubt on,
    It's sutthin' thet's—wha' d' ye call it?—divine,—
An' the slaves thet we ollers *make* the most out on
    Air them north o' Mason an' Dixon's line,"
        Sez John C. Calhoun, sez he;—
            "Fer all thet," sez Mangum,
            "'T would be better to hang 'em,
        An' so git red on 'em soon," sez he.

"The mass ough' to labor an' we lay on soffies,
    Thet 's the reason I wan' to spread Freedom's aree;
It puts all the cunnniest of us in office,
    An' reelises our Maker's original idee."
        Sez John C. Calhoun, sez he;—
            "Thet 's ez plain," sez Cass,
            "Ez thet some one 's an ass,
        It's ez clear ez the sun is at noon," sez he.

"Now don't go to say I 'm the friend of oppression,
    But keep all your spare breath fer coolin' your broth,
Fer I ollers hev strove (at least thet 's my impression)
    To make cussed free with the rights o' the North,"
        Sez John C. Calhoun, sez he;—
            "Yes," sez Davis o' Miss.,
            "The perfection o' bliss
        Is in skinnin' thet same old coon," sez he.

"Slavery 's a thing thet depends on complexion,
    It's God's law thet fetters on black skins don't chafe;
Ef brains wuz to settle it (horrid reflection!)
    Wich of our onnable body 'd be safe?"
        Sez John C. Calhoun, sez he;—
            Sez Mister Hannegan,
            Afore he began agin,
        "Thet exception is quite oppertoon," sez he.

"Gen'nle Cass, Sir, you need n't be twitchin' your
    collar,
Your merit 's quite clear by the dut on your knees,
At the North we don't make no distinctions o' color;
    You can all take a lick at our shoes wen you please,"
      Sez John C. Calhoun, sez he;—
      Sez Mister Jarnagin,
      "They wunt hev to larn agin,
    They all on 'em know the old toon," sez he

"The slavery question aint no ways bewilderin'.
    North an' South hev one int'rest, it's plain to a glance;
No'thern men, like us patriarchs, don't sell their childrin,
    But they du sell themselves, ef they git a good
        chance,"
      Sez John C. Calhoun, sez he;—
      Sez Atherton here,
      "This is gittin' severe,
    I wish I could dive like a loon," sez he.

"It'll break up the Union, this talk about freedom,
    An' your fact'ry gals (soon ez we split) 'll make head,
An' gittin' some Miss chief or other to lead 'em,
    'll go to work raisin' promiscoous Ned,"
      Sez John C. Calhoun, sez he;—
      "Yes, the North," sez Colquitt,
      "Ef we Southerners all quit,
    Would go down like a busted ballon," sez he.

"Jest look wut is doin', wut annyky 's brewin'
    In the beautiful clime o' the olive an' vine,
All the wise aristoxy is tumblin' to ruin,
    An' the sankylots drorin' an' drinkin' their wine,"
      Sez John C. Calhoun, sez he;—
      "Yes," sez Johnson, "in France
      They're beginnin' to dance
    Beelzebub's own rigadoon," sez he.

"The South 's safe enough, it don't feel a mite skeery
    Our slaves in their darkness an' but air tu blest
Not to welcome with proud hallylugers the cry
    Wen our eagle kicks yourn from the naytional nest,"
      Sez John C. Calhoun, sez he;—
      "O," sez Westcott o' Florida,
      "Wut treason is horrider
    Then our priv'leges tryin' to proon?" sez he.

"It's 'coz they're so happy, thet, wen crazy sarpints
    Stick their nose in our bizness, we git so darned riled;
We think it 's our dooty to give pooty sharp hints,
    Thet the last crumb of Edin on airth shan't be spiled,"
      Sez John C. Calhoun, sez he;—
      "Ah," sez Dixon H. Lewis,
      "It perfectly true is
    Thet slavery 's airth's grettest boon," sez he.

> *James Russell Lowell, "The Debate in the Sennit.*
> *Sot to a Nusry Rhyme," in his* The Biglow Papers,
> *edited by Homer Wilbur, 1848. Reprint by Ticknor*
> *& Fields, 1860, pp. 63-72.*

FREDERICK DOUGLASS   (essay date 1849)

[*One of the most distinguished black writers in nineteenth-century
American literature, Douglass escaped from slavery in 1838 and
subsequently devoted his considerable rhetorical skills to the abolitionist movement. Expounding on the theme of racial equality
in stirring, invective-charged orations and newspaper editorials
in the 1840s, 50s, and 60s, he was recognized by his peers as an
outstanding speaker and the foremost black abolitionist of his era.
In the excerpt below, Douglass attacks the institution of slavery
and illustrates the fallacies of Calhoun's argument in favor of
silencing the abolitionists. This essay was first published on February 9, 1849, in the* North Star, *a weekly abolitionist newspaper
that Douglass founded.*]

Better call [slavery] *Domestic Robbery Institution.* To buy and
sell, to brand and scourge human beings with the heavy lash—
to rob them of all the just rewards of their labor—to compel
them to live in ignorance of their relations to God and man—
to blot out the institution of marriage—to herd men and women
together like the beasts of the field—to deprive them of the
means of learning to read the name of God—to destroy their
dignity as human beings—to record their names on the ledger
with horses, sheep, and swine—to feed them on a peck of corn
a week—to work them under a burning sun in the rice swamp,
cottonfield, sugar plantation, almost in a state of nudity—to
sunder families for the convenience of purchasers—to examine
men, women, and children, on the auction block, as a jockey
would examine a horse—to punish them for a word, look, or
gesture—to burn their flesh with hot irons—to tear their backs
with the poisonous claws of a living cat—to shoot, stab, and
hunt humanity with bloodhounds,—for one class of men to
have exclusive and absolute power over the bodies and souls
of another class of human beings; this, the whole of this infernal
catalogue, is comprehended in the soft and innocent term,
"domestic institution." This is the established order of things
in Carolina; and Mr. Calhoun and his "forty thieves" would
have the same order of things in California. . . . [Calhoun] goes
the length of denying, on *moral* grounds, to any and every
person out of the State where slavery exists, the right of saying,
looking, or doing anything, directly or indirectly, for the overthrow of slavery.—According to this reasoning, it would be
immoral for Northern men to refuse to wear slave-grown cotton, or to eat slave-grown rice and sugar, since by pursuing
such a course, peradventure they might decrease the value of
the slaves, and thereby indirectly affect the permanence of
slavery. We are not to write, speak, or publish anything on
the subject of human slavery, lest it serve to darken the fame
of slavery, and lessen it in the popular estimation, and thereby
indirectly destroy slavery, by exalting liberty. To do so, would
necessarily be a flagrant aggression, a violation of the rights
of a State, and subversive of its government. For what we have
no right to do directly by legislation, we have no right to do
indirectly by any other means.—This is strange logic for one
of the most powerful minds and renowned statesmen that America affords. Coming from another quarter, it would demand
no answer or comment; but from such a man, endorsed by
such a company, read so universally, and put forth so impos-
ingly, and solemnly, aiming as it does, at the very foundation
of the antislavery moment, it may be proper to spend a few
thoughts upon it.

How completely has slavery triumphed over the mind of this
strong man! It holds full, complete, and absolute control in his
mind; so much so, that seeing it, he cannot and does not desire
to see anything else than slavery. The right of speech, the
freedom of the press, the liberty of assembling, and the right
of petition, have in his judgment no rightful existence in the
Constitution of the United States.

Slavery is there; he knows it to be there; it has a right to be
there; and anything inconsistent with it is wrong, immoral, and
has no right to be there. This is evidently the state of mind
which Mr. Calhoun brings to the consideration of this subject.

To reduce his reasoning to its real point and pith, it amounts to this—that where a people have no power to legislate for the overthrow of what *they think* an evil, they have no moral right to think, or speak, or do anything else which may induce those who have legislative power to exercise it for the removal of such evil. It is on this reasoning that he builds his complaint against the Northern states, as wanting in respect to the institutions and sovereignty of the Southern states; that they have not by legislative enactment silenced the voice of free speech, and suppressed the publications of the abolitionists. If Mr. Calhoun is right in his first position, he is right in his conclusion; but he is wrong in both. We have no legislative power to dethrone the Queen of England, but have we no moral right to say that England would be better under a republican form of government? We have no legislative right or power to alter or abolish the British tariff; but have we no moral right to say that it is unequal and oppressive, and that England would be better off without than with it. We have no legislative power to abolish the union between England and Ireland; yet is it not obviously our right to speak and write in favor of the repeal of the Union? Mr. Calhoun sinks the rights of the man in the duties of the citizen, and by confounding things which are separate and distinct, perpetrates a logical fallacy. Above and before all human institutions, stands the right of sympathizing with the oppressed and denouncing the oppressors of mankind.

Slavery is not only a wrong done to the slave, but an outrage upon man—not merely a curse to the South, but to the whole Union, and has no rightful existence anywhere.—Slaveholders have no rights.

Mr. Calhoun and his "forty thieves" see and clearly comprehend the moral forces now operating against slavery, and is too honest towards his fellow companions in crime to conceal the danger which besets, or to affect to despise that danger. He is proud, haughty, and bitter, but not defiant. He sees in the systematic agitation—the tracts, pictures, papers, pamphlets, and books—societies, lectures, and petitions, the most efficient means to bring about a state of things which will force the South into emancipation. (pp. 97-9)

> Frederick Douglass, in an extract from "Friends and Adversaries," in *John C. Calhoun, edited by Margaret L. Coit, Prentice-Hall, Inc.*, 1970, pp. 97-9.

HERMAN MELVILLE (essay date 1849)

[*A novelist, short story writer, poet, and critic, Melville was one of the major American literary figures of the nineteenth century. He is best known for* Moby-Dick, *his complex metaphysical novel of the quest for the white whale. The following excerpt is drawn from Melville's novel* Mardi and a Voyage Thither, *which begins as a travel narrative but becomes a combination of philosophical allegory and satire. In this passage Melville's voyagers, among them Yoomy, Babbalanja, Mohi, and Media, visit the southern part of Vivenza (the United States), where they encounter a ruthless slave driver named Nulli, who is generally believed to represent Calhoun.*]

It was a great plain where we landed; and there, under a burning sun, hundreds of collared men were toiling in trenches filled with the taro plant—a root most flourishing in that soil. Standing grimly over these, were men unlike them; armed with long thongs, which descended upon the toilers, and made wounds. Blood and sweat mixed; and in great drops fell.

'Who eat these plants thus nourished?' cried Yoomy.

'Are these men?' asked Babbalanja.

'Which mean you?' said Mohi.

Heeding him not, Babbalanja advanced toward the foremost of those with the thongs,—one Nulli: a cadaverous, ghost-like man; with a low ridge of forehead; hair, steel-gray; and wondrous eyes:—bright, nimble, as the twin corposant balls, playing about the ends of ships' royal-yards in gales.

The sun passed under a cloud; and Nulli, darting at Babbalanja those wondrous eyes, there fell upon him a baleful glare.

'Have they souls?' he asked, pointing to the serfs.

'No,' said Nulli, 'their ancestors may have had; but their souls have been bred out of their descendants; as the instinct of scent is killed in pointers.'

Approaching one of the serfs, Media took him by the hand, and felt of it long; and looked into his eyes; and placed his ear to his side; and exclaimed, 'Surely this being has flesh that is warm; he has Oro [God] in his eye; and a heart in him that beats. I swear he is a man.'

'Is this our lord the king?' cried Mohi, starting.

'What art thou?' said Babbalanja to the serf. 'Dost ever feel in thee a sense of right and wrong? Art ever glad or sad?—They tell us thou art not a man:—speak, then, for thyself; say, whether thou beliest thy Maker.'

'Speak not of my Maker to me. Under the lash, I believe my masters, and account myself a brute; but in my dreams, bethink myself an angel. But I am bond; and my little ones;—their mother's milk is gall.'

'Just Oro!' cried Yoomy, 'do no thunders roll,—no lightnings flash in this accursed land!'

'Asylum for all Mardi's thralls!' cried Media.

'Incendiaries!' cried he with the wondrous eyes, 'come ye, firebrands, to light the flame of revolt? Know ye not, that here are many serfs, who, incited to obtain their liberty, might wreak some dreadful vengeance? Avaunt, thou king! *thou* horrified at this? Go back to Odo, and right her wrongs! These serfs are happier than thine, though thine no collars wear; more happy as they are, than if free. Are they not fed, clothed, and cared for? Thy serfs pine for food: never yet did these; who have no thoughts, no cares.'

'Thoughts and cares are life, and liberty, and immortality!' cried Babbalanja; 'and are their souls, then, blown out as candles?'

'Ranter! they are content,' cried Nulli. 'They shed no tears.'

'Frost never weeps,' said Babbalanja; 'and tears are frozen in those frigid eyes.'

'Oh fettered sons of fettered mothers, conceived and born in manacles,' cried Yoomy; 'dragging them through life; and falling with them, clanking in the grave:—oh, beings as ourselves, how my stiff arm shivers to avenge you! 'Twere absolution for the matricide, to strike one rivet from your chains. My heart outswells its home!'

'Oro! Art thou?' cried Babbalanja; 'and doth this thing exist? It shakes my little faith.' Then, turning upon Nulli, 'How can ye abide to sway this curs'd dominion?'

'Peace, fanatic! Who else may till unwholesome fields, but these? And as these beings are, so shall they remain; 'tis right and righteous! Maramma champions it!—*I* swear it! The first blow struck for them dissolves the union of Vivenza's vales. The northern tribes well know it; and know me.'

Said Media, 'Yet if—'

'No more! another word, and, king as thou art, thou shalt be dungeoned:—here, there is such a law; thou art not among the northern tribes.'

'And this is freedom!' murmured Media; 'when heaven's own voice is throttled. And were these serfs to rise, and fight for it; like dogs, they would be hunted down by her pretended sons!'

'Pray, heaven!' cried Yoomy, 'they may yet find a way to loose their bonds without one drop of blood. But hear me, Oro! were there no other way, and should their masters not relent, all honest hearts must cheer this tribe of Hamo on; though they cut their chains with blades thrice edged, and gory to the haft! 'Tis right to fight for freedom, whoever be the thrall.'

'These South savannahs may yet prove battlefields,' said Mohi, gloomily, as we retraced our steps. (pp. 247-50)

> Herman Melville, "They Visit the Extreme South of Vivenza," in his Mardi and a Voyage Thither, Vol. II, 1849. Reprint by Constable and Company Ltd., 1922, pp. 247-52.

HENRY CLAY   (lecture date 1850)

[*Clay was a prominent Kentucky congressman during the first half of the nineteenth century. In Congress, he, Calhoun, and Daniel Webster formed what became known as the "great triumverate" of orator-statesmen of their day. Throughout his political career, Clay's primary aim was to preserve the Union; thus, although he viewed slavery as a moral evil, he advocated its perpetuation because he believed that abolition would destroy the Union. Clay considered Calhoun's intellectual intensity tiresome, but praised his genius as a statesman in an obituary tribute delivered in the Senate on April 1, 1850, and excerpted below.*]

Mr. PRESIDENT: Prompted by my own feelings of profound regret, and by the intimations of some highly esteemed friends, I wish . . . to add a few words to what has been so well and so justly said . . . of the illustrious deceased.

My personal acquaintance with him, Mr. President, commenced upwards of thirty-eight years ago. We entered at the same time, together, the House of Representatives. . . . The Congress of which we thus became members was that amongst whose deliberations and acts was the declaration of war against the most powerful nation, as it respects us, in the world. During the preliminary discussions which arose in the preparation for that great event, as well as during those which took place when the resolution was finally adopted, no member displayed a more lively and patriotic sensibility to the wrongs which led to that momentous event than the deceased whose death we all now so much deplore. Ever active, ardent, able, no one was in advance of him in denouncing the foreign injustice which compelled us to appeal to arms. Of all the Congresses with which I have had any acquaintance since my entry into the service of the Federal Government, in none, in my humble opinion, has been assembled such a galaxy of eminent and able men as were in the House of Representatives of that Congress which declared the war, and in that immediately following the peace; and, amongst that splendid constellation, none shone more bright and brilliant than the star which is now set. (pp. 8-9)

During the long session at which the war was declared, we were messmates, as were other distinguished members of Congress from his own patriotic State. I was afforded, by the intercourse which resulted from that fact, as well as the subsequent intimacy and intercourse which arose between us, an opportunity to form an estimate, not merely of his public, but of his private, life. . . . Such, Mr. President, was the high estimate I formed of his transcendent talents, that if, at the end of his service in the Executive Department, under Mr. Monroe's administration, the duties of which he performed with such signal ability, he had been called to the highest office in the Government, I should have felt perfectly assured that under his auspices, the honor, the prosperity, and the glory of our country would have been safely placed.

Sir, he has gone! No more shall we witness from yonder seat the flashes of that keen and penetrating eye of his, darting through this chamber. No more shall we be thrilled by that torrent of clear, concise, compact logic, poured out from his lips, which, if it did not always carry conviction to our judgment, always commanded our great admiration. Those eyes and those lips are closed forever!

And when, Mr. President, will that great vacancy which has been created by the event to which we are now alluding, when will it be filled by an equal amount of ability, patriotism, and devotion to what he conceived to be the best interests of his country?

Sir, this is not the appropriate occasion, nor would I be the appropriate person, to attempt a delineation of his character, or the powers of his enlightened mind. I will only say, in a few words, that he possessed an elevated genius of the highest order; that in felicity of generalization of the subjects of which his mind treated, I have seen him surpassed by no one; and the charm and captivating influence of his colloquial powers have been felt by all who have conversed with him. (pp. 9-10)

[Ought] we not to profit by the contemplation of this melancholy occasion? Ought we not to draw from it the conclusion how unwise it is to indulge in the acerbity of unbridled debate? How unwise to yield ourselves to the sway of the animosities of party feeling? How wrong it is to indulge in those unhappy and hot strifes which too often exasperate our feelings and mislead our judgments in the discharge of the high and responsible duties which we are called to perform? How unbecoming, if not presumptuous, it is in us, who are the tenants of an hour in this earthly abode, to wrestle and struggle together with a violence which would not be justifiable if it were our perpetual home!

In conclusion, sir, while I beg leave to express my cordial sympathies and sentiments of the deepest condolence towards all who stand in near relation to him, I trust we shall all be instructed by the eminent virtues and merits of [Mr. Calhoun's] exalted character, and be taught by his bright example to fulfil our great public duties by the lights of our own judgment and the dictates of our own consciences, as he did, according to his honest and best comprehension of those duties, faithfully and to the last. (p. 10)

> Henry Clay, in an extract from "Proceedings in the United States Senate," in The Carolina Tribute to Calhoun, edited by J. P. Thomas, Richard L. Bryan, 1857, pp. 8-10.

DANIEL WEBSTER   (lecture date 1850)

[*Webster established himself as a leading spokesman for Northern interests during his long and distinguished career as a United*

States congressman. Famous for his oratorical skills, he challenged Calhoun's theory of states' rights in a number of eloquent speeches in the Senate. Despite their political opposition, Webster greatly admired Calhoun. As the following excerpt indicates, much of this admiration was founded on what Webster termed Calhoun's "undoubted genius" and "unspotted integrity." Webster's comments were drawn from his obituary tribute to Calhoun delivered in the Senate on April 1, 1850.]

I made my first entrance into the House of Representatives in May, 1813, and there found Mr. Calhoun. He had already been in that body for two or three years. I found him then an active and efficient member of the assembly to which he belonged, taking a decided part, and exercising a decided influence, in all its deliberations.

From that day to the day of his death, amidst all the strifes of party and politics, there has subsisted between us, always, and without interruption, a great degree of personal kindness.

Differing widely on many great questions respecting the institutions and government of the country, those differences never interrupted our personal and social intercourse. I have been present at most of the distinguished instances of the exhibition of his talents in debate. I have always heard him with pleasure, often with much instruction, not unfrequently with the highest degree of admiration.

Mr. Calhoun was calculated to be a leader in whatsoever association of political friends he was thrown. He was a man of undoubted genius and of commanding talent. All the country and the world admit that. His mind was both perceptive and vigorous. It was clear, quick, and strong. (pp. 10-11)

[The] eloquence of Mr. Calhoun, or the manner of his exhibition of his sentiments in public bodies, was part of his intellectual character. It grew out of the qualities of his mind. It was plain, strong, terse, condensed, concise; sometimes impassioned, still always severe. Rejecting ornament, not often seeking far for illustration, his power consisted in the plainness of his propositions, in the closeness of his logic, and in the earnestness and energy of his manner. These are the qualities, as I think, which have enabled him, through such a long course of years, to speak often, and yet always command attention. (p. 11)

[He] had the basis, the indispensable basis, of all high character; and that was, unspotted integrity—unimpeached honor and character. If he had aspirations, they were high, honorable, and noble. There was nothing groveling, or low, or meanly selfish, that came near the head or the heart of Mr. Calhoun. Firm in his purpose, perfectly patriotic and honest, as I am sure he was, in the principles that he espoused, and in the measures that he defended, aside from that large regard for that species of distinction that conducted him to eminent stations for the benefit of the republic, I do not believe he had a selfish motive, or selfish feeling.

However, sir, he may have differed from others of us in his political opinions, or his political principles, those principles and those opinions will now descend to posterity under the sanction of a great name. He has lived long enough, he has done enough, and he has done it so well, so successfully, so honorably, as to connect himself for all time with the records of his country. He is now a historical character. Those of us who have known him here, will find that he has left upon our minds and our hearts a strong and lasting impression of his person, his character, and his public performances, which, while we live, will never be obliterated. We shall hereafter, I

am sure, indulge in it as a grateful recollection that we have lived in his age, that we have been his contemporaries, that we have seen him, and heard him, and known him. We shall delight to speak of him to those who are rising up to fill our places. And, when the time shall come when we ourselves shall go, one after another, in succession, to our graves, we shall carry with us a deep sense of his genius and character, his honor and integrity, his amiable deportment in private life, and the purity of his exalted patriotism. (p. 12)

> *Daniel Webster, in an extract from "Proceedings in the United States Senate," in* The Carolina Tribute to Calhoun, *edited by J. P. Thomas, Richard L. Bryan, 1857, pp. 10-12.*

THE SOUTHERN LITERARY MESSENGER (essay date 1850)

[In this excerpt from an obituary notice, the anonymous critic portrays Calhoun as a political prophet whose guiding inspiration was patriotism.]

In the last agony of Jerusalem, her woes and her fate were foretold long beforehand in solemn and mysterious forebodings by the last prophet which was vouchsafed to the doomed people of God. The seer was however spared the misery of witnessing the calamities he had so long predicted. Death smote him at his post, as he went his rounds on the ramparts of the fated city; and a kind Providence snatched him away as the evil days were breaking, which it had been his destiny to foresee, and his dread mission to announce.

So died Calhoun—the warrior in his harness—the sentinel at his station—the patriot in the performance of his duty—and the single statesman of his wide country whose eyes were not blinded by ambition, interest, or the desire of applause, but were sufficiently purified from the delusions of worldly weakness, to read with prophetic understanding the signs of the heavens, and the terrible miseries of the impending night.

What his far-reaching sagacity discovered, he had the boldness and the honesty to proclaim. His last speech,—denounced, misconstrued, misapprehended at the time of its delivery,—is already a voice from beyond the tomb. At the hour of its composition it was irradiated by that instinct of inspiration, which is breathed into the soul of man by the hallowing touch of the Angel of Death. Beneath the shadow of those sombre wings, the confused and intricate jugglery of worldly passions, the dark labyrinths of political intrigue, the hollow semblances of terrestrial plausibilities,—and the curious play of conflicting interests become transparent; and, as the mists of human error are lifted from before our sight, the horizon expands, and the future is revealed in proportions more distinct than the fleeting features of the passing time. As the glory of the rising sun, before the descending revolution of the globe has brought his orb to light, gilds the summits of the lofty mountains, so even before the hand of Death has struck, the radiance and celestial wisdom of the future world rest at times upon the great minds of earth which are hastening thither. It is with this feeling that the last speech of John C. Calhoun should now be read—and then it may be potent to avert the ruin which otherwise it might have only foretold. And so, let us hope, it will be regarded by his countrymen, for thus his country may be saved by the costly oblation, as Rome was redeemed by the voluntary sacrifice of Decius.

We cannot but trust that this great and immeasurable loss may be the means of our national safety. When we see Clay and

Webster [see excerpts dated 1850], his great co-evals, and the rivals of his fame, forgetting the animosities of political warfare, and the deep differences of long party opposition, and vieing with each other in offering earnest and cordial homage to the magnificent proportions of that mighty intellect which is eclipsed forever, and to the stainless integrity of that pure heart which beats no more—we must indulge the hope that sectional jealousies and the strife of factions will be freely sacrificed as the most grateful hecatomb to the manes of the illustrious dead. The keys of a conquered city, which had been won under the auspices of the corpse of Bertrand Du Guesclin, were laid upon his coffin—the last and most precious honour to a departed hero. May a more priceless trophy—the union of a divided nation—constitute the last homage to Calhoun: then may his bereaved country have a deeper and a juster pride in her dead son, than she can have in any of her living ones.

Calhoun's race was run and well run. His task was ended,—his work done—and his brilliant career was rounded off with a symmetrical perfection which has left no deficiency behind. His Treatise on the Constitution had received the finishing touch of his hand—and will remain for our instruction, the legacy of a patriot and statesman to his countrymen, which renders all posterity the inheritors of his profound wisdom. His last speech was the full outpouring of his sagacity and love of country: it was the last word of a statesman, which left nothing further to be said or done, until the nation had profited by that solemn warning. Had he lived, his countrymen might have turned a deaf ear to its instructions—cheated themselves into a dangerous disregard of its prophetic truth—and lulled themselve into a delusive security by the imputation of petty motives to their adviser, or the still more beguiling fallacies of party opposition. Now, it is the voice of one speaking almost in the presence of his God, and dying in the service of his country. (p. 301)

Doubted and denied as it may honestly be by many, Calhoun has been for a long series of years the great and almost sole bulwark between the Union and its dissolution. He stood between the living and the dead, and for a time arrested the plague. He could have done so no longer,—and he is gone. The will remained, but the means were denied him by the angry commotion of the times. His death may induce sobriety and moderation, and thus avert the doom which he apprehended, or at least will spare him the pang of witnessing the rupture of that noble fabric to which he clung with such fond tenacity, even while advocating a still more sacred cause. (p. 302)

The moral and intellectual attributes of Mr. Calhoun consorted well with his lofty pre-eminence. To the innocence and purity of a child he added the wisdom of a consummate statesman, and the far-reaching sagacity of a prophet. His mind was vast and comprehensive, and his acute reasoning powers were exercised upon an immense array of valuable acquisitions. He was more of a political philosopher than of a politician. His acquaintance with men was perhaps limited, but his knowledge of the springs and processes of national and social development was exact and universal. The love of truth, of justice, of freedom, and of his country, constituted his ruling passions, and were accompanied by a thorough scorn of everything grovelling and base. . . . His temperament was ardent, and his whole soul was wrapped up in the cause to which his life and energies were devoted. His powers of generalization were very conspicuous yet his logic was as keen and as nicely tempered as a Damascus blade, and it was as strictly and minutely concatenated as the chain of proofs in mathematical demonstration.

But his intellect was too clear and unclouded not to shoot far beyond the range of inferior minds,—and what mind was equal to his own? The eagle may gaze with unsheltered eye on the meridian sun, but weaker eyes can rest on it only in its decline. Thus Mr. Calhoun was ever so far in advance of his age and countrymen, that he never could retain, as he never desired, a party. His political deductions possessed the prophetic character of exact science—but they were so rapid and spontaneous as to require some interpreter between him and his fellow citizens. Truth which appeared in its naked simplicity to his clear vision was not recognized without some outward garniture by others. The only adequate interpreter of his wisdom was the slow instruction and verification of time. Hence Mr. Calhoun's most profound and valuable suggestions were frequently presented at a premature and unseasonable moment, when the country was not yet prepared for them, and rejected by those who could not recognize their bearing or appositeness. It is an error which could only occur to an intellect of the highest order, but it is frequent with truly great minds, and is the last from which they can completely extricate themselves. On this principle the supposed vacillations and changes of Mr. Calhoun become intelligible as the regular processes in the orderly development of a great mind. The discovery of to-day was merely the stepping stone for the conclusions of to-morrow, which in their turn served as the scaffolding to a further and equally rapid advance. But others toiled slowly and painfully after him, and when they had reached his first position, they charged to inconsistency the still-existing and even widened discrepance which in reality was due to his own more rapid progress. (pp. 302-03)

> *"John C. Calhoun,"* in The Southern Literary Messenger, *Vol. XVI, No. 5, May, 1850, pp. 301-03.*

THE SOUTHERN LITERARY MESSENGER (essay date 1854)

[*This anonymous critic reviews a single-volume edition of the* Disquisition *and* Discourse, *commenting upon Calhoun's successful blending of fact and theory and his sagacious political opinions.*]

[Mr. Calhoun's *"A Disquisition on Government"* and *"A Discourse on the Constitution and Government of the United States"*] furnishes a worthy sequel to the former labours of its distinguished author. The last of the rich productions of his intellect it embodies and embalms the ripe experience and profound speculation of his previous life. Elaborated with all that exactness which a rigid discipline of the faculties enabled him to attain—this crowning monument of his greatness forms an ornament well fitted to surmount the peerless marble of his fame. To the admirers of Mr. Calhoun this work possesses a mournful interest from the fact that its pages glow with the last rays of his declining but still unclouded intellect. To the completion of this task was consecrated the latest inspiration of his genius, and like the traditional responses of the Sybils, the volume of its revelations is the more to be appreciated, because the oracle which gave them utterance is stamped with the seal of an eternal silence. The voice which echoed the teachings of his wisdom is hushed; but the living spirit of his genius still breathes through these pages, and weaves its spell of conviction in the mind of the reader. For the successful accomplishment of the task so faithfully executed in the work before us, no man could have pledged abilities of a higher or more peculiarly appropriate order than the great political philosopher of Carolina. Analysis was the peculiar province of his intellect. His mind was a vast crucible in which every idea was resolved into its constituent elements—subjected to the infallible test of truth, and arranged with all the accuracy of scientific investigation. To trace every stream of thought back to the fountain from which its sparkling waters sprung—to ascertain its source and trace its devious wanderings toward the great ocean of knowledge, was at once the natural impulse and the necessary law of his mental organization. To powers peculiarly adapted to his enterprize, he added as the fruits of studious thought and laborious experience, in public affairs, a knowledge of the science of Government, in its relations both abstract and concrete, which few ever possessed in an equal— none in a greater—degree.

It has been the misfortune of most eminent writers, upon the theory of Government, that they have failed to combine a knowledge of practical legislation with the spirit of speculative enquiry.... To this objection, at least, the work of Mr. Calhoun is not liable.... For thirty years he lived in contact with the institutions of which he wrote; and every revolution of the complex machinery of our federal system evolved some new principle—some hidden clue to the mystery of Government,— which, under the powerful lens of his intellect, kindled into a blaze of discovery. The opportunities for observation thus afforded are amply sufficient to relieve this *Disquisition* from the imputation of mere theorism. It forms the common altar upon which speculation and experience combine to offer votive incense to truth. (pp. 321-22)

The two works of Mr. Calhoun, immediately under our notice, are so inseparably connected both in subject-matter and in mode of treatment, as to justify us in regarding the one as the preliminary of the other—the *Disquisition* as the preface to the *Discourse on the Constitution.* The former is the demonstration of a great moral problem—the latter is the corollary which results with the accuracy of truth, with the infallibility of intuition. Both are eminently characteristic of the mind of the author. And upon this consistency between the works and their author, we apprehend will be founded the objections of those who deny the correctness of his reasoning. The charge of *abstractionism* is one from which the admirers of Mr. Calhoun have always found it their duty to defend their leader. There is a class of persons who profess to be startled by every proposition not verified by the ordinary teachings of every-day-life, who reject as false every deduction not sanctioned by the positive experience of passing events.... By such persons this volume will be rejected as abounding in theory, but barren in fact—teeming with solutions of metaphysical phenomena, but destitute of the practical wisdom of experience. To this we reply, that the nature of some subjects is such as to require the application of the strictest rules of metaphysical analysis. (pp. 323-24)

Of that sort of speculation which reasons from known facts to irresistible conclusions, which starting from the vantage-ground of established phenomena, and following the elusive thread of truth in all its mazy windings through the labyrinth of error, emerges into the cloudless daylight of discovery, this volume furnishes many striking illustrations. It is profoundly metaphysical and still eminently practical—metaphysical because the nature of his subject imposed that necessity upon its author—practical because by the crystallizing process of intense thought the whole theory of government has been compressed into a form alike accessible to all. (p. 324)

Of the elaborate train of reasoning through which the author passes to establish the federal organization of our system, in contradistinction to its *national* bearings, we speak no ordinary

Calhoun as secretary of war.

praise in pronouncing it worthy of the genius which produced and the judgment which sanctioned it. Irresistible in logic, it is faultless in style. The modifications in the constitution, suggested by Mr. Calhoun, as essential to preserve the equality of the States furnish the only points upon which we shall have occasion to dissent from his views.... To an honest zeal for the advancement of that section to whose service the best energies of his life were devoted, we attribute the fact that our author seems to have overestimated the danger to which Southern institutions are exposed. We do not deny the expediency of these alterations if the necessity upon which they are contended for, be once established. We do not challenge his reasoning, if his premises be once correctly made out. Mr. Calhoun recognized in domestic slavery the corner-stone of the wealth, the prosperity, the civilization of the South. He regarded it as the palladium of our modern Troy, and he never ceased to warn his brethren lest some cunning Diomed—some crafty Ulysses, should steal upon them and wrest it from their possession. He believed that an organized effort was aiming at its destruction. Measuring the attempt more by the fatality of its probable consequences, than by the prospect of its possible accomplishment, he sought to provide, by the aid of constitutional amendment, a shield for the protection of the South, which self-interest had already furnished from the inexhaustible armory of its peaceable defence. Slavery has nothing to fear from its enemies either secret or avowed. It is sectional in its character, but national in its relations—local in its situation, but world-wide in its influences. Its strength is not in written constitutions. Its might is not in armed force. Its power is in the manufactures which it sustains—the commerce which it supports—the industry which it employs—the sentiments which it nurtures—the civilization which it upholds. Self-advancement is the main-spring of human action. When mankind ceases to need the staples of Southern climates, the South will have ceased to need the labour which produces them. (pp. 326-27)

[Mr. Calhoun's] doctrines were misconceived. His principles were misconstrued. But it is the part of folly to censure what it does not understand. It has been the fortune of some men to live in advance of the age in which they have flourished. They are not contented to bring up the rear, or advance with the main body, in the grand march of progress. They must head the van. They must lead its columns. Such men are the videttes of science—the avant-couriers of knowledge. And it is not until the great mass of mankind reach the same elevation upon which they have stood, that the value of the information which they have transmitted is fully appreciated. . . . [Mr. Calhoun's] opinions must . . . await their meed of applause at the hands of a more distant generation. His sagacity sought to anticipate good by foreseeing evil. His eyes had been touched with the precious ointment of Oriental fable, and his expanded vision ranged beyond the narrow boundaries of the present, to the limitless horizon of the future. Posterity will do justice to his fame when experience shall have verified his teachings. . . . The day is not far distant when his country will claim, as the common treasure of a Nation, the tomb which Carolina now guards as the sacred emblem of a mother's pride. The morning of his triumph will yet succeed the dubious darkness of is partial eclipse. Until that time shall arise, those who have failed to appreciate his wisdom may profit by his example—those who cannot equal his merits may imitate his virtues—those whose bosoms do not respond to his high morality and lofty sentiment, may at least attempt to practise the precepts of the one and emulate the chivalry of the other. (pp. 329-30)

"Works of Calhoun," in The Southern Literary Messenger, *Vol. XX, No. 6, June, 1854, pp. 321-30.*

JAMES PARTON (essay date 1865)

[*During the second half of the nineteenth century, many hostile reviewers, particularly in the northern United States, viewed the Civil War as the outcome of Calhoun's plotting. The following excerpt from the Boston-based* North American Review *is representative of this position: Parton labels Calhoun a "traitor to the Union," accuses him of lying, and holds him personally responsible for instigating the war.*]

[Mr. Calhoun] has been styled the most inconsistent of our statesmen; but beneath the palpable contradictions of his speeches, there is to be noticed a deeper consistency. Whatever opinion, whatever policy, he may have advocated, he always spoke the sense of what Mr. Sumner used to call the Southern oligarchy. If *it* changed, *he* changed. If he appeared sometimes to lead it, it was by bending it in the direction in which it wanted to go. He was doubtless as sincere in this as any great special pleader is in a cause in which all his powers are enlisted. Calhoun's mind was narrow and provincial. He could not have been the citizen of a large place. As a statesman he was naturally the advocate of something special and sectional, something not the whole. (pp. 389-90)

We have the written testimony of an honorable man, still living, Commodore Charles Stewart, U.S.N., that John C. Calhoun was a conscious traitor to the Union as early as 1812. In December of that year, Captain Stewart's ship, the *Constitution*, was refitting at the Washington Navy Yard, and the Captain was boarding at Mrs. Bushby's, with Mr. Clay, Mr. Calhoun, and many other Republican members [of Congress]. Convers-

ing one evening with the new member from South Carolina, he told him that he was "puzzled" to account for the close alliance which existed between the Southern planters and the Northern Democracy.

> You [said Captain Stewart] in the South and Southwest, are decidedly the aristocratic portion of this Union; you are so in holding persons in perpetuity in slavery; you are so in every domestic quality, so in every habit in your lives, living, and actions, so in habits, customs, intercourse, and manners; you neither work with your hands, heads, nor any machinery, but live and have your living, not in accordance with the will of your Creator, but by the sweat of slavery, and yet you assume all the attributes, professions, and advantages of democracy.

Mr. Calhoun, aged thirty, replied thus to Captain Stewart, aged thirty-four:—

> I see you speak through the head of a young statesman, and from the heart of a patriot, but you lose sight of the politician and the sectional policy of the people. I admit your conclusions in respect to us Southrons. That we are essentially aristocratic, I cannot deny; but we can and do yield much to democracy. This is our sectional policy; we are from necessity thrown upon and solemnly wedded to that party, however it may occasionally clash with our feelings, for the conservation of our interests. It is through our affiliation with that party in the Middle and Western States that we hold power; but when we cease thus to control this nation through a disjointed democracy, or any material obstacle in that party which shall tend to throw us out of that rule and control, we shall then resort to the dissolution of the Union. The compromises in the Constitution, under the circumstances, were sufficient for our fathers, but, under the altered condition of our country from that period, leave to the South no resource but dissolution; for no amendments to the Constitution could be reached through a convention of the people under their three-fourths rule.

Probably all of our readers have seen this conversation in print before. But it is well for us to consider it again and again. It is the key to all the seeming inconsistencies of Mr. Calhoun's career. He came up to Congress, and took the oath to support the Constitution, secretly resolved to break up the country just as soon as the Southern planters ceased to control it for the maintenance of their peculiar interest. The reader will note, too, the distinction made by this young man, who was never youthful, between the "statesman" and the "politician," and between the "heart of a patriot" and "the sectional policy of the people."

Turning from this loathsome and despicable exposition to the Congressional career of Mr. Calhoun, we find no indication there of the latent traitor. He was merely a very active, energetic member of the Republican party; supporting the war by assiduous labors in committee, and by intense declamation. . . . In all his speeches there is not a touch of greatness. He declared that Demosthenes was his model,—an orator who was a master of all the arts, all the artifices, and all the tricks by which a mass of ignorant and turbulent hearers can be kept attentive, but who has nothing to impart to a member of Congress who honestly desires to convince his equals. Mr. Calhoun's harangues in the supposed Demosthenean style gave him, however, great reputation out of doors, while his diligence, his dignified and courteous manners, gained him warm admirers on the floor. He was a messmate of Mr. Clay at this time. Besides agreeing in politics, they were on terms of cordial personal intimacy. Henry Clay, Speaker of the House, was but five years older than Calhoun, and in everything but years much younger. Honest patriots pointed to these young men with pride and hope, congratulating each other that, though the Revolutionary statesmen were growing old and passing away, the high places of the Republic would be filled, in due time, by men worthy to succeed them.

When the [War of 1812] was over, a strange thing was to be noted in the politics of the United States: the Federal party was dead, but the Republican party had adopted its opinions. The disasters of the war had convinced almost every man of the necessity of investing the government with the power to wield the resources of the country more readily; and, accordingly, we find leading Republicans, like Judge Story, John Quincy Adams, and Mr. Clay, favoring the measures which had formerly been the special rallying-cries of the Federalists. Judge Story spoke the feeling of his party when he wrote, in 1815: "Let us extend the national authority over the whole extent of power given by the Constitution. Let us have great military and naval schools, an adequate regular army, the broad foundations laid of a permanent navy, a national bank, a national bankrupt act," etc., etc. The strict-constructionists were almost silenced in the general cry, "Let us be a Nation." In the support of *all* the measures to which this feeling gave rise, especially the national bank, internal improvements, and a protective tariff, Mr. Calhoun went as far as any man, and farther than most; for such at that time was the humor of the planters.

To the principle of a protective tariff he was peculiarly committed. It had not been his intention to take part in the debates on the Tariff Bill of 1816. On the 6th of April . . . , Mr. Samuel D. Ingham of Pennsylvania, his particular friend and political ally, came to him and said that the House had fallen into some confusion while discussing the tariff bill, and added, that, as it was "difficult to rally so large a body when once broken on a tax bill," he wished Mr. Calhoun would speak on the question in order to keep the House together. "What can I say?" replied the member from South Carolina. Mr. Ingham, however, persisted, and Mr. Calhoun addressed the House. An amendment had just been introduced to leave cotton goods unprotected, a proposition which had been urged on the ground that Congress had no authority to impose any duty except for revenue. On rising to speak, Mr. Calhoun at once, and most unequivocally, committed himself to the protective principle. He began by saying, that, *if the right to protect had not been called in question, he would not have spoken at all*. It was solely to assist in establishing *that* right that he had been induced, without previous preparation, to take part in the debate. He then proceeded to deliver an ordinary protectionist speech; without, however, entering upon the question of constitutional right. He merely dwelt upon the great benefits to be derived from affording to our infant manufactures "immediate and ample protection." That the Constitution interposed no obstacle, was assumed by him throughout. He concluded by observing, that a flourishing manufacturing interest would "bind together more closely our widely-spread republic," since "it will greatly increase our mutual dependence and intercourse, and excite an increased attention to internal improvements,—a subject every way so intimately connected with the ultimate attainment of national strength and the perfection of our political institutions." He further observed, that "the liberty and union of this country are inseparable," and that the destruction of either would involve the destruction of the other. He concluded his speech with these words: "Disunion,—this single word comprehends almost the sum of our political dangers and against it we ought to be perpetually guarded."

The time has passed for any public man to claim credit for "consistency." A person who, after forty years of public life, can truly say that he has never changed an opinion, must be either a demigod or a fool. We do not blame Mr. Calhoun for ceasing to be a protectionist and becoming a free-trader; for half the thinking world has changed sides on that question during the last thirty years. A growing mind must necessarily change its opinions. But there *is* a consistency from which no man, public or private, can ever be absolved,—the consistency of his statements with fact. In the year 1833, in his speech on the Force Bill, Mr. Calhoun referred to his tariff speech of 1816 in a manner which excludes him from the ranks of men of honor. He had the astonishing audacity to say: "I am constrained in candor to acknowledge, for I wish to disguise nothing, that the protective principle was recognized by the Act of 1816. How this was overlooked at the time, it is not in my power to say. *It escaped my observation,* which I can account for only on the ground that the principle was new, and that my attention was engaged by another important subject." The charitable reader may interpose here, and say that Mr. Calhoun may have forgotten his speech of 1816. Alas! no. He had that speech before him at the time. Vigilant opponents had unearthed it, and kindly presented a copy to the author. We do not believe that, in all the debates of the American Congress, there is another instance of flat falsehood as bad as this. It happens that the speech of 1816 and that of 1833 are both published in the same volume of the *Works of Mr. Calhoun.* . . . We advise our readers who have the time and opportunity to read both, if they wish to see how a false position necessitates a false tongue. Those who take our advice will also discover why it was that Mr. Calhoun dared to utter such an impudent falsehood: his speeches are such appallingly dull reading, that there was very little risk of a busy people's comparing the interpretation with the text. (pp. 392-96)

[Calhoun's] endowments were not great, nor of the most valuable kind; and his early education, hasty and very incomplete, was not continued by maturer study. He read rather to confirm his impressions than to correct them. It was impossible that he should ever have been wise, because he refused to admit his liability to error. Never was mental assurance more complete, and seldom less warranted by innate or acquired superiority. If his knowledge of books was slight, his opportunities of observing men were still more limited, since he passed his whole life in places as exceptional, perhaps, as any in the world,—Washington and South Carolina. From the beginning of his public career there was a canker in the heart of it; for, while his oath, as a member of Congress, to support the Constitution of the United States, was still fresh upon his lips, he declared that his attachment to the Union was conditional and subordinate. He said that the alliance between the Southern planters and Northern Democrats was a false and calculated compact, to be broken when the planters could no longer rule by it. While he resided in Washington, and acted with the Republican party in the flush of its double triumph, he appeared a respectable character, and won golden opinions from eminent men in both parties. But when he was again subjected to the narrowing and perverting influence of a residence in South Carolina, he shrunk at once to his original proportions, and became thenceforth, not the servant of his country, but the special pleader of a class and the representative of a section. And yet, with that strange judicial blindness which has ever been the doom of the defenders of wrong, he still hoped to attain the Presidency. There is scarcely any example of infatuation more remarkable than this. Here we have, lying before us at this moment, undeniable proofs, in the form of "campaign lives" and "campaign documents," that, as late as 1844 there was money spent and labor done for the purpose of placing him in nomination for the highest office.

Calhoun failed in all the leading objects of his public life, except one; but in that one his success will be memorable forever. He has left it on record . . . that his great aim, from 1835 to 1847, was to force the slavery issue on the North. "It is our duty," he wrote in 1847, "to force the issue on the North." "Had the South," he continued, "or even my own State, backed me, I would have forced the issue on the North in 1835"; and he welcomed the Wilmot Proviso in 1847, because, as he privately wrote, it would be the means of "enabling us to force the issue on the North." In this design, at length, when he had been ten years in the grave, he succeeded. Had there been no Calhoun, it is possible—nay, it is not improbable—that that issue might have been deferred till the North had so outstripped the South in accumulating all the elements of power, that the fire-eaters themselves would have shrunk from submitting the question to the arbitrament of the sword. It was Calhoun who forced the issue upon the United States, and compelled us to choose between annihilation and war. (pp. 432-34)

James Parton, "John C. Calhoun," in The North American Review, Vol. CI, No. CCIX, October, 1865, pp. 379-434.

H. VON HOLST   (essay date 1882)

[*The following excerpt is drawn from Von Holst's biography of Calhoun, which is faulted by many twentieth-century scholars for its bias against the southern United States. Von Holst challenges Calhoun's theory of states' rights, labeling it "neither more nor less than the systematization of anarchy," and argues that his defense of slavery is flawed by his blindness to the Constitution's protection of individual liberties.*]

[The] name of Calhoun already conveys a much more definite idea to the American people than that of either Webster or Clay, and . . . this difference will be steadily increased in his favor. The simple explanation of this remarkable fact is, that Calhoun is in an infinitely higher degree the representative of an *idea,* and this idea is the pivotal point on which the history of the United States has turned from 1819 to nearly the end of the first century of their existence as an independent republic. From about 1830 to the day of his death, Calhoun may be called the very impersonation of the slavery question. From the moment when he assumes this character, his figure towers far above all his contemporaries, even Jackson not excepted; while up to that time he is, in spite of his uncommonly brilliant career, only an able politician of the higher and nobler order, having many peers and even a considerable number of superiors among the statesmen of the United States. (p. 7)

The tariff of 1828 gave birth to his first great political manifesto, the so-called *South Carolina Exposition.* The document

issued by the legislature of that State does not concern us here; we have only to deal with Calhoun's original draft of it. Nor is it now of any interest whether his economical reasoning was correct or fallacious; only the political conclusions which he drew from his economical premises are of historical importance. The essential point of these economical premises is that, according to him, there is a *permanent* conflict of interest with regard to the tariff policy between the "staple States" and the rest of the Union. The reason of this is simply that the staple States are exclusively devoted to agriculture, and will forever remain purely agricultural communities, because "our soil, climate, habits, and *peculiar labor* are adapted" to this "our ancient and favorite pursuit." This was the wizard's wand which worked such an astonishing metamorphosis in the mind of Calhoun that one is tempted to believe that a new man, whom we have never met before, has stepped upon the stage. In the beginning of his career . . . [he was] praised as absolutely free from sectional prejudices; and . . . he, indeed, judged everything from a national point of view, hardly deigning to answer the objections which legal quibbles, party passion, and local interests raised against what the welfare and the honor of the "nation" demanded. But now he speaks of "our political system resting on the great principle involved in the recognized diversity of geographical interests in the community," and adopts this for the rest of his life as the basis of all his political reasoning and his whole political activity. The *Exposition* fills fifty-six printed pages, but it does not contain a single sentence bearing directly on the national interest. This point is only incidentally mentioned, with the assertion that the pretended unconstitutional usurpation of the Federal government, which has called forth the *Exposition,* seriously endangers the political morality and the liberty of the republic. The national statesman is transformed into the champion of the interests and the rights of the minority, and the reason of the change is that the minority is a geographical section with a "peculiar labor" system, which creates a "recognized diversity" of interests. His first question is no more, What ought the Federal government to do, and what has it the right to do? but, What effect has the policy of the Federal government on the staple States in their peculiar situation, and what constitutional means have they for counteracting the pernicious effects of the Federal policy? The corner-stone of the political edifice of the United States is henceforth to him no more the principle that the majority is to rule, but that the minority has the right and the power to checkmate the majority, whenever it considers the Federal laws unconstitutional; in other words, whenever different views are entertained about the powers conferred by the Constitution upon the Federal government, those of the minority were to prevail, provided it was deemed worth while to have recourse to the last "constitutional" resort.

The Articles of Confederation had been supplanted by the Constitution in order to render the Union "more perfect." If this purpose was to be fulfilled, the Union must continue to grow more perfect, for where life is there is also development. Either it was an illusion that the historical destiny of the North American continent could be fulfilled by welding it into one Union composed of many republican commonwealths, and then the Union would, sooner or later, fall to pieces, no matter what the Constitution said; or the authors of the Constitution had correctly understood the genius of the American people, and had skilfully adapted their work to the peculiar natural conditions of the country, and in that event the States would steadily go on growing together as the parts of an organic whole, no matter what this or that man, or even this or that section, might be pleased to proclaim as the correct interpretation of the constitution. Calhoun had been so well aware of this fact that a favorite argument of his in support of the policy advocated by him had been the favorable effect it would have upon the "consolidation of the Union." Now there was in the whole political dictionary no term more abhorred by him than this. The sovereignty of the States, in the fullest sense of the term, is declared to be *the* essential principle of the Union; and it is not only asserted as an incontestable right, but also claimed as an absolute political necessity in order to protect the minority against the majority. The authority quoted for this opinion is not any section of the Constitution, but the Virginia and Kentucky resolutions, with their doctrine, that the States have the right "to interpose" when the Federal government is guilty of a usurpation, because, as there is no common judge over them, they, as the parties to the compact, have to determine for themselves whether it has been violated. This theory is brought by Calhoun into the more precise formula that each State has the right to "veto" a Federal law which it deems unconstitutional. Whether such a veto is to be an injunction against the execution of the law throughout the Union, or only in the individual State, and, in the latter case, what is to become of the principle that different Federal laws cannot prevail in different parts of the Union, we do not learn from the *Exposition*. We are only told that the veto ought to be pronounced by a convention as representing the sovereignty of the State, but it is left undecided whether it might not also be done by the legislature.

Calhoun was very far from having completely killed the old national Adam in his bosom. He therefore could not entirely suppress the feeling that, if this theory were to be put into practice, it might lead after all to very strange consequences with regard to the legislative activity of the Federal government; nay, with regard to the life of the Union itself. So he hastened to show that the veto was by no means so terrible a thing as it might appear at the first glance. In adopting the Constitution the States had so far abandoned their sovereignty that three fourths of them could change the compact as they pleased. If, therefore, it was desired that the Federal government should have the contested power, it was only necessary that three fourths of the States should say so, and all the damage done would be that the exercising of the power had been postponed for a while. How was it that these penetrating eyes failed to see that the Federal legislation might thereby be turned into a bulky machine, more fatal to healthy political life than Juggernaut's car to the fanatical worshippers? But leaving this practical objection aside, how was it that he failed to see that thereby one fourth of the States would get the power to change the Constitution at will? Suppose—and the case might certainly very easily happen—that the Federal government exercises a power which has been actually granted to it by the Constitution, and that a State sees fit to veto the law, that the question, as must be the case, is submitted to all the States, and the objecting State is supported by one fourth of the whole number. Is any dialectician sharp enough to disprove the fact that, in such a case, the Constitution, though not a single letter is either added or erased, has been actually changed by one fourth of the States, though that instrument expressly requires the consent of at least three fourths to effect the slightest change? Working in defence of the peculiar interests of the slave-holders with the lever of the state sovereignty, Calhoun thus begins to subvert the foundation of the whole fabric of the Constitution.

The practical conclusion to which Calhoun came was, "that there exists a case which would justify the interposition of this State, in order to compel the general government to abandon an unconstitutional power, or to appeal to this high authority [the States] to confer it by express grant." He, however, deemed it "advisable" "to allow time for further consideration and reflection, in the hope that a returning sense of justice on the part of the majority, when they come to reflect on the wrongs which this and the other staple States have suffered, and are suffering, may repeal the obnoxious and unconstitutional acts, and thereby prevent the necessity of interposing the veto of the State."

Daniel Webster wrote on April 10, 1833, to Mr. Perry, "In December, 1828, I became thoroughly convinced that the plan of a Southern confederacy had been received with favor by a great many of the political men of the South." If this suspicion was well founded the above-quoted sentence of the *Exposition* proves that Calhoun, at all events, was not privy to such a plot. He not only had no desire to force a crisis upon the country, but he had strong hopes that it would be avoided, and he plainly stated his reasons for these hopes. He was "further induced, at this time, to recommend this course, under the hope that the great political revolution, which will displace from power on the 4th of March next those who have acquired authority by setting the will of the people at defiance, and which will bring in an eminent citizen, distinguished for his services to the country and his justice and patriotism, may be followed up, under his influence, with a complete restoration of the pure principles of our government." But it is to be noted that he meant exactly what he said, neither more nor less. He *hoped* that by the influence of Andrew Jackson the protectionists would be defeated, but he did not feel quite sure of it; and if his hopes should not be realized, he had explicitly stated what, in his opinion, ought to be done. In order to leave no doubt whatever on this point, he followed up the last-mentioned sentence with the declaration that, in thus recommending delay, he wished it "to be distinctly understood that neither doubts of the rightful power of the State nor apprehension of consequences" constituted the smallest part of his motives. (pp. 75-83)

As soon as all hope had to be given up that the protective system could be destroyed with Jackson's help in the regular parliamentary way, Calhoun resumed the contest at the point where he had left it with the *South Carolina Exposition*. His second manifesto—*Address to the People of South Carolina*, dated Fort Hill, July 26, 1831—was published in the *Pendleton Messenger*. The whole question of the relation which the States and the general government bear to each other, *i.e.*, of state sovereignty, was reargued. The key-note of his whole argument and of his whole subsequent political life is the assertion, "The great dissimilarity and, as I must add, as truth compels me to do, contrariety of interests in our country . . . are so great that they cannot be subjected to the unchecked will of a majority of the whole without defeating the great end of government, without which it is a curse,—justice." This is the real broad foundation of his doctrine that the Union could never have a safe foundation upon any other legal basis save state sovereignty, which enables the minority to defend themselves against usurpations. No new argument is adduced either on the constitutional or on the economical question, but the whole reasoning is closer and the language is more direct and bolder. The Federal government has dwindled down to a mere "agent" of the "sovereign States," and the veto power of these is termed "nullification."

Calhoun had, of course, not expected to convince his adversaries. What he wanted was to mark off the old, widely trodden road with the utmost precision, so that in future no gap could be reasoned into it, and to consolidate his own party, and to inspire it with resolution to live up to its profession of faith. The apprehension that this would be done was great enough to dampen the ardor of the protectionists when the tariff question came again before Congress. The duties were considerably reduced, but the plantation States were not satisfied either with the amount or with the manner in which the reduction was effected. South Carolina received the new tariff as a declaration that the protective system was "the settled policy of the country," and on August 28, 1832, Calhoun issued his third manifesto, determined to have the die cast without further delay. [His *Letter to Governor Hamilton on the Subject of State Interposition*] is the final and classical exposition of the theory of state sovereignty. Nothing new has ever been added to it. All the later discussions of it have but varied the expressions and amplified the argument on particular points. Thirty years later the programme laid down in it was carried out by the South piece by piece, and the justification of the Southern course was based, point by point, upon this argument.

The late champion of a *national* policy and of *consolidating* measures now takes for his starting-point the assertion that, "so far from the Constitution being the work of the American people collectively, no such political body, either now or ever, did exist." The historical review by which he tried to prove this assertion contains two seemingly slight, but in fact very important, errors. The colonies did not "by name and enumeration" declare themselves free and independent States, nor is the Constitution declared "to be *binding* between the States so ratifying," but Article VII. of the Constitution reads, "The ratification of the conventions of nine States shall be sufficient for the *establishment* of this Constitution between the States so ratifying." From these historic "facts" he draws the conclusion "that there is no direct and immediate connection between the individual citizens of a State and the general government." Strange indeed! for the authors and the advocates of the Constitution thought that the most important change effected in the political structure of the Union, by substituting the Constitution for the Articles of Confederation, was exactly the establishment of direct and immediate connections between the individual citizens and the Federal government; and not a single day passed in which a great number of citizens were not actually brought into contact with the Federal government, in the courts, in the custom-houses, in the departments, etc., without being reminded in any way whatever that they were citizens of this or that particular State. If the relation between the individual citizen and the Federal government were, in fact, exclusively through the State, then, indeed, it might have been true that "it belongs to the State as a member of the Union, in her sovereign capacity in convention, to determine definitely, as far as her citizens are concerned, the extent of the obligation which she has contracted; and if, in her opinion, the act exercising the power [in dispute] be unconstitutional, to declare it null and void, which declaration would be obligatory on her citizens." The Federal government is floating in the air without a straw of its own to rest upon, the sport of the sovereign fancies of the States. "Not a provision can be found in the Constitution authorizing the general government to exercise any control whatever over a State by force, by veto, by judicial process, or in any other form,—a most important omission, designed, and not accidental." And the actual state of the case corresponds with the right, for "it would be impossible for the general government, within the limits of the States, to execute, legally, the act nullified, while, on the other hand, the State would be able to enforce, legally and peaceably, its declaration

of nullification." Yet nullification is declared to be "the great conservative principle" of the Union.

Undoubtedly, there is method in this madness, but madness it is nevertheless; for the whole theory is neither more nor less than the systematization of anarchy. The Union is constructed upon the principle that the essence of the idea *State,* the supremacy of the will which has to act for the whole,—that is, in a free State, the government of the laws,—is by principle excluded from its structure. If there ever was an illustration of the "tragedy of Hamlet with the part of Hamlet left out," here it is. This vast republic, to which the future belonged more than to any other state of the globe, was to be a shooting star, a political monster without a supreme will, because this could be lodged nowhere with safety. The resort to force—"should folly or madness ever make the attempt"—would be utterly vain, if at all possible, for "it would be . . . a conflict of moral, not physical, force." This moral force, however, was also but a rope of sand, if a sovereign State should so will it. Even a decision by three fourths of the States would by no means be unconditionally binding upon all the members of the Union. "Should the other members undertake to grant the power nullified, and should the nature of the power be such as to defeat the object of the association or union, at least as far as the member nullifying is concerned, it would then become an abuse of power on the part of the principals, and thus present a case where secession would apply." The Union was to have laws only so long and just so far as *every* constituent member of it was pleased to submit to them. In his great political testament, the *Disquisition on Government,* Calhoun directly says, "Nothing short of a negative, absolute or in effect, on the part of the government [!] of a State can possibly protect it against the encroachments of the united government of the States, whenever [!] their powers come in conflict." And as even this might prove not to be a sufficient protection, each State was to have, in the form of the right of secession, a most absolute veto against all its co-States. What a nice checker-board the United States might become, if the exercise of this right should get to be the political fashion! Suppose the States at the mouths of the great streams, and four or five others commanding a part of their navigable waters, should secede, what a pretty picture the map of the United States would present! Why, the German *Bund* of bygone days would have had a most formidable rival. Calhoun himself would have turned with disgust and contempt from the idea of thus bridging over the craggy actualities of life with the cobwebs of an over-subtle logic, if he had conceived the possibility of his theory being ever put into practice in *this* manner. It seemed to him so plausible *only* because he was fully conscious of the fact that, if it were ever put to the test, the Union would split into *two solid geographical sections*. Never would he have stultified his intellect by this ingenious systematization of anarchy, if he could not have written,—

> Who, of any party, with the least pretension to candor, can deny that on all these points [the great questions of trade, of taxation, of disbursement and appropriation, and the nature, character, and power of the general government] so deeply important, no two distinct nations can be more opposed than this [the staple States] and the other sections?

(pp. 95-102)

In the Senate the floodgates of debate [on the slavery question] were opened by Calhoun's motion (January 7, 1836) not to receive two petitions for the abolition of slavery in the District of Columbia. (p. 123)

That the attack of the abolition petitions was not directed against slavery in the States, but merely against slavery in the District, was, though not from the legal point of view, yet as to the ultimate practical result, matter of absolute indifference. If, as all the petitions asserted, the nature of slavery made its existence in the District a national disgrace and a national sin, the same disgrace and the same sin weighed down every Southern State. Calhoun's assertion, therefore, could not be refuted, that "the petitions were in themselves a foul slander on nearly one half of the States of the Union." If the national legislature now, in any way, offered its assistance to brand the peculiar institution of one half of the constituent members of the Union, it certainly violated the spirit of the Constitution; for the Constitution, as everybody admitted, not only tacitly recognized slavery as a fact which the States exclusively had power to deal with, but moreover served in many essential respects as its direct support and protection. Calhoun was therefore unquestionably right when he said that, unless an undoubted provision of the Constitution compelled them to receive such petitions, it was their duty to reject them at the very threshold; and he proved that there was no such absolute compulsion by an undoubted constitutional provision. On the other hand, however, inasmuch as some obligations were imposed upon the whole Union with regard to slavery, the existence of slavery in some of the States was actually and legally also a concern of those States in which it did not exist. And in respect to whatever actually and legally concerned the people, they had a constitutional right to demand that their representatives should listen to their wishes and grievances presented in the form of petitions. Besides, no ingenuity could reason out of the Constitution the power of Congress over slavery in the District; for somewhere the power had to be lodged, and the legislative power of Congress over the District was expressly declared to be "*exclusive* in all cases whatsoever." To lay down the principle that Congress was in duty bound to shut its door against all anti-slavery petitions was therefore most certainly an abridgment of the right of petition. The opponents of Calhoun were, in fact, no less right than he. Not their arguments, but the facts, and the Constitution, which had been framed according to the facts, were at fault. The founders of the republic had been under the necessity of admitting slavery into the Constitution, and the inevitable consequence was that conclusions which were diametrically opposed to each other could be logically deduced from it by starting the argument *first* from the fact that slavery was an acknowledged and protected institution, which, so far as the States were concerned, was out of the pale of the Federal jurisdiction; and *then* from the no less incontestable fact that the determining principle of the Constitution was liberty, and that the spirit and the whole life of the American people fully accorded with the Constitution in this respect.

The flaw in all the reasoning of Calhoun on the slavery question was, that he took no account whatever of the latter fact. The logical consequence of this was that his constitutional theories were of a nature which rendered the acquiescence of the North in them an utter impossibility. He never became fully conscious of this fact, which rendered all his exertions to obtain absolute safety for slavery *in the Union* as vain as the pouring of water into a cask without a bottom. His reasoning on the dangers which threatened slavery in the actual Union, under the actual Constitution, was, however, not in the least affected by it. From the first he saw them with such an appalling clearness that his predictions could not but seem hallucinations of a

diseased mind so long as the people, both at the North and at the South, had not been taught by bitter experience that the conflict was irrepressible, because a compromise between antagonistic principles is *ab initio* an impossibility. From the first he saw, predicted, and proved that, unless his constitutional doctrines were accepted, slavery could not be safe in the Union, and that therefore the slave States would have to cut the ties which bound them to the North. (pp. 124-28)

On February 12, 1847, he had said in the Senate, "If I know myself, if my head was at stake, I would do my duty, be the consequences what they might." It was his solemn conviction that throughout his life he had faithfully done his duty, both to the Union and to his section, because, as he honestly believed slavery to be "a good, a positive good," he had never been able to see that it was impossible to serve at the same time the Union and his section, if his section was considered as identical with the slavocracy. In perfect good faith he had undertaken what no man could accomplish, because it was a physical and moral impossibility: antagonistic principles cannot be united into a basis on which to rest a huge political fabric. Nullification and the government of law; state supremacy and a constitutional Union, endowed with the power necessary to minister to the wants of a great people; the nationalization of slavery upon the basis of states-rightism in a federal Union, composed principally of free communities, by which slavery was considered a sin and a curse; equality of States and constitutional consolidation of geographical sections, with an artificial preponderance granted to the minority,—these were incompatibilities, and no logical ingenuity could reason them together into the formative principle of a gigantic commonwealth. The speculations of the keenest political logician the United States had ever had ended in the greatest logical monstrosity imaginable, because his reasoning started from a *contradictio in adjecto*. This he failed to see, because the mad delusion had wholly taken possession of his mind that in this age of steam and electricity, of democratic ideas and the rights of man, slavery was "the most solid foundation of liberty." More than to any other man, the South owed it to him that she succeeded for such a long time in forcing the most democratic and the most progressive commonwealth of the universe to bend its knees and do homage to the idol of this "peculiar institution;" but therefore also the largest share of the responsibility for what at last did come rests on his shoulders.

No man can write the last chapter of his own biography, in which the *Facit* of his whole life is summed up, so to say, in one word. If ever a new edition of the works of the greatest and purest of proslavery fanatics should be published, it ought to have a short appendix,—the emancipation proclamation of Abraham Lincoln. (pp. 349-51)

> *H. Von Holst, in his* John C. Calhoun, *1882. Reprint by Houghton Mifflin Company, 1899, 374 p.*

JEFFERSON DAVIS (essay date 1887)

[*Davis represented Mississippi in the United States Senate from 1847 to 1851 and served as secretary of war during Franklin Pierce's administration. He was reelected to the Senate in 1857, but resigned to become president of the Confederacy. In the following excerpt, Davis defends Calhoun against charges that he was a sectionalist and a disunionist.*]

No public man has been more misunderstood and misrepresented than Mr. Calhoun. Not unfrequently he has been described as a "hair-splitting abstractionist," a "sectionist" and

A cartoon drawn during the presidential campaign of 1832. The politicians Calhoun, Clay, Wirt, and Jackson play poker; Clay has just won the hand with his three aces.

a "disunionist." That he was eminently wise and practical, that his heart and his mind embraced the whole country, that he was ardently devoted to the Union of the constitution as our Fathers made and construed it, his official acts and published speeches clearly demonstrate. (p. 246)

He entered the House of Representatives in 1811, a period of intense excitement, of depredations upon our commerce, and upon the rights of seamen, citizens of the United States, which had aroused a just spirit of resistance. The policy of non-intercourse no longer satisfied the prouder spirits among our people; but, timidity and selfishness magnifying the danger of conflict with Great Britain, contended both in and out of Congress for further toleration of the ills we had, sooner than brave "those we knew not of." It was such a time as this that naturally brought forward men who loved their country, their *whole* country, and who would as soon fight for the commerce and sailors of New England as if they had belonged to their own State or section; and thus it was that, foremost of those who advocated defiance to Great Britain, and war with all its consequences, stood Calhoun of South Carolina and Clay of Kentucky. So ardent and effective were Calhoun's invocations as to cause a jeer to be thrown at those advocating the protection of our sailors, as "backwoodsmen who never saw a ship till convened here." Mr. Calhoun claimed that such sympathy was commendable, and said: "It constitutes our real Union, the rest is form; the wonder is, in fact, on the other side. Since it cannot be denied that American citizens are held in foreign bondage, how strange that those who boast of being neighbors and relations should be dead to all sympathy." In his speech

December 12th, 1811, he put to his opponents the searching question: "Which shall we do, abandon or defend our commercial and maritime rights and the personal liberties of our citizens employed in exercising them?" Again he answered to the excuse of those who opposed preparation for war by representing the defenseless state of the country for which the majority, not the minority, was to be held responsible, and said: "It is no less the duty of the minority than a majority to endeavor to defend the country. For that purpose we are sent here and not for that of opposition." In the same spirit of broad patriotism, he rebuked those who were pleading against the necessary expense which would attend armed opposition. "But it may be, and I believe was said, that the people will not pay taxes, because the rights violated are not worth defending; for that the defense will cost more than the gain. Sir, I enter my solemn protest. . . . There is, sir, one principle necessary to make us a great people—to produce not the form, but the real spirit of union—and that is to protect every citizen in the lawful pursuit of his business."

After the war of 1812 had been successfully ended, to which success Calhoun, in civil life, and his compatriot, Jackson, in the army, had been recognized as mainly contributing, we see him laboring with the same zeal, though under different form, for the general welfare and common defense.

On January 31st, 1816, referring to the condition and future prospects of the country, he thus spoke: "We are now called upon to determine what amount of revenue is necessary for this country in time of peace. This involves the additional question, What are the measures which the true interests of the country demand?'' Treating of the defense of the country on land, he advocated a regular draft from the body of the people in preference to recruiting an army by individual enlistment, and of the latter said: ''Uncertain, slow in its operation, and expensive, it draws from society only its worst materials, introducing into our army, of necessity, all the severities which are exercised in that of the most despotic governments. Thus composed, our armies, in a great degree, lose that enthusiasm with which citizen soldiers, conscious of liberty and fighting in defense of their country, have ever been animated.'' Then, with the same deep concern for every interest of the broad Union to which he was proud to belong, he proceeded to discuss material questions as follows: ''I shall now proceed to a point of less, but still of great importance—I mean the establishing of roads and the opening of canals through various parts of the country.'' Referring to the widely dispersed condition of our population, and the difficulty in the then condition of the country of collecting the military means at a menaced point, he said: ''The people are brave, great, and spirited, but they must be brought together in sufficient numbers, and with a certain promptitude, to enable them to act with effect. . . . Let us make great permanent roads; not like the Romans, with views of subjecting and ruling provinces, but for the more honorable purpose of defense and of connecting more closely the interests of various sections of this great country.'' This he enforced by reference to the embarrassments felt for the want of facilities in transportation during the preceding war, and then proceded to consider what encouragement could properly be given to the industry of the country. He said: ''In regard to the question, How far manufactures ought to be fostered, it is the duty of this country, as a means of defense, to encourage its domestic industry, more especially that part of it which provides the necessary materials for clothing and defense. . . . Laying the claims of manufacturers entirely out of view, on general principles, without regard to their interests, a certain encouragement should be extended at least to our woollen and cotton manufactures.'' After the war of the Revolution, it will be remembered that President Washington recommended special encouragement for the manufacture of materials requisite in time of war, and indicated the payment of bounties for the same. A like experience of the sufferings of the defenders of the country during the suspension of foreign trade suggested to both the propriety of guarding against such want in the future. Mr. Calhoun, in the same speech, called attention to the preparation which should be made for the defense of our coast and navigable rivers, and answered the argument which was opposed to the taxation which would be required, that it would impair the moral power of the country, and in that connection said: ''Let us examine the question, whether a tax laid for the defense, security, and lasting prosperity of a country is calculated to destroy its moral power, and more especially of this country. If such be the fact, indispensable as I believe these taxes to be, I would relinquish them; for of all the powers of the Government, the power of a moral kind is most to be cherished. We had better give up all our physical power than part with this. But what is moral power? The zeal of the country and the confidence it reposes in the administration of its government.''

After stating the obligation of the representatives as agents of the people, and their duty to influence their constituents to agree to whatever sacrifices were necessary for the security and prosperity of the country, he said: ''I know of no situation so responsible, if properly considered, as ours. We are charged by Providence, not only with the happiness of this great and rising people, but, in a considerable degree, with that of the human race. We have a government of a new order, perfectly distinct from all others which have preceded it—a government founded on the rights of man; resting, not on authority, not on prejudice, not on superstition, but reason. If it shall succeed, as fondly hoped by its founders, it will be the commencement of a new era in human affairs.'' To men of the present day, the full significance of the argument of Mr. Calhoun for the encouragement of the manufactures which had grown up under the necessities of the war may not be appreciated in their antisectional character; it may, therefore, be not inappropriate to say that it was before the invention of steamships and steam locomotives, and that the manufactures were almost exclusively in the Northern States, and it would have required prophetic vision to foresee their introduction into the land of Calhoun. Commerce was then conducted on the sea and in sailing vessels. A wide plain lay between the mountains of South Carolina and the sea. If the water-power at the base of the mountains had been utilized for purposes of manufacture, the transportation across the plain would have been too slow and expensive for a profitable commerce. Therefore, the agricultural products, chiefly in the country near to the sea, were transported in ships to places where the water-power was near to a harbor, and thus it will be seen that to advocate encouragement to the manufacturers was to benefit, not the people of his own section, but those far away from it, and that in this, as well as in his zealous efforts for the vindication of the rights of sailors, he rose above any considerations of sectional interest or feeling, and stood forward as the champion of his countrymen, to whatever State they might belong. I now submit it to any candid and intelligent reader whether I have not disproved the charge of sectionalism as made against Calhoun. (pp. 247-50)

In the beginning of Mr. Calhoun's career we find him the champion of the honor and independence of the United States, and subsequently advocating a policy of a tariff and internal improvements as a means of providing for the common defense. His patriotism and generosity caused him to overlook the danger which lurked beneath measures which, distorted from their real purpose, could be made to serve the aggrandizement of one section, the impoverishment of another, and taxation, not for common defense, but for the benefit of individuals and corporations. In this, as in other instances of his public career, we find evidence of the extent to which his broad patriotism, generosity, and purity engendered a confidence which never proved misplaced. When abuses, progressing in geometrical ratio, warned him of the evils which threatened the perpetuity of the Union, he labored assiduously, even unto the end of his life, to point out the danger and invoke the application of appropriate remedies. It is but justice to him to say that his ardent devotion to the Union of the Constitution was the source of whatever his friends will admit were the errors of his political life, and it is a tribute to his elevated nature that he did not anticipate all that sordid avarice and narrow selfishness would build on the small foundation which patriotic credulity had laid.

Imposts designed to provide revenue, like the costs of transportation from foreign countries, were of advantage, and served to encourage home manufactures, and in so far as the benefit thus resulted to individuals in any of the States, Mr. Calhoun did not object; but when duties were made, not to provide the means necessary for the support of government, but were discriminations intended solely for the profit of particular classes—*this* was not the scheme to which he had ever given favor; and then he invoked the Constitution as the shield of the minority to protect it against oppression. In pointing out the landmarks of the fathers, and showing how they were being obliterated, and the tendency of such crime to produce disunion, he was not expressing a thought which originated in desire, but warning those who, he hoped, would, like himself, recoil from the approach of so great a disaster, that they might, in time, retrace their steps, and, before it was too late, avert the theatrical calamity. He was too wise to ignore how many and grievous would be the consequences of disrupting the bonds which held the States together; not only the compact, but the traditions, memories, and historical glories which cemented them as a family together. To those who know him well, and remember how regardless he was of his personal safety, when, with a disease that was rapidly carrying him to the grave, he rejected all solicitation to remain quietly at home, and came, at an eventful period, to renew his labors in defense of the Constitution and the preservation of the Union, it must seem absurdly strange that currency could have been obtained for a report that he desired to destroy a confederation to which his life had been devoted, and in the annuals of which all his glories were recorded. This may, perhaps, be due to the fact that the unreflecting have confounded nullification with disunion, when, in point of fact, the idea of nullification, so far as South Carolina is concerned, was adopted as a remedy *within* the Union. The hope was, by State interposition, to induce the call of a convention of States, to which would be submitted the constitutional question of laying duties; otherwise, imposing taxes upon the whole people for the benefit of a particular class. The question to be presented was, What was the proper limit of the powers delegated by the States to the general government? All else was expressly reserved to the States or the people. The phrase "the people" necessarily meant the people of the several States, as there were no other people known to the Constitution. The language must have been intended to convey the State governments and the people of the States so far as they possessed rights and powers with which their governments had not been invested. The whole proceeding of South Carolina was on the ground that the Constitution did not authorize the general government to impose and collect duties on imports for the benefit of manufacturers, *i.e.*, a protective, not a revenue tariff. In this connection Mr. Calhoun referred to the constitutional provision for amendment, and it as in the nature of his profound intellect to believe that, if the States were assembled in convention, any imperfection which experience had proved to exist would be remedied, and additional safeguards provided to protect the people from the usurpations of government. It would be needless to inquire, in the light shed by the experience of 1860 and 1861, especially of the peace congress, whether that hope would have been realized. I am now treating of the question as it was presented to his mind and that of his associates. Thus it is evident that their remedy looked, not to a dissolution of the Union, but to the purification of its general government, the happiness and contentment of the people, and the perpetuity of their fraternal relations. No more dangerous and vicious heresy has grown up than the supposition that ours is a government made and controlled by a majority of the people of the Untied States *en masse*.

Let us now examine the odious and unfounded accusation that he was a disunionist.

To the clear understanding of the charge it is necessary, in the first place, to define the true meaning of the word "union." The history of its formation irrefutably proves that it was a confederation of Sovereign States, each acting separately and for itself alone. The States so agreeing to unite entered into a compact styled The Constitution of the United States of Amer-

ica. This constitution was declared to be binding between the States ratifying the same, and that "The ratification of the conventions of nine States shall be sufficient for the establishment of the constitution between the states so ratifying the same."—Art. VII.

The men who founded our constitutional government were too profound as statesmen and philosophers, after having achieved their independence of Great Britain, to transfer the liberties they had acquired to the control of a majority of the people, *en masse*. The most careless reading of the Constitution, and the laws enacted to carry out its provisions, will show there is not a department or officer of the Federal Government who derives power and authority from a majority of the people of the United States. The power of amending the Constitution was given to the States, not to the people collectively. From the speech of Mr. Calhoun delivered in the Senate February 15th and 16th, 1833, I make the following extract:

> To maintain the ascendency of the Constitution over the law-making majority is the great and essential point on which the success of the system must depend. Unless that ascendency can be preserved, the necessary consequence must be that the laws will supersede the Constitution; and finally, the will of the executive, by the influence of his patronage will supersede the laws; indications of which are already perceptible. This ascendency can only be preserved through the action of the States as organized bodies, having their own separate governments, and possessed of the right, under the structure of our system, of judging of the extent of their separate powers, and of interposing their authority to arrest the unauthorized enactments of the general government within their respective limits.

Additional evidence could be abundantly offered that nullification was intended to conserve, not to destroy the Union, and in the manner proposed to secure a remedy short of secession. It would be unfair to judge of the practicability of the plan by the state of the country at a subsequent date, and we must presume that it was more feasible in 1833 than it was in 1860.

In 1850, during the long and exciting debate over what was known as the compromise measures of that year, Mr. Calhoun was generally confined to his lodgings, being too ill and debilitated to occupy his seat in the Senate. In that condition he wrote the speech read for him to the Senate on March 4th, 1850. It was the effort of a dying man whose affections clung so tenaciously to the Union he had long and faithfully served, that, though unable to deliver the speech, he submitted the MSS. to the Senate. To him earthly ambition was a thing of the past, but the love of truth and justice, devotion to the cause of liberty, and hopes for the people's welfare and happiness under the Constitution, all of which could not die, sustained his sinking frame for this last supreme effort in his country's cause. (pp. 252-55)

No one has so fully and clearly expounded the Constitution, no one has so steadily invoked a strict observance of it, as the means of securing the blessings of liberty to ourselves and our posterity, for which the more perfect Union was formed. It required neither his dying assertion nor the testimony of others to exculpate him from the charge of desiring to destroy our

Constitutional Union. His whole life speaks trumpet-tongued denial. (pp. 256-57)

Jefferson Davis, "Life and Character of the Hon. John Caldwell Calhoun," in The North American Review, *Vol. CXLV, No. CCCLXX, September, 1887, pp. 246-60.*

HENRY CABOT LODGE (lecture date 1910)

[*Lodge was an American politician, historian, and author who co-edited the* North American Review *with Henry Adams from 1873 to 1876 and who later served as associate editor of the* International Review. *His remarks below are drawn from his "Speech on the Acceptance of the Statue of John C. Calhoun Delivered in the Senate of the United States March 12, 1910." In this excerpt from his address, Lodge pays tribute to Calhoun's penetrating intellect and dismisses the commonly held belief that he was an inconsistent political thinker.*]

[Mr. Calhoun] had an intellect of great strength, a keen and penetrating mind; he thought deeply and he thought clearly; he was relentless in reasoning and logic; he never retreated from a conclusion to which his reasoning led. And with all this he had the characteristic quality of his race, the "perfervidum ingenium," the intensity of conviction which burned undimmed until his heart ceased to beat. Thus endowed by nature and equipped with as good an education as could then be obtained in the United States, Mr. Calhoun entered public life at the moment when the American people were smarting under the insults and humiliations heaped upon them by France and England, and were groping about for some issue from their troubles and some vindication of the national honor and independence. Calhoun and his friends, men like Henry Clay, and like Lowndes and Cheves, from his own State, came in on the wave of popular revolt against the conditions to which the country had been brought. Wavering diplomacy, gunboats on wheels, and even embargoes, which chiefly punished our own commerce, had ceased to appeal to them. They had the great advantage of knowing what they meant to do. They were determined to resist. If necessary, they intended to fight.

They dragged their party, their reluctant President, and their divided country helplessly after them. The result was the War of 1812. With war came not only the appeal to the national spirit, which was only just waking into life, but the measures without which war cannot be carried on. The party which had opposed military and naval forces, public debts, tariffs, banks, and a strong central government now found themselves raising armies, equipping and building a navy, borrowing money, imposing high import duties, sustaining the bank, and developing in all directions the powers of the government of the United States. The doctrines of strict construction, which had been the idols of the ruling party, looked far less attractive when invoked by New England against their own policies, and the Constitution, which Jefferson set aside, as he thought, to acquire Louisiana, became most elastic in the hands of those who had sought to draw its bands so tightly that the infant nation could hardly move its limbs. Mr. Calhoun, with his mind set on the accomplishment of the great purpose of freeing the United States from foreign aggression, and thus lifting it to its rightful place among the nations of the earth, did not shrink from the conclusions to which his purpose led. His mind was too clear and too rigidly logical to palter with or seek to veil the inevitable results of the policy he supported. As he wished the end, he was too virile, too honest in his mental processes, not to wish the means to that end. The war left a legacy of

debts and bankruptcy, and in dealing with these problems it was Calhoun who reported the bill for a new Bank of the United States, who sustained the tariff of 1816, defended the policy of protection to manufactures, and advocated a comprehensive scheme of internal improvements. (pp. 170-72)

In 1825 Mr. Calhoun was elected vice-president, and was re-elected four years later. In 1832 he resigned the vice-presidency to become senator from South Carolina. His resignation, followed by his acceptance of the senatorship, marks his public separation from the policies of his earlier years and the formal devotion of his life to the cause of states rights and slavery. The real division had begun some years before he left the vice-presidency. His change of attitude culminated in his support of nullification and in his bitter quarrel with Jackson. . . . (p. 175)

I have thus referred to the change in Mr. Calhoun's position solely because of its historical significance, marking, as it does, the beginning of a new epoch in the great conflict between the contending principles of nationalism and separatism. In his own day he was accused of inconsistency, and the charge was urged and repelled with the heat usual to such disputes. Nothing, as a rule, is more futile or more utterly unimportant than efforts to prove inconsistency. It is a favorite resort in debate, and it may therefore be supposed that it is considered effective in impressing the popular mind. Historically, it is a charge which has little weight unless conditions lend it an importance which is never inherent in the mere fact itself. If no man ever changed his opinions, if no one was open to the teachings of experience, human progress would be arrested and the world would stagnate in an intellectual lethargy. . . . Mr. Calhoun defined inconsistency long before the day when the charge was brought against him with that fine precision of thought which was so characteristic of all his utterances.

He said in the House in 1814:

Men cannot go straight forward but must regard the obstacles which impede their course. Inconsistency consists in a change of conduct when there is no change of circumstances which justify it.

Tried by this accurate standard, Mr. Calhoun is as little to be criticised for his change of position as Mr. Webster for his altered attitude in regard to the system of protection. With the new conditions and new circumstances both men changed on important questions of policy, and both were justified from their respective points of view in doing so. That Mr. Calhoun went further than Mr. Webster, changing not only as to a policy, but in his views of the Constitution and the structure of government, does not in the least affect the truth of the general proposition. The very measures which he had once fostered and defended had brought into being a situation which he felt with unerring prescience portended the destruction of the fundamental principles in which he believed and of a social and economic system which he thought vital to the safety and prosperity of the people whom he represented. The national force which he had helped to strengthen, the central government which he had so powerfully aided to build up, seemed to him to have become like the creation of Frankenstein, a monster which threatened to destroy its creators and all he personally held most dear. It was inevitable that he should strive with all his strength to stay the progress of what he thought would bring ruin to the system in which he believed. Once committed to this opinion, he was incapable of finding a half-way house where he could rest in peace or a compromise which he could accept with confidence. His reason carried him to the inevitable end which his inexorable logic demanded, and to that reason and that logic he was loyal with all the loyalty of strong conviction and an honest mind. There is no need to discuss either the soundness or the validity of the opinions he held. That is a question which has long since passed before the tribunal of history. All that concerns us to-day is to recall the manner in which Calhoun carried on his long struggle of twenty-five years in behalf of principles to which he was utterly devoted. He brought to the conflict remarkable mental and moral qualities, deep conviction, an iron will, a powerful mind, an unsparing logic, and reasoning powers of the highest order. Burr said that any one who went onto paper with Alexander Hamilton was lost. Any one who admitted Mr. Calhoun's premises was lost in like fashion. Once caught in the grasp of that penetrating and relentless intellect, there was no escape. You must go with it to the end. (pp. 176-78)

We do well to place here a statue of Calhoun. I would that he could stand with none but his peers about him and not elbowed and crowded by the temporarily notorious and the illustrious obscure. His statue is here of right. He was a really great man, one of the conspicuous figures of our history. In that history he stands out clear, distinct, commanding. There is no trace of the demagogue about him. He was a bold as well as a deep thinker, and he had to the full courage of his convictions. The doctrines of socialism were as alien to him as the worship of commericalism. He "raised his mind to truths." He believed that statesmanship must move on a high plane, and he could not conceive that mere money-making and money-spending were the highest objects of ambition in the lives of men or nations.

He was the greatest man South Carolina has given to the nation. That in itself is no slight praise, for from the days of the Laurenses, the Pinckneys, and the Rutledges, from the time of Moultrie and Sumter and Marion to the present day, South Carolina has always been conspicuous in peace and war for the force, the ability, and the character of the men who have served her and given to her name its high distinction in our history. But Calhoun was much more even than this. He was one of the most remarkable men, one of the keenest minds, that American public life can show. It matters not that before the last tribunal the verdict went against him, that the extreme doctrines to which his imperious logic carried him have been banned and barred, the man remains greatly placed in our history. The unyielding courage, the splendid intellect, the long devotion to the public service, the pure unspotted private life, are all there, are all here with us now, untouched and unimpaired for after ages to admire. (pp. 184-85)

Henry Cabot Lodge, "John C. Calhoun," in his The Democracy of the Constitution and Other Addresses and Essays, *Charles Scribner's Sons, 1915, pp. 160-85.*

WILLIAM E. DODD   (essay date 1911)

[*In the following excerpt from an essay first published in 1911, Dodd takes issue with the notion that Calhoun was a disunionist.*]

It has been customary in American history-writing to treat Calhoun from 1833 to his death in 1850, as an arch-conspirator, seeking the overthrow of the government which he served and upon which he had bestowed the best years of his life. I am constrained to view him differently. Calhoun was a nationalist at heart to the day of his death and in the intimacy of private

correspondence he spoke of a severed nation "bleeding at every pore"—a state of things which he said he could not think of encouraging. What he was striving for during the last seventeen years of his life was the building of a "solid" South which should follow his teaching implicitly and which, cast into the scales of national politics, would decide all great questions in its favor. And it cannot be doubted that he expected to be elevated to the presidency as a natural result. . . . It was not his aim to break up the Union but to dominate it.

His method of uniting the people of the South was to show them that without such union the greatest interest of their section, slavery, was doomed. Calhoun sought to weld together his people on a basis of economic interest just as Clay had sought to build a "solid" North on the basis of a high tariff. . . . The South, regardless of party lines, had come to regard slavery as either a good thing or an evil which could not, and ought not, to be eradicated; Whigs vied with Democrats in asseverating their loyalty to the "peculiar institution." Slavery was uglier in outward appearance than protection, but in principle negro servitude and a protective tariff were alike—each meant the exploitation of the weaker and more ignorant classes of society by the wealthier and more intelligent. As a matter of morals there was no difference between the demand of the Western Reserve that a prohibitive tariff in favor of their wool be maintained by the federal government and that of South Carolina that negro slavery should be forever guaranteed. A high tariff on wool compelled the poor white man to give his labor to others wihtout recompense; slavery compelled the negro to work for his master without reward. (pp. 133-35)

[Calhoun] had begun, the son of a small planter, whose father had been an anti-slavery man, had become a slaveholder through no fault of his own, married a lady of the aristocratic régime in Charleston and turned his attention to national politics. He became at once an ardent nationalist, impelled onward by the sectionalism of New England, and was one of the great figures of that period of reconstruction which followed the second war with England. Compelled by the injustice and bad faith of a personal and despotic party leader, he turned his matchless genius to the invention of a doctrine which should reconcile nationality with particularism, and became at once the champion of slavery and cotton, the money interests of the South. From 1833 to 1850 he taught the South that property in negro slaves was more sacred than the rights and ideas so eloquently defended by his own great teacher, Jefferson. He died, the greatest reactionary of his time. (pp. 166-67)

William E. Dodd, "John C. Calhoun," in his Statesmen of the Old South; or, From Radicalism to Conservative Revolt, *Macmillan, 1911, pp. 91-170.*

CHARLES EDWARD MERRIAM   (essay date 1914)

[*Merriam explicates the political philosophy underlying Calhoun's pronouncements on nullification, slavery, and secession.*]

It is the purpose of this paper to examine the political theory of John C. Calhoun—the foremost of Southern jurists and the ablest expounder of Southern political theory as well as of Southern constitutional law. The views of this great authority upon the constitutional questions involved in nullification, secession, and slavery are well known; but the political theory upon which these opinions rested is, unfortunately, far less familiar, although equally essential to a proper understanding of Calhoun's position. The work in which Calhoun's ideas are best expressed is *A Disquisition on Government,* accompanied by *A Discourse on the Constitution and Government of the United States* one of the most notable American treatises on political theory that appeared during the first half of the past century. This, taken in connection with the numerous public utterances of Calhoun, affords a basis for the study of his political philosophy (p. 319)

The "social contract" theory which had long held sway in America was not accepted as a fitting foundation for the political system of Calhoun. He condemned in no uncertain terms the time-honored hypothesis of a pre-civil "state of nature" and the origin of government by means of a contract. This had been the theory of the revolutionists in the seventeenth and eighteenth centuries, and continued to be the prevailing American doctrine even in the nineteenth. In fact, this hypothesis of an original "state of nature" and the contractual character of government had been one of the leading principles of "the fathers"; the theory of contract had even been extended from individuals to the relations between the states; it was recognized in many of the state constitutions; adopted by men of all parties, aristocrats as well as democrats; and was generally accepted as the correct theory of the origin of political institutions. In the politics of Calhoun, however, there was no place for the assumptions of the *Naturrecht* philosophy, and he had no sympathy with its interpretation of the nature of government. The "state of nature" he regarded as a mere fiction, an unwarrantable hypothesis. As he says:

> Instead of being the natural state of man, it is,
> of all conceivable states, the most opposed to
> his nature, most repugnant to his feelings, and
> most incompatible with his wants. His natural
> state is the social and political.

Government is not artificial and unnatural, but perfectly natural in the sense that it is necessary to the development and perfection of human powers. Government is not a matter of choice, depending for its origin and continuance on the caprice of the individual; on the contrary, it is a primary necessity of man, and, "like breathing, it is not permitted to depend on our volition." There are, reasons Calhoun, two fundamental elements in the constitution of man: one the selfish, the other the social, instinct or tendency. Of these two, however, the stronger is the selfish tendency, and, as a consequence, there arises conflict between individuals which must be in some way controlled. The instrument by means of which this control is effected is government—a necessity arising out of the essential nature of man. *Society* is necessary to man; *government* is necessary to society. But government itself contains the germs of evil, and must in its turn be controlled or balanced. To this end is erected a constitution intended to hold in check the destructive tendencies found in government. This constitution bears the same relation to government as government does to society; as government restrains the selfish tendencies of the individual, so the constitution checks the selfish tendencies of the government. There is this difference to be noted, however, that government is of divine origin, whereas the constitution is a human device and construction. There *must* be a government; there *may* a constitution.

The organization of the constitution Calhoun regards as one of the greatest of political problems. How can the government be the members of the society? Calhoun's answer to this perennial problem is that there must be created an *organism* "by which resistance may be systematically and peaceably made on the part of the ruled, to oppression and abuse of power on the part of the rulers." This result may be effected by establishing the

responsibility of the rulers to the ruled through the exercise of the right of suffrage—the primary principle in the establishment of constitutional government. Yet this principle alone is inadequate to afford the necessary protection; "it only changes the seat of authority, without counteracting, in the least, the tendency of the government to oppression and abuse of its powers." We are still confronted by the imminent danger that the majority of the electors will prove to be tyrannical, and oppress the weaker minority as intolerably as the most irresponsible government.

Calhoun enters, therefore, on a vigorous polemic against the despotism of the majority. He asserts that the tendency of the majority is to identify itself with the whole people, and hence to assume all the rights belonging to the people. Although only a fraction, they regard themselves as the whole, and act as if the whole people; while, on the other hand, the minority is treated as if it were nothing at all. Again, Calhoun points out the probability that great political parties will arise, that their organization will become increasingly centralized, and that stricter party discipline will prevail. Offices will come to be regarded as the legitimate reward of the victorious party, while recognition of other than paritsans will be excluded. Party strife will become fiercer and fiercer as it becomes more factional, and will finally result in an appeal to force and the establishment of absolute government. The rule of the numerical majority is hence regarded by Calhoun as inevitably tending toward oppressive and absolute government.

Calhoun anticipated the development of the modern party and spoils system. The intensity of the party struggle, he said, "must lead to party organization and party caucuses and discipline; and these, to the conversion of the honors and emoluments of the government into means of rewarding partisan service, in order to secure the fidelity and increase the zeal of the members of the party." The government of the party will gradually pass from the hands of the majority into those of its leaders. As the struggle becomes more bitter "principles and policy would lose all influence in the elections; then cunning, falsehood, deception, slander, fraud and gross appeals to the appetites of the lowest and most worthless portions of the community would take the place of sound reason and wise debate."

On the floor of Congress Calhoun declared: "When it comes to be once understood that politics is a game, that those who are engaged in it but act a part, that they make this or that profession not from honest conviction or intent to fulfill it, but as the means of deluding the people and through that delusion to acquire power, when such professions are to be entirely forgotten, the people will lose all confidence in public men and they will be regarded as mere jugglers."

Nor is there any way by which this inherent tendency may be effectively restrained. It may be urged that a sufficient check is found in the power of public opinion to keep party spirit within reasonable limits. But to this Calhoun is not ready to assent. He concedes the great power of public sentiment, particularly the public sentiment of modern times in its highly developed form, but does not consider it even now as an effective barrier against the tendencies of the majority. Public opinion itself may be just as despotic as the majority party, just as radical and unreasonable, and consequently as uncertain a defender of the rights of the minority. Nor are constitutional restrictions or the separation of powers of sufficient force against the majority. All restrictions must be interpreted, all requirements carried out, by the prevailing party, and if not in accord

Calhoun in middle age.

with their tendencies will be practically made of no effect. The minority is helpless and must submit to any adjustment of constitutional balances that may commend itself to the majority.

The "tyranny of the majority" is, then, one of the fundamental propositions in the theory of Calhoun. Majority rule is always liable to abuse at the hands of a party, an interest, or a section, which interprets consitutional law, determines public opinion, arrogates to itself the right and privilege properly belonging only to the whole people.

With dramatic power Calhoun pictures the inevitable advance of majority encroachment and aggression.

Application of this principle is made in reference to a question of taxation. Under the operation of the numerical majority, says Calhoun, a party or section obtaining power may easily abuse and oppress another section found in the minority. Taxes may be levied by the majority section which fall upon the minority section; not only this, but these taxes are actually returned by the minority to the majority, virtually as bounties paid by the weaker to the stronger party. The case in point was that of the protective tariff which he considered to be levied for the benefit of the North at the expense of the South. It seemed to him, therefore, an excellent illustration of the "majority tyranny" upon which so much emphasis had been laid.

In place of the dangerous "*numerical* majority," Calhoun presents his doctrine of the "*concurrent* majority." The basis for this is found in the existence of varied and diverse interests, which under the law of the absolute or numerical majority are liable to suffer from governmental oppression. "All constitutional governments," says Calhoun, "take the sense of the community by its parts, each through its appropriate organ." On the other hand, those governments in which power is cen-

tered in an individual or a body of individuals, including the majority of all individuals, may be regarded as absolute governments. The principle upon which they rest is, in last analysis, force, in contrast to the principle of constitutional governments, which is that of compromise. Under the "concurrent" or "constitutional" majority system this principle of compromise will be made effective by giving "each interest or portion of the community a negative on the others." Without a "concurrent majority" there can be no negative; without a negative there can be no constitution. Calhoun declares that—

> It is this negative power—the power of preventing or arresting the action of the government—be it called by what term it may—veto, interposition, nullification, check, or balance of power—which, in fact, forms the constitution.

The positive power makes the *government*, but the negative power makes the *constitution*. The essence of the "concurrent majority" is, then, the veto power granted to the various separate interests. Governmental action is conditioned, not upon the consent of a *majority of individuals*, but upon that of *all interests*.

The advantages of such a system are presented with great enthusiasm. With a "concurrent majority" there will be a greater degree of attachment to the state than is otherwise possible. Attention will be attracted not so much to party as to country. Public policy will not be directed against any one interest or group, and hence there will be no violent resentment and animosities aroused, such as always arise under the rule of the absolute majority. Consequently there will result a higher development of "common devotion." Politically and morally there must follow, according to Calhoun, loftier standards of conduct under the régime of compromise than under that of force. Moreover, under this system there may be obtained a higher degree of liberty. Government will be effectually restrained from arbitrary and oppressive conduct by the veto power of the various interests, and thus political freedom will be guaranteed. In any other government, indeed, liberty can be little more than a name; the "constitutional majority" alone makes it a reality. By the same logic, civilization and progress are fostered by the system of compromise, for under it are secured liberty and harmony—two of the greatest stimulators of civilized development. On the whole, Calhoun would conclude that the "organism" known as the "concurrent" or "constitutional" majority is eminently adapted to realize the great ends of government included under the protection and perfection of society.

Two objections may be raised against the proposed system, Calhoun concedes; namely, its complexity and its ineffectiveness. To the first of these he replies that undoubtedly the simplest of all governments are absolute and that all free governments are of necessity complex in their nature. Hence this style of argument applies to the whole philosophy and practice of free governments which he does not consider it necessary to defend. The objection to the effectiveness of the proposed system is not regarded as serious. Calhoun maintains that in times of real stress the compromise principle is not hostile to the passage of necessary measures, and that any policy agreed upon is far more enthusiastically supported than if compelled by force. Obedience will be rendered, not from a selfish or sectional motive, but from a higher sense of obligation to country. An analogy to the compromise principle is discovered in the unanimity required of a jury before decisive action can be taken. As necessity leads the jurors to a unanimous decision, so the far more imperious necessities of government will lead to a compromise and agreement in the affairs of state. (pp. 319-26)

It is now evident that Calhoun's argument all leads up to the defense of a particular theory of public law in the United States. ''Concurrent'' or ''constitutional'' majority is simply the prolegomena to nullification. The interests to be consulted and given a veto power are the separate states of the union. The tyranny to be averted is the enforcement of protective tariff laws or the passage of laws unfavorably affecting slavery interests.

Upon this foundation of political theory is erected a structure of public law famous in the history of the American union. This is the doctrine of nullification as expounded by Calhoun, its most powerful advocate. The individual states of the union are to enjoy a veto on the proceedings of the general government, thus establishing the principle of action through the concurrent instead of the numerical majority. A state may reject any measure of the general government regarded as inconsistent with the terms of the constitution; may, in other words, nullify the proposed action of the federal government. If three-fourths of the states support the action of the government, the nullifying state must either yield or withdraw from the union. Thus a constitutional means of defense is possessed by each state; there is no possibility of tyrannical conduct on the part of the ''numerical majority''; and the action of the ''concurrent majority'' is assured. Nullification, in Calhoun's eyes, was not only a theory of the relation of the states to the union, but it was a theory of constitutional government in general; founded not merely in the particular process by which the United States came to be, but equally essential in the framework of any free constitution.

Calhoun does not limit the application of this principle to the field of interstate affairs in the United States. It is also recommended as a sound basis for government within the individual states. In South Carolina, for example, he points out, representation in the legislature is distributed on the basis of property, population, and territory. Representation in the senate is based on election districts, and thus gives to the southern part of the state the predominance in that body; the house is based on property and population, thus giving the northern part of the state the majority there. As the governor, the judges, and all important officers are elected by the legislature, there is established an equilibrium between the sections. ''Party organization,'' says Calhoun, ''party discipline, party proscription, and their offspring, the spoils principle, have been unknown to the state.'' The same principle and similar methods might well be introduced, he thinks, into other states and there be followed by like beneficent results. As already stated, nullification as conceived by Calhoun was not simply a theory applicable to the American Union, but a fundamental doctrine of free government. (pp. 326-27)

A further departure of Calhoun from the traditional American theory is found in his defense of slavery. He it was who formulated most clearly the doctrine which served as a justification for the subjection of the negro. Tolerated rather than approved in the early days of the republic, slavery had never been looked upon with any degree of pride. It had been regarded, not as a positive good, but as a necessary and temporary evil. The growing profitableness of slavery made it, however, economically desirable; the passionate assaults of the abolitionists upon the institution aroused a spirit of resentment against such sweeping

condemnation of a ''domestic institution,'' and finally the early feeling of toleration for slavery was transformed into an opinion that, after all, it was really a beneficent arrangement. Slavery no longer seemed to be a stumbling-block; it became the ''corner-stone of free government.'' As Calhoun said, ''the discussion over the subject has compelled us of the South to look into the nature and character of this great institution and to correct any false impressions that even we had entertained in relation to it.'' Out of this inquiry into the nature and character of slavery there came a theoretical defense of the system—a renaissance of the Aristotelian doctrine.

To construct such a theory it was, of course, desirable to overthrow certain propositions made in 1776. It has already been shown that Calhoun disposed of the theory of the social contract; we are now concerned with the attack on the theorem that ''all men are created equal.'' The assault was carried on by Calhoun in the most vigorous style. ''Taking the proposition literally,'' said he, ''there is not a word of truth in it. It begins with 'all men are born,' which is utterly untrue. Men are not born. Infants are born. They grow to be men.'' He thought that ''it is indeed difficult to explain how an opinion so destitute of all sound reason ever could have been so extensively entertained, except on the hypothesis of a state of nature,'' which he utterly rejects. Not only, reasons Calhoun, are men not equal, but their very inequality must be regarded as one of the essential conditions of the progress of civilization. There have always been, and must always be, a front rank and a rear rank in the onward march of humanity; to reverse or confound their order would check the advance of the race. The fact that individuals or races are unequal is not an argument against, but rather in favor of, social and political advancement. Calhoun asserted that ''there has never yet existed a wealthy and civilized society in which one portion of the community did not, in point of fact, live on the labor of the other.'' Menial tasks are unsuited to the nature and occupations of free citizens, and are best performed by a slave class, thus freeing the higher class from the necessity of degrading drudgery. As in the Greek states, such a democracy is less extensive, but more intensive; and in Calhoun's estimation a purer and higher type of free government results. On the whole, this relation between the higher and the lower class may be regarded ''as the most solid and durable foundation on which to rear free and stable political institutions.''

It may be objected that this is an unwarranted interference with human liberty. But to this the answer is that liberty is not a right to which all are alike entitled. On the contrary, it is ''a reward reserved for the intelligent, the patriotic, the virtuous, and deserving—and not a boon to be bestowed on a people too ignorant, degraded, and vicious to be capable either of appreciating or of enjoying it.'' Liberty may be had only by those who are fit for it; if forced on an unfit people, it leads directly to anarchy, the greatest of all curses. Liberty is not for all, and therefore to take it away from those who are unfit for its exercise is no injustice to them, but in reality the most equitable kind of treatment.

Such was the theory upon which Calhoun defended the institution of slavery. He skilfully used the early argument of Aristotle, that some men are slaves by nature; but ignored that of Montesquieu when he said that in modern times ''the demand for slavery is the demand of luxury and pleasure, and not that of love for the public welfare.''

The philosophic basis for nullification and for slavery was thus stated by Calhoun. It remains to show the theory upon which rested secession, the third in the series of propositions which he expounded with such keenness and power. The germ of the argument for secession is inherent in Calhoun's doctrine of sovereignty. Here again is a point of departure from the prevalent political theory. In the early years of the republic it had been generally held that in the United States there existed a divided sovereignty. The states were sovereign in certain matters, the national government sovereign in certain others. If any ultimate sovereign was thought of, it was "the people," as contrasted with the government. "The people," however, was a term of indefinite import, as later became evident when it was urged by one party that "the people" were the people of the several states, and by the other that "the people" were the people of the nation. So far as there was any legal sovereignty, this was held to be divided between two sets of authorities, the local and the general. (pp. 328-31)

Calhoun, however, was wholly intolerant of any theory of divided sovereignty. To him such a condition appeared logically impossible and contradictory. He reasoned that in its very nature sovereignty must be indivisible. "To divide is to destroy it"; sovereignty must be one, or it is not at all. There can be no state partly sovereign and partly non-sovereign; there can be no association composed of half-sovereign states on the one hand and a half-sovereign government on the other. The vital principle of the state, its life and spirit, cannot be sundered; it must remain one and indivisible. All compromise is rejected, and the doctrine of the indivisibility of sovereignty is presented in its clearest and most striking light.

Applying this argument to the nature of the union, Calhoun asserts that the states were originally sovereign, and that they have never yielded up their sovereignty. They could not surrender a part and retain another part, but they must either have given up all or have retained all; the states must be fully sovereign or fully subject. This was the alternative which Calhoun urged with relentless logic. Given the original sovereignty of the states, and the indivisibility of sovereignty, either the states must be sovereign communities and the United States a mere agent, or the United States must be sovereign and the states subordinate. In Calhoun's theory there was no opportunity given for a division of the field between the states and the union; such a compromise was excluded. It is true, he concedes, that the central government enjoys the right to exercise sovereign power, but it does not have the true sovereignty from which these powers are only emanations. The central government acts as a sovereign, but it is not a sovereign. It wears the robes of authority only by sufferance of the legitimate owner, the states.

To the central government there are delegated by the states certain attributes of sovereignty, such as the war power, the taxing power, the power to coin money; but these powers do not constitute sovereignty. In Calhoun's theory the attributes of sovereignty may be divided and the supreme authority itself remain unimpaired. Thus the states do not surrender the sovereignty; they merely forego the exercise of certain of its attributes, and these, moreover, are liable to recall at any moment by the state from which derived.

In Calhoun's theory, in fact, neither federal nor state *government* is supreme, for there is a determining power back of them. One must distinguish, he maintains, between the constitution-making power and the law-making power; the former alone is sovereign, and to its act is due the formation and organization of the government. The constituent power in any state concedes both to the state government and to the national government certain powers or attributes of sovereignty, but,

as it may recall the power granted to the state government, so with equal right it may recall the authority delegated to the central government. Throughout this process the sovereign power remains as undisturbed and intact as ever. The practical conclusion which he draws is, naturally, that the states may at any time rightfully assert their sovereign prerogative and withdraw from the union. (pp. 331-32)

The foregoing paragraphs have, it is hoped, made clear the political philosophy underlying the three great issues that agitated this country down to the Civil War. Nullification was based on the theory of the "concurrent" or "constitutional" majority, applied to the general government; slavery was based on the Aristotelian theory of natural and necessary individual and race inequality; secession, on the doctrine of the indivisibility of sovereignty. The clearest exposition of these doctrines was made by Calhoun, although from this we might possibly except the argument upon slavery, which was defended with great dialectical cleverness by several other writers. Of the influence of Calhoun there is no question. He was easily the first in rank among the theorists of his school; his doctrines dominated the South, and under their influence the "irrepressible conflict" was at last precipitated. (p. 336)

In conclusion, what estimate should be made of Calhoun as a political theorist? Certainly upon many points his political theories were skilfully wrought. This is notably true in regard to his repudiation of the *Naturrecht* theory of an original state of nature and a social contract antecedent to the establishment of government. His assertion of the unity and indivisibility of sovereignty is also in accord with the doctrine now generally accepted by political scientists. On these questions he reasoned with great clearness and force. From another point of view, however, his reasoning, though keen and strong, was narrow and cramped. Calhoun seemed to lack the proper historical perspective. Thus he saw that an inferior and a superior race can with difficulty coexist on the same territory on terms of entire equality, but he applied this doctrine in defense of the institution of slavery long after its death-knell had been sounded throughout the civilized world. The argument from the inequality of races could not justify the complete denial of civil and political rights to the lower race, in the nineteenth century and in the United States. Calhoun saw clearly what De Tocqueville and Bryce have pointed out; namely, the danger of party or majority despotism in a democracy, but he failed to see the impracticability under the given conditions of such a scheme as the "concurrent majority" or nullification. He perceived the difficulty involved in a divided sovereignty, but he overlooked the nationalizing influences that were at work in the United States, and hence failed to see that this very doctrine of the divisibility of sovereignty was the safeguard of states' rights, and that, if conflict were precipitated, the one and indivisible sovereignty would fall to the nation. Granting, for the sake of argument, his favorite premise that the states were originally sovereign, it did not follow socially, economically, politically that they were still so situated. Calhoun's reasoning was keen and acute, rather than broad and comprehensive. Logic seemed to overbalance the historical and social sense; his conclusions, therefore, were brilliant examples of dialectics, but ill adapted to the time and place in which he lived.

Yet, when all is considered, one must rank Calhoun as among the strongest of American political theorists in the first half of the nineteenth century. Clear in his style of expression, keen and vigorous in the use of logic, Calhoun developed a formidable body of political and constitutional theory, not easy to attack and overthrow. His influence in determining the course of Southern political thought was very great and entitles him to the first place among the theorists of his school. This is as true of his political philosophy as of his public law; for in both Calhoun's influence was predominant. (pp. 337-38)

> Charles Edward Merriam, "The Political Philosophy of John C. Calhoun," in Studies in Southern History and Politics, *Columbia University Press, 1914, pp. 319-38.*

CHRISTOPHER HOLLIS (essay date 1927)

[*In the excerpt below, the British historian Hollis defends Calhoun's position on slavery.*]

In January, 1836, two petitions were presented [in the U.S. Senate] for the abolition of slavery in the District of Columbia. There was no question that, if received, they would be overwhelmingly defeated. Yet Calhoun passionately demanded that they be not even received. Senators from the North assured him that there was no intention to touch the institution of slavery. Senators from the South assured him that, if ever slavery were touched, they would rally to his side in its defence. Neither the one class nor the other could see that there was here any justification for the refusal to receive a citizen's petition, a refusal the legality of which was very doubtful. How much better, they argued, that the petition be received and overwhelmingly defeated in order to teach to abolitionists a lesson not thus foolishly to waste their time.

Calhoun would not admit such reasoning. He rounded on his Southern colleagues, who had said that "whenever the attempt shall be made to abolish slavery they will join with me to repel it. . . . The attempt is now being made," he cried. The petition called the existence of slavery in the District of Columbia "a national disgrace and a national sin." If it was a national disgrace and a national sin in Washington, why was it not also such throughout all the Southern States? "The most unquestionable right," he said, at another time, "may be rendered doubtful, if once it be admitted to be a subject of controversy."

If we admit his purpose, Calhoun was right to go out and meet every attack upon slavery. To allow it to be spoken of as a thing only to be tolerated was the first step to its being spoken of as a thing not to be tolerated. Yet here he probably blundered. The only hope for the preservation of slavery and of Southern life lay in a rigid adherence to every letter of the Constitution. Calhoun could only expect this strictest interpretation when it suited him, if he also gave the same strictest interpretation when it did not suit him.

Calhoun was from the opening of this battle under very little doubt concerning its end. Wealth and the spirit of the age, going, as they usually do go, hand in hand, may be despised but they cannot be resisted. Yet Calhoun saw that slavery would stand no chance if the moral case against it was allowed to go by default and the South to appear as a land of heartless ogres, taking advantage of legal quibbles in order to stand upon intolerable rights. The constitutional guarantees of slavery could only be maintained if a case for it, apart from constitutional guarantees, was shown to exist.

Calhoun was willing to undertake such a task. Slavery even "in the abstract," he said, was not an evil. It was "a good—a positive good." "Many in the South," he was afterwards to admit, used to think slavery "a moral and political evil," but "that folly and delusion are gone." He based his defence of it upon two principles—one historical, one biological. On the one hand "the relation which now exists between the two races in the slave-holding States has existed for two centuries. It has grown with our growth and strengthened with our strength. It has entered into and modified all our institutions, civil and political. None other can be substituted." On the other hand, "to destroy the existing relations would be to destroy this prosperity" (of the Southern States) "and to place the two races in a state of conflict, which must end in the expulsion or extirpation of one or the other. No other can be substituted compatible with their peace and security. The difficulty is in the diversity of the races. So strongly drawn is the line between the two in consequence and so strengthened by the force of habit and education, that it is impossible for them to exist in the community, where their numbers are so nearly equal as in the slave-holding States, under any other relation than that which now exists. Social and political equality between them is impossible. No power on earth can overcome the difficulty. The causes lie too deep in the principles of our nature to be surmounted. But, without such equality, to alter the present condition of the African race, were it possible, would be but to change the form of slavery."

Only prejudice can deny that there is much force in both these arguments. It is an easy and terrible thing to destroy a society. And therefore there is always much to be said for the maintenance of any institution which happens to exist, even though it be not theoretically the best. If it must be changed, it must be changed carefully. Conservatism is never ridiculous, even if Conservatives frequently are. On the other hand, real as is the equality of man, yet when a country is inhabited by two races, approximately equal in numbers and so different as to make intermarriage between them repugnant, the society must either live in chaos or the one race must be the ruler of the other. And it is very arguable that, the more definite the arrangement of superiority and inferiority, the happier the condition of both races. Slavery is the most definite of all such arrangements.

There is very little reason to think that the negro-race has at all benefited by the abolition of slavery. The negroes, in the time of slavery, used, it is true, to look forward to a great day of freedom from captivity and found their main spiritual comfort in the Book of Exodus. It was much as the schoolboy vaguely looks forward to a fine, free life, which awaits him as soon as he is rid of the tyranny of school-rules and able to push out into the world. The reality has been found to have probably about as much, and as little, of the dream in the former case as in the latter.

I have heard negroes spontaneously appealing back to "seventy years ago"—the end of the slavery-time—as to one "when de niggers all was good," and contrasting it with the evil present "when de devil, he go up and down in Montgomery County." There is probably about as much truth in this as in the reverse picture. Certainly there were cruel slave-owners—in the West, mostly, on the Mississippi, in the country brought newly under slavery—though a witness as little favourable to the South as Mrs. Beecher Stowe admits that the worst slave-owners were often Northerners and Lowell's grotesque, "Birdofreedum Sawin," was, for what he was worth, of New England origin. But in the old slave States of the East, where the slave-owners were a special class, trained up to their responsibility, the descendants of five generations of slave-owners, where "slavery has grown with our growth and strengthened with our strength," there was too high a sense of honour among owners for much cruelty to be tolerated. As a lady once said to Calhoun, "Your plantation is a more eloquent argument for slavery than all your orations." At law the slave had no rights, but public opinion made the master not only master but also protector of his slave. To change the legal, without changing the psychological, relation between the two races would be, as Calhoun said with penetrating truth, but to "change the form of slavery." You have not to-day abolished slavery in the United States. You have merely abolished slave-owners. You have robbed the negro of his protector. Booker Washington, himself, spoke of "the immense amount of help rendered the negro during the period he was a slave." By whom is that help rendered to-day?

When Calhoun said that slavery was "the most solid foundation of liberty," he did not speak merely in the tedious and sophistical paradox of rhetoric. The negro, unable to recognise the equality of man or to think in terms other than those of master or of servant, is, if free, a menace to the general liberty and equality of society. (pp. 130-34)

> *Christopher Hollis, "John Caldwell Calhoun," in his* The American Heresy, *Sheed & Ward, 1927, pp. 99-169.*

VERNON LOUIS PARRINGTON (essay date 1927)

[*An American historian, biographer, and critic, Parrington is best known for his unfinished literary history of the United States,* Main Currents in American Thought. *Though modern scholars disagree with many of his conclusions, they view Parrington's work as a significant first attempt at fashioning an intellectual history of America based on a broad interpretive basis. In the following excerpt from* Main Currents, *Parrington examines the historical and intellectual traditions that shaped Calhoun's theory of constitutional government. Pointing out that Calhoun suggested safeguards against two potential evils of democratic government that have since become reality—consolidation in politics and despotic rule by the majority—Parrington argues that he has been unjustly overlooked by later political thinkers. Margaret L. Coit, the author of a Pulitzer Prize-winning biography of the statesman (see excerpt dated 1950), termed Parrington's remarks "a landmark in Calhoun historiography" for their emphasis on the continuing relevance of Calhoun's system for defending the rights of minorities.*]

John C. Calhoun [was] a man who set his face like flint against every northern middle-class ambition, and with his dream of a Greek democracy steered his beloved South upon the rocks. A truly notable figure was this ascetic Carolinian. In the passionate debates over slavery he daily matched powers with Webster and Clay and proved himself intellectually the greatest of the three. He is the one outstanding political thinker in a period singularly barren and uncreative. His influence was commanding. Tall, lean, eager, with no humor, no playfulness, lacking the magnetic personality of Clay and the ornate rhetoric of Webster, speaking plainly and following his logic tenaciously, this gaunt Scotch-Irishman became by virtue of intellect and character, driven by an apostolic zeal, the master political mind of the South, an uncrowned king who carried his native Carolina in his pocket like a rotten borough. Long before his death he had expanded a political philosophy into a school of thought. What he planned a hundred disciples hastened to execute. Like Jefferson he was a pervasive influence in shaping men's opinions. It was impossible to ignore him or to escape the admonitory finger that pointed at every weak and shuffling compromiser.

Whatever road one travels one comes at last upon the austere figure of Calhoun, commanding every highway of the southern mind. He subjected the philosophy of the fathers to critical analysis; pointed out wherein he conceived it to be faulty; cast aside some of its most sacred doctrines, provided another foundation for the democratic faith which he professed. And when he had finished the great work of reconstruction, the old Jeffersonianism that had satisfied the mind of Virginia was reduced to a thing of shreds and patches, acknowledged by his followers to have been a mistaken philosophy, blinded by romantic idealism and led astray by French humanitarianism. To substitute realism for idealism, to set class economics above abstract humanitarianism, was the mission to which Calhoun devoted himself. He undid for the plantation South the work of his old master. Speaking in the name of democracy, he attacked the foundations on which the democratic movement in America had rested, substituting for its libertarian and equalitarian doctrines conceptions wholly alien and antagonistic to western democracy, wholly Greek in their underlying spirit.

Calhoun's career was linked indissolubly with slavery. He was the advocate and philosopher of southern imperialism, and in defense of that imperialism he elaborated those particularist theories which prepared the way for the movement of secession. Born and bred in South Carolina, he was enveloped from infancy in the mesh of southern provincialism. Except for two years at Yale, where he graduated in the class of 1804, and eighteen months reading law in Connecticut, his life was spent between Washington and his plantation. He was in temperament a Puritan, of that Scotch-Irish strain which, scattered along the wide American frontier, greatly modified the American character and gave to the South such different leaders as Stonewall Jackson and Jefferson Davis. It was a hard, stern race—that Scotch-Irish—little responsive to humanitarian appeal; and Calhoun was harder and sterner than most. He held his emotions in strict subjection to his reason. Intent on thinking every problem through from premise to conclusion, concerned always with fundamental principles, he would have become, in an environment congenial to humanistic thought, a distinguished intellectual. His mind would have lost its rigidity and become pliable from contact with diverse streams of theory, and his speculations would have found new horizons from more generous intellectual acquisitions. But unhappily there was nothing either at Washington or in South Carolina that tended to liberalize his thinking. He had not gone to school, as Jefferson had done, to the great thinkers of Europe; he had not found an intellectual stimulus in revolutionary systems of philosophy. He dwelt all his life in the arid world of politicians. His two years at Yale may even be accounted a calamity. Timothy Dwight and Calhoun were cut out of the same cloth. The South Carolina Puritan would only be confirmed in his dogmatisms by the most dogmatic of Yankee Puritans; and in consequence his career, like Jonathan Edwards', suffered from a narrow, ingrowing intellectualism. He was a potential intellectual whose mind was unfertilized by contact with a generous social culture. (pp. 65-7)

Calhoun's contribution to political theory—a contribution that elevates him to a distinguished place among American political thinkers—was the child of necessity, and received its particularist bias from the exigencies of sectional partisanship. With the rapid expansion of the nation westward, and the consequent augmenting of a potentially hostile free-soil power, the South was doomed to become increasingly a minority voice in the councils of government; and if it were to preserve its peculiar institution it must find more adequate means of self-protection than it had enjoyed hitherto. The tendencies most to be feared, in his judgment, were the spontaneous drift towards consolidation, and an uncritical faith in numerical majorities. He was convinced that America had too thoughtlessly accepted the principle of political democracy as a sufficient safeguard against the danger of arbitrary government. Soon or late it must discover, what the South already was discovering, that numerical democracy, unrestrained by constitutional limitations on its will, is no friend to political justice. The critical test of every government is the measure of protection afforded its weakest citizen; and judged by this test a democratic state, when power has come to be centralized in few hands, may prove to be no other than a tyrant. Irresponsible in its unrestraint, the majority vote may easily outdo an Oriental despot in arbitrary rule, and the more power it wields the more ruthless will be its disregard of minority opinion. The political philosopher who proposes to formulate an ideal democratic system of government, therefore, must deal critically with this fundamental problem of political justice, for upon the solution will turn the excellence and permanence of every democracy. It was to this baffling problem that Calhoun addressed himself.

In seeking a constitutional defense for the threatened southern interests, he drew from the two great reservoirs of American constitutional theory. From the Jeffersonian Republicans he derived his familiar doctrine of states rights in opposition to the consolidating principle; from the Federalists of the Montesquieu school he drew his theory of static government, resulting from exactly balanced powers; and from the amalgamation of these diverse theories he formulated a new principle. Both schools of earlier thought, he had come to believe, had been sound in their major premises, but both had gone astray in certain important deductions. The experience of forty years, with the democracy constantly augmenting its powers, had demonstrated to Calhoun's satisfaction both the grave danger that lay in the principle of consolidation, and the insufficiency of existing checks on the Federal government. The prime mistake of the Jeffersonians, he conceived, was their belief that the democratic majority will necessarily serve the cause of political justice; and the miscalculation of the Federalists resulted from the belief that the division of powers provided in the Constitution was adequate to prevent arbitrary government. He now proposed to correct these two mistakes by providing an additional check through the simple expedient—as logical as it was efficacious, granted his premises—of recognizing the veto power of the individual commonwealth upon an act of the Federal government. Stripped of its states-rights limitation, this was in germ the principle of the referendum, modified, however, by certain suggestive provisions. (pp. 68-70)

The perennial problem of constitutional government, then, in Calhoun's philosophy, remains what it was seen to be by the Federalist followers of Montesquieu—the problem of restraining government by constitutional checks to the end that it be kept just. Existing machinery having demonstrated its inadequacy, it remained to provide more effective. Freedom Calhoun regarded as the crown jewel of civilization, hardly won, easily lost. But freedom was not to be measured by *habeas corpus* acts and similar legal restraints on tyranny; it was freedom from legal exploitation and statutory dictatorship. "The abuse of delegated power, and the tyranny of the stronger over the weaker interests, are the two dangers, and the only two to be guarded against; and if this be done effectually, liberty must be eternal. Of the two, the latter is the greater and most difficult to resist." . . . In more definite terms the problem is thus stated:

Two powers are necessary to the existence and preservation of free States: a power on the part of the ruled to prevent rulers from abusing their authority, by compelling them to be faithful to their constituents, and which is effected through the right of suffrage; and a power to compel the parts of society to be just to one another, by compelling them to consult the interest of each other—which can only be effected . . . by requiring in the concurring assent of all the great and distinct interests of the community to the measures of the Government. . . .

In elaboration of the second phase of the problem Calhoun contributed the principle on which his reputation as a political thinker must rest—the doctrine of a concurrent majority. He found his solution in an expansion of the principle of democracy—recovering the true principle, he was fond of insisting—by superimposing upon the consolidated, indiscriminate numerical majority the will of a geographical majority; or in other words, by a special form of sectional referendum. (p. 72)

[In speculating] on the possibility of achieving political justice by the machinery of representation, Calhoun was face to face with a revolutionary conception—the conception of proportional economic representation. The idea was implicit in his assumption of an existing economic sectionalism that must find adequate expression through political agencies. He had come to understand the futility of a miscellaneous numerical majority; he had only to go back to eighteenth-century philosophy and substitute economic classes for economic sectionalism, finding his social cleavages in economic groups instead of geographical divisions, to have recast the whole theory of representation. Clearly, he had made enormous strides in his thinking. He had long since put behind him the philosophy of Jefferson. He had subjected the principle of democracy to critical scrutiny. But instead of rejecting it as an unworkable hypothesis, as the Hamiltonian Federalists had done, he proposed to establish it on a sound and permanent basis. The ideal of democracy he conceived to be the noblest in the whole field of political thought, but misunderstood and misapplied as it had been in America, it had become the mother of every mischief. This betrayal of democracy he laid at the door of the Jeffersonians. They had accepted too carelessly the romantic dogmas of the French school, and had come to believe that democracy was synonymous with political equalitarianism.

It was this false notion that had debased the noble ideal, and delivered it over to the hands of the mob. To assert that men are created free and equal is to fly in the face of every biological and social fact. The first business of the true democrat, therefore, was to reëxamine the nature of democracy and strip away the false assumptions and vicious conclusions that had done it incalculable injury. The Greeks, he pointed out, understood its essential nature better than the moderns. Democracy assumes a co-partnership among equals. Its only rational foundation is good will, and it can function only through compromise. From this it follows that in a society composed of high and low, capable and weak, worthy and unworthy—as every historical society has been composed—a universal democracy is impractical. The numerous body of social incompetents will suffer one of two fates: they will be exploited by the capable minority under the guise of free labor, or they will be accepted as the wards of society and protected by the free citizens—they must inevitably become either wage slaves or bond slaves, in either case incapable of maintaining the rights of free members of the commonwealth. Democracy is possible only in a society that recognizes inequality as a law of nature, but in which the virtuous and capable enter into a voluntary co-partnership for the common good, accepting wardship of the incompetent in the interests of society. This was the Greek ideal and this ideal had created Greek civilization. (pp. 73-4)

It was the persuasive ideal of a Greek democracy in the plantation states that lay back of Calhoun's defense of slavery—a defense that thrusts into sharp relief the change of southern attitude in the decade of the thirties. The earlier Jeffersonian attitude had been fairly expressed by a Georgia representative in the debate on the Missouri question:

> Believe me, sir, I am not a panegyrist of slavery. It is an unnatural state; a dark cloud which obscures half the lustre of our free institutions! . . . Would it be fair; would it be manly; would it be generous; would it be just, to offer contumely and contempt to the unfortunate man who wears a cancer in is bosom, because he will not submit to cautery at the hazard of his existence? . . .

But with slavery put upon its defense, the southern spokesmen passed from apology to praise. From the first, Calhoun accepted the system implicitly, but now he subjected it to critical analysis in the light of his theory of a Greek democracy. Over against it he set the northern system of wage labor, and he came to the conclusion that the latter was more brutal and inhumane than the former. He was convinced that heretofore the South had made a serious mistake in apologizing for its peculiar institution, and in expecting its eventual extinction. In this matter the fathers had been wrong. No serious-minded Southerner any longer believed that slavery was on the way to natural extinction. It was spreading daily and must be permitted to spread. The hopes of southern civilization were bound up with it. The North must be brought to recognize it as a beneficent institution, necessary to a free, cultivated democracy, the only alternative to those fierce conflicts between wage and capital which already in the manufacturing states were threatening the permanence of American institutions. (pp. 75-6)

[In] the end the political philosopher turns partisan to a cause. His fruitful speculations on the theory of representation, his inquiry into the economic basis of politics, remained incomplete, the larger reaches only half explored. Espousing the ideal of democracy, he yielded to the seductions of a Greek republic. Beginning as a Jeffersonian, he ended as the philosopher of a slave aristocracy, from whose principles men like Governor McDuffie of South Carolina deduced the dictum that "the laboring population of no nation on earth are entitled to liberty, or capable of enjoying it." It was a curious dream, yet no more curious than his faith in an obsolete article in the Constitution to withstand the advance of a hostile economy. There is something almost tragic in the self-deception of this clear-minded realist in his appeal to a paper defense against economic forces. "The Constitution—no interference—no discrimination," he cried passionately in repudiating the right of Abolition petition. "These are the grounds on which the battle may be safely fought. . . . You must tell these deluded fanatics, you have no right to intermeddle in any form or shape. . . . Expediency, justice, plighted faith, and the Constitution: these, and these only, can be relied on to avert conflict." . . . (p. 77)

Lost faiths and repudiated prophets go down to a common grave. The living have little inclination to learn from the dead.

The political principles of Calhoun have had scant justice done them by later generations who incline to accept the easy opinion that the cause which triumphs is altogether the better cause. What Calhoun so greatly feared has since come about. He erected a last barrier against the progress of middle-class ideals—consolidation in politics and standardization in society; against a universal cash-register evaluation of life: and the barrier was blown to pieces by the guns of the Civil War. Historically he was the last spokesman of the great school of the eighteenth century, the intellectual descendant of John Adams. The two men were much alike in the broad principles of their political philosophy, and identical necessities brought them to identical conclusions. They agreed in the fundamental principle that property will rule by reason of its inherent power, and that political justice is attainable only by a nicely calculated system of checks and balances, which provides each important group with a defensive veto. But in the social experience on which Adams founded his doctrine, political antagonism was potential in rival classes, and justified a division of powers on the model of the British constitution. In the intervening years, however, the economic alignment had become sectional, the rise of party government had created a new problem, and the earlier division of powers seemed to demand a supplementary veto if the nice balance contemplated in the Constitution were to be maintained. This was the kernel of the states-rights doctrine which Calhoun elaborated with such skill. That he should have associated the principle with a cause that was doomed was disastrous to the just fame of Calhoun. More, it was disastrous to the vital democratic principle of decentralized powers. In championing a Greek democracy Calhoun affronted the latent idealism of America, and the harm he did to agrarian democracy was incalculable. (pp. 77-8)

> *Vernon Louis Parrington, "Winds of Political Doctrine," in his* Main Currents in American Thought, an Interpretation of American Literature from the Beginnings to 1920: The Romantic Revolution in America, 1800-1860, Vol. 2, *Harcourt Brace Jovanovich, Inc., 1927, pp. 63-93.*

HERBERT L. CURRY (essay date 1943)

[Curry examines the structure and style of Calhoun's speeches, focusing on his methods of argumentation.]

Most of Calhoun's speeches now available were presented before legislative bodies. . . . None of the Great Nullifier's speeches before the bench nor any of those presented to popular audiences have achieved fame. Only a limited number of his occasional speeches are extant, and none of his legal efforts have been preserved. A legislative occasion preceded by adequate preparation seems to have been the speaking situation which he preferred.

This preference manifests itself in the structure and style of his speeches, which follow the classical pattern of organization. The introductions are of the short, factual, reference-to-theme type which are unemotional and lack attention-getting power. The thesis statement is likely to be found in the body of the speech rather than between the introduction and the body. They are not accurately stated and are dull. The body of the speech is generally organized on a deductive logical basis, although a combination logical-topical method may be employed. The conclusions are generally of the appeal-to-emotions type, but the simple rounding-out-of-the-thought type does occur. Much

Calhoun's house at his Fort Hill plantation.

of the emotional appeal of the speech is likely to be found in the conclusion.

Almost every known logical device may be found in Calhoun's speeches. He consistently employed causal reasoning and showed a fondness for the cause-to-effect form. Enthymemes, particularly of the hypothetical and residual disjunctive type, were used frequently. Authority, specific instance, and analogy were employed upon occasion. Seldom is an argument supported by only one device; rather several are used.

Reductio ad absurdum, turning the tables, and the dilemma were his favorite forms of refutation, but counterargument was used frequently. These weapons may seem ponderous, but Calhoun was a constructive builder rather than a destroyer of arguments. A keen appreciation of both the proper position and the space allowed for refutation is evident. The technique was to state an opponent's argument, then to state its refutation. Neither the effect of the refutation nor its relation with the argument as a whole is considered, with the result that the refutatory technique does not compare with that used in constructive argument.

The pathetic proof is blunt, heavy, and abstract. Bald references to duty, honor, justice, right, truth, and fairness are frequently used and indicate that the classical scholars had considerable influence on Calhoun's technique. These proofs

are poorly used; they do not even approach the facility which characterized his use of logical proof.

The same type of criticism applies to Calhoun's use of ethical proof. It is formal, stilted, obvious, and limited, in general, to the process of attempting to establish his character, intelligence, capacity, and vision. Severe criticism may be leveled at an opponent's argument, but rarely is the personality of an opponent subject to attack. His opponents were assumed to be gentlemen, in which class he placed himself, and among such persons name calling was deprecated.

The formal elements of unity, emphasis, and coherence are rigidly observed. A precise definition of position, a nice partition of his subject matter, a thorough analysis, and close adherence to his issues characterized the Carolinian's speeches. Issues and subissues are frequently stated as questions, answers are made, and summaries of the points given. This use of internal summaries is supplemented by external summaries. The whole process from analysis to final summary does produce rigidity, but there are few byways traversed in the process of making a speech.

Calhoun's speeches are a study in the use of language. Short, easily understood words thrown into simple, compound, and complex sentences make for ease of understanding. Figurative language, illustration, analogy, or words used merely for effect are rare. In this respect he offers a sharp contrast to the florid style which Webster displayed, particularly in his occasional addresses, and to the vituperative style which Benton employed.

The total effect of Calhoun's methods was to produce speeches characterized by dry intellectuality. He seems to have been more interested in displaying intellectual processes than in moving men to accept his point of view.

For more than a quarter of a century the Great Nullifier was ranked as one of the nation's finest speakers. Yet he rarely achieved the ends which he sought, particularly when he spoke before the Senate. It must be admitted that as a good politician he probably asked for more than he expected to receive; his relative failure to achieve all that he demanded may have been more apparent than real. One can think of but few measures which resulted as Calhoun desired; he was defeated on nullification (the South claimed a victory on this one, since Clay's compromise reduced tariff duties), the banks, the Mexican War, internal improvements, abolition petitions, and the slavery issue. International affairs were settled as he advocated: war with England in 1812, a compromise agreement on the Oregon question, annexation of Texas, and a defeat of the Yucatan proposal.

His defeats, however, must not be charged against his speaking. In the nullification controversy he faced an embittered and hostile audience which because of personal and political affiliations could never have voted to support him. The Senate in 1850 was not so preponderantly in opposition as had been the case in 1833, but a strong majority was opposed—so opposed that the mighty Webster could do nothing with it.

Calhoun's function as a speaker was to present and keep alive a minority viewpoint. That he succeeded is indicated by the prominence which he achieved as a speaker and as a politician. The causes which he favored were doomed to defeat by the catastrophic changes produced by the impact of the Industrial Revolution upon the social, economic, and political patterns of American culture. (pp. 659-61)

> Herbert L. Curry, "John C. Calhoun," in A History and Criticism of American Public Address, Vol. II, edited by William Norwood Brigance, McGraw-Hill, 1943, pp. 639-64.

PETER F. DRUCKER (essay date 1948)

[*A German-born American economist, educator, and journalist, Drucker has written extensively on political issues and on the problems of industrial management. In the excerpt below, he maintains that Calhoun's "rule of the concurrent majority" is the foundation of America's pluralistic political system. After examining the practical operation of Calhoun's theory in American government, Drucker delineates the strengths and weaknesses of political pluralism.*]

The American party system has been under attack almost continuously since it took definite form in the time of Andrew Jackson. The criticism has always been directed at the same point: America's political pluralism, the distinctively American organization of government by compromise of interests, pressure groups and sections. And the aim of the critics from Thaddeus Stevens to Henry Wallace has always been to substitute for this "unprincipled" pluralism a government based as in Europe on "ideologies" and "principles." But never before—at least not since the Civil War years—has the crisis

been as acute as in this last decade; for the political problems which dominate our national life today: foreign policy and industrial policy, are precisely the problems which interest and pressure-group compromise is least equipped to handle....

Yet, there is almost no understanding of the problem—precisely because there is so little understanding of the basic principles of American pluralism. Of course, every politician in this country must be able instinctively to work in terms of sectional and interest compromise; and the voter takes it for granted. But there is practically no awareness of the fact that organization on the basis of sectional and interest compromise is both the distinctly American form of political organization and the cornerstone of practically all major political institutions of the modern U.S.A. (p. 412)

To find an adequate analysis of the principle of government by sectional and interest compromise we have to go back almost a hundred years to John C. Calhoun and to his two political treatises [*Disquisition* and *Discourse*].... Absurd, you will say, for it is practically an axiom of American history that Calhoun's political theories, subtle, even profound though they may have been, were reduced to absurdity and irrelevance by the Civil War. Yet, this "axiom" is nothing but a partisan vote of the Reconstruction Period. Of course, the specific occasion for which Calhoun formulated his theories, the Slavery issue, has been decided; and for the constitutional veto power of the states over national legislation, by means of which Calhoun proposed to formalize the principle of sectional and interest compromise, was substituted in actual practice the much more powerful and much more elastic but extra-constitutional and extra-legal veto power of sections, interests and pressure groups in Congress and within the parties. But *his basic principle itself: that every major interest in the country, whether regional, economic or religious, is to possess a veto power on political decisions directly affecting it,* the principle which Calhoun called—rather obscurely—"*the rule of concurrent majority,*" has become the organizing principle of American politics. And it is precisely this principle that is under fire today.

What makes Calhoun so important as the major key to the understanding of American politics, is not just that he saw the importance in American political life of sectional and interest pluralism; other major analysts of our government, Tocqueville, for instance, or Bryce or Wilson, saw that too. But Calhoun, perhaps alone, saw in it more than a rule of expediency, imposed by the country's size and justifiable by results, if at all. He saw in it a basic principle of free government.

> Without this (*the rule of concurrent majority based on interests rather than on principles*) there can be ... no constitution. The assertion is true in reference to all constitutional governments, be their forms what they may: It is, indeed, the negative power which makes the constitution,—and the positive which makes the government. The one is the power of acting;—and the other the power of preventing or arresting action. The two, combined, make constitutional government.
>
> ... it follows, necessarily, that where the numerical majority has the sole control of the government, there can be no constitution ... and hence, the numerical, unmixed with the

concurrent majority, necessarily forms, in all cases, absolute government.

> . . . The principle by which they (governments) are upheld and preserved . . . in constitutional governments is *compromise;*—and in absolute governments is *force.* . . .

(pp. 413-14)

[However] much the American people may complain in words about the "unprincipled" nature of their political system, by their actions they have always shown that they too believe that without sectional and interest compromises there can be no constitutional government. If this is not grasped, American government and politics must appear not only as cheap to the point of venality, they must appear as utterly irrational and unpredictable.

Sectional and interest pluralism has molded all American political institutions. It is the method—entirely unofficial and extra-constitutional—through which the organs of government are made to function, through which leaders are selected, policies developed, men and groups organized for the conquest and management of political power. In particular it is the explanation for the most distinctive features of the American political system: the way in which the Congress operates, the way in which major government departments are set up and run, the qualifications for "eligibility" as a candidate for elective office, and the American party structure.

To all foreign observers of Congress two things have always remained mysterious: the distinction between the official party label and the "blocs" which cut across party lines; and the power and function of the Congressional Committees. And most Americans though less amazed by the phenomena are equally baffled.

The "blocs"—the "Farm Bloc," the "Friends of Labor in the Senate," the "Business Groups," etc.—are simply the expression of the basic tenet of sectional and interest pluralism that major interests have a veto power on legislation directly affecting them. For this reason they must cut across party lines—that is, lines expressing the numerical rather than the "concurrent" majority. And because these blocs have (a) only a negative veto, and (b) only on measures directly affecting them, they cannot in themselves be permanent groupings replacing the parties. They must be loosely organized; and one and the same member of Congress must at different times vote with different blocs. The strength of the "blocs" does not rest on their numbers but on the basic mores of American politics which grant every major interest group a limited self-determination—as expressed graphically in the near-sanctity of a senatorial "filibuster." (pp. 414-15)

The principle of sectional and interest compromise leads directly to the congressional committee system—a system to which there is no parallel anywhere in the world. Congress, especially the House, has largely abdicated to its committees because only in the quiet and secrecy of a committee room can sectional compromise be worked out. The discussion on the floor as well as the recorded vote is far too public and therefore largely for the folks back home. But a committee's business is to arrive at an agreement between all major sectional interests affected; which explains the importance of getting a bill before the "right" committee. In any but an American legislature the position of each member, once a bill is introduced, is fixed by the stand of his party which, in turn, is decided on grounds that have little to do with the measure itself but are rather

dictated by the balance of power within the government and by party programs. Hence it makes usually little difference which committee discusses a bill or whether it goes before a committee at all. In the United States, however, a bill's assignment to a specific committee decides which interest groups are to be recognized as affected by the measure and therefore entitled to a part in writing it ("who is to have standing before the committee"), for each committee represents a specific constellation of interests. In many cases this first decision therefore decides the fate of a proposed measure, especially as the compromise worked out by the committee is generally accepted once it reaches the floor, especially in the House.

It is not only Congress but every individual member of Congress himself who is expected to operate according to the "rule of concurrent majority." He is considered both a representative of the American people and responsible to the national interest and a delegate of his constitutents and responsible to their particular interests. Wherever the immediate interests of his constituents are not in question, he is to be a statesman; wherever their conscience or their pocketbooks are affected, he is to be a business agent. This is in sharp contrast to the theory on which any parliamentary government is based—a theory developed almost two hundred years ago in Edmund Burke's famous speech to the voters at Bristol—according to which a member of Parliament represents the commonweal rather than his constituents. (pp. 415-16)

The principle of sectional and interest pluralism also explains why this is the only nation where Cabinet members are charged by law with the representation of special interests—labor, agriculture, commerce. In every other country an agency of the government—any agency of the government—is solemnly sworn to guard the public interests against "the interests." In this country the concept of a government department as the representative of a special interest group is carried down to smaller agencies and even to divisions and branches of a department. (pp. 416-17)

But the central institution based on sectional pluralism is the American party. Completely extra-constitutional, the wonder and the despair of every foreign observer who cannot fit it into any of his concepts of political life, the American party (rather than the states) has become the instrument to realize Calhoun's "rule of the concurrent majority."

In stark contrast to the parties of Europe, the American party has no program and no purpose except to organize divergent groups for the common pursuit and conquest of power. Its unity is one of action, not of beliefs. Its only rule is to attract—or at least not to repel—the largest possible number of groups. It must, by definition, be acceptable equally to the right and the left, the rich and the poor, the farmer and the worker, the Protestant and the Catholic, the native and the foreign-born. (p. 417)

As soon as it cannot appeal at least to a minority in every major group (as soon, in other words, as it provokes the veto of one section, interest or class) a party is in danger of disintegration. Whenever a party loses its ability to fuse sectional pressures and class interests into one national policy—both parties just before the Civil War, the Republican Party before its reorganization by Mark Hanna, both parties again today—the party system (and with it the American political system altogether) is in crisis.

It is, consequently, not that Calhoun was repudiated by the Civil War which is the key to the understanding of American politics but that he has become triumphant since.

The apparent victors, the "Radical Republicans," Thaddeus Stevens, Seward, Chief Justice Chase, were out to destroy not only slavery and states rights but the "rule of the concurrent majority" itself. And the early Republican Party—before the Civil War and in the Reconstruction Period—was indeed determined to substitute principle for interest as the lodestar of American political life. But in the end it was the political thought of convinced pluralists such as Abraham Lincoln and Andrew Johnson rather than the ideologies of the Free Soilers and Abolitionists which molded the Republican Party. And ever since, the major development of American politics have been based on Calhoun's principle. To this the United States owes the strength as well as the weaknesses of its political system.

The weaknesses of sectional and interest compromise are far more obvious than its virtues. . . . (pp. 417-18)

There is, first of all, the inability of a political system based on the "rule of the concurrent majority" to resolve conflicts of principles. All a pluralist system can do is to deny that "ideological" conflicts (as they are called nowadays) do exist. Those conflicts, a pluralist must assert are fundamentally either struggles for naked power or friction between interest groups which could be solved if only the quarreling parties sat down around a conference table. Perhaps, the most perfect, because most naive, expression of this belief remains the late General Patton's remark that the Nazis were, after all, not so very different from Republicans or Democrats. (Calhoun, while less naive, was just unable to understand the reality of "ideological" conflict in and around the slavery problem.)

In nine cases out of ten the refusal to acknowledge the existence of ideological conflict is beneficial. It prevents fights for power, or clashes of interests, from flaring into religious wars where irreconcilable principles collide (a catastrophe against which Europe's ideological politics have almost no defense). It promotes compromise where compromise is possible. But in a genuine clash of principles—and, whatever the pluralists say, there *are* such clashes—the "rule of concurrent majority" breaks down; it did, in Calhoun's generation, before the profound reality of the slavery issue. A legitimate ideological conflict is actually aggravated by the pluralists' refusal to accept its reality: the compromisers who thought the slavery issue could be settled by the meeting of good intentions, or by the payment of money, may have done more than the Abolitionists to make the Civil War inevitable.

A weakness of sectional and interest pluralism just as serious is that it amounts to a principle of inaction. . . . [No] nation, however unlimited its resources, can have a very effective policy if its government is based on a principle that orders it to do nothing important except unanimously. Moreover, pluralism increases exorbitantly the weight of well organized small interest groups, especially when they lobby *against* a decision. Congress can far too easily be high-pressured into emasculating a bill by the expedient of omitting its pertinent provisions; only with much greater difficulty can Congress be moved to positive action. This explains, to a large extent, the eclipse of Congress during the last hundred years, both in popular respect and in its actual momentum as policy-making organ of government. Congress, which the Founding Fathers had intended to be the central organ of government—a role which it fulfilled up to Andrew Jackson—became the compound representative of sections and interests and, consequently, progressively incapable of national leadership.

Pluralism gives full weight—more than full weight—to sections and interests; but who is to represent the national welfare? Ever since the days of Calhoun, the advocates of pluralism have tried to dodge this question by contending that the national interest is equal to the sum of all particular interests, and that it therefore does not need a special organ of representation. But this most specious argument is contradicted by the most elementary observation. In practice, pluralism tends to resolve sectional and class conflicts at the expense of the national interest which is represented by nobody in particular, by no section and no organization.

These weaknesses had already become painfully obvious while Calhoun was alive and active—during the decade after Andrew Jackson, the first President of pluralism. Within a few years after Calhoun's death, the inability of the new system to comprehend and to resolve an ideological conflict—ultimately its inability to represent and to guard the national interest—had brought catastrophe. For a hundred years and more, American political thought has therefore resolved around attempts to counteract if not to overcome these weaknesses. Three major developments of American constitutional life were the result: the growth of the functions and powers of the President and his emergence as a "leader" rather than as the executive agent of the Congress; the rise of the Supreme Court, with its "rule of law," to the position of arbiter of policy; the development of a unifying ideology—the "American Creed."

Of these the most important—and the least noticed—is the "American Creed." In fact I know of no writer of major importance since Tocqueville who has given much attention to it. Yet even the term "un-American" cannot be translated successfully into any other language, least of all into "English" English. In no other country could the identity of the nation with a certain set of ideas be assumed—at least not under a free government. This unique cohesion on principles shows, for instance, in the refusal of the American voter to accept Socialists and Communists as "normal" parties, simply because both groups refuse to accept the assumption of a common American ideology. (pp. 418-20)

In the United States ideological homogeneity is the very basis of political diversity. It makes possible the almost unlimited freedom of interest groups, religious groups, pressure groups, etc.; and in this way it is the very fondament of free government. (It also explains why the preservation of civil liberties has been so much more important a problem in this country—as compared to England or France, for instance.) The assumption of ideological unity gives the United States the minimum of cohesion without which its political system simply could not have worked.

But is even the "American dream" enough to make a system based on the "rule of the concurrent majority" work today? Can pluralism handle the two major problems of American politics—the formulation of a foreign policy, and the political organization of an industrial society—any more successfully than it could handle the slavery issue? Or is the American political system as much in crisis as it was in the last years of Calhoun's life—and for pretty much the same reasons?

A foreign policy can never be evolved by adding particular interests—regional, economic or racial—or by compromising among them; it must supersede them. If Calhoun's contention that the national interest will automatically be served by serving the interests of the parts is wrong anywhere, it is probably wrong in the field of foreign affairs.

A foreign policy and a party system seem to be compatible only if the parties are organized on programmatic grounds, that is on principles. For if not based on general principles, a foreign policy will become a series of improvisations without rhyme or reason. In a free society, in which parties compete for votes and power, the formulation of a foreign policy may thus force the parties into ideological attitudes which will sooner or later be reflected in their domestic policies too.

This was clearly realized in the early years of the Republic when foreign policy was vital to a new nation, clinging precariously to a long seaboard without hinterland, engaged in a radical experiment with new political institutions, surrounded by the Great Powers of that time, England, France and Spain, all of them actually or potentially hostile. This awareness of foreign policy largely explains why the party system of the Founding Fathers—especially of Hamilton—was an ideological one; it also explains why the one positive foreign-policy concept this country developed during the entire nineteenth century—the Monroe Doctrine—was formulated by the last two politically active survivors of the founding generation, Monroe and John Quincy Adams. No matter how little Calhoun himself realized it, his doctrine would have been impossible without the French Revolution and the Napoleonic Wars which, during the most critical period of American integration, kept its potential European enemies busy. By 1820, the country had become too strong, had taken in too much territory, to be easily attacked; and it was still not strong enough, and far too much absorbed in the development of its own interior, to play a part in international affairs. Hence Calhoun, and all America with him, could push foreign policy out of their minds. . . . (pp. 421-22)

But today foreign policy is again as vital for the survival of the nation as it ever was during the administrations of Washington and Jefferson. And it has to be a foreign *policy,* that is, a making of decisions; hence neither ''isolationism'' nor ''internationalism'' will do. (For ''internationalism''—the search for formulae which will provide automatic decisions, even in advance—is also a refusal to have a foreign policy; it may well have done this country, and the world, as much harm as ''isolationism''—perhaps more. To survive as the strongest of the Great Powers, the United States might even have to accept permanently the supremacy of foreign policies over domestic affairs, however much this may go against basic American convictions, and indeed against the American grain. But no foreign policy can be evolved by the compromise of sectional interests or economic pressures; yet neither party, as today constituted, could develop a foreign policy based on definite principles.

The other great national need is to resolve the political problems of an industrial society. An industrial society is by nature ultrapluralistic, because it develops class and interest groups that are far stronger, and far more tightly organized, than any interest group in a pre-industrial age. A few big corporations, a few big unions, may be the actually decisive forces in an industrial society. And these groups can put decisive pressure on society: they can throttle social and economic life.

The problem does not lie in ''asocial behavior'' of this or that group but in the nature of industrial society which bears much closer resemblance to feudalism than to the trading nineteenth century. Its political problems are very similar to those which feudalism had to solve—and failed to solve. It is in perpetual danger of disintegration into virtually autonomous fiefs, principalities, ''free cities,'' ''robber baronies'' and ''exempt bish-oprics''—the authority and the interest of the nation trampled underfoot, autonomous groups uniting to control the central power in their own interest or disregarding government in fighting each other in the civil conflict of class warfare. And the alternative to such a collapse into anarchy or civil war—the suppression of classes and interest groups by an all-powerful government—is hardly more attractive.

An industrial society cannot function without an organ able to superimpose the national interest on economic or class interests. More than a mere arbiter is needed. The establishment of the ''rules of civilized industrial warfare,'' as was done by both the Wagner Act and the Taft-Hartley Act, tries to avoid the need for policies by equalizing the strength of the conflicting sections; but that can lead only to deadlock, to collusion against the national interest or, worse still, to the attempt to make the national authority serve the interest of one side against the other. In other words, an industrial society cannot fully accept Calhoun's assumption that the national good will evolve from the satisfaction of particular interests. An industrial society without national policy will become both anarchic and despotic.

Small wonder that there has been increasing demand for a radical change which would substitute ideological parties and programmatic policies for the pluralist parties and the ''rule of the concurrent majority'' of the American tradition. (pp. 422-23)

[Yet] reformers not only fail to ask themselves whether an ideological system of politics would really be any better equipped to cope with the great problems of today—and neither the foreign nor the industrial policy of England, that most successful of all ideologically organized countries, look any too successful right now; the critics also never stop to consider the unique strength of our traditional system.

Our traditional system makes sure that there is always a legitimate government in the country; and to provide such a government is the first job of any political system—a duty which a great many of the political systems known to man have never discharged.

It minimizes conflicts by utilizing, rather than suppressing conflicting forces. It makes it almost impossible for the major parties to become entirely irresponsible: neither party can afford to draw strength from the kind of demagogic opposition, without governmental responsibility, which perpetually nurtures fascist and communist parties abroad. Hence, while the two national parties are willing to embrace any movement or any group within the country that commands sufficient following, they in turn force every group to bring its demands and programs into agreement with the beliefs, traditions and prejudices of the people.

Above all, our system of sectional and interest compromise is one of the only two ways known to man in which a free government and a free society can survive—and the only one at all adapted to the conditions of American life and acceptable to the American people.

The central problem in a free government is that of factions, as we have known since Plato and Aristotle. Logically, a free government and factions are incompatible. But whatever the cause—vanity and pride, lust for power, virtue or wickedness, greed or the desire to help others—factionalism is inherent in human nature and in human society. For 2000 years the best minds in politics have tried to devise a factionless society. . . . But to creat the factionless free society is as hopeless as to set up perpetual motion. From Plato to Rousseau, political thought has ended up by demanding that factions be suppressed, that is, that freedom, to be preserved, be abolished.

The Anglo-American political tradition alone has succeeded in breaking out of this vicious circle. Going back to Hooker and Locke, building on the rich tradition of free government in the cities of the late middle ages, Anglo-American political realism discovered: that if factions cannot be suppressed, they must be utilized to make a free government both freer and stronger. (pp. 423-25)

But—and this is the real discovery on which the Anglo-American achievement rests—factions can be used constructively only if they are encompassed within a frame of unity. A free government on the basis of sectional interest groups is possible only when there is no ideological split within the country. This is the American solution. Another conceivable solution is to channel the driving forces, the vectors of society, into ideological factions which obtain their cohesion from a program for the whole of society, and from a creed. But that presupposes an unquestioned ruling class with a common outlook on life, with uniform mores and a traditional, if not inherent, economic security. Given that sort of ruling class, the antagonist in an ideological system can be expected to be a "loyal opposition," that is, to accept the rules of the game and to see himself as a partner rather than as a potential challenger to civil war. (p. 425)

In this country, the ruling-class solution was envisaged by Alexander Hamilton and seemed close to realization under the presidents of the "Virginia Dynasty." Hamilton arrived at his concept with inescapable consistency; for he was absorbed by the search for a foreign policy and for the proper organization of an industrial society—precisely the two problems which, as we have seen, pluralism is least equipped to resolve. But even if Hamilton had not made the fatal mistake of identifying wealth with rulership, the American people could not have accepted his thesis. A ruling class was incompatible with mass immigration and with the explosive territorial expansion of nineteenth-century America. It was even more incompatible with the American concept of equality. And there is no reason to believe that contemporary America is any more willing to accept Hamilton's concept. . . . This country as a free country has no alternative, it seems, to the "rule of the concurrent majority," no alternative to sectional pluralism as the device through which factions can be made politically effective.

It will be very difficult, indeed, to resolve the problems of foreign and of industrial policy on the pluralist basis and within the interest-group system, though not provably more difficult than these problems would be on another, ideological, basis. It will be all the harder as the two problems are closely interrelated; for the effectiveness of any American foreign policy depends, in the last analysis, on our ability to show the world a successful and working model of an industrial society. But if we succeed at all, it will be with the traditional system, horse-trading, log-rolling and politicking all included. An old saying has it that this country lives simultaneously in a world of Jeffersonian beliefs and in one of Hamiltonian realities. Out of these two, Calhoun's concept of "the rule of the concurrent majority" alone can make one viable whole. The need for a formulated foreign policy and for a national policy of industrial order is real—but not more so than the need for a real understanding of this fundamental American fact: the pluralism of sectional and interest compromise is the warp of America's

political fabric—it cannot be plucked out without unravelling the whole. (pp. 425-26)

Peter F. Drucker, "A Key to American Politics: Calhoun's Pluralism," in The Review of Politics, *Vol. 10, No. 4, October, 1948, pp. 412-26.*

RICHARD HOFSTADTER   (essay date 1948)

[*A distinguished American historian and social critic, Hofstadter was one of the first to challenge and reinterpret the works of the Progressive historians. In his studies, Hofstadter applied a pluralistic, inquisitive, and skeptical approach to historical investigation. During his lifetime, he was the recipient of two Pulitzer Prizes: in 1956 for* The Age of Reform: From Bryan to F. D. R. *and in 1964 for his* Anti-Intellectualism in American Life. *In his* The American Political Tradition and the Men Who Made It, *first published in 1948 and excerpted below, Hofstadter argues that Calhoun's ideas on class structure, which underlay his interpretation of the sectional controversy between the North and the South, prefigured the theories of Karl Marx.*]

Calhoun, representing a conscious minority with special problems, brought new variations into American political thinking. Although his concepts of nullification and the concurrent voice have little more than antiquarian interest for the twentieth-century mind, he also set forth a system of social analysis that is worthy of considerable respect. Calhoun was one of a few Americans of his age—Richard Hildreth and Orestes Brownson were others—who had a keen sense for social structure and class forces. Before Karl Marx published the *Communist Manifesto*, Calhoun laid down an analysis of American politics and the sectional struggle which foreshadowed some of the seminal ideas of Marx's system. A brilliant if narrow dialectician, probably the last American statesman to do any primary political thinking, he placed the central ideas of "scientific" socialism in an inverted framework of moral values and produced an arresting defense of reaction, a sort of intellectual Black Mass. (pp. 68-9)

In 1788 Patrick Henry, arguing against the federal Constitution, asked: "How can the Southern members prevent the adoption of the most oppressive mode of taxation in the Southern States, as there is a majority of the Northern States?" This anxiety about the North's majority ripened like the flora of the Southern swamplands. As the years went by, the South grew, but the North grew faster. In 1790, when Calhoun was eight years old, populations North and South were practically equal. By 1850, the year of his death, the North's was 13,527,000, the South's only 9,612,000. This preponderance was reflected in Congress. Although Southern politicians held a disproportionate number of executive offices, federal policy continued to favor Northern capital, and Southern wealth funneled into the pockets of Northern shippers, bankers, and manufacturers. Of course, the greater part of the drain of Southern resources was the inevitable result of a relationship between a capitalistic community and an agrarian one that did little of its own shipping, banking, or manufacturing. But a considerable portion too came from what Southerners considered an "artificial" governmental intrusion—the protective tariff. It was tariffs, not slavery, that first made the South militant. Planters were understandably resentful as the wealth of the Southern fields; created by the hard labor of the men, women, and children they owned, seemed to be slipping away from them. "All we want to be rich is to let us have what we make," said Calhoun.

Southern leaders began to wonder where all this was going to stop. Given its initial advantage, what was to prevent the North from using the federal government to increase the span between the political power of the sections still further, and then, presuming upon the South's growing weakness, from pushing exploitation to outrageous and unbearable extremes? Humiliated by their comparative economic backwardness, frightened at its political implications, made uneasy by the world's condemnation of their ''peculiar institution,'' Southern leaders reacted with the most intense and exaggerated anxiety to every fluctuation in the balance of sectional power. How to maintain this balance was Calhoun's central problem, and for twenty-two years his terrible and unrelenting intensity hung upon it. ''The South,'' he lamented as early as 1831, ''. . . is a fixed and hopeless minority,'' and five years later he declared in significant hyperbole on the floor of the Senate: ''We are here but a handful in the midst of an overwhelming majority.'' In 1833, speaking on the Force Bill, he saw the South confronted with ''a system of hostile legislation . . . an oppressive and unequal imposition of taxes . . . unequal and profuse appropriations . . . rendering the entire labor and capital of the weaker interest subordinate to the stronger.''

After 1830, when abolitionism began to be heard, the South's revolt was directed increasingly against this alleged menace. There is little point in debating whether fear of abolition or fear of further economic exploitation was more important in stimulating Southern militancy and turning the Southern mind toward secession. The North, if the balance of power turned completely in its favor, could both reduce the planter class to economic bondage and emancipate its slaves. Southern leaders therefore concentrated on fighting for the sectional equilibrium without making any artificial distinctions about their reasons. As Calhoun put it in 1844, ''plunder and agitation'' were ''kindred and hostile measures.'' ''While the tariff takes from us the proceeds of our labor, abolition strikes at the labor itself.''

Of course, voluntary emancipation was out of the question. To understand the mind of the Old South it is necessary to realize that emancipation meant not merely the replacement of slave labor by hired labor, but the loss of white supremacy, the overthrow of the caste system—in brief, the end of a civilization. Although Calhoun once condemned the slave trade as an ''odious traffic,'' there is no evidence that he ever shared the Jeffersonian view of slavery, widespread in the South during his youth, that slavery was a necessary but temporary evil. During a conversation with John Quincy Adams in 1820 he revealed how implicitly he accepted the caste premises of slavery. Adams spoke of equality, of the dignity and worth of human life. Calhoun granted that Adam's beliefs were ''just and noble,'' but added in a matter-of-fact way that in the South they were applied only to white men. Slavery, he said, was ''the best guarantee to equality among the whites. It produced

A political cartoon drawn in 1847. Calhoun, with his characteristic goatee, is seen standing off his enemies in the Senate.

an unvarying level among them . . . did not even admit of inequalities, by which one white man could domineer over another.''

Calhoun was the first Southern statesman of primary eminence to say openly in Congress what almost all the white South had come to feel. Slavery, he affirmed in the Senate in 1837, ''is, instead of an evil, a good—a positive good.'' By this he did not mean to imply that slavery was always better than free labor relations, but simply that it was the best relation between blacks and whites. Slavery had done much for the Negro, he argued. ''In few countries so much is left to the share of the laborer, and so little exacted from him, or . . . more kind attention paid to him in sickness or infirmities of age.'' His condition is greatly superior to that of poorhouse inmates in the more civilized portions of Europe. As for the political aspect of slavery, ''I fearlessly assert that the existing relation between the two races in the South . . . forms the most solid and durable foundation on which to rear free and stable political institutions.''

The South thought of emancipation as an apocalyptic catastrophe. In a manifesto prepared in 1849 Calhoun portrayed a series of devices by which he thought abolitionists would gradually undermine slavery until at last the North could ''monopolize all the territories,'' add a sufficient number of states to give her three fourths of the whole, and then pass an emancipation amendment. The disaster would not stop with this. Since the two races ''cannot live together in peace, or harmony, or to their mutual advantage, except in their present relation,'' one or the other must dominate. After emancipation the ex-slaves would be raised ''to a political and social equality with their former owners, by giving them the right of voting and holding public offices under the Federal Government.'' They would become political associates of their Northern friends, acting with them uniformly, ''holding the white race at the South in complete subjection.'' The blacks and the profligate whites that might unite with them would become the principal recipients of federal offices and patronage and would ''be raised above the whites of the South in the political and social scale.'' The only resort of the former master race would be to abandon the homes of its ancestors and leave the country to the Negroes.

Faced with such peril, the South should be content with nothing less than the most extreme militancy, stand firm, meet the enemy on the frontier, rather than wait till she grew weaker. Anything less than decisive victory was unthinkable. ''What! acknowledged inferiority! The surrender of life is nothing to sinking down into ackowledged inferiority!''

It was one of Calhoun's merits that in spite of his saturation in the lore of constitutional argument he was not satisfied with a purely formal or constitutional interpretation of the sectional controversy, but went beyond it to translate the balance of sections into a balance of classes. Although he did not have a complete theory of history, he saw class struggle and exploitation in every epoch of human development. He was sure that ''there never has yet existed a wealthy and civilized society in which one portion of the community did not, in point of fact, live on the labor of the other.'' It would not be too difficult ''to trace out the various devices by which the wealth of all civilized communities has been so unequally divided, and to show by what means so small a share has been allotted to those by whose labor it was produced, and so large a share to the non-producing classes.'' Concerning one such device he had no doubts; the tariff was a certain means of making ''the poor

poorer and the rich richer.'' As early as 1828 he wrote of the tariff system in his *Exposition and Protest*:

> After we [the planters] are exhausted, the contest will be between the capitalists and operatives [workers]; for into these two classes it must, ultimately, divide society. The issue of the struggle here must be the same as it has been in Europe. Under the operation of the system, wages must sink more rapidly than the prices of the necessaries of life, till the operatives will be reduced to the lowest point,—when the portion of the products of their labor left to them, will be barely sufficient to preserve existence.

In his *Disquisition on Government* Calhoun predicted that as the community develops in wealth and population, ''the difference between the rich and poor will become more strongly marked,'' and the proportion of ''ignorant and dependent'' people will increase. Then ''the tendency to conflict between them will become stronger; and, as the poor and dependent become more numerous in proportion there will be, in governments of the numerical majority, no want of leaders among the wealthy and ambitious, to excite and direct them in their efforts to obtain the control.''

Such arguments were not merely for public consumption. In 1831 a friend recorded a conversation in which Calhoun ''spoke of the tendency of Capital to destroy and absorb the property of society and produce a collision between itself and operatives.'' ''The capitalist owns the instruments of labor,'' Calhoun once told Albert Brisbane, ''and he seeks to draw out of labor all the profits, leaving the laborer to shift for himself in age and disease.'' In 1837 he wrote to Hammond that he had had ''no conception that the lower class had made such great progress to equality and independence'' as Hammond had reported. ''Modern society seems to me to be rushing to some new and untried condition.'' ''What I dread,'' he confessed to his daughter Anna in 1846, ''is that progress in political science falls far short of progress in that which relates to matter, and which may lead to convulsions and revolutions, that may retard, or even arrest the former.'' During the peak of the Jacksonian bank war he wrote to his son James that the views of many people in the North were inclining toward Southern conceptions. They feared not only Jackson's power, but ''the needy and corrupt in their own section. They begin to feel what I have long foreseen, that they have more to fear from their own people than we from our slaves.''

In such characteristic utterances there is discernible a rough parallel to several ideas that were later elaborated and refined by Marx: the idea of pervasive exploitation and class struggle in history; a labor theory of value and of a surplus appropriated by the capitalists; the concentration of capital under capitalistic production; the fall of working-class conditions to the level of subsistence; the growing revolt of the laboring class against the capitalists; the prediction of social revolution. The difference was that Calhoun proposed that no revolution should be allowed to take place. To forestall it he suggested consistently—over a period of years—what Richard Current has called ''planter-capitalist collaboration against the class enemy'' [see Additional Bibliography]. In such a collaboration the South, with its superior social stability, had much to offer as a conservative force. In return, the conservative elements in the North should be willing to hold down abolitionist agitation; and they would do well to realize that an overthrow of slavery in the South would prepare the ground for social revolution in the North. (pp. 77-82)

Calhoun had an ingenious solution for the sectional problem: in return for the South's services as a balance wheel against labor agitation, the solid elements in the North should join her in a common front against all agitation of the slavery issue. His program for the tariff problem was best expressed in a letter to Abbott Lawrence in 1845: Northern manufacturers should join the planters in producing for the export market. At best it would be impossible for manufacturers to attain prosperity in the home market alone; "the great point is to get possession of the foreign market," and for that the high-duty tariff is nothing but an obstruction. The North should emulate English manufacturers by lowering duties, importing cheap raw materials, and competing aggressively for foreign trade. "When that is accomplished all conflict between the planter and the manufacturer would cease."

During the last seven years of Calhoun's life the sectional conflict centered more and more on the acquisition of new territory and its division between slave and free society. Nullification had failed for lack of unity within the South. The alliance with the West was unstable and uncertain. The proposed alliance with Northern capital Calhoun could not bring about. Hence the problem of defense turned increasingly upon the attempt to acquire new slave territory in Texas, Mexico, and the vast area wrested from Mexico by war, and keeping the North from taking the West for free labor.

Calhoun's interest in Texas was defensive in intent, but exorbitantly aggressive in form. Great Britain, eager for a new market and an independent source of cotton, was encouraging Texas to remain independent by offering financial aid and protection. During 1843, when Lord Brougham and Lord Aberdeen both openly confessed Britain's intent to foster abolition along with national independence in Texas, Calhoun, then Secretary of State, stepped forward in alarm to link the annexation issue with a thoroughgoing defense of slavery. Southerners feared that another refuge for fugitive slaves and the example of an independent, free-labor cotton-producing country on their border would be a grave menace to their social structure. Britain, Calhoun frankly told the British Minister, was trying to destroy in Texas an institution "essential to the peace, safety, and prosperity of the United States"! In 1844 he published an interpretation of Britain's motives. Having freed the slaves in her own colonial empire, he charged, she had lost ground in world production of tropical products, including cotton, had endangered the investment in her empire, and had reduced it to far poorer condition than such areas as the Southern United States and Brazil, where slavery survived. Britain, in her effort "to regain and keep a superiority in tropical cultivation, commerce, and influence," was desperately trying to "cripple or destroy the productions of her successful rivals" by undermining their superior labor system.

Ardent as he had been for annexation of Texas, Calhoun was frightened during the war with Mexico by sentiment in the South for conquest and annexation of all Mexico. If Mexico were taken, he feared that the necessity of controlling her would give the executive tremendous powers and vast patronage, bring about precisely the centralization of federal power that he so feared, and finally destroy the constitutional system. He predicted that conflict between North and South over disposition of the acquired territory might easily disrupt the Union. "Mexico is for us the forbidden fruit; the penalty of eating it would be to subject our institutions to political death."

In 1846 the introduction of the Wilmot Proviso, which banned slavery from all territory to be taken from Mexico, excited the South as nothing had before. Calhoun felt that it involved a matter of abstract right upon which no compromise should be considered, even though it was unlikely that slavery would go into the territories in question. In December he told President Polk that he "did not desire to extend slavery," that it would "probably never exist" in California and New Mexico. Still he would vote against any treaty that included the Wilmot Proviso, because "it would involve a principle."

Calhoun became obsessed with the North's tendency to "monopolize" the territories for free labor. In 1847, when Iowa had entered the Union and Wisconsin was ready for statehood, he expressed his fear that the territories would yield twelve or fifteen more free states. The South was fast losing that parity in the Senate which was its final stronghold of equality in the federal government. In March of that year he called for a united Southern party to force a showdown on Southern rights. In his last great speech, which was read to the Senate for him because he was dying, he declared with finality that the balance of power had already been lost. The South no longer had "any adequate means of protecting itself against . . . encroachment and oppression." Reviewing the growth of Northern preponderance, the exploitation of the South, and the progressive disintegration of the moral bonds of Union, Calhoun warned that the nation could be saved only by conceding to the South an equal right in the newly acquired Western territory and amending the Constitution to restore to her the power of self-protection that she had had before the sectional balance was destroyed.

An amendment to the Constitution would be a guarantee of equality to the South. Calhoun demanded that this guarantee should take the form of the concurrent majority, which was the king pin in his political system. All through his sectional phase Calhoun had been preaching for the concurrent majority. He expressed it as early as 1833 in his speech on the Force Bill and last formulated it in the ***Disquisition on Government,*** published after his death. Government by numerical majorities, he always insisted, was inherently unstable; he proposed to replace it with what he called government by the whole community—that is, a government that would organically represent both majority and minority. Society should not be governed by counting heads but by considering the great economic interests, the geographical and functional units, of the nation. In order to prevent the plunder of a minority interest by a majority interest, each must be given an appropriate organ in the constitutional structure which would provide it with "either a concurrent voice in making and executing the laws or a veto on their execution." Only by such a device can the "different interests, orders, classes, or portions" of the community be protected, "and all conflict and struggle between them prevented."

Time had persuaded Calhoun that a dual executive would be the best means of employing the concurrent majority in the United States. The nation should have two presidents, each representing one of the two great sections, each having a veto power over acts of Congress. No measure could pass that did not win the approval of the political agents of both sections. The equality between sections that had existed at the beginning of the government would thus be restored.

Calhoun's analysis of American political tensions certainly ranks among the most impressive intellectual achievements of American statesmen. Far in advance of the event, he forecast an alliance between Northern conservatives and Southern reactionaries, which has become one of the most formidable aspects of American politics. The South, its caste system essentially intact, has proved to be for an entire century more resistant to change than the North, its influence steadily exerted to retard serious reform and to curb the power of Northern labor. Caste prejudice and political conservatism have made the South a major stronghold of American capitalism.

But prescient and ingenious as Calhoun was, he made critical miscalculations for the sectional struggle of his own time. He had a remarkable sense for the direction of social evolution, but failed to measure its velocity. His fatal mistake was to conclude that the conflict between labor and capital would come to a head before the conflict between capital and the Southern planter. Marx out of optimism and Calhoun out of pessimism both overestimated the revolutionary capacities of the working class. It was far easier to reconcile the Northern masses to the profit system than Calhoun would ever admit. He failed to see that the expanding Northern free society, by offering broad opportunities to the lower and middle classes, provided itself with a precious safety valve for popular discontents. He also failed to see that the very restlessness which he considered the North's weakness was also a secret of its strength. "The main spring to progress," he realized, "is the desire to individuals to better their condition," but he could not admit how much more intensely free society stimulated that essential desire in its working population than his cherished slave system. . . . (pp. 84-8)

Calhoun, in brief, failed to appreciate the staying power of capitalism. At the very time when it was swinging into its period of most hectic growth he spoke as though it had already gone into decline. The stirrings of the Jackson era particularly misled him; mass discontent, which gained further opportunities for the common man in business and politics, and thus did so much in the long run to strengthen capitalism, he misread as the beginning of a revolutionary upsurge. Calhoun was, after all, an intense reactionary, and to the reactionary ear every whispered criticism of the elite classes has always sounded like the opening shot of an uprising.

Calhoun's social analysis lacked the rough pragmatic resemblance to immediate reality that any analysis must have if it is to be translated into successful political strategy. He never did find a large capitalist group in the North that would see the situation as he did. Although he joined the Whig Party for a few years after his disappointment with Jackson, a long-term alliance with such firm spokesmen of capitalist tariff economics as Clay and Webster was unthinkable. Under the Van Buren administration he returned to the Democratic fold on the subtreasury issue, and there he remained. During the late thirties, while he was still appealing to Northern conservatives to join hands with the planters, he admitted that the Whig Party, the party most attractive to Northern capital, was more difficult than the Democrats on both the tariff and abolition. (pp. 88-9)

The essence of Calhoun's mistake as a practical statesman was that he tried to achieve a static solution for a dynamic situation. The North, stimulated by invention and industry and strengthened by a tide of immigration, was growing in population and wealth, filling the West, and building railroads that bound East and West together. No concurrent majority, nor any other principle embodied in a parchment, could stem the tide that was measured every ten years in the census returns. William H. Seward touched upon the South's central weakness in his speech of March 11, 1850, when he observed that what the Southerners

wanted was "a *political* equilibrium. Every political equilibrium requires a physical equilibrium to rest upon, and is valueless without it." In the face of all realities, the Southerners kept demanding that equality of territory and approximate equality of populations be maintained. "And this," taunted Seward, "must be perpetual!"

Moreover, the Calhoun dialectic was so starkly reactionary in its implications that it became self-defeating. There was disaster even for the South in the premise that every civilized society must be built upon a submerged and exploited labor force—what Hammond called a "mud-sill" class. *If* there must always be a submerged and exploited class at the base of society, and *if* the Southern slaves, as such a class, were better off than Northern free workers, and *if* slavery was the safest and most durable base on which to found political institutions, then there seemed to be no reason why *all* workers, white or black, industrial or agrarian, should not be slave rather than free. Calhoun shrank from this conclusion, but some Southerners did not. George Fitzhugh won himself quite a reputation in the fifties arguing along these lines. The fact that some Southerners, however few, followed Fitzhugh was an excellent one for Northern politicians to use to rouse freemen, especially those who were indifferent to the moral aspects of slavery, to take a stand against the spread of the institution.

Calhoun could see and expound very plausibly every weakness of Northern society, but his position forced him to close his eyes to the vulnerability of the South. Strong as he was on logical coherence, he had not the most elementary moral consistency. Here it is hard to follow those who, like Professor Wiltse, find in him "the supreme champion of minority rights and interests everywhere." It is true that Calhoun superbly formulated the problem of the relation between majorities and minorities, and his work at this point may have the permanent significance for political theory that is often ascribed to it. But how can the same value be assigned to his practical solutions? Not in the slightest was he concerned with minority rights as they are chiefly of interest to the modern liberal mind—the rights of dissenters to express unorthodox opinions, of the individual conscience against the State, least of all of ethnic minorities. At bottom he was not interested in any minority that was not a propertied minority. The concurrent majority itself was a device without relevance to the protection of dissent, but designed specifically to protect a vested interest of considerable power. Even within the South Calhoun had not the slightest desire to protect intellectual minorities, critics, and dissenters. Professor Clement Eaton, in his *Freedom of Thought in the Old South*, places him first among those politicians who "created stereotypes in the minds of the Southern people that produced intolerance" [see Additional Bibliography]. Finally, it was minority privileges rather than rights that he really proposed to protect. He wanted to give to the minority not merely a proportionate but an *equal* voice with the majority in determining public policy. He would have found incomprehensible the statement of William H. Roane, of Virginia, that he had "never thought that [minorities] had any other *Right* than that of freely, peaceably, & *legally* converting themselves into a *majority* whenever they can." This elementary right Calhoun was prompt to deny to any minority, North or South, that disagreed with him on any vital question. In fact, his first great speeches on the slavery question were prompted by his attempt to deny the right of petition to a minority.

Calhoun was a minority spokesman in a democracy, a particularist in an age of nationalism, a slaveholder in an age of advancing liberties, and an agrarian in a furiously capitalistic country. Quite understandably he developed a certain perversity of mind. It became his peculiar faculty, the faculty of a brilliant but highly abstract and isolated intellect, to see things that other men never dreamt of and to deny what was under his nose, to forecast with uncanny insight several major trends of the future and remain all but oblivious of the actualities of the present. His weakness was to be inhumanly schematic and logical, which is only to say that he thought as he lived. His mind, in a sense, was *too* masterful—it imposed itself upon realities. The great human, emotional, moral complexities of the world escaped him. . . . (pp. 89-92)

> *Richard Hofstadter, "John C. Calhoun: The Marx of the Master Class," in his* The American Political Tradition and the Men Who Made It, *1948. Reprint by Vintage Books, 1954, pp. 68-92.*

MARGARET L. COIT (essay date 1950)

[*The following excerpt is drawn from Coit's Pulitzer Prize-winning biography, widely hailed for humanizing Calhoun. Here, Coit contends that by the end of his life, Calhoun had repudiated the doctrine of states' rights because it was not a viable pattern upon which to frame a federalist system of government.*]

Behind [Calhoun] when he died, unfinished but blocked out, were his two books—*A Disquisition on Government* and *A Discourse on the Constitution of the United States*—to which he had literally given his last days and almost his last hours. Upon them his claim to fame is assured. For here, stripped of the day-to-day issues of his own time, is the essence of his entire political philosophy, the sum of all his living and thinking. Here is what latter-day critics would hail as perhaps the most powerful defense of minority rights in a democracy ever written. (p. 518)

The first book is superior to the second, which is diffuse, repetitive, clearly showing the illness of its author. Yet even the second is extraordinary. It is too much to claim, as do the most fervid Southern enthusiasts, that these books rank with Aristotle's, but with the single exception of the *Federalist Papers,* they represent America's most remarkable contribution to political thought.

In the *Disquisition* Calhoun outlined what he conceived to be the principles of government in general, and of democratic government in particular. In the *Discourse* he illustrated these principles by means of the Constitution and the American federal theory—and here is where the difficulties begin. For none knew better than Calhoun how vastly America had outgrown the federal pattern; and that the interests, once represented by states and later by sections, would soon be scattered across the entire country. By 1850, Calhoun had realized that although politically states' rights were a safeguard, economically they were not enough. Von Holst points out how in the end Calhoun repudiated what had been supposed to be his entire political philosophy; fifteen years after his passing, a generation of Southern young men would die in the name of states' rights, mistakenly supposing that they were dying in the name of Calhoun.

For passionate as was Calhoun's love for South Carolina; convinced as he was that the state was the unit upon which America was built, this organization still, to Calhoun, was a means and not an end. He was fighting, not for the original American pattern, but for the general federal theory; but this not even his most devoted admirers could understand. And not the fed-

eral theory alone, but the justice which the federal theory was devised to maintain, was to Calhoun the essence of America. America had outgrown states' rights—the usurpations of majority rule proved this—thus the theory must be reworked upon a new pattern.

This explains the confusion that distorts the second volume of Calhoun's mighty work. How could a country, which had embodied its theory in a pattern, maintain the theory without the pattern? Yet Calhoun's very recognition of this dilemma is the measure of his greatness as a statesman. It was not the Union that mattered so much as the purpose behind it. Calhoun was not doctrinaire; his aim was to make democracy work.

The purpose of his book was threefold: to save the South, to save the Union, to save the federal principles of the Union. All, he knew, were indispensable, one to the other. He knew that 1850 was the last chance for the South and West to rally behind a constitutional amendment which he thought would 'protect the South forever against economic exploitation.' He knew that ten years later would be too late. Within the Union, unconquered, the South could form a barrier against the final triumph of industrial centralization and unchecked majority rule; without, all would be lost.

Thus, in his last days, with haunted vision and in agony of spirit Calhoun had thrust against the forces which challenged the Union. The right to secede, as a last resort, hopeless as secession might be, he did not deny: 'That a State, as a party to the constitutional compact, has the right to secede . . . cannot be denied by anyone who regards the Constitution as a compact—if a power should be inserted by the amending power, which would radically change the character of the system; *or if the former should fail to fulfill the ends for which it was established*.' Yet, practically, he knew that the South's only hope was in the Union.

Calhoun saw the country politically as 'a democratic Federal republic, democratic not aristocratic, federal not national . . . of states, not of individuals.' He saw it as a government, not of the numerical majority, but of the concurrent majority—with each major group in society having a voice in the legislation affecting it, as in the legislation affecting the whole.

Economically, his ideal was not an agrarian, but a balanced, economy. The numerical supremacy of factory workers over farmers, of industrialists over planters, he considered had nothing to do with the rights and powers belonging to each group. The one was not the slave of the other; all were essential to the maintenance of a sound and healthy economic system.

For Calhoun, America was a protest against the European spirit, against an aristocracy of birth, against the artificial aristocracy of accumulated wealth 'and the decadence of men.' The South, although conservative, static, at odds with the dynamic and expanding North, he saw as the symbol of this protest. Already the South was an anachronism, a minority voice against the majority will, but still the last barrier against the rising, middle-class, standardized civilization which was sweeping the world in the wake of the Industrial Revolution.

Future events would prove to many how terribly right he had been. A century later Harold Laski would find an America committed to the evaluation of men by what they had rather than what they were—to the pursuit of wealth rather than of happiness as the chief end of man.

To Calhoun the American system was an experiment in diversity. It was based upon the right of peoples to choose their own way of life, economic and social, and to live it, regardless of the majority pattern. America's freedom was in her differences. Under the federal political system, as written, different civilizations, granting that they could agree on principles involving the common interest and common safety of all, could live together.

In the South a special civilization had developed. It was a Southern civilization, common only to that region and representative of it. Yet it was under the American system that it had grown to fruition; and it was authentically American.

With the secession of the South, the great American experiment would be at an end. As a political philosopher and as a patriot, Calhoun could not bear to see it end. Furthermore, in the American system Calhoun saw principles applicable to the entire world, to all mankind. One of the earliest advocates of 'One World,' he was, however, wise enough to know that there could never be one pattern of culture for the world. In a world where 'progress in matter,' as he had long foreseen, had outstripped moral development, you may say that you must have one standard of values to exist, but it does not follow either that you will have the values or continue to exist. As a practical statesman, Calhoun was not so much interested in what you have to have, or should have, as in what you could have.

Any government, national or world-wide, that crushes men into a single pattern, he deemed a despotic government. This was the principle invoked by every conqueror through time; and for the United States, for example, to impose on the world one system of industrial capitalism, whether good or evil, would be adoption of the tyrannical belief that the world could only exist under one system. Half a century before Adolf Hitler was born, Calhoun had the wisdom to know that although men may agree on general principles of safety, a world system based upon one country's concept of freedom, denies others the very right of choice which is essential to freedom.

A world federal government, Calhoun might see as desirable and possible. But he would have laughed at what the world, or the post-Civil War United States, considered to be a federal government. Federal, as a working word in the American vocabulary, has indeed been dead since the Civil War. For federal involved the rights of peoples to control their own affairs in their own localities; and the same federal principle which protected the South as a minority voice in the United States could be readily invoked in a world federal government today.

Governments, Calhoun had always contended, were formed to protect minorities; majorities could look after themselves. As written, the Constitution had been an attempt to protect minority rights. In a federal Union the South was a constant conservative check against the national advances of 'liberalism' and 'progress.' Thus, for the majority, it was necessary to strip her of the power to say how the Constitution was written. It was necessary to abolish the federal theory, and what could not be done by law was finally done by war.

The demolition work was complete. 'Conquered and subjugated,' the Southern people, as a latter-day statesman pointed out, were relegated to be 'drawers of water and hewers of wood.' The war that was to 'free' the Negro had left a backwash of eleven million Southern men and women, both black and white, who eighty years after the guns of Sumter and Shiloh were still, were living on cash incomes of less than two hundred and fifty dollars a year. The South, which knew that democracy flourished only under an economy in which 'private property

was widely distributed, individually owned, and personally managed,' had become the country of which it could be said that '85 per cent of Georgia is owned by people outside.'

By the twentieth century, the 'Colonial status of the South,' sensed by the suspicious 'Pat' Calhoun and his backwoodsmen, phophesied and out-lined by John Calhoun, had become a recognized, and, it was to be feared, a permanent status. By near the half-century mark, John Gunther could report that more Southern industries and more Southern resources were 'being transferred to Northern control month by month.'

War had left a whole people despoiled, a whole land laid waste. Yet hand in hand with the Northern victory came the grimmest, most ironic joke of all. For by bleeding and defrauding the South, if finally became evident that the industrialists were bleeding and defrauding themselves. High tariffs had walled out their world markets, and their greatest home market could not afford to buy what they made. The seed of future depressions was sown in the Southern states, as was foreseen by Franklin D. Roosevelt when he warned that the 'economic unbalance in the Nation as a whole' was 'due to this very condition of the South.' Here, indeed, was proof of Calhoun's doctrine that only by aiding, not by subjecting his fellows to his will, can man assure prosperity for himself.

'The South . . . the poor South . . .' Not even in his wildest imaginings had Calhoun foreseen the desolation that became the truth. But he sensed it, nevertheless. He had seen the beginning of the end, and his life's struggle had been to avoid that end. He had warned; and his warnings were heeded too late. And viewing the grim lesson of the 'Colonial' South today, bleeding still from wounds unhealed after eighty years, would have filled Calhoun with fear as to the fate of 'backward' minority peoples under the rule of a world government unless it were firmly based on the federal principle. It is fortunate, perhaps, for the peoples of the world that America developed a philosopher who believed that superior to progress was the right of individuals to choose whether they would be progressive or not; and that federalism was a system—and not a word. (pp. 519-23)

Margaret L. Coit, in her John C. Calhoun: American Portrait, *Houghton Mifflin Company, 1950, 593 p.*

CHARLES M. WILTSE (essay date 1951)

[*Wiltse's three-volume biography of Calhoun, comprised of* John C. Calhoun: Nationalist, 1782-1828, John C. Calhoun: Nullifier, 1829-1839, *and* John C. Calhoun: Sectionalist, 1840-1850, *is considered the most comprehensive and thorough study of the statesman's life and thought. In the excerpt below, drawn from Wiltse's third volume, he traces the development of Calhoun's political philosophy as expressed in its final form in the* Disquisition *and the* Discourse. *Wiltse also underscores the lasting significance of Calhoun's analysis of the relationship between liberty and power.*]

If Calhoun's library had been preserved it might be possible to trace the germ of his political ideas in his reading, but we know enough of his preference in books to give a general idea of his intellectual antecedents. We know that he knew Plato and Aristotle, Machiavelli and Hobbes and Locke; we know that he studied institutional history, particularly that of the Greeks and Romans and Hebrews, the history of the Italian republics and of Great Britain; we knew that he had high admiration for Burke. He was thoroughly steeped in the literature of political controversy produced in his own country, from the

Revolutionary pamphlets through the *Federalist*, the State Rights controversy that preceded Jefferson's rise to power, John Taylor of Caroline, and the constitutional commentaries and glosses of his own time; and he was on familiar terms with the economic doctrines that had burgeoned since the days of Adam Smith. (p. 420)

His reading undoubtedly entered into his thinking, but the quality of his intellect led Calhoun almost inevitably to generalize from his experience, and to set up his generalizations in the form of universal laws. His unshakable self-confidence, his unquestioning certainty that he was right, led him to evaluate the actions of others and in large measure to determine his own on the basis of these general principles. His own political philosophy, in short, was a framework on which he hung his reading of history and in terms of which he interpreted the economic and political forces of his time. By the same token it is also a pattern which gives consistency and direction to a career that appeared to his enemies and often to his friends to be erratic and without principle. His course was not determined by simple reactions to people and events but was rather derived from a system of philosophy into which people and events had first been neatly fitted and arranged.

Calhoun belonged to an age of revolution, of intellectual ferment, of political and economic experimentation. He was born before the close of the American struggle for independence. When he was a precocious lad of six his father opposed ratification of the new Constitution of the United States because it gave too much power to a central government. The French Revolution was the overshadowing fact of his youth. He was nearing maturity when Virginia rebelled against the autarchy of the Alien and Sedition Acts, and he had already entered preparatory school when the explosive force of that rebellion carried Thomas Jefferson to the Presidency. He was in college when Bonaparte completed the transition from successful military commander to First Consul to Emperor, and we know from his letters that the young Carolinian watched the process and its aftermath with interest and concern.

Equally suggestive of conflict and upheaval is Calhoun's early political career. He entered public life at a time when his country was being forced to choose sides in a world-wide struggle for power. He sat in a war Congress and grappled there with the problems of foreign invasion and internal revolt. He saw, and encouraged, the rise of industry in the Northern and Middle states, but in the process he had amply opportunity to observe the interaction of economic forces and political events. From the vantage point of a Cabinet seat he witnessed the rising sectional tension between North and South, and he recognized the Missouri Compromise for what it was—an internal balance of power. It was an age of wonderful technological advances, which seemed to go hand in hand with crumbling social institutions: an age when active minds went back to fundamentals, and thinking men sought new interpretations of the world order.

Calhoun's own search for first principles undoubtedly began at an early stage of his career, but it was not until the summer and fall of 1828, when he made his first intensive study of the Constitution in search of an answer to the tariffs that were eating away the prosperity of his native state, that the broad outline of the political theory ultimately refined and perfected in the *Disquisition* and *Discourse* was worked out. The first statement of it came in the *South Carolina Exposition and Protest* of that year, with refinements and amplifications being added as the nullification controversy unfolded, to conclude

with the great debate with Webster on the Force Bill and on the nature of the Constitution.

There was further enlargement of the doctrine in the course of the three-year controversy with Jackson over the removal of the deposits from the Bank of the United States, in the course of which the focus shifted from legislative to executive power. The reports on incendiary publications and on executive patronage of 1835 and 1836 built up the background. The return of the Whigs to power with the election of 1840 led Calhoun to consider the whole question of centralization in the general context of a Hamiltonian program, while the Dorr rebellion in Rhode Island showed him how an unchecked numerical majority might operate. By 1842, when the tariff compromise was swept aside at the bidding of local interests, an understanding of the forces that were changing the whole scope and structure of government as they changed the face of nature had begun to loom more important in his eyes than even the Presidency itself. It was then that he conceived the idea of writing a book on government and prepared to rest his place in history on his analysis of the political process.

He anticipated many of the arguments of the *Discourse* in his speech on the veto power in 1842. By the summer of 1843, when he probably began the tentative blocking out of the systematic treatises, the precise ideas of the *Disquisition* and some of its phrasing began to appear in his speeches and in his familiar writings. The analysis of man in relation to society first appeared in his letter to William Smith on the Rhode Island controversy, dated July 1843. In the State Department the following year he became fully aware for the first time "of the immense influence, which may be exerted through it on foreign and domestic relations"; and before he left the Cabinet he was talking of "concurrent majorities" as being the "essence of the constitution."

In retirement and at work on his treaties once more, he reflected sharply in his private letters on the influence of patronage as he had seen it grow in the Tyler administration. "The truth is," he explained to J. R. Matthews in August of 1845, "that the office holders & the office seekers govern the country, & the struggles between the parties have degenerated into a mere contest for the spoils, without a particle of regard on either side for principles or country." He enlarged on the theme the following spring, in the midst of the battle for the Walker tariff, in terms such as might have gone into the *Disquisition.* "I have seen enough of publick men," he wrote to his brother-in-law in May 1846, "to come to the conclusion, that there are few, indeed, whose attachment to self is not stronger, than their patriotism, and their friendship." He was prepared, however, to make allowances, comparing this personal self-love to the friction in a machine. "We must take men as they are, and do the best we can with them. . . . If all were disinterested patriots, there would be very little difficulty in constructing or managing the political machine; and very little merit in doing either." It was later that same year that he prepared his elaborate exposition of the constitution of South Carolina as a perpetual balance of interests.

His speeches and writings on the Mexican War, and on the territorial and slavery questions growing out of it from 1847 on, display the theory pretty much in its final form, with the language used being the same or very similar to that in which the posthumous treatises are expressed. His starting point in 1828 had been the defense of a conscious minority against exploitation by a legislature in the hands of a stronger interest. Twenty years later he was still defending that same minority,

Calhoun, as depicted in a political cartoon in 1848. The Granger Collection, New York.

now relatively weaker than before, against not mere exploitation but destruction at the hands of a numerical majority fired with crusading zeal. In the interval he had broadened and enriched and universalized his principles as he watched them work themselves out with almost mathematical precision to ends he had foreseen.

What Calhoun was actually doing was rationalizing the government process as he had seen it at work in his own time. From his own experience he generalized that certain basic premises would always be true—that governments tend to become absolute, that rulers tend to abuse their powers, that the honors and emoluments of government are in themselves enough to fix party lines and to precipitate a struggle for power. All these propositions were deductions from the nature of man, but they were far more than that to the grim-visaged realist from South Carolina. They were also obvious facts that anyone could see for himself in the day-to-day operations of the government of the United States. The history of his own country was both the source and the practical proof of his theory.

In making the generalizations on which his political theory rested, Calhoun was not concerned with the motives or morals of individuals, nor with those by-products of the process that have seemed good to later historians, steeped in an altogether different social philosophy. He did not look on the extension of the franchise as a forward step in raising the condition of the common man; he saw it as one of the means by which irresponsible power passed to a numerical majority, to be wielded by a small group of politicians for partisan ends. He did not see in the destruction of the Bank of the United States any popular victory over entrenched privilege and private monopoly; to him it represented a dangerous extension of executive

power, more potent for evil than for good. He did not regard the protective tariff as a means of building up industry, increasing the national wealth, and raising the standard of living for the masses; he saw it rather as a tremendous engine of political bribery whereby the stronger was permitted to exploit the weaker interest in return for votes. In his eyes the anti-slavery agitation and the Wilmot Proviso were not elements in a great moral crusade; they were simply the final proof that constitutional guarantees and property rights were alike worthless in the face of a hostile majority.

Contemporary history as he wrote his treatises only made Calhoun's case seem the stronger. The popular revolutionary governments in Europe gave way to new and more powerful absolutisms almost before the tumult died, because the weaker interests had not been clothed with power to protect themselves. And the election of Zachary Taylor to the Presidency of the United States offered only another illustration of the political process in action. Democrats dissatisfied with Polk's administration, some of them friends and erstwhile followers of his own, went over to the Whigs to swell the margin to victory. Taylor Democrats they called themselves, and made their case on principles; but what were they in reality but partisans who had failed to get what they wanted in the way of office, or special legislation, or protection for some special interest? They thought of themselves as standing for truth and justice against political corruption, but was not their concept of truth and justice, in reality, only their own self-interest?

From the hot August day in 1846 on which the Wilmot Proviso made its first appearance it became increasingly evident with each session of Congress and with each election that a sectional majority in the Northern states would not permit slaves to be carried into any territory of the United States. To the South, already a minority in numbers and in wealth, sensitive because world opinion condemned her labor system and on the defensive because of the long crusade her co-partners in the Union had been waging against it, the Proviso could mean only one thing. Slaveholders were to be held rigidly within their existing bounds, while the millions of acres acquired by the common military effort were to be applied to making the stronger interest stronger still.

True, Northern spokesmen denied over and over again that there was any intention, then or ever, of interfering with slavery in the states where it existed; but how could a man who read history as Calhoun read it have any illusions on that score? Politicians of both parties in the North had been forced step by step to follow the abolitionists, and the abolitionists had declared that slavery must go. It was inherent in the political process itself, which in turn was an inescapable concomitant of human nature, that the stronger interest would abuse its power at the expense of the weaker. There could be only one possible answer: power to resist; a concurrent veto to be applied by a united South through the Nashville Convention, or by state interposition, or by the threat to secede from the Union. A numerical majority in control of the general government had defined the powers of that government as sovereign. From that claim, if it were allowed to stand, would flow not only the abolition of slavery and the economic ruin of the South, but also the practical destruction of political liberty in the United States.

The problem with which Calhoun came to grips was the perennial problem of government—how to achieve a working adjustment between liberty and power. Liberty was the goal, because it was the liberty of the individual to seek his own betterment, to develop his own talents and skills, to realize his own fullest potentialities, that led to every advance in civilization and thereby improved the condition of the whole society. But power was necessary to curb the conflicts arising out of the inherent selfishness of men. Because of that inherent selfishness, however, power was inevitably subject to abuse, which could be curbed only by power itself. The answer, in the abstract terminology of political theory, was a kind of pluralism, whereby the sovereignty lay not in the whole but in the parts or classes or elements of which the whole was composed. In the language of governmental structure it was a form of federalism, geographical in the terms of Calhoun's time and place but functional in concept, since he thought of the states and sections as economic interests rather than as mere areas of land.

The concurrent veto in operation is a negative variation of the pressure-group approach, which persists in one form or another in all diverse societies. Is it not in this fashion that we have come in our time to the public purchase and destruction of foodstuffs in order to raise prices to fantastic levels in the interest of a special group? Is it not thus that we have come to pay wages for work unperformed, and rent for land unused? Is it not in these terms that we have raised the cost of government beyond the wildest nightmares of our ancestors and bought partisans to keep in power the generous patrons of our own selfishness? The effectiveness of the approach clearly depends on the relative power of the opposing interests, with the weaker being compelled to make up in organization and unity what it lacks in strength. The Southern movement of 1849-1850 was just such an attempt of a weaker to bargain with a stronger interest. The power of the individual states, as nullification had shown, was purely negative, and could be easily crushed by a majority. But if the Southern states could be brought to unite they could perhaps save their institutions, their way of life, their source of livelihood. Remember Calhoun and his fellow planters were quite sure that the South was economically more necessary to the North than the North was to them.

The real issue of constitutional interpretation—of liberty against power—has been obscured by the fact that the test was made in defense of an unworthy cause. Let us, therefore, assume a hypothetical case. Let us assume that manufacturing has been concentrated in a dozen states, with no more than a third of the population; and that the physical conditions are such as to preclude its extension to other localities. If for any reason the rest of the Union gradually became imbued with the idea that the private ownership of manufacturing was immoral, and launched a vigorous agitation aimed at nationalization with a distribution of the profits pro rata among the whole population, would not the manufacturing states react exactly as the South reacted to the abolitionist crusade? Would not the manufacturers fall back on constitutional limitations, on group pressure, and ultimately on secession from the Union?

In retrospect, Calhoun's policy for the South, leading as it did to civil war, seems suicidal, and his defense of slavery, to use the mildest term, amoral. Yet what were the alternatives? It seems indisputable that Southern acquiescence in the kind of legislation being introduced at every session of Congress by the Northern majority would, as Calhoun argued, have ended in the abolition of slavery. Suppose, then, that Calhoun had accepted abolition as inevitable, and had persuaded the South to free her slaves without waiting to have the inevitable forced upon her. Would that have changed the Northern majority in Congress, or prevented the passage of laws in the interest of

the dominant section? Surely the history of Reconstruction, of the postemancipation tariffs, of railroad rate discrimination and other forms of economic exploitation, proves the contrary. The picture of the stonger interest abusing the powers of government to exploit the weaker has been materially altered only as major economic interests have come to transcend state and regional boundaries. Even this alteration does not change the substance, but only poses the original problem in a different form.

If we accept Calhoun's estimate of human nature, it is difficult to escape his conclusion that the majority will always exploit the minority unless the weaker portion has power to protect itself. The concurrent veto was to give them that power. The theory remains today what Calhoun himself conceived it: a defense of the minority—any minority—against the arbitrary exercise of power. It was, and is, effective to precisely the degree that the moral and physical cost of coercion seems to the majority to outweigh the gain. The great South Carolinian was defending an eighteenth-century form of society that had already been rendered obsolete by the technological developments of his own time. But his basic fear of power was justified, and the scientific advances that he failed to take into full account have only accelerated the tendency he recognized for governments to become absolute. As he clearly saw, an issue may be compromised only so long as both sides are strong. When one is weak, no matter how noble its cause, it will be crushed: for men are still moved by love of gain, and power still corrupts. Let us not forget that the accretions of power we yield to government to promote our safety and our welfare may also be used for our destruction. (pp. 420-27)

Calhoun's genius lay in his awareness of the problem his country faced, and his greatest contribution was his long and patient effort to explain it in terms that would make a peaceable solution possible. The United States was the first great modern nation in which agriculture and industry were both major interests. Calhoun more than any other man drove home the point that policies designed to foster and encourage the one would be ruinous to the other, and we have come at last, though by a different route, to his position. We have recognized the necessity, in a nation embracing many economic interests, for equalizing what he called the burdens and bounties of government. We have done it by direct action through taxation and subsidies, and in the process we have made the central government powerful beyond Calhoun's most gloomy fears; but we have at least recognized the problem with which he struggled, and we have arrived at a solution, however tentative, within the framework of the Constitution—not the Constitution he so painstakingly limited lest the society he cherished be destroyed, but one better suited to the needs of a more complex age and perhaps not less responsive to the welfare of those who are governed by it.

The federation of sovereign states that seemed to Calhoun the only practical way to reconcile the conflicting demands of agriculture and industry was essentially static, without adequate room for the development of a dynamic society. The concurrent veto was negative, defensive, designed to preserve the order of things as they were. In action it could only obstruct, until obstruction became intolerable and had to be swept aside. Thoroughgoing conservative that he was, Calhoun came at last to place security for his class above all other considerations, and when security becomes an end in itself the society is doomed.

In his rejection of the democratic dogma, and in his failure to appreciate the moral values in the antislavery crusade, Calhoun was following out the premises of his own mechanistic theory of society. His estimate of human nature was low, but his analysis of the political process is still largely valid, and is nowhere better illustrated than in his own career. His defense of the minority against the weight of numbers is timeless in its application, and his insistence that the power of government must somehow be controlled is a universal condition of human freedom.

For himself and in his own time his path was marked by repeated failures, but his place in history cannot be determined in terms of his own political fortunes. As statesman he came to grips with the basic problems of government, and clarified the issues for a half century of partisan conflict. As political theorist he showed more clearly than any other American has ever done how the political process works. (pp. 483-84)

> *Charles M. Wiltse, in his* John C. Calhoun: Sectionalist, 1840-1850, *1951. Reprint by Russell & Russell, 1968, 592 p.*

LOUIS HARTZ (essay date 1952)

[*Hartz, a professor of political science, was awarded both the Woodrow Wilson Prize and the Lippincott Prize for his* The Liberal Tradition in America, *which is considered an influential work for its fresh insight into American history. In the following excerpt from an essay first published in 1952, Hartz points out contradictions in Calhoun's thought regarding the legal, social, and moral issues associated with nullification. According to Hartz, the greatest of these contradictions involved Calhoun's advocacy of slavery.*]

In the summer of 1832 a bitterly contested election was held in South Carolina. Voters were bribed and kidnapped, street violence was on the verge of breaking out, and both sides were secretly collecting arms in the event of civil war. The issue was whether the "sovereign" state of South Carolina should take it upon itself to nullify the tariff legislation of the federal government. Few South Carolinians supported the tariff, but the state had had a vigorous tradition of nationalism, and there were many who looked with horror on the "revolutionary" policy of nullification. The election went against them. Spurred on by the legal logic of Calhoun and the wild oratory of McDuffie, a strange but effective pair of influences, the Nullifiers swept the state and achieved an objective they had failed to achieve two years before: a legislative majority sufficiently large to call a constituent convention. After that there was no stopping the headlong rush toward nullification. Governor Hamilton called a special session of the legislature, the legislature immediately called a convention, and by November South Carolina's famous Ordinance of Nullification had been issued. The Tariff Acts of 1828 and 1832 were "null, void, and no law."

The Nullifiers, however, had rushed into a situation they did not quite foresee. If you had asked them before nullification what was going to happen afterward, you would not have received a very clear answer, except possibly from Calhoun. The reason was that they were relying on such overwhelming support from other Southern states and even from President Jackson himself that they did not believe that their action would seriously be challenged by the federal government. As it turned out, however, this was precisely the support they did not get. Every Southern state condemned the Ordinance of Nullification. Jackson denounced it as "treason." A force bill was introduced in Congress to put its provisions down. Wherever they turned the Nullifiers faced the bitter pill that passionate

men again and again have to swallow in politics: the realization that even their friends are not as passionate as they. Instead of putting South Carolina at the head of a glorious movement against "consolidation," they had isolated it from the Union, and left it facing alone the imminent threat of civil war.

It has been said of a certain French politician of the nineteenth century that he followed the formula of Danton except for one variation: he believed in audacity, audacity and then *no* more audacity. One might say the same thing, if it were not a bit too cruel, about the South Carolina Nullifers. Of course, when they saw the drift of events, they began to drill a volunteer army, and to set up arsenals throughout the state, but in the process they silently searched their souls. Eleven days before the Ordinance of Nullification was supposed to go into effect, on the very day that the Force Bill was reported in the Senate, that search came to a spectacular end. A large meeting of Nullifiers gathered at the Circus in Charleston and, saying that reform of the tariff was imminent, they virtually suspended the Nullification Ordinance. Nothing could hide the panic that went into this assembly. It was composed of private citizens, not of legislators or members of a constituent convention. The setting aside of the action of a sovereign state by such a body must surely be ranked as one of the hastiest forms of "nullification" that has ever been devised. (pp. 231-33)

This essay will concern itself with the theory of nullification, and after the events just described, the point I intend to make about it is bound to seem perverse. I intend to agree with Calhoun that the theory was a "conservative" theory. It is a tribute to Calhoun's gloomy genius as a political prophet that it is possible to stress his view again today. For it is, of course, in light of the Civil War that came after Calhoun died that the nullification idea takes on conservative significance. In the perspective of the Civil War the Harpers and McDuffies of 1832 cease to be "revolutionaries," cease to be "jacobins." They become men of peace, trying to solve by legal means the only problem in American history that has shattered completely the framework of our legal institutions.

In that perspective, too, our traditional approach to the theory of nullification has to be turned around a bit. What becomes even more important than the way the Nullifiers tried to limit the national government is the way they tried to limit themselves. It is easy to overlook this second matter. The Nullifiers could have chosen the path of secession, and indeed some of their opponents in South Carolina, like William Drayton and Langdon Cheves, would have gone along with them if they had. They could have appealed to a Jeffersonian right of revolution, as the violent McDuffie came close to doing on many occasions. But they did not want to secede and they did not want to revolt. The whole purpose of their philosophy was to construct a legal framework within which the battle between North and South could be contained, a peaceful "preservative," as Calhoun put it, of the American federal system. If their action symbolizes a trigger-happy impulse on the part of Americans to resist oppression, it symbolizes also something else that has been its curious counterpart: perhaps the most sensitive legal conscience in the world.

Here, indeed, was the root of their philosophic troubles. They would not have had to agonize themselves to justify secession or revolution. The premise of state "sovereignty" from which they began led directly to the most radical conclusions. What actually bothered them was how to bring a state conceived as supreme and uncontrollable into any sort of binding relationship with other states that, of course, were as supreme and uncontrollable as it was. It was this question that inspired the elaborate apologetics in which they engaged, the labyrinthine subtleties that few men outside of Calhoun and Chancellor Harper, even in South Carolina, were able to follow. If South Carolina was sovereign, why bother with the tariff at all? Why trouble yourself over the opinion of other states? The Nullifiers were astride the wild horse of Bodin and Hobbes, and it was not their radicalism that was illogical but their conservatism.

The North, however, was not quite in a position to make the most of this embarrassment. The Nullifiers argued that in 1878 South Carolina had entered into a "compact" with other "sovereign" American states for the purpose of creating a federal government that was the "joint agent" of them all. Now the real problem in this argument is that when you impose a binding compact on sovereign states you have bound them *too much:* technically they cannout be bound at all. But what troubled Daniel Webster was that South Carolina had not been bound *enough,* and so instead of pointing out that the conclusions of the Nullifiers did not match their premises, he assailed both as empirically false. This reduced the argument to a historical plane where, because the evidence was sufficiently vague, an endless stream of charge and countercharge became the order of the day. Webster denied that the Constitution was a "compact"; they asserted it. He asserted that a compact could create a vital American nation; they denied it. He insisted that the nation had acted in 1787; they insisted that the states had acted. The central logical flaw of nullification, its attempt to limit at all an illimitable sovereign, was removed from the spotlight of controversy.

Calhoun saved his logic, but in the process he virtually lost his constitutional "preservative." It has been said of Calhoun that he is the most rigorous thinker in American political thought; but his rigor, I suggest, was the rigor of John Stuart Mill: he tried to unite antitheses as logically as any man could. In [his *Letter to Governor Hamilton on the Subject of State Interposition*], in which he insisted on the "total dissimilarity" between secession and nullification, he outlined the course a sovereign state should take after it had nullified an act of the "joint agent." Solemnly obeying legal process, it would wait for the issue to be submitted to the other sovereign states, but three quarters of them would be required for a decision against it, since that is the number needed for amending the Constitution. It is shocking to think what would happen to the federal government under such a procedure, but it is puzzling to see why a sovereign state should bother to embark upon it. What if three quarters of the states actually do go against it? Is it any less sovereign then? Calhoun is too honest to evade this question. And so he tells Governor Hamilton, quite by the way: "Nullification may, indeed, be succeeded by secession." In other words, two things that are "totally dissimilar" on one page blend into another on the next as if nothing at all has happened.

The truth is, nothing has happened. The state was sovereign to begin with and it was sovereign to end with. What is curious is the elaborate ritual of legalism that has intervened in the middle. But there is no use laboring this point further. It would be possible to follow the struggle with "sovereignty" out at length in the nullification literature, and to show how it finally mastered its verbal limitations in the claims for independence that came with the Civil War. But the Civil War was not brought about because the sixteenth century had fashioned a concept that the American Southerners insisted on using in the nineteenth. If we want to get at some of the deeper causes of

the breakdown of Calhoun's constitutional conservatism, it would be well to turn to the social aligments of the age, and to Calhoun's attempt to deal with them.

It is a commonplace of American history that the theory of states' rights has followed the course of economic interest. What makes the process bizarre is that at the same time the theory has been developed with infinite logical labor, so that one gets the odd impression that Hegel is proving himself on the American scene while Marx is doing so too. If the pure metaphysical passion is to be found in American political thought at all, where would we place it if not in the men who have struggled so heroically with the categories of state and nation? And yet everyone knows that Jefferson tended to forget his metaphysics at the time of the Louisiana Purchase and that the New England Federalists tended to discover theirs at the time of the Embargo. The same principle holds true of the South Carolina Nullifiers. Before Calhoun became concerned over the tariff and slavery, he had denounced the notion of strict constitutional construction, and McDuffie, who joined the nullification movement late, had said things that were even worse. He had said that politicians who exalted the states were inferior men who did so because the could not win a place on the national scene.

The fact that the Nullifers misunderstood their economic ills does not alter the fact that we are dealing here with a genuine problem in the politics of economic interest. Basically the troubles of South Carolina did not come from the tariff: they came from concentration on the production of cotton at a time when the settlement of new lands in the Southwest was forcing the price of that commodity down. But whatever might be said about cotton, or the slave economy on which it rested, South Carolina was pretty well destined to be an agricultural state, and above all it would be absurd to insist on a classical pattern of perfect rationality in the behavior of economic interests. If such a pattern were the normal thing, the record of American history would read a good deal differently from the way it does. It would read a good deal differently on the score of the tariff itself, and not because of the kind of enlightenment South Carolina needed. It is reasonable to suspect that more economic mistakes have been made in the process of supporting the American tariff than have been made in the process of opposing it.

Calhoun's defense of the South as an economic interest represents the same failure of conservatism that we find in his defense of the South as a collection of states. In terms of theory, to be sure, this is not entirely true. When in his political speeches and in the *Disquisition on Government* Calhoun substitutes "minorities" and "interests" for "states" and gives them the power of nullifying national policy, he releases himself from the wild theoretical horse he is trying to ride on the legal plane. Minorities and interests can hardly be called "sovereign," and Calhoun does not call them that. But all that Calhoun really accomplishes by this is to remove his problem from the realm of logic and put it in the realm of social fact. In social fact the Southern minority that Calhoun starts with has been torn away from the rest of the American nation as effectively as the concept of sovereignty would ever tear it away. It is a grim and isolated group, engaged in a war it cannot win, whose secession he actually predicted before he died. Under such circumstances preserving the Union by the simple technique of the "concurrent majority," if not legally illogical, is at any rate practically impossible.

Calhoun's method was to shatter the fabric of American community and then to attempt to restore it by a purely mechanical device. But this was to overlook a very important truth: mechanical devices are only as strong as the sense of community that underlies them. And yet his error was not unprecedented in American thought. The Founding Fathers had made it too. In the minds of many of them, Adams and Hamilton and Morris for example, the American scheme of checks and balances was designed to control a destructive war between proletarians on the one hand and artistocrats on the other. This war, which in the case of Adams was deduced largely from the irrelevant experience of ancient Greece and the Renaissance city-states, would surely have shattered the American Constitution as quickly as the struggles of France after the Restoration shattered the Charter of 1814. Happily such war has not been a general characteristic of American life, which has been permeated by a sense of social agreement that has been the wonder of foreign critics since the time of Tocqueville, and so the wrongness of the premises of the Founding Fathers has been obscured by what seems to be the "rightness" of their conclusions. But the case of Calhoun, alas, was somewhat different. The desperate struggle that he was describing was actually becoming a fact. He was making the mistake of the Founding Fathers at the only time in our history when it could readily be exposed. Of course, the "concurrent majority" was not adopted, and neither was his scheme of a dual executive, which embodied it. But if it had been, is it fair to assume that the North would have found it tolerable?

Notice, however, that Calhoun does not merely accept the scheme of Adams: the "concurrent majority" goes beyond it and supplements political checks with economic-interest checks. A threefold division of the functions of government on the national plane is not enough, because a single party can gain control of them simultaneously. Calhoun, in other words, is busily piling up checks in face of the very situation that is going to explode them all. This seems strange but, given the premises of the eighteenth century, is it? Once you concede that mechanical devices can serve as a substitute for the spirit of community which permits them to function, are you not automatically embarked on such a course? There is logic here, even if of a rather inverted kind: the more conflict you have, the more checks you need, and the more certain it is that no checks will work. Calhoun, like some tragic hero, was fated to bring the tradition of Adams to a climax in American thought at the moment it collapsed completely.

This is just another version of the paradox that Mr. Peter Drucker should recently rediscover Calhoun as the chief philosopher of our free and easy system of pressure politics [see excerpt dated 1948]—Calhoun who wrote on the eve of the Civil War. It is possible, I think, to carry Mr. Drucker's point too far. Weak as party discipline is in America, single interests do not have a veto on public policy, as real estate knows in connection with rent control and labor in connection with the Taft-Hartley Act. But the relevance of the "concurrent majority" principle to the pulling and hauling of interests on the American political scene is striking enough, and it reveals again the strange tragedy of Calhoun's nullification conservatism. The system of American logrolling is a system of "checks and balances" that bears a curious resemblance to the one our Founding Fathers had in mind, but instead of being imposed on the fabric of the American community, it has largely risen out of it. It has had many causes, one of which is the constitutional scheme itself, but no one can doubt that the social unity of American life has been among the most important. Societies frozen by deep and

permanent conflict have never inspired the easy barter of individual interests.

But what Calhoun was doing, if he is to be considered a philosopher of our interest-group system, was offering it as a substitute for the social unity on which it rests. Of course, if we were to agree with what he often implies, that the struggles between the North and South were simply the result of using the device of the "numerical majority," there would be nothing fantastic about this procedure. Legislating the logrolling technique into existence would be a perfectly reasonable act. But the sectional struggle obviously came from deeper sources, as he himself practically admits when he declares the South to be a permanent and hopeless minority. Minorities cannot be permanent unless there is some profound division of interest to make them so. And under such circumstances not even legislation can produce the spirit of pressure-group adjustment. For that spirit is ordinarily possible precisely because the nation is not split into warring social camps, because majorities and minorities are *fluid* and the groups that make them up know that they can easily exchange places on another issue or at another time. Calhoun said that the "concurrent majority" produced the spirit of compromise. What was actually the case, however, was that the spirit of compromise produced the "concurrent majority."

Nothing shows up the anguish of the man more clearly than this perpetual putting of the cart before the horse. Looked at from one angle, his mood is the authentic mood of irrational desperation: not merely because he clings to the form of compromise while its substance is disappearing, but because he has convinced himself that an exaggeration of its form will somehow compensate for a loss of its substance. Mr. Drucker's point, as I have said, ought not to be taken too literally: we have never had the "concurrent majority" in American politics. The spirit of compromise Calhoun calls for outdoes in amiability even the spirit that pervades a Congressional cloakroom in a time of high profits and high wages. As he himself puts it, each interest will "promote its own prosperity by conciliating the good will, and promoting the prosperity of others." There will be a "rivalry to promote the interests of each other." There will be "patriotism, nationality, harmony, and a struggle only for supremacy in promoting the common good of the whole." All of this when the country is on the brink of civil war, and simply by extending a notch the logic of John Adams! One is tempted to wonder whether the keenest pathos of the compromise spirit before the Civil War lies in the speeches of Henry Clay, or whether it lies right here, in Calhoun, dreaming up out of the South's own bitterness a mirage of social peace the like of which even a peaceful nation has never experienced.

At the time in which Calhoun was writing, however, neither South Carolina nor the South as a whole was quite in the position he made it out to be. There is one problem that Calhoun and other Nullifiers were careful to avoid: the problem of the minority within the minority—the problem, in other words, of the Unionists in South Carolina. It is not strange, given the treatment the Unionists received, that they should blast the Ordinance of Nullification with the very language the Nullifiers used to defend it, that they should call it "the mad edict of a despotic majority." How were the Calhounians to meet this charge? It would have been suicidal for the Nullifiers to give their opponents a veto, but let us suppose, out of passion for logic that they did. There was also a minority within the Unionist minority, and a minority within that. Were these minorities to be given a veto too? The point I am making is the fairly obvious one that if the minority principle is carried to its logical conclusion it unravels itself out into Locke's state of nature where separate individuals execute the law of nature for themselves. Locke's acceptance of majority rule was by no means ill considered.

But this is merely a logical victory over Calhoun, and it is likely to lead us away from rather than closer to the central problem to be faced. In politics most principles break down when carried to their "logical conclusion," and if a man is brave enough to match his mind against reality, provided he does not use concepts like "sovereignty," which make it impossible, he ought to be given the privilege of silently drawing a few lines. The real significance of the Unionist minority lies in another place. It lies not in the fact that it was a minority but in the fact that it was *Unionist*. And the reason why this is important is that it reveals an important mechanism by which groups are held together in a political community: the mechanism of crisscrossing allegiances. Had the South Carolinians been one hundred per cent in favor of Nullification, or had the Unionist minority simply been indifferent to the question, they would hardly have given up so quickly their challenge to the federal government. But Jackson was in direct negotiation with the Unionist minority—he had promised them all the aid they needed—and this was a very sobering piece of knowledge for the Nullifiers to have. In other words, the fact that South Carolina was not a monolithic entity, as the Calhounian terms of "state" or "interest" or "minority" might imply, had a lot to do with uniting it to the rest of the nation.

If Calhoun's concern with a national "preservative" had transcended everything else, he would have welcomed this empirical defect in his premises. And as a matter of fact, there is a certain amount of evidence, on the wider plane of the struggle between North and South, to suggest that he actually did. With a number of other Southerners, as the Civil War approached, he suggested an alliance between Northern capitalists and Southern planters to keep both the slaves and the free working-class down. This alliance presumably would have helped to save the Union by exploiting common tensions within the sectional interests he usually described in monolithic terms. But Calhoun was in general no philosopher of intrasectional conflict, for the obvious reason that he was too embittered a Southerner. Instead of welcoming this imperfection in his premises, he glossed it over. Which, of course, made it harder than ever for him to reach his conservative conclusions.

History, as usual, was on the side of his premises. The drift toward civil war was a drift toward the consolidation of North and South into increasingly monolithic interests. Intersectional allegiances, one by one, began to disappear. America approached what is probably the most dangerous moment in the political life of any community: the moment of the almost perfect *rationalization* of its internal conflict. This made Calhoun's simplistic antithesis of majority and minority a real one, but what it did for the mechanical approach to politics is a matter of the obvious record. Once again, as in the case of his states'-rights legalism, Calhoun had laid a foundation that exploded the structure he tried to build upon it.

I have discussed nullification as a legal issue and as an issue of social interest. There was also a moral question in the crisis of 1832, the question of slavery, which already, at the hands of Harper and Senator Smith, had begun to produce that massive defense of a stratified society which flowered in the South before the Civil War. As this argument evolved, fed by the attack of Northern abolitionism, it did as much as anything else to produce the sectional intransigence that shattered Calhoun's nullification conservatism, but it challenged nullification in another way as well: philosophically. For the doctrine of nullification was, as I have shown, an exaggerated version of the mechanical rationalism of the eighteenth century, while the theory of slavery was a romantic revolt against it. Even if they had not had Burke, Disraeli, and Carlyle to read, the logic of their attack on Jefferson would have impelled the Southerners to discover that the Social Contract was a myth, that governments were divinely inspired, and that coercion was a law of life. But if this was so, how could the Constitution be a "compact," and why should minorities be so diligently defended? The philosophy of slavery struck hammer-blows at the finespun rationalism of nullification, and because Calhoun contributed to it he found himself caught in the most painful contradiction of his strange career, more painful even than the conflict between "sovereignty" and "preservative" or, on the plane of practice, between the war of the sections and the "concurrent majority."

Interestingly enough, it is this devotion of Calhoun to the theory of slavery that has given him his familiar reputation as a "conservative." In terms of what I have been saying, it is precisely this devotion that is "radical," that challenges his clinging to the Union. One is tempted now to give up Calhoun's own Nullification Act terminology. For while a case can be made for abolishing the term "conservative" from the study of American thought as a whole, it is precisely in connection with the theory of slavery that it has its most legitimate use. That theory, with its predominantly feudal image, comes as close to the authentic mood of the Western reaction as anything America has ever turned up. But though it does not pay to quibble over terms, provided the substance of an issue is clear, a word can still be said for Calhoun's claim that the rationalist theory of nullification was "conservative," and not merely in the obvious political sense that it sought to preserve the Union, but in the philosophic sense as well. For the "reaction" that the defense of slavery inspired in Southern thought was strangely enough an Enlightenment, since the philosophy of Jefferson was the vested theoretical interest that men like Bledsoe and Harper were forced to assail. This miraculous inversion of the European pattern, which gave to the Southern disciples of Burke the spirit of iconoclastic discovery we might expect to find in Diderot, confounds the issue of terminology so badly that we can even call rationalism reactionary. We can say, at any rate, that it was an older thing than the "feudal conservatism" it confronted.

Mixing nullification with "feudal conservatism" was like mixing water with oil. Things could not have been worse. What is inevitably the *bete noire* of any reactionary attack is precisely what the Nullifiers had to advance: the idea of the manmade constitution. Fitzhugh branded it as "absurd." Calhoun, courageous to the end, drew a distinction between "constitution" and "government," as if by keeping Sieyes and Maistre in watertight compartments he might be able to enjoy them both. Governments were natural and divinely inspired, but constitutions, which controlled them, were not. It was a tenuous enough distinction. Can it reasonably be argued that what governs government is any less governmental than government itself?

The clash between the Englightenment and the reaction became even more vivid when the question of "rights" came up. There is a happily unconscious paradox in a lot of Southern oratory:

slavery is excellent, but Southerners will die rather than be "slaves" of the North. Of course, as long as the defense of slavery grounds itself in racial theory concerning the Negro, this is a paradox easily resolved. But Southern thought, as in the case of men like Hughes, Holmes, and Fitzhugh, refused to stop at the color line, insisting that slavery or something like it was the ideal system of life for whites as well as blacks. Even here, to be sure, the "slavery" of the South is not automatically justified, since slaves ought to be inferior men and Southern gentlemen are certainly not in that class. But once again the bottom falls out of the Southern position. The definition of justifiable slavery is the mysterious status quo ordained by a mysterious Providence, and only wild Jeffersonian "metaphysicians" would dare to overturn it. If this is true, the enslavement of the South by the tariff would seem to be just as valid as the enslavement of the slave by the lash. The Hegelian type of conservatism, which young Thomas Dew brought back to Virginia from Germany, has burnt many fingers in the history of social thought.

One of the reasons the Southerners would not stop their defense of slavery at the racial line was that they wanted to belabor the "wage-slavery" of the North and to insist that their own system of labor, suitably defined by Henry Hughes and others as a kind of feudal "warranteeism," was actually superior to it. There was a movement of thought, partially inspired by the Young England philosophy of Disraeli, in which iron laws of capitalist oppression and proletarian revolt were contrasted with sentimental laws of paternal care and social peace. Calhoun himself contributed something to this movement, which gave him a curious resemblance to the European "feudal socialists" whom Marx so bitterly derided. But the main point for us to grasp is the strikinng way in which this philosophy clashed with the rational mechanics of nullification. If the corporate ideal of the plantation is to be maintained, how can one also maintain a theory of minority rights which logically unravels itself out into Locke's state of nature? An anonymous critic of the "concurrent majority" in *DeBow's Review* assailed Calhoun for deserting the great slave truth that the best type of rule was the "natural" rule of the "despot." He was, alas, on solid ground.

These contradictions were bad enough, but what was even worse, from the angle of Calhoun's nullification conservatism, was that the romantic theory of slavery itself threatened to resolve them. Men who have read Burke and Scott do not need to rely on constitutional apologetics in order to defend their sectional life. They are led automatically to another type of claim: the blood-and-soil claim of any ancient culture. This claim solved Calhoun's problem at a single stroke. It absorbed into the organicism of his defense of slavery the very sectional plea that had impelled him to repudiate it. It made Burke do the job of Adams as well. And as time passed, and the cult of "Southernism" defined itself in contrast to the commercialism of Yankeedom, it grew enormously in the Southern mind. . . . But the question is, what did it do to Calhoun's "preservative" of the nation? Didn't it pack even more explosive power than the concept of "sovereignty" itself?

It is strange that this idea should begin to evolve in the South and not the North, for it was of course the basic idea of modern nationalism—in its liberal form, the passionate thesis of Rousseau and Mazzini. Webster could surely have used it. A charge of Burkian or Rousseauian romanticism would have lifted his concept of the American "people" to a high ground where the constitutional exegesis of the Nullifiers could not have undermined it. But Webster, the great philosopher of American "nationalism," remains as dry and legalistic as Marshall. The ironic fact was that the liberal romanticism of the North did not lead to the nationalism of Rousseau as the conservative romanticism of the South led to the nationalism of Burke or Scott. With the exception of a few men like Barlow and perhaps Emerson, it led in other directions: radical individualism, as in Thoreau, or radical cosmopolitanism, as in Garrison. The South, the home of "particularism," became in a curious sense the originator of romantic nationalism in American political theory.

It is not hard to see that the idea of blood-and-soil nationalism was more explosive than either the idea of "sovereignty" or the idea of "minority." Sovereignty was an uncontrollable concept, but it was at any rate a concept, a rational abstraction, something you could argue about. So was "minority." But there was really no arguing with the spirit of Southern culture, for by definition its ethos was irrational and its claim divine. As the romantic philosophy of slavery swept forward it not only corroded the mechanical premises of nullification but it advanced in their place a sectional plea colored with the most frightening overtones. Fitzhugh, with his "organic nationality," with his bitter attack on the "Calhoun school," was the great philosopher of this movement. He is the man, I suggest, who ought to have the reputation for theoretical consistency which Calhoun has attained. (pp. 233-44)

This was the end of Calhoun's constitutional conservatism, this swallowing up of the Southern argument into the romantic logic of reactionary thought. Of course, the South was never as logical as Fitzhugh wanted it to be. It continued to divide its time between the world of Burke and the world of Jefferson, as indeed it still does. Even in 1861, after all of Fitzhugh's lessons, it appealed to a Jeffersonian right of revolution. But there is no doubt that the rise of the naturalistic authoritarianism that Fitzhugh represented did as much as anything else in the South to discredit the reasoning of Calhoun. And the irony of it, as usual, was that Calhoun himself had helped its rise along. (p. 244)

Louis Hartz, "A Conservation Prophet in the Romantic South," in Intellectual History in America: Contemporary Essays on Puritanism, the Enlightenment, and Romanticism, Vol. I, *edited by Cushing Strout, Harper & Row Publishers, 1968, pp. 213-44.*

GERALD M. CAPERS (essay date 1960)

[*In the following excerpt from his* John C. Calhoun, Opportunist: A Reappraisal, *Capers portrays Calhoun as a man largely motivated by personal ambition.*]

[In the pages of John Quincy Adams' diary (see Additional Biography)] every action of the Carolinian was recorded as that of a self-seeking, hypocritical, and scheming politician. This diary was published in the 1870's and used by Hermann Von Holst as the basis for his hostile biography of the famous southerner [see excerpt dated 1882]. Thus in the Reconstruction Era, Calhoun seen through Adams' biased eyes became the personification of the unprincipled and wicked South plotting rebellion years before she tried it.

Most of Calhoun's later biographers have portrayed him as the symbol of the purity of southern motives. In their eyes both

An illustration of, from left to right, Webster, Clay, and Calhoun.

Calhoun and the South are above reproach, never motivated but by the loftiest incentives. Calhoun the man has remained in the clouds, symbolic of the Lost Cause. As a natural consequence the fiction persists that his great contemporaries, Jackson, Clay, and Webster, were ambitious men who used every means within their power to attain the presidency. But the Carolinian, willing in his high patriotism to accept high office because he so conspicuously had the interests of the whole nation and not himself at heart, never stooped to low personal ambition nor to any of the sordid methods of his rivals.

The letters and papers of Calhoun lend a superficial support to this thesis, but there is a much stronger case for a contrary interpretation. Calvinistic in mental habit and temperament, as was Adams, Calhoun could never admit personal ambition but had to rationalize his policies and his every political act exclusively in terms of national interest. His shift in the middle of his career from extreme nationalism to an extreme state-rights position made rationalization all the more essential, not merely for his own mental comfort but also to convince the nation of his intellectual integrity. Webster made an identical shift in the opposite direction about that same time, yet he was not subject, in any such degree, to an urge for self-justification. Jackson and Clay, since their appeal was more to men's hearts, never bothered themselves about the matter of consistency. While much of this rationalizing on Calhoun's part was unconscious, it satisfied his peculiar complex and it has been accepted by his biographers for the most part at face value. But why should he not be exposed to the same critical philosophy of human behavior with which biographers have approached his contemporaries? To explain his career in terms of englightened self-interest can be regarded as condemnation only by those who persist in identifying the fleshless symbol with the man.

Clay, it is generally admitted, wanted all his life to become President and took practical measures to achieve that objective. When in sectional crises he threw the whole weight of his influence and energy into successful efforts at compromise to save the Union, his patriotic course enhanced as much as it hindered his chances for the highest office. Calhoun, it might similarly be argued, equally wanted the presidency all his life and within the limits of his own inhibitions took what he regarded as practical steps towards that end. That he frequently differed with Clay by no means proved that he was any less patriotic or less desirous of preserving the Union—in fact he argued that acceptance of his proposals was the only sure method of such preservation. At no stage in his career can it be clearly proved that he consciously placed his own fortunes above those of the nation. Yet he was always able to convince himself that the course most convenient to his own aspirations was also best suited for the general welfare of all the American people.

Gerald M. Capers, in his John C. Calhoun, Opportunist: A Reappraisal, *University of Florida Press, 1960, 275 p.*

RICHARD N. CURRENT   (essay date 1963)

[A professor of United States history, Current has written a number of books on nineteenth-century American political figures. In the following excerpt from his study of Calhoun, Current identifies the source of Calhoun's enduring relevance, rejecting the argument that the statesman's theory of the concurrent majority is the working model for twentieth-century American government.]

By the beginning of the twentieth century, Calhoun had lost practically all relevance for living Americans. In 1911 the historian William E. Dodd, himself a Southerner, could write: "No political party looks back to Calhoun as its founder or rejuvenator, no group of public men proclaim allegiance to his doctrines, no considerable group of individuals outside of South Carolina profess any love for his name and ideals."

Suddenly, nearly a hundred years after his death, his reputation recovered and took on new aspects. By the middle of the twentieth century a Calhoun revival was under way. He and his theory seemed timely again.

New biographies came out. . . . His *Disquisition on Government* was reissued again and again, in various editions. A project for publishing his complete writings, in twelve to fifteen volumes, was announced. He was made the subject of dozens of essays, and these were given space not only in learned journals but also in popular periodicals. . . . (p. 137)

More remarkable than the quantity of this writing was the theme of much of it. The authors treated Calhoun as no antiquarian curiosity but a political philosopher with an enduring message and a unique relevance for their time. (pp. 137-38)

[For example, Peter F. Drucker (see excerpt dated 1948)] elaborated upon "Calhoun's pluralism" as a "key to American politics." . . . Drucker contended that "for the constitutional veto power of the states over national legislation, by means of which Calhoun proposed to formalize the principle of sectional and interest compromise, was substituted in actual practice the much more powerful and much more elastic but extra-constitutional veto power of sections, interests, and pressure groups." (p. 140)

Though he made the most elaborate presentation of the new Calhounism, Drucker did not originate it. Before him, Charles M. Wiltse had put forth the thesis in a couple of published essays [see Additional Bibliography]. . . . Even earlier, V. L. Parrington had suggested the idea [see excerpt dated 1927]. (p. 141)

The illustrations the neo-Calhounites use, to demonstrate the "veto" by each interest or each minority today, are plausible but unconvincing. Here is one [by John Fischer]: "For sixteen years [1932-48] the Republicans lost much of their standing as a truly national party because they had made themselves unacceptable to labor." Thus labor's "veto" did seem to have some effect during those years, but it failed to operate against the Taft-Hartley Act (1947), which the Republican Congress passed despite the last-ditch opposition of labor leaders, who denounced it as a "slave-labor law." And what had happened to labor's "veto" during the preceding twelve years of Republican supremacy? Another example [from Fischer]: "Similarly, the Democrats during the middle stage of the New Deal incurred the wrath of the business interests." What became of the *business* "veto" during those sixteen (ultimately twenty) years that the New Dealers were in power? The explanation is offered that President Franklin D. Roosevelt had set aside the "veto" by his appeal to the needs of the "temporary emergency" which the depression had brought. But what does a "veto" amount to if it can be charmed away by a couple of magic words, such as "temporary emergency"? Surely this is not the kind of negative power that Calhoun had in mind!

A third illustration, which the neo-Calhounites use to support their argument, does further damage to their own case. [According to Drucker]: "By 1946 . . . labor troubles could be resolved only on a basis acceptable to both labor and employer: higher wages *and* higher prices." Now, this may illustrate a "veto" by labor and by employer, but it also shows the lack, in this instance, of a "veto" by consumer or by farmer. What the wage-price agreement here amounts to, in fact, is a deal between two interests at the expense of the rest of the community. It is not an agreement arrived at through consultation of all interests.

No doubt this sort of bargaining *is* fairly typical of what actually goes on in the United States. Together with the other examples mentioned, it demonstrates the fact that politicians and pressure groups normally do not appease every minority (not even every big one), do not allow each interest a "veto," do not arrive at action on the basis of unanimity. Instead, they construct a working majority through the combination of several (but not necessarily all) minorities. When, to form the combination, the support of a particular group is needed, the demands of that group, the positive or negative demands, are respected. To the extent, then, that any interest or minority can get concessions from other interests or minorities in the process of forming the majority, to that extent the "veto" of the interest or minority is effective. But only to that extent. The process is familiar enough, and so is the word for it—"logrolling."

This practice is far from new in the history of American politics. In Calhoun's own time there were blocs, lobbies, and factions, and there was logrolling among them. Calhoun himself was aware, painfully aware, of the concessions that both Whig and Democratic politicians were prone to make to tariff lobbyists or to the antislavery or free-soil bloc. He knew from bitter experience what "availability" meant in the choosing of a presidential candidate. He was acquainted with the struggle, essentially the same then as now, by which contending groups sought to get control of the government. "If no one interest be strong enough, of itself, to obtain it," he wrote, "a combination will be formed between those whose interests are most alike—each conceding something to the others, until a sufficient number is obtained to make a majority." That was the essence of the process in his day, and it remains the essence of the process in ours.

But this was not and is not what Calhoun advocated. Quite the contrary. He condemned that kind, the familiar kind, of politics. He thought that by its inevitable tendency "principle and policy would lose all influence in the elections; then cunning, falsehood, deception, slander, fraud, and gross appeals to the appetites of the lowest and most worthless portions of the community would take the place of sound reason and wise debate." Certainly he had no use for the kind of trading that went on at party conventions. He opposed allowing minorities, such as the abolitionists, to exercise any kind of veto on presidential nominations. For example, as he looked forward, in 1847, to the election of the following year, he thought there was a scheme by which slaveholders and abolitionists would be "coerced into nominating and supporting the same candidate" on the Democratic ticket.

> Should it succeed—should the party machinery
> for President-making prove strong enough to

force the slaveholding States to join in a convention to nominate and support a candidate who will be acceptable to the abolitionists, they will have committed the most suicidal act that a people ever perpetrated. I say acceptable; for it is clear that the non-slaveholding States will outnumber in convention the slaveholding, and that no one who is not acceptable to the abolitionists can receive their votes; and, of course, the votes of the States where they hold the balance; and that no other will be nominated, or, if nominated, be elected.

Calhoun went on to denounce all nominating conventions as "irresponsible bodies" which were unknown to the Constitution. He urged Southerners to renounce the forthcoming Democratic convention of 1848 and to unite in a strictly Southern party. The election of the President, he added, ought to be left strictly to the electoral college, as the framers of the Constitution had intended. He refused to be satisfied with the combination of interests upon policy unless *all* interests (that is, all property-owning interests and, in particular, the slavery interest) were consulted and their approval gained. "I am," he declared, "in favor of the government of the whole; the only really and truly popular government—a government based on the concurrent majority—the joint assent of all the parts, through their respective majority of the whole." He insisted upon essential *unanimity* as the condition for governmental action.

This requirement, for all the assertions of the neo-Calhounites, does not exist today. It did not exist when Calhoun was alive. He looked for some means of imposing it; he found the means, constitutionally, in his theory of state rights and, politically, in his plan for creating a sectional party or at least a sectional faction—the solid South. Except when his own presidential hopes were active and his own chances appeared to be good, he was inclined to turn away from the game of politics as it was customarily played—and still is.

In sum, the new interpreters of Calhoun have been careless in their reading of his philosophy and superficial in their description of current politics. They have attributed to him the very political principles and practices which he detested and for which he sought quite different alternatives. Without realizing it, they have misused the term "concurrent majority" so as to make it mean essentially what he himself meant by the term "numerical majority," that is, a combination of the majorities of many or even most *but not all* interests.

It might, or might not, be a good thing if the United States actually had institutions to give effect to the kind of "political pluralism" that the neo-Calhounites admire. It might be desirable, for instance, to set up a third house as a supplement to Congress, a third house in which economic, sectional, religious, racial, and other groups would be represented as such; and in which each of them could exercise a veto. Possibly this would work, and possibly it could be considered as a Calhounian solution—but only if certain passages are isolated from his works, unrestrained inferences are drawn from these passages, and the rest of his writings and his career itself are ignored.

On the whole, he seems to have taken a dualist, not a pluralist, view of politics. Though he mentioned the existence of various interests in society, he made no attempt to list and describe them, and certainly he never specified racial or religious mi-

norities, or the working class, as deserving of the veto power. Generally he ignored the variety of possible groupings. When he got down to theorizing, he really thought about only two groups at a time, not several. On occasion he dealt with the duality of capital and labor. Most often he had in mind the twofold grouping of North against South, free states against slave states. These were, to him, the majority and the minority, and this was the minority he sought to protect—the minority of slaveholders.

It is farfetched to say that his "insights remain vital for any minority." This might be remotely true if his theory were abstracted enough, but the theory would have to be stretched to the point where it had only the most tenuous connection with what Calhoun actually thought and said. The assumption would have to be made that, somehow, the case for the onetime master has been, or at least can be, converted into a case for the onetime slave. This assumption has yet to be proved. Perhaps the National Association for the Advancement of Colored People ought to peruse Calhoun's works for means of protecting Negro rights. If the N.A.A.C.P. should do so, the news would be startling, and if the search were successful, the news would be amazing.

Surely the spirit of Calhoun is not to be found in the meetings of today's minority groups, of whatever creed or color. Nor is it to be discovered in all the political bargaining of the lobby, the congressional bloc, the executive department, or the smoke-filled room. We of the twentieth century must look elsewhere if we are to find the genuine ghost of the Great Nullifer. (pp. 142-47)

Wherever a White Citizens' Council meets in Mississippi, or a similar group in another of the Southern states, *there* is to be sought, nowadays, the true spirit of Calhoun. It is to be sought in the activities of conservative—or reactionary—Southern whites. The way *they* use the lobby, the bloc, the party convention, and other political devices can be considered as essentially Calhounian.

These white Southerners now face a problem quite similar to the one that Calhoun faced more than a hundred years ago. They talk of maintaining white supremacy and he talked of protecting slavery. The problem remains that of defending, against external attack, institutions based upon a belief in human inequality.

One of Calhoun's proslavery arguments was this: that to turn the Negroes loose without giving them full civic rights (which he thought them by nature unfitted for) would only be to change the form of their bondage—they would cease to be the property of individual masters but would become the slaves of the community as a whole. As applied to the group servitude which Calhoun thus foresaw, abolition continues to be a live issue in the South. In the New Deal days, for example, the W.P.A. was an antislavery agency to the extent that it provided, at comparatively high pay, alternative employment for previously dependent "colored help." During the Second World War the manpower shortage and the Fair Employment Practices Commission brought additional job opportunities, and these also had an abolitionist effect. So did the wartime propaganda directed against racist notions and, as in the Four Freedoms slogan, in favor of human rights. Since the war, the emancipationist trend has been continued and accelerated by the civil-rights program of the Truman Administration, the diplomatic requirements of the Cold War, and the Supreme Court's reinterpretation of the Thirteenth and Fourteenth Amendments, especially in the historic case of *Brown* v. *Topeka* (1954), requiring desegregation of public schools.

In the face of the new abolitionism, Southern leaders of the present have responded in much the same way that Calhoun responded to the antislavery movement of his time. . . . [He] resorted to the doctrine of state rights and to political devices, such as nullification, with which to implement the doctrine. He maintained that a "union" of Southerners would benefit the Union itself, that it was essential to the smooth working of the machinery of the federal Constitution. "The machine never works well when the South is divided," he said, "nor badly when it is united." Not only, then, did he call upon Southerners to unite; he also strove to win Northern sympathy and support for his united South. If such a combination had been attainable on his terms, he would have preferred an alliance of Northern and Southern conservatives. He withdrew temporarily from the party of Andrew Jackson, and on two occasions (1832 and 1836) when he disapproved both major parties and their presidential candidates, he advised that South Carolina cast her electoral votes for a third, irregular ticket. Finally he rejoined the Democratic party, but for reasons of expediency, not principle. He continued to hope that events ultimately would bring the conservatives of both sections into a single national party.

Recently, many Southern politicians have resorted to tactics that are reminiscent of Calhoun's. Within Congress, these politicians have formed blocs and, by means of them, have exercised a kind of concurrent veto at times, as in the Senate filibusters against civil-rights legislation in 1949 and subsequent years. Repeatedly, in presidential elections, the more extreme Southerners have threatened to withhold from the Democratic candidate the electoral votes of their states. In 1948 South Carolina and a few others actually did so, throwing their votes to the irregular, Dixiecratic candidate, J. Strom Thurmond. . . . (pp. 148-50)

The Dixiecrats, legitimate heirs of Calhoun, relied in the 1940's, as he had done in the 1840's, on the hope that labor troubles in the North would bring Northern conservatives to the Southern cause. This dream of a party realignment, one that would bring together the property interests of both sections within a single organization, has recurred from time to time in the minds of both Northerners and Southerners during the years since Calhoun's death.

For a quarter of a century the sectional conflict and the Civil War made impossible the realization of the dream. Then, in the Compromise of 1877, by which the Southerners agreed to the seating of Rutherford B. Hayes as President, despite his dubious electoral majority, the Hayes Republicans attempted to replace their Negro and carpetbagger allies with substantial white men, especially the old Whigs, in the South. This was, as C. Vann Woodward has termed it, a scheme of "reunion and reaction." It had only a limited and temporary success.

At last, in 1952, exactly a hundred years after Daniel Webster had proposed a new party of Northern and Southern conservatives, a party of that kind seemed to be in the making, with Dwight D. Eisenhower as its chief. Two years later the Charlestonian Herbert Ravenel Sass contended that the American republic had already adapted itself to Calhounian principles but must adapt itself still further. "It is now in the process of adapting itself," Sass wrote, "and this further and far-reaching adaptation to Calhoun's blueprint reflects the revolution in political philosophy of which the Eisenhower victory of 1952 was

a symptom. It is a counter-revolution against the national socialism which is the inevitable sequel of the concept of the republic as a single standardized equalitarian unit." Without accepting all of Sass's implications, one can agree that the Eisenhower election, to the extent that it actually represented a conservative North-South reaction against current trends, exemplified the materialization, at least incipient, of Calhounian hopes.

During the presidency of Eisenhower and also that of John F. Kennedy, conservative Democrats from the South and conservative Republicans from the North have cooperated again and again in Congress. Still, in opposing the integration of schools and other public facilities, the Southern bloc has not, of itself, provided the sort of veto that Calhoun envisaged in nullification. Some of the Southerners have revived the idea of nullification itself, though they call it "interposition"—an alternative term that Calhoun also used. For instance, the *Richmond News Leader,* in 1955, devoted a special supplement to this theme. The editors called for "Interposition Now!" They reprinted Jefferson's and Madison's Kentucky and Virginia resolutions and, filling five columns, one of Calhoun's statements of "the right of interposition." The editors, asserting that the right still existed, called attention to his view of it as the fundamental principle of our system, resting on facts historically as certain as our revolution itself, and deductions as simple and demonstrative [demonstrable] as that of any political or moral truth whatever." Several of the Southern states later passed interposition resolutions, though none of the states actually attempted to interpose against, or nullify, the Supreme Court's decision of 1954 or any of the federal measures intended to give effect to the decision.

The die-hard defenders of segregation are thoroughly justified in thinking of themselves as successors and inheritors of Calhoun. It remains to be seen whether they can succeed any better than he did in making state rights a barrier to human rights. (pp. 150-52)

> *Richard N. Current, in his* John C. Calhoun, *Washington Square Press, Inc., 1963, 182 p.*

WILLIAM W. FREEHLING   (essay date 1965)

[*An American historian and educator, Freehling is the author of the award-winning* Prelude to Civil War: The Nullification Controversy in South Carolina, 1816-1836 *(see Additional Bibliography). In the following excerpt from an essay on Calhoun, Freehling challenges those critics who view the statesman as a "thoroughgoing economic determinist," highlighting his dual emphasis on the problems of conflicting economic interests and corrupt spokesmen. These "twin obsessions," according to Freehling, are responsible for the inconsistencies in Calhoun's political theory.*]

Over a century after his death John C. Calhoun is still considered one of America's outstanding political theorists. In a culture which has usually exalted the doctrine of majority rule, he stands out as an entrenched defender of minority rights. The South Carolinian's political theory has been equally renowned for its emphasis on economic interests, and even detractors heap praise on his insight into the economic roots of political events. Political scientists term him a founding father of pressure group theory, while historians point to him with pride as an American counterpart of the great European theorists of economic determinism. (p. 25)

No one would deny that the clash of pressure groups alarmed Calhoun. But he was far from a thoroughgoing economic determinist. The crucial reason why his political philosophy is hopelessly inconsistent is that he had only a sporadic commitment to an economic interest theory of history.

First of all, Calhoun had a morbid appreciation of the political power of antislavery ideology. For the last two decades of his life the abolitionist campaign was Calhoun's master concern, and he feared the antislavery "fanatics"not because they appealed to northern pocketbooks but because they engaged the nation's conscience. Calhoun often reiterated his conviction that "a large portion of the northern states believed slavery to be a sin," and he always dreaded the moment when the Yankees would feel "an obligation of conscience to abolish it." The notion that ideas can be the decisive force in politics makes Calhoun a rather milktoast Marxist, and marks his first important step away from a thoroughly economic conception of history.

The dangers wrought by corrupt spoilsmen, Calhoun's second deviation from an economic interest theory of politics, is even more significant in his political thought. To a Marxist, or to any consistent believer in economic determinism, the politician's quest for the spoils of office is of minor importance. Politicians are the tools of the interests they represent, and the commands of the interests—not the intrigues of the spoilsmen—form the driving force of the historical process. But Calhoun always believed that demagogic spoilsmen could delude the rabble, control popular elections, ignore the desires of the great communal interests, and turn the political scene into a mere scramble for patronage. As a disdainful patrician in the age when the two-party system first became an American fixture, he feared that democracy could not survive the race for the spoils. This alarm about emergent spoilsmen is the neglected theme in the thought and career of the Carolinian.

Calhoun's concern with corrupt politicians is particularly evident in *A Disquisition on Government*, the most systematic statement of his political philosophy. The *Disquisition* has long been regarded as Calhoun's definitive formulation of, and solution to, the problem of warring economic interests. However, to read the *Disquisition* in this way is to miss half of Calhoun's intention. The *Disquisition* presents a picture of democracy gone to seed. Corruption in government has been a prime cause of its swift decline; spoilsmen feuding over patronage will soon bring on anarchy and revolution; the unscrupulous political boss will emerge the despotic victor. Calhoun's concern with the war of selfish economic interests is no more acute than his very different concern with the clash of scheming political spoilsmen. These twin obsessions, inseparable yet irreconcilable, produce a political theory which can best be termed a mass of contradictions.

For the purpose of analysis the two theories which are intertwined in the *Disquisition* have been termed the "theory of interests" and the "theory of spoilsmen." The theory of interests designates Calhoun's contention that the leading interest groups—the different classes, separate sections, various economic groups—dominate political events. The theory of spoilsmen deals with his contention that corrupt demagogues control the democratic process. (pp. 25-7)

Before turning to the theory of spoilsmen, it would be well to underscore the assumptions upon which the theory of interests is based. The problem posed by warring interests and the solution achieved by the concurrent majority both assume that the legislators perfectly represent the desires of their constituents. Discord in Congress merely reflects conflict between

economic interests. When the pressure groups are neutralized, the legislative feuds will cease. The new objectives of the economics interests even produce the growing quality of political leadership. As the pressure groups' thirst for plunder gives way to the necessity for compromise, statesmen inevitably replace politicos at the head of the state. The major economic interests are the guiding, primal force in the political drama. The men who sit in the halls of Congress are mere servants who speak, maneuver, and vote as their constituents direct.

The theory of spoilsmen, like the theory of interests, is based on the primordial selfishness of human nature. However, the focus shifts from the economic interests to their politicians, and the servants become masters. Spoilsmen, breaking free from the control of the interests which selected them, emerge as the primary historical force. This time, the pot of gold which turns men into plunders is the spoils of office rather than the riches of minorities. Since nations—like individuals and economic interests—are primarily selfish, governments must maintain "vast establishments" to deter aggressive enemies. The politicians who are elected to the higher offices in the government control the hiring, paying, and firing of the thousands of employees which such huge military preparations require. Since politicians—like almost everyone else—are self-interested, they will employ every effective method to gain a monopoly of the spoils.

The spoilsmen have the supreme weapon of demagoguery at their disposal. Calhoun assumed that the average voter is a greedy and gullible creature who will respond to inflammatory appeals to his passions. Demagogues bent on securing patronage need only make full use of "cunning, falsehood, deception, slander, fraud, and gross appeals to the appetites of the lowest and most worthless portions of the community." Soon the nation will be "thoroughly debased and corrupted." Demagogic spoilsmen will completely control their depraved constituents.

Meanwhile the party structure will be refined and extended. Patronage will be used to control wayward legislators, and the party boss will demand absolute obedience from his immediate subordinates. As Calhoun's dirge unfolds, politicians forget their constituents and engage in the most violent struggle for patronage. Those "seeking office and patronage would become too numerous to be rewarded by the offices and patronage at the disposal of the government"; the disappointed would shift their allegiance causing the control of the government to "vibrate" between the factions until "confusion, corruption, disorder, and anarchy" become so destructive that all social interests seek peace from their politicians by turning to a military despot. Thus in the imminent destruction of democracy spoilsmen rather than interests will tear down the last walls of the republic.

Nothing better shows the extent of Calhoun's fear of spoilsmen than the historical examples he developed in the *Disquisition*. Calhoun believed that the Romans and the English had experimented with the concurrent majority, and he employed their histories to demonstrate his principles. The resulting narratives bear little resemblance to historical truth, but they supply an excellent illustration of Calhoun's own logic and fears. With both Rome and England, Calhoun viewed his historical material through the perspective of his social theory. And in each narrative the war of spoilsmen poses the greatest threat to the concurrent majority.

In ancient Rome, argued Calhoun, two distinct classes of interest existed, the patricians and the plebeians. A violent conflict between the two classes was at last resolved by giving the Tribune, controlled by the plebeians, the power to veto all laws that the Senate, controlled by the patricians, passed. But the concurrent majority soon broke down. The enormous wealth gained in conquest caused.

> the formation of parties, (irrespective of the old division of patricians and plebeians,) having no other object than to obtain the control of the government for the purpose of plunder. . . . Under their baneful influence, the possession of the government became the object of the most violent conflicts; not between patricians and plebeians,—but between profligate and corrupt factions. They continued with increasing violence, until, finally, Rome sank, as must every community under similar circumstances, beneath the strong grasp, the despotic rule of the chieftain of the successful party;—the sad but only alternative which remained to prevent universal violence, confusion and anarchy.

Thus the concurrent majority, introduced to end a bloody conflict of class interests, was itself overturned by the equally violent strife of political spoilsmen. However, the concurrent majority wins its vindication in Calhoun's panegyric on the political genius of the English. For in Calhoun's England the concurrent majority successfully ends the supremacy of spoilsmen.

The miraculous success is gained by totally ignoring the conflict of pressure groups. Calhoun's visionary England is undisturbed by controversies between classes or occupations or sections. The sole problem revolves around the spoils of office. The prime contestants include the citizens who pay the taxes, the monarch who dispenses the patronage, and the lords who receive the offices. Each of the disputants controls a segment of the government, and each segment has a veto on all legislation. The House of Commons represents "the great tax-paying interest by which the government is supported." The King is "the conduit through which, all the honors and emoluments of the government flow." The conflict between Commons and King would necessarily "end in violence and an appeal to force" were it not for the stabilizing influence of the House of Lords. Whereas the King dispenses the patronage, the Lords receive the spoils. Since the members of the House of Lords are "the principle recipients of the honors, emoluments, and other advantages derived from the government," their most profound desire is to preserve the system. Thus the Lords interpose to maintain the equilibrium between Commons and Kings.

The genius of the system, continued Calhoun, is most evident when the British kingdom expands. Rome collapsed because the bounty gained in conquest inspired a resurgence of spoilsmen. But in England an increase in patronage only adds stability to the system: "the greater the patronage of the government, the greater will be the share" which the House of Lords receives; "the more eligible its condition, the greater its opposition to any radical change" in governmental form. No matter how lush the spoils become, the Lords, Commons, and King will go on checking each other, thus preventing a war over patronage and demonstrating the supreme virtue of the concurrent majority.

In both the Roman and English narratives, then, corruption in government emerges as Calhoun's prime concern. In Rome, the concurrent majority checked the clash of interests and then succumbed to a conflict of spoilsmen. In England, communal pressure groups are nowhere to be found, and the system is devised to avert a war over patronage. These historical fantasies reveal once again how profoundly Calhoun was disturbed by the intrigues of the spoilsmen.

Calhoun never really explained how the success of the concurrent majority in England points the way toward a cure for the disease of spoilsmen in a democracy. As Calhoun described it, the alleged absence of spoilsmen in England depends as much on the principle of monarchy as on the doctrine of the concurrent majority. Spoilsmen do not develop in England, he wrote, partly because the dispenser of patronage is an hereditary king rather than an elected politician, which prevents "in consequence of its unity and hereditary character, the violent and factious struggles to obtain the control of the government,—and, with it, the vast patronage which distracted, corrupted, and finally subverted the Roman Republic." Calhoun was hardly proposing that a democratic nation save itself by adopting a king. The question remains, how could the concurrent majority cure the disease of spoilsmen in a democracy?

First of all, Calhoun believed that governmental revenues would inevitably shrink when each minority interest could veto any tax bill. Reduced taxes would result in diminished patronage, thereby removing the cause of the clash between spoilsmen. On the other hand, under a government of the numerical majority, the minority interests would continually be forced to pay higher taxes, thereby increasing patronage and stimulating spoilsmen.

But, as Calhoun indirectly admitted, minority veto would never reduce patronage enough to discourage the spoilsmen for long. Calhoun is remembered today more for his later years as a determined sectionalist than for his early career as an ardent nationalist. Yet the fundamental premise of the early Calhoun, the assumption that strong national military preparations alone insure lasting peace, is what destroys his later political theory. Calhoun could legitimately expect that minority veto would remove one of the two causes of huge bureaucracy, a majority's systematic perversion of the power of taxation to exploit the minority. However, the South Carolinian hoped and believed that no interest would veto the necessary expenses for national defense—the second reason for vast government—and he maintained that legitimate appropriations for military survival would alone produce a government large enough to stimulate violent conflicts between spoilsmen.

Thus Calhoun's first solution to the problem of spoilsmen fails because, even under the concurrent majority, patronage will be extensive enough to attract demagogues. But Calhoun did not rely solely on reducing the spoils to put down the politicians. He also believed that the very nature of government under the concurrent majority would elevate to power men of enlarged and enlightened views. Since pressure groups would have to cooperate instead of conflict, they would elect disinterested statesmen rather than scheming politicians. The concurrent majority would effectively force interests to destroy the spoilsmen.

The difficulty with this solution to the problem of spoilsmen is that it rests on the premises of the theory of interests; it assumes that pressure groups control their politicians. But the theory of spoilsmen assumes that demagogues can delude the rabble and break free from all control. If the concurrent majority would force interests to elect statesmen, the spoils of office would continue to call forth the demagoguery of the spoilsmen. Since the "vast" military establishments would still offer rich patronage harvests, corrupt politicians would have no reason to cease their electioneering. And since the masses would remain as gullible as ever, statesmen would still have little chance of defeating demagogues in a popular election. Thus the need for disinterested compromisers, like the reduction in the size of government, may slow down but cannot stop the rise of spoilsmen. In both cases the "vast" military establishment remains to invite the resurgence of demagogues. Under the concurrent majority in the future, no less than under the numerical majority in the past, the supremacy of spoilsmen will continue to threaten the republic.

The concurrent majority's failure to end the disease of spoilsmen is serious enough in itself. The race for patronage alone leads to revolution and dictatorship. However, the continued supremacy of political spoilsmen also has a disastrous effect on an ultimate reconciliation of economic interests. Critics of the *Disquisition* have always maintained that minority veto would destroy a democratic system by completely paralyzing the governmental process. . . . Calhoun conceded the overriding importance of this consideration, but he countered with the assertion that the concurrent majority would inevitably produce compromise because enlightened statesmen would be elevated to power. With "representatives so well qualified to accomplish the object for which they were selected," argued Calhoun,

> the prevailing desire would be, to promote the common interests of the whole; and, hence, the competition would be, not which should yield the least to promote the common good, but which should yield the most . . . herein is to be found the feature, which distinguishes governments of the concurrent majority so strikingly from those of the numerical. In the latter, each faction, in the struggle to obtain the control of the government, elevates to power the designing, the artful, and unscrupulous, who, in their devotion to party,—instead of aiming at the good of the whole,—aim exclusively at securing the ascendency of party.

It is hardly necessary to trace the ultimate defect in Calhoun's theory. The concurrent majority, to be successful in conciliating interests, must result in compromise; statesmen are likely—but by Calhoun's own admission, spoilsmen unlikely—to seek the general interest; the concurrent majority fails to stop the war of spoilsmen; hence politicos, not the wise and virtuous, will be elected; thus governmental deadlock and social anarchy are likely to ensue; therefore the concurrent majority cannot successfully end the clash of interests.

The failure of the concurrent majority is the result of the fundamental contradiction in Calhoun's political philosophy. The concurrent majority, expressly designed to end political strife by preventing clashes between different portions of the community, assumes that the interests control their politicians. The theory of spoilsmen rests on the premise that demagogues control their constituents. The concurrent majority, in curing the disease of the interests, will not affect the intrigues of the demagogues. Even a completely disinterested government will supply enough patronage to whet the appetites of the spoilsmen. Thus corrupt demagogues will still use the rabble to obtain

Calhoun toward the end of his life.

high office and use high office to enrich themselves. And the continued success of unscrupulous politicians will undermine the chance of a disinterested compromise between communal interests. In the end, Calhoun's attempt to unite in one theory two irreconcilable conceptions of political causation topples the entire logical structure.

The central importance of the theory of spoilsmen in the *Disquisition* leads to the obvious question, why was Calhoun so distressed about political corruption? The answer comes from two directions. First of all, as a political philosopher well versed in the ideology of the Founding Fathers, Calhoun inherited that strain of late eighteenth-century thought which considered democratic politics the pursuit of gentlemen and disdained legislative cabals and mass parties. Secondly, as the political leader of the South Carolina planters during the Age of Jackson, Calhoun had special reasons to deplore the emerging spoils system. (pp. 28-34)

Although sensitive souls throughout the country were disgusted with the emerging spoils system in the Age of Jackson, the South Carolina aristocrats shrieked the longest and the loudest. The rise of the political manager upset their delicately balanced, limited democracy and produced some of the evils they most feared—a passion for federal patronage, the rule of party hacks, the rise of inferior demagogues. South Carolina's participation in the political parties was occasional and superficial. The Calhounites, quickly disillusioned by their bitter experience with the early Jackson movement, usually remained aloof from national coalitions. And when Calhoun sporadically and suspiciously rejoined the Democratic party, he always insisted that taxes should be lowered so that the party would be based on principles rather than spoils.

However, Calhoun's attempt to reform the Democratic party was not solely the disinterested campaign of a South Carolina patrician to reestablish the ideals of the Founding Fathers. His rhetoric on executive patronage also probably reflects the bitter disappointment of a brilliant and supremely ambitious young man who climbed with incredible speed to the higher ranks of federal power and then never achieved his ultimate goal. Political maneuvering had destroyed his presidential prospects in 1832 and threatened to produce a life of personal frustration. Calhoun may well have realized that his marked superiority at political reasoning was somewhat offset by his notorious failings as a practical politician. In this sense, he may have hoped that reduced executive patronage would produce a nation where the Calhouns rather than the Van Burens, the philosopher statesmen rather than the party managers, would once again have a chance to be President of the United States.

But Calhoun's obsession with political corruption was more than a response to unfulfilled ambition, more than a patrician's distrust of the new political managers. It was also one expression of that violent South Carolina radicalism in the crisis of the 1830s which produced both the nullification crusade against the tariff and the gag rule fight against the abolitionists. The South Carolinians, morbidly aware of their own weaknesses—depressed economically, frightened by recurrent slave conspiracies, able to defend slavery only with the doctrine that bondage was a "necessary evil" (and secretly believing that necessary or not the evil was grave)—found themselves faced for the first time with a mounting abolitionist attack and a high protective tariff, both of which seemed to threaten slavery and the future of southern white civilization. The planters devised (and tried to believe) a proslavery argument, developed a closed, rigid, restrictive society, and even endeavored (a bit lamely) to acquire some of that Yankee spirit of commercial enterprise which they held in such contempt. But for their ultimate salvation they turned to national politics. Convinced that their only hope lay in the most rigid adherence to principle, the South Carolina aristocrats were made desperate by the apathy of natural allies throughout the nation. Many southerners seemed content to compromise with the abolitionists. Most Democrats, both North and South, refused to engage in an uncompromising fight against Clay's American System. There could be only one explanation. Politicians were compromising with abolitionists and monopolists to keep their party together and to increase their chances of grabbing a share of the spoils of office. If the American System could be destroyed and patronage reduced, the South might be brought to defend itself in time and the Democrats brought to stand steadfast on the only principles which could save the union. And surely Calhoun's belief that politicians often ignore their constituents in their race for the spoils originated in part with what he considered the shame of the spoilsmen in the 1830s.

Thus, in his practical career as in his political theory, Calhoun's concern with spoilsmen was as important as his fear of interests. By exorcising the new political brokers Calhoun could hope to bring the republic back to the enlightened rule of disinterested patricians, fulfill his presidential ambitions, and develop national political movements based on principals rather than spoils. When statesmen replaced spoilsmen, the clash between fundamental interests over the American System and over abolition could also be resolved.

Yet Calhoun's practical program was vitiated by the same logical contradiction between the theory of interests and the theory of spoilsmen which destroyed his political philosophy. The South Carolinian was again unable to decide whether pressure groups or politicians caused historical events. On the one hand, Calhoun held that the Democratic party would be run by spoilsmen rather than statesmen until the American System ceased to supply patronage. On the other hand, he maintained that the American System would only be destroyed when statesmen replaced spoilsmen at the head of the Democratic party. If interests could be neutralized, spoilsmen would disappear. Yet spoilsmen must disappear before interests could be neutralized. The reformer hardly knew where to begin. As Calhoun saw the dilemma in a more practical situation, Jackson's Democratic politicos—although elected by interest groups opposed to Clay's brainchild—compromised with an American System which fed them patronage, thereby frustrating their constituents.

Nullification was, among other things, a desperate way out of the vicious circle. South Carolina, by nullifying high duties, could at once neutralize interests and reduce patronage. For a time in the late 1830s Calhoun was almost sanguine. But even nullification was no real escape, for by Calhoun's own admission the unnullified military establishments remained to invite the resurgence of spoilsmen. More important, in the 1840s, with nullification discredited, the South Carolinian was again trapped in his own logical nightmare. Thus when Democrats like Thomas Ritchie and Van Buren compromised a bit with the American System and with the abolitionists, Calhoun's profound bitterness was the logical culmination of the inconsistencies in his own political program.

The *Disquisition*, written in the late 1840s, reflects Calhoun's despair as his career drew to a close. The increasingly angry controversy between northern and southern interests seemed disastrous enough in itself. But in addition the vast federal patronage seemed certain to perpetuate the regime of the spoilsmen. With unscrupulous politicians in power the North and South would never find grounds for reconciliation. Thus the *Disquisition* represents one of Calhoun's later desperate attempts to restrain the interests and spoilsmen which together seemed destined to break up the republic.

In one sense, the *Disquisition* is a justly celebrated contribution to the American democratic tradition. Calhoun was a political realist who ranks with James Madison and John Adams in his mordant analysis of the defects of a democracy. As Calhoun endlessly reiterated, entrenched majorities can ignore constitutional restraints and pay little heed to minority rights. The South Carolinian was also clearly right that the clash of interests and the intrigues of spoilsmen often threaten the efficiency of a democratic government.

The problem with the *Disquisition* lies not in its diagnosis but rather in its exaggeration of the weaknesses in a republic. Calhoun's critics have often argued that the theory of interests overstates both the helplessness of democratic minorities and the selfishness of economic interests. It must now be added that the theory of spoilsmen magnifies the threat posed by scheming politicans. Ambitious demagogues may sometimes exert more political influence than the economic determinists like to think. But Calhoun surely overestimated the spoilsmen's capacity to delude the masses and overthrow the system. Indeed Calhoun's rhetoric on the evils of patronage often sounds suspiciously like that of a late nineteenth-century mugwump, fighting his curious crusade to save democracy by enacting civil service reform. The combination of this exaggerated fear of spoilsmen and Calhoun's exaggerated fear of interests simply posed problems too grave for the concurrent majority, or any constitutional reform, to solve. The resulting inconsistencies in the *Disquisition* must create renewed doubts as to whether Calhoun deserves his reputation as America's most rigorous political logician. It would be closer to the truth to call the author of the *Disquisition* one of the more confused political philosophers in the American tradition.

The contradictions in Calhoun's *Disquisition* provide a particularly revealing illustration of that ambivalence toward democratic principles which so often marked the political thought of the more aristocratic southern slaveholders. As historians have often reminded us in the past two decades, the clash between American politicians has characteristically taken place within a consensus of belief in democratic government. Calhoun paid his personal testimonial to this pervasive American concensus by straining to remain both a statesman and a theorizer of the democratic persuasion. But the deeper significance of Calhoun's tragic career is that despite his fascination with abstract political argument he could not put together a consistent democratic theory. The key to Calhoun's thought is not just his concern with class or any other kind of economic interests, not just his concern with moral fanatics, not just his concern with demagogic spoilsmen. Rather, the secret of his political philosophy—the reason why it is inevitably inconsistent—is that Calhoun distrusted democracy for so many exaggerated and contradictory reasons. An eighteenth-century elitist increasingly disillusioned with the emerging political order in the Age of Jackson, Calhoun by the end of his career no longer quite believed in American democracy. (pp. 38-42)

> *William W. Freehling, "Spoilsmen and Interests in the Thought and Career of John C. Calhoun," in* The Journal of American History, *Vol. LII, No. 1, June, 1965, pp. 25-42.*

PAUL F. BOLLER, JR.   (essay date 1978)

[*Boller contends that Calhoun's theory of liberty was in essence a "philosophy of inequality" designed to justify not only slavery but also rule by the aristocracy.*]

One of the most famous confrontations in American history took place between President Andrew Jackson and Vice-President John C. Calhoun, at a Jefferson birthday dinner in Washington on April 13, 1830. When it came time for the President to propose a toast, Jackson, determined to meet head-on the nullificationist threat within the Democratic party, stood up, faced the vice-president, and, looking him straight in the eye, thundered: "Our Federal Union—it must be preserved." While the banqueters watched breathlessly, Calhoun, his hand trembling, proposed firmly in his turn: "The Union—next to our liberty the most dear."

Liberty was one of Calhoun's favorite words, and it is not surprising that one of his biographers declared: "With Milton he was ready to say, 'Where liberty dwells, there is my country'" [see entry for Styron in the Additional Bibliography]. But Calhoun's liberty had little in common with Milton's; it was in fact quite compatible with slavery. For Calhoun liberty was not a natural right possessed by every individual; it was a social privilege, and it was reserved for peoples and groups he regarded as superior. . . . He was not an individualist, and he regarded the natural-rights philosophy as both false and dangerous because of its individualistic emphasis.

Though he rejected natural rights, Calhoun placed liberty, as he conceived of it, high in his hierarchy of values. "With me," he once told the Senate, "the liberty of the country is all in all. If this be preserved, every thing will be preserved, but if lost, all will be lost." From his earliest days in public life on the eve of the War of 1812 until his last days during the sectional crisis following the Mexican War, Calhoun looked upon liberty as his primary guide for public policy. His letters, reports, and speeches were filled with the catchphrases of freedom: blessings of liberty, personal liberty, free country, free people, the liberties of mankind. (pp. 81-2)

Calhoun defined liberty the way Locke (whom he studied as a young man) and Edwards did: as absence of external obstacles to voluntary action. But despite the Scotch-Irish Presbyterian background and his experience as an undergraduate at Calvinist Yale, he at no time in his life evinced any interest in the free-will question. Nor was he ever much interested in the Lockean liberty of individual action that Paine and Emerson thought was so important. From almost the beginning of his public career Calhoun tended to regard the notion of an individual as apart from his society as a foolish and even dangerous fiction. The southern states, he said time and again, were aggregates of communities, not of individuals, and the United States itself was an aggregate of states. This meant that individual liberty was intimately linked with the liberty of the community (nation, section, state) and was always subordinate to it where vital issues were at stake. Denouncing proposals to keep states without antislavery constitutions out of the Union, Calhoun angrily told the Senate on February 19, 1847:

> It is proposed, from a vague, indefinite, erroneous, and most dangerous conception of *private individual liberty,* to override this *great common liberty* which the people have of framing their own constitution! Sir, the right of framing self-government on the part of individuals is not near so easily to be established by any course of reasoning, as the right of a community or a State to self-government. And yet, Sir, there are men of such delicate feelings on the subject of liberty—men who cannot possibly bear what they call slavery in one section of the country . . . —that they are ready to strike down the *higher right of a community* to govern themselves, in order to maintain the *absolute right of individuals,* in every possible condition to govern themselves!

Calhoun simply did not believe in "the absolute right of individuals" to govern themselves. He put the "great common liberty"—the right of a political community to sovereignty, independence, security, and material well-being—far above the rights and liberties of individuals. He was no Hegelian; but he came close at times to dissolving the freedom of individuals in that of the collectivity. The great common liberty, he said repeatedly, was the *sine qua non* for whatever liberties people making up the community possessed and thus a "higher right" which might necessitate restrictions on liberty for individual citizens. Calhoun's inclination, throughout his career, was to relate every important public issue with which he was concerned to its bearing on liberty conceived in this fashion. Like the Founding Fathers, Calhoun once said, his first reaction when questions of magnitude came before him was to ask: "Is it constitutional?" "Is it consistent with our free, popular institutions?" "How is it to affect our liberty?" But he never meant individual freedom to take precedence over communal liberty. It was misleading and, in fact, downright irresponsible, he thought, to look upon liberty as an "absolute right of individuals." He was never at heart a real individualist, and he was not much attracted to Paine's philosophy even in his younger Jeffersonian days. He loved liberty, but he was not a civil libertarian. (pp. 82-3)

[Liberty], according to Calhoun, was not a natural right; . . . it was a civil right created by the people out of social experience. Calhoun, like Burke (whom he admired), denied that all men are born free and equal possessing inalienable rights like liberty. Infants, he said, are not born free; they are subject to their parents, guardians, and to older people generally; and only gradually, as they develop into mature, responsible persons, do they acquire the civil and political rights prevailing in their society. Human rights are never natural; they are always conventional or customary rights existing within and inseparable from the social order. Every right which individuals possess is the product of long history and is based on social utility; it has proven itself to be conducive to the welfare of the community as a whole.

But if Calhoun thought the ultimate sanction for individual rights was societal welfare, he also thought that the needs of society dictated an unequal enjoyment of these rights by different members of the community. Some people, he said, are superior, mentally and morally, and it benefits society to have them exercise certain rights freely; but other people are inferior in natural endowments, and it would detract from the well-being of society to bestow any rights on them.

Calhoun favored giving people he regarded as superior preferential rights and privileges. In every society, he maintained, there are gifted individuals who are eager to improve themselves; the "desire of individuals to better their condition" is the fountainhead of social advance. By improving themselves, these people at the same time benefit the community, and it is society's obvious interest to see to it that they have liberty to get ahead in life and security in the possession of the fruits of their exertions. Calhoun regarded individual liberty and private property as necessary inducements to individual enterprise and therefore indispensable to social progress. But private property, like liberty and the suffrage, is an acquired, not a natural, right; it is justified by its contribution to the material welfare of society. Since individuals differ in native ability, health, strength, and ambition, and some accumulate more worldly goods than others, the protection of private property means the maintenance of inequality in property holdings. But economic inequality is natural and proper and should be upheld by government. The same is true of liberty. Calhoun regarded inequality in the enjoyment of liberty as both necessary and desirable.

The question of who gets liberty and how much liberty he gets was for Calhoun the great problem of government. Government must be strong enough to protect society against internal and external dangers, but it must also permit enough liberty for people with ability to get ahead in life. Calhoun wanted able individuals to have as much freedom as possible, consonant with law and order, to better their condition, and he came to favor laissez-faire on the federal level. But he did not think it was possible to lay down any hard and fast rules regarding the proper balancing of liberty and authority. Societies vary considerably in intelligence, historical experience, and social and economic circumstances, and what is possible in one community may be neither possible nor desirable in another. Some communities, Calhoun pointed out,

> require a far greater amount of power than others to protect them against anarchy and external dangers; and, of course, the sphere of liberty in such must be proportionally contracted. The causes calculated to enlarge the one and contract the other are numerous and varied. Some are physical—such as open and exposed frontiers surrounded by powerful and hostile neighbors. Others are moral—such as the different degrees of intelligence, patriotism, and virtue among the mass of the community, and their experience and proficiency in the art of self-government. Of these, the moral are by far the most influential. A community may possess all the necessary moral qualifications in so high a degree as to be capable of self-government under the most adverse circumstances, while, on the other hand, another may be so sunk in ignorance and vice as to be incapable of forming a conception of liberty or of living, even when most favored by circumstances, under any other than an absolute and despotic government.

Calhoun insisted that no people could possess for long more liberty than that to which they were fairly entitled. If people lack the character and training to exercise their liberties wisely, they will probably descend into license and anarchy. Genuine liberty depends on virtue and enlightenment, and if people show little promise of being able to behave decently, it is absurd to grant them liberty. Liberty, in short, is

> a reward to be earned, not a blessing to be gratuitously lavished on all alike—a reward reserved for the intelligent, the patriotic, the virtuous and deserving, and not a boon to be bestowed on people too ignorant, degraded, and vicious to be capable either of appreciating or of enjoying it.

Like Calhoun, Paine . . . linked liberty with virtue and thought it had to be earned. Unlike Calhoun, though, he insisted that all human beings, including blacks, had a right to earn it.

Needless to say, Calhoun, as a white supremacist, thought that the Negro lacked the requisite capacity for freedom and that his natural inferiority, physical, mental, and moral, justified all the restraints imposed on him by the institution of slavery. Calhoun made extensive use of the Census of 1840 (despite its proven errors) in order to show that the free black in the North was far worse off in every respect than the Southern slave because he did not know what to do with his freedom. In the free states, Calhoun contended, the blacks had "invariably sunk into vice and pauperism, accompanied by the bodily and mental afflictions incident hereto—deafness, blindness, insanity and idiocy—to a degree without example." But in the South, where the states "retained the ancient relation" between the races, the blacks had "improved greatly in every respect—in number, comfort, intelligence, and morals." Abolishing slavery, he warned, would not "raise the inferior race to the condition of freemen," but rather would "deprive the negro of the guardian care of his owner, subject to all the depression and oppression belonging to his inferior condition." It would also lead to "deadly strife between the two races" and eventually a "war of races" throughout the Western hemisphere.

By means of slavery, the South, Calhoun was convinced, had achieved a proper balance between liberty and authority: it extended liberty to those worthy of it (whites) and withheld it from the undeserving (blacks). It was a fair, just, stable, and contented society, in Calhoun's opinion, and he wanted to keep it free from outside interference. The South's major problem, as he saw it, was to protect its "constitutional liberty," that is, its freedom under the U.S. Constitution to order its internal affairs as it saw fit. Since the South was part of a Union in which majority rule prevailed at the federal level, Calhoun was naturally alert to threats to the South's "constitutional liberty" posed by majority rule and anxious to suggest devices by which the southern states might retain their freedom within the American system to preserve slavery. In *Disquisition,* therefore, Calhoun had something quite specific in mind: the desire to safeguard the liberty of the southern slaveowner (not that of Negro, Indian, or poor white) against any majority that threatened to interfere with his way of life. But he discussed the question throughout in only the most general terms, and his *Disquisition* has been regarded as an astute analysis of the dangers to individual liberty and minority rule presented by representative institutions in general. It is so, however, only if the liberties of all individuals and the rights of all minorities and not just of a privileged few are taken into account. (pp. 93-6)

In *Disquisition* and *Discourse on the Constitution,* Calhoun said almost nothing about slavery directly. His propensity, even in Senate speeches, was to talk in abstract terms, and he was, not surprisingly, charged by contemporaries with being too "metaphysical." Calhoun's powers of logical analysis, given his premises, were indeed of a high order, but they frequently led him to prefer scoring a point to coming to grips with an issue. His *Discourse,* in particular, resembles an interminably involved scholastic exercise in logic-chopping, full of brilliant reasoning but utterly remote from the realities of American life. In all of Calhoun's lofty ruminations on society and government there was an unstated but fundamental premise: the indispensability of slavery to American civilization. The Union, he thought, could endure only half slave and half free. At the heart of his philosophy, shaping all that he thought and said about liberty, was an unshakable belief in racial inequality. Calhoun was not exceptional in believing the black man inferior to the white; in varying degrees most whites in Calhoun's day believed this. But that slavery followed logically from this assumption as the proper status for the Negro seemed a preposterous deduction for increasing numbers of whites in Europe and America after the eighteenth century.

Unlike many southerners before 1830, Calhoun is never known to have favored working for a gradual end to slavery. In a speech in Congress in 1816, it is true, he referred to the slave trade as an "odious traffic" and in 1820 he supported the Missouri Compromise delimiting slavery. But he came to regret the Missouri Compromise and by the mid-1830s he was praising slavery as an unqualified good. When he talked, as he did ceaselessly, about protecting the liberty of the minority against the tyranny of the majority, he was never thinking of the Negro, the most abused, exploited, and helpless minority in Calhoun's America. In Calhoun's system the black was to have no rights of nullification, concurrence, or secession to defend himself against oppression. Calhoun may have been quite right about human nature: people may be incurably self-centered, and it may be society's primary task to find ways of keeping the human lust for power and pelf in check. But what was Calhoun's whole philosophy itself but an elaborate, self-interested

effort to justify the abuse of power by the dominant majority in his own state and section over a defenseless minority?

Calhoun's philosophy of inequality included whites as well as blacks, for there were large qualifications on his respect even for people of his own race. Though he accepted popular sovereignty in principle and sometimes referred to the United States as a "constitutional democracy," he actually had little faith in the competency of the majority of white people. In justifying slavery in the South, Calhoun was led (partly, no doubt, for polemical reasons) to sketch a theory of society in which the majority of people everywhere, regardless of color, are always kept in a distinctly subordinate status. There has "never yet existed," he declared, "a wealthy and civilized society in which one portion of the community did not, in point of fact, live on the labor of the other." Social progress, in his view, comes about only by exploitation; the advance of civilization has always depended on the exploitation of the many by the few. In every community, he said, there is a master class which appropriates a sizable share of the fruits of the labor of working people for its own use. By exploiting the laboring classes, members of the master class achieve an economic security which frees them from manual labor and provides them with the wealth and leisure to cultivate the civilized arts and engage in public service. This is just as true in the North, where capital exploits labor, he said, as in the South; and he attempted to win the support of northern businessmen for slavery by arguing that the equalitarian natural-rights views of the abolitionists, when spread among the lower classes, were as threatening to the property rights of northern capitalists as to those of southern planters.

In some respects, though the point can be overstated (Calhoun's economic analysis is very broad and sketchy and full of simplisms), Calhoun was saying what Karl Marx was saying, though Calhoun, of course, favored exploitation of the workers by the nonproducing classes, while Marx wanted them to revolt. Calhoun thought that rule by a superior elite was necessary for social, economic, and intellectual progress in every society. In the end, he wanted more than a concurrent voice for his privileged minority; he was asking for domination. In Calhoun, concern for "the great common liberty" of the nation had given way to a concern for the liberty of section and state and finally to preoccupation with the liberty of the aristocratic few. Like George Fitzhugh, he had come to believe that liberty was "the privilege of the few—not the right of the many." He refused to entertain Paine's idea that liberty was a privilege which people of all races and classes had a right to achieve.

Abraham Lincoln readily saw the catch in Calhoun's view of liberty. "We all declare for liberty," he observed in a speech on April 18, 1864,

> but in using the same *word* we do not all mean the same *thing*. With some the word liberty may mean for each man to do as he pleases with himself, and the product of his labor; while with others the same word may mean for some men to do as they please with other men, and the product of other men's labor.

For Lincoln, the liberty which Calhoun came to celebrate was in reality tyranny; it was the liberty of the wolf to plunder the sheep. But the Declaration of Independence, on which Calhoun poured so much scorn, repudiated this kind of liberty; it "gave promise," said Lincoln, "that in due time the weights should be lifted from the shoulders of all men, and that *all* should

A depiction of Calhoun's last appearance in the Senate. The Bettmann Archive, Inc.

have an equal chance.'' Lincoln looked upon this promise as the central idea of American politics. He tended to view liberty and equality as twentieth-century liberal democrats do: not as natural rights existing as actual facts in a past state of nature, but as worthy moral ideals to be endlessly striven for in the present and future; and he thought that apologists for slavery, in rejecting these ideals, rejected the very meaning of American civilization.

In his later years Calhoun said that he wanted the United States to return to what it had been in its pristine purity in 1789. But he would have had to go farther back than that to find what he wanted, for, like Lincoln, most of the founders of the Republic regarded liberty as a promise for all rather than as a privilege for a few. Though Calhoun regarded himself as a conservative, he died, as William E. Dodd has written, ''the greatest reactionary of his time'' [see excerpt dated 1911]. And though his view of liberty as an achievement of the social process rather than as a gift of nature places him closer to contemporary thought than Jefferson and Paine, the uses he made of his insight make his philosophy relevant to authoritarians in the contemporary world rather than to lovers of individual liberty. Calhoun talked continually about liberty, but it was his ''sweet land of slavery'' that he came finally to prize most highly. His motto, at the end, should have been: ''The Union—next to our Slavery, the most dear.'' (pp. 102-05)

Paul F. Boller, Jr., ''John C. Calhoun on Liberty as Privilege,'' in his Freedom and Fate in American Thought: From Edwards to Dewey, *SMU Press, 1978, pp. 81-105.*

ADDITIONAL BIBLIOGRAPHY

Adams, John Quincy. *Memoirs of John Quincy Adams, Comprising Portions of His Diary from 1795 to 1848.* Edited by Charles Francis Adams. 12 vols. Philadelphia: J. B. Lippincott & Co., 1874-77.

> Contains numerous references that document Adams's drastic change of attitude toward Calhoun. Two of Adams's diary entries are considered particularly illuminating in this respect: in the first, dated October 1821, he praises Calhoun's nonpartisanship, while in the second, dated May 1844, he denounces Calhoun as a ''slavemonger.''

Anderson, James L., and Hemphill, W. Edwin. ''The 1843 Biography of John C. Calhoun: Was R.M.T. Hunter Its Author?'' *The Journal of Southern History* XXXVIII, No. 3 (August 1972): 469-74.

> Presents newly discovered evidence supporting the critics' contention that R.M.T. Hunter is the author of the 1843 *Life of John C. Calhoun* (see annotation below).

Anderson, John M. Introduction to *Calhoun: Basic Documents,* by John C. Calhoun, edited by John M. Anderson, pp. 9-26. State College, Penn.: Bald Eagle Press, 1952.

Focuses on Calhoun's analysis of the problem of safeguarding minority rights. Anderson praises him as one of the few early nineteenth-century political thinkers who recognized the interdependence of society and government.

Bancroft, Frederic. *Calhoun and the South Carolina Nullification Movement.* Baltimore: Johns Hopkins Press, 1928, 199 p.

A history of the nullification controversy.

Basso, Hamilton. "John Calhoun of Fort Hill: The American as Aristocrat." In his *Mainstream,* pp. 44-63. New York: Reynal & Hitchcock, 1943.

Centers on Calhoun's early Calvinistic education and its effect on his thought and character. Basso hypothesizes that if Calhoun had received a liberal education, he might have constructed a more humanistic—and more enduring—political philosophy.

Benton, Thomas Hart. *Thirty Years' View; or, A History of the Working of the American Government for Thirty Years, from 1820 to 1850,* Vol. II. New York: D. Appleton and Co., 1856, 788 p.

Includes commentary on Calhoun's political career. A Missouri senator from 1820 to 1850, Benton was one of Calhoun's bitterest enemies.

Bradford, Gamaliel. "John Caldwell Calhoun." In his *As God Made Them: Portraits of Some Nineteenth-Century Americans,* pp. 87-127. Boston: Houghton Mifflin Co., Riverside Press, 1929.

Portrays Calhoun as a "thinking apparatus," examining how his reliance on reasoning and analysis affected both his public and private lives.

Coit, Margaret L. "Calhoun and the Downfall of States' Rights." *The Virginia Quarterly Review* 28, No. 2 (Spring 1952): 191-208.

Holds that by 1850, Calhoun had rejected the doctrine of states' rights as a practical solution to the problem of protecting the rights of minorities. Coit's essay is an elaboration of an argument advanced in her earlier biography of Calhoun (see excerpt dated 1950).

———, ed. *John C. Calhoun.* Great Lives Observed. Englewood Cliffs, N.J.: Prentice-Hall, Spectrum Books, 1970, 174 p.

A three-part introduction to Calhoun's life and thought containing extracts from his writings, extracts from contemporary appraisals of his career, and extracts from important twentieth-century essays on the statesman. Annotations preface the excerpts.

Current, Richard Nelson. "John C. Calhoun, Philosopher of Reaction." *The Antioch Review* III, No. 2 (June 1943): 223-34.

Argues that Calhoun's ideas on class structure anticipated those of Karl Marx. According to the Calhoun scholar Margaret L. Coit, Current was the first critic to formulate this opinion. Current incorporated this essay in a slightly different form in his 1963 book-length study of Calhoun (see excerpt above).

Curry, J.L.M. *Principles, Acts, and Utterances of John C. Calhoun, Promotive of the True Union of the States.* Chicago: University of Chicago Press, 1898, 30 p.

Argues against the theory that Calhoun was a disunionist.

Eaton, Clement. "The Calhoun Influence." In his *The Freedom-of-Thought Struggle in the Old South,* rev. ed., pp. 144-61. New York: Harper & Row, Publishers, Torchbooks, 1964.

Contends that Calhoun's importance lies in his role as an agitator on the slavery issue.

Freehling, William W. *Prelude to Civil War: The Nullification Controversy in South Carolina, 1816-1836.* New York: Harper & Row, Publishers, 1966, 395 p.

A detailed examination of the nullification crisis that contains an extended discussion of Calhoun's role in the controversy. Freehling attempts to show that the South Carolinians' nullification crusade was not only a reaction to high tariff rates but also an attempt to halt anti-slavery agitation.

Gabriel, Ralph Henry. "A Footnote on John C. Calhoun." In his *The Course of American Democratic Thought: An Intellectual History since 1815,* pp. 103-10. Ronald Series in History, edited by Robert C. Pinkley and Ralph H. Gabriel. New York: Ronald Press Co., 1940.

Determines that Calhoun's ideas on progress, liberty, nationalism, and the nature of government accord with "the American democratic faith." Gabriel emphasizes Calhoun's prescience in recognizing that the protection of sectional interests is a precondition to national unity.

Garson, Robert A. "Proslavery as Political Theory: The Examples of John C. Calhoun and George Fitzhugh." *The South Atlantic Quarterly* 84, No. 2 (Spring 1985): 197-212.

Rebukes scholars for dismissing the political ideas of Calhoun and George Fitzhugh as outmoded proslavery arguments. According to Garson, both men constructed important political theories that transcend the issue of the sectional controversy between the North and the South.

Heckscher, Gunnar. "Calhoun's Idea of 'Concurrent Majority' and the Constitutional Theory of Hegel." *The American Political Science Review* XXXIII, No. 4 (August 1939): 585-90.

Compares Calhoun's ideas on government to those of the German political philosophers Georg Wilhelm Friedrich Hegel and F. J. Stahl.

Hubbell, Jay B. "John C. Calhoun." In his *The South in American Literature: 1607-1900,* pp. 413-24. Durham, N.C.: Duke University Press, 1954.

Outlines the fundamentals of Calhoun's political philosophy, concentrating on his doctrine of the concurrent majority.

Hunt, Gaillard. *John C. Calhoun.* American Crisis Biographies. Philadelphia: George W. Jacobs & Co., 1908, 335 p.

A biography in which Calhoun emerges as a selfless political leader who consistently subordinated his own interests to those of the South.

Jenkins, John S. *The Life of John Caldwell Calhoun.* Auburn, N.Y.: James M. Alden, 1850, 454 p.

An early examination of Calhoun's life and thought. Jenkins relies heavily on Calhoun's speeches and devotes much of his discussion to the nullification controversy.

Kirk, Russell. "Southern Conservatism: Randolph and Calhoun." In his *The Conservative Mind from Burke to Santayana,* pp. 130-60. Chicago: Henry Regnery Co., 1953.

Examines the careers of Calhoun and John Randolph within the context of the Southern conservative political tradition. Kirk describes the primary characteristics of this tradition as "a half-indolent distaste for alteration; a determination to preserve an agricultural society; a love of local rights; and a sensitivity about the negro question."

Lander, Ernest McPherson, Jr. *Reluctant Imperialists: Calhoun, the South Carolinians, and the Mexican War.* Baton Rouge: Louisiana State University Press, 1980, 189 p.

Investigates South Carolina's involvement in the Mexican War. Calhoun's opposition to the war is of particular interest to Lander.

———. *The Calhoun Family and Thomas Green Clemson: The Decline of a Southern Patriarchy.* Columbia: University of South Carolina Press, 1983, 275 p.

Deals with the family lives of Calhoun and Thomas Green Clemson, the husband of Calhoun's daughter Anna Maria.

Lerner, Ralph. "John C. Calhoun." In *American Political Thought: The Philosophical Dimension of American Statesmanship,* edited by Morton J. Frisch and Richard G. Stevens, pp. 99-124. New York: Charles Scribner's Sons, 1971.

A detailed examination of Calhoun's political philosophy. Lerner discusses Calhoun's theory of the concurrent majority and remarks on the ambiguous nature of the concept of "the common good," which Calhoun used in formulating this theory.

Life of John C. Calhoun: Presenting a Condensed History of Political Events from 1811 to 1843. New York: Harper & Brothers, 1843, 76 p.

The first book-length biography of Calhoun, written to promote his candidacy for the presidency in 1844. The authorship of this anonymously published campaign document is a source of contention. While some critics attribute the work to Calhoun's friend R.M.T. Hunter, others maintain that it is autobiographical; still others contend that it is the joint production of Hunter and Calhoun's daughter Anna Maria.

Marmor, Theodore R. "Anti-Industrialism and the Old South: The Agrarian Perspective of John C. Calhoun." *Comparative Studies in Society and History* IX (1966-67): 377-406.
A "case study" of Calhoun's thoughts on Southern agriculture. Marmor asserts that it is a mistake to assume that Calhoun opposed industrialism because he was a leading spokesman for his section's agrarian interests.

Meigs, William M. *The Life of John Caldwell Calhoun.* 2 vols. New York: G. E. Stechert & Co., 1925?
A commendatory biography that urges the validity of Calhoun's interpretation of the Constitution. Meigs makes extensive use of Calhoun's correspondence.

Oliver, Robert T. "Behind the Word, Studies in the Political and Social Views of the Slave-Struggle Orators: John Caldwell Calhoun." *The Quarterly Journal of Speech* XXII, No. 3 (October 1936): 413-29.
Argues that all of Calhoun's political ideas were consonant with his devotion to slavery and to the Union.

Pinckney, Charles Cotesworth. "John C. Calhoun, from a Southern Standpoint." *Lippincott's Monthly Magazine* LXII (July 1898): 81-90.
A personal reminiscence of Calhoun by one of his neighbors in Pendleton, South Carolina.

Pinckney, Gustavus M. *Life of John C. Calhoun: Being a View of the Principal Events of His Career and an Account of His Contributions to Economic and Political Science.* Charleston, S.C.: Walker, Evans & Cogswell Co., 1903, 251 p.
A sympathetic treatment of Calhoun's political career that is largely comprised of quotations from his works. Pinckney downplays the slavery issue, concentrating instead on Calhoun's ideas regarding commerce, finance, and minority rights.

Pritchett, John Perry. *Calhoun: His Defense of the South.* Poughkeepsie, N.Y.: Printing House of Harmon, 1937, 38 p.
Discusses the Southern social values Calhoun defended against attacks by Northerners. Pritchett's study is designed for general readers rather than historians.

Schlesinger, Arthur M., Jr. *The Age of Jackson.* Boston: Little, Brown and Co., 1945, 577 p.
A study of Jacksonian democracy that contains frequent and oftenquoted comments on Calhoun. Schlesinger contends that while Calhoun's concurrent majority theory was immediately designed to protect the rights of Southern slaveholders, it was "in the end . . . a brilliant study of modern society, whose insights remain vital for any minority."

Schultz, Harold S. "A Century of Calhoun Biographies." *The South Atlantic Quarterly* L, No.2 (April 1951): 248-54.
Assesses the various biographies of Calhoun published between 1843 and 1950.

Spain, August O. *The Political Theory of John C. Calhoun.* 1951. Reprint. New York: Octagon Books, 1968, 306 p.
In Spain's words, "a comprehensive exposition of the political theory of John C. Calhoun." In addition to describing Calhoun's political ideas, Spain discusses their historical origins, their applicability during the statesman's era, and their significance in the twentieth century.

Styron, Arthur. *The Cast-Iron Man: John C. Calhoun and American Democracy.* New York: Longmans, Green and Co., 1935, 426 p.
Uses Calhoun's political ideas to condemn the social reformers and capitalists of the North in the first half of the nineteenth century.

Thomas, J. P., ed. *The Carolina Tribute to Calhoun.* Columbia, S.C.: Richard L. Bryan, 1857, 409 p.
A collection of obituary tributes to Calhoun. The volume incorporates speeches, eulogies, and sermons delivered by South Carolinians and an account of congressional proceedings on the statesman's death.

Thomas, John L., ed. *John C. Calhoun: A Profile.* American Profiles, edited by Aïda DiPace Donald. New York: Hill and Wang, 1968, 228 p.
A collection of important essays on Calhoun's life and thought. Critics represented include Jefferson Davis, Charles M. Wiltse, Margaret L. Coit, Peter F. Drucker, and Louis Hartz.

Trent, William P. "John Caldwell Calhoun." In his *Southern Statesmen of the Old Régime: Washington, Jefferson, Randolph, Calhoun, Stephens, Toombs, and Jefferson Davis,* pp. 153-93. Library of Economics and Politics, edited by Richard T. Ely, no. 13. New York: Thomas Y. Crowell & Co., 1897.
Follows the course of Calhoun's political career, concentrating on his shift from a nationalist to a sectionalist position. While generally sympathetic to his subject, Trent finds that Calhoun's lack of foresight precludes him from ranking as a great statesman.

Wiltse, Charles M. "Calhoun and the Modern State." *The Virginia Quarterly* 13, No. 3 (Summer 1937): 396-408.
Views Calhoun's doctrine of state sovereignty as the foundation of economic pluralism in twentieth-century American government.

———. "Calhoun's Democracy." *The Journal of Politics* 3, No. 2 (May 1941): 210-23.
Examines within a historical context Calhoun's constitutional defense of the concurrent majority theory.

Nikolai (Vasilyevich) Gogol

1809-1852

(Born Nikolai Gogol-Yanovsky; also transliterated as Nikolay; also Vasilevich, Vasil'yevich, Vasilievich, and Vasilyevitch; also Gogol' and Gógol; also wrote under the pseudonyms of V. Alov and Rudy Panko) Russian novelist, dramatist, short story writer, essayist, critic, and poet.

The following entry presents criticism of Gogol's *Revizor* (*The Inspector General;* also published in English as *The Government Inspector*). For additional information on Gogol's career and *The Inspector General,* see *NCLC,* Vol. 5.

Considered one of the most brilliant and enigmatic writers in Russian literature, Gogol was the author of multifaceted works that combine elements of realism, romanticism, satire, fantasy, and farce and that often exhibit a deep concern with spiritual values, as well as the eccentricities of the author's own personality. The complexity of such acknowledged masterpieces as *Mërtvye dushi (Dead Souls)* and "Shinel" ("The Overcoat") has inspired an enormous range of critical interpretations, from the early view of his writings as naturalistic social commentaries to later, less orthodox readings, including explications of his works as arcane systems of symbols and as exercises in linguistic innovation. This diversity particularly characterizes discussion of Gogol's most important drama, *The Inspector General,* which many critics regard as the greatest comedy in Russian theater. Realistic in style, the play was widely perceived at the time of its first production as a politically motivated attack on the corrupt bureaucracy of nineteenth-century Russia; however, the work's ostensibly authentic portrayal of Russian life belies its complexity, which has prompted further analyses of the play as moral and spiritual allegory, vaudevillian farce, and absurdist commentary on human existence.

According to Gogol, the situation that served as the basis for *The Inspector General* was provided by Alexander Pushkin in response to an appeal by Gogol for a "purely Russian" anecdote. "Do me a favor," Gogol wrote, "give me a subject; I will instantly make a five-act comedy of it, and it will be funnier than hell." Pushkin replied with a story of mistaken identity, which Gogol quickly transformed into the promised comedy. In Gogol's version, the prominent figures of a provincial Russian town are alerted that a government inspector will be arriving incognito to assess municipal affairs. An impecunious traveler named Khlestakov is mistaken for the expected official, is bribed and fêted, attempts to seduce the mayor's wife and daughter, becomes betrothed to the latter, and departs shortly before the arrival of the real inspector. In this simple plot, constructed within the framework of perverse logic that is typical of his works, Gogol combined mockery of Russian officialdom and parody of literary conventions with fantasy and grotesque comedy.

The play is largely based in theatrical tradition, utilizing the ancient device of mistaken identity, stock characters from eighteenth-century Russian comedy, and elements of vaudevillian slapstick, while adhering closely to the classical unities of time, place, and action. Unencumbered by subplots, *The Inspector General* is often praised for its dramatic structure, in which

Sovfoto

the action develops frenetically between a startlingly brief exposition and an equally startling final scene. In the words of Vladimir Nabokov, "the play begins with a blinding flash of lightning and ends in a thunderclap. In fact it is wholly placed in the tense gap between the flash and the crash." The play is also admired for its exceptionally rich rendering of spoken Russian, in which nuances of speech reflect aspects of character and suggest deeper meanings. *The Inspector General* departs from theatrical tradition in its farcical parody of the love intrigue common to Russian comedy, as well as in its rejection of the conventional dichotomy between virtuous and villainous characters. Gogol's characters are devoid of attractive features, embodying instead such qualities as ignorance, snobbery, and malice. Nevertheless, they are not generally described as villains, but rather as caricature-like depictions of insignificance and insubstantiality. In the words of Jesse Zeldin, the play "is a remarkable achievement . . . of the portrayal of nothingness, of soullessness. These are all little men who aren't there."

Completed in December 1835, *The Inspector General* was initially denied production by government censors, who objected to Gogol's satiric portrayal of bureaucratic corruption. At the behest of the poet Vasily Zhukovsky, however, Czar Nicholas I read the play, and he personally overruled that decision. In April 1836 he attended the play's premiere, where he was reported to have laughed heartily and to have remarked, "Everyone has got his due, and I most of all." In contrast to the czar, the audience as a whole reacted with bewilderment and disapproval. Pavel Annenkov noted that at the end of the play "some people called for the author because they thought he had written a comic masterpiece, others because some of the scenes showed talent, but most because it had made them laugh. The general opinion, . . . however, was that 'this is impossible, this is libel, this is farce'." Subsequent performances of the play caused a sensation in the theater world and engendered heated controversy among critics, who were largely divided upon partisan grounds over the issue of the play's realism and social relevance. While conservative critics denounced *The Inspector General* as a crude, unrealistic farce and a libel against the Russian government, liberal critics praised the play as an artistic rendering of unpleasant social realities. Gogol was deeply offended by both readings: devastated by the criticism of reactionary commentators, he was equally distressed that his defenders similarly viewed the play as a narrow social and political commentary. His immediate reaction was to declare the play utterly devoid of social relevance. He eventually modified his position several times, maintaining that *The Inspector General* was indeed implicitly critical of social institutions and was therefore a bad play; that *The Inspector General* was an incisive commentary on social ills and therefore a great work of literature; and that *The Inspector General* was expressly written as an allegorical representation of humanity's moral condition. Elaborating on the latter interpretation, the author designated the town in which the play is set as "our spiritual city," the real inspector as "our awakening conscience" sent "by command of the Almighty," and the other characters as "the passions residing in our souls." However, critics agree that the play is free from moral didacticism and dismiss this interpretation as a product of the religious and moral fanaticism of Gogol's later years.

Since Gogol's death, the focus of commentary on *The Inspector General* has shifted away from the controversy over the play's realism. Although Soviet critics have continued to regard the work as a social document indicting corruption and injustice under czarist rule, most recent commentators have interpreted the work instead as an intensely subjective artistic creation. Some scholars, stressing the play's fantastic and grotesque elements and atmosphere of unreality, have described *The Inspector General* as an absurdist portrayal of human existence. Formalist critics, who consider Gogol the first great Russian prose stylist, approach his play as primarily an exercise in linguistic manipulation. Another reading has been offered by those who note the play's numerous religious and spiritual elements: while denying that *The Inspector General* contains the didactic element asserted by Gogol, many commentators have seen diabolic connotations in the character of Khlestakov and biblical parallels in the play as a whole. Some have discussed *The Inspector General* as a parody of judgment day and Khlestakov as a symbolic false messiah, while others have portrayed Khlestakov as the Antichrist or his agent.

This multiplicity of interpretations notwithstanding, critics are unanimous in their praise of *The Inspector General*. The play has also remained popular with readers and audiences throughout the world, despite its basis in a social milieu that has been largely forgotten. As Henry Ten Eyck Perry concluded, many qualities have contributed to the enduring appeal of *The Inspector General*: "Its plot has artistic structure without being rigidly formal. Its texture is a happy combination of individuality and universal truth. Its vitality is extraordinary; its in-

ventiveness seems never to flag; it has the creative quality of life; it lacks only the consistent intellectual meaning which life itself so often seems to lack."

NIKOLAI GOGOL [WITH DAVID MAGARSHACK]   (essay date 1842)

[*The following excerpt is taken from "After the Play," a dramatic dialogue in which Gogol sought to defend himself against the widespread criticism with which* The Inspector General *was received. In the dialogue, various characters leaving a theater after a performance of the play share their impressions of the production, with some voicing views similar to those of Gogol's critics and others presenting the author's rebuttals. "After the Play" was written in 1836 and revised for publication in 1842. The following excerpt, which was taken from a version reprinted in the biographical study* Gogol *by David Magarshack, includes comments and summarized passages by Magarshack.*]

> *A Middle-Aged Civil Servant* (*coming out with hands out-spread*): This is goodness only knows what! Such a—Such a—It's—it's terrible! (*Goes out.*)
>
> *A Gentleman a Little Careless about Literature* [Bulgarin] (*addressing another*): It's a translation, isn't it?
>
> *The Other:* Good heavens, no. The action takes place in Russia. It's our customs and even our ranks.
>
> *A Gentleman a Little Careless about Literature:* I seem to remember something of the kind in French, not altogether of the same kind, though.

Bulgarin, whom Gogol characterized in a letter to Danilevsky from Rome on the 13th of May 1838, as 'a man whom it is as revolting to thrash as to kiss', next appears in the guise of two literary gentleman. In one scene he is addressed by A Nondescript Gentleman.

> *A Nondescript Gentleman:* I am no judge of literary merit, sir, but the play has wit. Yes, sir, it's witty, witty.
>
> *A Literary Gentleman:* Good heavens, what's so witty about it? What low people, what a low tone! Most trivial jokes. Why, it's obscene.
>
> *A Nondescript Gentleman:* Well, sir, that's a different matter. I said I am no judge of literary merit. I only observed that the play was funny. I enjoyed it.
>
> *A Literary Gentleman:* It's not funny at all. Good heavens, what's so funny about it and how could you have enjoyed it? A most improbable subject. Full of the most absurd and unlikely situations. No plot, no action, no understanding.
>
> *A Nondescript Gentleman:* Of course, that may be. So far as literature is concerned, you're quite right. It may not be amusing from a literary point of view, but from any other point of view it is.

A Literary Gentleman: Is it? Good heavens, even from any point of view there's nothing amusing in it. What dialogue! Who talks like that in high society? Tell me yourself, do we talk like that?

A Nondescript Gentleman: That's true, sir. You're very clever to have noticed that. I thought so myself. There's no nobility in the dialogue. None of the characters seems to be able to conceal his low origin—that's true.

A Literary Gentleman: Well, there you are! And you're praising it.

A Nondescript Gentleman: Who's praising it? I'm not. I can see myself now that the play's rubbish. I'm afraid I'm no judge of literature.

(*Both go out.*)

Another Literary Gentleman (*comes in accompanied by several people whom he addresses, brandishing his arms*): Believe me, I am an authority on this sort of thing: it's a disgusting play! A sordid, sordid play! Not a single life-like character, all caricatures! There's nothing like it in life. Believe me, there isn't. I know, I'm a writer myself. . . . His play isn't a comedy even. It's a farce, a farce, and a very unsuccessful farce. Compared with it, the silliest comedy by Kotzebue is like Mont Blanc before Pulkov Hill. I'll prove it to them, prove it to them mathematically. It's simply his friends who have praised him up to the skies and I shouldn't be in the least surprised if he didn't think he was a Russian Shakespeare. It's always a man's friends who give him big ideas about himself. Take Pushkin. Why does the whole of Russia talk about him now? It's all because of his friends: they shouted, shouted and now the whole of Russia is shouting with them. (*Goes out with his friends.*)

He is followed by two army officers, one of whom agrees with him that Gogol's play is a farce. 'But', objects the other, 'didn't you say that you had never laughed so much in your life?' But his friend merely repeats Bulgarin's arguments, claiming that his laughter had nothing to do with it. Gogol then brings on 'two art lovers', one of whom, referring to Bulgarin's criticisms, declares that only people 'who talk of drawing-rooms but are admitted no further than the entrance hall' condemn the play as sordid. His objection to the play is that it has no real plot.

Second Art Lover: Yes, that's true; if by plot we understand what is generally understood by it, that is, love interest, then it has no plot. But it seems to me it is time we stopped regarding this particular kind of plot as important. All you have to do is to look around you. Everything in the world has changed. The important theme in a plot now is the desire to obtain a good job, to eclipse your rival by your brilliant wit, to avenge yourself for being disregarded or laughed at. Does not rank, capital or an advantageous marriage mean more today than love?

First Art Lover: That's all very well, but even then I can't see a good plot in the play.

Gogol's reply to this sort of criticism, which he puts into the mouth of the Second Art Lover, is that people are merely used to the conventional type of play ending in marriage. A plot that revolves round two characters, however, is no longer interesting; its subject must be of vital concern to all the characters. 'In such a play', he claims, 'everyone is a hero. . . . It is the idea, the thought behind the play that ought to govern its action. . . . At the beginning, comedy was the creation of a whole people. Such, at least, Aristophanes took it to be. It was much later that the love interest gained predominance in it, but how weak is such a plot even in the hands of the best playwrights, how insignificant are these stage lovers with their cardboard love!' It is the social element in comedy that the Second Art Lover, that is, Gogol himself, considers of the utmost importance. 'Can't comedy and tragedy', he argues, 'express the same lofty idea? Doesn't absolutely everything about a mean and dishonest person show us what an honest man ought to be like? Does not all this accumulation of base actions, all this miscarriage of law and justice, give us a clear idea what law, duty and justice require of us? . . . In the hands of a man of talent', he concludes, 'everything can serve as an instrument of the Beautiful, provided it is guided by the high ideal to serve the Beautiful.'

A third and a fourth art lover appear on the scene.

Fourth Art Lover: What can serve as an instrument of the Beautiful? What are you discussing?

First Art Lover: We are discussing comedy. We were all talking about comedy in general. No one has as yet said anything about the new comedy. What do you say?

Fourth Art Lover: What I say is that you can see that the playwright has talent, that he knows life, that his play is very amusing, true and taken from life but, on the whole, there seems to be something lacking in it. . . . It is strange that our writers of comedies can't do without the government. No comedy ends without it.

Third Art Lover: That's true. But on the other hand, it is quite natural. We all belong to the government, we almost all serve the government, and the interests of us all are connected with the government. It's therefore no wonder that this fact is reflected by our writers.

Fourth Art Lover: True enough, but in that case this connexion must be felt. The funny thing is that no play can possibly end without the interference of the government. Is is sure to appear, just as Fate did in ancient tragedy.

Second Art Lover: Well, you see, this is therefore something that is natural to all our writers of comedies, and that represents the distinguishing character of our comedy. A sort of secret faith in our government is rooted deep in all our hearts. Well, there is nothing wrong in that: God grant that our government should always and everywhere live up to its calling to be the representative of Providence on earth, and that we should believe in it as the ancients believed in Nemesis which overtook the evil-doers.

This identification of the government with Providence was, of course, one of Gogol's basic beliefs, indeed, almost an article of faith with him, and that is why it never occurred to him that by exposing the vices of the government officials he also exposed the viciousness of the régime of which they were an inseparable part. To the officials themselves, however, any sort of exposure was tantamount to an attack on the government itself, and that is why they never hesitated to express their hatred of Gogol's works, and this in the end became the official attitude of the government, too.

Gogol's defence against this attitude is summarized by the Very Modestly-Dressed Man, the first of his thoroughly 'good' characters which he was to draw so unconvincingly in the second part of *Dead Souls*. He is a provincial official and he refuses the offer by Mr. A. of an important post in Petersburg because he fears that some corrupt official might take over his humble post in the provinces. Laughter, the Modestly-Dressed Man declares, is the best way of exposing hypocrisy.

> I confess [*he says*] I felt glad when I saw how absurd well-meaning words sound on the lips of a rogue, and how laughably absurd everyone from the gallery to the stalls thought the mask he put on. And after this there are people who say that one ought not to allow it to be put on the stage! I overheard a remark made, I believe, by a very respectable man who wondered what the common people would say if they saw that such terrible abuses exist among us.
>
> *Mr. A.:* I confess that I, too, asked myself the question what the common people would say if they saw all this.
>
> *Very Modestly-Dressed Man:* What the common people would say? (*Steps aside.*)
>
> (*Two persons in drab peasants' coats pass by.*)
>
> *The Blue Coat (to the grey one):* I dare say our governors were lively enough in the old days, but they all took fright when the Tsar's justice caught up with them.
>
> (*Both go out.*)
>
> *Very Modestly-Dressed Man:* That's what the common people will say. Did you hear?
>
> *Mr. A.:* What?
>
> *Very Modestly-Dressed Man:* I dare say our governors were lively enough in the old days, but they all took fright when the Tsar's justice caught up with them. Do you hear how a man's natural feelings never lead him astray? How true is the judgment of the simple person if it is not clouded over by theories and ideas taken out of books, but is based on an understanding of man's nature. Why, isn't it quite clear that after a performance like this the common people's faith in the government will increase? Yes, they need such performances. Let them dissociate the government from the bad servants of the government. Let them see that abuses do not originate with the government, but with

those who do not understand its demands, those who do not want to give an account to the government. Let them see that their government is actuated by noble sentiments, that its unslumbering eye watches equally over everyone, that sooner or later it will catch up with the violators of the law, honour and sacred duty of man, that those whose conscience is not clear will pale before it. Yes, they ought to see these performances; believe me [Gogol, carried away by his specious argument, did not seem to realise that he was now ascribing to the Russian people an attitude of mind that was becoming more and more characteristic of his own attitude in the 'forties], even if they happened to be the victims of injustice and oppression themselves, they would come out comforted after such a performance, with firm faith in the unslumbering supreme law. . . . It's a good thing there isn't an honest man in the play [he concludes]. Man is vain: show him one good trait of character among many bad ones and he will leave the theatre feeling proud of himself. Yes, it is a good thing that only exceptions and vices are exhibited on the stage, for they are such a thorn in the flesh of every honest man that he is ashamed to confess that such things are possible.

Having thus driven the argument in defence of his play to its logical and at the same time absurd conclusion, Gogol turns to the question whether serious subjects should be discussed in a comedy. The argument for and against is carried on first by three men who leave the theatre together, and then by a young society lady and her husband.

The first man declares that vices and abuses are not a fit subject for comedy, the second replies that there are hundreds of light comedies and there is no reason why one or two serious comedies should not exist. 'I must say,' he goes on to voice Gogol's own predicament, 'I should not like to be in the author's shoes. How is he to please the public? If he chooses some trivial society subject everyone will say: "He writes nonsense, his play lacks a deep moral purpose"; if he chooses a subject which has some serious moral purpose they will say: "It's not his business, let him write nonsense."'

The young society lady enjoyed the play, finding that everything in it was true. She laughed—and again Gogol is speaking through her mouth—because the villainy and baseness exposed in the play would remain villainy and baseness however dressed up and wherever found.

> *Mr. N. (going up to the lady):* A clever woman told me just now that she, too, had laughed, but the play had made her feel sad in spite of that.
>
> *Young Lady:* I don't care what your clever woman felt. My nerves are not so sensitive, and I'm always glad to laugh at what is intrinsically funny. I know that some of us are ready to have a good laugh at a man's crooked nose, but haven't the courage to laugh at a man's crooked soul.

With this parting shot, Gogol winds up his argument against the detractors of his great play, though he carries it on for a few more pages, in which several more people make unflattering remarks about him as 'an utter ignoramus' who had been sacked from his job, and about his play as 'just an amusing fairy-tale'. He ends with a long monologue by the author of the play, in which he again considers the nature of laughter in *The Government Inspector.*

> I regret [he writes in reply to the many criticisms that there is not one positive character in his play] that no one has noticed the honest character in my play. This honest and noble character is—laughter. It is noble because it decided to appear in spite of the low esteem in which it is held in the world. . . . Laughter is more significant and more profound than people think. Not the laughter which is aroused by temporary irritation and a morbid and jaundiced disposition; nor that light laughter which serves for the idle amusement and entertainment of people, but the laughter which issues from man's serene nature . . . the laughter which deepens everything, draws attention to what might have passed unnoticed, and without whose penetrating force man would have been disheartened by life's trivialities and emptiness. . . . No, they are unjust who say that laughter arouses our indignation. It is only the dark aspects of life that arouse our indignation, but laughter is bright. . . . They are unjust who say that laughter makes no impression on those against whom it is directed and that a rogue will be the first to laugh at a rogue whom he sees exposed on the stage: the rogue of a later age will laugh, but the contemporary rogue will not have the nerve to laugh . . . for even he who is not afraid of anything in the world is afraid of ridicule. . . . The world says that what is amusing is low, and only that which is uttered in a stern voice is described as high. But, good Lord, how many people one meets daily, for whom there is nothing high in the world! Everything created by inspiration is just nonsense, just amusing fairy-tales to them: Shakespeare's works are just amusing fairy-tales; the sacred emotions of one's heart are just amusing fairy-tales. No, it is not my injured pride that makes me say that. I am not saying that because my weak and immature works have just been called amusing fairy-tales. . . . Centuries have passed, cities and peoples have vanished from the face of the earth . . . but the "amusing fairy-tales" are alive and are read today. . . . The world would have gone to sleep without such "fairy-tales", life would have grown shallow, and the souls of men would have been covered with slime and mildew. Amusing fairy-tales, indeed! Oh, may the names of those who listened sympathetically to these "amusing fairy-tales" remain for ever sacred to posterity; the wondrous hand of Providence was always stretched out over the heads of their creators. In times of trouble and persecutions all who were noblest among nations became their patrons: the crowned monarch sheltered them behind his imperial shield from the height of his unapproachable throne.

> Onward with a stout heart! [Gogol concludes]. And let not my soul be downcast by censure, but receive thankfully any indication of faults, without despairing even when denied the possession of high impulses and sacred love of humanity! The world is like a whirlpool: opinions and idle talk move about in it everlastingly, but time puts everything in its true perspective. Like husks, the false values fly off and, like hard seeds, the immutable truths remain. . . .

(pp. 140-48)

Nikolai Gogol [with David Magarshack], in an extract from Gogol: A Life *by David Magarshack, Grove Press, Inc., 1957, pp. 140-48.*

NIKOLAY GOGOL   (essay date 1846)

[*Gogol's "Denouement of* The Government Inspector," *excerpted below, was his second explication in dramatic form of that work. Here, the character "First Comic Actor" discusses the play as a spiritual allegory. This piece was written in 1846.*]

FIRST COMIC ACTOR. . . . Take a close look at the town depicted in the play. Everyone agrees that no such town exists in all of Russia; a town in our country where all the officials are monsters is unheard of. You can always find two or three who are honest, but here—not one. In a word, there is no such town. Do you agree? Now suppose this town is actually our spiritual city and is to be found in each of us? No, let's not look at ourselves through the eyes of a man of the world (after all, it's not he who will pronounce judgment upon us); let us look, as well as we can, with the eyes of Him Who will call all men to account, before Whom the best of us—mark it well—will cast down their eyes in shame. Let us see who will then have enough courage to ask, "Is my face crooked?" Pray we are not alarmed by our own crookedness, just as we felt no fear upon seeing the crookedness of those officials. . . . No, Semyon Semyonych, it's not our beauty that ought to concern us but the fact that our lives, which we are in the habit of regarding as comedies, might very well end in the same sort of tragedy that concluded this comedy. Say what you will, the inspector who awaits us at the portals of the grave is terrible. Can you really be ignorant of this inspector's identity? Why deceive ourselves? He is our awakening conscience, who will force us, once and for all, to take a long hard look at ourselves. Nothing will remain hidden from this inspector, for he is sent by command of the Almighty. There will be no turning back when his coming is heralded. Suddenly horrors to make a man's hair stand on end will be revealed about and within us. Far better to examine ourselves at the beginning of our lives than at the end. Instead of engaging in idle self-centered chatter and self-congratulation, let us now visit our deformed spiritual city, a city several times worse than any other, where our passions run amuck like hideous officials plundering the treasury of our souls! At the beginning of our lives, let us take an inspector by the hand and examine all that lies within us—a true inspector and not a counterfeit! Not Khlestakov! Khlestakov is a mediocrity; he is the frivolous conscience of the world, venal and deceitful. The passions residing in our souls will buy him off in an instant. Arm in arm with Khlestakov, we will see nothing of our spiritual city. Note how in conversing with him, each official cleverly wriggled out of his difficulties and justified himself. They emerged almost sanctified. Don't you think our every passion, or even a trivial vulgar habit, has more cunning to it than does a swindling official? . . . No, you will not discern anything in yourselves with the superficial conscience of the world: [our passions] will deceive it, and it will deceive them, as Khlestakov duped the officials, and then it will vanish without leaving a trace. You will be in the position of the mayor turned fool, who let his imagination run away with him, began worming his way into a general's rank, announcing he was certain to be top man in the capital, promising positions to others, when he suddenly saw that he had been hoodwinked and played for a fool by a young whippersnapper, a featherbrain bearing no resemblance to the true inspector. No . . . gentlemen, . . . fling aside your worldly conscience. Examine yourselves, not through the eyes of Khlestakov, but those of the true inspector! I vow, our spiritual city is worth the same thought a good ruler gives to his realm. As he banishes corrupt officials from his land sternly and with dignity, let us banish corruption from our souls! There exists a weapon, a scourge, that can drive it out. Laughter, my worthy countrymen! Laughter, which our base passions fear so! Laughter, created so that we might deride whatever dishonors the true beauty of man. Let us restore to laughter its true significance! Let us wrest it from those who have turned it into a frivolous worldly blasphemy that does not distinguish between good and evil! Just as we laughed at the abominations of others, let us laugh at those abominations we uncover in ourselves! Not only this comedy, but everything that ridicules the ignoble and depraved, no matter who the author, must be understood as referring to ourselves, as if written about us personally. . . . Let us not swell with indignation if some infuriated mayor or, more correctly, the devil himself whispers: "What are you laughing at? Laugh at yourselves!" Proudly we shall answer him: "Yes, we are laughing at ourselves, because we sense our noble Russian heritage, because we hear a command from on high to be better than others!" Countrymen! Russian blood flows in my veins, as in yours. Behold: I'm weeping. As a comic actor, I made you laugh earlier, and now I weep. Allow me to think that my calling is as honest as yours, that I serve my country as you do, that I'm not a light-headed jester created for the amusement of frivolous people, but an honorable functionary of God's great kingdom, and that I awakened laughter in you—not that dissolute laughter stemming from the empty vanity of idle hours by which man mocks man, but laughter born of love for man. Together we shall prove to the world that everything in the Russian land, from small to great, strives to serve Him Whom all things should serve, and that whatever exists in our land is surging upwards (*glancing up*) to the Supreme Eternal Beauty! (pp. 188-90)

> *Nikolay Gogol, in an extract in his* The Theater of Nikolay Gogol: Plays and Selected Writings, *edited by Milton Ehre, translated by Milton Ehre and Fruma Gottschalk, The University of Chicago Press, 1981, pp. 188-90.*

P. KROPOTKIN   (essay date 1905)

[*Kropotkin was a Russian sociologist, philosopher, geographer, essayist, and critic. Born of an aristocratic family, he became an anarchist in the 1870s and later fled to Europe, where he composed several of his best-known works. Chief among these is* Memoirs of a Revolutionist, *which is considered a monumental autobiographical treatment of the revolutionary movement in Russia. Kropotkin also wrote several literary histories, including* Russian Literature, *which was drawn from a series of lectures he gave in the United States. In the following excerpt from* Russian Literature, *Kropotkin outlines the plot of* The Inspector General *and praises the play's literary and dramatic qualities.*]

Gógol's prose-comedy, *The Inspector-General* (*Revizór*), has become, in its turn, a starting point for the Russian drama—a model which every dramatic writer after Gógol has always kept before his eyes. "Revizór," in Russian, means some important functionary who has been sent by the ministry to some provincial town to inquire into the conditions of the local administration—an Inspector-General; and the comedy takes place in a small town, from which "you may gallop for three years and yet arrive nowhere." The little spot—we learn it at the rising of the curtain—is going to be visited by an Inspector-General. The local head of the Police (in those times the head of the Police was also the head of the town)—the Gorodníchiy or Governor—has convoked the chief functionaries of the place to communicate to them an important news. He has had a bad dream; two rats came in, sniffed and then went away; there must be something in that dream, and so there is; he has just got this morning a letter from a friend at St. Petersburg, announcing that an inspector-general is coming, and—what is still worse—is coming incognito! Now, the honourable Governor advises the functionaries to put some order in their respective offices. The patients in the hospital walk about in linen so dirty that you might take them for chimney sweeps. The chief magistrate, who is a passionate lover of sport, has his hunting apparel hanging about in the Court, and his attendants have made a poultry-yard of the entrance hall. In short, everything has to be put in order. The Governor feels very uncomfortable. Up to the present day he has freely levied tribute upon the merchants, pocketed the money destined for building a church, and within a fortnight he has flogged the wife of a non-commissioned officer, which he had no right to do; and now, there's the Inspector-General coming! He asks the postmaster "just to open a little" the letters which may be addressed from this town to St. Petersburg and, if he finds in them some reports about town matters, to keep them. The postmaster—a great student of human character—has always indulged, even without getting this advice, in the interesting pastime of reading the letters, and he falls in with the Governor's proposal.

At that very moment enter Petr Iványch Dóbchinsky and Petr Iványch Bóbchinsky. Everyone knows them, you know them very well: they play the part of the town Gazette. They go about the town all day long, and as soon as they have learnt something interesting they both hurry to spread the news, interrupting each other in telling it, and hurrying immediately to some other place to be the first to communicate the news to someone else. They have been at the only inn of the town, and there they saw a very suspicious person: a young man, "who has something, you know, extraordinary about his face." He is living there for a fortnight, never paying a penny, and does not journey any further. "What is his object in staying so long in town like ours?" And then, when they were taking their lunch he passed them by and looked so inquisitively in their plates—who may he be? Evidently, the Governor and all present conclude, he must be the Inspector-General who stays there incognitio. . . . A general confusion results from the suspicion. The Governor starts immediately for the inn, to make the necessary enquiries. The womenfolk are in a tremendous excitement.

The stranger is simply a young man who is travelling to rejoin his father. On some post-station he met with a certain captain—a great master at cards—and lost all he had in his pocket. Now he cannot proceed any farther, and he cannot pay the landlord, who refuses to credit him with any more meals. The young man feels awfully hungry—no wonder he looked so inquisitively into the plates of the two gentlemen—and resorts to all sorts of tricks to induce the landlord to send him something for his dinner. Just as he is finishing some fossil-like cutlet enters the Gorodníchiy; and a most comic scene follows, the young man thinking that the Governor came to arrest him, and the Governor thinking that he is speaking to the Inspector-General who is trying to conceal his identity. The Governor offers to remove the young man to some more comfortable place. "No, thank you, I have no intent to go to a jail," sharply retorts the young man. . . . But it is to his own house that the Governor takes the supposed Inspector, and now an easy life begins for the adventurer. All the functionaries appear in turn to introduce themselves, and everyone is only too happy to give him a bribe of a hundred roubles or so. The merchants come to ask his protection from the Governor; the widow who was flogged comes to lodge a complaint. . . . In the meantime the young man enters into a flirtation with both the wife and the daughter of the Governor; and, finally, being caught at a very pathetic moment when he is kneeling at the feet of the daughter, without further thought he makes a proposition of marriage. But, having gone so far, the young man, well-provided now with money, hastens to leave the town on the pretext of going to see an uncle; he will be back in a couple of days. . . .

The delight of the Governor can easily be imagined. His Excellency, the Inspector-General, going to marry the Governor's daughter! He and his wife are already making all sorts of plans. They will remove to St. Petersburg, the Gorodníchiy will soon be a general, and you will see how he will keep the other Gorodníchies at his door! . . . The happy news spreads about the town, and all the functionaries and the society of the town hasten to offer their congratulations to the old man. There is a great gathering at his house—when the postmaster comes in. He has followed the advice of the Governor, and has opened a letter which the supposed Inspector-General had addressed to somebody at St. Petersburg. He now brings this letter. The young man is no inspector at all. . . . (pp. 73-6)

In short, the letter produces a great sensation. The friends of the Governor are delighted to see him and his family in such straits, all accuse each other, and finally fall upon the two gentlemen, when a police soldier enters the room and announces in a loud voice: "A functionary from St. Petersburg, with Imperial orders, wants to see you all immediately. He stays at the hotel." Thereupon the curtain drops over a living picture of which Gógol himself had made a most striking sketch in pencil, and which is usually reproduced in his works; it shows how admirably well, with what a fine artistic sense, he represented to himself his characters.

The Inspector-General marks a new era in the development of dramatic art in Russia. All the comedies and dramas which were being played in Russia at that time (with the exception, of course, of *Misfortune from Intelligence*, which, however, was not allowed to appear on the stage) hardly deserved the name of dramatic literature: so imperfect and puerile they were. *The Inspector-General,* on the contrary, would have marked at the time of its appearance . . . an epoch in any language. Its stage qualities, which will be appreciated by every good actor; its sound and hearty humour; the natural character of the comical scenes, which result from the very characters of those who appear in this comedy; the sense of measure which pervades it—all these make it one of the best comedies in existence. If the conditions of life which are depicted here were not so exclusively Russian, and did not so exclusively belong to a bygone stage of life which is unknown outside Russia, it would

have been generally recognised as a real pearl of the world's literature. (pp. 77-8)

> *P. Kropotkin, "Gógol," in his* Russian Literature, *1905. Reprint by Benjamin Blom, 1967, pp. 67-87.*

V. V. GIPPIUS (essay date 1924)

[*Gippius was a prominent Russian translator and critic best known for his writings on Gogol. He was the first general editor of the fourteen-volume edition of Gogol's collected works, and his* Gogol, *published in Russian in 1924, is considered the best critical study of the author in any language. In the following excerpt from that work, Gippius discusses the importance of the phantasmal to the dramatic action in* The Inspector General *and examines Gogol's deliberate rejection of verisimilitude and traditional romantic intrigue.*]

The dramatic action of *The Inspector General* follows the same "old principle" that Gogol had noted as early as 1832: "He is just about to get something and grasp it with his hand when suddenly there is some obstacle and the desired object is removed to an enormous distance." Here this applies to the mayor, in his various ambitions and aspirations for rank, fine food, etc., as well as to Maria Antonovna in her hopes for love and marriage. In his notebook Gogol was of course only outlining the "principle." We might flesh it out as follows: a "desired object" is not only "removed to an enormous distance" but proves to be a phantom; that fact becomes apparent, after which everything returns to where it was in the beginning, as in the fairy tale of the fisherman and the fish. Belinsky, during his Hegelian period, interpreted Gogol in these terms: the mayor's dream about the rats is the beginning of "a series of phantoms which comprise the reality of the comedy"; Khlestakov is "a creation of the mayor's frightened imagination, a phantom or shade of his conscience." This interpretation coincided with the one that Gogol himself made in 1842, and it perhaps helped him understand himself as a writer: Khlestakov, he says, is "a phantasmagoric figure who, mendacious deception incarnate, speeds off in the troika Lord knows where." The effect of Act V depends on the return from the world of phantoms to the world of reality. The reading of a letter characterizing each of the people present is not a new device for a denouement, but Gogol introduces an unexpected touch: the gendarme bearing news of the arrival of a real inspector general.

In **"Leaving the Theater after the Performance of a New Comedy,"** Gogol himself said that this denouement had the same significance as "inescapable fate in the tragedies of the ancients." Here too he called laughter the only honest character in the play [see excerpt dated 1842]. But Vyazemsky came just as close to what Gogol had in mind when he called the government the only honest character. The moral and social idea of the comedy is revealed in the appearance of a representative of the government at the end. If there is no triumph of virtue here, as there is in Kvitka's play, where the officials themselves are essentially virtuous and where there are "positive" types as such, then there is at least the punishment of vice, as in Molière's *Tartuffe,* Fonvizin's *The Minor,* and Kapnist's *Chicanery.* The following remark, in **"Leaving the Theater,"** alludes to this tradition: "It is strange that our writers of comedies cannot get along at all without the government; there is not one of our comedies that develops without it." But Gogol made a bold break with tradition in another way: not only did he not introduce virtuous heroes, he even denied his heroes any attractive features whatever, deliberately eschewing verisimilitude in order to present "the contemptible and the insignificant" with "terrible, almost caricature-like intensity." As is evident from this statement, Gogol was not afraid of either a lack of verisimilitude or of caricatures. When The First Member of the Audience in **"Leaving the Theater"** demands "respectable" heroes, saying that "if the comedy is to be a picture and mirror of our social life, it ought to reflect that life in all faithfulness," the Author, speaking through the Second Member of the Audience, replies: "You see, the setting and the scene of action are imaginary. Otherwise the author would not have perpetrated such blatant inaccuracies and anachronisms, he would not even have let certain characters make speeches that are inappropriate, considering their nature and their place in society." The first drafts of **"Leaving the Theater"** were made when Gogol's impressions of the premiere of *The Inspector General* were still fresh in his mind. In 1842 he made it the concluding piece in his collected works, and his theories of drama are therefore of special importance.

Gogol's statement about the imaginary nature of the setting of *The Inspector General* ought to eliminate the kind of guesswork that attempts to determine just which real-life impressions produced the text of this play. Also, they ought to explain why it is that scholars who are unfamiliar with the psychology of creativity fail to understand how Gogol could have written this play without ever having lived in a provincial town. Bulgarin thought that the character-types in the play were Ukrainian (surprisingly, this view was supported by Vengerov); but this does not stand up under critical scrutiny either (in order to defend it, Vengerov was forced to ascribe a "highstrung" nature to Ukrainians).

Gogol resolutely rejected the one feature of plot that was fundamental to the comedy which in our day is called "classical" and in his day was called "romantic" (in contrast to the comedy of antiquity): the love-intrigue. In his treatise on esthetics, Galich defines the "romantic" comedy as one that takes place "not in a social but a domestic circle, revolving around its immovable point—marriage." The surviving fragments of *The Order of St. Vladimir* do not enable us to judge what role was played by the love between the *virtuous* heroes—the idealistic Misha and the "poor but honest" Odosimova—and whether their marriage would have occurred, threatened as it was by the mother's scheme of making a profitable match for her son. But Gogol detected the changes taking place in that stratum of society which provided the models for his comic lampoons; and in **"Leaving the Theater"** he suggested another scheme for a comic plot, which still included the idea of profitable marriage, but not love. "Everything in the world has long since changed. Now a stronger element in the plotting of drama is the desire to obtain a profitable position, to shine and eclipse someone else at all costs, to take revenge for the contempt and the ridicule one has suffered. Is there now not more electricity in rank, in money-capital, in a profitable marriage, than in love?" This is the scheme of *The Order of St. Vladimir,* and, in some particulars, of *Marriage* (the electricity of a profitable marriage), of *The Inspector General* (the electricity of rank), and of *The Gamblers* (the electricity of money-capital). It also looks ahead to the basic scheme of Nikolay Ostrovsky's plays, which did not, however, ignore the theme of the electricity of love. But for Gogol, these "theatrical lovers with their cardboard love" are not only insignificant, but cannot possibly be made into anything more than cardboard. In the words of the Second Lover of the Arts (**"Leaving the Theater"**), the introduction of a love-intrigue destroys "the significance of social comedy," which was just what Gogol set particular store by

A watercolor by the actor Karatygin of Gogol during a rehearsal of The Inspector General. *Photo Flammarion.*

during those years when he was keenly aware of his mission as a writer. It is essential to recognize that there is a hidden psychological reason why Gogol departed so decisively from the tradition in just this respect, a reason which biography, psychology and psycho-pathology have so far been incapable of revealing in all its aspects.

In *The Inspector General,* Gogol presents a parody of the love-intrigue. The unity of time required a rapid tempo, yet afforded sufficient scope within the confines of the five acts and the twenty-four hours in which the action of the play unfolds. As if making fun of this rule, Gogol inserts two declarations of love, a misunderstanding due to a rivalry, and a proposal and engagement into the span of half an act and several minutes, only to laugh at this "phantom" too in the final act. Senkovsky advised Gogol to liven up the comedy with a love-intrigue—to have Khlestakov running after some young provincial lady and to picture her in turn as being jealous of Maria Antonovna, the mayor's daughter. But this lame piece of advice unwittingly underscored Gogol's bold originality. (pp. 85-8)

V. V. Gippius, in his Gogol, *edited and translated by Robert A. Maguire, Ardis, 1981, 216 p.*

JANKO LAVRIN (essay date 1926)

[*Lavrin is an Austrian-born British essayist, biographer, and critic who is best known for his studies of nineteenth- and twentieth-*

century Russian literature. These include An Introduction to the Russian Novel, *in which he combined literary criticism with an exploration into the psychological and philosophical background of an author. Lavrin is also the author of two critical studies of Gogol:* Gogol *and* Gogol (1809-1852): A Centenary Survey. *In the following excerpt from the former work, he discusses* The Inspector General *as a realistic social satire.*]

[Gogol's *Revizor* is not] a merely exhilarating comedy, but a satire full of gall and hidden indignation. It is saturated with all that "malice, laughter and salt" which he had to suppress when giving up the plan for his *Vladimir.* And as to its technique, it is a work made of one piece. Everything in it is inevitable. Each situation, each figure, is an organic part of the whole. The play abounds in grinning irony and indirect indictments; yet being moral in the best sense as all true art always is, it is not in the least moralizing; there is not a single puppet spluttering out "ideas" and moral recipes. Apart from this, each character speaks a language of his own and, as in *The Marriage,* the comicality of the characters strengthens that of the situations. Together with Griboyedov's *Gore ot Uma (The Mischief of Being Clever), The Revizor* belongs to the favourite plays of the Russian stage. And it certainly deserves this honour. (p. 137)

The genesis of *The Revizor* is due to an anecdote told by Pushkin of how he himself had been mistaken in Nizhny Novgorod for a high official from Petersburg who had arrived incognito in order to inspect the order of the town. Such a *qui-pro-quo* is in itself only funny. Gogol's imagination, however, transmuted also this incident in such a way as to make it a pretext for showing the whole of Russian life in its most pessimistic aspect—under the mask of fun and laughter. (p. 138)

Gogol said later, in his **"Author's Confession":** "I saw that in my former works I laughed for nothing, uselessly, without knowing why. If it is necessary to laugh, then let us laugh at that which really deserves to be laughed at by all. In my *Revizor* I decided to gather in one place and deride all that is bad in Russia, all the evils which are being perpetrated in those places where the utmost rectitude is required from man."

Corruption, snobbery, stupidity, malice—the whole compendium of vices which could be found in a stagnant provincial existence is focussed in *The Revizor* and whipped with merciless laughter. Gogol never moralizes nor does he indulge in direct indictments. He does not even pretend to swing the whip in his own hands, but makes his characters whip themselves without knowing it, as it were, especially when they talk of their own abuses with a kind of childlike innocence. He never speaks for the facts, because he is a great enough artist to understand that facts must always speak for themselves. He is perhaps at his best when putting on the mask of an *ingénu* and talking with a most serious countenance about things which are taken seriously only by his characters and not by the reader. His irony consists in his pretending not to see any irony at all, although indirectly he makes us feel the wide gap between his own standpoint and that of his characters. The less he himself emphasizes this gap and pretends to be on the same level as his characters, he greater the comic-satirical atmosphere of the play. This atmosphere grows and grows; but having reached its highest pitch, it suddenly bursts of itself and dissolves into the sinister last chord, whose effect is all the stronger because of the previous comicality. True, Gogol sometimes achieves his effects by various traditional "tricks"; but in his case they are convincing because he knows how to motivate them psychologically. At the same time, the strictest artistic economy

is preserved throughout, both in the construction and the details of the play. "In *The Revizor* there are no scenes to which the word 'better' can be applied, because none of them is inferior to the rest," wrote Bielinsky; "they are all excellent; they are the necessary parts forming one artistic whole, which is rounded up not only by its external form, but also by its inner contents; and so it is a self-sufficient world of its own." (pp. 150-52)

The play in itself is not a "realistic" copy of Russian provincial life, but an exaggerated picture of all those vices on which Gogol wished to vent his own indignation. It was his conscious craving for a higher form of life that severed him all the more from actual existence. It was his strong but unsatisfied need of reverence coupled with his utter incapacity to revere anything with genuine abandonment and passion that made him all the more aggressive. Hence he indulged at least in his *negative passion*—the passion of indictment, of anger, of laughter through tears. Having collected the necessary objective facts, he modified them according to his own inner need and constructed out of them a picture which he himself took for a mirror of real life. In fact, Gogol had to do so, because this was the only way in which he could attack and refute the reality he loathed. Once more he asserted himself against it—through his art. (pp. 152-53)

In order to clear up certain misunderstandings with regard to his *Revizor,* he published in its new edition of 1846 a kind of epilogue called **"The Dénouement of the Revizor"** [see excerpt dated 1846]. Owing to various influences which he had undergone abroad, Gogol made here an attempt at interpreting the whole piece in an allegorical way. The shabby town in which the gorodnichy ruled supreme he suddenly declared to be the town of our soul. Khlestakov was transmuted into a symbol of our volatile worldly conscience, and the Inspector-General himself into that of our true conscience which everyone will have to confront after death, etc. Such interpretation is of course ridiculous and entirely unconvincing.

But if it obscures the piece, it shows certain new and disturbing features in Gogol himself. . . . [We] must say a few words about the importance of *The Revizor*'s success for his personal destiny.

The strong effect produced by this play was bound to influence Gogol's further activities. Before that, he was not quite sure of his true vocation simply because he did not know in which direction he could assert his talents and ambitions to their utmost. In spite of all his triumphs, he seemed still to be groping and experimenting, as it were, with his own fate. Together with literature he had tried also pedagogic activities (his professorship). His *Arabesque* shows how divided his interests were between literature proper and various quasi-scientific and pedagogic propensities. He planned a big History of Little Russia, and an even bigger History of the Middle Ages—"in eight or perhaps in nine volumes". *The Revizor* however, put an end to it all. He saw what a great influence could be exercised by a writer who would tackle the realities of Russia and "describe manners". This stimulated both his "realistic" and his ethical veins. In short, he took leave of all romantic fancies and concentrated his efforts upon what he considered his true mission. Being sincerely convinced that he was a realist, he turned his eyes once more towards the actual Russia of that time. (pp. 156-57)

Janko Lavrin, in his Gogol, *E. P. Dutton & Co., 1926, 263 p.*

BORIS BRASOL   (essay date 1934)

[*Brasol was a Russian-born American critic. Here, he examines the character Khlestakov as a manifestation of the demonic.*]

Khlestakov, as conceived by Gogol, is a vanishing "neither this nor that" type, one which can be met anywhere, or to put it differently—*everywhere*. Like the source of gossip, Khlestakov evades localization: the microbe of the trivial plague, invisible though it be, penetrates everything, knowing neither barriers nor destination. In this sense, Khlestakov is *omnipresent*. But he is more than that—he is *omnipotent*. In his eloquent tirades he boasts of his many wonderful achievements; according to him, he is the real author of practically every famous novel and an intimate friend of every great writer. Carried on the wings of his imagination, inspired by the lie for its own sake, he paints this glowing picture:

> I am acquainted with pretty actresses, . . . and I am meeting writers quite frequently. I am on a friendly footing with Poushkin. I used to say to him quite often: 'Well, brother Poushkin, how do things stand?'—'Why, fairly well, brother', he would say,—'Just so-so'. . . . Oh, he is a great eccentric! . . . Yes, I am contributing to magazines. . . . By the way, I have written a number of books: *The Marriage of Figaro, Robert the Devil, Norma*—why, I can't even remember all the titles. . . . Everything comes to me by accident. I didn't want to write, but the theatrical manager insisted: 'Oh, please, do write something, old boy!'—So I said to myself, 'Why, all right, old fellow!' And then I think it was on that same evening I wrote everything and thrilled everybody. The buoyancy of my thoughts is extraordinary. . . .

Khlestakov hypnotizes his audience by the blooming nonsense which he is twittering in a perfectly effortless manner.

> "Khlestakov"—says Gogol—"is by no means lying frigidly, swaggeringly or in a theatrical style. He lies with sentiment, his eyes express delight which is derived from the act itself of lying. Altogether, these are the happiest and most poetic moments in his life—they almost amount to inspiration."

(pp. 138-40)

Khlestakov succeeds in everything: he can write wonderful books; the government machine is under his thumb; the human mind, to him, is an open book; he is welcome everywhere; he has reached the top rung of the social ladder; he is an habitué in the Imperial Palace; he is the first candidate for the rank of Field Marshal, and, were it not for the untimely slip, he might—who knows?—have been promoted to the office of the Czar himself.

In other words, Gogol claims that Khlestakov is everywhere, or *omnipresent;* that he knows everything, which means that he is *omniscient;* that he is capable of achieving anything, and this makes him *omnipotent*. Thus, the three properties of Divinity are also possessed by Khlestakov—the primordial symbol of the commonplace—perhaps the Devil himself—who, in this neutral guise, must appeal to the "neither this nor that" human type, decaying in an environment of self-conceited mediocrity.

Lermontov has once defined his Demon as something that is "neither day nor night, neither light nor darkness",—a twilight, deprived of either shape or color. Such is also Khlestakov: an immortal being with neither past nor future. No one knows whence he came and whither he goes; he is simply there—omniscient, omnipotent and omnipresent. Indeed, his existence is equivalent to the refutation of the universal law of evolution. Notwithstanding this, he is in a state of perpetual mobility, or incongruous agitation, like some of those tiny colloidal particles in the strange phenomenon of the Brownian movement. His triumphs, though petty, are lasting; they are accepted as something positively granted and forever imbedded in the living tissues of the social order; they are acclaimed by that majority which, if Ibsen be right, is always wrong.

It seemed to Gogol that Khlestakov—the eternal impostor—is much more than a mere sociological phenomenon: he is the incarnation of Evil itself, and as such, he grows to the proportion of a moral issue predicated upon religion. In Khlestakov, the three Divine attributes appear as though in an inverted mirror.

Gogol never doubted the existence of God, but, likewise, he firmly believed in the reality of the Devil, while the coexistence of these two primary principles, mutually excluding each other, gave birth to that metaphysical antinomy which began to torture our author's conscience long before that mind of his had reached the point of final disintegration.

Besides, there was another problem to be solved—one with which theodicy has been hopelessly struggling ever since the Manichaean times, when the ancient Persians expounded their dualistic doctrine of Ahriman and Ormazd: What is the source and purpose of Vice and Evil in a world whose destinies are preordained by God, the Cause of Good and Virtue?—

The facile answer of a Leibnitz that the existence of wickedness is justified as a necessary condition of the greatest moral good, was altogether repugnant to the mentality of Gogol, who, at least in his early days, was firmly convinced that the greatest moral good can be achieved only on condition that Evil be overcome by the free will of man. If so, what was the means of conquering the Devil?— To this Gogol—not the moralist, but the artist governed less by logic than emotion—could have given but one answer: Evil is deprived of its corrupting lure if it is laughed at.

> "Your words"—Gogol once wrote to Sheviriév—"relating to the question of how one can make a fool of the Devil are in complete accord with my own thoughts. For a long time, I have been endeavouring to achieve but one end, namely, that man, after reading my works, should begin to laugh heartily at the Devil."

Gogol knew that La Rochefoucauld was right when he said that "ridicule dishonors more than dishonor itself." It was for this reason that Gogol chose the comedy form for his *Reviser.*

Of course, the term "comedy" should be used here with reservations, for the nature of Gogol's laughter can scarcely be compared with that which sounds in the political satires of Aristophanes, or in the grateful creations of Molière, or in the merry plays of Shakespeare, or in Beaumarchais' immortal farce: Gogol's is decidedly a pathological laughter, a "laughter through tears", as he himself called it. While he does ridicule Khlestakov, trying to make a fool of him, still Khlestakov, the fool, fatally makes the other characters in the play appear as even greater fools. To this extent, then, in creating *The Reviser,* Gogol has defeated his own purpose. (pp. 141-44)

Boris Brasol, ''Gogol,'' in his *The Mighty Three: Poushkin-Gogol-Dostoievsky, A Critical Trilogy, William Farquhar Payson,* 1934, pp. 117-90.

HENRY TEN EYCK PERRY (essay date 1939)

[*Perry offers a general assessment of* The Inspector General, *focusing on characterization and the dramatic function of various figures in the play.*]

In 1836 Nikolay Vasilyevich Gogol produced his famous comedy *The Inspector-General* (*Revizor*). In it he did not attempt to show the nobility and the landed gentry, or the peasants and the serfs, but concentrated his attention upon typical middle-class citizens of an undistinguished sort. They are the Chief of Police, the Superintendent of Schools, the Judge, the Postmaster, and the District Physician, men who are responsible for the welfare of their fellow citizens and who pride themselves on their public offices. They are drawn in rough outlines, with the gusto and verve which has caused Gogol to be called the father of Russian realism.

If he is the father of Russian realism, his realism is built upon a romantic basis. Beneath it is the same idealism that underlies Griboyedov's *Woe from Wit,* a hope that social conditions may be improved throughout Russia as a result of clearer insight and sounder culture. Griboyedov put his violent views into the mouth of his protagonist, Chatsky, rather too obviously; Gogol, with what seems like deliberate self-restraint, has no character in *The Inspector-General* formally express the author's own sentiments. He is unwilling to commit himself to a definite attitude towards the problem he has taken up, but he does attempt to present all sides of the subject. His determined effort to be impersonal is shown by the ''Notes for the Actors'' which he prefixed to his drama. In them he describes the bodies, clothes, and mannerisms of the principal characters, with a minute power of observation that reminds one of Ben Jonson's detailed description of men and their habits. By the time *The Inspector-General* is over we know a great deal about the lives of a number of small Russian officials, where they get their money and how they spend it, their relations with their neighbors and their families, their amusements and their hypocrisies. The fact that they have their transparent hypocrisies introduces the element of judgment from an ideal standpoint, which lies concealed behind the numerous persons and incidents in the foreground of Gogol's work.

The weakness of realism is that the numerous physical facts it presents may distract attention from the underlying meaning of a work of art. Its strength is that the emphasis on these same physical facts may stimulate the spectator to a new awareness of the physical limitations of mankind. The more petty objects there are in the world, the more necessary it is that they should be arranged with delicacy and skill to serve some useful purpose. The appearance of a single integrated personality is an excellent way of displaying the absurdity of people whose houses and minds are cluttered up with too many pieces of useless bric-a-brac. In Kotzebue's *The German Provincials* a man from the city is introduced into the restricted atmosphere of a small German town and succeeds in exposing its narrow-minded superstitions. Kotzebue's hero is a rather unpleasantly smug person. It would have been quite as easy for the dramatist to satirize him as to ridicule his environment. Gogol did not wish to run the risk of having the sympathy in his story lie in

the wrong quarters. As the disturbing influence in his comedy he took a young man who is quite as much of a rascal as the townspeople among whom he finds himself. He is more successful, because he has had a wider experience and because circumstances play into his hands more easily, but one feels convinced that his triumphs will be hollow and short-lived.

The plot of *The Inspector-General* is supposed to be based upon a story that Pushkin told Gogol of how he had once been mistaken for a government inspector in a small Russian town. Gogol imagined an impecunious and unprincipled junior clerk in such a position, and the result is the character of Khlestakov. Khlestakov has lost all his money by playing cards with an infantry captain and is about to be put in jail by an indignant innkeeper. He is not a bad sort of fellow. Though easygoing and pleasure-loving, he is appreciative of life's experiences and endowed with a lively imagination. ''The more sincerity and simplicity the actor puts into this role,'' Gogol wrote, ''the better he will play it.'' He is attended by his elderly and taciturn manservant, who likes to lecture his master behind his back, but who takes a part in his disreputable schemes and extricates him from his precarious position before it is too late. These two persons appear in only the three central acts of the play. They are used by the dramatist to point out the weaknesses of his other characters, and yet they themselves have the failings of the average sensual man. The world is made up of people like that, Gogol seems to say, and on the title page of his comedy he prints the significant motto, ''Don't blame the looking-glass if your face is crooked.''

Khlestakov has a confidant in a friend of his who does not appear upon the stage but to whom he writes a letter describing his experiences as the supposed inspector-general. This letter, which is intercepted by the Postmaster and read in the last act after Khlestakov's departure, contains the essence of the play. Khlestakov describes to his friend how all the inhabitants of the town, thinking him to be an inspector-general, have bribed and flattered him; for the two days he has lived there, he has been treated like a king by a pack of knaves. He comments on the stupidity and amorousness of the townspeople, their drunkenness and bestiality, the foul odors that come from them, and the bad manners that they display. Still he regards them all as hospitable and kindhearted. These are the people of whom Gogol says, ''Their prototypes may be found in almost any community.'' They have been tricked by Khlestakov, but only because of his greater poise; he can criticize the food given him at the inn more volubly than the Chief of Police can apologize for its inadequacy. The first scene between these two important characters is an excellent example of Gogol's plan and method. In it Khlestakov thinks that he is being arrested for debt and the Chief of Police believes that his dishonesty is being investigated by a higher official. Each man is a rogue with certain pardonable weaknesses, each supposes the other to be more respectable than he really is, and each is afraid that his own true character will be detected by his opponent.

Gogol's exposure of personal insincerity and official corruption reaches into every department of governmental activity. Each one of the town's magistrates is eager to offer money secretly to the supposed inspector, on the understanding that he as an individual will not be reported upon unfavorably. The Chief of Police, who is virtually the major of the city, is the principal target for satire. He is a self-made man, who has arrived at his present position by taking bribes and by persecuting mercilessly those who cannot or will not pay him for his patronage. Within limits, he is a clever man, or he could not have risen so far in the world. There is little doubt that, after the fiasco of Khlestakov's visit has been forgotten, he will retrieve himself and again solidify his position with the dishonest members of the community.

The members of the family of the Chief of Police, his vain wife and his ignorant daughter, provide the only feminine element in a play which is too occupied with the framework of society to devote much attention to matters of sex. Both mother and daughter are coquettish in their different ways, and each is much interested in clothes and fashions. They are jealous of each other's place in Khlestakov's affections. Their rivalry brings about an amusing scene, when the daughter finds Khlestakov on his knees before her mother. This situation is highly farcical, but, like many other ridiculous incidents in the play, it is also a revelation of character. When the Superintendent of Schools lights his cigar at the wrong end, when the Chief of Police puts a hatbox instead of a hat on his head, when Khlestakov slips and almost falls in his drunkenness, one laughs, but one is made acutely aware of the Superintendent's nervousness, the Chief of Police's excitement, or Khlestakov's carelessness, as the case may be.

The two minor characters in *The Inspector-General* who perhaps best exhibit the peculiar quality of Gogol's art, on a small scale, are the landed proprietors, Dobchinsky and Bobchinsky, a close parallel to Tweedledum and Tweedledee. They are both described as being short and stocky; they both speak very fast and use many gestures. Dobchinsky, the taller and the more serious, wants to legitimatize his eldest son, who was born out of wedlock. Bobchinsky, the more expansive and lively, has the great ambition of wishing to be talked about in St. Petersburg. When Dobchinsky is chosen by the Chief of Police to be present at the first interview with Khlestakov, Bobchinsky follows them, peeps through a crack of the door off and on during the conversation, and finally, when the door falls off its hinges, is catapulted into the room. The result is that his nose is severely scratched, and he appears throughout the rest of the play with a ludicrous plaster on it. Bobchinsky and Dobchinsky vie with each other for the credit of having been the first person to suppose that Khlestakov was the expected inspector-general. At the end each is anxious to disclaim the responsibility for the false identification. They present a pitiable picture of amazement and futility in the final tableau, when it is announced that the real inspector-general has just arrived to investigate conditions in the town.

Dobchinsky and Bobchinsky are rather like flies on the wheel of the comedy's action. In this respect they are not unlike the more important characters in the plot. There is a suggestion throughout the play that the individual life is not significant compared with the social fabric of which it is a part. Inspectors may come and inspectors may go, it is implied, but the little town with its corrupt magistrates will continue, and the world is made up of thousands of such small communities. By exposing the follies of this particular town Gogol laid himself open to the Chief of Police's gibe that authors are dangerous Liberals. Gogol was more liberal than the Liberals, however, when, on being hailed by them as their spokesman and champion, he insisted that he was not working for any one narrow political party. He hated the dishonest officialdom in the Russia of his day, but he also realized that under every uniform there was a human being as simple and inoffensive as Dobchinsky or Bobchinsky. *The Inspector-General* not only shows the difference between what men seem to be in public and what they are in private life, but in an indirect and tantalizing way it hints

vaguely at the mystery of what human beings are really like at bottom.

Gogol makes the Chief of Police declare that all men have their little failings, and it is God himself who has arranged it so, whatever Voltaire and his followers may say to the contrary. This statement expresses Gogol's central position very fairly. He is a satirist up to a certain point, beyond which he is a humanitarian. He has found that farce, which is only an exaggerated kind of realism, is artistically a happy medium between the extremes of ridicule and sympathy. These two opposing attitudes, which had been struggling in the work of eighteenth-century writers like Goldoni and Lessing, came to a sort of comic synthesis in the rough horseplay of *The Inspector-General*. The same uproarious mixture of criticism and understanding suffuses Gogol's great comic narrative, *Dead Souls,* written a few years later. In it the writer's appreciation of humanity has, if anything, increased, and his indignation at social abuses is no less intense; but the projected scope of this novel is too vast to be fully realized, and *The Inspector-General* must be considered Gogol's most finished literary production. It compresses into the five acts of one play its author's sensitive interpretation of his experience on earth. (pp. 319-24)

The Inspector-General rises superior to the limitations of realism. It stands by itself among the dramatic works of Gogol and all other Russian writers, and it has sometimes been called the best play written in the Russian language. On its own ground it has certainly never been surpassed. Everything about this unique comedy grows upon one with continued acquaintance. One must interpret its profuse material for oneself and not be disconcerted to find that it is by turns a farce, a satire, and a sentimental comedy. Its plot has artistic structure without being rigidly formal. Its texture is a happy combination of individuality and universal truth. Its vitality is extraordinary; its inventiveness seems never to flag; it has the creative quality of life; it lacks only the consistent intellectual meaning which life itself so often seems to lack. (p. 325)

Henry Ten Eyck Perry, "Crosscurrents in Russia: Gogol, Turgenev, and Chekhov," in his Masters of Dramatic Comedy and Their Social Themes, *Cambridge, Mass.: Harvard University Press, 1939, pp. 314-58.*

VLADIMIR NABOKOV   (essay date 1944)

[*A Russian-born American man of letters, Nabokov was a prolific contributor to many literary fields, producing works in both Russian and English and distinguishing himself in particular as the author of the novels* Lolita *and* Pale Fire. *Nabokov was fascinated with all aspects of the creative life, and his works frequently explore the origins of creativity, the relationships of artists to their work, and the nature of invented reality. In the following excerpt from his biographical and critical study* Gogol, *Nabokov discusses the importance of secondary characters and inanimate objects in* The Inspector General *and briefly evaluates the play's artistic merit.*]

The epigraph to [*The Government Inspector*] is a Russian proverb which says "Do not chafe at the looking glass if your mug is awry." Gogol, of course, never drew portraits—he used looking glasses and as a writer lived in his own looking glass world. Whether the reader's face was a fright or a beauty did not matter a jot, for not only was the mirror of Gogol's own making and with a special refraction of its own, but also the reader to whom the proverb was addressed belonged to the same Gogolian world of goose-like, pig-like, nothing-on-earth-like facial phenomena. Even in his worst writings Gogol was always good at creating his reader, which is the privilege of great writers. Thus we have a circle, a closed family-circle, one might say. It does not open into the world. Treating the play as a social satire (the public view) or as a moral one (Gogol's belated amendment) meant missing the point completely. The characters of *The Government Inspector* whether subject or not to imitation by flesh and blood, were true only in the sense that they were true creatures of Gogol's fancy. Most conscientiously, Russia, that land of eager pupils, started at once living up to these fancies—but that was her business, not Gogol's. In the Russia of Gogol's day bribery flourished as beautifully as it did, and does, anywhere on the Continent—and, on the other hand, there doubtless existed far more disgusting scoundrels in any Russian town of Gogol's time than the good-natured rogues of *The Government Inspector*. I have a lasting grudge against those who like their fiction to be educational or uplifting, or national, or as healthy as maple syrup and olive oil, so that is why I keep harping on this rather futile side of *The Government Inspector* question.

The play begins with a blinding flash of lightning and ends in a thunderclap. In fact it is wholly placed in the tense gap between the flash and the crash. There is no so-called "exposition." Thunderbolts do not lose time explaining meteorological conditions. The whole world is one ozone-blue shiver and we are in the middle of it. The only stage tradition of his time that Gogol retained was the soliloquy, but then people do talk to themselves aloud during the nervous hush before a storm while waiting for the bang to come. The characters are nightmare people in one of those dreams when you think you have waked up while all you have done is to enter the most dreadful (most dreadful in its sham reality) region of dreams. Gogol has a peculiar manner of letting "secondary" dream characters pop out at every turn of the play (or novel, or story), to flaunt for a second their life-like existence (as that Colonel P. who passed by in **"Shponka's Dream"** or many a creature in *Dead Souls*). In *The Government Inspector* this manner is apparent from the start in the weird private letter which the Town-Mayor Skvoznik-Dmukhanovsky reads aloud to his subordinates—School Inspector Khlopov, Judge Lyapkin-Tyapkin (Mr. Slap-Dash), Charity Commissioner Zemlyanika, (Mr. Strawberry—an overripe brown strawberry wounded by the lip of a frog) and so forth. Note the nightmare names so different from, say, the sleek "Hollywood Russian" pseudonyms Vronsky, Oblonsky, Bolkonsky etc. used by Tolstoy. (The names Gogol invents are really nicknames which we surprise in the very act of turning into family names—and a metamorphosis is a thing always exciting to watch.) After reading the important part of the letter referring to the impending arrival of a governmental inspector from Petersburg the Mayor automatically continues to read aloud and his mumbling engenders remarkable secondary beings that struggle to get into the front row.

"... my sister Anna Kyrillovna and her husband have come to stay with us; Ivan Kyrillovich [apparently a brother, judging by the patronymic] has grown very fat and keeps playing the violin."

The beauty of the thing is that these secondary characters will not appear on the stage later on. We all know those casual allusions at the beginning of Act I to Aunt So-and-so or to the Stranger met on the train. We all know that the "by the way" which introduces these people really means that the Stranger with the Australian accent or the Uncle with the comical hobby would have never been mentioned if they were not to breeze

in a moment later. Indeed the "by the way" is generally a sure indication, the masonic sign of conventional literature, that the person alluded to will turn out to be the main character of the play. We all know that trite trick, that coy spirit haunting first acts in Scribia as well as on Broadway. A famous playwright has said (probably in a testy reply to a bore wishing to know the secrets of the craft) that if in the first act a shot gun hangs on the wall, it must go off in the last act. But Gogol's guns hang in midair and do not go off—in fact the charm of his allusions is exactly that nothing whatever comes of them.

In giving his instructions to his subordinates in view of preparing and repairing things for the arrival of the Government Inspector, the Mayor refers to the Judge's clerk.

"... a knowing fellow, I daresay, but he has such a smell coming from him—as if he had just emerged from a vodka distillery.... I meant to mention it to you [to the Judge] long ago but something or other kept putting it out of my head. Remedies may be found if, as he says, it is his natural odor: you might suggest to him a diet of onions or garlic, or something of that kind. In a case like this Christian Ivanovich [the silent District Doctor of German extraction] might help by supplying this or that drug."

To which the Judge retorts:

"No, it is a thing impossible to dislodge: he tells me that his wet nurse dropped him when he was a baby and that there has been a slight smell of vodka hanging about him ever since."

"Well [says the Mayor] I just wanted to draw your attention to it, that is all." And he turns to another official.

We shall never hear about that unfortunate clerk again, but there he is, alive, a whimsical, smelly creature of that "injured" kind over which Gogol smacked his lips.

Other secondary beings have no time to come out in full attire, so impatient are they to jump into the play between two sentences. The Mayor is now drawing the attention of the School Inspector to his assistants:

"One of them, for instance, the one with the fat face ... can't think of his name ... well, every time he begins his class, he simply must make a grimace, like this [shows how] and then he starts to massage his chin from under his cravat. Of course if he makes faces only at the boys, it does not much matter—it may be even necessary in his department for all I know of those things; but consider what might happen if he did it in front of a visitor—that would be really dreadful: His Excellency the Government Inspector or anybody else might think it was meant for him. Goodness only knows what consequences that might have."

"What on earth am I to do with him, pray? [replies the School Inspector]. I have spoken to him several times already. Only the other day when our Marshal of Nobility was about to enter the classroom he went into such facial contortions as I have never yet seen. He did not mean anything, bless his kind heart, but *I* got a wigging: suggesting revolutionary ideas to youth, that's what they said."

Immediately afterwards another homunculus appears (rather like the little firm heads of witch doctors bursting out of the body of an African explorer in a famous short story). The Mayor refers to the history teacher:

"He is a scholar, no doubt, and has acquired loads of learning, but there—he lectures with such vehemence that he loses all self-control. I happened to hear him once: so long as he was talking about the Assyrians and the Babylonians it was—well, one could stand it; but when he got to Alexander the Great, then—no, I simply can't describe his state. Lord, I thought the house was on fire! He dashed out of his desk and banged a chair against the floor with all his might! Alexander the Great was a hero, we all know that, but is this a reason to break chairs? It is wasting Government property.''

''Ah yes, he is vehement [admits the School Inspector with a sigh] I have mentioned it to him several times. He answers: whether you like it or not, I can't help forfeiting my own life in the cause of learning.''

The Postmaster, to whom the Mayor talks next, asking him to unseal and read the letters that pass through his office (which the good man had been doing for his own pleasure for years), is instrumental in letting out another homunculus.

''It's a great pity [he says to the Mayor] that you don't read those letters yourself: they contain some admirable passages. The other day for instance a lieutenant was writing to a friend and describing a ball he had been to—in a most waggish style. . . . Oh, very, very nice: 'My life, dear friend,' he wrote, 'floats in empyrean bliss: lots of young ladies, band playing, banner galloping . . .'—all of it written with great, great feeling.''

Two quarrelsome country squires are mentioned next by the Judge, Cheptovich and Varkhovinsky, neighbors, who have taken proceedings against each other which will probably last all their lives (while the Judge merrily courses hares on the lands of both). Then as Dobchinsky and Bobchinsky make their dramatic appearance with the news that they have discovered the Government Inspector living incognito at the local inn, Gogol parodies his own fantastic meandering way (with gushes of seemingly irrelevant details) of telling a story: all the personal friends of Bobchinsky come bobbing up as the latter launches upon the report of his and Dobchinsky's sensational discovery: ''So I ran to see Korobkin [Mr. Box] and not finding Korobkin at home [Jack-in-the-box had left it], I called on Rastakovsky [Mr. Blankety-Blank], and not finding Rastakovsky at home . . . [of all the homunculi only these two will appear as visitors at the end of the last act by special request of the stage management].'' At the inn where Bobchinsky and Dobchinsky see the person whom they wrongly suspect to be the Government Inspector they interview the inn-keeper Vlass— and here—among the gasps and splutters of Bobchinsky's feverish speech (trying to tell it all before his double, Dobchinsky, can interrupt him) we obtain this lovely detailed information concerning Vlass (for in Gogol's world the more a person hurries the more he loiters on the way):

''. . . and so Dobchinsky beckoned with his finger and called the inn-keeper—you know, the inn-keeper Vlass—his wife has borne him a child three weeks ago—such a smart little beggar— will keep an inn just like his father does. . . .''

Note how the newborn Anonymous Vlassovich manages to grow up and live a whole life in the space of a second. Bobchinsky's panting speech seems to provoke an intense fermentation in the backstage world where those homunculi breed.

There are some more to come. The room where Khlestakov— the sham Government Inspector—dwells is identified by the fact that some officers who had also chanced to pass through that town some time before had a fight there over cards. One of the Mayor's men, the policeman Prokhorov, is alluded to in the following way.

The Mayor, in blustering haste to the policeman Svistunov: ''Where are the others? . . . Dear me, I had ordered Prokhorov to be here, too. Where is Prokhorov?''

The Policeman: ''Prokhorov is at the police station, but he cannot be put to any good use.''

The Mayor: ''How's that?''

The Policeman: ''Well, just as I say: he was brought in this morning in a carriage dead drunk. Two buckets of water have been poured over him already, but he has not come round yet.''

''But how on earth did you let him get into such a state?'' the Mayor asks a moment later, and the Police Officer (incidentally called Ukhovyortov—a name which contains the idea of ''viciously hitting people on the ear'' all in one word) replies: ''The Lord knows. There was a brawl in the suburb yesterday— he went there to settle matters and came back drunk.''

After this orgy of secondary characters surging at the close of the first act there is a certain lull in the second which introduces Khlestakov. True, a gambling infantry captain, who was great at piling up tricks, appears to the echoes of cheerful card-slapping as Khlestakov recalls the money he lost to him in the town of Pensa; but otherwise the active, ardent Khlestakov theme is too vigorous in this act (with the Mayor visiting him at the inn) to suffer any intruders. They come creeping back in the third act: Zemlyanika's daughter, we learn, wears a blue frock—and so she floats by in between the speeches, a pink and blue provincial maiden.

When upon his arrival at the Mayor's house Khlestakov, in the most famous scene of the Russian stage, starts showing off for the benefit of the ladies, the secondary characters that come tumbling out of his speech (for at last they had been set rolling by Khlestakov's natural garrulousness and the Mayor's wine) are of another race, so to speak, than those we have already met. They are of a lighter, almost transparent texture in keeping with Khlestakov's own iridescent temperament—phantoms in the guise of civil servants, gleeful imps coming to the assistance of the versatile devil ventriloquizing through Khlestakov. Dobchinsky's children, Vanya, Lisanka, or the inn-keeper's boy existed somewhere or other, but these do not exist at all, as such. The allusions have become delusions. But because of the crescendo of lies on Khlestakov's part the driving force of these metaphysical creatures is more felt in its reaction upon the course of the play than were the idyllic gambols of the little people in the background of Act I.

''Ah, Petersburg!'' exclaims Khlestakov. ''That is what I call life! Perhaps you think I am just a copying clerk? [which he was]. No, Sir, the head of my section is right chummy with me. Has a way, you know, of slapping me on the shoulder and saying: 'Come and have dinner with me, old chap.' I only look in at the office for a couple of minutes, just to tell them: 'Do this, do that.' And then the copying clerk, old rat, goes with his pen—trrk, trrk, scraping and scribbling away. [In long drawn accents] It was even suggested that I be made a Collegiate Assessor. [Again trippingly] But thought I to myself, what's the use? And there is the office boy [these are bearded men in Russia] running up the stairs after me with a brush— 'Allow me, Sir,' he says, 'I'll just give a bit of shining to your shoes.''' Much later we learn that the office ''boy's'' name was Mikhey, and that he drank like a fish.

Further on, when, according to Khlestakov, soldiers rushed out of the guardhouse as he passed and gave the grand salute: ''Their officer whom I knew very well said to me afterwards:

'Well, well, old boy, I am damned if we did not take you for the Commander-in-Chief!'''

When he starts talking of his Bohemian and literary connections, there even appears a goblin impersonating Pushkin: ''I hobnob with Pushkin. Many a time I have said to him: 'Well, old Push, how are things going?'—'As usual, my dear fellow,' he says, 'very much as usual.' Quite a character!''

Then other bigwigs come jostling and buzzing and tumbling over each other as Khlestakov rushes on in an ecstasy of invention: Cabinet Ministers, Ambassadors, Counts, Princes, Generals, the Tsar's Advisors, a shadow of the Tsar himself, and ''Messengers, messengers, messengers, thirty-five thousand messengers,'' spermatozoids of the brain—and then suddenly in a drunken hiccup they all fade; but not before a real allusion (at least real in the same sense as the little people of Act I were ''real''), the ghost of needy clerk Khlestakov's slatternly cook Mavroosha peeps out for a dreadful instant through a chink of Khlestakov's speech in the midst of all those golden ghosts and dream ambassadors—to help him out of his skimpy overcoat (that carrick, to be exact, which later on Gogol was to immortalize as the attribute of a transcendental ''chinovnik'').

In the next act, when one by one the nervous officials present their respects to Khlestakov, who borrows money from each (they think that they are bribing him) we learn the names of Zemlyanika's children—Nicholas, Ivan, Elizabeth, Mary and Perepetuya: it was probably gentle Perepetuya who wore the pale blue frock. Of Dobchinsky's three children, two have been mentioned already by the Mayor's wife as being her godchildren. They and the eldest boy are uncommonly like the Judge who visits Mrs. Dobchinsky every time her poor little husband is away. The eldest boy was born before Dobchinsky married that wayward lady. Dobchinsky says to Khlestakov: ''I make bold to ask your assistance in regard to a most delicate circumstance. . . . My eldest son, Sir, was born before I was married. . . . Oh, it is only a manner of speaking. I engendered him exactly as though in lawful wedlock, and made it perfectly right afterwards by sealing the bonds, Sir, of legitimate matrimony, Sir. Well, now I want him to be, in a manner of speaking, altogether my legitimate son, Sir, and to be called the same as I: Dobchinsky, Sir.'' (The French ''sauf votre respect,'' though much too long, would perhaps better render the meaning of the humble little hiss—an abbreviation of ''Soodar''—''Sir,'' which Dobchinsky adds to this or that word at the fall of his sentences.)

''I would not have troubled you,'' he goes on, ''but I feel sorry for him, seeing his many gifts. The little fellow, you see, is something quite special—promises a lot: he can recite verses and such like things by heart, and whenever he happens to come across a penknife he makes a wee little carriage—as clever as a conjuror, Sir.''

One more character appears in the background of the act: it is when Khlestakov decides to write about those weird provincial officials to his friend Tryapichkin (Mr. Ragman) who is a sordid little journalist with mercenary and pamphleteering inclinations, a rascal with a knack of making laughing stocks of those he chooses to chastise in his cheap but vicious articles. For one instant he winks and leers over Khlestakov's shoulder. He is the last to appear—no, not quite the last, for the ultimate phantom will be the gigantic shadow of the real Government Inspector.

This secondary world, bursting as it were through the background of the play, is Gogol's true kingdom. It is remarkable that these sisters and husbands and children, eccentric school teachers, vodka-bewitched clerks and policemen, country squires quarreling for fifty years over the position of a fence, romantic officers who cheat at cards, wax sentimental over provincial balls and take a ghost for the Commander-in-Chief, these copying clerks and fantastic messengers—all these creatures whose lively motion constitutes the very material of the play, not only do not interfere with what theatrical managers call ''action'' but apparently assist the play, to be eminently playable.

Not only live creatures swarm in that irrational background but numerous objects are made to play a part as important as that of the characters: the hatbox which the Mayor places upon his head instead of his hat when stamping out in official splendor and absent-minded haste to meet a threatening phantom, is a Gogolian symbol of the sham world where hats are heads, hatboxes hats, and braided collars the backbones of men. The hurried note which the Mayor sends from the inn to his wife telling her of the exalted guest whom she must get ready to receive gets mixed up with Khlestakov's hotel bill, owing to the Mayor having used the first scrap of paper that came to hand: ''I hasten to tell you, my dearest, that I was in a most sorry plight at first; but thanks to my trusting in the mercy of God 2 salted cucumbers extra and ½ a portion of caviare, 1 rouble 25 kopeks.'' This confusion is again a piece of sound logic within Gogol's world, where the name of a fish is an outburst of divine music to the ears of gourmets, and cucumbers are metaphysical beings at least as potent as a provincial town mayor's private deity. These cucumbers breed in Khlestakov's eloquent description of his ideal of noble living: ''On the table for instance there is a watermelon [which is but a sublimated cucumber]—not an ordinary watermelon but one that costs 700 roubles.'' The watery soup ''with feathers or something floating in it'' [instead of golden eyelets of shimmering fat] which Khlestakov has to be content with at the inn is transformed in the speech referring to his life in the capital into a *potage* that comes in a pan ''straight from Paris by steamer,''—the smoke of that imaginary steamer being as it were the heavenly exhalation of that imaginary soup. When Khlestakov is being made comfortable in his carriage the Mayor has a blue Persian rug brought from the store room (which is crammed with the compulsory offerings of his bearded subjects—the town merchants); Khlestakov's valet adds to this a padding of hay—and the rug is transformed into a magic carpet on which Khlestakov makes his volatile exit backstage to the silvery sound of the horse-bells and to the coachman's lyrical admonition to his magical steeds: ''Hey you, my winged ones!'' (''Hey vy, zalyotnye!'' which literally means, ''the ones that fly far''): Russian coachmen are apt to invent fond names for their horses—and Gogol, it may be assumed (for the benefit of those who like to know the personal experiences of writers) was to acquire a good deal of viatic lore during the endless peregrinations of his later years; and this gust of poetry, in which Khlestakov—the dreamy infantile swindler—fades out seems to blow open the gates for Gogol's own departure from the Russia he had invented towards distant hazy climes where numberless German watering towns, Italian ruins, Parisian restaurants and Palestine's shrines were to get mixed up in much the same way as Providence and a couple of cucumbers did in the distracted Mayor's letter.

It is amusing to recall that this dream play, this ''Government Specter,'' was treated as a skit on actual conditions in Russia. It is still more amusing to think that Gogol in his first dismal effort to check those dangerous revolutionary allusions to his play pointed out that there was at least one positive character in it: Laughter [see excerpt dated 1842]. The truth is that the play is not a "comedy" at all, just as Shakespeare's dream-plays *Hamlet* or *Lear* cannot be called "tragedies." A bad play is more apt to be good comedy or good tragedy than the incredibly complicated creations of such men as Shakespeare or Gogol. In this sense Molière's stuff (for what it is worth) is "comedy" i.e. something as readily assimilated as a hot dog at a football game, something of one dimension and absolutely devoid of the huge, seething, prodigiously poetic background that makes true drama. And in the same sense O'Neill's *Mourning Becomes Electra* (for what *that* is worth) is, I suppose, a "tragedy."

Gogol's play is poetry in action, and by poetry I mean the mysteries of the irrational as perceived through rational words. True poetry of that kind provokes—not laughter and not tears—but a radiant smile of perfect satisfaction, a purr of beatitude—and a writer may well be proud of himself if he can make his readers, or more exactly some of his readers, smile and purr that way.

Khlestakov's very name is a stroke of genius, for it conveys to the Russian reader an effect of lightness and rashness, a prattling tongue, the swish of a slim walking cane, the slapping sound of playing cards, the braggadocio of a nincompoop and the dashing ways of a lady-killer (minus the capacity for completing this or any other action). He flutters through the play as indifferent to a full comprehension of the stir he creates, as he is eager to grab the benefits that luck is offering him. He

is a gentle soul, a dreamer in his own way, and a certain sham charm hangs about him, the grace of a petit-maître that affords the ladies a refined pleasure as being in contrast with the boorish ways of the burly town worthies. He is utterly and deliciously vulgar, and the ladies are vulgar, and the worthies are vulgar—in fact the whole play is (somewhat like *Madame Bovary*) composed by blending in a special way different aspects of vulgarity so that the prodigious artistic merit of the final result is due (as with all masterpieces) not to *what* is said but to *how* it is said—to the dazzling combinations of drab parts. As in the scaling of insects the wonderful color effect may be due not to the pigment of the scales but to their position and refractive power, so Gogol's genius deals not in the intrinsic qualities of computable chemical matter (the "real life" of literary critics) but in the mimetic capacities of the physical phenomena produced by almost intangible particles of recreated life. (pp. 41-56)

> *Vladimir Nabokov, in his* Nikolai Gogol, *1944. Reprint by New Directions Books, 1959, 172 p.*

VSEVOLOD SETCHKAREV (essay date 1953)

[*In the following excerpt from a biographical and critical study of Gogol originally published in German in 1953, Setchkarev discusses the oppressive effect resulting from the moral mediocrity that pervades* The Inspector General.]

[In] "**Confession of the Author,**" Gogol declares that he received the anecdote serving as the basis for *The Inspector-General* from Pushkin. (p. 168)

The anecdote which Pushkin gave him and which is said to have happened to himself is simple. In a remote provincial town, a vain fop who happens to be passing through is mistaken for the incognito inspector general, whose imminent arrival has been announced. The authorities overwhelm him with servility and displays of respect, and he tolerates it with thoughtless audacity. After his departure, the mistake is revealed.

This plot corresponded to Gogol's wishes. He was extremely dissatisfied with the usual stereotyped techniques of comedy and rightly considered them outmoded. Always the same situations, always the same love intrigues—from this dead end the road could lead only to a complete renewal, which would have to be preceded by the elimination of the old stereotypes.

First of all, the deliberate omission of the love intrigue was decisive: in the four scenes of Act IV it is only parodied. Secondly, the utter lack of any didacticism; and thirdly, connected with this, an absolute refusal to divide the characters into good and bad.

Gogol's dismal view of the world—meaninglessness thought to be meaningful, against an ominous background—is also illustrated in this strange "comedy." The world is a curious confusion of misunderstandings; but the worst misunderstanding lies in the fact that the overwhelming majority of people believe that they are achieving something positive, something important, that they are something special, and also that they act in all good faith with the certain conviction that they are in the right—and thus only further the hopeless confusion. The forced attempts to stamp *The Inspector-General* as a social satire, a social pamphlet, attempts which from its first performance to this day have not subsided, do not get at its true meaning. The work reflects the world—not a Russian provincial town at a certain time. Like the characters, the abuses exist only as symbols. The bribes taken by the mayor, the corruption of the officials, and the hint of an embezzlement

A montage of the cast of the 1909 Moscow Art Theater production of The Inspector General. *From* The Pictorial History of the Russian Theatre, *by Herbert Marshall. By permission of Herbert Marshall.*

are of course the only real crimes of which there is mention, but they have no structural function at all. Neither oppression of the innocent, nor interference with justice, nor any other shocking crime worthy of punishment play a role. There can be no question of social sympathy, for the "oppressed" (here the group of merchants and citizens not holding official positions) are either first-class swindlers themselves, like the merchants, or they are stupid and without dignity, like the non-commissioned officer's widow; and the only one who could possibly arouse our sympathy, the locksmith's wife, considerably dampens the growing positive feelings toward her by her classic cannonade of insults.

In the very first scene it becomes perfectly clear that none of the characters is in his proper place. Yet the fates of other men depend on these men. None of them is really bad, but also none of them is really good. A dreadful, life-killing middle way, a cosmic mediocrity wafts toward the audience. Every individual is extremely satisfied with himself and with the whole: a stagnating confusion.

Into this atmosphere explodes Khlestakov, the false inspector general. While the upright, average men of the town are convinced of their importance, Khlestakov represents a second dismal possibility for a human type: he is convinced of nothing at all—and of everything, depending on the situation. He is a complete nonentity, a dummy without any center of gravity in himself whatsoever, for whom the border between reality and imagination is easily blurred; he is able to trip along over the waves of confusion which he himself has set in motion precisely because of his empty weightlessness. It was a brilliant move on Gogol's part to represent his hero as completely passive. He is by no means a conscious deceiver or a rogue—just a nothing, and this nothing prospers, this nothing attains glory. "I love good food. After all, one lives in order to pluck the flowers of pleasure." This sentence of Khlestakov's, both in form and content, characterizes him perfectly. What sort of world is it in which people of this kind live well and end well? The hero's instability is clarified by the structure. In the last scene, his simultaneous betrothal and departure are conclusively motivated psychologically in two independent parallel passages; the fact that the sum of these motivations, united in one person, results in a paradox both brands the character and proves anew the irrationality of existence. The mayor sees himself confronted with an incomprehensible discrepancy: he simultaneously experiences the greatest success and the greatest failure in his life (Khlestakov's betrothal and departure).

The whole comedy takes place in one day; the events develop with breathtaking speed, and only in this way is the delusion of the officials comprehensible and likely, for in their fear they leave themselves no time to reflect.

One man's senseless fear of another must necessarily lead to disaster—not the words of conscience are listened to, but the words of the authorities. Dobchinsky makes the following generalization: "When a high official speaks, one is frightened." And the whole play moves in this atmosphere of fear.

The plot is imbedded, as it were, between a flash of lightning and the thunderclap that one feels approaching inevitably and that is presented by Gogol in a technically very original manner. In deliberate contrast with Tartuffe, no punishment is imposed on stage. The gendarme merely reports the fact of the arrival of the real inspector general, and there follows only a sudden shift in the positions of the characters and then a minute-long silence.

The thunderbolt neither clarifies nor solves anything, and therefore its effect is all the more dreadful. Gogol later attempted to read into his comedy the idea of fatal retribution; the government, therefore, is supposed to be its tool—obviously a farfetched interpretation, for we see only a new increase of fear and nothing more. Why should the mayor not succeed in getting out of the situation this time too, as, according to his own statement, he has so often done before? The inspector general, as genuine as he now may be, comes, of course, from the same world; we have no cause to conclude that he is to be an ideal type. The lightning which strikes the morass does not have the triumph of justice as a consequence, as in Molière. Everything remains as uncertain and as threatening as in the beginning.

The wretched mediocrity of *all* the characters produces the oppressive effect of *The Inspector General*. Gogol does not describe individual wickedness and its evil action on good people, but a solid collective being with morals, habits, and customs in common that hold each one captive and from whose net there is no escape. He purposely leaves out the catharsis, and when he writes at a later date that the only honest and noble character in the play is laughter itself, it is at best a surface laughter, as in his previous works; not a liberating laughter of release, but a laughter over funny details that does not touch on the essentials.

At the very beginning, the mayor's ominous dream, which he associates with the inspector general, has a weirdly comic tinge: "Just as if I had had a presentiment: all night long last night I dreamed of two unusual rats. Really, I have never seen the like: black, of unnatural size! they came, sniffed about,—and went away again." Any farcical tone is neutralized by the fear in the background; the piece should never be allowed to pass over into burlesque. With sure good taste, Gogol softens the tone again and again and emphasizes in his stage directions that exaggeration would be the death of the whole performance—an author's wish rarely heeded by foreign stage directors. Strangely enough, they think that they can convey a "Russian milieu" by simply raising the volume, and not only do they fail to accomplish this but they also completely miss the point of this supranational comedy. Scenes like the mutual misunderstanding and fear between the mayor and Khlestakov, Bobchinsky's fall, the letter on the bill—all of this should be staged as if in passing, not for its own sake. Khlestakov's great scene with its brilliant, fireworklike crescendo of lies can only produce its full effect if it is spoken as if improvised. Khlestakov believes everything that happens to come into his mind during his torrent of words, becomes enthusiastic about his own lies, and finally goes into raptures, and the madder his hyperboles, the more overwhelmed is his stage audience with their naive authenticity. A conscious awareness in his speeches would destroy the effect. The requests for loans from the officials and the continual declarations of love to the mayor's daughter and wife likewise take place without any reflection; they simply develop from the situation. His clichés ("How I wish I were your kerchief, madam, that I might clasp your lily-white neck . . .") turn little by little into downright nonsense: a series of formulae without contents. To Anna Andreyevna's remark that she is married, "in a manner of speaking," he replies: "That doesn't make any difference! Love knows no distinctions; and Karamzin has said: 'The laws condemn.' We shall withdraw into the shade of fountains. Your hand, I beg of you, give me your hand!'"

The ardor of this nonsense sweeps everyone along. Although Gogol has brilliantly individualized his characters, each one is seized with fear; each one has reason to be afraid. They stand before us as if they were alive, but Gogol avoids building any subplots on them. Zemlyanika's attempt to blacken the character of his colleagues comes to naught; the action is advanced by the least sharply delineated characters (Bobchinsky, Dobchinsky, the Postmaster). Gogol makes use of this procedure so that he can develop a second plot alongside the main action: the conflict between the officials and the exploited (although also dishonest) citizens, which maintains its tension thanks to Khlestakov's unpredictable behavior. This second line gave the comedy its social aspect, and because of its exaggeration by critics, *The Inspector-General* has been labeled an exposé, a militant period piece. For Gogol, however, it was nothing more than an attempt at a mixture of styles (harmless comedy and satire); the customary tragic view of the petty world was to be the product of this combination. (pp. 168-72)

Vsevolod Setchkarev, in his Gogol: His Life and Works, *translated by Robert Kramer, New York University Press, 1965, 264 p.*

PAUL DEBRECZENY (essay date 1966)

[*Debreczeny is a Hungarian-born American critic who specializes in nineteenth-century Russian literature. In the following excerpt he surveys critical reaction to early performances of* The Inspector General, *emphasizing the polarization of the work's reception that resulted from an intellectual rivalry between critics associated with the journal* Severnaya pchela (Northern Bee), *edited by F. V. Bulgarin, and those associated with* Sovremennik (The Contemporary), *edited by Alexander Pushkin.*]

The first performance of *The Government Inspector* was in April, 1836. The timing was unfortunate, for the first issue of *The Contemporary* had just appeared carrying Gogol's article on the development of journalistic literature, which, according to Panayev's testimony, was producing great controversy. Bulgarin had already shown displeasure over Belinsky's article on "The Russion Story . . ." and his *Northern Bee* had turned against Gogol's *Arabesques* and *Mirgorod;* but he had not yet launched a full-scale critical attack on Gogol when *The Government Inspector* appeared. Bulgarin, of course, like Belinsky, was not to know who had written the anonymous article, and his anger naturally turned primarily against Pushkin. Gogol's closeness to the new periodical, however, was sufficiently demonstrated even if his authorship of the article was unknown. This same first issue of *The Contemporary* contained his dramatic fragment *The Morning of a Man of Business* and his short story "The Carriage," as well as Pushkin's praise of *Mirgorod* and *Arabesques.* Under these circumstances Bulgarin could no longer restrain himself. Even at the price of self-contradiction, he decided to vent his anger on *The Government Inspector.* Thus the play, as the first major work produced by a member of *The Contemporary* circle after the launching of that journal, was doomed on purely partisan grounds to have a bad reception in the enemy camp.

In his review of the play, Bulgarin did not even attempt to conceal his party spirit when he wrote:

. . . By no means do we wish to take up arms against the author's talent. He is, indeed, a talented writer of whom we should expect a lot of good, if only the literary circle to which he now belongs, and which is in a desperate want of talent, did not overpraise him.

Added to the purely partisan controversies was the circumstance that Belinsky had detected in Gogol's earlier works a realistic quality which, in political terms, amounted to liberalism. Bulgarin examined the new play from this point of view and the suspicion of a liberal tendency alone—quite apart from the author's closeness to *The Contemporary*—would have sufficed to set the critic against *The Government Inspector.* The Emperor had applauded the play on the first night, but Bulgarin, blessed with the "scent" of a police agent, knew better who the enemies of the government were. He wrote:

Is this a comedy? No. It is impossible to ground a true comedy upon administrative malpractices. What are needed are counteractions, a plot, verisimilitude, and nature, but none of these are present in *The Government Inspector.* It will be a great pity if someone from the audience, unfamiliar with our provinces, thinks that such morals really exist in Russia, and that there is such a city where you can find neither an honest soul nor a reasonable mind.

Bulgarin could not censure Gogol for the same unadorned representation of reality that had evoked Belinsky's praise, for to deplore the play on the grounds of its realism was to admit that the corruption represented was in fact an ugly reality. Bulgarin's tactic, therefore, was to declare that the play was *un*realistic; that it was counterfeit art, whose pretense to realism constituted a libel against Russia and her government. Even granting that some corruption did exist, the play did not represent it realistically, Bulgarin said:

You can travel in Russia far and wide and you will not hear the word "bribe." They accept, but cleverly; and the offers are even subtler.

But realistic or not, what was disturbing was that the play was running successfully and had stirred up public opinion to an extent that none of the usual run of the generally poor Petersburg repertory could ever have done. Bulgarin's explanation of the success was:

This is a hilarious farce, a series of funny caricatures, which cannot but make you laugh.

The play's appeal was enhanced, he added, by the fact that the characters had the outward appearance of Russian officials and bore civil service ranks, which superficial resemblance amused the public.

That the play was unrealistic farce, then, was Bulgarin's basic argument, but it apparently did not satisfy even the reviewer himself, for he scattered through the article a good deal of supplementary argument—obviously an attempt to buttress a weak central idea.

He argued at the beginning of the article, in order to forestall the idea that national life was reflected in the play, that the trick of the *incognito* was an age-old international device. If, however, the play was a mere anecdote, based on an international theme, it is not clear why he took the trouble of elaborating a passionate denial of its Russian implications.

In another part of the review he argued that Gogol had based the play on the Russian reality of Fonvizin's time, or an even earlier period. In imitating Fonvizin, he forgot that society had changed since the days of the classical satirist. Bulgarin evidently did not notice that this argument contradicted the previous one about the international nature of the plot.

Still not satisfied, the reviewer offered yet another solution:

> The author wished to depict a Russian pro-
> vincial town with its mores, but succeeded in-
> stead in depicting a Ukrainian or White Russian
> one. His merchants are not Russians; they are
> simply Jews. The feminine coquetry is not Rus-
> sian at all. No—and the mayor himself could
> not have allowed himself such liberties, in a
> Great Russian town, among serving or retired
> noblemen.

This strongly resembles what Polevoy had said about the *Evenings:* that the base, cynical humor of that volume reflected a
Ukrainian and not a Russian mind. Once more, Bulgarin did
not notice that his third argument canceled out the previous
two.

Bulgarin's objections to the play as a whole, diverse as they
were, all referred to socio-political questions. They were accompanied by remarks on various artistic aspects of the play,
such as character-drawing, language, and construction. His
objection to the characters was that they were exaggerated to
the point of caricature:

> He based his comedy not on similarity, nor on
> likelihood, but on unlikeliness and impossibil-
> ity. In some tiny town, with which Sodom and
> Gomorrah compare as roses with thistles, live
> these people whom the author has deprived of
> every human faculty, except the ability to speak;
> but even this ability is used only for idle twad-
> dle.

He developed this idea in some "advice" to Gogol's "friends":

> They should tell him not to exaggerate his char-
> acters' ridiculous and defective qualities be-
> yond credulity; i.e., to portray his characters
> according to nature and not in a caricaturish
> manner—if he wants to write comedies and not
> farces.

And further:

> What impression is made by *The Government
> Inspector?* An unpleasant one! It is distressing
> to sit through five acts and to hear no sensible
> word, only crude raillery and abuse; to see not
> a single noble feature of the human heart. If
> the evil were mixed with the good, then the
> heart of the spectator could, after a just indig-
> nation, at least be refreshed; but *The Govern-
> ment Inspector* provides food neither for the
> mind nor for the heart; it contains neither thought
> nor feeling.

Here was an argument about the proper balance between the
"positive" and the "negative" in literature—an argument that
was to be used in Russian periodicals whenever bureaucrats
were to interfere with art—not only in Gogol's time.

Bulgarin also repeated about *The Government Inspector* what
had been said in both *Northern Bee* and *Library for Reading*
about the immoral, tasteless, vulgar nature of *Mirgorod*. The
rivalry between Anna Andreyevna and her daughter hurt his
moral feelings. Such behavior, he declared, was worthy of the
savages of the Sandwich Islands described by Captain Cook.
The characters' immoral behavior, he continued, found its expression in such vulgar language as would make even Narezhny

and Paul de Kock blush; indeed, the latter two authors appeared
as innocent maidens in comparison with Gogol. On this account, the following advice was offered to Gogol's friends:

> The friends of the author of *The Government
> Inspector* would render him and the public a
> great service if they could persuade him to for-
> sake the cynicism of his language. . . . We have
> never seen such cynicism either on the Russian
> stage or in Russian literature. It is inexcusable
> that a young author, who has a conception of
> decency, should resort to such dirty equivo-
> cations as are contained in *The Government In-
> spector.*

Finally, with respect to the plot, Bulgarin found that the May-
or's mistake in taking Khlestakov for an inspector was not
sufficiently motivated: it was unlikely that an experienced,
shrewd bureaucrat, as the Mayor was portrayed to be, should
fall a prey to the silly young Khlestakov. (pp. 17-18)

It was only to be expected that the scapegoat of the article in
The Contemporary, Senkovsky, would follow in Bulgarin's
steps in reviewing Gogol's comedy. Indeed, Senkovsky's review turned out to be a reiteration of most of Bulgarin's comments. It leveled, for instance, the same charge against Gogol's
"friends" (i.e., against *The Contemporary*): they would ruin
Gogol's career by disproportionate praise. Their laudation of
the young author was so inordinate, Senkovsky complained,
that some even talked of a comparison between Gogol and
Baron Brambeus!

To be sure, Senkovsky had been antagonized as never before
by the anonymous article on journalism, and, like Bulgarin,
he was determined to vent his annoyance with *The Contemporary* on Gogol's comedy. Yet his review was by no means
as crude or straightforward as Bulgarin's. He kept a condescending rather than an angry tone and employed his usual
editorial skill. (p. 18)

His criticism was interspersed with encouraging phrases, and
he praised the humor of such scenes as Osip's conversation
with Khlestakov at the inn (2: ii), and the extraction of a meager
"loan" from Dobchinsky and Bobchinsky (4: vii). In this way
he achieved an impression of objectivity, and his attack, for
attack it was, did not seem so obvious.

Even though his objections to the play were essentially the
same as Bulgarin's, Senkovsky's restraint saved him from the
self-contradiction Bulgarin had committed in piling argument
upon argument in a nervous hurry. The author, he argued,
offered no message in the play. Indeed, no message was possible, since *The Government Inspector* was simply a dramati-
zation of an international anecdote. The characters, as figures
of an anecdote, were not based on observations of social morals; they were all crooks and fools whose actions were not
inspired by human passions and whose vices could only be
interpreted as individual ones, with no social implications. The
mistake of simply adapting an anecdote for the stage, the reviewer continued, led also to a complete lack of plot and of
dénouement. The Government Inspector, therefore, was not a
comedy. However, it did not pass for an amusing farce either,
because of its gross indecency.

> Beauty and squalor are growing in his works
> with equal force, so much so that he has never
> produced anything more amusing yet more filthy
> than his latest play. How can he pile so much

dirt on so much pure gold! A respect for our readers prevents us from quoting those passages which should be censured most—so revolting are they to pure taste and society manners. They transgress the limits of the crudest farce.

Senkovsky, like Bulgarin, was bent on giving valuable advice to young authors. He concluded his analysis of Gogol's play with the suggestion that another female character should be introduced into it. She could meet Khlestakov while he was still staying at the inn; he could fall in love with her, which would provide the play with a plot; and finally, the reviewer shrewdly advised, many amusing situations could be got out of a possible jealousy between this new character and Marya.

Grech, the third member of the reactionary triumvirate, joined his colleagues somewhat later in a criticism of *The Government Inspector.* He, like Senkovsky, allowed the play a "liveliness and sharpness" but regarded it as "not a comedy, but a caricature in dialogue." His conclusion was:

> The plot is not original, nor is it likely or possible; from its beginning to its end there is not one noble, elevated notion; not a single idea.

Bulgarin's and Senkovsky's reviews represented the immediate reception of *The Government Inspector* by the hostile literary camp. They were followed, although not immediately, by four reviews in defense of Gogol. The first of these appeared in *The Moscow Observer.* . . . [V. Androsov, the journal's editor-in-chief], reviewed the Moscow performance of May, 1836. His low opinion of that performance did not prevent him from appreciating the comedy itself.

His theoretical approach betrayed his affinity with the Moscow literary circle. There were, in his view, two kinds of comedy. In the first, light comedy, individual failings were ridiculed, and the audience experienced a rather mean pleasure in laughing at the misfortunes of the characters. The second kind, social comedy, aimed its arrows at socially significant, common vices, and therefore the laughter it aroused was mingled with self-recognition and shame. This second kind of comedy, to which Androsov said Gogol's play belonged, grew out of a development of social consciousness, and its rules changed as society changed. Therefore, he concluded, aiming no doubt at Senkovsky's criticism, it was unjust to demand of a new comedy complete adherence to the classical conception of plot, love-intrigue, and *dénouement.* The rules of classicism reflected a different social structure from that which Gogol was portraying. New circumstances demanded new methods. After this answer to Senkovsky, Androsov made a further sub-division of comedy: some social comedies expressed the truth of the real, while others reflected the truth of the possible. *The Government Inspector,* the reviewer said, belonged to the second sub-division; it contained the socially possible, essential and typical, rather than the strictly real. Androsov summed up his argument thus:

> . . . A comedy attempts to express the essential, or typical, features of people; to express not what a person thought, said, or did in one situation or another, but what the person, by virtue of his character, *could* or *should* have felt, thought, or done under the given circumstances.
>
> . . . Our author [Gogol] has succeeded in expressing the *essence* of those people who make up the diverse picture of our provincial mores.

With this contention, however, Androsov had run into difficulty. Like Bulgarin and Senkovsky, he was aware that to approve Gogol's play as social comedy was both to admit that it reflected an unflattering Russian reality and to concur in the criticism of it. Such indeed were Androsov's inclinations, but it was dangerous to say so. To escape so delicate a conclusion, he ended his argument by asserting that Gogol's characters were exceptional; that indeed there were few such people in Russia; and that ridiculing a few high-ranking individuals did not show disrespect towards the social system as a whole.

Androsov thus entangled himself in the intricate problem of the "typicality of the exceptional." It is hard to say how far he was aware of his sophistry; but it certainly aided him in praising Gogol's work without committing himself to politically dangerous conclusions.

The second favorable review of *The Government Inspector* was written by Prince P. Vyazemsky and published in the second issue of *The Contemporary* for 1836. . . . Vyazemsky, with aristocratic aloofness, declared at the beginning of the article that the reviewers of periodicals were too vulgar and stupid to merit his attention; he was rather replying to remarks on the play made in literary *salons.* In spite of this declaration, the article was a refutation, point by point, of Bulgarin's and Senkovsky's arguments. (pp. 19-20)

The play had been attacked, Vyazemsky stated, on three planes—literary, moral, and social—all of which he would examine.

The first literary objection—that the play was a farce rather than a comedy proper—he considered unimportant: there existed poor comedies and brilliant farces, and the merit of a play did not depend on its particular genre. Neither was it important if Gogol's characters were caricatures: a caricaturish tendency did not decrease the value of Teniers's pictures. Vyazemsky conceded that *The Government Inspector* was not a "high" comedy of the type of *The Misanthrope,* but then Gogol had not intended it to be, as his choice of provincial characters showed. The choice of characters, Vyazemsky continued, predetermined the language, which would not be characteristic if it were not vulgar. Further, the lack of "positive heroes" only enhanced the artistic value of the play. The presence of such heroes had weakened Fonvizin's *The Hopeful Young,* and it was no wonder that Catherine the Great had ordered Starodum's monologues to be left out when she listened to a reading of that play. It was no great harm, the article went on, if Gogol's comedy lacked historical concreteness and trueness to life—qualities that could hardly be expected of a light comedy. The Mayor's foolish mistake regarding Khlestakov's identity, which Bulgarin had found beyond credulity, was explained by Vyazemsky with the aid of a Russian proverb—"Fear has big eyes." Vyazemsky attested that he had himself heard of a similar case.

Under the heading of moral objections, the reviewer returned to the question of the play's coarse language, and observed that only lower-class journalists who wished in vain to enter good society were so over-anxious to protect its tone. Those who naturally belonged to the best circles used language freely and were not ashamed to say "This soup stinks" (Khlestakov's expression, 2: vi). (p. 20)

Proceeding to defend Gogol against another moral objection, namely that the play lacked a moral message, he argued that *The Government Inspector* did not incite to immoral behavior; it simply portrayed such behavior in a cold, detached manner. True, no moral was appended to it, but after all it was not a tale for children. A painting of robbers did not have to contain virtuous men as well just for the sake of a moral.

Replying to objections on the social plane, Vyazemsky conceded that there probably was no such town in Russia as the one portrayed in *The Government Inspector,* but he argued that this was irrelevant. Gogol had found one of his characters in one town and another in a different town and had placed them all together in an exaggerated but artistically true environment. Such selection was normal in art: a statue of Venus was a combination of several women's beautiful features. But in any case there was no harm in Gogol's characters, the reviewer concluded; they were stupid and ridiculous rather than wicked.

The last remark was an attempt to take Gogol for what he was: a magnificent humorist. This attempt was supported by the reviewer for *Literary Supplements to Russian Invalid,* who wrote:

> A man with weak nerves should fear fits; the chagrined and the melancholy should rush to the theater when *The Government Inspector* is played. The comedy will cure many sorrows, will disperse many a spleen.

Such interpretations of the play, however, remained isolated endeavors. As we have seen, Bulgarin and Senkovsky had rejected the play on socio-political grounds and Androsov had praised it for its socially significant types. Even Vyazemsky, who regarded Gogol's characters as harmless creatures of literature and the problem of trueness-to-life as a question of literary form rather than social content, was forced by the other critics into a discussion of typicality.

That the attention was focused on social problems was largely due to Belinsky's essay "The Russian Story and Mr. Gogol's Stories," after which it became virtually impossible to regard Gogol from a purely literary point of view. Belinsky further emphasized social relevance when he reviewed the first issue of *The Contemporary* and the two pieces by Gogol published in it. One of them, "**The Carriage,**" he said,

> . . . is no more than a joke, although a highly brilliant one. It demonstrates Mr. Gogol's dexterity in capturing both society's prominent features and those nuances which everyone sees around himself every minute yet Gogol alone can catch. . . .
>
> (pp. 20-1)

It was only to be expected that Belinsky would receive *The Government Inspector* in the same spirit. He, like Androsov, reviewed the play on the basis of the Moscow performance. He wrote:

> They are wrong who think that this comedy is merely funny. Yes, it is funny, so to speak, externally; but inside it is all grief and sorrow.
>
> . . . His [Gogol's] original view of things, his capacity for capturing the characters' features and putting the stamp of the typical on them, his inexhaustible humor—all this gives us a hope that our theater will rise from the dead. Moreover, we can hope that we shall have our own national theater, which will regale us not with unnatural grimaces in a foreign manner, not with borrowed wit, nor with remodeled

monstrosities, but with an artistic representation of our social life.

The emphasis was on the socially typical. Belinsky, Androsov, Bulgarin, and Senkovsky, radically opposed as they were otherwise, were all guided by the same demand for a social message in works of literature. The first two critics hailed Gogol's works because they corresponded, the critics thought, to their conception of society; the second two rejected them for the opposite reason. The social criterion remained predominant in both cases. (p. 21)

> *Paul Debreczeny, ''Nikolay Gogol and His Contemporary Critics,'' in* American Philosophical Society, *n.s. Vol. 56, No. 3, 1966, pp. 5-68.*

SIMON KARLINSKY　(essay date 1969)

[Karlinsky identifies elements of the absurd in The Inspector General.*]*

The first performance of Nikolai Gogol's comedy *The Inspector General* took place in April of 1836 with the expressed approval and encouragement of the reigning monarch, Nicholas I. Although not very successfully staged, the play created an effect that neither the emperor nor the playwright had foreseen. To Gogol's horror, much of the popular opinion of the day and a considerable segment of the press saw in his play a wholesale indictment of Russian reality. Those who favored such an indictment hastened to stress the realistic nature of the new comedy and insisted on seeing in it a precisely recorded, unvarnished transcript of what life was really like in a provincial Russian town. Monarchist-minded critics, such as the notorious Faddei Bulgarin and other defenders of the régime, on the other hand, stressed the unreal, improbable, even fantastic nature of the comedy's characters and situations. The Russia depicted by Gogol, those status-quo defenders argued, existed only in the author's imagination.

Throughout the nineteenth century the anti-establishment interpretation of *The Inspector General* as a soberly realistic satire prevailed. Twentieth-century critical views, however, suggest that, whatever their political motivations at the time, both sides had valid arguing points. With its drab, provincial setting, with its portrayal of the lives of lesser government officials shown in specific and precise detail, *The Inspector General* falls indeed within the new realistic trends of the 1830's and 40's. But Gogol's contemporaries (except for those who attacked the play on political grounds) failed to discern other, equally important strains in the play: the grotesque and surrealistic forms of its humor, the deliberate stretching of logic, the strange sexual overtones and the strong admixture of the absurd in the motivations and actions of the central character, Khlestakov.

Gogol's use of alogism can be illustrated in its basic form by citing the remark made by the Judge in the very first scene of the play. Defending one of his subordinates against the charge of constantly smelling of alcohol, the Judge explains that the man can't help it: his nurse dropped him when he was a baby and since then he has emitted a slight odor of vodka. The explanation, accepted with equanimity by the Mayor and other characters, is quintessentially surrealistic, with its deliberate juxtaposition of two prosaic, believable facts (the dropped baby and the smell of vodka) to support a patently absurd explanation. Equally surrealistic is the Mayor's note to his wife, scribbled on a restaurant bill, so that she is puzzled to read of her husband's hope for Divine mercy in exchange for two dill pickles and a half-portion of caviar. The long sequence of bribery scenes dissolves into absurdity when, after accepting thousands of rubles from town officials and merchants, the false inspector and his servant settle for smaller sums (always insisting that these are loans, not bribes), then for a silver tray, a loaf of sugar and, finally, for a worthless piece of string.

Absence of the traditional love interest in *The Inspector General* was a deliberate stratagem on Gogol's part and it puzzled his contemporary audiences. The conservative critic Osip Senkovsky demonstrated his misunderstanding of this aspect of the comedy when he chided Gogol for not including among his characters some young woman, a friend or an enemy of the Mayor's daughter, with whom Khlestakov could become romantically involved, "thus adding interest to the entire play." The whole point of Khlestakov's frantic and simultaneous courtship of the Mayor's wife and daughter, which replaces the customary love intrigue, is a parodistic *reductio ad absurdum* of that particular literary convention. In the 19th century, Khlestakov's mindless and unmotivated courtship of the two women was interpreted as further evidence of his flighty, irresponsible character. But if Gogol is satirizing anything here, it is the automatic expectations of the audience (and, as we see, one of the leading critics of the time fell into his trap). Khlestakov proposes marriage to the Mayor's daughter without any mercenary (he has already acquired his loot) or other discernible motivation; he has certainly no desire or intention of marrying her. Simultaneously, he seeks the hand of her mother. To the mother's objection that she is already married, Khlestakov retorts with a wildly inappropriate quotation ("The laws condemn . . .") from Karamzin's morbid gothic tale "The Isle of Bornholm," where these words refer to tragic consequences of incest. Similarly, while flirting with the Mayor's daughter, Khlestakov reinforces his advances with a passage from Lomonosov's "Ode from the Book of Job," about the futility of complaining against Divine Providence. The patent, preposterous unsuitability of these literary references (which were easily identifiable by Gogol's contemporary audience) leaves little doubt that parody of literary conventions, rather than any realistic depiction of character, was the object of these scenes of unmotivated double courtship.

Literary historians have discovered numerous plays in Russian literature and in other literatures which use a basic situation similar to the one in *The Inspector General* and which may have served Gogol as models or precedents. But in all of those plays the young man mistaken for a person of importance and authority is inevitably a clever swindler, a rogue or a picaro, who manipulates the misunderstanding to achieve personal gain and prestige. Next to such clearly and unequivocally motivated traditional characters, Gogol's Khlestakov seems a kind of bouncy, energetic sleepwalker, whose only identifiable motivation is the pleasure that he derives from telling lies. The material gain and ego-gratification he enjoys during the play come to him through the gullibility and stupidity of other characters, rather than through any planning or machinations of his own. Cast in the traditional situation of a picaro and endowed with the requisite energy and the gift of gab, Khlestakov nevertheless plays a remarkably passive, almost somnambulistic role in the action of the comedy. He owes his successful final escape to the foresight of his clever servant, without whose advice he would have stayed on until ignominiously exposed. Viewed from the angle of Khlestakov's success—achieved despite lack of intelligent planning or discernible motivation—the entire plot of *The Inspector General* can be read as a commentary on the absurdity of human endeavor and human existence, a com-

mentary whose implications go far deeper than any exposure of bribery or corruption in the civil service which may have interested Gogol's contemporaries. (pp. 147-48)

Simon Karlinsky, "The Alogical and Absurdist Aspects of Russian Realist Drama," in Comparative Drama, Vol. III, No. 2, Fall, 1969, pp. 147-55.

A. DE JONGE (essay date 1973)

[*An English translator and critic, de Jonge has written studies of French, Russian, and German literature and history. In the following assessment of* The Inspector General *as an allegory, de Jonge outlines its principal themes and dramatic techniques, including construction, language, and characterization.*]

Although his two major farces *The Gamblers (Igroki)* and *Marriage (Zhenit'ba)* are masterpieces of their kind it is *The Inspector General (Revizor))* that makes Gogol' the greatest comic playwright since Molière, with whose work the piece bears comparison both in terms of its use of farce and its projection of moral values. It is with this play that Gogol', notably in later years, makes his first overt claims to a moral purpose. Although this accords with his ever-increasing tendency to preach, we should not dismiss his suggestion that the town be seen as our mental town, the characters as the passions that pillage our souls [see excerpt dated 1846]. Of course such an allegorical interpretation does not provide an entirely satisfactory reading, any more than would the suggestion that the piece was simply the indictment of contemporary bureaucratic corruption. The truth lies to one side of these interpretations and yet it includes them both. Perhaps the greatest strength of the mature Gogol' is his ability to write in a way that is both directly narrative, vivid and realistic, and at the same time general to the point of allegory. Both here and in *Dead Souls* allegory seems to lurk beneath the surface, constantly on the point of emerging without ever quite doing so. Gogol' induces a moral awareness in his readers but is too skilled an artist ever to moralize in so many words by moving onto an allegorical level as such.

It is important to establish from the outset that whatever the town may or may not be, it is not a real place in the sense that St Petersburg was real. Gogol' had little direct experience of Russian provincial life. His creation is essentially the product of his hearsay reality. All we know is that it is in the centre of Russia—one can ride for three years in any direction and not reach a frontier. There is something unreal, dreamlike, about its location. In his epilogue (**"Teatral'nyy raz'ezd"**) he emphasizes that it is a collective place, that his characters are universals and not specific satirical targets [see excerpt dated 1842]. One of the ways in which he hints at this allegorical level without realizing it is by means of a blend of generality of conception and specificity of detail. The town may be anywhere but its inhabitants have definite characteristics. Like the people of *Dead Souls,* they are realistic characters in a setting that has a strangely unrealistic, almost mythic, feel to it.

That Gogol' is once again offering a portrait of negative values is confirmed by a passage in the epilogue which explains that he omitted to introduce a single positive character as a source of relief, lest this destroy the realism of the negative ones. Thus he is anxious to secure our belief in his inventions as representing life as it is: a belief we would all too gladly shake off. However he admits to the presence of one positive character, namely laughter. His conception of the aesthetic role of humour has progressed from the self-directed therapy of *The*

Evenings to become a moral force. He suggests in the epilogue that it is our ability to laugh that renders the triviality and emptiness of existence terrifying, and that without laughter the world would go to sleep. Thus laughter is a means of preserving our humanity and our moral consciousness. It is a form of criticism, an instrument of moral judgment, and this explains its role in both *The Inspector General* and *Dead Souls*.

Such a view accords well with the importance that the theme of judgement held for Gogol' and with its role in this piece. We, as a laughing audience, stand in judgement on the characters. Moreover, the theme of injustice is an essential element of the play itself. Even as mayors go, say the merchants, this one is a monster of injustice. It is significant that the most prominent minor character is Lyapkin-Tyapkin the judge, who is more interested in dogs than in justice, and who confesses that he can never sift truth from falsehood when hearing evidence. When the mayor describes the state of the town he refers to venial sins (*greshki*). He is himself 'in many ways a sinner' and Zemlyanika he knows to be a sinner, since he's an intelligent man. But despite his awareness of corruption, the mayor's projects for reform are only concerned with appearance. He has no sense of the inner man, freely admitting in Act 1, Scene 1 that he can say nothing about the 'inner order'. This absence of any spiritual sense is one of the most important features of Gogol''s indictment. Indeed sin and judgement play a vital role in this play. Gogol' seems to echo Biblical rhetoric when the mayor says that the Inspector can 'come at any hour'. The play itself is the account of a pseudo-judgement at the hands of Khlestakov. The officials make the cardinal error of assessing him on appearance, and are finally only too pleased to be judged by him, because such judgement is easy. But the whole piece stands with reference to the awesome figure of the real Inspector who is by definition everything Khlestakov is not; the embodiment of absolute justice. He has powerful allegorical connotations—perhaps the reason why he never appears on stage—and the play concludes in a kind of temporal paradox whereby he remains for ever about to appear in the next second. If, as Merezhkovsky suggests, Khlestakov is Antichrist, then the Inspector is the genuine article. But rather than impose an unequivocally allegorical interpretation of his identity it would appear more likely that Gogol''s imaginative construction has been shaped by the pattern of false Messiah and Last Judgement. To say that he has used a Biblical code is not to say that he intended a Biblical message. He has written a play not a parable.

As with all his best work the play's construction is remarkably simple. It is of course based on the device of mistaken identity. But where comic playwrights tend to use a device to create a series of complications in the plot, Gogol' is more concerned with an analysis of the mistake itself. The play proper begins with Dobchinsky and Bobchinsky announcing the arrival of a young man who must, for irrefutable reasons—he won't leave his room or pay his bill, he is young—be the Inspector General. The play ends with the mayor's asking himself how he could ever have mistaken for an Inspector General a coxcomb who was in every way his opposite. It is on this diametric opposition between 'is' and 'appears' that the drama is founded. The familiar theme of the confusion of reality and fantasy is here turned to comic effect, since it is the officials' guilty conscience that reduces their sense of reality to the point where they will accept the first stranger in town for his very opposite. Gogol''s exploration of their mistake takes the shape of a detailed examination of the phenomenon of non-communication. So panic-stricken are they that they interpret events in terms of the most

extraordinary patterns of cause and effect: the thought of impending judgement has destroyed their grasp on reality. Thus both judge and postmaster see the Inspector's advent as a sign that Russia is about to declare war on Turkey. Bobchinsky and Dobchinsky deduce Khlestakov's identity from the fact that he stared at their food. The persistent misinterpretation of Khlestakov's every action is a continual source of comedy. When he offers Luka Lukich a cigar in Act 4 the gesture is so pregnant with significance that the poor man is quite unnerved by the decision should he accept it or not. The officials cannot understand Khlestakov even when he tells the truth. When he tells them that he was almost made a collegiate assessor, a rank only halfway up the ladder, they all stand to attention out of respect. They cannot understand him, only hearing what they expect to hear. Thus the mayor's first encounter with Khlestakov is a model of non-communication. They never succeed in exchanging thoughts, they can only swap noises. So obsessed with his own problems is each character that he is unable to grasp what the other is saying. For Khlestakov is as confused as anyone. It is only comically late in the play that he suspects a mistake. In earlier episodes he expresses surprise and delight at his reception, and, a typical Gogolian device, he finds the mayor's hospitality to visitors perfectly credible, only saying that he welcomed the local practice of showing travellers round; in other towns he was shown nothing.

The characters' minimal grasp on reality again emerges when, in the heat of the moment, they offer the most delightful and absurd justifications. When the mayor believes that he has been denounced by the N.C.O.'s wife whom he had had flogged, he blurts out that she had flogged herself. A similar reluctance to allow reality to obstruct the pleasure principle emerges in the mayor's wife's hesitant rejoinder to Khlestakov's avowal of instant timeless passion: 'Excuse me, but I am to some extent . . . married.' The whole pattern of non-communication and misunderstanding is ironically summed up by the mayor who unconsciously points to the cause of his misfortune when, in the last act, he says: 'Words cannot hurt'. For this is precisely what they have done throughout this play. It is words and not deeds that have brought about the officials' collective undoing.

For Khlestakov consists of nothing but words. At the beginning of the play he is an empty windbag. The officials inspire him, make him what they want him to be. They give him the breath of life, creating him in the image of their guilty conscience. Gogol' is to employ the same device in *Dead Souls* when each official in the town of N will interpret Chichikov's non-existent purchases in terms of his particular sense of guilt. In both instances the characters reveal themselves by imparting significance to a person or concept originally by definition almost without significance. This emerges in Gogol''s instructions as to how Khlestakov is to be played. He is not a stock character from knock-about farce, to be played as 'braggarts and scapegraces are played'. The actor must play him with as much simplicity and sincerity as possible. He is not a confidence trickster or villain in an active sense. It is his situation that turns him into an unconscious confidence trick.

He has no personality or will of his own, is quite incapable of concentrated thought. This is clear from Gogol''s description of how he speaks. 'His speech is jerky, words come out quite unexpectedly . . . He is simply stupid; he babbles only because he sees that they are disposed to listen; he lies because he has had a hearty dinner and drank a considerable quantity of wine. He is frivolous only when he approaches the ladies. The scene in which he starts lying at random should receive special at-

Vsevolod Meyerhold and Erast Garin modeling a pose for the dumb scene in Meyerhold's 1926 production of The Inspector General. *From* Meyerhold on Theatre, *translated and edited by Edward Braun. Hill and Wang, 1969. Copyright © 1969 by Edward Braun. Reprinted by permission of Hill and Wang, a division of Farrar, Straus and Giroux, Inc.*

tention. His every word . . . is a completely unexpected impromptu, and therefore should be expressed abruptly'. He is thus largely created by circumstances. There is no consistency to him unless it be *poshlost'* [mean-spirited vulgarity, mediocrity], *khamstvo* [boorishness]. His ambitions consist entirely of false needs, they concentrate exclusively on appearance. A windbag, he is bold till faced with reality, whereupon he is instantly deflated. But you can't keep a good balloon down: he rapidly adapts to fresh circumstances and is soon inflated by the attentions of the mayor and his colleagues. In the boasting scene image succeeds image until all sense of proportion is lost. His soup arrives hot from Paris, 35,000 couriers speed to his door, and he finally achieves a sinister ubiquity, 'I am everywhere, everywhere' he cries. His keynote is bluster and one of the principal sources of the comedy is that for once he is in a situation in which bluster pays off and is taken at its face value. In his first encounter with the mayor he interprets the offer of a change of quarters as a threat of imprisonment. His first reaction is a panic-stricken blustering that puts the fear of God into the luckless mayor. Finally his complete lack of consistency, the fact that he lives solely from moment to moment, emerges in his farcical and idiosyncratic courtship of the mayor's wife and daughter.

But of course Khlestakov is not just a comic character. He has sinister not to say diabolic connotations. These are brought to a head in the last act when Zemlyanika says 'It's as if some kind of fog confused us, it was the devil's doing.' More sinister, if less obvious, is Osip's answer to Khlestakov's question, how can it be that the other guests at the inn are eating wheras he is not, as if he were not like them. Osip replies 'But of course they are not like you'. Although he goes on to point out that the other guests pay, the reply has more sinister undercurrents. Thus Gogol' once described 'our mutual friend the devil' as 'a blusterer [who] consists entirely of hot air', a description that fits Khlestakov well. His particular brand of devilry takes the shape of a complete lack of substance; insignificant and mediocre, he is nothing but froth and it is what others project into him that swells him to monstrous proportions. He is moreover a parody of humanity. He has the capacity to ape and hence devalue the spiritual dimension. An unconscious hypocrite, he says he hates two-faced behaviour. He alone in the play touches on the spiritual. He has a remarkable literary talent, producing instant masterpieces because his thoughts have an 'extraordinary lightness'. His soul 'thirsts for enlightenment', and finally he describes himself in his letter, in a terrible parody of Gogol''s own aspirations, as longing for spiritual sustenance, needing to take up some noble cause. That Gogol' had much in common with his hero emerges in his own correspondence. 'It is time, it is time at last to do something serious, oh, what an incomprehensibly amazing significance all the incidents and circumstances of my life have had! How salutary all the unpleasantnesses and disappointments were for me! They had something elastic in them; touching them it seemed to me, *I bounded higher'*. All Khlestakov is here, even the extraordinary lightness. The same quality emerges in another letter which opens with a spiritual admonition, only to proceed to try to touch its recipient for 18,000 roubles. Indeed Gogol' recognizes this quality in himself, notably with respect to his last book *Selected Passages,* of which he writes: 'Really there is something Khlestakovian in me.''

Gogol' constructs the play in a manner similar to *Dead Souls;* the arrival in town of a sinister stranger acts as a device that brings out the true nature of a whole rogue's gallery set in a world of diabolical provincial mediocrity. He shows remarkable technical skill in revealing the failings of each character. For, strictly speaking, the others are scarcely involved in the action of the play which consists of a continuing confrontation between Khlestakov and the mayor. The other officials are made to form a kind of dynamic tableau, a chorus of reactions. This emerges very clearly in Act 4, in which they each appear in turn. The structure of every scene is the same, but so skilfully does Gogol' vary the pace and speech characterization that there is no sense whatsoever of static repetition. Instead the act moves very gently into an ever-increasing atmosphere of vague irreality culminating with the populace calling to Khlestakov through the window with their bristling forest of petitions. Indeed a great proportion of the play could be considered a kind of dynamic picture, and it is of course as a direct contrast to this, its most important compositional quality, that Gogol' ends the piece with a sustained static freeze.

The author's highly developed sense of his medium is perhaps to be explained in part by his family association with amateur dramatics, partly by his own gifts of mimicry. But be that as it may he displays here, as elsewhere indeed, a remarkable gift for stagecraft. He has a great awareness of the dramatic medium as such, with an eye not just on the actors but also on the producer. Not only does he give careful instructions as to how his characters behave, particularly as to how they should come on and go off, he has also written the parts in a way that gives the actors great scope to embroider them with gesture and expression, and to use the stage as a physical space, for example in the kind of grouping and re-grouping required by the action of Act 4, Scene 1. Moreover he makes much use of farcical stage business. It is Bobchinsky and Dobchinsky who act as the centre of the knockabout aspect of the piece, usually serving as the springs of visual action. Moreover the author supplies the kind of detail that normally has to be provided by a producer. We are told when and how Bobchinsky looks in on the mayor's first interview with Khlestakov; this piece of business is built to a climax as he falls into the room, and is later picked up when we see Bobchinsky with a plaster on his nose on his next entrance. More scope for stage business is created as the various officials take it in turns to read extracts from Khlestakov's letters, stopping as it comes to mention, and to judge, the reader in question. Like Molière he uses farcical elements to lend verve to his play, to give it the pace that will carry the audience, helping the actors to maintain a *rapport* with them, and indeed to make them laugh.

Gogol''s other great comic resource remains of course his language. He has a remarkable talent for the recreation of the rhythm and idiom of direct speech in a way that appears less a direct reproduction than its amplification. His dialogue is so true to life yet so much larger than life that it borders on the grotesque. This emerges in the speech of the mayor, which serves as a superb means of characterization. He has a wide range of tones; when talking to his colleagues his speech is composed of authoritative instruction cloaked in a form of heavy-handed and ironic politeness as he dwells on their sundry failings. Beneath this blend of authority and delicacy lies a strong undercurrent of fear which emerges in flashes of impatience. When talking to Khlestakov he uses a deferential tone which disguises an ever-increasing measure of alarm, while his asides show him seeking his opponent's measure. However, his normal tone is pithy, highly coloured and idiomatic, employing *pogovorki* [sayings] without ever lapsing into cliché. Thus after Khlestakov's boasting scene, when the mayor's wife is irritating enough to inform her husband that far from being frightened she simply felt herself to be in the presence of a gentleman, the mayor snaps back:

> Oh you women! That's done it! That one word's all we needed! .. All you've got to do is blurt something out—you'll just get flogged, but the husband—well, he's as good as dead.

What is most striking about this style is the prominence that Gogol''s use of language imparts to verbs. Although this is a characteristic of the Russian language as such, it would be fair to say that if there is one specific feature that focuses the particular flavour of Gogol''s style, it is the verb. Time and again it is this that gives a particular phrase its richness. Gogol' has an extraordinary command over the range and nuance that formation by prefixation gives to Russian verb forms. Although, as was suggested, this is an intrinsic feature of Russian, so that one must beware of describing as peculiarly Gogolian turns of phrase that are part of a common linguistic heritage, the fact remains that Gogol''s style does give prominence to what is at least potentially one of the most important features of the language. This is perhaps one of the reasons why his

style conveys the peculiar effect of having realized essential Russianness, of having created a model of the Russian language writ large. It is principally the speech of the mayor that brings out this quality to the full. Thus he has two tirades in Act 5, one cursing the merchants in Scene 2, the other cursing Khlestakov in the final scene, in which he gives full tongue. The speeches consist almost entirely of exclamations, and are so loaded with idiom that they provide what amounts to an illustration of Russian invective, and are hence, by definition, quite impossible to translate.

Khlestakov's speech stands in oppositional contrast to that of the mayor. It is at its most characteristic when he is flirting—a mixture of ill-assimilated gallicism and a parody of the rhetoric of passion. In his letter he employs a combination of racy slang, *obchistil menya krugom* [cleaned me out] and phoney French *zhuiruyu* [*je jouis*]. But on the whole his language is neutral and conventional, the product of circumstance. Where the mayor's speech is peculiar to him, one of his most striking characteristics, Khlestakov speaks in a purely conventional way, precisely because he has no character. His speech also contrasts with that of Osip, the only character in the play who understands the situation from the start. Osip, by his language, emphasizes his grasp on reality, for it is idiomatic and very much to the point. He uses ambiguity to avoid answering embarrassing questions; thus when the mayor's servant asks him whether his master is really a general he replies: 'He's a general, but not the kind you know' (*General, da tol'ko s drugoi storony*). Because Gogol' wishes to show him as being in control of the situation he never devalues his language by excessive eccentricity or rhetoric. It remains vivid and down-to-earth.

Speech characterization is also used to effect with the merchants and harridans of Act 4. He creates a view of them through their language. The presence of the merchants is justified dramatically by the way in which their language fills out the picture by creating an atmosphere of 'merchantness'. The N.C.O.'s wife similarly introduces a proletariat dimension, notably through the phonetic transcription of her speech—*necha* and *shtraft* for *nichego* [nothing] and *shtraf* [fine], and the highly-coloured language in which she expresses herself.

Gogol''s play is ostensibly about the fate of a number of petty officials in a town in the middle of nowhere, yet it has wider implications. These emerge in certain passages that touch on the play's relation to the audience. Not the least of these is the epigraph: 'Don't blame the mirror if you see an ugly mug.' Whom is the author addressing? The characters? Hardly, since the epigraph stands outside the play. It is more likely that he is addressing his potentially critical public. The implication is that the play is a mirror in which we see ourselves. It is we who are responsible for the blackness of what we see. This creates a strange involvement whereby we actually become part of the play, an involvement that re-emerges in the last act, notably in the mayor's angry cry to the audience: 'What are you laughing at? You're laughing at yourselves!' It emerges more subtly in the preceding scene. There has, as usual, been talk of pigs in this play. Zemlyanika, envying the apparent good fortune of the mayor's family, talks of happiness crawling into a pig's mouth. Another character criticizing the new-found dignity of the mayor's wife says: 'Seat her at table and she'll put her feet on it.' (A variant of the Russian saying: Seat a pig at table and it puts its feet up.) Gogol' employs a piggy rhetoric to bring out the awfulness of his characters. But, when the mayor realizes Khlestakov's identity, and stares around him in a panic-stricken fog, he says: 'I can't see a thing, just pigs' snouts instead of faces.' Whose snouts are these? It does not take much imagination, in the light of the epigraph, to visualize the mayor once again turning to the audience and seeing across the footlights, not a sea of faces, but a sea of snouts. Gogol' emphasizes our involvement yet a third time when, a few lines later, the mayor says that all that is now needed is for some miserable liberal scribbler to turn the whole adventure into a play. The effect of this remark is to turn the piece into a kind of perpetual motion machine; every time we reach the conclusion we learn that the action we have just witnessed will, subsequently, become the subject of a play. This is of course the play we shall see or read next time we begin at Act 1, Scene 1. An appropriate image for this self-perpetuating cycle would be the infinity of ugly faces created by the juxtaposition of two Gogolian mirrors. But the mayor goes on to prophesy how a future audience will react; they will grin and clap, which is precisely what the audience should be doing as he makes his speech. But the mayor uses a future tense, the audience *will*, i.e. at a future date; so what are we doing, and who are we? Gogol' suggests that although the episode will eventually acquire the status of a purely aesthetic reality, a fiction performed by actors for an audience, it is for the moment something else—an implication strengthened by the fact that it is directly after this that the mayor warns us we are laughing at ourselves. Perhaps we are real protagonists in a real action, as likely in our own way as any mayor to mistake Khlestakov for the Inspector General. (pp. 106-17)

A. de Jonge, "Gogol'," in Nineteenth-Century Russian Literature: Studies of Ten Russian Writers, *edited by John Fennell, University of California Press, 1973, pp. 69-129.*

JESSE ZELDIN (essay date 1978)

[*An American critic specializing in Russian literature, Zeldin is the editor and translator of Gogol's* Selected Passages from Correspondence with Friends. *He is also the author of* Nikolai Gogol's Quest for Beauty: An Exploration into His Works, *in which he argued that "Gogol was primarily interested in the nature of reality, which he identified with beauty." In the following excerpt from that work, Zeldin examines falsity as the essence of* The Inspector General.]

One of the difficulties with *The Inspector General,* as well as one of its marks of greatness, is its susceptibility to a variety of interpretations. Depending on the critic's particular bias, these interpretations range from social criticism, to a political attack, to Freudian complexes, to metaphysical revelations, to good, not-always-so-clean, fun. In the context of Gogol's own interests, prejudices, and statements, however, it is still highly likely that he remained concerned with his vision of truth and beauty as immaterial absolutes to be sought, rather than as concrete manifestations. Satan continues to be the father of lies.

This is not to imply, as Evdokimov, for one, does, that Khlestakov is an agent of the devil, a deceiver who, Mephistopheles-like, attempts to entrap people. His role is catalytic rather than deliberate, for what happens, happens because of decisions to falsify, decisions that have been made long before the play opens. In other words, Gogol is not dealing here with people as they are in reality, but as they have falsified themselves. For this reason, he could with justice claim that not one character in the piece was based on anything in the real world. He does not mean for the audience to see itself on stage as it really

is, but as it might convince itself it is. It is all a lie, in short, but so obviously one that the truth should be revealed. This is the reason that no one in the play acts in consciousness of either himself or of his relations with others. Yet each person's ego is of vital importance to him, although in reality no one has a true self, only an obsession. Instead of being real, these selves are imaginary. In this sense, the events of the play constitute a fantasy, constructed by the imaginations of those within it— a diary of madmen.

It seems to me that this imaginary quality in the play is the crux of the matter, for the implication is that the world that is presented on stage—the world that some members of Gogol's audience in outrage identified themselves with; the world of deceit, which they thought real; the one that they thought they lived in—is not real at all. It is entirely fantastic, not only for the author of *The Inspector General* and for the characters in his play, but for those in the orchestra, loge, and balcony who, being less perspicacious than the author, failed to realize how far off the mark, how false, that world is. The joke was on those who thought they saw the joke. This is an imaginary world, further, because it is a man-made world, one based on refusal to comprehend, rather than the real created world, which is true and beautiful. Thus, what we are faced with in *The Inspector General* is not only the triviality and banality—the *poshlost'* that Gogol himself referred to and that Nabokov, among others, made so much of—but also a much deeper ugliness. What Gogol was doing was holding up a mirror to his audience's imagination, not to what they are but to what they think they are; this is what *we* imagine reality to be, not what Gogol does, for he did not believe that he had any imagination at all. Like many imaginary constructions, further, this is a parody, a turning upside down. Gogol's hope was that once the parody was exposed for what it was, it would be abandoned as being too ridiculous, too laughable, and too much at variance with what is known to be true for it any longer to be taken seriously and indulged in. Consequently, this lie that imagination had made would be discarded, and men would return to their proper harmonious home.

Hence Gogol's emphasis upon the living-statue scene at the end and upon the character—or lack of it—of Khlestakov. Surely Gogol was experienced enough in the theater to know that a minute and a half of immobility on stage, which is what he called for, is a very long time. The scene is there for additional clarification, to inscribe the point as emphatically as he could, despite its difficulty dramatically. Because Gogol is so precise in the way that he stations his characters, he must have thought that the audience needed the time in order to realize what the scene meant. In his note preceding the first scene of the play he wrote:

> The actors must pay attention in particular to the last scene. The last word pronounced [by the policeman, that another Inspector General has arrived] should produce a sudden electric shock among them all. The whole group should change position in the twinkling of an eye. An astonished sound should escape all the women at once, as though from a single breast. If these directions are not followed, the whole effect may be lost. . . .

The last scene itself is described as follows:

> The Mayor in the middle like a post, with arms outstretched and head thrown back. On his right

side, his wife and daughter, concentrated upon him by the inclination of their bodies; behind [or beyond] them the Postmaster, reduced to a question mark addressed to the audience; behind [or beyond] him Luka Lukich, lost in utter innocence; behind [or beyond] him, at the very edge of the stage, three lady visitors, leaning towards one another with the most satirical expressions on their faces aimed straight at the Mayor's family. On the Mayor's left side: Zemlyanika, his head bent somewhat to the side as though he were listening to something; behind [or beyond] him the Judge, with arms spread wide, squatting almost to the ground and making a movement with his lips as though he were going to whistle or declare, "That's all we needed!"; behind [or beyond] him, Korobkin, turned to the audience with eyes screwed up, caustically hinting at the Mayor; behind [or beyond] him, at the very edge of the stage, Bobchinsky and Dobchinsky, their hands reaching out to each other, mouths wide open and goggle-eyed at each other. The other visitors simply remain like posts. For almost a minute and a half the petrified group holds this position. . . .

(pp. 70-2)

Following Gogol's directions, there are two possible ways that the main characters could be positioned, either of which is suggestive:

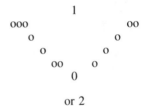

First, and most obvious, is the fact that Gogol gives directions for precisely twelve persons, plus the central figure (carefully made central) of the Mayor. Second, the characters are not arranged evenly: there are five on the Mayor's left hand, and seven on his right; in addition the groupings are slightly different. All this is sufficient to make the whole picture seem somewhat uneven, somewhat discordant, as though something, somewhere, somehow has gone wrong. The elements are deliberately not arranged to compose a harmonious whole. Certainly, the number of persons (twelve plus one) chosen for the tableau was a conscious decision (the policeman, for example, could easily have been included, thus making an even fourteen. But this would have made the Christ and Disciples analogy impossible). Given the expressions on people's faces and the attitudes of their bodies, we have, in arrangement 1, the Crucifixion; or, in 2, the Last Supper, but in parodic rather than real form. The scene itself is a deception, but is meant to be seen as such. These are a false god and false disciples, all of them living in a false world. And instead of the harmonious reconciliation that either of the events should signify, with the promise of the eternally beautiful life to come, we know that the announcement of a new Inspector General, who may or may not be a genuine one, means a return to the cacophonous

falsity that has reigned throughout the play. The parody remains exactly that.

When we turn to Khlestakov, we find ourselves in the same unreal world. He is not only a parody of an inspector general, he is also a parody of a human being. Gogol describes him as follows in the character sketch preceding the comedy:

> A young man of twenty-three years, thin, slight, somewhat foolish and stupid, one of those people who in offices is called "good-for-nothing." He speaks and acts at random. He is incapable of concentrating on any thought for any length of time. His speech is jerky, and words fly out of his mouth completely unexpectedly. The more the one filling this role shows sincerity and simplicity, the more he will succeed. Fashionably dressed. . . .

In his "Letter to a Writer" of 1836, complaining about how Khlestakov had been played, Gogol described him thus:

> Khlestakov is not a swindler at all; he is not a liar by profession; he himself forgets that he is lying and almost himself believes what he is saying. . . . To lie means to speak a line in a tone so close to the truth, so naturally, so naïvely, that it could only be done when speaking nothing but the truth. . . . Khlestakov does not at all lie coldly, nor as a theatrical braggart; he lies with feeling; his eyes bespeak the pleasure he gets from it. It is the best, the most poetic moment of his life, almost a kind of inspiration. . . .

And in 1841, in a description that was not published until the edition of 1889, Gogol said:

> Khlestakov in himself is a worthless person. . . . But the strength of the general fear has made a remarkable comic person out of him. . . . He who had hitherto been thwarted and snubbed in everything . . . felt elbow room and suddenly expanded, when he least expected it himself. Everything in him is surprise and unexpectedness. He cannot even guess why he is getting so much attention and respect. . . . The further he goes, the more wholeheartedly does he enter into what he is saying. . . . It seems to him that he really has done all these things. . . . Having himself been repeatedly blasted, he knows the speech for it perfectly; he feels a special pleasure in blasting others, even if only in tales. . . . On waking, he is the same Khlestakov he was before. He does not even remember that he frightened them all. As before, there is no understanding in him; there is the same stupidity in all his actions. . . .

(pp. 72-4)

It is quite clear, then, that Khlestakov is a figment of the imagination, a kind of wish fulfillment, an Inspector General who corresponds to preconceived fantasies, both his and others', rather than a reality in himself. There is little doubt, further, that the new Inspector General announced by the policeman, regardless of what he really is, will also immediately be transformed, in a parody of transfiguration, into an imaginary being who will fit the fears, desires, and prejudices of the imaginary inhabitants of the town. Reality, whatever it may be, will once again be refused; the cacophonous ugliness of death (itself a parody) will once again usurp the place of harmonious beauty.

The horror to Gogol was that his play and the characters in it were taken to be portrayals of the world as it really is, while he knew that it was Annunziata who was real, not Khlestakov. From Gogol's point of view, his critics were in the same position as those who find Milton's Satan powerful and his Christ pale; Dante's *Inferno* more impressive than his *Paradiso;* Dostoevsky's Ivan more alive than his Father Zosima.

Gogol's comment that Khlestakov's lies took on the semblance of truth, even for him, further emphasizes the parodic nature of the play. Khlestakov, too, is a joke—but a very serious one, because he does not know he is. In this he goes beyond a Tartuffe, who at least has the virtue of hypocrisy, so that, avoiding parody, Tartuffe remains human. Khlestakov, on the contrary, being parodic, is imaginary; he only gives the semblance of a man. It is no answer to say that Khlestakov in actuality is some irresponsible clerk from Petersburg who just happened to be passing through, because that does not clothe him in any more flesh and blood nor give him any more soul than he had before. Even the letter at the end, by which the townspeople learn that Khlestakov is a fake, is of little help, for there is no revelation of truth in it at all, just that he is not what they thought he was. No one knows any better what he is.

The strange and shocking thing about the play is the persistence of the townspeople, their utter refusal to see anything in any light but the one that they themselves have provided. Their deception is thus entirely self-deception. Nobody foisted Khlestakov off on them; they foisted him off on themselves, as each of them foists himself off on the others. From this point of view, it is appalling that the information about Khlestakov's falsity does not result in a realization of their own falsity. They discover—perforce—that he is imaginary, but not that they themselves are. Indeed, one is struck by the remarkable stubbornness of these people, who are not in themselves terribly stupid. Gogol says as much of the Mayor, who is "very shrewd in his own way," while Zemlyanika, we are told, is a "wily scoundrel." The only one who we are definitely informed is stupid is Khlestakov himself. Untruth is not embraced because of a lack of reason; it arises, curiously enough, out of too great a trust in reason. The Mayor's tirade in act 5, for example, focusses on the original mistake made in taking Khlestakov for an inspector general; but neither he nor anyone else finds that the conclusions and actions based on that premise are amiss. If Khlestakov had been an inspector general, whatever was said and thought—all the townspeople's actions—would have been, to their way of thinking, perfectly proper. Not only do they lack substance; they do not even know that they lack substance. Khlestakov is not the only one who is worthless (Gogol also calls him "empty"); we have one example after another of egoism and conviction of rectitude (this applies even to the shopkeepers who bring complaints against the Mayor; we discover that they, too, are false) attached to vacuums, to substancelessness.

The absence of substance is pointed out twice in the course of the play, both times in reference to Khlestakov, and both times inadvertently. The first time this happens is in scene 4 of act 3. Osip, Khlestakov's servant, is asked if his master is not a general. He replies, "Oh, yes—he's a general. But in reverse." In answer to whether that makes him more or less than a genuine general, he says, "More." . . . The second instance is in scene 8 of act 5. The Postmaster, asked *what* (not *who*) he thinks Khlestakov is, responds in kind: "Neither this nor that; the devil knows what it is!". . . . In both cases we learn that it is whatness that is of interest rather than whoness—a thing rather than a person. In this connection, we also note (Osip has passed the information on to the audience in a soliloquy) that Khlestakov is a collegiate registrar (the lowest grade on the Table of Ranks). Osip's speech makes a point of this. The reader, or audience, has a right to ask *why* this particular rank is ascribed to him, since most of Gogol's officials are of more middling grade. There are two reasons for the choice: first, to make the enormity of the parody clear (how many television comedies have made comic hay out of the second lieutenant impersonating the general, or the shipping room clerk passing himself off as head of the company); the second is involved with the question of what a registry clerk does: he notes down, files away, "statisticizes," if I may coin a word. In short, his job, his vocation—if Khlestakov can be said to have one—is to abstract persons, to dehumanize them. And this is precisely what he does, by his presence alone, not by his action, in the course of the play. The trick that Gogol accomplished was to create a character who is unaware of his function even while receiving total cooperation in the exercise of that function. He who wishes to lose his soul loses it. Much of the greatness of the comedy rests on this ground of Khlestakov's unawareness; as Gogol pointed out, he doesn't know what is going on. He doesn't even know what he is doing while doing it, as his letter to his friend in which he describes the people of the town indicates. As others imagine him, so he imagines others, no more aware than they of this imaginary quality. According to the letter, in Khlestakov's "judgment" the Mayor is "as stupid as a grey gelding," and the "grey gelding" is repeated; the Postmaster is the "image of the porter Mikheyev; the scoundrel probably also hits the bottle"; Zemlyanika is "a pig in a skull cap"; Luka Lukich "stinks of onions"; the Judge, Lyapkin-Tyapkin, "is as *mauvais ton* as you can get." . . . None of these descriptions really does any more than file its subject away and register it without concern for reality, for the descriptions do not really apply to anyone at all; they are as deceptive as their subjects.

Gogol in this play accomplished two very original things. First, he managed a play about deception without using a conscious deceiver. In such comedies about mistaken identity (and their number is legion), the trickster is usually a conscious rogue; one need but refer to the comedies of Plautus, Shakespeare, Jonson, and Molière for examples. In *The Gamblers,* Gogol wrote in this tradition. There, everyone is a conscious cheat. In *The Inspector General,* no one is, because no one, as we have noted, is a hypocrite. It is a remarkable achievement, in this sense, of the portrayal of nothingness, of soullessness. These are all little men who aren't there.

From this point of view, Gogol was indeed acting as a teacher and prophet, giving warning of the pit that yawns and the fate that awaits those who see this as a real depiction of a real world: these are not persons; they are parodies of persons. Nowhere within the play is there a portrayal of the harmonious beauty that Gogol held so dear. On the contrary, he presents us with a discordant ugliness, the only release from which is laughter. In a return to an image for ugliness that he had used so often in the Little Russian tales, he has the Mayor say, when the full extent of the mistake that he has made has been borne in upon him, "I see only pig snouts instead of faces, nothing more," . . . thus repeating a remark made by Khlestakov and unconsciously putting himself in Khlestakov's class. . . . Furthermore, the remark is not addressed to anyone in particular, or it is addressed to everyone in general. There are no stage directions to indicate whether the Mayor is speaking to the other members of the cast, to the audience, or to his own imagination. For this one brief flash, Gogol holds out the possibility of redemption from the ugly and false, for the Mayor has just said that he has "been killed, utterly killed." Unfortunately, this is only a glimpse of the truth regarding others, not the truth about himself. Like everyone else, he cannot discard his mask, because there is only a void behind it. Gogol is more worried about his audience, however, than he is about the imaginary creatures of the play: those in the comedy have no future, but the audience may have, since Gogol still believed that the reality of the latter might be asserted. At this point, the future is still outside the work of art, on the other hand, rather than inside it. Only as *Dead Souls* developed did he realize that as he wrote, he must carry his readers into the future if his vision was to be communicated, if the quest was to involve them as well as himself.

The ugliness, and hence falsity (or falsity, hence ugliness), within the play is reinforced by the discordancy that we meet at every turn—it is a reversal of the harmony that Gogol felt to be essential: no one is interested in anything save his own skin; each tries to gain favors for himself, to maintain his face, to be regarded, to be singled out, not for what he is, but for what he imagines himself to be, just as Proprishchin, Kovalyov, and Akaky Akakyevich did. The Mayor's wife and daughter, Anna Andreyevna and Maria Antonovna, imagine that they are highly seductive females and that they are persons who are capable of holding their own in the most exalted circles; the Mayor imagines that he is a general, with a decoration on his breast, giving orders; Luka Lukich, the superintendent of schools, imagines that he is a clever boulevardier, superior to these country yokels; the Judge, Lyapkin-Tyapkin, imagines that he is a man of independent, well-considered thought; the Postmaster imagines that he is a man who keeps up with events, one who knows what is going on; Zemlyanika, the administrator of charitable institutions, imagines that he is a down-to-earth practical man; Dobchinsky and Bobchinsky, Gogol's Tweedledum and Tweedledee, imagine that they are persons of probity and intelligence; and so forth and so on. One cannot imagine what these imaginings have to do with reality. As with Poprishchin, Kovalyov, and Akaky Akakyevich, fantasy has usurped the place of truth. Like the Inspector General himself, everyone in the play—with the possible exception of Osip—is traveling incognito. It is not that the forms assumed are in themselves bad; indeed, . . . all the disguises make perfectly good sense in the unreal world in which the characters live. They fail because, although x plus y may equal z, or two plus two may equal four, they are only registrations without meaning.

For Gogol—and this applies to his view of the world as well as to his view of art—form without substance (and substance here is *not* a synonym for matter) is empty, is meaningless. In fact, the forms taken by these persons are material—x, y, and z notwithstanding—not spiritual. It is precisely spirit that is lacking in *The Inspector General*. To put it another way, this is a play without a soul: persons are not like this for the very good and sufficient reason that these are not persons. Indeed, to criticize *The Inspector General* on realistic grounds is to miss the point entirely, as Gogol himself was well aware. He was always careful to avoid the mistake of confusing fiction with truth (both Hanz Kuechelgarten and Piskaryov made that mis-

take and may serve as warnings of its consequences). The play may be the thing; but as in *Hamlet,* to indicate the truth, not to be the truth. Gogol, one of the greatest handlers of the Russian language, also knew that telling the truth is not so easy as many assume. The oath "I swear to tell the truth, the whole truth, and nothing but the truth" probably appeared to him as irresistibly comic, as, indeed, it is. We can imagine what would have happened if Pushkin had given *that* idea to Gogol!

Material (or rank, riches, esteem, prerogatives) is the mask that the dramatis personae assume; therefore, we may say that what they actually do, so far as Gogol is concerned, is deform themselves, which answers the question we asked above about to whom the Mayor's remark, "I see only pig snouts," is addressed: it is addressed to all who have exchanged spirit for matter. Not only was this image used to characterize ugliness in the Little Russian tales, we remember; it was also used in specific reference to nonhuman monsters, all of whom are, from man's point of view, deformed (this gives them their grotesque quality, and from this their horror arises). They are also, therefore, soulless. Without hanging the entire interpretation of *The Inspector General* on one phrase, I think we can safely conclude that this comedy is Gogol's greatest horror story, so much so that it is bearable only because it is funny, and it is funny only because it is not real. This is not the laughter of Homer's gods whose wounds are healed overnight while men die, nor is it the objective laughter of Mozart shaking his head at mere folly. For Gogol, nothing could surpass the terror that he felt at the sight of deformed material emptiness, of chaos; his laughter is an exorcism of that terror, for the soulless, he believed, were without—or beyond—hope; and not to laugh would have been to condemn himself to black despair and deny his vision—that is, to become one of the characters on stage. What a blow, then, it must have been when some members of the audience protested that Gogol had put them on stage, while others praised him for giving a "realistic" picture of conditions in Russia. For both were casting the prophet-teacher—who was attempting to turn men's eyes to truth and beauty and thus to save them—in the role of a satanic destroyer. "For the sake of Heaven," one can hear him cry, "don't you realize that this is *not* what you are!" (pp. 74-80)

Jesse Zeldin in his Nikolai Gogol's Quest for Beauty: An Exploration into His Works, *The Regents Press of Kansas, 1978, 244 p.*

MILTON EHRE   (essay date 1980)

[*Ehre analyzes the structure of* The Inspector General *and examines Gogol's use of dramatic technique in order to define the nature of the play's comic effect, demonstrating its skillful combination of comedy and apocalyptic terror.*]

Gogol's labored apologias for his great play, written in anxious defense against the miscomprehensions of critics, have been largely ignored or ridiculed. In the nineteenth century they were dismissed as the rantings of a religious fanatic; in the twentieth, when our habit is to convert moral judgements into clinical diagnoses, as the symptoms of pathology. The strained style Gogol adopted whenever he felt threatened should not deceive us. He was an acute student of the arts, alert to his own purposes. Any examination of his work must take his views into account.

For Gogol, *The Government Inspector* was a play that should arouse terror as well as laughter. Such is the common thread of his two most important statements about the play, the dramatized essays **"Leaving the Theater After a Performance of a New Comedy,"** probably written shortly after the historic première of 1836 [see excerpt from the revised version dated 1842], and the **"Dénouement of *The Government Inspector*,"** written a full decade later [see excerpt dated 1846]. He had not intended a balanced "portrait" of contemporary society, he writes in **"Leaving the Theater . . . ,"** but a heightened image of what he found wrong in Russia: "From all over, from the four corners of Russia, what has been excluded from the truth, moral failings and abuses, have flocked together . . ." in an "ideal" place of assembly so that the audience might experience "an intense, noble disdain for whatever is ignoble." The viewer "shudders in the depths of his being. . . . He must be constantly on guard . . ." lest the objects of his laughter "burst into his soul." These terrifying images should "incessantly haunt the imagination . . ." of the audience.

Though his overwrought rhetoric places him squarely in the Romantic age, Gogol's interpretation of 1836 can still be read in the context of classical theories of comedy, whose purpose was, in a leading Russian classicist's paraphrase of Boileau, "to correct manners through ridicule, / . . . to amuse and serve." The function of comedy is social. It enlightens the public to the ways of the world and acts as a moral prophylactic. . . . The final emphasis is on the liberating power of laughter. Proper laughter is "good-natured" and indicates a "magnanimous soul." It frees us from self-righteousness and leads to forgiveness and "reconciliation." The theater creates a community, as "all men come together, like brothers," in a single shared "spiritual motion."

In the 1846 **"Dénouement . . ."** the emphasis turns from society to the self, from reconciliation and community to preparation for the world's end. Christian allusions had resonated through the metaphors of the 1836 piece; the play is now read as Christian allegory. The earlier "place of assembly," which offered a microcosm of Russian wrongdoing, has become our common "spiritual city." The town's officals are identified with our human passions and "trivial vulgar habits." Khlestakov, the fake government inspector, represents "the frivolous conscience of the world." He blinds us to the identity of the true inspector, who is "our awakening conscience." The religious imagination of the **"Dénouement . . ."** is, as the title tells us, entirely turned to last things, to death and the grave. Where Gogol saw comedy in **"Leaving the Theater . . ."** as inhibiting vice and softening self-righteousness, thereby bringing about reconciliation between men here on earth, he now describes an audience that feels "no desire to be reconciled to the characters, but, on the contrary, wishes to repel them unhesitatingly. . . ." Laughter has been transformed from an instrument of community to "a weapon, a scourge" that will drive corruption from our souls and purify us before Last Judgment. . . . (pp. 137-38)

These two readings—the play as social and as apocalyptic satire—anticipate the two tendencies of Gogol criticism: the nineteenth-century (and Soviet) view that locates his art in the actualities of Russian society, and the modernist revision that highlights its demonic aspects (while often ignoring the religious motives, so that Gogol becomes an archetypal "absurdist"). As is often the case in such polemics, the antagonists are responding to different sides of the same object. *The Government Inspector* may be read as social comedy (Gogol's 1836

reading) and as a kind of metaphysical comedy centered on the radical imperfection of human nature (his 1846 revision). It mocks the way of the world but its mockery is part of an effort to obliterate the world as a prelude to final judgement. Nor are the two views mutually exclusive. Apocalyptic terrors result from a sense of social dissolution—even in the **"Dénouement . . . ,"** where the primary concern is spiritual salvation, Gogol still speaks of "terror at our social chaos." Moreover, his apocalypse is comical, and comedy treats the actualities of human life, which always have a social context. Gogol creates his comic apocalypse by organizing his play so as to reveal the illusory pursuits of his people, the insubstantial character of their society, and the resulting chaos. He brings his world to the brink where final judgment waits. In the following pages we shall examine that organization and, then, the issues posed by a comic apocalypse.

Few who write on *The Government Inspector* fail to point to the brilliance of the opening two lines: "Gentlemen! I've summoned you here because of some very distressing news. A government inspector is on his way." The obligatory exposition of classical comedy has been compressed into a stunning fifteen words (in Russian). Here is the dramatic situation that governs the entire play, the ineluctable presence that hovers over it from beginning to end. What follows, however, is not an elaboration of that situation, a working out of motive to final resolution as in most drama before Gogol. The situation remains constant for most of the play; the government inspector is a given, an inescapable fact, who elicits, instead of an evolving intrigue, a series of frenzied responses:

> A government inspector?
>
> An inspector?
>
> • • • • •
>
> As if we didn't have enough troubles!
>
> Good God! And with secret instructions!

The work ends on analogous accents of inexorable destiny:

> His Excellency the government inspector has arrived from the capital. In the name of the emperor he demands your immediate presence at the inn.

In Nabokov's felicitous words: "The play begins with a blinding flash of lightning and ends in a thunderclap. In fact it is wholly placed in the tense gap between the flash and the crash" [see excerpt dated 1944].

However, it is not only that these lines are dramatically effective, which they are. They also define the structure of the play. The impending arrival of the government inspector is announced in the opening two sentences; he arrives in the final two. These symmetrical pairs, echoing each other in their official bombast and note of irrevocable fact, comprise the only events with the potential to affect the lives of the characters. As a result, the gap between the flash and the crash, which is the duration of the play, acquires a curious status. The life of the play is dislodged from fact, or reality—the true inspector, and shifted to a realm of illusion—the pursuit of a specter: Khlestakov, the unwitting imposter, the False Pretender, a character who, in Gogol's words, is "phantasmagorical."

"Hurry, hurry, for God's sake, hurry" are the last words of Act I, and much of the play is saturated with words of haste,

A scene from the Meyerhold production of The Inspector General. From Meyerhold on Theatre, translated and edited by Edward Braun. Hill and Wang, 1969. Copyright © 1969 by Edward Braun. Reprinted by permission of Hill and Wang, a division of Farrar, Straus and Giroux, Inc.

as the townspeople rush headlong to discover the nature of their visitor or cater to his whims.

> MAYOR. Quick, get the police captain. No, wait. [. . .] Tell someone out there to hurry and bring the police captain. [. . .] Go out to the street . . . no, wait! Go get. [. . .] My God! My God! . . . Quick, go to the street; no, wait, first run to my room—do you hear! [. . .] Run, quick; take some men and have each of them grab a . . . Oh hell, the sword's scratched [. . .] Have each of them grab a street—what the!—grab a broom. [. . .] (I, iii-iv.)

• • • • •

> ANNA. Later? That's a fine piece of news! Later! I don't want your later. Just tell me, what's his rank? Is he a colonel? [. . .]

> MARYA. Oh Mama! It doesn't matter. We'll know in a few hours.

> ANNA. A few hours! Thank you very much. That's brilliant. Why not a month while you're at it. Avdotya! Avdotya! What have you heard? Has someone arrived? . . . What? They rushed off? You should have run after them. Go now.

> Hurry! [. . .] Run—ask where they've gone. Find out the details. Who is he, is he handsome? Do you hear [. . .] And come right home. [. . .] Hurry, hurry, for God's sake, hurry! (I, iv.)

The activity on stage rushes along, like Khlestakov's mind, at breakneck speed: policemen and servants rush on stage to receive their orders; Bobchinsky and Dobchinsky tumble on to it with their extraordinary news; the officials slink on to bribe the putative inspector; Khlestakov flits across like a phantom.

But all this rushing is toward an illusion, the false inspector, who in turn won't sit still, whose mind leaps with "extraordinary lightness" from one fabrication to another until he finally flies off in his troika, as if vanishing into thin air. The object of this frenzied bustle is a man without substance, a creature of pure improvisation who can only respond to the signals of the moment, "a nobody and a nothing" in the words of the postmaster (V. viii). Khlestakov's exceptional vacuity has been the subject of much metaphysical and psychological speculation, but it has a dramatic function. Because he lacks character, the townspeople can project their own fears and fantasies upon him. In a sense he is their creation: Khlestakov is "the most empty of men," Gogol wrote, ". . . but the force of general terror has made him into a remarkable comic character." What makes him so comic is the enormous discrepancy between his own inconsequentiality and the importance the terrified town places upon him. Conversely, the frantic rush of the townspeople to placate this illusory phantom deprives their experience of substance. We get the inconsequential in pursuit of the inconsequential; so to speak, nothing heaped upon nothing.

The Gogolian annihilation of experience is particularly thorough-going in the seduction scenes. It has often been said that Gogol's innovation in the tradition of comedy was in eliminating the conventional love story. This is not so. The love story is present, and it is at the center of the play. The action of the "gap" turns around the seeming change in the mayor's fortunes, which is marked by the course of Marya's and Khlestakov's courtship. Before the betrothal the mayor felt himself in danger of destruction; afterwards he is for an instant on top of the world. Instead of dispensing with the conventions of love, Gogol trivializes them so that they become ludicrous. He draws his conventions, not from high comedy, but from popular farce and vaudeville: the ingénue of high comedy is converted into an imbecilic provincial, the paramour into a featherbrained fake, the action into automatized mime. "... comedy should cohere spontaneously, . . ." he wrote, and the love scenes are decomposed into a series of hurried accidental gestures, abrupt and unmotivated. Marya wanders aimlessly on to the stage, "going nowhere in particular"; Khlestakov blurts out in his inimitable fashion, "And why, may I ask, weren't you going anywhere in particular?"; he steals a kiss; she is indignant; he falls to his knees to beg forgiveness; Mama bursts in exclaiming, "Oh good heavens"; Khlestakov, not one to be easily put off, again falls to his knees, this time to make a pass at Mama; the daughter walks in with another "Oh good heavens," and so it goes. By reducing action to the quick-paced and bare gestures of farce, Gogol turns his love story into a parody of a love story. The language of love is likewise a parodic *reductio ad absurdum:* "My life hangs by a thread. If you reject my undying love, I no longer deserve to dwell in this vale of tears. My heart ablaze, I ask your hand" (IV, xii-xiv). These inspired words of Khlestakov are addressed not to Marya but to her mother! Such displacements are of course a standard ploy of farce.

If the "love story" goes virtually unnoticed, it is because it was meant to. In **"Leaving the Theater . . ."** Gogol expressed his disdain for plots that centered on love or "private" life; these were like "a precise little knot at the corner of a handkerchief." Instead he wanted a plot that would tie together all the characters, the whole of society. The "lovers" of *The Government Inspector,* unlike the ingénues and gallants of traditional comedy, offer no alternative image to the comedic world about them. They are as inane as the more conventional comic figures: the gruff and highhanded mayor, his coquettish wife, the bumbling and corrupt officials, all of whom have their prototypes in Russian eighteenth-century comedy. Gogol's great innovation was not to eliminate the love story but to incorporate it into the comic pattern. Instead of two worlds—one fallen; the other of good sense, decorous and decent—he gives us a single universe, tied into "one great knot," all of it ludicrous.

The same integrating power sweeps Khlestakov into the vortex of the play. As classical comedy opposed the comically nonsensical to men and women of good sense, it divided the virtuous and misguided from its authentic villains. *The Government Inspector* is a play without virtuous characters, and it is also a play without villains. Khlestakov comes out of a venerable line of charlatans and imposters, but, as Gogol tirelessly

repeated, he is not to be identified with the "braggarts and theatrical rogues" of comedy for the simple reason that he has no idea he's lying. Khlestakov, for Gogol, was a dreamer, a fantasist, for whom imagination and reality have become interwoven into a crazy quilt of illusion. Exposing the ludicrousness of the world about him, he is himself ludicrous. Neither virtuous nor evil, the characters of Gogol's comic works (the melodramas are something else) are merely ridiculous. They reside in a halfway house between redemption and damnation— a comic purgatory.

Besides rushing, the play's other mode is one of performance. Action is speeded up and automatized so that it loses all substance; at the same time, action is transformed into acting, an illusory makebelieve, again lacking in substance. The departure from tradition is once more striking. Where comic masquerades before Gogol divided neatly into deceivers and deceived, confidence men and their gulls, in *The Government Inspector* almost everyone is an impersonator, an actor.

> MAYOR. . . . He wants to remain incognito. Fine. We can bluff too, act as if we don't have a hint who he is. (II, viii.)

> • • • • •

> ANNA. Osip, dear, I imagine many counts and princes call on your master?

> OSIP, *aside.* What do I say? They fed me fine now, and it can only get better. (*Aloud.*) Yes, ma'm, counts and everything. (III, x.)

> • • • • •

> KHLESTAKOV. The place is crawling with officials. . . . Seems they've taken me for someone from the ministry. I must have laid it on thick yesterday. (IV, viii.)

Even in those rare moments when Khlestakov is not acting, his every word is taken as performance. The comic routines between him and the mayor are built on this principle: the mayor putting on a show while taking Khlestakov's pedestrian responses for merely another show:

> MAYOR. [. . .] Pyotr Ivanovich Dobchinsky and I—Dobchinsky here is one of our local landowners—well, since we were in the neighborhood on official business, we made a point of stopping in to determine whether the guests are being treated properly. Some mayors may not concern themselves with the welfare of others, but I, I . . . insist that a good reception be extended to all persons. Not only because my position demands it, but also out of Christian love for humanity. And now, as if in reward, fortune has afforded me such a pleasant acquaintance.

> KHLESTAKOV. I'm also glad. If not for you, I might have been stranded here for ages. I was racking my brains how to pay the bill.

> MAYOR, *aside.* Sure, tell it to the birds! Didn't know how he'd pay, did he? (*Aloud.*) May I be so bold as to ask to what parts you are bound?

> KHLESTAKOV. Saratov. I'm on my way home.

MAYOR, *aside, an ironic expression on his face.* Saratov, eh? And without a blush! Oh, you've got to be on your toes with him. (*Aloud.*) A most worthy enterprise, sir. (II, viii.)

More fequently the impersonations are duets, as two characters perform ballet-like verbal dances of pretense.

KHLESTAKOV, *bowing.* How delighted I am, madam, to have the pleasure of your acquaintance.

ANNA. It's even more of a pleasure for us to meet you.

KHLESTAKOV, *posturing.* Oh no, madam, not at all. It's far more pleasant for me.

ANNA. How can you say that, sir! You're only trying to flatter us. Please be seated.

KHLESTAKOV. Standing near you, madam, is joy itself. But if you insist, I'll sit. . . . How delighted I am at last to be sitting beside you.

ANNA. Oh my! I dare not dream your compliments are intended for me. . . . I imagine, after the capital traveling through the provinces must have been quite disagreeable.

KHLESTAKOV. Exceedingly so. Accustomed as I am, *comprenez-vous,* to moving in the best society, and suddenly to find myself on the road—filthy inns, the dark gloom of ignorance . . . I must say, if not for the good fortune . . . (*glancing at* ANNA ANDREEVNA *and posturing*) that has rewarded me for all my trials and tribulations . . .

ANNA. Indeed, how disagreeable it must have been.

KHLESTAKOV. At this moment, madam, everything is most agreeable.

ANNA. You can't mean that, sir! You do me too much honor. I'm not worthy.

KHLESTAKOV. Why aren't you worthy? Madam, you *are* worthy.

ANNA. I live in the country.

KHLESTAKOV. Yes, but the country has its hillocks, its rivulets. (III, vi.)

The characters of the play rush after an illusion—the false inspector—and when they catch up with him, they in turn metamorphose into illusory characters, masked selves performing stylized rituals of impersonation.

The ironies of the Discovery and Peripety revolve around metaphors of life as performance. As the town's officials come to the realization that they have foisted an identity upon Khlestakov, that under his mask there is nothing and nobody, the mayor is overcome by the dread that he too may lack substantial identity, that he may be only an actor in a performance.

Oh you thick-nosed idiot! Taking that squirt, that worm, for an important person! . . . He'll turn you into the laughing stock of all Russia. What's more, some cheap hack will stick you

into a comedy. That's what hurts. [. . .] And they'll all grin and clap. [. . .](V, viii.)

Though the play is unremitting in its comic vision, it gives us momentary glimpses of suffering underlying its comedy. Its pathos stems from this sense of loss of selfhood. The townspeople's deepest fears are that they too may be nothings and nobodies:

BOBCHINSKY. [. . .] Your Excellency. I have a very humble request.

KHLESTAKOV. What about?

BOBCHINSKY. I humbly beg you, sir, when you return to the capital, tell all those great gentlemen—the senators and admirals and all the rest—say, "Your Excellency or Your Highness, in such and such a town there lives a man called Pyotr Ivanovich Bobchinsky." Be sure to tell them, "Pyotr Ivanovich Bobchinsky lives there."

KHLESTAKOV. Very well.

BOBCHINSKY. And if you should happen to meet with the tsar, then tell the tsar too, "Your Imperial Majesty, in such and such a town there lives a man called Pyotr Ivanovich Bobchinsky."

KHLESTAKOV. Fine. (IV, vii.)

When [the] performance collapses, when the Discovery unmasks Khlestakov and the townspeople as actors in a comedy of mutual deception, the mode of rush returns. But where the earlier rush was a linear movement toward an end, however illusory, the stage now witnesses a tornado-like whirl of recrimination and abuse. Deprived of an end to action, the townspeople turn upon themselves. As we move from the mayor's expansive rhetorical outbursts—the wider end of our tornado's funnel—the language narrows, phrasing becomes terser and hence quicker, compressing finally to one or two-word expletives before Dobchinsky's and Bobchinsky's last effort to get off the hook. (pp. 139-46)

The action between the flash and the crash concludes in an image of social dissolution. The society of the play has pursued an illusion, and in the end its fabric is rent. The message of the gendarme, in Gogol's stage directions, "strikes like a thunderbolt." The frenzied whirlwind stops, and all freeze in terror in the dumb scene. The intervention of the central government to set straight a world out of joint provided a standard resolution of comedy before Gogol, but Gogol's inspector is much different from his predecessors. He has no presence in the life of the play. . . . He never appears on stage, and is not even given a name. Though dispatched by the emperor, he is heralded in an (untranslatable) official formula that avoids mention of the word emperor or tsar. More than government or tsar, he represents a generalized and abstract Nemesis finally overtaking a society that has been trivialized into nothingness, its members shown as deceptive masks pursuing illusory goals. It is a society without the cement of affection, kindness, or loyalty. Gogol's apocalypse—his vision of disaster—is not directed toward some external agency. His world is doomed by its own fragmented and insubstantial nature.

"Doom," "apocalypse" are strong words, and we may ask whether comedy can bear their weight. A classic definition of comedy [in Aristotle's *Poetics*] reads as follows: "As for Comedy, it is . . . an imitation of men worse than the average: worse, however, not as regards any and every sort of fault, but only as regards one particular kind, the Ridiculous, which is a species of the Ugly. The Ridiculous may be defined as a mistake or deformity not productive of pain or harm to others.'' The genius of Aristotle's definition is that it is purely formal: it refrains from prescribing a subject for comedy, so that anything may be comical—hypocrisy, pretension, death, slipping on a banana peel, the apocalypse.

The key phrase is ''not productive of pain or harm to others.'' Comic actions cannot have serious consequences for the observer. The potential for seriousness must be present—the agents make ''mistakes'' or possess ''deformities'' of character that may lead to disasters like those of tragedy. We are concerned for their fate, but at some point in the course of the action the grounds of our concern are removed. Pity and terror and other painful emotions are as much part of comedy as of tragedy; in comedy, however, they are provoked only to be shown as baseless. The agent must resemble us in some ways—otherwise he would be monstrous, not ridiculous. Nevertheless, his error or deformity is so gross as to make him worse than we are. The pity of tragedy is for undeserved misfortune; its terror, for the fate of one like ourselves. In comedy misfortune is shown as deserved; the terror we feel as unwarranted, even if only in retrospect, because the agent is too unlike ourselves. The pity and terror of tragedy are lived through until they resolve in purgation; pity and terror in comedy, since they are shown to be baseless, resolve in a ''relaxation of concern.'' Unburdened of pity and dread, we laugh. To cite a popular example: Sancho Panza hangs over the edge of a shallow ditch mistaking it for a precipice. In order to laugh we cannot be indifferent to Sancho's fate, for the indifferent do not react in any way. We must have the capacity for a sympathetic apprehension of his terror, and, in addition, the normative knowledge that precipices are indeed dangerous. Perceiving his error, we are released from our anxiety and are free to laugh. The more Sancho writhes in pain, the funnier it gets.

What then is the status of a comic apocalypse? At the end of *The Government Inspector* the world collapses before our eyes and we smile: ''What are you laughing at? Laugh at yourselves!'' the mayor cries out at us even as everything goes to pieces. The terrors of ultimate disaster remain real for the characters. Their terror is communicated to us, but as the grounds of our concern are removed it dissolves into laughter. The double vision characteristic of comedy comes into play: we witness the heralding of the arrival of the true inspector who, in Gogol's description, is ''to destroy them all, obliterate them completely, wipe them from the face of the earth,'' while we are simultaneously made aware that their catastrophe is as trivial as their lives. What after all has actually happened? A bumbling and foolish mayor has lost his chance to become a bumbling and foolish general; a vain and feather-brained coquette will not realize her ambition to move to the capital; a crowd of corrupt officals may finally receive the punishment they so richly deserve. Both the terror and the laughter are extreme. Like much great comedy *The Government Inspector* veers perilously close to the opposite of comedy, achieving a complexity denied to lesser and more timid talents. It is no great achievement to make comedy out of a slip on a banana peel—it is a supreme achievement to take us to the edge of the abyss and make us laugh. Gogol's comic genius pushes to a point where comic triviality threatens to shade into a void of meaninglessness, which is a prelude to apocalyptic terror. But his apocalypse also loses substance before the force of his

comedy. His characters are ultimately too ridiculous for us to take even their disaster seriously. To borrow Kant's famous formula for explaining laughter, our terror is ''a strained expectation'' reduced suddenly to ''nothing.''

We do not, however, laugh at nothing. ''Nothing'' and ''Nothingness'' are valid metaphors for what we experience, but there must be objective facts to compel our reactions. We laugh at something, at distinctively human ''mistakes'' and ''deformities'': vanity, arrogance, misplaced ambition, self-serving rationalizations, plain silliness. Comedy is necessarily rooted in the vagaries of actual human life. Without the presence of the recognizably human there would be no concern, and hence no cause for laughter. Remorselessly Gogol has reduced his characters to absurdity, and yet they survive his onslaught to convey a mirror image, however crooked, of the human condition. As such his apocalypse takes on the aspect of an admonition. It was Bergson who pointed out that the human mind cannot conceive of ''Nothing,'' that it will always see something, even if only a black spot. In moral life ''negation aims at someone. . . . It is is of a pedagogical and social nature. It sets straight or rather warns. . . . Thus the ''nothings'' of *The Government Inspector* are convertible into imperatives of ''No'' or ''Don't.'' ''Don't live like this,'' the play tells us; say ''No'' to illusory ambition, false vanity, envy and enmity, or else catastrophe will ensue. Though the 1846 **''Dénouement . . .''** pointed us to the apocalyptic character of the play, we must conclude that the 1836 **''Leaving the Theater . . .''** was closer to the mark after all, and comedy is incorrigibly social, ''illuminating'' the ways of the world, and implying positive values through its negative images. If comedy derives from human error and ugliness, we could never recognize these without a knowledge of the true and the beautiful. We laugh at what is because we sense what ought to be, and it is of what ought to be that *The Government Inspector,* like all significant comedy, would remind us. The disaster may be final for the characters but it cannot be so for us, for that would be painful, not pleasurable, and laughter is a pleasant thing. Also Gogol tells us that in laughing we reach ''reconciliation''—tolerance and forgiveness born of acceptance of our flawed human natures. (pp. 146-49)

Milton Ehre, ''Laughing through the Apocalypse: The Comic Structure of Gogol's 'Government Inspector','' in The Russian Review, *Vol. 39, No. 2, April, 1980, pp. 137-49.*

NICK WORRALL   (essay date 1982)

[*In this interpretation of* The Inspector General, *Worrall examines language, characters, dramatic technique, and principal themes.*]

Gogol's reputation as a world dramatist rests almost entirely on *The Government Inspector,* a play which, it is generally acknowledged, is very difficult to translate adequately and is, therefore, only known in, at best, unsatisfactory translations. It is, therefore, worth noting the variations in the kinds of language which the characters are given in the original—for example, the limited cunning and portentousness of the mayor's speech combined with a terrific command of expletive; the postmaster's naïveté and slow-wittedness which are part of his phraseology; Anna Andreyevna's mannered preciosity mixed with vulgar colloquialism. None before Gogol, and few since, have managed to weld colloquial Russian into such a uniquely expressive and essentially dramatic medium, possessing the power and resourcefulness of verse.

The beginnings of Gogol's plays are always significant. This comedy begins with a figure of Authority surrounded by its satellite representatives of Enlightenment, Health, Justice and Charity. The play also begins with a characteristic set of repetitions. The word *revizor* is repeated four times in the first four lines and the word is associated with something unknown, 'incognito', and secret. The mayor then goes on to talk about a dream. The world of dream is especially significant for Gogol as it stands opposed to the surface world of calculation, time, money, cause and effect. Even someone like the mayor still possesses the power to dream and, through it, to penetrate to another kind of reality even though, in doing so, that reality begins to take on overtones of the comic grotesque. Nevertheless, the dream stands for something significant. The key terms of the account of the dream are 'intuition', 'night', 'blackness' and 'rats'. Superficially comic, it alerts our attention to a deeper level of nightmare with connotations of finality, corpses, nothingness. Then follows an interesting stage direction as the mayor 'mutters in a low voice as he runs through the letter'. Much depends on the way this is treated in performance but there is a strong suggestion that Gogol intends it to sound like a reading from a holy text, muttered in church, with the significant sections emphasized: 'to inform you' (repeated) 'the whole province . . . especially our district'. Another interesting stage direction follows: 'He raises his finger aloft significantly.' Again, depending on performance, there is a clear indication that this is both a naturalistic gesture and, in another key, is also the finger of judgement raised slowly over the heads of those present which can descend 'Shast!', just like that, as he says later when the doors burst open to admit Bobchinski and Dobchinski, but also, through them, the spectre of Judgement. The key words and phrases which follow seem clearly related to final judgement and death. The talk is of 'sins'. He can 'arrive at any time'—'incognito'. These, it would seem, are the parameters of the play—this life seen in relation to the absolute fact of death and judgement. If this is the case, then the pattern of the play is perfectly formed. It begins with the finger raised and ends with the finger brought down, crushingly, on the quick and the dead.

Another part of the pattern is also present in this opening. The 'truth' is received in the form of the written word and is accepted as 'biblical' truth (Chmykhov's letter). It is also dissolved through the written word (Khlestakov's letter). The play is testament to the extraordinary power which the written word possesses. It travels to the ends of the earth (by post). Words, when written down, have almost magical powers: 'Ah well, if you've got a letter—there won't be war with the Turks'. Therefore, the *quality* of the written word is important. Chmykhov in his letter, the correspondents whose secrets the postmaster shares, Tryapichkin, even Khlestakov, partake of its power and its magic but only succeed in distorting and perverting its essence. The Bible is the word incarnate, the intermediary between this world and the next, with the priest a kind of spiritual postmaster. But instead of a 'visionary' we have a 'spier' in the figure of Ivan Kuzmich Shpyokin.

Gogol presents us with yet another version of the division of labour. Health is the province of Gibner (*gibnut'* = to perish). Education is the province of Khlopov (*khlopat'* = to slam or slap). 'Caritas' is the province of Zemlyanika. Justice is the province of Lyapkin-Tyapkin. 'Language' also seems to be the province of Gibner, as the mayor suggests when he asks that a sign be placed above each patient's bed on which something should be written in Latin, or some such language: 'That's your department', he says, addressing the doctor. It is interesting that, in the early versions of the play, Gibner could at least speak. Here he, the linguist, can only utter inarticulate sounds. It is not just a joke at the expense of Germans who cannot speak Russian. The Healer is called Christian, but his patients are dying in droves. (They 'get well like flies'.) It is the doctor who should be in charge of what the mayor describes as 'internal arrangements'—that area which, in the letter from Chmykhov, is said to contain the 'litttle sins'. The words which Gogol carefully chooses establish a spiritual dimension to the world which is unfolding and also point to the significance of the doctor, whose virtual nonexistence becomes a spiritual vacuum at the centre of the play. They also point to a total lack of a spiritual dimension within the inhabitants of the drama as a whole. There is not a man 'without sin', says the mayor and accuses the judge of never going to church, whereas he, the mayor, is 'firm in my faith'; this invokes a typically Gogolian irony of 'going to church every Sunday'—an act of meaningless ritual, habit and superstition.

Education—the world of the great teachers, which includes Christ, as well as Plato and Socrates—has evolved (seemingly via the judge's explanation of the Creation) to produce a group of grotesques who are only capable of pulling faces. The mayor's description of their activities suggests that the words they use have become a dead letter, meaningless. They mug, grimace, smooth their beards from under their cravats and, in a marvellous parody of bygone heroism, imitate the actions of Alexander the Great by smashing school furniture. As the mayor remarks prophetically, 'the devil knows what will become of it'.

His warning about what might flow from that 'damned incognito' sounds like a roll-call at the Last Judgement as each is called before some higher authority before being consigned to the flames: 'And who is the judge?—Lyapkin-Tyapkin—Bring forth Lyapkin-Tyapkin! . . .' and so on. The devil is already potentially present, unnoticed, amidst the general disorder in the judicial offices, or in the squalor of the Charitable Institution, in the ignorance and disarray of the classroom. He has entered the Postal Department through the half-opened flap of a letter. He may be a petty devil, but the evils which flow from his admission grow to mammoth proportions. The implication is that the smaller involves the greater, not only in the abstract terms of good and evil, but also in the social pattern in which this town is connected to the larger unit of St Petersburg. It is the evil which emanates from 'the internal condition', social and personal, which knows no boundaries.

Gogol appears to imply that the admission of evil carries retribution with it. Once the hunting whip has been allowed into the office to a place on top of the cupboard of official papers, this cannot just be tidied away temporarily and then put back again once there has been an inspection. The whip carries retribution with it. Gogol describes it as an *okhotny arapnik*, literally 'a hunting whip', but he means it to stand for Khlestakov (the whipper). He is the retributive hunting *arapnik*, already peeping out of the files and half-opened letters ready to give the perpetrators of folly a sound swingeing which cannot be forgotten as soon as he leaves.

The arrival of Bobchinski and Dobchinski introduces another theme in the play, one which connects internal and external worlds and which relates to the health of the individual and the health of society—that of food. The world of *The Government Inspector* consists of the grossly over-fed and the starving. Gogol refers in his character delineations at the beginning of the play to the 'potbellies' of Bobchinski and Dobchinski. The

Actors Garin and Raikh as Khlestakov and Anna Andreevna in Meyerhold's production of The Inspector General. *From* Meyerhold: The Director, *by Konstantin Rudnitsky. Ardis, 1981. Reprinted by permission of Ardis Publishers.*

latter has a delicate stomach and needs to eat salmon. All the town officials are well-fed and the mayor's dream of St Petersburg embroiders a fantasy of even rarer delicacies. Khlestakov is starving and indulges in the fantasies of the hungry—soup from Paris and a 700-rouble melon. Osip is also starving and, as is clear, usually has to make do with his master's leavings. His fantasy of St Petersburg life also includes food. The play is full of references to food and drink and over-indulgence, so that virtually all the town officials become figures in a mediaeval panorama depicting gluttony. The one exception is Luka Lukich, whose nerves have caused him to waste away. The stomach, *zheludka*, becomes a centre of well-being. Dobchinski's 'disorder' is seen to derive from over-eating. This is paralleled by a form of mental disorder in Bobchinski, derived from an overactive, because starved, imagination which mistakes impoverished clerks for dignitaries and which hungers for the imaginative food of other worlds, but can only peer through cracks in doors (as in the scene at the inn) a metaphorical equivalent of peeking under letter flaps. In his wish that Khlestakov remind the Tsar of his existence, Bobchinski connects us with the themes of hunger and, especially, neglect. In an Act 4 stage direction added by Gogol to the final version of the play, the hands of petitioners wielding their paper complaints and seeking redress of grievances, are seen through a window. This is then succeeded by a vision of universal poverty, violence, starvation and neglect as the rear doors open to reveal a figure 'in a frieze greatcoat with an unshaved chin, a swollen lip and a bandaged cheek'. To which Gogol added: 'Behind him is seen a vista of others'.

Khlestakov connects the internal and external worlds in arriving from outside. He is, so to speak, consumed by the town and gives rise to internal disorder. Fear begins to take over from the moment Bobchinski and Dobchinski have told of their encounter at the inn in Act 1. The mayor begins to echo Bobchinski's mistake of taking one thing for another. First of all he instructs the orderly to tell everyone to 'grab a street', when he means 'a broom'. The judge has already said that the chaos in the judicial department is such that truth cannot be distinguished from falsehood. This symptomatic casualness is shown to have wider and far-reaching consequences, once again of a retributive nature. The mayor's *lapsus linguae* is followed by the famous moment of the hatbox, donned in mistake for a hat, which was retained from the first version of the play and which most commentators describe as part of a tendency on Gogol's part to rely for comic effect on elements of vaudeville. The same is said of the collapsing door at the inn. Nothing could be further from the truth. The mayor's mistaking the hatbox for the hat is a metaphorical demonstration of his tendency, under the influence of fear, to be unable to distinguish with his customary certainty between what is true and what is false. The 'vaudeville' stunt anticipates the confrontation with Khlestakov and justifies, psychologically, his acceptance of this 'hatbox' of a clerk for the 'hat' of a government inspector, despite all appearances to the contrary. 'The box is a box. The devil take it', says the mayor, when we have just seen him take it for something else.

'Go and look through a crack and find out everything', shrieks Anna Andreyevna to the serving girl, Avdotya. 'In two hours' time we shall know everything', says her daughter. This is an extraordinary world in which the secret of the universe seems available to those who diligently peer under letter flaps, through a crack in the door, or through the keyhole, or for whom minutes and hours are ample time for ultimate revelation. Bobchinski peers round a door at the inn and glimpses a meeting between two 'christian mortals', in the mayor's words. What is Khlestakov frightened of at first? It is the turning of the door-handle, indicated in a stage direction. He is terrified of the door which opens into himself, into his own emptiness. 'I'm a . . . I'm . . . I'm . . .' he stutters inarticulately as he searches for self-definition. The mayor is more confident of his own inner identity, which he controls by being two people at once. He believes he can shuttle between the two versions of himself, the inner private person and the outer public person, and still retain control of truth and illusion. Instead, the opposite happens. Appearance and reality grow further and further apart, as do the two sides of his nature.

At the end of the scene between Khlestakov and the mayor, there is another of those strange moments in this extraordinary play when, as Dobchinski goes to open the door:

> . . . it tears itself off its hinges and Bobchinski, who has been listening from the other side, flies on to the stage together with it ['her' in Russian, that is, the door]. Everyone lets out a shout.

It is very like the final dumb scene, which is prefaced by a simultaneous exhalation of breath from everyone on stage in response to the shock, but here the action continues. What *has* happened? This is no vaudeville stunt. While the door has fallen off its hinges because of Bobchinski's weight against it, at the same time some external force has entered the play. It is so powerful it resembles a gigantic blast which not only tears the door off its hinges but lifts Bobchinski up bodily and hurls him, and the door he has been making love to, physically on to the stage. The only sign that anything out of the ordinary has happened is a 'small bruise—just above the nose', and the conventional cure is one of Christian Ivanovich's plasters. But, just as if what has been admitted through the crack in the door has struck everyone a massive blow on the head, everything which follows takes place in a daze of confusion which the 'Healer' is powerless to minister to. The devil himself has entered the play and blinded everyone. His mark is there, on the floor, 'spread out, like the devil knows what', as the mayor remarks to the contrite Bobchinski, indicating the place of his 'fall' and the seemingly indelible stain of its sprawled, and spreading, image. It is from this dark room, under the stairs, that the devil himself emerges like a shadow presence accompanying all the characters and, like a shadow, is gigantic in proportion to the conventional size of the human figures.

An hour has passed between Acts 1 and 3 but, during the scene at the inn, time has stopped and people are frozen in an eternal moment, which anticipates the final tableau. Anna Andreyevna and Marya Antonovna have remained, seemingly immobile, at the window through which we are treated to a vision glimpsed on two levels—of a deserted street and of a dead world: '. . . there's not a soul about; as if everyone's dead'. The only sign of life is Dobchinski. Or *is* it Dobchinski? It is also a little man in a frock coat, the shape of the contemporary devil—

two things at the same time. 'Not very tall . . . in a frock coat . . . who is it?'

A note announces the 'government inspector's' arrival. It also pronounces judgement on the utter banality of a world where the mercy of God is conflated with pickled cucumbers and half a portion of caviare for 1 rouble 25 kopecks. Anna and Marya exit, and the sound of the rubbish they are talking wafts on from the wings. It is given physical embodiment in the rubbish which Misha sweeps on from off-stage, a manifestation of verbal trash in a world in which rubbish as a fact of existence, piled behind fences, overrunning the streets, begins to assume Beckettian proportions.

In his drunken speech, Khlestakov provides us with another vision of life—composed this time of an undifferentiated mass of insect-like creatures, buzzing and scratching, kept in thrall by a power which is itself experienced as a fact of nature, like the 'earthquake' produced by Khlestakov's presence among them. In their turn, the townspeople tremble before Khlestakov as before the might of nature itself. He, in his turn, is carried away on a self-abandoning tempest of rhetoric, striking fear and terror into the hearts of his auditors. It is both comic and terrifying. Th devil has become, like Brecht's vision of an ambitious greengrocer in *Arturo Ui*, a little man with a moustache. 'It is terrifying, simply terrifying', says Artemi Filipovich, 'but I don't know why.' 'Oh, isn't he nice! What a dear little nose he's got. He's so sweet. . .' chorus Anna Andreyevna and Marya Antonovna. The significance of noses in Gogol's work does not need labouring.

The money in the judge's hand during the bribe scene is burning like fire. 'Oh God, I'm under the hand of judgement and the cart has come to take me away', he declares. People believe money can do anything. They can purchase their innocence, but their exemption from judgement. Everything can become a transaction. One by one, the automatons, with their hands down the seams of their trousers in military fashion, file past and offer their financial sacrifice on the altar of officialdom to appease the Gods of Authority. Khlestakov can humiliate them, degrade them, insult them, flatter them—it makes no difference. Someone, like Artemi Filipovich, will seek the opportunity to turn the situation to his own advantage and betray his colleagues. He is the one with inheritors. 'What are your children called?' asks Khlestakov, and the vision of endless repetitions of little versions of Artemi Filipovich unfurls: 'Nikolai, Ivan, Elizaveta, Marya and Perepetuya' (and perpetua and perpetua and perpetua . . .). It is a vision of despair and Khlestakov finds it amusing—something for Tryapichkin to scribble about in the papers. And yet this is 'living', as Bobchinski wants the Tsar to note.

The attempted seduction of Marya Antonovna is in a different key. Something in her has not quite been destroyed. She feels insulted and humiliated and says so, if rather stupidly. The mother has long since crossed the divide between innocence and experience. What is a little potential incest with a son-in-law after all? As she declares, with devastating ambiguity when Khlestakov is on his knees before her: 'Get up, get up, the *pol* [floor/sex] here isn't clean'.

The 'phantasmagorical' figure of Khlestakov, like the personified image of deception, takes himself off in his troika, 'God knows whither'. This was how Gogol described him in the "Advance Notice To Actors." This description has led to a tendency to see Khlestakov as something of a positive force, serving to reveal the town to itself, then taking off into the purer elements of air and space. Certainly he is going 'out there', but his armaments in his battle with the elements are money, sugar loaves, a silver tray and a bit of rope. His only protection is a cover and some straw as he submits to being packed into the troika like an egg in transit, fragile, and likely to be smashed by the first real bump. But he sits there, we imagine, like a dog in straw, or a pig in muck, as the coachman urges on his semi-ethereal steeds.

From one pig in muck Gogol turns to others, as the mayor and his wife contemplate wallowing in the swill of the Petersburg good life. The world is metamorphosing before our eyes into the one which the mayor subsequently sees, when enlightened, as composed of 'pigs' snouts'. The menagerie arrives to congratulate this forerunner of Napolean Pig on his success. They give their blessing. At this juncture, with the departure of Khlestakov, the fog in which everyone has been groping is suddenly dispelled. It is signalled by the mayor's sneezing, twice. We are returned to the beginning of the play with the repetitions of *revizor*, prefixed, now by the negative *nye*, as the postmaster (prompted he suggests, by some 'devilish' power) leads us out of that maze through the reading of the unsealed letter.

The mayor, in a frenzy of passion, offers to do violence to his other self by threatening that self with his fist and grinding it under his heel. The process is cyclical and retributively self-destructive while embracing us all. 'What are you laughing at? You're laughing at yourselves.' The mayor makes the point that shadow and substance are inseparable. The final, alienated action is to look for scapegoats. These are physically objectified in the 'doubleness' of Dobchinski and Bobchinski, as the rest of the characters seek to avenge themselves on the false duality they have created and of which they are victims.

At this point, the emissary of Judgement appears and announces that the final reckoning, in the shape of the real government inspector, awaits them . . . at the very same inn which harboured Khlestakov! In this world there is judgement, of a sort, but no salvation. God, like the devil, is necessarily short in stature and dressed in a frock coat. (pp. 91-102)

> *Nick Worrall, " 'The Government Inspector'," in his* Nikolai Gogol and Ivan Turgenev, *1982. Reprint by Grove Press, Inc., 1983, pp. 81-115.*

ADDITIONAL BIBLIOGRAPHY

Coleman, Arthur P. "Humorous Dialogue" and "Humorous Types." In his *Humor in the Russian Comedy from Catherine to Gogol*, pp. 50-8, pp. 59-88. 1925. Reprint. New York: AMS Press, 1966.
    Examines comic dialogue and characters in *The Inspector General*, relating the play to Russian comic tradition.

Ehre, Milton. Introduction to *The Theater of Nikolay Gogol: Plays and Selected Writings*, by Nikolai Gogol, edited by Milton Ehre, translated by Milton Ehre and Fruma Gottschalk, pp. ix-xxvi. Chicago: University of Chicago Press, 1980.
    Discusses Gogol's career as a dramatist and the place of his works in the Russian theatre.

Erlich, Victor. "The Importance of Being a Comedy Writer." In his *Gogol*, pp. 98-111. New Haven: Yale University Press, 1969.
    Outlines the plot of *The Inspector General*, its most salient features, and its initial critical reception.

Fanger, Donald. "Confronting a Public, I." In his *The Creation of Nikolai Gogol*, pp. 125-42. Cambridge: Harvard University Press, Belknap Press, 1979.
    Considers various social, psychological, and aesthetic features of *The Inspector General*.

Finch, Chauncey E. "Classical Influence on N. V. Gogol." *The Classical Journal* XLVIII, No. 8 (May 1953): 291-96.
    Suggests that Aristophanes influenced *The Inspector General*.

Gorelik, Mordecai. "The Tsar Laughed." In *Theatre and Drama in the Making*, Vol. 2, edited by John Gassner and Ralph G. Allen, pp. 743-52. Boston: Houghton Mifflin Co., 1964.
    An eyewitness account of Vsevolod Meyerhold's production of *The Inspector General*, which is considered one of the most important theatrical productions of the twentieth century.

Ivanov, Vyacheslav. "Gogol's *Inspector General* and the Comedy of Aristophanes." In *Gogol from the Twentieth Century: Eleven Essays*, edited and translated by Robert A. Maguire, pp. 200-14. Princeton: Princeton University Press, 1974.
    Analyzes elements common to *The Inspector General* and classical Greek comedy, offering suggestions for a production of Gogol's play.

Keshokov, Alim. "Laughter That Evokes the People's Wrath." *Soviet Literature* 4, No. 433 (1984): 198-200.
    Discusses an Ethiopian production of *The Inspector General*, noting the popular appeal of Gogol's social and moral satire in post-revolutionary Ethiopia.

Kott, Jan. "The Eating of *The Government Inspector*," translated by Joanna Clark. *Theatre Quarterly* V, No. 17 (1975): 21-9.
    Examines the obsession with food in *The Inspector General* and considers it as a prototypical element of "tragic farce," a dramatic genre in which absurdity, reality, comedy, and nightmare are freely intermingled.

Lavrin, Janko. "Gogol the Playwright." In his *Nikolai Gogol (1809-1852): A Centenary Survey*, pp. 78-94. London: Sylvan Press, 1951.
    Surveys plot, theme, and technique in *The Inspector General*.

Magarshack, David. "The Mature Artist." In his *Gogol: A Life*, pp. 113-49. New York: Grove Press, 1957.
    Reviews critical reaction to early performances of *The Inspector General*, the devastating effect of that reaction on Gogol, and Gogol's own views of the play as discerned from subsequent published writings.

Peace, Richard. "Theatre." In his *The Enigma of Gogol: An Examination of the Writings of N. V. Gogol and Their Place in the Russian Literary Tradition*, pp. 151-205. Cambridge: Cambridge University Press, 1981.
    A detailed examination of *The Inspector General*, including an analysis of the play's characters, themes, comedy, structure, and technical devices.

Rowe, William Woodin. "Plays." In his *Through Gogol's Looking Glass: Reverse Vision, False Focus, and Precarious Logic*, pp. 135-54. New York: New York University Press, 1976.
    Examines reality and illusion in *The Inspector General*, the typically Gogolian reversals and negations, and the associations between Khlestakov and the devil.

Varneke, B. V. "Gogol." In his *History of the Russian Theatre: Seventeenth through Nineteenth Century*, edited by Belle Martin, translated by Boris Brasol, pp. 298-316. New York: Macmillan Co., 1951.
    Notes similarities between *The Inspector General* and works by other European dramatists, offers a brief critical assessment of the play, and discusses its critical reception and stage history.

Worrall, Nick. "Meyerhold Directs Gogol's *Government Inspector*." *Theatre Quarterly* II, No. 7 (July-September 1972): 75-95.
    Attempts to "reconstruct" from firsthand sources Vsevolod Meyerhold's production of *The Inspector General*.

Thomas Chandler Haliburton

1796-1865

Canadian humorist, essayist, short story writer, and editor.

Haliburton was a pioneer in the development of Canadian and American humorous literature. He is best known for his creation of the character Sam Slick, a glib, irreverent braggart and shrewd peddler from New England. Haliburton is also remembered for his strong political views, which he expressed in his stories about Sam Slick as well as in lesser-known works—his miscellaneous fictional sketches and letters about Nova Scotian and New England life and his political and historical writings. Today, critics chiefly praise Haliburton for his creative rendering of dialects and satirical descriptions of various social classes.

Born in Windsor, Nova Scotia, Haliburton studied at nearby King's College. He married Louisa Neville in 1816 during a trip to England and then returned to Nova Scotia to complete the law studies he had begun under the tutelage of his father, a provincial judge. In 1826, after practicing law for several years, Haliburton became a Tory member of the provincial parliament and, upon his father's death in 1829, was appointed to serve out his term on the local Court of Common Pleas. Haliburton was named in 1841 to the Supreme Court of Nova Scotia. He retired from this position in 1856 and shortly afterwards moved to England, where he married his second wife, Sarah Williams. He also won election to the House of Commons, retaining his seat for a number of years. Haliburton died at Isleworth at the age of sixty-nine.

Throughout his legal career, Haliburton produced a variety of works that fall into four categories: historical and political writings, edited anthologies, miscellaneous fictional sketches and letters, and sketches featuring the Yankee character Sam Slick. Most commentators believe Haliburton began his literary career with *A General Description of Nova Scotia*, although his authorship of the history has never been confirmed. Both this work and Haliburton's *An Historical and Statistical Account of Nova Scotia* present the province's history, its natural resources, and its economic potential for prospective settlers. In his political treatises, *The Bubbles of Canada, A Reply to the Report of the Earl of Durham*, and *Rule and Misrule of the English in America*, Haliburton expressed his conservative views concerning Canada's prospective form of government, insisting that a constitutional democracy based on the American system would not be in the best interests of either Canada or Great Britain. In addition, Haliburton's interest in the influence of frontier humor on literature led him to collect and edit the works of other writers for two anthologies: *Traits of American Humor* and *The Americans at Home*. Haliburton also wrote miscellaneous fictional sketches and letters in which he commented humorously on social and political themes. In these pieces, collected in *The Letter-Bag of the Great Western, The Old Judge,* and *The Season-Ticket*, Haliburton's characters give their opinions on nations, social and political institutions, and their acquaintances and neighbors; their pithy comments are worded in the dialects for which Haliburton has become noted.

Haliburton's historical and political writings, edited anthologies, and miscellaneous fictional sketches and letters never

The Granger Collection, New York

attained the popularity or critical attention enjoyed by the Sam Slick stories. These sketches, collected in the three series of *The Clockmaker*, the two series of *The Attaché, Sam Slick's Wise Saws and Modern Instances*, and *Nature and Human Nature*, represent Haliburton's attempts to combine his conservative philosophy with humorous storytelling. Called the author's "mouthpiece" by critics, Sam provided Haliburton with a colorful means to effect a didactic purpose. That avowed purpose was to prod his fellow Nova Scotians into improving their work habits in order to compete with what the author believed to be the more vigorous and efficient Americans. In the first two series of *The Clockmaker*, the Yankee Sam Slick travels to Nova Scotia. There he meets a Squire, who travels with him, recording Slick's adventures on the road and his comments on such issues as women's rights and the political situation of the Canadian provinces. The third series is set in England, where Sam's negative comments about the country are countered by the Squire and another American, the Reverend Hopewell. In the two series of *The Attaché*, Sam holds a post at the American Legation in England. He returns to Nova Scotia in *Sam Slick's Wise Saws and Modern Instances* to examine the state of the province's fishing industry for the president of the United States. In *Nature and Human Nature*, the last work in which Haliburton described the Yankee's experiences, Sam continues his investigations for the president and expounds on the condition of humankind, the state of female education, and the superiority of Americans over the English. Throughout these stories, Haliburton expressed his distrust of American democracy and advocated the loyalist view that the Canadian provinces needed strong ties with the British government.

The enduring interest of the Sam Slick sketches is due, in part, to their presentation of Haliburton's political philosophy. But more importantly, by creating the character of the Yankee clock peddler, Haliburton became one of the originators of a brand of humor that is based on frontier life. This humor often takes the form of blunt observations on the American and British systems of government, delivered in Sam's characteristically caustic language. Sam Slick is considered a master of "soft sawder," his term for language meant to manipulate others, and his skills as a trader and speaker allow him to convince customers that they not only desire but need what he has to sell. Though some commentators have faulted as caricature his representations of the speech patterns of his Yankee peddler, Haliburton has been credited with popularizing many colorful and descriptive phrases and words, including "hot foot" for hurrying, "gumption" for courage, and "jawbreakers" for multisyllabic words. Through his use of language, many critics agree, Haliburton had a substantial influence on the genre of humorous writing.

Critics have generally focused on Haliburton's sketches about Sam Slick, though some consider his historical and political writings interesting artifacts of one man's concern for his native country, fascination with his adopted country, and ambivalence toward his American neighbors. Contemporary reception of Haliburton's first two series of *The Clockmaker* was favorable, but the sketches that followed were significantly less popular: reviewers claimed that they were repetitious and that Haliburton had exhausted his material. According to most commentators, *The Attaché* and his subsequent works mark the beginning of the decline in Haliburton's creative powers. Today, while virtually unread by the general public, his work receives attention from critics who discuss both its political message and comic elements. By creating the Sam Slick sketches, Haliburton earned a place as an important figure in the history of humorous literature.

(See also *Dictionary of Literary Biography*, Vol. 11: *American Humorists, 1800-1950*)

PRINCIPAL WORKS

A General Description of Nova Scotia   (history)   1823
An Historical and Statistical Account of Nova Scotia
   (history)   1829
*The Clockmaker; or, The Sayings and Doings of Samuel
   Slick, of Slickville, first series*   (sketches)   1836
*The Clockmaker; or, The Sayings and Doings of Samuel
   Slick, of Slickville, second series*   (sketches)   1838
The Bubbles of Canada   (treatise)   1839
A Reply to the Report of the Earl of Durham   (treatise)
   1839
*The Clockmaker; or, The Sayings and Doings of Samuel
   Slick, of Slickville, third series*   (sketches)   1840
The Letter-Bag of the Great Western; or, Life in a Steamer
   (fictional letters)   1840
The Attaché; or, Sam Slick in England, first series
   (sketches)   1843

The Attaché; or, Sam Slick in England, second series
   (sketches)   1844
The Old Judge; or, Life in a Colony   (sketches)   1849
Rule and Misrule of the English in America   (treatise)
   1851
*Sam Slick's Wise Saws and Modern Instances; or, What He
   Said, Did, or Invented*   (sketches)   1853
Nature and Human Nature   (sketches)   1855
The Season-Ticket   (sketches)   1860
Selections from Sam Slick   (sketches)   1923
The Sam Slick Anthology   (sketches)   1969

[C. W. UPHAM]   (essay date 1830)

[*In the following excerpt from a review of Haliburton's* An Historical and Statistical Account of Nova Scotia, *Upham commends the work.*]

Mr. Haliburton, the author of these volumes, we understand, is a citizen of Annapolis in Nova-Scotia, a young lawyer of respectability, and a member of the House of Assembly. He has given us a history and description of his native province, which not only do great credit to himself, and to Nova-Scotia, but will safely bear a comparison with any of the works of a similar kind, that have appeared in the United States. (p. 121)

Mr Haliburton has added much to the value of his work, by prefixing to it a large and well executed map of Nova-Scotia, by inserting several plates, representing the aspect and outlines of places of interest, and by some very useful and instructive statistical tables. Among the latter is one giving a view of the religious opinions of the people of Nova-Scotia, as they were ascertained by means of a census. Among the principal evils of a colonial condition, is the want of a stirring spirit of enterprise in the mass of the people, and the degradation of the civil and professional pursuits, produced by the glare and glitter of an elegant and imposing military life, as it is exhibited in the finely arrayed British regiments, that are quartered in the provincial garrisons.

In closing our remarks upon Mr Haliburton's work, we would . . . recommend it to those who are interested in American history. It is written with clearness, spirit, industrious accuracy, and with great candor and justice. It needs a more copious index, and is perhaps rather deformed, than improved by the chronological table of events from 1763 (where the history terminates) to 1828. It must necessarily be very defective, and, brief as it is, it contains much useless matter. What connexion, for instance, is there between the history of Nova-Scotia, and the fact, that 'Ernest Augustus, Duke of Cumberland, was born June 5, 1771.' Still, notwithstanding these slight blemishes, the ***Historical and Statistical Account of Nova-Scotia*** is a valuable work, honorable to its author, and worthy of the thanks of his native province. . . . (p. 134)

> [*C. W. Upham*], "*Haliburton's History of Nova-Scotia,*" *in* The North American Review, *n.s. Vol. XLI, January, 1830, pp. 121-35.*

[GEORGE CROLY]   (essay date 1837)

[*Croly praises Haliburton's creation of the character Sam Slick as well as the humor in the first series of* The Clockmaker.]

We have always had a great respect for our brethren of the United States, in a certain way. We regarded them, for instance, as a remarkable steam-boat people, as remarkably ready at amusing themselves with the simplicity of English brains, and as equally remarkable for thinking themselves the first shots, soldiers, sailors, philosophers, and legislators under the moon. But their glory is about to set, their laurel about to wither, their "stars," twenty-six as they are, are about to be lost in the dawn of a genius, provokingly close to their own frontier, a neighbour, with all the dangerous superiority of wit, sharpened by the gratification of local rivalry;—even an Englishman, writing in Nova Scotia the happiest of all burlesques, with the best of all intentions, at once to raise an imperishable, but not ill-tempered laugh at the Yankees, and to excite the languor of his Nova Scotian friends—to tell Jonathan in perfect good-humour that the most professional of all sneerers may be made the subject of the most acute of all ridicule—and to teach the people of that vast and capable colony, Nova Scotia, that they have something worth struggling for—something to desire, and a multitude of things to mend. Such a volley coming from Nova Scotia on the flank of their clever, and rather self-satisfied friends, the New England States, must have astonished them as much as the Spartans were astonished at the visit of a *Theban* invasion, or all Greece when it saw Pindar shooting up like a meteor from *Boeotia*.

The volley is given from the masked battery of the ***Clockmaker, or Sayings and Doings of Samuel Slick of Slickville.***

To let our readers a little into the character of the hero, we should mention that in America the clockmaker is professionally, what the pedlar, the blue beadsman, or the travelling tinker of England was a hundred years ago, a very important personage among the old farmers and their old wives, the carriers of London news, the tellers of old stories, and the general circulators of all sorts of the smaller trades among the remote and quiet villages, where neither a stage-coach was seen, nor a Sunday paper dreamt of. But the clockmaker of the "States" exhibits the improvement of the age. He is of a higher grade, yet with nearly the same profession. His business is undoubtedly to sell his wooden clocks; but his practice is to be the general conduit of all opinions going at the time, and thus exhibiting all the peculiarities of the native character in their most prominent point of view, to serve, as circumstances may determine, for the portrait or the caricature of the Yankee. The stories told in America of the dexterity of the clockmaker tribe in taking in purchasers, in getting off their wares, and in general object of hoodwinking the vigilance of mankind, are numberless, and some of them capital. But Mr Slick's talents must, for the present, stand in place of our memories, and we must suffer the world to make acquaintance with the greatest original existing on its surface. (p. 673)

> [*George Croly*], *"The World We Live In, No. XIII,"*
> in Blackwood's Edinburgh Magazine, *Vol. XLII, No.*
> *CCLXX, November, 1837, pp. 673-92.*

THE SPECTATOR   (essay date 1839)

[*This critic reviews Haliburton's* The Bubbles of Canada, *calling it the work of a "furious partisan" who draws heavily from other writers and adds nothing new to the issues he discusses.*]

Having written a clever, satirical, humorous, and sensible work on Nova Scotia, in which colony he seems to have been a resident, the author undertakes [in ***The Bubbles of Canada***] to do something on Canada, where, for aught that appears, he

has never been, and of which he knows nothing beyond what records open to any one can teach. Armed with these and his reputation, he pounces upon Canada as an interesting subject; he steals a titlepage from Head; he concocts a dull party pamphlet in the shape of a volume; and, we conceive, imposes upon his publisher, for Mr. Bentley would never have been so inconsiderate as to print the book, had he been, at starting, fully aware of its nature and character.

These are harsh charges; and we proceed to substantiate them by an analysis of the volume.

The apparent object of the author was to give a history of the peoples, governments, and constitutions of Canada, from its conquest by Wolfe to the present day; in order to inform the British public of the cause of the late outbreak, and thus to indicate the true nature of the remedy to be applied. With such judgment and industry does he set about his task, that out of 330 pages, 130 are mere bodily reprints of state papers; namely,

> 26 pages A despatch of Lord Goderich, pp. 104-130;
> 54 ——A string of Resolutions of the Canadian House of Assembly, pp. 135-189;
> 25 ——A minute of Lord Aberdeen, pp. 193-218;
> 25 ——A *virtual,* if not positively a *verbatim* reprint of a despatch of Lord Glenelg's; but printed without the usual marks of quotation, so as to deceive an incautious reader, pp. 221-246.
>
> ——
> 130

Besides these, the volume (for its parts cannot be called by any literary term implying workmanship) is stuffed with other quotations. Their extent we have not taken the trouble to reckon, but we should conceive full one third, perhaps one half. They consist of extracts, interwoven with the author's text, from addresses of the House of Assembly, speeches and despatches of Governors and Ministers; a quotation from the Abbé Raynal, another from the Duke De la Rochefoucault Liancourt, besides innumerable passages from American and Canadian writers and pamphleteers, and from speeches by English Lords and Commoners. And what is worse than all, they are neither apt nor useful; throwing no *new* and no *true* light upon any point in dispute. "*Facts* and not theories are wanted," says the writer in his introduction: but there is not a single fact in the book which is necessarily the result of personal observation; scarcely one which is not taken from public records or generally accessible documents; whilst it abounds, not in theories, but in the notions of a furious partisan inflated to intoxication by success in a narrow provincial sphere.

The plan of the book was not injudicious, had the writer possessed the requisite qualifications for carrying it into execution. The period treated of is divided into five epochs; the first embracing the time from the conquest of the colony to 1791, when the Constitutional Act was brought into operation; the second the conduct of the House of Assembly (with, at starting, thirty-five French and fifteen British members—the latter subsequently reduced to three,) till 1818, when a Civil List was first demanded; the third closes with 1828, and the appointment of the Parliamentary Committee to inquire into Canadian grievances; 1834 is the limit of the fourth epoch, when another Committee was appointed; the fifth comes down to this "present time of writing."

Throughout so long a period, the only epochs that have a particle of what may be called information, are the first two; and what they contain is of a scant and general nature,—being a brief sketch of the various and conflicting laws of Canada; an account of the seigneurial tenures, with the obstacles they of necessity throw in the way of all improvement; and something like a proof that the true *origin* of the discontent is the rivalry of the races. After admitting . . . what it is the aim of the book to deny, that there were grievances to complain of, and that the Legislative Council was far from immaculate, this author shows, by his account of the earlier proceedings of the House of Assembly, (1791-1818,) that the French Canadians were actuated by a hatred of the British settlers, envying their prosperity, throwing every obstacle in its way that they could, and resisting every change that tended to promote immigration into the country or settlement in their own districts; whilst they pursued their plans of depressing the British interests as much as possible, and absorbing the whole power of the colony, with a systematic cunning for their immediate purpose, but a very profound ignorance of their true interest, and their own strength, measured either against America or Great Britain. This conclusion is of course drawn from the one-sided statement of an enraged partisan, who gives symptoms of suppressing records which might make against him; and the French Canadians could probably tell another tale. But this is now of little consequence. The doom of the Red Indian seems impending over "la nation Canadienne"—they will be *absorbed* by the Britishers or the Americans.

Of literary merit the volume has not a particle, except occasionally a clear, rapid, slashing style; and the first few pages of introduction have a neat and trenchant sarcasm, with an indiscriminateness of attack that reminded one of a reverend satirist, and induced a hope that we were going to enjoy the Letters of a Canadian "Peter Plymley."

> *A review of "The Bubbles of Canada," in* The Spectator, *Vol. 12, No. 551, January 19, 1839, p. 64.*

THE MONTHLY REVIEW, LONDON (essay date 1840)

[*In the following excerpt, the reviewer praises the satire in Haliburton's* The Letter-Bag of the Great Western, *yet contends that the author overworks well-known jokes and, too often, neglects to focus on the absurdities of the characters and their situations.*]

[*The Letter Bag of the Great Western* is another] of Mr. Haliburton's attempts in the guise of a *jeu d' esprit,* to give publicity to his party sentiments, and raise a laugh at the expense of those whose policy he impugns, and of that which he deems ridiculous in national manners, or characteristic of the frailities, follies, and habits of individuals. While admitting that there are many happy satirical hits, not a few home-thrusts, and numerous two-edged jokes, we must say that there is also a vast deal of phrase-mongery, and playing upon words when the joke is either but common-place or not over-delicate, and an offensive prominence of *self:* all which detract from the weight and smartness of the strokes. His wit has more of slang than humour in it,—his sentiments are forced rather than natural. What he represents the "Traveller, before he had travelled," to be, may be very truly said of himself, viz., that there is a want of reality, of acquaintance, of deep insight concerning the characters and things attempted to be pungently set off,—imagination, fireside-writing, and a laboured use made of what he has read, being very frequently apparent, were it merely from the hammering that is practised on single and not very characteristic points. Besides, the deficiency of dramatic power, preventing the author from making the most of his points, and when the plan of the book admits of every variety, is most obvious. He makes the reader much oftener laugh, than to have a clear conception of the peculiarity, or the absurdity meant to be exposed and caricatured; the labour is always fully as manifest as the joke.

The plan of the book is this,—a number of the passengers in the "Great Western,"—twenty-eight of them—of both sexes, and of almost every degree and description, write to their friends characteristic letters, the illustrious "Sam" himself being one of the voyagers and correspondents; and the occasion and contrivance of this fictitious correspondence is intended sometimes to serve the purpose of ridiculing the English, chiefly of the inferior or strongly-marked middle classes,—others have a fling at the *modes* of the vessel and *steaming-it* in general,—and others again have a *shy* at former voyagers, such as *Fanny Kemble,* who have favoured the world with their opinions and sketches of what occurred to them, or of what they saw and felt in crossing the Atlantic and among the Yankees.

Of course a work of this kind admits of no other sort of criticism than that of the most general kind, such as we have already offered, to be illustrated by some specimens: nor can we be more fortunate in our selection, nor more favourable to the author, than by quoting first of all portions of the Dedication to Lord John Russell, the occasion serving to let many things be said in joke than have a serious meaning: as thus,—"I have selected your lordship as my Mecaenas, not on account of your quick perception of the ridiculous, or your powers of humour, but solely on account of the very extensive patronage at your disposal. Your lordship is a colonial minister, and I am a colonial author." The author of **Bubbles from Canada,** and other whimsical works, under the name of Samuel Slick the "Clockmaker," goes on to say that the connexion of the *minister* and *author* is so intimate and so natural, that the latter has not only a claim to the former's protection, but a right to his support; and that the work is inscribed to his Lordship, not for the purpose of paying him a compliment, but that a very substantial compliment may be paid to Mr. "Sam," as in the case of Eastern present-giving. Then comes more fooling, but it is fooling to the purpose, and serious after all; for he cuts smartly at the policy and practice hitherto pursued of showering honours and preferring to offices all but colonists, on notable occasions, such as the Coronation:—

> In your humid climate it never rains but it pours; but in the colonies, as in Egypt, it never rains at all. Even the dew is wanting.—What is the necessary qualification for advancement? Is it talent and industry? Try the paces and bottom of the colonists, my Lord, and you will find they are not wanting. Is it humbug? There are some most accomplished and precious humbugs in all the provinces, men who would do credit to any government, and understand every popular pulsation, and can accelerate or retard its motion at will.

> (pp. 306-08)

Much labour, without force, or manifest satire is bestowed on the **"Journal of an Actress,"** affording a striking proof of the author's inability to fathom character, to reach beyond outside verisimilitude, or to perform the master-work of development by a few happy touches. There is character and fidelity, however, in the following,—

Wrote journal, mended a pair of silk stockings, hemmed a pocket-handkerchief, night-capped, and went to bed—to dream, to idealise, to build aërial castles, to get the hysterics, and to sleep.

Altered my petticoats, added two inches for Boston Puritans, and the Philadelphia Quakers; took off two for the fashionables of New York, three for Baltimore, and made kilts of them for New Orleans.

(pp. 308-09)

The Abolitionist, the Lawyer's Clerk, the Shareholder, the Professor, Moses Levi, the American Citizen, &c., furnish occasion for ample variety of satire, which, however, as already hinted, is often mere word-making or phrase-playing, that becomes dull from overworking, and that is frequently feeble in its nature, or extravagant as a caricature. (p. 312)

A review of "The Letter Bag of the Great Western," in The Monthly Review, *London, Vol. I, No. III, March, 1840, pp. 306-14.*

THE SPECTATOR   (essay date 1840)

[*In reviewing the third series of* The Clockmaker, *the critic maintains that Haliburton has exhausted his material.*]

[**The Clockmaker,** third series] is inferior in interest and attraction to its predecessors, partly from the difficulty of continuing a subject to fulfill the expectations of the reader, but still more from the exhaustion of the proper theme. In the first volume every thing was apt and natural as well as new. Samuel Slick, the travelling Yankee clockmaker, was a proper figure, as the painters say, for the landscape of Nova Scotia; the natives were fitting accessories; the colonial subjects discussed were those which such a person would be most likely to handle, and in a quaint and homely way; whilst the cant words in Slick's mouth, if not possessing inherent wit, had that taking character which makes phrases pass current for a time. When he was carried, as in the second volume, into his own country, and discussed the religion, slavery, and many other matters of the United States, with a passing commentary upon the outbreak in Canada and its future prospects, the scene was enlarged, but its general characteristics were pretty much the same. In the third series, not only are many of the topics less fitted for the discussion of Sam Slick, but they are such as no one greatly cares to hear discussed at all; whilst the slang in which they are conveyed, having no peculiar fitness, looks forced and out of place. Mr. Haliburton has committed the same error as in his **Bubbles of Canada,** and the **Letter-Bag of the Great Western**—traded upon his name. He seems to think that a pointed style and a sarcastic humour, which no doubt enable him to make frequent hits, are a valid substitute for subjects and matter. The partly adventitious reputation he has achieved, owing much of its currency to the cant phrases of "human natur" and "soft sawdur," seems also to have inflated him; and, to use cognate illustrations, "he does not think small beer of himself," nor is above "showing his thought." (p. 1073)

Although the author indicates that this is most likely Mr. Slick's last appearance, there is no doubt that if skillfully managed in England—*his* remarks being confined to such subjects as appertain to him, or treated, when they are above him, in the style becoming such a person, and other characters being introduced for higher themes—the **Clockmaker** in London would

be a telling publication, if Mr. Haliburton has gathered any thing to tell. (p. 1074)

A review of "The Clockmaker—Third Series," in The Spectator, *Vol. 13, No. 645, November 7, 1840, pp. 1073-74.*

THE MONTHLY REVIEW, LONDON   (essay date 1840)

[*This reviewer faults the weakened humor of the third series of* The Clockmaker.]

In the first Series the Clock-maker carried us to Nova Scotia, and discoursed in his Yankee slang and sarcastic manner shrewdly and bitingly concerning a variety of matters, all naturally connected with the country and suitable to man. In the second, taking us to the United States, his native land, he was equally at home, and not less amply supplied with materials which were apt and weighty enough to bear humours and sarcastic discussing, even wordy loaded as is Sam's fashion, without seeming to be overdone. Still, his quaint and funny style began to grow tiresome, for it had more the form of forced point than the reality of wit, and was calculated rather to excite a passing laugh than to leave a permanent impression. After reading any of the volumes, perhaps hardly a single phrase, and certainly not one of the ideas verbosely communicated, abode on the reader's mind, thus shewing that there was little which was strikingly original, or tersely and brilliantly uttered, so as at once to fix the imagination and establish a valuable sentiment or truth. But in this third series [of **The Clock-Maker**], while one is getting still more tired of the droll style and the repetitions of cant Yankeeisms, the subjects are far sought for, and for the most part without obvious substance; the reader all the while still rising in his demand for novelty of matter, and a keener-edged and more laughable use of Slickism.

In spite of all these drawbacks, however, this series abounds with smart and pithy ideas and sayings; the humour is often happily wedded to sound and pungent sense; while both in the droller and more serious passages there is to be found powerful sentiment, although the intervals be for the most part filled up at best with but smart hits, the labour to be smart being too obvious.

The territorial scope which this series takes is still transatlantic, keeping between Halifax, the starting post of the travellers,— that is of Slick and the Squire, who acts the part of chronicler, and holding on till they reach New York, whence they are about to embark, for England, where the author, Mr. Haliburton, will no doubt make the Clock-maker and his companion amusing and instructive mouth pieces. (pp. 497-98)

A review of "The Clock-Maker," in The Monthly Review, *London, Vol. III, No. IV, December, 1840, pp. 497-504.*

THE MONTHLY REVIEW, LONDON   (essay date 1843)

[*In commenting on* The Attaché, *the reviewer welcomes Haliburton's focus on English society.*]

Welcome Yankee wooden-clock maker to our shores, whether as pedlar or diplomatist; for there are lots of things and manners here to exercise the sharpest and most humorous of thy "Sayings and Doings," and good service thou mayest perform for the subjects of Queen Victoria,—and, for that matter too, in behalf of thine own *almighty nation,* were it but in setting up the follies and vanities of the Britishers as a warning beacon to the *great republic*. Thy nonsense as well as thy serious talk has a purpose in it; and though thou art not free from prejudice and not particularly distinguished for penetration, yet there is health in thy nature, with pungency in thy strictures which must render these volumes extremely popular, both on account of the laughter which they provoke, and the pointed instruction which they convey!

[In *The Attaché*], Sam comes amongst us in the character of an *attaché* to the American legation at the court of St. James; in the volumes before us proposing to record whatever he has witnessed and heard, having a piquant nature. We may observe, however, that unless he means to extend his observations and sayings he will have left unnoticed very many things amongst us that ought to be exposed and made the object of criticism, and not seldom of laughter or contempt. Slick's satire has healing in it, for it is honestly bestowed, at the same time that it is heartily felt. Let him therefore proceed boldly with what he has begun; although it would be better were he to be less lavish of phraseology, and more abundantly racy in regard to matter and occasion. (p. 475)

Slick, on directing his diplomatic eyes towards our shores, fortifies himself with two friends; the one an old American church minister, whose flock has suddenly deserted him, running off to the Unitarian folds; and squire Poker, a retired provincial barrister. The book is to be considered the writing principally of the lawyer, who however carefully notes down the discourse of the diplomatist and the congregationless pastor, making their talk buttress as far as possible his own ultra-toryism. The political creed of the book may be inferred from the few short sentences which we quote. "He said he could tell a man's politicks by his shirt. A Tory, sir, is a gentleman every inch of him, stock, lock, and barrel; and he puts a clean frill shirt on every day. A Whig, sir, is a gentleman every other inch of him, and he puts an unfrilled one on every other day. A Radical, sir, ain't no gentleman at all, and he only puts one on of a Sunday. But a Chartist, sir, is a loafer; he never puts one on till the old one won't hold together no longer, and drops off in pieces."

A shorter and directer test of political principle need not be asked for. The fact is that Sam, even when travelling with his clocks, was never more self-possessed than we find him in his new and diplomatic capacity; although the great variety of situations and scenes with which he was beginning for the first time to form an acquaintanceship might well have discomposed and bewildered him. Yet it is not so; for, if possible, he is more sharply observant, more acutely quaint, more humorously descriptive than on any former occasion. (pp. 476-77)

> *A review of "The Attaché; or, Sam Slick in England," in* The Monthly Review, *London, Vol. II, No. IV, August, 1843, pp. 475-83.*

[C. C. FELTON]   (essay date 1844)

[In the following excerpt from a review of The Attaché, *the critic faults Haliburton's depictions of both American and English characters and his attempts at humor.]*

The author of *The Attaché*, understood to be one of the Nova Scotian judges, has acquired considerable reputation by the humorous sketches he has published under the pseudonym of Sam Slick. These sketches have been widely circulated both in England and America, and have been praised more than they

deserve. They show a perception of the ludicrous, and sometimes a talent for witty description. Mr. Slick is designed by the author to be a representative of the common New England character. The keen pursuit of gain, the eagerness for driving a bargain, the resort to trickery and even downright fraud, which have been charged upon the Yankee, are drawn out at great length in the character of Mr. Samuel Slick, the pedler. That very apocryphal personage, the Yankee pedler, with his clocks and wooden nutmegs, is the most common object of the jeers and jokes of our Southern brethren, whose mythical and highly imaginative notions of the men of the North it seems quite impossible to correct. These myths have been taken up, apparently in good faith, by the provincial judge, and, with a still more poetical coloring, drawn from the gentleman's own lively fancy, presented in the person of Mr. Slick. No doubt, there is some foundation for these representations; something approaching a type, by the gross exaggeration of which these distorted and scarcely recognizable images are produced. The New England trader, pedler, or whatever he may be, is, doubtless, sharp at a bargain, and shrewd to turn his opportunities of gain to excellent account; but not more so than the corresponding classes of men elsewhere. Sam Slick is no proper representative of the Yankees. He is badly conceived; his character is an incongruous mixture of impossible eccentricities. His sayings are sometimes not destitute of wit; but his language is a ridiculous compound of provincial solecisms, extravagant figures, vulgarities drawn from distant sources, which can never meet in an individual, and a still greater variety of vulgar expressions, which are simply and absolutely the coinage of the provincial writer's own brain. On this point we speak with some confidence. We can distinguish the real from the counterfeit Yankee, at the first sound of the voice, and by the turn of a single sentence; and we have no hesitation in declaring, that Sam Slick is not what he pretends to be; that there is no organic life in him; that he is an impostor, an impossibility, a nonentity.

A writer of genius, even if he write from imperfect knowledge, will, as it were, breathe the breath of life into his creations. Sam Slick is an awkward and highly infelicitous attempt to make a character, by heaping together, without discrimination, selection, arrangement, or taste, every vulgarity that a vulgar imagination can conceive, and every knavery that a man blinded by national and political prejudice can charge upon neighbors whom he dislikes. (pp. 211-12)

The author of this work is a Tory of the most violent description. A provincial always exaggerates the opinions, manners, and fashions of the parties at home, to whom he would fain assimilate himself. There is something belittling in his condition, and in the influences to which he is subjected. He has not the lofty consciousness of belonging to a great nation,—of being, among his fellow-subjects, a peer among equals. He has, on the contrary, an uncomfortable sense of inferiority. . . . (pp. 212-13)

It seems almost incredible, that a man of ordinary powers of observation and discernment can gravely repeat the antiquated political absurdities, which this writer appears to have treasured in his very soul, as the quintessence of all political wisdom. This is a striking example of . . . the belittling effects of the colonial system on the intellects of colonists. (p. 214)

But to return to the work before us. The lovers of light literature have read the former books, which record the sayings and doings of Sam Slick, and some have been entertained by what they mistook for wit and humor. At any rate, their circulation has been such as to tempt the writer to work the vein still further. How far the blame of this proceeding is to be laid to the long ears of a "discerning public," or to the suggestions of a partially successful author's vanity, we shall not undertake to say; but thus much is quite certain, that the vein, such as it was, gave out long before the author did; that all the humor, poor as it was, in the conception of Sam Slick's character, was exhausted long before the end of the first week of his official existence as *Attaché* to the American Legation at the court of St. James. In making out the plot of this work, the author was driven to adopt the most improbable absurdities; not simple extravagancies, which genius may clothe with originality, and exalt into brilliant conceptions, by its kindling power; but absurdities unredeemed by ingenuity or novelty, plausibility or wit. The supposition, that a person like Major Jack Downing could have been the intimate friend and adviser of the President of the United States, was an extravagance; yet the originality and truth of the Major's character, the sagacity of his observations, the felicity and idiomatic point of his language, and the argumentative wit of his illustrations, redeemed the improbability of the first conception, and gave a wide and immediate popularity to his letters, almost unexampled in America. The idea of Sam Slick, the *Attaché,* is evidently borrowed from our friend the Major; but the improbable part was taken, and all the wit was left behind. Sam Slick, the *quondam* pedler, is represented as appointed to a place on the most important foreign mission, with every possible vulgarity of thought, speech, and action in full blossom. He appears in England, is invited about in English society, associates with the statesmen and noblemen of that proud monarchy, and communicates to our author the results of his observations. All this is violently improbable. It is, in the first place, impossible for any such person, even in our abused and long-suffering democracy, to receive an appointment like that; and, secondly, if we could get over this impossibility, it would still be impossible for such an individual to obtain any access to the society which he is described as frequenting. Here, then, we have two stubborn impossibilities to start with. But we might pardon even these, if the character of the *Attaché* had been drawn with any truth and liveliness; if his language had been other than coarse and gross, and false to the spirit of the American idioms. But nothing can equal the falsehood and vulgarity of the book, even after we have got over the outrageous extravagance of the main circumstances of the plot, except its incredible dulness. A writer of genius would certainly have the means, in the rich contrasts between the various phases of English life, and between English life as a whole and American life, to present a series of pictures at once amusing and instructive, even though the framework of the story were absurdity itself; and, in some passages, this author has shown feeble glimpses of a power to appreciate the capabilities of the subject. In some parts of Mr. Slick's description of what it is the author's pleasure to make him call a "juicy day," we see faint intimations of a sense of the humorous bearings of the scene. It is clumsily overwrought, and outrages in nature and probability; but some of the points are seized, and tolerably managed. (pp. 215-16)

Mr. Slick, like Mr. Sam Weller, is very fond of these illustrative stories; in this respect, he doubtless imitates his illustrious predecessor. But we cannot often award him the praise of a successful imitation. His stories are too long, and very often dull. In the eighth chapter, for example, the attempt at an amusing sketch of Mr. Rufus Dodge's visit to Niagara Falls is too strained to excite any other feeling than a sense of weariness, and a sincere regret, that the author should have cudgelled his brains so hard to so little purpose. The absurdity of the whole representation is so great, that we can only say, "*Incredulus odi,*" to every word of it. As to being entertained by such a tasteless and awkward effort to be funny, the coarsest and broadest laugher would read it without the slightest peril to his gravity.

One of the prominent characters in the work is Mr. Hopewell, an aged clergyman of the American Episcopal Church. The author has evidently an affection for this prosy old gentleman, his politics, and his general views of men and things. His lectures to Sam on manners and conversation, on the propriety of using and the impropriety of omitting titles, and his Latin and Greek quotations to that erudite functionary, are truly edifying; and it is surprising, that Sam, having for many years enjoyed the valuable instructions of the reverend gentleman, should have derived so little benefit from them. In truth, the conception of this character is feeble, and we soon weary of it. Mr. Hopewell's doings and sayings, both on board ship, and after his arrival in England, are not those which a man of ordinary sense would do and say, there or anywhere else. We recognize in the delineation the same infirmity of hand, the same inability to draw and sustain a consistent character,—a character that shall act like a human being, with the motives, feelings, and senses of a human being,—which we have noted in the other personages of the story. The scene in the cottage, described in the eleventh chapter, is quite mawkish and silly; and nearly as much so is the twelfth chapter, entitled, "Stealing the Hearts of the People," wherein the clergyman is represented as preaching in an English church against all the reforms of the times, and portraying the blessings enjoyed by the poor in that happy country, especially the blessings derived from an Established Church, with such irresistible force and energy, that he convinced William Hodgins, a sturdy radical, of the sin of the Chartist agitation, saved him from ruin, and made his wife a happy woman. It requires but the simplest statement, to show the extravagant absurdity of this representation. It needed the exaggerated loyalty, the high wrought Toryism of a provincial, to venture to make it, in the face of the existing evils in the condition of the English poor, the oppressiveness of the English Established Church, and its utter inadequacy to the religious or secular instruction of the body of the people. No Englishman of any party would have risked his character for sanity, by gravely putting forth such unreal mockeries, in this nineteenth century. (pp. 220-22)

> [C. C. Felton], "'The Attaché; or, Sam Slick in England'," in The North American Review, *Vol. LVIII, No. 122, January, 1844, pp. 211-27.*

THE SPECTATOR   (essay date 1844)

[*In the following excerpt from a negative review of the second series of* The Attaché, *the critic emphasizes its similarities to Haliburton's earlier works.*]

This second series of the Clockmaker's adventures in England is varied by a change in the externals of Sam Slick; who, entranced with his reception in high life, turns dandy. But little is produced by the metamorphosis beyond an occasional display of weakness. The arrival of his father, Colonel Slick—a hero of Bunker's Hill, full of Yankee prejudices, but without Sam's shrewdness or knowledge of the world—is a better contrivance. His coming horrifies his son, on account of the ridicule that will be produced in the fashionable circles, and torments him for a long time, because he cannot make out what the Colonel's business is; till at last it comes out that he has been persuaded by a swindler that he is the heir to a title in England, and, despite of Republicanism, he has come over to pursue the claim. . . .

Beyond the peculiarities of the Colonel this series does not greatly differ from the previous volumes of the *Attaché or Sam Slick in England*. The matter is not very deep, the topics very novel, or the views very striking. Mr. Slick and the Squire, when out walking, meet a ladies boarding-school; which gives rise to a diatribe by Slick upon the evils of these establishments: but his example is run-away matches, which are the exception, not the rule—the real evils are of another character. The party go to Blackwall, to eat white bait; and the sight of Greenwich Hospital enables the minister, Mr. Hopewell, to pass a panegyric upon the British character, the British constitution, and above all upon the Anglican Church Establishment; and this leads to a comparative discussion on the Pulpit and the Press of England and America. "Responsible Government" for Colonies is debated on another occasion; and the old story of the exclusive monopoly of Colonial patronage by Englishmen is powerfully and sensibly argued, with some good because real illustrations. The subject is further pursued in the "The Canadian Exile," a tale of a Loyalist's miseries—not so good, because too extreme. A railway-ride with a person who holds some stock in the American Non-paying States induces a rhapsody against the Ballot and Repudiation; but not the slightest novelty either of view or information is imparted. . . .

The *mannerism* is less, probably, than in the former volumes, because Slick himself occasionally drops it, and the Colonel appears with a difference. But the want of real substance in matter, the opinionated confidence in the writer's own views, with the imperfect knowledge on which he jumps to conclusions, and the mode by which he often makes mere writing in the graver parts, or the "funny way" of Slick, do duty for substantial qualities, is more clearly visible than in the former works, and renders it judicious to have closed the exhibition.

> *A review of "Sam Slick in England, Second Series,"*
> *in* The Spectator, *Vol. 17, No. 854, November 9,*
> *1844, p. 1073.*

THE CHURCH REVIEW   (essay date 1852)

[*In the following excerpt from a review of* Rule and Misrule of the English in America, *the critic censures Haliburton for relying heavily on the works of other historians without giving them due credit and for basing his argument on incomplete factual information.*]

It is the object of Judge Haliburton's new book [*Rule and Misrule of the English in America*] to show that however government on the democratic republican plan may have succeeded in the late English colonies, now the United States of America, it is not adapted to the colony of Canada, and cannot succeed there; and still less in Great Britain or France.

As grounds for this conclusion, he undertakes to establish, by a review of the colonial history of the United States, two propositions; first, that those States were always republican in spirit, and independent in fact for many years after their first plantation, so that the revolution which separated them from the mother country was not a sudden outburst, but a progressive growth, which sprang from seeds planted at the beginning; second, that the existing political system of the United States, instead of dating from the American revolution, dates back to the very commencement of the colonies, being wholly based

upon ideas and institutions familiar to the colonists from the earliest times, or introduced and firmly established long previous to the revolution.

The commencement of the first chapter seems to imply that this is the first attempt at any such generalization. But that is very far from being the case. While the American revolution was yet in progress, the first of Judge Haliburton's two leading ideas, was started by George Chalmers, who had been a lawyer in Maryland under the proprietary government, and who, on being driven away by the declaration of independence, had obtained a clerkship under the Board of Trade. He published at London in 1781 his well known *Political Annals,* a quarto volume, in which the history of the colonies is traced from their settlement to the English revolution of 1689, for the very purpose, among others, of showing their rebellious temper from the beginning. This same idea was followed up and still more exclusively, in another work, containing a summary or abridgment of the *Political Annals,* and carrying down the political history of the colonies to the conquest of Canada. This latter work was partly printed by Chalmers, but suppressed for some unknown reasons, nor was it published till 1845, when it was issued from a Boston press. Both these works, though disfigured by absurd attempts at imitating Gibbon's fashion of telling things by implication instead of directly, and by a grandiloquence little suited to the subject, are yet exceedingly valuable for the mass of extracts which they contain from unpublished papers in the colonial office, from which Chalmers, with great industry and good judgment, has selected such portions as suited his purpose. The *Political Annals* have long been familiar to all students of American history; and our American writers, viewing the charge of early republicanism, and impatience under external control which Chalmers brought in the spirit of accusation, as in fact a high compliment to our ancestors, have not failed to give a full development to that idea.

Nor is the other leading suggestion of this book, that the existing political institutions of America are a natural growth from colonial times without any violent changes or sudden innovations, at all more original. This was in fact a favorite idea of the old Federal Party, more or less distinctly expressed in general terms, by many writers; and very fully brought out in all its particulars, and with many curious and remarkable details, in the first three volumes of Mr. Hildreth's new *History of the United States,* published in 1849. In this part of Judge Haliburton's book, and indeed throughout the whole of it, he is under much greater obligations to Mr. Hildreth's *History* than he has thought it necessary to acknowledge. He has treated it in fact very much as the ruins of the old temples and other public buildings at Rome used to be treated by the modern inhabitants, digging into it without remorse, as if it were a mere quarry, and quietly carrying off and working into his own edifice, stones squared and polished, and columns shaped by an industry not his own. This may be well enough in case of ruins abandoned and deserted; but whether a house which has a living tenant in it, can fairly be treated in this way, is another question. . . . [There are many] passages extracted from Mr. Hildreth's *History,* verbatim, or with very trifling alterations, for which no acknowledgment is made, which is the more remarkable, as the Judge, lawyer-like, does profess to give his authorities, and does several times refer to, and purport to quote from Mr. Hildreth's *History of the United States.* . . . Mr. Hildreth writes, "they voted a present to the king, of cranberries," "special good samp," and "codfish." Judge Haliburton copies thus—"a present to the king of some cranberries, a *special good samp.,* as they were designated, and also some codfish;''—seeming to take ''samp'' as a contraction of sample; and not knowing that it was only another Indian name for the same dish known further South as hominy.... [Judge Haliburton has appropriated] entire paragraphs, or series of paragraphs, to the extent sometimes of a page or more. Considering this very free appropriation of unacknowledged passages, we are not surprised that by way of introduction to one of the few paragraphs admitted to be borrowed, . . . Mr. Hildreth is spoken of ''as decidedly the most able and impartial of American historians.'' The question being to set out a table with borrowed meats, it is but natural that one should help himself to the best, or what he esteems such. But whether this casual compliment, apparently paid rather to serve a purpose of his own in giving additional weight to a particular observation, than out of any feeling of obligation or disposition to acknowledge it, will be, or ought to be, entirely satisfactory to the author, whose labors are thus freely appropriated, does not seem to us quite so clear.

Having thus referred to the sources whence Judge Haliburton has derived his leading ideas, most of his facts, and a large part of his very language, we are obliged to add that his method of stating and maintaining the argument, leaves his readers, such of them as depend upon him for their information, entirely in the dark, as to whether or not there is any force in it, or grounds for the conclusion which he seeks to draw. Everybody who knows any thing of America, knows that Massachusetts and the New England States are not the only States in the Union. It was not by those States alone that the revolution was sustained, and the Federal Constitution formed, nor have they alone enjoyed the benefits of self-government. Everybody who knows any thing of American history, knows that the Union included, from the beginning, two other groups of States, in many respects exceedingly different both from New England and from each other. The group of Middle States, (New York, New Jersey, Pennsylvania, and Delaware,) differed from the New England States in several particulars, to which, in his argument, Judge Haliburton ascribes great importance. The inhabitants were not of ''common origin, speaking the same language.'' They included Dutch, Germans in very considerable numbers, Scotch and Scotch-Irish, immigrants from England, and immigrants from New England, very discordant materials, and by no means free from prejudices and antipathies of race and class. There was a much less degree of that social equality, which prevailed in New England, and to which so much importance is ascribed in the argument. There were no free schools, and a large part of the population was entirely uneducated. There was a large class of indented servants, or those who had been so; there was a body of wealthy landed proprietors, forming a natural aristocracy; then, as to religion, another point to which a great political importance is ascribed, there was no public religious establishment of any sort, or but a very partial one; and the people were divided among a multitude of sects, not without the jealousies, hostilities and rivalries naturally growing out of such a state of things. Thus the mutual rivalry of the Episcopalians and Presbyterians produced a strong effect on the politics of New York.

The group of Southern States, (Maryland, Virginia, North Carolina, South Carolina, and Georgia,) presented a very different aspect. Here there was still less of social equality or means of general education. Nearly half the population, in some districts more than half, were slaves. There was a large body of indented servants or their descendants. In the back settlements of the Carolinas, there was as great a mixture of races as in Pennsylvania—a large proportion of them recent immigrants from Europe. In their religious ideas and establishments, these Southern States differed greatly from those further North. (pp. 523-27)

Now our author has simplified the argument,—but at the same time totally destroyed the force of it,—by leaving the middle and Southern States entirely out of the account. He has confined himself to New England, and even to Massachusetts. From the great length at which he goes into the Puritan church system, and the stress which he lays upon it in the argument, one would suppose him to think that none but Puritans could ever make republicans, and that only dissenters and fanatics are capable of self-government.

But here arises this pregnant question, which every thoughtful reader will be apt to put, and to which the book before us furnishes no answer whatever: How happened it then that the Cavaliers and Churchmen of Virginia were just as forward and as active in the work of the revolution, as the Puritans of New England? Patrick Henry was a Churchman, and Samuel Adams a son and representative of the old Puritans; but both were as decided in politics as in their religious opinions. Who more steady and unyielding in most trying times than John Jay? The religious body that adhered as a body, as well as by its individual members to the side of the mother country, was not the Church of England, but the society of Quakers. The wild Scotch Highlanders and the German population proved far more adhesive than those of English descent. Indeed, the native born Britons, resident in the colonies, furnished a supply of active and conspicuous leaders, very large in proportion to their whole number. It is plain then that Judge Haliburton's collection of facts is not broad enough to sustain the argument founded upon it. He shows, or attempts to show, how and why republicanism sprang up and grew in New England, and why it succeeds there; and if New England were the whole of the United States; or if Puritanism, education by common schools, equality of ranks, and all the peculiarities which he dwells on in his book, had been, or were now, common to all the rest of the States, then his argument would be entitled to weight. But vulnerable and defective as it stands, it will, we very much fear, have but little influence with those inclined to republican innovations; and just as little with the British ministry and parliament, to induce them, which seems to be one chief object of it, abandon the system of ''responsible government'' lately introduced into the principal British colonies, very much as it appears to Judge Haliburton's disgust.

Did occasion call for it, we think we could make an historical argument quite equal, at least, to any thing brought forward in this book, tending to show that this very system of ''responsible government'' is not only the strongest possible political assimilation between the social system of the colonies and that of the mother country, but is altogether the most promising method yet suggested of continuing with comfort and satisfaction to both parties their political connection; a connection which, for various reasons, we desire to see continued for at least a considerable period; not only out of our friendly regard for both the parties more immediately interested, but also out of special motives of our own, as citizens of the United States. (pp. 528-29)

But while our author will fail, we fear, to make much impression either upon advocates for republicanism, whether in Europe or America, or upon the British government, we are somewhat apprehensive, lest in the order of his zeal, he may have got himself personally into a predicament, or if not personally, at least in his capacity as an author. He has fairly thrown down the glove to our New England brethren of Puritan descent and sympathies, attacking their fathers as to their doings both in Church and State, with very little of moderation. Now, if the Judge did not know it already, at least his shrewd old friend, Sam Slick, might have whispered in his ear, that the Yankees of the present day, like their Puritan progenitors, are men with whom one may not safely get into a quarrel, whether to be decided by blows or words, without good preparation; and even then he must be pretty adroit at fencing who shall escape wholly unscathed. We think the Judge himself refers to an uncomfortable practice early introduced into Massachusetts of "whipping and cropping the ears of such as slandered the government and churches, or otherwise gave a bad report of the country." Now we do not suppose that the Judge's back or his bodily ears are in any great danger, even should he be caught, like another Morton of Merry Mount, walking the streets of Boston, or even attempting, like that eminent worthy, to set up a maypole in that vicinity,—an exploit to which the Judge refers with gusto,—though, should he undertake to carry out the precedent by "broaching a cask of wine and a hogshead of ale," and should the Maine temperance law be enacted in the mean time in Massachusetts, which is not improbable, we cannot tell how that attempt might turn out. But we do look, every day, with fear and trembling, expecting to see our unfortunate friend stuck fast, nailed up by the ears in some critical New England pillory. And we must privately tell him, without going into particulars here, lest it might give an advantage to the enemy, that in the excess of his zeal against dissent and disloyalty, and out of a very unnecessary and superfluous effort to gild the refined gold and to paint the lily of Puritanism, he has fallen into some unfortunate mistakes and misrepresentations as to matters of fact, and quite unwarranted inferences as to motives, which one who knows how to make so good a use of Mr. Hildreth's "able and impartial history," ought to have avoided; and which we are afraid may, first or last, expose their author to some pretty severe critical castigation. That painful duty falls not to us. It would indeed be a great work of supererogation, not to say of impertinence, to interfere on behalf of those so abundantly able to defend themselves and their own. . . . Yet we cannot quit this topic without suggesting to the Judge the safety and expediency, as well as the justice, of giving even the —— his due. (pp. 530-31)

> *"Haliburton and Hildreth, and the 'North American Review'," in* The Church Review, *Vol. IV, No. 4, January, 1852, pp. 523-48.*

[THOMAS CHANDLER HALIBURTON] (essay date 1854)

[*In this excerpt from his preface to an English edition of* Sam Slick's Wise Saws and Modern Instances, *Haliburton explains his purpose in writing these sketches.*]

The original design in writing the sketches known as the *Sayings and Doings of the Clock-maker,* which has never since been lost sight of, was to awaken Nova Scotians to the vast resources and capabilities of their native land, to stimulate their energy and enterprise, to strengthen the bond of union between the colonies and the parent State, and by occasional reference to the institutions and governments of other countries, to induce them to form a just estimate and place a proper value on their own. That I have succeeded in effecting much good for those for whom they were designed, I have had the most gratifying proofs. To effect my object, it was necessary to appeal to the mass of the people; I have, therefore, written in a colloquial style, and called in the aid of a humorous itinerant American (Mr Slick), to propound, in his own peculiar way, the moral lessons I was desirous of enforcing. That this humour and these worldly maxims should have been so favourably received and so much approved, on this side of the Atlantic (notwithstanding their local application), is indeed to me a source of very great pleasure, and calls for my most warm and grateful acknowledgements. (p. iv)

> [*Thomas Chandler Haliburton*], *in a preface to his* Sam Slick's Wise Saws and Modern Instances; or, What He Said, Did, or Invented, *second edition, Hurst and Blackett, Publishers, 1854, pp. iii-iv.*

THE ATHENAEUM (essay date 1855)

[*In the following excerpt from a review of* Nature and Human Nature, *the critic asserts that Haliburton's talent remains strong.*]

How far either Yankee or Nova-Scotian nature—how far that wider humanity which is the same "from China to Peru"—are represented in [*Nature and Human Nature*], we are not in a humour to determine dogmatically. The Author of 'Sam Slick' has established a manner—a dialect—a form of sentiment, as well as a form of sarcasm—which are as consistent in their interdependence and separately as complete as the links of a perfectly fashioned chain. We are not in the very best case for maintaining that an artist's pictures are truthful, because, having become used to his hand, we thoroughly enjoy and relish them. Turner-worshippers, we know, after rhapsodizing on the scriptural, poetical, geological, and meteorological fidelity to nature of their idol, will talk of the painter's "scarlet grass," in substantiation of his exactness and in justification of their own implicit faith,—but Slick-sympathy does not carry us so far. We suspect there may be in his case exaggeration, as well as vitality. We could hint, even, that there is something like Sterne's faded sentimentality and falseness in the Clockmaker's pathetics. In short, we do not swear by our old friend, though we enjoy his company—accepting him for what he is and *as* he is—with unabated relish. It is fair, however, to let the world hear how cleverly he characterizes and defends himself as something different from the person we have just indicated.—

> "I am just a nateral man. There is a time for all things, and a way to do 'em too. If I have to freeze down solid to a thing, why then, ice is the word. If there is a thaw, then fun and snow-ballin' is the ticket. I listen to a preacher, and try to be the better for his argufying, if he has any sense, and will let me; and I listen to the violin, and dance to it, if it's in tune, and played right. I like my pastime, and one day in seven is all the Lord asks. Evangelical people say he wants the other six. Let them state day and date, and book and page for that, for I won't take their word for it. So I won't dance of a Sunday; but show me a pretty gall, and give me good music, and see if I don't dance any other day. I am not a droll man, dear, but I say what I think, and do what I please, as long as I know I ain't saying or doing wrong. And if that ain't poetry, it's truth, that's all."

These two new volumes, like their predecessors, are a rattling, random miscellany of proverbs, sharp sayings, stories and hard hits, without plan or moral. . . .

There are touches in [*Nature and Human Nature*] that Hood himself might have signed. (p. 286)

A capital chapter tells how the Clockmaker, in his salad days, got into trouble by saving the life of a child who was drowning,—but it is rather long and a little broad in its humour. Chapter the second in volume the second—entitled "Female Colleges"—may be recommended as another excellent article,—not merely in right of its educational caricatures, and because it satirizes that indelicate hyper-delicacy which Mrs. Trollope and Capt. Marryat denounced as a plant of diseased growth in America,—but because our author keeps the balance true, and after having shown us a silly, sentimental, shallow pretender, exhibits her satirist as smaller than the victim of his satire, when he pains her by a practical joke, which, though play to himself, is death to the poor woman. (pp. 286-87)

[The] above . . . will suffice to show the reader that this chip of the old block is handsomely cut—also, that the old block is not so worn down as to be excused further chipping. The Author of 'Sam Slick' has the air in this book of taking leave of his public. So did Mrs. Siddons when she thought she had enough of the stage, but she took leave some dozen times,—and the public never had enough of Mrs. Siddons so long as she was able to appear. We will not, then, say "good bye" to Master Samuel. Let his faults be ever so patent, let his humour be ever so largely mixed up with stage-alloy, there are few sinners or sayers in the book-market worthier of gathering a crowd to observe and to listen than 'Sam Slick.' (p. 287)

A review of "Nature and Human Nature," in The Athenaeum, No. 1428, March 10, 1855, pp. 286-87.

THE ATHENAEUM (essay date 1865)

[*In this eulogy to Haliburton, the critic praises his story-telling ability, observation of character, and originality.*]

"Sam Slick," the name so much more familiar to us than the more formal, but real, Mr. Justice Haliburton, died on Sunday, at Gordon House, Isleworth. As a writer, he may be said to have amused his peculiar world during one generation of men. It is thirty years since *The Clock-maker; or, the Sayings and Doings of Sam Slick of Slickville,* appeared in a collected form, and founded the reputation of its author. At that time he was thirty-eight years of age, and, it may be added, at the height of his powers both of imagination and of memory. We say "of memory," for many of his stories were of older manufacture, but admirably re-cast, exquisitely moulded, and set on high for the world to admire. (p. 309)

As may be supposed from his 'Sam Slick' series of books, he was an excellent story-teller; but he was as pleased to listen to a good story as he was himself skilled in the art of telling one. His observation of national and personal character was so acute, correct and humorous, that in the delineation of them he rose to the rank of an artist who had no second in his peculiar vocation, nor, indeed, any competitor deserving of the name. He was the thoroughly original, and all imitations of an originality that defied being imitated, were execrable. In 'Sam Slick' he portrayed national character beyond the Atlantic. In his *Letter-bag of the Great Western,* he gave life-like portraits of individuals, their manners, style, feelings and expressions. Perhaps the most faultless of these papers is the **"Journal of an Actress,"** in which the cleverness and audacity, refinement and coarseness, modesty and bounce, pretty humility and prettier arrogance of Miss Fanny Kemble were touched off in a style which all the world could identify, and the lady herself not turn her lip at, except to smile at the skill with which her literary merits and affectations were imitated so as to be like

reality. Few writers have showered more innocent mirth on our generation than the late Mr. Haliburton. (pp. 309-10)

"Mr. Haliburton," in The Athenaeum, No. 1975, September 2, 1865, pp. 309-10.

F. BLAKE CROFTON (essay date 1892)

[*In the following excerpt from his survey of Haliburton's works, Crofton outlines the elements of humor through which Haliburton attempted to highlight the faults of his countrymen. The critic attributes Haliburton's fame to his sketches about Sam Slick.*]

The author of Sam Slick has suffered some loss in fair appreciation by the very success of his best known book. The avidity with which readers of *The Clockmaker* adopted the central figure in that satirical work as a type of the Yankee people, and their enjoyment of his keen sayings, caused them to overlook the prime intention of his creator. . . . (p. 355)

This past neglect of Haliburton in Nova Scotia was probably due in part to the distasteful truths he told its inhabitants, and in part to the fact that he left his native province to reside abroad. But the lack of due appreciation for the judge among his countrymen savored strongly of ingratitude; for he has advertised Nova Scotia widely and permanently. . . . [Haliburton] has done more to make [Acadia] known than any writer except Longfellow, who was indeed largely indebted to Haliburton's [*An Historical and Statistical Account of Nova Scotia*] for his material when composing *Evangeline*. Besides writing the history of his country, Haliburton described her scenery, the features of her climate, and her natural resources faithfully and fully. He sketched her social life of half a century ago in *The Old Judge* and other works. Above all, he drew the attention of his countrymen to their remediable weaknesses. He found among them too much self-satisfaction and too much politics, and too little enterprise and industry. Too many of them were waiting inertly for political panaceas, or wasting their energy in clamoring for them. He strove, shrewdly, to cure these defects by the wholesome example and the caustic comments of a very live Yankee. As a politician, he thought it expedient to tell his countrymen unpalatable truths through the lips of a foreigner. For the clockmaker's satiric utterances—so often grotesquely and perhaps purposely exaggerated—his constituents could not hold him responsible. "A satirist," says Sam Slick, in *Nature and Human Nature*, speaking of his previously published sayings and doings,—"a satirist, like an Irishman, finds it convenient sometimes to shoot from behind a shelter."

That the judge's vicarious sarcasms bore some good fruit in Nova Scotia there can be little doubt. But they had not then, and they have not yet, produced the signal results which Sam Slick complacently notes in *Nature and Human Nature*. "I have held the mirror up to these fellows," he says, "to see themselves in, and it has scared them so they have shaved slick up and made themselves decent. . . . The blisters I have put on their vanity stung 'em so, they jumped high enough to see the right road, and the way they travel ahead now is a caution to snails."

As a humorist, Haliburton's chief qualifications were a keen appreciation of the ludicrous, an excellent memory for absurdities, the faculty of hitting off quaint and fancy-tickling phrases, and a most lively imagination. All these characteristics are copiously illustrated in the multitudinous yarns which his characters spin upon the smallest provocation. Indeed, it is evident that he often moots a subject merely to introduce an anecdote; and the very slight main plot of each of the four books narrating Mr. Slick's career is little more than a thread to string his tales and talks upon. The same may be said of *The Old Judge* and *The Season Ticket.*

Artemus Ward was not without warrant in terming Haliburton the founder of the American school of humor, for most of its forms and phases are illustrated in the pages of this pioneer humorist. Specimens of affected simplicity, Mark Twain's characteristic, occur in the second chapter of *Nature and Human Nature,* and elsewhere. Undeveloped prototypes of Mrs. Partington may be found in Mrs. Figg, in the female servant in the *Letter Bag,* and in an old woman in *The Season Ticket.*

Several modern jests and jocular phrases were anticipated by Haliburton, if they have not been borrowed from him. In *The Old Judge,* an Indian explains to the governor, who expresses surprise at seeing him drunk so soon again, that it is "all same old drunk." "Fact, I assure you," the pet phrase of the liar in Brass, is often used by a character in *The Old Judge,* and by another in *The Season Ticket.* Mr. Locke (Petroleum V. Nasby) told me that he made a hit in a stump speech by dividing his hearers into "men with clean shirts and Democrats." I wonder whether he had read the definitions quoted by Sam Slick of a Tory ("a gentleman every inch of him, . . . and he puts on a clean shirt every day") and of a Whig ("a gentleman every other inch of him, and he puts on an unfrilled shirt every other day")? Fifteen years before Topsy's famous phrase appeared in *Uncle Tom's Cabin,* a country girl in *The Clockmaker,* being asked where she was brought up, replied: "Why, I guess I was n't brought up at all. *I growed up.*"

The temptation to distort words, which led the judge occasionally to perpetrate a *double-entendre,* also led him into endless punning. How strong this temptation must have been may be gathered from his making a speaker pun while earnestly protesting against the shabby treatment of the loyalists in the little Canadian rebellion of 1837-38, a subject on which Haliburton felt very deeply indeed, and to which he often recurs. "He who quelled the late rebellion amid a shower of balls," he makes a colonist complain, "was knighted. He who assented, amid a shower of eggs, to a bill to indemnify the rebels was created an earl. Now, to pelt a governor-general with eggs is an overt act of treason, for it is an attempt to throw off the *yolk!*" Punning, good, bad, and indifferent, was a feature of his conversation as well as of his anecdotal works.

Haliburton's sarcasm was usually pointed at types and classes, seldom at individuals. He saw an unoccupied field for a satirist at home, and he took possession of it. "The absurd importance attached in this country to trifles," one of his characters observes, "the grandiloquent language of rural politicians, the flimsy veil of patriotism under which selfishness strives to hide, . . . present many objects for ridicule and satire."

Haliburton used dialogue largely in his humorous books, with the definite object of making them popular. "Why is it," says Mr. Slick in *Wise Saws,* "if you read a book to a man, you set him to sleep? Just because it is a book, and the language ain't common. Why is it, if you talk to him, he will sit up all night with you? Just because it's talk, the language of natur'." And written chat, Haliburton thought, was the next best medium to oral chat for holding the attention of all classes. His dialogue, however, is not always consistently suited to his characters, either in matter or in manner. Even the spelling which he uses to represent local mispronunciations is carelessly or capriciously varied.

The fame of Haliburton, as we have intimated, depends largely upon the freaks and tales of his most popular creation, Sam Slick of Slickville. This inconsistent personage is evidently meant to be a typical, wide-awake Yankee. Although not so uniformly representative of New England as Hosea Biglow, in many respects Mr. Slick corresponds to his type. He is full of shifts and dodges. He devises an effective lure to get a passenger on a steamer to leave a comfortable seat, and when the latter reclaims his chair he feigns ignorance of the English language. He has a fast horse in Boston, which will not cross a bridge because it has once fallen through one. He manages to sell it at a high figure,—advertising, with literal truth, that he would not sell it at all if he did not want to leave Boston. When there is a duty of thirty per cent on lead, and no duty on works of art, he makes a large profit by investing in leaden busts of Washington, and melting the Father of his Country after he has passed the custom house. Sam Slick loves to "best" anybody in a "trade,"—particularly when the other party thinks himself knowing. To take in another smart "Down-Easter" is an intense joy to him: he compares it to coaxing a sly fish to take the bait. He wants to turn everything to practical use: at Niagara, he is struck first by the water-power, and secondly by the grandeur of the falls. If he flatters and "soft-sawders" everlastingly, he cringes to no man. If he sometimes abuses his country himself, he never lets others do so with impunity. He is especially hard upon tourists in search of facts to verify their prejudices against America, and he loves to "bam" them by shocking tales of "gouging-schools" and "black stoles,"—garments made of "nigger-hide," and used to punish refractory slaves, who are "etarnally skeered" at being dressed in dead men's skins, and can be heard screeching a mile away. Self-conceited, Mr. Slick is too sublimely so to be conscious of the failing. He boasts, of course, but sometimes with a peculiar object. "Braggin' *saves advertisin',*" he remarks; "it makes people talk and think of you, and incidentally of your wares. I always do it, for, as the Nova Scotia magistrate said, 'what's the use of being a justice, if you can't do yourself justice?'" Mr. Slick is a cyclopædia of slang, and his sayings are widely quoted, to illustrate colloquialisms, all through *Bartlett's Dictionary of Americanisms.*

But in some of his characteristics Sam Slick is far from being a typical New Englander. He satirizes both abolitionists and prohibitionists. He believes that women require "the identical same treatment as horses." He has an extreme contempt for mock modesty or squeamishness, from which New Englanders, in his time, were not supposed to be specially exempt. He repeatedly casts ridicule upon it. He has little appreciation for Puritanism. "Puritans," he observes in *Nature and Human Nature,* "whether in or out of church, make more sinners than they save, by a long chalk. They ain't content with real sin. . . . Their eyes are like the great magnifier at the Polytechnic, that shows you awful monsters in a drop of water, which were never intended for us to see, or Providence would have made our eyes like Lord Rosse's telescope."

To believe that any human being, much less one who starts life under considerable disadvantages, could know all that Mr. Slick says he knows would tax one's credulity overmuch. He is equally at home in the politics of England, Canada, and the United States. He paints, he plays the piano and the bugle, he dances, he is skilled in woodcraft and angling, he rows and paddles neatly, he shoots like Leather-Stocking or Dr. Carver. He can speculate in all lines with equal success. He has a fair smattering of medicine and chemistry. He offers a hawker of patent cement a much better receipt, of his own invention. He has been in almost every country, including Poland, South America, and Persia. In the latter country he has learned the art of stupefying fishes and making them float on the surface. He dyes a drunken hypocrite's face with a dye which he got from Indians in "the great lone land;" and when the hypocrite repents he has a wash ready to efface the stain. "I actilly larned French in a voyage to Calcutta," he says, "and German on my way home." He knows a little Gaelic, too, which he has learned from a pretty girl, on a new and agreeable system.

At Rome, in Juvenal's time, it was the "hungry Greek," in Johnson's London it was the "fasting monsieur," who knew all the sciences; and let it be granted that the typical Jack-of-all-trades in this century and on this continent is the inquisitive and acquisitive Yankee. Yet Sam Slick beats the record of his shifty countrymen. He has been wherever a lively reminiscence can be located, and he is endowed with any art or attainment which comes in handy "to point a moral or adorn a tale," to snub a snob or help a friend. He understands every phase of human nature, male and female, black, white, and red, high and low, rich and poor. He is equally familiar with every social stratum. In *Nature and Human Nature* he minutely describes two picnics. At one the belles are Indian half-breeds; at the other they are fashionable Halifax young ladies. If the ex-clockmaker has obtained the *entrée* into the illogically exclusive society of Halifax, it is the first time that talent, unaided by modish manners or a scarlet uniform, has ever succeeded in doing so. (pp. 355-59)

The mottoes of his *Wise Saws* and *Nature and Human Nature* avow that the author's study was mankind; that his subjects, like Juvenal's, were human joys, griefs, powers, passions, and

Sam Slick greeting a customer.

pursuits. And in spite of the careless inconsistencies in Sam Slick, Haliburton was an apt student and sound judge of character. His knowledge of human nature is displayed in many of his aphorisms, and the sententious remarks, such as the following, which are made by several of his personages: "No man nor woman can be a general favorite and be true." "Nothing improves a man's manners like running an election." "There is a private spring to every one's affections." "A woman has two smiles that an angel might envy: the smile that accepts the lover before words are spoken, and the smile that alights on the first-born baby and assures it of a mother's love."

For a man who began life as a provincial lawyer and politician, Haliburton's horizon was remarkably, almost phenomenally wide. He intuitively recognized the tendencies of the age, noted all the currents of public opinion, and gauged their volume and force with approximate exactness. Indeed, the time may come when his fame as a political and ethical thinker, and forecaster of events and movements, may exceed his fame as a humorist. (p. 360)

F. Blake Crofton, "Thomas Chandler Haliburton," in The Atlantic Monthly, Vol. LXIX, No. CCCCXIII, March, 1892, pp. 355-63.

RAY PALMER BAKER (essay date 1920)

[*In this excerpt from a historical study of the relationship between Canadian, American, and English literature, Baker focuses on the four categories of Haliburton's works: his historical and political treatises, the sketches in the Slick series, his other fiction, and his edited anthologies. In a portion of the essay not included below, Baker details Haliburton's critical and popular reception in Canada, the United States, and England.*]

Haliburton represents more accurately than any other Pre-Confederation writer the main tendencies of Canadian life and literature, tendencies inextricably connected with developments south of the Border, and therefore American even in the narrower sense of the word, yet as undoubtedly English as the people of this Continent were English in thought and speech after the Revolution. It is true that the inhabitants of the United States, influenced by European ideals, have diverged more widely from the New England norm than have their cousins in the Canadas; but the divergence is not so great as commonly supposed. A hundred and fifty years count for little in the life of kindred peoples. The work of Haliburton, therefore, is, in many respects, as much of the United States as of Canada, and as much of Great Britain as of either. (p. 69)

His work, completed sometime before his death, falls into four divisions: historical and political treatises which place him among the pamphleteers; the *Slick* series, in which the satiric tendency of the Loyalist tradition finds supreme expression; miscellaneous fiction, in which the *Slick* methods are further developed; and, finally, compilations to meet the demand for Yankee stories.

In 1829 he began his literary career with the publication, in two volumes, of *An Historical and Statistical Account of Nova Scotia*. . . . Though the narrative, which is carried down to 1763, was reviewed favorably in England and the United States, it follows closely the sources indicated by the writer. With usual complacency Haliburton, who did not discover the papers relating to the Expulsion of the Acadians, remarks "that the particulars of this affair seem to have been carefully concealed." From a few hints he therefore constructs an idyllic description of the Acadians, whose banishment reminds him of the Mantuan shepherd driven from his patrimony by the soldiers of Augustus; but in spite of this sympathetic picture he defends those responsible for the operation, and thus reveals the bias which renders his historical monographs so inconclusive. Regarding the value of the *Account* scholars in Canada are now agreed. Though it represents much conscientious labor, Haliburton was handicapped by his inability to consult the necessary documents. No longer authoritative, it may still be read with profit. Its lucidity shows that the author had acquired a clear, attractive style, and that he was capable of continuous narrative. It shows also that he was impelled by the national curiosity which was manifesting itself in many directions; but it shows little else. Though there is evidence of reading and literary taste, there is nothing to justify the praise which the book has received. Haliburton himself, who was no mean critic, was under no delusion as to its merit. In *The Clockmaker* he refers to it as "Haliburton's *History of Nova Scotia,* which, next to Mr. Josiah Slick's *History of Cattyhunk* in five volumes, is the most important account of unimportant things I have ever seen."

Much less readable are his contributions to the political literature arising from the enunciation of various theories regarding the future of British North America. The first of these controversial pamphlets—for they are such in spirit, if not in bulk—is *The Bubbles of Canada* . . . , a series of letters on colonial relations. Though purporting to be by Sam Slick, who had already made his *début,* it has none of his peculiarities of diction. Nevertheless, it ran through two English editions and later appeared in Philadelphia and Paris. As a reply to the Earl of Durham's *Report,* it attracted wide attention. In it Haliburton maintains, with some show of reason, that the people of the Maritime Provinces, who were happy and contented, should not have their happiness and contentment jeopardized by union with the disaffected French-Canadians; and, with less reason, that the latter had no grievances which were not due to political incapacity. To establish these points he summarizes the acts affecting Lower Canada. Though illuminating, the summary degenerates into mere compilation where it is difficult to find the Swift-like humor and biting sarcasm apparent to Tory critics. Even the clear, slashing, trenchant style praised by his opponents cannot counterbalance his offensive partisanship. Those reviewers who accused the author of trading on his reputation were not entirely unjustified. (pp. 75-7)

Rule and Misrule of the English in America . . . , the last of Haliburton's treatises, cannot be dismissed . . . cavalierly. In spite of the fact that only one edition was issued on each side of the Atlantic, it has acquired a reputation which commands respect. Like *The Bubbles* it is really an argument to prove that responsible government would fail if introduced into Canada. Because a republican system has succeeded in the United States, it does not follow, argues Haliburton, that it will succeed elsewhere. . . . It was unsuited to the ignorance, poverty, and sloth of the *habitants,* and was contrary to the predilections of the English immigrants. Though the outline of colonial history leading to these conclusions is a careful synopsis of the rise of British power in America, the application of the principles involved is of dubious value. By periodicals like the *Naval and Military Gazette* and the extreme Tory reviews Haliburton's thesis was received with enthusiasm. It probably did something to explain the "origin, formation, and progress" of the United States; but it is doubtful if those who read it on the advice of the *Quarterly Review* had any clearer understanding of "the elements of American society." Nevertheless, its reception has given rise to a school of criticism which professes to find it a

"profoundly philosophic and prophetic work." Such an estimate appears to be due to misinformation. No one, it is true, will question Haliburton's theory of political development or his belief that representative systems cannot be acquired and maintained by revolution. Still, the ideas, which were neither new nor profound, can be traced to Burke and other eighteenth century writers with whom he was familiar. To say that he foretold the collapse of the French Republic and the rise of Communism means little more than that he was influenced by conservative opinion. His "thoughtfully reasoned theories of colonial government" fail to account for the growth of liberal institutions in his native land, and recent investigations have shown the fallacies in his view of the Revolution. Those who would have him accepted as a political philosopher tend to obscure his real merits and to detract from his well-deserved fame.

Although the extent of his historical work has given it an exaggerated importance, it is valuable chiefly as an index of the culture to be found in Canada at the beginning of the Victoria Era and as a residuum of the party opinion which Haliburton represented. His *Address on the Present Condition, Resources, and Prospects of British North America,* published at Montreal and London in 1857, and his speech in the House of Commons in 1860, **"The Repeal of the Differential Duties on Foreign and Colonial Wood,"** add nothing to the theories that he had previously advocated. The *fin-de-siècle* reaction against democracy and the recent pessimism in Europe and America regarding the success of popular government have influenced Canadians in their estimation of Haliburton's propaganda. No student of affairs can ignore its effect. Yet, though an historian cannot avoid reference to Haliburton's treatises, he is bound to show that they spring from a limited range of ideas; that they are polemical in tone; that they lack sympathy and moderation; that they are wanting in the facts of history; that their imaginative power is not sufficient to give them rank as literature; and, finally, that they are of interest because they reflect the spirit of a substantial part of the Canadian people at the period when they were written, and because they indicate the temper which made possible the *Slick* series, on which Haliburton's reputation must eventually rest. (pp. 77-9)

The mood of the *Slick* series . . . was general among the people of Acadia. . . . [The] literature of the Loyalists during the Revolution was mainly satirical in tone. The Tories, representing the wealthiest and most aristocratic families of the Thirteen Colonies, looked with scorn on the plebeian instigators of rebellion. Political satire was thus based on class distinctions.

Hatred of gentlemen like Washington who associated themselves with the radical movement was more intense because their championship implied a kind of disloyalty to their caste. This feeling dominated the thirty thousand Loyalists who made their homes in the Maritime Provinces, and colored their literature for the next eight decades. . . . Although [Haliburton's] sketches differ little in aim from the tirades of the party journals, his sense of humor gives them a human quality hitherto lacking in Loyalist prose.

Since the cardinal principle of the Loyalist Tradition was, and is, the maintenance of British connection, the value of its continuance became Haliburton's principal thesis. By reference to the government of the United States he attempts to prove the superiority of English institutions and to induce the colonists to form a just estimate of their own. In every respect his work is typical of his party and of his time: of his party in his scorn of the masses, who reciprocated his detestation; of his time in his endeavor to make known the resources of his native land. Though Haliburton had all the narrowness and complacency which he satirized in his countrymen, he was observant enough to recognize the commercial stagnation due to their insularity and their dependence on the government. Against their lack of initiative he waged unrelenting warfare. . . . [He] never ceased to proclaim the advantages of Nova Scotia. To arouse his countrymen to an appreciation of its possibilities he introduces the Yankee peddler, the despised of despised, to comment on their foibles and to gull them with his wares. The acuteness of his observations shows how much New England has contributed to the Nova Scotian temperament. That *The Clockmaker* has been able to overcome the immediate anger aroused by Sam's animadversions is a sure index of the author's genius. Though they may not have yielded the results to which he laid claim, he would be rejoiced, if he could return to the flesh, to witness the vitality of the imperialistic feeling which he did much to strengthen.

In its advocacy he did not confine himself to the *Slick* series as he had promised in *The Attaché.* The first of his miscellaneous works of fiction appeared in 1840. *The Letter Bag of the Great Western; or Life in a Steamer,* a series of twenty-eight letters by passengers from Bristol to New York on the ship which gives its name to the title, is well adapted to Haliburton's manner. One of the cleverest skits is the "**Journal of an Actess,**" which is written with the gaiety and vivaciousness of a Becky Sharp, and, like *Vanity Fair,* hovers on the border of the mysterious world of diamonds and after-theatre suppers so alluring to the heart of the uninitiated. Equally delightful is Rebecca Fox in her self-revelation entitled "**From One of the Society of Friends to her Kinswoman.**" Her little vanities are all dramatically effective; but even they are marred by the typification which renders most of the personages mediocre. This is especially true when the conversation turns on any of Haliburton's pet theories. The constant interjection of his own opinions detracts from the [merit of the book]. . . . (pp. 83-5)

It was followed in 1849 by *The Old Judge; or Life in a Colony.* . . . The scheme is not original. An English traveller is introduced to Mr. Justice Sanford, a retired judge of the Supreme Court of Judicature; is shown around Halifax, and, with his host, is storm bound at Mount Hope, where they meet Stephen Richardson, whose stories help to pass the time. The tales, which are valuable for their illuminating glimpses of colonial life, abound in brilliant descriptive passages; but the value of Haliburton's material throws into relief his lack of constructive skill and overemphasis of detail. It is unfortunate that a work of merit in its portrayal of early Canadian scenes and customs should suffer from these disadvantages. (p. 85)

It is now necessary to speak of Haliburton's editorial labors. Rightly or wrongly, he considered himself the apostle of American humor. In 1852 he issued his *Traits of American Humor. By Native Authors,* a collection of sketches culled from the work of a dozen writers, chief of whom is James Russell Lowell. The compilation is valuable because it reveals the compiler as a student of American literature. His analysis of the differences among the people of the various sections—differences due to climate and occupation—shows no little acumen. The *Traits* was followed in 1854 by a companion volume, *The Americans at Home; or Byways, Backwoods, and Prairies.* Like its predecessor it was published in the United States, but secured its greatest vogue across the Atlantic. . . . [It] is interesting to note that the reviews of both anthologies recognize Haliburton as the chief agent in the rapprochement

between England and the United States. The dominant note is the fact of kinship. In the Yankee stories reviewers professed to find a reflection of Anglo-Saxon characteristics, customs, and modes of thought. In the lingo of the Atlantic seaboard they traced the ancient forms of the common tongue. (p. 86)

[It] is possible to examine Haliburton's claims to remembrance. Most of his books may be discarded; the political treatises disappear, the miscellaneous fiction is too uneven to be of permanent value. *Slick,* however, remains. The illustrations by Hervieu and Leech helped to establish Uncle Sam in Great Britain. To Canadians the shifty peddler, as the popular etymology of the work *Yankee* indicates, has become the typical New Englander. To thousands who have never read the book he is a creature of flesh and blood. Indeed, his sharpness at driving bargains has had much to do with the latent distrust of the United States. Moreover, the minor characters are occasionally well drawn; the incidents, though monotonous, are full of life. The humor, however, is often due to temporal causes, and is, therefore, transitory in appeal. Nothing changes so rapidly as a nation's idea of what constitutes fun. *Tom Sawyer* and *Huckleberry Finn* no longer tickle the schoolboy. The *Innocents* is being rapidly forgotten. Haliburton likewise is suffering from the sentence of time. Of the *Slick* series *The Clockmaker* alone has sustained its early reputation. And there is reason. Its pictures of manners and customs and its glimpses of road and forest will always arouse the curious. Some of these miniatures—scenes of the Canadian countryside—have never been excelled. Equally attractive are the essay-like paragraphs in which the author turns aside to chat of himself. He knows what he wants to do. He risks the dangers—the hackneyed subjects and the repetitions. "The only attraction they are susceptible of is the novelty of a new dress." If his readers like prolixity, they may have it: artistic damnation is a small price to pay for moral salvation. Yet the lessons, which are trite enough, are gladly forgotten in a day when few people read for edification. Didacticism even in humor is doomed. *The Clockmaker,* by a common trick of fate, is remembered by everything except by that for which it was written. That it has been read for almost a century proves that its virtue is not single. (pp. 92-4)

Ray Palmer Baker, "Thomas Chandler Haliburton and the Loyalist Tradition in the Development of American Humor," in his A History of English-Canadian Literature of the Confederation: Its Relation to the Literature of Great Britain and the United States, *Cambridge, Mass.: Harvard University Press, 1920, pp. 68-97.*

JOHN DANIEL LOGAN   (essay date 1924)

[*In the following excerpt from an assessment of Haliburton as a humorist and of his place in Canadian, English, and American literature, Logan calls the author the "first systematic humorist and satirist of the Anglo-Saxon peoples."*]

During the lifetime of Thomas Chandler Haliburton, both the people and the intellectual leaders in British North America, in the United States, and in England were thinking parochially. Haliburton thought for them in continents. The Anglo-Saxon peoples in the United Kingdom and in the new world knew in their inner hearts that they were all one great family. Haliburton was the first man to discover that, though one family, they lacked the family spirit, and he was the first writer of prominence to attempt to engender in them that spirit. This was his peculiar and unique apostolate. How well he succeeded in creating this family spirit amongst the Anglo-Saxon peoples, is a secondary problem. How he came to conceive of his being called to a peculiar apostolate in the world, and by what methods as a man of letters he attempted to fulfil his mission, is of primary importance.

Haliburton was the first systematic humorist and satirist of the Anglo-Saxon peoples. He was, moreover, a humorist "with a thesis." Several distinctions in literary classification are involved in those dicta. Let it not be objected that Jonathan Swift was the first systematic humorist and satirist of the British peoples. When he wrote, *The Tale of a Tub* . . . , *The Battle of the Books,* and that definitively social and political satire, *Gulliver's Travels* . . . , his thought was wholly on the English people, and as far away as possible from the English colonists in America.

Further, the truth is that only quantitatively was Swift a systematic satirist. That is to say, Swift wrote, *as occasion demanded of him,* certain occasioned *pièces-a-thèse* in satire. He did not consciously set out, from the beginning of his career, to be a satirist: he had the gifts; and when occasion arose, he employed his gifts in irony. Haliburton, on the other hand, consciously launched himself on a literary career as a satiric humorist, having a single and definite purpose. Systematically, through twenty-five years . . . and in eight volumes (*The Clockmaker* and Sam Slick series and his miscellaneous humorous fiction), he kept at his thesis, that the Anglo-Saxon peoples were one in origin, speech, ideals and customs, and should, realizing the unnaturalness of separation, by free and constitutional means, establish a Zollverein of autonomous Anglo-Saxon nations. Haliburton's great purpose as a man of letters was to "correct the vision" of the Anglo-Saxon peoples. Though the immediate reference is only to a section of the Anglo-Saxons, still it may be made inclusive. Says Sam Slick: "I have held the mirror up to these fellows to see themselves in. . . . The blisters I have put on their vanity stung 'em so they jumped high enough to see the right road, and the way they travel ahead now is a caution to snails."

There was, of course, no comic characterization in Swift's satires, whereas Haliburton's humorous works contain a gallery of comic characters, and, as has been truly said, "no type of humour since My Uncle Toby Sterne's *Tristram Shandy* has been so thoroughly worked out as Sam Slick." For the same reason that we have applied to Swift, Sterne cannot be regarded as a systematic humorist in the Haliburton range and method. Dickens, however, definitively addressing the English people in England, aimed to produce, in *The Pickwick Papers,* literature of mere humorous or comic characterization. He is primarily a novelist. A novel implies plot in the development of the narrative and analysis of character. He is a humorist only by virtue of his gallery of comic characters; and his humorous characterization is meant to create sympathy and pathos as well as smiles and laughter. In other words, he is not a satirist; for in all satire there is a distinct aim to cause pain as a remedial measure. The laughter begotten of satire is harsh and malicious, startling and painful, like "the crackling of thorns under a pot." Swift was a satirist; Dickens was a gentle, kindly, sympathetic humorist.

There is a third species: the satiric humorist. Haliburton, as he discloses his genius, art and aim, for instance, in the latest *Clockmaker* series, uses no plot, but keeps his work unified by a single character or "spokesman" and his speeches—Sam Slick of Slickville, "his sayings and doings." Or if anyone insists that Haliburton does employ plot, he should add that

there is no development in the plot; but it is a "mere thread on which to string facts, jests, and opinions." Here it must be observed that the facts and opinions are primary, and are satiric in intent, but that Haliburton put in his jests, as a humorist, both for the sake of the intrinsic fun of them and, chiefly, to "soft sawder" (to use his colloquial metaphor) the satire. His humour, expressed best in aphorisms and epigrams, is, as one of his earliest critics has said, "the sunny side of common-sense," and was designed to relieve the pain of the satiric truth, as the comic episodes in Shakespeare's tragedies relieve the emotional poignancy of the tragic strain.

Haliburton's works in satiric humour were not designed to be literature as such. He was, as we have said, a humorist with a thesis, a propagandist, and this was uppermost in his mind. He did, however, create at least one immortal character and innumerable aphorisms and epigrams which have become part of the stock speech of the English-speaking peoples. But, as a writer, he made the implications of his thought, even when addressing his Nova Scotian compatriots, reach out to all the Anglo-Saxon peoples.

Another distinction belongs to Haliburton, which shall be merely mentioned here. As a systematic humorist and satirist he was the progenitor, not the originator, of the *method* employed by all these mere "funsters" who have on the American continent written humour in dialect. That is to say, as Ray Palmer Baker aptly puts it, Haliburton's works "naturalized" the conversational and dialectical method of humorous narrative and "smart sayings," employed first and best by Sam Slick, though it must be remembered that aphoristic humour and satire in America were originated by Benjamin Franklin.

Haliburton's method of humour in dialect did not become "naturalized" in England, but his humorous and satiric works had greater popular vogue and appreciation in England than in the United States. What was "naturalized" in England was the conception of the Haliburton humour as the typical American method. This "naturalization" of a New England character-type and of a dialectical method of humour and satire, accomplished by the works of Haliburton, both in America and in England, is what was meant to be conveyed by Artemus Ward and others when they asserted that Haliburton is the "father" or "Ferander" of American humour. (pp. 95-101)

The assertion that Haliburton was "the father (or founder) of *American* humour" as well as "the creator of the *American* type in literature," is based on misleading ambiguities. And it is unmistakably misleading to credit Haliburton with being "the *first American* in literature." Nor is it at all true that Sam Slick is "the typical American."

What they who make these distinctions in the case of Haliburton mean to say is: First, Haliburton naturalized a method of humour in dialect which became the method of his successors (Ward, and others, in diction and figures of speech; Mark Twain, and others, in humorous mendacity or exaggeration and in comic characterization). Secondly, Haliburton popularized in both England and Europe this method of humour in the dialect and character of Sam Slick, until they became accepted as peculiarly American, the one as the only original American method of humour, and the other as the typical New Englander, whom the English cartoonists transmuted in caricature into "Uncle Sam." Thirdly, though other native-born United States men of letters had a vogue in England and Europe, Haliburton had produced satiric comedy and comic characterizations which were not only un-English in method and conception, but also so original as to be altogether unlike any other humorous characterization which had appeared in the world. In short, the world popularization of the chief phases of what has become accepted as American humour of thought, speech, and character; this is the great literary achievement of Haliburton as a writer. (pp. 116-17)

Cooper's and Richardson's romances were read by the educated classes in England, and in the United States, so that the English reading public were familiar with the characters of American and Canadian fiction before they ever read a line of Haliburton. . . . The readers of England were familiar enough with the culture and civilization of the United States to know that Cooper's and Haliburton's American characters were class portraits of the typical pioneer New Englander. But assuming that the English cultivated public did not know this, two facts make it impossible that the English people should accept Sam Slick as the typical American.

The first fact is that from 1820 (the year after the publication of Irving's *Sketch-Book*) to 1840 (the year of the publication of the third series of **The Clockmaker**), the English professional classes decided to get a first-hand knowledge of American and British North American civilization and culture. A new discovery of the New World was undertaken. English travellers annually visited the New World, and on returning home published reminiscences of those whom they had met and of what they had seen and heard. (pp. 120-22)

The second fact is that while the uncritical population of the "Down East" States actually believed that there existed amongst them an original character (literary pseudonym, Sam Slick), at the same time the cultivated American, naturally self-conscious, feared that Sam Slick would be accepted by the popular English mind as the typical American, and consequently, resented what really had not happened, namely, the English acceptance of Haliburton's chief character, Sam Slick, as the American national type. There was no possibility that cultivated English men and women would accept the slangy, irreverent, conceited, yet shrewd creature, Sam Slick, as the typical American, any more than the cultivated people of the United States would accept the London Cockney, Sam Weller, as the typical Englishman. And so the early attack of C. C. Felton, in the *North American Review* [see excerpt dated 1844], and the later attack of George William Curtis, in *Harper's Magazine*, on Haliburton, for having burlesqued and caricatured American character, culture, and civilization were really unwarranted. Yet what did happen is precisely *what Haliburton himself had wished to happen*—namely, that the English people and other peoples *would* accept his Sam Slick and his sayings and doings as *typical Americanism*, and as a *reductio ad absurdum* or *refutation of republican and democratic institutions and civilization*.

The truth is that Haliburton did not mean Sam Slick to be a mere character type at all, but an epitome of the characteristics of an essentially experimental and, as he believed, dangerous and self-centred civilization. And so Haliburton made Sam Slick a person of many characteristics, many distinct and contradictory traits, impossible in a single person, that might in a single character personify a *people*, and thus satirize the versatile genius and limitations of Republican Democracy. Sam Slick is, therefore, an absolute creation, and as such was to be the spokesman of Haliburton as a social and political critic of the civilization of all the Anglo-Saxon peoples. But to the people of a monarchical democracy, as the English, Sam Slick was not a social and political critic; he was taken by them to be an absolute creation in comic characterization, and his sayings and doings as a fresh and original species of humour. That such an uncultured and disreputable creature as Sam Slick should appear in the world as the acutest and most sagacious critic of Anglo-Saxon civilizations on both sides of the Atlantic struck the English imagination as richly humorous; and it was in general due to this strictly humorous appreciation of Sam Slick and his sayings and doings that Haliburton's works had unprecedented popularity overseas. Hitherto America had looked to England for its literary entertainment; with the advent of Sam Slick, England, for the first time, looked to America for literary entertainment. Really, it was Haliburton, not English travellers returned home from America, that had made a new discovery of the New World to Europeans.

We get at the root of Haliburton's genius by asking, not where or how he got his conception of Sam Slick as a character; but why he chose an uncultured and disreputable creature to be the critic of the faults and foibles of the people of the Maritime Provinces and the United States. Why did he not choose someone socially and intellectually higher? To be sure, there are amongst Haliburton's characters representatives of genuine Nova Scotian and American culture; the Squire, Reverend Mr. Hopewell, and even a real person, Mr. Everett (who was none other than Edward Everett, president of Harvard and diplomat). Still, these are largely interlocutors and "foils" to the supreme character, Sam Slick, himself *sui generis*.

The satiric mood or temper of the Loyalists in pre-revolutionary days "flowered" for the last time in Haliburton. The Loyalists scorned the masses. Haliburton also scorns the masses; but he rubs in his scorn by using a member of the masses, to be the critic, not only of his equals, but also of his superiors in social and intellectual status. His Border Scots humour tempted him to over-indulge his sense of the ludicrous, with the result that Sam Slick appeared so ridiculously amusing that the people of Nova Scotia and the United States, both the cultured and the uncultured, even when they winced and resented a criticism, forgot the satire in laughter.

This, then, is the essential formula of Haliburton's genius; a subtle satiric perception of social values, tempered and humanized by an irrepressible sense of the ludicrous, of plebian humour. And this is his real and greatest achievement as an original satiric humorist; the invention or absolute creation of a socially and intellectually inferior character, who is not a single type but many characters, to be the critic of his social and intellectual superiors, and the mouthpiece of wisdom to them. Never before had there appeared in literature such fresh, novel, piquant and exuberant humour, which was aimed at types and classes, and seldom at individuals, and which, as an early Victorian critic has aptly said, combines the shrewd, caustic qualities of the Scots humour with the hearty, mellow spirit of the English humour, "the sunny side of common-sense."

Turning now to the concrete appreciation of Haliburton, we shall best obtain such an appreciation of his powers and qualities as a satirist, humorist, aphorist, descriptive writer, or *raconteur*, if we remember that in all of his humorous fiction he is almost all of these, though saliently one or another in a given work. While there is no development of his powers in writing, there is in any given work a predominance of a certain gift or power. In general, then, a practical method of "reading" Haliburton is to approach him thus: First, the humorous *story-telling* and *aphoristic* genius of Haliburton predominate in the first and second series of **The Clockmaker** and in **Nature and**

Human Nature. Secondly, the *narrative and descriptive* genius of Haliburton predominates in the third series of **The Clockmaker, The Attaché,** and most notably in **The Old Judge.** Thirdly, the character-delineating and nature-painting genius of Haliburton, his ingenious invention, his powers of imagination, narrative and descriptive gifts, and his extraordinary relish of the humorous and ludicrous are found in their most satisfying form, for all classes of readers, in **The Old Judge; or Life in a Colony.** (pp. 123-27)

Despite Haliburton's signal achievements in descriptive prose, he does not rank as a great artist. The reason for this is not because of the infrequent achievements of distinction in descriptive prose on the part of Haliburton, but is based on other general considerations, chiefly on Haliburton's lack of power to individualize each of his characters, his lack of technical skill, and of literary style.

We can best understand Haliburton's alleged weakness in character drawing by thinking of any of the outstanding characters of Dickens. Dick Swiveller, for instance, is always, unmistakably, Swiveller, identified by a single moral quality. He has character. Sam Slick, on the other hand, is never any *one* character, any one Slick; he is several characters, a *promiscuity* of moral and intellectual qualities. *We,* not the author, put together the opposite characters, and call them one; but the truth is that if we heard the one Slick speaking, and next examined a speech of a different quality which we did not know was uttered by Slick, we would not say, "That's just like Slick." He might have uttered both of them, and he might not. Precisely; it is the promiscuousness of Slick's character that compels the critic to say that as a character he is not a unity, and therefore not well-drawn. Or, take Reverend Joshua Hopewell. He is a moral unity, consistent throughout; but he is intellectually two or more persons, an Englishman, a Provincial, and an American. He has an incredible knowledge, for a rural and untravelled clergyman, about life and manners in the United States and Canada, and about life and men and politics in Britain. So that as a character there is the same promiscuousness about Reverend Mr. Hopewell as about Sam Slick, only in less degree. The trouble was that Haliburton used Slick or Hopewell or the Squire, whenever his thought demanded a spokesman, whether his ideas were suited logically to the character or not. In short, none of these characters is a spiritual unity, or consistently drawn.

As a character delineator, as a structural artist, and as a stylist, Haliburton's work corresponded to his thought, which was prolix and too full of detail. As there is no unity to his major characters, so there is no plot to his works. And yet, as Haliburton himself tells us in **The Old Judge,** this is not a defect at all. The purpose of his writings was not literary, but rather to inform and to amuse while informing. He therefore needs characters and the unity of their speeches as the thread on which to string facts, ideas, and opinions. Consequently, there will be repetitions, digressions, diffuseness, and an over-wealth of detail, particularly of humour, jests, and anecdotes, to sugarcoat the pills of his social and political ideas. The noble and wistful "Apologia" which concludes the second series of **The Attaché,** shows that Haliburton consciously adopted this style as the one best suited to his matter. (pp. 141-43)

Thirty years before Herbert Spencer published his *Philosophy of Style* . . . , Haliburton anticipated him by publishing his psychology of conservational prose style (*Wise Saws* . . .). Haliburton, as Spencer after him, based particular styles on the conversation of mental energies (attention). Haliburton, too,

arranges the structure and rhythm of his sentences that by their very length, abrupt endings or transitions they compel interest. He employs a conversational style, because, as he says, "the test of a real genuine book is that it is read in the parlour and the kitchen." "Why is it," asks Sam Slick, "if you *read* a book to a man you set him to sleep? Just because it is a book and the language aint common. Why is it if you *talk* to him he will sit up all night with you? Just because it's talk, the language of natur'." This, then, is the psychology of that "written chat," the conversational style, of Haliburton. Haliburton thus had two styles, one colloquial and humoristic, the other consciously artistic; and in both Haliburton was a master.

Matthew Arnold, perhaps the greatest of English critics, once said to his master in criticism, Sainte-Beuve, that Lamartine was not an important author. To Arnold the French master-critic replied: "Lamartine is not important absolutely, or from the world point of view, but he is important, to *us.*" What Sainte-Beuve saw, and what Arnold missed perceiving, was that Lamartine, as the sole representative of a type of poetry, a type which was more frequently represented in English poetry, filled a place in French literature that otherwise would have been vacant. From the cosmopolitan point of view, Lamartine does not bulk large; but from the French point of view he is important. His poetry is distinctly valuable to French literature as a whole. Similarly, many an outstanding Canadian writer, from Goldsmith and Richardson to the present, may not bulk large judged by world standards; but they are all important to *us* as Canadians. Fortunately for us as Canadians, Haliburton is both a great Canadian prose writer and one of the world's great writers, judged both by cosmopolitan standards and by his influence. We may best appreciate the genius and distinction of Haliburton by briefly sketching his influence on three literatures, Canadian, English, and American.

(1) It is commonly said that Haliburton's influence on Canada and Canadian literature was predominantly political, not literary. What is true is that he was unread in Canada, so far as his humour was concerned, and that he has had no successors in his native country. Stephen Leacock is not a successor, since he has not followed the method of Haliburton, but rather that of Mark Twain. On the other hand, it was Haliburton who, along with Joseph Howe, ushered in the New Era of Prose in Canada, and thereby issued the declaration of the literary independence of British North America. This is why he is important both to us as Canadians and also to the world. Not only was he the first to give us the foundation-stone for our temple of original Canadian prose, but he was also the first to give us a significant and permanent place in English and world literature.

(2) The vogue of Irving, Cooper and Richardson was largely due to the fact that the English people were enjoying *new matter* written, however, in the manner of Goldsmith and of Sir Walter Scott. On the other hand, Haliburton's satiric comedy and comic characterization startled the quiescent literary society of England. Here was something *not* English, something not English-American or English-Canadian, but a sheer literary novelty, absolutely *American.* Hitherto, even up to the time of the vogue of Irving, Cooper, and Richardson, the continent of America had depended upon England for literary sustenance and for its models. With the advent of Haliburton, England, *for the first time in history,* looked across to the American continent for fresh and original literature. Moreover, even English humoristic literature, at least in one instance, modelled itself on Haliburton. There is no necessity to argue the matter.

The fact is that Dickens' *Pickwick Papers,* which appeared serially, two years later than *The Clockmaker* sketches (which in serial form were copied widely by the American press) betrays some imitation of Haliburton, and that Sam Weller is an English version of Sam Slick. Haliburton has had an unprecedented popularity in England, which remains to this day. His chief character, Sam Slick, has been accepted by the English as comparable to Sterne's Uncle Toby, Dickens' Swiveller, Thackeray's Marquis of Steyne, Cervantes' Don Quixote, Daudet's Tartarin, and Twain's Huckleberry Finn, or, say, the enduring comic characters of fiction. Moreover, Haliburton's aphorisms and epigrams have become part of the colloquialisms of English speech and popular literature.

(3) The influences of Haliburton on American literature are wide and pervasive. Haliburton introduced in Sam Slick and other characters the new Englander and similar American types into their own and world literature. In a double sense, Haliburton is the "apostle of American humour." (a) He is the progenitor of the method of all those who in the United States have written the humour of dialect. (b) By his editorial labours on behalf of the distribution of American humour amongst the people, as in his compilations, *Traits of American Humour* and *The Americans at Home,* Haliburton influenced the fiction, especially the humorous fiction, written in the United States. There can be no doubt of his influence on Artemus Ward, Josh Billings, and other American "dialect" humorists writing in prose, and on Mark Twain. Haliburton produced his humorous effects more frequently by grotesque conceits and ludicrous situations than by dialect and tricks of construction. Lowell, writing in verse, felt the full force of Haliburton's influence, for in *The Biglow Papers* not only dialect, but also situations in *The Clockmaker* series, have been imitated if not actually borrowed by Lowell. It must be admitted that Haliburton's influence on Longfellow was wholly accidental. Whether Longfellow got the "story" of Evangeline from Hawthorne, or from his own pastor, who got it from an aunt of Haliburton, or from reading Haliburton's account of the expulsion of the Acadians, is of no moment. It is, however, interesting to know that Haliburton in one way or another furnished the matter and the inspiration of the best example of American romantic poetry. But what is more important is the fact that Francis Parkman derived his romantic method of writing history from his reading of Haliburton's *Historical and Statistical Account of Nova Scotia.*

The journalism of Haliburton's time felt the Nova Scotia humorist's influence. The newspapers printed "Yankee Yarns" and "Yankee Stories" in the manner of Sam Slick. Finally, authors found it profitable to write imitations and burlesques of Sam Slick, and to put them on the market as being the work of Sam Slick.

Thomas Chandler Haliburton's aims were noble. His methods were according to his illumination. His genius was indisputably original and unique. His influence on literature was immense and lasting. As the first systematic humorist of the Anglo-Saxon peoples, his work is not for an age, but for the world and for all time. (pp. 144-51)

> *John Daniel Logan, in his* Thomas Chandler Haliburton, *The Ryerson Press, 1924, 176 p.*

V. L. O. CHITTICK (essay date 1924)

[*In this excerpt from the conclusion to his study of Haliburton, Chittick discusses the author's dual nature: the "forward-looking, respect-compelling Haliburton" and the "backward-looking, contempt-provoking Haliburton."*]

Two entirely distinct Haliburtons, each thoroughly inconsistent with the other, seem bound to emerge into clearness as the result of this study, as they must from any impartial examination of the life and works of its subject. On the one hand is the forward-looking, respect-compelling Haliburton. . . . [This was a man] who served his country for years with patriotic devotion, both as public servant and private citizen; who conferred a lasting benefit upon his fellow colonists by fearlessly satirizing their fatal habits of shiftlessness and despondency, and by constantly holding before them the glowing prospects of their future prosperity; who in season and out preached the doctrine of Imperial unity and Empire solidarity; who professed a philosophy of cheerfulness and expounded the gospel of an optimistic outlook. . . . (pp. 645-46)

On the other hand there is the backward-looking, contempt-provoking Haliburton. This was the man who at the time he finally retired from public life was chiefly conspicuous for his stubborn and almost unique adherence to, and advocacy of, the principles of an outworn and utterly discredited type of Toryism . . . ; [who] increasingly exemplified throughout his whole life a spirit of gloom, foreboding, and disillusion; who because of a contemptible indulgence in venomous satire threatened to disrupt one of his dearest and closest friendships; who held himself aloof from the "common people" in an irascible and unsociable pretension of class or family superiority; who was notoriously deficient in his comprehension of the underlying drift and meaning of the popular movements going on around about him; who uttered dull commonplaces, cheap puns, and vulgar *double entendres;* who often, though perhaps unwittingly, taught what was based neither on expediency nor morality; and who commanded . . . scant respect . . . within barely over a decade beyond his death. . . . (pp. 646-48)

Extremes indeed meet, as Haliburton himself was frequently given to saying. The truth about him, moreover, lies in no convenient compromise between the two extremities of fact and opinion here presented. It includes them both. Recent estimates of him, nevertheless, have as a rule tended only to consider the former, and wholly to ignore the latter. The result has been the creation of a partial myth about the "Foremost writer of British North America," concerning whom in the process it has been stated extravagantly that, "He wrote not for an age, but for all time" [according to T. G. Marquis]; and erroneously that he was, "a man of whom his coevals spoke in no slighting terms—whether as an orator, a legislator, a writer, a judge, or a citizen" [according to A. H. O'Brien (see Additional Bibliography)]; and both extravagantly and erroneously that he was, "the first and only creator of a unique and distinct species of fictional characterisation and speech and humour," "in his day the supreme aphorist and epigrammatist of the English speaking peoples," and one whose "wit and wisdom remain part of the warp and woof of modern world literature" [according to J. D. Logan]. But Haliburton's fame needs no enhancement by credit for what he neither was nor did. Haliburton never achieved greatness, though he occasionally approached it. Nor was he from any point of view a genius of the first order. What he lacked in higher qualities, however, he went far towards making good by the uses to which he put his extraordinary gifts of mental alertness and ingenuity. He contributed nothing to the store of the world's enduring thought, but he contrived to instruct and entertain an international audience for the better part of a full half century. Cut off from the main currents of intellectual stimulus, he had the curiosity to enlighten himself on nearly every question of considerable importance in his time, and the ability to discourse on each with an oracular power that always found for him attentive listeners. The amount of informing small talk he acquired on subjects of a somewhat more trivial nature was truly amazing. Much that he wrote was crude and careless, tiresome, sentimental, and labored, yet with all this that was inferior in his numerous volumes there was also sufficient of popular appeal, and of solid worth as well, to justly obtain for him, a resident of a despised colony still in the pre-confederation era of Canadian development, and with native literature only in its infancy there, a more general and more cordial recognition as a man of letters than has been secured by any other colonial author before or since. While his first published venture in humor was doubly fortunate in falling into the hands of a friend eager to promote its circulation, and in appearing at the precise moment ripe for its hearty reception, there was unquestionable merit in a performance which, with its sequels, could fairly eclipse the wide-spread favor of the models from which it was copied. Undeniable composite though he was, Sam Slick was no mere imitation, but quite different enough from his predecessors in the tradition to which he belonged to fully deserve in his own right all the renown long accorded him, save only that of being the first of his kind. The days of "Sam Slick sez" are now definitely over, but there is the testimony of incontrovertible evidence in plenty to show that he had his period of notable triumph, and that it was not brief.

While Haliburton as a maker of wise saws—and it was in that rôle ordinarily that as Sam Slick he was once so freely quoted—enjoyed a vogue that lasted well down to the present, his furious and protracted opposition to anything that might terminate in a democratic control of the colonies, either from within or without, rendered unavoidable his prompt and decisive rejection as a political theorist. (pp. 651-52)

To match his unusual knowledge of the topographical and commercial features of the colonies, he had a remarkably detailed acquaintance with the manifold aspects of colonial life common everywhere about him—which is by no means the same thing as saying he had the profound insight into human nature he is repeatedly asserted to have possessed, largely through his early reviewers having blundered into ascribing to him personally what he himself expressly attributed to Sam Slick. Of immeasurably greater value to his abiding reputation was the rare facility he had of making memorable what he knew of the colonials by hitting it off in vivid caricature. In utilizing this his most precious talent to impress his various lessons in thrift and diligence, politics and government, he produced a series of pictures unsurpassed as an accurate revelation of the manners and customs of his contemporaries. The element of comic exaggeration necessarily incident to this kind of drawing emphasizes rather than obscures the essential fidelity of his descriptions. Together with his realistic, though equally graphic, record of persons and scenes familiar to him through everyday contact they constitute decidedly his most skillful and most finished work as a writer. If he continues to retain his position of eminence in provincial literature, it will not be by virtue of all the didactically applied wit of his humorous anecdotes, nor by all the brilliant fire and clever invective of his serious arguments, but because he has left to posterity these faithful and painstaking delineations of his people and their environment. Little else that the bequest of his diligent pen affords can ever again prove attractive to the average reader, though obviously to the historically-minded there is much besides in his books

that will always appeal as a dependable and unfailing source of antiquarian information. In certain other respects, to be sure, his literary endeavors should make him gratefully remembered, if not extensively read. It was he, for instance, who conducted the pioneer exploration of his country's annals, and it was he, too, who first revealed the wealth of romantic and tragic happenings in its absorbing story, and showed the way to its possibilities for fiction. For the rest, the greater portion of his writings, he has already paid the inevitable penalty of the political propagandist. In spite of his many services in their behalf, his countrymen have never as yet erected any substantial memorial to perpetuate the name of their earliest noteworthy author, or the titles of his once popular compilations. For those who may resent or regret this striking, and significant, failure to honor so celebrated, though often mistaken, a prophet in his own land there is at least the consolation of Sam Slick's pertinent inquiry, "Who the devil cares for a monument that actilly desarves one?" (pp. 653-54)

> *V. L. O. Chittick, in his* Thomas Chandler Haliburton ("Sam Slick"): A Study in Provincial Toryism, *Columbia University Press, 1924, 695 p.*

D. C. HARVEY (essay date 1937)

[*Harvey examines Haliburton's purpose in writing the Sam Slick stories and outlines his political message.*]

Thomas Chandler Haliburton [was the] creator of Sam Slick, that composite character which won for its author international fame in the world of letters.

Both his college and his province have reason to be proud of the fact that a native Nova Scotian, writing from a little town in an obscure colony, could stamp this figure upon the imagination of the English-speaking world and, in so doing, could reveal something of that struggle which was being waged to manufacture a Nova Scotian from American and British raw material. The secret of his power lies in the fact that he wrote under the spur of local patriotism about matters within the immediate range of his own observation, and set down faithfully his own varying reactions to the conflicting moods and ideas of his own generation. With such a background and such an experience as his, none but a composite character could have reflected the conflicting ideas and emotions that warred within his own soul; nor, as the range of his observation increased, could even the versatile Sam meet all his needs. Hence he was compelled to adopt other characters and other devices.

Sprung from Loyalist and pre-Loyalist stock, born into the official class, educated at King's College in the days of its most unpopular exclusiveness, representing a constituency that prided itself on the romance and antiquity of its history, living and moving as a judge on circuit amongst a stiff-necked Puritan people who had been transplanted from the four colonies of New England, responsive to the intellectual movement that stirred his native province during his youth, it is little wonder that Haliburton at first became a mirror of many moods and conflicts, and only gradually discovered a central position from which to pour the stream of his humour upon the fires of an ever-present controversy. Naturally, too, he chose his chief mouthpieces from the predominating strain in his immediate environment: the Connecticut Clockmaker for shrewdness in business, and the Connecticut Minister for a compromise between Puritanism and Anglicanism. (pp. 429-30)

At King's College Haliburton had been well-grounded in the classics; and, if one may judge from his quotations and allusions, he was acquainted with Juvenal, Martial, and Horace. Further, the Loyalist literary group in Nova Scotia had sought in satire relief from the monotony of life in what they called "Nova Scarcity", and had written *longo intervallo* in the style of the English Augustans. It is not surprising, then, to find that Haliburton chose satire as a vehicle for his ideas.

Now, the great Dryden divided English satirists into two classes: the followers of Horace, men of the world who assailed the enemies of common-sense with the weapons of humour and sarcasm, and the followers of Juvenal, the prophets who assailed vice and crime with passionate indignation and invective. With this classification in mind, it is possible to argue that Haliburton was of the school of Horace and his followers in 18th century England, rather than of the school of Juvenal: but whilst Haliburton was acquainted with both the ancient and the modern Augustans, it is obviously futile to attempt to classify him as one of them. As heir of all the ages, he no doubt found inspiration in many masters; but, though he adorns his pages with verses or couplets from both the Roman and the English classics, he himself hints that his closest literary affinity was with Fielding and Smollett; and the inference is that he learned from these authors not so much a literary form as a literary function. This function was to hold the mirror up to nature, to depict the life and manners of the age. It is in this light, then, as the Fielding and Smollett of America, that he must be considered, or, as Sam said, "You can't measure me by English standards. You must take an American one, and that will give you my length, breadth, height and weight to a hair." (pp. 431-32)

The place for the Yankee Clockmaker had been prepared by *The Club* which met regularly in [Joseph] Howe's home, 1828-32, and planned weekly sketches in dialect on local men and movements. When *The Club* was disbanded, owing to diverging views of Howe and Haliburton, the latter aspired to deal with his public in his own way through the Yankee dialect of Sam Slick. In this respect, as in his desire to be anonymous, Haliburton was the child of his age. In Nova Scotia an earlier reformer, John Young, as *Agricola,* had written a brilliant series of articles on agriculture for which he was publicly recognized by Lord Dalhousie. In justifying his anonymity, Young wrote: "The regular attack upon the prejudices and habits of a people exposed a writer to much resentment. For that reason, I resolved on acting behind the curtain and shutting myself from the gaze of the public." There is more than a chance resemblance between this statement of Agricola and the Clockmaker's defence of his incognito: "A satirist, like an Irishman," says Sam, "finds it convenient sometimes to shoot from behind a shelter. Like him, too, he may occasionally miss his shot, and firing with intent to do bodily harm is almost as badly punished as if death ensued. And, besides, an anonymous book has a mystery about it."

In this passage Haliburton, who is frequently his own interpreter, definitely calls himself a satirist; and on another occasion he playfully compared his satiric function to that of his brother, the doctor, in the words: "You cut up the dead and I cut up the living." But a satirist to be effective must have a central position and a serious purpose; and his merits must be determined as much by the worthiness of his purpose as by the skill with which he handles the peculiar and dangerous vehicle that he has chosen. Haliburton, himself, does not leave even the most casual of his readers in doubt as to the fundamental

seriousness of his writing. Apart from the freqent iteration and elucidation of his leading ideas on sound pedagogical priniciples, an iteration which caused one reviewer to say that he had reached "the poorest of all repetitions, that of repeating himself," Haliburton insists both directly and indirectly that he must not be regarded as a vain trifler. In the *Letter Bag of the Great Western* he says: "Although I am one of the merriest fellows of my age to be found in any country, yet I am a great approver of the old maxim of 'being merry and wise', being, after my own fashion, a sort of laughing philosopher, and . . . I most indulge in that species of humor that has a moral in it." Similar ideas may be found in *The Attaché* and *Wise Saws,* all of which insist that he never lost sight of his original design, to awaken Nova Scotians to the vast resources and capabilities of their native land, to depict the worst features of the United States in order to show them that they might be better off at home, to vindicate the superiority of British character and institutions, and to stir up Great Britain to a consciousness of the importance of her colonies so that she would blot out the word *colonial,* make Englishmen of the Nova Scotians, incorporate them in her body of citizens and make them feel that they were an integral part of a great nation. This is the great purpose which Haliburton pursues, however devious his pathway and however faulty his methods.

The first series of *The Clockmaker* deals mainly with local conditions, although Haliburton's ideas of America and Great Britain are introduced occasionally and indirectly. The purpose of the volume is to acquaint the Nova Scotians with their resources and to stimulate them into activity. (pp. 433-34)

In the second and third series of *The Clockmaker,* Haliburton gropes toward a solution of the wider problem: how to prevent the Nova Scotians from imitating the republican institutions of the Americans, and how to awaken the British to a sense of the importance of their colonies. His theory is that the Americans are abandoned to democracy and destined to civil war as a nemesis for the Revolution, and abandoned to atheism through their insistence upon the voluntary system of religion in preference to an established church.

But he finds himself in something of a quandary, because he can hardly expect Sam, who regards his nation as "the greatest nation atween the poles", to become the champion of monarchy and of Anglicanism. Fortunately he had prepared a way out of his difficulty through Sam's tutor, Rev. Joshua Hopewell, who had been educated at Harvard before the Revolution and, though he stayed with his flock from a sense of duty, was a hearty admirer of British institutions. Consequently Sam quotes him when he must criticize American institutions, although he frequently saves his face by saying, "I don't go the whole figur' with Minister, though I opinionate with him in part." In this way Haliburton is able to present British institutions in a more favourable light through Mr. Hopewell and, as Sam cannot be kept in the background, he is made to boast so outrageously about the virtue of American institutions as to achieve the same effect. (pp. 435-36)

The Clockmaker's message for England was twofold: She must recognize that on the day she loses her colonies she ceases to be a first-rate power, and that in order to retain them the Colonial Office must bestir itself and become acquainted with the true desires and needs of those for whose destinies it is responsible. To the Little Englanders and to the people of England in general he points out, what Chatham had told the King's Friends before the American Revolution, that, although they might not be able to look for direct taxation from the colonies, they drew a large if invisible revenue from the monopoly of their trade. In an elaborate essay called **"Snubbing a Snob"** Sam points out to a muddle-headed Englishman that "wood, water, stone and airth" are the only things for which the Nova Scotian does not send to England.

On the other hand, Haliburton's remedy for the discontent in the colonies as expressed through Mr. Hopwell was not responsible government, but a career for the ablest colonials in the imperial service:

> The restlessness in the colonies proceeds not from grievances, for, with the exception of a total absence of patronage, they do not exist; but it is caused by an uneasiness of position, arising from a want of room to move in. There is no field for ambition, no room for the exercise of distinguished talent in the provinces. The colonists, when comparing their situation with that of their more fortunate brethren in England, find all honour monopolised at home, and employment, preferments, and titles liberally bestowed on men frequently inferior in intellect and ability to themselves, and this invidious distinction sinks deeper into the heart than they are willing to acknowledge themselves.

But it was Sam who insisted that the Colonial Office must not listen to every colonial who calls himself a patriot, for there are five different kinds of patriots to be found in the colonies: the *rebel patriot*, who talks better than he fights; the *mahogany patriot*, who wants to take his betters' mahogany away from them; the *spooney patriot*, who thinks the world can be reduced to squares like a draftboard, and governed by systems; the *place patriot*, who is a rogue; the *true patriot*, who is neither a sycophant to the government nor a tyrant to the people, but manfully opposes either when they are wrong, supports existing institutions as a whole, but is willing to mend or repair any part that is defective.

Here then, as briefly as one can give it, while illustrating both form and matter, was Haliburton's central idea. *The Attaché* is but an elaboration of this main thesis, though showing a little more sympathy with the Americans and some slight development towards a definite remodelling of the Colonial Office, so as to make it a real imperial board comprising experienced colonials or Englishmen with long experience in the colonies. In it he also insists on wiping out the name Colonial and making Englishmen of all. "If you don't make Englishmen of us, the force of circumstances will make Yankees of us." This sentence written in 1843 shows that Haliburton is still haunted by the fear that he expressed in private correspondence nineteen years earlier, the fear of American Annexation.

In *Wise Saws,* written in 1853, Haliburton uses the Clockmaker to disclose the danger of American poaching upon the Nova Scotian fisheries. Though Sam has frequently boasted that Connecticut beats all the world for "geese, gals and onions", when he decides to marry he returns to Nova Scotia for a bluenose gal, a daughter of a Loyalist. Here he learns of American skill in coaxing fish beyond the three mile limit, applies his knowledge of clocks to a noiseless invention for catching fish without bait, and discourses on how to evade customs laws without smuggling.

In *Nature and Human Nature,* which should be read as Haliburton's *apologia pro vita sua,* he explains his ideas once more,

defends his methods and in a sense bids Nova Scotia farewell, for he is going to the centre of the Empire to implement his central idea.

In *The Season-Ticket,* written in England, when confederation talk was in the air, he interests himself in the resources of Vancouver, emphasizes the imperial necessity of a transcontinental railway for British North America, and reluctantly drops the idea of imperial federation in favour of Canadian federation. (pp. 437-39)

Though Haliburton worked as an historian, an editor, a political pamphleteer, and a satirist, his international reputation was made on his humour as manifested in Sam Slick. (p. 439)

By careful elimination, . . . as well as by casual observation, we are brought back to the Slick series for that quaint combination of Humanism and Puritanism which enabled Haliburton to become an American in the larger sense, to scale the heights of European conventionality, and to win favour there. His Humanism appears in the depth and range of his interest in men as men, and in his capacity for making every man speak for himself. His Puritanism is seen in his desire to remake his countrymen in his own image, to warn them off the political field while playing the political game himself with a clear eye upon the main chance, and in the compensation that he found for his repressions in coarseness of humour.

Through *Samuel Slick of Slickville, Onion County, Connecticut,* Haliburton caught the ear of his generation and gave it an illuminating commentary upon the passing events of twenty years throughout the entire English speaking world, at a time when every day threatened some new attack upon the existing order of society. (p. 440)

> *D. C. Harvey, "The Centenary of Sam Slick," in* The Dalhousie Review, *Vol. XVI, No. 4, January, 1937, pp. 429-40.*

ARTHUR L. PHELPS (essay date 1951)

[*In treating Haliburton as one of the first Canadian writers, Phelps states that the author's fame rests on his Sam Slick series, which broke with the English literary tradition.*]

To talk about Thomas Chandler Haliburton as our first distinctively Canadian writer is to suggest paradox and fate's whimsy. For Haliburton, who did so much in his writings and in the tradition he created, to discover and nourish an individualized Canadianism, was against that Confederation whose logic has led to the Statute of Westminster and the progressive withering of colonialism. Haliburton disliked and distrusted the Yankee theories of democracy and independence: he wanted the bond with Britain tight and obvious. . . . Haliburton did not want the Canadas of the early nineteenth century to go the way of the thirteen Colonies. He wanted no absorption into the United States of America. It was natural that he should see in Canadian Confederation, among other things, a trend away from the motherland. Yet the very delight and pride he took in his native province, Nova Scotia, nourished by implication the large Canadianism whose road was to be the road towards independence. Today, however, in 1951, Haliburton's spirit might be reassured after all. If ghosts can grin, he might grin at the sardonic whimsy by which the Canadianism which threw off British colonialism yesterday becomes nourishment for the protest against absorption by the United States today. (pp. 19-20)

In that young colony in the first half of the nineteenth century there was a good deal of conscious and unconscious kinship with the literary and social traditions of the eighteenth century. Joseph Howe, one of the great figures in the great debates that led to Confederation, gathered about himself a group of well-read, cultivated and sharp-minded men who called themselves *The Club*. Haliburton was drawn into this group and helped to make it lively. . . . In creating Sam Slick, the peripatetic Yankee clockmaker, with his droll talk in drawled dialect, full of homely wisdom and incisive comment, Haliburton had begun the making of Canadian literature. Somehow Haliburton was able to make his reports of the doings of Slick and the sayings of Slick combine two elements that give body and spirit to what we call good writing: local flavour and human verity. It is scarcely proper to say that Haliburton added to these two elements humour. Rather, he found and expressed the humour which is always, to the friendly and discerning eye, embedded alike in the local and the universal. And that humour of course included the wry, the ironic, the grotesque—all that makes the business of being alive on the earth fascinating and inexplicable, homely and miraculous. (pp. 21-2)

[The] fame of Haliburton the writer rests on the Sam Slick series, published again and again in successive editions in England, the United States, France and Germany. Sam Slick the clockmaker takes his place in literature alongside Mark Twain's Tom Sawyer and Dickens' Sam Weller.'

Of course the reader of today may find Haliburton old fashioned, lumbering, and, in the end, merely tedious. Selections from his writings, however, under astute editing, have persuaded many who might otherwise miss him that there are delights still to be found in the work of a man who touched the funny bones and sharpened the wits of his own generation. The fact is that Haliburton knew human nature and, without too much illusion or disillusion, loved it. (pp. 23-4)

It is Haliburton himself of course who is the droll boy as he goes on, page after page, revealing Sam, revealing his native Nova Scotia, revealing the new, raw, shrewd America as exemplified in Sam; revealing as well, when his story takes Sam as American attaché to the Court of St. James, the shams, mannerisms and hypocrisies of the older culture. (pp. 25-6)

I could be tempted to go on and on. Suffice to say this (I paraphrase an American critic): at a time when on this side of the Atlantic the writers of prose fiction whose work counted at all—Irving, Cooper, Richardson—wrote as Englishmen wrote, Thomas Chandler Haliburton wrote as an American—that is, as an American in the continental sense.

We Canadians say he wrote as a Canadian. Thomas Chandler Haliburton is part of our tradition. (pp. 26-7)

> *Arthur L. Phelps, "Thomas Haliburton," in his Canadian Writers, McClelland and Stewart Limited, 1951, pp. 19-27.*

DESMOND PACEY (essay date 1952)

[*In this brief introduction to Haliburton's work, excerpted from a historical survey of Canadian literature that was originally written in 1952, Pacey focuses on* The Clockmaker.]

[With the publication of the first series of *The Clockmaker*], Thomas Chandler Haliburton had found his *métier;* Nova Scotia had found its wittiest prophet; and Canada had found its first great humourist.

The appearance of *The Clockmaker* was no freak or accident. It arose in answer to the immediate demands of the province, and it embodied attitudes which had long been maturing in the mind of the author. To a provincial society which seemed about to lose faith in its own destiny, it proclaimed that its salvation lay in its own perseverance and ingenuity; to those members of that society who were tempted to emigrate to the United States (and many emigrated at this period) it held up to ridicule the cheapness and shallowness of American society. The book spoke to them, moreover, in their own language, in an idiomatic prose which combined the witty antitheses of eighteenth century English with the dialectal ingenuity of North America.

The Clockmaker is not, perhaps, a great book, but it is an astonishingly good book to have come from a small provincial society in the throes of depression. Like all significant works of art, it blends the particular and the universal; even today, when many of the issues to which it alludes have been forgotten, there is scarcely a page of it which does not hold our interest or arouse our amusement. It exhibits practically every form of humour known to man, and in particular those humorous devices which have come to be labelled, ironically enough in view of Haliburton's prejudices, as "typically American". There is the humour of dialect, in phrases such as "soft sawder" and "a pretty considerable smart horse". There is comic exaggeration, of the type later beloved by Mark Twain: "As for the people on the shore, they know so little of horses that a man from Aylesford once sold a hornless ox there, whose tail he had cut and nicked, for a horse of the Goliath breed". There are puns aplenty: much of the first chapter, for example, consists of various puns on the word "circuit". There is the comedy of situation: Haliburton can turn an anecdote as neatly as he turns a phrase. There is irony in abundance: almost every statement which Haliburton makes can be interpreted in several ways, and many of his sentences are like many-edged weapons which cut us whichever way we turn them. There is, of course, satire: satire at the expense of the shiftless farmers of Nova Scotia, of the lawyers who exploit their credulity and of the Yankee smart alecks who gull them. Above all, there is the humour of character.

The Clockmaker swarms with memorable characters. Caricatures they may be, but with a few sure strokes they are drawn and we never forget them. There is, for example, Elder Stephen Gran whose face was "as long as the moral law, and perhaps an inch longer" and who felt that "he had conquered the Evil One and was considerable well satisfied with himself". Greatest of them all, of course, is Sam Slick. He has the ambivalence of so much of the book: Haliburton at once detests and admires him. He is crude, coarse, arrogant, ignorant and downright dishonest, the representative and inevitable product, in Haliburton's eyes, of a republican democracy; but at the same time he is shrewd, practical, self-reliant and inventive, and in this respect the embodiment of an ideal which Haliburton would have his fellow Nova Scotians emulate.

With the publication of the first series of *The Clockmaker*, Haliburton's greatest work came to an end. Even the second series, published two years later, shows a marked decline in his powers. He has become less concrete and more theoretical; the natural flow of his racy idiom is impeded by self-consciousness; the positive aspect of the first series—Haliburton's effort to arouse Nova Scotians from their lethargy—is almost wholly crowded out by his crusade against colonial democracy; there is less wit and more vulgarity; the book is altogether more diffuse and superficial. The faults of the first series—disor-

Sam Slick selling a clock in The Clockmaker, *first series. Illustration by C. W. Jefferys from* Sam Slick in Pictures: The Best of the Humor of Thomas Chandler Haliburton, *edited by Lorne Pierce. The Ryerson Press, 1956.*

derliness of presentation, repetition and redundancy, lapses into mere facetiousness—are here magnified and made more apparent.

Much of Haliburton's later life was spent in England where, until his death on the eve of Confederation, he devoted his energies to a vain attempt to stem the tide of responsible government and colonial autonomy. . . . To the very end of his life he retained the capacity to turn a witty phrase and to tell an amusing anecdote, but his later books will not stand comparison with *The Clockmaker.* (pp. 16-18)

> *Desmond Pacey, "The Colonial Period (1750-1867),"*
> *in his* Creative Writing in Canada: A Short History
> of English-Canadian Literature, *revised edition, The*
> *Ryerson Press, 1961, pp. 1-34.*

JOHN PENGWERNE MATTHEWS (essay date 1962)

[*In his description of the development of Canadian literature, Matthews discusses the moral lessons Haliburton included in* The Clockmaker *series and the sources from which he drew the character Sam Slick.*]

[In writing *The Clockmaker* series], Haliburton, possessed by a fierce local patriotism, strongly imbued with the traditions of Tory aristocracy, made no secret of his double purpose: of

arousing his countrymen to new energy and ambition in fulfilling the potentialities of the colony, and at the same time of convincing the Colonial Office that the settlement was not, and did not deserve to be treated as, the Cinderella of the Empire. To accomplish this aim he succeeded in blending two traditions with such originality that his work marks the first genuine contribution of Canadian letters to literature in English.

Haliburton set out to portray, by a series of sketches, his views on the social, political, and economic problems of Nova Scotia. In carrying out his intention of attacking what he considered the dangerous concern for reform prevailing in the colony, Haliburton drew upon the English traditions of Swift and Burke. Nova Scotians would do well to attend more to their own immediate practical problems, and not waste their time and energies pursuing political will-o'-the-wisps. To point the moral, Haliburton created the figure of the irrepressible Yankee, Sam Slick. It was a far cry from the polished admonishments of Swift and Burke to the rough sophistry of a New England pedlar, and in making the adaptation, Haliburton drew upon a second, this time American, tradition.

There was already a rapidly developing American mythology of folk-heroes. Davy Crockett had become the centre of one such collection of legends, involving tall tales and feats of heroic proportions. Buffalo Bill, Paul Bunyan, and Kit Carson were to succeed him in later decades as representatives of American civilization advancing westward into the unknown. Jacksonian democracy had emphasized the virtues of the "natural" man, and the self-conscious aspects of frontier life had been elevated to a type of authenticity by the employment of certain genuine pioneers as symbols of the new "natural" Everyman, or, more accurately, the new Superman.

Accompanying the element of exaggeration in American humour was the element of fraud. Life was highly competitive and it was necessary to outwit others or be outwitted oneself. This in turn led to a high regard for "smartness" or "slickness" as a factor determining one's place in frontier society. Charles Dickens complained in the eighteen-forties that in America smartness was extolled at the expense of honesty, and Trollope later found the same thing. He was told: "On the frontier a man is bound to be smart. If he ain't smart he's better go back East; perhaps as far as Europe. He'll do there." Frauds and swindles were the basis for delighted appreciation. (pp. 36-7)

In *The Clockmaker* can be found the Canadian compromise, the epitome of this "slickness" used for a moral purpose, developing a subtlety that contrasts strongly with the more blatant dishonesty openly praised in the frontier tales of the United States. The Yankee pedlar with his wooden nutmegs was a well-known figure in American humour by the beginning of the nineteenth century, and in such a character Haliburton found the goad he could apply to the inert elements of Nova Scotia life. (p. 37)

Sam Slick . . . represented all those traits of bumptiousness which Haliburton so detested, and while his self-confidence and ingenuity are characteristics that Nova Scotians would do well to copy, he is the caricature of a national prototype that Haliburton did not admire. But as Will Honeycomb provided the *Spectator* with many opportunities for criticizing the traditions of morality and breeding surviving from Restoration days, remaining himself a not unsympathetic character, so Sam Slick provided Haliburton with a means of combining his social message with entertainment.

Haliburton's combination of the particular and the universal brought him great success not only within the bounds of Nova Scotia, for Haliburton gave his English readers a picture of the type of American they had already visualized. He confirmed and brought to life their own prejudiced conception of the typical Yankee. At the same time, the sketches were expressed with such easy and apparently appropriate wit that English readers began to believe that a new and original form of creative writing was emerging from their colony in North America. Ironically, from this impression that at last there was a book authentically North American in spirit, rather [than] pseudo-European, sprang the association of Sam Slick's humour with the United States and its literature, rather than with a Canadian commentary upon it. The nature of the humour of Sam Slick has been discussed so often that recapitulation would serve no useful function here; it is more to the point to insist upon the synthesis between the tradition of entertaining sketches joined to a didactic purpose, and the already established New England tradition of "wisecracks" and "smart alecks."

Haliburton concerned himself with the middle classes in Nova Scotia: the educated, the merchants, and the yeomanry. Unlike Brackenridge, he did not call upon every "Tom, Dick, and Harry" as the hope of the colony. His was not an emotional appeal to the masses, but a reasoned plea for each member of society to play his part in the station of life in which he found himself. Inevitably, he found his greatest audience among the middle classes. (pp. 38-9)

Nova Scotian, or rather Halifax, society at the turn of the eighteenth century had already assumed the elements of stratification to be found in English provincial circles, and had developed a degree of sophistication, security, and leisure sufficient for the development of an appreciation of cultural values. This was ground prepared for easy adaptation of the English tradition. This tradition joined the native pungency of the North American tradition which contrasted strongly with the more rigid social climate of Halifax, and produced the originality of Haliburton. *The Clockmaker* series mark more than a starting point in Canadian letters, for in some ways they mark an end as well. Haliburton's Sam Slick marks the beginning of a true integration of the British and the North American traditions. Unfortunately, for some considerable time, he also marks the end. . . . The way had been prepared for a distinctively Canadian literary tradition, but no one followed the lead. It was for Mark Twain to follow on, and to annex for American literature the type of character that Haliburton had created. Canadian critics could not see the difference between the synthesis that Haliburton had created and the unadulterated American slick humour south of the border. As a result, Canadian writers and critics drew back in well-bred horror from the distasteful crudities of the frontier, and looked, more resolutely than ever, eastward across the Atlantic to the source of all good things. (pp. 39-40)

John Pengwerne Matthews, "The Eighteenth-Century Inheritance," in his Tradition in Exile: A Comparative Study of Social Influences on the Development of Australian and Canadian Poetry in the Nineteenth Century, *University of Toronto Press, 1962, pp. 28-48.*

L.A.A. HARDING   (essay date 1965)

[*Harding investigates Haliburton's rendering of folk language in the Sam Slick series, particularly focusing on his use of farm imagery.*]

A great deal of the freshness of Haliburton's comic view of life comes from his turn of phrase and imagery describing the world of Sam Slick, as the latter sees it, in earthy, colloquial language which comes from the farm, the workshops, the kitchens and the wharves. It *smells* of the farm, the workshops, the kitchens and the wharves, and provides much of the reason for the enormous Sam Slick vogue, which made Haliburton a notable rival of Dickens. It is no longer the imagery of today, which may explain why few read Sam Slick now. It is the common language of not-so-ordinary men; men who had had to struggle with the unpromising soil in an unpromising climate and who enjoyed their own salty, free-and-easy form of conversation and words for their own sake. It is the folk language of the time, strong, apt and often beautifully bathetic. It rarely tells a round, unvarnished tale, but it often delivers a character neatly and humorously revealed. Sam's character and attitude is plain, for instance, in ". . . Britishers won't stay in a house, unless every feller gets a separate bed. . . ." Haliburton's New Englanders and Nova Scotians had their own (very similar) idiom just as distinctively as Synge's Irishmen or Burns' Scotsmen. Consider, for instance, Sam's approach to a professor from whom he wishes a quick summary of a learned work: ". . . now larned men in a general way are all as stupid as owls, they keep a devil of a thinkin', but they don't talk. So I stirs up old Hieroglyphic with a long pole; for it's after dark, lights is lit, and it's time for owls to wake up and gaze."

One sees the comic force of this idiom, when Sam says to the Reverend Hopewell, who has been shocked at Sam's typically materialistic reaction on his first sight of the grandeur and majesty of Niagara Falls which to the minister represent the voice of Nature and the power of God:

> . . . it does seem kinder grandlike—that 'are great big lake does seem like an everlastin' large milk-pan with a lip for pourin' at the falls, and when it does fall head over heels, all white froth and spray like Phoebe's syllabub, it does look grand, no doubt, and it's nateral for a minister to think on it as you do; but still, for all that, for them that ain't preachers, I defy most any man to see it without thinkin' of a cotton mill.

Haliburton here uses with great effect the language of the farm, the kitchen and the workshop, when he makes Sam talk of "an everlastin' large milk pan with a lip for pourin'", "Phoebe's syllabub", and observes the obvious connection to an industrially-minded Yankee of "that voice of Nature in the wilderness", as the Reverend Hopewell had called it, with a "cotton mill". Each man thinks in terms of his character and experience. Commonsense furthermore says that a roar is a roar and that Niagara and a cotton mill have at least that in common. Haliburton knew very well the value of contrast to communicate his comic view of life, and the above example illustrates the part played in it by his use of down-to-earth folk language and imagery (in dialect of course). The total result is more than mere amusement at the unexpected comparisons of Niagara with "an everlastin' large milk-pan" and "Phoebe's syllabub", and at the idea suggested by the awe-inspiring power in front of Sam's eyes flowering into a "cotton mill". A cotton mill roaring with all its machinery going at full speed is the poetry and song of the industrialist, the practical, cynical and acquisitive man.

It is however far more comprehensive than that. The characters of the two men are also thrown into relief; the spiritual old man with a sense of beauty who sees the power of God in all Nature, and the Yankee materialist who immediately sees industry and profits. By means of such imagery one sees in a flash, in the exchange between Sam and the Reverend Hopewell, two types of humanity, both of which have had a great part in the founding and development of the United States (not to mention Canada) and without either of which it would have been a very different country. One feels that these two kinds of American had a greater effect upon the national character than any two similar representative types from the South. These are both strong and influential characters, frequently met with in the early days. One sees also that both are basically good men, though their views and opinions and characters are widely divergent, if not opposite. One is interested in this world, the other in the next. There is in fact a thumbnail sketch here of the whole early history of the United States in the language, reactions, and characters of these two men. Furthermore there is undoubtedly a touch of satire on both humanity in general and the New England character in particular.

The effect of the homely simile, which in Sam's language often involves animals, either farm or wild, is well illustrated by Sam's indignation at Dr. Abernethy, the fashionable doctor at the court of St. James in London. The latter had been too outspoken at the expense of the Hon. Alden Gobble, the American Secretary to the Legation in London, when the latter went to the doctor for a cure for indigestion, or bolting his "vittles". One notes the skilful, humorous build-up which shows Alden Gobble as a very wide-awake Yankee diplomat, almost sharp enough to cut himself. He could "hide his trail like an Indian". Sam angrily tells the tale:

> The Hon. Alden Gobble was dyspeptic, and he suffered great oneasiness arter eatin', so he goes to Abernethy for advice. "What's the matter with you?" said the doctor, jist that way, without even passing the time o' day with him: "What's the matter with you," said he. "Why," says Alden, "I presume I have dyspepsy." "Ah!" said he, "I see; a Yankee swallered more dollars and cents than he can digest?" "I am an American citizen," says Alden, with great dignity: "I am Secretary to our Legation at the Court of St. James". "The devil you are," said Abernethy; "then you'll soon get rid of your dyspepsy." "I don't see that 'are inference," said Alden. "It don't foller from what you predicate at all—it an't a natural consequence, I guess, that a man should cease to be ill because he is called by the voice of a free and enlightened people to fill an important office." (The truth is you could no more trap Alden than you could an Indian. He could see other folks' trail, and made none himself; he was a raal diplomatist, and I believe our diplomatists are allowed to be the best in the world.) "But I tell you it does foller," said the doctor; "for in the company you'll have to keep, you'll have to eat like a Christian."

Sam's indignation at this slight to one of his fellow, free-and-enlightened citizens is expressed in the strong farm imagery of a dog and hog:

> . . . I'd a fixed his flint for him, so that he'd think twice afore he'd fire such another shot as that 'are again. I'd a made him make tracks, I

guess, as quick as a dog does a hog from a potato field. He'd a found his way of the hole in the fence a plaguy sight quicker than he came in, I reckon.

This farm imagery, even though the joke is on the Hon. Alden Gobble and Sam Slick rather than on the rude and vitriolic Dr. Abernethy, nevertheless reduces the fashionable London doctor, in Sam's bruised Yankee soul at least, and to some extent in ours, to the undignified and even grotesque image of a horrified hog scuttling squealing from a forbidden potato field with the farm dog snapping at his heels. The doctor pictured as a panicking pig trying to get back out through a hole in the farmer's fence is a strong comic image. The Hon. Alden Gobble has been made to look like a loutish lumberjack and therefore Sam, in patriotic and purely imaginary revenge, makes Dr. Abernethy look like the disappearing rearend of a pig, caught in the potatoes and conscious of error.

Sam's imagery is powerful and, though his triumph is purely imaginary, his point well made; but his anger at the insolence of Abernethy inadvertently betrays his comic character when one of the much despised but secretly somewhat respected English (with regard to superficial *savoir faire* at least—they quibbled, for instance, about spitting in the sawdust and took an hour to eat a ten-minute meal) gets in a wicked thrust and an unsporting one, at an important, dignified and highly respected "free-and-enlightened citizen" of the greatest republic the sun even shone on. Sam is surprised and angry, and when we see a man surprised and angry about a small point, then there is one of the unfailing elements of comedy. As a result all three men involved, Sam, the Hon. Gobble and Dr. Abernethy, are comically transmogrified into the small boys they once were; we see them in a new light; there is something incongruous, and they become figures of fun. We look down upon them from the godlike height of comedy as three little quarreling human beings, with their quirks and their pride and their tempers. Sam, who almost always is the master of every situation, who always scores off everybody else and gets the last laugh, is ruffled and riled, and the reader sees him for once unable to do much but nurse his damaged national dignity and invent revenges—a schoolboy again. He then adds darkly, his mind still running on pigs, that the Hon. Alden Gobble would "a 'taken the bristles off his hide as clean as the skin of a spring shote of a pig killed at Christmas", if the doctor had not slipped out of the door as he fired such a skilful Parthian shot. However, the doctor had scored his point; unsportingly perhaps, he has, with no more than his periscope showing, torpedoed the elusive Gobble. He has told him that he is a pig, but that he is safe now that he is free of his old associates and then he makes an agile exit—chuckling.

One comic element in this exchange is undoubtedly that of the biter being bit. The famous doctor is undeniably rude (though we see Sam frequently being rude, or offensively nationalistic, or both); he is furthermore rude to a clever man who is in a high diplomatic position and, what is worse to Sam, the smartest of smart Yankees, who could "catch a weasel asleep" any day in the week; then, to add insult to injury, the doctor, slipping away betimes from fields where glory does not stay, deprives the Hon. Alden Gobble, and therefore Sam, vicariously, of the opportunity of retaliation. There is nothing so irritating as being deprived of the last word. Both these outraged Americans are open-mouthed with surprise at this rudeness coming from so unexpected, so unfair a quarter, as a fashionable society doctor, to such an elevated, dignified and wide-awake personage as the Honourable Secretary to the American Legation at the Court of St. James.

Rudeness is often funny, probably because of the unexpectedness of it in a world where we cannot afford to be rude and also where we are trained from childhood to be polite, frequently against our real feelings. Politeness, in fact, is often a necessary hypocrisy. This is well illustrated by the great success of that rather over-rated comedy, *The Man Who Came to Dinner,* where the consistent rudeness, so startling in our society, defeats itself in the end because it is so consistent that there is no surprise left. Children of course are naturally and honestly rude. "Kiss the lady, Tommy," says Mother. "No, she's prickly", replies the young citizen of the future, with a complete honesty which he will learn to hide in his next ten years. In fact in one sense a child is not rude at all, since he does not mean to be, but merely honest; however, when a full-grown man, like Sam Slick, or the Hon. Gobble, or Dr. Abernethy, acts like a child, that is funny.

Another instance of farm language used for satirical effect is seen where Sam, still smarting patriotically from the slight to the Honourable Secretary to the Legation at the Court of St. James, turns for revenge on the nearest Britishers, the lacksadaisical Bluenoses with their country ways and their contemptible horseflesh:

> . . . the nasty yo'-necked, cat-hammed, heavy-headed, flat-eared, crooked-shanked, long-legged, narrow-chested, good-for-nothing brutes; they ain't worth their keep one winter. I vow I wish one of those blue-noses, with his go-to-meetin' clothes on, coat tails pinned up behind like a leather blind of a shay, an old spur on one heel, and a pipe stuck through his hat-band, mounted on one of those limber-timbered critters, that moves its hind legs like a hen a-scratchin' gravel, was sot down in Broadway, in New York, for a sight. Lord! I think I hear the West Point Cadets a-larfin' at him: "Who brought that 'are scarecrow out of standin' corn and stuck him here?"

The description of scrub stock in the way of horseflesh is good, cumulative invective—suggestive of Prince Hal telling Falstaff what he thinks of him or Kent giving Oswald a thumbnail sketch of himself—and, mounted contentedly on such an inferior steed, poor farmer Bluenose seems to lose caste by mere association. The man takes on the quality of the "cat-hammed", "heavy-headed" Rosinante he is riding; he after all chose it and sits contentedly on the unfortunate and dejected animal. The man appears something of a donkey. To underline this, Sam adds the reference to the coat-tails pinned up behind "like a leather blind of a shay", the old and solitary spur, the pipe in the hat-band, and the ignoble animal with the action (at least of the hind legs) of "a hen a-scratchin' gravel". This is a sufficiently graphic picture of a simple countryman in any age, at least until the nineteen-ten era of the first flivvers; but then the final rural image, of Bluenose being brought out of "standin' corn" like a scarecrow, and "sot down in Broadway", clinches it, with the additional nice contrast of Broadway and the farm, and the neat and shining West Point cadets and the shabby, happy, Bluenose farmer on his tottering Dobbin.

The equine metaphor is varied in the mordant description of Marm Pugwash, the bad-tempered but beautiful hostess of the inn at Amherst, who is brought to us in flesh and blood colours by means of typical Haliburton farm imagery.

Sam and the Squire reach the inn late; so late that Marm Pugwash is not at all pleased. She is irritably sweeping up the ashes and banking up the coals for the night and would just as soon not see them, or their money either. Sam, just before they get there, forewarns the Squire of the erratic service they may expect:

> . . .Marm Pugwash is onsartin in her temper as a mornin' in April; it's all sunshine or all clouds with her, and if she's in one of her tantrums, she'll stretch out her neck and hiss like a goose with a flock of goslings. I wonder what on earth Pugwash was a-thinkin' on when he signed articles of partnership with that 'are woman; she's not a bad-lookin' piece of furniture, neither. . . .

This kind of Medusan shock-effect is achieved by the simultaneous double image of a beautiful woman and a hissing goose. It is vivid comic imagery. (pp. 37-43)

Sam's farm imagery again clearly presents a character—this time the feminine one of Marm Pugwash discontentedly ruling the small and frustrating world of an Amherst inn in uneasy harness with Mr. Pugwash, whose weaknesses she probably came to recognize early, but after marriage. One feels, in the words of the old folk saying that the grey mare was the better horse, and that she knew it. There she stands, like Browning's Duchess, looking as though she were alive; the effect is achieved by a goose, sour apples and a skittish, temperamental mare.

Another instance of farm imagery, which is masterly in its combination of humour and pathos, occurs in Sam's account of the broken heart of a New England Paul Bunyan, one Washington Banks. This W. Banks was tall, so tall that he could spit down on the heads of British Grenadiers, or nearly wade across the Charleston river, and he was furthermore as strong as a towboat. Sam lets us know just how tall he was: "I guess he was somewhat less than a foot longer than the moral law and catechism too." He was the observed of all observers, particularly the feminine ones, who would rush to the "winders" exclaiming "bean't he lovely!" Well, poor Banks died of a broken heart, the only poor soul Sam had ever heard of who had actually succumbed to this romantic malady. Women, of whom Haliburton took a strongly unromantic view, never did:

> The female heart, as far as my experience goes, is just like a new india-rubber shoe; you may pull and pull at it until it stretches out a yard long, and then let go, and it will fly right back to its old shape. Their hearts are made of stout leather, I tell you; there is a plaguy sight of wear in 'em.

However, men have died, and worms have eaten them too, but not for love, says Sam. Nor did W. Banks die for love; he died from lifting the heaviest anchor of the *Constitution* on a bet, of all the foolish things to do, with his prospects. Sam meets this huge, long-legged, sad-eyed hero a month or two before his death, and finds him quite, quite down, in fact "teetotally defleshed":

> "I am dreadfully sorry," says I, "to see you Banks, lookin' so peeked: Why, you look like

a sick turkey hen, all legs; what on airth ails you?''

Now probably the only sick, wild bird which might convey the impression of a very tall, powerful, Bunyanesque figure in his decline would be a heron, crane or stork, but the farm image of the ''sick turkey hen'' is far better. It combines the pathetic and ridiculous in such a way as to surprise the reader into a rueful smile at humanity, which will lightly lift frigate anchors for no very good reason.

In another typical passage Sam Slick describes conditions in the States in the 1830's, by the use of an extraordinary cluster of seven farm or animal images. (The italics are Haliburton's.)

> *The Blacks and the Whites* in the States show their teeth and snarl, they are jist ready to fall to. The *Protestants and Catholics* begin to lay back their ears, and turn tail for kickin'. The *Abolitionists* and *Planters* are at it like two bulls in a pastur'. *Mob-law* and *Lynch-law* are workin' like yeast in a barrel and frothin' at the bunghole. *Nullification* and *Tariff* are like a charcoal pit, all covered up, but burnin' inside, and sendin' out smoke at every crack enough to stifle a horse. . . . *Surplus Revenue* is another bone of contention; like a shin of beef thrown among a pack of dogs, it will set the whole on 'em by the ears.

These terms and this imagery are so essential to Haliburton that one wonders how he would have written without them. And if this imagery succeeds with us in making his characters and incidents and anecdotes vivid, how much more effective must it have been in his day, when the farm and the country were much closer to every man and everyone was at least familiar with the ubiquitous cab-horse? With Haliburton, as this passage shows, the animal imagery comes naturally. Men are interpreted through the animals, usually to describe disorder satirically in the supposedly ordered world of men, or at least to show conduct which falls below the rational level. If there is something amiss Sam immediately thinks of a dog or a rat or a pig, or a bull, or a heifer, or a mare, or a weasel, or a lobster, or a frog, or a sick turkey hen. His animal images come pouring out as ''thick as toads arter rain''. (pp. 43-6)

It would be hard to find another writer who expresses his view of life with such a debt as Haliburton to the farm, the wharf, the kitchen and Noah's ark in general. . . . Sam talks, for instance, in farm and kitchen terms of another young lady at an inn where he was staying who was ''as blooming as a rose and as chipper as a canary bird,'' but who was also, he quickly discovered on attempting a kiss, ''as smart as a fox-trap and as wicked as a meat-axe,'' in fending off Yankee boarders. He finds however that it is all a feminine bluff and he gets his kiss in the end, which causes him to ruminate: ''. . . if you haven't turned out as rosy a rompin', larkin', light-hearted a heifer as ever I see'd afore, it's a pity.''

Shakespeare, originally a country boy, sometimes uses similar feminine imagery. One thinks, for instance, of one of the supreme comic images of literature, which gives the very subjective view of an old soldier, who was not at all impressed with her, of one of history's most interesting women. Scarus, liking Antony and blaming Cleopatra for Antony's downfall, describes her flight, from the famous sea-battle where she left her navy gazing, as being like that of a ''cow in June'', across the meadow, thundering hooves, tail erect—with a horse-fly

after her. Antony might have preferred a kinder simile, but the anti-romantic Haliburton, like Scarus, was a heifer man at heart, with a touch of the meat-axe in his nature. (p. 46)

> *L.A.A. Harding, ''Folk Language in Haliburton's Humour,'' in* Canadian Literature, *No. 24, Spring, 1965, pp. 37-46.*

TOM MARSHALL   (essay date 1976)

[*Marshall discusses the ambivalence in Haliburton's work toward American and British cultures.*]

The first very memorable character in Canadian literature is a stage-American, his creator an ardent Tory imperialist who went ''home'' to die in the British House of Commons. He wrote of the ''white nigger'' more than a hundred years before Norman Mailer and Pierre Vallières. (p. 134)

The first Sam Slick sketch appeared in Howe's newspaper *The Novascotian* in 1835. Sam was designed to reach a larger audience than Haliburton's history had done. The purpose was propaganda. . . . Sam was intended to demonstrate both the undesirable and the desirable qualities of the Yankee in order to make the Nova Scotians rouse themselves from their lethargy for long enough to institute certain material reforms. The result is a series of sketches, each with moral appended, an approximation of picaresque. As in *Don Quixote*, and in *Tom Sawyer* and *Huckleberry Finn* later on, a pair of contrasted heroes is presented for our inspection. Each embodies an aspect of his creator and makes an appeal to something in the intended audience.

The squire, tolerant, relaxed and reasonable, is akin to Haliburton himself. He epitomizes British virtues. Sam Slick, as many have observed, is a type of the Yankee pedlar, braggart and con-man. Naïve and cunning at the same time, he has the exaggerated self-confidence and childlike chauvinism that the British attributed to the Americans:

> I allot you had ought to visit our great country, Squire, said the Clockmaker, 'afore you quit for good and all. I calculate you don't understand us. The most splendid location atween the poles is the United States, and the first man alive is Gineral Jackson, the hero of the age, him that's skeered the British out of their seven senses. Then there's the great Daniel Webster; its generally allowed he's the greatest orator on the face of the airth, by a long chalk; and Mr. Van Buren, and Mr. Clay, and Amos Kindle, and Judge White, and a whole raft of statesmen, up to everything and all manner of politics; there ain't the beat of 'em to be found anywhere. If you was to hear 'em I consait you'd hear genuine pure English for once, anyhow; for it's generally allowed we speak better English than the British. They all know me to be an American citizen here, by my talk, for we speak it complete in New England.

Sam is as charming or as obnoxious as Muhammed Ali.

He has, as one would expect, a firm belief in manifest destiny:

> The Nova Scotians must recede before our free and enlightened citizens, like the Indians; our folks will buy them out, and they must give place to a more intelligent and ac-*tive* people.

They must go to the lands of Labrador, or be located back of Canada; they can hold on there a few years, until the wave of civilization reaches them, and then they must move again as the savages do. It is decreed; I hear the bugle of destiny a-soundin' of their retreat, as plain as anything. Congress will give them a concession of land, if they petition, away to Alleghany's backside territory, and grant them relief for a few years; for we are out of debt, and don't know what to do with our surplus revenue.

Here is the American attitude to other cultures and peoples (and, by implication, to the natural environment) perceived and expressed as plainly as by any Canadian nationalist of the 1970's. And yet, paradoxically, Sam is assigned the task of telling the Nova Scotians what is wrong with them. His own deficiencies of moral and spiritual insight do not invalidate his criticisms.

Slick combines the dialect and characteristics of the New Englander with those of the western American folk-hero: the rustic superman; Davy Crockett; Daniel Boone. He is a Canadian parody of the American folk-hero, the teller of "tall-tales" about Paul Bunyan and others. As John Matthews has observed, the invention of Sam involves the harnessing of the Yankee love of the "smart" con-man to a moral purpose [see excerpt dated 1962].

If Sam is intended, as he is, to represent a social barbarism, then why is he made so attractive, so charming? How is it he can be so acute in his criticism of the Bluenoses? What is Haliburton's attitude to him?

The answer to such questions is known instinctively to sensitive Canadians, so much so that we do not normally bother to ask them. We live quite naturally with a kind of doublethink about America and Americans. It is a truism that we are appalled at many things American, and yet cannot help but admire American inventiveness and energy. Envy, admiration, amusement, disapproval, even horror—these are the mixed feelings aroused by the antics of our close kinfolk to the south. To deny our cultural kinship with them, and our necessarily very ambivalent feelings about the United States, however, is to distort the essential (and continuing) task of defining our very real differences. It is hypocrisy not to admit that there is an "American" within us all.

The learned and respectable judge Haliburton was also a man of the new world. A questioner once received from him this reply: "I am Sam Slick, says I, at least what is left of me." He had roots in New England as well as old England. He is reported to have had a strong streak of coarseness in his nature, loving bawdy jokes and the company of "hostlers and fishermen rank with the obscenities of the stable and the dory." He loved the taproom and excelled in the art of telling unprintable stories. He seems to have been (not altogether unlike Al Purdy) an interesting mixture of roistering good fellow, on the one hand, and scholar and gentleman on the other, i.e. the squire and pedlar combined. The two heroes reflect two aspects of his character, and *The Clockmaker* itself expresses the "Canadian tension" between the ways of old world and new.

Haliburton deplores American social disorder, and predicts the civil war. But he also supplies Sam with a speech attacking the conceit and condescension of the Englishman visiting North America: "He swells out as big as a balloon; his skin is ready to burst with wind—a regular walking bag of gas . . ." As for the Nova Scotians, they are described as "a cross of English and Yankee, and therefore first cousins to us both." Their country is "like this night; beautiful to look at, but silent as the grave—still as death, asleep, becalmed." The unrealized nature of the place and people (here confused, as if they had achieved a union) is seen in terms of "a long heavy swell, like the breathin' of the chist of some great monster asleep". The image of the sleeping giant, who embodies our sense of space, was always appropriate. In their refusal to confront or engage this mysterious space, the people condemn themselves to a species of paralysis that mirrors the land's apparent emptiness.

The Americans, of course, have confronted the wilderness, but in a fashion so aggressive and destructive that we should be reluctant to emulate it. Slick is moved to observe that Nova Scotia is a happy backwater—in fact, "one of the happiest sections of all America"—but he feels that it could be one of the richest as well if the Bluenoses would abandon political agitation between reformers and Tories in order to concentrate on the development of natural resources. It would, I suppose, be smug of us (with our jaundiced hindsight) to ask whether Haliburton mightn't have been aware of the eventual problems and excesses of growth, of pushing clocks on the timeless. That is asking too much of a man of his time (unless he be Malthus). Sam's job was to teach the Bluenoses "the value of time." They were not supposed to acquire any of the less desirable American characteristics in the process.

Haliburton's politics are pragmatic. The reformers are characterized as misinformed and overcome with passion, and Haliburton's own Tories are not spared, since Sam warns them of "the prejudices of birth and education" and remarks shrewdly that "power has a natural tendency to corpulency".

In all of this one can see the ability to see two or more sides to every question, a pragmatic rather than a reactionary conservatism, an ability to live with uncertainties and antagonistic philosophies, an awareness of shifting perspectives. This is "Canadian". On the subject of systems of government Haliburton's mouthpiece Mr. Hopewell opines:

> When I look at the English House of Lords . . .
> and see so much larning, piety, talent, honour,
> vartue, and refinement collected together, I ax
> myself this here question: Can a system which
> produces and sustains such a body of men as
> the world never saw before and never will see
> ag'in, be defective? Well, I answer myself,
> perhaps it is, for all human institutions are so,
> but I guess it's e'en about the best arter all. It
> wouldn't do here now, Sam, nor perhaps for a
> century to come; but it will come sooner or
> later with some variations. Now the Newtown
> pippin, when transplanted to England, don't
> produce such fruit as it does in Long Island,
> and English fruits don't preserve their flavour
> here neither; allowance must be made for dif-
> ference of soil and climate . . . So it is . . . with
> constitutions; our'n will gradually approximate
> to their'n, and their'n to our'n. As they lose
> their strength of executive, they will varge to
> republicanism, and as we invigorate the form
> of government (as we must do, or go to the old
> boy), we shall tend towards a monarchy. If this
> comes on gradually, like the changes in the
> human body, by the slow approach of old age,
> so much the better; but I fear we shall have

fevers and convulsion-fits, and colics, and an everlastin' gripin' of the intestines first; you and I won't live to see it, Sam, but our posteriors will, you may depend.

Hopewell is an American clergyman, but surely he suggests here what Haliburton wants for Nova Scotia, i.e. a British system of government well adapted to North American conditions. This is the practical Canadian via media. Ironically, here is also an accurate prophecy of the American monarchical presidency.

Few (if any) of my observations here are very original, but my purpose is to suggest a situation and a pattern that persists in later Canadian writing. I am not aware that this pattern has ever been very fully examined as it emerges from the styles, textures and formal structures of our major works of literature. One finds in Haliburton's comedy a certain ambivalence; the things Canadian, American and British that he criticizes are inside him as well as outside him; one senses divided loyalties, ironic undertones. Similar but more complex and subtly developed ambivalences may be observed in the best humorous or satirical work of Leacock, Klein, Purdy, Mordecai Richler, Robertson Davies and Leonard Cohen.

Personally, I find *The Clockmaker* just a bit tedious as reading-matter, but it is the first notable attempt to articulate Canada, and therefore a good place to begin. (pp. 134-38)

> Tom Marshall, "Haliburton's Canada," in Canadian Literature, Nos. 68-9, Spring-Summer, 1976, pp. 134-38.

FRED COGSWELL (essay date 1976)

[*In this excerpt from a survey of Haliburton's works that primarily focuses on the Sam Slick series, Cogswell treats Haliburton as a humorist.*]

There runs throughout Haliburton's career a supreme irony; men read him for his humour and disregarded what to him was the *raison d'être* of everything he ever wrote.

Haliburton began his writing to make Nova Scotians and the rest of the world aware of the heritage and resources of the colony. He partly accomplished his purpose with the publication of *A General Description of Nova Scotia* . . . and *An Historical and Statistical Account of Nova Scotia.* . . . Both books are praiseworthy pioneering ventures, well proportioned in arrangement and dignified and straightforward in style, and they represent a vast amount of individual research. They brought Haliburton only a local reputation, although *An Historical and Statistical Account* was, many years later, to provide the theme for Longfellow's poem *Evangeline.* It was *The Clockmaker; or, The Sayings and Doings of Samuel Slick, of Slickville* . . . that launched Haliburton upon his literary career. (pp. 109-10)

The economic distress of the 1820's [in Nova Scotia] culminated in political agitation. Haliburton saw the Reform movement as a cloak for the ambitions of those who wished to supplant the present office-holders in their revenues. The salvation of Nova Scotia could only come, he felt, through a marked change in the habits of its people. He would have them emulate the thrift, hard work, and ingenuity of their Yankee neighbours, and his principal reason for writing *The Clockmaker* was to persuade them to do so. (p. 110)

The Clockmaker, like a picaresque novel, is episodic. The narrator, a thinly disguised Haliburton, and Sam Slick, a Yankee clockmaker, travel about Nova Scotia, and their seemingly chance encounters and observations provide the material for anecdote and conversation. There is no development of plot within the work as a whole, but each chapter is unified in that its incidents and comments exemplify a theme. Each chapter is a lay sermon illustrated by pointed anecdote and often culminating in a homely but original and apt epigrammatic text. With no rising curve of suspense to attract and hold attention, *The Clockmaker* has nevertheless gone through at least seventy editions since the first was published in 1836, and has appeared in the United States, in England, and on the Continent. It has done so as a result of its author's brilliant use of characterization, anecdote, language, and point of view.

Only one of the characters in *The Clockmaker* really counts. The Squire and Mr. Hopewell are either foils to Sam Slick or pegs on which to hang Tory arguments, and the characters met intermittently are types who can usually be summed up in a surname. Human interest is sustained in chapter after chapter of a very long narrative by the vanity, resourcefulness, and linguistic ability of that Yankee jack-of-all-trades, Sam Slick.

The character of Slick has been objected to on the grounds that his attitude and actions are not consistent throughout Haliburton's several works about him, that his speech reflects the dialects of many localities rather than one, that he is in fact paste rather than diamond, a stage character and not a credible human being. It is quite true that the Sam Slick of *The Clockmaker* is not the Sam Slick of *The Attaché; or, Sam Slick in England* . . . , intended for a different audience. In the latter book, the peaceful Yankee pedlar has become a thin-skinned, pugnacious braggadocio. Perhaps critics of the change have not sufficiently noticed that Americans abroad are not always the same as Americans at home. Both Sam Slicks are consistent within the limits of the books in which they appear. In point of fact, Sam Slick's versatility is an artistic reflection of the spirit of New England. The Yankees were the Greeks of the New World, and Slick is a folk hero, an Odysseus of their commercial frontier. In their excursions by land and sea, the Yankees not only acquired knowledge of men and affairs, but they also picked up their language where they found it, appropriating picturesque phrases much as they appropriated ideas that could later be turned into dollars and cents. In Haliburton's time, Slick was a credible New Englander; if he is a stage character today, he is one at least in the same brilliant sense as the characters of Molière and Dickens.

By his use of Sam Slick in *The Clockmaker,* Haliburton preserves a fine balance in assessing Americans, British, and Nova Scotian colonists. His judgments, like those of most great humorists, are essentially ambivalent. He admired the British for their institutions, achievements, and because he was of their stock. He disliked them because they refused to alter traditional ways of doing things and because they patronized colonists. He disliked the Americans because of their bragging, their opportunism, and because they had beaten the British. He admired their thrift, industry, shrewdness, and practicality. Haliburton saw in the Nova Scotians a people of essentially British virtues. They were, however, ruining themselves by extravagance and by sacrificing their private affairs to the pursuit of pleasure, politics, and religion. Sam Slick serves both as an unconscious example of American crudity and as a model to demonstrate to Nova Scotians how they should employ themselves. His praise of Britain is usually confined to secondhand accounts of the opinions of his clergyman and is often qualified by his own disagreement. Out of Sam Slick's comment and action in *The Clockmaker* emerges an ideal Nova Scotian life founded upon Burkean principles and unified by practicality and common sense. The satire becomes universal because individual and local personalities are kept subordinate to the central theme.

Whether of character, situation, or language, the humour in *The Clockmaker* depends upon the reader's enjoyment of the exposure of human weakness or incongruity. Although often coarse, it is not savage or cruel. Despite its theme, *The Clockmaker* is an essentially happy book. At this stage in his life, Haliburton was secure in his enjoyment of life and in his faith that his gospel for Nova Scotia would ultimately prevail.

Haliburton united two incongruous elements in the style of *The Clockmaker*. The narrative parts are written in the formal English of eighteenth-century prose. In Sam Slick's conversations, Haliburton becomes a prose poet, daring in metaphor, building up adjectival climaxes without fear of barbarisms, and utilizing all the local resources of dialect. The use of dialect did for Haliburton what the use of lowland Scots did for Burns. It gave him his crowning touch of individuality and lifted him above the ruck of popular writers like Theodore Hook and Charles Lever whose works superficially resemble his own.

The Clockmaker was Haliburton's most popular book. He followed it . . . with *The Attaché; or, Sam Slick in England,* which contained much hard-hitting criticism of English society. Haliburton's British audience proved much less disposed to laugh at themselves than they had been to laugh at Nova Scotian colonists and Yankees. Less popular still, but deservedly so, were the final Sam Slick books: *Sam Slick's Wise Saws and Modern Instances; or, What He Said, Did, or Invented* . . . and *Nature and Human Nature.* . . . (pp. 111-13)

All four books keep the same structure and for their interest depend upon Sam Slick, the freshness of their anecdotes, and the justice of the viewpoint displayed in them. Few readers can absorb more than sixteen hundred pages of almost continuous monologue by one character without becoming weary of his mannerisms. Few writers can fill up as many pages with humorous anecdote and remain fresh and funny. Haliburton told his best stories first, and after *The Attaché* there is a considerable decline in the quality of the anecdotes presented. Still worse, Haliburton gradually lost the perspective necessary to the humorist. In *The Clockmaker,* he could allow himself to be worsted by Sam Slick and laugh. In less than ten years, his consciousness that his political ideals were doomed prevented Haliburton from further self-laughter. The more strongly the forces of history turned against Toryism, the more extreme became his satire in its favour until the effect of his humour was vitiated by partisan distortion. *The Attaché,* good as it is, is marred by extreme statement. Worst of all, in the last two Sam Slick books, Haliburton shows signs of exchanging the role of social critic for that feeblest of vaudeville roles—the mere teller of funny stories.

Although the Sam Slick books made Haliburton's reputation, they do not comprise all his fiction. Two books in which the professional humorist triumphs over the deeper satirist of human society are *The Letter-Bag of the Great Western; or, Life in a Steamer* . . . and *The Season Ticket* . . . , the latter published after his move to England.

The first of these reminds one of Smollett's *Humphrey Clinker* and Galt's *The Ayrshire Legatees.* It is a collection of letters purporting to have been written by passengers aboard the *Great Western* en route from Liverpool to Halifax. Haliburton's avowed purpose was to popularize steam travel between England and Nova Scotia, but he completely fails to bring his imagination to this task, so that *The Letter-Bag* throughout remains as crude propaganda. He spends his ingenuity instead on rather juvenile "high jinks" and on burlesquing the national and religious mannerisms which Anglo-Saxons of a certain type automatically assign to "foreigners." Although it contains some fine comic passages, *The Letter-Bag* is too extreme in its caricature and too gross in its humour to rank very high as literature.

Railway travel in the British Isles is the matter of *The Season Ticket.* Here the subject is treated with more understanding and depth and is enlarged to include the whole subject of transportation within the British Empire. Haliburton saw improved transportation as vital to the unification and development of the Empire and advocated, among other projects of a far-seeing nature, the building by the British government of a railway to link the isolated British North American colonies. *The Season Ticket* is by far a more considerable book than *The Letter-Bag.* At the same time, neither incidents nor characters are so lively and entertaining as those of the Sam Slick books.

The Old Judge . . . is Haliburton's valedictory to a Nova Scotia he failed to convert to his own way of thinking. Sombre, realistic, balanced in its judgments, it is the most satisfying of all Haliburton's books although it lacks the surface brilliance of *The Clockmaker.* It is constructed upon a pattern similar to that of *The Clockmaker* but more diversified. Nova Scotia is seen through the eyes of an educated British tourist who visits his friend, the Old Judge, and is squired around Nova Scotia by another friend, Lawyer Barclay. The tourist's observations and encounters are supplemented by the observations and reminiscences of his friends and the other characters who are incidentally introduced. The most interesting of these last is Stephen Richardson, a Nova Scotian eccentric. In the sketches of men and women, in the account of melodramatic events at lonely frontier outposts, and in his background descriptions, Haliburton unveils in *The Old Judge* an unsuspected facet of romantic feeling and talents of a high order for serious fiction. Had he considered it worthwhile, he might have become Canada's first major novelist.

Although *The Old Judge* is not lacking in the political bias and humour that characterized Haliburton's work, it is a sad book—full of regret for a way of life that was passing and masking its bitterness with ironic dignity. In its range, it is easily the best portrait of early nineteenth-century life in British North America; in human insight and interest, it is matched only by Susanna Moodie's *Roughing It in the Bush.* (pp. 113-14)

Much of Haliburton's work is dated. Many of his favourite mannerisms, like the pun, have gone out of style. The smart Yankee is no longer a novelty to readers. There are, however, in his best work enough humour and wise comment of a universal nature to make it worth reading today. Haliburton must continue to vie with Stephen Leacock as Canada's greatest humorist. (p. 115)

Fred Cogswell, "Haliburton," in Literary History of Canada: Canadian Literature in English, Vol. I, edited by Carl F. Klinck, second edition, University of Toronto Press, 1976, pp. 106-15.

BEVERLY RASPORICH (essay date 1982)

[*The following excerpt is from a feminist discussion of the Canadian humorists Thomas McCulloch, Haliburton, and Stephen Leacock.*]

The female student and critic of Canadian literary humour writes doubly from the underground. Not only do some members of the largely male-directed Can. Lit. Club dismiss her subject matter as trivial, but the contents and face of Canadian humour are remarkably masculine. Its profile—composed of the likes of McCulloch's Mephibosheth Stepsure, Haliburton's Sam Slick, Leacock's "little man" in the bank, Davies' Samuel Marchbanks, Richler's Boy Wonder, Mitchell's Jake and the kid, and Kroetsch's studhorse man—is adequate proof of modern psychology's conclusion that traditionally women have not been allowed, or have not chosen to be, purveyors of humour. As I see it, the female critic has two choices. She can, like Thomas Haliburton's "white niggers," the Bluenoses, lazily acquiesce to the status quo, adopt the established literary aesthetic of humour which from Socrates to Freud to Wayne C. Booth's *A Rhetoric of Irony* has had a masculine vocabulary and bias and assist in her own continuing literary colonization, but prove the place of a Canadian humorous tradition; or she can take the imperial bull by the horns, look him squarely in the eye, and insist on his co-operation in liberating humour into a brave new world. Although my feminist friends might scoff at the first choice, on the one hand, as a good natured female critic, my inclination is to nurture the nation's infant laughter, regardless of its sex. On the other hand, the second choice has to be considered; not only because I am a woman, but because I am a Canadian, and the utopian New Eden dream which is the very heart of the Canadian Psyche and His masculine humour belongs equally to me.

In assessing the early comic tradition in English Canada, it is fair to say that it flourished suddenly in nineteenth century Nova Scotia with Thomas McCulloch and Thomas Haliburton, died, and was revived some hundred years later by the internationally celebrated Stephen Leacock. (pp. 227-28)

Some critics might argue that Canadian humour . . . began with the Nova Scotian Thomas Haliburton, a nineteenth-century Tory judge . . . whose fictional character Sam Slick, an audacious, peddling, comic Yankee, was in his time extremely popular, earning his author the rather paradoxical title of the "Father of American Humour." Although the raw, republican character and humour of Sam Slick, duping the Nova Scotia locals as a southern peddler in *The Clockmaker* . . . and upsetting old world decorum in *The Attaché* . . . , was a portrait of early American frontier fun, at least one critic, R. E. Watters, has begun to see in Haliburton's fiction the beginning of a native Canadian position. In Haliburton's ambivalent treatment of the fast-talking, fast-selling "cipherin" Sam as both satiric object and a vigorous standard of comparison to the lazy bluenosers, Watters identifies the characteristic Canadian love-hate attitude towards the American; and in his perceptive analysis of the alternate voice in Haliburton's humour, the character of Squire Poker, who was introduced as a British traveller but in later revisions became the native Nova Scotian, Watters uncovers the quiet, double-edged ironic mode of humour which is typical of the Canadian as "fifth business," of Haliburton and later, of Stephen Leacock, as he stands *in media res* between two aggressive parent cultures, Uncle Sam and John Bull. For Haliburton, Squire Poker expressed the Canadian's final ironic self-knowledge of being caught between two parent cultures and of not so easily shaking off the influence of aggressive America. (p. 232)

Recognizing the Canadian's intermediary position is important because it is the very condition of the humour of such Anglo-Canadian nationally-minded writers as Haliburton and Lea-

The Squire, Sam Slick, and Reverend Hopewell at an English laborer's cottage in The Attaché, *first series. Illustration by C. W. Jefferys from* Sam Slick in Pictures: The Best of the Humor of Thomas Chandler Haliburton, *edited by Lorne Pierce. The Ryerson Press, 1956.*

cock. And while they have been capable of turning the sandwiched position to advantage in the British-American marketplace, by playing, as Haliburton's Squire does, the devious, ironic middle man, or as Leacock does in his famous essay "Oxford As I See It" by cleverly, simultaneously lambasting both British and American systems of education, the collision between old world and new world values as it affects their own country is their first motivation to satire and irony. More precisely, in the case of Haliburton, Leacock (and later, Robertson Davies), it is their allegiance to an imperial, genteel British ideal of Canada as anglicized New Eden in conflict with the democratic ordinary realities of Canadian life and the infectious, vulgar spirit of American republicanism which forces their humour. Certainly, this is the underlying tension and *raison d'être* of Haliburton's *The Clockmaker*. For Haliburton, as a Tory aristocrat descended from an old New England family who fled the American revolution, the New Eden dream for Nova Scotia, in conrast to the reformer Joseph Howe's vision of responsible government, was based on British ideals and allegiance. Haliburton's New England legacy was the Loyalist view that by preserving the British connection in political subservience, social ideals, and intellectual culture, "the descendants of the exiled Tories would grow into a great nation in the Northern regions." This idealism lies behind *The Clockmaker;* its satire is born of the distance Haliburton perceived between the ideal of a superior country of British gentlemen and the reality of the coarse Bluenosers, many of whom had emigrated out of New England before the revolution and were as ridiculously Yankee to Haliburton as Sam Slick himself, who so easily duped them. (pp. 233-34)

While collapsing idealism is generally the source of both irony and satire, in early Canadian humour the dream of a new world utopia meeting reality is a steady invitation to satire; and an escape into pastoral memory and convention a constant ironic fancy. A classic expression of the latter, the ironic retreat as comic métier, is Haliburton's later humorous work on his colony, *The Old Judge.*

The Old Judge, written after Joseph Howe had obtained responsible government and Haliburton had lost his "anti-democratic" battle with him for Nova Scotia, is a fine chronicle of manners, full of descriptive interest and not without humour. Significantly, however, the utopian hope which led to satire in *The Clockmaker* is replaced in *The Old Judge* by a nostalgia for a lost Eden and a benevolent irony of defeat and acceptance. Although as the author explains, "You will, perhaps, smile at the idea of antiquities in a country which is universally called a new world," he celebrates the Nova Scotian past, including its picturesque beauty; Fred Cogswell nicely summarizes the thrust of the fiction when he explains: "Although *The Old Judge* is not lacking in the political bias and humour that characterized Haliburton's work, it is a sad book—full of regret for a way of life that was passing and masking its bitterness with ironic dignity" [see excerpt dated 1976].

The vision of paradise to be and then lost, and its ultimate mode of humour, the ironic dignity of the gentleman, necessarily affects the status of women in Haliburton's humour. Looking backwards in *The Old Judge* to the Golden Age of Nova Scotia in the late eighteenth century meant to Haliburton the resurrection of conservative thought, of Burkean idealism and spirit, and of the doctrine of sentimentalism which, among other things, claimed that the truly aristocratic and ideal woman was morally superior and more sensitive than the male. The obscene joke, then, which Haliburton was fond of in male company, was not fit for the ears of innocent Eves and aristocratic mothers whose maternal "divinity within her" in *The Old Judge* "sympathizes with the celestial, and invests it with the attributes of a ministering angel." . . . Humour, in fact, really could only embrace woman when she fell from her pedestal and became thereby a proper object of satire and reform. Since immigrants were not universally British gentility, Haliburton had plenty of material. In *The Old Judge,* he explains: "Nothing astonishes the inhabitants of these colonies more than the poverty, ignorance and degradation of the people who are landed upon their shores, from the passenger ships that annually arrive from Europe." . . . The natural outcome of these rough settlers and the primitive frontier fact was a savage comedy of sexual battle which Haliburton articulated through Sam Slick and his taming of women, a comedy which in his Tory-minded attitude towards women he could not help approve of, although he distanced himself from its primitive "republican" excesses as the civilized Squire. A significant portion of Sam Slick's humour then is based on subjugating and "beatin womankind," on putting the "spring-stop" to her tongue and in demonstrating through such savage comedy as the flaying of Marm Porter by Sam in "Taming a Shrew" that " 'A woman, a dog, and a walnut / The more you lick them the better they be'." . . . (pp. 234-36)

While some thoughtful male critics like R. E. Watters worry about women as the butt of the sadistic joke, most do not. Moreover, it would seem that Christian culture and its metaphor of lost Eden due to female fault (When Adam delved and Eve span / Who then was the gentleman?) is a firm first psychological premise of Canada's gentleman humorists, Haliburton, Leacock, and Davies, whose comic personas retreat into an ideal world of civilized male order and authority, venturing out only to belittle women from a distance for falling from grace (into vulgar equality); or, in the case of the old judge, to report with irony a gaudy, plebian, tasteless caste of women cavorting about in what ought to be genteel society:

> Oh! Look at that old lady, with a flame-coloured satin dress, and an enormous bag hanging on her arm, with tulips embroidered on it, and a strange looking cap, with a bell-rope attached to one side of it, fanning a prodigious bouquet of flowers in her belt . . . Oh, observe that member woman, that lady from the rural districts, habited in a gaudy-coloured striped silk dress, trimmed all over with little pink bows, having yellow glass buttons in the centre; a cap without a back, stuffed full of feathers like Cinderella's godmother; and enormously long gloves, full of wrinkles, like the skin of an elephant! They are both happy, but it is the happiness of fools.
>
> (p. 236)

The quest for Eden, the quarrel with Eden, and Eden regained, may not be the absolute, stringent pattern of a national humour (or even exclusively Canadian) but certainly, the ideal of an arcane garden place, parodied, or presented as a hopeful model in social satire or in ironic comedy, persists in Canadian letters. (p. 239)

The reasons for the pastoral preoccupation are no doubt various, but they would seem to include the longstanding effects of a clerical and colonial paternalism which promotes both Christian metaphor and myth. As well, the New Eden ideal meeting, if not the reality, at least the mythology of nation as vast, formidable frontier establishes the basic incongruity of much of our humour. In any case, for many of our twentieth-century humorists, virtue continues to exist in the country, vice in the town and city, while women as picaresque adventurers or satiric sages exist hardly at all. It seems to me that in order for the comic tradition in Canada to become more than, in the words of Sam Slick, "small potatoes and few in a hill," women need to join, as equal jovial participants, that laughing company of men dubbed by Mark Twain "the belly and the members." Otherwise, we will never boast of a progressive, full-bodied tradition of literary humour in this country. It may very well be, too, that this will not be accomplished until the serious moral mythology of Eden with the female as seductive destroyer of the garden dream completely recedes from or is happily revised in the Canadian comic imagination. Certainly our laughter will persist at the comic novels and humorous sketches written from a male point of view but without an alternate, genuine female perspective, I venture to say that for literary women, at least, it can only be half-hearted. (pp. 239-40)

Beverly Rasporich, "The New Eden Dream: The Source of Canadian Humour, McCulloch, Haliburton, and Leacock," in Studies in Canadian Literature, *Vol. 7, No. 2, 1982, pp. 227-40.*

KATHERINE MORRISON   (essay date 1984)

[*Morrison discusses* The Old Judge *as a serious commentary by Haliburton on politics and society, deeming it his best work.*]

Thomas Chandler Haliburton was the most famous writer in nineteenth-century British North America. In spite of his renown the book that many modern scholars consider Haliburton's finest, *The Old Judge or Life in a Colony* . . . , is almost unknown, neglected in its day because of the absence of the author's popular comic character, the Yankee pedlar Sam Slick. Twentieth-century lack of interest in Haliburton's works rests upon three assumptions: Sam Slick is no longer very amusing; Haliburton's right-wing Tory views are offensive to modern readers; and Haliburton's writings are not in the mainstream of Canada's literary tradition. Few would disagree with the first of these, but the second and third need to be examined in light of *The Old Judge*. This book shows aspects of Haliburton and his art which are not present in his other works.

Most of the stories in *The Old Judge* are told by Judge Sandford, Haliburton's serious and thoughtful persona. An English visitor, as narrator, and Lawyer Barclay, an additional story teller, maintain and extend the Judge's point-of-view during their travels through Nova Scotia. The Judge's reminiscences integrate the past with the observations of the travellers in a unified colonial setting. The three are educated, astute, and share their author's Tory sympathies. (p. 58)

The humorist and Tory polemicist are augmented by a compassionate paternalist and a patriot eager to preserve the Nova Scotian past. In addition, Fred Cogswell found "an unsuspected facet of romantic feeling and talents of a high order for serious fiction" [see excerpt dated 1976]. In *The Old Judge* Haliburton used all of his skills as an author in the service of a central message: the Loyalist ideals should not be rejected and forgotten in favour of a more "American" and democratic society.

Haliburton was familiar with the prevailing ideals of the United States and wanted no part of them in Nova Scotia. Jefferson's famous words to Madison, " '*that the earth belongs in usufruct to the living*': that the dead have neither powers nor rights over it," was never "self-evident" to Haliburton or his compatriots. The concept of a new and morally superior nation, which was free of a feudal past, had wide popularity in the United States of the early nineteenth century. . . .

Jefferson's statement means that the institutions of the past are escapable. Haliburton's American contemporary, Ralph Waldo Emerson, went much further, arguing that all human institutions are suspect. (p. 59)

Haliburton must have found these Americans naïve. We can imagine his answering Jefferson on the past and Emerson on society with Burke's words that the social contract is "a partnership not only between those who are living, but between those who are living, those who are dead and those who are to be born." In *The Old Judge* he stressed the often disastrous consequences of attempts to shed the past or to live in isolation, both stemming from a disdain for communalism and glorification of the individual: "alas," he said, "man in America is made for himself."

Haliburton, while he admired American efficiency and inventiveness, wanted a community-based and hierarchically structured society, firmly in that eighteenth-century tradition which rested upon centuries of faith in a Great Chain of Being. He was a latter-day Augustan, spiritually akin to Samuel Johnson.

Haliburton expressed a Burkean faith in a sense of tradition as the basis for keeping those in authority wise and responsible. His satiric barbs, directed at irresponsibility in the upper-classes and insubordination among the lower, suggest that *noblesse oblige*, a valued part of those Loyalist ideals, must be kept alive and healthy. (p. 60)

By the time he wrote *The Old Judge* Haliburton probably realized that his desired social structure would never prove acceptable in a land where the poorest immigrant had reason to hope that he might soon become a landowner. Judge Sandford claims membership in "the good old Tory party, the best, the truest, the most attached and loyal subjects her Majesty ever had. . . . There are only a few of them now surviving, and they are old and infirm men, with shattered constitutions and broken hearts . . . doomed to inevitable martyrdom." The elegiac note merges with the author's still undiminished powers as a humorist.

In spite of his commitment to the British Empire, Haliburton was not an unquestioning Anglophile. In *The Old Judge* he spoke with bitterness of a British tendency to denigrate colonials. Both an effete aristocracy and the levelling and socially fragmenting tendencies of the United States were to be resisted. The very act of writing *The Old Judge* indicates how eager Haliburton was to defend, extol, and preserve the traditions and history of his native Nova Scotia. It was an outpost of Empire, which he wished to see governed with the accumulated wisdom of British history.

Three tales near the beginning of *The Old Judge* present Judge Sandford as a Johnsonian social critic. "Asking a Governor to Dine," "A Ball at Government House," and "The Old Admiral and the Old General" make such extensive use of the dinner party and ball as a setting for situational irony and didactic humour that they evoke Jane Austen's writings. In addition, there is the common theme of wise-versus-foolish governing and the presence in all of Governor Hercules Sampson. This good-natured man's effectiveness is weakened by the requirement that he treat everyone as an equal. He is the "Old General" of the last of the three stories, whose frustrating position is contrasted to that of the "Old Admiral" where naval traditions permit no such nonsense. Haliburton, probably contemplating that favourite eighteenth-century concept, "the ship of state," made the case that the colony would be better off if viewed as a ship and "governed" by a "captain" than by its present inefficient, semi-democratic machinery.

The situation is presented in microcosm in "Asking a Governor to Dine." Captain Jones, the only navy man at a dinner party given by a wealthy merchant for Governor Sampson, arrives late. "He was dressed in an old shabby frock-coat with a pair of tarnished epaulettes, his hands bore testimony to their familiarity with the rigging, and he had not submitted himself to a barber for two days, at least." Governor Sampson's arrogant young aide-de-camp, the Honourable Mr. Trotz, makes an audible comment on the strange-looking guest:

> "Pray," said Trotz . . . to his neighbour, but loud enough to be distinctly heard, "who is that old quiz? Is he a colonist?"
>
> "Captain Jones, of H.M. ship Thunderer, sir; very much at your service!" said the sailor with a very unmistakable air and tone.
>
> Trotz quailed. It was evident that, though a good shot, he preferred a target to an antago-

nist, and wanted bottom. True courage is too noble a quality to be associated with swaggering and insolant airs.

Trotz, who appears again in "A Ball at Government House," represents the decadent aspects of aristocracy, where irresponsible behaviour weakens the traditional hierarchy and encourages the trend toward social and political equality. Captain Jones' rough exterior counters a widespread belief that persons of authority in hierarchical societies do not work, but live on the energies of their underlings. Haliburton, by showing the inability of someone like Trotz to stand up to a man like Captain Jones, is saying that those who are courageous, hard-working, responsible, and intelligent do, in fact, rise to the top. Trotz is a travesty of *noblesse oblige;* Captain Jones is fulfilment.

In "The Old Admiral and the Old General," Governor Sampson envies the Admiral for having "'no turbulent House of Assembly to plague him.'" The Admiral "is not altogether able to understand [the legislature] . . . whose remonstrances look very like mutiny to him, and always suggest the idea of arrest and court-martial." These two highest officials in the colony have "each their little empire to rule. The one is a despotic and the other a constitutional monarch." . . . The Admiral, a larger edition of Captain Jones, "converses . . . freely," while the General, "compelled to be ceremonious," is unable to perform effectively as Governor of Nova Scotia.

By describing their entertainments, Haliburton strengthens his position with dramatic irony. A typical party of the General's, "A Ball at Government House," is a huge and heterogeneous assemblage of people. "Sir Hercules, with great good humour" attempts a conversation: . . .

> "What a pity it is there is no theatre at Halifax."
>
> "Yes, sir—very, sir—for them as sees no harm in 'em, sir—yes, sir."

At the other end of the social scale we have the female counterpart of the Honourable Mr. Trotz. A social climber instructs a young girl:

> "I will introduce [Captain Beech and Lieutenant Birch] to you; they are both well connected and have capital interest. Take my arm, but don't look at those country members, dear, and then you won't have to cut them, for Sir Hercules don't like that. . . . Keep close to me, now, and I'll take you among the right set. . . ."

The Admiral never has such entertainments; his training and experience forbid toadying and self-serving. He chooses his guests without regard to local politics:

> People are expected to speak above a whisper, or they cannot be heard, and to be at home, or they cannot be agreeable. The dinner itself has . . . a higher seasoning, . . . while the forbidden onion lurks stealthily concealed under the gravy. . . . The conversation, also, is unlike that at the palace. . . . You hear nothing of the Merrygomish Bridge, the election at Port Medway, or the alteration of the road at Aspatangon, to which the Governor is compelled to listen, and, at each repetition, appear as much interested as ever.

The Governor is now "compelled to listen." Presumably he is also compelled to retain the services of Mr. Trotz, whom the Admiral, like Captain Jones, would dispose of summarily.

There is a sharp contrast between the petty materialism and parochial "pork-barrelling" of the General's guests and the wide-ranging interests of the Admiral's. The intensity of the social irony in these three stories shows an author deeply concerned with the source and wielding of political power.

Two stories which show Haliburton in a more overtly serious vein, concerned with the human need for a sense of community, are "The Lone House" and the two-part "Horse-Shoe Cove; or, Hufeisen Bucht." Both highlight Haliburton's preoccupation with the effect of the past on the living; both reveal his "anti-Emersonian" attitude toward nature.

The introduction to "Horse-Shoe Cove" is a succinct expression of Haliburton's moral outrage at the individualistic trend in North America:

> There are no hamlets, no little rural villages. . . . No system of landlord and tenant, or farmer and cotter, and, consequently, no motive or duty to protect and encourage on the one hand, or to conciliate and sustain on the other. No material difference in rank or fortune . . . and hence no means to direct or even to influence opinion; and, above all, no unity in religious belief; and, therefore, no one temple in which they can all worship together, and offer up their united prayers and thanksgivings as members of one great family to their common Father in Heaven.

The Judge's "good-old" Toryism is spelled out in this quotation, stressing the religious basis he believed to be necessary to a viable community. His disapproval of these tendencies to leave home and dwell in isolation does not, however, include the spearheading of a new settlement:

> Follow any new road into the wilderness, and you will find a family settled there, miles and miles from any house. But imagination soon fills up the intervening space with a dense population, and you see them in the midst of a well-cultivated country, and enjoying all the blessings of a civilized community. They are merely pioneers.

The events at Horse-Shoe Cove illustrate the dangers inherent in real isolation. This is layered history, where successive occupants—Indian, French, German, and British—of a beautiful cove are haunted by "ghosts" of former inhabitants. These ghosts succeed in evicting the trespassers, suggesting that the dead have not only rights but also power over the living. The American concept of a "virgin land" without predecessors is implicitly, but strongly, denied.

A German named Nicholas Spohr, exploring south of Lunenberg, finds a cove, "concealed by two hooded promontories, that gave to the Cove a striking resemblance to a horse-shoe." "Hooded" sounds an ominous note countering the good-luck implied by the horse-shoe. There were forty cleared acres, buildings of hewn timbers, a large bell, a neglected orchard and garden, a spring, and a rustic table with "Pierre and Madeline, 1740" and two clasped hands carved into the corner. These clasped hands are an extended ironic symbol in this tale of banishment.

Nicholas lays a claim and moves his family to this beautiful estate, where he begins to fancy himself a landed gentleman and ceases to do much work. Indians arrive to bury a deceased chief in their ancient burial-ground. They look upon him as an intruder and temporarily mar his joy. The stress on Nicholas' "happiness" in his unearned wealth suggests that Haliburton may have been implicitly critical of Jefferson's "pursuit of happiness" as a human right. Later, Nicholas returns from Halifax to find his wife and children slaughtered and scalped. He had cut trees in the Indian burial-ground to sell for cordwood and to open his estate to the admiring gaze of travellers. In "prostrating these ancient trees, he had unintentionally committed sacrilege, and violated the repose of the dead—an offence that, in all countries and in all ages, has ever been regarded with pious horror or implacable resentment."

Nature provides an illusion of happiness to the ill-fated Nicholas Spohr, who thinks of Horse-Shoe Cove as "a world of wonders." He returns in the full splendour of autumn to discover his slaughtered family:

> He had never beheld anything like this in his own country. . . . [Here] death was cruel as well as impatient, and, like a consumptive fever, beautified its victim with hectic colour before it destroyed it. . . . When he entered the little placid Cove, which lay glittering like a lake of molten silver beneath the gaze of the declining sun, he was startled at beholding his house reversed and suspended far and deep in its pellucid bosom, and the trees growing downwards with their umbrageous branches or pointed tops, and all so clear, so distinct, and perfect, as to appear to be capable of corporeal touch. And yet, strange to say, far below the house, and the trees, and other earthly objects, was the clear, blue sky with its light, fleecy clouds that floated slowly through its transparent atmosphere, while the eagle was distinctly visible soaring in unrestrained liberty in the subterranean heavens.

Haliburton intended close links between this scene of magnificence and the grisly spectacle awaiting.

Losing his reason, Nicholas dies on the graves of his wife and children, becoming a ghost to the local inhabitants. The Cove is now a terrifyingly haunted place, where Indians bury their dead with strange incantations and rotting timbers expose the bell which tolls on windy nights. The first alien inhabitants to be evicted from the Cove were the French; Nicholas and his family become the next.

The second part of the story occurs a generation later. A Captain John Smith arrives with the Loyalists, buys and renovates Horse-Shoe Cove, but finds himself isolated for the local German inhabitants fear and resent him as an intruder and magician. When a young indentured servant runs to the nearest town and charges Smith with the murder of a pedlar, the jury convicts him in spite of a lack of evidence. Smith escapes and hides until the remains of the pedlar and a bear are found. Though he is now exonerated, joy in Horse-Shoe Cove is gone and the Smiths depart for England; the third to be driven forth.

The Indians and Germans of this story appear to be an extension of nature: human society in prescriptively controlled communities. An intruder is never welcomed by such a society, but is usually tolerated until perceived to do violence to the group's customs or beliefs. Neither Nicholas nor Captain Smith was guilty of any wrongdoing according to those who look upon man as an individual free to discard his past and inherited institutions. According to Haliburton, however, by leaving the protection and moral support of his own community, each wanderer brought his troubles on himself.

The conclusion stresses Haliburton's strong sense of the past:

> The land comprised within the grant of poor Nicholas Spohr . . . remained derelict for many years; but as it was covered with valuable timer, cupidity in time proved stronger than superstition. . . . The story of Nicholas and Captain Smith is only known to a few old men like myself, and will soon be lost altogether, in a country where there is no one likely to found a romance on the inmates and incidents of the "Hufeisen Bucht."

Judge Sandford is once more the martyred old Tory dying of a broken heart, but he makes a valid point by suggesting that the land has again been violated. The cupidity that disdained respect for the Indians' sacred ground is paralleled by a shortsightedness which fails to preserve the community's history. It cannot see beyond possession of the land by the living.

The Lent family of "The Lone House" provides a different illustration of the sad consequences of human isolation, for here there are no former inhabitants. The family dwells upon a desolate spot near the Atlantic coast, surrounded by "enormous bogs . . . in an undulating country of granite formation." There is enough soil to sustain only one family and the government and nearest neighbours provide a small subsidy for maintaining a way-station and possible haven on a barren stretch of the coastal road. There was a benevolent motive in the Lents' decision to settle here and provide a much-needed service, but man "was not made to live alone; . . . natural wants, individual weakness, and common protection require that, though we live in families, our families must dwell in communities."

John Lent, the husband and father, is caught in a blizzard, frozen in a sitting position, returned to his family by the mailman, and left unburied with his widow and little girls. Again Haliburton casts nature as a seductive yet dangerous beauty, for the Judge is reminded of this grim story as the narrators admire an ice storm:

> There had been . . . a slight thaw accompanied by a cold fine rain that froze . . . into ice of the purest crystal. Every deciduous tree was covered with this glittering coating, and looked in the distance like an enormous though graceful bunch of feathers; while on a nearer approach, it resembled . . . a dazzling chandelier. The open fields . . . glistened in the sun as if thickly strewed with the largest diamonds; and every rail of the wooden fences . . . was decorated with a delicate fringe of pendant ice, that radiated like burnished silver. . . . The . . . rays of the sun . . . invested them with all the hues of the prism. It was a scene as impossible to describe as to forget, . . . and its effects are as well appreciated as its beauty. The farmer foresees . . . serious injury to his orchard, the woodsman a pitiless pelting of ice, . . . the huntsman a barrier to his sport, and the traveller an omen of hard and severe weather; and yet such was the

glory of the landscape, that every heart felt its magic.

There is no pantheism here. This Burkean concept of the Sublime is one more aspect of *The Old Judge* which identifies Haliburton with Canada's literary tradition.

The bereaved widow of John Lent temporarily loses her reason but the outcome of "The Lone House" is a contrast to that of "Horse-Shoe Cove," for here the survivors are not driven away. God, plus the spirit of her dead husband, provide the widow with a mystical community to hold her to her lonely outpost. She is possessed, not rejected, by the land:

> God had never failed them. . . . She . . . and her children had been fed in the wilderness, like the chosen people of the Lord. . . . It would be ungrateful and distrustful in her to leave a place He had selected for her. . . . And, besides, she said, there is my old man; his visits now are dearer to me than ever; he was once my companion—he is now my guardian angel. I cannot and will not forsake him while I live; and when it is God's will that I depart hence, I hope to be laid beside him, who, alive or dead, has never suffered this poor dwelling to be to me a "Lone House."

The widow, a responsible member of the Family of Man, continues her husband's work of succouring the traveller and providing a haven for the shipwrecked mariner. Haliburton paid a moving tribute to the strength of woman, who "successfully resists afflictions that overpower the vigour and appal the courage of man." He is all patriotism and compassion in this story; no humorist or outraged Tory is in evidence.

The Old Judge is like an ancient treasure chest into which a few have glanced, but whose gems have not been carefully examined. Among these are comic characters comparable to Leacock's best and enough tales of the supernatural to suggest that the Canadian literary tradition has a plentiful supply of ghosts. It is said that Haliburton left us only one book of such high quality, for there are indications near the end of *The Old Judge* that he planned to continue writing stories about life in a colony. Professor Watters believes that he would have done so had he received any encouragement from his readers. He did not. Haliburton bowed to his public and returned to Sam Slick: an overworked parody of an American, who successfully turned *The Old Judge* into "a *forgotten* masterpiece." (pp. 60-7)

> Katherine Morrison, "In Haliburton's Nova Scotia: 'The Old Judge or Life in a Colony'," in Canadian Literature, *No. 101, Summer, 1984, pp. 58-68.*

ADDITIONAL BIBLIOGRAPHY

Avis, Walter S. "Further Lexicographical Evidence from *The Clockmaker*." *American Speech* XXVIII, No. 1 (February 1952): 16-18.
　　A list of words for which the first known appearance in writing occurs in the speech of Haliburton's character Sam Slick.

Bailey, Richard W. "Haliburton's Eye and Ear." *The Canadian Journal of Linguistics* 26, No. 1 (Spring 1981): 90-101.
　　Discusses the work done by linguist Walter S. Avis concerning the speech patterns of Haliburton's characters and examines Haliburton's use of English dialects.

———. "The English Language in Canada." In *English as a World Language,* edited by Richard W. Bailey and Manfred Görlach, pp. 134-76. Ann Arbor: University of Michigan Press, 1982.
　　Includes a discussion of Haliburton's use of different varieties of Canadian and American English.

Baker, Ray Palmer. "Thomas Chandler Haliburton." In *Sam Slick,* by Thomas Chandler Haliburton, edited by Ray Palmer Baker, pp. 13-28. New York: George H. Doran Co., 1923.
　　Praises the freshness of Haliburton's Sam Slick stories and the author's skill at characterization and description.

Bengtsson, Elna. *The Language and Vocabulary of Sam Slick: I.* Upsala Canadian Studies, edited by S. B. Liljegren, vol. V. Upsala: A.-B. Lundequistska Bokhandeln, 1956, 52 p.
　　A study of the language used in the Sam Slick series.

Bissell, Claude T. "Haliburton, Leacock and the American Humourous Tradition." *Canadian Literature,* No. 39 (Winter 1969): 5-19.
　　Examines the attitudes of Haliburton and Stephen Leacock toward Canada and the United States and their effect on the two authors' approach to humor.

Chisholm, Mary P. F. "'Sam Slick' and Catholic Disabilities in Nova Scotia." *Catholic World* LXIV, No. 382 (January 1897): 459-65.
　　Discusses Haliburton's efforts to secure political emancipation for Canadian Catholics.

Chittick, V.L.O. "The Pervasiveness of Sam Slick." *Dalhousie Review* 33, No. 2 (Summer 1953): 88-101.
　　Examines the literary tradition behind the stock character Sam Slick and its effect on Haliburton's works.

———. "The Gen-u-ine Yankee." In *Masks of Fiction: Canadian Critics on Canadian Prose,* edited by A. J. M. Smith, pp. 53-80. A New Canadian Library Original. Aylesbury: McClelland and Stewart, 1961.
　　An analysis of the sources Haliburton used to create the character Sam Slick.

———. "The Hybrid Comic: Origins of Sam Slick." *Canadian Literature,* No. 14 (Autumn 1962): 35-42.
　　Cites Seba Smith's fictional character Jack Downing as the model for Haliburton's Sam Slick.

Davies, Richard A. "'Not at all the man that we have imagined': Mr. Justice Haliburton in England (1835-65)." *Dalhousie Review* 59, No. 4 (Winter 1979-80): 683-95.
　　Examines the author's life in England.

Harding, L. A. A. "Yankee at the Court of Judge Haliburton." *Canadian Literature,* No. 39 (Winter 1969): 62-73.
　　Explores the ways in which Haliburton handled anecdotes in order to reveal irony, delineate his characters, and express his misgivings about American democracy.

———. "Compassionate Humour in Haliburton." *Dalhousie Review* 49, No. 2 (Summer 1969): 224-28.
　　Contrasts Haliburton's gentle portrait of "Aunt Thankful" with the author's usually satirical view of women.

———. "The Commodore of the Mackerel Fleet; or, The Brine in Haliburton." *Dalhousie Review* 50, No. 4 (Winter 1970-71): 517-27.
　　Examines Haliburton's images of the sea and sailors as keys to understanding his view of the Maritime Provinces and New England.

Jeffreys, C. W. *Sam Slick in Pictures: The Best of the Humour of Thomas Chandler Haliburton.* Edited by Lorne Pierce, parallel text by Malcolm G. Parks. Toronto: Ryerson Press, 1956, 205 p.
　　A collection of Jeffreys's illustrations for Haliburton's works, with explanatory text by Parks.

Kelly, Darlene. "Thomas Haliburton and Travel Books about America." *Canadian Literature,* No. 94 (Autumn 1982): 25-38.
　　Describes Haliburton's satirical arguments against contemporary, uninformed British views of America.

Liljegren, S. B. *Canadian History and Thomas Chandler Haliburton: Some Notes on Sam Slick,* Pts. I, II, and III. Upsala Canadian Studies, edited by S. B. Liljegren, vols. VIII, IX, and X. Upsala: A.-B. Lundequistska Bokhandeln, 1969-70.
    A study of Canadian history as presented in the works of Haliburton.

McDougall, Robert L. "Thomas Chandler Haliburton." In *Our Living Tradition, second and third Series,* edited by Robert L. McDougall, pp. 3-30. Toronto: University of Toronto Press, 1959.
    Discusses Haliburton's reputation, philosophy, and place in Canadian literature.

O'Brien, A. H. *Haliburton ("Sam Slick"): A Sketch and Bibliography.* 2d ed. Montreal: Gazette Printing Co., 1909, 26 p.
    A biographical sketch and detailed bibliography of Haliburton's works.

Percy, H. R. *Thomas Chandler Haliburton.* The Canadians, edited by Robert Read. Don Mills, Ontario: Fitzhenry & Whiteside, 1980, 64 p.
    An illustrated profile of Haliburton's life and works.

Trent, W. P. "A Retrospect of American Humor." *The Century Magazine* LXII, n.s. XLI (November 1901-April 1902): 58-9.
    A brief look at Haliburton's place in the development of American humor.

Wood, Ruth Kedzie. "The Creator of the First Yankee of Literature." *The Bookman* XLI, No. 2 (April 1915): 152-60.
    A biographical sketch and remarks concerning the reception of Haliburton's work by his contemporaries.

Letitia Elizabeth Landon

1802-1838

(Later Letitia Elizabeth Maclean; also wrote under pseudonyms of L. and L.E.L.) English poet, novelist, journalist, dramatist, and editor.

Considered a promising poet by her contemporaries, Landon achieved widespread popularity during the early nineteenth century. Her poetry, with its exotic settings and effusive, passionate style, strongly appealed to readers of the Romantic age. A prolific writer, Landon also wrote novels, critical reviews, and a drama; of these prose works, only her novels gained any recognition. While her poetry and novels were well received in her own era, Landon's reputation has declined, and her works are virtually unknown today.

Landon was born in Chelsea and attended the day school of Miss Rowden, the poet who had instructed Mary Russell Mitford and Lady Caroline Lamb. An imaginative child, Landon reveled in the adventure tales of *Robinson Crusoe* and the *Arabian Nights* and invented endless stories for her younger brother. In 1815 the Landon family moved to Old Brompton, where they lived next door to William Jerdan, editor of the newly founded *Literary Gazette.* Jerdan was impressed by Landon's poetry and began publishing it in 1820, first under the initial "L." and later under "L.E.L." This anonymous manner of publication stirred great interest in the youthful author and contributed to the growing popularity of her works. Encouraged by Jerdan's support and favorable public reception, Landon continued to write and soon revealed her identity.

Landon became a well-known figure in the literary circles of her day. Partially in an effort to support her mother and clergyman brother, she worked prodigiously: in addition to composing several volumes of poetry and novels, she helped edit the *Literary Gazette,* wrote reviews, and even attempted a drama, *Castruccio Castracani.* From the onset of her career, however, she was accused of having affairs with the illustrator Daniel Maclise and the journalists Jerdan and William Maginn, both of whom wrote favorable reviews of her work that some readers considered mere puffery. Many of Landon's contemporaries were also intrigued by what they saw as an enactment of the passionate themes of her writings in her own life. Whether these rumors of affairs were true remains unclear, but they attracted a great deal of attention to her work. Many commentators believe that the allegations also led Landon to break her engagement to the journalist John Forster, hoping to spare him from the scandal that might attend their marriage. Shortly after, she met and secretly married George Maclean. In 1838, the couple sailed for a three-year stay in Cape Coast Castle, Africa, where Maclean served as colonial governor. Soon after their arrival, Landon was found dead in her room with a vial of prussic acid, a highly poisonous substance that she had claimed to be taking for medicinal purposes. Various theories about her death were proffered: suicide, murder by Maclean or his mistress, and accidental overdose. The circumstances of Landon's death were never satisfactorily explained, and readers of her day came to regard her as a tragic figure whose melancholy works were eerily prophetic.

Commentators have generally disregarded Landon's critical works and play, focusing instead on her novels and poetry.

Landon achieved some success in her own time as a novelist, particularly for *Ethel Churchill,* which is set in the age of George II. While this three-volume, unfinished work is sometimes praised for its sympathetic depiction of poverty and the plight of young artists, it is often faulted for its profuseness and convoluted plot. Clearly, Landon's contemporary popularity rested on her poetry, which was admired for its fluency and sentimental treatment of forlorn love. In the title poem of *The Fate of Adelaide,* for example, the heroine, Adelaide, is deserted by her lover, Orlando, who marries an Eastern woman, and she and Adelaide are later buried side by side. Landon's next work, a collection entitled *The Improvisatrice,* presents the impassioned outpourings of an Italian woman. Critics have noted that this work reflects both the Romantic emphasis on spontaneous expression of feeling and the author's distaste for revision. Landon's major poetic collections include *The Troubadour, The Golden Violet,* and *The Venetian Bracelet*—all of which are extemporaneous treatments of unhappy love. As a contributor to many of the popular annuals of her day, Landon also composed a large number of lyric poems; "Erinna" and "Monody on the Death of Mrs. Hemans" are generally regarded as two of her best. "Erinna," a blank-verse monologue, realistically depicts a young female poet in ancient Greece, while "Monody on the Death of Mrs. Hemans" is notable as a skillful and generous tribute to a poet who was Landon's contemporary and, at times, her literary rival.

After her death, the appeal of Landon's work swiftly faded. Contemporary critics, who were fascinated by her early anonymity and tragic demise, praised the spontaneity, fluency, and sentimentality of her poetry. Many later nineteenth-century critics, however, viewed its sentimentality as maudlin and its spontaneity as a lack of emendation. Critical response in the twentieth century has been negligible. The few modern critics who discuss Landon echo their predecessors in pointing out the conventional nature of her writings, though their explanations range from financial pressures that forced her to write quickly, to inept literary advice from friends, to her own lack of artistic skill. Today, Landon is considered a minor literary figure, yet her works are generally noted as an accurate expression of early nineteenth-century attitudes and tastes.

PRINCIPAL WORKS

The Fate of Adelaide (poetry) 1821
The Improvisatrice, and Other Poems (poetry) 1824
The Troubadour, Catalogue of Pictures, and Historical Sketches (poetry) 1825
The Golden Violet with Its Tales of Romance and Chivalry, and Other Poems (poetry) 1827
The Poetical Works of L. E. L. 3 vols. (poetry) 1827
The Venetian Bracelet, The Lost Pleiad, A History of the Lyre, and Other Poems (poetry) 1829
Romance and Reality (novel) 1831
Francesca Carrara (novel) 1834
Ethel Churchill; or, The Two Brides (novel) 1837
The Zenana, and Minor Poems of L. E. L. (poetry) 1839
Castruccio Castracani [first publication] (drama) 1841; published in *Life and Literary Remains of L.E.L.*
Lady Anne Granard; or, Keeping up Appearances (novel) 1842
The Poetical Works of L. E. Landon (poetry) 1880

LETITIA ELIZABETH LANDON (essay date 1824)

[*In the following excerpt from her introductory remarks to* The Improvisatrice, *Landon describes the work. This piece was first published in 1824. For additional commentary by Landon, see excerpt dated 1829.*]

Poetry needs no preface: if it do not speak for itself, no comment can render it explicit. I have only, therefore, to state that *The Improvisatrice* is an attempt to illustrate that species of inspiration common in Italy, where the mind is warmed from earliest childhood by all that is beautiful in nature, and glorious in art. The character depicted is entirely Italian,—a young female with all the loveliness, vivid feeling and genius of her own impassioned land. She is supposed to relate her own history; with which are intermixed the tales and episodes which various circumstances call forth.

> *Letitia Elizabeth Landon, from an advertisement to "The Improvisatrice," in her* The Poetical Works of Miss Landon, *E. L. Carey and A. Hart, 1838, p. 6.*

[WILLIAM MAGINN] (essay date 1824)

[*One of the most prominent journalists in England during the first half of the nineteenth century, Maginn wrote prolifically for a variety of English periodicals. He was a principal early contributor, under the pseudonym of Morgan O'Doherty, to* Blackwood's Edinburgh Magazine. *Many critics believe that Maginn invented* Noctes Ambrosianae, *a series of witty dialogues that first appeared in* Blackwood's *in which contemporary issues and personalities are treated with levity, gravity, and pungent satire. In the following excerpt, drawn from an installment of the* Noctes *that was originally published in August 1824, Maginn discusses* The Improvisatrice *with Christopher North, a fictional character based on the Scottish critic and essayist John Wilson. Maginn's close friendship and alleged affair with Landon has caused some critics to question his critical objectivity.*]

Odoherty. Literary Gazettes!—What a rumpus all that fry have been keeping up about Miss Landon's poetry—the *Improvisatrice,* I mean.

North. Why, I always thought you had been one of her greatest admirers, Odoherty. Was it not you that told me she was so very handsome?—A perfect beauty, I think you said.

Odoherty. And I said truly. She is one of the sweetest little girls in the world, and her book is one of the sweetest little books in the world; but Jerdan's extravagant trumpeting has quite sickened every body; and our friend Alaric has been doing rather too much in the same fashion. This sort of stuff plays the devil with any book. Sappho! and Corinna, forsooth! Proper humbug!

North. I confess you are speaking pretty nearly my own sentiments. I ran over the book—and I really could see nothing of the originality, vigor, and so forth, they all chatter about. Very elegant, flowing verses they are—but all made up of Moore and Byron.

Odoherty. Nay, nay, when you look over the *Improvisatrice* again, I am sure you will retract this. You know very well that I am no great believer in female genius; but nevertheless, there is a certain feminine elegance about the voluptuousness of this book, which, to a certain extent, marks it with an individual character of its own.

North. I won't allow you to review this book, my dear Standard-bearer, for I perceive you are half in love with the damsel concerned; and under such circumstances, a cool and dispassionate estimate is what nobody could be expected to give—least of all you, you red-hot monster of Munster. (pp. 466-67)

> [*William Maginn*], *from an essay in* Noctes Ambrosianae, *Vol. I by John Wilson and Others, revised edition, 1863. Reprint by W. J. Widdleton, 1870, pp. 466-67.*

WINTHROP MACKWORTH PRAED (poem date 1824)

[*In the poem excerpted below, written in 1824, Praed apostrophizes the unknown "L. E. L."*]

I have a tale of Love to tell;
Lend me thy light lute, L. E. L.
Lend me thy lute! what other strings
Should speak of those delicious things,
Which constitute Love's joys and woes
In pretty duodecimos?
Thou knowest every herb and flower,
Of wondrous name, and wondrous power,
Which, gathered where white wood-doves nestle,
And beat up by poetic pestle,
Bind gallant knights in fancied fetters,

And set young ladies writing letters:
Thou singest songs of floods and fountains,
Of mounted lords and lordly mountains,
Of dazzling shields and dazzling glances,
Of piercing frowns and piercing lances,
Of leaping brands and sweeping willows,
Of dreading seas and dreaming billows,
Of sunbeams which are like red wine,
Of odorous lamps of argentine,
Of cheeks that burn, of hearts that freeze,
Of odors that send messages,
Of kingfishers and silver pheasants,
Of gems to which the Sun makes presents,
Of miniver and timeworn walls,
Of clairschachs and of atabals.
Within thy passion-haunted pages
Throng forward girls—and distant ages,
The lifeless learns at once to live,
The dumb grows strangely talkative,
Resemblances begin to strike
In things exceedingly unlike,
All nouns, like statesmen, suit all places,
And verbs, turned lawyers, hunt for cases.

(pp. 334-35)

•　•　•　•　•

Vain, vain!—take back the lute! I see
Its chords were never meant for me.
For thine own song, for thine own hand,
That lute was strung in Fairy-land;
And, if a stranger's thumb should fling
Its rude touch o'er one golden string,—
Good-night to all the music in it!
The string would crack in half a minute.

(p. 336)

Winthrop Mackworth Praed, in a preface to The
Poems of Winthrop Mackworth Praed, Vol. I, *revised edition, W. J. Widdleton, 1865, pp. 334-37.*

THE WESTMINSTER REVIEW　(essay date 1825)

[*This commentator dismisses the homage paid to Landon by the*
Literary Gazette, *but concedes that* The Improvisatrice *exhibits
some poetic skill on Landon's part.*]

We imagine very few of our readers know, that, within the
last twelve months, there has appeared [*The Improvisatrice*],
on which the following decision has been pronounced: "as far
as our poetical taste and critical judgment enable us to form
an opinion, we can adduce no instance ancient or modern, of
similar talent and excellence." The ancients are out done, and
the moderns are surpassed by an English poet of the year of
our Lord 1824, and this is the first moment that the news has
come to our ears! That poet, too, the same critic informs us,
is "a young female."

Our readers, no doubt, are restless with curiosity to learn the
name of the critic, and the name of the poet: when we mention
the London *Literary Gazette,* as the work in which the criticism
appeared, probably we have given to all, who are acquainted
with this weekly journal, a sufficient criterion of the worth of
the criticism.

We are afraid that having informed our readers that "the poetical taste and critical judgment" which pronounce the eulogium upon this poet, are those of the *Literary Gazette,* we
shall have entirely quenched their curiosity to learn any thing
about the writings of the young female; and most probably
have excited a strong prejudice against them. Assuredly few
have more reason to apply the Italian proverb to themselves,
than she has:

　　Da chi mi fido, mi guarda Dio:
　　Da chi non mi fido, mi guarderò Io.

thus rendered in homely language by a writer of the 16th century:

　　From him I trust God help me at my neede:
　　Of him I trust not, myself will take heede.

As we may have done harm, therefore, to L. E. L. (for she is
the poetess to the talent and excellence of whose *Improvisatrice*
and other poems, the critic of the *Literary Gazette* can find no
parallel ancient or modern), by quoting the eulogium of her
panegyrist, we will endeavour to atone for it, by assuring our
readers, that her poems are better than such a criticism from
such a critic might lead them to expect. (pp. 537-38)

All languages have metaphors and similes: the English language is also very rich in poetical terms; words, that, having
always been set apart for poetry, have, as mere words, poetical
associations, and no associations connected with common life,
conversation, or literature. To a real poet, one who has poetical
thoughts, such a language affords great facilities and advantages: it enables him to transmit, in their undiminished sublimity, beauty, or pathos, all that his imagination or his feelings
create in his own breast. But, to a person who is not a poet in
thought, the English language is an evil, not a blessing; its
richness in poetical terms conceals from him his own poverty
in poetical thought; and because he has at command a string
of poetical expressions he foolishly imagines himself a poet.

L. E. L. has, with multitudes of others at all times, and more
especially in the present day, fallen into this mistake: and she
has fallen into it the more readily and deeply, because nearly
all her poetry relates to love, a topic, for every thing connected
with which there are nearly as many forms of expression and
words as there are in Arabic for a lion; and on which we would
engage to manufacture a poet out of any young person, particularly a female, by supplying her with a dictionary of love
phrases, similes, &c., with as little exertion of intellect, as is
employed in manufacturing a stocking in the loom. (pp. 538-
39)

[Our] authoress is capable of better things, . . . [for] amidst
very much that is mere verbiage, and pages filled with puny
and sickly thoughts clothed in glittering language that draws
the eye off from their real character and value, there are indications of poetical talent. . . . To conclude; our serious and
well-meant advice to L. E. L. is, to free herself as much as
possible from her poetical vocabulary, to nurse her poetical
thoughts, to avoid the subject of love, a topic so full of words
and so barren of thought, and, above all, not to be elated by
the praise, or guided by the "poetical taste and critical judgment" of the *Literary Gazette,* if she wish that her reputation
as a poet should rest on a solid and permanent foundation.
(p. 539)

*A review of "The Improvisatrice, and Other Poems,"
in* The Westminster Review, *Vol. III, No. VI, April,
1825, pp. 537-39.*

LETITIA ELIZABETH LANDON   (essay date 1829)

[*In this excerpt from her preface to* The Venetian Bracelet, *published in 1829, Landon discusses her poetic intention and offers reasons for her use of the theme of love. For additional commentary by Landon, see excerpt dated 1824.*]

Diffidence of their own abilities, and fear, which heightens the anxiety for public favour, are pleas usually urged by the youthful writer: may I, while venturing for the first time to speak of myself, be permitted to say they far more truly belong to one who has had experience of both praise and censure. The feelings which attended the publication of the *Improvisatrice,* are very different from those that accompany the present volume. I believe I *then* felt little beyond hope, vague as the timidity which subdued it, and that excitement which every author must know: *now* mine is a "farther looking hope;" and the timidity which apprehended the final verdict of others, is now deepened by distrust of my own powers. Or, to claim my poetical privilege, and express my meaning by a simile, I should say, I am no longer one who springs forward in the mere energy of exercise and enjoyment; but rather like the Olympian racer, who strains his utmost vigour, with the distant goal and crown in view. I have devoted my whole life to one object: in society I have but sought the material for solitude. I can imagine but one interest in existence,—that which has filled my past, and haunts my future,—the perhaps vain desire, when I am nothing, of leaving one of those memories at once a good and a glory. Believing, as I do, in the great and excellent influence of poetry, may I hazard the expression of what I have myself sometimes trusted to do? A highly cultivated state of society must ever have for concomitant evils, that selfishness, the result of indolent indulgence; and that heartlessness attendant on refinement, which too often hardens while it polishes. Aware that to elevate I must first soften, and that if I wished to purify I must first touch, I have ever endeavoured to bring forward grief, disappointment, the fallen leaf, the faded flower, the broken heart, and the early grave. Surely we must be less worldly, less interested, from this sympathy with the sorrow in which our unselfish feelings alone can take part. And now a few words on a subject, where the variety of opinions offered have left me somewhat in the situation of the prince in the fairy tale, who, when in the vicinity of the magic fountain, found himself so distracted by the multitude of voices that directed his way, as to be quite incapable of deciding which was the right path. I allude to the blame and eulogy which have been equally bestowed on my frequent choice of love as my source of song. I can only say, that for a woman, whose influence and whose sphere must be in the affections, what subject can be more fitting than one which it is her peculiar province to refine, spiritualize, and exalt? I have always sought to paint it self-denying, devoted, and making an almost religion of its truth; and I must add, that such as I would wish to draw her, woman actuated by an attachment as intense as it is true, as pure as it is deep, is not only more admirable as a heroine, but also in actual life, than one whose idea of love is that of light amusement, or at worst of vain mortification. With regard to the frequent application of my works to myself, considering that I sometimes pourtrayed love unrequited, then betrayed, and again destroyed by death—may I hint the conclusions are not quite logically drawn, as assuredly the same mind cannot have suffered such varied modes of misery. However, if I must have an unhappy passion, I can only console myself with my own perfect unconsciousness of so great a misfortune.

> *Letitia Elizabeth Landon, in a preface to "The Venetian Bracelet," in her* The Poetical Works of Miss Landon, *E. L. Carey and A. Hart, 1839, p. 102.*

[EDWARD LYTTON BULWER]   (essay date 1831)

[*Landon's friend Bulwer, a popular and versatile writer, commends* Romance and Reality. *This flattering review provoked ridicule among Bulwer's enemies because he unwittingly praised a novel whose major characters were largely patterned after his wife and himself.*]

The Author of [*Romance and Reality*] is a lady of remarkable genius. We remember well when she first appeared before the public in the pages of *The Literary Gazette.* We were at that time more capable than we are now of poetic enthusiasm; and certainly that enthusiasm we not only felt ourselves, but we shared with every second person we then met. We were young, and at college, lavishing our golden years, not so much on the Greek verse and mystic character to which we ought, perhaps, to have been rigidly devoted, as

> Our heart in passion and our head in rhymes.

At that time, poetry was not yet out of fashion, at least with us of the cloister; and there was always, in the Reading Room of the Union, a rush every Saturday afternoon for *The Literary Gazette,* and an impatient anxiety to hasten at once to that corner of the sheet which contained the three magical letters of "L. E. L." And all of us praised the verse, and all of us guessed at the author. We soon learned it was a female, and our admiration was doubled, and our conjectures tripled. Was she young? Was she pretty? and—for there were some embryo fortune-hunters among us—was she rich? We ourselves, who, now staid critics and sober gentlemen, are about coldly to measure to a prose work the due quantum of laud and censure, then only thought of homage, and in verse only we condescended to yield it. But the other day, in looking over some of our boyish effusions, we found a paper superscribed to "L. E. L." and beginning with "Fair Spirit." We need scarcely add that we have burnt the weed that we then intended as an offering, and fancied might be mistaken for a flower. These early proofs of the genius of our Poetess are, indeed, singularly beautiful: they have gone far towards producing a new school— a school, in truth, which we do not admire, and in which the proselytes have done their possible to copy the faults, without the merits of the founder. But, despite the beauty of the poems we refer to, Miss Landon has greatly improved in poetical taste of late. Something more vigorous, staid, and thoughtful than belonged to her early poetry, has dignified the grace and sweetness of that last published. And though we think that severe and stern study is yet wanting to complete the full extent of her powers, those powers have given a promise—more especially in her blank verse ("**Erinna,**" for instance,) and her smaller pieces—which can only be duly kept by performances, not of the soft and gentle only, but of the noblest and most enduring order. And now we come to the volumes on our table.

Romance and Reality is a novel of great merit. Its beauties and its faults are those of genius. (pp. 546-47)

The talent to delineate character, and the talent to deduce observation from the portrait, are wholly distinct. In the one lies Scott's genius; in the other, Godwin's. In the latter faculty, Miss Landon is the more especially felicitous. The whole work abounds with passages of equal eloquence and truth—in aphorisms of pointed originality, in descriptions adorned by a singular richness and power of diction. Yet in the reflexions there is sometimes an affectation of imagery, or of novelty, which we do not like, and which we entreat our Author to avoid for the future. For instance:—"Youth is the French Count, who takes the Yorick of Sterne for that of Shakspeare; it combines better than it calculates; its wishes are prophecies of their own fulfilment.'' Now the discerning reader will perceive at once that the above image is too strained, ''too peregrinate,'' as Master Holofernes would say; and he will also perceive that the fault is one which no stupid person could commit. It is the fault of youth and fancy—a fault of an order to which true criticism is always lenient. Another fault to which we should be disposed to be less indulgent, were it not of very unfrequent occurrence, is, that instead of aspiring from the level road of genius, our Author sometimes stoops below it, and sullies her wings among the flippancies of a class of writers so immeasurably beneath her, that she ought only to know them in order to avoid. We allude to passages against such harmless vulgarities as ''blue coats and brass buttons.'' All those toilet severities do very well for the *''flunkies,''* as Blackwood expresses himself, but not for the Poetess of *''***Erinna.***''*

The story continues through romance and reality, through love, reflection, criticism, ambition, travel, and death. We will not abridge it. The reader must fly to the book itself; and if he read it once for the story, he must read it twice for the wit and the eloquence, for the style, the reflections, and the moral. Miss Landon's prose contains the witness of some faculties not visible in her poetry—acute liveliness, and playful, yet deep observation. It contains also the same one fault, which we shall call the want of art, and on which we shall add a word or two of explanation and advice. When an actor first begins to speak in public, let his voice be ever so full and musical, it is ten to one but that it seems weak and overstrained. Why? Because he has not learnt to manage it. The voices that seem the strongest and the richest, are often the least so by nature. Practice and management are the secrets by which the orator or the actor obtains his effects. Exactly so in fictitious composition: it is not the power only, but the knowledge of those places in which the power should be cast, that makes the novelist or the poet thrill and command his readers at his will. . . . Whenever we moralise where we should paint, we may be equally clever—nay, cleverer in a higher order of merit, but we are not equally successful in gaining our end, and enforcing our moral. Thus the Author of the book before us often prefers to tell us the character of a person than to throw the person into scenes in which the character would be far more instantaneously and vividly bodied forth. This, since she has the two faculties chiefly requisite for creating dramatic effect—a ready power to enter into various character, and a great command and variety of language, is a deficiency, not of nature, but of art. How is that deficiency alone to be remedied? By a deep and earnest study of the Drama! . . . The trick of the boards, the scenic effect, the life of the stage, is what a novelist possessed of Miss Landon's powers should intently study. It will teach her never to narrate, where she can act, her story; and while as thoughtful, as reflective, as analysing as ever, to be so only in the right moment, and with the most effect. We need not say that we should not have given this advice to a writer of moderate genius; nor should we have given it to a novelist of long standing. It *is* given as a proof that we form from the present performance great hopes for the future. And now, passing over unmentioned, on the one hand, a few slight inaccuracies and petty blemishes, and on the other, a whole host of delicate and subtle beauties of composition, we consign our Author to the popularity she will doubtless obtain, and most richly deserve. When we consider her accomplishments, her versatility, her acute observation, her graceful fancy, her powers both in the actual world and the ideal, her habit of thought, and her command of language; and when we remember also how much she has yet done, and how young she yet is, we

speak advisedly when we recommend to her the highest models and the severest study. Such a recommendation could only be given to one capable, if she do justice to herself, of achieving those triumphs which, as her critics, we anticipate, and as her admirers, we predict. (pp. 549-51)

> [*Edward Lytton Bulwer*], *in a review of "Romance and Reality," in* The New Monthly Magazine, *Vol. XXXII, No. CXXXII, December, 1831, pp. 545-51.*

[JOHN WILSON] (essay date 1832)

[*A Scottish critic, essayist, novelist, poet, and short story writer, Wilson is best known as Christopher North, the name he assumed when writing for* Blackwood's Edinburgh Magazine, *a Tory periodical to which he was a principal contributor for over twenty-five years. In the following excerpt from an essay in* Noctes Ambrosianae *that was originally published in* Blackwood's *in February 1832, Wilson and the fictional character Timothy Tickler enthusiastically praise Landon as a promising artist.*]

Tickler. I love L. E. L.

North. So do I—and being old gentlemen, we may blamelessly make the public our confidante. There is a *passionate purity* in all her feelings that endears to me both her human and poetical character. She is a true enthusiast. Her affections overflow the imagery her fancy lavishes on all the subjects of her song, and color it all with a rich and tender light which makes even confusion beautiful, gives a glowing charm even to indistinct conception, and when the thoughts themselves are full-formed and substantial, which they often are, brings them prominently out upon the eye of the soul in flashes that startle us into sudden admiration. The originality of her genius, methinks, is conspicuous in the choice of its subjects—they are unborrowed—and in her least successful poems—as wholes—there is no dearth of poetry. Her execution has not the consummate elegance and grace of Felicia Hemans—but she is very young, and becoming every year she lives more mistress of her art—and has chiefly to learn now how to use her treasures, which, profuse as she has been, are in abundant store; and, in good truth, the fair and happy being has a fertile imagination,—the soil of her soul, if allowed to lie fallow for one sunny summer, would, I predict, yield a still richer and more glorious harvest. I love Miss Landon—for in her genius does the work of duty—the union of the two is ''beautiful exceedingly''—and virtue is its own reward; far beyond the highest meed of praise ever bestowed by critic—though round her fair forehead is already wreathed the immortal laurel.

Tickler. Her novel [*Romance and Reality*] is brilliant.

North. Throughout.

> This morning gives us promise of a glorious day.

> [*John Wilson*], *from an essay in* Noctes Ambrosianae, *Vol. V, by John Wilson and Others, revised edition, 1863. Reprint by The H. W. Hagemann Publishing Co., 1894, p. 28.*

[FRANCIS MAHONY] (essay date 1833)

[*Mahony extols Landon's work, finding her theme of love particularly fitting for a woman writer. For additional commentary by Mahony, see poem dated 1836.*]

Letitia Elizabeth Landon! Burke said, that ten thousand swords ought to have leaped out of their scabbards at the mention of the name of Marie Antoinette; and in like manner we maintain, that ten thousand pens should leap out of their ink bottles to pay homage to L. E. L. . . .

In which quarter of our literary world is not L. E. L. known and admired? From her *Improvisatrice* (a word puzzling to pronounce to the average natives of Cockney-land, and which she, not having the fear of Della Crusca before her eyes, spelt with a single *v*, thereby deluding into that practice many ingenious young gentlemen and ladies), which, we believe, was her first work published in the substantive shape of a volume, to her last illustrations of the gatherings of Fisher or Heath, through the verse of her *Golden Violet* and the prose of her *Romance and Reality*, all her works have been favourites with every body, but especial pets of the press. We do not doubt that the forthcoming *Francesca Carrara* will receive an *accueil* equally favourable.

There is too much about love in them, some cross-grained critic will say. How, Squaretoes, can there be too much of love in a young lady's writings? we reply in a question. Is she to write of politics, or political economy, or pugilism, or punch? Certainly not. We feel a determined dislike of women who wander into these unfeminine paths; they should immediately hoist a mustache—and, to do them justice, they in general do exhibit no inconsiderable specimen of the hair-lip. We think Miss L. E. L. has chosen the better part. She shews every now and then that she is possessed of information, feeling, and genius, to enable her to shine in other departments of poetry; but she does right in thinking that Sappho knew what she was about when she chose the tender passion as the theme for woman.

> *[Francis Mahony], "Miss Landon," in* Fraser's Magazine, *Vol. VIII, No. XLVI, October, 1833, p. 433.*

ALLAN CUNNINGHAM (essay date 1834)

> *[Cunningham hails Landon as one of the most successful poetesses of the era.]*

[Letitia Elizabeth Landon is], next to "Sister Joanna," the most successful poetess of our day. She is the L. E. L. of many a pretty poem: nor has she sung only a tender ditty or two, and then shut her lips to listen to the applause they brought; she has written much; sometimes loftily, sometimes touchingly, and always fluently and gracefully. She excels in short and neat things; yet she has poured out her fancy and her feelings through the evolutions of a continuous narrative and intricate story. The flow of her language is remarkable; her fancy is ever ready and never extravagant. Her chief works are *The Improvisatrice,* and *The Venetian Bracelet;* nor has she hesitated to try her hand in prose also, and in a long story: *Romance and Reality* displays ready wit, much sprightliness, and an extensive acquaintance with the world. She is young; pleasing, too, in company, and lively without effort.

> *Allan Cunningham, "British Poetry: Letitia Elizabeth Landon," in his* Biographical and Critical History of the British Literature of the Last Fifty Years, *Baudry's Foreign Library, 1834, p. 115.*

FATHER PROUT [PSEUDONYM OF REV. FRANCIS MAHONY] (poem date 1836)

> *[Writing under the pseudonym of Father Prout, Mahony hails Landon in the following poem as "The Angel of Poetry." For additional commentary by Mahony, see excerpt dated 1833.]*

Lady! for thee a holier key shall harmonise the chord—
In Heaven's defence Omnipotence drew an avenging sword;
But when the bolt had crush'd revolt, one angel, fair though frail,
Retain'd his lute, fond attribute! to charm that gloomy vale.
The lyre he kept his wild hand swept; the music he'd awaken
Would sweetly thrill from the lonely hill where he sat apart forsaken:
There he'd lament his banishment, his thoughts to grief abandon,
And weep his full. 'Twas pitiful to see him weep, fair Landon!

He wept his fault! Hell's gloomy vault grew vocal with his song;
But all throughout derision's shout burst from the guilty throng:
God pitying view'd his fortitude in that unhallow'd den;
Free'd him from hell, but bade him dwell amid the sons of men.
Lady! for us, an exile thus, immortal Poesy
Came upon earth, and lutes gave birth to sweetest minstrelsy;
And poets wrought their spellwords, taught by that angelic mind,
And music lent soft blandishment to fascinate mankind.

Religion rose! man sought repose in the shadow of her wings;
Music for her walked harbinger, and Genius touch'd the strings:
Tears from the tree of Araby cast on her altar burn'd,
But earth and wave most fragrance gave where Poetry sojourn'd.
Vainly, with hate inveterate, hell labour'd in its rage,
To persecute that angel's lute, and cross his pilgrimage;
Unmov'd and calm, his songs pour'd balm on sorrow all the while;
Vice he unmask'd, but virtue bask'd in the radiance of his smile.

O where, among the fair and young, or in what kingly court,
In what gay path where Pleasure hath her favourite resort,
Where hast thou gone, angelic one? Back to thy native skies?
Or dost thou dwell in cloister'd cell, in pensive hermit's guise?
Methinks I ken a denizen of this our island—nay,
Leave me to guess, fair poetess! queen of the matchless lay!
The thrilling line, lady! is thine; the spirit pure and free;
And England views that angel muse, Landon! reveal'd in THEE!

(pp. 314-15)

> *Father Prout [pseudonym of Rev. Francis Mahony], "The Angel of Poetry: To L. E. L.," in his* The Reliques of Father Prout, *edited by Oliver Yorke [pseudonym of Rev. Francis Mahony], 1836. Reprint by George Bell & Sons, 1875, pp. 314-15.*

TAIT'S EDINBURGH MAGAZINE (essay date 1837)

> *[This critic praises* Ethel Churchill *as Landon's best work but faults its "exuberance and restlessness," noting that the profusion*

of characters, dialogues, and scenes would be sufficient for three novels.]

Francesca Carrara affords only a faint type of some aspects of *Ethel Churchill,* which, in the higher qualities that distinguish fictitious writing, far surpasses its romantic predecessor. . . . [Miss Landon displays] greater maturity of understanding, an enlarged and more subtle comprehension of character, and a firmer grasp, in dealing both with the hard realities of life, and the play of the interests and passions which stir up its mysterious depths, or alternate in light and shadow on its varied surface:—and the ripening fruits of knowledge and experience still glow amidst the luxuriant blooms, or sparkle in the fresh dews of fancy and poetry. Description, sentiment, flights of imagination, and those nameless, brilliant, and evanescent graces, which were the charm of Miss Landon's greener works, adorn or relieve the more powerful pictures before us, though in subservience to more potent agencies. For the first time—although she has not wholly dismissed the gay or the passionate beings that flutter between the imaginative and the real—the authoress of *Ethel Churchill* has presented us with some of the genuine creatures of stern reality, whom, though never met before, we at once recognise as partakers of our human nature, in all its beauty and strength, weakness and error. These new personages are neither the ideal creations of pure invention, nor yet those characters of historical romance, which, in ordinary hands, are true only in the few outward and visible signs, and shew nothing individual or distinctive. Miss Landon has, we think, been most true and successful where she was not tied down to walk by the card. The coquette, Lavinia Fenton, the original Polly, of whom she could know little or nothing from books, is moulded into a truer representation of character than the Lady Mary Wortley, of whom she

A portrait of Landon by Daniel Maclise.

has read a great deal; and the young poet, Walter Maynard, who is the pure offspring of her reflection and observation, is more of "a true man" than Pope, whose image she had seen reflected in twenty volumes of memoirs and letters, and was condemned to take at second-hand, and render as tamely as he is given. Writers of original power succeed best when dealing with more yielding substances than history presents to them; unless they triumph, by boldly setting its dicta at defiance, and draw the historical personages brought forward after their own truer conception. Thus, we consider the historical scenes and characters of *Ethel Churchill,* the tamest and least successful, though such may not be the general impression; nor are we sure that the author who, for our entertainment, resuscitates the great or the celebrated dead, whose images are stamped in our memory, and about whom we have made up our minds, does not place a stumbling block in his own path—unless he possessed the plastic energy, the potent mastery of Shakspeare or Scott, to exorcise the ancient idol, before he fill the vacant fancy with something felt at once as more beautiful and more true. But these, if failures at all, are those of laudable ambition. The work has other and greater faults. The pain it inflicts is not always compensated by the instruction it conveys. It is at the same time most real in passion and feeling, and often improbable in motive and incident; and, on the whole, is more to be regarded as an earnest of what its author must achieve, and a sign of a commanding advancement, than the realization of a perfect romance. (p. 745)

The main fault of this romance, as a work of art, is exuberance and restlessness. The reader finds no repose—no quiet, breathing intervals, occupied with dull dialogue or tame retrospect. One brilliant character, one agitating scene, rapidly succeeds another; while the rich materials of at least three romances are profusely heaped up, in description, sentiment, striking situations, and subtle analysis of passion and motive.

At present, *Ethel Churchill* is, out of sight, Miss Landon's most artistical work, none of her poetry excepted. She has poured into it the rich treasury of long-brooding thought, of ripened experience, a deeper pathos, and more sustained and expansive imagination than can be traced in any of her earlier compositions. But if, at present, her most brilliant achievement, we entertain the hope that *Ethel Churchill* will not always remain her most *perfect* work; and that we shall, from the same pen, have something more cheerful, serene, and temperate; and, with as much of the romance and poetry of life, a freer mingling of its sober, household virtues, every-day trials, and quiet enjoyments. (p. 756)

"Ethel Churchill," in Tait's Edinburgh Magazine, *n.s. Vol. IV, No. XLVIII, December, 1837, pp. 745-56.*

ELIZABETH BARRETT BROWNING   (poem date 1838)

[*A leading poet in Victorian England, Browning is best known for her cycle of love poetry,* Sonnets from the Portuguese. *In the following excerpt from a poem written in 1838, "L. E. L.'s Last Question," Browning eulogizes Landon as an English poet of love.*]

"Do you think of me as I think of you?"
From her poem written during the voyage to the Cape.

''Do you think of me as I think of you,
My friends, my friends?''—She said it from the sea,
The English minstrel in her minstrelsy,
While, under brighter skies than erst she knew,
Her heart grew dark, and groped there as the blind
To reach across the waves friends left behind—
''Do you think of me as I think of you?''

                                        (p. 208)

· · · · ·

Love-learnëd she had sung of love and love,—
And like a child that, sleeping with dropt head
Upon the fairy-book he lately read,
Whatever household noises round him move,
Hears in his dream some elfin turbulence,—
Even so suggestive to her inward sense,
All sounds of life assumed one tune of love.

And when the glory of her dream withdrew,
When knightly gestes and courtly pageantries
Were broken in her visionary eyes
By tears the solemn seas attested true,—
Forgetting that sweet lute beside her hand,
She asked not,—''Do you praise me, O my land?''
But,—''Think ye of me, friends, as I of you?''

Hers was the hand that played for many a year
Love's silver phrase for England, smooth and well.
Would God, her heart's more inward oracle
In that lone moment might confirm her dear!
For when her questioned friends in agony
Made passionate response, ''We think of thee,''
Her place was in the dust, too deep to hear.

                                        (p. 209)

> *Elizabeth Barrett Browning, ''L. E. L.'s Last Question,'' in her* Elizabeth Barrett Browning's Poetical Works, Vol. II, *Dodd, Mead, and Company, 1884, pp. 208-10.*

SAMUEL LAMAN BLANCHARD   (poem date 1841)

[*Blanchard included the following poem in his biography,* Life and Literary Remains of L. E. L., *published in 1841 (see Additional Bibliography).*]

> How have I wonder'd what ye meant,
>   Ye alphabetic Graces!
> And so you really represent
>   One of dear Nature's faces!
>
> The sage, the schoolboy, both can tell
>   The worth of L. S. D.
> But, then, the worth of L. E. L.!
>   All *letters* told in three!
>
> Life to her lays! However Fame
>   'Mongst brightest names may set hers,
> These three initials—nameless name—
>   Shall never be *dead letters*!

                                        (pp. 44-5)

> *Samuel Laman Blanchard, in a poem, in* The Adventurous Thirties: A Chapter in the Women's Movement *by Janet E. Courtney, Oxford University Press, London, 1933, pp. 44-5.*

WILLIAM HOWITT   (essay date 1847)

[*In the following excerpt from his survey of Landon's writings, Howitt outlines some merits and faults of her poetry and prose, noting the correlation of love and adversity throughout the works.*]

The subject of L. E. L.'s first volume [*The Fate of Adelaide*] was love; a subject which, we might have supposed, in one so young, would have been clothed in all the gay and radiant colours of hope and happiness; but, on the contrary, it was exhibited as the most fatal and melancholy of human passions. With the strange, wayward delight of the young heart, ere it has known actual sorrow, she seemed to riot and to revel amid death and woe; laying prostrate life, hope, and affection. Of all the episodical tales introduced into the general design of the principal poem, not one but terminated fatally or sorrowfully; the heroine herself was the fading victim of crossed and wasted affections. The shorter poems which filled up the volume, and which were mostly of extreme beauty, were still based on the wrecks and agonies of humanity.

It might be imagined that this morbid indulgence of so strong an appetite for grief, was but the first dipping of the playful foot in the sunny shallows of that flood of mortal experience through which all have to pass; and but the dallying, yet desperate pleasure afforded by the mingled chill and glittering eddies of the waters, which might hereafter swallow up the passer through; and the first real pang of actual pain would scare her youthful fancy into the bosom of those hopes and fascinations with which the young mind is commonly only too much delighted to surround itself. But it is a singular fact, that, spite of her own really cheerful disposition, and spite of all the advice of her most influential friends, she persisted in this tone from the first to the last of her works, from that time to the time of her death. Her poems, though laid in scenes and times capable of any course of events, and though filled to overflowing with the splendours and high-toned sentiments of chivalry; though enriched with all the colours and ornaments of a most fertile and sportive fancy,—were still but the heralds and delineations of melancholy, misfortune, and death. Let the reader turn to any, or all, of her poetical volumes, and say whether this be not so, with few, and in most of them, no exceptions. The very words of her first heroine might have literally been uttered as her own:—

> Sad were my shades; methinks they had
>   Almost a tone of prophecy—
> I ever had, from earliest youth,
>   A feeling what my fate would be.
>   —*The Improvisatrice*
>   (p. 439)

This is one singular peculiarity of the poetry of L. E. L., and her poetry must be confessed to be peculiar. It was entirely her own. It had one prominent and fixed character, and that character belonged wholly to itself. The rhythm, the feeling, the style, and phraseology of L. E. L.'s poetry were such, that you could immediately recognise it, though the writer's name was not mentioned. Love was still the great theme, and misfortune the great doctrine. It was not the less remarkable, that, in almost all other respects, she retained to the last the poetical tastes of her very earliest years. The heroes of chivalry and romance, feudal pageants, and Eastern splendour, delighted her imagination as much in the full growth, as in the budding of her genius.

I should say, that it is the young and ardent who must always be the warmest admirers of the larger poems of L. E. L. They are filled with the faith and the fancies of the young. The very scenery and ornaments are of that rich and showy kind which belongs to the youthful taste;—the white rose, the jasmine, the summer garniture of deep grass and glades of greenest foliage; festal gardens with lamps and bowers; gay cavaliers, and jewelled dames, and all that glitters in young eyes and love-haunted fancies. But amongst these, numbers of her smaller poems from the first dealt with subjects and sympathies of a more general kind, and gave glimpses of a nobility of sentiment, and a bold expression of her feeling of the unequal lot of humanity, of a far higher character. Such in the *Improvisatrice,* are "The Guerilla Chief," "St. George's Hospital," "The Deserter," "Gladesmure," "The Covenanters," "The Female Convict," "The Soldier's Grave," &c. Such are many that might be pointed out in every succeeding volume. But it was in her few last years that her heart and mind seemed every day to develop more strength, and to gather a wider range of humanity into their embrace. In the latter volumes of the *Drawing-room Scrap Book,* many of the best poems of which have been reprinted with the **Zenana,** nothing was more striking than the steady development of growing intellectual power, and of deep, generous, and truly philosophical sentiments, tone of thought, and serious experience.

But when L. E. L. had fixed her character as a poet, and the public looked only for poetical productions from her, she suddenly came forth as a prose writer, and with still added proofs of intellectual vigour. Her prose stories have the leading characteristics of her poetry. Their theme is love, and their demonstration that all love is fraught with destruction and desolation. But there are other qualities manifested in the tales. The prose page was for her a wider tablet, on which she could, with more freedom and ampler display, record her views of society. Of these, **Francesca Carrara,** and **Ethel Churchill,** are unquestionably the best works, the latter preeminently so. In these she has shown, under the characters of Guido and Walter Maynard, her admiration of genius, and her opinion of its fate; under those of Francesca and Ethel Churchill, the adverse destiny of pure and high-souled woman.

These volumes abound with proofs of a shrewd observation of society, with masterly sketches of character, and the most beautiful snatches of scenery. But what surprise and delight more than all, are the sound and true estimates of humanity, and the honest boldness with which her opinions are expressed. The clear perception of the fearful social condition of this country, and the fervent advocacy of the poor, scattered through these works, but especially the last do honour to her woman's heart. These portions of L. E. L.'s writings require to be yet more truly appreciated.

There is another characteristic of her prose writings which is peculiar. Never were the feelings and experiences of authorship so cordially and accurately described. She tells us freely all that she has learned. She puts words into the mouth of Walter Maynard, of which all who have known anything of literary life must instantly acknowledge the correctness. The author's heart never was more completely laid open, with all its hopes, fears, fatigues, and enjoyments, its bitter and its glorious experiences. In the last hours of Walter Maynard, she makes him utter what must at that period have been daily more and more her own conviction.

> I am far cleverer than I was. I have felt, have thought so much! Talk of the mind exhausting itself!—never! Think of the mass of materials which every day accumulates! Then experi-

ence, with its calm, clear light, corrects so many youthful fallacies; every day we feel our higher moral responsibility, and our greater power.

They are the convictions of "higher moral responsibilities and greater power," which strike us so forcibly in the later writings of L.E.L.

But what shall we say to the preparation of prussic-acid, and its preservation by Lady Marchmont? What of the perpetual creed of L. E. L., that all affection brings woe and death?

Whether this melancholy belief in the tendency of the great theme of her writings, both in prose and poetry,—this irresistible annunciation, like another Cassandra, of woe and desolation,—this evolution of scenes and characters in her last work, bearing such dark resemblance to those of her own after experience,—this tendency, in all her plots, to a tragic catastrophe, and this final tragedy itself,—whether these be all mere coincidences or not, they are still but parts of an unsolved mystery. Whatever they are, they are more than strange, and are enough to make us superstitious; for surely, if ever

> Coming events cast their shadows before,

they did so in the foreboding tone of this gifted spirit. (pp. 439-41)

> *William Howitt, "L. E. L.," in his* Homes and Haunts of the British Poets, *1847. Reprint by George Routledge and Sons, Limited, 1894, pp. 433-45.*

D. M. MOIR   (lecture date 1850-51)

[*Moir notes the progressive improvement in Landon's work, attributing many of her poetic failings to inexperience. This piece was originally part of a series of lectures delivered in 1850-51.*]

In this brilliant constellation of female genius, which gained its culminating point about twenty-five years ago, and which numbered, with the names [Joanna Baillie, Felicia Hemans, and Caroline Bowles], those also of Mary Russell Mitford, Maria Jewsbury, and Mary Howitt, Letitia Elizabeth Landon succeeded in obtaining that popularity which was second only to Mrs Hemans. Like her, she was brought out as a juvenile prodigy, with much flourish of critical trumpets, and, while yet in her teens, produced **The Improvisatrice,** to prove that such encomiums, however exorbitant they might seem, were not altogether misplaced; for it unquestionably exhibited a liveliness of fancy, store of poetical ideas, command of language, and an ear attuned to the varied cadences of verse. Its prime fault was diffuseness—a fault of inexperience, and less prominent in her subsequent appearances, **The Troubadour, The Golden Violet,** and **The Venetian Bracelet,** which are all distinguished by greater concentration of thought and style. Her earlier writings exhibited a peculiar constitution of genius. She arrayed her portraitures in the brilliant costume of Moore, and exhibited them against the gloomy background of Byron; always, at the same time, preserving enough of individuality to make and keep them distinctively her own. Like the former, her earth was too full of roses and singing-birds, and love: like the latter, her skies were too often the theatre of whirlwind, of lightning, thunder-cloud, and storm. She was always in extremes—either in the seventh heaven of ecstasy, or in the lowest depths of hypochondriacal sadness. She "no trite medium knew;" but her walk was her own, although she might be said to differ from some of her contemporaries less in distinctive excellencies than in distinctive peculiarities. Her deficiency alike in judgment and taste made her wayward and capricious, and her efforts seemed frequently impulsive. Hence she gave to the public a great deal too much—a large part of her writings being destitute of that elaboration, care, and finish essentially necessary in the fine arts, even when in combination with the highest genius, to secure permanent success; for the finest poetry is that which is suggestive—the result as much of what has been studiously withheld as of what has been elaborately given. It is quite apparent, however, that L. E. L. had opened her eyes to these her defects, and was rapidly overcoming them; for her very last things—those published in her *Remains,* by Laman Blanchard—are incomparably her best, whether we regard vigorous conception, concentration of idea, or judicious selection of subject. Her faults originated in an enthusiastic temperament and an efflorescent fancy; and showed themselves, as might have been expected, in an uncurbed prodigality of glittering imagery,—her muse, untamed and untutored, ever darting in dalliance from one object to another, like the talismanic bird in the Arabian story. Alas! that on such a sunny noon should have instantaneously descended an eve so dark and so dismal! (pp. 273-75)

D. M. Moir, "Lecture VI: Letitia Elizabeth Landon," in his Sketches of the Poetical Literature of the Past Half-Century, *third edition, William Blackwood and Sons, 1856, pp. 273-75.*

WILLIAM JERDAN (essay date 1853)

[Jerdan, editor of the Literary Gazette *and Landon's chief supporter, dedicated his* The Autobiography of William Jerdan *to L. E. L., "to whose genius the* Literary Gazette *was, during many years, indebted for its greatest attractions." Jerdan maintains that an awareness of Landon's "dual individuality" is necessary to understand her writings.]*

I found in L. E. L. a creature of another sphere, though with every fascination which could render her most loveable in our every-day world. The exquisite simplicity of childhood, the fine form of womanhood, the sweetest of dispositions, the utmost charm of unaffected manners, and, above all, an impassioned ideal and poetical temperament which absorbed her existence and held all else comparatively as nothing. . . . From day to day and hour to hour, it was mine to facilitate her studies, to shape her objects, to regulate her taste, to direct her genius, and cultivate the divine organisation of her being. For the divine part was in Her! . . . [Unless] it can be comprehended that there are two almost distinct yet inseparably united faculties to be traced in human nature—the one celestial and the other terrestrial—I must confess it to be impossible for me by any description to convey an accurate idea of the dual individuality of L. E. L. In exoteric society she was like others; but in her inmost abstract and visioned moods (and these prevailed) she was the Poet, seen and glorified in her immortal writings.

And immortal they will be, despite of the critical censures which may justly be bestowed upon immature blots and careless errors: so long as love and passion animate the breast of youth, so long as tenderness and pathos affect the mind of man, so long as glowing imagery and natural truth have power over the intellect and heart, so long will the poetry of L. E. L. exert a voice to delight, touch, refine, and exalt the universal soul.

I have endeavoured to explain this subject, not metaphysically, but absolutely and truly, in order that what follows may not be mistaken for self-assumption.

It is the very essence of the being I have so faintly portrayed, not to see things in their actual state, but to imagine, create, exaggerate, and form them into idealities; and then to view them in the light in which vivid fancy alone has made them appear. Thus it befel with my tuition of L. E. L. Her poetic emotions and aspirations were intense, usurping in fact almost every other function of the brain; and the assistance I could give her in the ardent pursuit produced an influence not readily to be conceived under other circumstances or upon a less imaginative nature. The result was a grateful and devoted attachment; all phases of which demonstrate and illume the origin of her productions. Critics and biographers may guess, and speculate, and expatiate for ever; but without this master-key they will make nothing of their reveries. With it, all is intelligible and obvious, and I have only to call on the admirers of her delicious compositions to remember this one fact to settle the question of their reality or romance—that they are the effusions of passionate inspiration, lighted from such unlike sources, and not uncommon events, and that they must be attributed to the spirit which clothed them according to its own unreal dreams, and not to the apparent cause. (pp. 169-71)

William Jerdan, "L. E. L.," in his The Autobiography of William Jerdan, Vol. III, *Arthur Hall, Virtue, & Co., 1853, pp. 169-83.*

[THEODOSIA YARROW] (poem date 1855)

[The following poem, "A Lament for L. E. L.," was attributed by R. R. Madden to Theodosia Yarrow.]

The sweet singer departed—the summer bird gone from
   the garden of his love—it hath waited for him—will
   he not come again?

A dirge for the departed! bend we low,
   Around the bed of her unwakening rest
Still be the hoarse voice of discordant woe,
   Still as the heart within her marble breast,
      Which stirs not at the cry of those she loved the best.

A dirge—Oh weave it of low murmurings,
   And count the pauses by warm dropping tears,
Sweeter, yet sadder than the woodlark sings,
Amid the shower of April's fitful wings
      Be the faint melody; the name it bears
      Shall thrill our England's heart for many linked
         years.

Out far-off England! oft times would she sit,
   With moist eyes gazing o'er the lustrous deep,
Through distance, change, and time; beholding it
   In its green beauty, while the sea did keep
      A whispering noise, to lull her spirit's visioned sleep.

And fondly would she watch the evening breeze
   Steal, crushing the smooth ocean's sultry blue,
As 'twere a message from her own tall trees,
Waving her back to them, and flowers, and bees,
      And loving looks, from which her young heart drew
      Its riches, and all the joys her winged childhood
         knew.

And smiling in their distant loveliness,
   Like phantoms of the desert—till the tide
Of passionate yearnings burst in wild excess
   Over her gentle heart: the home sick bride
   Whelming both lute and life, and the sweet minstrel
     died.

Spring shall return to that beloved shore,
   With health of leaves, and buds, and wild wood
     songs,
But hers the sweetest with its tearful lore,
Its womanly fond gushes come no more,
   Breathing the cadenced poesy that throngs
   To pure and fervid lips unstained by cares and
     wrongs.

Oh! never more shall her benignant spell
   Fan those dim embers in a worldly heart,
Which once were love and sympathy—nor tell
   Of griefs borne patiently with such sweet art
   As wins e'en selfish pain from brooding o'er his
     smart.

Oh never more! the burden of the strain,
   Be those sad hopeless words!—then make her bed
Near shadowy boughs, that she may dwell again
   Where her own English violets bloom and fade,
   The sole sweet records clustered o'er her head
In this strange land—to tell where our beloved is
     laid.

                    (pp. 303-04)

[*Theodosia Yarrow*], "A Lament for L. E. L.," in The Literary Life and Correspondence of the Countess of Blessington, Vol. II *by R. R. Madden, second edition, T. C. Newby, 1855, pp. 303-04.*

J. CORDY JEAFFRESON (essay date 1858)

[*Jeaffreson praises Landon as a talented poet, defending her against claims that she did not adequately revise her work.*]

Miss Landon's fame was won by her poetry; it was in her metrical compositions that her genius displayed itself: her prose-writings are lively, dramatic, forcible, but they contain nothing distinctive,—differing as they do but little from the productions of many other artists far less richly endowed, and marked by no signs of that passion and depth of pathetic feeling which inspired her melodious verse. Still her novels are interesting, and bristle with the indications of rare intellect; and they will long continue to be read, both for their own merits, and because every fact connected with the sad history of their author will for many a day be attractive. (p. 182)

[Miss Landon's] first effusions in the *Literary Gazette* . . . made all readers capable of appreciating poetry, aware that "L. E. L." was no common rhymester. Week by week the verses poured forth, eloquent of deep feelings, possessing a melody that Moore never in his sweetest lyrics surpassed, and rolling on with a lawless strength that showed plainly they flowed because they could not be withheld. They were covered with faults, want of polish, carelessness, redundancy of metaphor and ornament; but these very artistic failings were overlooked, nay admired—for they were the proofs and insignia of youthful and impetuous genius. Within the unknown poet's breast swelled a power that was not to be trifled with, an irrepressible force that must have its way like electricity;—how should she pause to count numbers, refer to the rules of Syntax for enlightenment on a dubious

expression, or debate on the artistic proprieties, when thoughts, feelings, fancies, images followed in quick succession, struggling for utterance and defying reflection. Here was the secret of "L. E. L.'s" power; poetry was the natural expression of her ardent feelings; she, like the nightingale which "crowds and hurries and precipitates with thick fast warbling his delicious notes," poured forth her soul into song, because it was the only way nature permitted her to disburthen herself of her ungovernable emotions. Song with her was not a mere mental exercise, an art,—it was a passion, an instinct. It is absurd to say she might have done greater things if she had taken more care, more "pains," as if the production of poetry were much the same thing as the manufacture of a gauze-bonnet. The conditions of her genius denied her the faculty of composing with cold critical deliberation; just in proportion as she "took pains" her power deserted her and her virtue departed from her; with her, faultlessness would have necessitated the absence of all the elements of her poetic excellence, and would have been the greatest of all faults. (pp. 184-85)

J. *Cordy Jeaffreson, "Letitia Elizabeth Landon," in his* Novels and Novelists: From Elizabeth to Victoria, *Vol. II,* Hurst and Blackett, Publishers, 1858, pp. 182-97.

CHRISTINA ROSSETTI (poem date 1859)

[*Rossetti is ranked among the finest English poets of the nineteenth century. Her poetry treats such opposing forces as sensuality and asceticism, human passion and divine love, and love of life and anticipation of death. The following poem, "L. E. L.," was written in 1859.*]

"Whose heart was breaking for a little love."

Downstairs I laugh, I sport and jest with all:
   But in my solitary room above
I turn my face in silence to the wall;
   My heart is breaking for a little love.
     Tho' winter frosts are done,
     And birds pair every one,
And leaves peep out, for springtide is begun.

I feel no spring, while spring is wellnigh blown,
   I find no nest, while nests are in the grove:
Woe's me for mine own heart that dwells alone,
   My heart that breaketh for a little love.
     While golden in the sun
     Rivulets rise and run,
While lilies bud, for springtide is begun.

All love, are loved, save only I; their hearts
   Beat warm with love and joy, beat full thereof:
They cannot guess, who play the pleasant parts,
   My heart is breaking for a little love.
     While beehives wake and whirr,
     And rabbit thins his fur,
In living spring that sets the world astir.

I deck myself with silks and jewelry,
   I plume myself like any mated dove:
They praise my rustling show, and never see
   My heart is breaking for a little love.
     While sprouts green lavender
     With rosemary and myrrh,
For in quick spring the sap is all astir.

Perhaps some saints in glory guess the truth,
  Perhaps some angels read it as they move,
And cry one another full of ruth,
    "Her heart is breaking for a little love."
      Tho' other things have birth,
      And leap and sing for mirth,
When springtime wakes and clothes and feeds the earth.

Yet saith a saint: "Take patience for thy scathe;"
  Yet saith an angel: "Wait, for thou shalt prove
True best is last, true life is born of death,
  O thou, heart-broken for a little love.
      Then love shall fill thy girth,
      And love make fat thy dearth,
When new spring builds new heaven and clean new
  earth."

                                    (pp. 153-55)

Christina Rossetti, "L. E. L.," in The Complete
Poems of Christina Rossetti, Vol. I, *edited by R. W.
Crump, Louisiana State University Press, 1980, pp.
153-55.*

HENRY FOTHERGILL CHORLEY   (essay date 1872?)

*[Chorley criticizes Landon's literary friends for encouraging her
to write prolifically without revision. Chorley's death date of 1872
has been assigned to the following excerpt because the actual
date of composition is not certain.]*

In spite of the miserably low standard of her literary morality,
Miss Landon (for awhile put forward as Mrs. Hemans's rival)
was meant for better things. She was incomplete, but she was
worthy of being completed; she was ignorant, but she was
quick, and capable of receiving culture, had she been allowed
a chance. If she was unrefined, it was because she had fallen
into the hands of a coarse set of men—the Tories of a provincial
capital—such as then made a noise and a flare in the *Noctes
Ambrosianae* of *Blackwood's Magazine,* second-hand followers of Lockhart and Professor Wilson, and Theodore Hook;
the most noisy and most reprehensible of whom—and yet one
of the cleverest—was Dr. Maginn. Not merely did they, at a
very early period of the girl's career, succeed in bringing her
name into a coarse repute, from which it never wholly extri-
cated itself, but, by the ridiculous exaggeration of such natural
gifts as she possessed, (no doubt accompanied by immediate
gain), flattered her into the idea that small further cultivation
was required by one who could rank with a Baillie, a Tighe,
a Hemans—if not their superior, at least their equal. (pp. 249-50)

As years went on, the ephemeral success of Miss Landon's
verses subsided: and, indeed, she had rendered herself next to
incapable of anything like a sustained effort, though some of
her smaller lyrics were more earnest and more real in their
sentiment and sweetness than her earlier love-tales and ditties
had been. There was amendment, too, in her versification. She
attempted drama, in the tragedy, I think, of *Castruccio Cas-
trucani,* but without the smallest success. She wrote a volume
of sacred verse, which was sentimental rather than serious.
She took Annuals in hand, but the result was the same, and it
must have been felt so by herself. At last she began to write
imaginative prose; and the coterie who supported her blew the
trumpet before her first novel, *Romance and Reality,* as no one
would do now-a-days were a new Dickens, or a new Bulwer,
on the threshold. (pp. 250-51)

Henry Fothergill Chorley, "Miss Landon," in Henry
Fothergill Chorley: Autobiography, Memoir, and

Letters, Vol. I, *edited by Henry G. Hewlett, Richard
Bentley and Son, 1873, pp. 249-52.*

ERIC S. ROBERTSON   (essay date 1883)

*[Describing the early favorable response to Landon and her works,
Robertson attempts to analyze her reaction.]*

[Verse] writers, especially the more modern ones, have not
held [Letitia Landon] in high esteem. There has been a natural
jealousy about her, and the real truth is that this jealousy was
not irrational. "L. E. L." was a spoiled woman.

Not pretty enough to be a beauty, not patient enough to be a
clear thinker, not inspired enough to be a fine poet, not sincere
enough to be steadfast in her affections; a little of the flirt and
gadabout, so hungry for applause that she hasted too eagerly
to win it,—she was doomed to the early disappointment which
her curious foreboding disposition seemed to court for itself.
On the other hand, if not beautiful, she was graceful; if not
inspired, she had such a taste as came very near the true poetical
nature; if not possessed of that great-hearted sincerity which
makes the highest lives a succession of long calms and a few
great storms, she was possessed of sweet amiability, and that
longing to be loved constantly betraying itself even in feeble
natures, though with an appeal that is often touching. There
was nothing to make her early days miserable, but from childhood her style of thought, so far as it was expressed in literary
form, was sickly. Ere she had become a full-grown woman,
the world did everything it could to help her on. A kindly editor
opened up to her the glory of print as soon as she could write
facile verses; the public repaid her with its courtesy. At the
Oxford Union there was a rush of young students whenever a
new number of the magazine containing her poems appeared.
Emolument came to her with more ease than it has come to
almost any woman-writer of our own times. . . . With many
sensibilities, but no distinct aim, Letitia Landon allowed the
circumstances of her first success to master her. Finding that
money and flattery could be had in abundance by such facile
productions as her pen had produced for the *Literary Gazette,*
she devoted her powers to endless contributions for *Books of
Beauty, Keepsakes,* and all such ephemera of the time. (pp.
212-13)

From their first appearance the numerous contributions to the
Gazette which were signed "L. E. L." piqued the public curiosity. They were evidently the work of a young lady; and as
they were romantic and a little sad though sweet in tone, speculation as to their authorship became quite a popular topic.
(p. 216)

[In] 1830-31 a hastily-written novel, called *Romance and Reality,* came from the pen of "L. E. L.", and a sounder experiment
in prose fiction, *Francesca Carrara,* in 1834, compelled the
critics to acknowledge that besides a knack for writing troubadour verses, Miss Landon was capable of writing capital
prose analyses of female character, and of penning descriptions
of set scenes in very effective prose. Indeed, anyone who
wishes to see "L. E. L.'s" powers at their best will find them
exhibited, not in the wearily musical moan of her poetry, but
in the sparkling paragraphs which light up not only the novel
just alluded to, but the subsequent prose works of the author.
(pp. 218-19)

Eric S. Robertson, "L. E. L. and Others," in his
English Poetesses: A Series of Critical Biographies,
Cassell & Company, Limited, 1883, pp. 212-54.

S. M. ELLIS (essay date 1928)

[In the following excerpt from a review of D. E. Enfield's L.E.L.: A Mystery of the Thirties *(see Additional Bibliography), Ellis discusses Landon's poetic style.]*

[The] biographical stockpot has lately received the remains of the once famous L.E.L., and after a vigorous stewing down, and whitewashing before serving, quite a presentable meal is the result.

The author of this book has adopted the staccato, "realistic" manner, with here and there some imaginary scraps of conversation. As a rule, I abominate this style in biography—certainly when it is applied to great personalities; but in this case it is successful, and an acceptable medium for presenting the "agreeable rattle" character of Letitia Landon, that artificial but hard-working young woman who, without any genius of her own, succeeded in making her contemporaries accept her (after Byron's death) as the pre-eminent poet of passionate and blighted love, with an ensuing early grave—"blighted feelings, hopes destroyed. . . ."

> The maiden grew beside the tomb,
> Perhaps 'twas that which touched her bloom . . .
> I ever had, from earliest youth, a feeling what my fate
>   would be. . . .

If L.E.L. were living at the present time she would be one of those industrious, omniscient ladies who write the "Pages for Women" in weekly papers—articles combining love, sentiment, household recipes, and rhapsodies on London sunsets or autumn leaves. But L.E.L. differs from these generally anonymous females in that she secured contemporary fame and posthumous remembrance by "living" and "dying" her particular brand of literary work. She left a trail of amorous adventure in the London Society of her time, and then went off to Cape Coast Castle to meet, at the age of thirty-six, that strange, sudden death which remains a mystery to this day and so entirely in keeping with her poetical imaginings. (pp. 854-55)

> *S. M. Ellis, "L.E.L., Mrs. Carlyle, Chelsea," in*
> The Fortnightly Review, *Vol. CXXIV, No. DCCXLIV,*
> *December 1, 1928, pp. 854-56.*

JANET E. COURTNEY (essay date 1932)

[Courtney assesses the value of Landon's poetry, contending that her artistic growth was thwarted by critics and readers who encouraged her to write voluminously without revision.]

When [Letitia] was about thirteen the Landons returned to London, and there they chanced to have as neighbour, William Jerdan, the editor of the newly founded *Literary Gazette,* a very influential paper in its day. He was an amiable man and seems to have been captivated by the clever little girl, even to the point of publishing some of her verses, and she was hailed by a wide circle as the "Child of Song."

Child she was indeed, not much more than fourteen, but she was already scribbling faster than she could think, encouraged rather unwisely by critics who ascribed to her "an elegance of mind peculiarly graceful in a female." It would have been better for her if they had judged her as a poet and not as a young woman, instead of speeding her upon a career of elegant and quite undiscriminating versification, exhibiting all Byron's melancholy with none of his strength. At eighteen she brought out a long poem, **"The Fate of Adelaide,"** which even her partial friend, Laman Blanchard, had to admit had more of

promise than of performance. Adelaide, a Swiss maiden, is beloved by Orlando; but he departs to the Crusades and marries an Eastern lady. Both his ladies die of love and are buried side by side, whilst he is left, hanging sad and pensive, over their sister graves:

> They laid
> Zoraide (for so she wish'd it) by the side
> Of her sweet rival.

Sad rubbish, but typical of much that followed and really little inferior to the later poems, though it was never republished and does not appear in the Collected Works of the poetess. It showed, like all her early work, what a French critic, M. Jules Lefevre-Deumier, has called "la grace, ou plutôt la négligence melodieuse," characteristic of all her poetry, and it played with passions which a girl of eighteen could know nothing about, but which in her ignorance, or in her audacity—one hardly knows by what name to call it—she thought poetic "genius" could divine without ever experiencing them. (pp. 328-29)

It was, perhaps, unfortunate that *Adelaide* was followed by a volume entitled *The Improvisatrice and Other Poems,* for the very title encouraged its author in her dangerous habit of improvising. In the name-poem, "a young female" ("L.E.L." herself, idealized?) "with all the loveliness, vivid feeling, and genius of her own impassioned land" (Italy) "is supposed to relate her own history"—needless to say a history of dying for love:

> Oh, mockery of happiness!
>   Love now was all too late to save—
> False Love. Oh, what had you to do
>   With one you had led to the grave?
> A little time I had been glad
>   To mark the paleness on my cheek,
> To feel how, day by day, my step
>   Grew fainter, and my hand more weak.

And so on, and so on, luxuriating in her sorrow, whilst the tardy, though true lover, when the grave has finally closed over his fair and fragile lady, is supposed to devote the rest of his mortal life to mourning her, as thus:

> There is a lone and stately hall,
> Its master dwells apart from all.
>
>   • • • • •
>
>   He was young,
> The castle's lord, but pale like age;
> His brow, as sculpture beautiful,
>   Was wan as Grief's corroded page.
> He had no words, he had no smiles,
>   No hopes—his sole employ to brood
> Silently over his sick heart
>   In sorrow and in solitude.

All very pretty and Byronic and full of a "wilful sadness," which "L.E.L.'s" impressionable public insisted on taking seriously—so seriously that when, in **"Sappho's Song,"** she wrote:

> It was my evil star above,
>   Not my sweet lute that wrought me wrong;
> It was not song that taught me love,
>   But it was love that taught me song.

they immediately concluded that the young poetess was speaking from the depths of a broken heart, whereas, as a matter of fact, she was then a lively and cheerful young woman, going about freely in society and enjoying to the full the fame that her poetry had won for her.

Did this fame bring her happiness? It is hard to say. Her poems are steeped in melancholy, but that was the fashion of her time. Moreover, the poet, as such, may "sit above the clang and dust of Time," even if he has not, as certainly she had not, "the world's secret trembling on his lip." One cannot be a poet, even a middling one, says M. Lefevre-Deumier, without being in some sort the confidant of posterity, without catching some whisper of Destiny—and Destiny had in store for poor "L.E.L." no happier future than it held for the greater poet lately dead. So that when a world in mourning for Byron was in such haste to acclaim his feminine re-incarnation, it omitted to notice that "l'aigle mort renaissait papillon."

Perhaps it wouldn't have minded, if it had. It was obsessed by the phenomenon of a young woman pouring out her soul in a flood of melodious verse enriched with a wealth of imagery. It was ready to welcome whatever she chose to give it. So, encouraged by critics who should have sternly checked her faults, she went on in the same vein and gave it *The Troubadour, The Golden Violet, The Venetian Bracelet,* all more or less on the same pattern, collections of lyrical stories, supposed to be the effusions of competitors in feasts of song, but never individualised—just "L.E.L." relating this or that tale of unhappy love, this or that story of sentimentalized passion. To read one is to read all, and having read, to forget. And the pity of it is that she had real poetic talent, if she could but have been persuaded to give herself time for a little reflection. But she prided herself on being equal to anything, and she didn't discriminate. (pp. 330-31)

Her own conception of her calling was no mean one. She has expressed it at its highest in "**Erinna**," a poem dedicated to the young Greek poetess who died in her eighteenth year and whose sepulchral epigram by Antipater appears in the Greek Anthology:

> Oh, glorious is the gifted poet's lot
> And touching more than glorious: 'tis to be
> Companion of the heart's least earthly hour;
> The voice of love and sadness, calling forth
> Tears from their silent fountain: . . .
>
> From the first moment when a falling leaf,
> Or opening bud or streak of rose-touch'd sky
> Waken'd in me the flush and flow of song,
> I gave my soul entire unto the gift
> I deem'd mine own, direct from heaven; it was
> The hope, the bliss, the energy of life;
>
> · · · · ·
>
> My songs have been the mournful history
> Of woman's tenderness and woman's tears;
> I have touch'd but the spirit's gentlest chords;—
> Surely the fittest for my maiden hand;—
> And in their truth my immortality.

But that was just the pity of it. Suffused as they were with gentle sentiment, seldom as direct and sincere in expression as the passage above quoted, her songs did not achieve immortality or anything like it. They achieved a passing vogue and a short *réclame*, due to the mystery of her fate, which barely survived her contemporaries. . . . Much that she wrote

deserved this oblivion; it is scarcely up to the level even of *Keepsakes* and *Annuals,* and no ballad of hers will live as long as Mrs. Hemans' *Casabianca.* But amongst her later poems are a few that show considerable command of metre and true poetic feeling. (pp. 336-37)

But she has no staying power, no sustained excellence. When she gets a good stanza, it is followed almost immediately by one of pedestrian banality. Take "**New Year's Eve**":

> There is no change upon the air,
>   No record in the sky;
> No pall-like storm comes forth to shroud
>   The year about to die.
>
> A few light clouds are in the heaven
>   A few far stars are bright;
> And the pale moon shines as she shines
>   On many a common night.

An admirable start, but turn the page and you come upon:

> Sad the mere change of fortune's chance,
>   And sad the friend unkind;
> But what has sadness like the change
>   That in ourselves we find?

Could anything be more trite? Again in "**The Nameless Grave**" she starts very badly:

> I will not pause beside a tomb
>   Where nothing calls to mind
> Aught that can brighten mortal gloom,
>   Or elevate mankind.

but at the end, remembering Shelley and Keats, she achieves two quite tolerable stanzas:

> He who hath sung of passionate love,
>   His life a feverish tale:—
> Oh! not the nightingale, the dove
>   Would suit this quiet vale.
>
> See, I have named your favourite two—
>   Each had been glad to crave
> Rest 'neath this turf's unbroken dew,
>   And such a nameless grave.

But the gold is too rare and the dross too plentiful. It is difficult to reckon her amongst even lesser literary lights. (p. 338)

Janet E. Courtney, "Alphabetical Graces," in The London Mercury, *Vol. XXVI, No. 154, August, 1932, pp. 326-38.*

LIONEL STEVENSON (essay date 1947)

[*Stevenson was a respected Canadian literary critic and biographer. Here, he evaluates Landon's work, describing it as "the perfect epitome of the transition from Romanticism to Victorianism."*]

"The disappearance of Shelley from the world," wrote Thomas Lovell Beddoes in 1824, "seems, like the tropical setting of that luminary . . . to which his poetical genius can alone be compared with reference to the companions of his day, to have been followed by instant darkness and owl season; whether the vociferous Darley is to be the comet, or tender, full-faced L.E.L. the milk-and-watery moon of our darkness, are questions for the astrologers."

Cape Coast Castle, where Landon died mysteriously. From Maclean of the Gold Coast: The Life of George Maclean, 1801-1847, *by G. E. Metcalfe. Oxford University Press, 1962. Reprinted by permission of the publisher.*

The modern reader, on the basis of his unfamiliarity with both of the nominees, is likely to feel that Beddoes—if he was not indulging in unmitigated sarcasm—must have been a particularly inept soothsayer. George Darley is represented in the anthologies by two or three melodious lyrics, and mentioned in the handbooks along with Beddoes himself in discussions of the abortive pseudo-Elizabethan dramatic efforts of the twenties; and his other candidate, Miss Letitia Elizabeth Landon, is usually ignored by anthologies and handbooks alike.

If, however, one attempts to propose substitute names, one realizes the amazing hiatus in English poetry during the third decade of the nineteenth century. . . . To fill the interval between the death of Byron and the emergence of Tennyson, we are reduced to suggesting such names as Barry Cornwall and James Montgomery. Recourse to contemporary records proves that the outstandingly successful and popular poet was incontrovertibly the "tender, full-faced L.E.L." Her poetical career coincides precisely with the six-year hiatus; the sales of her books reflect her immense appeal to the public; and the remarks of her contemporaries indicate how much they were impressed. (p. 355)

The reasons for this amazing success are not hard to find. . . . She began to write just at the moment when Romanticism had

become popular to the extent of becoming vulgarized, and she provided a lush and effusive romanticism exactly suited to the taste of the young and the plebeian. She had picked up all the obvious traits from the work of Byron and Keats and Leigh Hunt—ornate descriptions of highly colored Italianate scenes, tragic episodes in vaguely medieval or renaissance palaces, a morbid enjoyment of melancholy and self-pity. She might be described, in short, as a female Byron, with the same fluently extemporizing style and the same insistence upon a sensitive soul blasted by the rude touch of the common world, but with Byron's violence and "Satanism" toned down to a sweet lady-like pathos.

In appearance, therefore, her work closely resembled the great poetry of the era, but beneath its surface was a disconcerting absence of two qualities that are essential for making poetry great—technical skill and personal perception. Like most woman versifiers, she had a receptive ear for the melodies of words and stanzas, and could reproduce them lavishly. The ease with which her lyrics flowed from her pen, and the chorus of praise which acclaimed her from the beginning, conspired to obviate hard work and self-discipline. The only advice that she received was from Jerdan, whose taste was so commonplace that his emendations were probably detrimental, being in the direction of triteness. As a result, her poems are peculiarly soporific:

the reader's mind soon gives up the effort to grasp a single clear-cut, original image or genuine emotion, and drifts with the stream of hackneyed phrases and inevitable rhymes. (p. 358)

An example both of [Landon's] poetic style and of the innocently egotistic note that pervaded her work may be quoted from an autobiographic digression that closes *The Troubadour*. She describes the sunny June morning when the poem was conceived in "rainbow dreams":

> And I was happy; hope and fame
> Together on my vision came,
> For memory had just dipp'd her wings
> In honey dews, and sunlit springs,—
> My brow burnt with its early wreath,
> My soul had drank its first sweet breath
> Of praise, and yet my cheek was flushing,
> My heart with the full torrent gushing
> Of feelings whose delightful mood
> Was mingled joy and gratitude.
> Scarce possible it seem'd to be
> That such praise could be meant for me.—
> Enured to coldness and neglect,
> My spirit chill'd, my breathing check'd,
> All that can cow and crush the mind,
> Friends, even more than fate unkind,
> And fortunes stamp'd with the pale sign
> That marks and makes autumn's decline. . . .

She goes on to express her gratitude to the critics "who made my way a path of light":

> Thanks for the gentleness that lent
> My young lute such encouragement,
> When scorn had turn'd my heart to stone,
> O, theirs be thanks and benison!

This is followed by an equally extraverted account of her grief over the recent death of her father. (p. 360)

In [*The Golden Violet*] appeared what is perhaps her best poem, a long dramatic monologue entitled "**Erinna.**" In portraying the character of the ancient Greek poetess, she waxed especially autobiographic. The poem is in blank verse, instead of her customary tetrameter couplets, and as a picture of a young woman poet's mental development it is undeniably convincing. Its tragedy of frustration arises solely from temperamental sources and not from external misfortune. "I have not attempted to write a classical fiction," she explained in her preface; "feelings are what I wish to narrate, not incidents; my aim has been to draw the portrait and trace the changes of a highly poetical mind, too sensitive perhaps of the chill and bitterness belonging even to success." The poem has distinct affinities with the psychological monologues written subsequently by Tennyson and Browning. (p. 361)

The significance of Miss Landon's poetry, then, resides in its being the perfect epitome of the transition from Romanticism to Victorianism. Imaginative escape to overcolored scenes of far away and long ago, mingled with egocentric emotional analysis, and written in an extemporizing style that ignored technical precision—these are the traits of the Romantics, popularized into a formula. On the other hand, her invincible sentimentality and her taste for earnest moralizing clearly foreshadow some of the most famous (if least profound) poems of Elizabeth Barrett and Alfred Tennyson. (pp. 362-63)

Lionel Stevenson, "Miss Landon: 'The Milk-and-Watery Moon of Our Darkness', 1824-30," in Modern Language Quarterly, *Vol. 8, No. 3, September, 1947, pp. 355-63.*

GERMAINE GREER   (essay date 1982)

[*A noted Australian feminist critic, Greer is best known for her* The Female Eunuch. *Greer's basic argument, as explained in the book's introduction, is that women's "sexuality is both denied and misrepresented by being identified as passivity." She explains that women, urged from childhood to live up to an "Eternal Feminine" stereotype, are valued for characteristics associated with the castrate—"timidity, plumpness, languour, delicacy and preciosity"—hence the book's title. From the viewpoint of this primary assumption, Greer examines not only the problems of women's sexuality, but also their psychological development, their relationships with men, their social position, and their cultural history. In the following excerpt from an article explaining the aims of The Tulsa Center for the Study of Women's Literature, Greer discusses the historical neglect of women writers, citing Landon as an example of a "lost" female author.*]

We have not reached the moment when we may generalize about women's work, because no generalization which is not based upon correct understanding of individual cases can be valid. It is only by correct interpretation of individual cases that we can grasp what we have in common with the women who have gone our chosen way before us. . . . If our study of the fortunes of women writers of the past saves us time and pain and shows us the importance of new strategies, they shall not have lived in vain, and the sneering, dismissive entries in biographical sourcebooks may have to be revised.

Just how much work has to be done and what bearing it may have upon our understanding of our own predicament may be illustrated by citing one example. Laetitia Elizabeth Landon is the kind of woman writer about whom a little is known and nothing understood. She was not only one of the most famous women writers of her generation but one of the most famous writers of either sex; yet she died in voluntary exile, probably by her own hand, at the age of thirty-six, and the work of her short lifetime followed her into obscurity. (pp. 14-15)

[Much] of what was written about L.E.L. [is characterized by the review of *The Improvisatrice* in the *Westminister Review* (see excerpt dated 1825)]. . . . *The Improvisatrice* is a very interesting contribution to the literature of female genius. Its theme may derive from Madame de Staël's *Corinne*, which may itself be derived from the real life case of Corilla Olimpica, the *improvvisatrice* who was crowned with laurel in the Campidoglio in 1774. The significance of Italy not only in the writings of L.E.L. but also in those of her contemporary, Mrs. Hemans, and their younger contemporary, Elizabeth Barrett Browning, is inextricably connected with the persistent idea that the climate of Italy fostered female genius and rewarded it with passionate (sexual) admiration. The English version, however, early established the stereotype of the woman of genius suffering in a Byronic fashion from the inadequacy and petty tyranny of the men in her life. L.E.L. may have read the novel *A Woman of Genius*, which appeared anonymously in 1822, full of a kind of rage that we now find familiar without realizing how many times it has appeared on earth before:

> Not content with thus clipping the wings of her ambition man would even confine her on those points in which he affects to admit her to a participation with himself. She may love; he not only *permits*, he *requires*, that she shall love: but how? in silence, in sighs, in agony,

without complaint; in torture without the alle-
viation of appearing to suffer.

L.E.L. did not voice her frustrations quite so clearly, for she
had not the shield of anonymity; instead she cloaked them in
a series of masochistic stereotypes in which the heroine con-
summates her passion in death even when her lover's arms are
available. Because L.E.L. thought of herself as an *improvvisatrice* (for she would have been quite incapable of any kind
of revision of her work) the elements of her governing fantasies
are almost embarrassingly obvious; the same motifs recur in
the work of her female contemporaries but are more efficiently
veiled. The twisted eroticism of L.E.L.'s writing was half-
perceived by some of her contemporaries who occasionally
accused her of impropriety and morbidness, to her great distress. (p. 16)

Nowadays we would respect L.E.L. more if we could uncover
what Blanchard was afraid of revealing [in his biography (see
Additional Bibliography)]. It is harder for us to respect a woman
who seems to have capitulated so utterly to the sexual double
standard, to the publishers and their crude demands, to the
Tories and their ruthless factionalism, and to the vapidity of
the literary coteries, than it is for us to pardon unchastity or
duplicity. L.E.L. herself made a strong appeal to posterity to
plead her case, and left behind a key to the puzzle:

> I live among the cold, the false,
>   And I must seem like them;
> And such I am, for I am false
>   As those I most condemn.
>
> I teach my lip its sweetest smile,
>   My tongue its softest tone;
> I borrow others' likeness, till
>   Almost I lose my own.
>
> I pass through flattery's gilded sieve,
>   Whatever I would say;
> In social life, all, like the blind,
>   Must learn to feel their way. . . .
>
> I hear them speak of love, the deep,
>   The true, and mock the name;
> Mock at all high and early truth,
>   And I too do the same. . . .
>
> And one fear, withering ridicule,
>   Is all that I can dread;
> A sword hung by a single hair
>   For ever o'er the head.
>
> We bow to a most servile faith,
>   In a most servile fear;
> While none among us dares to say
>   What none will choose to hear.
>
> And if we dream of loftier thoughts,
>   In weakness they are gone;
> And indolence and vanity
>   Rivet our fetters on. . . .
>
> I have such eagerness of hope
>   To benefit my kind;
> And feel as if immortal power
>   Were given to my mind. . . .
>
> Why write I this? Because my heart
>   Towards the future springs,
> That future where it loves to soar
>   On more than eagle wings. . . .

> I am myself but a vile link
>   Amid life's weary chain;
> But I have spoken hallow'd words,
>   Oh do not say in vain!
>
> My first, my last, my only wish,
>   Say will my charmed chords
> Wake to the morning light of fame,
>   And breathe again my words? . . .
>
> Let music make less terrible
>   The silence of the dead;
> I care not, so my spirit last
>   Long after life has fled

One of the best poems L.E.L. ever wrote was a monody on
the death of Mrs. Hemans; the generosity of a spirit which
could be touched to one of its finest issues by the death of a
rival with whom she was always unfavorably compared is worth
recording. Elizabeth Barrett Browning paid L.E.L.'s monody
the supreme compliment of imitating it in a reply that she
addressed to L.E.L. [see excerpt dated 1838]. In life, the snub-
nosed Brompton Sappho could not associate with these grander
ladies, yet spiritually both were very much aware of her. Flashy,
exposed, exaggerated, and occasionally absurd as she was, she
helped to push back the limitations on women writers. Without
her slipshod improvisation with its haphazard assonances and
liquid syntax, in which the clauses simply run into each other
to make a seamless whole with no irritable adversities of coordination, we could not have had the language of that essentially female form, the verse novel, of which *Aurora Leigh* is
the greatest but by no means the only example.

If only L.E.L. had been discouraged from publishing, she
might have accomplished more and suffered less. Her poems
might have languished in tiny hand-sewn books hidden away
in drawers, but they would have borne the mark of no pressure
but her own eagerness to set down the fantasy, instead of the
dreary imprint of poetry by the foot. On the other hand, she
and her family might simply have starved to death. Until we
have restored L.E.L.'s historical situation to something resembling its actual complexity, we cannot successfully interpret
it. (pp. 21-3)

*Germaine Greer, "The Tulsa Center for the Study
of Women's Literature: What We Are Doing and Why
We Are Doing It,"* in Tulsa Studies in Women's
Literature, *Vol. 1, No. 1, Spring, 1982, pp. 5-26.*

ADDITIONAL BIBLIOGRAPHY

Ashton, Helen. *Letty Landon.* New York: Dodd, Mead & Co., 1951,
306 p.
    A fictionalized reconstruction of Landon's life.

Blanchard, Samuel Laman. *Life and Literary Remains of L.E.L.*
2 vols. London: H. Colburn, 1841.
    A biography of Landon that also contains some of her previously
    unpublished works.

Bushnell, George Herbert. "The Husband of L.E.L." In his *From
Papyrus to Print: A Bibliographical Miscellany*, pp. 169-77. London:
Grafton & Co., 1947.

A brief summary of George Maclean's life that recounts the investigations into Landon's death.

Elwood, Mrs. "Mrs. Maclean." In her *Memoirs of the Literary Ladies of England,* Vol. II, pp. 304-32. 1843. Reprint. New York: AMS Press, 1973.
    An anecdotal biography of Landon containing an overview of her works.

Enfield, D. E. *L.E.L.: A Mystery of the Thirties*. London: L. and V. Woolf, 1928, 201 p.
    A biographical study of Landon.

Madden, R. R. "Notice and Letters of L.E.L." In his *The Literary Life and Correspondence of the Countess of Blessington,* Vol. II, 2d ed., pp. 264-316. London: T. C. Newby, Publisher, 1855.
    Chronicles Landon's life and the circumstances surrounding her death. Madden, a physician, conducted an informal investigation into Landon's death at her husband's request.

Rosenblum, Dolores. "Christina Rossetti's Religious Poetry: Watching, Looking, Keeping Vigil." *Victorian Poetry* 20, No. 1 (Spring 1982): 33-49.
    Notes the "aesthetic of pain" common to both Landon's and Christina Rossetti's poetry.

Stevenson, Lionel. "Romanticism Run to Seed." *The Virginia Quarterly Review* 9, No. 4 (October 1933): 510-25.
    Views the "riotous improvisation" that characterizes English literature of the late 1820s and 1830s as an inevitable result of the Romantics' defiance of traditional rules of theme and technique. According to Stevenson, the writings of Landon, William Maginn, John Wilson, John Gibson Lockhart, Theodore Hood, and Francis Sylvester Mahony typify English literature of this period.

Thrall, Miriam M. H. "The Story of L.E.L." In her *Rebellious "Fraser's": Nol Yorke's Magazine in the Days of Maginn, Thackeray, and Carlyle,* pp. 193-207. New York: Columbia University Press, 1934.
    Recounts Landon's role at the *Literary Gazette* and her relationship with Maginn.

Wharton, Grace, and Wharton, Philip [pseudonyms of Katharine Thomas and Anthony Thomas]. "Letitia Elizabeth Landon (L.E.L.)." In their *The Queens of Society,* Vol. I, pp. 259-320. Philadelphia: Porter & Coates, 1890.
    A detailed biography of Landon by two of her close friends.

Henry Crabb Robinson

1775-1867

English diarist and critic.

Robinson is remembered as an insightful and outspoken commentator on the literary world of nineteenth-century London. Chronicled in his *Diary, Reminiscences, and Correspondence,* his recollections provide an astute assessment of literary trends and society during his lifetime. Robinson is praised both for his writings about his contemporaries and for his role in helping to introduce German literature to England.

Born and raised in Bury St. Edmunds, England, Robinson studied law as a youth and moved to London in 1796. There he worked as a clerk in a law office until, in 1798, he came into a minor inheritance. Robinson then put aside his legal career for several years and traveled to Germany, where he studied literature and philosophy at the University of Jena. He quickly made the acquaintance of several important literary figures, including Johann Wolfgang von Goethe, Johann Friedrich von Schiller, and Johann Gottfried von Herder. Robinson's command of the German language enabled him to fully appreciate their writings. In particular, Robinson recognized the genius of Goethe's works and determined to make them known to others in England.

Having enjoyed his stay in Germany, Robinson returned in 1805 to London, where he worked for several years as a war correspondent and editor for the *Times*. He found editorial work unfulfilling, however, and in 1811 he made two significant decisions: to study for the bar and to keep a diary. Two years later Robinson passed the bar and began practicing law, but continued to write for journals on a free-lance basis. Through his work as a journalist, he became friends with many members of the London literary community, most notably the poet William Wordsworth and the essayist Charles Lamb. Robinson's friendship with Wordsworth, in fact, became one of the pivotal relationships in his life. Over the course of thirty years, Robinson wrote extensively on Wordsworth, and his day-to-day record of the poet's methods and philosophies, included in the *Diary,* is now considered one of the most valuable sources of information about Wordsworth. In turn, Wordsworth thought highly of Robinson and dedicated sections of several poems to him. Robinson's popularity evidently derived not only from his great conversational abilities but also from his inherent generosity: he both encouraged authors and, on many occasions, helped them financially.

In addition to his social interests, Robinson was strongly committed to literature. He frequently composed journal articles, including an influential and illuminating series on Goethe for the *Monthly Repository.* Yet the majority of Robinson's remarks on literature are found in his *Diary,* for which he is best known today. There, he recorded the Shakespearean lectures of the poet Samuel Taylor Coleridge; Robinson's transcripts of these speeches, in fact, provide one of the few complete collections of Coleridge's criticism, and Robinson's own critical comments, which are interspersed throughout, are admired for their insight and objectivity. Indeed, scholars frequently note Robinson's impartiality, even in regard to such a cherished friend as Wordsworth. While Robinson greatly admired the

poet's work, he also noted its occasional weaknesses. Because Robinson extensively reported on contemporary figures and events, most critics consider his *Diary* a significant contribution to nineteenth-century literary criticism and a valuable historical document.

Though he had successfully managed to integrate his literary interests with a law career, Robinson became financially independent in 1828 and retired to read, write, and socialize. In addition, he also became a political activist and philanthropist; he helped found London University and participated in the antislavery movement. He also hosted extremely popular Sunday morning breakfast parties for his literary contemporaries, though several complained about his tendency to monopolize conversations. In fact, according to one story, an acquaintance once noted, "If there is anyone here who wishes to say anything, he had better say it at once, for Crabb Robinson is coming." Despite his alleged verbosity, Robinson endured as a beloved social figure. He continued to read voraciously throughout his long life and made his last diary entry only five days before his death at age ninety-one. While writing about Matthew Arnold, he broke off in mid-sentence, "But I feel incapable to go on."

Several collections of extracts from Robinson's diary have appeared, but together they constitute only a small portion of its over one hundred volumes. The first collection, his *Diary, Reminiscences, and Correspondence*, was published two years after his death. Upon its appearance, critics praised the work's scope, readability, and historical value, though a few commentators labeled it mere gossip. Later modified editions have focused on such specific areas as literary criticism, German scholarship, and drama. As more of Robinson's writings reach publication, scholars continue to commend his critical acumen and foresight: in addition to helping introduce German literature to England, he championed the Romantic poets Wordsworth and John Keats and the novelist Sir Walter Scott. Robinson's diaries are also valued for his detailed interviews with a number of his contemporaries. In particular, his discussions with the poet and artist William Blake have been termed by Edith Morley "the most revealing contemporary interpretations we possess of the mystic poet-painter and his personality." Today, most critics value Robinson's extensive comments on literature and society both as a reflection of contemporary taste and as an intimate record of the English literary circles of the nineteenth century.

PRINCIPAL WORKS

Diary, Reminiscences, and Correspondence of H. C. Robinson. 3 vols. (diary, memoirs, and letters) 1869
Blake, Coleridge, Wordsworth, Lamb, Etc.: Being Selections from the Remains of H. C. Robinson (criticism) 1922
The Correspondence of Henry Crabb Robinson with the Wordsworth Circle, 1808-1866. 2 vols. (letters) 1927
Crabb Robinson in Germany, 1800-1805 (letters) 1929
Henry Crabb Robinson on Books and Their Writers. 3 vols. (criticism) 1938
The London Theatre, 1811-1866: Selections from the Diary of Henry Crabb Robinson (criticism) 1966
The Diary of Henry Crabb Robinson: An Abridgement (diary) 1967

HENRY CRABB ROBINSON   (diary date 1811)

[*Here, Robinson declares his intention to record his recollections and experiences in a diary.*]

This year I began to keep a *Diary*. This relieves me from one difficulty, but raises another. Hitherto I have had some trouble in bringing back to my memory the most material incidents in the proper order. It was a labor of *col*lection. Now I have to *se*lect. When looking at a diary, there seems to be too little distinction between the insignificant and the important, and one is reminded of the proverb, "The wood cannot be seen for the trees."

> *Henry Crabb Robinson, in a diary entry of 1811, in his* Diary, Reminiscences, and Correspondence, *Vol. I, edited by Thomas Sadler, 1869. Reprint by Fields, Osgood, & Co., 1870, p. 204.*

WILLIAM WORDSWORTH   (poem date 1814)

[*An English poet and critic, Wordsworth was central to the English Romantic movement. According to several sources, Words-*

worth *wrote this section of his unfinished epic poem,* The Excursion, *with Robinson in mind.*]

> A Man he seems of cheerful yesterdays
> And confident to-morrows,—with a face
> Not worldly-minded; for it bears too much
> Of Nature's impress,—gaiety and health,
> Freedom and hope; but keen, withal, and shrewd.
> His gestures note,—and hark! his tones of voice
> Are all vivacious as his mien and looks.

> *William Wordsworth, in an extract from his* The Excursion: Being a Portion of 'The Recluse', a Poem, *Longman, Hurst, Rees, Orme, and Brown, 1814, p. 335.*

HENRY CRABB ROBINSON   (essay date 1833)

[*In the following excerpt, Robinson discusses three classes of literary works, the epic, the dramatic, and the lyric, and outlines both his philosophy of poetry and his conception of beauty. Robinson abbreviated many words and phrases, each of which has been given its full form here and placed in brackets. His remarks were first published in the* Monthly Repository *in 1833.*]

The epic is marked by this character of style,—that the poet presents his *object* immediately and directly, with a total disregard of his own personality. He is, as it were, an indifferent and unimpassioned narrator or chronicler; he relates his tale in one uniform tone; he never hurries and never stops; dwells as long on the description of a warrior's dress or of a meal, as in the statement of the most momentous incident.... The opposite class of poetry is the *lyric*, in which the poet gives mainly objects as they are reflected in the mirror of his own individuality. And this certainly is the essential character of odes, elegies, songs, &c. These same classes, designated generally, as the *objective* and *subjective*, were called by Schiller the naive and the sentimental, and they have also been named the real and the ideal. In general, modern poets belong to the subjective class; ... we add, for the sake of completeness, that the dramatic poet must unite the powers of both in an equal degree. In the plan of his drama, in the relation of the characters to each other, all in subordination to the purpose of the work, he must have the epic impartiality; but in the execution, he is lyric. (pp. 210-11)

· · · · ·

A splendid moral [Sentiment] or happy [thought] in rhythmical [Language]: is *not* poetry— ... A million of fine passages does not make a poem—It is the *Whole* as a *Whole*—The general [exhibition] of Man & Life which the poet lays open to us—It is a great rule—abstract thoughts & [general reflections] are anti poetical for poetry is addressed not to the [understanding] but to the Sense—*Sensible* [exhibition] is essential to poetry—Many of the noble moral tirades of Shakespeare— are *in themselves* mere pieces of rhetorick & this is the only merit [which] the vulgar are sensible of—but these same pieces (for instance Hamlets Monologues) are highly poetical as parts of a whole—Those who read with pleasure the Beauties of Shakespeare & who gape over his pieces may be said never to have understood or rather felt Shakespeare— ... In all [descriptions] beauty & the *sense of beauty* must predominate [where] this is [effected] by music or [painting] that is by the [awakening] distinct images in the fancy or rousing indefinite & vague sensations—is indifferent—The [Sensation] must be raised where it is raised generally—there can be no dispute This sense of Beauty say the modern Critics is the object of the fine Arts who in their perfect purity admit of no other feeling—And this, they say, is the essential difference [between] the antient grecian classical poetry & the modern romantic poetry—This leading notion is carried by the new school to such an extreme that the leading authors do not hesitate to say that perfect beauty ought not to *interest* & ought to leave the Mind in repose—... Hence say the critics the poet ought not to be in earnest he must *play* with his [subject] And be himself—*cold* tho' thro' his Art he makes his readers warm—... these views—I hold them to be true beyond dispute.... A *poet ought not to interest* The genuine Poet scorns to press the [*curiosity*] of the Reader into his Service. (pp. 211-12)

> *Henry Crabb Robinson, in an extract from "Retirement and Controversial Writings," in* Henry Crabb Robinson of Bury, Jena, "The Times," and Russell Square *by John Milton Baker, George Allen & Unwin Ltd., 1937, pp. 210-12.*

HENRY CRABB ROBINSON   (diary date 1867)

[*The following excerpt, drawn from Robinson's* Diary, *contains his final critical commentary, which he was unable to complete.*]

During the last two days I have read the first essay [of Matthew Arnold's *Essays in Criticism*] on the qualifications of the present age for criticism. The writer resists the exaggerated scorn of criticism, and maintains his point ably. A sense of creative power he declares happiness to be, and Arnold maintains that genuine criticism is. He thinks of Germany as he ought, and of Goethe with high admiration. On this point I can possibly give him assistance, which he will gladly—

But I feel incapable to go on.

(p. 503)

> *Henry Crabb Robinson, in a diary entry on January 31, 1867, in his* Diary, Reminiscences, and Correspondence, Vol. II, *edited by Thomas Sadler, 1869. Reprint by Fields, Osgood, & Co., 1870, pp. 503-04.*

THOMAS SADLER   (essay date 1869)

[*Sadler was the editor of Robinson's* Diary, Reminiscences, and Correspondence, *which was first published in 1869. In this excerpt from his introduction, Sadler provides a brief sketch of Robinson's personality and interests and focuses on his religious beliefs.*]

Mr. Robinson was a voracious devourer of books. He read before he got up, and after he went to bed. On his journeys, whether on foot or on a stage-coach, he was in the habit of spending much of his time in reading. The most attractive scenery had to share his attention with a book. He said: "I could have no pleasure at the seaside without society. That is the one great want of my life, or rather the second,—the first being books." In a Christmas visit to Rydal, for a month or five weeks, he would read from ten to twenty volumes of such works as those of Arnold, Whately, and Isaac Taylor. Nor was he one of those who think they have read a work when they have only skimmed through it, and made themselves acquainted with its general contents. Sometimes he gives, in the *Diary,* an account of what he read, and there is a large bundle of separate papers, containing abstracts of books, plots of stories, and critical remarks.

In his case, however, there was no danger of becoming so absorbed in literature as to lose his interest in men. He was eminently *social.* But he liked to have to do with persons who had some *individuality.* It was an affliction to him to be obliged to spend several hours with one of those colorless beings who have no opinions, tastes, or principles of their own. Writing from Germany to his brother, he said, "I love *characters* extremely." The words, "He is a character," are frequently the prelude to an interesting personal description. Of one whom he knew, he says: "All his conversation is ostentatious egotism; and yet it is preferable to the dry talk about the weather, which some men torment me with. The revelations of character are always interesting." (pp. viii-ix)

Mr. Robinson's name is widely known as that of a capital talker. There is a saying that a man's strength is also his weakness, and in this case there are not wanting jokes about his taking all the conversation to himself. It is reported that one day at a breakfast-party at Sam Rogers's, the host said to those assembled: "O, if there is any one here who wishes to say anything, he had better say it at once, for Crabb Robinson is coming." But there is no subject on which he more frequently reproaches himself, than with this habit of taking too large a share of the talk. When his strength was beginning to fail, his friend Edwin Field urged him in a letter to refrain from talking "more than two hours consecutively." He notes this in the *Diary,* and adds: "Is this satire? It does not offend me." Yet he was too candid not to acknowledge that conversation was the one thing in which, in his own estimation, he excelled. It was, he said, his power of expression which enabled him to make his way as a barrister, notwithstanding his deficiencies in legal attainment. He not only had a copious vocabulary, but could also convey much meaning by his manner, and by a playful exaggeration in his words. (pp. ix-x)

It is not too much to say, that to the great majority of those who were in the habit of meeting him his conversation was a real delight. The Editor well remembers the secret pleasure with which he invariably saw him come into the room, and the feeling which the announcement of his death caused, as of a loss which, in kind, could never be made up. There were veins in his conversation, from which more good was to be gained in a pleasant hour after dinner, than from many a lengthened serious discourse.

Throughout life Mr. Robinson was a man of unusual activity. He himself would hardly have admitted this. A title that suggested itself to him for his *Reminiscences* was, "Retrospect of an Idle Life." When on one occasion he was told by his medical attendant that he had been using his brain too much, he exclaimed, "That is absurd." He would say of himself, that while he talked too much he *did* nothing. But, in truth, men "who have nothing to do" are very serviceable members of society, if they only know how to employ their time. (pp. x-xi)

Mr. Robinson used to lament that he had not the faculty of giving a graphic account of the illustrious men with whom he came into contact. He had, at all events, one qualification for interesting others,—he was interested himself. The masters of style have no arts which can take the place of a writer's own enthusiasm in his subject. Mr. Robinson's descriptions are often all the more effective from their very naturalness and simplicity. The Italian tour, with Wordsworth, may be cited as an example. What was written on the journeys is, on the whole, hardly equal to the ordinary home *Diary.* Nor is that tour one of the best, so far as the record is concerned. And yet the few notes jotted down day by day are admirably illustrative of Wordsworth's mind and character, and are strikingly confirmed by the "Memorials" written by him afterwards. The poet's love for natural beauties rather than works of art, for the country rather than the towns, for fresh life in bird, or flower, or little child, rather than for the relics of the things of old,—his annoyance at the long streets at Bologna,—his eagerness to depart from the fashionable watering-place of Ischl,—the wide difference in his interest in those places which have influenced the character and works of a great man, and those which have only been outwardly associated with him,— his being allured by the sound of a stream, and led on and on till midday, notwithstanding that he was expected back to breakfast, and the relief his anxious friend felt as soon as he heard the same sound, knowing that it would be likely to be irresistible to the truant, and tracking him out by this clew,— these and kindred touches of character have in them the material and coloring of genuine biography. (pp. xiv-xv)

To those who were not intimate with Mr. Robinson what he says respecting religion may sometimes be puzzling. There are occasions when his words seem to imply that with him belief was rather hoped for than an actual possession. He thought there was more real piety in the exclamation of the anxious father in the Gospels, "Lord, I believe; help thou mine unbelief," than in the confident and self-satisfied assertion of the longest creed. His sympathy in opinions was with those who have exercised the fullest liberty of thought. He had traversed far and wide the realms of theological speculation, and in every part he had found sincere and devout men. But he was always interested and touched by genuine religious feeling, wherever he found it,—whether in the simple and fervent faith of the Moravians at Ebersdorf, or in the blessings which the old Catholic woman at Bischoffsheim poured upon Christian Brentano, or in the vesper service at the wayside inn in the Tyrol, or in the family worship at Ambleside, where "sweet Jessie" Harden "read the prayers." He thoroughly entered into the sentiment of the author of the "Religio Medici,"—"I cannot laugh at, but rather pity, the fruitless journeys of pilgrims, or condemn the miserable condition of friars; for though misplaced in circumstances, there is something in it of devotion. I could never hear the Ave Mary bell without an elevation, or think it a sufficient warrant, because they erred in one circumstance, for me to err in all,—that is, in silence and contempt. Whilst, therefore, they directed their devotions to her, I offered mine to God, and rectified the errors of their prayers by rightly ordering mine own." Looking to the church of the future, he hoped there would be found in it "the greatest quantity of religion founded on devotional sentiment, and the least quantity of church government compatible with it, and consistent with order." The concluding paragraph of his obituary of his friend Anthony Robinson, written in 1827, is strikingly applicable to himself: "Could Mr. Robinson be justly deemed a religious man? If religion be a system of confident conclusions on all the great points of metaphysical speculation, as they respect the universe and its author,—man and his position in the one, and relation to the other,—it must be owned Mr. Robinson laid no claim to the character. But if the religious *principle* be that which lays the foundations of all truth deeper than the external and visible world; if religious *feeling* lie in humble submission to the unknown Infinite Being, who produced all things, and in a deep sense of the duty of striving to act and live in conformity with the will of that Being; if, further, Christianity consist in acknowledging the Christian Scriptures as the exposition of the Divine will, and the guide of human conduct,—then, surely, he may boldly claim to be a member of that true Christian Catholic Church, according to his own definition of it,—'An association of men for the cultivation of knowledge, the practice of piety, and the promotion of virtue.'"

Mr. Robinson was an earnest thinker on the profoundest and most difficult religious subjects. This was especially the case in his old age. As we like to look up to the stars, though we may not be able to tell their magnitude or their distance, and to behold the majesty of the sea, though we may not be able to fathom its depths, so he seemed to be attracted to the great problems of religion, as if he liked to feel their infinitude, rather than hoped to find their solution. He stated as his experience, that "Religion in age supplies the animal spirits of youth." His old age had its pathetic side, as, indeed, every old age must have.

Those who, in his later years, met him in society, and saw how full of life he was, with what zest and animation he told his old stories, merely requiring, now and then, help as to a name or a date, may easily have imagined his strength greater than it really was.

But though few, perhaps, have ever so closely watched the approach of infirmity, and though he was in the habit of saying, "Growing old is like growing poor, a sort of going down in the world," his frequent expression was, "This does not make me melancholy." And when, at last, "everything seemed to tire," there was, with this feeling of mortal weariness, another feeling, which was that he was

> On the brink of being born.

> (pp. xvi-xviii)

Thomas Sadler, in a preface to Diary, Reminiscences, and Correspondence, Vol. I *by Henry Crabb Robinson, edited by Thomas Sadler, 1869. Reprint by Fields, Osgood, & Co., 1870, pp. v-xix.*

AUGUSTUS De MORGAN (essay date 1869)

[*De Morgan was a close friend of Robinson. In the following excerpt from an appendix to the 1869 edition of the* Diary, *De Morgan describes Robinson's talent for conversation and elaborates on two of his favorite subjects: German literature and the works of Wordsworth.*]

As a master of the art of conversation,—that is, of power of conversation without art,—H. C. R. was a man of few rivals. He could take up the part of his friend Coleridge, whom Madame de Staël described to him as tremendous at monologue but incapable of dialogue. If any one chose to be a listener only, H. C. R. was his man; he had always enough for two, and a bit over. And he appreciated a listener, and considered the faculty as positive, not negative, virtue. But this did not mean that he cared little whether he was talking to a man or a post, and only wanted something which either had no tongue to answer, or would not use it. Coleridge, or some one like him, is said to have held a friend by the button until the despairing listener cut it away, and finished his walk. On his way back he found his talking friend, holding up the button in his hand, and still in the middle of his discourse. This would not have happened to H. C. R., who took note of his auditor. "I consider—," he said, "as one of the most sensible young men I ever knew."—"Why! he hardly says anything."—"Ah! but I do not judge him by what he says, but by *how* he listens." But H. C. R. could and did *converse*. . . . H. C. R. was one of those who keep alive the knowledge that there is such a thing as conversation, and what it is. In our day, what between the feuds of religion, politics, and social problems, and the writers who think that issuing a book is giving hostages to society never to be natural again, conversation is almost abandoned to children. (p. 510)

The elements of conversational power in H. C. R. were a quick and witty grasp of meaning, a wide knowledge of letters and of men of letters, a sufficient, but not too exacting, perception of the relevant, and an extraordinary power of memory. His early education was not of a very high order of the classical, nor did his tastes induce him to cultivate ancient literature: in truth, his German and Italian opportunities *used up* his love of letters, which was very decided. He was fond of the drama, and of ballad compositions. For his profession, the law, he had more turn than taste. With his memory, he got ample knowledge for a practitioner cheaper than most; and his mind was able to form and argue distinctions. So he was a successful barrister: he made the law a good horse, but never a hobby.

His intercourse with the school of Coleridge, Wordsworth, Southey, Charles Lamb, &c., and with the German school, from Goethe and Schiller downwards, to say nothing of others, gave him a wide range of anecdote and of comparison. By the time he died the tablet of his memory had more than sixty years of literary recollections painted upon it; and painted with singular clearness. He had a comical habit of self-depreciation, which, though jocose in expression, took its rise in a real feeling that his life had been thrown away. It had, in fact, been of a miscellaneous character, and, save only in his legal career, had nothing to which a common and understood name could be attached. Accordingly it was, "I speak to you with the respect with which a person like myself ought to speak to a great—." Here insert scholar, mathematician, physician, &c., as the case might be. Or, perhaps, "I am nothing, and never was anything, not even a lawyer." Sometimes, "Do not run away with the idea that I know that or anything else." But the climax was reached when, after giving an account of something which involved a chain of anecdotes, running back with singular connection and clearness through two generations, he came at last to a loss about some name. It would then be, "You see that my memory is quite gone; though that is an absurd way of talking, for I never had any."

His memory was very self-consistent. Those who watched his conversation would find that, though at different times the same anecdote would occur in very different illustrative duties, it was always the same. And this continued to the very last. (pp. 510-11)

H. C. R. had also a remarkable power of close verbal quotation, orally given. The writer has verified this by books, and judges that the memory was equally good at repeating conversations. He also noticed that an anecdote, containing a retort or a *bon-mot,* was always given in the same words. There are men who are strong in recollection of the substance of what was said, but who synonymize, not merely words, but idioms and proverbs. You end with, "It was six of one and half a dozen of the other," and are reported as pronouncing, "It was all of a piece." You say, "He will come to the gallows," and "He will die in his shoes" is carried away. Of such paronomasia H. C. R. was incapable. (p. 513)

Those who have breakfasted and dined with H. C. R. will find it impossible to describe the charm of those social meetings. We have heard of a difficult host, whose parties were celebrated for unrestrained association, which was accounted for by a saturnine guest as follows: "O, any two persons who can get on with him are sure to be able to get on with one another!" In this case, however, assimilation was powerfully aided by the genial good-humor of the host, and effectually prepared by his choice of associates. For there was nothing like *general society* at his table; the guests were a cluster of persons whose minds had affinities with his own. We all know that an English convivial meeting will, about as often as not, have its barricades erected by one set and another against those of the wrong set. It is not quite the majority of cases in which all the guests unfeignedly believe in the power of the host to choose the proper collection. But at the house of H. C. R. (that all who frequented it knew the secret is more than the writer will undertake to say), each man felt the assurance that every guest would be—in the opinion of a discerning and experienced host, who cultivated acquaintance only according to liking—a man whose society was personally agreeable to that host. . . . As to H. C. R. himself, at the head of his table, he managed to secure attention to his guests without the guests themselves feeling that they were on his mind. It is a great drawback on many pleasant parties, that one unfortunate individual—the one whom every other would wish to feel at ease—seems to be but a director of the servants, indulged with a seat at the table. It would sometimes have been a comfort to the writer if he could have been made sure that his host had had, before dinner, what the tale calls a "snack by way of a damper." But this uneasiness never arose with respect to H. C. R., who made his meal and carried on his conversation, while, somehow or other,—the most satisfactory way in which many things can happen,—his guests were perfectly well served, as he knew and saw. And so these parties were too pleasant in all details to allow any remembrance of one part by its contrast with another. The writer would find great difficulty in any attempt at closer description: he was far too agreeably engaged to take note of particulars. To be inserted between two conversible fellow-guests is destructive of the power and the will to watch many other details: that can only be done with effect by a person who is seated between his foe and his bore. (pp. 514-15)

If there were two subjects upon which he was apt to be *huffed,* they were German literature generally and Wordsworth. And yet he certainly showed no striking adhesion to German doctrines in philosophy, and no remarkable—certainly no exclusive—adoption of German tone of thought. These things had opened his mind, for his first real studies were in Germany, and in German: but they did not block up the gateway. Real business, that of a reporter from the scene of a campaign, of a newspaper writer, of a well-employed lawyer, probably shaped modes of thought which prevented the speculative from usurping the whole field, and even from entire occupation of any part of it.

As to Wordsworth and his poetical comrades, it is certain that the soul of H. C. R. was not that of a Lake-poet. Had he written verse, the writer feels sure, without pronouncing upon the exact place, that he would have come nearer to Hudibras than to the *Excursion.* He admired and appreciated, and saw all that was to be seen; whether, in the meaning of the enthusiasts, he felt all that was to be felt, may be hung up for further inquiry. It may be suspected that, both as to the German and the English schools, his admiration was for the writings, and his affection for his friends: *fiat mixtura* was the prescription. It is worth noting, that both his great objects of enthusiasm, both the points on which his temper was occasionally assailable, were connected with deep personal regards and long friendships. If, then, it be true which was whispered, namely, that under irritation at an assault on Wordsworth, he in former time told a literary lady that she was an "impertinent old maid,"—no doubt in that joco-serious tone in which he often launched a hard word; it was followed by a letter of apology,—it must have been for his friends he spoke, and not for their doctrines.

The writer, who knows little of the German language, and has little sympathy either with their recent philosophy or their historical criticism, *exceptis excipiendis,* and who is not capable of more than a percentage of Wordsworth, did not abstain from either subject, and spoke his mind with freedom on both. There was never any appearance of annoyance; the worst was: "You're a mathematician, and have no right to talk about poetry. I wonder whether I could ever have been a mathematician; I think not: to be sure, I never tried. I have often thought whether it would have been possible for a creature like myself, without a head to put anything into, to have a notion given to him of a mathematical process." Such a sparring-match one day ended in the writer undertaking to give an idea of the way in which arithmetic acts in problems of chance. The attempt was very successful; and H. C. R. made several references on future occasions to his having obtained one idea on mathematics.

As to German, the writer one day ventured to bring forward what he has long called the seven deadly sins of excess of that language: 1. Too many volumes in the language; 2. Too many sentences in a volume; 3. Too many words in a sentence; 4. Too many syllables in a word; 5. Too many letters in a syllable; 6. Too many strokes in a letter; 7. Too much black in a stroke. It was all frankly admitted, as it would probably be by most of the Germans themselves. The serious truth is, that the German mind has this kind of tendency to excess, entirely independent of the language. Free, strong, and earnest thought desires to get to the bottom of everything; and what it cannot find it makes. It asks, What is the universe? but this is poor measure for a transcendental intellect. It then inquires how it is to be proved, *a priori,* that a universe is possible. And it is much to be feared that it will come at last to a serious attempt to find out what, if existence had been impossible, we should have had in its place. This, and more, was brought forward by the writer to vex the spirit of the German scholar. He even ventured to ask the like of whether if *Werden,* while transmuting *Nichts* into *Seyn,* had been brought before the Absolute for coining spurious Existence, he would have been able, with Hegel's help, to prove that Existence and Non-existence are all one. Things like these were brought forward when there appeared any languor. It would be: "Well! how are you today, Mr. R.?"—"O, a poor creature; my head's not fit for anything; it never *was* good for much!" If a discussion was thereupon brought about, the head would be roused, all the power would be wakened in five minutes, and a small course of anecdote, beginning with Wieland, and ending with yesterday's visit from—, or perhaps *vice versa,* would send all megrim to the rightabout.

The last of the Lake School—for, though H. C. R. did not serve at the altar, he was free of the Inner Court—was, strange to say, not a poet, not apparently enthusiastic about poetry, more interested in the real life than in the ideal, tolerably satirical in thought and phrase, and a man whose very last wish would have been for the "peaceful hermitage" to end his days in. This is the report of one: how was it with others? Did the mind of H. C. R. take color from that of the person with whom he conversed? Would he have been other things to other men? Such a power, or tendency, or what you please, may go a little in aid of the writer's impression that he was fit for success in anything,—in different degrees for different things, but with sufficient for utility and note. In whatever he tried, he gained opinion, whether in what he liked, or in what he disliked. It is much to be regretted that he had not an absorbing literary pursuit; but there are instances enough in which the peculiar

talents which are best displayed in conversation have turned the others to their own purpose. (pp. 516-18)

The elements of his power of conversation have been enumerated, but all put together will not explain the charm of his society. For this we must refer to other points of character which, unassisted, are compatible with dulness and taciturnity. A wide range of sympathies, and sympathies which were instantaneously awake when occasion arose, formed a great part of the whole. This easily excited interest led to that feeling of communion which draws out others.

Nothing can better illustrate this than reference to the old meaning of *conversation.* Up to the middle of the last century, or near it, the word never meant *colloquy* alone; it was a perfect synonyme for *companionship.* So it was with Crabb Robinson; his conversation was companionship, and his companionship was conversation. (p. 519)

> *Augustus De Morgan, in an appendix to* Diary, Reminiscences, and Correspondence, Vol. II *by Henry Crabb Robinson, edited by Thomas Sadler, 1869. Reprint by Fields, Osgood, & Co., 1870, pp. 509-19.*

F. D. MAURICE (essay date 1869)

[Maurice discusses the qualities of Robinson's personality, as reflected in his Diary, *that make his writing so appealing.]*

[The] *Diary,* it need scarcely be remarked to any one who knew Mr. Robinson, was not written chiefly to commemorate his own acts and thoughts. There is a very pleasant image of him in it, but it is the image of a man who thought first of the people whom he saw, and among whom he dwelt, of himself chiefly as one who could learn from them or show them kindness. He mixed with too many people to be a Boswell. He had no special hero, and was far from a retailer of any man's opinions. On the other hand, he offended no one's prejudices, was tolerant of all the peculiarities which he encountered, never seems to have quarrelled with any of his acquaintances, and did his best to reconcile their quarrels. He was of humble birth, and was utterly free from any desire to conceal it, as well as from any envy of those who possessed an ancestry. He had too little ambition, and no avarice; he went to the Bar late, left it as soon as he had reached a fair competence, indulged in few luxuries, except the great one of helping those who needed help. He never took the least pains to penetrate the circles of the upper ten thousand. But among men of letters in England, France, and Germany he was a welcome and familiar guest. He was able to converse with them on all the subjects which interested them most, never affected to know more than he did know, was always able to give an intelligible account of what they said, and to make a reasonable guess at what they meant. A more agreeable narrator it would be difficult to find. There are no rough edges in his reminiscences; he is always cheerful, never out of sorts with his friends or the world. . . . [He] sees the best side in his friends; is very desirous of their good opinion, yet can risk it for the sake of correcting their false impressions of each other. He makes mistakes about facts, as every man must do who travels over such an extent of ground. Every reader will probably detect some circumstance which has been stated carelessly. But his errors are never malicious; three volumes of anecdotes with so little spite perhaps never issued from the press of any country. They have not therefore the kind of attraction which belongs to the memoirs of Horace Walpole or Lord Hervey. But for the literary—I do not say, of course, for the political or aristocratic—history of the nineteenth century, they are far more valuable than those are for that of the eighteenth century; more valuable than Evelyn and Pepys are for the seventeenth.

Of politics Mr. Robinson was not an indifferent observer. He was a Liberal and a Dissenter, but as much opposed to Napoleon as Southey or Wordsworth; a foreign correspondent of the *Times* when Copenhagen was bombarded. Still politics, on the whole, make little show in his *Diary*. He passes over the Queen's Trial and the Reform Bill much more rapidly than would have seemed possible for a man frequenting clubs as much as he did. In one sense he more deserves to be credited with "pure literature" than Landor. Though he was not himself a maker of books (he always wished, he says, like the high-born lady who was compelled for her livelihood to sell muffins, that no one might hear the cry of any little pamphlet which he published), he reverences the makers of books above any class of the community. (pp. 361-62)

Many of us can recollect how people in the humbler Liberal ranks—the inspiration being no doubt received originally from the sublime circle in Holland House—spoke of Southey as selling himself for a "butt of malmsey." Mr. Robinson lived among those who were sure to repeat this witticism, with others of the same kind. From the first he treated it as vulgar and false. He saw in Southey the true-hearted, self-denying man that he was; he was sure that his changes of opinions were honest changes of that; in heart he was always an earnest social reformer; a man who, instead of selling himself to a party, was using up his strength and his brain that he might support himself and do service to others. No parts of the *Diary* are more wise and hearty than those which refer to this excellent man.

Mr. Robinson was present at Coleridge's lectures on Shakespeare, and listened to his conversation at Highgate. He did not profess always to understand him, but he does not, like most writers of his time, compliment himself on his incapacity. He was puzzled with Coleridge's theology, and differs from it when he was not puzzled. But he never suspected him of playing false with others or with himself. (pp. 362-63)

Wordsworth, Coleridge, Lamb, Flaxman, Landor,—these alone would make a considerable gallery of portraits. And being exhibited separately and together, in different days of their lives, not as subjects for discussion and criticism, but in friendly converse, and in all moods of joy and grief, we know much of them which formal biographies do not tell. Nearly as vivid, if not quite as interesting, are Robinson's recollections of Madame de Staël, when she met him in Germany, and eagerly welcomed him as a dragoman to bring German philosophy (which he made no great boast of understanding) within the reach of her French intellect; again, when she was the idol of English society. No fresh light perhaps is thrown upon the authoress or the woman, but our previous impressions of both are made clearer and deeper. (p. 363)

Much as we ought to value such records as these for their own sake, it is impossible to separate them from the friendly, cordial man who has bestowed them upon us. Those who have never seen him or shared his hospitality will become well acquainted with him through this *Diary;* they must feel towards himself much personal gratitude and regard. Personal,—for he too was personal. . . . He cared much more for persons themselves than either for opinions or for truth as truth. His want of any strong conviction or fervent zeal is what he most laments in himself. It was no morbid self-accusation; he was not the least inclined

to be morbid; he was singularly healthy in body and happy in his spirits. He felt inwardly that it was a want: a very interesting and pathetic letter to Benecke shows that he longed for some satisfaction of it. The discovery of such a craving in a man of his social and cheerful temperament is very impressive, and even startling. (p. 364)

> F. D. Maurice, "Walter Savage Landor and Henry Crabb Robinson," in Macmillan's Magazine, Vol. XX, No. 118, August, 1869, pp. 355-65.

[HERMAN MERIVALE] (essay date 1869)

[Merivale discusses Robinson's religious beliefs.]

Many who knew Crabb Robinson in person, as well as others who were familiar with him only by report, will perhaps feel a little surprised at finding so many entries in the *Diary and Reminiscences* devoted to recording his very transitory religious impressions. There was not really substance enough in the worthy writer's intellect to affix any value to those records in themselves. But they are curious, if we may so express ourselves, even from their commonplace character. Mr. Robinson's mind was, in this matter, the type of that of thousands of Englishmen, constituted and educated like himself, but less in the habit of noting down their fleeting changes of sentiment, and with less *abandon* in their self-disclosures.

Early in life he got into a loose way of free-thinking, insomuch that no less a personage than Robert Hall took the trouble of addressing him a course of letters to point out the error of his ways. But this youthful tendency was soon worn out. He became, and remained through life, fond of religious talk and reading, full of lamentations over his own deficiencies, and interest in the more robust convictions of others. But he could fix his mind steadily on nothing. All his days he was catching at one solution after another of the obvious difficulties which occurred to his mind, throwing it aside with dissatisfaction, and then regretting that he could not arrive at any certainty of faith. There was, no doubt, something in his religious education which contributed to this result. He was . . . brought up a Dissenter, under strict forms of Puritanism; but it was that peculiar Puritanism of the last century which, under the training of Doddridge and his school, softened into a more expansive doctrine, which finally landed many in Unitarianism. (pp. 535-36)

Mr. Robinson diverted himself all his life, intending through the whole of it to make himself a master of religious controversy when he found leisure. On Dec. 23, 1815, . . . he reports: 'I read several chapters of *Paley's Evidences of Christianity*, having resolved to read attentively and seriously that and other works on a subject transcendently important, and which I am ashamed thus long to have delayed studying.' The value of his sceptical opinions may be judged of from the fact that he had never taken the trouble to examine the most elementary of English writers on the other side.

> I have never attempted to conceal from you (he says to his friend Mr. Benecke, who became early in life a serious convert), that my mind is very unsettled on the great points of religion, and that I am still what the Quakers call a seeker. I was very ill educated, or rather I had no regular instruction, but heard what are called orthodox notions preached in my childhood, when I, like other children, believed all that I heard uncontradicted. But before I was twenty years

old I met with anti-religious books, and had nothing to oppose to sceptical arguments. I sprang at once from one extreme to another, and from believing everything I believed nothing. My German studies afterwards made me sensible of the shallowness of the whole class of writers, whom I before respected; and one good effect they wrought on me; they made me conscious of my own ignorance, and inclined me to a favourable study of religious doctrines. . . . Whenever I take my residence for a time near you, I shall request your aid in not merely this matter (justification by faith), but generally in the study of the great Christian scheme in all its bearings, about which I have been talking—and talking very idly, and sometimes very lightly—all my life, without studying it as I ought. I am anxious, as I said before, to remove this reproach from me; for, whether true or false, it is sheer folly on my part to have given it so little attention, or rather to have attended to it in so desultory a way.

(pp. 536-37)

[As] his acquaintance with the world at large extended, he grew less and less satisfied with the narrow sectarianism of many of those early associates whom he had been at first tempted to admire. 'I prefer Dissent to the Church,' he says, in his later years; 'but I like Churchmen better than Dissenters.'

But with all this apparent levity of religious judgment, it is plain that he was seriously haunted, especially in advanced life, by real perplexities and doubts which he could neither solve nor dash aside. He started on his path of inquiry with a resolution not to believe anything he did not like—that is to say, in his own phraseology, what did not satisfy his own 'moral sense.' 'I cannot extend belief to pretended revelation which is repugnant to my moral sense.' But then, lawyer and logician as he was, however superficial, there came home to him the crushing reply, 'Natural religion, if you receive it at all, forces you to admit doctrines contrary to your moral sense; and if natural religion, why not revelation?' It is the old perplexity, in which Butler plunges human reason on purpose; and from which neither Mill nor Maurice, neither modern latitudinarianism nor modern sentiment, have been able to rescue it. Given a God omniscient and all-benevolent, and the existence of evil is (in the ordinary sense) impossible. Yet it does exist. And the eternal perdition of a soul is, fundamentally, not a whit more irreconcilable with those attributes of the Deity than is the suffering of a moment's pain. It is curious to note how the sense of the magnitude of this difficulty grows on our honest if somewhat simple inquirer. He is contented at first with the merest platitudes of his Dissenting school. 'Antony,' his brother, 'remarked that the amount of pain here justifies the idea of pain hereafter. But I remarked that evil and pain here may be considered as means towards an end.' In later life, the giant, whom the first stone from the brook once seemed sufficient to overthrow, looks in on him with terribly menacing proportions. (pp. 537-38)

It was rather a singular accompaniment of this kind of well-meaning half-scepticism, that Robinson should have had all his life a great tendency to associate with people whom the world called fanatics, and to make what he could out of their oracular sayings. 'It is strange,' he says of himself, 'that I, who have no imagination nor any power beyond that of a logical

understanding, should yet have great respect for religious mystics.' Wonderfully diversified is the religious matter of this kind on which he seems to have fed. He chronicles, page after page, the crazy maunderings of poor Blake the artist, listens with equal interest and respect to the rather vapid outpourings of Flaxman the sculptor, the revelations of Williamson the Swedenborgian, the rant of Edward Irving, half enthusiast and half impostor, the maudlin softnesses of Faber the popular convert to Romanism, and the Biblical paradoxes of the very emancipated Professor Donaldson. To him such people acted as magnets, and he could not refrain, as soon as he came home from talking with them, from noting down his recollections of their inspiration, although sometimes he complains of his inability to comprehend it, and at other times cannot resist the temptation to a little slyly sarcastic commentary.

For the rest, the 'life of the old man,' to use the Horatian expression, remains recorded in these volumes as in a 'votive tablet.' And no reader can rise from them without a kindly feeling for the genial, amiable, active-minded gossip whom they portray; a Londoner of the Londoners, very familiar with men and things, and yet with that kind of hearty freshness about him which one is inclined to attribute specially to men of unspoilt habits and few ideas. (pp. 538-39)

[*Herman Merivale*], "Diaries of Henry Crabb Robinson," in The Edinburgh Review, *Vol. CXXX, No. CCLXVI, October, 1869, pp. 509-39.*

WALTER BAGEHOT   (essay date 1869)

[*Bagehot is regarded as one of the most versatile and influential authors of mid-Victorian England. He was also a close companion of Robinson. In the following excerpt from an essay written in 1869, Bagehot assesses Robinson's skill as a writer, conversationalist, critic, lawyer, and speaker.*]

Perhaps I should be ashamed to confess it, but I own I opened the three large volumes of Mr. Robinson's [*Diary, Reminiscences, and Correspondence*] with much anxiety. Their bulk, in the first place, appalled me; but that was by no means my greatest apprehension. I knew I had a hundred times heard Mr. Robinson say that he hoped something he would leave behind would 'be published and be worth publishing.' I was aware too—for it was no deep secret—that for half a century or more he had kept a diary, and that he had been preserving correspondence besides; and I was dubious what sort of things these would be, and what—to use Carlyle's words—any human editor could make of them. Even when Mr. Robinson used to talk so I used to shudder; for the men who have tried to be memoir-writers and failed, are as numerous, or nearly so, as those who have tried to be poets and failed. A specific talent is as necessary for the one as for the other. But as soon as I had read a little of the volumes, all these doubts passed away. I saw at once that Mr. Robinson had an excellent power of narrative-writing, and that the editor of his remains had made a judicious use of excellent materials.

Perhaps more than anything it was the modesty of my old friend (I think I may call Mr. Robinson my old friend, for though he *thought* me a modern youth, I *did* know him twenty years)—perhaps, I say, it was his modesty which made me nervous about his memoirs more than anything else. I have so often heard him say (and say it with a vigour of emphasis which is rarer in our generation even than in his),—'Sir, I have no literary talent. I cannot write. I never *could* write anything, and I never *would* write anything,'—that being so taught, and so vehemently, I came to believe. And there was this to justify my creed. The notes Mr. Robinson used to scatter about him—and he was fond of writing rather elaborate ones—were not always very good. At least they were too long for the busy race of the present generation, and introduced Schiller and Goethe where they need not have come. But in these memoirs (especially in the **Reminiscences** and the **Diary**—for the moment he gets to a letter the style is worse) the words flow with such an effectual simplicity, that even Southey, the great master of such prose, could hardly have written better. Possibly it was his real interest in his old stories which preserved Mr. Robinson; in his letters he was not so interested and he fell into words and amplifications; but in those ancient anecdotes, which for years were his life and being, the style, as it seems to me, could scarcely be mended even in a word. And though, undoubtedly, the book is much too long in the latter half, I do not blame Dr. Sadler, the editor and biographer, for it, or indeed blame anyone. Mr. Robinson has led a very long and very varied life, and some of his old friends had an interest in one part of his reminiscences and some in another. (pp. 291-92)

[There] are some men who cannot be justly described quite gravely; and Crabb Robinson is one of them. A certain grotesqueness was a part of him, and unless you liked it you lost the very best of him. He is called, and properly called, in these memoirs Mr. Robinson; but no well-judging person ever called him so in life. He was always called 'old Crabb,' and that is the only name which will ever bring up his curious image to me. He was, in the true old English sense of the word, a 'character;' one whom a very peculiar life, certainly, and perhaps also a rather peculiar nature to begin with, had formed and moulded into something so exceptional and singular that it did not seem to belong to ordinary life, and almost moved a smile when you saw it moving there. 'Aberrant forms,' I believe, the naturalists call seals and such things in natural history; odd shapes that can only be explained by a long past, and which swim with a certain incongruity in their present *milieu.* Now 'old Crabb' was (to me at least) just like that. You watched with interest and pleasure his singular gestures, and his odd way of saying things, and muttered, as if to keep up the recollection, 'And *this* is the man who was the friend of Goethe, and is the friend of Wordsworth!' There was a certain animal oddity about 'old Crabb' which made it a kind of mental joke to couple him with such great names, and yet he was to his heart's core thoroughly coupled with them. If you leave out all his strange ways . . . , you lose the life of the man. (pp. 293-94)

[A] main part of Mr. Robinson's conversation was on literary subjects; but of this, except when it related to persons whom he had known, or sonnets to 'the conception of which he was privy,' I do not think it would be just to speak very highly. He spoke sensibly and clearly—he could not on any subject speak otherwise; but the critical faculty is as special and as peculiar almost as the poetical; and Mr. Robinson in serious moments was quite aware of it, and he used to deny that he had one faculty more than the other. (p. 300)

Still less do I believe that there is any special value in the expositions of German philosophy in these volumes, or that there was any in those which Mr. Robinson used to give on such matters in conversation. They are clear, no doubt, and accurate, but they are not the expositions of a born metaphysician. He speaks in [the **Diary**] of his having a difficulty in concentrating his 'attention on works of speculation.' And such books as Kant can only be really mastered, can perhaps only

be usefully studied, by those who have an unusual facility in concentrating their mind on impalpable abstractions, and an uncommon inclination to do so. Mr. Robinson had neither; and I think the critical philosophy had really very little effect on him, and had, during the busy years which had elapsed since he studied it, very nearly run off him. There was something very curious in the sudden way that anything mystical would stop in him. At the end of a Sunday breakfast, after inflicting on you much which was transcendental in Wordsworth or Goethe, he would say, as we left him, with an air of relish, 'Now I am going to run down to Exeter Street to hear Madge. I shall not be in time for the prayers; but I do not so much care about that; what I do like is the sermon; it is so clear.' Mr. Madge was a Unitarian of the old school, with as little mystical and transcendental in his nature as any one who ever lived. There was a living piquancy in the friend of Goethe—the man who *would* explain to you his writings—being also the admirer of 'Madge;' it was like a proser, lengthily eulogising Kant to you, and then saying, 'Ah! but I do love Condillac; he is so clear.'

But, on the other hand, I used to hold—I was reading law at the time, and so had some interest in the matter—that Mr. Robinson much underrated his legal knowledge, and his practical power as a lawyer. What he used to say was, 'I never knew any law, sir, but I knew the practice. . . . I left the bar, sir, because I feared my incompetence might be discovered. I was a tolerable junior, but I was rising to be a leader, which I was unfit to be, and so I retired, not to disgrace myself by some fearful mistake.' In these Memoirs he says that he retired when he had made the sum of money which he thought enough for a bachelor with few wants and not a single expensive taste. The simplicity of his tastes is certain; very few Englishmen indeed could live with so little show or pretence. But the idea of the gross incompetence is absurd. No one who was so ever said so. There are, I am confident, plenty of substantial and well-satisfied men at the English bar who do now know nearly as much law as Mr. Robinson knew, and who have not a tithe of his natural sagacity, but who believe in themselves and in whom their clients believe. On the other hand, Mr. Robinson had many great qualifications for success at the bar. He was a really good speaker: when over seventy I have heard him make a speech that good speakers in their full vigour would be glad to make. He had a good deal of the actor in his nature, which is thought, and I fancy justly thought, to be necessary to the success of all great advocates, and perhaps of all great orators. He was well acquainted with the petty technicalities which intellectual men in middle life in general cannot learn, for he had passed some years in an attorney's office. Above all, he was a very thinking man, and had an 'idea of business'—that inscrutable something which at once and altogether distinguishes the man who is safe in the affairs of life from those who are unsafe. I do not suppose he knew much black-letter law; but there are plenty of judges on the bench who, unless they are much belied, also know very little—perhaps none. And a man who can intelligently read Kant, like Mr. Robinson, need not fear the book-work of English law. A very little serious study would have taught him law enough to lead the Norfolk circuit. He really had a sound, moderate, money-making business, and only a little pains was wanted to give him more.

The real reason why he did not take the trouble I fancy was that, being a bachelor, he was a kind of amateur in life, and did not really care. He could not spend what he had on himself, and used to give away largely, though in private. And even more, as with most men who have not thoroughly worked when young, daily, regular industry was exceedingly trying to him.

No man could be less idle; far from it, he was always doing something; but then he was doing what he chose. Sir Walter Scott, one of the best workers of his time, used always to say that 'he had no temptation to be idle, but the greatest temptation, when one thing was wanted of him, to go and do something else.' Perhaps the only persons who, not being forced by mere necessity, really conquer this temptation, are those who were early broken to the yoke, and are fixed to the furrow by habit. Mr. Robinson loitered in Germany, so he was not one of these.

I am not regretting this. It would be a base idolatry of practical life to require every man to succeed in it as far as he could, and to devote to it all his mind. The world certainly does not need it; it pays well, and it will never lack good servants. There will always be enough of sound, strong men to be working barristers and judges, let who will object to become so. But I own I think a man ought to be able to be a 'Philistine' if he chose; there is a sickly incompleteness about people too fine for the world, and too nice to work their way in it. And when a man like Mr. Robinson had a real sagacity for affairs, it is for those who respect his memory to see that his reputation does not suffer from his modesty, and that his habitual self-depreciations—which, indeed, extended not only to his powers of writing as well as to those of acting—are not taken to be exactly true. (pp. 300-03)

[The great part of Mr. Robinson's] life was spent in society where his influence was always manly and vigorous. I do not mean that he was universally popular, it would be defacing his likeness to say so. 'I am a man,' he once told me, 'to whom a great number of persons entertain the very strongest objection. Indeed he had some subjects on which he could hardly bear opposition. Twice he nearly quarrelled with me: once for writing in favour of Louis Napoleon, which, as he had caught in Germany a thorough antipathy to the first Napoleon, seemed to him quite wicked; and next for my urging that Hazlitt was a much greater writer than Charles Lamb—a harmless opinion which I still hold, but which Mr. Robinson met with this outburst: 'You, sir, YOU prefer the works of that scoundrel, that odious, that malignant writer, to the exquisite essays of that angelic creature!' I protested that there was no evidence that angels could write particulary well, but it was in vain, and it was some time before he forgave me. Some persons who casually encountered peculiarities like these, did not always understand them. In his last years, too, augmenting infirmities almost disqualified Mr. Robinson for general society, and quite disabled him from showing his old abilities in it. Indeed, I think that [the *Diary*] will give almost a new idea of his power to many young men who had only seen him casually, and at times of feebleness. After ninety it is not easy to make new friends. And, in any case, this book will always have a great charm for those who knew Mr. Robinson well when they were themselves young, because it will keep alive to them the image of his buoyant sagacity, and his wise and careless kindness. (pp. 303-04)

*Walter Bagehot, "Henry Crabb Robinson (1869),"
in his* Literary Studies, *Vol. 2, E. P. Dutton & Co.,
Inc., 1911, pp. 291-304.*

LEON H. VINCENT   (essay date 1898)

[*In the following excerpt, Vincent provides an appreciative overview of Robinson's life and career.*]

The inscription on [Crabb Robinson's] tomb records the names of eight men of renown to whom he had sustained the relation of "friend and associate." The eight names are Goethe, Wordsworth, Wieland, Coleridge, Flaxman, Blake, Clarkson, and Charles Lamb. The list is striking, and clearly indicates the wide range of Crabb Robinson's sympathies. To each of these men he rendered the tribute of a hearty and discriminating admiration. His place in the world of literature and art was peculiar. He had a strong masculine regard for men of genius because they were men of genius, but no measure of self-interest mixed with this regard. He had not the creative power himself, but he understood that power in others. He was not a mere satellite, for he held distinctly a critical attitude at times; and no commonplace moon ever thinks of passing strictures upon the central sun. We need a word to express the relation. To men of genius he gave the encouragement and stimulus of a dignified admiration based on solid reasons. To the general reading public he was a sort of mentor; his good sense in other matters awakened confidence in the soundness of his judgment; his catholicity of taste operated to allay that prejudice which the mob always conceives against a poet who is both new and queer. (pp. 806-07)

Crabb Robinson justified his existence if only by the services he rendered Wordsworth. He was an early and discriminating admirer. He championed Wordsworth's poetry at a time when champions were few and not influential. It must have been with special reference to the needs of poets like the author of *Lyrical Ballads* that the saying "Woe unto you when all men shall speak well of you" was uttered. Yet I am not sure but there is a measure of woe in the condition of him of whom all men speak ill. At a time when critical disapprobation was pretty nearly unanimous Crabb Robinson's was one of the few voices in commendation. It was not a loud voice, but it was clear and impressive. (p. 810)

Crabb Robinson's way of paying homage was very delicate. . . . He liked Wordsworth's poetry, and he did his unostentatious best to make others like it. He did not cry aloud from the housetop that the messiah of English verse had at last arrived, neither did he found a society. He spoke to people of Wordsworth's verse, got them to read it, occasionally read poems himself to receptive listeners. If people balked at Louisa in the Shade, or were unsympathetic in attitude toward the Spade, with which Wilkinson hath till'd his Lands, he urged upon them the necessity and the wisdom of judging a man by the noble parts of his work, and not by the less fortunate parts. If they had read Wordsworth only to laugh at him, he insisted upon reading to them those poems which compelled their admiration; for there are poems with respect to which the public cannot hold a noncommittal attitude. The public must either admire, or else consent to stultify itself by not admiring.

By this method he did more to advance Wordsworth's reputation than if he had written a dozen eulogistic articles in the great reviews. (pp. 810-11)

I believe that the evidence of the *Diary* goes to show that Crabb Robinson was able to pronounce upon new poetry. This is one of the most difficult and delicate of undertakings. People with that gift are few. With respect to poetry, most of us follow the hue and cry raised in the newspapers and literary journals. We are able to admire what we are told is admirable. When the road is pointed out for us we can travel it, but we are not able to find the road ourselves. Crabb Robinson places himself upon record more than once. The most notable entry concerns Keats.

In December, 1820, he wrote, "I am greatly mistaken if Keats do not very soon take a high place among our poets."

Of many good books which a man may read, if he will, this *Diary* of Henry Crabb Robinson is one of the "sweetest and most fortifying." It is a fine illustration of literary sanity. Literary sanity is not entirely fashionable just now, and a perusal of these thirty-years-old volumes may be good for us. Certainly, it is well for us to know about the Diarist himself. A life like his is among the most potent influences for culture. (p. 812)

Leon H. Vincent, "A Successful Bachelor," in The Atlantic Monthly, Vol. LXXXI, No. CCCCLXXXVIII, June, 1898, pp. 805-12.

EDITH J. MORLEY (essay date 1922)

[*Morley edited several collections of Robinson's writings and wrote the biography* The Life and Times of Henry Crabb Robinson *(see excerpt dated 1935). In this excerpt from her introduction to* Blake, Coleridge, Wordsworth, Lamb, &c.: Being Selections from the Remains of Henry Crabb Robinson, *Morley assesses Robinson as a literary critic and conversationalist.*]

Dr. Sadler's edition of the *Diary, Reminiscences, and Correspondence*—the only one hitherto available—confessedly does not include more than a twenty-fifth or thirtieth part of the whole. From 1811 to 1867 there is a detailed daily journal; from 1790 to 1843 there are four huge volumes of *Reminiscences,* averaging 450 folio pages; there are 32 volumes of correspondence, each containing some 160 letters—for the most part to or from himself—many of them very long. These range over Robinson's whole life, some of them being family letters of earlier date. In addition there are 28 volumes containing "**Journals of Tours**," and various volumes and bundles of miscellanea. We know from the *Diary* that, nevertheless, much time was spent by Robinson towards the end of his life in the destruction of papers and of letters which he thought would prove valueless to posterity. It cannot be claimed that everything which is preserved merits publication. Inevitably, much in so detailed a *Diary* must for us who come after be unprofitable reading. People of importance in their day, or events and discussions which once loomed large, have ceased to be interesting. We do not want to know exactly where Robinson visited and dined on every one of 365 days every year. The part he took as a young man in debates, or later on in lawsuits as a practising barrister, or in discussions throughout his life; his services as mediator between his friends, or as adviser and guide to all and sundry; his errors, real and imaginary, of omission and commission—some of this indubitably could be spared with advantage. But the man who emerges from this mass of material is, nevertheless, a lovable personality—no Boswell certainly, but one who possessed a genuine gift for characterization, an instinct for friendship, and the power to stamp himself and his experience with extraordinary vividness on his pages. This is no mere prosy raconteur, unable to distinguish between small things and great; no shorthand reporter taking indiscriminate notes of what passes before his eyes. The man has a mind of his own; he has critical ability and the power to estimate the worth of new works, prose or poetry, good as well as bad. In 1820 he was already hailing Keats as a great poet; he at once recognized the value of Macaulay's history; long before he knew the name of their author he, like the rest of the world, was devouring the *Waverley Novels,* but, unlike most people, with an instinctive preference for the more successful of them. *Kenilworth* and *Ivanhoe,* for example, are

recognized as definitely inferior to the *Heart of Midlothian* and *Rob Roy.* But, above all, it is as the admirer and missionary of Wordsworth among English men of letters that Crabb Robinson is best remembered, and to him and his readings and quotations in early days Wordsworth owed a large proportion of his first audience, fit though few. Moreover, as his German friends recognized, Crabb, for so he was always called by his intimates in later life, was one of the earliest to popularize German literature and to introduce German philosophy into England. The man who, as a student at Jena, had been introduced to Goethe, had heard Schelling lecture upon Methodology, and had successfully impersonated Fichte, never ceased to acclaim, to read, and to write about the first-named, never forgot to sing the praises of Kant, to magnify the Schlegels, and to spread the gospel of transcendentalism. (pp. xii-xiv)

Remembering these friendships and these achievements, reading as we may in his *Diary* and letters of Robinson's innumerable acts of kindness, many of which involved not only trouble and self-sacrifice, but also the power to give valuable help in business and in family difficulties, we may as soon believe in Macaulay's strange theory of the "inspired idiot," as in H.C.R.'s own estimate of his character, ability, and influence. He is curiously detached in his self-criticism, as also in his judgments on the criticisms passed upon him by other people. (p. xiv)

Robinson has too frequently been taken at his own valuation, but it is certain that his self-depreciation and extraordinary modesty do him scant justice. W. S. Landor wrote of him early in their acquaintance, in 1831: "He was a barrister, and notwithstanding, both honest and modest—a character I never heard of before," and this genuine humility is apparent in his estimates of himself. To take two examples as typical of many. His *Diary* is written in a simple, unassuming, direct style which at first may lead the unwary to ignore this narrative power and unusual gift for reporting conversation, and thereby revealing the character of the speakers. He does not understand Blake; he thinks him indubitably mad. But H. C. R.'s account of his interviews with Blake are the most revealing contemporary interpretations we possess of the mystic poet-painter and his personality. Many people have written well of Lamb, whose lovable self is an inspiration to his critics. But who has said more in a single sentence than H. C. R. has included in the following comment: "Lamb, who needs very little indulgence for himself, is very indulgent towards others"? . . . What force of judgment there is in all his criticisms, and some of these are adverse, on the character of Wordsworth, whom he worshipped this side idolatry as much as any; how well he depicts Coleridge in those "innings-for-one that he called conversation." These character sketches—and the *Diary* bristles with them, great men and small, poets, statesmen, revolutionaries, criminals in the dock, lawyers on circuit, judges on the bench, chance acquaintances picked up on the road—these are not mere lucky flukes. "True ease in writing comes from art, not chance," and there is the genuine art, which conceals itself, in H. C. R.'s achievements. The statement that he "never *could* write anything" is abundantly disproved on his own evidence.

Similarly with the assertion that he never had any memory. There is no need to go to the testimony of Professor De Morgan or of Bagehot [see excerpts dated 1869], the friends of his last years, when he might well be excused had his faculties failed him. But once more his oft-repeated complaint is incontrovertibly contradicted by his own writings—even by the least interesting of these, the journals of his tours, or by the reminiscences of his experiences as boy and man. No doubt the daily journal helped him with the latter, but even the *Diary* was not always filled up day by day; sometimes a week's doings were inserted in the small hours after a long day in the courts, and the *Diary* is frequently supplemented thirty years later by incidents it was not considered fitting to include—even in cipher—at the time of their occurrence. To get a complete picture it is often necessary to consult both the first draft and the later, the very much later, working-up.

Crabb Robinson's chief gift was, however, for conversation. Essentially a "clubbable" man, he was, and felt himself to be, pre-eminently at home at the Athenæum, of which he was one of the earliest members and where much of his time was passed, especially as he grew older. But everywhere his sociability and genius for getting on with all sorts and conditions of men and women stood him in good stead. An excellent whist player, he frequented Lamb's parties; he played chess with Mrs. Barbauld, and regaled her and the Aikens with the poems of Wordsworth—which they did not invariably appreciate—or of Southey, or even of the free-thinking, wicked Lord Byron. He was equally at home in Unitarian and Dissenting circles, in the Anglican atmosphere of Rydal Mount or Fox How, or with Roman Catholic O'Connell or Quillinan. He was profoundly interested in religious speculation, but the essentials of his own creed, as expounded in more than one place in his *Diary* and letters, he worked out for himself. It was, above all, a tolerant creed, as might be expected from so tolerant a man. Nothing, for instance, more repelled him than the conception of eternal damnation for unbelievers, and there is a long letter on this subject to his friend Richmond, then on the point of being ordained minister in the Episcopalian Church of America.

Crabb Robinson's acquaintances were of every social class and of very various capacity. Though he dearly loved a "lion," there was nothing of the intellectual snob about him, and he mixed freely with all kinds of people.... [He had] an enormous repertory of anecdotes, and, if we may believe the rather sharp (but affectionately admiring) account of Bagehot, in his old age his pet stories did duty rather too often. There is, however, no doubt of his mastery of the art of conversation, and it was partly for this reason that his company was so eagerly sought. As a young man and in middle life he was constantly invited out: in his old age his breakfast-parties were institutions. He complains that he neglects necessary work for desultory amusement and unprofitable talk, that his days are spent to no purpose, and that he gets through nothing of importance. But in this, as in so many of his self-reproaches, there is little substance. Literally he added to the gaiety of nations—by what he was, as well as by what he said. He was, in addition, an admirable man of business, and, in spite of his assertions to the contrary, a competent and successful barrister with a sound practice. (pp. xvi-xxi)

He could be prosy and dull and self-assertive. His society manners were not always above reproach; for instance, even as a young man he frequently fell asleep in company when he did not find it amusing, or when there was music which he could not appreciate. His views on politics, too, were very pronounced, and he was unable to brook contradiction on certain matters both political and literary. Above all, he had character, personality, mind; and such a man was unlikely, considering the number of his acquaintances and the variety of his pursuits, to pass through life without making enemies. But he had a genius for friendship, and social gifts which have outlasted him. Not only do his *Diary* and the other jottings-down

of his leisure moments revivify the men whom he knew and loved. They create for him new friends in his readers, who owe to him what is almost a personal acquaintance with many they had otherwise vainly wished to know in their habit as they lived. And "old Crabb" himself moves among his comrades, still, as in a society which has long since passed away, active, vivacious, sympathetic, understanding, and intensely alive, cheering them by [in Wordsworth's phrase] his "buoyant spirit." (pp. xxii-xxiii)

> *Edith J. Morley, in an introduction to* Blake, Coleridge, Wordsworth, Lamb, & c.: Being Selections from the Remains of Henry Crabb Robinson *by Henry Crabb Robinson, edited by Edith J. Morley, Manchester University Press, 1922, pp. xi-xxiii.*

F. W. STOKOE (essay date 1926)

[*Stokoe evaluates Robinson's influence on English opinion of German literature. In a portion of the essay not excerpted below, Stokoe includes Robinson among propagandist English reviewers of German literature in the nineteenth century.*]

[Henry Crabb Robinson] published translations from German and articles on German literature, but his chief influence was personal. As the friend of Coleridge, Wordsworth, Lamb, Carlyle, as a welcome guest in literary and artistic circles, he brought his influence to bear immediately upon the intellect and imagination of England. The efficacy of his propaganda in favour of German literature, and particularly of its chief Goethe, though not an easily calculable factor, must be reckoned among those which contributed to the better understanding of the subject. If its quantity may be rated low, its quality is, in more than one respect, of a high order. In the first place, Robinson's knowledge of Germany and German literature is clearly in advance of that of any of his English contemporaries whose utterances on the subject are recorded in this earliest stage of German studies in England; even Carlyle fell short of him in respect of general knowledge and grasp of things German. In the second place, his influence was backed by his intelligent enthusiasm and by the weight and charm of his personality. A review casually read may leave us very cool towards the subject of its eulogy. But when clever, agreeable Mr Robinson, leaning towards us confidentially over the walnuts and the wine, quotes *Faust* with an authentic German accent, and, translating his quotation, illustrates it by an anecdote from his personal reminiscences of the celebrated author (whose name, we learn on his authority, is not, as we had supposed, to be pronounced like the archaic or poetical form of the third person singular indicative of the verb "to go"), we are moved to take a more sympathetic interest in German literature, brought close to us in this insinuating and even flattering manner.

Robinson was not a creative artist, not primarily an original thinker; he was, in perhaps the noblest sense of the word, a dilettante. (pp. 53-4)

If we read Crabb Robinson's published *Diary* with a view to ascertain along what lines this influence was chiefly exercised, we receive the impression that the light of Goethe's genius shone so brightly to Robinson's eyes that it almost eclipsed all fainter luminaries. He is, among Englishmen of note, the first to realise clearly the literary importance of Goethe; on the aesthetic side, indeed, he has perhaps a more intelligent appreciation of him than any English writer previous to 1830, with the single exception of Shelley. (p. 57)

On reading *Faust, Erster Teil* (which, surprisingly, he did not do till November 1811) he betrays some agitation along with his delight. Robinson . . . was not above social prejudices; and although his foreign experience must have accustomed him to theological and ethical speculations of a bolder type than those current in England at the beginning of the nineteenth century, yet in these matters also he shared some prejudices with his English contemporaries; though in Robinson these appear as honest and respectable scruples. (p. 58)

> [Nov. 10, 1812]. On my walk to Camberwell [Robinson in later years seldom walked alone without taking a book with him] read Goethe's new *Faust;* a most astonishing performance on which I have no leisure now to speak. It is a most pregnant, and equally delightful and disgusting performance. A masterpiece of genius before which I bow with humility, and the beauties of which are so ravishing that I am ashamed and afraid to allow myself to feel offended by its moral and aesthetic deformities.
>
> Nov. 11 . . . Read *Faust* with delight on my walk.
>
> Nov. 23. The day was fine, and on my walk finished that wonderful poem *Faust*. The Scene in the Brocken, the Walpurgis Nacht is very wonderful, but that, as well as the whole poem, leaves much to wonder at, as well as to admire. However a cold thinker in the closet may tolerate a speculation concerning the Supreme Being, which even supposes the possibility of his Nonentity, yet a poem addressed to the people, which treats of the deepest subjects in a style that supposes the utmost indifference to the result of the speculation . . . cannot well be justified . . . The poetic worth of the new scenes, more especially of Margaretha in person, is transcendent Goethe here as elsewhere maintains his character as the inimitable and incomparable poet.
>
> (pp. 58-9)

[Here] we have the expression of that sense, almost universal among Englishmen, even of the most liberal culture, of that day, that Goethe's speculative daring and licence of description were at times of a dangerous tendency.

The idea emerges again in a letter of Robinson's to Wordsworth of July 1832 . . . :

> Thinking of old age, and writing to you, I am, by a natural association of ideas, reminded of the great poet lately dead in Germany. As one of his great admirers, I wished but for one quality in addition to his marvellous powers—that he had as uniformly directed those powers on behalf of the best interests of mankind, as you have done. . . .

With these misgivings in his mind, he turned with relief to that one of Goethe's longer works where speculation has perhaps least part, to the large, serene, noble simplicity of *Hermann und Dorothea:*

> March 10, 1833. I went on reading *Hermann und Dorothea*, which I have just finished (we must of course take this to refer to a reperusal

of the work). I hold it to be one of the most delightful of all Goethe's works. Not one of his philosophical works, which the exclusives exclusively admire, but one of the most perfectly moral as well as beautiful. It realises every requisite of a work of genius. I shed tears over it repeatedly, but they were more tears of tenderness at the perfect beauty of the characters and sentiments. Incident there is none.
>
> (p. 59)

There is much evidence in his *Diary* that Robinson was by no means disposed to keep his knowledge and opinions of German literature to himself; that he delighted to impart to others . . . the treasures to which he held the key; and although the range of his propagandist activity was limited, it was highly important, lying as it did about the very focus of the English intellectual world. (p. 60)

> *F. W. Stokoe, "Periodical Literature, 1788-1818, and Two Propagandists, William Taylor and Henry Crabb Robinson," in his* German Influence in the English Romantic Period: 1788-1818, *Cambridge at the University Press, 1926, pp. 33-60.*

HERBERT G. WRIGHT (essay date 1927)

> [*Wright discusses Robinson's commentary on the Romantic poet and artist William Blake.*]

Readers of Crabb Robinson's diary . . . will be aware of the fact that Robinson was a keen student of Blake, and in his eagerness to make his work known abroad wrote an essay on him for a German periodical. As it is one of the earliest attempts at an appreciation of Blake and almost certainly the first to appear in any foreign tongue, this study is of an unusual interest and deserves more detailed consideration than it has hitherto received. (p. 137)

At the time when Robinson wrote [his **"Essay on Blake"**] he had not yet made the acquaintance of Blake and consequently we have in the essay no such shrewd personal observations of the poet as he noted down in later years. It is evident, however, that he was attracted by this strange genius and made an honest attempt to understand the mystic who differed so greatly from his own eminently sane and cool-headed self. To Robinson Blake was a singular phenomenon and though the poet's way of thinking at times passed his comprehension, he sought to familarise himself with all that he had painted or written. In the essay he speaks of Blake's illustrations to children's books, to Young's *Night Thoughts* and to Blair's *Grave,* not with the vague remoteness of a superficial dilettante but with the accurate comment of one who knew them well. The same holds good of his remarks on *Poetical Sketches* and *Songs of Innocence and of Experience,* on *Europe* and *America*. He describes in detail not merely the contents of these books, but their appearance and the unusual processes applied in their production. No doubt he is puzzled like one who has strayed into a weird and unknown world, but at least he talks with intimate knowledge. Moreover, Robinson had learned what he could about Blake from the few sources then available. (pp. 139-40)

Robinson regards Blake as an extraordinary man, a combination of genius and madness, demanding esteem because of his abilities and pity by reason of his claim to be gifted with supernatural powers. He evidently finds something to admire in Blake's defiance of accepted doctrines in art and in the courage and steadfastness with which he pursued his own course in spite of poverty and the derision of critics. Robinson perceives quite rightly that Blake's confidence and firmness of purpose were due to his faith in supernatural guidance. Hence the blank negation with which Blake met his opponents. Robinson sympathises with Blake's indignation when Schiavonetti was allowed to engrave the designs for Blair's *Grave* in a manner contrary to their author's most cherished artistic beliefs. But at the same time he views Blake with a critical eye. He clearly rejects his fixed ideas on the infamy of oil-painting and disapproves of his sweeping condemnation of the Dutch and Venetian masters. He also notes the incoherent arrangement of the *Catalogue* and the frequent ambiguity and obscurity of Blake's work. So much so that he generally prefers to let Blake explain his own views or to quote the appreciation of some authority like Fuseli. More than once Robinson confesses his inability to interpret Blake's intention. . . . It is perhaps in speaking of the illustrations to Young's *Night Thoughts* that he expresses his own opinions of Blake's designs most fully, and incidentally he gives us some valuable details concerning them. He tells us that although only thirteen years had elapsed since the publication of the work, it has already disappeared from the bookshops and become extremely rare. Robinson had also heard that the publisher had withheld from the public three-quarters of the drawings made by Blake for this subject and had likewise refused to sell them, even though offered a considerable sum. As for those published, Robinson finds them of unequal value. 'At times the inventions of the artist vie with those of the poet; often, however, they are merely an absurd translation of them, through the unhappy idea, peculiar to Blake, that everything with which the imagination dazzles the spiritual eye, flashing back, must be given to the bodily eye to be tasted (*sic*). Thus Young is literally translated and his poems tranformed into a picture.' (pp. 140-41)

In his essay Robinson also comments on Blake's religious views. He says that at times his position seems to be that of the orthodox Christian but on the other hand his attitude towards ancient mythology, as expressd in the *Catalogue,* appears distinctly unorthodox. On occasion Blake speaks like a zealous monotheist denouncing idolatry and yet his statement that 'the antiquities of every Nation under Heaven, is no less sacred than that of the Jews' savours of the tolerance and indifference of paganism rather than of the essential strictness of Christianity. Robinson mentions Blake's admiration for Swedenborg but points out that he refused to join the Swedenborgians under Proud. He is therefore driven to the conclusion that Blake was not a regular devotee of any Church and that in religion, as in everything else, he was a law unto himself.

The latter part of Robinson's study is concerned with Blake's poetry. In the first place it deals with the *Poetical Sketches* and here it must be admitted that Robinson does scant justice to the excellence of some of these early poems. After his customary remark as to their inequality, he continues: 'The structure of the verse is for the most part so loose and negligent that it displays a complete ignorance of art and at the same time most of the pieces are of outrageous crudeness and very repellent.' Robinson's ear was evidently not attuned to the fresh cadence of Blake's lyric measures. Nor is anyone nowadays likely to join in the lavish praise that he bestows on the dramatic fragments in this volume, which he considers to display 'a wildness and grandeur of imagination that bear witness to genuine poetic feeling.' His judgment is, however, not altogether at fault, for as an illustration of Blake's powers at this stage he chooses the poem "To the Muses." Passing to the *Songs*

of Innocence and of Experience, he again finds a strange mixture of good and bad. Some of the poems in the earlier book he describes as 'childlike songs of great beauty and simplicity,' while others seem to him extremely childish. He is more puzzled by the *Songs of Experience,* 'metaphysical riddles and mystical allegories,' which, though they contain pictures of the greatest beauty and sublimity, are full of poetic fancies that could be intelligible only to the initiated. Robinson shows his insight by the poems that he quotes—first, the introductory "Piping down the valleys wild" and "Holy Thursday" and then as a contrast to this 'tender and simple poem' the 'truly singular and sublime description' of "The Tiger." Of the allegorical songs he cites "The Garden of Love," because he thinks that he understands it, whereas others are 'completely incomprehensible.' Perplexed as Robinson is by some of these allegories, he is still more bewildered by *America* and *Europe* and confesses himself incapable of giving an account of them. He finds their form as baffling as their meaning. *Europe* he calls a 'mysterious, unintelligible rhapsody' which 'seems to be in verse.' Before bringing his essay to a close Robinson comments on the fact that in 1810 Blake's poems were but little known, apparently even less than his paintings and engravings. 'These prophecies,' he says, 'like the songs, do not seem to have come to the knowledge of the general public.'

Summing up, Robinson declares that Blake indisputably possesses all the elements of greatness, though in unequal proportions. He suggests that in art he will perhaps never create perfect and immortal work nor in poetry flawless masterpieces, but for all that he considers that Blake well repays attention. Amid all his wildness and extravagance Robinson notes occasional flashes of reason. In this connexion he makes a remark which has its interest. In Blake's *Catalogue,* he says, 'one finds many expressions which one would rather have expected from a German than an Englishman,' and in the concluding lines of his essay he insists that the personality of Blake is likely to make a greater appeal to the German than to the English people. Robinson probably had in mind not the innate leaning of the German towards metaphysical speculation but rather the different character of English and German literature at the time when he was writing. It does not appear, however, that Robinson's essay gave any particular stimulus to the study of Blake in Germany. . . . [The] essay had no widespread influence. Perhaps its publication [in 1811] at a time when Germany was in a ferment of patriotic emotion and political agitation accounts for its passing unnoticed. The sweet melodies of Blake were lost in the hoarse roar of cannon. (pp. 141-43)

> *Herbert G. Wright, "Henry Crabb Robinson's 'Essay on Blake',"* in The Modern Language Review, *Vol. XXII, No. 2, April, 1927, pp. 137-54.*

CHARLES FREDERICK HARROLD (essay date 1928)

[*Harrold explores Robinson's relationship to several major literary figures and interprets the* Diary *as a reflection of the author. According to Harrold, the* Diary *indicates that Robinson had "apparently but three enthusiasms: the quest for theological certainty, the formation of great friendships and exhilarating acquaintanceships, and the uninterrupted reading of books."*]

As a man, Robinson united a mysterious faculty of charming the great spirits of the age with a singular and conscious physical oddity that amounted to ugliness. Of "old Crabb" in his final years, one might be pardoned for reflecting, "And *this* is the man who was the friend of Goethe and is the friend of Wordsworth!"—or whispering with Clough, after one of Robinson's breakfasts, ''Not at all the regular patriarch!'' The portrait by Scharf (1860) is obviously something between an over-realistic sketch and a caricature. We see the profile of a seemingly little man, sitting hunched-up at a little writing table, his large gray head sunken between his shoulders, his long thin hair falling nearly to the lapel; his high forehead, flat nose, and protruding under-jaw forming an amused and quizzical expression, enhanced by his spectacles, as he writes with what seems to be an impotent little hand. But he capitalized his ugliness much as Lamb utilized his stammering; he often punctuated the climax of an anecdote by suddenly thrusting out his prominent chin and slowly drawing it back as the significance of the story got about. No doubt it was partly because of this happy ability to reconcile an unprepossessing exterior with a genial and anecdotic soul that Robinson won his way into the heart of nearly every noted person of a half century.

Another paradox presents itself when we reflect that, wide as his literary acquaintance was, he left behind him, except his **Remains**, nothing but a small volume on Gall and Spurzheim's *Craniology* . . . , and a translation of a German fairy tale, *Amatonda*, by Anton Wall . . . , both of which were flat failures. Rather than attempt original literary work he seems to have preferred aiding others in contributing, for example, valuable material to Gilchrist's *Life of Blake*, Mrs. Austin's *Characteristics of Goethe*, and Talfourd's *Final Memorials of Charles Lamb*. (p. 48)

What made Robinson so successful in his intimacies with such men as Goethe, Wordsworth, Coleridge, Lamb, Blake, Flaxman? The answer is probably two-fold: his power of conversation and his charming modesty. The first depended largely on his wide reading and his prodigious memory. It is perhaps not too much to surmise that he read all of the important English and German books of his time. He apparently was that joy of every author's heart: a curious, sympathetic, creative reader. Backed up by a vast store of information and reminiscence, his comical habit of self-depreciation must have endeared him to all his associates. He seems always to be intimating that he has thrown his life away and rejoices in the permission to live vicariously in the happiness of others. His manner of address often took the form of, ''I speak to you with the respect with which a person like myself ought to speak to a great—''. Here insert, says De Morgan, *scholar, mathematician*, etc., as the case may be [see excerpt dated 1869]. In an age of social decorum, such careful self-effacement meant much. Or he might suddenly state, ''I am nothing, never was anything, not even a lawyer''. But perhaps the most striking modesty came when, at the end of several anecdotes related with astonishing clearness, running back through two generations, he would admit, when at a loss regarding a name, ''You see that my memory is quite gone; though that is an absurd way of talking, for I never had any''. However, his humility could at times yield to a disarming and disconcerting candor. It was his candor that won Madame de Staël. To her characteristically sudden and bald question, ''Are you rich?'' he replied instantly, ''As you please to take it; I am either a rich man of letters or a poor gentleman.'' (pp. 49-50)

There is no record of any of his conversations degenerating into argument. If pressed, he probably preferred a conversational argument to an argumentative conversation. Before he became a figure and a ''character,'' he undoubtedly had the secret of the perfect listener. . . . [Nowhere] in the **Diary** is his delicate curiosity and careful effort at sympathetic understanding so manifest as in the entries for December, 1825, and

January, 1826. The entry for December 10 begins with a significant question, ''Shall I call Blake artist, genius, mystic, or madman? Probably he is all. I will put down without method what I can recollect of the conversation of this remarkable man.'' For several pages we behold Robinson skillfully drawing Blake out, putting a careful question here, tentatively expressing an opinion there, and in general winning his way into Blake's confidence as far, perhaps, as any of Blake's friends ever went.

Later in life, when he had entered upon his inevitable career as talker, he tended more and more to live up to Madame de Staël's remark about Coleridge, that he was ''very great in monologue, but that he had no idea of dialogue.'' He tended to value a friend by his capacity to listen. His anecdotes cascaded everywhere. The breakfasts to which he invited the brighter students of University College grew cold as he dwelt over a reminiscence of Wieland or Herder and forgot to permit the appearance of the next course. . . . But these instances are perhaps unrepresentative of the conversational powers that in time made Robinson one of the most venerable and most sought-after men of the period. (pp. 50-2)

His **Diary** is the mirror of its writer. While it lacks the richness of personality and the vivid narrative to be found in Pepys' *Diary*, it is less stern and restrained than Evelyn's. It can in no real sense of the term be called literature. Of his limitations as a writer Robinson was quite thoroughly aware. ''I early found,'' he said, ''that I had not the literary ability to give me such a place among English authors as I should have desired; but I thought that I had an opportunity of gaining a knowledge of many of the most distinguished men of the age, and that I might do some good by keeping a record of my interviews with them.'' He became in time sufficiently aware that he even lacked in an eminent degree the ''Boswell faculty.'' But if his **Diary** lacks the genius of Pepys or Boswell, it compensates in some measure by an overflow of enthusiasm and animal spirits, and by the conscious effort at insight which he brought to bear upon whatever interesting mind he met. On the whole it is a meticulous and sober account, with only an infrequent flash of humor or irony. (p. 52)

Perhaps the richest anecdotic material is that relating to Goethe and Wordsworth, the two great subjects of his reminiscent conversations and discourses. Robinson first met Goethe in 1801, in Weimar. The meeting was short, and the young Englishman lapsed instantly into awed gazing while Goethe conversed with a friend. We learn that Goethe ''was about fifty-two years of age, and was beginning to be corpulent. He was,'' says Robinson, ''one of the most oppressively handsome men I ever saw.'' Once outside, and the interview successfully over, Robinson sighed in relief, ''Gott sei Dank!'' (pp. 52-3)

He has an amusing anecdote about Wordsworth's fame in 1816, eighteen years after the *Lyrical Ballads*. After a Mr. Hutton had conferred with Wordsworth about the sale of Richard Wordsworth's land, Robinson was drawn aside and asked, ''Is it true,—as I have heard reported,—that Mr. Wordsworth ever wrote verses?'' He relates also that Rogers once said to the poet, ''If you would let me edit your poems, and give me leave to omit some half-dozen, and make a few trifling alterations, I would engage that you should be as popular a poet as any living'', whereupon Wordsworth replied, ''I am much obliged to you, Mr. Rogers; I am a poor man, but I would rather remain as I am''. Yet Robinson was among the first to perceive Wordsworth's shortcomings, even to agree with Jeffrey that *The White Doe of Rylstone* was ''the very worst poem ever written.'' He early saw that *The Excursion,* "too mystical to be popular," would have few readers and would bring the "imputation of dullness" upon its author. No doubt it was Wordsworth the man as well as Wordsworth the poet that held Robinson's affection and loyalty. (pp. 54-5)

Leafing through the *Diary,* one is amazed at the rich stream of *bon mots,* anecdotes, and amusing reflections which whirl and sparkle through a dark current of ephemeral political problems and theological preoccupations.... We read on, to the passage about Coleridge's discourse on *action* as the end of all, and learn that Robinson himself turned a very touching *bon mot:* some one said of Coleridge's remarks, "This is a satire on himself"; "No", replied Robinson, "it is an elegy".

There is little of interest to us now in those portions of the *Diary* devoted to tours or to theological discussion. We yawn and leave behind us pages of discourse on Unitarianism, the Trinity, the Atonement, and pages given to tours in which Robinson, always partly the child of the eighteenth century, saw practically nothing of interest in nature, and everything in the personal traits of men. There is very little more richness in those entries reflecting the great political problems of the time. We read more about the Test and Corporation Act than about Waterloo. On June 23, 1815, he recorded, "I went to the Surrey Institution to read the detailed account of the glorious victory at Waterloo ... After nine o'clock I walked to Ayrton's. The illuminations were but dull, and there were scarcely any marks of public zeal or sympathy. I stayed at Ayrton's till past one. Lamb, Alsager, etc., were there, but it was merely a card party".

Here and there we encounter an entry of a humorous, ironic, or bizarre nature. Frequently it is obvious that such an effect was not intended. Yet what shall we say about the following?: "*January 9th* (1816)—(At Norwich). This morning I went immediately after breakfast to a Jew dentist, C...., who put in a natural tooth in the place of the one I swallowed yesterday. He assured me it came from Waterloo, and promised me it should outlast twelve artificial teeth". And how are we to "take" Robinson's assertion that Lamb had the finest collection of shabby books he ever saw? ... And so the entries run,— a cataract of impressions, gossipy anecdotes, records of unexpected meetings, of wise and witty observations overheard at table, a stream now turning muddy with speculations on eternal damnation or deism, flashing with a pun that convulsed one of Rogers' "breakfasts", now rising in quaint dignity over a stiff *bon mot* that no longer thrills, flowing gently and sedately in a long passage of rumination over a minor political crisis, damning up momentarily with a thick agglomeration of memories of such a long-forgotten personage as Mrs. Clarkson or Mrs. Barbauld ... Truly a droll world, from this distance, a world full of a piety that is now quaint, of longings for a new dispensation, of momentary Byronic sneers, of echoes from Horace Walpole and Boswell, of Jane Austen heroines and the *Mysteries of Udolpho,* of interminable teas and endless conversations, of hysterical enthusiasms over German "tales of horror" and the majesty of Goethe, of delicate young ladies musing over the poems of Cowper, of thunderous *Reviews* shaking the literary heavens, of the mystery and magic of the Waverley novels, on Coleridge's mad and magnificent lectures, of Fraser's installments of an impudently unintelligible work called *Sartor Resartus* ...

The most unconsciously charming feature of Robinson's work is the casual manner in which his entries often deal with men who have since his day gained classic significance. On January

10, 1824, he dined at Lamb's and heard a Mr. C.... "Break out at last by an opposition to Mr. (Edward) Irving, which made the good man so angry that he exclaimed: 'Sir, I reject the whole bundle of your opinions.' Now it seemed to me," adds Robinson, "that Mr. C.... had no opinions, only words, for his assertions seemed a mere *galimatias*". The Mr. C...., of course, was young Thomas Carlyle, recently the translator of *Wilhelm Meister,* and as yet only a poor tutor. (pp. 55-7)

In the latter sections of the *Diary* we find him encountering Daniel Webster's "air of Imperial strength, such as Caesar might have had"; dining with "Rogers, the Dean of the poets," ... and meeting Alfred Tennyson of "eminent talent"; going "with a feeling of predetermined dislike" to meet Emerson at Lord Northampton, and finding his dislike vanishing instantly before the "most interesting countenance" full of "a combination of intelligence and sweetness"; dining with "Mrs. Browning, the late Miss Barrett,—not the invalid I expected"—with a "handsome oval face, a fine eye," and a husband with a "very amiable expression" and a "singular sweetness about him".—What a magnificent list of friends and acquaintances! (pp. 58-9)

Robinson had apparently but three enthusiasms: the quest for theological certainty, the formation of great friendships and exhilarating acquaintanceships, and the uninterrupted reading of books. The narrow dogmatism of his Dissenting parents never ensnared him; he once defined the Church in his own terms as "An association of men for the cultivation of knowledge, the practice of piety, and the promotion of virtue". His liberal tendency to doubt hardened and closely formulated opinions he carried over into politics, and called himself a liberal conservative or a conservative liberal. He looked with distrust on the universal conservative reaction to the French Revolution, showed no apparent admiration for Napoleon, and shared in the spirit of 1830 and of 1848. But, as a spectator of life, he never fully gave himself to any cause. International in his interests, he lived in a world of ideas and memories and humane hopes. Just philosophical enough to enjoy reading skillful theological discourses, he was never quite metaphysician enough to follow Hegel or Fichte, and saw no incongruity in turning from an elucidation of Kant to a rhapsody over the excellent expository power of Madge, his favorite Unitarian minister. During a visit of five weeks at Rydal Mount in the winter of 1839 he read carefully (after his characteristic fashion) Carlyle's *French Revolution,* Arnold's *Rome,* Gladstone's *Church and State,* part of Cicero's *Letters to Atticus,* and three formidable theological works by Isaac Taylor, besides several "things from Ben Jonson" and some German with Miss Harden and the Arnolds. For him, reading meant thoughtful study, entries in his *Diary,* abstracts of plots, outlines of books, extended critical notes in his letters to friends. Because the classical side of his education had never been adequate, his taste for ancient literatures was considerably stunted, and his omnivorous reading in English, German, and Italian soon prevented any careful retrievement of his loss. But, hearty in his love of the present and its living writers, he devoured the books of his friends almost as fast as they left the press. (pp. 59-60)

His *Diary* is singularly free of remarks about his health. The vast well of memories continued to bubble-up to within a few days before his death. As an old man of exceptional hardihood he was inclined to over-estimate his strength and had to be warned not to talk for more than two hours.... On January 31, five days before the end, he records, "During the last two days I have read the first essay on the qualifications of the present age for criticism. The writer maintains his point ably. A sense of creative power he declares happiness to be, and Arnold maintains that genuine criticism is. He thinks of Germany as he ought, and of Goethe with high admiration. On this point I can possibly give him assistance, which he will gladly—But I feel incapable to go on" [see excerpt dated 1867]. Thus ends the last entry, a little incoherent in phrasing but representative of his never-satisfied intellectual curiosity. "On this point I can possibly give him assistance"—with these characteristic words Robinson's *Diary* closes. One remembers his aid in Gilchrist's *Life of Blake,* in Mrs. Austin's *Characteristics of Goethe,* and the tireless encouragement and friendship which he lavished among the literary workers of some sixty years. At the last, the memory of *John Gilpin* mingled with the ideas of Matthew Arnold and a new age. (pp. 60-1)

> Charles Frederick Harrold, "A Spectator of Life: Henry Crabb Robinson," in The Sewanee Review, Vol. XXXVI, No. 1, Winter, 1928, pp. 46-61.

B. J. MORSE (essay date 1931)

[*Morse outlines Robinson's role in the introduction of German literature to English readers and assesses Robinson's critical response to Goethe's works. This essay was written in 1931.*]

Henry Crabb Robinson was a man of extremely catholic tastes and had a unique gift for accommodating himself to any new intellectual movement or tendency which he encountered in his wide and varied wanderings in the chief countries of Europe. At a time when all nations were subject to the political and intellectual domination of France, when the mind of England was completely bounded by the limits of her shores, and stultified by her so called splendid isolation, Robinson was slowly but surely making good his claims to be considered a citizen of Europe, and seeking to understand and propagate the ideas at the root of the movements that were to become the corner stones upon which the intellectual life of our days was to be founded. He was what Goethe would have called a "Weltbürger", and devoted all his energies to teach to others that conception of a "Weltliteratur" which the great German poet was assiduous in teaching to all who came in contact with him. Despite the manifold duties of a busy private and professional life, Robinson did all that lay in his power to enlighten his immediate circle as to the merits of German literature and philosophy, which were then held in great disesteem. His great hero was Goethe, then less appreciated than he is now (if that be possible), and he was never tired of discussing his works, and, when this was possible, of disseminating his ideas. Robinson's work as a mediator was accomplished amongst some of the most important circles of the day, and his influence determined the development of many of the most influential English men of letters of the period. It is consequently of great value, and none the less so for having been done by word of mouth. (p. 199)

It is customary to regard Crabb Robinson as a mere dilettante in the arts. . . . If we persist in accepting Robinson's own modest estimation of his work as a labourer for German literature in England, we shall certainly do him wrong, especially in regard to his propaganda work for Goethe in England. Arriving in Germany at a time when Goethe's name was only mentioned with abhorrence in England as one of the most destructive and immoral influences of the age, Crabb Robinson's mind was elastic enough to overcome the insular prejudices of his fellow-countrymen, and to be critically appreciative in a degree that we may look in vain for until the publication of the works of Carlyle and George Henry Lewes. This in itself was a feat of no small importance, and points to an understanding of the literary currents in Germany that was unique at the time, and remained so for many years to come. Generally speaking, there was no contemporary who could have vied with Robinson in knowledge of things German; and the number of his acquaintanceships with the most distinguished and important German men of letters could not easily have been rivalled. (pp. 201-02)

Robinson's first detailed account of his opinions and impressions of Goethe was communicated in a letter dated 11 May 1801. These remarks are very important as documentary evidence for the progress which he was making under the influence of his surroundings and the tutelage of his German friends, for it contains in a concise form all the main ideas of contemporary German critics concerning Goethe. He states that Goethe is the idol of the German literary world, and tells his brother to be very careful how he takes the poet's name in vain. "The Critics of the New School assert that since the Existence of Letters, there have only been four of those exalted Geniuss on whom Nature & Art have showerd down all their Gifts to form that perfection of Intellect,—A Poet—Virgil, Milton, Wieland, Klopstock, Ariosto, Ossian, Tasso &c. &c. are Singers of various and great excellence but the sacred fire has been possessed in its perfection only by Homer, Cervantes, Shakespeare and Göthe—Nay some of this new School have even asserted that the three great *Tendencies* of the late Century are the french revolution, the Fichtean Philosophy and *Wilhelm Meisters Lehrjahre.*" This letter also contains a reference to his intention of introducing "*Wilhelm Meisters Apprenticeship* . . . a Novel certainly of first rate excellence" to the English public. He states that he has read the book with more delight than any other German novel that has come his way, and singles out for special praise the profound criticism of the drama which it contains. . . . (pp. 206-07)

Goethe he considered the most oppressively handsome man he had ever seen, and in his presence he was painfully impressed by the majesty and dignity of his commanding figure. He gives high praise to *Werter,* and comparing it to *La Nouvelle Heloïse* he is forced to the opinion that the German novel is the better one, for in it "all is Passion, there are no languid passages the stream of [sentiment] flows wildly and boisterously till it rushes in the Vortex of destruction." He is of the opinion that the book is a perfect work of art, and that it is a "sort of philosophical System displayed in one all comprehensive Image—Werter is personified Sensibility", a sentence which reappears later in one of the apocryphal utterances of Coleridge. But Robinson does not think this to be Goethe's strength: on the contrary, the celestial repose and the solemn tranquility of the characters in *Iphigenie* please him more, being to him, indeed, the chief of his qualities. "And this is in my mind the characteristic of Göthe—His better and more perfect Works are [without] disorder and tumult they resemble Claude Lorraine's Landscapes and Raphael's Historical pieces—Göthes Songs and Ballads and Elegies all have the same [Character] his ballads in particular have a wildness of fancy [which] is [fascinating] but [without] turbulence—No Hurry Scurry as in Burgers Lenora." And again, "His pieces breathe a sort of etherial softness and repose." Like most of his contemporaries in England Crabb Robinson censured a certain want of moral delicacy in some of the works and the private life of Goethe; but it should also be noticed that his strictures were not based on the narrow-mindedness current in England at the time, but in accordance with the standards of morality which he deduced from the works of Goethe. He thought that the author of *Werter, Iphigenie in Tauris,* and *Torquato Tasso* ought to have been animated by higher moral standards than those evident in some of his works and practised in his private life, Robinson's remarks concerning Christiane Vulpius are harsh and unworthy of him, although they represent the view of the average Englishman.

Before making this call on Goethe, Robinson told his companion that he wished to converse with Wieland, but only to look at Goethe; and according to his own account he sat with Goethe for a quarter of an hour without saying a word, although he is careful to state that this was not due to the German poet's deportment, which was courteous enough, but to his own self-consciousness. He informs us that Goethe was beginning to grow corpulent at this time, but that his features were still very handsome and reminded him of the figure of Kemble in *Measure for Measure.*

Robinson's opinion that the characteristic trait in Goethe's poetical work is its calm repose is very curious, for contemporary English critics generally asserted the contrary. The distinction which he draws between the spirits of Bürger's ballads and Goethe's is also unique, and shows a marked advance on the critical views then current in England; but his views regarding Goethe's morality are quite in keeping with the traditional opinions of English critics in general. Even Carlyle, who was very keen on stressing the moral tendencies in Goethe's productions, had to admit that Goethe did not always put his moral teachings as clearly as he wished him to. (pp. 208-10)

Goethe, [Robinson] says, is one of the few man of the age whose names will be of importance to after ages, and this is sufficient to pardon the garrulity of anyone describing a visit to him, and recording even the most insignificant matters connected with him. "I have seen him in his familiar moments, as stript of disguise as he can be And quite himself . . . Göthe said nothing which *un de nous autres* could not have said too And you may say does an insignificant thing become important because it falls from the Tongue of a great Man? I answer, in a truly great Man everything is important." In explanation of this passage he proceeds to make clear what he means by the term "a great man", and his remarks on this head are important because they foreshadow some of the conceptions of Thomas Carlyle. Carlyle has often been accredited with having introduced the idea of the Great Man into English literature and philosophy, but this view is not a true one, for the conception appears in one form or another in the writings of Hobbes, Samuel Rogers, Cowper, Wordsworth, Byron and Shelley. The explanation of the idea given by Robinson has more in common with Carlyle's theory than with that of any of the above named writers. Robinson distinguishes clearly between a great man and a man of talents. Goethe is a great man but Schlegel, who was also present, he calls a man of talents. The latter related witty anecdotes, recited epigrams, strove his best to shine to gain a reputation as a brilliant talker. Goethe did not shine, and made no effort to do so, but everything he said was in keeping with himself, indicating his habitual feelings and sentiments. "Göthe is a Great Man not merely because he has produced masterpieces of poetry rivelling (sic) the best works of antiquity; but that he is distinguished by habitual manliness, consistency, vigour, truth, & health of Opinion & sentiment. He is a Man of practical wisdom." The most admirable characteristic of Goethe's intellectual life he finds in the universality of his tastes; he respects all things, despising nothing but fri-

volity. Robinson thought that Goethe's powerful mind was more suited to study the nature of things and to represent human nature through the medium of poetry than to teach moral truths. He found in Goethe "an abstract of all intellectual powers combined—And then employed in the common concerns of life". The conversation turned on Oriental literature, and Robinson was surprised to discover that Goethe was much averse to it; and indeed such a statement from the lips of the author of the "West-Östlicher Diwan" was astonishing. This antipathy to Oriental literature in general confirmed an opinion that Robinson had long held, viz., that Goethe's aversion to Christian views was merely a matter of taste, and that his religion had affinities with the "[splendid] heroic poetic religion of the Antients." (pp. 213-14)

Robinson was acquainted with most of the celebrated English men of letters of the day, and his labours for German literature in England were therefore of great importance. Most critics have avoided an attempt to trace and estimate the real extent of his influence on the formation of the opinions of his literary friends, considering it to be too indefinite to be proved, because it was effected by word of mouth and not by published writings. It is true that Robinson published but little, and even this little is not of great importance because it was not published until long after the appearance of the work of the writers who had been influenced by him. And for this reason it is not necessary to examine them here. This does not lessen the importance of his influence on his literary friends and through them on the mind of the English public in general. (p. 216)

The influence of Robinson's conversation and advice on Carlyle's publications is difficult to determine, but a close examination of their published works will establish much in favour of the view that this influence is greater than is generally admitted. In cases where ideas and views common to both are to be found in Robinson's letters, we are justified in supposing a fairly strong case for an influence on the part of Robinson, especially when they are not in agreement with the views of contemporary critics. One of the most striking ideas common to both is the distinction they make between a great man and a man of talents. It is true that Carlyle applies the distinction to manufacturers and creators, artists and artizans, the true poet and the mere writer, but fundamentally they come to the same thing. "I distinguish very pointedly a great Man from a Man of great Talents", says Robinson, for "this class of Men whose Talents are something they possess (a property, a thing foreign from & attached to themselves), is very different from that of those, of whom it should not be said that they *have genius* but that they *are genius's*". The same idea is to be found in Carlyle, although certain elements of his theory are certainly due to the influence of Fichte.

Their opinions of the intellectual and private character of Goethe are almost identical, as the careful reader will not fail to notice. Robinson thinks Goethe a great man not merely because he is a great writer, but because he is also distinguished by a habitual consistency, manliness, truth, and vigour. He finds Goethe's ballads, elegies, *Hermann and Dorothea, Torquato Tasso,* and *Iphigenie* to be but "different expressions or energies of the same soul". (pp. 224-25)

In 1802, prognosticating the judgment of some future critic of his labours for German literature in England, Crabb Robinson wrote down the following remarks, "One of those who made the first public attempts to attract the notice of the literati of this period to philosophy which had already risen to great splendour in Germany was Robinson a man who seems to have had little more than a [presentiment] of the supreme worth of science, & a conviction of the absolute nothingness of the now forgotten works of Locke &c but who wanted clearness of [Understanding] & sharpness of penetration of comprehend the whole field before him—The little pieces he wrote now appear to be highly insignificant but still it is impossible to say that they did not in some slight degree contribute to further the study of science here''. With all respect to Robinson's own opinion we cannot agree with this verdict, for it is manifestly unjust. As an interpreter of German literature in England Robinson deserves a much higher place. He was a sturdy and indefatigable pioneer whose labours did much to turn the tide of critical opinion in favour of a more correct appreciation of Goethe's works, and his sympathetic accounts of Goethe certainly helped to prepare the way for Carlyle and George Henry Lewes. (p. 227)

> *B. J. Morse, ''Crabb Robinson and Goethe in England,'' in* Englische Studien, *Vol. 67, No. 2, 1932-33, pp. 199-227.*

JOHN MIDDLETON MURRY   (essay date 1931)

[*Murry was a noted English essayist, magazine editor, and literary critic during the first half of the twentieth century. In the following excerpt from his critique of* The Correspondence of Henry Crabb Robinson with the Wordsworth Circle, *Murry discusses Robinson's relationship with Wordsworth.*]

Probably the best thing yet written about Henry Crabb Robinson is Walter Bagehot's vivid essay [see excerpt dated 1869]. In it we see and hear the man, forgetting to make the tea at his breakfast-parties, keeping his unprepared guests ('the more astute used to breakfast before they came') hungry while he made them 'undergo the bust', pointing his familiar anecdotes with an out-thrust of his chin. 'Old Crabb' is there, with his 'slovenly' nose, his inability to remember names, which gave Bagehot the sly excuse to convey in a single remark—a triumph of narration—both 'old Crabb's' tone and young Matthew Arnold's manner:

> Probably the most able, and certainly the most consequential, of all the young persons I know. You know which it is. The one with whom I could never *presume* to be intimate. The one whose father I knew so many years.

But Bagehot is a little cruel; he seemed to have forgotten that 'old Crabb' was once young, and that the garrulous last twenty of a life of ninety years might not reveal, even to a critic of genius, the whole secret of a personality which great men had loved and trusted. Besides being a little cruel, Bagehot is also a little unfair. We would not willingly forgo the picture of 'the wonderful and dreary faces' which Clough used to make while he listened perforce to Crabb Robinson's reading of Wordsworth's poems; but we cannot admit the implication that the old man did not truly appreciate the poet, while the young one did. Both of them revered Wordsworth, in different ways and perhaps for different qualities; but Clough's reverence was barely this side idolatry, whereas old Crabb had known, and knew that he had known, a greater man—Goethe. In our slightly changed perspective, Crabb Robinson's appears the sounder judgement.

Professor Edith Morley's admirable edition [*The Correspondence of Henry Crabb Robinson with the Wordsworth Circle*] of all those of Crabb Robinson's papers which are concerned with

the Wordsworth circle puts an end to all doubts of his critical understanding of Wordsworth's poetry. It contains two careful letters written by him to a young correspondent who found the approach to Wordsworth's poetry none too easy. They prove that, even if, as Bagehot says, the old man did not read the best of Wordsworth's poems at his breakfast-parties—and Bagehot does not tell us which he read—he knew perfectly well which were the best. Matthew Arnold himself could hardly have improved on his selection. And Bagehot's suggestion that he was impervious to mysticism is pointedly answered by his brief comment on the *Intimations* ode:

> This is the grandest of Wordsworth's smaller poems, as it is perhaps the grandest ode in the English language. But let it be passed over for the present. It is, as some say, mystical. It treats of a mystery, certainly.

Evidently Crabb Robinson was, like many other good men, shy of the word 'mystical'; he was mistrustful of high-falutin; and very probably he was not, as Bagehot hints, the kind of man to draw out the philosophical implications of Wordsworth's poetry. But neither was Wordsworth himself. One of the most critically valuable letters in Professor Morley's collection is one of Wordsworth's, dated 1814, carefully copied by Crabb Robinson, with a due sense of its importance, in which the poet struggles, vehemently and awkwardly, with the charge that he did not distinguish 'between Nature as the work of God and God Himself'. It is a charge which a precise theologian must inevitably bring against Wordsworth's poetry; and later on we find Crabb Robinson reporting to the poet a very definite condemnation of his heresy by a Puseyite clergyman. Crabb found, we think, a certain satisfaction in communicating the charge, for he had no sympathy with Wordsworth's evolution towards orthodoxy. And Professor de Sélincourt's recent publication of the early version of *The Prelude* has clearly shown how uncomfortable Wordsworth was about his own youthful Pantheism, and how carefully he tried to cover up its traces. (pp. 188-90)

[Crabb Robinson]—if he was anything—was a Unitarian. . . . But, in truth, he was simply a Wordsworthian: the difficulty was that he wanted to believe that the early Wordsworth was the real Wordsworth, and Wordsworth did not. Common to them both was a disinclination and an inaptitude for thinking out the theological position; but Wordsworth was resolved on being orthodox, while Crabb Robinson—in this, perhaps, not unmindful of Goethe—was content to remain where he was. Like a good many others, he preferred Wordsworth as poet to Wordsworth as Tory and High Churchman. (p. 191)

Crabb Robinson had been one of those to whom *Lyrical Ballads* came as a revelation. Wordsworth had done something for him, and he never forgot it. Looking back, at the end of his life, when he had outlived all his friends, he wrote:

> A poem is worth nothing that is not a companion for years, and this is what distinguishes Wordsworth from the herd of poets. He *lasts*. I love him more than I did fifty years ago. You will see few men advanced in life who will say the same of Lord Byron, even though they once loved him, that is, as I did Wordsworth, from the beginning. . . . In my youth I fell in with those of his works then just published, and became a passionate lover. I knew many by heart, and on my journeys was always repeating or

reading them. I made many converts. Wordsworth had to create his public. He formed the
taste of the age in great measure. . . . The cause
of the opposition . . . lies in the *simple style,*
on which every abuse was lavished. Wordsworth was of opinion that posterity will value
most those lyrical ballads which were most
laughed at. He may be partial in this opinion;
certainly they are the most characteristic.

(pp. 191-92)

Professor Edith Morley, in her preface, will not admit that
Wordsworth was quick to condemn and slow to admire his
contemporaries. She will have no spots on the sun. But no
idiosyncrasy of Wordsworth's is better authenticated than this;
and none is more frequently alluded to in the letters of his
intimates and admirers. . . . Crabb Robinson saw [this] defect
in proportion. In his admirable letters to Landor, to dissuade
him from publishing his satire against Wordsworth—letters in
which his discernment is as apparent as his loyalty—he wrote:

> What matters it that he is insensible to the as-
> tonishing powers of Voltaire or Gothe—He is
> after all W.: In all cases I care little what a man
> is not—I look to what he is.—And W. has
> written a hundred poems, the least excellent of
> which I would not sacrifice to give him that
> openness of heart you require—Productive power
> acts by means of concentration—With few ex-
> ceptions those only love everything who like
> me can do nothing.

That may be Crabb Robinson at his best; but not a sentence
in any letter in these volumes is inconsistent with that rare
combination of devotion and detachment. (pp. 193-94)

[Personal] affection was what he felt and valued; betrayal of
friendship was ever for him the worst of crimes. . . . He cared
for persons, not principles. He had the mind to recognize great
men; but, more rare, the heart to love them. Like a true lover
he could keep his eyes fixed not on what they were not, but
on what they were. It was no wonder that great men were glad
of him. (pp. 198-99)

> *John Middleton Murry, "Crabb Robinson and the
> Wordsworths," in his* Countries of the Mind: Essays
> in Literary Criticism, second series, *Oxford Univer-
> sity Press, London, 1931, pp. 188-99.*

EDITH J. MORLEY   (essay date 1935)

[*In the following excerpt from Morley's biography of Robinson,
the critic analyzes Robinson's taste in literature. According to
Morley, early nineteenth-century literary trends can be discerned
by studying Robinson's commentary on his readings. For further
criticism by Morley, see excerpt dated 1922.*]

Throughout his life an omnivorous reader, Crabb Robinson's
choice of books is representative of the educated taste of his
period, and it would be possible to trace the trends of opinion
in literature in the first half of the nineteenth century by a
careful study of his notes on his reading—with the proviso,
always, that he was usually somewhat in advance of the age,
and that his opinions were those of a man of judgment and
discrimination, who neither accepted nor rejected at the behest
of fashion or of the critics. Naturally his friendships with Lamb
and with Wordsworth and Coleridge stimulated and to some
extent moulded his taste, but they never dominated it—partly

no doubt because the intimacies were formed when he was
already mature and had had the advantage of the self-discipline
and inspiration which he had derived from his stay in Germany
and his wide knowledge of a second literature and language.
Crabb Robinson . . . never ceased to regret that he had missed
the benefits of a severe classical training, but it is certain that,
while he was in no sense an exact scholar, he had read widely
and with enjoyment, in both Latin and Greek; and that, later
on, he added to these many of the chief works—poetry, drama,
fiction, criticism and philosophy—in French, Italian, and Spanish, as well as German and English. To his reading he brought
the 'spirit and judgment, equal or superior,' which enabled him
to temper his book-learning with his knowledge of men and
of affairs. Nor, it must be remembred, did his provincial,
middle-class, dissenting upbringing imply in his case ignorance, even in his youth, of what was going on in English
letters. . . . He never lost his youthful admiration for Pope,
and, in 1843, he wrote to Quillinan: 'Before I had heard of
the *Lyrical Ballads,* which caused a little revolution in my taste
for poetry, there were four poems which I used to read incessantly; I cannot say which I then read the oftenest or loved the
most. They are of a very different kind, and I mention them
to show that my taste was *wide.* They were *The Rape of the
Lock, Comus, The Castle of Indolence* and *The Traveller.* Next
to these were all the ethic epistles of Pope; and, with respect
to these, they were so familiar to me, that I never for years
looked into them—I seemed to know them by heart. I ought,
perhaps, to be ashamed to confess that at that period I was
much better acquainted with the *Rambler* than the *Spectator.*'

The habit of literary discussion in correspondence indicated by
this extract is apparently common to Crabb Robinson and to
all his acquaintance, so that one is able to get a good idea of
the books and poems that were in vogue in different parts of
the country and in different types of society. (pp. 140-41)

Crabb Robinson is among the earliest to recognize the new era
inaugurated by the Great Unknown, and he punctually records
the appearance of the various Waverley Novels, which he reads
and usually estimates at their worth. The writer of *Waverley,*
he thinks, 'has united to the ordinary qualities of works of
prose fiction, excellencies of an unusual kind,' and 'there is
more than the usual portion of good sense in this book.' Dalgetty, 'a glorious exhibition of a most inglorious personage,'
is 'the only finished character' in *The Legend of Montrose,* 'by
no means one of the great works of the author.' *Guy Mannering*
is a work 'of higher interest than *Waverley,*' the 'comic painting
being excellent,' while, rather surprisingly, 'There are scenes
of terror hardly inferior to Mrs. Radcliffe's.' (p. 145)

In later days Crabb Robinson is equally ready to welcome the
great Victorian novelists and to distinguish between the worth
of their work and the weaknesses of some of their immediate
predecessors and contemporaries. For example, 'Ainsworth is
another of these popular writers whose vices are the source of
their sad celebrity. Worse novels in most senses cannot be
conceived than *Jack Sheppard,* [etc.]—having all the faults of
Dickens with very little of his genius (*13th September 1844*).
Crabb Robinson objects particularly to the sensationalism of
Ainsworth, and to his exaltation of a picaresque hero. Fenimore
Cooper does not attract him because 'to an English reader the
improbability of the incidents [in *The Pilot.* He is writing in
1836] is offensive.' And even Landor's praise of G. P. R.
James as 'the equal of Walter Scott,' only wrings from Crabb
Robinson the half-hearted praise that 'He certainly is one of
the best of Scott's disciples as a maker of historical novels and

he has contrived to deviate less from history than his competitors. . . . James is a scholar and a good historian, but I know not that I shall read more of his books.' Lady Morgan (Sydney Owenson) 'shows power of observation and is sensible where she does not strive to be wise'; Galt's *Annals of the Parish* is 'well-executed,' interesting as a historical document of social changes, and, above all, as giving a true picture of Scottish life in a country village. Similarly, *Rab and his Friends* is 'delightful,' and Crabb Robinson re-reads it with pleasure. (pp. 145-46)

Crabb Robinson has something stronger than dislike for any book the moral trend of which he considers doubtful: for example, he condemns George Sand, though she extorts his unwilling admiration. He can stand and even enjoy an amount of preaching which to-day would be found intolerable, but his taste is too sound to permit him to accept a mere sermon in the guise of fiction, whether this be intended for juvenile or for adult consumption. Thus he refuses to read *The Wide Wide World* in spite of the praise generally accorded it, and though he thinks *Peg Woffington* (Charles Reade) a capital story, he finds that 'it has too much religious cant' in it. The one exception to his condemnation of pure didacticism in novel-form is when he reads any book dealing with the evils of slavery. Not merely *Uncle Tom's Cabin*, but also Mrs. Stowe's *Dred*, a much inferior book, come in for a most unfair share of appreciation. For once his principles overpower his judgment and he is incapable of an unbiased opinion.

This is in marked contrast to his attitude to *Mary Barton*, which, though 'good and edifying and honourable to Mrs. Gaskell who wrote it,' is dismissed with the remark that 'the moral tendency is far better than the artistic merit,' and that it is unrelieved by any touch of imagination. One wishes that he had been acquainted with *Cranford*, which he would certainly have appreciated, but he seems to have missed it, to his own loss and to ours. *Ruth* he considers a great improvement on *Mary Barton*. 'Indeed,' he writes to his brother (*12th February 1853*) it is 'one of the most exquisitely beautiful specimens of moral painting, treating a most delicate and difficult subject with unsurpassable refinement.'

The novels of Miss Manning, Mrs. Oliphant, Miss Edgeworth, Wendell Holmes (whose *Elsie Venner* 'is not to my taste'), Hawthorne (*The Scarlet Letter* is 'an admirable piece of portrait-painting') are all commented on in turn, as are very many books of more ephemeral interest. As late as 1864, when near his ninetieth birthday, Crabb Robinson reproached himself because he 'could not recover from [his] reading mania,' so it may be supposed that he did not allow much to escape his notice in his more receptive years. Soon after making the above complaint, there is an entry in his diary apropos of *Pendennis* which summarises pretty accurately his opinion of the relative attraction of Dickens and Thackeray. 'There is a free and easy fun in [Dickens] which gives [him] a gaiety I do not find in Thackeray. There is however more of depth, more of design in Thackeray.' And then: 'I like *Pendennis* as little as ever, though I admire it more.' 'It is more clever than pleasant.' One gathers that this represents his general attitude to the two greatest Victorian novelists. 'Thackeray has great skill in the representation of entirely selfish and worthless characters'; 'Becky Sharp is a gem from the beginning,' but 'odious morally.' Crabb Robinson finds it depressing to stay too long in vanity fair, and though he recognises Thackeray's genius and reads his books, he is happier in the company of Dickens. But here again he distinguishes. Thus (. . . *10th April 1842*) *Bleak*

House 'begins well, and like his former tales will probably exhibit great ability in painting *scenes,* without the like faculty of connecting these scenes into one great act.' He cannot 'comprehend the praise given to' *Great Expectations*, for example; it is 'one of the least agreeable of his books,' while *Hard Times* is 'by no means one of the best.' On the other hand, *David Copperfield* is 'superior in truth to most of Dickens's novels and less extravagent in its incidents.' As for *Barnaby Rudge*— a much earlier work—he decides when he has finished all of it 'yet published' (*5th August 1841*) 'I will read no more till the story is finished. . . . I will not expose myself to further anxieties.' That is the proper spirit, and speaks of his unmistakable delight in the great delineator of the 'characters' which always charmed Crabb Robinson whether in real life or in literature. It is for her delineation of these that he admires George Eliot. Maggie's aunts in *The Mill on the Floss* resemble the creations of Jane Austen, and are 'exquisitely drawn,' though nothing in the book quite comes up to Mrs. Poyser, and *Silas Marner* is 'perhaps George Eliot's best novel.' So, too, when he criticises *Barchester Towers,* or *The Bertrams,* or *The Warden:* the comic scenes are excellent, and show Trollope at his best. In *Villette,* again, 'a book of very superior ability,' but 'an uncomfortable book,' it is in the 'character sketches' that the author excels; but there is 'too much preaching.' Four years earlier, in 1849, he had 'sat up till one, reading *Jane Eyre,*' which gave him 'very great pleasure indeed; it is an extraordinary work.' To his credit be it said, that he found nothing to justify the verdict that it was 'a wicked book.'

It is not only in novel-reading that Crabb Robinson keeps abreast of all that is published. He comments, for example, on the historians, Froude, Maitland, and Macaulay, as their works appear, and usually with just appreciation. He reads Carlyle and refuses to be put off by Wordsworth's dislike for his style. He enjoys the *French Revolution* and rightly estimates the worth of *Sartor Resartus.* Though he dislikes much in the man, and at one period is estranged from him, it is he who helps Carlyle in the selection of German novels to be translated, the letters asking for his advice being carefully preserved. Later on, he welcomes the early work of Ruskin and endeavours to understand his opinions about the Pre-Raphaelites as well as to fathom how Venetian architecture can justly be said to typify decadence of morals. *The Two Paths* arouses his admiration, and he is duly impressed by the author himself.

In poetry, too, his love and reverence for Wordsworth do not prevent him from reading everything else that appears, and he is seldom at fault in estimating its value. Thus, while he is avowedly not able to appreciate Blake's 'designs,' he ventures to rank his lyrics with those of Shakespeare. As is well-known, he was among the first, if not the earliest, to discover Blake's poetic genius and he was justly proud of his share in obtaining public recognition for it.

Byron's poetry Crabb Robinson fails altogether to appreciate, partly, no doubt, because of his prejudice against the man, and partly also because he judges him chiefly by his tales in verse and by his dramas. But he obstinately refuses sufficiently to admire the *Vision of Judgment* in spite of Goethe's praise, and the subject-matter of *Don Juan,* and particularly its picture of London society in the time of the Regency, suffice to distort his view of its achievement. (pp. 147-50)

References to Tennyson are . . . appreciative, and, on the whole, discriminating. Thus, while he considers the *Idylls of the King* contains 'beautiful passages,' he adds that not one of them is 'as pleasing as the *Morte d'Arthur* in an earlier volume.' On the other hand, he dismisses *Maud* as a 'disagreeable poem' with 'spasmodic brilliance.' But already in 1845 he had written of Tennyson as 'by far the most eminent of the young poets. His poems are full of genius.' According to Crabb Robinson, however, they are also 'enigmatical' and 'many of his most celebrated pieces are really poetic riddles.' Thus, while he enjoys and admires *In Memoriam* (which he prefers to *Adonais*), he finds it very hard to understand.

With Matthew Arnold, Crabb Robinson was familiar from his boyhood, but on the whole he liked him less than his brothers and sisters and very much less than his parents, though, on at least one occasion, a meeting with him at the Athenaeum is mentioned as productive of pleasant conversation. His poetry does not receive adequate notice, but the last entry in the diary refers appreciatively to his *Essay on the Function of Criticism:* 'He thinks of Germany as he ought, and of Goethe with high admiration. On this point I can possibly give him assistance, which he will gladly——' [see excerpt dated 1867]. But here the pen falls from his hand and the untiring diarist has written his last comment on men and books. (p. 151)

[Crabb Robinson] read almost everything that appeared, verse and prose, was an indefatigable student of the reviews and quarterlies and weeklies, while *The Times* is described as being as necessary to him as his daily meals. The *Saturday Review* and the *Athenæum* were his favourite literary papers, but he read regularly, contributed articles, and subscribed to many of the solid Nonconformist journals, and, except when in company, and not always then, was seldom without some printed matter in his hand. He read when he took his long walks in town and country, read on stage-coaches and in the railway, at meals and in bed, and he was always pleased to discuss books and articles either with his friends or with chance acquaintances. When an audience failed him, he wrote down his opinions in his diary or letters, so that these serve to enlighten the reader about what caused a stir in literary circles for three-quarters of a century. Crabb Robinson frequently reproached himself for spending undue time over worthless books and essays. Modern students, however, owe him much for the detailed critical comments which enable them to visualise the successive literary fashions of his long life. No later historian can have the same first-hand knowledge of how writers struck their contemporaries and of what appeared of importance in its own day. (p. 152)

> *Edith J. Morley, in her* The Life and Times of Henry Crabb Robinson, *J. M. Dent & Sons Limited, 1935, 212 p.*

JOHN MILTON BAKER   (essay date 1937)

[*The following excerpt is from Baker's* Henry Crabb Robinson of Bury, Jena, ''The Times,'' and Russell Square, *a detailed study of Robinson's life and works. Here, Baker analyzes Robinson's treatment of Goethe's works and outlines Robinson's concept of poetics.*]

[Crabb Robinson's series on Goethe for the *Monthly Repository* is] informative, critically and historically important, and, what is more, interesting. If there were no other reason, the articles would hold the reader because of the subject-matter; Goethe himself is such an attractive figure that no one can fill a large number of pages with ungarnished facts about him without including much good reading matter. Few, however, are able to write simple unadorned prose about this man, most of those who approach him dissolve in a cloud of aesthetic technicalities

or liquify into a saccharine torrent of praise. Crabbe lacks the glitter of style which characterizes the usual output about Goethe, but he has gathered together many engaging things about his author which he tells without any pretence or pother about form, as if he were talking to the reader from a red plush armchair at the Athenaeum. And, like animated but leisurely conversation, at times the words fit into a very pretty pattern and at other moments there is a let-down which makes his diction seem barren. Here as elsewhere one frequently feels that Robinson is attempting to apply some of Wordsworth's theories in particularizing; revealing his vast subject seriatim with a pocket flash-light, as a railway detective inspects an express train in the yard at night. The whole extends before one glowing from its own dim lights, but whatever he pauses upon stands out in full relief.

His attention is directed to details of all sorts. Goethe is made to appeal to an Englishman as a substantial man of the world and also as a person full of intriguing ideas. To accomplish this he picks out facts of political, sociological, and even religious appeal. His process of selection in itself involves critical ability which is further exercised in his comments on the work, his own assumptions to the contrary. He devotes too little space to *Werther,* for example, but he sees in its hero a type-figure representing the oppressed bourgeois and hence makes it symbolize the aspirations of the age. He uses skill in noting the better of Goethe's lyrics; on the other hand, he underrates Scott's *Lady of the Lake* and narrative poetry in general. He is full of unexpected suggestions. He has, for example, a penchant for the poetical riddle, which after centuries of disfavour, he would revive. As a true romanticist he is fired with enthusiasm for the *West-Eastern Divan,* building up background for the reader and delighting in its enigmatic quality.

He is at his best in his treatment of the dramatic works, which he discusses as closet plays, yet voicing appreciation of the moments when their theatric effectiveness shows through. Although he was more pressed for space as the series progressed, his workmanship improved as he went along. He elevated *Tasso* to the position it deserves, an innovation for England, and he recognized Shelley's genius in the poet's translation of a fragment of *Faust.*

He slighted Goethe's critical writing, failing to treat the author's outstanding ideas about literature and art. It is probable that space limitations combined with literary diffidence prevented him from undertaking a discussion of aesthetics and also from giving more of a view of Goethe's philosophy. He looked upon the poet's works as a great reservoir from which the reader could gather facts about life. An outstanding contribution of the series was its attack on exaggerated prudery. In the *Roman Elegies* and in his discussion of the work on Cellini, which, though but a translation, he thought important, he made an appeal for greater frankness in literature.

One can obtain considerable real entertainment, however, by reading the series in the light of impressionistic criticism. Crabb had a way of dwelling on the passages which he liked. The beating of the drums when Egmont goes to his death, the great scene in which Faust sits alone in his study, the charm of Marianne, Iphigenie, and Princess Leonora, the dry realism of *Reinecke Fuchs,* the lyric power of the *Erl König,* the romantic delirium of the Walpurgis-Night scene are brought vividly before the reader.

At the time Crabb was writing his résumé there were three of Goethe's major plays and one less-important work which had been made available for readers of English. Sir Walter Scott had translated *Götz*, William Taylor *Iphigenie*, and Lord Leveson Gower *Faust*. In addition there was an English version of *Clavigo* and *Stella*, and Joseph Mellish had provided a recension of *Palaeophron and Neoterpe*. Gower deliberately omitted parts of *Faust* as unworthy morally. Scott's *Götz* had a limited influence. Consequently, William Taylor's *Iphigenie* was the only work of significance which in an unqualified way had revealed Goethe's dramatic genius. Taylor considered *Iphigenie* as the greatest of the plays, belittling *Tasso, Egmont, Die Natürliche Tochter*, and many smaller things were virtually unknown.

Robinson's study presented for the first time in England the whole of Goethe's dramatic works. *Tasso* he pronounced a personal favourite which would need a Mrs. Siddons to make it more than a closet drama. To *Faust* he devoted most space, rating some of its passages as among the loftiest poems ever written. *Egmont* he ranked high, and defended vigorously against Schiller's criticism. *Götz* was given its due as an engaging early work; interest was created in *Clavigo*, though he put the play on a lower plane as bourgeoise melodrama, and he called attention to the nearly unknown *Natürliche Tochter*.

Wilhelm Meister is "the great work which holds the same preeminent place among Goethe's prose writings which *Faust* does among his poems" and "in our judgment, the single work which Germany has to exhibit in emulation of the acknowledged masterpieces of Spain, France, and our own country." He called it a "psychological or rather pedagogical novel." The work delighted him because it presented a great body of evidence regarding life from which one could draw one's own philosophical conclusions. He chose for quotation passages in which Goethe appears to break down the old idea of a struggle between the good and the bad in man and to substitute an expansive altruism, only controlled by Love. In his discussion of the *Wanderjahre* section of the novel, Robinson contributed little that was of new or of outstanding interest. He noted that in one place a single year of wandering is mentioned and later the duration of the journeying is extended over several years without explanation. Further, he objected to the way characters appear and disappear at random and mysteries are left unexplained.

His review of *Rameau's Neffe* occasioned a spirited attack on Diderot, whom he said Goethe contemplated with peculiar complacency. Diderot, according to H.C.R.,

> was one of the worst men of the age, thoroughly profligate in life and utterly unprincipled, unless a passionate, and consistent, and uniform hatred of certain opinions can be dignified with the name of principle.

Hermann und Dorothea he slighted, although he spoke of it as "one of the most original and characteristic of our author's poems." (pp. 200-04)

In the course of his treatment of *Hermann und Dorothea*, in his final article on Goethe's Works in the *Monthly Repository* for 1833 Robinson made a digression on poetics [see excerpt dated 1833]. He connected the German poetical theory with metaphysics and outlined Schiller's classification of poetry as the naïve and the sentimental. The Schlegels were mentioned as writers of the new school. He discussed the three classes of work, the epic, the lyric, and the dramatic. (p. 210)

Poetry, Crabb argued, when he was a resident in Germany, has its value in a singleness of impression and in the general exhibition of man and life presented. A poet ought not to interest, he should be cold, he should scorn to press the curiosity of the reader into his service. H.C.R. seemed to consider a poem as a mere magic-lantern device, in its form of no importance but only of value for the image it projects into the mind of the reader. (p. 211)

In the quarrel of the ancients and moderns Crabb allied himself with the ancients, granting the moderns superiority only in the experimental sciences for which he elsewhere expressed little use.

> The Immortal remains of antient Literature demonstrate that we are far below the Greeks in all that respects taste, speculative science, & heroic virtue—While we believe ourselves their superiors in the experimental sciences.

One feels that he is right to the extent that the Greeks had a somewhat clearer theory of poetry than Henry Crabb Robinson. For his application of his critical ideas presents elements of inconsistency. In regard to a large class of magnificent poems neglected by his contemporaries his doctrines and his taste approach agreement. He recognized the true greatness of Wordsworth's odes and sonnets and of works such as Goethe's *Tasso*. The pieces of literature mentioned convey an image of the heights of human virtue and the energies of human nature, each is artistically complete in itself. But Robinson fails to conform entirely to his dogma, for the authors are hardly playful and indifferent but deeply in earnest. Further, although they have a dignified simplicity of language, they are far removed from prose. Another group of significant poems violates his theory but includes his favourites. *The Prelude* has little value as a whole but is rich in passages of striking beauty. Robinson treated the work as such in his review of it in the *Christian Reformer*.

Samson Agonistes, another favourite, is conscious art. It glitters before one with its plain grandeur like a newly chiselled marble statue. It is neither simple nor prosaic, and the author has developed it with a serious purpose. In addition, when H.C.R. strictly applies his theory he overrates poems that are good enough in their way, but not of the first order. Among such were short epigrams with a whimsical twist to them, naïve poems, and formless, fanciful absurdities like Schlegel's *Paradan*, charming soap-bubble creations like *Cupid as a Landscape Painter*, and Charles Lamb's verses to a whale. He copied the poems mentioned several times in different notebooks and took the greatest delight in them. Finally, a great work of the imagination like the *Ancient Mariner* failed to impress him. When he received *Lyrical Ballads* in Germany, he praised many of Wordsworth's contributions, but said nothing of Coleridge's masterpiece. Later he expressed surprise that Lamb thought the poem to be greater than anything Wordsworth had written. (pp. 212-13)

Robinson professed to have been interested in content rather than in form, and in light of his own theory he would have hailed the *Ancient Mariner* rather than *Samson Agonistes* as a supreme achievement. H.C.R.'s own translations, *Tasso, Paradan, Drops of Nectar, Cupid as a Landscape Painter, The Wanderer, Mahomet's Song, Prometheus, Ganymede, The Bounds of Humanity, The Nightingale, Gesang Der Geister Über den Wassern, Der Fischer*, and *Anacreon's Grave* show depth and breadth of feeling, and fancy on his part. Many of them are interesting reading. Others fail, however, because he took too literally the theories of *Lyrical Ballads* and the Schlegels. In *Prometheus, Mahomet's Song,* parts of *Tasso,* and elsewhere there are enough smooth, well-cadenced lines to show that he might have turned out pleasant verse if he had gone to school to Dryden instead of to the German critics. He seems to have selected for translation pieces adapted to reading aloud, and in turning them to English appears to have made an attempt to break away from "sing-song." He was successful in oral reading, entertaining his friends by reciting hundreds of lines of poetry. He read Miss Maling *Iphigenie* and Goethe *Samson Agonistes.* Mellish's translation of *Palaeophron and Neoterpe* "is not bad—The Only thing is that *no one knows how to read it.*" His comment on Mellish held equally true of his own work. He expressed horror of "falling into a bell man's tone." In the same letter he remarked,

> Seems as if *we* have [neglected] the Art of [reading] & declamation so much that we do not know how to feel & apply the metrical capacities of our [language]: We are lazy bigots in our [Amusements] who will not seek after new pleasures.

His observations on reading aloud provide the essential factor in his appreciation of poetry. He enjoyed sweeping, well-turned lines like those of Milton and whimsical selections to cause a smile like *Cupid as a Landscape Painter.* He admired lofty sonnets on which he could linger in making people feel the outstanding idea. But he did not fully appreciate the *Ancient Mariner* because it has too much rhythm for easy oral recitation. (pp. 213-14)

> John Milton Baker, in his Henry Crabb Robinson of Bury, Jena, "The Times," and Russell Square, *George Allen & Unwin Ltd.,* 1937, 256 p.

JANET ADAM SMITH   (essay date 1938)

[*Smith interprets Robinson's diary as a revealing portrait of the author.*]

[*Henry Crabb Robinson on Books and Their Writers* gives] us excellent pictures of the outstanding writers between 1800 and 1860; they throw a good deal of light on the Wordsworth-Coleridge quarrel, and on the relations between Wordsworth's family and his French daughter ("I liked everything about her except that she called Wordsworth 'father,' which I thought indelicate"). But the most interesting picture of all is that of Crabb Robinson himself.

He was "the enlightened reader" the author dreams of. He bought new books (and paid for them), he attended lectures, he subscribed to limited editions, he contributed generously to testimonials and tombstones; when he liked a new book he went round and read extracts from it to his friends. But writers could count on him not only for a loan of five guineas or a good start to a subscription list, but also for an alert and intelligent reading of their books. His remarks were sometimes penetrating (as on Coleridge's *Aids to Reflection*—"a book which excited feelings that will probably never ripen and doubts that will remain unresolved") and sometimes commonplace; but whether he was talking of the Waverley Novels, *Uncle Tom's Cabin,* Miss Porden's *Veils* or *Endymion,* he always showed a sense of responsibility. It was worth while sorting out his impressions of each new book he read, and it was worth while re-reading a good book three or four times and over-

hauling his views on it. There was nothing priggish in his attitude, but he realized that the enjoyment of books is not a passive condition, and that only by constantly exercising his critical faculties could he keep his powers of appreciation keen. His remarks on Dickens, Hawthorne, F. D. Maurice, Emerson and Hans Andersen show that he lost none of his critical awareness with age, and at ninety-two he was still capable of reading *Essays in Criticism* with pleasure. His passion for Goethe and Wordsworth did not prevent him liking *The Woman in White* and *Hajji Baba;* but he did not confuse the enjoyment he got from a readable novel with that given by an original imaginative work. "Just good enough to engage my attention, but hardly enough to justify it" is a characteristic entry (on *Cecil, a Peer*). He went to publishers' parties, and he liked hearing what Lady Blessington earned by her pen, how many copies of Macaulay's *History* had been sold, and what the *Edinburgh Review* paid its contributors; but he knew that an interest in literature is not the same thing as a taste for literary gossip.

He was sharp to notice lapses from his own high standard of attention ("I was, however, so drowsy that I read this poem without comprehending it"), and he recognized his limitations as a reader. He had no ability for abstract reasoning; he liked an author's morality to square with his writings, and was upset to discover that the author of the excellent *Adam Bede* was Miss Evans who lived with Lewes: "Such a fact destroys all comfortable notions of right and wrong, true and false, as they make the writer quite independent of personal character." There are several entries to show that he recognized and allowed for the natural conservatism of age: "I ought to be suspicious perhaps of my own declining judgment"; "A warm eulogy of Miss Barrett's poems. I must read them, I fear, though I dread new poems." He had none of the arrogance of the I-know-what-I-like reader; he could not make head or tail of most of Blake's ideas ("he went off upon a rambling statement of a union of sexes in man as in God—an androgynous state in which I could not follow him"), but it never occurred to him to make a joke of them. If he found a poem obscure, he did not jump to the conclusion that it was the poet's fault, but read it a second and third time. *Bracebridge Hall* was "flimsy and shallow," John Wilson's *Isle of Palms* "an *attenuation* of Wordsworth's poetry," Campbell "wrote *down* to the mediocrity of the age," *Westward Ho!* "has been produced by the wish to produce a vulgar hatred of Popery."

There is much to smile at in Crabb Robinson: his annoyance when his programme was upset (on a friend's recommendation he read *The Two Noble Kinsmen* and "it filled my mind with the subject so that I could not go on with my regular reading"), his smugness ("I can relish novelty"), and his conscientious précis of novels which he knew to be worthless. But there is a great deal more to admire in the man who did not leave it to posterity to sort out Wordsworth from Samuel Rogers, or to see through Washington Irving and Thomas Campbell; who made his judgments not in the spirit of a tipster (he showed no complacency at having anticipated popular opinion), but as a man who always thought it worth while to bring all his wits to bear on every book he read. (pp. 85-6)

> Janet Adam Smith, "The Uncommon Reader," in The London Mercury, *Vol. XXXIX, No. 229, November, 1938, pp. 85-6.*

ELUNED BROWN   (essay date 1958)

[*Brown examines Robinson's response to contemporary theater and focuses on his reaction to two prominent actors of the era, J. P. Kemble and Edmund Kean.*]

The chief interest of the diary lies in Crabb Robinson's account of his friendships with leading Romantic writers and his reactions to their writings, but it is also a rich source for recreating the theatrical performances of the early nineteenth century. (p. 14)

Crabb Robinson had occasionally acted as a theatrical critic for *The Times* in 1807-8, but for most of his life he was an enthusiastic theatre-goer without a professional concern. He did not devote much attention to "getting up", although critics like Leigh Hunt were commenting intelligently at this date on theories of costume and decor. (p. 15)

Crabb Robinson's chief concern, in Romantic fashion, was with the interpretation of character and with the acting style. He often judged the playing of Shakespearian characters with his conversations with Coleridge in mind:

> Dowton looked Falstaff well, but did not give the joviality of the [character]. He was almost a querulous man his humour was constrained Nor did he display the easy cunning & self possession & address [which] Coleridge justly considers as the peculiar features of this [character].

His reactions to the two actors who dominated the early nineteenth century theatre, J. P. Kemble and Edmund Kean, are then especially interesting: he was not overwhelmed by the spectacular productions of Kemble and his knowledge of Shakespeare made him an acute critic of the interpretation of character. He disliked Kemble's style and manner, although he usually expressed himself more moderately than Hunt. In 1811, before Kean's appearance in London, Robinson condemned Kemble's style:

> A[myot] & I then went together to [Covent Garden: *Richard III*] gave me no pleasure Kembles Richard is by no means a fine piece of acting. Excepting two or three moments of energy he was tame & flat.

This charge of tameness and lack of fire was made again in 1812 when Young's performance in *Julius Caesar* was compared favourably with Kemble's whose acting was condemned as "stiff and pedantic". Even his acting in *Henry VIII* as Wolsey, one of his most successful parts, was disliked and here Sadler gives a false impression for the extract ends: "Kemble in the scene of his disgrace was greatly applauded." But Robinson continued:

> but I thot even in that scene his acting was as often absolutely bad as good, the expression being utterly mistaken & without any truth of sentiment whatever

Actors who possessed a more "natural" style were commended and contrasted with Kemble:

> Elliston a less presumptuous, but still imperfect Hostspur He has the necessary vivacity & warmth, but not the dignity of the noble Percy Perhaps after all rather better than that cold-spur Kemble.

Crabb Robinson's judgment on Kean is the more interesting because of his rejection of the artificial rhetoric of Kemble's style. His opinion hardened against Kean more than has been realised. . . . Nevertheless, he admired Kean's style and verve, although his expectations were disappointed and he particularly regretted Kean's "want of a commanding figure and powerful voice." (pp. 15-16)

[Robinson] discussed Kean's manner of playing death scenes in some detail when he wrote about Miss O'Neill's performance in *Isabella:*

> She also died well—Her last motions were a convulsive [movement] of her hands as if in search of her child after she had lost her sight in the agonies of death This trick she had learnt of Kean And now the idea is known it will become the common property of the profession Hitherto actors when they died thought they had only bodily suffering to represent—And he who [could] strain the muscles of the throat the most frightfully was the hero—Kemble & Mrs. Siddons excelled in this art But Kean has happily changed this idea altogether—he has performed dying scenes on this principle that even in the last moments the ruling passion & the personalities of the character are not to be lost in the general idea of human suffering.

But Robinson found Kean's method too realistic and horrifying and concluded:

> I incline to think after all the old system is the truest and that the man who has received a mortal wound of which he is to dye in 5 minutes is a mere animal

He then analysed some of Kean's dying scenes:

> In Macbeth when mortally wounded he poises himself for a second staggers totters & falls— He revives crawls after his sword & as his fingers reach it he dyes In Richard when his sword is beaten out of his hands he continues fighting with his fist as if he had a sword Perhaps this [would] have become Macbeth better than Richard but the latter character was the first performed and he [could] not afford to reserve his best conception for the fitter occasion

Crabb Robinson, however, became increasingly critical of Kean and by 1816 his attitude had hardened. (pp. 16-17)

It is an over-easy judgment that Kean was the actor for the Romantic writers because he overthrew the artificaly rhetorical style of Kemble. Many writers saw him as the "natural" actor, with great force of passion and energy, and with added ferocity perhaps the successor of Garrick, who in his turn overthrew the artificiality of Quin. The critics who were the leaders of the Romantic movement in journalism and *belles-lettres*—Hazlitt, Hunt and Lamb—welcomed Kean's style and rejected Kemble's even before 1814. But there were always important qualifications: Hazlitt disagreed with Kean's interpretations and found fault with his restless passionate manner when it was not part of the character but a trick of style; Hunt was disappointed when he first saw Kean because he did not find the truly spontaneous style he expected. Not many of the leaders of critical opinion were as adulatory as Keats.

Crabb Robinson's reactions show a hardening in attitude to Kean rather early. He too rejected and disliked Kemble's style and applauded rivals of Kemble's who seemed to adopt a less rhetorical style, although none of them challenged Kemble sufficiently powerfully. Crabb Robinson applauded Kean's energy, but then came to consider this as mannered as Kemble's cold rhetoric. His objection was not based on the fact that, as Hazlitt pointed out, a "natural" style is as studied as an artificial, but that he found Kean's tricks of style in the name of passion merely tricks and mannerisms incapable of expressing a wide range of emotion, and he failed to find in him the true exponent of romantic ideals. It is interesting that Robinson did not share the disappointment that many of Kean's more enthusiastic supporters felt in his King Lear. Robinson thought that Lear demanded passion alone and not "vigour and grace", so that "Kean's defects are lost in this character and become almost virtues". (pp. 17-18)

> Eluned Brown, "A Note on Henry Crabb Robinson's Reactions to J. P. Kemble and Edmund Kean," in Theatre Notebook, Vol. XIII, No. 1, Autumn, 1958, pp. 14-18.

G. SINGH (essay date 1966)

[*Singh provides a detailed survey of Robinson's knowledge of Italian literature and assesses his critical commentary on a variety of Italian dramatists, poets, historians, and other writers. According to Singh, Robinson's views of Italian literature reflect the importance of Italian culture to nineteenth-century English writers.*]

A self-made and self-educated man, if ever there was one, Crabb Robinson saw to it that his own cultural equipment and range of knowledge was by no means less rich and varied than the circle of his friends. Besides English literature, he knew German literature intimately well—so well indeed that Carlyle turned to him for advice in his own studies and translations from German,—and he made assiduous, though rather desultory, efforts most of his life to master as much as he could French, Italian and Spanish languages and literatures as well. That he himself was not gifted with creative powers did not prevent him from enjoying—and what is more, from critically assessing—the literary merits and achievements of those who were formidably superior to him. His powers of critical discrimination and evaluation, not only of books and works of literature, but also of the moral and psychological character of the people he knew, are evident from the numerous comments interspersed throughout his published and unpublished writings.

It was for example Crabb Robinson who suggested to Wordsworth that he

> could have found room for Filicaja in your happy enumeration in the prefatory Sonnet. There are several also among his, so perfect and delicious that I wish you could perform on them what you have satisfactorily done thrice for Michael Angelo. Let me set down one: 'Qual madre i figli con pietoso affetto.'

It is this remarkably wide horizon of literary and imaginative sympathies that makes Crabb Robinson differ from and criticise Landor for his "indiscriminate censure of modern Italian poetry." On certain questions Crabb Robinson's own literary reactions and critical judgments are more enlightened than even those of Blake, Wordsworth or Coleridge. For instance, he found—and quite rightly so—Blake's view of Wordsworth's "Essay Supplementary to the Preface" "very commonplace," in so far as Blake thought that the Prefaces are "very mischievous, and indirectly contrary to Wordsworth's own practice." And Crabb Robinson's explanatory-cum-critical com-

ment is that "this Preface is not the defence of his own style, in opposition to what is called *poetic diction,* but a sort of historic vindication of the *unpopular* poets."

Crabb Robinson's critical taste, however, was not always to be easily satisfied. For instance, he dismissed Macaulay's article on Machiavelli as no good: "Read the praised article in the *Edinburgh Review* on Machiavelli by Macaulay, which I thought little of;" a paper by Bagehot on Shakespeare was summarily disposed of as being "wild, paradoxical and somewhat pretentious;" and of Edgar Allan Poe's poems Crabb Robinson tells us that "The Raven" is the only poem

> that has much impressed him. He has in an essay on "The Philosophy of Composition" (foolish heading), explained the instruments of effect and thereby lessened its impression. His prose tales are all of the same kind. He is fond of imagining mysteries and puzzles, and then of solving them, and of hyperbolical and extravagant descriptions. . . . I begin to tire of Poe and wish I had not begun his writings.

All these tokens of an independent critical judgment and taste clearly show that Crabb Robinson's extraordinary success in the art of making and keeping friends—friends so bewilderingly different one from the other in character and temperament as Wordsworth and Goethe, Blake and Hazlitt, Carlyle and Landor,—was not simply a matter of personal amiability and disinterested instinct to bestow praise where it was due, but also a matter of his possessing—a fact too often lost sight of in assessing Crabb Robinson's personality—in an uncommon degree the capacity to feel intelligent sympathy with the works of art and genius, coupled with an unfailing knack of discerning them.

Now, one of the subjects Crabb Robinson made it his business to acquire as thorough a knowledge of as possible was Italian literature—a subject which, after English and German literature, seems to have attracted him most, and to the study of which he devoted a rather considerable part of his socially and even otherwise busy life. The vogue of Italy with the romantics and, later on, keen general interest in Italy's political destiny, art and culture must have strengthened his instinctive desire to widen his cultural horizons. Moreover, as a literary pilgrim across Europe—Goethe called him "a sort of missionary on behalf of English poetry"—and in fact being, though not in the same way, as Coleridge, the wandering Jew, not merely of English, but of European literature as a whole, "moving about in worlds not realized," in spite of his best efforts to realize them, Crabb Robinson was, generally speaking, not satisfied with his visit, and especially his stay in a foreign country, unless he had made friends with, or had met at least once, and if possible more than once, the authors and *letterati* of that country. Thus, during his travels to Italy—and once he was there in the company of no less a man than Wordsworth himself—Crabb Robinson met people like Niccolini, Leopardi, Giordani, Ranieri and Vieusseux. In the thirty-three volumes and odd of his diary, the three volumes concerning his travels to Italy, and the three volumes of his reminiscences—all to be found in MS in Dr. William's Library, London,—we find Crabb Robinson's views and impressions, literary opinions and judgments concerning the people he met and the books he read, set down almost with the ease, frankness and intimacy of a Pepysian diary. These views, apart from their intrinsic or historical and cultural importance, are interesting in so far as they are the views of a man with such a singularly rich culture and social and literary contacts, as Crabb Robinson. Moreover, they throw light on what a cultivated foreigner thought about the contemporary state of affairs in social and literary Italy.

From Crabb Robinson's impressions we get an interesting picture of the sort of literary repute a particular book or author enjoyed in contemporary Italy and England, the kind of literary fashions and criteria in vogue, the representative cultural currents and critical attitudes of at least two—if not three—literary generations, the romantic, the early Victorian and the mid-Victorian age. As to the very nature of his critical evaluations, whether or not they are sound according to our own criterion to-day—even though subsequent scholarship and criticism have gone far by way of corroborating them for the most part—they have almost invariably about them the same breadth and humanity, the same qualities of commonsensicalness and unacademic realism and sincerity, that one usually associates with Dr. Johnson's literary criticism. Indeed, like Dr. Johnson, Crabb Robinson usually refers the issues and problems of literary criticism to the broader and more fundamental issues of life itself—of human nature and human conduct. (pp. 404-07)

The first time Crabb Robinson began the study of Italian was somewhere in 1809, but it was not until almost twenty years later that he seriously took it up again, and spent much time and labour on it. Among the very first authors he seems to have read are Alfieri and Goldoni.... Commenting on the second volume of Alfieri's *Vita* he says:

> The worthless, indolent, ignorant, self-willed Lord exhibits himself in the second volume of his life as an incipient poet, but furnishes no means to the stranger of his writing, of judging how far he was really a poet. He was at all events . . . a late-wise as the Greeks called self-educated men. But his history also shows perhaps that to leave the mind like a soil barren for a time is less pernicious in the end than to load it with a worthless crop which may exhaust without enriching the land. If Alfieri instead of galloping over Europe, flying from himself, had set down to Law or any other pursuit in his Youth, could he then have at last risen to be a great dramatist poet? I should suppose not. Yet by reading nothing in his youth he did not become the creator of any new form of poetry. He was the servile imitator of ancient tragedy in its economy. His natural delicacy of feeling as to music facilitated his power of Versification. And being an Enthusiast in certain notions, which before the Revolution were the signs of a superior mind, he probably became a poet more to express polemically certain moral and political notions than from any genuine love for poetic conceptions, as such. This I guess only not knowing his Works. From his life I should not suspect him to have been a real poet, though I should suppose him capable to be the eloquent versifier of grand sentiments. An Italian Schiller without Schiller's profound thought and habits of study.

In a brief compass like this, and with the handicap of having read Alfieri's writings only in translation, it is quite remarkable how Crabb Robinson can lay his finger on so many essential and characteristic aspects of Alfieri's work and powers as a poet and dramatist. In this passage Crabb Robinson also dis-

plays his own capacity and attitude as a critic, even if he modestly disclaims that title. The sort of questions he raises—for instance, the relation between a poet's reading and his art, between his practical experience of life and his artistic development, and the subtle but important difference between the kind of learning and knowledge which are so essential to a poet, and the sort of "pernicious crop which may exhaust without enriching the land," that is to say the important difference between "a real poet" and an "eloquent versifier of grand sentiments," as well as the one between "moral and political notions" on the one hand, and "the poetic conceptions as such" on the other—are significantly indicative of Crabb Robinson's own critical bent of mind. The reference to Alfieri's "galloping over Europe, flying from himself," instead of setting down to the pursuit of law, has an autobiographical undertone, inasmuch as Crabb Robinson himself had to take to the study of law in order to occupy himself and thus to fill up the void he may have felt in view of the fact—and none could have realized it with such severe honesty and courage as Crabb Robinson himself—that his own literary powers were not strong enough to carry him very far in the profession of letters. What Crabb Robinson himself, however, did not recognize is that one's interest in law, when it is deliberately cultivated as an expedient to fill one's time, is itself a means of flying from oneself. Such an interest may indeed often interfere with one's "perception in matters of taste," as Crabb Robinson points out apropos of the thirteenth canto of Tasso's *Gerusalemme liberata,* when he observes that if it made "a faint impression" on him, it might well have been due to the fact "that my law study injures my perception in matters of taste." (pp. 407-09)

Crabb Robinson's interest in Alfieri's plays led him to the study of his poetry in which, he says, "I take great pleasure, tho' the verse is not liked by the Italians." This itself shows that even where a foreign literature was concerned, in which his linguistic equipment was at times far from adequate, Crabb Robinson did not hesitate to adopt an independent attitude, and he did so sometimes in the face of the prevalent official or conventional view of the matter. He preferred, for instance, Alfieri the poet to Alfieri the dramatist. . . . Crabb Robinson also read Alfieri's *Filippo* and *Misogallo.* Of the latter he says that "it better deserves the epithet of the sublimity of hatred than Lord Byron's epitaph on the King which Goethe so denominated." He also read Alfieri's treatise *Della tirannide* which was recommended to him by Landor, and he alludes to the chapter on religion as being specially admirable. Herein he finds the demonstration that "the Catholic religion is incompatible with liberty" to be perfect. Crabb Robinson's critical attitude to Catholicism comes to be seen also in his reaction to Alfieri's *Life,* where he finds the account of Alfieri's childhod "very interesting" in so far as it shows "how powerful an agent confession is in the education of Catholic children—and how easy but dangerous it is to punish by exciting shame." It seems that it was religion together with political despotism and the lack of many first-rate contemporary writers, or, as he put it, "no living poets but Manzoni, Leopardi and Niccolini"—that landed Crabb Robinson more or less in the same conflicting attitude towards Italy as the one which was Landor's or the Brownings' or that of the English men of letters in general who had at all any interest in Italy, namely, admiration of Italian as a language, and of Italy as a country—with its natural scenery, landscape and all that—and a scarcely concealed "disesteem of Italians" and contemporary Italian literature. Another curious trait in Crabb Robinson's attitude towards Italian was that he, as he himself said, liked "the expatriated Italians better than the Italians at home."

Other Italian playwrights Crabb Robinson studied are Goldoni, Maffei, Niccolini and Gozzi. Niccolini was a personal friend of his as well as of Landor. It is worth noting that even though Crabb Robinson was impressed by the literary knowledge and scholarship of Landor as well as by his creative talent—Landor, concerning whom Ezra Pound rightly wonders if England has ever produced an all-round man of letters of equal stature—and though he listened to him with interested curiosity, he was not prepared to accept Landor's opinions on many things, including Italian literature, both past and contemporary, which he felt he had better judge for himself. It is the extremely unfavourable and negative character of some of Landor's literary views that makes Crabb Robinson record them in his diary. But the act of recording itself does not imply that Crabb Robinson shared or approved of those views. Indeed, they are recorded with an implicit tone of disapproval, if anything. (pp. 410-12)

In Crabb Robinson's own judgement neither Goldoni nor Niccolini qualifies for particularly high praise. The popularity of Goldoni, whom Crabb Robinson primarily studied with a view to learning Italian (since Goldoni is considered to be a dramatist "admirably suited to that object"), is taken as an indication of "the fallen state of the drama in Italy, as that of his superior in the same style, Kotzebue, had lately been doing in Germany. But the plays—properly sentimental comedies—fairly exhibited the national condition and feeling in the last generation." If, however, Goldoni was still listened to in Italy, it was, Crabb Robinson observes, "for want of a better author." Crabb Robinson mentions *Pamela* and *Locandiera* as the two plays by Goldoni he read: the latter is regarded as a "piece of character" and something "that might be adapted to our stage."

Niccolini receives a closer attention and a more sympathetic treatment. Not that Crabb Robinson, because of his personal friendship with the author, is blind to Niccolini's faults as a dramatist. Of Niccolini's play *Nabucco*, for instance, he says:

> It is, like all his tragedies, declamatory, without passion or character. Niccolini made no secret of his liberal opinions; but he was an anxious, nervous, timid man, unfit for action. His tragedy of *The Sicilian Vespers*, though made as little political as possible, being a domesitc tragedy, could not but contain passages capable of dangerous application. . . . Niccolini's dramatic works all belong to the Classical school. He is a stylist, and very hostile to the Romantic school.

(p. 412)

In Crabb Robinson's criticism of Niccolini's dramas we have the criticism of one with a practical grasp of the psychological problems and requirements of a stage capable of satisfying the demands of a contemporary theatre-goer. (p. 413)

As to Crabb Robinson's reading in Italian non-dramatic literature, its range is much wider, including both major and minor writers, poets and historians ancient as well as modern. In fact, it was poetry, more than any other form of literature, that he had the greatest and most natural predilection for. Dante was for him, and for the German philosophers he met in the university town of Erlangen, one of the "triple glory of modern poetry," the other two being Shakespeare and Goethe. In fact, in spite of Landor's observation—and Crabb Robinson had considerable regard for Landor, although he found him "a man of very decided tastes, and his dislikings, personal and literary . . . expressed with offensive force''—that in Dante there was only about a seventieth part good, in Ariosto a sixth and in Tasso not a line worth anything, Crabb Robinson made at least the study of Dante and Ariosto just as important a part of his Italian studies and culture as the rest of Italian literature. His diary contains entries regarding his readings in the particular cantos of the *Divine Comedy* together with his brief comments. For instance: "Read the fifth canto of *Paradiso* . . . no part of the *Inferno* or *Purgatorio* more charming"—"Read the 11th delightful canto of *Purgatorio*"—"The rest of the morning I devoted to a Canto of the *Paradiso* . . . the 10th very difficult but beautifully written." On the whole—and here again Crabb Robinson asserts his independence of judgment in matters of taste—he preferred *Paradiso* to *Inferno* or *Purgatorio*.

It is, however, while criticising Boccaccio for what he considered to be an ill-written and ill-conceived life of Dante, that Crabb Robinson pays tribute to the author of the *Divina Commedia*. Boccaccio had merely subjected Dante to a superstitious interpretation; Crabb Robinson criticises such an approach:

> Read today a disagreeable book, only because it was the life, by a great man, of one still greater—by Boccaccio, of Dante. I did not expect, in the voluminous *conteur*, an extraordinary degree of superstition, and fantastic hunting after mystical qualities in his hero. He relates that Dante's mother dreamt she lay in of a peacock, and Boccaccio finds in the peacock four remarkable properties, the great qualities of the *Divina Commedia*: namely, the tail has a hundred eyes, and the poem a hundred cantos; its ugly feet indicate the mean *lingua volgare;* its screaming voice the frightful menaces of the *Inferno* and *Purgatorio;* and the odoriferous and incorruptible flesh the divine truths of the poem.

(pp. 414-15)

Although, together with Goldoni Tasso was among the very first writers Crabb Robinson studied with a view to acquiring "a little of this delightful language," and even though he kept reading Tasso off and on since then, he was not particularly interested in Tasso's poetry. In fact, when Landor expressed his opinion that only a seventieth part of Dante was good and no more than a sixth of Ariosto, Crabb Robinson reports to have interposed with: "But little of Tasso"—to which Landor replied: "Not a line worth anything—yes one line". Thus so far as Tasso was concerned, Crabb Robinson may well have agreed this time with Landor. This does not, of course, mean that Crabb Robinson had not made an attempt to read Tasso. For instance what he says about Wordsworth's attitude to Tasso's tomb—an attitude in such marked contrast with that of Leopardi—shows that both Wordsworth and Crabb Robinson were familiar with Tasso's poetry:

> Wordsworth is no hunter after sentimental relics. He professes to be regardless of places that have merely a connection with a great man, unless they had also an influence on his works. Hence he cares nothing for the burying-place of Tasso, but he has a deep interest in Vaucluse. The distinction is founded on just views and real, not affected sympathy . . .

On the other hand, Ariosto interested Crabb Robinson a good deal more, and there is a more detailed and more critical comment on him. For instance, while praising the tale of Ariodante in the fifth canto of *Orlando Furioso,* "who is willing to fight on behalf of the mistress whom he thinks guilty," as "charming," Crabb Robinson observes that "the refinement of generosity is above the level of Ariosto's age and country." While noting some of the "most beautiful and also of the coarsest passages in *Orlando Furioso,*" and how the sufferings of Angelica are most feelingly related, Crabb Robinson justly wonders why all that should have been "polluted by the disgusting scene with the hermit." But the nineteenth canto is considered to be "in Ariosto's style," since Ariosto's "gaiety becomes him better than his military spirit." . . . "Certainly one of the most splendid and popular works of poetic genius," *Orlando Furioso* was also one of the few long poems (Goethe's *Faust,* Wordsworth's *Prelude,* and Byron's *Don Juan* being, in varying degrees, others) which Crabb Robinson really enjoyed reading. And for him the enjoyment of the inherent beauties of what he read—whether those beauties appertained to style, story, incidents or plot—was just as important as the moral or philosophical meaning. His praise and defence of *Orlando Furioso* and of the critical spirit and attitude behind that praise should be evaluated in the light of his comments on Goethe's new *Faust:*

> On my walk read Goethe's new *Faust.* . . . It is a most pregnant and equally delightful and disgusting performance. A masterpiece of genius before which I bow with humility. And the beauties of which are so ravishing that I am ashamed and afraid to allow myself to feel offended by its moral and aesthetic deformities.

There is no better proof of Crabb Robinson's critically sound discrimination than his arguments in favour of those very extravagances, both moral and aesthetic, in Ariosto, which he condemns in Goethe, or his distinction between one work of poetic genius, which is at once splendid and popular, and another which is more splendid than popular and which presupposes the working of a more powerful poetic genius, and consequently the possession of a higher degree of imaginative and critical maturity in the reader. (pp. 416-18)

In addition to these major classics of Italian poetry, Crabb Robinson had also read Michelangelo's *Rime* and Poliziano's poetry. Gabriello Chiabrera, Salvatore Rosa, Vincenzo de Filicaia and Alessandro Guidi. He knew these poets—and especially Chiabrera and Filicaia—well enough to be able to communicate his interest to Wordsworth and to pronounce upon the merit of Wordsworth's translations from these poets. (p. 419)

Among the later poets, Crabb Robinson knew the works of Alfieri, Monti, Metastasio, Parini, Foscolo, Niccolini, Berchet, Pindemonte, Manzoni and Leopardi. It is in the relative evaluation of some of these poets that Crabb Robinson is seen upholding views which are no longer tenable today, and which ill-accord with the general tenour of Crabb Robinson's views on literature. Part of the explanation may be that so far as contemporary Italian literature is concerned Crabb Robinson's views may have been influenced by the prevalent opinion and vogue of those poets whom he so much admires, but whose poetry is at best good second class poetry. A glaring example of this lack of critical vigilance, or a faulty critical response is Crabb Robinson's high opinion of Monti as a poet, his preference of Monti's poetry to Leopardi's, and his taking Niccolini seriously as a poet. (p. 420)

Parini is another poet Crabb Robinson read—and read him both as a poet and as a prose writer. Running over the prose works by Parini—such as *Discorso nell'aprimento della nuova cattedra di belle lettere* and *Programmi di belle arti*—Crabb Robinson justly evaluated them as "a sort of elementary work of young people," and the author as "the echo of public opinion." For the sake of information, or, as he says, so that "the list will serve to suggest enquiries," he copied out all the names of the 16th century writers whom Parini classified as the Italian classics. Much of what was on Parini's list was gradually mastered by Crabb Robinson in the course of his studies. It was again through Parini—and his prose work *Delle cagioni del presente decadimento*—that he came to know that "after the death of the three great men of the 14th century—Dante, Petrarch and Boccaccio—there a deep decline of (Italian) letters."

But it is doubtful if Crabb Robinson really understood the nature or the causes of this decline, for not only does he speak of Chiabrera and Felicaia as poets of the first rank, but he is equally enthusiastic about the first-rate quality of Monti's and Niccolini's poetry. "Spent two hours lounging over the contents of Monti's works and also the first Canto of *Basvillian*"—so runs one of the entries in his diary concerning Monti. . . . In spite of his rather low opinion of Monti as a man, Crabb Robinson was able to do justice to him as a writer. The beginning of *Mascheroniana* is, Crabb Robinson points out, "among the most pleasant of modern poetry," and of "that very delightful poem by Monti the 'Bellezza dell'universo,'" he says that it is "only too delicate and soft. Surely there can be nothing more so in Metastasio." Monti's *Dialoghi* he found to be "a very clever book, but I am too poor an Italian scholar or too little alive to the delicacies of Italian humour to derive pleasure from the second dialogue which I read today." Of Monti's prose note on the satiric poets Crabb Robinson says that it is "a capital piece of criticism, resembling the critical prefaces of Dryden."

Not only did Crabb Robinson find Leopardi inferior to Monti, but also to Foscolo. Of the *Sepolcri,* we are told that there are in it "some striking thoughts, but the poem on the whole difficult and no great pleasure in it." And as to Foscolo's admiration for Dante—an admiration not unmingled with patriotic sentiment—Crabb Robinson says that Foscolo "would rather suffer martyrdom than acknowledge Milton to be the equal of Dante."

Crabb Robinson's literary estimates are frequently blended with reflections and comments on the social and political conditions of contemporary Italy, to which he ascribed, in part, the kind of defects or shortcomings he found in the writer's work or personal character. . . . [Crabb Robinson] shows himself to be fully imbued with the moral-cum-political liberalism that was so powerful an influence in the age of Wordsworth, Hazlitt and Byron.

He undoubtedly considered social and political justice and liberty not only infinitely superior to any literary or artistic achievement, but also indispensable requisites for that very achievement. His comments on Botta's *History of Italy,* for instance, illustrate Crabb Robinson's line of critical thought:

> An eloquent book which for its style has obtained great reputation. It is too declamatory and has more rhetorical than historical worth. The writer is reproached for abandoning his principles. I acquit him of this charge. He declares against public deliberative bodies for Italy, and I incline to think with sufficient reason. Whilst he inveighs with great indignation against

the cruelties of the old government, the oppression of the Papal power and also the iniquities practised by Buonaparte and the French, I do not see why he is to be censured. His imitation of the ancients and imaginary speeches is a piece of old fashioned pedantry, but these speeches after all chiefly interested me.

Among the classics of Italian prose however, it is Machiavelli who arouses Crabb Robinson's deepest interest and curiosity. Inasmuch as he almost always combined his interest in a literary work with his interest in the author's personality—and that is one reason why Crabb Robinson's remarks on literature, even when they are ostensibly unsound, are never pedantically arid or abstruse—the more controversial and complicated an author's character was, the more fascinating and worth study, as a rule, he found his work to be. No author, thus, could have lent himself so irresistibly to Crabb Robinson's scholarly and literary curiosity and psychological interest as the author of *Il principe*. It was during his stay at Florence in 1830 that Crabb Robinson happened to read it for the first time, and took occasion to discuss it with his friend Niccolini and other Italian friends. He had, however, his own personal and independent reaction to record in his diary:

> Now I have finished the *Principe,* I must say that I am unable to agree with those who assert that Machiavelli wrote his book in order to open the eyes of the people as to the nature of the kingly government as Samuel did to the Jews when they lusted after the king. I should be glad to believe it if I could. It is unpleasant to contemplate the union of great talents with an utter want of principles, but have we not witnessed this often, and particularly in France. Men may have an acute perception of the evils of tyranny, hypocricy and bigotry, and yet have no objection to be the instrument when they can profit by it. Diderot would have been a tool of the court, if they would have trusted him probably. Of Machiavelli's personal lust and character I know nothing. . . . It seems to me probable that Machiavelli wrote his *Principe* for the private eye only of Lorenzo to whom he dedicated it, in the hope that he should be taken into the confidential service of the Prince.

In spite of his avowed lack of knowledge of the personal life and character of Machiavelli—and it was not long after that he managed to read the *Life of Machiavelli* as he happens to note in 1835, but this does not seem to have made him alter his opinion of Machiavelli's character—Crabb Robinson's appraisal of his character and of the underlying motives of his thought and conduct is remarkably sound. But even before he had finished reading the *Principe,* he happened to know, generally speaking, enough about the main drift of Machiavelli's masterpiece to be able to judge and rather dismiss "the praised article in the *Edinburgh Review* on Machiavelli by Macaulay, which I thought little of." In his own analysis of the moral character and influence of the *Principe* Crabb Robinson combines, in a witty and convincing way, past and contemporary history, moral reflections and historical assessment, commonsense and a sharply logical mind. . . . (pp. 421-25)

It seems that as a prose writer Crabb Robinson set store by Machiavelli more than by Boccaccio. And yet, of course, he knew his Boccaccio—and that is not simply as the biographer of Dante but as the first prose writer in Italian and as the author of *Decameron.* As early as 1803 when he saw the performance of Lessing's *Nathan der Weise* at Weimer his judgment of the performance included a knowledgeable reference to Boccaccio. "But the work has no dramatic worth. All one recollects of it is the tale of the rings, which was borrowed from Boccaccio." Similarly after reading Keats's *Pot of Basil*—"a pathetic tale delightfully told"—Crabb Robinson went on to the source in Boccaccio: "I afterwards read the story in Boccaccio—each in its way excellent." However, it seems that Boccaccio did not satisfy him according to his expectation. After finishing the first volume of Boccaccio he tells straightforwardly that this "celebrated work does not equal my expectation." (pp. 425-26)

Besides Boccaccio and Machiavelli, other Italian prose writers whom Crabb Robinson studied are Guicciardini, Vico, Beccaria, Cuoco, Caro, Filangieri, Pecchio, Manzoni, Giordani, Botta. He approached literature as he approached other forms of human contact and experience, friendships, travels, discussions etc. as so many ways of understanding the total pattern—social, cultural and artistic—of a country's present and past life. And what is more, not being a specialist in a particular field, with a particular bias and self-imposed limitations, Crabb Robinson's was a truly open and catholic mind, and in virtue of the sort of culture he possessed and the way he attained to it he may be regarded as one of the founders of what is now known as liberal education.

And just as in the case of contemporary English and German literature, so also in the case of Italian literature and culture Crabb Robinson read as many books as he could, but at the same time, he also met and discussed matters with as many people as it was possible to do. He knew practically all the Italian exiles resident in London who had any cultural or literary pretensions at all—starting from the most distinguished of them all—Antonio Panizzi, Carlo Pepoli, Mazzini—to other less important ones, or "minor notabilities" as he called them, like Carlo Arrivabene, Gioacchino Prati, Evasio Radice, Luigi Angeloni, Antonio Gallenga, Giuseppe Pecchio, Fortunato Prandi etc. And in Italy itself he met a good many of all the important writers living, including Ranieri, Giordani and Poerio, besides those already mentioned.

From Crabb Robinson's observations and reflections on Italy and Italian literature of his time what emerges is an account—an authentic and first-hand literary chronicle—of the age—and of the part Italian literature, history and culture—both past and contemporary—played in the liberal education of an English writer, poet or man of letters in the 19th century. (pp. 426-27)

> *G. Singh, "Henry Crabb Robinson on Italian Literature," in Italica, Vol. XLIII, No. 4, December, 1966, pp. 404-28.*

ADDITIONAL BIBLIOGRAPHY

Behler, Diana I. "Henry Crabb Robinson as a Mediator of Early German Romanticism to England." *Arcadia* 12, No. 2 (1977): 117-55.
    Analyzes Robinson's role in introducing German literature to English readers.

Benson, Adolph B. "Fourteen Unpublished Letters by Henry Crabb Robinson: A Chapter in His Appreciation of Goethe." *PMLA* XXXI, n.s. XXIV, No. 3 (September 1916): 395-420.

Discusses correspondence by Robinson in which he expresses his critical response to Goethe.

Blunden, Edmund. "A Pattern for Intellectuals." *The London Mercury* XVII, No. 100 (February 1928): 413-17.
    Recounts Robinson's friendship with Wordsworth.

Brewer, Edward V. "A Pre-Carlylean Critic and Translator of Jean Paul Richter." *The Germanic Review* IV, No. 3 (July 1929): 248-59.
    States that Robinson, rather than Thomas De Quincey, first translated the works of the German author Jean Paul into English.

Gilbert, Mary E. "Two Little-Known References to Henry Crabb Robinson." *The Modern Language Review* XXXIII, No. 2 (April 1938): 268-71.
    A discussion of two references to Robinson in works by the German authors Bettina von Arnim and Clemens Th. Perthes.

Hudson, Derek. Introduction to *The Diary of Henry Crabb Robinson: An Abridgement,* by Henry Crabb Robinson, edited by Derek Hudson, pp. vii-xix. London: Oxford University Press, 1967.
    Details Robinson's upbringing and career.

King, R. W. "Crabb Robinson's Opinion of Shelley." *The Review of English Studies* IV, No. 14 (April 1928): 167-72.
    Considers Robinson's views towards the Romantic poet Percy Bysshe Shelley.

Larg, D. G. "Henry Crabb Robinson and Madame de Staël." *The Review of English Studies* V, No. 17 (January 1929): 22-35.
    Examines the relationship between Robinson and the French author Madame de Staël, whom he befriended in Germany.

Morley, Christopher. "'No Crabb, No Christmas.'" In his *Letters of Askance,* pp. 293-301. Philadelphia: J. B. Lippincott, 1939.
    An overview of Robinson's life and interests as presented in the *Diary.*

Morley, Edith J. "Carlyle in the *Diary, Reminiscences, and Correspondence of Henry Crabb Robinson*." *The London Mercury* VI, No. 36 (October 1922): 607-18.
    Notes the relationship between the critic Thomas Carlyle and Robinson as an indication of "Carlyle's growing preoccupation with German literature."

Norman, F. *Henry Crabb Robinson and Goethe: Parts I and II.* Publications of the English Goethe Society, edited by J. G. Robertson, n.s. vols. VI, VIII. 1930. Reprint. London: Wm. Dawson & Sons, 1966.
    An account of Robinson's relationship with Goethe as outlined in the *Diary.*

Pearson, Hesketh. "A Hazlitt-Hater." *The English Review* LX (May 1935): 619-20.
    Assesses Robinson's character by examining his sentiments toward the other literary figures with whom he associated.

Richardson, Joanna. "Henry Crabb Robinson, 1775-1867." *History Today* XXIX (August 1979): 538-41.
    A biographical study that includes a number of anecdotes about Robinson's contemporaries.

Sackville West, Edward. "Literary Gossip." *The Spectator* 154, No. 5570 (29 March 1935): 538.
    Analyzes the merits of Robinson's *Diary.*

Wellens, Oskar. "Henry Crabb Robinson: Reviewer of Wordsworth, Coleridge, and Byron in the *Critical Review,* Some New Attributions." *Bulletin of Research in the Humanities* 84, No. 1 (Spring 1981): 98-120.
    Outlines Robinson's contributions to the *Critical Review.*

Williams, Marjorie. "Crabb Robinson and Others." *The Contemporary Review* CLXXXVI, No. 1068 (December 1954): 357-61.
    Discusses Robinson's active social life within the literary community of his era.

August Wilhelm von Schlegel

1767-1845

German critic, translator, and poet.

A prominent figure in the German Romantic movement, Schlegel distinguished himself as an influential exponent of Romantic aesthetic theory and as an illustrious translator of William Shakespeare's plays. As a critic, Schlegel was instrumental in advancing the philosophy formulated by his brother Friedrich von Schlegel and other members of the Romantic circle at Jena. By systematizing their ideas and eloquently applying them to a variety of national literatures in such works as *Ueber dramatische Kunst und Litteratur* (*A Course of Lectures on Dramatic Art and Literature*), he played a key role in disseminating the principles of Romanticism throughout Europe and England. Schlegel was equally influential as the author of a popular and critically acclaimed translation of Shakespeare's dramatic works.

Schlegel was the son of Johann Adolf Schlegel, a noted hymn writer and fabulist, and the nephew of the dramatist and critic Johann Elias Schlegel. He was educated at Göttingen University, studying under the poet Gottfried August Bürger and the classical philologist Christian Gottlob Heyne, and subsequently worked in Amsterdam as a private tutor. In approximately 1796, the year of his marriage to the intellectually gifted Caroline Böhmer, Schlegel moved to Jena, where he was appointed to a professorship in literature and aesthetics and became part of a group of Romantic writers that included his brother Friedrich, Ludwig Tieck, and Novalis. In 1798, the brothers established *Das Athenäum,* a periodical disseminating Romantic thought, and August Wilhelm also made extensive contributions to such periodicals as the *Allgemeine Literatur-Zeitung* and Johann Christoph Friedrich von Schiller's *Die Horen.* Schlegel oversaw the publication of the majority of his Shakespeare translations at this time as well. With some initial assistance from his wife, he issued translations of sixteen Shakespeare dramas between 1797 and 1801; he published his seventeenth and final translation in 1810, the remaining plays in the Shakespearean canon being subsequently translated by Wolf Heinrich Baudissin and Dorothea Tieck.

The Jena Romantic circle dissolved in about 1800, as did Schlegel's marriage to Caroline, who had fallen in love with the philosopher Friedrich Wilhelm Joseph von Schelling. Shortly thereafter, Schlegel delivered a series of lectures in Berlin (published posthumously as *A. W. Schlegels Vorlesungen über schöne Litteratur und Kunst*) in which he summarized the doctrines that had previously been only fragmentarily articulated by Friedrich and the Jena Romantic group. Noted for their deft presentation of difficult concepts, the lectures thus helped to clarify and popularize Romantic aesthetic theory, enhancing Schlegel's position as a spokesperson for the Romantic movement as well. In 1804, he became the traveling companion of the French writer Madame de Staël, and it was during the course of their extensive European tour that he delivered in Vienna his *Lectures on Dramatic Art and Literature.* Published in German in 1809-11 and soon translated into many languages, this Romantic survey of ancient and modern European drama obtained wide circulation and became the cornerstone of Schlegel's influence and reputation as a critic. His fame was far-ranging and probably contributed to his appointment as sec-

retary to the crown prince of Sweden in 1813. Schlegel subsequently rejoined de Staël, staying with her until her death in 1817, and was named professor of art and literature at the University of Bonn the following year. He retained this post for the rest of his life; despite experiencing the disappointment of another failed marriage, he distinguished himself professionally in his remaining years by pioneering in the field of Oriental philology.

Schlegel was one of the most erudite critics of his age. Although commentators agree that his learning overwhelmed his artistry in such creative works as his *Gedichte* and the Classical tragedy *Ion,* Schlegel's scholarship contributed greatly to the distinction and appeal of his criticism. Schlegel's most representative and influential critical production was *Lectures on Dramatic Art and Literature.* Integrating his extensive knowledge with Romantic criticism, it comprised an account of the development of Western drama in which he elaborated such key concepts in Romantic aesthetic theory as the distinction between mechanical and organic form and the dichotomy between Classical and Romantic art. Schlegel discriminated between artificial formal attributes and innate form determined by the content of the work itself; his contention that theological differences between ancient and modern cultures had caused significant formal discrepancies between their respective art forms provided the basis for his division of art into Classical and Romantic categories. Although he did not necessarily originate these and other Romantic ideas in his dramatic criticism, Schlegel was quite successful in elucidating and applying them. In particular, he used the concepts of organic form and Romantic drama in defending the artistic integrity of Shakespeare's plays. The dramatist had hitherto been considered a child of nature whose works lacked conscious artistic form, and Schlegel's criticism played a crucial role in improving Shakespeare's critical reputation in Europe and England.

As set forth in his *Lectures on Dramatic Art and Literature, Vorlesungen über schöne Litteratur und Kunst,* and other works, Schlegel's theories concerning the nature and development of Western literature sometimes had a limiting impact on his criticism. As many commentators have noted, the rigid division that he posited between Classical and Romantic drama prevented him from appreciating formal eclecticism in general and such "hybrid" literatures as French Neoclassical drama in particular. Indeed, his treatment of French dramatists was so severe that Hugh Swinton Legaré claimed that Schlegel hoped to destroy Gallic drama through his criticism. This antipathy appears to be the most flagrant example of what William Taylor described as a predilection for *a priori* criticism that occasionally led Schlegel to "blame or praise [writers] *en masse.*" Nonetheless, he is often admired for producing well-informed commentary and for invoking a definite set of literary standards in his critical writings.

In addition to his critical acumen, Schlegel was an extraordinarily gifted translator who brought his superior linguistic skills to bear on his German translations of Dante Alighieri, Pedro Calderón de la Barca, and other authors. It was as a translator of Shakespeare, however, that he exercised his greatest influence on German literature. Critics generally agree that by providing verse versions of the plays that featured exquisitely rendered, line-for-line translations approximating the sense and rhythm of Shakespeare's originals, Schlegel improved immensely on the prose texts of previous translators, giving Germany a sound basis for the appreciation and study of the English dramatist's works. As many commentators have observed, such intellectual luminaries as Gotthold Ephraim Lessing, Johann Gottfried von Herder, and Johann Wolfgang von Goethe had prepared for the reception of Shakespeare in Germany during the eighteenth century; Schlegel's translation served as both a culmination of their efforts and a stimulus to the subsequent acceptance of Shakespeare's works into the very core of modern German culture and aesthetics.

While advances in linguistic and textual scholarship have made Schlegel's Shakespeare translations vulnerable to obsolescence, modern commentators regard them as his greatest achievement. This contrasts with his earlier reputation, for during his lifetime Schlegel was recognized primarily for his criticism. As Goethe and other contemporaries remarked, however, Schlegel could be haughty and harsh, exercising with Friedrich a kind of "critical club-law" that kindled resentment among his peers. They in turn insinuated that he was an opportunist who had overreached himself in his egoistic zeal for recognition, and they also occasionally ridiculed his notorious vanity and love of finery. This reaction was especially evident late in Schlegel's life, when Heinrich Heine described him as an "incredibly ridiculous personage" and George Henry Lewes disparaged him as a "coxcomb" and "foolish petit-maître." Lewes sounded a more telling note concerning Schlegel's reputation when he asserted that Schlegel had merely reaped the

glory of intellectual battles that had been initiated and won by Lessing. Similar doubts about Schlegel's originality have persisted into the twentieth century: although rarely censorious, modern critics have generally focused on Schlegel's role as the popularizer rather than as the progenitor of Romantic aesthetic theory. As René Wellek has pointed out, however, Schlegel's historical importance in popularizing Romantic theory was enormous, standing with his Shakespeare translations as his lasting legacy to German literature.

PRINCIPAL WORKS

"Etwas über William Shakspeare bei Gelegenheit *Wilhelm Meisters*" (essay) 1796; published in periodical *Die Horen*
"Ueber Shakspeares *Romeo und Julia*" (essay) 1797; published in periodical *Die Horen*
Shakspeare's dramatische Werke. 9 vols. [translator] (dramas) 1797-1810
Gedichte (poetry) 1800
Ion [first publication] (drama) 1803
Blumensträusse italiänischer, spanischer, und portugiesischer Poesie [translator] (poetry) 1804
Schauspiele von Don P. Calderon de la Barca [translator] (dramas) 1809; published in *Spanisches Theater*
Ueber dramatische Kunst und Litteratur. 2 vols. (lectures) 1809-11
  [*A Course of Lectures on Dramatic Art and Literature,* 1815]
August Wilhelm von Schlegel's sämmtliche Werke. 12 vols. (lectures, essays, poetry, and translations) 1846-47
A. W. Schlegels Vorlesungen über schöne Litteratur und Kunst (lectures) 1884
Briefe von und an August Wilhelm Schlegel. 2 vols. (letters) 1930
A. W. Schlegel's Lectures on German Literature from Gottsched to Goethe: Given at the University of Bonn and Taken Down by George Toynbee in 1833 (lectures) 1944
Kritische Schriften und Briefe. 7 vols. (essays and lectures) 1962

MADAME DE STAËL-HOLSTEIN (essay date 1810)

[*De Staël, a French critic and novelist, is credited with inculcating the theories of Romanticism into French literary and political thought. Schlegel had long been engaged as her traveling companion and literary adviser when, in 1810, she published* De l'Allemagne, *a work that introduced German Romanticism in France and inspired new modes of thought and expression in that country. As the following excerpt indicates, de Staël highly praised Schlegel's erudition, insight, and enthusiasm as a critic in her book but censured him and his brother for their prejudiced view of French literature.*]

[As] his knowledge of literature is uncommon even in Germany, [W. Schlegel] is led continually to application by the pleasure which he finds in comparing different languages and different poems with each other; so general a point of view ought almost to be considered as infallible, if partiality did not sometimes impair it; but this partiality is not of an arbitrary kind, and I will point out both the progress and aim of it;

nevertheless, as there are subjects in which it is not perceived, it is of those that I shall first speak.

W. Schlegel has given a course of dramatic literature at Vienna, which comprises every thing remarkable that has been composed for the theatre from the time of the Grecians to our own days: it is not a barren nomenclature of the works of the various authors; he seizes the spirit of their different sorts of literature with all the imagination of a poet; we are sensible that to produce such consequences extraordinary studies are required; but learning is not perceived in this work except by his perfect knowledge of the *chefs-d'oeuvre* of composition. In a few pages we reap the fruit of the labor of a whole life; every opinion formed by the author, every epithet given to the writers of whom he speaks, is beautiful and just, concise and animated. W. Schlegel has found the art of treating the finest pieces of poetry as so many wonders of nature, and of painting them in lively colors which do not injure the justness of the outline. . . . (p. 92)

An analysis of the principles on which both tragedy and comedy are founded, is treated in W. Schlegel's course of dramatic literature with much depth of philosophy; this kind of merit is often found among the German writers; but Schlegel has no equal in the art of inspiring enthusiasm for the great geniuses he admires; in general he shows himself attached to a simple taste, sometimes bordering on rusticity, but he deviates from his usual opinions in favor of the opinions of the inhabitants of the South. Their *jeux de mots* and their *concetti* are not the objects of his censure; he detests the affectation which owes its existence to the spirit of society, but that which is excited by the luxury of imagination pleases him in poetry as the profusion of colors and perfumes would do in nature. Schlegel, after having acquired a great reputation by his translation of Shakspeare, became equally enamored of Calderon, but with a very different sort of attachment from that with which Shakspeare had inspired him; for while the English author is deep and gloomy in his knowledge of the human heart, the Spanish poet gives himself up with pleasure and delight to the beauty of life, to the sincerity of faith, and to all the brilliancy of those virtues which derive their coloring from the sunshine of the soul.

I was at Vienna when W. Schlegel gave his public course of lectures. I expected only good sense and instruction where the object was only to convey information; I was astonished to hear a critic as eloquent as an orator, and who, far from falling upon defects, which are the eternal food of mean and little jealousy, sought only the means of reviving a creative genius. (pp. 92-3)

The Schlegels have been strongly accused of not doing justice to French literature; there are, however, no writers who have spoken with more enthusiasm of the genius of our troubadours, and of that French chivalry which was unequalled in Europe, when it united in the highest degree, spirit and loyalty, grace and frankness, courage and gayety, the most affecting simplicity with the most ingenuous candor; but the German critics affirm that those distinguished traits of the French character were effaced during the course of the reign of Louis XIV; literature, they say, in ages which are called classical, loses in originality what it gains in correctness; they have attacked our poets, particularly, in various ways, and with great strength of argument. The general spirit of those critics is the same with that of Rousseau in his letter against French music. They think they discover in many of our tragedies that kind of pompous affectation, of which Rousseau accuses Lully and Rameau, and

they affirm that the same taste which gives the preference to Coypel and Boucher in painting, and to the Chevalier Bernini in sculpture, forbids in poetry that rapturous ardor which alone renders it a divine enjoyment; in short, they are tempted to apply to our manner of conceiving and of loving the fine arts, the verses so frequently quoted from Corneille:

> "Othon à la princesse a fait un compliment,
> Plus un homme d'esprit qu'en véritable amant."

W. Schlegel pays due homage, however, to most of our great authors; but what he chiefly endeavors to prove, is, that from the middle of the seventeenth century, a constrained and affected manner has prevailed throughout Europe, and that this prevalence has made us lose those bold flights of genius which animated both writers and artists in the revival of literature. In the pictures and bas-reliefs where Louis XIV is sometimes represented as Jupiter, and sometimes as Hercules, he is naked, or clothed only with the skin of a lion, but always with a great wig on his head. The writers of the new school tell us that this great wig may be applied to the physiognomy of the fine arts in the seventeenth century: an affected sort of politeness, derived from factitious greatness, is always to be discovered in them.

It is interesting to examine the subject in this point of view, in spite of the innumerable objections which may be opposed to it; it is however certain that these German critics have succeeded in the object aimed at, as, of all writers since Lessing, they have most essentially contributed to discredit the imitation of French literature in Germany; but from the fear of adopting French taste, they have not sufficiently improved that of their own country, and have often rejected just and striking observations, merely because they had before been made by our writers.

They know not how to make a book in Germany, and scarcely ever adopt that methodical order which classes ideas in the mind of the reader; it is not, therefore, because the French are impatient, but because their judgment is just and accurate, that this defect is so tiresome to them; in German poetry fictions are not delineated with those strong and precise outlines which insure the effect, and the uncertainty of the imagination corresponds to the obscurity of the thought. In short, if taste be found wanting in those strange and vulgar pleasantries which constitute what is called *comic* in some of their works, it is not because they are natural, but because the affectation of energy is at least as ridiculous as that of gracefulness. "I am making myself lively," said a German as he jumped out of window: when we attempt to make ourselves any thing, we are nothing: we should have recourse to the good taste of the French to secure us from the excessive exaggeration of some German authors, as on the other hand we should apply to the solidity and depth of the Germans to guard us against the dogmatic frivolity of some men in France.

Different nations ought to serve as guides to each other, and all would do wrong to deprive themselves of the information they may mutually receive and impart. There is something very singular in the difference which subsists between nations; the climate, the aspect of nature, the language, the government, and above all, the events of history, which have in themselves powers more extraordinary than all the others united, all combine to produce those diversities; and no man, however superior he may be, can guess at that which is naturally developed in the mind of him who inhabits another soil and breathes another air: we should do well then, in all foreign countries, to welcome foreign thoughts and foreign sentiments, for hospitality of this sort makes the fortune of him who exercises it. (pp. 97-9)

> *Madame de Staël-Holstein, ''Of the Literary Treasures of Germany, and of Its Most Renowned Critics, A. W. and F. Schlegel,'' in her* Germany, *Vol. II, edited by O. W. Wight, H. W. Derby, 1861, pp. 89-99.*

[SIR JAMES MACKINTOSH]   (essay date 1813)

> [*Mackintosh questions the soundness of the Schlegel brothers' advocacy of national originality in literature, noting the danger of artificial primitivism and commending the use of universal aesthetic principles. The critic's comments were originally published as part of a review of Mme. de Staël's* De l'Allemagne *in the October 1813 issue of the* Edinburgh Review.]

The general tendency of the literary system of [William and Frederick Schlegel], is towards the manners, poetry, and religion of the middle age. They have reached the extreme point towards which the general sentiment of Europe has been impelled by the calamities of a philosophical revolution, and the various fortunes of a twenty years' universal war. They are peculiarly adverse to French literature; which, since the age of Louis XIV has, in their opinion, weakened the primitive principles common to all Christendom, as well as devested the poetry of each people of its originality and character. Their system is exaggerated and exclusive. In pursuit of national originality, they lose sight of the primary and universal beauties of art. The imitation of our own antiquities may be as artificial as the copy of a foreign literature. Nothing is less natural than a modern antique.

In a comprehensive system of literature, there is sufficient place for the irregular works of sublime genius, and for the faultless models of classical taste. From age to age, the multitude fluctuates between various, and sometimes opposite fashions of literary activity. They are not all of equal value: But the philosophical critic discovers and admires the common principles of beauty, from which they all derive their power over human nature. (p. 301)

> [*Sir James Mackintosh*], ''De l'Allemagne, par Mad. de Stael,'' *in* The Analectic Magazine, *n.s. Vol. III, April 1814, pp. 284-308.*

JOHANN GOTTLIEB FICHTE [AS REPORTED BY K. A. VARNHAGEN VON ENSE]   (conversation date 1814?)

> [*In the following remarks Fichte, an influential nineteenth-century German philosopher, suggests that jealousy informs the Schlegels' criticism of great contemporary authors. In the absence of information concerning the exact date of his comments, which were made in a conversation reported by the writer Karl August Varnhagen von Ense, Fichte's remarks are here dated 1814, the year of his death.*]

I would not have you pin your faith to these Schlegels. I know them well. The elder brother wants depth, and the younger clearness. One good thing they both have—that is, hatred of mediocrity; but they have also both a great jealousy of the highest excellence; and, therefore, where they can neither be great themselves nor deny greatness in others, they, out of sheer desperation, fall into an outrageous strain of eulogizing. Thus they have bepraised Goethe, and thus they have bepraised me.

> *Johann Gottlieb Fichte [as reported by K. A. Varnhagen von Ense], in an extract from ''Frederick Schlegel'' in* Blackwood's Edinburgh Magazine, *Vol. LIV, No. CCCXXXV, September, 1843, p. 311.*

[WILLIAM HAZLITT]   (essay date 1816)

> [*Hazlitt, an English critic and journalist, is considered one of the most important commentators of the Romantic age. He is best known for his descriptive criticism in which he stressed that no motives beyond judgment and analysis are necessary on the part of the critic. Though he wrote on many subjects, Hazlitt's most important critical achievements are his Romantic interpretation of characters from Shakespeare's plays, influenced by Schlegel, and his revival of interest in such Elizabethan dramatists as John Webster, Thomas Haywood, and Thomas Dekker. In the following excerpt, Hazlitt assesses Schlegel's* Lectures on Dramatic Art and Literature, *presenting a sympathetic account of the critic's pivotal distinction between Classical and Romantic art and discussing aspects of his commentary on Greek and European drama and dramatists. Hazlitt's remarks on Schlegel's Shakespeare criticism are detailed and largely complimentary: while he charges him with excessive partisanship, Hazlitt also credits Schlegel with bringing superior knowledge and discernment to bear on his criticism of the dramatist's works.*]

[In his *Lectures on Dramatic Literature,* Schlegel unfolds] that which is the *nucleus* of the prevailing system of German criticism, and the foundation of his whole work, namely, the essential distinction between the peculiar spirit of the modern or *romantic* style of art, and the antique or *classical*. There is in this part of the work a singular mixture of learning, acuteness and mysticism. We have certain profound suggestions and distant openings to the light; but, every now and then, we are suddenly left in the dark, and obliged to grope our way by ourselves. We cannot promise to find a clue out of the labyrinth; but we will at least attempt it. The most obvious distinction between the two styles, the classical and the romantic, is, that the one is conversant with objects that are grand or beautiful in themselves, or in consequence of obvious and universal associations; the other, with those that are interesting only by the force of circumstances and imagination. A Grecian temple, for instance, is a classical object: it is beautiful in itself, and excites immediate admiration. But the ruins of a Gothic castle have no beauty or symmetry to attract the eye; and yet excite a more powerful and romantic interest from the ideas with which they are habitually associated. If, in addition to this, we are told that this is Macbeth's castle, the scene of the murder of Duncan, the interest will be instantly heightened to a sort of pleasing horror. The classical idea or form of any thing, it may also be observed, remains always the same, and suggests nearly the same impressions; but the associations of ideas belonging to the romantic character, may vary infinitely, and take in the whole range of nature and accident. (p. 70)

Schlegel somewhere compares the Furies of Æschylus to the Witches of Shakespear—we think without much reason. Perhaps Shakespear has surrounded the Weird Sisters with associations as terrible, and even more mysterious, strange, and fantastic than the Furies of Æschylus; but the traditionary beings themselves are not so petrific. These are of marble,—their look alone must blast the beholder;—those are of air, bubbles; and though 'so withered and so wild in their attire,' it is their spells alone which are fatal. They owe their power to 'metaphysical aid:' but the others contain all that is dreadful in their corporal figures. In this we see the distinct spirit of the classical and the romantic mythology. The serpents that twine round the head of the Furies are not to be trifled with, though they implied no preternatural power: The bearded Witches in *Macbeth* are [not] in themselves grotesque and ludicrous, except as this strange deviation from nature staggers our imagination, and leads us to expect and to believe in all incredible things. They appal the faculties by what they say or do;—the others are intolerable, even to sight.

Our author is right in affirming, that the true way to understand the plays of Sophocles and Æschylus, is to study them before the groupes of the Niobe or the Laocoon. If we can succeed in explaining this analogy, we shall have solved nearly the whole difficulty. For it is certain, that there are exactly the same powers of mind displayed in the poetry of the Greeks as in their statues. Their poetry is exactly what their sculptors might have written. Both are exquisite imitations of nature; the one in marble, the other in words. It is evident, that the Greek poets had the same perfect idea of the subjects they described, as the Greek sculptors had of the objects they represented; and they give as much of this absolute truth of imitation, as can be given by words. But, in this direct and simple imitation of nature, as in describing the form of a beautiful woman, the poet is greatly inferior to the sculptor: It is in the power of illustration, in comparing it to other things, and suggesting other ideas of beauty or love, that he has an entirely new source of imagination opened to him; and of this power, the moderns have made at least a bolder and more frequent use than the ancients. (p. 71)

The description of the soldiers going to battle in Shakespear, 'all plumed like estriches, like eagles newly bathed, wanton as goats, wild as young bulls,' is too bold, figurative, and profuse of dazzling images, for the mild, equable tone of classical poetry, which never loses sight of the object in the illustration. The ideas of the ancients were too exact and definite, too much attached to the material form or vehicle in which they were conveyed, to admit of those rapid combinations, those unrestrained flights of fancy, which, glancing from heaven to earth, unite the most opposite extremes, and draw the happiest illustrations from things the most remote. The two principles of imitation and imagination indeed, are not only distinct, but almost opposite. For the imagination is that power which represents objects, not as they are, but as they are moulded according to our fancies and feelings. Let an object be presented to the senses in a state of agitation and fear—and the imagination will magnify the object, and convert it into whatever is most proper to encourage the fear. It is the same in all other cases in which poetry speaks the language of the imagination. This language is not the less true to nature because it is false in point of fact; but so much the more true and natural, if it conveys the impression which the object under the influence of passion makes on the mind. (pp. 71-2)

The great difference, then, which we find between the classical and the romantic style, between ancient and modern poetry, is, that the one more frequently describes things as they are interesting in themselves,—the other for the sake of the associations of ideas connected with them; that the one dwells more on the immediate impressions of objects on the senses—the other on the ideas which they suggest to the imagination. The one is the poetry of form, the other of effect. The one gives only what is necessarily implied in the subject; the other all that can possibly arise out of it. The one seeks to identify the imitation with an external object,—clings to it,—is inseparable from it,—is either that or nothing; the other seeks to identify the original impression with whatever else, within the

range of thought or feeling, can strengthen, relieve, adorn or elevate it. Hence the severity and simplicity of the Greek tragedy, which excluded every thing foreign or unnecessary to the subject. Hence the unities: for, in order to identify the imitation as much as possible with the reality, and leave nothing to mere imagination, it was necessary to give the same coherence and consistency to the different parts of a story, as to the different limbs of a statue. Hence the beauty and grandeur of their materials; for, deriving their power over the mind from the truth of the imitation, it was necessary that the subject which they made choice of, and from which they could not depart, should be in itself grand and beautiful. Hence the perfection of their execution; which consisted in giving the utmost harmony, delicacy, and refinement to the details of a given subject. Now, the characteristic excellence of the moderns is the reverse of all this. As, according to our author, the poetry of the Greeks is the same as their sculpture; so, he says, our own more nearly resembles painting,—where the artist can relieve and throw back his figures at pleasure,—use a greater variety of contrasts,—and where light and shade, like the colours of fancy, are reflected on the different objects. The Muse of classical poetry should be represented as a beautiful naked figure: the Muse of modern poetry should be represented clothed, and with wings. The first has the advantage in point of form; the last in colour and motion. (pp. 72-3)

The object of modern tragedy is to represent the soul utterly subdued as it were, or at least convulsed and overthrown by passion or misfortune. That of the ancients was to show how the greatest crimes could be perpetrated with the least remorse, and the greatest calamities borne with the least emotion. Firmness of purpose, and calmness of sentiment, are their leading characteristics. Their heroes and heroines act and suffer as if they were always in the presence of a higher power, or as if human life itself were a religious ceremony, performed in honour of the Gods and of the State. The mind is not shaken to its centre; the whole being is not crushed or broken down. Contradictory motives are not accumulated; the utmost force of imagination and passion is not exhausted to overcome the repugnance of the will to crime; the contrast and combination of outward accidents are not called in to overwhelm the mind with the whole weight of unexpected calamity. The dire conflict of the feelings, the desperate struggle with fortune, are seldom there. All is conducted with a fatal composure. All is prepared and submitted to with inflexible constancy, as if Nature were only an instrument in the hands of Fate.

It is for deviating from this ideal standard, and for a nearer approximation to the frailty of human passion, that our author falls foul of Euripides without mercy. There is a great deal of affectation and mysticism in what he says on this subject. Allowing that the excellences of Euripides are not the same as those of Æschylus and Sophocles, or even that they are excellences of an inferior order, yet it does not follow that they are defects. The luxuriance and effeminacy with which he reproaches the style of Euripides might have been defects in those writers; but they are essential parts of his system. In fact, as Æschylus differs from Sophocles in giving greater scope to the impulses of the imagination, so Euripides differs from him in giving greater indulgence to the feelings of the heart. The heart is the seat of pure affection,—of involuntary emotion,—of feelings brooding over and nourished by themselves. In the dramas of Sophocles, there is no want of these feelings; but they are suppressed or suspended by the constant operation of the senses and the will. Beneath the rigid muscles by which the heart is there braced, there is no room left for those bursts of uncontrolable feeling, which dissolve it in tenderness, or plunge it into the deepest woe. In the heroic tragedy, no one dies of a broken heart,—scarcely a sigh is heaved, or a tear shed. Euripides has relaxed considerably from this extreme self-possession; and it is on that account that our critic cannot forgive him. The death of Alcestes alone might have disarmed his severity. (pp. 84-5)

M. Schlegel decidedly prefers the *Hippolytus* of Euripides to the *Phaedra* of Racine. His reasons he gives in another work, which we have not seen; but we are not at a loss to guess at them. His taste for poetry is just the reverse of the popular: He has a horror of whatever obtrudes itself violently on the notice, or tells at first sight; and is only disposed to admire those retired and recondite beauties which hide themselves from all but the eye of deep discernment. He relishes most those qualities in an author which require the greatest sagacity in the critic to find them out,—as none but connoisseurs are fond of the taste of olives. We shall say nothing here of the choice of the subject; but such as it is, Racine has met it more fully and directly: Euripides exhibits it, for the most part, in the background. The *Hippolytus* is a dramatic fragment in which the principal events are given in a narrative form. The additions which Racine has chiefly borrowed from Seneca to fill up the outline, are, we think, unquestionable improvements. The declaration of love, to which our author particularly objects, is, however, much more gross and unqualified in Racine than in Seneca. The modern additions to the *Iphigenia in Aulis,* by Racine, as the love between Achilles and Iphigenia, and the jealousy of Eriphile, certainly destroy the propriety of costume, as M. Schlegel has observed, without heightening the tragic interest. In other respects, the French play is little more than an elegant, flowing, and somewhat diffuse paraphrase of the Greek. (pp. 85-6)

Aristophanes, of course, is an immense favourite with Schlegel—though it requires all his ingenuity to gloss over and allegorize his extravagance and indecency. . . .

The comedies of Aristophanes, we confess, put the *archaism* of our taste, and the soundness of our classic faith to a most severe test. The great difficulty is not so much to understand their meaning, as to comprehend their species—to know to what possible class to assign them—of what nondescript productions of nature or art they are to be considered as anomalies. According to Schlegel, who might be styled the Œdipus of criticism, they are the perfection of *the old comedy*. There is much virtue, we are aware, in that appellation: But to us, we confess, they appear to be neither comedies, nor farces, nor satires—but monstrous allegorical pantomimes—enormous practical jokes—far-fetched puns, represented by ponderous machinery, which staggers the imagination at its first appearance, and breaks down before it has answered its purpose. They show, in a more striking point of view than any thing else, the extreme subtlety of understanding of the ancients, and their appetite for the gross, the material, and the sensible. Compared with Aristophanes, Rabelais himself is plain and literal. (p. 87)

The account which is given of the *old,* the *middle,* and the *new comedy,* is very learned and dogmatical. The different styles and authors rise in value with the critic, in proportion as he knows nothing of them. He likes that, which some old commentator has praised, better than what he has read himself; and that still better, which neither he himself, nor any one else, has read. Diphilus, Philemon, Apollodorus, Menander, Sophron, and the Sicilian Epicharmus, whose works are lost, are pro-

digiously great men; and the author 'tries conclusions infinite' respecting their different possible merits. On the contrary, Terence is only half a Menander, and Plautus a coarse buffoon. In spite, however, of this fastidiousness, he cannot deny the elegant humanity of the one, nor the strong native humour of the other. (p. 88)

M. Schlegel very ably exposes the incongruities which have arisen from engrafting modern style and sentiments on mythological and classical subjects in the French writers.

> In *Phaedra,* . . . this princess is to be declared regent for her son till he comes of age, after the supposed death of Theseus. How could this be compatible with the relations of the Grecian women of that day?—It brings us down to the times of a Cleopatra.—When the way of thinking of two nations is so totally opposite, why will they torment themselves with attempts to fashion a subject, formed on the manners of the one to suit the manners of the other?—How unlike the Achilles in Racine's *Iphigenia* to the Achilles of Homer! The gallantry ascribed to him is not merely a sin against Homer, but it renders the whole story improbable. Are human sacrifices conceivable among a people, whose chiefs and heroes are so susceptible of the most tender feelings?

> Corneille was in the best way in the world when he brought his *Cid* on the stage; a story of the middle ages, which belonged to a kindred people; a story characterized by chivalrous love and honour, and in which the principal characters are not even of princely rank. Had this example been followed, a number of prejudices respecting tragical ceremony would of themselves have disappeared; tragedy, from its greater truth, from deriving its motives from a way of thinking still current and intelligible, would have been less foreign to the heart; the quality of the objects would of themselves have turned them from the stiff observation of the rules of the ancients, which they did not understand; in one word, the French tragedy would have become national and truly romantic. But I know not what unfortunate star had the ascendant. Notwithstanding the extraordinary success of his *Cid,* Corneille did not go one step farther; and the attempt which he made had no imitators.
> (pp. 91-2)

Our author prefers Racine to Corneille, and even seems to think Voltaire more natural: But he has exhausted all that can be said of French tragedy in his account of Corneille; and all that he adds upon Racine and Voltaire, is only a modification of the same general principles. He has been able to give no general character of either, as distinct from the original founder of the French dramatic school; Corneille had more pomp, Racine more tenderness; Voltaire aimed at a stronger effect: But the essential qualities are the same in all of them; the style is always French, as much as the language in which they write.

> It has been often remarked, that, in French tragedy, the poet is always too easily seen through the discourses of the different personages; that he communicates to them his own presence of

mind; his cool reflection on their situation; and his desire to shine upon all occasions. When we accurately examine the most of their tragical speeches, we shall find that they are seldom such as would be delivered by persons, speaking or acting by themselves without any restraint; we shall generally discover in them something which betrays a reference, more or less perceptible, to the spectator. Rhetoric, and rhetoric in a court dress, prevails but too much in many French tragedies, especially in those of Corneille, instead of the suggestions of a noble, but simple and artless nature: Racine and Voltaire have approximated much nearer to the true conception of a mind carried away by its sufferings. Whenever the tragic hero is able to express his pain in antitheses and ingenious allusions, we may safely dispense with our pity. This sort of conventional dignity is, as it were, a coat of mail, to prevent the blow from reaching the inward parts. On account of their retaining this festal pomp, in situations where the most complete self-forgetfulness would be natural, Schiller has wittily enough compared the heroes in French tragedy to the kings in old copperplates, who are seen lying in bed with their mantle, crown, and sceptre.

(p. 93)

M. Schlegel speaks highly of Racine's comedy, *Les Plaideurs;* and thinks that if he had cultivated his talents for comedy, he would have proved a formidable rival of Moliere. He might very probably have succeeded in imitating the long speeches which Moliere too often imitated from Racine; but nothing can (we think) be more unlike, than the real genius of the two writers. In fact, Moliere is almost as much an English as a French author,—quite a *barbare,* in all in which he particularly excels. He was unquestionably one of the greatest comic geniuses that ever lived; a man of infinite wit, gaiety, and invention,—full of life, laughter, and observation. But it cannot be denied that his plays are in general mere farces, without nature, refinement of character, or common probability. Several of them could not be carried on for a moment without a perfect collusion between the parties to wink at impossibilities, and act in defiance of all common sense. (p. 94)

The French critics contend, we think without reason, that their own [style of drama] is exclusively good, and all others barbarous.

Not so our author. If Shakespear never found a thorough partisan before, he has found one now. We have not room for half of his praise. He defends him at all points. His puns, his conceits, his anachronisms, his broad allusions, all go, not indeed for nothing, but for so many beauties. They are not something to be excused by the age, or atoned for by other qualities; but they are worthy of all acceptation in themselves. This we do not think it necessary to say. It is no part of our poetical creed, that genius can do no wrong. As the French show their allegiance to their kings by crying *Quand meme!*—so we think we show our respect for Shakespear by loving him in spite of his faults. Take the whole of these faults, throw them into one scale, heap them up double, and then double that, and we will throw into the opposite scale single excellences, single characters, or even single passages, that shall outweigh them all! All his faults have not prevented him from

showing as much knowledge of human nature, in all possible shapes, as is to be found in all other poets put together; and that, we conceive, is quite enough for one writer. (pp. 98-9)

[Schlegel's] observations on Shakespear's language and versification . . . are excellent. We cannot, however, agree with the author in thinking his rhyme superior to Spenser's: his excellence is confined to his blank verse; and in that he is unrivalled by any dramatic writer. Milton's alone is equally fine in its way. The objection to Shakespear's mixed metaphors is not here fairly got over. They give us no pain from long custom. They have, in fact, become idioms in the language. We take the meaning and effect of a well known passage entire, and no more stop to scan and spell out the particular words and phrases than the syllables of which they are composed. If our critic's general observations on Shakespear are excellent, he has shown still greater acuteness and knowledge of his author in those which he makes on the particular plays. They ought, in future, to be annexed to every edition of Shakespear, to correct the errors of preceding critics. In his analysis of the historical plays,—of those founded on the Roman history,—of the romantic comedies, and the fanciful productions of Shakespear, such as, the *Midsummer Night's Dream,* the *Tempest,* &c. he has shown the most thorough insight into the spirit of the poet. His contrast between Ariel and Caliban; the one made up of all that is gross and earthly, the other of all that is airy and refined, 'ethereal mould, sky-tinctured,'—is equally happy and profound. He does not, however, confound Caliban with the coarseness of common low life. He says of him with perfect truth—'Caliban is malicious, cowardly, false and base in his inclinations; and yet he is essentially different from the vulgar knaves of a civilized world, as they are occasionally portrayed by Shakespear. He is rude, but not vulgar. He never falls into the prosaical and low familiarity of his drunken associates, for he is a poetical being in his way; he always, too, speaks in verse. But he has picked up every thing dissonant and thorny in language, of which he has composed his vocabulary.'

In his account of *Cymbeline* and other plays, he has done justice to the sweetness of Shakespear's female characters, and refuted the idle assertion made by a critic, who was also a poet and a man of genius, that

stronger Shakespear felt for man alone.

Who, indeed, in recalling the names of Imogen, of Miranda, of Juliet, of Desdemona, of Ophelia and Perdita, does not feel that Shakespear has expressed the very perfection of the feminine character, existing only for others, and leaning for support on the strength of its affections? The only objection to his female characters is, that he has not made them masculine. They are indeed the very reverse of ordinary tragedy-queens. In speaking of *Romeo and Juliet,* he says, 'It was reserved for Shakespear to unite purity of heart, and the glow of imagination, sweetness and dignity of manners, and passionate violence, in one ideal picture.' The character of Juliet was not to be mistaken by our author. It is one of perfect unconsciousness. It has nothing forward, nothing coy, nothing affected, nothing coquettish about it:—It is a pure effusion of nature. (pp. 102-04)

In treating of the four principal tragedies, *Othello, Macbeth, Hamlet* and *Lear,* he goes deeper into the poetry and philosophy of those plays than any of the commentators. (p. 104)

The remarks on the doubtful pieces of Shakespear are most liable to objection. We cannot agree, for instance, that Titus

Andronicus is in the spirit of Lear, because in his dotage he mistakes a fly which he has killed for his black enemy the Moor. *Thomas Lord Cromwell,* and *Sir John Oldcastle* which he praises highly, are very different. *Pericles, prince of Tyre,* is not much to our taste. There is one fine scene in it, where Marina rouses the prince from his lethargy, by the proofs of her being his daughter. Yet this is not like Shakespear. *The Yorkshire Tragedy* is very good; but decidedly in the manner of Heywood. The account given by Schlegel, of the contemporaries and immediate successors of Shakespear, is good, though it might have been better. That of Ben Jonson is particularly happy. He says, that he described not characters, but 'humours,' that is, particular modes of expression, dress and behaviour in fashion at the time, which have since become obsolete, and the imitation of them dry and unintelligible. . . . He is also very successful in his character of the plays of Beaumont and Fletcher. They describe the passions at their height, not in their progress—the extremes, not the gradations of feeling. Their plays, however, have great power and great beauty. The *Faithful Shepherdess* is the origin of Milton's *Comus. Rule a Wife and Have a Wife* is one of the very best comedies that ever was written; and holds, to this day, undisputed possession of the stage. Yet, as our critic observes, there is in the general tone of their writings a certain crudeness and precocity, a heat, a violence of fermentation, a disposition to carry every thing to excess, which is not pleasant. Their plays are very much what young noblemen of genius might be supposed to write in the heyday of youthful blood, the sunshine of fortune, and all the petulance of self-opinion. They have completely anticipated the German paradoxes. Schlegel has no mercy on the writers of the age of Charles II. He compares Dryden himself to 'a man walking upon stilts in a morass.' He justly prefers Otway to Rowe; but we think he is wrong in supposing, that if Otway had lived longer he would have done better. His plays are only the ebullitions of a fine, enthusiastic, sanguine temperament: and his genius would no more have improved with age, than the beauty of his person. Of our comic writers, Congreve, Wycherley, Vanburgh, &c. M. Schlegel speaks very contemptuously and superficially. It is plain that he knows nothing about them, or he would not prefer Farquahar to all the rest. If, after our earlier dramatists, we have any class of writers who are excellent, it is our comic writers.

We cannot go into our author's account of the Spanish drama. The principal names in it are Cervantes, Calderon, and Lope de Vega. Neither can we agree in the praises which he lavishes on the dramatic productions of these authors. They are too flowery, lyrical, and descriptive. They are pastorals, not tragedies. They have warmth; but they want vigour.

Our author may be supposed to be at home in German literature; but his doctrines appear to us to be more questionable there, than upon any other subject. What the German dramatists really excel in, is the production of effect: but this is the very thing which their fastidious countryman most despises and abhors. They really excel all others in mere effect; and there is no nation that can excel all others in more than one thing. *Werter* is, in our opinion, the best of all Goethe's works; but because it is the most popular, our author takes an opportunity to express his contempt for it. *Count Egmont,* which is here spoken highly of, seems to us a most insipid and preposterous composition. The effect of the pathos which is said to lie concealed in it, is utterly lost upon us. *Nathan the Wise,* by Lessing, is also a great favourite of Schlegel; because it is unintelligible except to the wise. As the French plays are composed of a tissue of common-places, the German plays of this stamp are a tissue

of paradoxes, which have no foundation in nature or common opinion,—the pure offspring of the author's fantastic brain. (pp. 104-06)

> [*William Hazlitt*], *"Schlegel on the Drama," in* The Edinburgh Review, *Vol. XXVI, No. LI, February, 1816, pp. 67-107.*

[WILLIAM TAYLOR]   (essay date 1816)

> [*In this review of* Lectures on Dramatic Art and Literature, *Taylor acknowledges the epochal nature of Schlegel's work, praising the eloquence and erudition that he displays in systematizing Romantic drama criticism, but questions the wisdom of his "a priori" depreciation of domestic tragedy and sentimental drama. Taylor's remarks were originally published in the October 1816 issue of the* Monthly Review.]

We shall run over the lectures [in *A Course of Lectures on Dramatic Art and Literature*], one by one: but, trusting to public perusal for a general dissemination of their contents, we shall not attempt a minute analysis, or a complete epitome; rather endeavouring to dwell on the questionable sentences of award, or portions of theory. Disposed to rationality more than to mysticism, we are apt to doubt when we do not understand; and some platonic flights of style, or system, in M. Schlegel, not being easily reduced to perspicuous definition, these we mistrust. We are not fond, moreover, of *a priori* criticism, which makes the guage first, and then tries the work by it. We think that it is possible to admire Shakspeare without deifying Calderon, although M. Schlegel's plan of panegyric applies equally to both; and our feelings allot a higher value to Euripides, to Diderot, and to Kotzebue, than these writers can be permitted to claim under a scheme of appreciation, which assigns to domestic tragedy and sentimental drama the lowest rank in art. *"Tous les genres sont bons, hors le genre ennuyeux,"* said Voltaire, liberally and justly; and, of course, we should praise or blame by the head, and not by the class. Greater power may be displayed by one artist in a secondary line of art, than by another in the first. (p. 477)

The ancients, and their imitators the Italians and French, are described [by M. Schlegel] as constituting the *classical* school of art, while the Spaniards, the English, and the Germans, belong to the *romantic*. The latter school appears to be the more natural of the two, and to include less of the local and conventional in its manner: since the *Sakontala,* a Hindoo drama, composed in complete disconnection with either the ancient or the modern literature of Europe, approaches much nearer in structure to a play of Shakspeare than to a play of Sophocles; and so does *The Orphan of China,* in its native form. If we remember rightly, it was Herder who, by his rhapsody on Shakspeare, first gave to the German critics the luminous idea, that the Gothic or romantic drama should be considered as a peculiar form of art, having laws and conditions of its own; and that it is not less beautiful, and is far more convenient and comprehensive, than the Greek plan of drama, which could not have included in one whole the representation of any great event, such as the usurpation of Macbeth, the conspiracy of Venice, or the revolution of Swisserland under William Tell. With a chorus of furies, Aeschylus could leap over the bounds of space and time in his *Orestes,* and yet observe sufficient probability: but, in general, the supposed presence of an unchanged chorus, during the entire action, confined nearly to one spot and to one day the incidents that were introduced into a Greek tragedy. Hence a scene of family-distress is commonly the utmost attainment of the classical poet; and a cluster of independent plays, a trilogy, was requisite to exhibit on the Athenian stage the events of a single Gothic drama.

The phenomena of nature, says M. Schlegel in his second lecture, flow into one another, and do not possess an independent existence; a work of art, on the contrary, must be a connected whole, and complete within itself. Certainly, great skill is requisite, in the dramatic poet, neatly to detach an historic incident from its causes and effects, so as to give it a beginning, a middle, and an end; and to round it gracefully into a plot separate and entire, and progressively interesting. The historical plays of Shakspeare do not always attain this perfection: sometimes the action wants unity, as in *Henry IV.,* from the admixture of extraneous characters and incidents; sometimes it wants wholeness, as in [*Henry IV., Part 2*], there being no proper catastrophe, or termination of the story; and sometimes it wants progressive interests, as in *Henry VIII.,* and is prolonged beyond the period which decided the fate of the principal personages. Too close an imitation of nature, or adherence to fact, has occasioned these faults.

We have also an explanation of the division of dramatic art into tragic and comic pieces, and the greater severity of the ancients is asserted in keeping each kind unmixed. It may be suspected, however, that we possess castrated Alexandrian editions of the ancient dramatists. Aristarchus is known to have struck out many idle passages from Homer; the managers of an Alexandrian theatre may have rejected many from Aeschylus; and we perhaps inherit only what the pruning knife of the critic has spared. In the *Prometheus,* the entrance of the crazy old maid Io must have been intended for comic effect: clad in a cow-hide, with horns, and in avowed search of a sublime husband, she must, with her mops and moes, have excited derision; and the chorus satirically tell her, that it would have been better to marry an artisan than to speculate on climbing the bed of a divinity. . . . The *Persians* of Aeschylus are throughout written in the mock-heroic spirit of Chrononhotonthologos. We are mortified to see critic after critic, and even M. Schlegel himself, mistaking comedy for tragedy. He professes to treat with contempt the translation of Father Brumoy, but he slips into the same blunder.

Lecture iii. is an excellent composition, describing the structure of the Greek stage with luminous clearness and learned research. . . . [It] deserves the attentive consultation of every classical scholar. Barthélémy is censured for comparing the ancient tragedy with the modern opera: since the delivery of the Greek actors resembled chant rather than recitative, and had principally for its object to render audible to vast crowds the words of the poet; while the chorus sang in unison, accompanied with simple instruments, rather intended to indicate and regulate the rhythm than to overpower the voices. The use of masks is ingeniously but not satisfactorily defended by M. Schlegel; it occasions a loss of pathetic expression and change of feeling, for which no physiognomical adaptation can be an indemnity: but for impassive beings, such as ghosts, gods, and the witches in *Macbeth,* masks might still perhaps be used with good effect.

M. Schlegel observes that the conception of the Greek tragedy was ideal; and that it aimed at heroic delineation, at a colossal majesty, and a grace beyond nature. This is true of Aeschylus, less true of Sophocles, and not at all of Euripides;—it is true of French tragedy generally, of Young among the English, and of Schiller among the Germans. What is the proper inference? Merely that the heroic is a praiseworthy branch of art; and that to excel in it has in all civilized ages and countries founded

permanent reputation. M. Schlegel, however, seems inclined to place the essence of art in this elevation more than human; on which principle Euripides, Shakspeare, and Goethe, the poets who are truest to nature and most various in their delineations, must be pushed back into the inferior ranks. Grandeur of manner, in the arts of design as in the dramatic art, is accomplished by the omission of detail, but truth of nature by the insertion of it: hence some incompatibility must always subsist between the ideal and the true; between the beautiful and the characteristic; between the heroic and the natural. Why not award equal degrees of praise to equal degrees of excellence in either department? (pp. 478-80)]

M. Schlegel's extensive commentary [in the fourth lecture on Aeschylus's trilogy of Agamemnon, the *Choephorae,* and the *Eumenides*] is an admirable critical diatribe; original, classical, and just. . . .

The panegyric of Sophocles, which is pronounced in this lecture, is truly beautiful, and more strictly just than that of Aeschylus. (p. 483)

The fifth lecture treats of Euripides, the favourite poet of Socrates and of Milton. Yet his dramas are valued low by M. Schlegel, who considers them as indicating the decline of art. Certainly, they have not the uniform loftiness of those of Aeschylus, nor the uniform beauty of those of Sophocles: but they include greater variety of character, of situation, and of emotion; they have more of nature, if they have less of stage-trick; and they abound with sentiments of a penetrating wisdom. . . . If Aeschylus be the Schiller, and Sophocles be the Racine, Euripides is the Shakspeare, of the Greeks; and it is inconsistent in M. Schlegel to assign to Euripides so low and to Shakspeare so high a rank. Neither of these writers pursues an ideal beauty, but both are distinguished for truth of nature. They do not aim, like Aeschylus and Schiller, at a grandeur beyond reality, at a majesty more than human; they are not to be classed among the heroic or ennobling poets: they do not, like Sophocles and Racine, subdue within the limits of grace and beauty every expression of feeling or passion: nor are they to be classed among the idealizing or embellishing poets: but it is for copying the impressive phaenomena of human kind with fidelity, for catching a striking likeness of men and events in a narrow compass, for giving an inherent vitality to their personages, and animating each with a soul of its own, that Euripides and Shakspeare must be applauded. If they too often sink into vulgarity, their bursts of feeling and of passion gush into the heart and thrill to the marrow; and they are omnipotent over the present impression, whether it be grave or gay.

In the sixth lecture, the author treats of comedy, which seems to have begun in the parody of tragedy. A high and (we think) a well-founded panegyric of Aristophanes is here undertaken; whose resources of fancy gave a variety to Greek comedy, of which the modern stage is in want of the return. (pp. 484-86)

The seventh lecture relates to the middle comedy of the Greeks, which more nearly resembles that of the modern world than the early comedy of Aristophanes. We here meet with an ingenious application of Xenophon's doctrine of two souls to criticism:

> There are other moral defects, which are beheld by their possessor with a certain degree of satisfaction, and which he has even resolved not to remedy, but to cherish and preserve. Of this kind is all that, without reference to selfish pretensions, or hostile inclinations, merely

originates in the preponderance of sensuality. This may, without doubt, be united to a high degree of intellect, and when such a person applies his mental powers to the consideration of his own character, laughs at himself, confesses his failings to others, or endeavours to reconcile them to them, by the droll manner in which they are mentioned, we have then an instance of the self-conscious comic. This kind always supposes a certain inward quality of character, and the superior half, which rallies and laughs at the other, has from its tone and its employment a near affinity to the comic poet himself. He occasionally delivers over his functions entirely to this representative, while he allows him studiously to overcharge the picture which he draws of himself, and to enter into a sort of understanding with the spectators, to throw ridicule on the other characters. We have in this way the *arbitrary comic,* which generally produces a very powerful effect, however much the critics may affect to under-rate it. In the instance in question, the spirit of the old comedy prevails; the privileged fool or buffoon, who has appeared on almost all stages under different names, and whose character is at one time a display of shrewdness and wit, and at another of absurdity and stupidity, has inherited something of the extravagant inspiration, and the rights and privileges of the free and unrestrained old comic writer; and this is the strongest proof that the old comedy, which we have described as the original species, was not founded alone in the peculiar circumstances of the Greeks, but is essentially rooted in the nature of things.

We do not, however, feel convinced that the critic can so easily teach a comic as a tragic poet. There is an instantaneous contagiousness in skilful ridicule, which must be learnt by practice, not from precept. In life, he who reasons about conduct before he acts is commonly a loser of opportunities; and he who must be jogged for a repartee will invent it too late for effect. The *painful* have not the rapidity of the *cheerful* emotions. (p. 486)

From the declension of Roman art [in the eighth lecture], M. Schlegel proceeds to the commencement of modern or Italian art; notices the pastoral drama as a peculiarity which had no classical model; and describes the masked comedy conducted by *improvisator* actors. Alfieri is criticized with severity: but we would assign to his *Conspiracy of the Pazzi,* a more elevated station than M. Schlegel allots.

The ninth lecture treats of the antiquities of the French stage, and of the influence of Aristotle and his supposed rules on the forms of French plays. The three unities are discussed; and the unity of action is alone defended.

Lecture the tenth criticizes the principal dramatic works of the French. To the *Cid* of Corneille a high rank is granted: but, though it has the merit of neglecting unity of place, and the earlier scenes are spirited, the interest is in anti-climax; and the love of Chimene almost acquires a comic character in the latter acts.—Of Racine's tragedies, *Athalie* and *Britannicus* are especially praised: but his Greek and Turkish plays violate all costume of manners. Among Voltaire's tragedies, *Alzire* is here preferred. We do not think, however, that the philosophic dia-

logues, which it includes, are placed with probability in the mouths of Peruvians: here is surely as gross a violation of the costume of manners as we find in the Achilles of Racine. In *Zaire,* the discovery of her relation to Lusignan, which occurs early in the play, is perhaps more interesting than the catastrophe, so that the anxiety of the spectator is in an inverted order; and the character of Orosman is not Sultanic, but French:— still we consider this tragedy as the most masterly and original of all those of Voltaire. The *Peré de Famille* of Diderot is grievously under-rated. Its fable, or plot, is perhaps the completest of any dramatic poem extant: the action is intricate, progressively interesting, and the solution or catastrophe is rapid and complete: the characters are various and well-discriminated; and, though the style is perhaps too declamatory, this poetic prose is the French substitute for metrical diction, even in epic writing, and must be taken, like recitative at the opera, as the condition of the appropriate frame of mind in the spectator. The situations are critical, picturesque, and ethically harassing, yet admirably probable; and all the unities are conquered without constraint. It is perhaps the only French play in which the exposition is accomplished without any narration: generally speaking, the French dramatist is as awkward as Euripides in his opening: but in the *Peré de Famille,* the necessary preliminary information is all communicated by implication, and wrought into the action. (pp. 486-87)

The eleventh lecture includes a survey of French comedy which is under-valued by M. Schlegel. In delicate embarrassment, and in teasing situation, which gratifies the *grinning passion* of our nature, the French comic writers excel. Something of malice and something of ridicule are mixed up in this passion; yet it is too good-natured not to sympathize with its object, and too polite to make a laughing-stock of it: no apt name exists for this state of mind, of which irony is an ebullition. An excellent piece of criticism is the comparison between the *Aulularia* of Plautus, and the *Avare* of Moliere.

Diderot's essay on Dramatic Poetry, which Lessing considered as the best specimen of criticism extant in French, is here placed unjustly low. It was perhaps too carefully directed to the defence of domestic tragedy and sentimental drama, in which line the author aspired to reputation: but surely it contains delicate, original, feeling, and profound remarks on art, and has the merit of trampling under foot every national prejudice. Such tragedies as *Othello,* the *Fatal Curiosity,* and the *Gamester,* must remain admirable works of poetry, whatever arguments be accumulated in favour of personages more heroic.

In the twelfth lecture, M. Schlegel compares and assimilates the English and the Spanish theatre. Shakspeare is nobly praised: perhaps excessively in some particulars. *Hamlet,* for instance, of which the first act excites high expectation, and of which the latter acts sink into romantic farce, is treated as a profound and complete work of art. Probably we possess in it an old play, of which Shakspeare re-wrote the first act at leisure, and then rashly hurried the whole before the public, with little retouching of the rest. (p. 488)

The thirteenth lecture continues the history of the English stage, and deservedly praises Marlow, whose works ought to be collected and regularly edited. If the plays of Beaumont were thrown out of the collection by Beaumont and Fletcher, the remainder would form a richer ore. Dryden's *Don Sebastian* is under-rated. Rowe is justly characterized. *George Barnwell* is properly cried down, and is far inferior to the *Arden of Feversham* and to the *Fatal Curiosity* of the same author. (pp. 488-89)

Kotzebue is, in our judgment, unfairly depreciated by M. Schlegel. His slightest pieces, comic or tragic, have succeeded on every European stage, from Moscow to Paris; and in theatrical effect, in rapidity of power over the feelings, he is without a living rival. Some of his plays may justly be accused of flattering dangerous inclinations: thus the *Stranger* seems to palliate adultery, *La Peyrouse* to extenuate bigamy, and *Brother Moritz* to excuse impure marriage with the concubine of another: but these dramas are nevertheless in a high degree impressive; and many of his tragedies superadd to a vehement interest a patriotic, sublime, moral, and liberal aim. Such is *Gustavus Vasa;* which, for every requisite of fable, of character, and of emotion, surpasses any Gothic drama of Goethe, and is inferior only to the *Wilhelm Tell* or the *Mary Stuart* of Schiller. (p. 489)

On the whole, M. Schlegel's lectures deserve to be considered as forming an epoch in the history of criticism. With an eloquence worthy of Plato, with a command of fact worthy of Aristotle, he has for the first time shaped into a system those new principles of decision respecting dramatic art, which Sulzer, Herder, and Lessing, had partially and severally evulgated in Germany; and which must naturally arise from that more extensive and comprehensive comparison of models, which this age of translation has placed within the power of all Europe. If any thing be wanting to the taste of M. Schlegel, it is some portion of tolerance and liberality towards those who have written domestic dramas, and have brought on the stage the polished men and women of modern life. (p. 490)

[*William Taylor*], "*Schlegel's Lectures on Dramatic Art,*" *in* The Port Folio, *Vol. III, No. VI, June, 1817, pp. 477-90.*

[GEORGE BANCROFT] (essay date 1828)

[*Bancroft briefly assesses Schlegel's achievement as a critic, creative writer, and translator, allowing him unalloyed praise only in the latter category.*]

[Schlegel] has done much in criticism; and his lectures on Dramatic Poetry are ingenious and interesting, containing bold vindications of distinguished men, and a more copious and intelligent admiration of Shakspeare, than had yet been given by any critic. Still the best of his opinions may be discerned in the works of Lessing, and the highest place belongs to Schlegel only in a subordinate class. Of invention, he is destitute. As a translator, his merit is extraordinary. Shylock, on the German stage, hardly yields to his prototype; and Romeo and Juliet delight as much in Berlin and Vienna, as in London and New-York. (p. 180)

[*George Bancroft*], "*German Literature,*" *in* American Quarterly Review, *Vol. IV, No. VII, September, 1828, pp. 157-90.*

[HUGH SWINTON LEGARÉ] (essay date 1831)

[*Legaré disputes Schlegel's contention that differences between ancient and modern religions necessitated the development of two formally distinct types of literature and art, i.e., the Classical and the Romantic. According to Legaré, the spirit of the times may have changed, but the ideal of beauty did not, its formal standards having been defined by the ancient Greeks.*]

A. W. Schlegel in his valuable *Lectures upon Dramatic Poetry,* makes [the distinction between the "classical" and "roman-

tic" styles] the basis of all his comparisons between the ancients and the moderns in that art. His main object is to account for the simplicity of the Greek drama, and its close adherence to the three unities, as well as the rigid exclusion from it of every thing comic and incongruous, on principles which shall explain the difference between that style and the complicated and irregular plots and tragi-comic mixtures of Calderon and Shakspeare, without supposing any inferiority in the latter. It was not enough for him to say, that ancient taste was too fastidious; or that ancient criticism was more severe, as the modern is more indulgent—that the former exacted of genius more than it can perform, at least without a sacrifice of much of its power and enthusiasm—while the latter unshackles "the muse of fire" and gives it full scope and boundless regions to soar in—and that this is the reason, in short, why *Macbeth* and *Othello* are so much better (as *we* say they are) than the *Orestiad* or the *Oedipus.* This did not suit with Schlegel's way of thinking, first, because he was a good scholar, and knew better; and next and principally, because he was a German philosopher, and therefore bound to explain the phenomenon by some subtle process of reasoning of his own invention. This he has attempted to do, and the result (as we understand it) is, that in all the arts of taste, the genius of modern times is *essentially* different from that of the Greeks, and *requires,* for its gratification, works of a structure totally distinct from those which he admits to have been the best imaginable models of the classic style.

The principle, by which it is attempted to account for this mighty revolution in art and criticism, is *religion.* That of the Greeks we are told was "the deification of the powers of nature and of earthly life." Under a southern sky, amidst the sweets of a genial and radiant climate, genius naturally dreams of joy and beauty, and the forms with which a poetical fancy peopled heaven, were fashioned upon those with which it was familiar on earth. A gay, sensual, and elegant mythology, grew up under its plastic hands—its visions of ideal perfection were embodied in the idols of superstitious worship,—and Venus, Apollo, Minerva, Hercules, &c. have been individualized as images of certain attributes, and identified with the conceptions of all mankind, by the master-pieces which they may be said to have patronized, since they were created to adorn their temples or to grace their festivals. But this system of religious adoration was confined to the present life, addressed itself exclusively to the *senses,* exacted of the worshipper only forms and oblations, and confirmed him in the tranquil self-complacency or the joyous spirit which the face of nature and the circumstances of his own condition inspired. Christianity was, in all these particulars, the very opposite of Paganism. It added to the material world, a mysterious world of spirits—it substituted the infinite for the finite, an endless future for the transitory present—at the end of every vista in life, it presents the grave, and it has shrouded the grave itself in a deeper gloom, and made death emphatically the King of Terrors. But Schlegel has expressed himself so well upon this subject, that we are tempted to quote a long passage from him:

> Among the Greeks, human nature was in itself
> all sufficient; they were conscious of no wants,
> and aspired at no higher perfection than that
> which they could actually attain by the exercise
> of their own faculties. We, however, are taught
> by superior wisdom, that man, through a high
> offence, forfeited the place for which he was
> originally destined: and that the whole object
> of his earthly existence is to strive to regain

that situation which if left to his own strength, he could never accomplish. The religion of the senses had only in view the possession of outward and perishable blessings; and immortality, in so far as it was believed, appeared in an obscure distance like a shadow, a faint dream of this bright and vivid futurity. The very reverse of all this is the case with the Christian: every thing finite and mortal is lost in the contemplation of infinity; life has become shadow and darkness, and the first dawning of our real existence is beyond the grave. Such a religion must awaken the foreboding, which slumbers in every feeling heart, to the most thorough consciousness, that the happiness after which we strive, we can never here obtain: that no external object can ever entirely fill our souls, and that every mortal enjoyment is but a fleeting and momentary deception. When the soul resting, as it were, under the willows of exile, breathes out its longing for its distant home, the prevailing character of its song must be melancholy. Hence the poetry of the ancients was the poetry of enjoyment, and ours is that of desire; the former has its foundation in the scene which is present, while the latter hovers between recollection and hope. Let us not be understood to affirm that every thing flows in one strain of wailing and complaint, and that the voice of melancholy must always be loudly heard. As the austerity of tragedy was not incompatible with the joyous views of the Greeks, so the romantic poetry can assume every tone, even that of the most lively gladness; but still it will always in some shape or other, bear traces of the source from which it originated. The *feeling of the moderns is, upon the whole, more intense, their fancy more incorporeal, and their thoughts more contemplative*.

Now, we are disposed to assent, in general, to the justness of these observations. . . . Certainly we are more given to *spiritualizing* than the Greeks were—sensible objects suggest moral reflections more readily—the external world is treated as if it were the symbol of the invisible, and the superiority of mind to matter, of the soul to the body, is almost as much admitted by the figures of rhetoric and poetry, as in the dogmas of philosophy. There were no Herveys and Dr. Youngs at Athens. The *spirit*, we repeat it is changed—the associations which natural objects suggest, are different, of course—but does this alter, in any essential degree, the *forms* of beauty? Does it affect the *proportions* which the parts of a work of art ought to bear to each other and to the whole? Does it so far modify the relations of things that what would be fit and proper in a poem, an oration, a colonnade, a picture, if it were ancient, is misplaced and incongruous now? In short, has the philosophy of literature and the arts, the reason, the logic—which controls their execution and results as much as it does the conclusions of science, though in a less palpable manner—undergone any serious revolution? Schlegel and the rest of the same school affirm that such a revolution has taken place. Their favourite illustration of it is, as we have already remarked, the drama and the unities; Shakspeare and Sophocles are the great representatives of the "romantic" and the "classical"—and they compare the former to painting which is various, the latter, to sculpture, which is of course characterized by singleness and

simplicity. "Why," say they "are the Greek and romantic poets so different in their practice, with respect to place and time." The question is an interesting one. Many solutions may be offered; and the very last we should adopt would be the following: which, indeed, so far as it is intelligible, is only a different way of asserting the same thing; in other words, a very palpable *petitio principii*.

> The principal cause of the difference is the *plastic* spirit of the antique and the *picturesque* spirit of the romantic poetry. *Sculpture* directs our attention exclusively to the groupe exhibited to us, it disentangles it as far as possible from all external accompaniments, and where they can be altogether dispensed with, they are indicated as lightly as possible. *Painting*, on the other hand, delights in exhibiting in a minute manner, along with the principal figures, the surrounding locality and all the secondary objects, and to open to us in the back ground, a prospect into a boundless distance; light and perspective are its peculiar charms. Hence the dramatic, and especially, the tragic art of the ancients annihilates in some measure, the external circumstances of space and time; while the romantic drama adorns by their changes its more diversified pictures. Or to express myself in other terms, the principle of antique poetry is ideal, that of the romantic mystical: the former subjects, space and time, to the internal free activity of the mind; the latter adores these inconceivable essences as supernatural powers, in whom something of the divinity has its abode.

(pp. 18-21)

M. Schlegel means to say (as he does affirm elsewhere) that this difference between ancient and modern genius, which is thus illustrated by sculpture and painting, or the *plastic* and the *picturesque*, pervades all the departments of literature and art, without exception. In music, for instance, the ancients are said to have preferred melody, the moderns, harmony—in architecture, compare the Parthenon or the Pantheon with Westminster Abbey, or the Church of St. Stephen at Vienna—even the sculpture of the moderns, according to the opinion of Hemsterhusius, is too much like painting, as the painting of the ancients was probably too much like sculpture. Now, in the first place, we deny the fact that the taste of the moderns *is* different from that of the Greeks in these particulars. As for the drama, *we* have no tragedies but Shakspeare's and if we had, his incomparable genius has settled that part of the controversy irreversibly, so far as popular opinion is concerned. But do not all scholars, without exception, admire and delight in the Greek tragedy? As for music, we suspect that melody is as much preferred now to harmony, as it ever was at Athens; but if it were not, it would be for time to decide, whether the taste of the day were not a transitory and false one. We know too little of the state of that art among the Greeks, to enable us to draw any sure inferences from it. Besides, the proper comparison would be not between melody and harmony, but between romantic melody or harmony, and classical melody or harmony, since both existed at each of the two great periods, and there can be no fair comparison but between things of the same kind. So with architecture. A Gothic cathedral has its beauties—it has its own peculiar proportions—it has fitness to the solemn purpose for which it was designed—it has gorgeous ornament, imposing massiveness, striking altitude, immense extent—its long-drawn aisle and fretted vault—its storied windows—the choir, the altar, the crucifixes, the confessional of the penitent, the stones of the pavement worn by the knees of pilgrims and crusaders, the air of venerable antiquity and religious gloom pervading the whole interior—a thousand interesting associations of the past and of the future, of history and the church, conspire to make it one of the most impressive objects that can be presented to the imagination of man. The origin of the style was in a dark age; but it has taken root, nor is it at all probable that, so long as Christianity shall endure, the modern world will ever be brought to think as meanly of these huge piles, as a Greek architect (if one were suddenly revived) possibly might. Still, there are very few builders of the present age who do not prefer the orders of Greece—and even if they did not, how would that prove that future ages would not? "Time will show," as Byron says, which taste is the more natural and reasonable: and time only, and the voice of the majority, can shew it conclusively.

Meanwhile, let us descend to details: suppose a particular object proposed to be painted or described in the strict sense of those words? Are there two ways of doing that perfectly, and yet as different from each other as the styles in question are supposed to be? A portrait, for instance,—is a classical likeness, a different thing from a romantic, and yet both good likenesses of the same thing? Suppose the object described to be twilight. If the pictures were confined to the *sensible phenomena*, it is obvious there *could not be* any variety in them, as any one who doubts what is so obvious to reason, may convince himself by comparing parallel passages in the ancient and modern classics—e.g. Milton's lines, "now came still evening on, and twilight gray"—Virgil's beautiful verses on midnight, in the fourth *Aeneid,* Homer's on moon-light in the eighth *Iliad.* The exquisite sketches of these objects executed by the great masters just mentioned, are all in precisely the same style, and if they were in the same language, might easily be ascribed to the same age of poetry. To be sure, if without, or besides describing the object, some striking association of ideas be suggested, that may make a very material difference, because such things are essentially accidental and mutable. For instance, Dante's famous lines on the evening, describe it, not as the period of the day when nature exhibits such or such phenomena, which must always be the same while her everlasting order shall be maintained, but by certain casual circumstances which may or may not accompany that hour—the vesper bell, tolling the knell of the dying day, the lonely traveller looking back with a heart oppressed with fond regrets, to the home which he has just left—very touching circumstances no doubt, to those who have a home or have lived in Catholic countries, but still extraneous, and it may be, transitory circumstances.

The same thing may be affirmed of any other particular object, either in the moral or the material world. A picture of conjugal love, for instance, as in Hector and Andromache—of maternal despair, as in Shakspeare's Blanche—of filial devotedness, as in the *Antigone.* We do not comprehend how it is possible to exhibit such objects in more than one style that shall be perfect—and that the *natural,* the universal, the unchangeable—quod semper, quod ubique, quod ab omnibus. And what is clearly true of the details, we take to be equally true of the combinations. The *spirit* may vary, the *associations,* the colouring or complexion; but substantially, there can be but one form of ideal beauty, with which human nature, that never changes, will rest forever satisfied.

We will borrow an illustration, on this subject, from the learned Michaelis. If any two systems of religion and poetry differ in their spirit, in the associations with which they surround the objects of their adoration and praise, and the effect they produce upon the mind of the votary, it is the Jewish and the Pagan—the one dwelling forever in its prophetic raptures, upon the sublime unity of the Godhead, filling immensity, whose invisible glory it was the guiltiest audacity to degrade by attempting to represent it in any sensible image; the other crowding all space with a mob of thirty thousand deities of every rank and shape. The sacred poetry of the Hebrews, besides, is the great fountain of modern inspiration, strictly so called. Yet differing as widely as it is possible in the very element of thought and character from which Schlegel deduces such important results, there is no essential difference in the *forms* of Hebrew and Classical poetry. The illustration we shall borrow from the learned author referred to, is the following. He remarks that as the Heathen assigned to Jupiter a chariot and horses of thunder, so the Hebrews have a similar fable, and the Cherubim are expressly the horses of Jehovah's chariot. He is frequently described as sitting upon the Cherubim. He thunders so that the earth shakes—or as Horace might have expressed it,

> Jehovah per caelum tonantes
> Egit equos, volucremque currum;
> Quo bruta tellus, et vaga flumina
> Quo Styx et invisi horrida Toenari
> Sedes, Atlanteusque finis
> Concutitur.

The same observation holds, in the strictest manner true, of Milton and Dante, the two most sublime poets of modern times, the most Christian in spirit, and the most classical and severe in style.

After all, this classification of styles may be only a more artificial and scholastic way of confessing, that those irregular works of modern genius which are designated as romantic, *par excellence,* in fact, deviate very materially from the Greek standard. Of this no one who has studied criticism in the works of the ancients, can have any doubt at all. Three things were considered as essential to all excellence in a composition of genius, perfect unity of purpose, simplicity of style, and ease of execution—and it is in these things that the literature and art of Greece, exhibit their matchless perfection. Other nations have produced works indicating as rare and fertile invention, as much depth of thought, as much vigour of conception, as much intensity of feeling—but no body of literature or of art can be compared to the *antique* for the severe *reason,* the close, unsparing *logic* of its criticism. Unity of design, especially, which is more immediately connected with the subject in hand, they rigorously exacted. They considered a work of art always as a *whole*—a sort of organized body—to the very structure of which certain parts and proportions, and none others, were essential, and in which the least violation of this fitness and harmony, was a deformity, more or less uncouth and monstrous. The details were sacrificed without mercy to the general effect. In an oration, for instance, they looked to the end which the speaker had in view, and whatever was not calculated to further that, however brilliant and impressive in itself, was rejected without reserve. The notion of Pythagoras, that the sublime order of the universe was maintained by the secret power of *proportion,* by the magic of mathematical relations, probably sprung out of this truly Greek idea of the perfection of art, applied by analogy to the works of creation. This unity of thought, this harmony in composition, this . . . necessary connexion, like that of cause and effect, between the parts, every thing being in its right place, following logically from what goes before it, leading inevitably to what comes after it, pervades all the monuments of genius which that wonderful race has left behind it. Their superiority in this exquisite *logic* of literature and the arts—a logic not a jot less exact and elegant than the demonstrations of their own unrivalled geometry—is, we fear, a lamentable truth, nor will it help us much to call our deformities, peculiarities, and to dignify what is only *not* art with the specious title of the 'romantic.' (pp. 22-6)

> [Hugh Swinton Legaré], in a review of "Letters and Journals of Lord Byron, with Notices of His Life," in Southern Review, *Vol. VII, No. XIII, May 1831, pp. 1-42.*

JOHANN WOLFGANG VON GOETHE   (essay date 1832?)

[Goethe is considered Germany's greatest writer and a genius of the highest order. A shaping force in the major literary movements of the late eighteenth and early nineteenth centuries in Germany, he is best known for his drama Faust and his novel Die Leiden des jungen Werthers. While Goethe states in the extract below that he has not been personally affected by the Schlegels' criticism, he notes his friend Schiller's animosity toward the brothers and provides a generally unflattering portrait of their contemporary influence and reputation. In the absence of information concerning the exact date of his comments, Goethe's remarks are here dated 1832, the year of his death.]

[The] Schlegels, with all their fine natural gifts, have been unhappy men their life long, both the one and the other; they wished both to be and do something more than nature had given them capacity for; and accordingly they have been the means of bringing about not a little harm both in art and literature. From their false principles in the fine arts—principles which, however much trumpeted and gospeled about, were in fact egotism united with weakness—our German artists have not yet recovered, and are filling the exhibitions, as we see, with pictures which nobody will buy. (p. 311)

As for their Sanscrit studies again, that was at bottom only a *pis aller*. They were clear-sighted enough to perceive that neither Greek nor Latin offered any thing brilliant enough for them; they accordingly threw themselves into the far East; and in this direction, unquestionably, the talent of Augustus William manifests itself in the most honourable way. All that, and more, time will show. Schiller never loved them: hated them rather; and I think it peeps out of our correspondence how I did my best, in our Weimar circles at least, to keep this dislike from coming to an open difference. In the great revolution which they actually effected, I had the luck to get off with a whole skin, . . . to the great annoyance of their romantic brother Novalis, who wished to have me *simpliciter* deleted. 'Twas a lucky thing for me, in the midst of this critical hubbub, that I was always too busy with myself to take much note of what others were saying about me.

Schiller had good reason to be angry with them. With their aesthetical denunciations and critical club-law, it was a comparatively cheap matter for them to knock him down in a fashion; but Schiller had no weapons that could prostrate them. He said to me on one occasion, displeased with my universal toleration even for what I did not like, 'Kotzebue, with his frivolous fertility, is more respectable in my eyes than that barren generation, who, though always limping themselves,

are never content with bawling out to those who have legs— Stop!' (pp. 311-12)

> Johann Wolfgang von Goethe, "Frederick Schlegel," in Blackwood's Edinburgh Magazine, *Vol. LIV, No. CCCXXXV, September, 1843, pp. 311-24.*

GEORGE TOYNBEE   (diary date 1833)

[Toynbee attended Schlegel's lectures at the University of Bonn in 1833. In addition to taking notes on the lectures that he later published in English translation, Toynbee made the following revealing remarks in his diary concerning Schlegel's great vanity and fame. See the excerpt dated 1838(?) for additional commentary by Toynbee.]

To-day I heard Schlegel. He is one of the chiefs of German literature. Perhaps since the death of Goethe the chief. Here he is held in less estimation on account of his personal vanity. But indeed the attention paid to him both at home and abroad [has] been enough to turn his head. His admirers have to thank themselves for rendering him less admirable. In France some Princes hung a chain round his neck and in England he was arm in arm with the Duke of Sussex. And now our great man thinks it incumbent on him not to forget all this. He covers himself with ribbons, medals and badges. If he had died young he would probably have been immortal. Now his fame will perhaps die before him. What a condition for a man who is as well known in his own country as Scott amongst us! (p. 9)

> George Toynbee, in an extract from a diary entry in A. W. Schlegel's Lectures on German Literature from Gottsched to Goethe by A. W. Schlegel, edited by H. G. Fiedler, Basil Blackwell, 1944, pp. 5-12.

HEINRICH HEINE   (essay date 1835)

[Heine, one of the most prominent literary figures in nineteenth-century Europe and his native Germany, is primarily remembered for his poetry—characterized by passionate lyricism and wry irony— as well as his distinctive commentaries on politics, literature, and society. Heine was acquainted with Schlegel and ridiculed him in an essay on the Romantic school published in 1835 in his book De l'Allemagne. In the following excerpt from that work, Heine disparages Schlegel and his work, focusing his literary remarks on Schlegel's comparative method of criticism.]

My conscientious scrupulousness as a writer impels me to mention that several Frenchmen have complained to me that my criticisms on the Schlegels, and especially on A. W. Schlegel, have been much too trenchant. I think, however, that a closer acquaintance with German literature would have prevented these objections. Many Frenchmen know nothing of A. W. Schlegel but what they have gathered from Madame de Staël, his noble patroness. To the majority he is only a name, and this name has a distinguished ring about it, something like the name of Osiris, of whom also they know nothing except that he is an outlandish sort of god, who was worshipped in Egypt. Of the other points of similarity between A. W. Schlegel and Osiris they know absolutely nothing. (p. 242)

Herr August Wilhelm Schlegel was born at Hanover, Sept. 5, 1767. This fact does not rest on his own authority; I was never so ungallant as to ask him his age. The date, if I mistake not, I found in Spindler's *Dictionary of German Authoresses*. According to it, Herr August Wilhelm Schlegel is sixty-four years old. Alexander von Humbolt and other naturalists maintain that he is older. Champollion shared this opinion. If I must speak of his literary services, I must . . . commend him principally as a translator. In this province he undoubtedly did some first-rate work. In particular, his translation of Shakespeare into German is masterly and unsurpassable. With the exception, perhaps, of Herr Gries and Count Platen, A. W. Schlegel is the first metrical expert in Germany. In all his other work he must take the second, if not the third rank. In higher criticism he has . . . no philosophical basis to build upon, and is far outstripped by other of his contemporaries, in particular by Solger. In Old German studies Jacob Grimm is a head and shoulders above him. Grimm's *German Grammar* was a death-blow to the superficiality with which Old German documents had been edited after the example of the Schlegels. Perhaps Schlegel might have made better work of Old German if he had not deserted it for Sanskrit. But Old German had gone out of fashion, and with Sanskrit he had a better chance of making a sensation. But even in Sanskrit he never got beyond the dilettante stage; the initiative he owed to his brother Friedrich; and for the solid and scientific part of his studies he is indebted, as everyone knows, to Lassen, his learned collaborateur. Our real Sanskrit scholar, the first in his own line, is Franz Bopp, of Berlin. As an historian Schlegel tried at one time to cling to the skirts of Niebuhr, whom he attacked, but if we compare him with the great Roman historian, or Johannes von Müller, or Heeren, or Schlosser, or men of like calibre, we can only shrug our shoulders.

But as a poet, what rank are we to assign him? This is hard to determine. Solomons, the violin player, who gave lessons to George III., once said to his illustrious pupil, "Violin players may be divided into three classes: to the first class belong those who cannot play at all; to the second class those who play very badly; to the third class good players. Your Majesty has already attained to the second class."

Does Schlegel belong to the first or the second class of poets? Some say he is no poet at all; others say he is a very bad poet. I may safely assert that he is no Paganini.

A. W. Schlegel owed his celebrity mainly to the unparalleled effrontery with which he attacked all the "powers that be" in literature. He tore their laurel crowns from the old bepowdered perriwigs and raised clouds of dust. His fame is the natural daughter of scandal. (pp. 246-48)

[The] criticism that Schlegel brought to bear on the literary authorities of his day had no philosophical basis. After recovering from our astonishment at his constant audacity, we recognize the utter barrenness of the so-called Schlegel criticism. For example, when he means to depreciate the poet Bürger, he compares his ballads with the Percy collection of Old English ballads, and shows that the latter are far more simple, naïve, and consequently more poetical. Schlegel could fully conceive the spirit of the past, especially of the Middle Ages, and he was thus able to point out to others this spirit as revealed in the artistic production of the past, and to demonstrate their beauties from this point of view. But of all that concerns the present he has not a conception; at best he only catches something of the physiognomy, a few of the salient features of the present, and those generally not the most pleasing; failing to grasp the spirit behind them, he sees in all our modern life only a prosaical daub. As a rule, only a great poet can appreciate the poetry of his own times. The poetry of a past age reveals itself to us with far less effort, and it takes less effort to make others appreciate it. No wonder then that with the common herd Herr Schlegel succeeded in glorifying the poems in which the past lies buried at the expense of the

poems in which the living present lives and breathes. But death is not more poetical than life. The Old English poems that Percy collected give the spirit of their age, and Bürger's poems give the spirit of our age. This spirit Schlegel cannot conceive; else he would have perceived in the passion with which this spirit at times bursts forth from Bürger's poems, something other than the wild scream of an uncultured dominie; he would have recognized the agonizing cries of a Titan tortured to death by an aristocracy of Hanoverian squires and school pedants. This was, indeed, the condition of the author of "Lenore," and the condition of so many other men of genius who were struggling and sinking and starving as private teachers at Göttingen. How could the illustrious protégé of illustrious patrons, the knighted, baronetted, decorated August Wilhelm von Schlegel understand the verses in which Bürger exclaims that a man of honour before begging favours of the great will sooner let himself starve? (pp. 248-49)

Everything in modern life necessarily seemed to him prosaic, and the poetry of France, the native soil of modern society, was for him a closed volume. Racine, to begin with, was to him absolutely unintelligible, Racine who stands forth as the herald of the modern age, beside the Grand Monarch with whom the modern age begins. Racine was the first modern poet, as Louis XIV. was the first modern king. In Corneille there still breathes the spirit of the Middle Ages; in Corneille and the Fronde there is still the taint of ancient chivalry; this is why he is often classed as a Romantic poet. But in Racine there is not a trace of mediaeval sentiment; he is instinct with modern feelings, the interpreter of a new society. In Racine, for the first time, we catch the scent of violets, the spring fragrance of modern life, and we may even mark in him the first sprouting of the laurels that have grown to such a height in these latest times. Who can tell how many deeds were begotten of Racine's tender verses? The French heroes who lie buried at the Pyramids, at Austerlitz, at Moscow, at Waterloo, they all had listened to Racine's verses; their Emperor had listened to them from the lips of Talma. Who can tell how many hundredweights of glory of the Vendôme Column are really Racine's? Whether Euripides is a greater poet than Racine I know not, but I do know that Racine was a wellspring of love and honour, whose living waters intoxicated, enchanted, inspirited a whole nation. What more can be expected of a poet? We are all mortal; we go down to the grave and leave behind our uttered word to fulfil its mission, and then return to the breast of God, the meeting-place of poets' words, the home of all harmonies.

Now if Schlegel had confined himself to asserting that Racine's mission was over, and that the coming age required very different poets, there would have been some justice in his criticism; but it was most unjust to attempt to prove Racine's weakness by comparing him with older poets. Not only was the infinite grace, the gentle playfulness, the profound charm which Racine inspires by dressing his modern French heroes in ancient costumes, and adding to the interest of modern passion the interest of a witty masquerade—not only was all this lost on Schlegel, but he was actually so dull as to mistake this stage money for coin of the realm, to assay the Greeks of Versailles by the standard of the Greeks of Athens, and compare Racine's Phaedra with the Phaedra of Euripides. This habit of using the past as a foot-rule whereby to measure the present had become such a second nature with Schlegel, that he was perpetually turning the laurels of some older poet into a rod for the back of a younger poet. Then, in order to set down Euripides in his turn, the only way he could devise was to compare him with the older dramatist Sophocles, or the still older Aeschylus.

It would carry me too far if I were to dwell on the monstrous injustice of Schlegel's depreciatory criticism on Euripides, as unfair as that of Aristophanes in his day. A close parallel might be drawn in this respect between the attitude assumed by Aristophanes and by the Romantic school. The same feelings and tendencies underlie his attack on Euripides; and if Tieck may be called a romantic Aristophanes, the parodist of Euripides and of Socrates might with equal justice be styled a classical Tieck. As Tieck and the Schlegels, in spite of their own scepticism, bewailed the downfall of Catholicism; as they sought to reinstate the old faith in the hearts of the masses; as with this view they attacked with mockery and abuse the Protestant Rationalists and Freethinkers, the honest even more virulently than the insincere; as they held in utter abhorrence the men who were establishing an honourable commonwealth in life and literature; as they made fun of this ideal commonwealth as a sort of hugger-mugger philistinism, and were never tired of holding up as their ideal the heroic life of mediaeval feudalism,—so, too, Aristophanes, though he himself poked fun at the gods, nevertheless hated the philosophers who were undermining the very foundations of Olympus; he hated the rationalizing Socrates, who preached a higher morality; he hated the poets, the representatives, as it were, of modern life, of a life as different from the preceding epoch of Greek gods, heroes, and kings, as the present time is from the times of mediaeval feudalism; he hated Euripides, who was no longer, like Aeschylus and Sophocles, intoxicated with the spirit of Greek mediaevalism, but was approximating to the *bourgeois* tragedy of common life. I doubt whether Schlegel was aware of the true grounds for his depreciation of Euripides in comparison with Aeschylus and Sophocles. I think he was guided by unconscious antipathy; in the old Greek tragedian he sniffed the modern democratical Protestant element, which had already raised the bile of the Athenian knight-errant, the Olympian Catholic Aristophanes.

But perhaps I am doing Schlegel too much honour in giving him credit for definite sympathies and antipathies. Possibly he had none. In his youth he had been a Hellenist, and only late in life became a Romanticist. He was the *choragus* of the new school; it took its name from him and his brother, and of all the Schlegel school he was perhaps the least in earnest. He supported it by his talents, he worked himself into its spirit, he was proud of it as long as it prospered, and when the school fell into disgrace, he applied himself again to a new line of study.

Although the school died a natural death, Schlegel's efforts were not lost upon our literature. He showed by his example how scientific subjects may be treated in elegant language. Before his time few German savants had ventured to write a scientific work in a clear and attractive style. Their German was dry and crabbed, reeking of tallow candles and tobacco smoke. Schlegel was one of the few Germans who did not smoke, a virtue he owed to the company of Madame de Staël. To the same lady he was mainly indebted for that polish of manner which he turned to such good account in Germany. In this respect the death of that distinguished Frenchwoman was a great loss to the German savant. In her salon he had enjoyed ample opportunities of learning the newest fashions, and as her companion he had seen the world of fashion in every capital of Europe, and caught the manners of the best European society. Such an education in manners had become for him so

necessary a luxury, that after the death of his noble protectress he was not disinclined to offer the famous Catalani his companionship on her travels. (pp. 250-53)

[In] the year 1819, while still a raw youth at the University of Bonn, I had the honour of seeing face to face the great poetic genius, Herr August Wilhelm Schlegel. He was, with the exception of Napoleon, the first great man I had ever seen, and I shall never forget the imposing spectacle. To this very day I feel the thrill of awe that passed through me when I stood before his professional chair and heard him speak. In those days I wore a rough white coat, a red cap over my long, light hair, and no gloves. Herr August Wilhelm Schlegel wore kid gloves, and was dressed in the newest Paris fashion; he exhaled the essence of good society and *eau de mille fleurs;* he was the personification of elegance and refinement, and, when he spoke of the Lord Chancellor of England, he added, "My friend the Chancellor." At his side stood his servant in the baronial livery of the house of Schlegel, and snuffed the wax lights which stood in a silver candelabra beside a glass of *eau sucrée* on the great professor's desk. A liveried servant! wax lights! silver candelabra; my friend the Lord Chancellor of England! kid gloves! *eau sucrée!* what unheard-of novelties in the lecture-room of a German professor! These splendours dazzled us young folks not a little, myself more than others, and I wrote at the time three odes to Herr Schlegel, each beginning "O thou that," &c.; but I should never have ventured except by a poetic licence to address so distinguished a man with the familiar *thou.* And in his outward appearance there was really a certain distinction. A long, lean head, on which still glittered a few silver hairs, a lean body, so emaciated, so transparent, that he seemed all spirit, almost a living embodiment of spiritualism.

In spite of this he had married; he, the leader of the Romanticists, married the daughter of the Heidelberg Church councillor, Paulus, the leader of the German Rationalists. It was a symbolical marriage; the betrothal, as it were, of Romanticism to Rationalism; but there was no issue. On the contrary, the split between Romanticism and Rationalism was widened; and on the very morning after the wedding, Rationalism ran home and would have nothing more to do with Romanticism. For Rationalism, showing her usual common sense, was not content with a purely symbolic marriage, and, on discovering the woodenness and nullity of Romantic art, ran away. I know that this is obscure, and I will try to make my meaning as explicit as is possible.

Typhon, the wicked Typhon, hated Osiris, who is, as you know, an Egyptian god, and on getting him into his power, he tore him to pieces. Isis, poor Isis, the wife of Osiris, painfully collected the bits, stitched them together, and succeeded in wholly restoring her dismembered spouse. *Wholly*, do I say? alas, one part was wanting which the poor goddess failed to find, and she was forced to do the best she could with wood. Poor Isis! Hence arose in Egypt a scandalous myth, and in Heidelberg a mystical scandal.

After this, the public lost sight of A. W. Schlegel, and forgot all about him. This cold neglect was more than Schlegel could stand, and he determined, after a prolonged absence, to revisit Berlin, the chief scene of his literary triumphs, and to give again a course of lectures on aesthetics. But he had learnt nothing new in the interval, and he now addressed a public which had received from Hegel a philosophy of art and a science of aesthetics. His audience laughed at him and shrugged their shoulders. He fared like an ancient actress who reappears, after twenty years' absence, on the stage where she once reigned as favourite, and wonders why the house laughs instead of applauding. A frightful change had come over him; for a whole month he kept Berlin amused by exposing his follies and absurdities. He had turned into an old fop, and allowed himself to be the laughing-stock of the town. The stories told against him are almost past belief.

I saw A. W. Schlegel once again in Paris, and it was to me a melancholy sight. I had no notion of the alteration I have described before my own eyes convinced me of it. This was just a year ago, shortly after my arrival in the capital. I was on my way to visit the house in which Molière lived. On my way there, not far from this sacred spot, I caught sight of a human form, and on scanning the wizened features I detected a resemblance with the man I knew as August Wilhelm Schlegel. I thought I saw his ghost. It was, however, only his body. The spirit is dead and the body still haunts the earth, and has even grown somewhat stout. The thin, spiritualized legs had put on flesh; there was actually something like a paunch, and above it hung a whole row of ribands and orders. The venerable silver hairs that I remembered were replaced by a flaxen wig. He was dressed in the latest fashion of the year in which Madame de Staël died. His face, too, wore the aged simper of an old lady mumbling a lump of sugar, and he tripped jauntily along like a coquettish child. He had, indeed, undergone a strange rejuvenescence; it was as though some wicked fairy had brought out a comical second edition of his youth; he seemed to have regained all his youthful bloom, and I was inclined to suspect the red of his cheeks of being not rouge, but the genuine irony of nature.

At that moment I could almost fancy I saw Molière restored to life, and smiling down upon me from his window as he pointed to the tragi-comic spectacle. It flashed upon me at once in all its absurdity; I caught the full humour of the joke; I perceived the entire comicality of that incredibly ridiculous personage, which, alas! has hitherto found no great comedian to adapt it for the stage. Molière alone would have been the man to present such a figure on the boards of the Théâtre Français; he alone had the genius for such a task; and August Wilhelm Schlegel even in his younger days had an uneasy consciousness of this, and hated Molière for the same reason that made Napoleon hate Tacitus. Just as Napoleon Bonaparte, the French Caesar, must have felt that the republican historian would have drawn no more flattering portrait of him than of his prototype,—so A. W. Schlegel, the German Osiris, had long surmised that had Molière been alive he would never have escaped the great comedian. Napoleon said of Tacitus, he was the calumniator of Tiberius, and A. W. Schlegel said of Molière, he was no poet, but only a buffoon.

Soon afterwards A. W. Schlegel left Paris, having first received at the hands of his majesty Louis Philippe the decoration of the Legion of Honour. The *Moniteur* has hitherto hesitated to announce officially this occurrence, but Thalia, the Muse of Comedy, at once made a note of it in her book of jests. (pp. 254-58)

Heinrich Heine, "The Romantic School," in his Travel-Pictures, *translated by Francis Storr, George Bell and Sons, 1887, pp. 189-344.*

GEORGE TOYNBEE (essay date 1838?)

[*Toynbee assesses Schlegel's stature, influence, and works, crediting him with establishing the current system of German criticism*

and underscoring his sensitive and impartial approach to the literatures of other nations and ages. Toynbee's remarks were originally published in approximately 1838; for additional commentary by the critic, see the excerpt dated 1833.]

August Wilhelm Schlegel is distinguished for critical rather than creative power. No original work of genius has issued from his mind. He is a master of comprehension and analysis. Few men have combined such immense learning as he possesses with such a fine sense of the beautiful, and such a rigorous critical system. He has been entitled, and not unjustly, the first critic of modern times. His classical acquirements are of the first order, and he has written imitations of the ancients which show that he was fully capable of embodying the spirit of old. With the literature of the Middle Ages, and also with that of our Elizabethan era, he is intimately acquainted. He seems to lose the character of his nation as soon as he passes her boundaries, and to assume that of any other country the literature of which he may examine, criticize, or translate. He is bound by no ties or associations, and acknowledges only a general standard of truth, beauty, and genius. He may be said to have established the critical system which at present obtains in Germany, and which is essentially superior to that which any other country possesses. (p. 48)

As a critic, Schlegel has always insisted on a rigorous definition, and an impartial judgment. He views the works of literature in connexion with the time and country which gave them birth. He holds that there are certain internal laws which ought to give its suitable form to a poem, and that, therefore, the construction of the latter can never be regulated by abstract dicta or philosophical conclusions. He compares the cramping of genius by rules to an attempt to mould a fruit into a different shape from that which Nature had given it. In the works of great authors he proves that an apparently irregular arrangement is demanded by the nature of the subject and by the spirit in which it is treated. He demonstrates that every scene in Shakespeare is necessary to the perfection of the whole, which must inevitably be injured by any alteration. He wages incessant war with the narrow-minded commentators, who are always quarrelling with the past because it is not the present. In fine, he can transport himself into all ages and countries, and thus familiarize himself with the spirit in which every national poem was written. He enters into its intimate constitution and feels, as it were, its creation anew. He divests himself of all preconceived notions and studies it as a natural philosopher would a new organization. (pp. 48-9)

The most important work of A. W. Schlegel is, perhaps, his ***Lectures on Dramatic Art and Literature,*** which contain a complete survey and critical history of the drama from its rise to the present day. No particular theory is predominant throughout, and no partial leaning is evident to any particular form. The Greek drama is thoroughly appreciated, and elevated far beyond the point to which mere philologers would raise it. No comparisons are made between subjects which have no right to be compared. No foreign rules are brought to bear on national productions. Sophocles and Shakespeare stand side by side, perfect and independent in their separate spheres. It is only with regard to one country that Schlegel would, at first, seem to be prejudiced. He is deaf to the dramatic and poetical pretensions of the French. With the solitary exception of the *Athalie* of Racine, he ridicules all their tragedies. Nor does the far-famed Molière find any favour at his hands. . . . Schlegel's work has been ably translated into English by Mr. John Black . . . , and, therefore, there is no occasion for us to mention here the fine analysis which it gives of the works of Shakespeare. The lyrical poems of Schlegel are more celebrated for beauty and elegance of form and correctness of expression than for force of original genius. (pp. 49-50)

> *George Toynbee, "Continuation to Heine," in* A. W. Schlegel's Lectures on German Literature from Gottsched to Goethe *by A. W. Schlegel, edited by H. G. Fiedler, Basil Blackwell, 1944, pp. 46-72.*

[GEORGE HENRY LEWES]   (essay date 1843)

[*Lewes was one of the most versatile men of letters in the Victorian era in England. Critics often cite his influence on the novelist George Eliot, to whom he was a companion and mentor, as his principal contribution to English letters, but they also credit him with acumen in his literary commentary, most notably in his dramatic criticism. The following excerpt is taken from a polemic that Lewes wrote attacking Schlegel's critical principles and practices. He assails Schlegel relentlessly, rejecting key concepts such as his distinction between Classical and Romantic art and underscoring their deficiencies as tools for judging individual works of art. For additional commentary by Lewes, see the excerpt dated 1849.*]

The reputation of A. W. Schlegel is not undeservedly European. He has 'done the state some service;' he has stimulated the minds of many thinking men, directing their attention to points of literary history which had before been overlooked; and he has been useful to the science of criticism, by his paradoxes which have roused discussion, no less than by his principles which have received assent. His works are distinguished amongst their class by a splendour of diction, a felicity of illustration, and attractiveness of exposition rarely equalled; nor has their popularity been injured by the affectation of philosophic depth of which they are guilty. Although more Rhetorician than Critic, his writings contain some valuable principles luminously expressed, much ingenuity and acuteness, and are, in spite of all their drawbacks, worthy of serious attention. But in merits and in faults he is essentially a popular writer, and stands, with us, in the very false position of an oracle. As a popular writer he is efficient, and merits all the applause he has received; but as an oracle—as a rational, serious, philosophic critic—he is one of the most dangerous guides the student can consult. Freely admitting that his influence in England has not been on the whole without good result, we are firmly convinced that it has been in many things pernicious. And while we are constantly deploring the evils he has caused, we as constantly see him held up to our admiration and respect as the highest authority on Dramatic Art. Whatever benefit it was in his power to confer has been already reaped; and now it is important that his errors should be exposed. We beg the reader therefore to understand this article as polemical rather than critical: not as an estimate of Schlegel's work, but as a protest against his method, and examination of his leading principles. (p. 160)

Schlegel's method we regard as the most injurious portion of his work; the more so as it dignifies itself with lofty names, and wishes to pass off easy theorizing for philosophic judgment. . . . Bad as [the criticism of the last century] was, it was more satisfactory, more instructive than much of what passes as philosophic in the present day. Ridiculous though it be to talk of the 'elegance and sublimity' of Homer, or the 'irregularity' of Shakspeare, we prefer it to the rhapsodies of Schlegel on Calderon, wherein he defends the glittering nonsense of his favourite upon the ground that it is 'a sense of the mutual attraction of created things to one another on account of their common origin, and this is a refulgence of the eternal love which embraces the universe.' If there is better criticism in the present day than in the last century, it is because knowledge of art is greater and taste more catholic; not because 'analysis' has given place to 'synthesis,' as many people maintain. (pp. 163-64)

The greatest of modern critics, Lessing and Winckelman, were men of great analytic power, and it is to them that we owe the best appreciation of works of art. They were not declaimers. They studied patiently and reasoned profoundly. One aspect, one limb, did not to them represent the whole. They strove to evolve the meaning *from* each work, and not to force some *à priori* meaning *on* the work. They were judges and not advocates. It will be the scope of our remarks to show that Schlegel's 'synthesis' is rash, and not founded on a due 'analysis:' that he is an advocate and not a judge.

The first principle of classification is to trace constant uniformities amidst varieties: applied therefore to works of art, it consists in ranging under one head all such various specimens produced by various nations as have some principle in common; so that the diversities of language, customs, and tastes, are set aside, and the real generic resemblance made the ground of classification. This would be the scientific method; but Schlegel in his celebrated classification of art into classic and romantic has acted in direct opposition to it. He has grounded his classification on a single diversity instead of a constant uniformity. Except for historical purposes, the division of art into ancient and modern is fatal: it is assuming that the spirit of art is entirely religious, whereas we hope to prove that it is *national*. The ground of classification must be ethnic not chronological: it is a question of races not of periods.

Struck with the revolution operated by Christianity in men's opinions, Schlegel and others have jumped to the conclusion, that it also operated a revolution in the *spirit* of art. This is tantamount to saying that a change of belief brings with it a change of nature and of organic tendencies. Great as must always be the influence of religion upon art, it can never entirely change its spirit. Let us be understood. By the spirit of art we do not mean *opinions*. As a distinction is made, and justly, between the mind and its beliefs, so we would distinguish between the spirit of art, and the ideas therein expressed. There is in every nation an organic character, which no changes of opinion can efface; this sets its impress upon all its works, so that we never confound them with the works of another. This impress is the sign of what we call the spirit or the national tendencies of art. It cannot therefore be true that the spirit of Art is dependant on religion; the more so as religion itself is modified by the national character. We do not here allude to sectarian distinctions, or to varieties of interpretation; we point to the fact, that Christianity becomes a *subjective* religion with a northern race, while with a southern race it becomes *objective*. . . . (pp. 164-65)

What we contend for is, that the division into pagan and Christian, classic and romantic, is unwarrantable; that the real distinction is national and not religious. The national distinctions are very broad. We believe they may be ranged under two general classes of objective and subjective, or of southern and northern; each class is of course to be subdivided, but the above two we regard as the most general. Let us for a moment examine the characteristics of two nations, the Italians and Germans, which may be taken as types of the two classes.

We use the word in no ill sense, when we call the Italian nature *sensuous;* neither do we imply any superiority when we call the German *reflective*. As far as single words can express such complex things, we believe these two express the distinctive characteristics of the nations; or we might call the former plastic and definite; the latter dreamy and vague. Every thing in Italian art is definite; in its plastic hands all things assume distinct form; Italian poetry has no *reverie*. Nothing like reverie is to be seen in the southern character; neither poetry nor music, though both so fitted to express this peculiar mental state, have been used by the southerns to express it. German art delights in it. But then the sensuous passionate nature of the Italian is averse to that dallying with thought which constitutes a reverie, while in the German it is the source of exquisite delight. The thoughts of the Italian grow quickly into passions; in the German, passions when not highly excited, have an irresistible tendency to weave themselves into thoughts: so that while in the one all ideas stimulate to action, his tendency being to throw every thing *out* of him; in the other, actions stimulate thoughts, his tendency being to connect all outward things with his inward life. (p. 166)

To state our notion in a few words, we should say that the southern climate generates a sensuous activity, a love of continuity and of definite form; and that the northern generates a reflective activity, and a love of variety and rapid transitions.

To the proof. What are the essential characteristics of Italian music? Continuity, simplicity, melody. It is full of 'linked sweetness *long drawn out.*' The melody alone is considered of importance: the harmonies are mere accompaniments, having no further meaning. In all the productions of Palestrina, Pergolesi, Caldara, Scarlatti, Porpora, Paisiello, Cimarosa, Rossini, Bellini, and the hundred lovely names that throng upon the memory, we may observe, amidst all the varieties, certain characteristics: and these are an uniform simplicity in the structure, which consists of a few large outlines, and the sensuous or passionate expression. If we then compare the works of Bach, Beethoven, Schubert, or Spohr, we shall at once perceive the opposite characteristics of complexity in structure, rapidity of transitions, and the greater importance of the harmonies; moreover the harmonies in German music have a meaning of their own. If an Italian air be played and the accompaniment omitted, the expression of the feeling will nevertheless be preserved; but to omit the harmonies of a German air is to destroy it altogether. (p. 167)

We have selected music as the fittest illustration of our views, but we could examine the other arts with the same result. This result we must repeat is,—that southern nations are sensuous, passionate, and plastic, in a word objective; and northerns reflective, dreamy, vague, in a word subjective.

It is obvious that the distinction here stated must, if correct, be of all the most fundamental, and consequently the one on which to ground a classification. We must range the various races under these two classes, and speak not of classic and romantic, but of objective and subjective: for although the latter terms are ambiguous, the former are meaningless. The Greeks, Italians, and Spaniards differ amongst themselves, but one spirit reigns above all differences; they belong to one genus and differ only in varieties; while from the Teutonic races they are separated by a distinction of genus.

The foregoing remarks, if they have not established our classification, have at least shown the incompatibility of Schlegel's. Let us add also that Schlegel who uses the words 'romantic spirit' as if they contained the key to all the problems of modern art, utterly fails in applying his classification. To

call the Greeks classic was easy enough, but the Italians puzzled him: he felt that they belonged to the same class, and felt also that in spite of Christianity they were not romantic. In one place he reproaches the Italian drama "with a total absence of the romantic spirit;" but he does not say that Italy was not Christian; how then, if Christianity is the source of the 'romantic spirit,' are Christian poets not romantic? This dilemma he seems never to have felt. Dilemmas and contradictions never trouble his 'synthetic mind.' Yet would a true philosopher have seen, in this case, either that the notion of Christianity being the cause of the 'romantic spirit' was erroneous; or else he would have investigated the causes of the apparent contradiction. (pp. 168-69)

We are . . . [also] told that the great distinction between ancient and modern art, arising from the opposite tendencies of polytheism and Christianity, consists in the one being the poetry of *enjoyment* while the other is that of *desire:* the former has its foundation in the scene which is the present, while the latter hovers betwixt recollection and hope. This is an antithesis fit to captivate a stronger head than Schlegel's; yet it is an antithesis and no more; facts are directly opposed to it. To talk of the Greeks having invented the poetry of gladness, is downright absurdity. Almost all poetry is the expression of a regret or a desire: enjoyment finds very little place in the poetry of any nation, and in that of the Greeks less perhaps than any. (p. 170)

Schlegel's idea is founded upon an *à priori* view of the consequences of such a religion as polytheism, not upon an examination of the facts. He thinks the Greeks were conscious of no wants, and aspired at no higher perfection than that which they could actually attain by the exercise of their faculties. We, however, are taught by a superior wisdom that man through a high offence forfeited the place for which he was originally destined: consequently that the Christian is more dissatisfied with this life, than the pagan is, and hence the poetry of desire. We reject this reasoning. It seems to us that if religion had the effect on art which he asserts, then would polytheism more than Christianity be the religion of sadness. The Christian dies but to be born into a higher life. This hope compensates him for much of this life's ills; and makes him look on death as a subject of rejoicing, not of grief. The polytheist has not such a hope. (pp. 170-71)

The part played by Destiny in the Greek drama, is another instance of that rash synthesis to which unphilosophic minds resort. "Inward liberty and outward necessity," [Schlegel] says, "are the two poles of the tragic world." . . . [He] subsequently says that the "necessity ought to be no natural necessity, but to lie beyond the world of sense in the abyss of infinitude; and it must consequently be represented as the invincible power of Fate; *(folglich stellt sie sich als die unergründliche Macht des Schicksals dar).*" This is plain enough; let us now confront it with the facts.

The part actually played by Destiny, in the Greek drama, is extremely small. It is to be seen there, of course, as the doctrine of immortality is in our drama; but in both cases this is only as a portion of the national creed, not as an artistic principle; it was not there the poet sought the elements of tragedy. Shakspeare is a Christian poet, and his works are addressed to Christian audiences; yet would it be a very absurd criticism which asserted that moral responsibility and a future state formed the groundwork of the tragedy of *Lear,* or *Othello.* Such, however, is the reasoning of Schlegel. He finds the Greeks believed in an irresistible Destiny, and forthwith declares Destiny to be the ground of tragedy. Bad as this logic is, it is not the weakest portion of his famous formula. Let any one examine the nature of the several Greek dramas extant, and he will find that, in scarcely a dozen of them, can Destiny be said to have any prominence; and that in the rest it has no place. It is to be observed that Schlegel lays down principles in his introductory lectures which he never afterwards applies; and having stated Destiny to be the ground of tragedy, he never, subsequently, points out the use made of it by the poets. (pp. 171-72)

[We may expose Schlegel's error by examining the *Prometheus,* of which he] says that "the other poems are tragedies, but this is tragedy itself: its purest spirit is revealed with all the annihilating and overpowering influence of its first unmitigated austerity." The subject of the *Prometheus* is too generally familiar to need any account of it here. The struggle is between Zeus and Prometheus. The chained Titan glories in his deed . . . he knows that Zeus himself must one day lose the sovereign power, and therefore he suffers proudly. Zeus is here a Tyrant, not the symbol of Destiny, since he himself is subject to it. The tragic ground is, therefore, the same as if the struggle were between a king and a subject, instead of between a Titan and a god, and in nowise the struggle of man's soul with Destiny. The more we meditate on this piece, the more we shall feel convinced that Schlegel's notion is unfounded. The strongest application of his notion is not in the *Prometheus,* but in the *Oedipus.* Here, indeed, we see a great mind 'struggling in vain with ruthless Destiny;' yet most men would have suspected *Oedipus* to be tragic on the same principle as *Lear* or *Othello,* and would have referred the cause to some eternal facts of human nature, rather than to any religious dogma. (pp. 172-73)

Schlegel's view of the Chorus next deserves our attention, as another instance of his vicious method. (p. 173)

Schlegel, in his usual 'synthetic' manner, pronounces the "Chorus a personification of opinion on the action which is going on" . . . "it represented first the national spirit, and then the general participation of mankind. In a word, the Chorus is *the ideal spectator.*" Confronted with facts, this explanation is incompetent. What had the personification of opinion to do with the singing and dancing? Yet singing and dancing formed such important elements in the Chorus, that Schlegel himself, in objecting to Schiller's employment of it in *Die Braut von Messina,* says "modern poets have often attempted to introduce the chorus in their pieces, but for the most part without a correct, and always without *a vivid idea of its destination. We have no suitable singing or dancing:* and it will hardly ever succeed therefore in becoming naturalized with us." We may further ask: what 'general participation of mankind' is there in a Chorus which becomes the approving confidant of treacherous designs, and which in one place is maltreated and knocked down? (Vide Euripides: we forget the precise play.) We would ask, How can the Chorus be at one and the same time both 'ideal spectator' and actor in the drama? For an actor in the Drama it assuredly was, according to the evidence of the plays, and the express authority of Aristotle. It is true that Schlegel holds Aristotle cheap; true he says in one place that "Aristotle has entirely failed in seizing the real genius and spirit of the Greek tragedy;" true that he pays little regard to facts; and yet we find it difficult to conceive how he could for an instant reconcile his view of the Chorus with any single specimen. If ever the 'personification of opinion' be indeed present, it surely only forms one element and not the whole? We cannot however believe that it is ever present. Moral reflections, plaints of

woe, exultations of joy, long narratives, and brilliant imagery, are there; and these may perhaps be construed into the 'general participation of mankind' by the cunning artifices of 'synthetic criticism,' as Dante's *Beatrice* has been construed into Theology, or as Shakspeare's plays have been construed into concrete expressions of German philosophy. But we openly avow our hostility to such jugglery. We can neither receive such an explanation as true of the Greek Chorus, nor as in accordance with the Greek spirit. (p. 174)

We have hitherto dealt with [Schlegel] as a man of rash generalization; we have now to speak of him as an advocate.

In his first lecture he has given a description of what a true critic should aspire to; and this passage is worthy of being transcribed in letters of gold. "No man can be a true critic who does not possess a universality of mind, who does not possess a flexibility which, throwing aside all personal predilections and blind habits, enables him to transport himself into the peculiarities of other ages and nations, and to feel them as it were from their central point." (p. 175)

We have full right to test Schlegel by his own standard; and according to that we say he has shown himself to be no 'true critic,' for he has failed in placing himself at the 'central point of view.' We will not stop to point out the errors of his very slovenly and inaccurate lectures on the Roman and Italian dramas; but his treatment of Alfieri cannot be passed over in silence.

Alfieri, the greatest of the Italian dramatists, is dismissed in five pages, which contain almost as many blunders as paragraphs. He is here an advocate against the poet, and very sophistical are the arguments he brings forward. "From the tragedy of the Greeks," he says, "with which Alfieri first became acquainted towards the end of his career, he was separated by a wide chasm." If this be meant as expressing that the form and purpose of the dramas of Alfieri differed from those of the ancients, it is a truism; if that the artistic spirit (such as we before defined it) is different, it is an absurdity. No nation so closely resembles the Greeks, in artistic spirit, as the Italians; no dramatist so closely resembles Aeschylus as Alfieri. "I cannot consider his pieces," continues our critic, "as improvements on the French tragedy:" why should he? Let us for an instant grant that Alfieri is the reverse of the Greeks, and no improvement on the French, what then? Does not the matter resolve itself into this; that being an Italian, and addressing Italians, Alfieri is to be judged without reference to Greece or France? His nationality is a quality, not a fault. Yet we are told "his pieces bear no comparison with the better French tragedies in pleasing and brilliant eloquence:" how should they when it was his express desire to avoid declamatory tirades, which he considered undramatic? Göthe has well said that there is a negative criticism which consists in applying a different standard from that chosen by the author, and in this way you are sure to find him wanting. This Schlegel perpetually uses. Alfieri hated the French, and never thought of imitating them.

It is in his account of the French drama that Schlegel most unblushingly assumes the advocate's robe. His object is evidently not to place himself at the 'central point,' but to make the French drama ridiculous. He endeavours to dwarf it by most irrelevant contrasts with the Greek and Shakspearian drama, and only succeeds in displaying his critical incompetence. Let it be remembered however in extenuation, that Schlegel's object was not without its use in his day, though worse than useless now. French taste had for years usurped the German stage. Gottlob Lessing struck the usurper down. By dint of rare acuteness, untiring wit, and his impetuous zeal, he won the battle for ever. Schlegel rode gracefully over the battle-field and counted the slain; then, retiring to the metropolis, published his bulletin. Beside the masculine intellect of a Lessing, clear as crystal and as solid too, Schlegel is a foppish *petit maître*. But he addressed *petits maîtres*. The battle had been won in open field, with sweat of brow and strength of hand; but it had to be recounted in drawing-rooms, and for this the hardy warrior, covered with dust and gore, was not so fitted as the perfumed Schlegel, master of small talk and gifted with rhetorical abundance. The warrior and the coxcomb each did his work. Nevertheless, had Lessing and others never lived, Schlegel perhaps would eloquently have expatiated on the beauties of Racine; but when once the breach was made in the citadel, it was so pleasant to ride in, gracefully triumphant!

It is most true that Racine was not a Greek; true that he did not write upon romantic principles; but what then? Was he not a Frenchman, a poet of the higher order, worthy even to be placed beside the illustrious few? Because a Deer is neither Horse nor Elephant, is it nothing? It is a strange synthesis that concludes so; yet, metaphor apart, such is the conclusion of our critic. He admits that we "shall be compelled to allow the execution of the French drama is *masterly, perhaps not to be surpassed;* but the great question is, how far it is in spirit and inward essence related to the Greek, and whether it deserves to be considered an improvement on it." Not so at all: it is a question every way superfluous, a standard utterly fallacious. The antique drama grew up out of the spirit and artistic feeling of the Greeks, under a set of conditions which can never be again. So also did the French drama grow up out of the national spirit, of which it was the expression. It borrowed a learned air because it addressed a pedantic age; and even in its imitation of the ancients it expressed one characteristic of its own time. So also it was tinctured with gallantry, as our own drama was with concetti, because this was the fashion of the day. (pp. 176-78)

The Lecture on Shakspeare has met with more approbation than any other portion of the work. We believe it has been vastly overrated; we believe that eloquence has been mistaken for criticism, and varied ingenious illustration for profound insight. The author has, we are willing to admit, 'said many excellent things *about Shakspeare;*' but that he has worthily treated this great subject, that he has at all pierced to the core of it, that he has given to the student any important light, we cannot believe. It is a panegyric, not a criticism: a masterly panegyric, which many years ago was of beneficial influence. Had reason—had analysis formed the staple, and eloquence only the ornament of this Lecture, it would have been as useful now as then; but Schlegel is a rhetorician by nature, and as such we should have left him in peace had not his admirers declared him to be a philosophic critic.

It is not, however, on the score of unlimited admiration that we think Schlegel's lecture so faulty; it is because he has used pompous phrases, which are empty sounds with him. He talks of Shakspeare's 'profound art,' yet he gives no example of it. Shakspeare *was* a profound artist; he would not otherwise have been the greatest poet that the world has seen; but how has Schlegel exhibited specimens of it? He spins phrases; he says fine things *about* Shakspeare; and too much 'about,' not enough to the purpose. Let any one compare his brief and meager notices of the separate plays with the highflown panegyric

which precedes them: it will then be seen how barren is this verbiage of philosophy, how useless are these bursts of rhetoric when face to face with details. We must repeat there is no style of criticism so easy as this of 'synthetical appreciation.' Observe the licence of imagination in such passages as these: "'Shylock' possesses a very determinate and original individuality; and yet we perceive a light touch of Judaism in every thing which he says or does. *We imagine we hear a sprinkling of the Jewish pronunciation in the mere written words.*" Surely, if critics are allowed to 'imagine' in this way, sane men will shut their ears. If criticism is to become a province of conjecture and imagination, not a science, the sooner it be abolished the better. To conjecture is easy, to know is difficult; therefore, unless we curb the vagabond licence of the former, the latter will grow into rusty disuse. That Schlegel has little knowledge, and abundant conjecture, we believe has been established during the course of this article. (pp. 180-81)

[*George Henry Lewes*], "Augustus William Schlegel," in The Foreign Quarterly Review, *Vol. XXXII, No. LXIII, October, 1843, pp. 160-81.*

THE NEW ENGLANDER   (essay date 1844)

[*In the excerpt below, the anonymous writer surveys Schlegel's literary career, commenting on the merit of his creative and critical works and assessing the effects of the Schlegel brothers' critical theories.*]

[Augustus William Schlegel] is a man whom perhaps half of our readers know only by name, a man whom Germany itself seems to have forgotten; and yet, if all that modern literature, which has long been distinguished by the epithet *romantic,* were grateful, it would erect statues to Schlegel; for he was, after Lessing, its first, its most vigorous and most illustrious champion. (pp. 185-86)

It was W. Schlegel, who first, agitating effectually the great question of liberty in art, and discussing, from a point of view much more elevated than that of La Mothe, the famous dramatic legislation attributed to Aristotle, traced with a bold hand the poetry of romanticism: it was he, who first brought into one view, Sophocles, Aeschylus, Euripides, Corneille, Racine, Voltaire, Shakspeare and Calderon, the ancient theater, the theater imitated from the ancient and the modern theater, claiming for the last the right to be governed only by principles, drawn from the genius, ideas and manners of modern nations. (pp. 186-87)

[Early in his literary career, Schlegel established], conjointly with his brother Frederic, the *Athenaeum,* a literary review, which exercised a great influence over the direction of ideas in Germany—an influence for which the two brothers Schlegel have been severely reproached by later critics, and of which it is necessary for us to say a few words. . . .

[Upon] the ruins of the French, Greek and English schools, [the brothers Schlegel] attempted to found a school of schools, a vast caravansary, open to all importations, where might meet, upon a footing of equality, all the manifestations of human poetry, from the commencement of the world to the present day. From aversion to the exclusive spirit in criticism, they carried eclecticism to its utmost limits, and preached a kind of aesthetic polytheism, confounding, in the same adoption, all the gods of all countries and of all ages. The advantages and the dangers of this theory may easily be conceived; it enlarged the sphere of inspiration, but destroyed all originality, by annihilating the conditions of time and place. In short, it was more injurious than useful, in the formation and development of a truly national literature. Moreover, there soon resulted from it a new rage for translations and imitations, no longer limited to certain favorite models, but extended without distinction to all foreign productions. The intentions of the Schlegels were good; they aspired to make of literary Germany a bee-nation, rifling indiscriminately all the flowers of the human mind, to compose its honey; and their cosmopolite theory, fortified by the example of Göthe, produced on the contrary a swarm of hornets, withering the flowers by their touch, and unable to extract aught, save the proof of their own impotence. (p. 188)

[In] their eclecticism, in point of tastes and manners, [the Schlegels] readily admired, as the criterion of the beautiful in poetry, elegance and harmony of verse. William Schlegel united practice with theory. His various poems, which have gone through several editions, present a curious mixture of inspirations, pagan, Christian, mythological, catholic, oriental, chivalric, serious, trifling, refined, simple. Odes, epistles, elegies, ballads, songs, epigrams, sonnets—every thing is found there, every thing, even to the severe Greek tragedy of *Ion*, . . . which there figures between a *choliambe* and a *triolet*. The pieces entitled, **"Arion," "Pygmalion," "Prometheus,"** the **"Legend of St. Lucas,"** the **"Ballad of Fortunatus,"** and the **"Elegy of Rome,"** dedicated to Madame de Staël, are remarkable fragments. Among the sonnets are some very beautiful [pieces], especially those suggested by the death of a young girl, Augusta Baehmer. But if the poems of Schlegel are cosmopolite in substance, they are still more so in form. The poet's aim seems to have been, to execute, in the German language, every kind of poetical feat. He displays, in his rhythmical combinations, a variety and flexibility, which often degenerate into affectation and puerile coquetry. Thus there are poems, where, in each stanza, the measure diminishes by one syllable in each line, and others, where the poet imposes upon himself at pleasure, nine rhymes in succession: sometimes the grave Schlegel disdains not to indicate in italics *bouts-rimés*, which he has filled up very agreeably. All this is curious, and evinces rare skill in the management of the language, a skill of which Schlegel made an excellent use in his translations of Shakspeare and Calderon; but in original poems, this excessive attention to the style can not fail to impair the truth or the energy of the idea.

Another charge, which has been brought against the two celebrated editors of the *Athenaeum*, refers to the general tone of their criticism, and to their enthusiasm for Göthe, carried even to adoration, and combined with a severity towards their adversaries, easily changing to aristocratic haughtiness and impertinence. Nevertheless the *Athenaeum*, and the other polemical writings of Schlegel, have had their share of good influences also. Endowed by nature with the perception of the ideal, the noble and grand, the powerful critic made war unto death against frivolity and immorality. Independent of the poetical pantheism of Göthe, German literature was then separated into two parties. The idyls of Gessner and the celebrated pastoral and domestic poem of "Louisa" by Voss, had produced a mass of imitations; . . . Voss and Gessner knew how to preserve a certain simple grace, but in the hands of their imitators, [the German pastoral muse] gradually assumed the form of a ruddy milkmaid, with coarse hands, tangled hair and naked feet. Others were inspired with a fondness for the most vulgar incidents of life: there was a profusion of hexameters upon the delights of the table, of coffee, beer, sour-krout, potatoes, pipes

and slippers. W. Schlegel directed, against this poetry of the poultry-yard and kitchen, the keen shafts of his criticism, and the torrent was arrested by his elegant *persiflage*.

In a different way, the famous Kotzebue formed another literary and dramatic sect. Possessing talent and genius, but wanting greatness of soul, Kotzebue had acquired the popular favor, by introducing into the drama a feeble and false style, a mixture of frivolity and sentiment, where the most complete moral skepticism is plainly discernible, amid the interest of scenic combinations. This manner of adorning, coloring and ennobling vulgarity and vice, was rudely attacked by Schlegel. He put to the sword that innumerable family of mean and pitiable villains, with whom Kotzebue filled all the theaters of Germany—a despicable family, who practice, profess or tolerate, with sensibility and decency, deceit, knavery and profligacy. Schlegel attacked these bastardly creations, from the three stand-points of art, truth and morality, with the weapons of reason and ridicule, in prose and in verse, with logic and with epigrams. His collection of poems contains a series of sonnets, entitled **"A Triumphal Arch, Erected in Honor of Kotzebue,"** and composed at this period. It is poetry of the burlesque kind, in which are not wanting words inelegant, but full of wit and sarcasm. (pp. 189-90)

[At] Vienna, in the spring of 1808, amid a concourse of hearers, [W. Schlegel commenced] that famous course of lectures on dramatic literature, which has since been published in three volumes, and translated into all languages, and which in many respects, deserves the reputation it has obtained. . . . In the opinion of Schlegel, there are but three truly original theaters, which under this title are the objects of a minute analysis: the Greek theater, from which are derived the Latin and French, and the two theaters, which he calls *romantic*, the Spanish and the English, which, although contemporary, have a peculiar physiognomy, independent of each other, and have served to form the German theater, the foundations of which were laid by Göthe and Schiller. The first volume [of *A Course of Lectures on Dramatic Art and Literature*] is devoted entirely to the Greek theater, and is unquestionably the most remarkable. Never before Schlegel, had criticism been raised to such a height, to such splendor; it is a rare mixture of profound science, of lofty and brilliant poetry. The critic speaks of Greece with enthusiasm; he comprehends it, as an artist and a poet, in its most minute details, as well as in the harmony of the whole; the picture which he draws of Greek society, is one of the most beautiful things we have ever read. The following is one passage of many equally beautiful.

> The moral culture of the Greeks was a natural education perfected; the offspring of a noble race, endowed with delicate organs and a clear understanding, they lived under a mild and pure sky, and, favored by the happiest circumstances, accomplished all which it is given to man, confined within the limits of life, to accomplish here below. All their arts and their poetry express the consciousness of this harmony of their different faculties. They realized the poetry of happiness.

In the same elevated tone, Schlegel proceeds to the analysis of Sophocles, Aeschylus, Euripides and Aristophanes. Sophocles is his favorite Greek dramatist. The Latin and Italian theaters are treated very summarily and with extreme severity. The French theater is examined more in detail, and this is undoubtedly owing to the desire of the critic to destroy the glory of this theater. Here Schlegel is inferior to himself: not that this portion of his work does not contain a great number of judicious ideas and observations, which are true and will remain so; but Schlegel is evidently under the influence of passion. It is the dictatorship of Napoleon, which he is attacking, in the dictatorship of the French theater, and this is proved by the instantaneous change in the tone and nature of his criticism. The professor, who but lately had contended, with as much eloquence as reason, against the old negative criticism, exclusively intent upon the discovery of defects, identifying himself with the men of all countries and of all ages, in order to see and feel like them, now creeps along in the old beaten track, and analyzes Racine much as Laharpe would have analyzed Shakspeare. He sees, in the French theater, nothing but an imitation of the Greek, and after having proved how far from exact this imitation is, he concludes that the copy is bad and inferior to the original, instead of concluding that it is another, and that this very difference constitutes its true originality. He praises Racine, when he approaches the Greek tragedy, and blames him, when he removes from it: instead of seeing in Racine a *romantic*, that is a chivalric and Christian poet, painting, under Greek names and with the severe forms of Greek tragedy, chivalric and Christian heroes; instead of discussing the advantages and disadvantages of this fusion of forms and ideas, more or less heterogeneous, he persists in reducing the author of *Phaedra* to this dilemma: you copy, therefore you are not an inventor, you invent, therefore you are a bad copyist.

In the examination of the French comedy, Schlegel is still more feeble; for example, when he says—"Molière succeeded best in burlesque comedy, and his talent, as well as his inclination, was for farces," what does he prove, but that the worthy German critic understood not a word of *Tartuffe* or the *Misanthrope*? In the analysis of Shakspeare, the admiration of Schlegel becomes fanaticism: it is throughout a perpetual hymn. He afterwards confessed with candor that the English, even the most *Shakspearian*, considered him as an *ultra*. Nevertheless, the examination of the English theater is, after that of the Greek theater, the most remarkable part of the work. The Spanish theater, of which Schlegel sums up the principal epochs, in the persons of Cervantes, Lope de Vega and Calderon, is analyzed more briefly, although with the same enthusiastic admiration. In the examination of the German theater, which he considers in its infancy, the critic shows himself more calm, perhaps even a little severe. (pp. 191-93)

[In the] latter part of his career, Schlegel, already versed in the knowledge of all the languages and all the literatures of Europe, devoted himself to the study of the oriental languages, especially of the Sanscrit. He is now one of the most distinguished Indian scholars of the age. After having established at Bonn a printing office *ad hoc*, he enriched this part of science with several important works; among others, two volumes, entitled the *Indian Library* . . . ; a volume . . . containing the Latin translation of an episode of the Sanscrit poem, *Mahâbhârata;* a French work with the title, **The Origin of the Hindoos** [*De l'origine des Hindous*]; a memoir, addressed to M. Sylvestre de Sacy, in which, contrary to the opinion of that orientalist, he maintains that the invention of the tales of a *Thousand and One Nights*, attributed to the Arabians, belongs to the Indians; and another memoir, entitled, **Reflections upon the Study of the Asiatic Languages** [*Réflexions sur l'étude des langues asiatiques*], dedicated to Mackintosh. (p. 193)

From all this the reader can not fail to recognize in Schlegel, a poet, critic, philologist, orientalist and translator, a man

whose name will live in the literary history of the last fifty years. If the limits of this sketch permitted, it would be interesting to inquire, wherein Schlegel has become obsolete in literature; which of his ideas Germany has accepted and which it has repudiated: to seek, not only in Germany, but also in France, the traces of the influence exercised by him over modern criticism, unquestionably superior to ancient criticism, if not in erudition, at least in the elevation of the point of view, the grandeur and the range of the ideas. The fault of Schlegel's criticism, we have already indicated: it is an excessive pretension to universality; to constitute oneself the supreme judge of the literatures of all nations, is an enormous and dangerous enterprise. "With regard to both poets and prose-writers," as M. Sainte Beuve has well remarked, "each nation is the best judge of its own: the flower-girl of Athens, or, to speak in the style of Paul Louis Courrier, the meanest woman of the *rue Chauchat*, knows more of certain indigenous faults, than the foreign man of genius."

When unmindful of this truth, we are in danger of committing strange mistakes: we are liable, like Göthe, to see in Du Bartas, one of the greatest poets of France, or like Schlegel, in Molière, only a vulgar harlequin. Another disadvantage of this too ambitious criticism, is that of enfeebling, by diffusing too widely, the powers of him who devotes himself to it. Schlegel appears to have felt, but too late, this injurious effect; for he concludes the preface to his last publication, with this expression, which will also serve us for a conclusion: "Those essays are like landmarks, planted along my literary career; at the end of which I must acknowledge to myself, that I have undertaken much and accomplished little." (p. 194)

"A Memoir of Augustus William Schlegel," in The New Englander, *Vol. II, No. VI, April, 1844, pp. 185-94.*

[GEORGE HENRY LEWES]   (essay date 1849)

[*Having previously published a polemic on Schlegel's critical principles and methods (see excerpt dated 1843), Lewes here applies his strictures to Schlegel's Shakespeare commentary, challenging both the originality and clarity of his observations.*]

The Schlegels are constantly mentioned in connexion with Shakspeare; and their merits are certainly great. It is but justice, however, to add that they . . . owe almost every thing to Lessing. All that they have done (translation apart) is but an offshoot from Lessing and Herder. When once Lessing had destroyed the reigning prejudices about art, and shown the narrowness of French principles, and the vital force and richness of Shakspeare, they who came after him had an easy task. If the Schlegels had but followed him in the spirit as well as in the novelties of his criticism, the world would have been spared a quantity of verbiage and fantastic speculation. A. W. Schlegel's 'Lectures' are wonderful *as* lectures, in which the rhetoric is always effective; but they have been singularly overrated as philosophical criticisms. Considered *as* rhetorical expositions, they have a clearness and an eloquence which has carried them over Europe; but we cannot compliment them on their depth or sagacity. The lecture upon Shakspeare contains a number of 'fine things' said *about* the poet; but it is rather a panegyric than a critique. The ideas, when there are ideas, have all the vagueness in which rhetoricians delight, and which philosophers condemn. Expanding an idea which is to be found in Lessing and in Morgann's "Essay on Falstaff" respecting organic and mechanical forms, Schlegel tells us with much emphasis that Shakspeare was an 'organic artist.' But in spite of his glowing praise of the poet's 'profound art,' we defy the most acute reader to divine *what* the precise nature of that art actually is. It may be comforting to know that Shakspeare 'worked upon certain profound principles;' but we should like the teacher to have told us what those principles were, and how we are to detect their 'working' in the plays. Lessing, on the contrary, though less profuse in displays of philosophical language, tells us plainly and forcibly in what Shakspeare's art consists, and in what it is superior to the art of Voltaire. Schlegel speaks finely and discriminatingly upon the masterly power of characterisation which Shakspeare exhibits; but *that* is a topic with regard to which there never has been a dispute, from Ben Jonson downwards. In other respects, and when he descends to details, he is lost; the heights of abstraction and cloudy vagueness alone are congenial to his spirit. We cannot indeed help suspecting the value of those 'profound principles of criticism' which lead a man to decry Molière, to despise Racine, to place Calderon on a level with Shakspeare,—and to proclaim that *Sir John Oldcastle* and *Lord Thomas Cromwell* are not only 'unquestionably written by Shakspeare,' but are 'deserving to be classed among *the best and maturest of his works!*' Nor can we hope to fathom principles which are to prove that Shakspeare's anachronisms 'were for the most part committed *purposely, and after great consideration*'—and that in Shylock 'we hear a sprinkling of the Jewish pronunciation in the mere written words—as we sometimes still find it in the higher classes notwithstanding their social refinement.' Dashing rhetoric carries the day throughout. You are authoritatively told that Shakspeare is an artist. So far so good. You are then further informed that the peculiarity of this Shakspearian art is 'its thorough realisation of the romantic spirit.' Here you begin to feel a haze descending; a modest misgiving steals upon your mind as to whether you clearly apprehend the nature of this same 'romantic spirit;' you wish to understand the distinction between classic and romantic. The wish is rational; and the philosopher is only too happy to enlighten you—in the following luminous sentences: 'The whole of ancient poetry and art is as it were a *rhythmical nomos* (law), an harmonious promulgation of the permanently established legislation of a world submitted to a beautiful order, and reflecting itself in the eternal images of things.' This is not very clear, perhaps; but it sounds well; and as, after all, you care little, perhaps, about ancient art, you hurry on to what is said about the modern—*There* at any rate he may be intelligible. Let us see. 'The romantic poetry, again, is the expression of the *secret attraction to a chaos, which is concealed between the regulated creation,* even in its very bosom, and which is perpetually striving after new and wonderful births; the animating spirit of original love hovers here anew over the waters.' We hope some of our readers may understand this: But for ourselves, we would only ask why, if Shakspeare is the realisation of the spirit above described, the critic has not undertaken to point out the 'secret attraction to chaos' and the 'love hovering over the waters' in Shakspeare's separate plays? But instead of this, he contents himself with meagre and somewhat common-place remarks upon the story and the characters. (pp. 66-7)

> [*George Henry Lewes*], "*Shakspeare's Critics: English and Foreign,*" *in* The Edinburgh Review, *Vol. XC, No. CLXXXI, July, 1849, pp. 39-77.*

MADAME L. DAVÉSIÉS DE PONTÈS (essay date 1858)

> [*With a pointed reference to Heine's essay (see excerpt dated 1835), Davésiés de Pontès suggests that Schlegel's reputation will survive the onslaughts of time and ridicule.*]

We must not allow the re-action which of late years has taken place in Germany, or the mischievous raillery of a writer equally clever and unscrupulous who respects nothing either divine or human, to blind us to William Schlegel's merits, to his lofty endowments or to the salutary influence which, on the whole, he exercised over his country and his age. He first thoroughly penetrated into the secret of ancient scenic art. To him it was no longer a thing of the past; it became a living and breathing reality. His analysis of Shakespeare is no less masterly than his translation, though here, as usual, when carried away by his feelings, he saw only the beauties as in Molière he beheld only the defects. In short, let Mr. Heine laugh at him as he will, Schlegel will probably be remembered for other reasons than his "Petite peruque blonde" and his "Ruban." (p. 377)

> *Madame L. Davésiés de Pontès, "William Schlegel, Frederick Schlegel, Tieck, La Motte Fouqué, Novalis, Schulze.," in her* Poets and Poetry of Germany: Biographical and Critical Notices, *Vol. II, Chapman & Hall, 1858, pp. 372-423.*

GEORGE BRANDES (essay date 1873)

> [*Brandes, a Danish literary critic and biographer, was the principal leader of the intellectual movement that helped to bring an end to Scandinavian cultural isolation. He believed that literature reflects the spirit and problems of its time and that it must be understood within its social and aesthetic context. Brandes's major critical opus,* Hovedstrømninger i det 19de aarhundredes litteratur, *won him admiration for his ability to view literary movements within the broader context of all of European literature. In the following excerpt from his discussion of the German Romantic school in that work, originally published in 1873, Brandes outlines the evolution of Schlegel's first translations of Shakespeare. Observing the influence of Bürger, Schiller, Goethe, and other contemporary and near-contemporary German writers on Schlegel's work, he characterizes the translations as a synthesis of "the intellectual history of a whole generation."*]

In 1797, August Wilhelm Schlegel, then aged thirty, published the first volume of his translation of Shakespeare. Rough drafts of several of the plays in this edition have been found, and these faded, dusty manuscripts not only enable us to follow the persevering, talented translator in his self-imposed task, but, when carefully read, give us direct insight into his and his wife's spiritual life, and indeed into the intellectual life of the whole period. (p. 49)

The manuscripts are not always in A. W. Schlegel's handwriting. He set to work upon *Romeo and Juliet* in the winter of 1795-96; in 1796 he married Caroline Böhmer; and we have a complete copy of the first rough draft of the play in Caroline's handwriting, with corrections in Schlegel's. In September 1797, as her letters show, she copied *As You Like It* from an almost illegible manuscript. And she was more than a mere copyist. She collaborated with Schlegel in his essay on *Romeo and Juliet,* which ranks next to Goethe's disquisitions on *Hamlet* in *Wilhelm Meister* as the best Shakespeare criticism produced in Germany up to that time. We recognise her now and again in some outburst of womanly feeling, or in a greater freedom of style than we are accustomed to in Schlegel. She had a far truer understanding than her contemporaries of the full significance of a work, the aim of which was the incorporation of Shakespeare in his unalloyed entirety into German literature. But her interest in the work and the labourer did not, as the manuscripts show us, survive the first year of her married life. At first it is her handwriting which predominates, and, though it is less frequently to be seen alongside of her husband's in the manuscripts of those plays with which he was occupied during the years 1797-98, her collaboration is still apparent. We find the last traces of her pen in the manuscript of the *Merchant of Venice,* which dates from the autumn of 1798. In October of that year, Schelling joined the Romanticist circle in Jena. Thenceforward no more of Caroline's handwriting is discoverable.

Among the manuscripts in question, two give us a very distinct idea of the progress of Schlegel's intellectual development. They are two different texts of the *Midsummer Night's Dream.*

Before A. W. Schlegel's time no one in Germany, or elsewhere, had attempted to translate Shakespeare line for line. The two tame prose translations by Wieland and Eschenburg were, in fact, all that existed. As a student in Göttingen, Schlegel made the first attempt to reproduce in German verse parts of the *Midsummer Night's Dream.* (pp. 49-50)

At this time Bürger [who was serving as a professor at the University of Göttingen] was still considered to be Germany's best lyric poet and most accomplished versifier. Schlegel placed himself under his tuition, and learned all his linguistic and metrical devices, all the methods of producing artistic effects by careful choice and arrangement of words and use of rhythm and metres. With his natural gift of imitation, he appropriated as many of Bürger's characteristics as were at all compatible with his entirely different temperament. His poem **"Ariadne"** might have been written by Bürger. Bürger had been particularly successful in the sonnet, a form of poetry which had lately come into vogue in Germany. So closely did the pupil follow in the footsteps of his master, that when, many years later, a complete edition of Schlegel's works was published, two of Bürger's sonnets were accidentally included among them. (pp. 50-1)

In collaboration with Bürger he now began a translation of the *Midsummer Night's Dream,* of which he did the greater part, Bürger merely revising. He was still completely under his master's influence; the manuscripts show that he always accepted Bürger's corrections and deferred to his predilection for sonority and vigour. As a translator, Bürger took no pains to reproduce Shakespeare's peculiarities as closely as possible; he only manifested his own peculiarities, by making all the coarse, wanton speeches, and the passages in which misguided passions run riot, as prominent as possible; he emphasised and exaggerated everything that appealed to his own liking for a coarse jest, and destroyed the magic of the light and tender passages. In spite of his own great and natural love of refinement, young Schlegel strove in this matter also to follow in his master's steps, with the result that he was not infrequently coarse and awkward where he meant to be natural and vigorous.

A better guide would have been Herder, who, long before this, in the fragments of Shakespeare plays in his *Stimmen der Völker,* had given an example of the right method of translating from English into German. If Schlegel had taken lessons from Herder in Shakespeare-translating, he would never have rendered five-footed iambics by Alexandrines, nor changed the metre of the fairy-songs. No one had realised the inadequacy of Wieland's translation more clearly than Herder. And now the spirit in which the latter aimed at Germanising Shakespeare descended upon Schlegel, who, in spite of the faults of his first attempts, soon surpassed Herder himself. (pp. 51-2)

In 1791, Schlegel, now no longer in Bürger's vicinity, but a tutor in Amsterdam, devoted much attention to the works of Schiller. His poetical attempts were henceforth more in the

style of that master; he wrote a sympathetic criticism of *Die Künstler;* and he was led to a higher conception of art by the perusal of Schiller's æsthetic writings. His metrical style began to acquire greater dignity. But Schiller was almost as incapable as Bürger of developing in Schlegel a true and full understanding of Shakespeare—Schiller, who, in his translation of *Macbeth,* had transformed the witches into Greek Furies, and changed the Porter's coarsely jovial monologue into an edifying song. If Bürger's realism was one danger, Schiller's pomposity was another.

But at the same time that Schiller enlightened Schlegel as to the high significance of art, the newly-published Collected Works of Goethe, whom he only now began to appreciate, stimulated his natural inclination to study, interpret, and make poetical translations. . . . [To] Schlegel's critical intellect, Goethe's wonderful many-sidedness was now revealed. He understood and appreciated the artist's capacity of forgetting himself for the moment, of surrendering himself entirely to the influence of his subject, which in Goethe's case produced forms that were never arbitrarily chosen, but invariably demanded by the theme. He understood that he himself, as a poetical translator, must practise the same self-abnegation and develop a similar capacity of intellectual re-creation. Two things were required of the translator, a feminine susceptibility to the subtlest characteristics of the foreign original, and masculine capacity to re-create with the impression of the whole in his mind; and both of these requirements were to be found in Goethe; for his nature was multiplicity, his name "Legion," his spirit Protean.

There still remained the technical, linguistic difficulties to overcome; and in this, above all, Goethe was an epoch-making model. He had remoulded the German language. In passing through his hands it had gained so greatly in pliability and compass, had acquired such wealth of expression both in the grand and the graceful style, that it offered Schlegel exactly the well-tuned instrument of which he stood in need. While under Bürger's influence he had looked upon technical perfection as a purely external quality, which could be acquired by indefatigable polishing; he now realised that perfect technique has an inward origin, that it is in reality the unity of style which is conditioned by the general cast of a mind. (pp. 52-3)

Now, too, Schlegel acquired a quite new understanding of Fichte, the friend and brother-in-arms whom the Romanticists had so quickly won for their cause. He realised that Fichte's doctrine of the Ego contained in extremely abstract terms the idea of the unlimited capacity of the human mind to find itself in everything and to find everything in itself. Round this powerful fundamental thought of Fichte's, August Wilhelm's pliable mind twined itself. (p. 54)

[He] put his translation of Shakespeare aside for a time, and turned his attention to the poets of the South. He experimented in all directions, translated fragments of Homer, of the Greek elegiac, lyric, dramatic, and idyllic poets, of almost all the Latin poets and many of the Italian, Spanish, and Portuguese. . . . He lingered longest over Dante, although he did not possess the mastery of form required to render the *terza rima;* he rhymed only two lines of each triplet, thus altering the character of the verse and doing away with the intertwining of the stanzas.

After this he turned to *Romeo and Juliet* and *Hamlet,* sending fragments of his translations to [his brother] Friedrich, who showed them to Caroline. Her judgment was favourable on the whole, but she found fault with the style as being rather antiquated; this she ascribed to Wilhelm's having been lately employed in translating Dante, his ear having thereby become accustomed to obsolete words and expressions. The fact was, that shortly before this he had awakened to the necessity of being on his guard against the elaborate polish which he had made his aim after giving up Bürger's style; he now fell into the other extreme, became archaic, rugged, and hard.

In 1797 Schlegel sent the first samples of *Romeo and Juliet* to Schiller. They were printed in *Die Horen;* and in the same periodical there presently also appeared his essay, **"Etwas über William Shakespeare bei Gelegenheit Wilhelm Meisters."** In *Wilhelm Meister* Goethe had proclaimed the endeavour to understand Shakespeare to be an important element in German culture. In its conversations on *Hamlet* he had refuted the foolish theory that the great dramatist was an uncultivated natural genius, destitute of artistic consciousness. Had such been the case, the exact reproduction of his style would not have been a matter of vital importance in a German translation. But with so great an artist as the Shakespeare presented to us in *Wilhelm Meister,* it was plain that the harmony between subject and form must not be deranged. And yet even Goethe himself had, without any feeling of unsuitability, given his quotations from *Hamlet* in the old prose translation; even he had not realised how inseparably matter and manner are connected.

Slowly and laboriously Schlegel progresses. His judgment is still so defective that he fancies it impossible to dispense with Alexandrines; in *Romeo and Juliet,* he retains the five-footed iambics only "as far as possible"; the scene between Romeo and Friar Laurence he renders in Alexandrines, excusing himself with the remark that this metre is less detrimental in speeches garnished with maxims and descriptions than in the dialogue proper of the drama. The result is the loss of Romeo's lyric fervour.

He feels this himself, and with iron industry and determined enthusiasm sets to work again, rejects the Alexandrines, and compels himself, in spite of the verbosity of the German language, to say in ten or eleven syllables what he had said before in twelve or thirteen. For long it appears to him an impossible task to reproduce each line by one line. The translation swells in his hands as it did in Bürger's. Fourteen English lines become nineteen or twenty German. It seems to him that it is impossible to do with less; until at last he gains true insight, and sees, from the very foundation, how Shakespeare raises the edifice of his art. Now he renounces all amplitude and all redundancy that is not in Shakespeare. Each line is rendered by a single line. He curses and bewails the prolixity and inadequacy of German: his language has such different limits, such different turns of expression from the English language; he cannot reproduce Shakespeare's style; what he produces is a stammer, a stutter, without resonance or fire—but he coerces himself, he coerces the language, and produces his translation. (pp. 55-7)

Having acquired complete mastery of the style, Schlegel now began to reap the fruits of his labour. He, the master, opened his hand, and between the years 1797 and 1801 let fall from it into the lap of the German people sixteen of Shakespeare's dramas, which, in spite of occasional tameness or constraint of style, might, in their new form, have been the work of a German poet of Shakespeare's rank.

Let us consider what this really means. It means not much less than that Shakespeare, as well as Schiller and Goethe, saw the

light in Germany in the middle of last century. He was born in England in 1564; he was born again, in his German translator, in 1767. *Romeo and Juliet* was published in London in 1597; it reappeared in Berlin as a new work in 1797.

When Shakespeare thus returned to life in Germany, he acted with full force upon a public which was in several ways more capable of understanding him than his original public, though it was spiritually less akin to him and though they were not the battles of its day which he fought. He now began to feed the millions who did not understand English with his spiritual bread. Not until now did Central and Northern Europe discover him. Not until now did the whole Germanic-Gothic world become his public.

But we have also seen how much went to the production of an apparently unpretending literary work of this high rank. In its rough drafts and manuscripts we may read a great part of the intellectual history of a whole generation. Before it could come into existence nothing less was required than that Lessing's criticism and Wieland's and Eschenburg's attempts should prepare the soil, and that a genius like Herder should concentrate in himself all the receptivity and ingenuity of surmise belonging to the German mind, and should, with the imperiousness characteristic of him, oblige young Goethe to become his disciple. But Goethe in his prose *Götz* only imitated a prose Shakespeare. There had to be born a man with the unique talent of A. W. Schlegel, and he, with his hereditary linguistic and stylistic ability, had to be placed in a position to acquire the greatest technical perfection of the period. Then he had to free himself, by the influence of Schiller's noble conception of art, from the tendency to coarseness which was the result of Bürger's influence, and at the same time to steer clear of Schiller's tendency to pomposity and dislike of wanton joviality, had to gain a complete understanding of Goethe, to enter into possession, as it were, of the language which Goethe had developed, and to attain to an even clearer conviction than his of the essentiality of the harmony of subject and style in Shakespeare. It was necessary, too, that he should be stimulated by the ardour of a kindred talent and assisted by the keen criticism of a woman. Hundreds of sources had to flow into each other, hundreds of circumstances to coincide, of people to make each other's acquaintance, of minds to meet and fertilise each other, before this work, in its modest perfection, could be given to the world; a small thing, the translation of a poet who had been dead for two hundred years, it yet provided the most precious spiritual nourishment for millions, and exercised a deep and lasting influence on German poetry. (pp. 57-8)

> *George Brandes, "A. W. Schlegel," in his* Main Currents in Nineteenth Century Literature: The Romantic School in Germany, Vol. II, *translated by Diana White and Mary Morison, The Macmillan Company, 1902, pp. 49-58.*

W. SCHERER (essay date 1883)

[*In the following excerpt, originally published in 1883 in his* Geschichte der deutschen Litteratur, *Scherer ranks Schlegel's Shakespeare translations with the works of such illustrious contemporary writers as Goethe and Schiller.*]

Wilhelm Schlegel was the first to apply those newly developed forces of German language and metrical art, which dated from the appearance of Goethe's first Iambic plays, to making a noble German version of the great English dramatist.

Between 1797 and 1801 he translated sixteen of Shakspeare's plays, and in 1810 there followed yet a further instalment. Schlegel's Shakspeare certainly surpassed Voss' Homer. It did not conceal the wide difference between creative and imitative art, but it showed the close kinship between one perfect work and another, and for this reason it may rank directly by the side of the works which Goethe and Schiller produced in the period of their common labours.

W. Scherer, "Science: A. W. Schlegel," in his A History of German Literature, Vol. II, edited by F. Max Müller, translated by Mrs. F. C. Conybeare, 1886. Reprint by Charles Scribner's Sons, 1899, p. 250.

CHARLES F. JOHNSON (essay date 1909)

[*Johnson assesses Schlegel's Shakespeare commentary in* Lectures on Dramatic Art and Literature, *faulting his "romantic" critical approach as nonscientific, yet acknowledging his "broad and generous comprehension of Shakespearean art."*]

Little more than one hundred pages [of Schlegel's **Lectures on Dramatic Art and Literature**] are directly concerned with Shakespeare, but the work is the first connected commentary on the plays in the [German] language. It exhibits the fault of the romanticist in giving general impressions in impassioned language, and not analyzing or establishing statements by quotations. It is true, these general propositions commend themselves to us except when he says that the three parts of *Henry VI* and *Richard III* 'were undoubtedly composed in succession, as is proved by the style and the spirit in the handling of the subject.' Confidence in his critical faculty receives a severe shock when we read of *Thomas Lord Cromwell, Sir John Oldcastle* (First Part), and *A Yorkshire Tragedy:* 'These three pieces are not only unquestionably Shakespeare's, but in my opinion they deserve to be classed among his best and maturest works.' He falls into another but less serious error in writing of *Othello:*—

What a fortunate mistake that the Moor (under which name in the original novel a baptized Saracen of the northern coast of Africa was unquestionably meant) has been made by Shakespeare *in every respect a negro:* we recognize in Othello the wild nature of that glowing zone, which generates the most ravenous beasts of prey and the most deadly poisons, tamed only in appearance by foreign laws of honor and by nobler and milder manners. His jealousy is not the jealousy of the heart which is compatible with the tenderest feelings and adoration of the beloved object; it is of that sensual kind which in burning climes has given birth to the disgraceful confinement of women and many other unnatural usages.

To us who know the docile, childlike nature of the negro and his indifference to female exclusiveness, the above seems absurd. It is the Arab, not the Ethiopian, who instituted the 'disgraceful confinement of women.' But Othello is in essentials an Elizabethan gentleman, of a 'free and noble nature,' driven to desperation by agony of soul from the conviction that the wife he loves has proved unfaithful. Again, it is India rather than Africa which 'generates the most ravenous beasts of prey and the most deadly poisons.' But, apart from the above errors, Schlegel shows a broad and generous comprehension of Shakespearean art. (pp. 214-15)

He holds emphatically that Shakespeare is 'a profound artist and not a blind and wildly extravagant genius,' and considers the opposite opinion 'a mere fable, a blind and extravagant error.' He notes the power of giving life to stage characters, declaring that the poet 'possesses a capability of transporting himself so completely into every situation, even the most unusual, that he is enabled as *plenipotentiary of the whole human race*, without particular instructions for each separate case, to act and speak in the name of every individual.'

The inconceivable element herein, and what, moreover, can never be learned, is that the characters appear neither to do or say anything on the spectator's account merely; and yet that the poet, simply by means of the exhibition, and without any subsidiary explanation, communicated to the audience the gift of looking into the inmost recesses of their minds. Hence Goethe has ingeniously compared Shakespeare's characters to watches with crystalline plates and cases, which, while they point out the hours as correctly as other watches, enable us at the same time to perceive the inward springs by which all this is accomplished.

The power of drawing character is as mysterious as character itself, and it is hardly possible to 'look into the inmost recesses of the minds' of the great Shakespearean characters—we only know that the 'recesses' are there. The romanticists are fond of ingenious and striking imagery. . . . Sometimes, as in the above [example] from Goethe, they are beautiful but do not illustrate the subject, for Shakespeare's great characters are by no means in transparent cases. Hamlet and Iago and Macbeth are mysterious even to themselves, because they are original centres of force and not merely motive-driven machines. Schlegel seems to recognize this indirectly in several passages. His defense of the mixture of the tragic and the comic, and the relation of each to the other as elements of dramatic art, is more philosophical than that which defends the combination merely because it is not uncommon in real life. It is at once the strength and the weakness of the German commentators that they instinctively base their criticism on some form of the peculiarly German science of æsthetics. They sometimes gain thereby systematic form at the expense of a firm hold of reality.

Goethe, in his criticism of Hamlet in *Wilhelm Meister*, which contains the beautiful simile of the oak tree planted in a porcelain vase, had said that Hamlet was a 'lovely, pure, and most moral nature, without the strength of nerve which forms a hero, sinking beneath a burden (of duty) which it cannot bear and must not cast away'—in other words, a sentimentalist, a weakling. Schlegel says:—

With respect to Hamlet's character; I cannot, as I understand the poet's views, pronounce altogether so favorable a sentence upon it as Goethe does. He is, it is true, of a highly cultivated mind, a prince of royal manners, endowed with the finest sense of propriety, susceptible of noble ambition, and open in the highest degree to an enthusiastic admiration of excellence in others of which he himself is deficient. . . . He is not solely impelled by necessity to artifice and dissimulation, *he has a natural inclination for crooked ways;* he is a hypocrite towards himself, his far-fetched scruples are often mere pretexts to cover his want of determination. . . . Hamlet has no firm belief either in himself or in anything else; from expressions of religious confidence he passes over to sceptical doubts. . . . It is a tragedy of thought; the whole is intended to show that a calculating consideration, which exhausts all the relations and possible consequences of a deed, must cripple the power of acting.

These views, or modifications of them, one gathers from reading the play as a whole, for they are the general impressions left on the mind. Hamlet does not act, therefore he is irresolute. Since the publication of Professor Bradley's *Shakespearean Tragedy,* they have merely an historical interest, for there the character is analyzed and referred to well-known though subtle elements of human nature, and the propositions are established by quotations from the play itself. In other words, Bradley's criticism is not merely an appreciation, it is also a scientific argument.

Schlegel seems to rank *Macbeth* as the greatest of the tragedies, in which opinion he is not alone. His discourse on Caliban is admirable, and his animadversions on Dr. Johnson will command general assent. (pp. 216-19)

> Charles F. Johnson, "Foreign Criticism of Shake-speare: Schlegel, Ulrici, Gervinus, Freytag, Voltaire, Anatole France, Taine," in his Shakespeare and His Critics, *Houghton Mifflin Company, 1909, pp. 209-41.*

OSKAR WALZEL   (essay date 1923)

[*In the excerpt below, originally published in the 1923 edition of his* Deutsche Romantik, *Walzel sheds light on Schlegel's stinging literary satire that appeared in the* Athenaeum.]

A considerable portion of the philosophy and aesthetics of romanticism is perhaps most clearly and keenly reflected in the products of that artistic capriciousness which took delight in amusing itself with the weaknesses of the opponents of romanticism. There is a collection of romantic epigrams, written exclusively in prose, that embodies theories of the utmost importance. These epigrams are indispensable in the presentation of German romanticism. They are the aphorisms, which among the early romanticists were generally simply referred to as *Fragmente.* They were a favorite form with Friedrich Schlegel, and his brother took delight in using them like a keen-edged sword with which to make graceful and subtle thrusts at his literary opponents. The *Fragmente* of the Schlegel brothers may appropriately be considered later counterparts of the *Xenien* [of Goethe and Schiller]. In form many of them compete quite successfully with the terse brevity and telling force of the exquisitely edged couplets of Goethe and Schiller. Others, again, are considerably expanded and assume the proportions of little essays which with unique compression dispose in the smallest possible space of an entire argument, a book, or some person. There is nothing in the later years of the nineteenth century nor yet in modern journalism which really approaches the conciseness of these *Fragmente.* (pp. 187-88)

In the [*Fragmente* appearing in the second volume of the *Athenaeum* of 1798, called the] *Athenaeumfragmente,* . . . Friedrich Schlegel formulated the germinal ideas of romanticism. He created winged words: "Good dramas must be drastic" (No. 42); "An historian is a reversed prophet" (No. 80); or the assertion—which occasioned much mirth—that the French

Revolution, Fichte's *Wissenschaftslehre,* and Goethe's *Lehrjahre* were the greatest tendencies of the age (No. 216); or the terse statements about marriage *à quatre* (No. 34). (p. 190)

Wilhelm Schlegel was less concerned than his brother with the larger aspects of things. He revealed himself in the *Fragmente* as the sensitive connoisseur. For this very reason he was prone to confine himself to certain individuals and hence his satire was, relatively speaking, of a more personal nature. "Klopstock is a grammatic poet and a poetic grammarian" (No. 127). "Hogarth painted ugliness and wrote about beauty" (No. 183). "In his history, Johannes Mueller often glances beyond Switzerland into world's history; less frequently, however, does he observe Switzerland with the eye of a cosmopolite" (No. 224). The rule, inherent in the distich—and hence, also, in the *Xenien*—which demands antitheses in the lines and which places hexameter and pentameter in juxtaposition to each other like question and answer, like blow and counterblow, also holds in these *Fragmente.* It is felt more strongly and is likewise more obvious here than in the utterances of his brother Friedrich. One seems to feel that the younger brother was primarily seeking a vehicle for a striking, clear-cut thought while the older brother sought the clear-cut expression for an opportune idea. (p. 191)

Parody was already used in a sort of continuation of the *Athenaeumfragmente* which may be found at the end of the second volume of [the *Athenaeum*] (1799), in the **"Literarischer Reichsanzeiger oder Archiv der Zeit und ihres Geschmacks"**. The **"Reichsanzeiger"** chose, out of the variety offered by the *Fragmente,* only those adapted to personal satire and adroitly concealed them in the form of booksellers' advertisements. Wilhelm Schlegel, who was practically the sole author, was able to give pleasing variety to his jest. The lack of consideration displayed in ridiculing prominent German writers resembles the *Xenien* far more than it does the style of the *Fragmente.* The climax of these malicious thrusts was reached at the close where, in keeping with the form of newspaper advertisements which had been adhered to throughout, a meeting of creditors was announced. Strictly in accordance with the custom of the day, upon the application of the poets whose intellectual property had been borrowed by the debtor, there was called under the heading *Citatio Edictalis* a meeting of creditors relative to the poetry of the aulic councillor and *Comes Palatinus Caesareus* Wieland, and any one who could *titulo legitimo* make similar claims was invited to come forward within due time and then forever afterward to hold his peace. (p. 193)

[Wilhelm Schlegel's] delicate ear readily perceived any peculiar quality in poems which he disliked and he spared himself no pains in imitating any such qualities whenever he was bent upon making writers with whom he was at odds appear ridiculous. What is unquestionably his masterpiece in this field is likewise to be found in the *Athenaeum*—the **"Wettgesang"** by the three poets, J. H. Voss, Mathisson, and Schmidt von Werneuchen. The poem is delightfully prefaced by a detailed discussion in which the essential characteristics and persistent mannerisms in the poetry of these men are amply illustrated by numerous quotations. Voss's domestic, Philistine complacence, Mathisson's superlative elegance and diligent daubing of landscapes, Schmidt's song of praise to the commonplace are duly ridiculed. The song itself starts with twelve six-line strophes, each strophe devoting two lines each to Voss, Mathisson, and Schmidt. Then there ensues a dialogue in six four-line stanzas in which the three of them bestow extravagant eulogies upon one another. Finally they burst out in unison in a closing six-line strophe. Not only the content but the very diction itself is derived from the weaknesses of each of these three victims. Voss outdoes himself with clumsy laconisms; Mathisson's language is smooth, oily, and flat; Schmidt is dry and uncouth. Mathisson's tendency to fuse, with utter lack of style, the commonplace with the piquant is by no means overlooked. His collection of poems bearing the pompous title *Bas-reliefs am Sarkophage des Jahrhunderts . . .* is duly scored against him. Voss begins:

> Mathisson, your delineation of nature,
> Sweet as honey, soft as wax,
> Will never cease to delight
> Until primitive Teutonic taste runs wild.

Mathisson answers:

> Beplanting its slopes with potato-bulbs
> You plow, oh Voss, into Pindus;
> Boiled, the fruit will delight
> Apollo in Elysium.

He is taunted by Schmidt:

> I admire whatever I understand of you,
> Mathisson! But your bas-reliefs
> Which sprout at the bier—
> Are they some sort of wall-pepper?

About this time Goethe, too, was experimenting in satirical mimicry of a similar nature. His "Musen und Grazien in der Mark," which came out with the *Xenien,* was also meant to imitate the work of Schmidt von Werneuchen. This parody, which now bears the title "Deutscher Parnass," . . . is, strange to say, incorporated among the *Cantatas.* Certain it is that this production by Goethe almost awakens the impression of having emanated from the time-worn lyre of the aged Gleim. But the very fact that the "Deutscher Parnass" was misinterpreted for decades and that its real meaning was not deciphered until almost a century had elapsed shows quite conclusively that in the field of mimic satire Goethe was no match for the facile translator, Wilhelm Schlegel. (pp. 194-95)

> *Oskar Walzel, "Romantic Satire," in his* German Romanticism, *translated by Alma Elise Lussky, G. P. Putnam's Sons, 1932, pp. 185-223.*

RALPH TYMMS   (essay date 1955)

> [*Tymms assesses Schlegel's contribution as a critic to the German Romantic movement and acknowledges the importance of his Shakespeare translations to the development of German literature.*]

[August Wilhelm and Friedrich Schlegel] were alike in starting out from a historical approach to literary criticism, and from study of the Ancient Greeks, and in some others of their tastes and ideals; but the differences between them are more interesting than the resemblances. For, though both were exceptionally gifted critics, quick to detect faults in the works they reviewed, Friedrich was undisguisedly swayed by personal likes and dislikes, whereas August Wilhelm was increasingly unpartisan and academic in his judgements, consistent and steady in his opinions, but lacking Friedrich's verve and revolutionary *bravura,* his philosophical pragmatism, and his essentially subjective, provocative, critical technique. Accordingly, Friedrich veered round from one extreme opinion to another, and was adroit with sharp sallies and barbed phrases, but August Wilhelm preferred systematic exposition, regularity and clarity in

exposition, and a factual and unemotional style, based on the Goethean model. In almost every respect then it appears that August Wilhelm does not conform to Friedrich's axioms in the *Athenäum* about the romantic writer as an arbitrary, supremely subjective personage; he was in fact temperamentally one of the least 'romantic' of the romantics, if by 'romantic' is meant the irresponsibility and caprice which Friedrich shows in *Lucinde,* or Tieck in the satirical comedies. Yet paradoxically he became the spokesman of the romantic æsthetic theory, in Friedrich's place, when he held his celebrated course of lectures in Berlin in 1801-1804 (*Vorlesungen über schöne Literatur und Kunst*). He brought out nothing strikingly new or original in them, but what he did do was to summarize with admirable clarity the ideas of the Jena circle, which Friedrich had first proliferated in his fragmentary, rhapsodic way, and which had then been developed by almost endless discussion over a period of years within the Jena group. The Berlin lectures were not published during August Wilhelm's lifetime, but they brought him at last into public view all the same, as Friedrich's successor. This primacy as the exponent of the romantic æsthetics was confirmed by the even greater success of his Vienna lectures of 1807-8 (*Ueber dramatische Kunst und Literatur*) published in 1809-11; they were in part a repetition of the ideas of the Berlin lectures, and in this way offered once again a masterly summing-up of the doctrines which had been bequeathed by the pioneer Jena group to the later 'generations' of romantically-minded writers and their readers.

As a critic, August Wilhelm often showed intuitive understanding of a poet's meaning, and his instinctive sympathy, or insight, also appears in his justly renowned translation of seventeen of Shakespeare's plays . . . and of five of the plays of Calderón (*Spanisches Theater*). . . . August Wilhelm took his time before he found precisely the technique of translating Shakespeare that would adequately suit his purpose, but he did find it and from that point made even further progress in facility. The superiority of his version over the existing eighteenth-century translation by Wieland and Eschenburg is immeasurable, and Shakespeare now became a major element in German thought and æsthetic theory: August Wilhelm had made a contribution of incalculable value to German literature, and one which was no doubt of greater importance to its development than any original poetic work the German romantics were able to produce themselves, even when allowance is made for the excellence of the best of their *Märchen,* lyrics and literary criticism. (pp. 141-43)

> *Ralph Tymms, "Friedrich Schlegel and August Wilhelm Schlegel," in his* German Romantic Literature, *Methuen & Co. Ltd., 1955, pp. 121-46.*

RENÉ WELLEK   (essay date 1955)

> [*Wellek's* A History of Modern Criticism, *excerpted below, comprises a major, comprehensive study of the literary critics of the last three centuries. His critical method, as demonstrated in* A History *and outlined in his* Theory of Literature, *is one of describing, analyzing, and evaluating a work solely in terms of the problems it poses for itself and how the writer solves them. For Wellek, biographical, historical, and psychological information are incidental. Here Wellek explicates Schlegel's literary and critical doctrines, discussing such topics as his theories of metaphor and symbolism, his ideas concerning organic form in literature, and his views on the role of literary history in criticism.*]

August Wilhelm Schlegel's work could be viewed as mainly an application and exposition of the ideas of his younger brother.

It would be possible to compile a long series of parallel passages in which August Wilhelm repeats and develops what has been said by his brother on the nature of poetry and criticism, the character of the main literary genres, the role of myth in literature, etc. In almost every case the priority seems to belong to Friedrich. We thus might be inclined to dismiss August Wilhelm as an unoriginal mind, a kind of middleman and even popularizer of the ideas of his brother. There is some truth in this view, though we would need to stress the enormous historical importance of August Wilhelm's mediating and popularizing role. To many Englishmen he became "our national critic," "the new Stagyrite," the one clear voice of criticism out of Germany. Precisely because he did not take part in Friedrich's turn toward Catholicism and because (in spite of all his professed enmity to the ideals of the Enlightenment) he kept away from the excesses of the mystical view of poetry, his effect without and within Germany was much greater and more lasting than Friedrich's.

But we must not succumb to the temptation of making August Wilhelm a mere reflex of his brother, to treat him as an undistinguishable twin.... Not only did August Wilhelm frequently write on topics his brother never touched and vice versa, not only are there psychological differences between the two, but there is also a distinct difference of doctrine which it will be our purpose to discern and define. Psychologically and temperamentally, the difference is very obvious and great: August Wilhelm, from the beginning of his career, had an air of judicious objectivity, the detachment of a learned man of the world, a tolerant historical spirit, which was mostly absent in the more volatile, more polemical and more incisive brother. At times August Wilhelm also indulged in polemics, satire, and jokes, but one cannot help feeling that he is awkward at a game which is essentially foreign to his nature. Still, the tone of restraint, the careful weighing of evidence, the clauses and limitations in the writings of August Wilhelm constitute at times (compared with his brother's pronouncements) the difference between truth and mere paradox, cautious hypothesis and hazardous assertion. (pp. 36-7)

In him there always remained a very strong vein of the technician, the metrist, the virtuoso who can look on meter and poetic diction with an eye almost exclusively trained on the detail.... Throughout his career August Wilhelm advocated strict rules for the writing of German verse modeled on classical metrics, and with equally pedantic ingenuity developed theories of the sonnet, ottava rima, terzina, and even the sestina and canzone. August Wilhelm's criticism of this kind ranges all the way from an application of rigid formulas to an extraordinarily subtle exploitation of his experiences as a translator. He can indulge in fanciful speculations about the geometrical analogies of squares and triangles to sonnet structure, but he can also sensibly and sensitively criticize the details of many German poetic translations. August Wilhelm has the true philologist's devotion to the word, to close examination and close reading. One of his first reviews was devoted to Schiller's poem "Die Künstler," whose consistency and coherence of metaphor and sentence structure he examined with minute care. This vein persisted throughout Schlegel's critical career: from his review of Voss's Homer and Herder's translations from the German Latin poet Jakob Balde, to Goethe's *Hermann und Dorothea* and German translations of Propertius, Aeschylus, and Ariosto.... On occasion the interest in technical metrical perfection blinded Schlegel's critical judgment. He made much of a now forgotten poem on mineral baths, W. V. Neubeck's *Gesundbrunnen,* because it appealed to him by its correct han-

dling of the German hexameter and its charming invention of details. The man who translated Spanish "trochees" with all their assonances and closely imitated the most elaborate verse-schemes of Italian canzoni and in his own poetry experimented with all kinds of meters could not help being a craftsman also in his criticism. There is hardly anything of this in his brother Friedrich.

The preoccupation with meter and diction of the young August Wilhelm was soon modified by his enthusiasm for the Herderian ideal of world literature, for literary cosmopolitanism, which subsequently runs like a leading motif through his lifework. When August Wilhelm introduced specimens of his metrical translations from Dante . . . , he formulated his ideal of "entering into the structure of a foreign being, to know it as it is, to listen to how it became." The very first words of the *Dramatic Lectures* are an expression of a need for a "universality of the spirit," a "flexibility which enables us, by renouncing personal predilection and blind habit, to transfer ourselves into the peculiarities of other nations and ages, to feel them, as it were, from their own center." Thus August Wilhelm can say, with a good conscience, that French criticism of his time lacks the "necessary knowledge of the universal history of poetry" and can recommend to the Germans universality of education as the only possible return to nature, for he felt this to be true of himself. (pp. 37-8)

[August Wilhelm] had an intense curiosity for the unexplored and unknown, which led him to the study of Old French, Italian, and Spanish literature, made him a pioneer in the study of Middle High German and the *Nibelungenlied,* and finally the initiator of Sanscrit studies in Germany. His late French dissertations on the language and literature of the Provençals and on the origin of chivalrous romances display a learning very unusual for their time, and his research on the *Nibelungenlied,* which included collation of manuscripts and elaborate speculations on the historical facts behind its theme, have to be mentioned honorably in any history of Old German scholarship. But one must admit that in a rigorous sense none of August Wilhelm's great scholarly projects (with the exception of the late Sanscrit editions and translations) came to fruition. He was, in each case, outstripped by rivals and disciples: in France by Raynouard and Fauriel; at Bonn by Diez, his friend and younger colleague, on the Provençals; and by von der Hagen and Lachmann on the *Nibelungen.* His stimulation and critical praise proved more important than his actual technical contributions. August Wilhelm was one of the first to extoll the world of Arthurian romance, at least in Germany, and to praise adequately as figures Tristan and Parzival, which since then have entered European imagination. He was one of the first to take seriously the dictum of Johannes Müller that the *Nibelungenlied* was a German *Iliad:* he analyzed and praised the characterization of the heroes and the composition in a way that opened the poem for the first time to modern readers. But he also anticipated the extravagances of praise which have since been showered on the poetic value of the *Nibelungenlied,* and unfortunately he also was so deeply impressed by Wolf's theory of the origins of the Homeric epics that he suggested and initiated the long aberration of *Nibelungen* scholarship which was concerned with speculations about collective authorship and composition from individual "ballads" by a later "collector." Also, Schlegel's view of Provençal and Old French poetry, though sound in its rejection of the extravagances of Fauriel's claims for Provence, errs in emphasizing Teutonic influences. Schlegel argues that the Charlemagne romances owe their remote origin to Germanic epic traditions, a view which since has been thoroughly refuted by Joseph Bédier. (pp. 39-40)

[Metaphor], symbol, and myth hold the central position in Schlegel's theory of poetry. Metaphor is constantly defended as the basic procedure of poetry. August Wilhelm even defended the "baroque" (as we would say today) style of poetry which was then generally despised. In discussing the German "secentists" (as he calls them) Hofmannswaldau and Lohenstein he says that "poetry cannot be too fantastic; in a certain sense it can never exaggerate. No comparison of the most remote, of the largest and the smallest, if it is only apt and meaningful, can be too bold." Metaphor has its justification not only in this restoration of original vision *(Anschauung)* and immediacy of perception, but also in a total conception of the system of nature and the universe. "All things are related to all things; all things therefore signify all things; each part of the universe mirrors the whole." The whole mutual concatenation of things is to be restored through constant symbolizing. Thus, metaphor suggests "the great truth that each is all and all is each." "Imagination removes this disturbing medium [commonplace reality] and plunges us into the universe, while making it move within us like a magic realm of eternal metamorphoses, where nothing exists in isolation, but everything rises out of everything by a most marvelous creation." Schlegel here propounds a theory of correspondences, of symbolism, which is practically identical with that of the much later French symbolist movement. It is quite genuinely a rhetoric of metamorphoses which follows from a conception of the universe. (pp. 40-1)

Schlegel clearly sees that a distinction must be drawn between the merely decorative and intellectual use of these devices of metaphor and symbolism and their legitimate poetic function. In a very early discussion of the *Divine Comedy* (1791) he defends Dante's allegory as being more than a mere concept of the understanding. Allegory must be lost in the sensuous shape, and shine through it only as a soul shines through its body. In Dante imaginary beings have coherence, independently of their hidden meaning; there is more in them than can be resolved into concepts. "We everywhere tread solid ground, surrounded by a world of reality and individual existence." Though we may doubt the complete justice of the praise, we must realize that the distinction here drawn is valid. August Wilhelm returned to it frequently; in discussing Aeschylus in the *Dramatic Lectures* he calls allegory "the personification of a concept, a fiction contrived only for this purpose; but [symbolism] is what the imagination has created for other reasons, or what possesses a reality independent of concept, what is at the same time spontaneously susceptible of a symbolic interpretation; indeed it even invites it."

Later, Schlegel came to prefer the German word "Sinnbild" to "symbol." All art must be "sinnbildlich," i.e. it must present meaningful images. Nature itself creates symbolically; it reveals the inner by the outer; each thing has its own physiognomy. The artist points up the physiognomy of things; he lends the reader his sense for the penetration of the inner core. Art is thus a way of knowledge through signs, a thinking in images. Poetry is "bildlich anschauender Gedankenausdruck," according to the almost untranslatable formula of the 1798 lectures on aesthetics. The Kantean and Fichtean term "Idea" is then introduced in the Vienna lectures. Poetry must present "Ideas," i.e. necessary and eternally true thoughts and feelings which soar above earthly existence, in images. Here and elsewhere Schlegel is in acute danger of falling into the

intellectualistic misunderstanding of art. The formula "thinking in images" made a great impression outside of Germany also: Belinsky must have derived it from some German source and Hegel's "sinnliches Scheinen der Idee" is substantially identical with it. Schlegel's critical practice usually keeps him firmly to his original view (derived from Herder) that poetry must be concrete, to which he adds only the necessity of a symbolic relationship with the whole universe: a microcosmic-macrocosmic parallelism which has its ultimate roots in neo-Platonism. A work of art has the "inexhaustibility of creative nature whose counterpart it is in miniature." (pp. 41-2)

This symbolist view of poetry, an analogy of the totality of the universe and its relationships, is a precarious position, which has to be guarded carefully against two dangers: intellectualism and mysticism. Schlegel has not entirely escaped either of them. Intellectualism tempted him most in the discussion of the didactic philosophical poem and in the shape of the false ideal of a union of poetry and philosophy. He believed that they strive for the same end by different means and that poetry could be called "exoteric philosophy" and philosophy "esoteric poetry." A fusion of philosophical and poetic enthusiasm seems to him the solution of the problem of a perfect philosophical poem. But to excuse these formulas, of course, we must think of philosophy not as a technical subject but in the sense in which the romantics understood it: a poetic philosophy, a thinking in symbols as it was practiced by Schelling or Jakob Böhme.

But while Schlegel, on occasion, seems near to this perilous identification of poetry and philosophy, he is much oftener subject to the danger of mysticism. From Schelling he drew the phrase "beauty is the infinite represented finitely" and modified it to read "beauty is the symbolic representation of the infinite." The infinite is meant to be not something completely beyond this world but rather the mystery behind appearances and the mystery in us: it is something cosmic, obscure, the "oracular verdict of the heart, these deep intuitions in which the dark riddle of our existence seems to solve itself."

These passages often seem written under the influence of his environment: of his brother, Schelling, Creuzer, or many others of his contemporaries. Centrally, August Wilhelm held a view of poetry which is neither intellectualistic nor mystical. Poetry is metaphor, symbol, and myth but not mysticism. Myth is the concept which holds the view together: man poetizing is neither a philosopher nor a mystic but a myth-maker. Myth is the system of symbols on which the poet draws and which he restores to consciousness. Schlegel accepts the view that man went through a state dominated by myth and that such a state is natural to him. . . . What is usually called Enlightenment should thus rather be called Darkening, because it means the extinction of the inner light of man. Myth is not merely raw material of poetry. It is nature itself in a poetical costume, it is poetry itself, it is a complete view of the world. Since myth is a transformation of nature, it is itself capable of endless poetic transformations. . . . Usually he understands that poetry is not identical with myth and that myth is not merely an inert reservoir of images, gods, and stories. He propounds the possibility of a new nature myth, a union of "physics" and poetry, where "physics" means the new Schellingian *Naturphilosophie*. He argues that myth can be favorable to poetry only if it is a living myth, if it arose as an unconscious fiction of mankind, by which nature can be humanized, and if it is a belief still existing among the people. (pp. 43-4)

August Wilhelm, while not deficient in taste for Scottish ballads, German folk songs, and even 16th-century chapbooks,
had a detached attitude toward them: he recognized them as
often being dim and remote echoes of genuine antiquity and
did not share the uncritical enthusiasm for every snatch of song
or romance that was common among his Teutonizing contemporaries. In his famous essay on Bürger . . . , which professedly
was to serve as a rebuttal to Schiller's harsh review, Schlegel
actually throws up the case of "popular" poetry rather lightly.
Throughout his life, however, he held the Herderian view that
poetry is a universal language of mankind and is thus possible
among all sorts and conditions of men, in all ages and in all
societies. But he sees no particular virtue in the merely popular,
nor does he see any particular vice in the sophisticated and
learned, addressed to a limited audience. (pp. 45-6)

Kant, according to Schlegel, makes genius a mere blind tool
of nature. It is true that there is something in art which cannot
be learned, but purpose and all motives which can incite our
free activity influence the exercise of art. Great works of art,
such as the Greek tragedies, have come about as the result of
competitions. All creation is simultaneously judging, all expression of creative power is linked with constant introspection.
Genius is the intimate union of the unconscious and the self-
conscious activity of the human spirit, of instinct and intention,
freedom and necessity. Genius embraces the whole inner man,
all his powers: not only his fancy (*Einbildungskraft*) and understanding (*Verstand*), but also his imagination (*Fantasie*) and
reason (*Vernunft*). In passing, Schlegel here draws the distinction between *Einbildungskraft* and *Fantasie*, with the last
clearly considered the higher power, associated with reason.
"Creative imagination" is both unconditionally free and lawful: there cannot be any lawlessness in it. "One must merely
know," Schlegel explains, "that imagination through which
the world first originated for us and through which works of
art are created, is the same power, only in diverse kinds of
activity." (p. 46)

Schlegel does not seem to realize that there is a contradiction
between this view of art—which identifies it if not with nature
at least with the creative processes of nature, the *natura naturans*—and his usual stress on the consciousness, the reflec-
tiveness of the artist. If he rejects the neoclassical and Aristotelian view of "imitation" and admits only that imitation
may mean that art "should create living works like nature
creating independently, organized and organizing," there seems
no room for the artist's self-reflection and self-criticism which
he otherwise stresses as necessary, especially for the poet of
his age. "Today's poet," he says, "must be clearer in his
knowledge of the nature of art than great poets of former ages
could be, whom we must therefore understand better than they
understood themselves: a higher reflection must in his works
submerge itself again in the Unconscious." Presumably, in the
Schellingian system here adopted the emergence of consciousness out of nature is conceived of as so continuous and gradual
that no dualism of consciousness and the unconscious in a strict
sense would be admitted: on the highest level, consciousness
and the unconscious, freedom and necessity are one. It is one
of the advantages of the dialectical method to have things both
ways. And frequently, as in the argument about inspiration
versus conscious purpose in the composition of poetry, the
solution which affirms that both are necessary is the right one;
it is verified by observation and introspection and a study of
the historical evidence. But such solutions say little about the
share and order of the two contradictory elements and while

disposing of false extremes do little to advance the cause of
knowledge.

The same is true of the solutions propounded for reconciling
the opposition of form and content, unity and variety, by means
of the magic words "whole" or "organism" so prominent in
Germany since Herder, Goethe, and the Schlegels. August
Wilhelm constantly appeals to the organism metaphor, pressing
it sometimes very far. . . . In criticizing Euripides' luxurious
versification and his use of the chorus as mere external ornaments [for example], Schlegel . . . draws the parallel between
a work of art and a living being very closely. "If works of art
are to be looked at as organized wholes, then the insurrection
of individual parts against the unity of the whole is exactly
what in the organic world is putrefaction, which is usually the
more horrible and repulsive the nobler the organic shape it
destroys, and it thus must fill us with the greatest disgust in
this most eminent of literary kinds [tragedy]. However, most
men are less sensitive to the impression of spiritual than to the
impression of bodily putrefaction."

These extreme formulas which identify a work of literature
with an animal have made less impression than Schlegel's
contrast between organic and mechanical form which he expounded at the very beginning of the third volume of the *Dramatic Lectures:* "The form is mechanical when through outside
influence it is imparted to a material merely as an accidental
addition, without relation to its nature (as e.g. when we give
an arbitrary shape to a soft mass so that it may retain it after
hardening). Organic form, on the other hand, is innate; it unfolds itself from within and acquires its definiteness simultaneously with the total development of the germ." Such forms
occur in nature, from the crystallization of salts and minerals
to plants and flowers and up to the human race. "Also in the
fine arts all genuine forms are organic, i.e. determined by the
content of the work of art. In a word, form is nothing but a
significant exterior, the speaking physiognomy of everything
which, undistorted by any disturbing accidents, bears true witness to its hidden nature." Here the analogy is extended to
minerals and plants and the contrast to an external super-
imposed mold is worked out very clearly. Coleridge was to
quote these formulas literally.

Schlegel usually emphasizes the "unity and indivisibility" of
a work of art, the "inner mutual determination of the whole
and the parts," the fact that in a real work of art everything
exists relative to the whole. A beautiful whole can never be
pieced together from beautiful parts; the whole must first be
posited absolutely and then the particular evolved from it.
Schlegel speaks of a work of art as ideal if "in it matter and
form, letter and spirit have interpenetrated so completely that
we are unable to distinguish them." (pp. 47-9)

In practice Schlegel often attends mainly to form or to "inner
form." In discussing Voss's famous translation of Homer he
asks whether Voss has actually hit upon "the form, the style,
the tone, the color of the Homeric poems, which is really the
most important matter, since it encompasses the whole and
since all the content of a poem is known only through the
medium of form." Such a wide conception of form is also at
the base of Schlegel's most practically effective discussion of
the three unities. They are discarded in favor of a 'much deeper
lying, more intimate, more mysterious unity," for which Schlegel
accepts the term "unity of interest," drawn from De La Motte,
an early 18th-century French critic. But Schlegel recognizes
the difference between his use and that of De La Motte, who

thought of the psychology of the audience. Schlegel's unity is rather "inner form," an idea, such as fate in Greek tragedy.

At times Schlegel seems to admit that there is some contradiction between form and matter even in good art. He praises the Spanish drama for the way Spanish poets transformed the merely marvelous and adventurous, breathed into it a "musical soul," wholly purified it of gross materiality, changed it to color and perfume. Schlegel finds an irresistible charm in this very contrast between matter and form, a formula which seems to abandon the purely organic theory of the whole. In discussing the didactic poem Schlegel makes an even further concession to the distinction between form and matter. He does not, it is true, recognize didactic poems as the highest poetry, because their whole is not poetic but is held together merely by logic. Still, he does not deny the possibility of the genuineness of the individual poetic elements. Poetry, he says now, has its spirit and its letter; it should be allowed at times to cultivate the letter in isolation, without the spirit. Here the virtuoso, the technician and experimenter, rebels against his own general theory.

It is remarkable how skillfully and consciously Schlegel can combine a "holistic," organic view of poetry with a recognition of a theory of genres. The concept of the completely self-sufficient unity of a work of art leads to the concept of its complete "uniqueness" and, in Croce and other moderns, to the logical consequence of rejecting the genre concept altogether. Not so with Schlegel, who holds firmly to the biological metaphor which would imply that every individual, however individual, also belongs to a species. "Genuine forms must be looked upon as species of organizations to which life is restricted, but which still give much leeway to individuality." "A certain law of form is the condition of free individuality in art just as in nature; for anything that does not belong to any species of organizations is monstrous." Monstrosity, hybridization is thus the objection to an improper mixture of genres which Schlegel always points out as disadvantageous to art. Aristotle is repeatedly criticized for trying to judge the epic by the laws of tragedy, and much of Schlegel's own criticism is straight genre criticism, which disapproves of any violation of the purity of genre and could thus be considered a survival of the neoclassical point of view. Nonetheless, in his actual conception of the genres Schlegel differs considerably from neoclassical doctrines. (pp. 49-50)

August Wilhelm's main interest among the genres was the drama, and the *Lectures on Dramatic Art and Literature* were the most sustained and influential of his published works. Tragedy interested him more than comedy. Greek tragedy, on the one hand, and Shakespearean and Spanish drama, on the other— their differences and contrasts are the pivots around which Schlegel's speculations revolve. He has little use for Aristotle's *Poetics,* though he praised it for suggesting the organic analogy. He not only rejects the three "Aristotelian" unities; he even decides that Aristotle did not understand the nature of tragedy at all. Aristotle's view of poetry is purely logical and physical. *Catharsis* conceals a purely moralistic theory. The other usual explanations of tragic pleasure are equally unconvincing. We do not enjoy seeing misfortune because we are safe ourselves and we are not improved by seeing poetic justice done and the evil-doers punished. Poetic justice, if it means a nice distribution of rewards and punishments, is not necessary to good tragedy. Tragedy can end with the defeat of the righteous man and the triumph of the wicked, provided our inner consciousness and a vista into the future restore the equilib-

rium. At most, poetic justice in the genuine sense of the word is only a "revelation of the invisible blessing or curse which hangs over human sentiments and actions." Tragedy thus must be explained differently. Clearly, Schlegel's theory derives from Kant's definition of the sublime. The tragic mood is man's recognition of his dependence on unknown powers, of the transience of pleasures, affections, and life itself. It is a feeling of inexpressible melancholy, for which there is no other defense than the consciousness of a vocation transcending the limits of earthly life. When this mood pervades the representation of violent revolutions in a man's fate, either subduing his will or calling forth his heroic fortitude, we can speak of tragic poetry. If one had to formulate the purpose of tragedy as a doctrine, one would have to say that earthly existence must be considered as nothing, that all suffering must be endured and all difficulties overcome merely in order to affirm the claims of the mind to the divine. In tragedy, thus, man's struggle with fate is resolved into harmony, but it need be only an ideal harmony.

Similarly, comedy is deduced from the comic mood. It means forgetting all the gloomy considerations in the pleasant feeling of present happiness. We are then inclined to view everything in a playful light. The imperfections and irregularities of man must no longer be objects of dislike or pity but must entertain and amuse. A comic poet must refrain from letting his characters excite moral indignation or real sympathy. In tragedy every emotion is channeled in one direction, in comedy there is an "apparent lack of purpose" and a breakdown of all limits in the use of our mental faculties. Comedy is the more perfect the more vivid is the illusion of our purposeless play and unlimited caprice. In comedy Schlegel approves the breaking of illusion, the address to the public, even the pointing at individual spectators in the audience. Comedy "seeks the most colorful contrasts and continually crossing opposites." It is obvious that Schlegel can have little sympathy for the comedy of manners and character: he specifically censures French critics for considering character comedy superior to the comedy of intrigue. With his usual, apparently unromantic preference for the pure genre, however romantic in itself the genre may be, Schlegel prefers the comedy of fantasy and caprice to the realistic comedy in which he sees an approach to seriousness and hence an impure genre. (pp. 51-3)

Schlegel holds a theory of criticism which is remarkably conscious of the cooperation and interpenetration of criticism and history, theory and practice. He argues that there cannot be history without theory, since history, if it is not to be a mere chronicle, requires a principle of selectivity. Each phenomenon of art can be assigned its true position only by relating it to the idea of art. On the other hand, no theory of art can exist without the history of art, for obviously history, especially art history, has to teach by examples. Schlegel recognizes the central difficulty of art history, which since his time Croce has made the main argument against all of art history. Each genuine work of art is perfect by itself; but if history means progress, approximation to perfection, then art history must be made up of imperfect phenomena which actually should not have a place in the realm of genuine art. Schlegel solves the dilemma by appealing to an art spirit (*Kunstgeist*) that always appears modified by its environment, a nation, a specific age. This spirit organizes its own shape and thus has a history. . . . Schlegel also disposes of the other common objection to art history or literary history: that art is created by geniuses and thus is a mere freak of nature, a series of chance events. He answers that phenomena are objectively necessary while subjectively accidental; the person of the artist is contingent, but the style of a time is essential and necessary. We can think of all individual geniuses as single parts and appearances of the *one* great genius of mankind which cannot perish and must rise again from its ashes. Art history thus must comprehend whole ages and great masses and ignore the learned and human detail. It must look on history as an organic whole.

In that way Schlegel is able to formulate our aim as leading art criticism to "the historical point of view, i.e. even though each work of art ought to be closed within itself, we must consider it as belonging to a series, and in terms of its origin and existence and comprehend it from what has preceded and what follows or is still following from it." Schlegel said much earlier (1795) that "by explaining how art became what it is, we show also in the most convincing manner what it should be." This is not, in Schlegel's view, mere historical determinism: all genetic explanation, e.g. by biography, does not absolve us from forming an independent judgment. The laws of the beautiful are valid everywhere and at all times. Thus biography is not decisive for criticism. A work of art "is as much detached from the person of its author as fruit which is being eaten is detached from its tree; and even if all the poems of a man represent his poetic biography and together form, as it were, an artistic personality in which the individuality of the real one is revealed more or less, directly or indirectly, we must still consider them as products of free will, even of caprice, and must leave it undecided whether a poet could not have mirrored his individuality in his works quite differently, if he had only willed to do so."

Criticism, in relation to theory and history, is conceived of as the mediating middle link. . . . He can speak ambitiously in the terminology of idealist philosophy of "construing a work in its totality according to its structure and nature" or he can, more moderately, define its function as "comprehending and interpreting the meaning of a work in a pure, complete, and sharply definite manner." The critic thus aims to raise less independent but susceptible spectators to the insight of his own point of view. The actual process of grasping the meaning of a work of art is described largely as the reproduction of a general or total impression. Parallel to his conception of the wholeness of a work of art Schlegel thinks of the critical act as a whole and contrasts the right criticism—which is of an organic nature in which the individual exists only through the whole—with atomistic criticism—which views the work of art as a mosaic, a painstaking combination of mere particles. (pp. 54-6)

Schlegel also faces the problem of the subjectivity of criticism. He first argues that some kind of objectivity is achieved by distinguishing between a total impression and a mere mood. Ideally a critic should be able to tune himself at will, i.e. be able at any moment to evoke the purest and liveliest susceptibility for any work of the mind. Merely by being conscious of our transitory mood we may raise ourselves above it or realize, at least approximately, how another mood would have affected us. Objectivity is enhanced by historical study, by a knowledge of art history, since the critic must know the most eminent works and they cannot be found in any one time and place. Objectivity is also increased by constant reference to theory. A judgment can be clarified and expressed only in concepts, and concepts assume distinctness only in an assumed system. "Critical reflection is thus a constant experimentation to discover theoretical statements." In the end we must, however, recognize that something subjective will remain in every critical judgment. One can do nothing else than be aware of

one's personality, "treat it liberally," express it by the manner of our communication. Thus Schlegel opposes colorless "dignified" criticism which suppresses everything that is characteristic. If criticism is to be individual in its matter it must be so in its form as well.

The fact that people disagree about works of art does not disturb Schlegel; we disagree with ourselves at different times in our life, but this does not justify general skepticism in matters of art. "Different people may very well have their eyes on the same center, but since each of them starts from a different point of the circumference, they inscribe also different radii." Here is stated a conception which has since been called "perspectivism" and which happily mediates between mere historicism and the old dogmatism. It does not give up the ideal of one poetry and yet does not deny the variety of its historical forms.

These are, one can say without exaggeration, still wonderfully pertinent reflections on the nature and procedure of criticism and its relations to theory and history. They are best exemplified in Schlegel's most famous distinction: that between the classic and the romantic. It oscillates, as Schlegel wanted it to do, between theory and history. It mediates, as a truly critical idea, between them. (pp. 56-7)

[The] first Berlin lectures (1801-02) contain the full proclamation of the contrast, praised as a recent discovery, whose function is to allow an impartial recognition of both antinomies. "The historian and theoretician should try to keep to the point of indifference between the two poles." If actually carried out, the implications of this professed impartiality are those of extreme historicism and of the view that there are two ideals of poetry, both equally valid but mutually incompatible. Toward the end of the course of lectures the contrast is formulated as one between the classical emphasis on purity of genre and the romantic mixture of all poetic elements. Romantic poetry strives for the infinite not only in an individual work of art but in the whole course of art. Saying that "romantic art is limitless progressivity," August Wilhelm echoes Friedrich's famous "fragment."

The second lecture course (1802-03) adds to the contrast the idea that classical poetry is plastic and architectonic, while modern poetry is picturesque. Only the third lecture course (1803-04) attempts a systematic survey of romantic literature. The theoretical formulation is, however, surprisingly meager: it stresses that romantic poetry has its own necessary course of development and the actual discussion concerns mainly the historical role of Christianity, chivalry, courtly love, etc. as explanation for the rise of modern (i.e. medieval) literature. The emphasis is on the historical approach. (pp. 57-8)

The Vienna *Lectures on Dramatic Art and Poetry* . . . contain the most systematic and influential discussion. There the whole history of the drama is based on the contrast between classical and romantic. The contrast is seen as all-pervasive, affecting the other arts as well. Schlegel appeals to Rousseau, who showed that "rhythm and melody are the ruling principle of ancient, and harmony of modern, music." Hemsterhuis is quoted as saying that the ancient painters were too much sculptors, the modern sculptors too much painters. The spirit of ancient art and poetry, Schlegel concludes, is plastic, that of modern art picturesque. The contrast between Gothic and classical architecture is then applied to literature in a famous comparison, used also by Coleridge. "The Pantheon is no more different from Westminster Abbey or St. Stephen's Church in Vienna than the structure of a tragedy by Sophocles is from that of a drama by Shakespeare.'' Schlegel then repeats his account of the origin and spirit of romantic literature. The Greeks lived in the limits of the finite. Their religion was a deification of natural forms and earthly life. They thus invented the poetry of joy. But with the advent of Christianity everything changed. Poetry became the poetry of the infinite. The poetry of possession yielded to the poetry of desire (*Sehnsucht*). Harmony yielded to inner division. Chivalry, courtly love, and honor, determined by the spirit of Christianity, shaped the new literature. "In Greek art and poetry there is an original unconscious unity of form and matter; in the modern, so far as they have remained true to their peculiar spirit [i.e. did not become neoclassical], a more intimate penetration of both as two opposites is sought for. The Greeks solved their task to perfection; the moderns can satisfy their striving for the infinite only by approximation." This exposition is then supplemented at the beginning of the third volume, which is devoted to the romantic drama. There all the stress is on the romantic mixture of genres. Romantic drama is neither tragedy nor comedy in the strict sense, but drama (*Schauspiel*). Romantic poetry differs from classical by its delight in insoluble mixtures of everything antithetical: nature and art, poetry and prose, earnest and jest, memory and intuition, spirituality and sensuality. "Ancient poetry and art is a rhythmical *nomos,* a harmonious promulgation of the eternal legislation of a beautifully ordered world mirroring the eternal Ideas of things. Romantic poetry, on the other hand, is the expression of a secret longing for the chaos which is perpetually striving for new and marvelous births, which lies hidden in the very womb of orderly creation ... [Greek art] is simpler, clearer, more like nature in the independent perfection of its separate works; [romantic art], in spite of its fragmentary appearance, is nearer to the mystery of the universe." Greek drama is then compared with a group sculpture, modern drama with a large painting.

If we analyze these passages we can easily recognize the diverse elements drawn from Schiller and Friedrich Schlegel, but all the distinctions are brought together and worked out in a historical context. The antithesis, mechanical—organic, plastic—picturesque, finite—infinite, closed or perfect—progressive and unlimited, pure in the distinction of genres—indulging in mixtures, simple—complex, or rather these reconciled contrasts and opposites, are memorably phrased and brought into relationship with the historical contrasts between the Gothic and the classical style in the fine arts and with the differences between pagan and Christian religion and pagan and Christian morality. Schlegel himself tried to preserve an impartial balance, at least in these theoretical pronouncements; his genuine admiration for antiquity is obvious from his writings, but in the bulk of his critical practice the scales are heavily weighted in favor of the romantic. To Schlegel's contemporaries in search of a loosely organized, complex, and Christian art, the terms "mechanical," "finite," "pagan," and "simple" must have sounded as a condemnation of the classical. It seems excessive, however, to charge Schlegel either with complete subordination of the classical to the romantic ideal or, from a different point of view, with an extreme theory of the bifurcation of poetry, a splitting up of its ideal into two equally valid concepts. Schlegel does neither. It is clear that his own sympathies are largely with the romantic, that his general conception of poetry, with its stress on metaphor and symbol, leans in that direction. On the other hand, he has so general a concept of poetry that he could find it exemplified in works belonging to the classical type. Fundamentally he did not quite face the issues raised by the recognition of the two types and was not entirely certain how to distinguish between a historical category and an ever-recurring type. He also could not quite separate the descriptive use from the normative and thus never quite solved the actual difficulties raised by historical relativism.

Nonetheless, in this very lack of sharp decision there was some critical virtue: unlike his successors in the 19th century Schlegel never succumbed to completely amorphous, opinionless, and directionless relativism, to the total passive comprehension of everything ever written, which inevitably led later to mere factualism, to the indiscriminate accumulation of information about everything at any time anywhere. In Schlegel the methods and assumptions of *Geistesgeschichte*—the view that all cultural activities are closely parallel, that, for instance, ancient architecture, sculpture, religion, philosophy, literature, etc. implicate each other—are anticipated, but again the method is not pressed to the fantastic extremes of the 20th century: it still illuminates and does not obfuscate, as it does in Spengler and many other German parallel hunters who conceive of history as a sequence of sharply defined ages and types and talk very glibly of the Gothic or the baroque man. The germ of this method is in Schlegel, but only the germ. Schlegel still remained a critic who preserved a positive frame of reference, who, in spite of all his theoretical and practical universality, kept the needs of his time and of creative art in mind, who knew how to judge according to an ideal of poetry and literature. It may have made him blind to many values and many authors, but it preserved him at least from losing his grip on a set of principles and norms. Without them a critic ceases to be a critic and becomes a mere antiquary. (pp. 58-61)

Novalis, writing to Friedrich Schlegel, expressly asks that he keep his judgment separate from that of his brother and then formulates the contrast between the two Schlegels: "yours is always individual—his historical and general." In retrospect it may seem that Novalis was right: the voice of Friedrich Schlegel is certainly more individual, more striking, his sensibility subtler, more precise. The voice of August Wilhelm is often that of the historian, the man of detachment, of tolerance, of universality. But one could also turn Novalis' dictum around: Friedrich Schlegel is the more speculative, more "general" thinker of the two, the critic who less frequently enters into a close discussion of technique, who rarely analyzes a work of art; while August Wilhelm can become absorbed in concrete detail, in aesthetic surface, in the craft of literature. Friedrich certainly is preoccupied with irony and paradox, while his brother is not. Friedrich's theory of criticism makes much more of the polemical, the incitory, anticipatory, forward-looking function of criticism. Friedrich was much more interested in the new novel, the synthetic genre of the future, than his brother. Friedrich's conception of poetry early acquired a religious tinge and finally became fused with religion and philosophy, an evolution which was not shared by August Wilhelm.

August Wilhelm, in his turn, elaborated much more clearly and systematically than his brother a theory of metaphor and symbolism which led him to a theory of symbolic correspondences, of art as the restoration of man's original animizing intuition. August Wilhelm also was much more consistently preoccupied with a theory of "organic" structure in literature; while Friedrich accepts the view, he is not so interested as Wilhelm in the term. Wilhelm defends it not only for the individual work of art but also for the great genres and the whole evolution of literature. August Wilhelm remained much more a follower of Herder than Friedrich: his view of literature permitted biological analogies, though his symbolism divorced him from all naturalism. August Wilhelm thought about the problem of literary history and its relation to criticism more consistently and systematically. He was more interested in the drama than his brother. But these differences of emphasis and tone as well as personal development should not obscure their profound agreement in all essentials during the time of their most intimate collaboration. The unity of their view seems to me only less striking than the general sanity of their position. The Schlegels, it seems, best formulated a view of literature and criticism which was transmitted by Coleridge to the English-speaking world and is, on many essential points, accepted by recent English and American criticism. (pp. 72-3)

> *René Wellek, "August Wilhelm Schlegel," in his* A History of Modern Criticism: The Romantic Age, 1750-1950, *Yale University Press, 1955, pp. 36-73.*

MARGARET E. ATKINSON (essay date 1958)

[*According to Atkinson, Schlegel maintained a close fidelity to the original in translating Shakespeare, yet he could not avoid the subtle transmutations that naturally occur in the act of translation. In the excerpt below, Atkinson traces these transmutations in* Julius Caesar, Hamlet, *and* Twelfth Night. *Line references are taken from* Shakespeare's dramatische Werke (1797-1810) *and* The Plays of William Shakespeare (1786 and 1790).]

In general the reproduction of the continual contrast and variation of sound and tempo in Shakespeare's plays is one of Schlegel's most remarkable achievements. As a matter of course he translates the prose passages into prose and the verse into verse, thus retaining, for instance, the basic contrast in sound between the two funeral orations in *Julius Caesar* and between the serious and humorous scenes in *Twelfth Night*. His prose, like Shakespeare's, ranges from a pompous ponderousness in the speeches of Malvolio to a swift sprightliness in the clown's witty sallies, from a heavy formal rhetoric in Brutus's oration to a laconic brusqueness in Casca's comments on the events at the Lupercalia. Similarly in the verse passages, the love-lorn plaints of Duke Orsino have, as in the original, a very different ring from the lines of the bluff Antonio or the smug and wordy Polonius. Yet although Schlegel succeeds magnificently in reproducing in broad outline the contrasts of tempo and verbal melody that make up the musical pattern of the plays, his version does not sound like Shakespeare. And, indeed, it is impossible that it should. The artist cannot produce the same result in a different medium; German cannot be made to sound like English.

One of the main reasons for the disparity is the comparative paucity in German of words of Latin origin. . . . In general, . . . English words of Latin origin are lighter in texture than their Germanic equivalents, and hence there is many a phrase in Schlegel's version that sounds heavy, even cumbersome, compared with the original, e.g. 'wohlbedacht in der Gefahr' for 'most provident in peril', 'unverwundbar wie die Luft' for 'as the air invulnerable', 'boshafter Hohn' for 'malicious mockery'. In the comedy speeches especially we miss the leaven of the Romance words. . . . In Polonius's lines:

> Having ever seen, in the prenominate crimes,
> The youth you breathe of, guilty,
>
> (*H.* ii, 1)

the very sound of the word *prenominate,* with the extra light syllable giving a trisyllabic foot, is amusingly indicative of the volubility of the speaker. This effect would be lost if *prenominate* were replaced by *aforesaid;* but the German language

offers no such choice and Schlegel must perforce be satisfied with *vorbenannt.* Shakespeare's use of a corruption of polysyllabic Romance words for comic effect also poses a most difficult problem; 'the very devil incardinate' and 'I did impeticos thy gratillity', for instance, might well baffle any translator. In the first case Schlegel ignores the joke and writes simply: 'der eingefleischte Teufel selbst' and in the second he attempts to catch something of the effect by importing a foreign word: 'Ich habe dein Präsent in den Sack gesteckt'; in both cases the sense is retained but the exuberant rhythmical ripple of the original is lost.

Effects of verbal sound that are inherent in the very nature of the language are beyond the reach of the translator; but those that are primarily due to the poet's art—effects of rhythm, enjambement and pause, assonance and rhyme, alliteration, vowel patterns and consonant clusters—form a challenge to his poetic skill. In this sphere Schlegel both achieves much and loses much. His most striking achievement lies in a frequent close approximation to a line-for-line reproduction of the sense within the same space as the original. In Viola's monologue (*T.N.* ii, 2), for instance, in the opening scene of *Hamlet,* the scene of the royal welcome to Rosenkrantz and Guildenstern and the subsequent conversation with Polonius and Voltimand (*H.* ii, 2), and in speech after speech in *Julius Caesar,* almost every phrase is reproduced by a phrase of similar length, so that the pauses and overlapping lines fall at exactly the same points as in the original. The sound pattern of Hamlet's frenzied exclamations after his dialogue with the ghost are closely matched in the German:

> O all you host of heaven! O earth! what else?
> And shall I couple hell? O, fie! Hold, hold, my heart;
> And you, my sinews, grow not instant old,
> But bear me stiffly up. Remember thee?
> Ay, thou poor ghost, while memory holds a seat
> In this distracted globe. Remember thee?
>
> (i, 5)

> O Heer des Himmels! Erde!—Was noch sonst?
> Nenn' ich die Hölle mit? O pfui! Halt, halt mein Herz!
> Ihr meine Sehnen, altert nicht sogleich,
> Tragt fest mich aufrecht!—Dein gedenken? Ja,
> Du armer Geist, so lang Gedächtniss haust
> In dem zerstörten Ball hier. Dein gedenken? . . .

[Where Schlegel] finds a slight expansion of the text unavoidable, he often achieves it so skilfully and unobtrusively that the naturalness of the effect obscures the virtuosity that goes to its attainment. Here and there, however, expansion results in loss of dramatic force. The solemn portentousness of the line: 'A little ere the mightiest Julius fell' (*H.* i, 1) is weakened when the end of the line no longer coincides with the end of the phrase: 'Kurz vor dem Fall des grossen Julius, standen / Die Gräber leer', and the line: 'Love make his heart of flint that you shall love' (*T.N.* i, 5) also loses much of its forcefulness when it is expanded to a line and a half, and so deprived of its formal balance: 'Die Liebe härte dessen Herz zu Stein / Den ihr einst liebt'. In much the same way, Schlegel slackens the tension of some of Cassius's words in the quarrel scene with Brutus, e.g.

> Hated by one he loves; brav'd by his brother;
> Check'd like a bondman; all his faults observ'd,
> Set in a notebook, learn'd, and conn'd by rote,
> To cast into my teeth.

Gehasst von einem, den er liebt; getrotzt
Von seinem Bruder; wie ein Kind gescholten.
Man späht nach allen meinen Fehlern, zeichnet
Sie in ein Denkbuch, lernt sie aus dem Kopf,
Wirft sie mir in die Zähne.

                                        (*J.C.* iv, 3)

In the original the note of self-pity and tense indignation is reinforced by the sharp staccato phrases of almost equal length, rapped out one after the other. The German version, spread out over an extra line, sounds smooth by comparison. Here there is no violent punctuation. Twice the caesural pause is delayed almost to the end of the verse; and twice the sense moves on over the end-line pause, binding the whole together. The fire of emotional excitement is thus damped down.

Schlegel also frequently expands the text across the incomplete lines of the original, supplying the missing feet so that the metrical pattern proceeds unbroken. This, too, sometimes results in the obliteration of a significant or dramatic pause.... [In *Twelfth Night*] at the end of Viola's impassioned speech, 'Make me a willow cabin at your gate', there is a pause of dramatic significance created by an incomplete line:

VIOLA   O, you should not rest
          Between the elements of air and earth,
          But you should pity me.
OLIVIA   You might do much: What is your parentage?

                                        (*T.N.* i, 5)

Here the break in versification that precedes Olivia's reply seems to mark the very moment when she first falls in love with Viola—when, as Viola later says, 'her eyes had lost her tongue'. Schlegel writes:

VIOLA   O ihr solltet mir
          Nicht Ruh geniessen zwischen Erd und
               Himmel,
          Bevor ihr euch erbarmt!
OLIVIA   Wer weiss, wie weit
          Ihrs bringen könntet! Wie ist eure Herkunft?

and the significant break in the original is obliterated. It is true that there is nothing to prevent the actor himself from making a pause at each of these dramatic moments, but even so the peculiar effect of tension which is created by a pause inherent in the very texture of the verse, is lost. A very similar effect, sometimes missed by Schlegel, is produced by the omission of a syllable within the line. For example, in Ophelia's

          As if he had been loosed out of hell,
          To speak of horrors—he comes before me,

                                        (*H.* ii, 1)

her almost breathless horror at what she has seen is suggested by the unexpected break after the word *horrors*—an effect that is lost in Schlegel's metrically regular version:

          Als wär' er aus ker Hölle losgelassen,
          Um Gräuel kund zu thun—so tritt er vor mich.

                                        (pp. 27-32)

Apart from the loss of special dramatic significance, such instances of the filling in of verse pauses and incomplete lines have also a cumulative effect; they form part of a general process of smoothing, tidying and levelling of the versification. For although Schlegel realizes in theory that 'even irregularities are expressive in Shakespeare's versification', yet in practice he tends to obliterate these and so to produce a more supple but less forceful and expressive line. Often, for instance, he

fails to reproduce Shakespeare's use of consecutive accented syllables and of metrical inversion. The introduction of two or more successive heavy syllables creates a momentary *ritardando,* and can thus be used as a purely auditory means of making the important points of a speech stand out from the rest. Valentine's first speech at the beginning of *Twelfth Night* provides a clear illustration of this. Here the metre is, on the whole, unusually regular, and this seems appropriate, since Valentine is making a report and his own emotions are not deeply involved. The few irregularities are the more striking by contrast, and pick out the very points that must be impressed on the audience:

          The element itself, till seven years heat,
          Shall not behold her face at ample view;
          But like a cloistress she will veiled walk,
          And water once a day her chamber round
          With eye-offending brine: all this, to season
          A brother's dead love, which she would keep fresh
          And lasting, in her sad remembrance.

The long drawn-out ending of the first line mirrors the intended persistence of Olivia's grief. This is the only irregularity in the actual message, which then flows gently on until its end is marked by the colon pause. With the secondary accent on *all* in the strong foot 'all this', a more emphatic personal note of astonishment enters the speech, and in the succeeding line the two main and contrasting ideas are made to stand out by the heavy syllables *dead love* and *keep fresh*. Schlegel's lines, with their more even beat, fail to produce this effect:

          Der Himmel selbst, bis sieben Jahr verglüht,
          Soll ihr Gesicht nicht ohne Hülle schaun;
          Sie will wie eine Nonn' im Schleyer gehn,
          Und einmal Tags ihr Zimmer rings benetzen
          Mit augenschmerzendem gesalznem Nass:
          All diess, um eines Bruders todte Liebe
          Zu balsamiren, die sie frisch und dauernd
          In traurigem Gedächtniss halten will.

Only *all this* is faithfully reproduced; the other irregularities are lost. Added to this the last three lines of the original are here expanded to four, and as a result, the colon pause coincides with the end-line pause, and so does not serve to strengthen the effect of the combination of stressed syllables as does a strong mid-line break. Similarly Hamlet's important lines:

          I doubt some foul play: would the night were come!
          Till then sit still, my soul: foul deeds will rise,
          Though all the world o'erwhelm them to men's eyes.

                                        (i, 2)

owe much of their impressiveness to the sequence of stressed syllables in the second line and to the parallel heavy phrases 'foul play' and 'foul deeds', which fall ominously on the ear, and prepare the audience for subsequent events. Schlegel's version runs comparatively smoothly, and there is nothing—neither repetition nor rhythmical impressiveness—to pick out the key phrases, which are rendered by 'argen Ränken' and 'schnöde Thaten'; admittedly a faithful reproduction of the rhythm seems impossible, since the adjectives must have inflectional endings.... In a number of passages where the German version seems to lack the vigour of the original at a point of climax, the comparative weakness can be traced, among other factors perhaps, to the loss of a succession of heavy syllables. In *Julius Caesar*, for example, it is the death of Cassius that first brings home to us the hopelessness of the situation for Brutus and his friends, and this sense of the inevitability of tragedy is summed up by Titinius in words weighted with significance:

> O setting sun!
> As in thy red rays thou dost sink to-night,
> So in his red blood Cassius' day is set;
> The sun of Rome is set! Our day is gone;
> Clouds, dews, and dangers come; our deeds are done!
>
> (v, 3)

Here the strong monosyllables 'red rays' and 'red blood' stand out luridly, the foot 'Clouds, dews' forms an imposing opening to the line of impressive finality in which the recurrent *d* falls dully on the ear, and the words *come, done,* half echo *sun, Rome, gone* in the previous line like the tolling of a bell. Schlegel's version runs:

> O Abendsonne!
> Wie du in deinen rothen Strahlen sinkst,
> So ging in Blut der Tag des Cassius unter,
> Die Sonne Roms ging unter; unser Tag
> Ist hingeflohn: nun kommen Wolken, Thau,
> Gefahren; unsre Thaten sind gethan.

These lines, too, have an incantatory power owing to the solemn measured pace and the skilful arrangement of vowels and consonants (roth, Blut, Rom; unter, unser; Thau, Thaten, gethan), but the salient words are not picked out as in the original by deviation from the regular rhythmical beat, and the enjambement also contributes to the smoother, less stark effect. Often Shakespeare uses the additional weight of successive stresses to give depth to an emotional outburst, as, for example, in Duke Orsino's line: 'Here comes the countess; now heaven walks on earth', in Laertes' tortured cry as he sees Ophelia enter and realizes that she is mad: 'O heat, dry up my brains! tears, seven times salt' and Messala's slow, sad, and at the same time admiring comment on Brutus's fortitude in bereavement: 'Even so great men great losses should endure'. Schlegel's lines, with their almost regular alternation of lift and dip, have a less vigorous impact: 'Die Gräfin kommt, der Himmel geht auf Erden', 'O Hitze, trockne / Mein Hirn auf! Thränen, siebenfach gesalzen . . .', 'So trägt ein grosser Mann ein grosses Unglück'. (pp. 33-6)

The slower tempo produced by successive heavy syllables is particularly apt for the expression of the Duke's languid lovesickness in *Twelfth Night.* 'If ever thou shalt love' he says to Viola, 'In the sweet pangs of it, remember me' (ii, 4) and in the two words 'sweet pangs', surrounded as they are by contrasting light syllables, the whole essence of the line, and of his love, seems concentrated. The German version: 'Gedenke meiner in den süssen Qualen' sounds pleasantly soft and harmonious, but lacks the peculiarly expressive rhythm of the original. Similarly Schlegel's line: 'Die übersatte Lust erkrank' und sterbe', despite the heavy vowel sounds, cannot compare with the falling cadence of Shakespeare's 'The appetite may sicken and so die' (i, 1). Another striking instance is the final couplet of the first scene of the play, which by its very sound epitomizes the love-lorn atmosphere and so forms a musical climax:

> Away before me to sweet beds of flowers:
> Love thoughts lie rich, when canopy'd with bowers.

Such lines may well daunt the translator. The German version runs:

> Eilt mir voran auf zarte Blumenmatten!
> Süss träumt die Liebe, wenn sie Lauben schatten.

Here Schlegel attains a certain measure of equivalence—the soft slow foot 'süss träumt' and the half echo of 'Liebe' by 'Lauben' are especially effective—but the subtle rhythmical give and take of the original and the lush voluptuousness of the four successive stressed syllables 'love thoughts lie rich' are only partially reproduced.

The loss of such sequences of accented syllables is the most striking rhythmical modification in Schlegel's version of the plays. But there are other deviations from the original which reveal the same tendency to smooth out irregularities. It is, for example, clear from the lines quoted above, that Schlegel is equally apt to avoid successive light syllables in favour of a regular alternation of lift and dip. Similarly, where Shakespeare loosens the metrical structure by interpolating an extra unaccented syllable within the line, Schlegel frequently restores the normal pattern. Even when an extra syllable is used to particular dramatic effect, for instance, to suggest the rising excitement of the speaker, it is usually lost in the German rendering; thus Laertes' line: 'To hell, allegiance! vows, to the blackest devil!' is translated as: 'Zur Hölle, Treu'! Zum ärgsten Teufel, Eide!'' Indeed, so rigidly bound is Schlegel by the metrical pattern, that in his rendering of the [following line from *Hamlet*]: 'With pestilent speeches of his father's death' he elides a syllable to avoid the slight irregularity which exists in the original, and writes: 'Mit gift'gen Reden von des Vaters Tod'. Metrical inversion, too, is frequently smoothed out; the resultant loss of rhythmical expressiveness is perhaps most noticeable in lines where the original irregularity serves to lend emphasis to a command, or a vehement asseveration or exclamation, such as Polonius's 'Grapple them to thy soul with hooks of steel' ('Mit ehrnen Haken klammr' ihn an dein Herz'), Brutus's 'Hide it in smiles, and affability' ('In Lächeln hüll' es und in Freundlichkeit') or Mark Antony's 'Judge, O you gods, how dearly Caesar lov'd him!' ('Ihr Götter, urtheilt, wie ihn Cäsar liebte!'). (pp. 36-7)

It is impossible by a mere enumeration of some of the more striking differences in versification to give a clear idea of the constant though sometimes barely perceptible smoothing out of irregularities. Only a quotation of long passages could illustrate how the cumulative effect of the many slight alterations in rhythm in Schlegel's version subdues the exuberant dramatic vitality of the blank verse dialogue, giving it an un-Shakespearian ring and making it here and there reminiscent of the more remote and harmonious line of Goethe's *Tasso* and *Iphigenie.*

In the songs, on the other hand, where the rhythmical variety lies in the basic metrical pattern, and not in deviation from it, the rhythm of the original is almost perfectly reproduced. The reason is not far to seek. Schlegel approached the songs from a musical point of view, in the full realization that the incantatory effect is of paramount importance and must be retained at all costs. 'Die eingestreuten Lieder', he wrote, 'sind meistens süsse kleine Spiele und ganz Gesang; man hört in Gedanken eine Melodie dazu, während man sie bloss lieset.' One of his most striking achievements in this field is his successful reproduction of the complex strophic structure of 'Come away, death' (*T.N.* ii, 4).

> Come away, come away, death,
> And in sad cypress let me be laid;
> Fly away, fly away, breath;
> I am slain by a fair cruel maid.

My shroud of white, stuck all with yew,
  O prepare it;
My part of death no one so true
  Did share it.

Not a flower, not a flower sweet,
On my black coffin let there be strown;
Not a friend, not a friend greet
My poor corpse, where my bones shall be thrown;
A thousand thousand sighs to save,
  Lay me, O, where
Sad true-lover ne'er find my grave,
  To weep there.

Komm herbey, komm kerbey, Tod!
Und versenk' in Cypressen den Leib.
Lass mich frey, lass mich frey, Noth!
Mich erschlägt ein holdseliges Weib.
Mit Rosmarin mein Leichenhemd,
  O bestellt es!
Ob Lieb' ans Herz mir tödlich kömmt,
  Treu' hält es.

Keine Blum', keine Blum' süss
Sey gestreut auf den schwärzlichen Sarg.
Keine Seel', keine Seel' grüss
Mein Gebein, wo die Erd' es verbarg.
Um Ach und Weh zu wenden ab,
  Bergt alleine
Mich, wo kein Treuer wall' ans Grab
  Und weine.

Only in the last line but one is the pattern slightly modified and the musical flow is interrupted by the awkward pause after *mich*. However, it is not the rhythm alone that makes the rendering sound so much like the original. After all, Herder had adhered almost as closely to the rhythmical pattern in both his translations, yet he did not so exactly capture the essence of the song. Schlegel not only retains the rhythm and rhyme scheme, but models the very lilt and cadence of his words on the original, keeping the repetition and even the word order as far as is linguistically possible. Even so something is inevitably lost. In the first strophe, for instance, the key-word *away*, which occurs four times, is so soft and free from confining consonants that it almost has the effect of a sigh. Schlegel's *herbey* is harder in sound, and he wisely does not keep to it in the third line, but replaces it by the rhyme *mich frey*. In the intervening line, the melancholy softness of the alliteration in *s* and *l* is lost, but the predominant voicelessness of the consonants remains. In Schlegel's second strophe the dark vowel sounds of the first line strike a note of gloom which then prevails throughout, whereas in the original, the more rarified atmosphere of sadness is maintained by means of soft light sounds, among which the hard words *black coffin* stand out starkly. Only with the long drawn-out assonance of the fourth line (bones, thrown) a more sombre tone prevails. But such discrepancies are of small account compared with the close correspondence of sound that Schlegel achieves. In the other songs too—both in *Twelfth Night* and in *Hamlet*—it is largely through his skill in reproducing the sound pattern that he succeeds in capturing the mood of the original. The tripping rhythm of 'O Schatz! auf welchen Wegen irrt ihr?' (*T.N.* ii. 3) comes close to the lighthearted grace of 'O mistress mine, where are you roaming?'; Ophelia's 'How should I your true love know / From another one?' (*H*. iv. 5) is echoed in 'Wie erkenn' ich dein Treulieb / Vor den andern nun?'; and in the double refrain of the final song of *Twelfth Night*: 'Hop heisa, bey Regen und

Wind!' ('With hey, ho, the wind and the rain') and 'Denn der Regen, der regnet jeglichen Tag' ('For the rain it raineth every day') the lilt of the model is neatly caught. Only rarely does Schlegel's hand seem to lose its cunning, e.g. we miss the wraith-like wistfulness of Ophelia's 'Hey no nonny, nonny hey nonny' (*H*. iv. 5) in his heavier rendering 'Leider, ach leider'; and the gay nonsense rhyme: 'I am gone sir / And anon sir' (*T.N.* iv. 2) so entirely defeats him, that in the first verse he alters both rhythm and content, and the second he omits altogether.

Clearly it is not only the rhythm that imposes exacting demands on the translator's verbal ingenuity and sensitiveness to the sound of words, but also the expressive power of vowel and consonant groupings, rhyme, echo and contrast of sound. Rhyme is faithfully retained by Schlegel wherever it occurs, both in the songs and the rhymed couplets. The proportion of feminine rhymes is, however, higher than in the original text. This is no doubt partly due to the large number of unaccented verbal, adjectival and nominal endings in German and partly to Schlegel's feeling that feminine rhyme is intrinsically the more beautiful. The effect of the replacement of masculine by feminine rhyme is usually a slight weakening of impact, and sometimes this occurs in Schlegel's version at a moment when clear-cut finality is the very purpose of the rhyme. For instance, the concluding couplet of Act i of *Twelfth Night* runs:

> Fate, shew thy force: Ourselves we do not owe;
> What is decreed, must be; and be this so!

Schlegel writes:

> Nun walte, Schicksal! niemand ist sein eigen;
> Was seyn soll, muss geschehn; so mag sich's zeigen,

and the extra light syllable at the end of each line seems to soften the effect of blunt finality. (pp. 38-41)

The task of reproducing by vowel and consonant grouping a general auditory impression comparable to the original one is extremely complex, and that any passage should, when compared with the original, entirely satisfy the ear, is little short of miraculous. There are, however, such passages in Schlegel's versions. The line: 'Mein Verlangen / Scharf wie geschliffner Stahl, hat mich gespornt', falls on the ear with almost exactly the same effect of forceful hardness as does Shakespeare's 'My desire, / More sharp than filed steel, did spur me forth' (*T.N.* iii. 3). In both the peculiar combination of vowel and consonant sounds produces a sensuous effect that appeals to the ear with the immediacy of music and is perfectly calculated to strengthen the impact made on the intellect by the logical content. Similarly, in the lines:

> Beugt euch, ihr starren Knie'! gestähltes Herz,
> Sey weich wie Sehnen neugebohrner Kinder!,

by a skilful use of consonant sound Schlegel goes far towards producing the contrast of hard and soft that distinguishes the sound (and the sense) of the original:

> Bow, stubborn knees! and, heart with strings of steel,
> Be soft as sinews of the new-born babe.

> (*H*. iii. 3)

But such equivalence of impression is rare. More often Schlegel creates the same sort of effect—whether of loudness or softness, discord or harmony—but to a limited degree; and, indeed, even this is an achievement. The line: 'Das starke Gift bewältigt meinen Geist' is appropriately quiet in tone, but lacks the subtle suggestion of overwhelming physical weakness produced by the sequence of voiceless consonants in the original: 'The po-tent poison quite o'er-crows my spirit' (*H*. v, 2). The couplet:

> Tauch meinen Sinn in Lethe, Fantasie!
> Soll ich so träumen, gern erwach' ich nie!,

though pleasantly harmonious, does not quite evoke the at-mosphere of dreamy irreality in Shakespeare's:

> Let fancy still my sense in Lethe steep;
> If it be thus to dream, still let me sleep!
>
> (*T.N.* iv, 1)

We miss, in the German, the sustained assonance, in *ee*, the alliterative *s* and the recurrent *l*. Nor does Schlegel quite suc-ceed in matching the incantatory effect of: 'With such dexterity to incestuous sheets' in his rendering: 'In ein blutschänder-isches Bett zu stürzen' (*H*. i, 2). The tongue-twisting grouping of vowel and consonant sounds reproduces most aptly the impression of indecent haste; but the heavier texture suggests not neat finesse but an ungainly scramble. The idea of dexterity is missing in the sound as in the content. There is a similar thickening of texture in the rendering of Hamlet's very first line: 'A little more than kin, and less than kind' by 'Mehr als befreundet, weniger als Freund' and this also results in a loss of dramatic significance. Shakespeare seems purposely to have made this line sound as unobtrusive and unemphatic as possible: the metre is regular, the vowels mainly short and thin and the consonants soft. Yet, paradoxically, these very features make it stand out in contrast to the pompous urbane diction of the king and the other speakers, just as in the visual sphere Ham-let's drab figure stands out amidst the brilliance of the court. In general, as we have seen, Schlegel tends to smooth out metrical variations, yet here, where the regular alternation of lift and dip is essential to the dramatic effect, he introduces metrical inversion, and this, together with the long vowel sounds and recurrent *r*, dulls the expressive contrast of the original. On the other hand, Shakespeare's most violent and strident effects are often toned down in the translation. An obvious instance is Duke Orsino's speech on meeting Antonio:

> That face of his I do remember well;
> Yet, when I saw it last, it was besmear'd
> As black as Vulcan, in the smoke of war.
> A baubling vessel was he captain of,
> For shallow draught, and bulk, unprizable;
> With which such scathful grapple did he make
> With the most noble bottom of our fleet
> That very envy, and the tongue of loss,
> Cry'd fame and honour on him.
>
> (*T.N.* v, 1)

The first line is quiet and thoughtful, but as the memory of Antonio's valour in the stress of battle comes back to the Duke's mind, and he tries to convey it to his hearers, the speed quickens and explosive consonant clusters (*bl, lk, ft, dr, pr*) mark the violence of his words. Combinations such as 'scathful grapple' suggest stress and effort even in the very process of pronun-ciation. Schlegel's rendering begins well:

> Auf diess Gesicht besinn' ich mich gar wohl;
> Doch als ich es zuletzt sah, war es schwarz
> Vom Dampf des Krieges, wie Vulkan, besudelt.

There is a similar softness in the opening words and a similar working up to a contrasting harsh line. But then the *crescendo* is not continued:

> Er war der Hauptmann eines winz'gen Schiffs,
> Nach Gröss' und flachem Bau von keinem Werth,
> Womit er sich so furchtbar handgemein

> Mit unserer Flotte stärksten Segeln machte,
> Dass selbst der Neid und des Verlustes Stimme
> Preis über ihn und Ehre rief.

The violence is tempered by the intermingling of softer sounds. Similarly the lines:

> Und wie er Züge Rheinweins niedergiesst,
> Verkünden schmetternd Pauken und Trompeten
> Den ausgebrachten Trunk,

for all their noisy explosiveness, do not equal the loud *cres-cendo* of the original, culminating in the strident climax 'bray out' which echoes the vowel sounds of 'drain . . . down' in the preceding line:

> And, as he drains his draughts of Rhenish down,
> The kettle-drum and trumpet thus bray out
> The triumph of his pledge.
>
> (*H*. i, 4)

Thus, though far from disregarding the incantatory aspect of words, Schlegel tends to narrow the range and limit the variety of Shakespeare's sound effects. (pp. 41-4)

> *Margaret E. Atkinson, in her* August Wilhelm Schle-gel as a Translator of Shakespeare, *Basil Blackwell, 1958, 67 p.*

ARTHUR M. EASTMAN (essay date 1968)

[*In the following excerpt, Eastman depicts Schlegel as an inno-vative and influential force in Shakespearean criticism.*]

Schlegel's Shakespearean efforts span many years; they include translations that became the German standards and critical ar-ticles aplenty; but from our standpoint his great work must be the ***Course of Lectures on Dramatic Art and Literature***. . . . Approximately one-fifth of this ambitious survey goes to Shakespeare. Schlegel comes before his audience inviting a wide tolerance, a sympathy transcending narrow esthetic fac-tionalism. Man is plastic; his art forms evolving, arriving at one perfection in classical antiquity, at another in medieval and Renaissance Europe.

> We will quarrel with no man for his predilection
> either for the Grecian or the Gothic. The world
> is wide, and affords room for a great diversity
> of objects. Narrow and blindly adopted pre-
> possessions will never constitute a genuine critic
> or connoisseur, who ought, on the contrary, to
> possess the power of dwelling with liberal im-
> partiality on the most discrepant views, re-
> nouncing the while all personal inclinations.

So genial and morally appealing is this doctrine that we may fail to see how striking it is. French neo-classical criticism has absolutely disappeared from the equation, and though Shake-speare is again to be seen as Gothic, as the English and French neo-classicists had seen him, the Gothic has now been elevated to a parity with the Grecian! ''The Pantheon is not more dif-ferent from Westminster Abbey . . . than the structure of a tragedy of Sophocles from a drama of Shakespeare . . . But does our admiration of the one compel us to depreciate the other? May we not admit that each is great and admirable in its kind?'' (pp. 37-8)

Schlegel's strategies of treating the moderns as at least the equals of the ancients and of measuring them against principles which are inferred from their own practice rather than borrowed from the codifications of Corneille, Horace, or Aristotle, prepare for a new acceptance of Shakespearean tragicomedy. Sidney and most neo-classicists had lamented the mingled mode of Shakespeare's plays. Johnson had vindicated Shakespeare logically and psychologically: tragicomedy imitates aspects of nature which neither tragedy nor comedy alone can imitate, and the mind quickly and easily adjusts to changes of mood—at least, under Shakespeare's manipulation. Lessing, however, had had doubts. Because the mind is finite, it sets up arbitrary limits to save attention from distraction. "If we are witnesses of an important and touching event, and another event of trifling import traverses it, we seek and evade the distractions of our attention thus threatened"—so in actuality, so in art. Only when high and low causally connect can drama justly break down the generic barriers: "if gravity provokes laughter, sadness pleasure or *vice versa,* so directly that an abstraction of the one or the other is impossible to us, then only do we not demand it from art and art knows how to draw a profit from this impossibility." Unfortunately, Lessing neglected to apply his standard to Shakespeare's plays. It is doubtful how many would have passed the test. But for Schlegel there is no test. For him, what Shakespeare does defines the romantic drama and validates it.

> [Romantic drama] delights in indissoluble mixtures; all contrarieties: nature and art, poetry and prose, seriousness and mirth, recollection and anticipation, spirituality and sensuality, terrestrial and celestial, life and death, are by it blended together in the most intimate combination.
>
> It embraces at once the whole of the checkered drama of life with all its circumstances; and while it seems only to represent subjects brought accidentally together, it satisfies the unconscious requisitions of fancy, buries us in reflections on the inexpressible signification of the objects which we view blended by order, nearness and distance, light and color, into one harmonious whole; and thus lends, as it were, a soul to the prospect before us.

These undifferentiated totalities, these indissoluble mixtures, these fusions of opposites in Schlegel's opinion are "not mere licenses, but true beauties in the romantic drama." (pp. 39-40)

Schlegel argues . . . not to abolish the unities but to deny them solely sovereign sway. They are perfectly valid as one kind of means to one kind of end . . . : they express the plastic or sculptural sense of antiquity, which Schlegel opposes to the picturesque sense of modernity.

> Sculpture directs our attention exclusively to the group which it sets before us, it divests it as far as possible from all external accompaniments, and where they cannot be dispensed with, it indicates them as slightly as possible. Painting, on the other hand, delights in exhibiting, along with the principal figures, all the details of the surrounding locality and all secondary circumstances, to open a prospect into a boundless distance in the background; and light and shade with perspective are its peculiar charms. Hence the dramatic, and especially the tragic art, of the ancients, annihilates in some measure the external circumstances of space

and time; while, by their changes, the romantic drama adorns its more varied pictures. Or, to express myself in other terms, the principle of the antique poetry is ideal; that of the romantic is mystical: the former subjects space and time to the internal free-agency of the mind; the latter honors these incomprehensible essences as supernatural powers, in which there is somewhat of indwelling divinity.

These things being so, the important unity for picturesque drama is none of the traditional ones but a unity of interest or impression. "The separate parts of a work of art . . . must not be taken in by the eye and ear alone, but also comprehended by the understanding. Collectively, however, they are all subservient to one common aim, namely, to produce a joint impression on the mind." (pp. 41-2)

[Schlegel] sees Shakespeare's plays as romantic drama, a genre separate from but equal to the ancient genres of tragedy and comedy, reflective of the picturesque or mystical propensities of the modern mind. Inevitably he regards the traditional assessment of Shakespeare as a wildly luxuriant genius as misguided: "I consider, generally speaking, all that has been said on the subject a mere fable." He rejects the analytical separation of genius and taste on which the traditional view was based. "Genius," he declares, "is the almost unconscious choice of the highest degree of excellence, and, consequently, it is taste in its highest activity." If the activity of genius seems unconscious,

> it by no means follows, that the thinking power had not a great share in it. It is from the very rapidity and certainty of the mental process, from the utmost clearness of understanding, that thinking in a poet is not perceived as something abstracted, does not wear the appearance of reflex meditation.

We recall Lessing's observation that "every genius is a born critic." The two men are using the same kind of language to make the same kind of point, which they do handsomely. The language, however, is a touch unsympathetic to their purposes. By naming, it separates the powers and activities of the mind which the criticism is trying to bring together. It sets or seems to set against each other mental imagination and judgment, genius and taste, nature and art. It is disjunctive. But Schlegel also finds a different, a conjunctive language in the enormously influential imagery of organic form.

> Organical form . . . is innate; it unfolds itself from within, and acquires its determination contemporaneously with the perfect development of the germ. We everywhere discover such forms in nature throughout the whole range of living powers, from the crystallization of salts and minerals to plants and flowers, and from these again to the human body. In the fine arts, as well as in the domain of nature—the supreme artist, all genuine forms are organical, that is, determined by the quality of the work. In a word, the form is nothing but a significant exterior, the speaking physiognomy of each thing.

This is the great central and seminal idea in Schlegel's new esthetic. Genius unites creativity and restraint. It issues in organic forms according to laws derivable from its own essence. Its works are connected wholes, complete and satisfactory within themselves. The multiple parts of any one work, however diverse superficially they may be, cooperate ''to produce a joint impression on the mind''; and the mind, responsive to the forces stamping upon it this unified impression, submits as in a waking sleep, voluntarily surrendering itself.

This esthetic of unity, creative and responsive, enables Schlegel to refute or dismiss various other traditional complaints against Shakespeare—for example, the anachronisms which Pope had endeavored, ''with more zeal than judgment,'' as Johnson put it, ''to transfer to [Shakespeare's] imagined interpolators.'' Shakespeare knew as well as we, says Schlegel, that Bohemia has no seacoast, but he is only faithful to factual details in his domestic stories—his stories placed in England.

> In the novels on which he worked, he avoided disturbing the associations of his audience, to whom they were known, by novelties—the correction of errors in secondary and unimportant particulars. The more wonderful the story, the more it ranged in a purely poetical region, which he transfers at will to an indefinite distance. These plays, whatever names they bear, take place in the true land of romance, and in the very century of wonderful love stories.

The argument builds dizzily. Shakespeare, with consummate tact, avoids disturbing his audience. He transports them to the land of romance, where anything may happen, where any conjunction of times and traits may occur. Shakespeare ''had not to do with a hairsplitting, hypercritical age like ours,'' grumbles Schlegel: ''his audience entered the theater, not to learn true chronology, geography, and natural history, but to witness a vivid exhibition.'' Then, the enthusiastic fit seizing him, Schlegel boldly undertakes ''to prove that Shakespeare's anachronisms are, for the most part, committed of set purpose and deliberately.'' The tone of modish modernity in *Hamlet* was necessary to make it credible that Hamlet be ''a philosophical inquirer.'' Richard III's mention of Machiavelli is only a shorthand reference to principles of government that ''have been in existence ever since the existence of tyrants.'' Perhaps Johnson would have judged of Schlegel's success no more favorably than he did of Pope's, but we note the insistence on the audience's submissiveness and the suggestion of artistic purpose. The hypothesis of unity receptive and creative turns the neo-classical sin, [violation of the traditional unities], at worst, into an irrelevance; at best, into a prudent stroke of artistry in the interest, paradoxically, of probability.

More usefully, perhaps, the esthetic of organic unity invites (or reflects) a series of structural awarenesses. Schlegel sees that Theseus and Hippolyta provide a frame for *A Midsummer Night's Dream,* that the choruses of *Henry V* provide a lyric enlargement of the theme of war that the stage itself could not legitimately provide, that the ''sententious rhymes full of antitheses'' help set off the play-within-the-play in *Hamlet,* that the banishment of Alcibiades parallels the rejection by his former friends of Timon: ''they are both examples of ingratitude.'' The second plot in *King Lear,* which Warton had condemned and which Johnson had justified by appeals to variety, to plot, and to the moral ''that villainy is never at a stop, that crimes lead to crimes, and at last terminate in ruin,'' Schlegel apprehends with an enlarging awareness:

> two such un-heard of examples taking place at the same time have the appearance of a great commotion in the moral world: the picture be-

comes gigantic, and fills us with such alarm as we should entertain at the idea that the heavenly bodies might one day fall from their appointed orbits.

Schlegel recognizes the use of foils: ''Shakespeare makes each of his principal characters the glass in which the others are reflected, and by like means enables us to discover what could not be immediately revealed to us.'' So Hamlet, Laertes, and Fortinbras reflect themselves and each other. So the ''ideal follies'' of the higher characters in *Twelfth Night* define and are defined by the ''naked absurdities'' of the low. Schlegel recognizes the parodic value of various comic scenes: we think of Pyramus and Thisbe in *A Midsummer Night's Dream* commenting on the love of the aristocratic young couples; of the Gadshill robbery in *Henry IV, Part I,* with its burlesquing of the rebellion, or of the ring business at the end of *The Merchant of Venice* ironically replaying the pound of flesh plot of contract, forfeit, humiliation, and forgiveness. Schlegel has an especially sharp eye for the way Shakespeare blends contrasting elements, or manipulates contrasting emotional responses in his audience, to achieve his harmonies. Shakespeare softens Hero's distress at the altar ''to prepare for a fortunate catastrophe.'' That is, against our distress at her embarrassment he pits our knowledge that Don John's plot has already been detected, and detected by the happily idiot Dogberry and Verges whose interrogation of the scoundrels delights us. Shakespeare blends with the apparent tragicality of Fidele's funeral in *Cymbeline* a musicality that mitigates the impression without weakening it. He presents in *Richard III* a repulsive villain yet engages our interest by endowing him with ''profound skill in dissimulation . . . wit . . . prudence . . . presence of mind . . . quick activity . . . valor.'' (pp. 43-7)

If one of [Schlegel's] traits is a fine sense of structure, particularly as it uses and unifies contraries, another is a moral sensibility. This prevents Schlegel from shrugging off Bertram's ''unfeeling pride and light-hearted perversity,'' though it lets him recognize in Bertram ''the good qualities of a soldier'' and, in the world, a phlegmatic acceptance of ''man's injustice to woman, if so-called family honor is preserved.'' . . . Schlegel sees ''the heartless littleness of Octavius'' in *Antony and Cleopatra;* the ''mixture of hardness, moderation, and prudence'' in Bolingbroke in *Richard II;* the fusion in Hotspur of ''rude manners, arrogance, and boyish obstinacy'' with ''the majestic image of his noble youth'': ''we are carried away by his fiery spirit at the very moment we would most censure it.'' After cataloguing Hamlet's virtues, Schlegel then turns toward his shortcomings, which he sees in a sharp moral light. Hamlet

> has a natural inclination for crooked ways; he is a hypocrite towards himself; his far-fetched scruples are often mere pretexts to cover his want of determination . . . he is too much overwhelmed with his own sorrow to have any compassion to spare for others . . . On the other hand, we evidently perceive in him a malicious joy . . . Hamlet has no firm belief either in himself or in anything else.

Not until Santayana and L. C. Knights is the melancholy Prince to receive such another scourging.

Without his moral sensitivity Schlegel could not begin to be the critic he is. Yet it limits his criticism where the criticism of another moralist, Johnson, is free. Johnson repines that

Shakespeare sacrifices virtue to convenience and neglects opportunities to instruct. He regards the plays as things in nature, in a sense, from which moral lessons may be drawn, but he does not treat the lessons as intentional.... Schlegel, on the other hand, both draws morals and attributes them to Shakespeare's intent. The result is a contraction or narrowing of his criticism that makes it seem, at times, both less than full and faintly corrupted by a doctrinaire Christianity. In *Macbeth,* he says, Shakespeare

> wishes to show that the conflict of good and evil in this world can only take place by the permission of Providence, which converts the curse that individual mortals draw down on their heads into a blessing to others. An accurate scale is followed in the retaliation.

The punishment, that is to say, fits the crime, the crimes themselves being nicely graded, and the fact of pain or suffering is, *ipso facto,* evidence of guilt. So "Banquo, by an early death, atones for the ambitious curiosity which prompted the wish to know his glorious descendants." When he comes to examine *King Lear* Schlegel seems free from the worst excesses of the doctrine of poetic justice—at least, he finds no fault with "Cordelia's heavenly beauty of soul," and sees her death, not as reflective of her moral nature but as instrumental in bringing Lear fitly to his own death. But then doctrine has its say:

> According to Shakespeare's plan the guilty, it is true, are all punished, for wickedness destroys itself; but the virtues that would bring help and succor are everywhere too late, or overmatched by the cunning activity of malice. The persons of this drama have only such a faint belief in Providence as heathens may be supposed to have; and the poet here wishes to show us that this belief requires a wider range than the dark pilgrimage on earth to be established in full extent.

If at times Schlegel's criticism of the individual plays wraps them thus in darkness visible, more often it illuminates the individual character or the nature of his hold upon our minds. Indeed, the moral criticism divorced from the doctrinal schema is immensely valuable. It expresses a perceptiveness broader-ranging than this discussion has yet indicated and of which the following brief samples may serve as final witness. A century and a half before Tillyard and Lily Bess Campbell, Schlegel perceives the histories as "one great whole . . . an historical heroic poem in the dramatic form," and he sees this heroic poem as a mirror for monarchs. Sidney had repudiated the imitation of war by stage tumults, and Johnson had neglected to comment on them.... With a smile Schlegel grants the absurdity of a "handful of awkward warriors in mock armor, by means of two or three swords, with which we clearly see they take especial care not to do the slightest injury to one another," deciding "the fate of mighty kingdoms"; but he recognizes that the effort on the stage to make battles seem real—by using cavalry, noise, throngs of actors—renders "the spectator incapable of bestowing that attention which a poetical work of art demands." He sees the need, then, of an artful middle course, a stagecraft that will suggest that the main business of battle is elsewhere, that we are witnessing momentarily "separate groups of an enormous picture." Schlegel recognizes the incredibility of the bond plot in *The Merchant of Venice* and the equal incredibility of the casket plot but

observes that "the one . . . is rendered natural and probable by means of the other." Schlegel emancipates *The Winter's Tale* from the claims of realism—"the calculation of probabilities has nothing to do with such wonderful and fleeting adventures"—and pleasantly consigns those who affect to be displeased at neglect of dramatic decorum in *As You Like It* "to the wise fool, to be led gently out of [the forest of Arden] to some prosaical region." In terms not unlike those of Mack and Levin some one hundred fifty years later, Schlegel says of *Hamlet* that it "resembles those irrational equations in which a fraction of unknown magnitude always remains, that will in no way admit of solution." Johnson had dismissed the histories from his considerations on the unities. Schlegel proposed that "under the apparent artlessness of adhering closely to history as he found it," Shakespeare concealed "an uncommon degree of art." Shakespeare "knows how to seize the true poetical point of view, and to give unity and rounding to a series of events detached from the immeasurable extent of history without in any degree changing them." Like Johnson before him and Bradley after, Schlegel tries to catch the special or unique quality of the individual plays, especially the tragedies. For him, as for how many after, *Hamlet* is a tragedy of thought, *Macbeth* of terror, *King Lear* of compassion.

Johnson has a happy comparison between a critic recommending Shakespeare by the citation of individual passages and the pedant "who, when he offered his house to sale, carried a brick in his pocket as a specimen." I confess to feeling like that pedant, trying to convey the range, the genial tolerance, and the sharp perceptiveness of Schlegel's critical mind. Perhaps if we recognize in it the union of many and precise percepts with large, liberating concepts we do him justice. Along with hundreds on hundreds of awarenesses that came to him about speeches, characters, episodes, and the individual plays as he translated and mulled over Shakespeare, Schlegel made his own and made applicable to Shakespeare a new esthetic, inclusive and organic. (pp. 47-51)

Arthur M. Eastman, "Lessing and Schlegel," in his A Short History of Shakespearean Criticism, Random House, 1968, pp. 35-51.

RALPH W. EWTON, JR.   (essay date 1972)

[In assessing Schlegel's contribution as a literary theorist, Ewton underscores his departures from Romantic poetics and challenges his reputation as a systematizer of Romantic theory.]

Schlegel, it has been suggested, was the [Romantic] circle's systematizer and its popularizer. He was also, as Körner has shown in his *Die Botschaft der deutschen Romantik an Europa,* the mediator between German Romanticism and the rest of Europe. With some qualifications concerning Schlegel's systematizing, these roles are all characteristic of his theoretical labors. There is, however, some question as to the extent to which Schlegel is really a true representative of romantic poetics.

There are many respects in which Schlegel's literary theories are romantic. His theory and criticism is to a large degree directed toward upholding the artistic claims of modern literature, especially of the *romantische Poesie* of the early modern period. Schlegel's description of romantic poetry's qualities are typical. These qualities are, furthermore, considered to be properly those of literature after the Renaissance insofar as it is distinctively modern and not inspired by an anachronistic classicism.

Schlegel's definitions of *Poesie* are essentially romantic. *Poesie* is not just literature. It is an intuition and revelation of the nature of things. *Poesie* reveals in plastic images the truths of transcendental philosophy. It is a natural outgrowth of human nature. *Poesie* appears in non-aesthetic forms (*Naturpoesie*) but it is also the highest artistic product of man's selfconscious activity. The expressive capabilities of *Poesie* are considered to be limitless.

The list of Schlegel's romantic formulations could be drawn out. But so too could a list of deviations by Schlegel from the poetic theories of Schelling, Novalis and Friedrich Schlegel. The principal non-romantic tendencies of Schlegel's theories must be noted.

First of all, it should be observed that Schlegel's descriptions of *romantische Poesie* reflect less personal involvement than do the theoretical statements of Friedrich Schlegel and Novalis. The concept of romantic poetry remains more a historical and critical one. Romantic poetry is something given by history which the critic must deal with. The concept is not broadened to include all *Poesie* as, for example, in Friedrich's statement, "Die romantische Dichtart ist die einzige, die mehr als Art und gleichsam die Dichtkunst selbst ist; denn in einem gewissen Sinn ist oder soll alle Poesie romantisch sein". At times Schlegel comes close to agreeing with this statement insofar as it is applied to the literature of the future. But his own theoretical statements are usually based on a higher idea of *Poesie* which embraces both classic and romantic. His theories of *romantische Poesie* are not, however, a program for the future but rather a basis for judging a literary type found in history. To a far greater extent than for his contemporaries, *romantische Poesie* for Schlegel means the writing of Dante, Petrarch, Boccaccio, Cervantes, Calderon and Shakespeare.

H. A. Korff describes an important aspect of romantic literary theory with the formula "Relativierung des Werkes". By this he means the poet's rising above his works and, as he puts it, the "Erlösung der in dem Gegenstande gleichsam verzauberten Poesie". The "Relativierung des Werkes" may be an important part of the experience of the romantic poet but not so for August Wilhelm Schlegel, the romantic critic. Korff is, of course, speaking of Friedrich Schlegel's theories of romantic irony. The subject is virtually unmentioned in August Wilhelm's writings. We have seen that his idea of *Poesie* does go far beyond the naive idea of 'poems', that is, specific literary works. For the critic and literary technician, however, works are not "relativiert". Schlegel views works of both classic and romantic art not as an artist conscious of the irony of casting a magical *Poesie* into mere words, but as a critic who must explain the content and form of given verbal structures.

Another departure from romantic poetics is Schlegel's failure to deal with what Korff calls its "Märchenideal" as it was formulated, above all, by Novalis. Korff sees the philosophic justification for the romantic preoccupation with dream and fairy tale in transcendental philosophy. [In his *Geist der Goethezeit,* he] contrasts Schiller and the romantics in their appropriations of transcendentalism. . . . Sometimes Schlegel . . . speaks of the world as a riddle, but *Poesie* is its solution, not just a further riddle. It is true that Schlegel speaks of romantic poetry as an approximation toward expressing the infinite. But when he speaks of actual literary works his general statements on the nature of poetry come closer to the ideals of German Classicism. The struggle between *Natur* and *Geist* must be resolved. Content and form become one united whole. Transcendental philosophy, for Schlegel, points not to the chaotic nature of the world so much as to the orderliness of man's experience of it. And this order is revealed, above all, in the highest literary art. Again it seems evident that Novalis and Friedrich Schlegel speak of *Poesie* as a personal experience, whereas August Wilhelm Schlegel speaks from his characteristic historical-theoretical-critical standpoint. *Poesie* is not a personal problem of adequately expressing a puzzling world. Rather it is, in most of his statements, something already accomplished: artistic works appearing within a historical framework and there to be evaluated critically within a theoretical system adequate to them.

Another departure from romantic poetics is in Schlegel's refusal to adopt any extreme doctrine of aestheticism. Friedrich Schlegel's famous *Athenaeum* fragment on *romantische Poesie* states, "[Die romantische Dichtart] allein ist unendlich, wie sie allein frei ist und das als ihr erstes Gesetz anerkennt, daß die Willkür des Dichters kein Gesetz über sich leide". For August Wilhelm Schlegel, however, aestheticism remains more problematical. He follows Kant and Schiller in their freeing art from all external goals. But he does not go far beyond the position that art requires a willful submission to aesthetic laws. Art, including romantic art, must be beautiful and this implies that it must be meaningful. Art never degenerates into riddles whose meanings are virtually the exclusive property of a completely autonomous poet.

This discussion of Schlegel's romanticism began by pointing out that his point of view is in fact largely romantic. The subsequent qualifications are not intended to deny Schlegel's romantic inclinations. Rather the purpose was to suggest that the critic's theories do not always reach the extremes of the theories of the poets. Schlegel cannot be called merely the systematizer of views formulated by his more talented contemporaries.

There are romantic elements in Schlegel's theories but they hardly constitute a systematization of romantic literary theory. The word 'popularization' suits Schlegel's romantic theorizing somewhat better. His lectures were popular and, in their printed form, widely read, as Körner has demonstrated in some detail in the case of the Vienna Lectures. Insofar as Schlegel's works had a deeper influence, it was not as an aesthetic system. The only writer of major importance who was influenced by Schlegel was Coleridge who borrowed a number of details from the Vienna Lectures. Later theorists pass over Schlegel. He is not mentioned in most histories of aesthetics. Neglect in such works is, in spite of Haym's arguments, not entirely unjust, for Schlegel's works do not constitute the romantic aesthetic system Haym sees in them. It is entirely appropriate that the most recent evaluation of Schlegel's theories, that of Wellek, is in a work entitled *A History of Modern Criticism* [see excerpt dated 1955].

Although Schlegel's theories are not a systematic romantic poetics, they are not lacking in coherence. The unifying themes are: 1) the relationship of literature to primordial poetry in its three forms: language, rhythm and myth; 2) the relationship of literature to the theory of language; 3) the relationship of literature to the philosophy of Kant, Fichte and Schelling. In the case of Fichte and Schelling this is done largely through the subject of language, which is both the mediator of consciousness and the medium of *Poesie*. 4) a number of recurrent related themes: poetry as a higher (*potenzierte*) mode of expression; the connection of poetry and philosophical speculation; art as a fictional world; the essential nature of the poetic genres; the classical themes of the reconciliation of *Natur* and

Geist and the harmony of matter and form in art; the attempt to justify the artistic claims of romantic art; 5) finally, and most important, the unity of history, criticism and theory.

The unified approach to literature through history, criticism and theory remains the most important characteristic of Schlegel's writings. As admirable as this approach may be, it would seem that in it lies part of the reason why Schlegel is so little read today. The philosophically inclined reader of Schlegel's lectures will find them lacking in systematic plan and logical execution. The historian will find Schlegel's views antiquated in some respects and, perhaps, too theoretical. Those interested in Schlegel's criticism will be more likely to turn to the shorter works where theory is more in the background. . . . [We] hope that the reader will examine the theories in the works in which they appear. Schlegel's poetic theories gain in persuasion by their setting in their original historical and critical context. The major interest in Schlegel will undoubtedly continue to be that of scholars of German Romanticism. Many of the problems he discusses, however, are still with us and his statements on myth, symbolism, organic form, meaning in literature and, in general, the nature of the relationship of the fictional world of poetry to the real world around us, are still relevant even when they are not completely satisfying. (pp. 112-16)

> *Ralph W. Ewton, Jr., in his* The Literary Theories of August Wilhelm Schlegel, *Mouton, 1972, 120 p.*

ADDITIONAL BIBLIOGRAPHY

Behler, Ernst. "The Reception of Calderón among the German Romantics." *Studies in Romanticism* 20, No. 4 (Winter 1981): 437-60.
    Includes a discussion of Schlegel's response to Calderón and its effect on the Spanish dramatist's reception among the German Romantics.

"Memoir of the Literary Life of Augustus William von Schlegel." In *Course of Lectures on Dramatic Art and Literature*, rev. ed., by Augustus William Schlegel, edited by A. J. W. Morrison, translated by John Black, pp. 7-15. 1846. Reprint. New York: AMS Press, 1973.
    A biographical sketch focusing on Schlegel's literary activities.

Goslee, Nancy M. "Plastic to Picturesque: Schlegel's Analogy and Keats's *Hyperion* Poems." *Keats-Shelley Journal* XXX (1981): 118-51.
    Uses Schlegel's distinction between the plastic spirit of ancient art and the picturesque spirit of modern art as a tool for explicating certain aspects of Keats's *Hyperion* and *The Fall of Hyperion*.

Helmholtz, Anna Augusta. "The Indebtedness of Samuel Taylor Coleridge to August Wilhelm von Schlegel." *Bulletin of the University of Wisconsin*, No. 163. Philology and Literature Series, Vol. 3, No. 4 (June 1907): 279-370.
    A detailed examination of Coleridge's alleged appropriation of key concepts and phrases from Schlegel's criticism.

Hirschberg, Edgar W. "G. H. Lewes and A. W. Schlegel: An Important Critical Relationship." *The University of South Florida Language Quarterly* V, No. 3-4 (Spring-Summer 1967): 37-40.
    Reviews the main points of agreement and disagreement between Schlegel and Lewes concerning critical principles and methods.

Hofe, Harold von. "August Wilhelm Schlegel and the New World." *The Germanic Review* 35, No. 4 (December 1960): 279-87.
    Underscores the prominence of the New World as a thematic component in Schlegel's works. Hofe emphasizes Schlegel's concern with the relationship between the Americas and the concept of world historical development as well as his views regarding the influence of the New World on the intellectual life of the West.

Hughes, Glyn Tegai. "Profusion and Order: The Brothers Schlegel." In his *Romantic German Literature*, pp. 41-60. New York: Holmes and Meier Publishers, 1979.
    A brief overview of Schlegel's accomplishments as a creative writer and critic. Hughes considers Schlegel's Shakespeare translations and Shakespeare criticism achievements of lasting value.

Orsini, G. N. G. "Coleridge and Schlegel Reconsidered." *Comparative Literature* XVI, No. 2 (Spring 1964): 97-118.
    Addresses the controversy surrounding Coleridge's alleged plagiarism of Schlegel's ideas, tracing the English writer's remarks on organic form back to Schlegel.

Pascal, R. Introduction to *Shakespeare in Germany, 1740-1815*, edited by R. Pascal, pp. 1-36. Cambridge: Cambridge University Press, 1937.
    Discusses Schlegel in the context of the development of Shakespeare criticism in Germany during the mid-eighteenth to early nineteenth centuries.

Pochmann, Henry A. *German Culture in America: Philosophical and Literary Influences, 1600-1900*. Madison: University of Wisconsin Press, 1961, 865 p.
    Contains brief references to Schlegel's influence on numerous nineteenth-century American literary figures.

Raysor, Thomas Middleton. Introduction to *Shakespearean Criticism*, rev. ed., by Samuel Taylor Coleridge, edited by Thomas Middleton Raysor, pp. xv-lii. London: Dent, Everyman's Library, 1960.
    Includes an important discussion of Schlegel's effect on Coleridge. Raysor maintains that "it is almost certain that the great influence of Schlegel confirmed and developed rather than suggested many of Coleridge's ideas."

"August Wilhelm Schlegel (1767-1845)." In *The Reception of Classical German Literature in England, 1760-1860: A Documentary History from Contemporary Periodicals*, Vol. 6, edited by John Boening, pp. 206-319. New York: Garland Publishing, 1977.
    Provides facsimiles of sixteen articles on Schlegel originally published in British periodicals during the nineteenth century.

Rose, Ernst. Review of *Shakespeare's Werke*, by William Shakespeare, translated by Rudolf Schaller. *The German Quarterly* L, No. 2 (March 1977): 161-65.
    Maintains that Rudolph Schaller's *Shakespeare's Werke* surpasses Schlegel's Shakespeare translations.

Sauer, Thomas G. *A. W. Schlegel's Shakespearean Criticism in England, 1811-1846*. Studien zur Literatur der Moderne, edited by Helmut Koopmann, vol. 9. Bonn: Bouvier Verlag Herbert Grundmann, 219 p.
    A comprehensive examination of Schlegel's effect on English Shakespearean criticism during the years 1811 to 1846.

Schilling, Hanna-Beate. "The Role of the Brothers Schlegel in American Literary Criticism as Found in Selected Periodicals, 1812-1833: A Critical Bibliography." *American Literature* XLIII, No. 4 (January 1972): 563-79.
    Reviews references to the Schlegels in selected American periodicals between 1812 and 1833. Schilling concludes from her research that the brothers' ostensible influence on American critics of that period "cannot be documented."

Sir Walter Scott

1771-1832

(Also wrote under pseudonym Jedediah Cleishbotham) Scottish novelist, poet, short story writer, biographer, historian, critic, and editor.

Scott exerted a profound influence on early nineteenth-century European literature. During his lifetime he was the most popular author the world had ever known, and modern scholars consider him both the inventor of the historical novel and the first best-selling novelist. As the anonymous and enormously prolific "Author of *Waverley*," Scott not only elevated the novel to a status equal to that of poetry but also helped shape the way history has been written and understood by subsequent generations of historians and novelists. Despite the unprecedented contemporary success of his novels and poetry, Scott's literary reputation and popularity following his death gradually underwent one of the most pronounced reversals in the history of English literature. Today his poetry is largely ignored, and his novels attract the interest primarily of scholars and literary historians.

Scott was born in Edinburgh to middle-class parents, the fourth surviving child of Walter Scott and Anne Rutherford. At the age of two, he suffered an attack of polio that rendered him lame for the rest of his life. Biographers point out, however, that in spite of his illness, Scott led an active outdoor life during his childhood and developed early on an appreciation for the picturesque scenery that later figured so prominently in his writings. As a child Scott also displayed a deep fascination with Scottish history and literature along with an ability to retain everything he learned about his country's past, whether it was the details of an important battle or the lines of a lengthy ballad. According to the critic Ian Jack, "It was Scott's good fortune as a boy to be surrounded by a sort of Greek chorus of Scots antiquaries" from whom he absorbed both knowledge and enthusiasm. Scott enrolled in Edinburgh High School in 1778 and five years later entered the University of Edinburgh, studying history and law. In 1786, he was apprenticed to his father's legal firm and was called to the bar in 1792. While serving his apprenticeship, Scott traveled extensively in the Scottish Border country and Highlands, where he delighted in the natural settings and rural inhabitants. In 1800 he was able to combine his love for Scottish lore and literature with his ongoing excursions into the countryside as he started collecting and editing ballads for his *Minstrelsy of the Scottish Border*. The *Minstrelsy* contained numerous Scottish ballads that had never before appeared in print, as well as imitation ballads written by Scott and others. Although it produced only modest sales, the collection enjoyed critical favor. More importantly, with the *Minstrelsy*, as John Lauber has pointed out, Scott "discovered his proper subject, Scottish history and tradition."

The positive reception of the *Minstrelsy* and the encouragement of his friends prompted Scott to attempt an original work based on Scottish themes. His efforts resulted in *The Lay of the Last Minstrel*, a narrative poem set in medieval times that, in Scott's words, was "intended to illustrate the customs and manners which anciently prevailed on the Borders of England and Scotland." The success of the *Lay* when it appeared in 1805 was immediate and substantial. Determined to earn a living through

his writings, Scott gave up the law as a full-time profession and beginning in 1808 with *Marmion* published a series of highly popular and remunerative poems with Scottish backgrounds and themes, including what is perhaps his best-known long poem, *The Lady of the Lake*. By the time *Rokeby* appeared in 1813, however, readers were beginning to lose interest in his poetry. In addition, the triumph of the first two cantos of Lord Byron's *Childe Harold* in 1812 had convinced Scott that he could not compete with the younger poet. Anxious to retain his audience and large income, Scott decided to revise and complete a fragment of a novel that he had begun ten years before.

Entitled *Waverley; or, 'Tis Sixty Years Since*, Scott's tale of an Englishman who travels to the Scottish Highlands and becomes caught up in the Jacobite rebellion of 1745 proved a popular sensation when published in 1814. *Waverley* quickly became the most successful work of its kind ever to appear, and the novel brought huge profits to Scott and his publishers. Buoyed by his first venture as a novelist, he began writing at a rapid pace that over the next seventeen years produced more than two dozen novels and tales in a series that has since become known as the *Waverley Novels*. He was able to keep up his prolific output not only because he never plotted out his works ahead of time and seldom revised his manuscripts, but also because he maintained strenuous work habits even when

247

gravely ill. In the *Waverley Novels,* most of which describe the lives of ordinary individuals who become involved in great historical events, Scott presented in lavish detail the speech, manners, and customs of past ages. In studying these works, critics have often divided them into three groups: the so-called "Scotch Novels," or those dealing with Scottish culture and history, including *Old Mortality* and *The Heart of Mid-Lothian;* those concerned with medieval history in England and Europe, including *Ivanhoe* and *Quentin Durward;* and those focused on the Tudor-Stuart era in England, including *Kenilworth* and *Woodstock.* Although the sales of the *Waverley Novels* varied, they were by and large a consistent success with the public, who eagerly awaited each new work. Because writing novels was not considered as respectable as writing poetry, he had chosen to publish *Waverley* anonymously. When he himself had altered the status of the novel with *Waverley* and its successors, he nevertheless chose to retain his anonymity for many years, a practice his biographers have traced both to his love of secrecy and to his perception that the mystery surrounding the novels contributed to their sales. Many of the novels were published as "by the Author of *Waverley,*" and he was often referred to simply as the "Great Unknown." Despite his policy of anonymous publication, numerous readers and critics knew of his authorship; he became the most popular writer in English and a highly respected and admired figure throughout Europe. In 1818 he accepted a baronetcy, becoming Sir Walter Scott.

Scott's expenditures increased as quickly as his income, and many critics and biographers have tied his enormous output directly to a desire for material gain. Scott had purchased a farm in 1811 and, after renaming the property Abbotsford, began devoting huge sums of money to building, planting, and collecting relics from Scotland's past. Thus, although his income was large, his financial situation was often precarious. In 1826, disaster struck when a publishing house in which he was a silent partner failed. His debt amounted to over one hundred thousand pounds. Instead of choosing to declare bankruptcy, Scott arranged to work off the debt through his writings. The remainder of his life was devoted to the increasingly difficult task of producing saleable works in a variety of genres. Beginning in 1830 he suffered a series of strokes as he labored to pay his creditors. A trip to the Mediterranean in 1831 to regain his health proved unsuccessful, and after further strokes and paralysis he died at Abbotsford in 1832.

The critical history of Scott's works has been summed up by Robin Mayhead's statement that "no major British author has suffered more from changing literary fashions." During his lifetime, Scott enjoyed tremendous acclaim. The novelty of his approach and subject matter captivated his early audience; indeed, his writings created a vogue for all things Scottish and even led to an increase in tourism in Scotland. Many contemporary critics, however, agreed that Scott's poetry and novels shared glaring deficiencies, including careless construction, prolixity, and bad grammar. Yet most early reviewers quickly acknowledged the superiority of his novels, arguing that their originality, vivid portrayal of history, and lively characters outweighed their faults. His ability to bring Scottish and English history to life—to capture the language, costumes, and settings of the past—as well as his understanding of the effects of social change upon the lives of ordinary people, were entirely new to English fiction.

By the end of Scott's career, the *Waverley Novels* had almost entirely eclipsed his poetry, and the history of his literary reputation following his death is with few exceptions that of Scott

the novelist. However, the most significant study of Scott that appeared during the nineteenth century was a monumental biography, *The Life of Sir Walter Scott,* published by his son-in-law, John Gibson Lockhart, in 1837-38. This work, which despite its inaccuracies and falsifications is still considered one of the greatest biographies in English, helped to make the relationship between Scott's life and works an important critical topic. Scott was seen by many early Victorians as an almost heroic figure whose exemplary life and courageous struggle to pay his debts were reflected in the morally irreproachable qualities of his works. Yet certain critics, prominent among them Thomas Carlyle, felt that Scott's life should not be confused with his works, which were shallow, lacking in true passion, and written largely for material gain. As the nineteenth century progressed, the increasingly sophisticated design and self-conscious art of the novel as practiced by such writers as George Eliot and Henry James caused numerous commentators to deride the disorganized plots and intellectual superficiality of Scott's fiction. Although his admirers countered by praising his enduring appeal as a storyteller and the entertainment value of the *Waverley Novels,* by the turn of the century many critics maintained that Scott could no longer be considered a major English novelist. His readership as well as his critical stock had been declining since mid century, and while the second half of the twentieth century would show mounting scholarly interest in his works, Scott, a writer who in his own day had been compared with William Shakespeare, would eventually be described by W. E. K. Anderson as the "Great Unread."

Twentieth-century critics have emphasized Scott's important role in English literary history as well as his considerable impact on nineteenth-century European literature. Literary historians have traced his influence on the masterpieces of novelists as diverse as Charles Dickens, Gustave Flaubert, Honoré de Balzac, and William Makepeace Thackeray. Scholars have also explored Scott's significant contribution—through his invention and development of the historical novel—to the history of ideas, specifically with respect to the modern concept of historical perspective. Modern studies of the *Waverley Novels* have consistently stressed the superiority of the "Scotch Novels" over the rest, and critics have given particular attention to *The Heart of Mid-Lothian,* often considered his finest novel. Scott's works have attracted increasing scholarly notice since the general proliferation of English literary scholarship that began in the 1950s, and recent commentators have explored such specific aspects of his novels as his passive heroes, his portrayal of the Middle Ages, and his depiction of the struggle between past and present. Other notable events in twentieth-century Scott studies include the publication of Sir Herbert Grierson's edition of the novelist's letters in 1932-37 and the appearance of Edgar Johnson's definitive modern biography in 1970. Despite admiration for his writings, even Scott's most enthusiastic proponents readily concede the flaws and limitations of his best works and the inconsistency of his output as a whole—drawbacks that exclude him from the first rank of English novelists. Although his works are now largely the concern of literary specialists, Scott nevertheless remains a crucial figure in the development of the English novel and a seminal influence on nineteenth-century European literature.

PRINCIPAL WORKS

Minstrelsy of the Scottish Border. 3 vols. [editor and
   contributor]   (poetry)   1802-03
The Lay of the Last Minstrel   (poetry)   1805

Marmion: A Tale of Flodden Field (poetry) 1808
The Lady of the Lake (poetry) 1810
The Vision of Don Roderick (poetry) 1811
The Bridal of Triermain; or, The Vale of St. John (poetry)
     1813
Rokeby (poetry) 1813
Waverley; or, 'Tis Sixty Years Since (novel) 1814
The Field of Waterloo (poetry) 1815
Guy Mannering; or, The Astrologer (novel) 1815
The Lord of the Isles (poetry) 1815
The Antiquary (novel) 1816
The Black Dwarf [as Jedediah Cleishbotham] (novel)
     1816; published in *Tales of My Landlord, first series*
Old Mortality [as Jedediah Cleishbotham] (novel) 1816;
     published in *Tales of My Landlord, first series*
Tales of My Landlord, first series [as Jedediah
     Cleishbotham] (novels) 1816
The Heart of Mid-Lothian [as Jedediah Cleishbotham]
     (novel) 1818; published in *Tales of My Landlord,
     second series*
Rob Roy (novel) 1818
Tales of My Landlord, second series [as Jedediah
     Cleishbotham] (novel) 1818
The Bride of Lammermoor [as Jedediah Cleishbotham]
     (novel) 1819; published in *Tales of My Landlord,
     third series*
A Legend of Montrose [as Jedediah Cleishbotham] (novel)
     1819; published in *Tales of My Landlord, third series*
Tales of My Landlord, third series [as Jedediah
     Cleishbotham] (novels) 1819
The Abbot (novel) 1820
Ivanhoe (novel) 1820
The Monastery (novel) 1820
The Poetical Works of Walter Scott. 12 vols. (poetry) 1820
Kenilworth (novel) 1821
The Fortunes of Nigel (novel) 1822
Peveril of the Peak (novel) 1822
The Pirate (novel) 1822
Quentin Durward (novel) 1823
Redgauntlet: A Tale of the Eighteenth Century (novel)
     1824
St. Ronan's Well (novel) 1824
*Tales of the Crusaders (novels) 1825
*Woodstock; or, The Cavalier: A Tale of the Year Sixteen
     Hundred and Fifty-One* (novel) 1826
**Chronicles of the Canongate, first series (short stories)
     1827
Chronicles of the Canongate, second series (novel) 1828
St. Valentine's Day; or, The Fair Maid of Perth (novel)
     1828; published in *Chronicles of the Canongate, second
     series*
Anne of Geierstein; or, The Maiden of the Mist (novel)
     1829
Waverley Novels. 48 vols. (novels) 1830-34
Castle Dangerous [as Jedediah Cleishbotham] (novel)
     1832; published in *Tales of My Landlord, fourth series*
Count Robert of Paris [as Jedediah Cleishbotham] (novel)
     1832; published in *Tales of My Landlord, fourth series*
Tales of My Landlord, fourth series [as Jedediah
     Cleishbotham] (novels) 1832
The Poetical Works of Sir Walter Scott. 12 vols. (poetry)
     1833-34
The Miscellaneous Prose Works of Sir Walter Scott. 30 vols.
     (biographies, essays, travel sketches, histories, and
     criticism) 1834-71

The Journal of Sir Walter Scott (journal) 1890
Waverley Novels. 25 vols. (novels) 1892-94
The Complete Poetical Works of Sir Walter Scott. 5 vols.
     (poetry) 1894
The Letters of Sir Walter Scott. 12 vols. (letters) 1932-37

*This work contains the novels *The Betrothed* and *The Talisman.*

**This work contains the short stories "The Highland Widow," "The
     Surgeon's Daughter," and "The Two Drovers."

FRANCIS JEFFREY (essay date 1805)

[*Jeffrey was a founder and editor of the* Edinburgh Review, *one
of the most influential magazines in early nineteenth-century England. A liberal Whig, Jeffrey often allowed his political beliefs
to color his critical opinions. He is nevertheless considered an
insightful contemporary critic of Scott's works. In the following
excerpt from an 1805 review of* The Lay of the Last Minstrel,
*Jeffrey discusses the relationship between the poem and the chi-
valric romances Scott had sought to imitate and improve upon.
The critic also comments on various aspects of the* Lay, *including
its episodic design, picturesque subject matter, and versification.*]

We consider [*The Lay of the Last Minstrel*] as an attempt to
transfer the refinements of modern poetry to the matter and the
manner of the ancient metrical romance. The author, enamoured of the lofty visions of chivalry, and partial to the strains
in which they were formerly embodied, seems to have employed all the resources of his genius in endeavouring to recall
them to the favour and admiration of the public; and in adapting
to the taste of modern readers a species of poetry which was
once the delight of the courtly, but has long ceased to gladden
any other eyes than those of the scholar and the antiquary. This
is a romance, therefore, composed by a minstrel of the present
day; or such a romance as we may suppose would have been
written in modern times, if that style of composition had continued to be cultivated, and partaken consequently of the improvements which every branch of literature has received since
the time of its desertion.

Upon this supposition, it was evidently Mr. Scott's business
to retain all that was good, and to reject all that was bad in
the models upon which he was to form himself; adding, at the
same time, all the interest and beauty which could possibly be
assimilated to the manner and spirit of his originals. It was his
duty, therefore, to reform the rambling, obscure, and interminable narratives of the ancient romancers—to moderate their
digressions—to abridge or retrench their unmerciful or needless
descriptions—and to expunge altogether those feeble and prosaic passages, the rude stupidity of which is so apt to excite
the derision of a modern reader. At the same time, he was to
rival, if he could, the force and vivacity of their minute and
varied representations—the characteristic simplicity of their
pictures of manners—the energy and conciseness with which
they frequently describe great events—and the lively colouring
and accurate drawing by which they give the effect of reality
to every scene they undertake to delineate. In executing this
arduous task, he was permitted to avail himself of all that
variety of style and manner which had been sanctioned by the
ancient practice; and bound to embellish his performance with
all the graces of diction and versification which could be reconciled to the simplicity and familiarity of the minstrel's song.
(pp. 359-60)

[Mr. Scott] has produced a very beautiful and entertaining poem, in a style which may fairly be considered as original; and which will be allowed to afford satisfactory evidence of the genius of the author, even though he should not succeed in converting the public to his own opinion as to the interest or dignity of the subject. We are ourselves inclined indeed to suspect that his partiality for the strains of antiquity has imposed a little upon the severity of his judgment, and impaired the beauty of the present imitation, by directing his attention rather to what was characteristic, than to what was unexceptionable in his originals. Though he has spared too many of their faults, however, he has certainly improved upon their beauties: and while we can scarcely help regretting, that the feuds of Border chieftains should have monopolised as much poetry as might have served to immortalise the whole baronage of the empire, we are the more inclined to admire the interest and magnificence which he has contrived to communicate to a subject so unpromising.

Whatever may be thought of the conduct of the main story, the manner of introducing it must be allowed to be extremely poetical. An aged minstrel who had "harped to King Charles the Good," and learned to love his art at a time when it was honoured by all that was distinguished in rank or in genius, having fallen into neglect and misery in the evil days of the usurpation, and the more frivolous gaieties or bitter contentions of the succeeding reigns, is represented as wandering about the Border in poverty and solitude, a few years after the Revolution. In this situation he is driven, by want and weariness, to seek shelter in the Border castle of the Duchess of Buccleuch and Monmouth; and being cheered by the hospitality of his reception, offers to sing "an ancient strain," relating to the old warriors of her family; and after some fruitless attempts to recall the long-forgotten melody, pours forth *The Lay of the Last Minstrel*, in six cantos, very skilfully divided by some recurrence to his own situation, and some complimentary interruptions from his noble auditors.

The construction of a fable seems by no means the *forte* of our modern poetical writers; and no great artifice, in that respect, was to be expected, perhaps, from an imitator of the ancient romancers. Mr. Scott, indeed, has himself insinuated, that he considered the story as an object of very subordinate importance; and that he was less solicitous to deliver a regular narrative, than to connect such a series of incidents as might enable him to introduce the manners he had undertaken to delineate, and the imagery with which they were associated. (p. 360)

[However well calculated the story] may be for the introduction of picturesque imagery, or the display of extraordinary incident, it has but little pretension to the praise of a regular or coherent narrative. The magic of the lady, the midnight visit to Melrose, and the mighty book of the enchanter, which occupy nearly one-third of the whole poem, and engross the attention of the reader for a long time after the commencement of the narrative, are of no use whatsoever in the subsequent development of the fable, and do not contribute, in any degree, either to the production or explanation of the incidents that follow. The whole character and proceedings of the goblin page, in like manner, may be considered as merely episodical; for though he is employed in some of the subordinate incidents, it is remarkable that no material part of the fable requires the intervention of supernatural agency. The young Buccleuch might have wandered into the wood, although he had not been decoyed by a goblin; and the dame might have given her daughter to the deliverer of her son, although she had never listened to

the prattlement of the river and mountain spirits. There is, besides all this, a great deal of gratuitous and digressive description, and the whole sixth canto may be said to be redundant. The story should naturally end with the union of the lovers; and the account of the feast, and the minstrelsy that solemnised their betrothment is a sort of epilogue, superadded after the catastrophe is complete.

But though we feel it to be our duty to point out these obvious defects in the structure of the fable, we have no hesitation in conceding to the author, that the fable is but a secondary consideration in performances of this nature. A poem is intended to please by the images it suggests, and the feelings it inspires; and if it contain delightful images and affecting sentiments, our pleasure will not be materially impaired by some slight want of probability or coherence in the narrative by which they are connected. The *callida junctura* of its members is a grace, no doubt, which ought always to be aimed at; but the quality of the members themselves is a consideration of far higher importance; and that by which alone the success and character of the work must be ultimately decided. The adjustment of a fable may indicate the industry or the judgment of the writer; but the Genius of the poet can only be shown in his management of its successive incidents. In these more essential particulars, Mr. Scott's merits, we think, are unequivocal. He writes throughout with the spirit and the force of a poet; and though he occasionally discovers a little too much, perhaps, of the "brave neglect," and is frequently inattentive to the delicate propriety and scrupulous correctness of his diction, he compensates for those defects by the fire and animation of his whole composition, and the brilliant colouring and prominent features of the figures with which he has enlivened it. . . .

In the very first rank of poetical excellence, we are inclined to place the introductory and concluding lines of every canto; in which the ancient strain is suspended, and the feelings and situation of the Minstrel himself described in the words of the author. The elegance and the beauty of this *setting*, if we may so call it, though entirely of modern workmanship, appears to us to be fully more worthy of admiration than the bolder relief of the antiques which it encloses; and leads us to regret that the author should have wasted, in imitation and antiquarian researches, so much of those powers which seem fully equal to the task of raising him an independent reputation. (p. 362)

The ancient romance owes much of its interest to the lively picture which it affords of the times of chivalry, and of those usages, manners, and institutions which we have been accustomed to associate in our minds, with a certain combination of magnificence with simplicity, and ferocity with romantic honour. The representations contained in those performances, however, are for the most part too rude and naked to give complete satisfaction. The execution is always extremely unequal; and though the writer sometimes touches upon the appropriate feeling with great effect and felicity, still this appears to be done more by accident than design; and he wanders away immediately into all sorts of ludicrous or uninteresting details, without any apparent consciousness of incongruity. These defects Mr. Scott has corrected with admirable address and judgment in the greater part of the work now before us; and while he has exhibited a very striking and impressive picture of the old feudal usages and institutions, he has shown still greater talent in engrafting upon those descriptions all the tender or magnanimous emotions to which the circumstances of the story naturally give rise. Without impairing the antique air of the whole piece, or violating the simplicity of the ballad style, he has contrived in this way, to impart a much greater dignity, and more powerful interest to his production, than could ever be attained by the unskilful and unsteady delineations of the old romancers. Nothing, we think, can afford a finer illustration of this remark, than the opening stanzas of the whole poem; they transport us at once into the days of knightly daring and feudal hostility; at the same time that they suggest, and in a very interesting way, all those softer sentiments which arise out of some parts of the description. (p. 363)

In [numerous] passages, the poetry of Mr. Scott is entitled to a decided preference over that of the earlier minstrels; not only from the greater consistency and condensation of his imagery, but from an intrinsic superiority in the nature of his materials. From the improvement of taste, and the cultivation of the finer feelings of the heart, poetry acquires, in a refined age, many new and invaluable elements, which are necessarily unknown in a period of greater simplicity. The description of external objects, however, is at all times equally inviting, and equally easy; and many of the pictures which have been left by the ancient romancers must be admitted to possess, along with great diffuseness and homeliness of diction, an exactness and vivacity which cannot be easily exceeded. In this part of his undertaking, Mr. Scott therefore had fewer advantages; but we do not think that his success has been less remarkable. (p. 364)

The whole night-journey of Deloraine—the opening of the wizard's tomb—the march of the English battle—and the parley before the walls of the castle, are all executed with . . . spirit and poetical energy, . . . and a great variety of short passages occur in every part of the poem, which are still more striking and meritorious, though it is impossible to detach them, without injury, in the form of a quotation. It is but fair to apprise the reader, on the other hand, that he will meet with very heavy passages, and with a variety of details which are not likely to interest any one but a Borderer or an antiquary. We like very well to hear ''of the Gallant Chief of Otterburne,'' or ''the Dark Knight of Liddisdale,'' and feel the elevating power of great names, when we read of the tribes that mustered to the war, ''beneath the crest of old Dunbar, and Hepburn's mingled banners.'' But we really cannot so far sympathise with the local partialities of the author, as to feel any glow of patriotism or ancient virtue in hearing of the *Todrig* or *Johnston* clans, or of *Elliots, Armstrongs,* and *Tinlinns;* still less can we relish the introduction of *Black John of Athelstane, Whitslade the Hawk, Arthur-fire-the-braes, Red Roland Forster,* or any other of those worthies who

> Sought the beeves that made their broth,
> In Scotland and in England both,

into a poem which has any pretensions to seriousness or dignity. The ancient metrical romance might have admitted those homely personalities; but the present age will not endure them: And Mr. Scott must either sacrifice his Border prejudices, or offend all his readers in the other parts of the empire.

There are many passages, as we have already insinuated, which have the general character of heaviness, such is the minstrel's account of his preceptor, and Deloraine's lamentation over the dead body of Musgrave: But the goblin page is, in our opinion, the capital deformity of the poem. We have already said that the whole machinery is useless: but the magic studies of the lady, and the rifled tomb of Michael Scott, give occasion to so much admirable poetry, that we can on no account consent to part with them. The page, on the other hand, is a perpetual burden to the poet, and to the reader: it is an undignified and

improbable fiction, which excites neither terror, admiration, nor astonishment; but needlessly debases the strain of the whole work, and excites at once our incredulity and contempt. He is not a ''tricksy spirit,'' like Ariel, with whom the imagination is irresistibly enamoured; nor a tiny monarch, like Oberon, disposing of the destinies of mortals: He rather appears to us to be an awkward sort of a mongrel between Puck and Caliban; of a servile and brutal nature; and limited in his powers to the indulgence of petty malignity, and the infliction of despicable injuries. Besides this objection to his character, his existence has no support from any general or established superstition. Fairies and devils, ghosts, angels, and witches, are creatures with whom we are all familiar, and who excite in all classes of mankind emotions with which we can easily be made to sympathise. But the story of Gilpin Horner can never have been believed out of the village where he is said to have made his appearance; and has no claims upon the credulity of those who were not originally of his acquaintance. There is nothing at all interesting or elegant in the scenes of which he is the hero; and in reading those passages, we really could not help suspecting that they did not stand in the romance when the aged minstrel recited it to the royal Charles and his mighty earls, but were inserted afterwards to suit the taste of the cottagers among whom he begged his bread on the Border. We entreat Mr. Scott to inquire into the grounds of this suspicion; and to take advantage of any decent pretext he can lay hold of for purging *The Lay* of this ungraceful intruder. We would also move for a *Quo Warranto* against the spirits of the river and the mountain; for though they are come of a very high lineage, we do not know what lawful business they could have at Branksome castle in the year 1550.

Of the diction of this poem we have but little to say. . . . [The] versification is in the highest degree irregular and capricious. The nature of the work entitled Mr. Scott to some licence in this respect, and he often employs it with a very pleasing effect; but he has frequently exceeded its just limits, and presented us with such combinations of metre, as must put the teeth of his readers, we think, into some jeopardy. He has, when he pleases, a very melodious and sonorous style of versification, but often composes with inexcusable negligence and rudeness. There is a great number of lines in which the verse can only be made out by running the words together in a very unusual manner; and some appear to us to have no pretension to the name of verses at all. What apology, for instance, will Mr. Scott make for the last of these two lines?—

> For when in studious mood he pac'd
> St. Kentigern's hall.

or for these?—

> How the brave boy in future war,
> Should tame the unicorn's pride.

We have called the negligence which could leave such lines as these in a poem of this nature inexcusable; because it is perfectly evident, from the general strain of his composition, that Mr. Scott has a very accurate ear for the harmony of versification, and that he composes with a facility which must lighten the labour of correction. There are some smaller faults in the diction which might have been as well corrected also: there is too much alliteration; and he reduplicates his words too often. We have ''never, never,'' several times; besides '''tis o'er, 'tis o'er''—''in vain, in vain''—'''tis done, 'tis done;'' and several other echoes as ungraceful.

We will not be tempted to say any thing more of this poem. Although it does not contain any great display of what is properly called invention, it indicates perhaps as much vigour and originality of poetical genius as any performance which has been lately offered to the public. The locality of the subject is likely to obstruct its popularity; and the author, by confining himself in a great measure to the description of manners and personal adventures, has forfeited the attraction which might have been derived from the delineation of rural scenery. But he has manifested a degree of genius which cannot be overlooked, and given indication of talents that seem well worthy of being enlisted in the service of the epic muse. (pp. 366-67)

> Francis Jeffrey, "Scott's 'Lay of the Last Minstrel'," in his Contributions to the Edinburgh Review, D. Appleton and Company, 1860, pp. 359-67.

MR. TWISS (essay date 1809)

[In this excerpt from a review of Marmion, Twiss provides an extended analysis of that work and of Scott's poetic methods in general. The critic discusses such topics as plot, structure, characterization, style, and grammar.]

Among the poets of the time we live in, few are more entitled to notice, either by their beauties or by their blemishes, than the author of [Marmion]: for while he possesses a genius that might adorn the best age of literature, he is reviving that vicious style, which has already operated, with so irresistible a weight, to sink the early writers in oblivion.

If, in order to ascertain the first source of these evils, a careful and public-spirited reader should examine into the reasons, which may have induced Mr. Scott to adopt so erroneous a system, this reader would be likely to conclude, that a want of precision in thinking may have been the cause of all the mischief. Mr. Scott informs us, that his course of study has led him to admire the writing of the ancient poets; and he has apparently failed to distinguish which amongst the ingredients in that writing have raised his admiration. Possibly he may not have perceived, that what has pleased him in such works, has pleased him rather in spite, than by favour, of the diction: and, having remarked uncouth expression almost universally coupled with the beautiful poetry of the early writers, perhaps he has involuntarily fancied, that where uncouth expression appeared, there beautiful poetry must always be found. The rude nature of the subjects, which he has chosen to treat, may be supposed to have promoted and strengthened the mistake: for the association between unpolished manners and unpolished language would naturally act upon the mind of an author, investigating and recounting such histories as those of the antient borderers. One may conceive Mr. Scott, before he became known as a poet, to have been strongly impressed with all these feelings, and to have been aware how great an attention was likely to be excited by a species of composition, which, if the foundations of it were not in the nineteenth century absolutely original, had at least been so long disused, and was now reproduced with so much new modulation of his own, as to bear the face of novelty. And, when all these probable reasons have been considered, his anomalies, though not at all more venial, may appear a little less unaccountable.

The great reputation that attended *The Lay of the Last Minstrel*, was unquestionably adapted, if its author were very sanguine, to flatter him into more such undertakings. But he should have considered, that all which had before been done by his genius and his novelty of style united, must thenceforward be done, if it could be done at all, by his genius alone. For the style no longer had its novelty: and unfortunately it is in itself so faulty, that, when it loses this, it loses its only charm. Many of the persons, who at first were its warmest admirers, have found, that its tripping irregularity, which is so easy writing, is easy reading too; and the poet, like the conjurer, is out of credit when his tricks are known. And justly enough: for there seems to be no reason why one man should be distinguished for doing what a hundred of others can do likewise: and though nothing is meritorious merely because it is difficult, yet nothing which is not difficult can long be thought meritorious. This ballad-poetry was admired at first, because it seemed to be both beautiful and difficult: beautiful, because it was new; and difficult, because the world did not immediately perceive, that many were capable of performing what nobody had happened to perform before. A cooler consideration has succeeded to the enthusiasm which greeted these errors at their outset: they now begin to appear in their true colors. Still they are treated with forbearance, in consideration of the beauties which Mr. Scott has united to them; and the branches of rotten wood escape the axe, because the vine has interwoven herself so luxuriantly among them.

While the public taste was already in this state of revolution, Mr. Scott, never perhaps imagining the possibility of such a change, produced his **Marmion**. Its reception has of course been less flattering than that of the former poem. But the story and the style of **Marmion** argue a defect of judgment, not a falling off of genius: it is in his deliberative, not in his executive powers, that Mr. Scott appears to fail. Yet every reader, when he beholds an imagination so vigorous and so fertile wasted on this injurious style, must feel a degree of indignation mingled with his regret; and while he laments to see the rich treasure sinking to the bottom of the deep, he cannot chuse but blame the careless owner, for having trusted such a cargo to a vessel that was not sea-worthy.

Though the first poem of Mr. Scott did excite unusual attention, and **Marmion** has some admirers, it may be doubted whether another work after the same manner would be read at all. Mr. Scott's fame is chiefly derived from his beautiful, and at the same time faulty, Lusus Musae, *The Lay of the Last Minstrel:* nor has this fame been yet materially diminished. But it is more than probable, that the very peculiarities, which assisted to acquire a reputation for his genius at first, will occasion the loss of that reputation at last. The new, short, royal road, which he has found out, and by which he has ascended to his present eminence, leads to fame; but it does not go on to immortality. The path ceasing, the traveller can pass no further: its soil is too slippery to let him long preserve the same station; and the necessary consequence will be, that he must make up his mind to descend. Every man who admires talent, must wish to see Mr. Scott return immediately and voluntarily to the safe track, for his powers are strong enough to bear him through the journey; but if he will continue to struggle in his original course, he may hereafter seek the beaten way in vain, and fall, like his own wanderer among the rocks of Helvellyn, a melancholy warning for the rashness of future adventurers. (pp. 82-5)

In considering the story of **Marmion**, it is difficult to find any ground for commendation. Since it does not pretend to the regularity of an Epic Poem, it ought at least to have had the interest of a tolerable Romance. Indeed Mr. Scott, by the advertisement prefixed, declares a hope, that his fable will be found captivating as a narrative; but probably, by this time, both he and his readers have felt the fallacy of all such expectation. In the first place, the plot is so confused, as to be almost unintelligible at a single perusal: for the author, in his eager desire of throwing his characters into unexpected situations at last, and exciting surprise in the reader, has reduced himself to more awkward evasions of explanation, than ever were invented by a perplexed schoolboy, endeavouring to conceal unlucky facts from his master. And, at last, the desired object fails: for the obscure hints, and mysterious descriptions, which introduce certain disguised characters, such as Constance and De Wilton, awaken a shrewd suspicion of the very facts which they are intended to veil: and, when they are in fine explained, puzzle the memory without moving the passions. An author, in his ambition of producing dramatic effects, should carefully observe the distinction between mystery and confusion, for an incident does not become interesting by being unintelligible.

What can we say of such an incident as Marmion's battle with De Wilton in the camp circle? There is certainly something exceedingly improbable in the Palmer's utterance of that "vulgar augury," *The death of a dear friend.* In order that we might be impressed with a mysterious idea of the Palmer's dignity, he had been made to preserve an uninterrupted silence for the whole day; and yet, when he did at length speak, he spoke, as he himself afterwards told Clara, "he knew not why!" However, though he did not know what he meant himself, Marmion did; and these idle words, which would have produced rather an extraordinary coincidence in any body's mouth, and which it seems absolutely impossible for that Palmer to have spoken, sent out the gallant Marmion on horseback in the night. And even if Marmion's excursion were credible to the reader, how did De Wilton, unless, indeed, he were endued with a gift of prophecy, contrive to discover Marmion's departure, to prepare himself, and to arrive on the ground in time for this fight? But, at last, what is the issue of the adventure? Why, that one knight is pushed down and gets up again, and the other rides away, content with the pleasure of boasting his victory. It may be said, that "it was necessary to bring Marmion safe into Edinburgh, in order that the abbess might there prove his guilt, by giving the packet to De Wilton, which she would otherwise have had no opportunity of doing." Yes, as the author has now constituted his poem, it was necessary; but why does an author constitute a poem in such a manner as to make it necessary that a principal incident shall be of such a nature as neither to promote nor to retard the catastrophe, nor, indeed, to produce any single assistance to his story, except a long and heavy explanation?—Again, how blameable is the introduction of the vision at Edinburgh! It is true that the Scottish historians mention some illusion of this kind; but a poet should not introduce such a thing in his fable, unless he explain it either as a trick, or as the work of some supernatural agent concerned in the plot of the poem. And even thus it would be of no use here, for, at last, it occasions nothing. Apparently it has been the author's chief aim to keep his readers in suspense, as to the event of his narrative. And certainly few persons are likely, before-hand, to know its event; but while it is true that they cannot know, it is no less true that they have no reason to care.

Yet, even if these incidents had been developed with all possible art, still, perhaps, the story would not have been captivating; for though it is a frequent usage, among dramatists and other poets, to crowd their works with incident, yet mere incident is nothing, unless it produce some interesting situation. Now there are very few situations into which a human being can be thrown, that are strong enough to be interesting in

themselves; and where a situation does interest powerfully, it becomes interesting, in most cases, by the characters of the persons concerned. It is, therefore, the first duty of a poet, to make his readers care about his heroes; and if he does not originally accomplish that important object, he will find a strange damp and flatness even in those situations which might have been rendered the most affecting. . . . [We] feel no sympathy with De Wilton and Clara, who, though they are the hero and heroine, have a thorough insipidity of character; and, as this sympathy is wanting, of course the troubles in which they are engaged do not at all affect our minds. Nay, it seems probable that most readers would not care for any of the agents in this work, so much as for Marmion himself. And him it is impossible to like very earnestly, when one considers his conduct toward Constance and Clara; for, however general may be a dishonourable behaviour to women, there is no sin which will not rather be excused in the hero of a romance—even the sneaking and unknightly trick of the forged letters would sooner be forgiven.

Perhaps, as far as the fable is concerned, the most praiseworthy invention is that of Constance's trial. There is something superior to the ordinary course of story-writing, something really dramatic in this situation of the unhappy girl with her judges and executioners; and it is almost the only portion of the Poem where any thing like a strong situation can be found. But even here, Mr. Scott, in attempting to surprise his readers, produces a very inconsistent series of effects on their minds. (pp. 96-9)

[It] is natural to expect that Constance is some innocent and amiable girl, resigning herself to unmerited, but unavoidable woe. A surprise takes place, to be sure, when she acknowledges herself to have broken her vows, committed forgery, and attempted murder; but the description of her manner is inconsistent with her character, and the surprise is not by any means agreeable. Though there is something pleasant in the surprise that we feel when the accused give glorious proof of innocence, yet, to find the most atrocious vice in a creature for whom we are preparing to interest ourselves, can never gratify the good feelings of our nature. The Sun delights us when he breaks through heavy clouds; but who is pleased to see a murky fog overspread the transparent azure of heaven?

Still, though the plot appears to be defective in these particulars—though the spark of poetry creeps through the greater part of the narrative with a chill and smouldering progress—yet, at the end of its course, it suddenly bursts into flame, and blazes with a splendour that seldom has been equalled. The English forces are opposed to their foes at Flodden; and Mr. Scott, rising with the grandeur of his subject, now sweeps the strings of his harp, in an almost uninterrupted strain of magnificence, even till his minstrelsy approaches its end. (pp. 100-01)

The grandeur of certain subjects is capable of more than one mode of poetical expression; and thus, situations of a nature strictly analogous are described in a most dissimilar manner by Milton and Shakspeare. If Milton describes a battle, he describes it by a general pomp of style, and an occasional introduction of magnificent passages. If Shakspeare has a battle to be described, he does not raise his expressions beyond that ordinary elevation which all serious poetry requires, and he inserts few passages that would be individually striking; but when the reader has perused the whole scene, he feels his mind interested, expanded, enraptured, by the Poet's power, and is delighted more by the easy and sustained beauty and greatness of the whole, than by the dazzling glories of single parts. In the description of Flodden fight, Mr. Scott has modelled himself rather by Shakspeare than by Milton; and he has made a choice admirably adapted both to the purest principles of taste, and to the display of his own peculiar talents. It would be extravagant praise to say that he is the equal of Shakspeare. Shakspeare, indeed, excelled in grand epic description, and so does Mr. Scott; both have shewn the noblest powers of historical painting; yet Shakspeare's poetry governed the breast, not only by a sort of concurrent jurisdiction with the art of historical painting, but by further and higher powers, by those additional and paramount advantages which the poet must be acknowledged to possess above the painter. Still, as far as the genius for this particular order of poetry extends, (and a wide, a glorious extent it surely has,) there will scarcely be any injustice in giving equal admiration, to the Dramatist of Bosworth-field and to the Minstrel of Flodden fight.

After an examination of the plot, it is the natural course to consider the characters as they stand distinguished from each other. This is an enquiry very different from that examination of character which was made with respect to the interest imparted by the agents to the plot, to the incidents, and to the situations: for it is possible that a great number of persons might be described in a poem, none of whom should be pleasing enough to excite that interest which ought to exist for the heroes of romance, and yet all of whom should be forcibly, subtilely, and naturally distinguished from each other in character. In this art of delineating character with accuracy and distinctness, Mr. Scott gives several examples of his ability; but he seems to have taken more pains with the characters of his episodical and inferior people, than with those of his principal agents. (pp. 104-05)

There is one great and glaring fault which pervades the whole of this work: and that fault is, the tiresome minuteness with which every object, however insignificant, is described. There is a certain degree of accuracy which may be very interesting; but it should be an accuracy which relates to an interesting object. When a principal character is introduced, as, for instance here, Lord Marmion, the greatest possible accuracy of description is allowable, and even admirable; but nobody wishes a writer to specify the dresses and appearances of all the heralds and yeomen who may have half a dozen words to say in a long poem. (p. 106)

On the same principles as those which ought to direct the details relating to characters, the details relating to places should also be directed. When, for the first time, a spot is mentioned, which is to become the scene of some great and striking event, as for instance here, the vault in which Constance is immured, accuracy of description increases the interest and reality of effect; but who desires to know whether Tantallon castle had square turrets, stony shields with bloody hearts and mullets, stairs, steps, parapets, platforms, bulwarks, bartisans, bastions, and vantage-coigns? An excellent artist has said, that the slightest circumstance which can assist the expression of a portrait, should be carefully preserved; but the same artist adds, that he who, in a landscape, introduces a figure angling, must not trouble himself to represent the float of cork at the point of the fishing-line. Details in an old work, though they may be tastelessly minute, are sometimes pleasant enough, because they elucidate ancient manners; but it has been well observed, that, in a modern story, they are of no value for the purpose of information, because they can be no longer authentic; and of no chivalrous interest, because they appertain to nothing above common matters, such as eating, drinking, and dressing, which are not at all peculiar to chivalry.

But there are, in *Marmion,* several descriptions, so strictly conducive to the general objects of the poem, and, at the same time, so strikingly beautiful, that Mr. Scott may almost be said to have here shewn still greater descriptive powers than those which he manifested in his last poem. (pp. 107-08)

The lines that recount the tolling of the bell, for the spirits of the victims, are certainly among the most beautiful passages of English poetry. . . . (pp. 108-09)

But perhaps the most sustained and perfect piece of description is the picture of Edinburgh and the Borough-Moor, as they are seen from the heights of Blackford. . . .

The sensations of Clara and De Wilton, at their unexpected interview, are very poetically told, and may serve to shew the powers of the author's imagination.

The same merit is conspicuous in the song that Fitz Eustace sings to Marmion at the inn.

In the course of the Poem occur also several passages of a sweet and tender feeling. Fitz Eustace's melody, for instance, is characterised in some lines, of which the only material fault is the inharmoniousness of the names; but of which the beauties must be too obvious to require a comment. (p. 109)

Mr. Scott must be blamed for his constant attempts at shewing his own thorough acquaintance with the lore of authors generally unknown, and with the topography of the north country. Instances of these errors will be found in the tedious tale of Sir David Lindesay, in the histories of St. Hilda, in the fable of St. Cuthbert's maritime coffin, in the minutes of the coasting voyage sailed by the nuns of St. Whitby, and in numerous other passages gratuitously introduced into the narrative of the poem. The allusions to old legends must be tiresome to every body except romance-readers, and the versified localities of the North must be disagreeable to all but Scotchmen and borderers. The other gentlemen of the North would do well in observing this hint; we have had quite enough of the river Tweed and the Cheviot mountains; and these names are now become as familiar as those of Highgatehill and the Paddington Canal. A romance is not to be estimated like a colonial discovery, by its abundance of wood and water. But it unfortunately happens, that an author often forms too narrow a notion of his readers, and expects that their bosoms will feel a concern for every thing that a casual association has made interesting to his own.

Mr. Scott has not been much more fortunate in the majority of the moral remarks with which his work is interspersed, and which really are sad common-place. (p. 110)

In speaking of Marmion's conscience, Mr. Scott remarks:

> Thus oft it haps, that when within
> They shrink at sense of secret sin,
> A feather daunts the brave;
> A fool's wild speech confounds the wise,
> And proudest princes vail their eyes,
> Before their meanest slave.
>
> (pp. 110-11)

The same sort of flat sentiment is to be found in the reflections on the Palmer's first appearance; in the parallel between lions and men, which is introduced during the relation of Constance's trial; in the invective against the Monk, by whom Constance is betrayed; in the soliloquy of Marmion at the hostel fire; in the apology that follows the description of Marmion's grave;

and in various other passages, where simplicity seems to have been intended.

The foregoing observations apply only to the matter of which this poem is composed; what immediately follows, is directed to the consideration rather of the manner in which the composition has been executed. And here will be seen, in its fullest extent, the radical viciousness of the barbarous style.

The instances of bad English, and bad grammar, are of almost unceasing occurrence, and are frequently occasioned merely by the affectation of the sing-song phraseology. We perpetually find such errors as—

> His sandals were with travel *tore*— . . .

Again:

> These executioners were *chose*— . . .

And there is a constant contortion of the imperfect, in the verbs which terminate in ''*ing*,'' as by the substitution of *sprung* for *sprang*.

The phrase, ''*in place*,'' means *instead;* but Mr. Scott employs it as if it meant *into a place:*

> The summoned Palmer came *in place.*
>
> (p. 111)

There is such an expression in our language, as *Woe is me:* which may perhaps be explained, *woe is to me,* the preposition *to* being understood, and the accusative case remaining; but what is the grammatical construction of

> Woe were *we* each one? . . .

Mr. Scott is in the habit of mixing present and past tenses, without the least remorse; as in this passage:

> 'Would,' *thought* he, as the picture *grows,*
> 'I on its stalk had left the rose!'
>
> (pp. 111-12)

The language is not only full of bad English and bad grammar, but it really is sometimes almost unintelligible. (p. 112)

Precedents may probably be found, and quoted as authorities for many of [Scott's] errors; but it is better to forget such precedents than to produce them.

The lovers of this style seem to have a notion, that words, like coins, are the more valuable, the longer they have ceased to be current: and Mr. Scott, in the true spirit of the sect, overwhelms us with *yode,* and *selle,* and *rede,* and *guerdon,* and *stowre,* and *sheen,* and *bowne,* and others of the same family: not unfrequently relaxing his muse with a whole sentence such as:

> Who enters at such griesly door,
> Shall ne'er, I ween, find exit more. . . .

There are some lines, that seem to have hardly any meaning at all; and these may be considered among the happiest imitations of the antique minstrelsy. Among them:

> The Thistle's knight-companions sate,
> Their banners o'er them *beaming.* . . .

To the same spirit of parody may probably be referred the tedious and insipid successions of bad prose versified, that stupify even if they do not absolutely offend. (p. 114)

The introductions have no relation to the main story. They are mere excrescences, and therefore have no claim to a formal

and detailed criticism; but it would be unjust to deny that they comprise some passages of great merit. (p. 115)

The notes are objectionably voluminous. To occasional poems, indeed, explanations are often requisite, and to these works of a historical cast, a few references may fairly be permitted; but a hundred and thirty-six quarto pages of notes are rather more than the most indulgent reader can allow. Mr. Scott makes a couple of pages, in one place, by an extract from Dryden's *Essay on Satire:* in another place, a page by Perkin Warbeck's story, and by a speech in Ford's dramatic *Chronicle of Perkin Warbeck:* in another place a page about his own grandfather, inviting somebody to dinner: and in another four pages about an old woman, and a silly Northumbrian ballad that she used to repeat. He gives among these notes a ballad of his own too, called **''The Spirit's blasted Tree:''** which is not so good as the generality of his similar ballads. The rest of the notes are almost uniformly heavy and needless in the same degree.

And now, after so long an examination of the powers displayed by Mr. Scott in his **Marmion,** it is time to conclude these remarks. **Marmion,** with all its demerits, declares itself most clearly to have been written by a man of genius: but the genius of Mr. Scott does not appear to be, in strictness of speaking, a genius of the highest class. For his poetry seldom rises above the descriptive: and though, on some occasions, he has been very successful in describing character, yet his descriptions in general are nothing more than paintings of external objects. An author who presents a beautiful picture to the mental vision, is undoubtedly a poet; but an author who does not perform something more, is hardly a poet of the highest order. (pp. 119-20)

Scott at age six.

It has been declared by some persons connected with Mr. Scott, that his next poem will be written on a totally different plan: and his real friends must surely rejoice, if this declaration shall be fulfilled. Let him only lay aside that worst of all affectations, the affectation of simplicity; that worst of all systems, the contempt of system: and there can be little doubt that his genius will procure him an immortal honour. But that fashion of style, which is founded on the caprice of an author, must always flit with the caprice of the public: and he alone who models his poetry upon those great works which have stood firm against the tides of time past, may hope to raise a pile that shall withstand the current of ages to come. (p. 121)

> *Mr. Twiss, in a review of "Marmion," in* The London Review, *Vol. 1, No. 1, February 1, 1809, pp. 82-121.*

SAMUEL TAYLOR COLERIDGE   (letter date 1810)

[*An English poet and critic, Coleridge was central to the English Romantic movement and is considered one of the greatest literary critics in the English language. In the following excerpt from a letter to the poet William Wordsworth, Coleridge focuses on what he sees as the shortcomings of* The Lady of the Lake, *quoting extensively from the work and italicizing words and phrases he finds defective. Coleridge also suggests that Scott may have taken a passage from Wordsworth's poem "Ruth" and inserted it in slightly altered form in* The Lady of the Lake. *For additional commentary by Coleridge, see excerpt dated 1834(?).*]

I am reading Scott's **Lady of the Lake,** having had it on my table week after week till it cried shame to me for not opening it. But truly as far as I can judge from the first 98 pages, my reluctance was not unprophetic. Merciful Apollo!—what an easy pace dost thou jog on with thy unspurred yet unpinioned Pegasus!—The movement of the Poem (which is written with exception of a multitude of Songs in regular 8 syllable Iambics) is between a sleeping Canter and a Marketwoman's trot—but it is endless—I seem never to have made any way—I never remember a narrative poem in which I felt the sense of Progress so languid—. There are (speaking of the first 90 pages) two or three pleasing Images—that of the Swan . . . is the best— the following seems to me to demand something more for it's introduction than a mere description for description's sake supplies—

> With boughs that *quaked** at every breath   *!
> Gray Birch and Aspen wept beneath;
> Aloft, the ash and warrior Oak
> Cast anchor in the rifted Rock—

I wish, there were more faults of this kind—if it be a fault— yet I think, if it had been a beauty, it would not have instantly struck a perplexed feeling in my mind—as it did, & continues to do—a *doubt*—I seem to feel, that I could have used the metaphor; but not in that way, or without other images or feelings in tune with it.—That the **Lady of the Lake** is not without it's peccadillos against the 8th Commandment a la mode of Messieurs Scott & Campbell, this may suffice—

> Some feelings are to mortals *given*
> *With less* of Earth in them than *Heaven.*
>
>   Vide "Ruth." . . .

In short, what I felt in **Marmion,** I feel still more in the **Lady of the Lake**—viz. that a man accustomed to cast words in metre and familiar with descriptive Poets & Tourists, himself a Picturesque Tourist, must be troubled with a mental Strangury, if

he could not lift up his leg six times at six different Corners, and each time p— a canto.—I should imagine that even Scott's warmest admirers must acknowlege & complain of the number of prosaic lines—PROSE IN POLYSYLLABLES, surely the worst of all prose for chivalrous Poetry—not to mention the liberty taken with our Articles, & pron. relatives such as—

> And Malcolm heard his Ellen's Scream
> *As faultered thro' terrific Dream.*
> Then Roderick plunged *in sheath* his sword
> And veiled his wrath *in scornful word*
> 'Rest safe, till morning! Pity, 'twere
> Such cheek should feel the midnight air.
> Then may'st thou to James Stuart tell
> Roderick will keep the Lake & Fell
> Nor lackey, with his free-born Clan,
> The pageant pomp of earthly man!—
> More would he of Clan Alpine know,
> Thou canst our Strength & Passes shew.
> Malise, what ho!'—his henchman came;
> 'Give our safe conduct to the Graeme!'
> Young Malcolm answered, calm and bold,
> [']Fear nothing for thy favourite hold.
> The Spot, an Angel deigned to grace,
> Is blessed, tho' *robbers* HAUNT THE PLACE;
> Thy churlish Courtesy for those
> Reserve, who fear to be thy foes.
> As safe to me the mountain way
> At midnight, as in blaze of Day,
> !!!Tho', with his boldest at his back,
> Even Roderick Dhu *beset the Track*!
> Brave Douglas—lovely Ellen—nay—
> Nought here of parting will I say.
> Earth does not hold a lonesome glen
> So secret, but we meet agen.
> Chieftain! we too shall find an hour.'
> He said, and left the sylvan Bower.—

On my word, I have not *selected* this Stanza—I do not say, that there are not many better, but I do affirm, that there are some worse, and that it is a fair specimen of the general style.— But that you may not rely on my Judgment I will transcribe the next Stanza likewise, the 36th—

> Old Allan followed to the Strand
> (Such was the Douglas's Command)
> And anxious told, how, on the morn,
> The stern Sir Roderick *deep had sworn,*
> The fiery Cross should circle o'er
> Dale, Glen, & Valley, Down, & Moor.
> Much were the Peril to the Graeme
> From those, who to the signal came;
> Far up the Lake 'twere *safest land,*
> Himself would row him to the Strand.
> He gave his Counsel to the wind,
> While Malcom did, unheeding, bind,
> Round Dirk & Pouch and broad-sword roll'd,
> His ample Plaid in tightened *fold,*
> And stripped his Limbs *to such array*
> As best might suit the watery way.

>   37

> Then spoke abrupt: 'Farewell to thee,
> Pattern of old Fidelity!'
> The Minstrel's hand he kindly prest,—
> 'O! could I *point a place* of rest!

My Sovereign holds in ward my land,
My Uncle leads my vassal band;
To tame his foes, his friends to aid,
Poor Malcolm has but heart & blade.[']

Poor Malcolm! a hearty Blade, that I will say for him!—

The Poem commences with the poorest Paraphrase-Parody of [your] ''Hart Leap Well''—.

I will add but one extract more, as an instance of the Poet's ear for lyric harmony—Observe, this a poem of the dark Ages, & admire with me the felicity of aiding the imagination in it's flight into the Ages past, & oblivion of the present by—God save the King! & other savory Descants. (pp. 290-94)

[Boat Song]

Hail to the Chief who in triumph advances,
Honour'd & blest be the evergreen Pine!
Long may the Tree in his banner that glances,
Flourish, the Shelter and grace of our line!
     Heaven send it happy dew,
     Earth lend it sap anew,
Gayly to bourgeon and *broadly to grow,*
     While every highland Glen
     Sends our shouts back agen,
'Roderigh Vich Alpine dhu, ho! ieroe!'

Now, that will tell! that last Gaelic Line is 'a damn'd hard Hit'—as Renyolds [*sic*] said of a passage in *King Lear*—I suppose, there is some untranslatable Beauty in the Gaelic words, which has preserved this one line in each stanza unenglished—even as the old Popish Translators left the Latin Words & Phrases of the Vulgate sticking, like raisins in a pudding, in the English Text.—

In short, my dear William!—it is time to write a Recipe for Poems of this sort—I amused myself a day or two ago on reading a Romance in Mrs Radcliffe's style with making out a scheme, which was to serve for all romances a priori—only varying the proportions—A Baron or Baroness ignorant of their Birth, and in some dependent situation—Castle—on a Rock—a Sepulchre—at some distance from the Rock—Deserted Rooms—Underground Passages—Pictures—A ghost, so believed—or—a written record—blood on it!—A wonderful Cut throat—&c &c &c—Now I say, it is time to make out the component parts of the Scottish Minstrelsy—The first Business must be, a vast string of patronymics, and names of Mountains, Rivers, &c—the most commonplace imagery the Bard gars look almaist as well as new, by the introduction of Benvoirlich, Uam Var,

          on copse-wood gray
That *waved & wept* on *Loch Achray,*
And mingled with the pine trees *blue*
On the bold Cliffs of Benvenue—

How should the Poet e'er give o'er,
With his eye fix'd on Cambus-More—
Need reins be tighten'd in Despair,
When rose Benledi's ridge *in air*
Tho' not one image grace the Heath,
It gain such charm from flooded Teith—
Besides, you need not travel far,
To reach the Lake of Vennachar—
Or *ponder refuge* from your Toil
By far Lochard or Aberfoil!—

Secondly, all the nomenclature of Gothic Architecture, of Heraldry, of Arms, of Hunting, & Falconry—these possess the same power of reviving the caput mortuum & rust of old imagery—besides, they will stand by themselves, Stout Substantives, if only they are strung together, and some attention is paid to the sound of the words—for no one attempts to understand the meaning, which indeed would snap the charm—3—some pathetic moralizing on old times, or any thing else, for the head & tail pieces—with a *Bard* (that is absolutely necessary) and Songs of course—For the rest, whatever suits Mrs Radcliffe, i.e. in the Fable, and the Dramatis Personae, will do for the Poem—with this advantage, that however threadbare in the Romance Shelves of the circulating Library it is to be taken as quite new as soon as told in rhyme—it need not be half as interesting—& the Ghost may be a Ghost, or may be explained—or both may take place in the same poem—Item—the Poet not only may but must mix all dialects *of all ages*—and all styles from Dr Robertson's to the Babes in the wood—

I have read only two Cantos out of six—it is not that it would be any act of self-denial to send you the Poem, neither is it for the pain, which, I own, I should feel, and shrink *at* but not *from,* of asking Southey to permit me to send it—that I do not send you the Poem to day—but because I think, you would not wish me to ask Southey, who perhaps would refuse, and certainly would grant it with reluctance & fear—& because I take for granted, that you will have a copy sent you shortly. . . . (pp. 294-96)

Samuel Taylor Coleridge, in a letter to William Wordsworth in October, 1810, in his Collected Letters of Samuel Taylor Coleridge: 1807-1814, Vol. III, *edited by Earl Leslie Griggs, Oxford at the Clarendon Press, Oxford, 1959, pp. 290-96.*

JANE AUSTEN   (letter date 1814)

[*As one of the supreme stylists of the nineteenth century, Austen secured a lasting place in English literature with such classic novels as* Pride and Prejudice, Emma, *and* Mansfield Park. *In the following excerpt from a letter to her niece, Austen writes playfully about Scott's transformation from poet to novelist with* Waverley.]

Walter Scott has no business to write novels, especially good ones.—It is not fair.—He has Fame and Profit enough as a Poet, and should not be taking the bread out of other people's mouths.—I do not like him, & do not mean to like *Waverley* if I can help it—but fear I must. (p. 404)

Jane Austen, in a letter to Anna Austen on September 28, 1814, in her Jane Austen's Letters to Her Sister Cassandra and Others: 1811-1817, Vol. II, *edited by R. W. Chapman, Oxford at the Clarendon Press, Oxford, 1932, pp. 403-06.*

MARIA EDGEWORTH   (letter date 1814)

[*A popular author in early nineteenth-century England, Edgeworth is remembered today for her role in the development of the English novel of manners. In the following excerpt from a letter addressed to ''The Author of* Waverley,'' *she describes the pleasure her family derived from reading the novel, offering at the same time comments on the work itself. In the final portion of her remarks, Edgeworth expresses her gratitude for Scott's praise of her works in his postscript to* Waverley.]

We have this moment finished **Waverley**. It was read aloud to this large family, and I wish the author could have witnessed the impression it made—the strong hold it seized of the feelings both of young and old—the admiration raised by the beautiful descriptions of nature—by the new and bold delineations of character—the perfect manner in which every character is sustained in every change of situation from first to last, without effort, without the affectation of making the persons speak in character—the ingenuity with which each person introduced in the drama is made useful and necessary to the end—the admirable art with which the story is constructed and with which the author keeps his own secrets till the proper moment when they should be revealed, whilst in the mean time, with the skill of Shakespeare, the mind is prepared by unseen degrees for all the changes of feeling and fortune, so that nothing, however extraordinary, shocks us as improbable; and the interest is kept up to the last moment. We were so possessed with the belief that the whole story and every character in it was real, that we could not endure the occasional addresses from the author to the reader. They are like Fielding; but for that reason we cannot bear them, we cannot bear that an author of such high powers, of such original genius, should for a moment stoop to imitation. This is the only thing we dislike, these are the only passages we wish omitted in the whole work; and let the unqualified manner in which I say this, and the very vehemence of my expression of this disapprobation, be a sure pledge to the author of the sincerity of all the admiration I feel for his genius.

I have not yet said half we felt in reading the work. The characters are not only finely drawn as separate figures, but they are grouped with great skill, and contrasted so artfully, and yet so naturally, as to produce the happiest dramatic effect, and at the same time to relieve the feelings and attention in the most agreeable manner. The novelty of the Highland world which is discovered to our view excites curiosity and interest powerfully; but though it is all new to us it does not embarrass or perplex, or strain the attention. We never are harassed by doubts of the probability of any of these modes of life; though we did not know them, we are quite certain they did exist exactly as they are represented. We are sensible that there is a peculiar merit in the work which is in a measure lost upon us, the *dialects* of the Highlanders and the Lowlanders, etc. But there is another and a higher merit with which we are as much struck and as much delighted as any true born Scotchman could be; the various gradations of Scotch feudal character, from the high-born chieftain and the military baron, to the noble-minded lieutenant Evan Dhu, the robber Bean Lean, and the savage Callum Beg. The *Pre*—the Chevalier is beautifully drawn—

A prince: aye, every inch a prince!

His polished manners, his exquisite address, politeness and generosity, interest the reader irresistibly, and he pleases the more from the contrast between him and those who surround him. I think he is my favorite character; the Baron Bradwardine is my father's. He thinks it required more genius to invent, and more ability uniformly to sustain this character than any one of the masterly characters with which the book abounds. There is indeed uncommon art in the manner in which his dignity is preserved by his courage and magnanimity, in spite of all his pedantry and his *ridicules*, and his bear and bootjack, and all the raillery of MacIvor. MacIvor's unexpected "bear and bootjack" made us laugh heartily.

But to return to the dear good baron; though I acknowledge that I am not as good a judge as my father and brothers are of

his recondite learning and his law Latin, yet I feel the humor, and was touched to the quick by the strokes of generosity, gentleness, and pathos in this old man, who is, by the bye, all in good time worked up into a very dignified father-in-law for the hero. His exclamation of "Oh! my son! my son!" and the yielding of the fictitious character of the baron to the natural feelings of the father is beautiful. (Evan Dhu's fear that his father-in-law should die quietly in his bed, made us laugh almost as much as the bear and bootjack.)

Jinker, in the battle, pleading the cause of the mare he had sold to Balmawhapple, and which had thrown him for want of the proper bit, is truly comic; my father says that this and some other passages respecting horsemanship could not have been written by any one who was not master both of the great and little horse.

I tell you without order the great and little strokes of humor and pathos just as I recollect, or am reminded of them at this moment by my companions. The fact is that we have had the volumes only during the time we could read them, and as fast as we could read, lent to us as a great favor by one who was happy enough to have secured a copy before the first and second editions were sold in Dublin. When we applied, not a copy could be had; we expect one in the course of next week, but we resolved to write to the author without waiting for a second perusal. Judging by our own feeling as authors, we guess that he would rather know our genuine first thoughts, than wait for cool second thoughts, or have a regular eulogium or criticism put in the most lucid manner, and given in the finest sentences that ever were rounded.

Is it possible that I have got thus far without having named Flora or Vich Ian Vohr—the *last Vich Ian Vohr!* Yet our minds were full of them the moment before I began this letter; and could you have seen the tears forced from us by their fate, you would have been satisfied that the pathos went to our hearts. Ian Vohr from the first moment he appears, till the last, is an admirably drawn and finely sustained character—new, perfectly new to the English reader—often entertaining—always heroic—sometimes sublime. The gray spirit, the Bodach Glas, thrills *us* with horror. *Us!* What effect must it have upon those under the influence of the superstitions of the Highlands? This circumstance is admirably introduced; this superstition is a weakness quite consistent with the strength of the character, perfectly natural after the disappointment of all his hopes, in the dejection of his mind, and the exhaustion of his bodily strength.

Flora we could wish was never called *Miss MacIvor,* because in this country there are tribes of vulgar Miss *Macs,* and this association is unfavorable to the sublime and beautiful of *your* Flora—she is a true heroine. Her first appearance seized upon the mind and enchanted us so completely, that we were certain she was to be your heroine, and the wife of your hero—but with what inimitable art you gradually convince the reader that she was not, as she said of herself, *capable of making Waverley happy;* leaving her in full possession of our admiration, you first make us pity, then love, and at last give our undivided affection to Rose Bradwardine—sweet Scotch Rose! The last scene between Flora and Waverley is highly pathetic—my brother wishes that *bridal garment* were *shroud;* because when the heart is touched we seldom use metaphor, or quaint alliteration; bride-favor, bridal garment.

There is one thing more we could wish changed or omitted in Flora's character. I have not the volume, and therefore cannot refer to the page; but I recollect in the first visit to Flora, when she is to sing certain verses, there is a walk, in which the description of the place is beautiful, but *too long,* and we did not like the preparation for *a scene*—the appearance of Flora and her harp was too like a common heroine, she should be far above all stage effect or novelist's trick.

These are, without reserve, the only faults we found or *can* find in this work of genius. We should scarcely have thought them worth mentioning, except to give you proof positive that we are not flatterers. Believe me, I have not, nor can I convey to you the full idea of the pleasure, the delight we have had in reading *Waverley,* nor of the feeling of sorrow with which we came to the end of the history of persons whose real presence had so filled our minds—we felt that we must return to the *flat realities* of life, that our stimulus was gone, and we were little disposed to read the "Postscript, which should have been a Preface."

"Well, let us hear it," said my father, and Mrs. Edgeworth read on.

Oh! my dear sir, how much pleasure would my father, my mother, my whole family, as well as myself have lost, if we had not read to the last page! And the pleasure came upon us so unexpectedly—we had been so completely absorbed that every thought of ourselves, of our own authorship, was far, far away.

Thank you for the honor you have done us, and for the pleasure you have given us, great in proportion to the opinion we had formed of the work we had just perused—and believe me, every opinion I have in this letter expressed was formed before any individual in the family had peeped to the end of the book, or knew how much we owed you. (pp. 239-44)

> *Maria Edgeworth, in a letter to Sir Walter Scott on October 23, 1814, in her* The Life and Letters of Maria Edgeworth, Vol. I, *edited by Augustus J. C. Hare, Houghton, Mifflin and Company, 1895, pp. 239-44.*

WILLIAM WORDSWORTH   (letter date 1815)

[*An English poet and critic, Wordsworth was central to English Romanticism. Wordsworth's literary criticism reflects his belief that neither the language nor the content of poetry should be stylized or elaborate and that the value of a poet was to feel and express the relation between man and nature. In the following excerpt from a letter to R. P. Gillies, Wordsworth comments on Scott's characterization and use of picturesque effects in* Guy Mannering *and* Waverley. *For additional commentary on Scott by Wordsworth, see excerpt dated 1844.*]

You mentioned *Guy Mannering* in your last [letter]. I have read it. I cannot say that I was disappointed, for there is very considerable talent displayed in the performance, and much of that sort of knowledge with which the author's mind is so richly stored. But the adventures I think not well chosen, or invented, and they are still worse put together; and the characters, with the exception of Meg Merrilies, excite little interest. In the management of this lady the author has shown very considerable ability, but with that want of taste which is universal among modern novels of the Radcliffe school; which, as far as they are concerned, this is. I allude to the laborious manner in which everything is placed before your eyes for the production of picturesque effect. The reader, in good narration, feels that pictures rise up before his sight, and pass away from it unostentatiously, succeeding each other. But when they are

fixed upon an easel for the express purpose of being admired, the judicious are apt to take offence, and even to turn sulky at the exhibitor's officiousness. But these novels are likely to be much overrated on their first appearance, and will afterwards be as much undervalued. *Waverley* heightened my opinion of Scott's talents very considerably, and if *Mannering* has not added much, it has not taken much away. Infinitely the best part of *Waverley* is the pictures of Highland manners at Mac Ivor's castle, and the delineation of his character, which are done with great spirit. The Scotch baron, and all the circumstances in which he is exhibited, are too peculiar and *outré.* Such caricatures require a higher condiment of humour to give them a relish than the author of *Waverley* possesses. (pp. 666-67)

> *William Wordsworth, in a letter to R. P. Gillies on April 25, 1815, in* The Letters of William and Dorothy Wordsworth, The Middle Years: August 1811-1820, Vol. II, *Oxford at the Clarendon Press, Oxford, 1937, pp. 666-67.*

[SIR WALTER SCOTT]   (essay date 1817)

[*The following excerpt is drawn from an anonymous review that Scott wrote of his own* Tales of My Landlord, *first series. This review, considered to be among Scott's most revealing statements about his own work, contains a defense of* Old Mortality, *which had drawn protests from many Scots who felt that the novelist had overemphasized the absurd behavior and fanaticism of the nationalist Covenanters. Scott also briefly discusses* The Black Dwarf. *For additional commentary by Scott on his writings, see excerpts dated 1822 and 1826.*]

These *Tales* belong obviously to a class of novels which we have already had occasion repeatedly to notice, and which have attracted the attention of the public in no common degree,— we mean *Waverley, Guy Mannering,* and the *Antiquary,* and we have little hesitation to pronounce them either entirely, or in a great measure, the work of the same author. Why he should industriously endeavour to elude observation by taking leave of us in one character, and then suddenly popping out upon us in another, we cannot pretend to guess without knowing more of his personal reasons for preserving so strict an incognito than has hitherto reached us. We can, however, conceive many reasons for a writer observing this sort of mystery; not to mention that it has certainly had its effect in keeping up the interest which his works have excited. (p. 430)

[The volumes before us] are entitled *Tales of my Landlord:* why so entitled, excepting to introduce a quotation from Don Quixote, it is difficult to conceive: for Tales of my Landlord they are *not,* nor is it indeed easy to say whose tales they ought to be called. There is a proem, as it is termed, supposed to be written by Jedediah Cleishbotham, the schoolmaster and parish clerk of the village of Gandercleugh, in which we are given to understand that these Tales were compiled by his deceased usher, Mr. Peter Pattieson, from the narratives or conversations of such travellers as frequented the Wallace Inn, in that village. Of this proem we shall only say that it is written in the quaint style of that prefixed by Gay to his Pastorals, being, as Johnson terms it, 'such imitation as he could obtain of obsolete language, and by consequence in a style that was never written nor spoken in any age or place.'

The first of the Tales thus ushered in is entitled the *Black Dwarf.* It contains some striking scenes, but it is . . . deficient in the requisites of a luminous and interesting narrative. . . . (pp. 441-42)

The domestic scene [at Hobbie Elliot's house] is painted with the knowledge of the language and manners of that class of society, which give interest to the picture of Dandie Dinmont and his family, in **Guy Mannering.** But we do not think it equal to the more simple sketch contained in the earlier novel. This must frequently be the case, when an author, in repeated efforts, brings before us characters of the same *genus*. He is, as it were, compelled to dwell upon the specific differences and distinctions instead of the general characteristics, or, in other words, rather to shew wherein Hobbie Elliot differs from Dandie Dinmont than to describe the former as he really was. (p. 443)

[The characters are] not numerous, yet the tale is far from corresponding in simplicity. On the contrary, it abounds with plots, elopements, ravishments, and rescues, and all the violent events which are so common in romance, and of such rare occurrence in real life. (p. 444)

[The] narrative is unusually artificial. Neither hero nor heroine excites interest of any sort, being just that sort of *pattern* people whom nobody cares a farthing about. The explanation of the dwarf's real circumstances and character, too long delayed from an obvious wish to protract the mystery, is at length huddled up so hastily that, for our parts, we cannot say we are able to comprehend more of the motives of this principal personage than that he was a mad man, and acted like one—an easy and summary mode of settling all difficulties. As for the hurry and military bustle of the conclusion, it is only worthy of the farce of the Miller and his Men, or any other modern melo-drama, ending with a front crouded with soldiers and scene-shifters, and a back scene in a state of conflagration. . . . (p. 445)

[We] will take our oaths that the narrative is the worst part of the **Black Dwarf,** and that if the reader can tolerate it . . . , he will find the work itself contains passages both of natural pathos and fantastic terror, not unworthy of the author of the scene of Stanie's burial, in the **Antiquary,** or the wild tone assumed in the character of Meg Merrilies.

The story which occupies the next three volumes [**Old Mortality**] is of much deeper interest, both as a tale and from its connexion with historical facts and personages. (pp. 445-46)

The author . . . has acted in strict conformity with historical truth (whether with propriety we shall hereafter inquire) in representing the convenanters or rather the ultra-covenanters, for those who gained the skirmish fell chiefly under this description, as a fierce and sanguinary set of men, whose zeal and impatience under persecution had destroyed the moral feeling and principle which ought to attend and qualify all acts of retaliation. The large body of Presbyterians, both clergy and people, were far from joining in these extravagances, and when they took up arms to unite themselves to the insurgents, were received with great jealousy and suspicion by the high-flyers of whom we have spoken. The clergy who had been contented to exercise their ministry by the favour of the government, under what was called the Indulgence, were stigmatized by their opponents as Erastians and will-worshippers, while they, with more appearance of reason, recriminated upon their adversaries that they meant, under pretence of establishing the liberty and independence of the kirk, altogether to disown allegiance to the government. The author of **Old Mortality** has drawn a lively sketch of their distracted councils and growing divisions, and has introduced several characters of their clergy, on each of whom religious enthusiasm is represented as pro-

ducing an effect in proportion to its quality, and the capacity upon which it is wrought. It is sincere but formal in the indulged Presbyterian clergyman Poundtext, who is honest, well-meaning, and faithful, but somewhat timorous and attached to his own ease and comfort. The zeal of Kettledrummle is more boisterous, and he is bold, clamorous, and intractable. In a youth called Mac Briar, of a more elevated and warm imagination, enthusiasm is wild, exalted, eloquent, and impressive; and in Habbakuk Mucklewrath it soars into absolute madness. (pp. 460-61)

One great source of the universal admiration which this family of Novels has attracted, is their peculiar plan, and the distinguished excellence with which it has been executed. The objections that have frequently been stated against what are called Historical Romances, have been suggested, we think, rather from observing the universal failure of that species of composition, than from any inherent and constitutional defect in the species of composition itself. If the manners of different ages are injudiciously blended together,—if unpowdered crops and slim and fairy shapes are commingled in the dance with volumed wigs and far-extending hoops,—if in the portraiture of real character the truth of history be violated, the eyes of the spectator are necessarily averted from a picture which excites in every well regulated and intelligent mind the hatred of incredulity. We have neither time nor inclination to enforce our remark by giving illustrations of it. But if those unpardonable sins against good taste can be avoided, and the features of an age gone by can be recalled in a spirit of delineation at once faithful and striking, the very opposite is the legitimate conclusion: the composition itself is in every point of view dignified and improved; and the author, leaving the light and frivolous associates with whom a careless observer would be disposed to ally him, takes his seat on the bench of the historians of his time and country. In this proud assembly, and in no mean place of it, we are disposed to rank the author of these works; for we again express our conviction—and we desire to be understood to use the term as distinguished from *knowledge*—that they are all the offspring of the same parent. At once a master of the great events and minuter incidents of history, and of the manners of the times he celebrates, as distinguished from those which now prevail,—the intimate thus of the living and of the dead, his judgment enables him to separate those traits which are characteristic from those that are generic; and his imagination, not less accurate and discriminating than vigorous and vivid, presents to the mind of the reader the manners of the times, and introduces to his familiar acquaintance the individuals of his drama as they thought and spoke and acted. We are not quite sure that any thing is to be found in the manner and character of the **Black Dwarf** which would enable us, without the aid of the author's information, and the facts he relates, to give it to the beginning of the last century; . . . his free-booting robber lives, perhaps, too late in time. But his delineation is perfect. With palpable and inexcusable defects in the *denouement,* there are scenes of deep and overwhelming interest; and every one, we think, must be delighted with the portrait of the Grandmother of Hobbie Elliot, a representation soothing and consoling in itself, and heightened in its effect by the contrast produced from the lighter manners of the younger members of the family, and the honest but somewhat blunt and boisterous bearing of the shepherd himself.

[**Old Mortality**] however . . . is more adapted to the talents of the author, and his success has been proportionably triumphant. We have trespassed too unmercifully on the time of our gentle readers to indulge our inclination in endeavouring to form an estimate of that melancholy but, nevertheless, most attractive period in our history, when by the united efforts of a corrupt and unprincipled government, of extravagant fanaticism, want of education, perversion of religion, and the influence of ill-instructed teachers, whose hearts and understandings were estranged and debased by the illapses of the wildest enthusiasm, the liberty of the people was all but extinguished, and the bonds of society nearly dissolved. Revolting as all this is to the Patriot, it affords fertile materials to the Poet. As to the *beauty* of the delineation presented to the reader in this tale, there is, we believe, but one opinion: and we are persuaded that the more carefully and dispassionately it is contemplated, the more perfect will it appear in the still more valuable qualities of fidelity and truth. . . . The opinions and language of the *honest party* are detailed with the accuracy of a witness; and he who could open to our view the state of the Scottish peasantry, perishing in the field or on the scaffold, and driven to utter and just desperation, in attempting to defend their first and most sacred rights; who could place before our eyes the leaders of these enormities, from the notorious Duke of Lauderdale downwards to the fellow mind that executed his behest, precisely as they lived and looked,—such a chronicler cannot justly be charged with attempting to extenuate or throw into the shade the corruptions of a government that soon afterwards fell a victim to its own follies and crimes.

Independently of the delineation of the manners and characters of the times to which the story refers, it is impossible to avoid noticing, as a separate excellence, the faithful representation of general nature. Looking not merely to the litter of novels that peep out for a single day from the mud where they were spawned, but to many of more ambitious pretensions—it is quite evident that in framing them, the authors have first addressed themselves to the involutions and development of the story, as the principal object of their attention; and that in entangling and unravelling the plot, in combining the incidents which compose it, and even in depicting the characters, they sought for assistance chiefly in the writings of their predecessors. Baldness, and uniformity, and inanity are the inevitable results of this slovenly and unintellectual proceeding. The volume which this author has studied is the great book of Nature. He has gone abroad into the world in quest of what the world will certainly and abundantly supply, but what a man of great discrimination alone will find, and a man of the very highest genius will alone depict after he has discovered it. The characters of Shakspeare are not more exclusively human, not more perfectly men and women as they live and move, than those of this mysterious author. It is from this circumstance that . . . many of his personages are supposed to be sketched from real life. He must have mixed much and variously in the society of his native country; his studies must have familiarized him to systems of manners now forgotten; and thus the persons of his drama, though in truth the creatures of his own imagination, convey the impression of individuals who we are persuaded must exist, or are evoked from their graves in all their original freshness, entire in their lineaments, and perfect in all the minute peculiarities of dress and demeanour. [*Old Mortality*] . . . is accordingly equally remarkable for the truth and the endless variety of its characters. The stately and pompous dignity of Lady Margaret Bellenden, absorbed in the consciousness of her rank;—the bustling importance and unaffected kindliness of Mrs. Alison Wilson, varying in their form, but preserving their substance, with her variations of fortune;—the true Caledonian prudence of Neil Blane;—we cannot stay to examine, nor point out with what exquisite skill their char-

acteristic features are brought to the reader's eye, not by description or enumeration, but by compelling him, as in real life, to observe their effect when forced into contact with the peculiarities of others. The more prominent personages it would be superfluous to notice. We must be pardoned, however, for offering one slight tribute of respect to the interesting old woman by whom Morton is directed to Burley's last retreat: she is portrayed as a patient, kind, gentle, and generous being, even in the lowest state of oppression, poverty and blindness; her religious enthusiasm, unlike that of her sect, is impressed with the pure stamp of the Gospel, combining meekness with piety, and love to her neighbour with obedience and love of the Deity. And the author's knowledge of human nature is well illustrated in the last glimpse he gives us of our early acquaintance, Jenny Dennison. When Morton returns from the continent, the giddy *fille de chambre* of Tillietudlem has become the wife of Cuddie Headrigg, and the mother of a large family. Every one must have observed that coquetry, whether in high or low life, is always founded on intense selfishness, which, as age advances, gradually displays itself in its true colours, and vanity gives way to avarice; and with perfect truth of representation, the lively, thoughtless girl has settled into a prudent housewife, whose whole cares are centered in herself, and in her husband and children, because they are *her* husband and children. Nor in this rapid and imperfect sketch can we altogether pass over the peculiar excellence of the *dialogue*. We do not allude merely to its dramatic merit, nor to the lively and easy tone of natural conversation by which it is uniformly distinguished: we would notice the singular skill and felicity with which, in conveying the genuine sentiments of the Scottish peasant in the genuine language of his native land, the author has avoided that appearance of grossness and vulgarity by which the success of every similar attempt has hitherto been defeated. The full value of this praise we, on this part of the island, cannot, perhaps, be expected to feel, though we are not wholly insensible to it. The Scottish peasant speaks the language of his native country, his *national* language, not the *patois* of an individual district; and in listening to it we not only do not experience even the slightest feeling of disgust or aversion, but our bosoms are responsive to every sentiment of sublimity, or awe, or terror which the author may be disposed to excite. Of the truth of all this, Meg Merrilies is a sufficiently decisive instance. The terrible graces of this mysterious personage, an outcast and profligate of the lowest class, are complete in their effect, though conveyed by the *medium* of language that has hitherto been connected with associations that must have altogether neutralized them. We could, with much satisfaction to ourselves, and much we fear to the annoyance of our patient readers, dilate on this part of the subject, and illustrate our views by quotations from some of the scenes that peculiarly struck ourselves; but we have trespassed much on their indulgence, and there is one not unimportant view we have still to open to them. This chiefly relates to the historical portraits with which the author has presented us. (pp. 466-70)

Most of the group are drawn in harsh colours, and yet the truth of the resemblances, when illustrated by historical documents, will scarcely be disputed, except by those staunch partizans whose religious or political creed is the sole gauge for estimating the good or bad qualities of the characters of past ages. (p. 470)

Admitting . . . that these portraits are sketched with spirit and effect, two questions arise of much more importance than any thing affecting the merits of the novels—namely, whether it is safe or prudent to imitate, in a fictitious narrative, and often with a view to a ludicrous effect, the scriptural style of the zealots of the seventeenth century; and secondly, whether the recusant presbyterians, collectively considered, do not carry too reverential and sacred a character to be treated by an unknown author with such insolent familiarity.

On the first subject, we frankly own we have great hesitation. It is scarcely possible to ascribe scriptural expressions to hypocritical or extravagant characters without some risk of mischief, because it will be apt to create an habitual association between the expression and the ludicrous manner in which it is used, unfavourable to the reverence due to the sacred text. And it is no defence to state that this is an error inherent in the plan of the novel. Bourdaloue, a great authority, extends this restriction still farther, and denounces all attempts to unmask hypocrisy by raillery, because in doing so the satirist is necessarily compelled to expose to ridicule the religious vizard of which he has divested him. Yet even against such authority it may be stated, that ridicule is the friend both of religion and virtue, when directed against those who assume their garb, whether from hypocrisy or fanaticism. (p. 474)

Still, however, we must allow that there is great delicacy and hesitation to be used in employing the weapon of ridicule on any point connected with religion. Some passages occur in the work before us for which the writer's sole apology must be the uncontroulable disposition to indulge the peculiarity of his vein of humour—a temptation which even the saturnine John Knox was unable to resist either in narrating the martyrdom of his friend Wisheart or the assassination of his enemy Beatson, and in the impossibility of resisting which his learned and accurate biographer [Dr. Macrie] has rested his apology for this mixture of jest and earnest.

> 'There are writers,' he says, (rebutting the charge of Hume against Knox,) 'who can treat the most sacred subjects with a levity bordering on profanity. Must we at once pronounce them profane, and is nothing to be set down to the score of natural temper inclining them to wit and humour? The pleasantry which Knox has mingled with his narrative of his (Cardinal Beatson's) death and burial is unseasonable and unbecoming. But it is to be imputed not to any pleasure which he took in describing a bloody scene, but to the strong propensity which he had to indulge his vein of humour. Those who have read his history with attention must have perceived that he is not able to check this even on very serious occasions.'
>
> (p. 475)

Indeed Dr. Macrie himself has given us a striking instance of the indulgence which the Presbyterian clergy, even of the strictest persuasion, permit to the *vis comica*. After describing a polemical work as 'ingeniously constructed and occasionally enlivened with strokes of humour,' he transfers, to embellish his own pages, (for we can discover no purpose of edification which the tale serves,) a ludicrous parody made by an ignorant parish-priest on certain words of a Psalm, too sacred to be here quoted. Our own innocent pleasantry cannot, in this instance, be quite reconciled with that of the learned biographer of John Knox, but we can easily conceive that his authority may be regarded in Scotland as decisive of the extent to which a humourist may venture in exercising his wit upon scriptural expressions without incurring censure even from her most rigid divines.

It may however be a very different point how far the author is entitled to be acquitted upon the second point of indictment. To use too much freedom with things sacred is a course much more easily glossed over than that of exposing to ridicule the persons of any particular sect. . . . [We believe] the best service we can do our author in the present case is to [state] . . . that the odious part of his satire applies only to that fierce and unreasonable set of extra-presbyterians, whose zeal, equally absurd and cruel, afforded pretexts for the severities inflicted on non-conformists without exception, and gave the greatest scandal and offence to the wise, sober, enlightened, and truly pious among the Presbyterians. (pp. 475-76)

[We] have no delight to dwell either upon the atrocities or absurdities of a people whose ignorance and fanaticism were rendered frantic by persecution. It is enough for our present purpose to observe that the present Church of Scotland, which comprizes so much sound doctrine and learning, and has produced so many distinguished characters, is the legitimate representative of the indulged clergy of the days of Charles II. settled however upon a comprehensive basis. That after the revolution, it should have succeeded episcopacy as the national religion, was natural and regular, because it possessed all the sense, learning, and moderation fit for such a change, and because among its followers were to be found the only men of property and influence who acknowledged presbytery. But the Cameronians continued long as a separate sect, though their preachers were bigoted and ignorant, and their hearers were gleaned out of the lower ranks of the peasantry. Their principle, so far as it was intelligible, asserted that paramount species of presbyterian church-government which was established in the year 1648, and they continued to regard the established church as erastian and time-serving, because they prudently remained silent upon certain abstract and delicate topics, where there might be some collision between the absolute liberty asserted by the church and the civil government of the state. The Cameronians, on the contrary, disowned all kings and government whatsoever, which should not take the Solemn League and Covenant; and long retained hopes of re-establishing that great national engagement, a bait which was held out to them by all those who wished to disturb the government during the reign of William and Anne, as is evident from the Memoirs of Ker of Kersland, and the Negotiations of Colonel Hooke with the jacobites and disaffected of the year.

A party so wild in their principles, so vague and inconsistent in their views, could not subsist long under a free and unlimited toleration. They continued to hold their preachings on the hills, but they lost much of their zeal when they were no longer liable to be disturbed by dragoons, sheriffs, and lieutenants of Militia.—The old fable of the Traveller's Cloak was in time verified, and the fierce sanguinary zealots of the days of Claverhouse sunk into such quiet and peaceable enthusiasts as Howie of Lochgoin, or Old Mortality himself. It is, therefore, upon a race of sectaries who have long ceased to exist, that Mr. Jedediah Cleishbotham has charged all that is odious, and almost all that is ridiculous, in his fictitious narrative; and we can no more suppose any moderate presbyterian involved in the satire, than we should imagine that the character of Hampden stood committed by a little raillery on the person of Ludovic Claxton, the Muggletonian. If, however, there remain any of those sectaries who, confining the beams of the Gospel to the Goshen of their own obscure synagogue, and with James Mitchell, the intended assassin, giving their sweeping testimony against prelacy and popery, The Whole Duty of Man and bordles, promiscuous dancing and the Common Prayer-

Scott, at about twelve years of age.

book, and all the other enormities and backslidings of the time, may perhaps be offended at this idle tale, we are afraid they will receive their answer in the tone of the revellers to Malvolio, who, it will be remembered, was something a kind of Puritan: 'Doest thou think because thou art virtuous, there shall be no more cakes and ale?—Aye, by Saint Anne, and ginger will be hot in the mouth too.' (pp. 479-80)

> [Sir Walter Scott], in a review of "Tales of My Land-lord," in The Quarterly Review, Vol. XVI, No. XXXII, January, 1817, pp. 430-80.

[SIR WALTER SCOTT]   (essay date 1822)

[The following excerpt from Scott's "Introductory Epistle" to The Fortunes of Nigel is cast in the form of a conversation between Scott (Author of Waverley) and Captain Clutterbuck, a fictitious person created by Scott and supposedly connected with the publication of The Monastery. In this imaginary dialog, Scott discusses the popularity of his writings and responds to critics' charges of carelessness, commercialism, and lack of proper concern for his literary reputation. These comments were first published in 1822. For additional commentary by the author on his own works, see excerpts dated 1817 and 1826.]

Author of **Waverley**. I was willing to see you, Captain Clutterbuck, being the person of my family whom I have most regard for, since the death of Jedediah Cleishbotham; and I am afraid I may have done you some wrong in assigning to you *The Monastery* as a portion of my effects. I have some thoughts of making it up to you, by naming you godfather to [my next novel]. . . . But first, touching *The Monastery*—how says the world? You are abroad and can learn.

Captain Clutterbuck. Hem! hem! The inquiry is delicate. I have not heard any complaints from the publishers.

Author. That is the principal matter; but yet an indifferent work is sometimes towed on by those which have left harbour before it, with the breeze in their poop. What say the critics?

Captain. There is a general—feeling—that the White Lady is no favourite.

Author. I think she is a failure myself; but rather in execution than conception. Could I have evoked an *esprit follet,* at the same time fantastic and interesting, capricious and kind; a sort of wildfire of the elements, bound by no fixed laws or motives of action, faithful and fond, yet teasing and uncertain—

Captain. If you will pardon the interruption, sir, I think you are describing a pretty woman.

Author. On my word, I believe I am. I must invest my elementary spirits with a little human flesh and blood: they are too fine-drawn for the present taste of the public.

Captain. They object, too, that the object of your nixie ought to have been more uniformly noble. Her ducking the priest was no Naiad-like amusement.

Author. Ah! they ought to allow for the capriccios of what is, after all, but a better sort of goblin. The bath into which Ariel, the most delicate creation of Shakspeare's imagination, seduces our jolly friend Trinculo, was not of amber or rose-water. But no one shall find me rowing against the stream. I care not who knows it, I write for general amusement; and, though I never will aim at popularity by what I think unworthy means, I will not, on the other hand, be pertinacious in the defence of my own errors against the voice of the public.

Captain. You abandon, then, in the [novel you are presently working on] . . . , the mystic, and the magical, and the whole system of signs, wonders, and omens? There are no dreams, or presages, or obscure allusions to future events?

Author. Not a Cock Lane scratch, my son—not one bounce on the drum of Tedworth—not so much as the poor tick of a solitary death-watch in the wainscot. All is clear and above board: a Scots metaphysician might believe every word of it.

Captain. And the story is, I hope, natural and probable; commencing strikingly, proceeding naturally, ending happily, like the course of a famed river, which gushes from the mouth of some obscure and romantic grotto; then gliding on, never pausing, never precipitating its course, visiting, as it were, by natural instinct, whatever worthy subjects of interest are presented by the country through which it passes; widening and deepening in interest as it flows on; and at length arriving at the final catastrophe as at some mighty haven, where ships of all kinds strike sail and yard?

Author. Hey! hey! what the deuce is all this? Why, 'tis Ercles's vein, and it would require some one much more like Hercules than I to produce a story which should gush, and glide, and never pause, and visit, and widen, and deepen, and all the rest on't. I should be chin-deep in the grave, man, before I had done with my task; and, in the meanwhile, all the quirks and quiddities which I might have devised for my reader's amusement would lie rotting in my gizzard, like Sancho's suppressed witticisms, when he was under his master's displeasure. There never was a novel written on this plan while the world stood.

Captain. Pardon me—*Tom Jones.*

Author. True, and perhaps *Amelia* also. Fielding had high notions of the dignity of an art which he may be considered as having founded. He challenges a comparison between the novel and the epic. Smollett, Le Sage, and others, emancipating themselves from the strictness of the rules he has laid down, have written rather a history of the miscellaneous adventures which befall an individual in the course of life than the plot of a regular and connected epopœia, where every step brings us a point nearer to the final catastrophe. These great masters have been satisfied if they amused the reader upon the road; though the conclusion only arrived because the tale must have an end, just as the traveller alights at the inn because it is evening.

Captain. A very commodious mode of travelling, for the author at least. In short, sir, you are of opinion with Bayes—'What the devil does the plot signify, except to bring in fine things?'

Author. Grant that I were so, and that I should write with sense and spirit a few scenes unlaboured and loosely put together, but which had sufficient interest in them to amuse in one corner the pain of body; in another, to relieve anxiety of mind; in a third place, to unwrinkle a brow bent with the furrows of daily toil; in another, to fill the place of bad thoughts, or to suggest better; in yet another, to induce an idler to study the history of his country; in all, save where the perusal interrupted the discharge of serious duties, to furnish harmless amusement—might not the author of such a work, however inartificially executed, plead for his errors and negligences the excuse of the slave, who, about to be punished for having spread the false report of a victory, saved himself by exclaiming—'Am I to blame, O Athenians, who have given you one happy day?'

Captain. Will your goodness permit me to mention an anecdote of my excellent grandmother?

Author. I see little she can have to do with the subject, Captain Clutterbuck.

Captain. It may come into our dialogue on Bayes's plan. The sagacious old lady—rest her soul!—was a good friend to the church, and could never hear a minister maligned by evil tongues without taking his part warmly. There was one fixed point, however, at which she always abandoned the cause of her reverend *protégé:* it was so soon as she learned he had preached a regular sermon against slanderers and backbiters.

Author. And what is that to the purpose?

Captain. Only that I have heard engineers say that one may betray the weak point to the enemy by too much ostentation of fortifying it.

Author. And, once more I pray, what is that to the purpose?

Captain. Nay, then, without farther metaphor, I am afraid this new production, in which your generosity seems willing to give me some concern, will stand much in need of apology, since you think proper to begin your defence before the case is on trial. The story is hastily huddled up; I will venture a pint of claret.

Author. A pint of port, I suppose you mean?

Captain. I say of claret—good claret of the monastery. Ah, sir, would you but take the advice of your friends, and try to deserve at least one-half of the public favour you have met with, we might all drink Tokay!

Author. I care not what I drink, so the liquor be wholesome.

Captain. Care for your reputation, then—for your fame.

Author. My fame! I will answer you as a very ingenious, able, and experienced friend, being counsel for the notorious Jem MacCoul, replied to the opposite side of the bar, when they laid weight on his client's refusing to answer certain questions, which they said any man who had a regard for his reputation would not hesitate to reply to. 'My client,' said he—by the way, Jem was standing behind him at the time, and a rich scene it was—'is so unfortunate as to have no regard for his reputation; and I should deal very uncandidly with the court should I say he had any that was worth his attention.' I am, though from very different reasons, in Jem's happy state of indifference. Let fame follow those who have a substantial shape. A shadow—and an [anonymous] author is nothing better—can cast no shade. (pp. xxviii-xxxi)

Captain. But allowing, my dear sir, that you care not for your personal reputation, or for that of any literary person upon whose shoulders your faults may be visited, allow me to say that common gratitude to the public, which has received you so kindly, and to the critics who have treated you so leniently, ought to induce you to bestow more pains on your story.

Author. I do entreat you, my son, as Dr. Johnson would have said, 'free your mind from cant.' For the critics, they have their business, and I mine; as the nursery proverb goes—

The children in Holland take pleasure in making
What the children in England take pleasure in breaking.

I am their humble jackal, too busy in providing food for them to have time for considering whether they swallow or reject it. To the public I stand pretty nearly in the relation of the postman who leaves a packet at the door of an individual. If it contains pleasing intelligence—a billet from a mistress, a letter from an absent son, a remittance from a correspondent supposed to be bankrupt—the letter is acceptably welcome, and read and re-read, folded up, filed, and safely deposited in the bureau. If the contents are disagreeable, if it comes from a dun or from a bore, the correspondent is cursed, the letter is thrown into the fire, and the expense of postage is heartily regretted; while all the time the bearer of the despatches is, in either case, as little thought on as the snow of last Christmas. The utmost extent of kindness between the author and the public which can really exist is, that the world are disposed to be somewhat indulgent to the succeeding works of an original favourite, were it but on account of the habit which the public mind has acquired; while the author very naturally thinks well of *their* taste who have so liberally applauded *his* productions. But I deny there is any call for gratitude, properly so called, either on one side or the other.

Captain. Respect to yourself, then, ought to teach caution.

Author. Ay, if caution could augment the chance of my success. But, to confess to you the truth, the works and passages in which I have succeeded have uniformly been written with the greatest rapidity; and when I have seen some of these placed in opposition with others, and commended as more highly finished, I could appeal to pen and standish that the parts in which I have come feebly off were by much the more laboured. Besides, I doubt the beneficial effect of too much delay, both on account of the author and the public. A man should strike while the iron is hot, and hoist sail while the wind is fair. If a successful author keep not the stage, another instantly takes his ground. If a writer lie by for ten years ere he produces a second work, he is superseded by others; or, if the age is so poor of genius that this does not happen, his own reputation becomes his greatest obstacle. The public will expect the new work to be ten times better than its predecessor; the author will expect it should be ten times more popular, and 'tis a hundred to ten that both are disappointed.

Captain. This may justify a certain degree of rapidity in publication, but not that which is proverbially said to be no speed. You should take time at least to arrange your story.

Author. That is a sore point with me, my son. Believe me, I have not been fool enough to neglect ordinary precautions. I have repeatedly laid down my future work to scale, divided it into volumes and chapters, and endeavoured to construct a story which I meant should evolve itself gradually and strikingly, maintain suspense, and stimulate curiosity; and which, finally, should terminate in a striking catastrophe. But I think there is a demon who seats himself on the feather of my pen when I begin to write, and leads it astray from the purpose. Characters expand under my hand; incidents are multiplied; the story lingers, while the materials increase; my regular mansion turns out a Gothic anomaly, and the work is closed long before I have attained the point I proposed.

Captain. Resolution and determined forbearance might remedy that evil.

Author. Alas! my dear sir, you do not know the force of paternal affection. When I light on such a character as Bailie Jarvie, or Dalgetty, my imagination brightens, and my conception becomes clearer at every step which I take in his company, although it leads me many a weary mile away from the regular road, and forces me to leap hedge and ditch to get back into the route again. If I resist the temptation, as you advise me, my thoughts become prosy, flat, and dull; I write painfully to myself, and under a consciousness of flagging which makes me flag still more; the sunshine with which fancy had invested the incidents departs from them, and leaves everything dull and gloomy. I am no more the same author I was in my better mood than the dog in a wheel, condemned to go round and round for hours, is like the same dog merrily chasing his own tail, and gambolling in all the frolic of unrestrained freedom. In short, sir, on such occasions I think I am bewitched. (pp. xxxii-xxxiv)

Captain. You are determined to proceed then in your own system? Are you aware that an unworthy motive may be assigned for this rapid succession of publication? You will be supposed to work merely for the lucre of gain.

Author. Supposing that I did permit the great advantages which must be derived from success in literature to join with other motives in inducing me to come more frequently before the public, that emolument is the voluntary tax which the public pays for a certain species of literary amusement; it is extorted from no one, and paid, I presume, by those only who can afford it, and who receive gratification in proportion to the expense. If the capital sum which these volumes have put into circulation be a very large one, has it contributed to my indulgences only? or can I not say to hundreds, from honest Duncan the paper-manufacturer to the most snivelling of the printer's devils, 'Didst thou not share? Hadst thou not fifteen pence?' I profess I think our Modern Athens much obliged to me for having established such an extensive manufacture; and when universal suffrage comes in fashion, I intend to stand for a seat in the House on the interest of all the unwashed artificers connected with literature.

Captain. This would be called the language of a calico-manufacturer.

Author. Cant again, my dear son: there is lime in this sack, too; nothing but sophistication in this world! I do say it, in spite of Adam Smith and his followers, that a successful author is a productive labourer, and that his works constitute as effectual a part of the public wealth as that which is created by any other manufacture. If a new commodity, having an actually intrinsic and commercial value, be the result of the operation, why are the author's bales of books to be esteemed a less profitable part of the public stock than the goods of any other manufacturer? I speak with reference to the diffusion of the wealth arising to the public, and the degree of industry which even such a trifling work as the present must stimulate and reward, before the volumes leave the publisher's shop. Without me it could not exist, and to this extent I am a benefactor to the country. As for my own emolument, it is won by my toil, and I account myself answerable to Heaven only for the mode in which I expend it. The candid may hope it is not all dedicated to selfish purposes; and, without much pretensions to merit in him who disburses it, a part may 'wander, heaven-directed, to the poor.'

Captain. Yet it is generally held base to write from the mere motives of gain.

Author. It would be base to do so exclusively, or even to make it a principal motive for literary exertion. Nay, I will venture to say that no work of imagination, proceeding from the mere consideration of a certain sum of copy-money, ever did, or ever will, succeed. So the lawyer who pleads, the soldier who fights, the physician who prescribes, the clergyman—if such there be—who preaches, without any zeal for his profession, or without any sense of its dignity, and merely on account of the fee, pay, or stipend, degrade themselves to the rank of sordid mechanics. Accordingly, in the case of two of the learned faculties at least, their services are considered as unappreciable, and are acknowledged, not by any exact estimate of the services rendered, but by a *honorarium*, or voluntary acknowledgment. But let a client or patient make the experiment of omitting this little ceremony of the *honorarium*, which is *censé* to be a thing entirely out of consideration between them, and mark how the learned gentleman will look upon his case. Cant set apart, it is the same thing with literary emolument. No man of sense, in any rank of life, is, or ought to be, above accepting a just recompense for his time, and a reasonable share of the capital which owes its very existence to his exertions. When Czar Peter wrought in the trenches, he took the pay of a common soldier; and nobles, statesmen, and divines, the most distinguished of their time, have not scorned to square accounts with their bookseller.

Captain. (Sings.)

> O if it were a mean thing,
>   The gentles would not use it;
> And if it were ungodly,
>   The clergy would refuse it.

Author. You say well. But no man of honour, genius, or spirit would make the mere love of gain the chief, far less the only, purpose of his labours. For myself, I am not displeased to find the game a winning one; yet while I pleased the public, I should probably continue it merely for the pleasure of playing; for I have felt as strongly as most folks that love of composition which is perhaps the strongest of all instincts, driving the author to the pen, the painter to the pallet, often without either the chance of fame or the prospect of reward. Perhaps I have said too much of this. I might, perhaps, with as much truth as most people, exculpate myself from the charge of being either of a greedy or mercenary disposition; but I am not, therefore, hypocrite enough to disclaim the ordinary motives, on account of which the whole world around me is toiling unremittingly, to the sacrifice of ease, comfort, health, and life. I do not affect the disinterestedness of that ingenious association of gentlemen mentioned by Goldsmith, who sold their magazine for sixpence a-piece, merely for their own amusement.

Captain. I have but one thing more to hint. The world say you will run yourself out.

Author. The world say true; and what then? When they dance no longer, I will no longer pipe; and I shall not want flappers enough to remind me of the apoplexy.

Captain. And what will become of [your poor family of characters]? . . . We shall fall into contempt and oblivion.

Author. Like many a poor fellow, already overwhelmed with the number of his family, I cannot help going on to increase it. ''Tis my vocation, Hal.' Such of you as deserve oblivion—perhaps the whole of you—may be consigned to it. At any rate, you have been read in your day, which is more than can be said of some of your contemporaries of less fortune and more merit. They cannot say but that you *had* the crown. It is always something to have engaged the public attention for seven years. Had I only written *Waverley,* I should have long since been, according to the established phrase, 'the ingenious author of a novel much admired at the time.' I believe, on my soul, that the reputation of *Waverley* is sustained very much by the praises of those who may be inclined to prefer that tale to its successors.

Captain. You are willing, then, to barter future reputation for present popularity?

Author. Meliora spero. Horace himself expected not to survive in all his works; I may hope to live in some of mine. *Non omnis moriar.* It is some consolation to reflect that the best authors in all countries have been the most voluminous; and it has often happened that those who have been best received in their own time have also continued to be acceptable to posterity. I do not think so ill of the present generation as to suppose that its present favour necessarily infers future condemnation.

Captain. Were all to act on such principles, the public would be inundated.

Author. Once more, my dear son, beware of cant. You speak as if the public were obliged to read books merely because they are printed; your friends the booksellers would thank you to make the proposition good. The most serious grievance attending such inundations as you talk of is that they make rags dear. The multiplicity of publications does the present age no harm, and may greatly advantage that which is to succeed us.

Captain. I do not see how that is to happen.

Author. The complaints in the time of Elizabeth and James of the alarming fertility of the press were as loud as they are at present; yet look at the shore over which the inundation of that age flowed, and it resembles now the Rich Strand of the *Faëry Queene*—

> Bestrew'd all with rich array,
> Of pearl and precious stones of great assay;
> And all the gravel mix'd with golden ore.

Believe me, that even in the most neglected works of the present age the next may discover treasures.

Captain. Some books will defy all alchemy.

Author. They will be but few in number; since, as for writers who are possessed of no merit at all, unless indeed they publish their works at their own expense, like Sir Richard Blackmore, their power of annoying the public will be soon limited by the difficulty of finding undertaking booksellers.

Captain. You are incorrigible. Are there no bounds to your audacity?

Author. There are the sacred and eternal boundaries of honour and virtue. My course is like the enchanted chamber of Britomart—

> Where as she look'd about, she did behold
> How over that same door was likewise writ,
> *Be Bold—Be Bold,* and everywhere *Be Bold.*
> Whereat she mused, and could not construe it;
> At last she spied at that room's upper end
> Another iron door, on which was writ—
> BE NOT TOO BOLD.

(pp. xxxvii-xli)

[*Sir Walter Scott*], *''Introductory Epistle,''* in his The Fortunes of Nigel, *edited by Frederick M. Link, University of Nebraska Press, 1965, pp. xxv-xli.*

[WILLIAM HAZLITT]   (essay date 1824)

[*One of the most important commentators of the Romantic age, Hazlitt was an English critic and journalist. He is best known for his descriptive criticism in which he stressed that no motives beyond judgment and analysis are necessary on the part of the critic. In the following excerpt, Hazlitt explores the popular appeal and salient characteristics of Scott's poetry and novels.*]

Sir Walter Scott is undoubtedly the most popular writer of the age—the ''lord of the ascendant'' for the time being. He is just half what the human intellect is capable of being: if you take the universe, and divide it into two parts, he knows all that it *has been;* all that it *is to be* is nothing to him. His is a mind ''reflecting ages past''—he scorns ''the present ignorant time.'' He is ''laudator temporis acti''—a ''prophesier of things past.'' The old world is to him a crowded map; the new one a dull, hateful blank. He dotes on all well-authenticated superstitions; he shudders at the shadow of innovation. His retentiveness of memory, his accumulated weight of prejudice or romantic association, have overlaid his other faculties. The cells of his memory are vast, various, full even to bursting with life and motion; his speculative understanding is rather flaccid, and little exercised in projects for the amelioration of his species. His mind receives and treasures up every thing brought to it by tradition or custom—it does not *project* itself beyond this into the world unknown, but mechanically shrinks back as from the edge of a prejudice. The land of abstract reason is to his apprehension like *Van Diemen's Land,* barren, miserable, distant, a place of exile, the dreary abode of savages, convicts, and adventurers. Sir Walter would make a bad hand of a description of the *millennium,* unless he could lay the scene in Scotland five hundred years ago, and then he would want facts and worm-eaten parchments to support his style. Our historical novelist firmly thinks that nothing *is* but what *has been;* that the moral world stands still, as the material one was supposed to do of old; and that we can never get beyond the point where we are without utter destruction, though every thing changes, and will change, from what it was three hundred years ago to what it is now—from what it is now to all that the bigoted admirer of the "good old times" most dreads and hates.

It is long since we read, and long since we thought of our author's poetry. It would probably have gone out of date with the immediate novelty, even if he himself had not made the world forget it. It is not to be denied that it had great merit, both of an obvious and intrinsic kind. It abounded in vivid descriptions, in spirited action, in smooth and flowing versification. But it wanted *character*. It was poetry "of no mark or likelihood." It slid out of the mind, as soon as read, like a river; and would have been forgotten, but that the public curiosity was fed with ever-new supplies from the same teeming, liquid source. It is not every man that can write six quarto volumes in verse, that shall be read with avidity, even by fastidious judges. But what a difference between *their* popularity and that of the Scotch Novels! It is true, the public read and admired the *Lay of the Last Minstrel, Marmion,* and so on; and each individual was contented to read and admire because the public did: but with regard to the prose-works of the same (supposed) author, it is quite *another-guess* sort of thing. Here every one stands forward to applaud on his own ground, would be thought to go before the public opinion, is eager to extol his favourite characters louder, to understand them better than every body else, and has his own scale of comparative excellence for each work, supported by nothing but his own enthusiastic and fearless convictions. It must be amusing to the *Author of Waverley* to hear his readers and admirers (and are not these the same thing?) quarrelling which of his novels is the best, opposing character to character, quoting passage against passage, striving to surpass each other in the extravagance of their encomiums, and yet unable to settle the precedence, or to do the author's writings justice—so various, so equal, so transcendant are their merits! His volumes of poetry were received as fashionable and well-dressed acquaintances: we are ready to tear the others in pieces as old friends. There was something meretricious in Sir Walter's ballad-rhymes; and like those who keep opera *figurantes,* we were willing to have our admiration shared, and our taste confirmed by the town: but the Novels are like the mistresses of our hearts, bone of our bone and flesh of our flesh, and we are jealous that any one should be as much delighted, or as thoroughly acquainted with their beauties as ourselves. For which of his poetical heroines would the reader break a lance so soon as for Jeanie Deans? What "Lady of the Lake" can compare with the beautiful Rebecca? We believe the late Mr. John Scott went to his death-bed (though a painful and premature one) with some degree of satisfaction, inasmuch as he had penned the most elaborate panegyric on the Scotch Novels that had as yet appeared! The Epics are not poems, so much as metrical romances. There is a glittering veil of verse thrown over the features of nature and of old romance. The deep incisions into character are "skinned and filmed over"—the details are lost or shaped into flimsy and insipid decorum; and the truth of feeling and of circumstance is translated into a tinkling sound, a tinsel *commonplace*. It must be owned, there is a power in true poetry that lifts the mind from the ground of reality to a higher sphere, that penetrates the inert, scattered, incoherent materials presented to it, and by a force and inspiration of its own melts and moulds them into sublimity and beauty. But Sir Walter (we contend, under correction) has not this creative impulse, this plastic power, this capacity of reacting on his materials. He is a learned, a literal, a *matter-of-fact* expounder of truth or fable: he does not soar above and look down upon his subject,

imparting his own lofty views and feelings to his descriptions of nature—he relies upon it, is raised by it, is one with it, or he is nothing. A poet is essentially a *maker;* that is, he must atone for what he loses in individuality and local resemblance by the energies and resources of his own mind. The writer of whom we speak is deficient in these last. He has either not the faculty, or not the will, to impregnate his subject by an effort of pure invention. The execution also is much upon a par with the most ordinary effusions of the press. It is light, agreeable, effeminate, diffuse. Sir Walter's Muse is a *modern-antique*. The smooth, glossy texture of his verse contrasts happily with the quaint, uncouth, rugged materials of which it is composed; and takes away any appearance of heaviness or harshness from the body of local traditions and obsolete costume. We see grim knights and iron armour; but then they are woven in silk with a careless, delicate hand, and have the softness of flowers. The poet's figures might be compared to old tapestries copied on the finest velvet: they are not like Raphael's *Cartoons,* but they are very like Mr. Westall's drawings, which accompany, and are intended to illustrate them. . . . As to the rest, and compared with the true and great poets—what is he to Spenser, over whose immortal, ever-amiable verse Beauty hovers and trembles, and who has shed the purple light of Fancy, from his ambrosial wings, over all nature? What is there of the might of Milton, whose head is canopied in the blue serene, and who takes us to sit with him there? Sir Walter has no voluntary power of combination: all his associations (as we said before) are those of habit or of tradition. He is a merely narrative and descriptive poet, garrulous of the old time. The definition of his poetry is a pleasing superficiality.

Not so of his "NOVELS AND ROMANCES." There we turn over a new leaf—another and the same—the same in matter, but in form, in power how different! The Author of *Waverley* has got rid of the tagging of rhymes, the eking out of syllables, the supplying of epithets, the colours of style, the grouping of his characters, and the regular march of events, and comes to the point at once, and strikes at the heart of his subject, without dismay and without disguise. His poetry was a lady's waiting-maid, dressed out in cast-off finery: his prose is a beautiful, rustic nymph, that, like Dorothea in *Don Quixote* when she is surprised with dishevelled tresses bathing her naked feet in the brook, looks round her abashed at the admiration her charms have excited. The grand secret of the author's success in these latter productions is that he has completely got rid of the trammels of authorship; and torn off at one rent (as Lord Peter got rid of so many yards of lace in the "Tale of a Tub") all the ornaments of fine writing and worn-out sentimentality. All is fresh, as from the hand of nature: by going a century or two back and laying the scene in a remote and uncultivated district, all becomes new and startling in the present advanced period. Highland manners, characters, scenery, superstitions, northern dialect and costume, the wars, the religion, and politics of the sixteenth and seventeenth centuries, give a charming and wholesome relief to the fastidious refinement and "over-laboured lassitude" of modern readers, like the effect of plunging a nervous valetudinarian into a cold-bath. (pp. 297-300)

Sir Walter has found out (oh, rare discovery!) that facts are better than fiction; that there is no romance like the romance of real life; and that, if we can but arrive at what men feel, do, and say in striking and singular situations, the result will be "more lively, audible, and full of vent" than the fine-spun cobwebs of the brain. With reverence be it spoken, he is like the man who having to imitate the squeaking of a pig upon the stage, brought the animal under his cloak with him. Our author

A page from the autograph manuscript of Waverley.

has conjured up the actual people he has to deal with, or as much as he could get of them, in "their habits as they lived." He has ransacked old chronicles, and poured the contents upon his page; he has squeezed out musty records; he has consulted wayfaring pilgrims, bedrid sibyls; he has invoked the spirits of the air; he has conversed with the living and the dead, and let them tell their story their own way; and by borrowing of others, has enriched his own genius with everlasting variety, truth, and freedom. He has taken his materials from the original authentic sources, in large concrete masses, and not tampered with or too much frittered them away. He is only the amanuensis of truth and history. It is impossible to say how fine his writings in consequence are, unless we could describe how fine nature is. All that portion of the history of his country that he has touched upon (wide as the scope is—the manners, the personages, the events, the scenery) lives over again in his volumes. Nothing is wanting—the illusion is complete. There is a hurtling in the air, a trampling of feet upon the ground, as these perfect representations of human character or fanciful belief come thronging back upon our imaginations. (pp. 300-01)

What a host of associations! What a thing is human life! What a power is that of genius! What a world of thought and feeling rescued (almost) from oblivion! How many hours of *wholesome* heartfelt amusement has our author given to the gay and thoughtless! How many sad hearts has he soothed in pain and solitude! It is no wonder that the public repay with lengthened applause and gratitude the pleasure they receive. He writes as fast as they can read, and he does not write himself down. He is always in the public eye, and they do not tire of him. His worst is better than any other person's best. His *backgrounds*

(and his latter works are little else but backgrounds capitally made out) are more attractive than the principal figures and most complicated actions of other writers. His works, taken together, are almost like a new edition of human nature. This is indeed to be an author!

The political bearing of the Scotch Novels has been a considerable recommendation to them. They are a relief to the mind, rarified as it has been with modern philosophy, and heated with ultra-radicalism. At a time also when we bade fair to revive the principles of the Stuarts, it was interesting to bring us acquainted with their persons and misfortunes. The candour of Sir Walter's historic pen levels our bristling prejudices on this score, and sees fair play between Roundheads and Cavaliers, between Protestant and Papist. He is a writer reconciling all the diversities of human nature to the reader. He does not enter into the distinctions of hostile sects or parties, but treats of the strength or the infirmity of the human mind, of the virtues or vices of the human breast, as they are to be found blended in the whole race of mankind. Nothing can shew more handsomely, or be more gallantly executed. There was a talk at one time that our author was about to take Guy Faux for the subject of one of his novels, in order to put a more liberal and humane construction on the Gunpowder Plot, than our "no Popery" prejudices have hitherto permitted. Sir Walter is a professed *clarifier* of the age from the vulgar and still lurking old-English antipathy to Popery and slavery. Through some odd process of *servile* logic, it should seem that in reviving the claims of the Stuarts by the courtesy of romance, the House of Brunswick are more firmly established in point of fact, and the Bourbons, doubtless, become legitimate! In any other point of view, we cannot possibly conceive how Sir Walter imagines "he has done something to restore the declining spirit of loyalty" by these novels. His loyalty is founded on *would-be* treason: he props the actual throne by the shadow of rebellion. Does he really think of making us enamoured of the "good old times" by the faithful and harrowing portraits he has drawn of them? Would he carry us back to the early stages of barbarism, of clanship, of the feudal system, as "a consummation devoutly to be wished?" Is he infatuated enough, or does he so doat and drivel over his own slothful and self-willed prejudices as to believe that he will make a single convert to the beauty of Legitimacy, that is, of lawless power and savage bigotry, when he himself is obliged to apologise for the horrors he describes, and even render his descriptions credible to the modern reader by referring to the authentic history of these delectable times? He is indeed so besotted as to the moral of his own story, that he has even the blindness to go out of his way to have a fling at *flints* and *dungs* (the contemptible ingredients, as he would have us believe, of a modern rabble) at the very time when he is describing a mob of the twelfth century—a mob (one should think) after the writer's own heart, without one particle of modern philosophy or revolutionary politics in their composition, who were to a man, to a hair, just what priests and kings and nobles *let* them be, and who were collected to witness (a spectacle proper to the times) the burning of the lovely Rebecca at a stake for a sorceress, because she was a Jewess, beautiful and innocent, and the consequent victim of insane bigotry and unbridled profligacy. And it is at this moment, when the heart is kindled and bursting with indignation at the revolting abuses of self-constituted power, that Sir Walter *stops the press* to have a sneer at the people, and to put a spoke, as he thinks, in the wheel of upstart innovation! This is what he "calls backing his friends"—it is thus he administers charms and philtres to our love of Legitimacy, makes us conceive a horror of all reform, civil, political, or religious, and would fain put down the "Spirit of the Age." The author of **Waverley** might just as well get up and make a speech at a dinner at Edinburgh, abusing Mr. MacAdam for his improvements in the roads on the reasoning that they were nearly *impassable* in many places "sixty years since;" or object to Mr. Peel's "Police Bill," by insisting that Hounslow-Heath was formerly a scene of greater interest and terror to highwaymen and travellers, and cut a greater figure in the Newgate Calendar, than it does at present. Oh! Wickliff, Luther, Hampden, Sidney, Somers, mistaken Whigs, and thoughtless Reformers in religion and politics; and all ye, whether poets or philosophers, heroes or sages, inventors of arts or sciences, patriots, benefactors of the human race, enlighteners and civilizers of the world, who have, so far, reduced opinion to reason and power to law, who are the cause that we no longer burn witches and heretics at slow fires, that the thumbscrews are no longer applied by ghastly, smiling judges, to extort confession of imputed crimes from sufferers for conscience sake, that men are no longer strung up like acorns on trees without judge or jury, or hunted like wild beasts through thickets and glens, who have abated the cruelty of priests, the pride of nobles, the divinity of kings in former times, to whom we owe it that we no longer wear round our necks the collar of Gurth the swineherd and of Wamba the Jester, that the castles of great lords are no longer the dens of banditti from whence they issue with fire and sword to lay waste the land, that we no longer expire in loathsome dungeons without knowing the cause, or have our right hands struck off for raising them in self-defence against wanton insult, that we can sleep without fear of being burnt in our beds, or travel without making our wills, that no Amy Robsarts are thrown down trap-doors by Richard-Varneys with impunity, that no Red-reiver of Westburn Flat sets fire to peaceful cottages, that no Claverhouse signs cold-blooded deathwarrants in sport, that we have no Tristan the Hermit or Petit-Andrè crawling near us like spiders, and making our flesh creep and our hearts sink within us at every moment of our lives; ye who have produced this change in the face of nature and society, return to earth once more and beg pardon of Sir Walter and his patrons, who sigh at not being able to undo all that you have done! Leaving this question, there are two other remarks which we wished to make on the Novels. The one was to express our admiration at the good-nature of the mottoes, in which the author has taken occasion to remember and quote almost every living author, whether illustrious or obscure, but himself—an indirect argument in favour of the general opinion as to the source from which they spring;—and the other was to hint our astonishment at the innumerable and incessant instances of bad and slovenly English in them; more, we believe, than in any other works now printed. We should think the writer could not possibly read the Manuscript after he has once written it, or overlook the press. (pp. 302-04)

> [William Hazlitt], "Sir Walter Scott," in The New
> Monthly Magazine, n.s. Vol. X, No. XL, April, 1824,
> pp. 297-304.

SIR WALTER SCOTT   (journal date 1826)

[In the following excerpt from his journal, Scott records his thoughts on the numerous imitations that the success of his novels had inspired, commenting on the works of his rivals and on his own methods and limitations. For additional commentary by Scott on his works, see excerpts dated 1817 and 1822.]

[October 17, 1826]

Read over [Harrison Ainsworth's] *Sir John Chiverton* and [Horace Smith's] *Brambletye House,* novels in what I may surely claim as the stile

> Which I was born to introduce
> Refined it first and showd it's use.

They are both clever books, one in imitation of the days of chivalry, the other by [Horace] Smith one of the authors of the *Rejected Addresses,* dated in the time of the civil wars and introducing historical characters. I read both with great interest. . . . (p. 213)

I am something like Captain Bobadil who traind up a hundred gentlemen to fight very nearly if not altogether as well as myself. And so far I am convinced of this that I believe were I to publish **Canongate Chronicles** without my name (*nomme de guerre* I mean) the event would be a corollary to the fable of the peasant who made the real pig squeak against the imitator while the sapient audience hissd the poor grunter as if inferior to the biped in his own language. The peasant could indeed confute the longeared multitude by shewing piggy, but were I to fail as a knight with a white and maiden shield and then vindicate my claim to attention by putting 'by the Author of **Waverley** in the title my good friend *Publicum* would defend itself by stating I had tilted so ill that my course had not the least resemblance to my former doings when indisputably I bore away the garland. Therefore I am as firmly and resolutely determined that I will tilt under my own cognizance. The hazard indeed remains of being beaten. But there is a prejudice (not an undue one neither) in favour of the original patentee and Joe Manton's name has borne out many a sorry gun-barrell—More of this tomorrow. . . . (pp. 213-14)

. . . . .

[October 18, 1826]

I take up again my remarks on imitations. I am sure I mean the gentlemen no wrong by calling them so and heartily wish they had followd a better model, but it serves to show me *veluti in speculo* my own errors or if you will those of the *Stile.* One advantage I think I still have over all of them. They may do their fooling with better grace but I like Sir Andrew Aguecheek do it more natural. They have to read old books and consult antiquarian collections to get their information—I write because I have long since read such works and possess thanks to a strong memory the information which they have to seek for. This leads to a dragging in historical details by head and shoulders, so that the interest of the main piece is lost in minute descriptions of events which do not affect its progress. Perhaps I have sin'd in this way myself—indeed I am but too conscious of having considerd the plot only as what Bayes calls the means of bringing in fine things so that in respect to the descriptions it resembled the string of the Showman's box which he pulls to show in succession Kings, Queens, the battle of Waterloo, Bonaparte at Saint Helena, Newmarket races and White-headed Bob floord by Jemmy from Town. All this I may have done, but I have repented of it, and in my better efforts while I conducted my story through the agency of historical personages and by connecting it with historical incidents I have endeavourd to weave them pretty closely together and in future I will study this more—Must not let the background eclipse the principal figures—the frame overpower the picture.

Another thing in my favour is that my contemporaries steal too openly. Mr. Smith has inserted in *Brambletye House* whole pages from De Foe's *Fire and Plague of London.* . . .

When I *convey* an incident or so I am [at] as much pains to avoid detection as if the offence could be indicted in literal fact at the Old Bailey.

But leaving this—hard pressd as I am by these imitators who must put the thing out of fashion at last I consider like a fox at his last shifts whether there be a way to dodge them—some new device to throw them off and have a mile or two of free ground while I have legs and wind left to use it. There is one way to give novelty—To depend for success on the interest of a well contrived story. But woe's me, that requires thought, consideration—the writing out a regular plan or plot—above all the adhering to [it]—which I never can do for the ideas rise as I write and bear such a disproportioned extent to that which each originally occupied at the first concoction, that cocksnowns! I shall never be able to take the trouble. And yet to make the world stare—and gain a new march ahead of them all !!! Well something we still will do. (pp. 214-15)

> *Sir Walter Scott, in journal entries of October 17 and 18, 1826, in* The Journal of Sir Walter Scott, *edited by W. E. K. Anderson, Oxford at the Clarendon Press, Oxford, 1972, pp. 213-14, 214-17.*

JOHANN WOLFGANG VON GOETHE [CONVERSATIONS WITH JOHANN PETER ECKERMANN] (conversation date 1828)

[*Goethe was a German writer who is considered one of the greatest figures in world literature. A genius of the highest order, he distinguished himself as a botanist, physicist, biologist, artist, musician, and philosopher. Excelling in numerous genres, Goethe was a shaping force in the major literary movements of late eighteenth- and early nineteenth-century Europe. In the following excerpt from Johann Peter Eckermann's recollections of his conversations with Goethe, they discuss the former's reading of* The Fair Maid of Perth. *Eckermann's account of Goethe's admiration for Scott is considered somewhat exaggerated.*]

[October 3, 1828]

"Walter Scott's *Fair Maid of Perth* is excellent, is it not?" [said Goethe]. "There is finish! there is a hand! What a firm foundation for the whole, and in particulars not a touch which does not lead to the catastrophe! Then, what details of dialogue and description, both of which are excellent.

"His scenes and situations are like pictures by Teniers; in the arrangement they show the summit of art, the individual figures have a speaking truth, and the execution is extended with artistical love to the minutest details, so that not a stroke is lost. How far have you read?"

"I have come," said I, "to the passage where Henry Smith carries the pretty minstrel girl home through the streets, and round about lanes; and where, to his great vexation, Proudfoot and Dwining met him."

"Ah," said Goethe, "that is excellent; that the obstinate, honest blacksmith should be brought at last to take with him not only the suspicious maiden, but even the little dog, is one of the finest things to be found in any novel. It shows a knowledge of human nature, to which the deepest mysteries are revealed."

"It was also," said I, "an admirable notion to make the heroine's father a glover, who, by his trade in skins, must have been long in communication with the Highlanders."

"Yes," said Goethe, "that is a touch of the highest order. From this circumstance spring the relations and situations most favorable for the whole book, and these by this means also obtain a real basis, so that they have an air of the most convincing truth. You find everywhere in Walter Scott a remarkable security and thoroughness in his delineation, which proceeds from his comprehensive knowledge of the real world, obtained by lifelong studies and observations, and a daily discussion of the most important relations. Then come his great talent and his comprehensive nature. You remember the English critic, who compares the poets to the voices of male singers, of which some can command only a few fine tones, while others have the whole compass, from the highest to the lowest, completely in their power. Walter Scott is one of this last sort. In the *Fair Maid of Perth* you will not find a single weak passage to make you feel as if his knowledge and talent were insufficient. He is equal to his subject in every direction in which it takes him; the king, the royal brother, the prince, the head of the clergy, the nobles, the magistracy, the citizens and mechanics, the Highlanders, are all drawn with the same sure hand, and hit off with equal truth." (pp. 267-68)

· · · · ·

[October 9, 1828]

"How do you get on with your *Fair Maid of Perth?*" [said Goethe]. "How far have you read? Tell me all about it."

"I read slowly," said I. "However, I am now as far as the scene where Proudfoot, when in Henry Smith's armor he imitates his walk and whistle, is slain, and on the following morning is found in the streets of Perth by the citizens, who, taking him for Smith, raise a great alarm through the city."

"Ay," said Goethe, "that scene is remarkable; it is one of the best."

"I have been particularly struck," said I, "with Walter Scott's great talent for disentangling confused situations, so that the whole separates itself into masses and quiet pictures, which leave on our minds an impression as if, like omniscient beings, we had looked down and seen events which were occurring at the same time in various places."

"Generally," said Goethe, "he shows great understanding of art; for which reason we, and those like us, who always particularly look to see how things are done, find a double interest and the greatest profit in his works.

"I will not anticipate, but you will find in the third volume an admirable contrivance. You have already seen how the prince in council makes the wise proposal to let the rebel Highlanders destroy one another in combat, and how Palm Sunday is appointed for the day when the hostile clans are to come down to Perth, and to fight for life or death, thirty against thirty. you will see with admiration how Scott manages to make one man fail on one side on the decisive day, and with what art he contrives to bring his hero Smith from a distance into the vacant place among the combatants. This is admirably done; and you will be delighted when you come to it.

"But, when you have finished the *Fair Maid of Perth,* you must at once read *Waverley,* which is, indeed, from quite a different point of view, but which may, without hesitation, be set beside the best works that have ever been written in this world. We see that it is the same man who wrote the *Fair Maid of Perth,* but that he has yet to gain the favor of the public, and therefore collects his forces so that he may not give a touch that is short of excellence. The *Fair Maid of Perth,* on the other hand, is from a freer pen; the author is now sure of his public, and he proceeds more at liberty. After reading *Waverley,* you will understand why Walter Scott still designates himself the author of that work; for there he showed what he could do, and he has never since written anything to surpass, or even equal, that first published novel. (pp. 270-71)

> *Johann Wolfgang von Goethe, in conversations with Johann Peter Eckermann on October 3rd and October 9th, 1828, in his* Conversations with Eckermann, *M. Walter Dunne, Publishers, 1901, pp. 267-69, 270-71.*

HEINRICH HEINE (essay date 1828)

[*One of the most prominent literary figures in nineteenth-century Europe and in the history of his native Germany, Heine is remembered for his poetry—characterized by passionate lyricism and wry irony—as well as his distinctive commentaries on politics, art, literature, and society. In the following excerpt, Heine offers a negative assessment of* The Life of Napoleon Bonaparte, *emphasizing the detrimental effect that Scott's need for money had on his later writings. Heine's remarks were first published in German in 1828.*]

Poor Walter Scott! Hadst thou been rich thou wouldst not have written [*The Life of Napoleon Buonaparte*], and so hadst not become a poor Walter Scott! But the trustees of the Constable estate met together, and reckoned up and ciphered, and after much subtraction and division, shook their heads, and there remained for poor Walter Scott nothing but laurels and debts. Then the most extraordinary of all came to pass, the singer of great deeds wished for once to try his hand at heroism, he made up his mind to a *cessio bonorum*, the laurels of the great unknown were taxed to cover great and well-known debts; and so there came to life in hungry haste in bankrupt inspiration, the *Life of Napoleon,* a book to be roundly paid for by the wants of the English people in general, and of the English Ministry in particular.

Praise him, the brave citizen! praise him, ye united Philistines of all the earth! praise him, thou beautiful shopkeeper's virtue, which sacrificest everything to meet a note on the day when it is due! only do not ask of me that I praise him too.

Strange! the dead Emperor is, even in his grave, the bane of the Britons, and through him Britannia's greatest poet has lost his laurels!

He *was* Britannia's greatest poet, let people say and imagine what they will. It is true that the critics of his romances carped and cavilled at his greatness, and reproached him that he assumed too much breadth in execution, that he went too much into details, that his great characters were only formed by the combination of a mass of minor traits, that he required an endless array of accessories to bring out his bold effects; but, to tell the truth, he resembled in all this a millionaire, who keeps his whole property in the form of small specie, and who must drive up three or four wagons full of sacks of pence and farthings when he has a large sum to pay. Should any one complain of the ill-manners of such a style of liquidation, with its attendant troubles of heavy lifting and hauling and endless counting, he can reply with perfect truth that, no matter *how* he gives the money, he still gives it, and that he is in reality just as well able to pay and quite as rich as another who owns nothing but bullion in bars; yes, that he even has an advantage greater than that of mere facility of transport, since in the vegetable market gold bars are useless, while every huckster woman will grab with both hands at pence and farthings when they are offered her. *Now* all this popular wealth of the British

poet is at an end, and he, whose change was so current that the duchess and the cobbler's wife received it with the same interest, has at last become a poor Walter Scott! His destiny recalls the legend of the mountain elves, who, mockingly benevolent, gave money to poor people, which was bright and profitable so long as they spent it wisely, but which turned to mere dust when applied to unworthy purposes. Sack by sack we opened Walter Scott's new load, and lo! instead of gleaming smiling pence, there was nothing but idle dust, and dust again! He was justly punished by those mountain elves of Parnassus, the Muses, who, like all noble-minded women, are enthusiastic Napoleonists, and who were consequently doubly enraged at the misuse of the spirit-treasure which had been loaned. (pp. 369-72)

We are all mortal, and the best of us may once in a while write a bad book. People then say that the thing is below criticism, and that ends the matter. But it is really extraordinary that in this new work we do not find a trace of Scott's beautiful style. The colourless commonplace strain is sprinkled in vain with sundry red, green, and blue words; in vain do glittering patches from the poets cover the prosaic nakedness; in vain does the author rob all Noah's ark to find bestial comparisons; and in vain is the Word of God itself cited to heighten the colour of stupid thoughts. Stranger still is it that Walter Scott has not here succeeded in a single effort to bring into play his inborn talent of sketching characters, and of catching the traits of the outer Napoleon. Walter Scott learned nothing from those beautiful pictures which represent Napoleon surrounded by his generals and statesmen, though every one who regards them without prejudice must be deeply moved by the tragic tranquillity and antique severity of those features, which contrast in such fearful sublimity with the modern, excitable, picturesque faces of the day, and which seem to announce something of the incarnate God. But if the Scottish poet could not comprehend the form, how much less capable must he have been of grasping the character of the Emperor! And I therefore willingly pardon his blasphemy of a divinity whom he never knew. And I must also forgive him that he regards his Wellington as a god, and in deifying him, falls into such excessive manifestations of piety, that, rich as he is in figures of beasts, he knows not wherewith to compare him. Everywhere on earth as men are so are their gods. Stupid black savages adore poisonous snakes; cross-eyed Baschkirs pray to ugly logs; idiotic Laplanders reverence seals. Sir Walter Scott, in nothing behind them, worships his Wellington.

But if I am tolerant towards Walter Scott, and forgive him the emptiness, errors, slanders, and stupid things in his book— nay, if I even pardon him the weariness and *ennui* which its reading caused me, I cannot, for all that, forgive him its tendency. This is nothing less than the exculpation of the English Ministry as regards the crime of St. Helena. "In this case of equity between the English Ministry and public opinion," as [a] Berlin reviewer expresses it, "Walter Scott makes himself judge of its merits;" he couples legal quibblings with his poetic talent, in order to distort both facts and history, and his clients, who are at the same time his patrons, may well afford, beside the regular fees, to privately press an extra *douceur* into his hand.

The English have merely murdered the Emperor—but Walter Scott sold him. (pp. 373-75)

> *Heinrich Heine, "The Life of Napoleon Buonaparte," in his* Pictures of Travel, *translated by Charles*

G. Leland, 1855. Reprint by William Heinemann, 1906, pp. 369-80.

SAMUEL TAYLOR COLERIDGE   (essay date 1834?)

[In the following excerpt, drawn from marginalia in Coleridge's copy of an edition of Scott's novels, the critic speculates on the reasons why he has never been able to finish reading Ivanhoe *and also comments briefly on* Guy Mannering *and* Old Mortality. *Coleridge's remarks, thought to have been written sometime during the middle or late 1820s, cannot be positively dated prior to his death in 1834. For additional criticism on Scott's works by Coleridge, see excerpt dated 1810.]*

I do not myself know how to account for it, but so the fact is, that tho' I have read, and again and again turned to, sundry chapters of **Ivanhoe** with an untired interest, I have never read the whole—the pain or the perplexity or whatever it was always outweighed the curiosity. Perhaps the foreseen hopelessness of Rebecca—the comparatively feeble interest excited by Rowena, the from the beginning foreknown bride of Ivanhoe—perhaps the unmixed atrocity of the Norman nobles, and our utter indifference to the feuds of Norman and Saxon (*N.B.* what a contrast to our interest in the Cavaliers and Jacobites and the Puritans, Commonwealthmen, and Covenanters from Charles I to the Revolution)—these may, or may not have been the causes, but **Ivanhoe** I never have been able to summon fortitude to read thro'. Doubtless, the want of any one predominant interest aggravated by the want of any one continuous thread of events is a grievous defect in a novel. Therefore the charm of Scott's **Guy Mannering,** which I am far from admiring the most but yet read with the greatest delight—spite of the *falsetto* of Meg Merrilies, and the absurdity of the tale. But it contains an amiable character, tho' a very commonplace and easily manufactured compound, Dandy Dinmont—and in all Walter Scott's novels I know of no other. Cuddy in **Old Mortality** is the nearest to it, and certainly much more of a *character* than Dinmont. But Cuddy's consenting not to see and recognise his old master at his selfish wife's instance, is quite inconsistent with what is meant by a *good heart.* No wife could have influenced *Strap* to such an act. I have no doubt, however, that this very absence of *heart* is one and not the least operative of the causes of Scott's unprecedented favour with the higher classes. (p. 329)

> *Samuel Taylor Coleridge, "Scott's Novels: 'Ivanhoe',"* in his *Coleridge's Miscellaneous Criticism, edited by Thomas Middleton Raysor, 1936. Reprint by The Folcroft Press, Inc., 1969, pp. 328-29.*

[THOMAS CARLYLE]   (essay date 1838)

[A noted nineteenth-century essayist, historian, critic, and social commentator, Carlyle was a central figure of the Victorian age in England. In his writings, he advocated a Christian work ethic and stressed the importance of order, piety, and spiritual fulfillment. Known to his contemporaries as the "Sage of Chelsea," Carlyle exerted a powerful moral influence in an era of rapidly shifting values. His review of Lockhart's Life, *from which the following excerpt is drawn, profoundly affected subsequent critics and is considered one of the most important commentaries on Scott written during the nineteenth century. In his remarks, Carlyle assesses Scott's place within the literary, philosophical, and cultural climate of early nineteenth-century Europe, discussing the author's enormous popularity, the strengths and failings of his works, and the connection between his prolific output and his worldly ambitions. Carlyle's commentary later served as the basis for an extensive essay on Scott by Stephen (see excerpt dated 1871).]*

Into the question whether Scott was a great man or not, we do not propose to enter deeply. It is, as too usual, a question about words. There can be no doubt but many men have been named and printed *great* who were vastly smaller than he; as little doubt moreover that of the specially *good* a very large portion, according to any genuine standard of man's worth, were worthless in comparison to him. He for whom Scott is great may most innocently name him so; may with advantage admire his great qualities, and ought with sincere heart to emulate them. At the same time, it is good that there be a certain degree of precision in our epithets. (p. 302)

Friends to precision of epithet will probably deny his title to the name "great." It seems to us there goes other stuff to the making of great men than can be detected here. One knows not what idea worthy of the name of great, what purpose, instinct or tendency that could be called great, Scott ever was inspired with. His life was worldly; his ambitions were worldly. There is nothing spiritual in him; all is economical, material, of the earth earthy. A love of picturesque, of beautiful, vigorous and graceful things; a genuine love, yet not more genuine than has dwelt in hundreds of men named minor poets: this is the highest quality to be discerned in him. His power of representing these things too, his poetic power, like his moral power, was a genius *in extenso,* as we may say, not *in intenso.* In action, in speculation, *broad* as he was, he rose nowhere high; productive without measure as to quantity, in quality he for the most part transcended but a little way the region of commonplace. It has been said, "no man has written as many volumes with so few sentences that can be quoted." Winged words were not his vocation; nothing urged him that way: the great mystery of existence was not great to him; did not drive him into rocky solitudes to wrestle with it for an answer, to be answered or to perish. He had nothing of the martyr; into no "dark region to slay monsters for us," did he, either led or driven, venture down: his conquests were for his own behoof mainly, conquests over common market labour, and reckonable in good metallic coin of the realm. The thing he had faith in, except power, power of what sort soever, and even of the rudest sort, would be difficult to point out. One sees not that he believed in anything: nay, he did not even disbelieve; but quietly acquiesced, and made himself at home in a world of conventionalities: the false, the semi-false, and the true were alike true in this, that they were there, and had power in their hands more or less. It was well to feel so; and yet not well! We find it written, "Wo to them that are at ease in Zion;" but surely it is a double wo to them that are at ease in Babel, in Domdaniel. On the other hand he wrote many volumes, amusing many thousands of men. Shall we call this great? It seems to us there dwells and struggles another sort of spirit in the inward parts of great men!

Brother Ringletub, the missionary, inquired of Ram-Dass, a Hindoo man-god, who had set up for godhood lately, What he meant to do, then, with the sins of mankind? To which Ram-Dass at once answered, he had *fire enough in his belly* to burn up all the sins in the world. Ram-Dass was right so far, and had a spice of sense in him; for surely it is the test of every divine man this same, and without it he is not divine or great,— that he *have* fire in him to burn up somewhat of the sins of the world, of the miseries and errors of the world: why else is he there? . . . A great man is ever, as the Transcendentalists speak, possessed with an *idea.* Napoleon himself, not the superfinest of great men, and ballasted sufficiently with prudences and egoisms, had nevertheless, as is clear enough, an idea to start with: the idea that Democracy was the Cause of Man, the right and infinite Cause. Accordingly he made himself "the armed soldier of Democracy;" and did vindicate it in a rather great manner. . . . Thus was Napoleon; thus are all great men: children of the idea; or, in Ram-Dass's phraseology, furnished with fire to burn up the miseries of men. Conscious or unconscious, latent or unfolded, there is small vestige of any such fire being extant in the inner-man of Scott.

Yet, on the other hand, the surliest critic must allow that Scott was a genuine man, which itself is a great matter. No affectation, fantasticality or distortion, dwelt in him; no shadow of cant. Nay withal, was he not a right brave and strong man, according to his kind? What a load of toil, what a measure of felicity, he quietly bore along with him; with what quiet strength he both worked on this earth, and enjoyed in it; invincible to evil fortune and to good! A most composed invincible man; in difficulty and distress, knowing no discouragement, Samson-like, carrying off on his strong Samson-shoulders the gates that would imprison him; in danger and menace, laughing at the whisper of fear. And then, with such a sunny current of true humour and humanity, a free joyful sympathy with so many things; what of fire he had, all lying so beautifully *latent*, as radical latent heat, as fruitful internal warmth of life; a most robust, healthy man! The truth is, our best definition of Scott

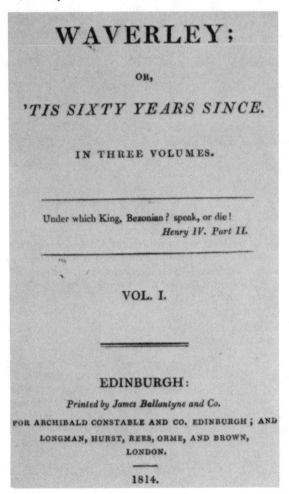

The title page of the first edition of Waverley.

were perhaps even this, that he was, if no great man, then something much pleasanter to be, a robust, thoroughly healthy, and withal, very prosperous and victorious man. An eminently well-conditioned man, healthy in body, healthy in soul; we will call him one of the *healthiest* of men. (pp. 303-05)

The *Minstrelsy of the Scottish Border* proved to be a well, from which flowed one of the broadest rivers. Metrical romances (which in due time pass into prose romances); the old life of men resuscitated for us: it is a mighty word! Not as dead tradition, but as a palpable presence, the past stood before us. There they were, the rugged old fighting men; in their doughty simplicity and strength, with their heartiness, their healthiness, their stout self-help, in their iron basnets, leather jerkins, jack-boots, in their quaintness of manner and costume; there as they looked and lived! It was like a new-discovered continent in literature; for the new century, a bright El Dorado,—or else some fat beatific land of Cockaigne, and paradise of Do-nothings. To the opening nineteenth century, in its languor and paralysis, nothing could have been welcomer. Most unexpected, most refreshing, and exhilarating: behold our new El Dorado; our fat beatific Lubberland, where one can enjoy and do nothing! It was the time for such a new literature; and this Walter Scott was the man for it. The *Lays,* the *Marmions,* the *Ladyes* and *Lords* of Lake and Isles, followed in thick succession, with ever widening profit and praise. (p. 315)

It was in this poetic period that Scott formed his connexion with the Ballantynes; and embarked, though under cover, largely in trade. . . . Viewed as it stood in the reality, as he was and as it was, the enterprise, since it proved so unfortunate, may be called lamentable, but cannot be called unnatural. The practical Scott, looking towards practical issues in all things, could not but find hard cash one of the most practical. If, by any means, cash could be honestly produced, were it by writing poems, were it by printing them, why not? Great things might be done ultimately; great difficulties were at once got rid of,—manifold higgling of booksellers, and contradiction of sinners hereby fell away. A printing and bookselling speculation was not so alien for a maker of books. Voltaire, who indeed got no copyrights, made much money by the war-commissariat, in his time; we believe, by the victualling branch of it. Saint George himself, they say, was a dealer in bacon in Cappadocia. A thrifty man will help himself towards his object by such steps as lead to it. Station in society, solid power over the good things of this world, was Scott's avowed object; towards which the precept of precepts is that of Iago: Put money in thy purse.

Here indeed it is to be remarked, that, perhaps, no literary man of any generation has less value than Scott for the immaterial part of his mission in any sense: not only for the fantasy called fame, with the fantastic miseries attendant thereon; but also for the spiritual purport of his work, whether it tended hitherward or thitherward, or had any tendency whatever; and indeed for all purports and results of his working, except such, we may say, as offered themselves to the eye, and could in one sense or the other be handled, looked at, and buttoned into the breeches-pocket. Somewhat too little of a fantast, this *vates* of ours! But so it was: in this nineteenth century, our highest literary man, who immeasurably beyond all others commanded the world's ear, had, as it were, no message whatever to deliver to the world; wished not the world to elevate itself, to amend itself, to do this or to do that, except simply pay him for the books he kept writing. Very remarkable; fittest, perhaps, for an age fallen languid, destitute of faith, and terrified at scepticism? Or, perhaps, for quite another sort of age, an age all in peaceable triumphant motion? But, indeed, since Shakespeare's time there has been no great speaker so unconscious of an aim in speaking. Equally unconscious these two utterances; equally the sincere complete product of the minds they came from: and now if they were equally *deep*? Or, if the one was living fire, and the other was futile phosphorescence and mere resinous fire-work? It will depend on the relative worth of the minds; for both were equally spontaneous, both equally expressed themselves unincumbered by an ulterior aim. Beyond drawing audiences to the Globe Theatre, Shakspeare contemplated no result in those plays of his. Yet they have had results! Utter with free heart what thy own *daemon* gives thee: if fire from heaven, it shall be well; if resinous firework, it shall be—as well as *it* could be, or better than otherwise!— The candid judge will, in general, require that a speaker, in so extremely serious a universe as this of ours, have something to speak about. In the heart of the speaker there ought to be some kind of gospel-tidings burning till it be uttered; otherwise it were better for him that he altogether held his peace. A gospel somewhat more decisive than this of Scott's—except to an age altogether languid, without either scepticism or faith! These things the candid judge will demand of literary men; yet withal will recognize the great worth there is in Scott's honesty if in nothing more, in his being the thing he was with such entire good faith. Here is a something not a nothing. If no skyborn messenger, heaven looking through his eyes; then neither is it a chimera with its systems, crotchets, cants, fanaticisms, and "last infirmity of noble minds,"—full of misery, unrest, and ill-will; but a substantial, peaceable, terrestrial man. Far as the Earth is under the Heaven does Scott stand below the former sort of character; but high as the cheerful flowery Earth is above waste Tartarus does he stand above the latter. Let him live in his own fashion, and do honour to him in that.

It were late in the day to write criticisms on those Metrical Romances: at the same time, the great popularity they had seems natural enough. In the first place, there was the indisputable impress of worth, of genuine human force, in them. This which lies in some degree, or is thought to lie, at the bottom of all popularity, did, to an unusual degree, disclose itself in these rhymed romances of Scott's. Pictures were actually painted and presented; human emotions conceived and sympathized with. Considering what wretched Della-Cruscan and other vamping-up of old worn-out tatters was the staple article then, it may be granted that Scott's excellence was superior and supreme. When a Hayley was the main singer, a Scott might well be hailed with warm welcome. Consider whether the *Loves of the Plants*, and even the *Loves of the Triangles*, could be worth the loves and hates of men and women! Scott was as preferable to what he displaced, as the substance is to the wearisomely repeated shadow of a substance. But, in the second place, we may say that the *kind* of worth which Scott manifested was fitted especially for the then temper of men. We have called it an age fallen into spiritual languor, destitute of belief, yet terrified at scepticism; reduced to live a stinted half-life, under strange new circumstances. Now vigorous whole-life, this was what of all things these delineations offered. The reader was carried back to rough strong times, wherein those maladies of ours had not yet arisen. Brawny fighters, all cased in buff and iron, their hearts too sheathed in oak and triple brass, caprioled their huge war-horses, shook their death-doing spears; and went forth in the most determined manner, nothing doubting. The reader sighed, yet not without a reflex solacement: "O, that I too had lived in those times, had never known these logic-cobwebs, this doubt, this sickliness; and been and felt myself alive among men alive!" Add lastly, that, in this

new-found poetic world there was no call for effort on the reader's part; what excellence they had, exhibited itself at a glance. It was for the reader, not an El Dorado only, but a beatific land of Cockaigne and Paradise of Donothings! The reader, what the vast majority of readers so long to do, was allowed to lie down at his ease, and be ministered to. What the Turkish bath-keeper is said to aim at with his frictions, and shampooings, and fomentings, more or less effectually, that the patient in total idleness may have the delights of activity,— was here to a considerable extent realized. The languid imagination fell back into its rest; an artist was there who could supply it with high-painted scenes, with sequences of stirring action, and whisper to it, Be at ease, and let thy tepid element be comfortable to thee. "The rude man," says a critic, "requires only to see something going on. The man of more refinement must be made to feel. The man of complete refinement must be made to reflect."

We named the **Minstrelsy of the Scottish Border** the fountain from which flowed this great river of Metrical Romances; but according to some they can be traced to a still higher obscurer spring: to Goethe's *Götz von Berlichingen with the Iron Hand;* of which . . . Scott in his earlier days executed a translation. (pp. 317-20)

How far *Götz von Berlichingen* actually affected Scott's literary destination, and whether without it the rhymed romances, and then the prose romances of the Author of **Waverley**, would not have followed as they did, must remain a very obscure question; obscure, and not important. Of the fact, however, there is no doubt but these two tendencies, which may be named *Götzism* and *Werterism,* of the former of which Scott was representative with us, have made, and are still in some quarters making, the tour of all Europe. In Germany too there was this affectionate half-regretful looking back into the past; Germany had its buff-belted watch-tower period in literature, and had even got done with it, before Scott began. Then as to *Werterism,* had not we English our Byron and his genus? No form of Werterism in any other country had half the potency: as our Scott carried chivalry literature to the ends of the world, so did our Byron Werterism. (p. 321)

British Werterism, in the shape of those Byron Poems, so potent and poignant, produced on the languid appetite of men a mighty effect. This too was a "class of feelings deeply important to modern minds; feelings which arise from *passion incapable of being converted into action,* which belong to an age as indolent, cultivated, and unbelieving as our own!" The "languid age without either faith or scepticism" turned towards Byronism with an interest altogether peculiar: here, if no cure for its miserable paralysis and languor, was at least an indignant statement of the misery; an indignant Ernulphus' curse read over it,—which all men felt to be something. Half-regretful lookings into the Past gave place, in many quarters, to Ernulphus' cursings of the Present. Scott was among the first to perceive that the day of Metrical Chivalry Romances was declining. He had held the sovereignty for some half-score of years, a comparatively long lease of it; and now the time seemed come for dethronement, for abdication; an unpleasant business; which however he held himself ready, as a brave man will, to transact with composure and in silence. After all, Poetry was not his staff of life; Poetry had already yielded him much money; *this* at least it would not take back from him. Busy always with editing, with compiling, with multiplex official, commercial business, and solid interests, he beheld the coming change with unmoved eye.

Resignation he was prepared to exhibit in this manner;—and now behold there proved to be no need of resignation. Let the Metrical Romance become a Prose one; shake off its rhyme-fetters, and try a wider sweep! In the spring of 1814 appeared *Waverley;* an event memorable in the annals of British literature; in the annals of British bookselling thrice and four times memorable. Byron sang, but Scott narrated; and when the song had sung itself out through all variations onwards to the *Don-Juan* one, Scott was still found narrating, and carrying the whole world along with him. All bygone popularity of chivalry lays was swallowed up in a far greater. What "series" followed out of *Waverley,* and how and with what result, is known to all men; was witnessed and watched with a kind of rapt astonishment by all. Hardly any literary reputation ever rose so high in our Island; no reputation at all ever spread so wide. Walter Scott became Sir Walter Scott, Baronet, of Abbotsford; on whom fortune seemed to pour her whole cornucopia of wealth, honour, and worldly good; the favourite of Princes and of Peasants, and all intermediate men. His *Waverley* series, swift-following one on the other apparently without end, was the universal reading, looked for like an annual harvest, by all ranks in all European countries. A curious circumstance superadded itself, that the author though known was unknown. From the first, most people suspected, and soon after the first, few intelligent persons much doubted, that the Author of *Waverley* was Walter Scott. Yet a certain mystery was still kept up; rather piquant to the public; doubtless very pleasant to the author, who saw it all; who probably had not to listen, as other hapless individuals often had, to this or the other long-drawn "clear proof at last," that the author was not Walter Scott, but a certain astonishing Mr So-and-so;—one of the standing miseries of human life in that time. But for the privileged author, it was like a king travelling incognito. All men know that he is a high king, chivalrous Gustaf or Kaiser Joseph; but he mingles in their meetings without cumber or etiquette or lonesome ceremony, as Chevalier du Nord, or Count of Lorraine: he has none of the weariness of royalty, and yet all the praise, and the satisfaction of hearing it with his own ears. In a word, the *Waverley Novels* circulated and reigned triumphant; to the general imagination the "Author of *Waverley*" was like some living mythological personage, and ranked among the chief wonders of the world. (pp. 322-23)

With respect to the literary character of these *Waverley Novels,* so extraordinary in their commercial character, there remains, after so much reviewing, good and bad, little that it were profitable at present to say. The great fact about them is, that they were faster written and better paid for than any other books in the world. It must be granted, moreover, that they have a worth far surpassing what is usual in such cases; nay, that if literature had no task but that of harmlessly amusing indolent, languid men, here was the very perfection of literature; that a man, here more emphatically than ever elsewhere, might fling himself back, exclaiming, "Be mine to lie on this sofa, and read everlasting Novels of Walter Scott!" The composition, slight as it often is, usually hangs together in some measure, and *is* a composition. There is a free flow of narrative, of incident and sentiment; an easy master-like coherence throughout, as if it were the free dash of a master's hand, "round as the O of Giotto." It is the perfection of extemporaneous writing. Farthermore, surely he were a blind critic who did not recognise here a certain genial sunshiny freshness and picturesqueness; paintings both of scenery and figures, very graceful, brilliant, occasionally full of grace and glowing brightness blended in the softest composure; in fact, a deep sincere love of the beautiful in nature and man, and the readiest faculty of expressing this by imagination and by word. No fresher paintings of nature can be found than Scott's; hardly anywhere a wider sympathy with man. From Davie Deans up to Richard Coeur-de-Lion; from Meg Merrilies to Die Vernon and Queen Elizabeth! It is the utterance of a man of open soul; of a brave, large, free-seeing man, who has a true brotherhood with all men. In joyous picturesqueness and fellow-feeling, freedom of eye and heart; or to say it in a word, in general *healthiness* of mind, these novels prove Scott to have been amongst the foremost writers.

Neither in the higher and highest excellence, of drawing character, is he at any time altogether deficient; though at no time can we call him, in the best sense, successful. His Bailie Jarvies, Dinmonts, Dalgettys (for their name is legion) do look and talk like what they give themselves out for; they are, if not *created* and made poetically alive, yet deceptively *enacted* as a good player might do them. What more is wanted then? For the reader lying on a sofa, nothing more; yet for another sort of reader, much. It were a long chapter to unfold the difference in drawing a character between a Scott and a Shakspeare, a Goethe! Yet it is a difference literally immense; they are of different species; the value of the one is not to be counted in the coin of the other. We might say in a short word, which means a long matter, that your Shakspeare fashions his characters from the heart outwards; your Scott fashions them from the skin inwards, never getting near the heart of them! The one set became living men and women; the other amount to little more than mechanical cases, deceptively painted automatons. Compare Fenella with Goethe's Mignon, which it was once said, Scott had "done Goethe the honour" to borrow. He has borrowed what he could of Mignon. The small stature, the climbing talent, the trickiness, the *mechanical case,* as we say, he has borrowed; but the soul of Mignon is left behind. Fenella is an unfavourable specimen for Scott; but it illustrates, in the aggravated state, what is traceable in all the characters he drew. To the same purport indeed we are to say that these famed books are altogether addressed to the every-day mind; that for any other mind, there is next to no nourishment in them. Opinions, emotions, principles, doubts, beliefs, beyond what the intelligent country gentleman can carry along with him, are not to be found. It is orderly, customary, it is prudent, decent; nothing more. One would say, it lay not in Scott to give much more: getting out of the ordinary range, and attempting the heroic, which is but seldom the case, he falls almost at once into the rose-pink sentimental,—descries the Minerva Press from afar, and hastily quits that course; for none better than he knew it to lead nowhither. On the whole, contrasting *Waverley,* which was carefully written, with most of its followers, which were written extempore, one may regret the extempore method. Something very perfect in its kind might have come from Scott; nor was it a low kind: nay, who knows how high, with studious self-concentration, he might have gone; what wealth nature had implanted in him, which his circumstances, most unkind while seeming to be kindest, had never impelled him to unfold?

But after all, in the loudest blaring and trumpetting of popularity, it is ever to be held in mind, as a truth, remaining true for ever, that literature *has* other aims than that of harmlessly amusing indolent, languid men: or if literature have them not, then literature is a very poor affair; and something else must have them, and must accomplish them, with thanks or without thanks; the thankful or thankless world were not long a world otherwise! Under this head, there is little to be sought or found in the *Waverley Novels.* Not profitable for doctrine, for reproof, for edification, for building up or elevating, in any shape! The sick heart will find no healing here, the darkly struggling heart no guidance: the Heroic that is in all men no divine awakening voice. We say, therefore, that they do not found themselves on deep interests, but on comparatively trivial ones, not on the perennial, perhaps not even on the lasting. In fact, much of the interest of these novels results from what may be called contrasts of costume. The phraseology, fashion of arms, of dress and life, belonging to one age, is brought suddenly, with singular vividness, before the eyes of another. A great effect this; yet by the very nature of it, an altogether temporary one. Consider, brethren, shall not we too one day be antiques, and grow to have as quaint a costume as the rest? The stuffed dandy, only give him *time,* will become one of the wonderfullest mummies. In antiquarian museums, only two centuries hence, the steeple-hat will hang on the next peg to Franks and Company's patent, antiquaries deciding which is uglier; and the Stulz swallow-tail, one may hope, will seem as incredible as any garment that ever made ridiculous the respectable back of man. Not by slashed breeches, steeple-hats, buff-belts, or antiquated speech, can romance heroes continue to interest us; but simply and solely, in the long run, by being men. Buff-belts and all manner of jerkins and costumes are transitory; man alone is perennial. He that has gone deeper into this than other men, will be remembered longer than they; he that has not, not. Tried under this category, Scott with his clear practical insight, joyous temper, and other sound faculties, is not to be accounted little,—among the ordinary circulating library heroes he might well pass for a demigod. Not little; yet neither is he great; there were greater, more than one or two, in his own age: among the great of all ages, one sees no likelihood of a place for him.

What then is the result of these *Waverley* romances? Are they to amuse one generation only? One or more. As many generations as they can, but not all generations: ah no, when our swallow-tail has become fantastic as trunk-hose, they will cease to amuse!—Meanwhile, as we can discern, their results have been several-fold. First of all, and certainly not least of all, have they not perhaps had this result: that a considerable portion of mankind has hereby been sated with mere amusement, and set on seeking something better? Amusement in the way of reading can go no farther, can do nothing better, by the power of man; and men ask, Is this what it can do? Scott, we reckon, carried several things to their ultimatum and crisis, so that change became inevitable: a great service, though an indirect one. Secondly, however, we may say, these historical novels have taught all men this truth, which looks like a truism, and yet was as good as unknown to writers of history and others, till so taught: that the bygone ages of the world were actually filled by living men, not by protocols, state-papers, controversies, and abstractions of men. Not abstractions were they, not diagrams and theorems; but men, in buff or other coats and breeches, with colour in their cheeks, with passions in their stomach, and the idioms, features, and vitalities of very men. It is a little word this; inclusive of great meaning! History will henceforth have to take thought of it. Her faint hearsays of "philosophy teaching by experience" will have to exchange themselves everywhere for direct inspection and imbodiment: this, and this only, will be counted experience; and till once experience have got in, philosophy will reconcile herself to wait at the door. It is a great service, fertile in consequences, this that Scott has done; a great truth laid open by him;— correspondent indeed to the substantial nature of the man; to his solidity and veracity even of imagination, which, with all

his lively discursiveness, was the characteristic of him. (pp. 334-38)

Scott's productive facility amazed everybody.... [His] rapidity is great, is a proof and consequence of the solid health of the man, bodily and spiritual; great, but unmiraculous; not greater than that of many others.... Admire it, yet with measure. For observe always, there are two conditions in work: let me fix the quality, and *you* shall fix the quantity! Any man may get through work rapidly who easily satisfies himself about it. Print the *talk* of any man, there will be a thick octavo volume daily; make his writing three times as good as his talk, there will be the third part of a volume daily, which still is good work. To write with never such rapidity in a passable manner is indicative not of a man's genius, but of his habits; it will prove his soundness of nervous system, his practicality of mind, and in fine, that he has the knack of his trade. In the most flattering view, rapidity will betoken health of mind; much also, perhaps most of all, will depend on health of body. Doubt it not, a faculty of easy writing is attainable by man! The human genius, once fairly set in this direction, will carry it far. (pp. 339-40)

Scott's career, of writing impromptu novels to buy farms with, was not of a kind to terminate voluntarily, but to accelerate itself more and more; and one sees not to what wise goal it could, in any case, have led him. Bookseller Constable's bankruptcy was not the ruin of Scott; his ruin was that ambition, and even false ambition, had laid hold of him; that his way of life was not wise. Whither could it lead? Where could it stop? New farms there remained ever to be bought, while new novels could pay for them. More and more success but gave more and more appetite, more and more audacity. The impromptu writing must have waxed ever thinner; declined faster and faster into the questionable category, into the condemnable, into the generally condemned. Already there existed, in secret, everywhere a considerable opposition party; witnesses of the *Waverley* miracles, but unable to believe in them, forced silently to protest against them. Such opposition party was in the sure case to grow; and even, with the impromptu process ever going on, ever waxing thinner, to draw the world over to it. Silent protest must at length have come to words; harsh truths, backed by harsher facts of a world-popularity overwrought and worn out, behoved to have been spoken;—such as can be spoken now without reluctance when they can pain the brave man's heart no more. Who knows? Perhaps it was better ordered to be all *otherwise.* Otherwise, at any rate, it was. One day the Constable mountain, which seemed to stand strong like the other rock-mountains, gave suddenly, as the icebergs do, a loud-sounding crack; suddenly, with huge clangour, shivered itself into ice-dust; and sank, carrying much along with it. In one day, Scott's high-heaped money-wages became fairy-money and nonentity; in one day the rich man and lord of land saw himself penniless, landless, a bankrupt among creditors.

It was a hard trial. He met it proudly, bravely,—like a brave proud man of the world. Perhaps there had been a prouder way still: to have owned honestly that he *was* unsuccessful then, all bankrupt, broken, in the world's goods and repute; and to have turned elsewhither for some refuge. Refuge did lie elsewhere; but it was not Scott's course, or fashion of mind, to seek it there. To say, Hitherto I have been all in the wrong, and this my fame and pride, now broken, was an empty delusion and spell of accursed witchcraft! It was difficult for flesh and blood! He said, I will retrieve myself, and make my point good yet, or die for it. Silently, like a proud strong man, he girt himself to the Hercules' task, of removing rubbish-mountains, since that was it; of paying large ransoms by what he could still write and sell. In his declining years too; misfortune is doubly and trebly unfortunate that befalls us then. Scott fell to his Hercules' task like a very man, and went on with it unweariedly; with a noble cheerfulness, while his life-strings were cracking, he grappled with it, and wrestled with it, years long, in death-grips, strength to strength;—and *it* proved the stronger; and his life and heart did crack and break: the cordage of a most strong heart! Over these last writings of Scott, his *Napoleons, Demonologies, Scotch Histories,* and the rest, criticism, finding still much to wonder at, much to commend, will utter no word of blame; this one word only, Woe is me! The noble warhorse that once laughed at the shaking of the spear, how is he doomed to toil himself dead, dragging ignoble wheels! Scott's descent was like that of a spent projectile; rapid, straight down;—perhaps mercifully so. It is a tragedy, as all life is; one proof more that Fortune stands on a restless *globe;* that Ambition, literary, warlike, politic, pecuniary, never yet profited any man. (pp. 341-43)

> *[Thomas Carlyle], in a review of "Memoirs of the Life of Sir Walter Scott, Baronet," in* The London and Westminster Review, *Vol. XXVIII, No. II, January, 1838, pp. 293-345.*

HONORÉ DE BALZAC   (letter date 1838)

[Balzac is often considered the greatest nineteenth-century French novelist. His importance rests on his vast work La comédie humaine, *consisting of more than ninety novels and stories in which he provides a comprehensive portrait of the French society of his day. In the following excerpt from a letter to Madame Hanska, his future wife, Balzac compares Scott with the English Romantic poet Lord Byron, emphasizing the diverse literary virtues of various works of Scott.]*

It is twelve years that I have been saying of Walter Scott what you have now written to me. Beside him Lord Byron is nothing, or almost nothing. But you are mistaken as to the plot of *Kenilworth.* To the minds of all makers of romance, and to mine, the plot of that work is the grandest, most complete, most extraordinary of all; the book is a masterpiece from this point of view, just as *St. Ronan's Well* is a masterpiece for detail and patience of finish, as the *Chronicles of the Canongate* are for sentiment, as *Ivanhoe* (the first volume, be it understood) is for history, *The Antiquary* for poesy, and *The Heart of Midlothian* for profound interest. All these works have each their especial merit, but genius shines throughout them all. You are right; Scott will be growing greater when Byron is forgotten, except for his form and his powerful inspiration. Byron's brain never had any other imprint than that of his own personality; whereas the whole world has posed before the creative genius of Scott, and has there, so to speak, beheld itself. (pp. 471-72)

> *Honoré de Balzac, in a letter to Madame Hanska on January 20, 1838, in his* The Letters of Honoré de Balzac to Madame Hanska: 1833-1846, *translated by Katharine Prescott Wormeley, 1900. Reprint by Little, Brown and Company, 1911, pp. 471-72.*

WILLIAM WORDSWORTH [CONVERSATIONS WITH MRS. DAVY AND LADY RICHARDSON]   (conversation date 1844)

[In the following extracts, the first drawn from reminiscences of Wordsworth's conversation by Mrs. Davy, the second from an account by Lady Richardson, the poet comments on the strengths and weaknesses of Scott's poetry and prose. For additional commentary on Scott by Wordsworth, see excerpt dated 1815.]

[July 11, 1844]

Mr. Wordsworth, in his best manner, with earnest thoughts given out in noble diction, gave his reasons for thinking that as a poet Scott would not live. 'I don't like,' he said, 'to say all this, or to take to pieces some of the best reputed passages of Scott's verse, especially in presence of my wife, because she thinks me too fastidious; but as a poet Scott *cannot* live, for he has never in verse written anything addressed to the immortal part of man. In making amusing stories in verse, he will be superseded by some newer versifier; what he writes in the way of natural description is merely rhyming nonsense.' As a prose writer, Mr. Wordsworth admitted that Scott had touched a higher vein, because there he had really dealt with feeling and passion. As historical novels, professing to give the manners of a past time, he did not attach much value to those works of Scott's so called, because that he held to be an attempt in which success was impossible. (pp. 442-43)

· · · · ·

[July 12, 1844]

[Wordsworth] discoursed at great length on Scott's works. His poetry he considered of that kind which will always be in demand, and that the supply will always meet it, suited to the age. He does not consider that it in any way goes below the surface of things; it does not reach to any intellectual or spiritual emotion; it is altogether superficial, and he felt it himself to be so. His descriptions are not true to Nature; they are addressed to the ear, not to the mind. He was a master of bodily movements in his battle-scenes; but very little productive power was exerted in popular creations. (p. 445)

> *William Wordsworth, in conversations with Mrs. Davy on July 11, 1844 and Lady Richardson on July 12, 1844, in his* The Prose Works of William Wordsworth: Critical and Ethical, *Vol. III, edited by Rev. Alexander B. Grosart, Edward Moxon, Son, and Co., 1876, pp. 442-43, 445.*

V. G. BELINSKY   (essay date 1844)

[Belinsky is considered the most influential Russian literary critic of the nineteenth century. He initiated a new trend in critical thought by combining literary appreciation with an exposition of progressive philosophical and political theory. In the following excerpt, Belinsky focuses on Scott's ability to capture in his novels the atmosphere of a given era. His comments were first published in 1844 in the journal Otechestvennye Zapiski.]

Among the men who have contributed most to the cultivation of a true view on history an honourable place belongs to the man who has written one very bad history and a multitude of excellent novels: we have in mind Walter Scott. The ignorant have proclaimed his novels to be the illegitimate product of the liaison of history with fiction. Evidently, the idea of history and fiction did not dovetail in their narrow conception. Thus, there are people who cannot for the life of them see any sense in opera as a production of art because the actors do not speak, but sing, and that does not happen in real life. Thus, there are people who consider verse as nonsense, rightly claiming that no one speaks in verse. There are different kinds of people and different kinds of narrow-mindedness! The people who are seduced by the blending of history with romance regard history as a military and diplomatic chronicle, from which point of view they are, of course, right. They do not understand that the history of customs and morals, which change with every new generation, is more interesting than the history of wars and treaties, and that the renovation of morals through the renovation of generations is one of the principal means by which Providence leads mankind to perfection. They do not understand that the historic and private lives of people are mingled together and fused like holidays with workdays. Walter Scott, as a man of genius, fathomed this with his instinct. Being familiar with the chronicles, he was able not only to read their lines, but between the lines. His novels are filled with a moving crowd, are alive with passions and seething interests great and small, base and lofty, and everywhere we feel the pathos of the epoch which the author has grasped with amazing skill. To read his novel is like living the age he describes, becoming for a moment a contemporary of the characters he portrays, thinking for a moment their thoughts and feeling their emotions. He was able, as a man of genius, to throw a retrospective glance at the sanguinary intestine disturbances of ancient England and turbulences of the new England which assumed the form of conservatism and opposition, and disclosed their meaning and significance in the strife of the Anglo-Saxon element with the Norman. That is why Guizot calls Walter Scott his teacher in history, and he himself explained the origin of the French revolution to be a result of *thirteen centuries* of strife between the Frank and Gallic elements. (pp. 305-06)

> *V. G. Belinsky, "'A Guide to the Study of Modern History' (Work by S. Smaragdov)," in his* Selected Philosophical Works, *Foreign Languages Publishing House, 1948, pp. 293-319.*

WALTER BAGEHOT (essay date 1858)

[*Bagehot is regarded as one of the most versatile and influential authors of mid-Victorian England. In addition to literary criticism, he wrote several pioneering works in the fields of politics, sociology, and economics. Bagehot's commentary on Scott is generally considered the most important mid-nineteenth-century assessment of the author. In the following excerpt, Bagehot provides an extended discussion of his achievement as a novelist, focusing on both the redeeming qualities and characteristic limitations of his works. The topics discussed by the critic include Scott's commonsensical approach to the world, romantic imagination, intellectual superficiality, and inability to create convincing heroines.*]

[The *Waverley Novels*] every where bear marks of a state of transition. They are not devoted with any thing like the present exclusiveness to the sentimental part of human life. They describe great events, singular characters, strange accidents, strange states of society; they dwell with a peculiar interest—and as if for their own sake—on antiquarian details relating to a past society. Singular customs, social practices, even political institutions which existed once in Scotland, and even elsewhere, during the middle ages, are explained with a careful minuteness. At the same time the sentimental element assumes a great deal of prominence. The book is in fact, as well as in theory, a narrative of the feelings and fortunes of the hero and heroine. An attempt more or less successful has been made to insert an interesting love-story in each novel. Sir Walter was quite aware that the best delineation of the oddest characters, or the most quaint societies, or the strangest incidents, would not in general satisfy his readers. He has invariably attempted an account of youthful, sometimes of decidedly juvenile, feelings and actions. The difference between Sir Walter's novels and the spe-

cially romantic fictions of the present day is, that in the former the love-story is always, or nearly always, connected with some great event, or the fortunes of some great historical character, or the peculiar movements and incidents of some strange state of society; and that the author did not suppose or expect that his readers would be so absorbed in the sentimental aspect of human life as to be unable or unwilling to be interested in, or to attend to, any other. There is always a *locus in quo,* if the expression may be pardoned, in the *Waverley Novels.* The hero and heroine walk among the trees of the forest according to rule, but we are expected to take an interest in the forest as well as in them. (pp. 446-47)

[No novel of Sir Walter Scott's] in any material degree attempts to deal with human affairs in all their spheres—to delineate as a whole the life of man. The canvas has a large background, in some cases too large either for artistic effect or the common reader's interest; but there are always real boundaries—Sir Walter had no *thesis* to maintain. Scarcely any writer will set himself to delineate the whole of human life, unless he has a doctrine concerning human life to put forth and inculcate. The effort is *doctrinaire.* Scott's imagination was strictly conservative. He could understand (with a few exceptions) any considerable movement of human life and action, and could always describe with easy freshness every thing which he did understand; but he was not obliged by stress of fanaticism to maintain a dogma concerning them, or to show their peculiar relation to the general sphere of life. He described vigorously and boldly the peculiar scene and society which in every novel he had selected as the theatre of romantic action. Partly from their fidelity to nature, and partly from a consistency in the artist's mode of representation, these pictures group themselves from the several novels in the imagination, and an habitual reader comes to think of and understand what is meant by "Scott's world;" but the writer had no such distinct object before him. No one novel was designed to be a delineation of the world as Scott viewed it. We have vivid and fragmentary histories; it is for the slow critic of after-times to piece together their teaching.

From this intermediate position of the *Waverley Novels,* or at any rate in exact accordance with its requirements, is the special characteristic for which they are most remarkable. We may call this in a brief phrase their *romantic sense;* and perhaps we cannot better illustrate it than by a quotation from the novel to which the series owes its most usual name. It occurs in the description of the court-ball which Charles Edward is described as giving at Holyrood House the night before his march southward on his strange adventure. The striking interest of the scene before him, and the peculiar position of his own sentimental career, are described as influencing the mind of the hero.

> Under the influence of these mixed sensations, and cheered at times by a smile of intelligence and approbation from the Prince as he passed the group, Waverley exerted his powers of fancy, animation and eloquence, and attracted the general admiration of the company. The conversation gradually assumed the line best qualified for the display of his talents and acquisitions. The gaiety of the evening was exalted in character, rather than checked, by the approaching dangers of the morrow. All nerves were strung for the future, and prepared to enjoy the present. This mood is highly favourable for the exercise of the powers of imagination, for po-

A modern photograph of Abbotsford. Courtesy of British Tourist Authority.

etry, and for that eloquence which is allied to poetry.

Neither 'eloquence' nor 'poetry' are the exact words with which it would be appropriate to describe the fresh style of the *Waverley Novels;* but the imagination of their author was stimulated by a fancied mixture of sentiment and fact very much as he describes Waverley's to have been by a real experience of the two at once. . . . Many historical novelists, especially those who with care and pains have 'read up' their detail, are often evidently in a strait how to pass from their history to their sentiment. The fancy of Sir Walter could not help connecting the two. If he had given us the English side of the race to Derby, he would have described the Bank of England paying in sixpences, and also the loves of the cashier.

It is not unremarkable in connection with this the special characteristic of the 'Scotch novels,' that their author began his literary life by collecting the old ballads of his native country. Ballad poetry is, in comparison at least with many other kinds of poetry, a sensible thing. It describes not only romantic events, but historical ones, incidents in which there is a form and body and consistence—events which have a result. . . . When Scott, according to his own half-jesting but half-serious expression, was 'beaten out of poetry' by Byron, he began to express in more pliable prose the same combination which his verse had been used to convey. As might have been expected, the sense

became in the novels more free, vigorous, and flowing, because it is less cramped by the vehicle in which it is conveyed. The range of character which can be adequately delineated in narrative verse is much narrower than that which can be described in the combination of narrative with dramatic prose; and perhaps even the sentiment of the novels is manlier and freer. . . . (pp. 447-50)

The sensible element, if we may so express it, of the *Waverley Novels* appears in various forms. One of the most striking is in the delineation of great political events and influential political institutions. We are not by any means about to contend that Scott is to be taken as an infallible or an impartial authority for the parts of history which he delineates. On the contrary, we believe all the world now agrees that there are many deductions to be made from, many exceptions to be taken to, the accuracy of his delineations. Still, whatever period or incident we take, we shall always find in the error a great, in one or two cases perhaps an extreme, mixture of the mental element which we term common sense. (p. 450)

The view which Scott seems to have taken of democracy indicates exactly the same sort of application of a plain sense to the visible parts of the subject. His imagination was singularly penetrated with the strange varieties and motley composition of human life. The extraordinary multitude and striking contrast of the characters in his novels show this at once. And even more strikingly is the same habit of mind indicated by a tendency never to omit an opportunity of describing those varied crowds and assemblages which concentrate for a moment into a unity the scattered and unlike varieties of mankind. . . . As in the imagination of Shakespeare, so in that of Scott, the principal form and object were the structure—that is a hard word—the undulation and diversified composition of human society; the picture of this stood in the centre, and every thing else was accessory and secondary to it. The old "rows of books," in which Scott so peculiarly delighted, were made to contribute their element to this varied imagination of humanity. From old family histories, odd memoirs, old law-trials, his fancy elicited new traits to add to the motley assemblage. His objection to democracy—an objection of which we can only appreciate the emphatic force, when we remember that his youth was contemporary with the first French Revolution, and the controversy as to the uniform and stereotyped rights of man—was, that it would sweep away this entire picture, level prince and peasant in a common *égalité*,—substitute a scientific rigidity for the irregular and picturesque growth of centuries,—replace an abounding and genial life by a symmetrical but lifeless mechanism. All the descriptions of society in the novels,—whether of feudal society, of modern Scotch society, or of English society,—are largely coloured by this feeling. It peeps out every where, and liberal critics have endeavoured to show that it was a narrow Toryism; but in reality it is a subtle compound of the natural instinct of the artist with the plain sagacity of the man of the world. (pp. 451-53)

The same thoroughly well-grounded sagacity and comprehensive appreciation of human life is shown in the treatment of what we may call *anomalous* characters. In general, monstrosity is no topic for art. Every one has known in real life characters which if, apart from much experience, he had found described in books, he would have thought unnatural and impossible. Scott, however, abounds in such characters. Meg Merrilies, Edie Ochiltree, Radcliffe, are more or less of that description. That of Meg Merrilies especially is as distorted and eccentric as any thing can be. . . . Her career in [*Guy Mannering*] corresponds with the strangeness of her exterior. "Harlot, thief, witch, and gipsy," as she describes herself, the hero is preserved by her virtues; half-crazed as she is described to be, he owes his safety on more than one occasion to her skill in stratagem, and ability in managing those with whom she is connected, and who are most likely to be familiar with her weakness and to detect her craft. Yet on hardly any occasion is the natural reader conscious of this strangeness. Something is of course attributable to the skill of the artist; for no other power of mind could produce the effect, unless it were aided by the unconscious tact of detailed expression. But the fundamental explanation of this remarkable success is the distinctness with which Scott saw how such a character as Meg Merrilies arose and was produced out of the peculiar circumstances of gipsy life in the localities in which he has placed his scene. He has exhibited this to his readers not by lengthy or elaborate description, but by chosen incidents, short comments, and touches of which he scarcely foresaw the effect. This is the only way in which the fundamental objection to making eccentricity the subject of artistic treatment can be obviated. Monstrosity ceases to be such when we discern the laws of nature which evolve it: when a real science explains its phenomena, we find that it is in strict accordance with what we call the natural type, but that some rare adjunct or uncommon casualty has interfered and distorted a nature which is really the same, into a phenomenon which is altogether different. Just so with eccentricity in human character; it becomes

a topic of literary art only when its identity with the ordinary principles of human nature is exhibited in the midst of, and, as it were, by means of, the superficial unlikeness. Such a skill, however, requires an easy careless familiarity with usual human life and common human conduct. A writer must have a sympathy with health before he can show us how, and where, and to what extent, that which is unhealthy deviates from it; and it is this consistent acquaintance with regular life which makes the irregular characters of Scott so happy a contrast to the uneasy distortions of less sagacious novelists.

A good deal of the same criticism may be applied to the delineation which Scott has given us of the *poor*. . . . His poor people are never coarse and never vulgar; their lineaments have the rude traits which a life of conflict will inevitably leave on the minds and manners of those who are to lead it; their notions have the narrowness which is inseparable from a contracted experience; their knowledge is not more extended than their restricted means of attaining it would render possible. Almost alone among novelists Scott has given a thorough, minute, life-like description of poor persons, which is at the same time genial and pleasing. The reason seems to be, that the firm sagacity of his genius comprehended the industrial aspect of poor people's life thoroughly and comprehensively, his experience brought it before him easily and naturally, and his artist's mind and genial disposition enabled him to dwell on those features which would be most pleasing to the world in general. In fact, his own mind of itself and by its own nature dwelt on those very peculiarities. He could not remove his firm and instructed genius into the domain of Arcadian unreality, but he was equally unable to dwell principally, peculiarly, or consecutively, on those petty, vulgar, mean details in which such a writer as Crabbe lives and breathes. Hazlitt said that Crabbe described a poor man's cottage like a man who came to distrain for rent; he catalogued every trivial piece of furniture, defects and cracks and all. Scott describes it as a cheerful but most sensible landlord would describe a cottage on his property: he has a pleasure in it. No detail, or few details, in the life of the inmates escape his experienced and interested eye; but he dwells on those which do not displease him. He sympathises with their rough industry and plain joys and sorrows. He does not fatigue, or excite their wondering smile by theoretical plans of impossible relief. He makes the best of the life which is given, and by a sanguine sympathy makes it still better. A hard life many characters in Scott seem to lead; but he appreciates, and makes his readers appreciate, the full value of natural feelings, plain thoughts, and applied sagacity.

His ideas of political economy are equally characteristic of his stong sense and genial mind. He was always sneering at Adam Smith, and telling many legends of that philosopher's absence of mind and inaptitude for the ordinary conduct of life. A contact with the Edinburgh logicians had, doubtless, not augmented his faith in the formal deductions of abstract economy; nevertheless, with the facts before him, he could give a very plain and satisfactory exposition of the genial consequences of old abuses, the distinct necessity for stern reform, and the delicate humanity requisite for introducing that reform temperately and with feeling. (pp. 453-56)

Many other indications of the same healthy and natural sense, which gives so much of their characteristic charm to the Scotch novels, might be pointed out, if it were necessary to weary our readers by dwelling longer on a point we have already laboured so much; one more, however, demands notice because of its importance, and perhaps also because, from its somewhat less obvious character, it might escape otherwise without notice. There has been frequent controversy as to the penal code, if we may so call it, of fiction; that is, as to the apportionment of reward and punishment respectively to the good and evil personages therein delineated; and the practice of authors has been as various as the legislation of critics. One school abandons all thought on the matter, and declares that in the real life we see around us good people often fail, and wicked people continually prosper; and would deduce the precept, that it is unwise in an art which should hold the "mirror up to nature," not to copy the uncertain and irregular distribution of its sanctions. Another school, with an exactness which savours at times of pedantry, apportions the success and the failure, the pain and the pleasure, of fictitious life to the moral qualities of those who are living in it—does not think at all, or but little, of every other quality in those characters, and does not at all care whether the penalty and reward are evolved in natural sequence from the circumstances and characters of the tale, or are owing to some monstrous accident far removed from all relation of cause or consequence to those facts and people. Both these classes of writers produce works which jar on the natural sense of common readers, and are at issue with the analytic criticism of the best critics. One school leaves an impression of an uncared-for world, in which there is no right and no wrong; the other, of a sort of Governesses' Institution of a world, where all praise and all blame, all good and all pain, are made to turn on special graces and petty offences, pesteringly spoken of and teasingly watched for. The manner of Scott is thoroughly different; you can scarcely lay down any novel of his without a strong feeling that the world in which the fiction has been laid, and in which your imagination has been moving, is one subject to *laws* of retribution which, though not apparent on a superficial glance, are yet in steady and consistent operation, and will be quite sure to work their due effect, if time is only given to them. Sagacious men know that this is in its best aspect the condition of life. Certain of the ungodly may, notwithstanding the Psalmist, flourish even through life like a green bay-tree; for providence, in external appearance (far differently from the real truth of things, as we may one day see it), works by a scheme of averages. Most people who ought to succeed, do succeed; most people who do fail, ought to fail. But there is no exact adjustment of "mark" to merit; the competitive examination system appears to have an origin more recent than the creation of the world;—"on the whole," "speaking generally," "looking at life as a whole," are the words in which we must describe the providential adjustment of visible good and evil to visible goodness and badness. And when we look more closely, we see that these general results are the consequences of certain principles which work half unseen, and which are effectual in the main, though thwarted here and there. It is this comprehensive though inexact distribution of good and evil, which is suited to the novelist, and it is exactly this which Scott instinctively adopted. Taking a firm and genial view of the common facts of life,—seeing it as an experienced observer and tried man of action,—he could not help giving the representation of it which is insensibly borne in on the minds of such persons. He delineates it as a world moving according to laws which are always producing their effect, never *have* produced it; sometimes fall short a little; are always nearly successful. Good sense produces its effect, as well as good intention; ability is valuable as well as virtue. It is this peculiarity which gives to his works, more than any thing else, the life-likeness which distinguishes them; the average of the copy is struck on the same scale as that of reality; an unexplained, uncommented-on adjustment works in the one,

just as a hidden imperceptible principle of apportionment operates in the other. (pp. 458-59)

[A] romantic tinge undeniably shows itself in Scott's pictures of the past. Many exceptions have been taken to the detail of mediaeval life as it is described to us in *Ivanhoe;* but one merit will always remain to it, and will be enough to secure to it immense popularity. It describes the middle ages as we should have wished them to have been. We do not mean that the delineation satisfies those accomplished admirers of the old church system who fancy that they have found among the prelates and barons of the fourteenth century a close approximation to the theocracy which they would recommend for our adoption. On the contrary, the theological merits of the middle ages are not prominent in Scott's delineation. "Dogma" was not in his way: a cheerful man of the world is not anxious for a precise definition of peculiar doctrines. The charm of *Ivanhoe* is addressed to a simpler sort of imagination,—to that kind of boyish fancy which idolises mediaeval society as the "fighting time." Every boy has heard of tournaments, and has a firm persuasion that in an age of tournaments life was thoroughly well understood. A martial society, where men fought hand to hand on good horses with large lances, in peace for pleasure, and in war for business, seems the very ideal of perfection to a bold and simply fanciful boy. *Ivanhoe* spreads before him the full landscape of such a realm, with Richard Coeur-de-Lion, a black horse, and the passage of arms at Ashby. Of course he admires it, and thinks there was never such a writer, and will never more be such a world. And a mature critic will share his admiration, at least to the extent of admitting that nowhere else have the elements of a martial romance been so gorgeously accumulated without becoming oppressive; their fanciful charm been so powerfully delineated, and yet so constantly relieved by touches of vigorous sagacity. One single fact shows how great the romantic illusion is. The pressure of painful necessity is scarcely so great in this novel as in novels of the same writer in which the scene is laid in modern times. . . . All sensible people know that the middle ages must have been very uncomfortable; there was a difficulty about "good food;"—almost insuperable obstacles to the cultivation of nice detail and small enjoyment. No one knew the abstract facts on which this conclusion rests better than Scott; but his delineation gives no general idea of the result. A thoughtless reader rises with the impression that the middle ages had the same elements of happiness which we have at present, and that they had fighting besides. We do not assert that this tenet is explicitly taught; on the contrary, many facts are explained, and many customs elucidated from which a discriminating and deducing reader would infer the meanness of poverty and the harshness of barbarism. But these less imposing traits escape the rapid, and still more the boyish reader. His general impression is one of romance; and though, when roused, Scott was quite able to take a distinct view of the opposing facts, he liked his own mind to rest for the most part in the same pleasing illusion. (pp. 460-61)

We may . . . sum up the indications of this characteristic excellence of Scott's novels by saying, that more than any novelist he has given us fresh pictures of practical human society, with its cares and troubles, its excitements and its pleasures; that he has delineated more distinctly than any one else the framework in which this society inheres, and by the boundaries of which it is shaped and limited; that he has made more clear the way in which strange and eccentric characters grow out of that ordinary and usual system of life; that he has extended his view over several periods of society, and given an animated description of the external appearance of each, and a firm representation of its social institutions; that he has shown very graphically what we may call the worldly laws of moral government; and that over all these he has spread the glow of sentiment natural to a manly mind, and an atmosphere of generosity congenial to a cheerful one. It is from the collective effect of these causes, and from the union of sense and sentiment which is the principle of them all, that Scott derives the peculiar healthiness which distinguishes him. There are no such books as his for the sick-room, or for freshening the painful intervals of a morbid mind. Mere sense is dull, mere sentiment unsubstantial; a sensation of genial healthiness is only given by what combines the solidity of the one and the brightening charm of the other.

Some guide to Scott's defects, or to the limitations of his genius, if we would employ a less ungenial and perhaps more correct expression, is to be discovered, as usual, from the consideration of his characteristic excellence. As it is his merit to give bold and animated pictures of this world, it is his defect to give but insufficient representations of qualities which this world does not exceedingly prize,—of such as do not thrust themselves very forward in it—of such as are in some sense above it. We may illustrate this in several ways.

One of the parts of human nature which are systematically omitted in Scott, is the searching and abstract intellect. This did not lie in his way. No man had a stronger sagacity, better adapted for the guidance of common men, and the conduct of common transactions. Few could hope to form a more correct opinion on things and subjects which were brought before him in actual life; no man had a more useful intellect. But on the other hand, as will be generally observed to be the case, no one was less inclined to that probing and seeking and anxious inquiry into things in general which is the necessity of some minds, and a sort of intellectual famine in their nature.... The desire to attain a belief, which has become one of the most familiar sentiments of heroes and heroines, would have seemed utterly incongruous to the plain sagacity of Scott, and also to his old-fashioned art. Creeds are *data* in his novels: people have different creeds, but each keeps his own. Some persons will think that this is not altogether amiss; nor do we particularly wish to take up the defence of the dogmatic novel. Nevertheless, it will strike those who are accustomed to the youthful generation of a cultivated time, that the passion of intellectual inquiry is one of the strongest impulses in many of them, and one of those which give the predominant colouring to the conversation and exterior mind of many more. And a novelist will not exercise the most potent influence over those subject to that passion if he entirely omit the delineation of it. Scott's works have only one merit in this relation: they are an excellent rest to those who have felt this passion, and have had something too much of it. (pp. 463-65)

The same limitation of Scott's genius shows itself in a very different portion of art—in his delineation of his heroines. The same blunt sagacity of imagination, which fitted him to excel in the rough description of obvious life, rather unfitted him for delineating the less substantial essence of the female character. The nice *minutiae* of society, by means of which female novelists have been so successful in delineating their own sex, were rather too small for his robust and powerful mind. Perhaps, too, a certain unworldliness of *imagination* is necessary to enable men to comprehend or delineate that essence: unworldliness of *life* is no doubt not requisite; rather, perhaps, worldliness is necessary to the acquisition of a sufficient ex-

perience. But an absorption in the practical world does not seem favourable to a comprehension of any thing which does not precisely belong to it. Its interests are too engrossing; its excitements too keen; it modifies the fancy, and in the change unfits it for every thing else. Something, too, in Scott's character and history made it more difficult for him to give a representation of women than of men. . . . It was rather late, according to his biographer, before Scott set up for "a squire of dames;" he was a "lame young man, very enthusiastic about ballad poetry;" he was deeply in love with a young lady, supposed to be imaginatively represented by Flora MacIvor, but he was unsuccessful. It would be over-ingenious to argue, from his failing in a single love-affair, that he had no peculiar interest in young ladies in general; but the whole description of his youth shows that young ladies exercised over him a rather more divided influence than is usual. Other pursuits intervened, much more than is common with persons of the imaginative temperament. . . . Scott's heroines, therefore, are, not unnaturally, faulty, since from a want of the very peculiar instinctive imagination he could not give us the essence of women, and from the habits of his life he could not delineate to us their detailed life with the appreciative accuracy of habitual experience. Jeanie Deans is probably the best of his heroines, and she is so because she is the least of a heroine. The plain matter-of-fact element in the peasant-girl's life and circumstances suited a robust imagination. There is little in the part of her character that is very finely described which is characteristically feminine. She is not a masculine, but she is an epicene heroine. Her love-affair with Butler, a single remarkable scene excepted, is rather commonplace than otherwise.

A similar criticism might be applied to Scott's heroes. Every one feels how commonplace they are—Waverley excepted, whose very vacillation gives him a sort of character. They have little personality. They are all of the same type;—excellent young men—rather strong—able to ride and climb and jump. They are always said to be sensible, and bear out the character by being not unwilling sometimes to talk platitudes. But we know nothing of their inner life. They are said to be in love, but we have no special account of their individual sentiments. People show their character in their love more than in any thing else. These young gentlemen all love in the same way—in the vague commonplace way of this world. We have no sketch or dramatic expression of the life within. Their souls are quite unknown to us. (pp. 465-68)

On the whole, and speaking roughly, [the] defects in the delineation which Scott has given us of human life are but two. He omits to give us a delineation of the soul. We have mind, manners, animation, but it is the stir of this world. We miss the consecrating power; and we miss it not only in its own peculiar sphere, which, from the difficulty of introducing the deepest elements into a novel, would have been scarcely matter for a harsh criticism, but in the place in which a novelist might most be expected to delineate it. There are perhaps such things as the love-affairs of immortal beings, but no one would learn it from Scott. His heroes and heroines are well dressed for this world, but not for another; there is nothing even in their love which is suitable for immortality. As has been noticed, Scott also omits any delineation of the abstract unworldly intellect. This too might not have been so severe a reproach, considering its undramatic, unanimated nature, if it had stood alone; but taken in connection with the omission which we have just spoken of, it is most important. As the union of sense and romance makes the world of Scott so characteristically agreeable,—a fascinating picture of this world in the light in which we like best to dwell in it, so the deficiency in the attenuated, striving intellect, as well as in the supernatural soul, gives to the ''world'' of Scott the cumbrousness and temporality, in short, the materialism, which is characteristic of the world. (p. 470)

Walter Bagehot, ''The 'Waverley Novels','' in The National Review, *London, Vol. VI, No. XII, April, 1858, pp. 444-72.*

H. A. TAINE (essay date 1863)

[*Taine was a French philosopher, critic, and historian who studied the influence of environment and heredity on the development of human character. In his well-known work,* Histoire de la littérature anglaise, *from which the following excerpt is drawn, Taine analyzes literature through a study of race and milieu. Here, he examines Scott's approach to history, discussing the relationship between his cultural background and his failure to delve into the deeper and darker aspects of human nature. Taine's commentary was first published in French in 1863.*]

The Lady of the Lake, Marmion, The Lord of the Isles, The Fair Maid of Perth, Old Mortality, Ivanhoe, Quentin Durward, who does not know these names by heart? From Walter Scott we learned history. And yet is this history? All these pictures of a distant age are false. Costumes, scenery, externals alone are exact; actions, speech, sentiments, all the rest is civilised, embellished, arranged in modern guise. We might suspect it when looking at the character and life of the author; for what does he desire, and what do the guests, eager to hear him, demand? Is he a lover of truth as it is, foul and fierce; an inquisitive explorer, indifferent to contemporary applause, bent alone on defining the transformations of living nature? By no means. He is in history, as he is at Abbotsford, bent on arranging points of view and Gothic halls. The moon will come in well there between the towers; here is a nicely placed breast-plate, the ray of light which it throws back is pleasant to see on these old hangings; suppose we took out the feudal garments from the wardrobe and invited the guests to a masquerade? The entertainment would be a fine one, in accordance with their reminiscences and their aristocratic principles. English lords, fresh from a bitter war against French democracy, ought to enter zealously into this commemoration of their ancestors. Moreover, there are ladies and young girls, and we must arrange the show, so as not to shock their severe morality and their delicate feelings, make them weep becomingly; not put on the stage overstrong passions, which they would not understand; on the contrary, select heroines to resemble them, always touching, but above all correct; young gentlemen, Evandale, Morton, Ivanhoe, irreproachably brought up, tender and grave, even slightly melancholic (it is the latest fashion), and worthy to lead them to the altar. Is there a man more suited than the author to compose such a spectacle? He is a good Protestant, a good husband, a good father, very moral, so decided a Tory that he carries off as a relic a glass from which the king has just drunk. In addition, he has neither talent nor leisure to reach the depths of his characters. He devotes himself to the exterior; he sees and describes forms and externals much more at length than inward feelings. Again, he treats his mind like a coal-mine, serviceable for quick working, and for the greatest possible gain: a volume in a month, sometimes in a fortnight even, and this volume is worth one thousand pounds. How should he discover, or how dare exhibit, the structure of barbarous souls? This structure is too difficult to discover, and

too little pleasing to show. Every two centuries, amongst men, the proportion of images and ideas, the mainspring of passions, the degree of reflection, the species of inclinations, change. Who, without a long preliminary training, now understands and relishes Dante, Rabelais, and Rubens? And how, for instance, could these great Catholic and mystical dreams, these vast temerities, or these impurities of carnal art, find entrance into the head of this gentlemanly citizen? Walter Scott pauses on the threshold of the soul, and in the vestibule of history, selects in the Renaissance and the Middle-age only the fit and agreeable, blots out plain spoken words, licentious sensuality, bestial ferocity. After all, his characters, to whatever age he transports them, are his neighbours, ''cannie'' farmers, vain lairds, gloved gentlemen, young marriageable ladies, all more or less commonplace, that is, steady; by their education and character at a great distance from the voluptuous fools of the Restoration, or the heroic brutes and fierce beasts of the Middle-age. As he has the greatest supply of rich costumes, and the most inexhaustible talent for scenic effect, he makes all his people get on very pleasantly, and composes tales which, in truth, have only the merit of fashion, though that fashion may last a hundred years yet.

That which he himself acted lasted for a shorter time. To sustain his princely hospitality and his feudal magnificence, he went into partnership with his printers; lord of the manor in public and merchant in private, he gave them his signature, without keeping a check over the use they made of it. Bankruptcy followed; at the age of fifty-five he was ruined, and one hundred and seventeen thousand pounds in debt. With admirable courage and uprightness he refused all favour, accepting nothing but time, set to work on the very day, wrote untiringly, in four years paid seventy thousand pounds, exhausted his brain so as to become paralytic, and to perish in the attempt. Neither in his conduct nor his literature did his feudal tastes succeed, and his manorial splendour was as fragile as his Gothic imaginations. He had relied on imitation, and we live by truth only; his glory is to be found elsewhere; there was something solid in his mind as well as in his writings. Beneath the lover of the Middle-age we find, first the ''pawky'' Scotchman, an attentive observer, whose sharpness became more intense by his familiarity with law; a good-natured man, easy and cheerful, as beseems the national character, so different from the English. (pp. 434-37)

In addition to a mind of this kind, he had all-discerning eyes, an all-retentive memory, a ceaseless studiousness which comprehended the whole of Scotland, and all classes of people; and we see his true talent arise, so agreeable, so abundant and so easy, made up of minute observation and gentle raillery, recalling at once Teniers and Addison. Doubtless he wrote badly, at times in the worst possible manner: it is clear that he dictated, hardly re-read his writing, and readily fell into a pasty and emphatic style,—a style very common in the present times, and which we read day after day in prospectuses and newspapers. What is worse, he is terribly long and diffuse; his conversations and descriptions are interminable; he is determined, at all events, to fill three volumes. But he has given to Scotland a citizenship of literature—I mean to the whole of Scotland: scenery, monuments, houses, cottages, characters of every age and condition, from the baron to the fisherman, from the advocate to the beggar, from the lady to the fishwife. When we mention merely his name they crowd forward; who does not see them coming from every niche of memory? The Baron of Bradwardine, Dominie Sampson, Meg Merrilies, the antiquary, Edie Ochiltree, Jeanie Deans and her father,—inn-

A portrait of Scott by Sir David Wilkie. Scottish National Portrait Gallery.

keepers, shopkeepers, old wives, an entire people. What Scotch features are absent? Saving, patient, "cannie," and of course "pawky;" the poverty of the soil and the difficulty of existence has compelled them to be so: this is the specialty of the race. The same tenacity which they introduced into everyday affairs they have introduced into mental concerns,—studious readers and perusers of antiquities and controversies, poets also; legends spring up readily in a romantic land, amidst time-honoured wars and brigandism. In a land thus prepared, and in this gloomy clime, Presbyterianism sunk its sharp roots. Such was the real and modern world, lit up by the far-setting sun of chivalry, as Sir Walter Scott found it; like a painter who, passing from great show-pictures, finds interest and beauty in the ordinary houses of a paltry provincial town, or in a farm surrounded by beds of beetroots and turnips. A continuous archness throws its smile over these interior and *genre* pictures, so local and minute, and which, like the Flemish, indicate the rise of well-to-do citizens. Most of these good folk are comic. Our author makes fun of them, brings out their little deceits, parsimony, fooleries, vulgarity, and the hundred thousand ridiculous habits people always contract in a narrow sphere of life. A barber, in *The Antiquary,* moves heaven and earth about his wigs; if the French Revolution takes root everywhere, it was because the magistrates gave up this ornament. He cries out in a lamentable voice: "Haud a care, haud a care, Monkbarns! God's sake, haud a care!—Sir Arthur's drowned already, and an ye fa' over the cleugh too, there will be but ae wig left in the parish, and that's the minister's." Mark how the author smiles, and without malice: the barber's candid selfishness is the effect of the man's calling, and does not repel us. Walter Scott is never bitter; he loves men from the bottom

of his heart, excuses or tolerates them; does not chastise vices, but unmasks them, and that not rudely. His greatest pleasure is to pursue at length, not indeed a vice, but a hobby; the mania for odds and ends in an antiquary, the archaeological vanity of the Baron of Bradwardine, the aristocratic drivel of the Dowager Lady Bellenden,—that is, the amusing exaggeration of an allowable taste; and this without anger, because, on the whole, these ridiculous people are estimable, and even generous. Even in rogues like Dirk Hatteraick, in cut-throats like Bothwell, he allows some goodness. In no one, not even in Major Dalgetty, a professional murderer, a result of the thirty years' war, is the odious unveiled by the ridiculous. In this critical refinement and this benevolent philosophy, he resembles Addison.

He resembles him again by the purity and endurance of his moral principles. His amanuensis, Mr. Laidlaw, told him that he was doing great good by his attractive and noble tales, and that young people would no longer wish to look in the literary rubbish of the circulating libraries. When Walter Scott heard this, his eyes filled with tears: "On his deathbed he said to his son-in-law: 'Lockhart, I may have but a minute to speak to you. My dear, be a good man—be virtuous, be religious—be a good man. Nothing else will give you any comfort when you come to lie here'" [see Additional Bibliography]. This was almost his last word. By this fundamental honesty and this broad humanity, he was the Homer of modern citizen life. (pp. 438-41)

> H. A. Taine, "Ideas and Productions," in his History of English Literature, Vol. III, *translated by H. Van Laun, 1889. Reprint by Henry Holt and Company, 1904, pp. 381-462.*

[HENRY JAMES]   (essay date 1864)

[*James was an American-born English novelist, short story writer, critic, and essayist of the late nineteenth and early twentieth centuries. He is regarded as one of the greatest novelists of the English language and is also admired as a lucid and insightful critic. In the following excerpt, James surveys Scott's accomplishments as a novelist, discussing his innovations, limitations, and enduring appeal as a storyteller.*]

Thirty years have elapsed since the publication of the last of the *Waverley* series. During thirty years it has been exposed to the public view. And meanwhile an immense deal has been accomplished in the department of fiction. A vast army has sprung up, both of producers and consumers. To the latter class a novel is no longer the imposing phenomenon it was in Sir Walter's time. It implies no very great talent; ingenuity is held to be the chief requisite for success. And indeed to write a readable novel is actually a task of so little apparent difficulty, that with many popular writers the matter is a constant trial of speed with the reading public. This was very much the case with Sir Walter. His facility in composition was almost as great as that of Mrs. Henry Wood, of modern repute. But it was the fashion among his critics to attribute this remarkable fact rather to his transcendent strength than to the vulgarity of his task. This was a wise conviction. Mrs. Wood writes three volumes in three months, to last three months. Sir Walter performed the same feat, and here, after the lapse of forty years, we still linger over those hasty pages. And we do it in the full cognizance of faults which even Mrs. Wood has avoided, of foibles for which she would blush. The public taste has been educated to a spirit of the finest discernment, the sternest exaction. No publisher would venture to offer *Ivanhoe* in the year 1864 as a novelty. The secrets of the novelist's craft have been laid bare; new contrivances have been invented; and as fast as the old machinery wears out, it is repaired by the clever artisans of the day. Our modern ingenuity works prodigies of which the great Wizard never dreamed. And besides ingenuity we have had plenty of genius. We have had Dickens and Thackeray. Twenty other famous writers are working in the midst of us. The authors of *Amyas Leigh*, of *The Cloister and the Hearth*, of *Romola*, have all overtaken the author of *Waverley* in his own walk. Sir Edward Bulwer has produced several historical tales, which, to use an expressive vulgarism, have "gone down" very extensively. And yet old-fashioned, ponderous Sir Walter holds his own.

He was the inventor of a new style. We all know the immense advantage a craftsman derives from this fact. He was the first to sport a fashion which was eventually taken up. For many years he enjoyed the good fortune of a patentee. It is difficult for the present generation to appreciate the blessings of this fashion. But when we review the modes prevailing for twenty years before, we see almost as great a difference as a sudden transition from the Spenserian ruff to the Byronic collar. We may best express Scott's character by saying that, with one or two exceptions, he was the first English prose story-teller. He was the first fictitious writer who addressed the public from its own level, without any preoccupation of place. . . . To posterity one of the chief attractions of *Tom Jones* is the fact that its author was one of the masses, that he wrote from the midst of the working, suffering mortal throng. But we feel guilty in reading the book in any such disposition of mind. We feel guilty, indeed, in admitting the question of art or science into our considerations. The story is like a vast episode in a sermon preached by a grandly humorous divine; and however we may be entertained by the way, we must not forget that our ultimate duty is to be instructed. With the minister's week-day life we have no concern: for the present he is awful, impersonal Morality; and we shall incur his severest displeasure if we view him as Henry Fielding, Esq., as a rakish man of letters, or even as a figure in English literature. *Waverley* was the first novel which was self-forgetful. It proposed simply to amuse the reader, as an old English ballad amused him. It undertook to prove nothing but facts. It was the novel irresponsible.

We do not mean to say that Scott's great success was owing solely to this, the freshness of his method. This was, indeed, of great account, but it was as nothing compared with his own intellectual wealth. Before him no prose-writer had exhibited so vast and rich an imagination: it had not, indeed, been supposed that in prose the imaginative faculty was capable of such extended use. Since Shakespeare, no writer had created so immense a gallery of portraits, nor, on the whole, had any portraits been so lifelike. Men and women, for almost the first time out of poetry, were presented in their habits as they lived. The *Waverley* characters were all instinct with something of the poetic fire. To our present taste many of them may seem little better than lay-figures. But there are many kinds of lay-figures. A person who goes from the workshop of a carver of figure-heads for ships to an exhibition of wax-work, will find in the latter the very reflection of nature. And even when occasionally the waxen visages are somewhat inexpressive, he can console himself with the sight of unmistakable velvet and brocade and tartan. Scott went to his prose task with essentially the same spirit which he had brought to the composition of his poems. Between these two departments of his work the difference is very small. Portions of *Marmion* are very good prose; portions of *Old Mortality* are tolerable poetry. Scott was never

a very deep, intense, poetic poet; his verse alone was unflagging. So when he attacked his prose characters with his habitual poetic inspiration, the harmony of style was hardly violated. It is a great peculiarity, and perhaps it is one of the charms of his historical tales, that history is dealt with in all poetic reverence. He is tender of the past: he knows that she is frail. He certainly knows it. Sir Walter could not have read so widely or so curiously as he did, without discovering a vast deal that was gross and ignoble in bygone times. But he excludes these elements as if he feared they would clash with his numbers. He has the same indifference to historic truth as an epic poet, without, in the novels, having the same excuse. We write historical tales differently now. We acknowledge the beauty and propriety of a certain poetic reticence. But we confine it to poetry. The task of the historical story-teller is, not to invest, but to divest the past. Tennyson's *Idyls of the King* are far more one-sided, if we may so express it, than anything of Scott's. But imagine what disclosures we should have if Mr. Charles Reade were to take it into his head to write a novel about King Arthur and his times.

Having come thus far, we are arrested by the sudden conviction that it is useless to dogmatize upon Scott; that it is almost ungrateful to criticise him. He, least of all, would have invited or sanctioned any curious investigation of his works. They were written without pretence: all that has been claimed for them has been claimed by others than their author. They are emphatically works of entertainment. As such let us cherish and preserve them. Say what we will, we should be very sorry to lose, and equally sorry to mend them. There are few of us but can become sentimental over the uncounted hours they have cost us. There are moments of high-strung sympathy with the spirit which is abroad when we might find them rather dull—in parts; but they are capital books to have read. Who would forego the companionship of all those shadowy figures which stand side by side in their morocco niches in yonder mahogany cathedral? What youth would willingly close his eyes upon that dazzling array of female forms,—so serried that he can hardly see where to choose,—Rebecca of York, Edith Plantagenet, Mary of Scotland, sweet Lucy Ashton? What maiden would consent to drop the dear acquaintance of Halbert Glendinning, of Wilfred of Ivanhoe, of Roland Graeme and Henry Morton? Scott was a born story-teller: we can give him no higher praise. Surveying his works, his character, his method, as a whole, we can liken him to nothing better than to a strong and kindly elder brother, who gathers his juvenile public about him at eventide, and pours out a stream of wondrous improvisation. Who cannot remember an experience like this? On no occasion are the delights of fiction so intense. Fiction? These are the triumphs of fact. In the richness of his invention and memory, in the infinitude of his knowledge, in his improvidence for the future, in the skill with which he answers, or rather parries, sudden questions, in his low-voiced pathos and his resounding merriment, he is identical with the ideal fireside chronicler. And thoroughly to enjoy him, we must again become as credulous as children at twilight. (pp. 583-87)

> *[Henry James], "Senior's Essays on Fiction," in* The North American Review, *Vol. XCIX, No. 205, October, 1864, pp. 580-87.*

[LESLIE STEPHEN]   (essay date 1871)

> *[Stephen is considered one of the most important English literary critics of the late Victorian and early Edwardian eras. In his criticism, which is often moralistic, Stephen argued that all lit-*

erature is nothing more than an imaginative rendering, in concrete terms, of a writer's philosophy or beliefs. In the following excerpt, Stephen offers a broad assessment of Scott's place in English literature, using Carlyle's review of Lockhart's Life *(see excerpt dated 1838) as a guideline for his remarks. The topics discussed here include Scott's desire to profit financially from his works, spontaneous method of writing, inability to depict profound thoughts and emotions, romantic imagination, and portrayal of the pleasures of the "healthy open-air life."*]

Various enthusiastic persons have recently been celebrating the centenary of Sir W. Scott's birth. Some people may possibly inquire whether there is any particular reason for remembering a man at the distance of precisely one hundred years from his first appearance in the world. Would not a more appropriate epoch be at the expiration of a similar period from the appearance of the *Lay of the Last Minstrel,* or of *Waverley*? And that suggests the further question whether the celebration, if postponed to the year 1905 or 1914, would produce any vivid enthusiasm. The doubt would have seemed profane a very few years ago; and yet we may already, perhaps, find some reason for suspecting that the great "Wizard" has lost some of his magic power, and that the warmth of our first love is departed. How many of those ladies and gentlemen who recently appeared in costume at the Waverley Ball were able to draw upon the stores of their memory, and how many were forced to cram for the occasion? A question, perhaps, not to be asked; but certainly one not to be answered with too much confidence by those who reflect upon the stock of information generally at the disposal of a well-educated English man or woman. We have heard it said—in private, be it understood, for such utterances do not so easily find their way into print, and least of all do they intrude into the speeches of centenary orators—that Scott is dull. People whisper dark hints of their hesitating allegiance to literary monarchs before the voice of rebellion swells into open expression. Yet even a muttered discontent sounds strange to middle-aged persons, who, in their schoolboy days, could spout the Death of Marmion or the Description of Melrose Abbey, till wise elders checked their undue excitement, or who followed with breathless interest the heroics of Meg Merrilies, and felt for the gallant Locksley almost as warm an enthusiasm as for the immortal Shaw the Lifeguardsman. Perhaps even the fame of that hero is growing dim. We don't talk about the Battle of Waterloo so much as formerly, and should rather blush to quote the "Up, Guards, and at them," even if historical criticism had not ruined that with so many other fine phrases. And yet, to couple the name of Scott with dulness sounds profane, especially when one remembers the kind of literature which is bought with avidity at railway bookstalls, and, for some mysterious reason, supposed to be amusing. If Scott is to be called dull, what reputation is to be pronounced safe? (p. 278)

Let us . . . take courage, and, with such impartiality as we may possess, endeavour to sift the wheat from the chaff. And, by way of following a safe guide, let us dwell for a little on the judgment pronounced upon Scott by one whose name should never be mentioned without profound respect, [Mr. Carlyle]. (p. 280)

The faults upon which he dwells are, of course, those which are more or less acknowledged by all sound critics. Scott, says Mr. Carlyle, had no great gospel to deliver; he had nothing of the martyr about him; he slew no monsters and stirred no deep emotions. He did not believe in anything, and did not even disbelieve in anything: he was content to take the world as it came—the false and the true mixed indistinguishably to-

gether. . . . He was a thoroughly healthy, sound, vigorous Scotchman, with an eye for the main chance, but not much of an eye for the eternities. And that unfortunate commercial element, which caused the misery of his life, was equally mischievous to his work. He cared for no results of his working but such as could be seen by the eye, and, in one sense or other, "handled, looked at, and buttoned into the breeches' pocket." . . . And then he fell into the modern sin of extempore writing, and deluged the world with the first hasty overflowings of his mind, instead of straining and refining it till he could bestow the pure essence upon us. In short, his career is summed up in the phrase that it was "writing impromptu novels to buy farms with"—a melancholy end, truly, for a man of rare genius. Nothing is sadder than to hear of such a man "writing himself out;" and it is pitiable, indeed, that Scott should be the example of that fate which rises most naturally to our minds. "Something very perfect in its kind," says Mr. Carlyle, "might have come from Scott, nor was it a low kind—nay, who knows how high, with studious self-concentration, he might have gone: what wealth nature implanted in him, which his circumstances, most unkind while seeming to be kindest, had never impelled him to unfold?"

There is undoubtedly some truth in the severer criticisms to which some more kindly sentences are a pleasant relief; and there is something too which most persons will be apt to consider as rather harsher than necessary. Is not the moral preacher intruding a little too much on the province of the literary critic? In fact we fancy that, in the midst of these energetic remarks, Mr. Carlyle is conscious of certain half-expressed doubts. The name of Shakspeare occurs several times in the course of his remarks, and suggests to us that we can hardly condemn Scott whilst acquitting the greatest name in our literature. Scott, it seems, wrote for money; he coined his brains into cash to buy farms. Well, and did not Shakspeare do pretty much the same? As Mr. Carlyle himself puts it, "beyond drawing audiences to the Globe Theatre, Shakspeare contemplated no result in those plays of his." (pp. 281-82)

To write for money was once held to be disgraceful; and Byron, as we know, taunted Scott, because his publishers combined

To yield their muse just half-a-crown a line;

whilst Scott seems half to admit that his conduct required justification, and urges that he sacrificed to literature very fair chances in his original profession. Many people might, perhaps, be disposed to take a bolder line of defence. Cut out of English fiction all that which has owed its birth more or less to a desire of earning money honourably, and the residue would be painfully small. The truth, indeed, seems to be simple. No good work is done when the one impelling motive is the desire of making a little money; but some of the best work that has ever been done, has been indirectly due to the impecuniosity of the labourers. When a man is empty he makes a very poor job of it, in straining colourless trash from his hardbound brains; but when his mind is full to bursting he may still require the spur of a moderate craving for cash to induce him to take the decisive plunge. Scott illustrates both cases. The melancholy drudgery of his later years was forced from him in spite of nature; but nobody ever wrote more spontaneously than Scott when he was composing his early poems and novels. If the precedent of Shakspeare is good for anything, it is good for this. Shakspeare, it may be, had a more moderate ambition; but there seems to be no reason why the desire of a good house at Stratford should be intrinsically nobler than the desire of a fine estate at Abbotsford. But then, it is urged, Scott allowed himself to write with preposterous haste. And Shakspeare, who never blotted a line? What is the great difference between them? Mr. Carlyle feels that here too Scott has at least a very good precedent to allege; but he endeavours to establish a distinction. It was right, he says, for Shakspeare to write rapidly, "being ready to do it. And herein truly lies the secret of the matter; such swiftness of writing, after due energy of preparation, is, doubtless, the right method; the hot furnace having long worked and simmered, let the pure gold flow out at one gush." Could there be a better description of Scott in his earlier years? He published his first poem of any pretensions at thirty-four, an age which Shelley and Keats never reached, and which Byron only passed by two years. *Waverley* came out when he was forty-three—most of our modern novelists have written themselves out long before they arrive at that respectable period of life. From a child he had been accumulating the knowledge and the thoughts that at last found expression in his work. He had been a teller of stories before he was well in breeches; and had worked hard till middle life in accumulating vast stores of picturesque imagery. The delightful notes to all his books give us some impression of the fulness of mind which poured forth a boundless torrent of anecdote to the guests at Abbotsford. We only repine at the prodigality of the harvest when we forget the long process of culture by which it was produced. And, more than this, when we look at the peculiar characteristics of Scott's style—that easy flow of narrative never heightening into epigram, but always full of a charm of freshness and fancy most difficult to analyze—we may well doubt whether much labour would have improved or injured him. No man ever depended more on the perfectly spontaneous flow of his narratives. . . . Scott skims off the cream of his varied stores of popular tradition and antiquarian learning with strange facility; but he had tramped through many a long day's march, and pored over innumerable ballads and forgotten writers before he had anything to skim. Had he not—if we may use the word without offence—been cramming all his life, and practising the art of storytelling every day he lived? Probably the most striking incidents of his books are in reality mere modifications of anecdotes which he had rehearsed a hundred times before, just disguised enough to fit into his story. . . . He was an impromptu composer, in the sense that when his anecdotes once reached paper, they flowed rapidly, and were little corrected; but the correction must have been substantially done in many cases long before they appeared in the state of "copy."

Let us, however, pursue the indictment a little further. Scott did not believe in anything in particular. Yet once more, did Shakspeare? There is surely a poetry of doubt as well as a poetry of conviction, or what shall we say to *Hamlet?* Appearing in such an age as the end of the last and the beginning of this century, Scott could but share the intellectual atmosphere in which he was born, and at that day, whatever we may think of this, few people had any strong faith to boast of. Why should not a poet stand aside from the chaos of conflicting opinions, so far as he was able to extricate himself from the unutterable confusion around them, and show us what was beautiful in the world as he saw it, without striving to combine the office of prophet with his more congenial occupation? Some such answer might be worked out; but we begin to feel a certain hesitation as to the soundness of our argument. Mr. Carlyle did not mean to urge so feeble a criticism as that Scott had no very uncompromising belief in the Thirty-nine Articles; for that is a weakness which he would share with many undeniably good writers. The criticism points to a different and more unfortunate deficiency. "While Shakspeare works from the heart outwards, Scott," says Mr. Carlyle, "works from the skin inwards, never getting near the heart of men." The books are addressed entirely to the every-day mind. They have nothing to do with emotions or principles, beyond those of the ordinary country gentleman; and, we may add, of the country gentleman with his digestion in good order, and his hereditary gout still in the distant future. The more inspiring thoughts, the deeper passions, are altogether beyond his range. If in his width of sympathy, and his vivid perception of character within certain limits, he reminds us of Shakspeare, we can find no analogy in his writings to the passion of *Romeo and Juliet,* or to the intellectual agony of *Hamlet.* The charge, we see, is not really that Scott lacks faith, but that he never appeals, one way or the other, to the faculties which make faith a vital necessity to some natures, or lead to a desperate revolt against established faiths in others. If Byron and Scott could have been combined; if the energetic passions of the one could have been joined to the healthy nature and quick sympathies of the other, we might have seen another Shakspeare in the nineteenth century. As it is, both of them are maimed and imperfect on different sides. It is, in fact, remarkable how Scott fails when he attempts a flight into the regions where he is less at home than in his ordinary style. (pp. 283-85)

As long as Scott keeps to his strong ground, his figures are as good flesh and blood as ever walked in the Salt-market of Glasgow; when once he tries his heroics, he manufactures his characters from the materials used by the frequenters of masked balls. There are, indeed, occasions, on which his genius does not so signally desert him. Balfour of Burley may rub shoulders against genuine Covenanters, and west-country Whigs without betraying his fictitious origin. The Master of Ravenswood attitudinizes a little too much with his Spanish cloak and his slouched hat; but we feel really sorry for him when he disappears in the Kelpie's Flow. And when Scott has to do with his own peasants, with the thoroughbred Presbyterian Scotchman, he can bring real tragic events from his homely materials. Douce Davie Deans, distracted between his religious principles and his desire of saving his daughter's life, and seeking relief even in the midst of his agonies, by that admirable burst of spiritual pride: "Though I will neither exalt myself nor pull down others, I wish that every man and woman in this land had kept the true testimony and the middle and straight path, as it were on the ridge of a hill, where wind and water steals, avoiding right-hand snares and extremes, and left-hand way-slidings, as well as Johnny Dodds of Farthy's acre and ae man mair that shall be nameless''—Davie, we say, is as admirable a figure as ever appeared in fiction. It is a pity that he was mixed up with the conventional madwoman, Madge Wildfire, and that a story most touching in its native simplicity, was twisted and tortured into needless intricacy. These pathetic passages, with others that might be mentioned, imply after all a rather narrow compass of feeling. The religious exaltation of Balfour, or the religious pigheadedness of Davie Deans, are picturesquely described; but they are given from the point of view of the kindly humorist, rather than of one who can sympathize with the sublimity of an intense faith in a homely exterior. And though many good judges hold the ***Bride of Lammermoor*** to be Scott's best performance, in virtue of the loftier passions which animate the chief actors in the tragedy, we are, after all, called upon to sympathize rather with the gentleman of good family who can't ask his friends to dinner without an unworthy device to hide his poverty, than with the passionate lover whose mistress has her heart broken. Surely this is the vulgarest side of the story. Scott, in short, fails unmistakeably in pure passion of all kinds; and for that reason his heroes are for the most part mere wooden blocks to hang a story on. . . .

[We] must confess that this is a considerable drawback from Scott's novels. To take the passion out of a novel is something like taking the sunlight out of a landscape; and to condemn all the heroes to be utterly commonplace is to remove the centre of interest in a manner detrimental to the best intents of the story.... We long to dismount these insipid creatures from the pride of place, and to supplant them by some of the admirable characters who are doomed to play subsidiary parts. And yet we may fairly assert that after many deductions there remains a whole gallery of portraits which could have been drawn by none but a master. If Scott has contributed no great characters, like Hamlet, or Don Quixote, or Mephistopheles, to the world of fiction, he is the undisputed parent of a whole population full of enduring vitality, and, if rising to no ideal standard, yet reflecting with unrivalled clearness the characteristics of some of the strongest and sturdiest of the races of man.

If, indeed, Scott, feeling instinctively that lofty passion was out of his reach, had confined himself to the ordinary daylight of common sense and common nature, he would have perhaps left more enduring work, though he would have produced a less marked impression at the time. Unluckily, or luckily,—who shall say which?—he took to that "buff-jerkin" business of which Mr. Carlyle speaks so contemptuously, and fairly carried away the hearts of his contemporaries by a lavish display of mediaeval upholstery. Lockhart tells us that Scott could not bear the commonplace daubings of walls with uniform coats of white, blue, and grey. All the roofs at Abbotsford "were, in appearance at least, of carved oak, relieved by coats-of-arms duly blazoned at the intersections of beams, and resting on cornices, to the eye, of the same material, but composed of casts in plaster of Paris, after the foliage, the flowers, the grotesque monsters and dwarfs, and sometimes the beautiful heads of nuns and confessors, on which he had doated from infancy among the cloisters of Melrose Abbey." That anecdote, recounted by the admiring Lockhart, gives the true secret of all Scott's failures. The plaster looks as well as the carved oak—for a time; but the day speedily comes when the sham crumbles into ashes, and Scott's knights and nobles, like his carved cornices, became dust in the next generation. It is hard to say it, and yet we fear it must be admitted that the whole of those historical novels, which once charmed all men, and for which we have still a lingering affection, are rapidly converting themselves into mere débris of plaster of Paris. Even our dear *Ivanhoe* is on the high-road to ruin; it is vanishing as fast as one of Sir Joshua's most carelessly painted pictures; and perhaps we ought not to regret it. (pp. 285-87)

[The] miserable taint of unreality threatens Scott's genius more than any other defect; and so far Mr. Carlyle's verdict can hardly be disputed. Already we have lost our love of buff jerkins and other scraps from mediaeval museums, and Scott is suffering from having preferred working in stucco to carving in marble. The mediaevalism of this day is perhaps deficient in any real vitality; yet we have got some way in advance of Strawberry Hill and Abbotsford and the carpenter's father of fifty years back. There is, however, something still to be said. *Ivanhoe* cannot be given up without some reluctance. The vivacity of the description—the delight with which Scott throws himself into the pursuit of his knickknacks and antiquarian rubbish, has something contagious about it. *Ivanhoe*, let it be granted, is no longer a work for men, but it still is, or still ought to be, delightful reading for boys.... But if *Ivanhoe* has rightly descended from the library to the schoolroom, we should not be ungrateful to Scott for wasting his splendid talents

on what we can hardly call by a loftier name than most amusing nonsense. We could not, without venturing into boundless fields of controversy, decide upon the good and the evil results of that romanticism of which Scott was the great English founder. This much may perhaps be safely said: a reaction from the eighteenth-century spirit of indiscriminating contempt for our past history, and specially for the "Dark Ages," was necessary and right. At a time when the public taste was too ill educated to distinguish between tinsel and genuine gold, it could only be attracted by that fast failing material which Scott offered for its acceptance. Had he taken a loftier tone he might have amused people more in the twentieth century, but he would have produced a smaller immediate effect on his own. Why should not a man stir a love of art by producing daubs when neither he nor his audience are capable of appreciating masterpieces? May we not at times accept with gratitude the sacrifice made by a genius which condescends to provide us with the only food that we can digest, as well as the sacrifice of temporary fame made by the man who works for our great grandchildren? It is a difficult problem, and one which we need not attempt to solve. Certainly, however, we must set against it that Scott contributed more than most people to that prevalent delusion of our times, that there is a hopeless divergence between the beautiful and the useful; that we cannot keep up historical associations except at the price of injuring our own generation, or do good now without making a clean sweep of all that appeals to the imagination. In so doing, he played into the hands of the purely obstructive people, who would not only live in a picturesque ruin, but build modern ruins to be like it; the end of which is, of course, that which they most dread, a final revolution by catastrophe, instead of a continuous development.

Scott, however, understood, and nobody has better illustrated by example, the true mode of connecting past and present. Mr. Palgrave, whose love of Scott's poetry is, perhaps, rather stronger than we can generally follow, observes in the notes to the *Golden Treasury* that the songs about Brignall banks and Rosabelle exemplify "the peculiar skill with which Scott employs proper names;" nor, he adds, "is there a surer sign of high poetical genius." The last remark might possibly be disputed; if Milton possessed the same talent, so did Lord Macaulay, whose ballads, admirable as they are, are not first-rate poetry; but the conclusion to which the remark points is one which is illustrated by each of these cases. The secret of the power is simply this, that a man whose mind is full of historical associations somehow communicates to us something of the sentiment which they awake in himself. Scott, as all who saw him tell us, could never see an old tower, or a bank, or the rush of a stream without instantly recalling a boundless collection of appropriate anecdotes. He might be quoted as a case in point by those who would explain all poetical imagination by the power of associating ideas. He is the poet of association. A proper name acts upon him like a charm. It calls up the past days, the heroes of the '41, or the skirmish of Drumclog, or the old Covenanting times, by a spontaneous and inexplicable magic. When the barest natural object is taken into his imagination, all manner of past fancies and legends crystallize around it at once.

Though it is more difficult to explain how the same glow which ennobled them to him is conveyed to his readers, the process somehow takes place. We catch the enthusiasm. A word, which strikes us as a bare abstraction in the report of the Censor General, say, or in a collection of poor-law returns, gains an entirely new significance when he touches it in the most casual manner. A kind of mellowing atmosphere surrounds all objects in his pages, and tinges them with poetical hues; and difficult as it is to analyze the means by which his power is exercised, though we may guess at its sources, this is the secret of Scott's most successful writing. Thus, for example, we have always fancied that the second title of *Waverley*—'*Tis Sixty Years Since,*—indicates precisely the distance of time at which a romantic novelist should place himself from his creations. They are just far enough from us to have acquired a certain picturesque colouring, which conceals the vulgarity, and yet leaves them living and intelligible beings. His best stories might be all described as *Tales of My Grandfather*. They have the charm of anecdotes told to the narrator by some old man who had himself been part of what he describes. Some people, who condemn the sham knights and nobles and the mediaeval upholstery of Scott's novels, have, by a natural reaction, taken a rather different view. There is a story of a dozen connoisseurs in the *Waverley Novels* who agreed that each should separately write down the name of his favourite story, when it appeared that each had, without concert, mentioned *St. Ronan's Well*. It has, indeed, the merit of representing modern life, and therefore giving no scope for the sham romantic. But the public is surely a wiser critic than any clique of connoisseurs; and, in this instance especially, we suspect that it is right. The ladies and gentlemen at the hotel are rather out of Scott's peculiar line, and excellent as Meg Dodds and the retired nabobs may be, they are scarcely equal to some of the old men and women in his less prosaic novels. If we were to give a list of the novels which to us appear to have the best chance of immortality, we should mention *Waverley, The Antiquary, Guy Mannering, Old Mortality,* and the *Bride of Lammermoor*. Some of the others— especially the *Heart of Midlothian*—contain passages equal to the best of these; but those we have noticed seem to be less defaced by Scott's inferior style, and they all of them depend, for their deep interest, upon the scenery and society with which he had been familiar in his early days, more or less harmonized by removal to what we may call, in a different sense from the common one, the twilight of history; that period, namely, from which the broad glare of the present has departed, and which we can yet dimly observe without making use of the dark-lantern of ancient historians, and accepting the guidance of Dryasdust. Dandie Dinmont, though a contemporary of Scott's youth, represented a fast perishing phase of society; and Balfour of Burley, though his day was past, had yet left his mantle with many spiritual descendants who were scarcely less familiar. Between the times so fixed Scott seems to exhibit his genuine power; and within these limits we should find it hard to name any second, or indeed any third.

When naturalists wish to preserve a skeleton, they bury an animal in an anthill and dig him up after many days with all the perishable matter fairly eaten away. That is the process which great men have to undergo. A vast multitude of insignificant, unknown, and unconscious critics destroy what has no genuine power of resistance and leave the remainder for posterity. Much disappears in every case, and it is a question, perhaps, whether the firmer parts of Scott's reputation will be sufficiently coherent to resist after the removal of the rubbish. We must admit that even his best work is of more or less mixed value, and that the test will be a severe one. Yet we hope, and chiefly for one reason, which remains to be expressed. Every great novelist describes many characters from the outside: but as a rule, even the greatest—and, with Mr. Carlyle's leave, we will add even Shakspeare—describes only one from the inside: and that, we need not say, is himself. We must add, indeed, to make the statement accurate, that every man is really

a highly complex personage, and, like Mrs. Malaprop's Cerberus, is at least three gentlemen in one. His varying moods, or the different stages of development through which he passes, may supply us with what we take to be different men, as Goethe utilized all the successive phases of his life, or as, to speak more conjecturally, Shakspeare in his cups was Falstaff, and Shakspeare melancholy was Hamlet. Not to work this out at length, or to supply the necessary qualifications, we may surely say that Scott has painted a full-length portrait of himself; and that no more loveable or in some respects more powerful nature was ever revealed to us. Scott, indeed, setting up as the landed proprietor at Abbotsford and solacing himself with painted plaster of Paris instead of carved oak, does not strike us any more than he does Mr. Carlyle, as a very noble phenomenon. To test Scott we may set aside such performances as *Ivanhoe, Kenilworth Castle,* the *Monastery,* and other stucco-work of a highly crumbling and unstable tendency. But luckily for us, we have also the Scott who must have been the most charming of all conceivable companions; the Scott who was idolized even by a judicious pig; the Scott, who, unlike the irritable race of literary magnates in general, never lost a friend, and whose presence diffused an equable glow of kindly feeling to the farthest limits of the social system which gravitated round him. He was not precisely brilliant; nobody, we know, ever wrote so many sentences and left so few that have fixed themselves upon us as established commonplaces; beyond that unlucky phrase about "my name being Macgregor and my foot being on my native heath"—which is not a very admirable sentiment—we do not at present remember a single gem of this kind. Landor, if we remember rightly, said that in the whole of Scott's poetry there was only one good line, that, namely, in the poem about Helvellyn referring to the dog of the lost man—

When the wind waved his garments, how oft didst thou start!

To judge either of poetry or prose on such principles is obviously unfair. Scott is not one of the coruscating geniuses, throwing out epigrams at every turn, and sparkling with good things. But the poetry, which was first admired to excess and then rejected with undue contempt, is now beginning to find its due level. It is not poetry of the first order. It is not the poetry of deep meditation or of rapt enthusiasm. Much that was once admired has now become rather offensive than otherwise. And yet it has a charm, which becomes more sensible the more familiar we grow, the charm of unaffected and spontaneous love of nature; but not only is it perfectly in harmony with the nature which Scott loved so well, but it is still the best interpreter of the sound healthy love of wild scenery. Wordsworth, no doubt, goes deeper; and Byron is more vigorous; and Shelley more ethereal. But it is, and will remain, a good thing to have a breath from the Cheviots brought straight into London streets, as Scott alone can do it. When Washington Irving visited Scott, they had an amicable dispute as to the scenery: Irving, as became an American, complaining of the absence of forests; Scott declaring his love for "his honest grey hills," and saying that if he did not see the heather once a year he thought he should die. Everybody who has refreshed himself with mountain and moor this summer should feel how much we owe, and how much more we are likely to owe in future, to the man who first inoculated us with his own enthusiasm, and who is still the best interpreter of the "honest grey hills." Scott's poetical faculty may, perhaps, be more felt in his prose than in his verse. The fact need not be decided; but as we read the best of his novels we feel ourselves transported to the

Scott's study at Abbotsford. © 1985 Jarrold Colour Publications.

"distant Cheviots blue;" mixing with the sturdy dalesmen, and the tough indomitable puritans of his native land; for their sakes we can forgive the exploded feudalism and the faded romance which he attempted in vain, as such an attempt must always be vain, to galvanize into life. The pleasure of that healthy open-air life, with that manly companion, is not likely to diminish; and Scott as its exponent may still retain a hold upon our affections which would have been long ago forfeited if he had depended entirely on his romantic nonsense. We are rather in the habit of talking about a healthy animalism, and try most elaborately to be simple and manly; indeed, we have endeavoured to prove that the cultivation of our muscles is an essential part of the Christian religion. When we turn from our modern professors in that line, who affect a total absence of affectation, to Scott's Dandie Dinmonts and Edie Ochiltrees, we see the difference between the sham and the reality, and fancy that Scott may still have a lesson or two to preach to this generation. Those to come must take care of themselves. (pp. 289-93)

[Leslie Stephen], "Some Words about Sir Walter Scott," in The Cornhill Magazine, Vol. XXIV, No. 141, September, 1871, pp. 278-93.

MARK TWAIN   (essay date 1883)

[*Twain, considered one of the most important shapers of modern American literature, broke with the genteel traditions of the nineteenth century by endowing his characters and narratives with natural speech patterns and colloquial language and by writing about subjects hitherto considered beneath serious art. In the* following excerpt, Twain insists that Scott's works had a reactionary and highly damaging influence on Southern society in the United States prior to the Civil War.]

Against the crimes of the French Revolution and of Bonaparte may be set two compensating benefactions: the Revolution broke the chains of the *ancien régime* and of the Church, and made a nation of abject slaves a nation of freemen; and Bonaparte instituted the setting of merit above birth, and also so completely stripped the divinity from royalty that, whereas crowned heads in Europe were gods before, they are only men since, and can never be gods again, but only figure-heads, and answerable for their acts like common clay. Such benefactions as these compensate the temporary harm which Bonaparte and the Revolution did, and leave the world in debt to them for these great and permanent services to liberty, humanity, and progress.

Then comes Sir Walter Scott with his enchantments, and by his single might checks this wave of progress, and even turns it back; sets the world in love with dreams and phantoms; with decayed and swinish forms of religion; with decayed and degraded systems of government; with the sillinesses and emptinesses, sham grandeurs, sham gauds, and sham chivalries of a brainless and worthless long-vanished society. He did measureless harm; more real and lasting harm, perhaps, than any other individual that ever wrote. Most of the world has now outlived good part of these harms, though by no means all of them; but in our South they flourish pretty forcefully still. Not so forcefully as half a generation ago, perhaps, but still forcefully. There, the genuine and wholesome civilization of the nineteenth century is curiously confused and commingled with the Walter Scott Middle-Age sham civilization, and so you have practical common-sense, progressive ideas, and progressive works, mixed up with the duel, the inflated speech, and the jejune romanticism of an absurd past that is dead, and out of charity ought to be buried. But for the Sir Walter disease, the character of the Southerner—or Southron, according to Sir Walter's starchier way of phrasing it—would be wholly modern, in place of modern and mediaeval mixed, and the South would be fully a generation further advanced than it is. It was Sir Walter that made every gentleman in the South a major or a colonel, or a general or a judge, before the war; and it was he, also, that made these gentlemen value these bogus decorations. For it was he that created rank and caste down there, and also reverence for rank and caste, and pride and pleasure in them. Enough is laid on slavery, without fathering upon it these creations and contributions of Sir Walter.

Sir Walter had so large a hand in making Southern character, as it existed before the war, that he is in great measure responsible for the war. It seems a little harsh toward a dead man to say that we never should have had any war but for Sir Walter; and yet something of a plausible argument might, perhaps, be made in support of that wild proposition. The Southerner of the American revolution owned slaves; so did the Southerner of the Civil War: but the former resembles the latter as an Englishman resembles a Frenchman. The change of character can be traced rather more easily to Sir Walter's influence than to that of any other thing or person. (pp. 327-29)

Mark Twain, "Enchantments and Enchanters," in his Life on the Mississippi, 1883. Reprint by Harper & Brothers Publishers, 1899, pp. 326-30.

G. K. CHESTERTON   (essay date 1903)

[*Chesterton was one of England's most prominent and colorful men of letters during the early twentieth century. Much of Ches-*

terton's work reveals his childlike joie de vivre *and reflects his pronounced Anglican and, later, Roman Catholic beliefs. His essays are characterized by their humor, frequent use of paradox, and chatty, rambling style. Although he is best known today as a detective novelist and essayist, he was also an eminent literary critic. In the excerpt below, Chesterton responds to Scott's detractors, defending his conception of the romantic novel and praising such facets of his work as its "spiritual adventurousness," its attention to the details of weapons and costumes, and its bombast.]*

It is said that Scott is neglected by modern readers; if so, the matter could be more appropriately described by saying that modern readers are neglected by Providence. The ground of this neglect, in so far as it exists, must be found, I suppose, in the general sentiment that, like the beard of Polonius, he is too long. Yet it is surely a peculiar thing that in literature alone a house should be despised because it is too large, or a host impugned because he is too generous. If romance be really a pleasure, it is difficult to understand the modern reader's consuming desire to get it over, and if it be not a pleasure, it is difficult to understand his desire to have it at all. Mere size, it seems to me, cannot be a fault. The fault must lie in some disproportion. If some of Scott's stories are dull and dilatory, it is not because they are giants, but because they are hunchbacks or cripples. Scott was very far indeed from being a perfect writer, but I do not think that it can be shown that the large and elaborate plan on which his stories are built was by any means an imperfection. He arranged his endless prefaces and his colossal introductions just as an architect plans great gates and long approaches to a really large house. He did not share the latter-day desire to get quickly through a story. He enjoyed narrative as a sensation; he did not wish to swallow a story like a pill, that it should do him good afterwards. He desired to taste it like a glass of port, that it might do him good at the time. The reader sits late at his banquets. His characters have that air of immortality which belongs to those of Dumas and Dickens. We should not be surprised to meet them in any number of sequels. Scott, in his heart of hearts, probably would have liked to write an endless story without either beginning or close.

Walter Scott is a great, and, therefore, mysterious man. He will never be understood until Romance is understood, and that will be only when Time, Man, and Eternity are understood. To say that Scott had more than any other man that ever lived a sense of the romantic seems, in these days, a slight and superficial tribute. The whole modern theory arises from one fundamental mistake—the idea that romance is in some way a plaything with life, a figment, a conventionality, a thing upon the outside. No genuine criticism of romance will ever arise until we have grasped the fact that romance lies not upon the outside of life, but absolutely in the centre of it. The centre of every man's existence is a dream. Death, disease, insanity, are merely material accidents, like toothache or a twisted ankle. That these brutal forces always besiege and often capture the citadel does not prove that they are the citadel. The boast of the realist (applying what the reviewers call his scalpel) is that he cuts into the heart of life; but he makes a very shallow incision, if he only reaches as deep as habits and calamities and sins. Deeper than all these lies a man's vision of himself, as swaggering and sentimental as a penny novelette. The literature of candour unearths innumerable weaknesses and elements of lawlessness which is called romance. It perceives superficial habits like murder and dipsomania, but it does not perceive the deepest of sins—the sin of vanity—vanity which is the mother of all day-dreams and adventures, the one sin that is not shared with any boon companion, or whispered to any priest.

In estimating, therefore, the ground of Scott's preeminence in romance we must absolutely rid ourselves of the notion that romance or adventure are merely materialistic things involved in the tangle of a plot or the multiplicity of drawn swords. We must remember that it is, like tragedy or farce, a state of the soul, and that, for some dark and elemental reason which we can never understand, this state of the soul is evoked in us by the sight of certain places or the contemplation of certain human crises, by a stream rushing under a heavy and covered wooden bridge, or by a man plunging a knife or sword into tough timber. In the selection of these situations which catch the spirit of romance as in a net, Scott has never been equalled or even approached. His finest scenes affect us like fragments of a hilarious dream. They have the same quality which is often possessed by those nocturnal comedies—that of seeming more human than our waking life—even while they are less possible. Sir Arthur Wardour, with his daughter and the old beggar crouching in a cranny of the cliff as night falls and the tide closes around them, are actually in the coldest and bitterest of practical situations. Yet the whole incident has a quality that can only be called boyish. It is warmed with all the colours of an incredible sunset. Rob Roy trapped in the Tolbooth, and confronted with Bailie Nicol Jarvie, draws no sword, leaps from no window, affects none of the dazzling external acts upon which contemporary romance depends, yet that plain and humourous dialogue is full of the essential philosophy of romance which is an almost equal betting upon man and destiny. Perhaps the most profoundly thrilling of all Scott's situations is that in which the family of Colonel Mannering are waiting for the carriage which may or may not arrive by night to bring an unknown man into a princely possession. Yet almost the whole of that thrilling scene consists of a ridiculous conversation about food, and flirtation between a frivolous old lawyer and a fashionable girl. We can say nothing about what makes these scenes, except that the wind bloweth where it listeth, and that here the wind blows strong.

It is in this quality of what may be called spiritual adventurousness that Scott stands at so different an elevation to the whole of the contemporary crop of romancers who have followed the leadership of Dumas. There has, indeed, been a great and inspiriting revival of romance in our time, but it is partly frustrated in almost every case by this rooted conception that romance consists in the vast multiplication of incidents and the violent acceleration of narrative. . . . In the truer romance of Scott there is more of the sentiment of "Oh! still delay, thou art so fair"! more of a certain patriarchal enjoyment of things as they are—of the sword by the side and the wine-cup in the hand. Romance, indeed, does not consist by any means so much in experiencing adventures as in being ready for them. How little the actual boy cares for incidents in comparison to tools and weapons may be tested by the fact that the most popular story of adventure is concerned with a man who lived for years on a desert island with two guns and a sword, which he never had to use on an enemy.

Closely connected with this is one of the charges most commonly brought against Scott, particularly in his own day—the charge of a fanciful and monotonous insistence upon the details of armour and costume. The critic in the *Edinburgh Review* said indignantly that he could tolerate a somewhat detailed description of the apparel of Marmion, but when it came to an equally detailed account of the apparel of his pages and yeomen the mind could bear it no longer. The only thing to be said about that critic is that he had never been a little boy. He foolishly imagined that Scott valued the plume and dagger of Marmion for Marmion's sake. Not being himself romantic, he could not understand that Scott valued the plume because it was a plume, and the dagger because it was a dagger. Like a child, he loved weapons with a manual materialistic love, as one loves the softness of fur or the coolness of marble. One of the profound philosophical truths which are almost confined to infants is this love of things, not for their use or origin, but for their own inherent characteristics, the child's love of the toughness of wood, the wetness of water, the magnificent soapiness of soap. So it was with Scott, who had so much of the child in him. Human beings were perhaps the principal characters in his stories, but they were certainly not the only characters. A battle-axe was a person of importance, a castle had a character and ways of its own. A church bell had a word to say in the matter. Like a true child, he almost ignored the distinction between the animate and inanimate. A two-handed sword might be carried only by a menial in a procession, but it was something important and immeasurably fascinating—it was a two-handed sword.

There is one quality which is supreme and continuous in Scott which is little appreciated at present. One of the values we have really lost in recent fiction is the value of eloquence. The modern literary artist is compounded of almost every man except the orator. Yet Shakespeare and Scott are certainly alike in this, that they could both, if literature had failed, have earned a living as professional demagogues. The feudal heroes in the *Waverley Novels* retort upon each other with a passionate dignity, haughty and yet singularly human, which can hardly be paralleled in political eloquence except in *Julius Caesar*. With a certain fiery impartiality which stirs the blood, Scott distributes his noble orations equally among saints and villains. He may deny a villain every virtue or triumph, but he cannot endure to deny him a telling word; he will ruin a man, but he will not silence him. In truth, one of Scott's most splendid traits is his difficulty, or rather incapacity, for despising any of his characters. He did not scorn the most revolting miscreant as the realist of to-day commonly scorns his own hero. Though his soul may be in rags, every man of Scott can speak like a king. (pp. 160-69)

Scott's bombast . . . will always be stirring to anyone who approaches it, as he should approach all literature, as a little child. We could easily excuse the contemporary critic for not admiring melodramas and adventure stories, and Punch and Judy, if he would admit that it was a slight deficiency in his artistic sensibilities. Beyond all question, it marks a lack of literary instinct to be unable to simplify one's mind at the first signal of the advance of romance. "You do me wrong," said Brian de Bois-Guilbert to Rebecca. "Many a law, many a commandment have I broken, but my word, never." "Die," cries Balfour of Burley to the villain in *Old Mortality*. "Die, hoping nothing, believing nothing—" "And fearing nothing," replies the other. This is the old and honourable fine art of bragging, as it was practised by the great worthies of antiquity. The man who cannot appreciate it goes along with the man who cannot appreciate beef or claret or a game with children or a brass band. They are afraid of making fools of themselves, and are unaware that that transformation has already been triumphantly effected. (pp. 173-74)

Of the faults of Scott as an artist it is not very necessary to speak, for faults are generally and easily pointed out, while there is yet no adequate valuation of the varieties and contrasts of virtue. We have compiled a complete botanical classification of the weeds in the poetical garden, but the flowers still flourish, neglected and nameless. It is true, for example, that Scott had an incomparably stiff and pedantic way of dealing with his heroines: he made a lively girl of eighteen refuse an offer in the language of Dr. Johnson. To him, as to most men of his time, woman was not an individual, but an institution—a toast that was drunk some time after that of Church and King. But it is far better to consider the difference rather as a special merit, in that he stood for all those clean and bracing shocks of incident which are untouched by passion or weakness, for a certain breezy bachelorhood, which is almost essential to the literature of adventure. With all his faults, and all his triumphs, he stands for the great mass of natural manliness which must be absorbed into art unless art is to be a mere luxury and freak. An appreciation of Scott might be made almost a test of decadence. If ever we lose touch with this one most reckless and defective writer, it will be a proof to us that we have erected round ourselves a false cosmos, a world of lying and horrible perfection, leaving outside of it Walter Scott and that strange old world which is as confused and as indefensible and as inspiring and as healthy as he. (pp. 175-76)

> *G. K. Chesterton, "The Position of Sir Walter Scott," in his* Varied Types, *Dodd, Mead and Company, 1903, pp. 159-76.*

ARTHUR SYMONS (essay date 1904)

[*Symons was a critic, poet, dramatist, short story writer, and editor who first gained notoriety in the 1890s as an English decadent. Eventually, he established himself as one of the most important critics of the modern era. In the following excerpt, Symons offers a highly unfavorable assessment of Scott's poetry, focusing on the mundane quality of his thought and his portrayal of nature.*]

[The] admirers of Scott have invariably spoken of his verse in praise that would be justified if the qualities for which they praise it were qualities supplementary to the essentially poetic qualities: they form no substitute. First Scott, and then Byron, partly in imitation of Scott, appealed to the public of their day with poems which sold as only novels have sold before or since, and partly because they were so like novels. They were, what every publisher still wants, "stories with plenty of action;" and the public either forgave their being in verse, or for some reason was readier than usual, just then, to welcome verse. (pp. 664-65)

Much has been claimed for Scott's poetry because of its appeal to unpoetical persons, who, in the nature of things, would be likely to take an interest in its subject matter; and it has been thought remarkable that poetry composed, like much of *Marmion,* in the saddle, by one "through whose head a regiment of horse has been exercising since he was five years old," should have seemed genuine to sportsmen and to soldiers. A striking anecdote told by Lockhart allows us to consider the matter very clearly [see Additional Bibliography]. "In the course of the day, when the *Lady of the Lake* first reached Sir Adam Ferguson, he was posted with his company on a point of ground exposed to the enemy's artillery, somewhere no doubt on the lines of Torres Vedras. The men were ordered to lie prostrate on the ground; while they kept that attitude, the captain, kneeling at the head, read aloud the description of the battle in Canto VI, and the listening soldiers only interrupted him by a joyous huzza when the French shot struck the bank close above them." "It is not often," says Mr. Hutton in his *Life of Scott* [see

Additional Bibliography], "that martial poetry has been put to such a test." A test of what? Certainly not a test of poetry. An audience less likely to be critical, a situation less likely to induce criticism, can hardly be imagined. The soldiers would look for martial sentiments expressed with clear and matter-of-fact fervor. They would want no more and they would find no more; certainly no such intrusion of poetry as would have rendered the speech of Henry V before the battle of Agincourt but partially intelligible to them, though there Shakespeare is writing for once almost down to his audience. Scott's appeal is the appeal of prose, the thing and the feeling each for its own sake, with only that "pleasurable excitement," which Coleridge saw in the mere fact of metre, to give the illusion that one is listening to poetry.

Let me give an instance from another art. If, on his return to England, you had taken one of Sir Adam Ferguson's soldiers into a picture gallery, and there had been a Botticelli in one corner, and a Titian in another, and between two Bellini altar-pieces there had been a modern daub representing a battle, in which fire and smoke were clearly discernible, and charging horses rolled over on their riders, and sabres were being flourished in a way very like the trooper's way, is there much doubt which picture would go straight home to the soldier? There, it might be said, is a battle-piece, and the soldier goes up to it, examines it, admires it, swears that nothing more natural was ever painted. Is that a "test" of the picture? Are we to say: this picture has been proved to be sincere, natural, approvable by one who has been through the incident which it records, and therefore (in spite of its total lack of every fine quality in painting) a good picture? No one, I think, would take the soldier's word for that: why should we take his word on a battlepiece which is not painted, but written?

A great many of the merits which people have accustomed themselves to see in Scott come from this kind of miscalculation. Thus, for instance, we may admit, with Mr. Palgrave, that Scott "attained eminent success" in "sustained vigour, clearness, and interest in narration." "If we reckon up the poets of the world," continues Mr. Palgrave, "we may be surprised to find how very few (dramatists not included) have accomplished this, and may be hence led to estimate Scott's rank in his art more justly." But is not this rather a begging of the question? Scott wrote in metre, and in some of his metrical narratives attained "sustained vigour, clearness, and interest in narration." But is there anything except the metre to distinguish these stories in verse from what, as Scott himself afterwards showed, might have been much better if they had been told in prose? Until this has been granted, no merit in narration will mean anything at all, in a consideration of poetry as poetry; any more than the noughts which you may add to the left of your figure 1, in the belief that you are adding million to million.

The fact is, that skill in story-telling never made any man a poet, any more than skill in constructing a drama. Shakespeare is not, in the primary sense, a poet because he is a great dramatist; he is a poet as much in the sonnets as in the plays, but he is a poet who chose to be also a playwright, and in measuring his greatness we measure all that he did as a playwright along with all that he did as a poet; his especial greatness being seen by his complete fusion of the two in one. And it is the same thing in regard to story-telling. Look for a moment at our greatest narrative poet, Chaucer. Chaucer tells his stories much better, much more pointedly, concisely, with much more of the qualities of the best prose narrative, than Scott; who

seems to tell his stories rather for boys than for men, with what he very justly called "a hurried frankness of composition, which pleases soldiers, sailors, and young people of bold and active dispositions." Chaucer is one of the most masculine of story-tellers, and if you read, not even one of the *Canterbury Tales,* but a book of *Troilus and Cressida,* you will find in it something of the quality which we applaud in Balzac; an enormous interest in life, and an absorption in all its details, because those details go to make up the most absorbing thing in the world. But in Chaucer all this is so much prose quality added to a consummate gift for poetry.... His whole vision of life is the vision of the poet; his language and versification have the magic of poetry; he has wisdom, tenderness, a high gravity, tinged with illuminating humor.... (pp. 665-67)

Now look at Scott: I do not say, ask Scott to be another Chaucer; but consider for a moment how much his admirers have to add to that all-important merit of "sustained vigour, clearness, and interest in narration." Well, it has been claimed, first and most emphatically, I think, by Sir Francis Doyle, that his poetry is "Homeric." Sir Francis Doyle says, in one of his lectures on Scott, given when Professor of Poetry at Oxford: "Now, after the immortal ballads of Homer, there are no ballad poems so full of the spirit of Homer as those of Scott." Homer, indeed, wrote of war and warriors, and so did Scott; Homer gives you vivid action, in swiftly moving verse, and so does Scott. But I can see little further resemblance, and I can see an infinite number of differences. No one, I suppose, would compare the pit-a-pat of Scott's octosyllabics with "the deep-mouthed music" of the Homeric hexameter. But Sir Francis Doyle sees in the opening of the *Lay of the Last Minstrel,* and not in this alone, "the simple and energetic style of Homer." Let me, then, take one single sentence from that battle in Canto VI of the *Lady of the Lake,* and set against it a single sentence from one of the battle-pieces in the *Iliad....* Here is Scott's verse:—

> Forth from the pass, in tumult driven,
> Like chaff before the wind of heaven,
> 　　The archery appear;
> For life! for life! their flight they ply,
> And shriek, and shout, and battle-cry,
> And plaids and bonnets waving high,
> And broadswords flashing to the sky,
> 　　Are maddening in the rear.

And here is Homer in English prose: "And as the gusts speed on, when shrill winds blow, on a day when dust lies thickest on the roads, even so their battle clashed together, and all were fain of heart to slay each other in the press with the keen bronze." Need I say more than these extracts say for themselves? What commonness and what distinction, what puerility of effort and what repose in energy!

Then there is Scott's feeling for nature. The feeling was deep and genuine.... There is a great deal of landscape painting in Scott's verse, and it has many good prose qualities: it is very definite, it is written "with the eye on the object," it is always sincere, in a certain sense; it is always felt sincerely. But it is not felt deeply, and it becomes either trite or generalized in its rendering into words.... Even in better landscape work, like the opening of the first introduction to *Marmion,* how entirely without magic is the observation, how superficial a notation of just what every one would notice in the scenery before him! To Ruskin, I know, all this is a part of what he calls Scott's unselfishness and humility, "in consequence of which Scott's enjoyment of Nature is incomparably greater than that of any other poet I know" [see Additional Bibliography,

1856]. Enjoyment, perhaps; but we are concerned, in poetry, with what a poet has made out of his enjoyment. Scott puts down in words exactly what the average person feels. Now it is the poet's business to interpret, illuminate, or at the least to evoke in a more exquisite form, all that the ordinary person is capable of feeling vaguely, by way of enjoyment. Until the poet has transformed enjoyment into ecstasy there can be no poetry. Scott's genuine love of nature, so profound in feeling, . . . was never able to translate itself into poetry; it seemed to become tongue-tied in metre. (pp. 667-68)

Ruskin's special praise of Scott, in his attitude toward nature, is that Scott did not indulge in "the pathetic fallacy" of reading one's own feelings into the aspect of natural things. This, in the main, is true, in spite of those little morals which Scott attaches to what he sees. But it is hardly more than a negative merit, at the best; and it is accompanied by no intimacy of insight, no revealing passion; aspects are described truthfully, and with sympathy, and that is all.

Throughout the whole of his long poems, and throughout almost the whole of his work in verse, Scott remains an improviser in rhyme, not a poet. But in a few of the songs contained in the novels, songs written after he had practically given up writing verse, flickering touches of something very like poetry are from time to time seen. In one song of four stanzas, **"Proud Maisie,"** published in 1818 in the *Heart of Midlothian,* Scott seems to me to have become a poet. In this poem, which is like nothing else he ever wrote, some divine accident has brought all the diffused poetical feeling of his nature to a successful birth. (pp. 668-69)

For the rest, all Scott's verse is written for boys, and boys, generation after generation, will love it with the same freshness of response. It has adventure, manliness, bright landscape, fighting, the obvious emotions; it is like a gallop across the moors in a blithe wind; it has plenty of story, and is almost as easily read as if it were prose. The taste for it may well be outgrown with the first realization of why Shakespeare is looked upon as the supreme poet. Byron usually follows Scott in the boy's head, and drives out Scott, as that infinitely greater, though imperfect, force may well do. Shelley often completes the disillusion. But it is well, perhaps, that there should be a poet for boys, and for those grown-up people who are most like boys; for those, that is, to whom poetry appeals by something in it which is not the poetry. (p. 669)

Arthur Symons, "Was Sir Walter Scott a Poet?" in The Atlantic Monthly, *Vol. XCIV, No. DLXV, November, 1904, pp. 664-69.*

VIRGINIA WOOLF (essay date 1924)

[A British novelist, essayist, and short story writer, Woolf is considered one of the most prominent figures of twentieth-century English literature. Like her contemporary James Joyce, with whom she is often compared, Woolf is remembered as one of the most innovative of the stream of consciousness novelists. Here, she provides an appreciative perspective on the Waverley Novels, *balancing their entertaining qualities, idiosyncratic attractions, and memorable characters against their artistic shortcomings. Woolf's remarks were written in 1924.]*

There are some writers who have entirely ceased to influence others, whose fame is for that reason both serene and cloudless, who are enjoyed or neglected rather than criticized and read. Among them is Scott. The most impressionable beginner, whose pen oscillates if exposed within a mile of the influence of

Stendhal, Flaubert, Henry James, or Chekhov, can read the *Waverley Novels* one after another without altering an adjective. Yet there are no books perhaps upon which at this moment more thousands of readers are brooding and feasting in a rapture of uncritical and silent satisfaction. And if this is the mood in which the *Waverley Novels* are read, the inference is perhaps that there is something vicious about such a pleasure; it cannot be defended; it must be enjoyed in secret. Let us run through *The Antiquary* again and make a note or two as we go. The first charge that is levelled against Scott is that his style is execrable. Every page of the novel, it is true, is watered down with long languid Latin words—peruse, manifest, evince. Old metaphors out of the property box come flapping their dusty wings across the sky. The sea in the heat of a crisis is 'the devouring element'. A gull on the same occasion is a 'winged denizen of the crag'. Taken from their context it is impossible to deny that such expressions sound wrong, though a good case might be made against the snobbery which insists upon preserving class distinctions even among words. But read currently in their places, it is difficult either to notice or to condemn them. As Scott uses them they fulfil their purpose and merge perfectly in their surroundings. Great novelists who are going to fill seventy volumes write after all in pages, not in sentences, and have at their command, and know when to use, a dozen different styles of varying intensities. The genteel pen is a very useful pen in its place. These slips and slovenlinesses serve as relaxations; they give the reader breathing space and air the book. Let us compare Scott the slovenly with Stevenson the precise. 'It was as he said: there was not a breath stirring; a windless stricture of frost had bound the air; and as we went forth in the shine of the candles, the blackness was like a roof over our heads.' One may search the *Waverley Novels* in vain for such close writing as this. But if we get from Stevenson a much closer idea of a single object, we get from Scott an incomparably larger impression of the whole. The storm in *The Antiquary,* made up as it is of stage hangings and cardboard screens, of 'denizens of the crags' and 'clouds like disasters round a sinking empire', nevertheless roars and splashes and almost devours the group huddled on the crag; while the storm in *Kidnapped,* for all its exact detail and its neat dapper adjectives, is incapable of wetting the sole of a lady's slipper.

The much more serious charge against Scott is that he used the wrong pen, the genteel pen, not merely to fill in the background and dash off a cloud piece, but to describe the intricacies and passions of the human heart. But what language to use of the Lovels and Isabellas, the Darsies, Ediths, and Mortons! As well talk of the hearts of seagulls and the passions and intricacies of walking-sticks and umbrellas; for indeed these ladies and gentlemen are scarcely to be distinguished from the winged denizens of the crag. They are equally futile; equally impotent; they squeak; they flutter; and a strong smell of camphor exudes from their poor dried breasts when, with a dismal croaking and cawing, they emit the astonishing language of their love-making.

'Without my father's consent, I will never entertain the addresses of anyone; and how totally impossible it is that he should countenance the partiality with which you honour me, you are yourself fully aware,' says the young lady. 'Do not add to the severity of repelling my sentiments the rigour of obliging me to disavow them,' replies the young gentleman; and he may be illegitimate, and he may be the son of a peer, or he may be both one and the other, but it would take a far stronger inducement than that to make us care a straw what happens to Lovel and his Isabella.

But then, perhaps, we are not meant to care a straw. When Scott has pacified his conscience as a magistrate by alluding to the sentiments of the upper classes in tones of respect and esteem, when he has vindicated his character as a moralist by awakening 'the better feelings and sympathies of his readers by strains of generous sentiment and tales of fictitious woe', he was quit both of art and of morals, and could scribble endlessly for his own amusement. Never was a change more emphatic; never one more wholly to the good. One is tempted, indeed, to suppose that he did it, half-consciously, on purpose—he showed up the languor of the fine gentlemen who bored him by the immense vivacity of the common people whom he loved. Images, anecdotes, illustrations drawn from sea, sky, and earth, race and bubble from their lips. They shoot every thought as it flies, and bring it tumbling to the ground in metaphor. Sometimes it is a phrase—'at the back of a dyke, in a wreath o' snaw, or in the wame o' a wave'; sometimes a proverb—'he'll no can haud down his head to sneeze, for fear o' seeing his shoon'; always the dialogue is sharpened and pointed by the use of that Scottish dialect which is at once so homely and so pungent, so colloquial and so passionate, so shrewd and so melancholy into the bargain. And the result is strange. For since the sovereigns who should preside have abdicated, since we are afloat on a broad and breezy sea without a pilot, the *Waverley Novels* are as unmoral as Shakespeare's plays. Nor, for some readers, is it the least part of their astonishing freshness, their perennial vitality, that you may read them over and over again, and never know for certain what Scott himself was or what Scott himself thought.

We know, however, what his characters are, and we know it almost as we know what our friends are by hearing their voices and watching their faces simultaneously. However often one may have read *The Antiquary*, Jonathan Oldbuck is slightly different every time. We notice different things; our observation of face and voice differs; and thus Scott's characters, like Shakespeare's and Jane Austen's, have the seed of life in them. They change as we change. But though this gift is an essential element in what we call immortality, it does not by any means prove that the character lives as profoundly, as fully, as Falstaff lives or Hamlet. Scott's characters, indeed, suffer from a serious disability; it is only when they speak that they are alive; they never think; as for prying into their minds himself, or drawing inferences from their behaviour, Scott never attempted it. 'Miss Wardour, as if she felt that she had said too much, turned and got into the carriage'—he will penetrate no further into the privacy of Miss Wardour than that; and it is not far. But this matters the less because the characters he cared for were by temperament chatterboxes; Edie Ochiltree, Oldbuck, Mrs. Mucklebackit talk incessantly. They reveal their characters in talk. If they stop talking it is to act. By their talk and by their acts—that is how we know them.

But how far then can we know people, the hostile critic may ask, if we only know that they say this and do that, if they never talk about themselves, and if their creator lets them go their ways, provided they forward his plot, in complete independence of his supervision or interference? Are they not all of them, Ochiltrees, Antiquaries, Dandy Dinmonts, and the rest, merely bundles of humours, and innocent childish humours at that, who serve to beguile our dull hours and charm our sick ones, and are packed off to the nursery when the working day returns and our normal faculties crave something tough to set their teeth into? Compare the *Waverley Novels* with the novels of Tolstoy, of Stendahl, of Proust! These comparisons of course lead to questions that lie at the root of fiction,

but without discussing them, they reveal unmistakably what Scott is not. He is not among the great observers of the intricacies of the heart. He is not going to break seals or loose fountains. But he has the power of the artist who can create a scene and leave us to analyse it for ourselves. When we read the scene in the cottage where Steenie Mucklebackit lies dead, the different emotions—the father's grief, the mother's irritability, the minister's consolations—all rise spontaneously, as if Scott had merely to record, and we have merely to observe. What we lose in intricacy we gain perhaps in spontaneity and the stimulus given to our own creative powers. It is true that Scott creates carelessly, as if the parts came together without his willing it; it is true also that his scene breaks into ruin without his caring.

For who taps at the door and destroys that memorable scene? The cadaverous Earl of Glenallan; the unhappy nobleman who had married his sister in the belief that she was his cousin; and had stalked the world in sables ever after. Falsity breaks in; the peerage breaks in; all the trappings of the undertaker and heralds' office press upon us their unwholesome claims. The emotions then in which Scott excels are not those of human beings pitted against other human beings, but of man pitted against Nature, of man in relation to fate. His romance is the romance of hunted men hiding in woods at night; of brigs standing out to sea; of waves breaking in the moonlight; of solitary sands and distant horsemen; of violence and suspense. And he is perhaps the last novelist to practise the great, the Shakespearean art, of making people reveal themselves in speech. (pp. 139-43)

Virginia Woolf, " 'The Antiquary'," in her Collected Essays, Vol. I, *Harcourt Brace Jovanovich, Inc., 1967, pp. 139-43.*

Scott after receiving his baronetcy, painted by Thomas Lawrence.

GEORG LUKÁCS (essay date 1937)

[*Lukács, a Hungarian literary critic and philosopher, is acknowledged as a leading proponent of Marxist thought. In the following excerpt, he provides a sociopolitical analysis of Scott's achievement as a historical novelist, focusing on his approach to portraying the past, on the cultural contexts in which he wrote, and on his attention to the life of the common people. Lukács's essay was first published in German in 1937.*]

It was the French Revolution, the revolutionary wars and the rise and fall of Napoleon, which for the first time made history a *mass experience*, and moreover on a European scale. During the decades between 1789 and 1814 each nation of Europe underwent more upheavals than they had previously experienced in centuries. And the quick succession of these upheavals gives them a qualitatively distinct character, it makes their historical character far more visible than would be the case in isolated, individual instances: the masses no longer have the impression of a "natural occurrence". One need only read over Heine's reminiscences of his youth in *Buch le Grand*, to quote just one example, where it is vividly shown how the rapid change of governments affected Heine as a boy. Now if experiences such as these are linked with the knowledge that similar upheavals are taking place all over the world, this must enormously strengthen the feeling first that there is such a thing as history, that it is an uninterrupted process of changes and finally that it has a direct effect upon the life of every individual. (p. 23)

These events, this transformation of men's existence and consciousness throughout Europe form the economic and ideological basis for Scott's historical novel. Biographical evidence of the individual instances which enabled Scott to become aware of these trends offers nothing of importance to the real history of the rise of the historical novel. The less so, as Scott ranks among those great writers whose depth is manifest mainly in their work, a depth which they often do not understand themselves, because it has sprung from a truly realistic mastery of their material in conflict with their personal views and prejudices.

Scott's historical novel is the direct continuation of the great realistic social novel of the eighteenth century. Scott's studies on eighteenth century writers, on the whole not very penetrating theoretically, reveal an intensive knowledge and detailed study of this literature. Yet his work, in comparison with theirs, signifies something entirely new. His great contemporaries clearly recognized this new quality. Pushkin writes of him: . . . "The influence of Walter Scott can be felt in every province of the literature of his age. The new school of French historians formed itself under the influence of the Scottish novelist. He showed them entirely new sources which had so far remained unknown despite the existence of the historical drama of Shakespeare and Goethe . . ." And Balzac, in his criticism of Stendhal's *La Chartreuse de Parme*, emphasizes the new artistic features which Scott's novel introduced into epic literature: the broad delineation of manners and circumstances attendant upon events, the dramatic character of action and, in close connection with this, the new and important role of dialogue in the novel.

It is no accident that this new type of novel arose in England. . . . The fact that England had fought out its bourgeois revolution in the seventeenth century and had from then on experienced a peaceful, upward development, lasting over centuries, on the basis of the Revolution's achievements, showed England to be the practical, model example for the new style of historical interpretation. The "Glorious Revolution" of 1688,

likewise, inevitably presented itself as an ideal to the bourgeois ideologists who were combating the Restoration in the name of progress.

On the other hand, however, honest writers, keenly observant of the real facts of social development, like Scott, were made to see that this peaceful development was peaceful only as the ideal of an historical conception, only from the bird's-eye view of a philosophy of history. The organic character of English development is a resultant made up of the components of ceaseless class struggles and their bloody resolution in great or small, successful or abortive uprisings. The enormous political and social transformations of the preceding decades awoke in England, too, the feeling for history, the awareness of historical development.

The relative stability of English development during this stormy period, in comparison with that of the Continent, made it possible to channel this newly-awoken historical feeling artistically into a broad, objective, epic form. This objectivity is further heightened by Scott's conservatism. His world-view ties him very closely to those sections of society which had been precipitated into ruin by the industrial revolution and the rapid growth of capitalism. Scott belongs neither with the ardent enthusiasts of this development, nor with its pathetic, passionate indicters. He attempts by fathoming historically the whole of English development to find a "middle way" for himself between the warring extremes. He finds in English history the consolation that the most violent vicissitudes of class struggle have always finally calmed down into a glorious "middle way". Thus, out of the struggle of the Saxons and Normans there arose the English nation, neither Saxon nor Norman; in the same way the bloody Wars of the Roses gave rise to the illustrious reign of the House of Tudor, especially that of Queen Elizabeth; and those class struggles which manifested themselves in the Cromwellian Revolution were finally evened out in the England of today, after a long period of uncertainty and civil war, by the "Glorious Revolution" and its aftermath.

The conception of English history in the novels of Scott thus gives a perspective (though not explicit) of future development in its author's sense. And it is not difficult to see that this perspective shows a marked affinity with that resigned "positivity" . . . in the great thinkers, scholars and writers of this period on the Continent. Scott ranks among those honest Tories in the England of his time who exonerate nothing in the development of capitalism, who not only see clearly, but also deeply sympathize with the unending misery of the people which the collapse of old England brings in its wake; yet who, precisely because of their conservatism, display no violent opposition to the features of the new development repudiated by them. Scott very seldom speaks of the present. He does not raise the social questions of contemporary England in his novels, the class struggle between bourgeoisie and proletariat which was then beginning to sharpen. As far as he is able to answer these questions for himself, he does so in the indirect way of embodying the most imporant stages of the whole of English history in his writing.

Paradoxically, Scott's greatness is closely linked with his often narrow conservatism. He seeks the "middle way" between the extremes and endeavours to demonstrate artistically the historical reality of this way by means of his portrayal of the great crises in English history. This basic tendency finds immediate expression in the way he constructs his plot and selects his central figure. The "hero" of a Scott novel is always a more or less mediocre, average English gentleman. He generally possesses a certain, though never outstanding, degree of practical intelligence, a certain moral fortitude and decency which even rises to a capacity for self-sacrifice, but which never grows into a sweeping human passion, is never the enraptured devotion to a great cause. Not only are the Waverleys, Mortons, Osbaldistons and so on correct, decent, average representatives of the English petty aristocracy of this kind, but so, too, is Ivanhoe, the "romantic" knight of the Middle Ages.

In later criticism this choice of hero was sharply criticized, for example by Taine [see excerpt dated 1863]. Such later critics saw here a sympton of Scott's own mediocrity as an artist. Precisely the opposite is true. That he builds his novels round a "middling", merely correct and never heroic "hero" is the clearest proof of Scott's exceptional and revolutionary epic gifts, although from a psychological-biographical point of view, no doubt his own personal, petty aristocratic-conservative prejudices did play an important part in the choice of these heroes.

What is expressed here, above all, is a renunciation of Romanticism, a conquest of Romanticism, a higher development of the realist literary traditions of the Enlightenment in keeping with the new times. As a form of opposition to the degrading, all-levelling prose of rising capitalism the "demonic hero" makes his appearance even in the writings of politically and ideologically progressive writers who frequently, though unjustly, have been treated as Romantics. This hero type, particularly as he appears in the poetry of Byron, is the literary expression of the social eccentricity and superfluity of the best and sincerest human talents in this period of prose, a lyrical protest against the dominion of this prose. But it is one thing to acknowledge the social roots or even the historical necessity and justification of this protest and another to make of it a lyrical-subjectivist absolute. On this latter basis an objective portrayal is impossible. The great realistic writers of a somewhat later period who portrayed this type, such as Pushkin or Stendhal, overcame Byronism differently from Scott and in a higher form. They interpreted the problem of the eccentricity of this type in a social-historical, objective-epic way: that is, they saw the present historically and revealed all the social determinants of the tragedy (or tragi-comedy) of this protest. Scott's criticism and rejection of this type does not go as deep as this. His recognition or rather sense of the eccentricity of this type has the result of eliminating him from the sphere of historical portrayal. Scott endeavours to portray the struggles and antagonisms of history by means of characters who, in their psychology and destiny, always represent social trends and historical forces. Scott also extends this approach to the processes of declassing, always regarding them socially and not individually. His understanding for the problems of the present is not sufficiently deep for him to portray the problem of declassing as it affects the present. Therefore he avoids this subject and preserves in his portrayals the great historical objectivity of the true epic writer.

For this reason alone, then, it is completely wrong to see Scott as a Romantic writer, unless one wishes to extend the concept of Romanticism to embrace all great literature in the first third of the nineteenth century. But then the physiognomy of Romanticism, in the proper, narrow sense, becomes blurred. And this is of great importance if we are to understand Scott. For the historical subject-matter of his novels is very close to that of the Romantics proper. However, . . . Scott's interpretation of this subject-matter is entirely opposed to that of the Romantics, as is his manner of portrayal. This contrast has its

first, immediate expression in the composition of his novels—with the mediocre, prosaic hero as the central figure.

Naturally, Scott's conservative philistinism is manifest here as well. Already Balzac, his great admirer and successor, took objection to this English philistinism. He says, for example, that with very few exceptions all of Scott's heroines represent the same type of philistinely correct, normal English woman; that there is no room in these novels for the interesting and complex tragedies and comedies of love and marriage. Balzac is right in his criticism, and it applies far beyond the erotic sphere which he stresses. Scott does not command the magnificent, profound psychological dialectics of character which distinguishes the novel of the last great period of bourgeois development. (pp. 31-4)

But the change which Scott effects in the history of world literature is independent of this limitation of his human and poetic horizon. Scott's greatness lies in his capacity to give living human embodiment to historical-social types. The typically human terms in which great historical trends become tangible had never before been so superbly, straightforwardly and pregnantly portrayed. And above all, never before had this kind of portrayal been consciously set at the centre of the representation of reality.

This applies to his mediocre heroes as well. They are unsurpassed in their portrayal of the decent and attractive as well as narrow-minded features of the English "middle class". And as central figures they provide a perfect instrument for Scott's way of presenting the totality of certain transitional stages of history. This relationship was most clearly recognized by the great Russian critic, Belinsky. He accepts that the majority of the minor characters are more interesting and significant as human beings than the mediocre main hero, yet he strongly defends Scott. "This has indeed to be the case in a work of purely epic nature, where the chief character serves merely as an external central hub round which the events unfold and where he may distinguish himself merely by general human qualities which earn our human sympathy; for the hero of the epic is life itself and not the individual. In epic, the individual is, so to speak, subject to the event; the event over-shadows the human personality by its magnitude and importance, drawing our attention away from him by the interestingness, diversity and multiplicity of its images."

Belinsky is quite right in emphasizing the purely epic character of Scott's novels. In the entire history of the novel there are scarcely any other works—except perhaps those of Cooper and Tolstoy—which come so near to the character of the old epos. (p. 35)

Nevertheless, Scott's works are in no way modern attempts to galvanize the old epic artificially into new life, they are real and genuine novels. Even if his themes are very often drawn from the "age of heroes", from the infancy of mankind, the spirit of his writing is nevertheless that of man's maturity, the age of triumphing "prose". This difference must be stressed if only because it is intimately connected with the composition of Scott's novels, with the conception of their "hero". Scott's novel hero is in his way just as typical for this genre as Achilles and Odysseus were for the real epopee. The difference between the two hero types illustrates very sharply the fundamental difference between epic and novel, moreover in a case where the novel reaches its closest point to the epic. The heros of the epic are, as Hegel says, "total individuals who magnificently concentrate within themselves what is otherwise dispersed in the national character, and in this they remain great, free and noble human characters''. Thereby ''these principal characters acquire the right to be placed at the summit and to see the principal event in connection with their individual persons''. The principal figures in Scott's novels are also typical characters nationally, but in the sense of the decent and average, rather than the eminent and all-embracing. The latter are the national heroes of a poetic view of life, the former of a prosaic one.

It is easy to see how these contrasting conceptions of the hero spring from the fundamental requirements of epic and novel. Achilles is not only compositionally the central figure of the epic, he is also a head taller than all his fellow actors, he really is the sun round which the planets revolve. Scott's heroes, as central figures of the novel, have an entirely opposite function. It is their task to bring the extremes whose struggle fills the novel, whose clash expresses artistically a great crisis in society, into contact with one another. Through the plot, at whose centre stands this hero, a neutral ground is sought and found upon which the extreme, opposing social forces can be brought into a human relationship with one another. (pp. 35-6)

Scott presents great crises of historical life in his novels. Accordingly, hostile social forces, bent on one another's destruction, are everywhere colliding. Since those who lead these warring forces are always passionate partisans of their respective sides, there is the danger that their struggle will become a merely external picture of mutual destruction incapable of arousing the human sympathies and enthusiasms of the reader. It is here that the compositional importance of the mediocre hero comes in. Scott always chooses as his principal figures such as may, through character and fortune, enter into human contact with both camps. The appropriate fortunes of such a mediocre hero, who sides passionately with neither of the warring camps in the great crisis of his time can provide a link of this kind without forcing the composition. (pp. 36-7)

This manner of composition is not the product of a ''search for form'' or some ingeniously ''skill'', it stems rather from the strengths and limitations of Scott's literary personality. In the first place Scott's conception of English history is, as we have seen, that of a ''middle course'' asserting itself through the struggle of extremes. The central figures of the Waverley type represent for Scott the age-old steadfastness of English development amidst the most terrible crises. In the second place, however, Scott, the great realist, recognizes that no civil war in history has been so violent as to turn the entire population without exception into fanatical partisans of one or other of the contending camps. Large sections of people have always stood between the camps with fluctuating sympathies now for this side, now for the other. And these fluctuating sympathies have often played a decisive role in the actual outcome of the crisis. In addition, the daily life of the nation still goes on amidst the most terrible civil war. It has to go on in the sheer economic sense that if it does not, the nation will starve and perish. But it also goes on in every other respect, and this continuation of daily life is an important foundation for the continuity of cultural development. Of course, the continuation of daily life certainly does not mean that the life, thought and experience of these non- or not passionately participant popular masses can remain untouched by the historical crisis. The continuity is always at the same time a growth, a further development. The ''middle-of-the-road heroes'' of Scott also represent this side of popular life and historical development.

But still further and very important consequences flow from this manner of composition. For instance what may sound paradoxical to the reader prejudiced by present-day traditions of the historical novel, but is nevertheless true, is the fact that Scott's incomparable ability to recreate the great figures of history was due to precisely this aspect of his composition. In Scott's life-work we meet with the most important personalities of English and even of French history: Richard *Coeur de Lion*, Louix XI, Elizabeth, Mary Stuart, Cromwell etc. All these figures appear in Scott in their real historical grandeur. Yet Scott is never prompted by a feeling of romantically decorative hero-worship à la Carlyle. For him the great historical personality is the representative of an important and significant movement embracing large sections of the people. He is great because his personal passion and personal aim coincide with this great historical movement, because he concentrates within himself its positive and negative sides, because he gives to these popular strivings their clearest expression, because he is their standard-bearer in good and in evil.

For this reason Scott never shows the evolution of such a personality. Instead, he always presents us with the personality complete. Complete, yet not without the most careful preparation. This preparation, however, is not a personal and psychological one, but objective, social-historical. That is to say, Scott, by disclosing the actual conditions of life, the actual growing crisis in people's lives, depicts all the problems of popular life which lead up to the historical crisis he has represented. And when he has made us sympathizers and understanding participants of this crisis, when we understand exactly for what reasons the crisis has arisen, for what reasons the nation has split into two camps, and when we have seen the attitude of the various sections of the population towards this crisis, only then does the great historical hero enter upon the scene of the novel. (pp. 37-8)

Scott thus lets his important figures grow out of the being of the age, he never explains the age from the position of its great representatives, as do the Romantic hero-worshippers. Hence they can never be central figures of the action. For the being of the age can only appear as a broad and many-sided picture if the everyday life of the people, the joys and sorrows, crises and confusions of average human beings are portrayed. The important leading figure, who embodies an historical movement, necessarily does so at a certain level of abstraction. Scott, by first showing the complex and involved character of popular life itself, creates this being which the leading figure then has to generalize and concentrate in an historical deed. (p. 39)

Scott's unequalled historical genius shows itself in the individual characteristics which he gives his leading figures so that they really concentrate in themselves the salient positive and negative sides of the movement concerned. The social and historical solidarity of leader and led in Scott is differentiated with extraordinary subtlety. Burley's single-minded, dauntless, heroic fanaticism marks the human summit of the rebellious Scottish Puritans at the time of Stuart Restoration, just as Vich Ian Vohr's peculiar, adventuresome compound of French courtly manners and clan patriarchalism represents the reactionary side of Stuart Restoration attempts after the ''Glorious Revolution'' which closely involved backward sections of the Scottish people.

This close interaction, this deep unity between the historical representatives of a popular movement and the movement itself is heightened compositionally in Scott by the intensification and dramatic compression of events. . . . The inclusion of the dramatic element in the novel, the concentration of events, the greater significance of dialogue, i.e. the direct coming-to-grips of colliding opposites in conversation, these are intimately linked with the attempt to portray historical reality as it actually was, so that it could be both humanly authentic and yet be re-liveable by the reader of a later age. It is a question of the concentration of characterization. Only bunglers have maintained (and continue to do so) that the historical characterization of people and events means the accumulation of single, historically characteristic traits.

Scott never under-estimated the importance of picturesque, descriptive elements of this kind. Indeed, he used them so much that superficial critics have seen here the essence of his art. But for Scott the historical characterization of time and place, the historical "here and now" is something much deeper. For him it means that certain crises in the personal destinies of a number of human beings coincide and interweave within the determining context of an historical crisis. It is precisely for this reason that his manner of portraying the historical crisis is never abstract, the split of the nation into warring parties always runs through the centre of the closest human relationships. Parents and children, lover and beloved, old friends etc. confront one another as opponents, or the inevitability of this confrontation carries the collision deep into their personal lives. It is always a fate suffered by groups of people connected and involved with one another; and it is never a matter of one single catastrophe, but of a chain of catastrophes, where the solution of each gives birth to a new conflict. Thus the profound grasp of the historical factor in human life demands a dramatic concentration of the epic framework. (pp. 40-1)

The colourful and varied richness of Scott's historical world is a consequence of the multiplicity of these interactions between individuals and the unity of social existence which underlies this richness. The problem of composition already discussed, the fact, that the great historical figures, the leaders of the warring classes and parties are only minor characters in the story, now takes on a new light. Scott does not stylize these figures, nor place them upon a Romantic pedestal; he portrays them as human beings with virtues and weaknesses, good and bad qualities. And yet they never create a petty impression. With all their weaknesses they appear historically imposing. The primary reason for this is, of course, Scott's deep understanding for the peculiarity of different historical periods. But the fact that he is able to combine historical grandeur with genuine human qualities in this way depends upon the manner of his composition. (p. 45)

[This] manner of composition certainly does not mean that Scott's historical figures are not individualized down to their smallest human peculiarities. They are never mere representatives of historical movements, ideas etc. Scott's great art consists precisely in individualizing his historical heroes in such a way that certain, purely individual traits of character, quite peculiar to them, are brought into a very complex, very live relationship with the age in which they live, with the movement which they represent and endeavour to lead to victory. Scott represents simultaneously the historical necessity of this particular individual personality and the individual role which he plays in history. What results from this peculiar relationship is not merely whether the struggle will end in victory or defeat, but also the special, historical character of the victory or defeat, its special historical *valeur*, its class timbre. (p. 47)

[The] truthfulness of historical atmosphere which we are able to relive in Scott rests on the popular character of his art. This popular character met with growing incomprehension during the literary and cultural decadence. Taine asserts quite erroneously that Scott's art propagated feudal attitudes. This false theory was taken over whole by vulgar sociology and further extended, the sole difference being that Scott was now conceived as the poet, not of the feudal world, but of the English merchants and colonizers of contemporary English imperialism. Such "theories" of the historical novel—devised in order to erect a Chinese wall between the classical past and the present and so to deny the Socialist character of our present-day culture à la Trotsky—see in Scott nothing but the bard of the colonizing merchants.

The precise opposite is true. And this was clearly recognized by Scott's immediate contemporaries and important successors. George Sand quite rightly said of him: "He is the poet of the peasant, soldier, outlaw and artisan." For . . . Scott portrays the great transformations of history as transformations of popular life. He always starts by showing how important historical changes affect everyday life, the effect of material and psychological changes upon people who react immediately and violently to them, without understanding their causes. Only by working up from this basis, does he portray the complicated ideological, political and moral movements to which such changes inevitably give rise. The popular character of Scott's art, therefore, does not consist in an exclusive portrayal of the oppressed and exploited classes. That would be a narrow interpretation. Like every great popular writer, Scott aims at portraying the totality of national life in its complex interaction between "above" and "below"; his vigorous popular character is expressed in the fact that "below" is seen as the material basis and artistic explanation for what happens "above". (pp. 48-9)

Scott sees and portrays the complex and intricate path which led to England's national greatness and to the formation of the national character. As a sober, conservative petty aristocrat, he naturally affirms the result, and the necessity of this result is the ground on which he stands. But Scott's artistic world-view by no means stops here. Scott sees the endless field of ruin, wrecked existences, wrecked or wasted heroic, human endeavour, broken social formations etc. which were the necessary preconditions of the end-result.

Undoubtedly, there is a certain contradiction here between Scott's directly political views and his artistic world picture. He, too, like so many great realists, such as Balzac or Tolstoy, became a great realist despite his own political and social views. In Scott, too, one can establish Engels's "triumph of realism" over his personal, political and social views. Sir Walter Scott, the Scottish petty aristocrat, automatically affirms this development with a sober rationality. Scott, the writer, on the other hand, embodies the sentiment of the Roman poet, Lucan: "Victrix causa diis placuit, sed victa Catoni" (the victorious cause pleased the gods, but the vanquished pleased Cato).

It would be wrong, however, to interpret this contrast all too rigidly, without interconnections: namely, to see in the sober affirmation of English reality, of the "middle way" of English development something purely negative, something which could only have hindered the unfolding of Scott's great historical art. On the contrary, we must see that this great historical art arose precisely out of the interaction, out of the dialectical interpenetration of both these sides of Scott's personality. It is precisely because of his character that Scott did not become a Romantic, a glorifier or elegist of past ages. And it was for this reason that he was able to portray objectively the ruination of past social formations, despite all his human sympathy for, and artistic sensitivity, to the splendid, heroic qualities which they contained. Objectively, in a large historical and artistic sense: he saw at one and the same time their outstanding qualities and the historical necessity of their decline.

This objectivity, however, only enhances the true poetry of the past. . . . [The] official representatives of earlier ruling classes by no means play the leading role in Scott's picture of history, quite contrary to the misrepresentations of later critics. Among the aristocratic figures of his novels—if one leaves out the correct "middle-of-the-road heroes", who can only very conditionally be called positive heroes—there are very few positively drawn figures. On the contrary, Scott very often shows in a humorous, satirical or tragic manner the weakness, the human and moral degeneration of the upper strata. Admittedly the Pretender in *Waverley*, Mary Stuart in *The Abbot*, even the Prince of Wales in *The Fair Maid of Perth* exhibit humanly attractive and winning features, but the chief tendency in their portrayal is to show their inability to fulfil their historic missions. In such cases Scott achieves his poetry by conveying to us the objectively historical, social reasons for this personal inability via the atmosphere of the whole, without pedantic analysis. Further, in a whole number of figures, Scott draws the repellently brutal sides of aristocratic rule (e.g. the Knight Templar in *Waverley*, etc.) as well as the already comic incapacity of the court nobility, increasingly severed from national life, to cope with the problems of their age. The few positive figures are made positive mostly by simple fulfilment of duty and gentlemanliness. Only a few great champions of historical progress, such as Louis XI in particular, are allowed historical monumentality.

In most cases where aristocratic figures play a positive role, whether completely positive or problematic, this rests upon their connection with the people, which of course usually takes the form of a living or, at least, not yet extinct patriarchal relationship (e.g. in the case of the Duke of Argyle in *The Heart of Midlothian*). The real life in Scott's historical reality is formed by the life of the people themselves. As an English petty aristocrat with strong ties both in tradition and individual habits of life with the bourgeoisie, Scott has a deep sympathy for the defiant self-assurance of the medieval English-Scots burgher and the independent, free peasant. In the character of Henry Gow in particular (*The Fair Maid of Perth*), he gives a fine picture of this medieval burgher courage and self-confidence. Henry Gow as a fighter is at least the equal of every knight, but he proudly declines the knighthood offered to him by the Earl of Douglas; burgher he is and free burgher he will live and die.

In Scott's life-work we find marvellous scenes and characters from the life of the serfs and the free peasants, from the fortunes of society's outlaws, the smugglers, robbers, professional soldiers, deserters and so on. Yet it is in his unforgettable portrayal of the survivals of gentile society, of the Scottish clans where the poetry of his portrayal of past life chiefly lies. Here in material and subject-matter alone, there is present such a powerful element of the heroic period of mankind, that Scott's novels at their height do indeed approach the old epics. Scott is a giant discoverer and awakener of this long vanished past. It is true that the eighteenth century already loved and enjoyed the poetry of primitive life. And in the wave of enthusiasm for Homer, in Homer's ousting of Virgil as the model, there is undoubtedly a dawning awareness of this infant period of mankind. Important thinkers such as Ferguson even saw the relationship between the Homeric heroes and the American Indi-

ans. Nevertheless this predilection remained abstract and moralizing in quality. Scott was the first actually to bring this period to life, by introducing us into the everyday life of the clans, by portraying upon this real basis both the exceptional and unequalled human greatness of this primitive order as well as the inner necessity of its tragic downfall.

In this way, by bringing to life those objective poetic principles which really underlie the poetry of popular life and history, Scott became the great poet of past ages, the really popular portrayer of history. Heine clearly understood this quality and saw, too, that the strength of Scott's writing lay precisely in this presentation of popular life, in the fact that the official big events and great historical figures were not given a central place. He says: "Walter Scott's novels sometimes reproduce the spirit of English history much more faithfully than Hume." The important historians and philosophers of history of this period, Thierry and Hegel, aspire to a similar interpretation of history. But with them it goes no further than a demand, a theoretical pronouncement of this necessity. For in the field of theory and historiography only historical materialism is capable of intellectually unearthing this basis of history, of showing what the childhood of mankind was really like. But what in Morgan, Marx and Engels was worked out and proved with theoretical and historical clarity, lives, moves and has its being poetically in the best historical novels of Scott. (pp. 54-6)

Georg Lukács, "The Classical Form of the Historical Novel," in his The Historical Novel, *translated by Hannah Mitchell and Stanley Mitchell, Merlin Press, 1962, pp. 19-88.*

DAVID DAICHES   (essay date 1951)

[*Daiches is a prominent English scholar and critic who has written extensively on English and American literature. In the following excerpt, he offers an extended assessment of what he considers to be Scott's best works, the "Scotch Novels." Daiches emphasizes how these novels reflect the ongoing conflict in Scott's mind between his passionate love for Scotland's past and his sober understanding of the historical inevitability of the union of Scotland with England. This essay was first published in* Nineteenth-Century Fiction *in September 1951.*]

The novels on which Scott's reputation as a novelist must stand or fall are his 'Scotch novels'—those that deal with Scottish history and manners—and not even all of those. *Waverley, Guy Mannering, The Antiquary, Old Mortality, The Heart of Midlothian, Rob Roy, The Bride of Lammermoor, A Legend of Montrose* and *Redgauntlet*—all, except *Redgauntlet*, earlier novels—constitute Scott's list of masterpieces. There are others of the *Waverley Novels* of which no novelist need be ashamed, many with excellent incidental scenes and memorable character studies, but this group of Scottish novels all possess Scott's characteristic virtues, and they represent his particular kind of fiction at its very best.

The fact that these novels are all concerned with Scottish history and manners is intimately bound up with the reasons for their being his best novels. For Scott's attitude to life was derived from his response to the fate of his own country: it was the complex of feelings with which he contemplated the phase of Scottish history immediately preceding his own time that provided the point of view which gave life—often a predominantly tragic life—to these novels. Underlying most of these novels is a tragic sense of the inevitability of a drab but necessary progress, a sense of the impotence of the traditional kind of heroism, a passionately regretful awareness of the fact that the Good Old Cause was lost forever and the glory of Scotland must give way to her interest.

Scott's attitude to Scotland, as Edwin Muir pointed out some years ago in a thoughtful and provocative study [see Additional Bibliography], was a mixture of regret for the old days when Scotland was an independent but turbulent and distracted country, and of satisfaction at the peace, prosperity and progress which he felt had been assured by the Union with England in 1707 and the successful establishment of the Hanoverian dynasty on the British throne. His problem, in one form or another, was the problem of every Scottish writer after Scotland ceased to have an independent culture of her own: how to reconcile his country's traditions with what appeared to be its interest. Scott was always strongly moved by everything that reminded him of Scotland's past, of the days of the country's independence and the relatively recent days when the Jacobites were appealing to that very emotion to gain support for their cause. He grew up as the Jacobite tradition was finally ebbing away, amid the first generation of Scotsmen committed once and for all to the association with England and the Hanoverian dynasty. He felt strongly that that association was inevitable and right and advantageous—he exerted himself greatly to make George IV popular in Scotland—yet there were strong emotions on the other side too, and it was these emotions that made him Tory in politics and that provided the greater blessing of leading him to literature and history. (pp. 90-2)

This conflict within Scott gave life and passion to his Scottish novels, for it led him to construct plots and invent characters which, far from being devices in an adventure story or means to make history look picturesque, illustrated what to him was the central paradox of modern life. And that paradox admitted of the widest application, for it was an aspect of all commercial and industrial civilizations. Civilization must be paid for by the cessation of the old kind of individual heroic action. Scott welcomed civilization, but he also sighed after the old kind of individual heroic action. Scott's theme is a modification of that of Cervantes, and specifically, *Redgauntlet* is Scott's *Don Quixote*. (p. 92)

The Jacobite movement for Scott was not simply a picturesque historical event; it was the last attempt to restore to Scotland something of the old heroic way of life. This is not the place for a discussion of the real historical meaning of Jacobitism—I am concerned at present only with how Scott saw it and how he used it in his novels. He used it, and its aftermath, to symbolize at once the attractiveness and the futility of the old Scotland. *That* Scotland was doomed after the Union of Parliaments of 1707 and doubly doomed after the Battle of Culloden in 1746; the aftermath of 1707 is shown in *The Heart of Midlothian* and of 1746 in *Redgauntlet*. In both novels, explicitly in the latter and murmuring in an undertone in the former, there is indicated the tragic theme (for it *is* tragic) that the grand old causes are all lost causes, and the old heroic action is no longer even fatal—it is merely useless and silly. One thinks of the conclusion of Bishop Hurd's *Letters on Chivalry and Romance:* 'What we have gotten by this revolution, you will say, is a great deal of good sense. What we have lost is a world of fine fabling.' But to Scott it was more than a world of fine fabling that was lost; it was a world of heroic ideals, which he could not help believing should still be worth something. He knew, however, even before it was brought home to him by Constable's failure and his consequent own bankruptcy, that in the reign of George IV it was not worth much—certainly not as much as novels about it.

Scott has often been presented as a lover of the past, but that is a partial portrait. He was a lover of the past combined with a believer in the present, and the mating of these incompatible characters produced that tension which accounted for his greatest novels. (pp. 93-4)

It is this ambivalence in Scott's approach to the history of his country—combined, of course, with certain remarkable talents which I shall discuss later—that accounts for the unique quality of his Scottish novels. He was able to take an *odi et amo* attitude to some of the most exciting crises of Scottish history. If Scott's desire to set himself up as an old-time landed gentleman in a large country estate was romantic, the activities by which he financed—or endeavoured to finance—his schemes were the reverse, and there is nothing romantic in James Glen's account of Scott's financial transactions prefixed to the centenary edition of his letters. He filled Abbotsford with historical relics, but they were relics, and they gave Abbotsford something of the appearance of a museum. He thus tried to resolve the conflict in his way of life by making modern finance pay for a house filled with antiquities. This resolution could not, however, eliminate the basic ambivalence in his approach to recent Scottish history: that remained, to enrich his fiction.

This double attitude on Scott's part prevented him from taking sides in his historical fiction, and Sir Herbert Grierson has complained, though mildly, of this refusal to commit himself. 'Of the historical events which he chooses for the setting of his story,' writes Sir Herbert, 'his judgment is always that of the good sense and moderated feeling of his own age. He will not take sides out and out with either Jacobite or Hanoverian, Puritan or Cavalier; nor does he attempt to transcend either the prejudices or the conventional judgment of his contemporaries, he makes no effort to attain to a fresh and deeper reading of the events.' Sir Herbert partly answers his own criticism later on, when he concedes that Shakespeare likewise concealed his own views and did not stand clearly for this or that cause. But there are two questions at issue here. One is whether Scott's seeing both sides of an historical situation is an advantage or a disadvantage to him as a novelist; the other is whether, as Sir Herbert charges, he accepts the prejudices or the conventional judgment of his contemporaries and 'makes no effort to attain to a fresh and deeper reading of the events'. I should maintain that his seeing both sides is a great advantage, and, as to the second point, that, in terms of his art, Scott *does* attain to a fresh and deeper reading of the events. I say in terms of his art, because I of course agree that there is no overt philosophizing about the meaning of history in Scott's novels. But the stories as told by Scott not only 'attain to a fresh and deeper reading of the events', but also, I submit, do so in such a way as to illuminate aspects of life in general. As this is the crux of the matter, it requires demonstration in some detail.

Let us consider first *Waverley,* Scott's initial essay in prose fiction, and a much better novel, I venture to believe, than most critics generally concede it to be. . . . [The] plot is built around an Englishman's journey into Scotland and his becoming temporarily involved in the Jacobite Rebellion on the Jacobite side. How does he become so involved and how are the claims of the Jacobite cause presented? First he becomes angry with his own side as a result of a series of accidents and misunderstandings (undelivered letters and so on) for which neither side is to blame. In this mood, he is willing to consider the possibility of identifying himself with the other side—the Jacobite side—and does so all the more readily because he is involved in friendly relations with many of its representatives.

He admires the heroism and the clan spirit of the Highlanders, and their primitive vigour (as compared with the more disciplined and conventional behaviour of the Hanoverian troops with whom he formerly served) strikes his imagination. He becomes temporarily a Jacobite, then, not so much because he has been persuaded of the justice of the cause, or because he believes that a Jacobite victory would really improve the state of Britain, but because his emotions have become involved. It has become a personal, not a national, matter.

It should be noted further that Waverley goes into the Highlands in the first place simply in order to satisfy a romantic curiosity about the nature of the Highlanders, and it is only after arriving there that he succumbs to the attractions of clan life. Not that his reason ever fully succumbs: though he comes to realize the grievances of the Highland Jacobites, he has no illusions about their disinterestedness or their political sagacity, and even when he does surrender emotionally he remains critical of many aspects of their behaviour. Thus it is emotion against reason, the past against the present, the claims of a dying heroic world against the colder but ultimately more convincing claims of modern urban civilization.

The essence of the novel is the way in which these conflicting claims impinge on Waverley. It is worth noting that Waverley, though he began his progress as a soldier in the army of King George, did not set out completely free of any feeling for the other side. Though his father had deserted the traditions of his family and gone over completely to the Government, his uncle, who brought him up, was an old Jacobite, and his tutor, too, though an impossible pedant who had little influence on Wa-

A painting by Eugène Delacroix of Rebecca's abduction in Ivanhoe.

verley, supported the old régime in both Church and State. Waverley thus belonged to the first generation of his family to begin his career under the auspices of the new world—specifically, to become a soldier of King George as a young man. That new world was not yet as firmly established in Scotland as it came to be during Scott's own youth: there was still a possibility of successful rebellion in Waverley's day, but none in Scott's. It was too late for Scott to become a Jacobite, even temporarily, except in his imagination, so he let Waverley do it for him. The claims of the two sides are a little more evenly balanced for Waverley than for Scott, yet even in the earlier period the issue is never really in doubt, and Waverley's part in the Jacobite rebellion must be small, and must be explained away and forgiven by the Government in the end. Above all, it must be a part entered into by his emotions on personal grounds rather than by his reason on grounds of national interest.

I have said that the essence of *Waverley* is the way in which the conflicting claims of the two worlds impinge on the titular hero. The most significant action there cannot concern the hero, but involves the world in which he finds himself. It is important, of course, that the hero should be presented as someone sensitive to the environment in which he finds himself; otherwise his function as the responsive observer could not be sustained. To ensure that his hero is seen by the reader as having the proper sensitivity, Scott gives us at the opening of the book several chapters describing in detail Waverley's education and the development of his state of mind. Waverley's education, as described in Chapter Three, is precisely that of Scott himself. By his undisciplined reading of old chronicles, Italian and Spanish romances, Elizabethan poetry and drama, and 'the earlier literature of the northern nations', young Waverley was fitted to sympathize with the romantic appeal of the Jacobite cause and its Highland supporters. This, as we know from Lockhart and from Scott's own account, was Scott's own literary equipment, and it qualified Waverley to act for him in his relations with the Scottish Jacobites. (pp. 95-8)

The subtitle of *Waverley* is ''Tis Sixty Years Since', and the phrase is repeated many times throughout the book. It deals, that is to say, with a period which, while distant enough to have a historical interest, was not altogether out of the ken of Scott's own generation. In the preface to the first edition of *The Antiquary,* his third novel, Scott wrote: 'The present work completes a series of fictitious narratives, intended to illustrate the manners of Scotland at three different periods. *Waverley* embraced the age of our fathers, *Guy Mannering* that of our youth, and the *Antiquary* refers to the last years of the eighteenth century.' (Scott, it will be remembered, was born in 1771.) As Scott comes closer to his own day, the possibilities for heroic action recede and the theme of the lost heir is introduced as a sort of substitute. It was with recent Scottish history that Scott was most concerned, for the conflict within himself was the result of relatively recent history. The Jacobite Rebellion of 1745 was the watershed, as it were, dividing once and for all the old from the new, and Scott therefore began his novels with a study of the relation between the two worlds at that critical time. It was not that the old Scotland had wholly disappeared, but that it was slowly yet inevitably disappearing that upset Scott. Its disappearance is progressively more inevitable in each of the next two novels after *Waverley.*

Guy Mannering is not in the obvious sense a historical novel at all. It is a study of aspects of the Scottish situation in the days of the author's youth, where the plot is simply an excuse for bringing certain characters into relation with each other. Once again we have an Englishman—Colonel Mannering, who, like Edward Waverley, shares many of his creator's characteristics—coming into Scotland and surrendering to the charm of the country. Scott has to get him mixed up in the affairs of the Bertrams in order to keep him where he wants him. Round Guy Mannering move gypsies, smugglers, lairds, dominies, lawyers and farmers, and it is to be noted that none of these characters, from Meg Merrilies to Dandie Dinmont, belongs to the new world: they are all essentially either relics of an earlier age, like the gypsies, or the kind of person who does not substantially change with the times, like that admirable farmer Dandie. These people are made to move around the Bertram family, or at least are brought into the story through some direct or indirect association with that family, and the family is decayed and impoverished. The lost heir is found and restored, and, largely through the benevolent offices of an English colonel, a Scottish landed gentleman is settled again on his ancestral acres. That is how things happen in the days of Scott's youth: no clash of arms or open conflict of two worlds, but the prophecies of gypsies, the intrigues of smugglers, the hearty activities of farmers, all set against the decay of an ancient family and all put to right in the end with the help of a gypsy, an English officer, and a Scottish lawyer. If the heroic element is less than in *Waverley,* the element of common life is greater, and the two virtues of honesty (in Dinmont) and urbanity (in Counsellor Pleydell) eventually emerge as those most worth while.

Counsellor Pleydell is a particularly interesting character because he represents that combination of good sense and humanity which Scott so often thought of as mediating between extremes and enabling the new world to preserve, in a very different context, something of the high generosity of the old. Pleydell is a lawyer, esentially middle class and respectable, but he is drawn with such sympathy that he threatens to remove most of the interest from the rather artificial main plot and share with Dandie Dinmont the reader's chief attention. If the gypsy Meg Merrilies provides something of the old-world romantic note—and she does so with great vigour and effectiveness—the lawyer and the farmer between them represent the ordinary man providing comfort for the future. The bluff courage and honesty of the farmer and the kindly intelligence of the lawyer dominate the story at the end. (pp. 101-03)

The scene of *The Antiquary* is the Scotland of Scott's own day. The external plot, which is once again that of the lost heir, is, as usual, not to be taken seriously: its function is to bring the faintly drawn Englishman Lovel into Scotland and so set the appropriate characters into motion. In three successive novels Scott begins by bringing an Englishman into Scotland, by sending forth an observer to note the state of the country at the time represented by the novel's action. Lovel, of course, is no more the hero of *The Antiquary* than Christopher Sly is the hero of *The Taming of the Shrew,* and his turning out at the end to be the lost heir of Glenallan is the merest routine drawing down of the curtain. The life of the novel—and it has abundant life—centres in the Scottish characters whom the plot enables Scott to bring together, and in their reactions to each other. (pp. 105-06)

The characteristic tension of Scott's novels is scarcely perceptible in *The Antiquary,* though I think it can be discerned by those who look carefully for it. In *Old Mortality* it is present continuously and is in a sense the theme of the story. In this novel Scott goes back to the latter part of the seventeenth century to deal with the conflict between the desperate and embittered Covenanters and the royal armies intent on stamping out a religious disaffection which was bound up with political disagreements. Though this was an aspect of Scottish history which, in its most acute phases at least, was settled by the Revolution of 1689, it represented a type of conflict which is characteristic of much Scottish history and which Scott saw as a struggle between an exaggerated royalism and a fanatical religion. It should be said at the outset that as a historical novel in the most literal sense of the word—as an accurate picture of the state of affairs at the time—this is clearly Scott's best work. Generations of subsequent research have only confirmed the essential justice and fairness of Scott's picture of both sides. The only scholar ever seriously to challenge Scott on this was the contemporary divine, Thomas McCrie, who made an attack on the accuracy of Scott's portrait of the Covenanters, but posterity has thoroughly vindicated Scott and shown McCrie's attack to have been the result of plain prejudice.

But we do not read *Old Mortality* for its history, though we could do worse. We read it, as Scott wrote it, as a study of the kinds of mentality which faced each other in this conflict, a study of how a few extremists on each side managed, as they so often do, to split the country into warring camps with increasing bitterness on the one side and increasing cruelty on the other. (pp. 107-08)

If Scotland had not torn itself in two before the issues presented in the eighteenth century were ever thought of, the fate of the country might have been different, and Scott's study of the last of the Scottish civil wars before the Jacobite Rebellions is thus linked with his major preoccupation—the destiny of modern Scotland. If moderate men on both sides could have won, the future would have been very different. But, though there were moderate men on both sides and Scott delighted to draw them, their advice in the moments of crisis was never taken. There is no more moving passage in the novel than the description of Morton's vain attempt to make his fanatical colleagues behave sensibly before the Battle of Bothwell Brig. There is a passion behind the telling of much of this story that is very different from the predominantly sunny mood of *The Antiquary.* The extremists prevail, the Covenanting army is destroyed, and a victorious Government takes a cruel revenge on embittered and resolute opponents. This is one novel of Scott's where the moderate men do not remain at the end to point the way to the future. (p. 109)

Harry Morton, the observer, the man who sees something good on both sides and is roped into the Covenanting side by a series of accidents, represents the humane, intelligent liberal in a world of extremists. *Old Mortality* is a study of a society which had no place for such a character: it is essentially a tragedy, and one with a very modern ring.

If *Old Mortality* is, from one point of view, Scott's study of the earlier errors which made the later cleavage between Scotland and her past inevitable (for it is true to say that after the Covenanting wars the English saw no way but a union of the two countries to ensure the perpetual agreement of the Scots to the king chosen by England and to prevent the succession question from being a constant bugbear), *Rob Roy* is a return to his earlier theme, a study of eighteenth-century Highland grievances and their relation to Scotland's destiny. It is, in a sense, a rewriting of *Waverley* and the main theme is less baldly presented. The compromise character here is the ever-delightful Bailie Nicol Jarvie, the Glasgow merchant who is nevertheless related to Rob Roy himself and, for all his love of peace and his commercial interests, can on occasion cross the Highland line into his cousin's country and become involved in scenes of violence in which, for a douce citizen of Glasgow, he acquits himself very honourably.

Rob Roy represents the old heroic Scotland, while the worthy Bailie represents the new. The Union of 1707 may have been a sad thing for those who prized Scotland's independence, but to the Bailie and his like it opened up new fields for foreign trade, and brought increased wealth.... Rob Roy is courageous and sympathetic, and Helen Macgregor, his wife, is noble to the verge of melodrama, but they represent a confused and divided Highlands and are, after all, nothing but glorified freebooters. Scott, in the person of Francis Osbaldistone, pities their wrongs and feels for their present state, but he knows that they and what they stand for are doomed—indeed, they admit it themselves—and throws in his lot with the prudent Bailie. (pp. 110-11)

There are two pivots to this novel; one is the relations between Francis Osbaldistone and his friends with Rob Roy and *his* friends, and the other is Francis's relations with his uncle and cousins. It is, I believe, a mistake to regard the family complications in *Rob Roy* as mere machinery designed to provide a reason for young Osbaldistone's journey into Scotland: they loom much too largely in the novel for that. They represent, in fact, a statement of the theme on which the Rob Roy scenes are a variation—the impossibility of the old life in the new world. Francis's uncle is an old-fashioned Tory Jacobite squire, completely gone to seed, and his sons are either fools or villains. This is what has become of the knights of old—they are either freebooters like Rob Roy, shabby remnants of landed gentry like Sir Hildebrand, or complete villains like Rashleigh. Francis's father had escaped from this environment to embrace the new world wholeheartedly and become a prosperous London merchant. He is at one extreme, Bailie Nicol Jarvie is the middle figure, and Rob Roy is at the other extreme. But the pattern is more complicated than this, for the novel contains many variations on each type of character, so much so, in fact, that it is an illuminating and accurate picture of Scottish types in the early eighteenth century. And through it all runs the sense of the necessity of sacrificing heroism to prudence, even though heroism is so much more attractive. (pp. 112-13)

Of *The Heart of Midlothian,* which most critics consider the best of Scott's works, I shall say nothing, since I have analysed it in accordance with the view of Scott here developed in the introduction to my edition of the novel.

The Bride of Lammermoor, which followed *The Heart of Midlothian,* presents the conflict between the old and the new in naked, almost melodramatic terms: the decayed representative of an ancient family comes face to face with the modern purchaser of his estates. The book is stark tragedy, for the attempted compromise—the marriage between the old family and the new—is too much for circumstances, and the final death of hero and heroine emphasizes that no such direct solution of the problem is possible. (pp. 113-14)

A Legend of Montrose—the companion piece of *The Bride of Lammermoor* in the third series of *Tales of My Landlord*—is a slighter novel than those I have been discussing: it lives through one character only, Captain Dugald Dalgetty, the only military figure in English literature beside whom Fluellen looks rather thin. But this one character is sufficient to illuminate the whole story, since, in a tale concerning the Civil War of the 1640s, he represents the most complete compromise figure—the mer-

cenary soldier, trained in the religious wars of the Continent, willing to fight on and be loyal to any side which pays him adequately and regularly. This is another novel of a divided Scotland—divided on an issue foreshadowing that which divides the two camps in *Old Mortality.* Here again we have Highland heroism presented as something magnificent but impossible, and the main burden of the novel falls on Dugald Dalgetty, mercenary and pedant (a most instructive combination to those interested in Scott's mind), the man of the future who, ridiculous and vulgar though he may be, has a firm code of honour of his own and performs his hired service scrupulously and courageously.

After *The Bride of Lammermoor* and *A Legend of Montrose* Scott turned to other fields than relatively recent Scottish history, and in *Ivanhoe* he wrote a straight novel of the age of chivalry without any attempt to relate it to what had hitherto been the principal theme of his prose fiction—the relations between the old heroic Scotland and the new Anglicized, commercial Britain.... But he returned later to the theme which was always in his mind, and in *Redgauntlet* produced if not certainly the best, then the most illuminating of his novels.

Redgauntlet is the story of a young Edinburgh man who becomes involved against his will in a belated Jacobite conspiracy some twenty years after the defeat of Prince Charlie at Culloden. The moving spirit of the conspiracy turns out to be the young man's own uncle (for, like so many of Scott's heroes, young Darsie Latimer is brought up in ignorance of his true parentage), who kidnaps him in order that, as the long-lost heir to the house of Redgauntlet, he may return to the ways of his ancestors and fight for the Pretender as his father had done before him. Darsie, of course, has no liking for this rôle so suddenly thrust upon him, and is saved from having to undertake it by the complete collapse of the conspiracy. That is the barest outline of the plot, which is enriched, as so often in Scott, with a galaxy of characters each of whom takes his place in the complex pattern of late eighteenth-century Scottish life which the novel creates.

As with most of the Scottish novels, the story moves between two extremes. On the one hand, there is the conscientious lawyer Saunders Fairford, his son Alan, who is Darsie's bosom friend and with whom Darsie has been living for some time before the story opens, and other characters representing respectable and professional Edinburgh. Saunders Fairford is Scott's portrait of his own father, and the figure is typical of all that is conventional, hard-working, middle-class, unromantic. At the other extreme is Darsie's uncle, a stern fanatical figure reminiscent of Balfour of Burley. Between the two worlds—that of respectable citizens who are completely reconciled to the new Scotland and that of fanatical Jacobites engaged in the vain task of trying to recreate the old—Scott places his usual assortment of mediating figures, from the blind fiddler, Wandering Willie, to that typical compromise character, the half-Jacobite Provost Crosbie. This is the Scotland in which Scott himself grew up and in which he recognized all the signs of the final death of the old order. For most of the characters Jacobitism is now possible only as a sentiment, not as a plan of action. But to Redgauntlet, who has dedicated his life to the restoration of the Stuarts, it is a plan of action, and the tragedy—for the novel is essentially a tragedy—lies in the manner of his disillusion. (pp. 114-16)

It is important for a proper understanding of Redgauntlet's character to note that his zeal is not only for the restoration of the Stuarts; it is, in some vague way, for the restoration of an independent Scotland, and his dominant emotion is Scottish nationalism rather than royalism. Scott made him a symbol of all that the old, independent Scotland stood for, and that is why his fate was of so much concern to his creator. . . . Scott, who burst into tears when he heard of old Scottish customs being abolished and who protested in horror when, at the uncovering of the long-hidden crown jewels of Scotland, one of the commissioners made as though to place the old Scottish crown on the head of one of the girls who were present—the Scott who, in his heart, had never really reconciled himself to the Union of 1707 (though he never dared say so, not even in his novels), was portraying in the character of Redgauntlet something of himself, something, perhaps, of what in spite of everything he wished to be. But as Darsie Latimer—who is clearly a self-portrait, though a partial one—he only touched the fringe of that tragedy, without becoming involved in it. (p. 118)

Basing Scott's claim on these Scottish novels, what then was his achievement and what is his place among British novelists? It might be said, in the first place, that Scott put his knowledge of history at the service of his understanding of certain basic paradoxes in human society and produced a series of novels which both illuminates a particular period and throws light on human character in general. His imagination, his abundant sense of life, his ear for vivid dialogue, his feeling for the striking incident, and that central, healthy sense of the humour of character, added, of course, essential qualities to his fiction. But it was his tendency to look at history through character and at character through the history that had worked on it that provided the foundation of his art. Scott's might be called a 'normal' sensibility, if such a thing exists. He has no interest in aberrations, exceptions or perversions, or in the minutiae of self-analysis—not unless they have played a substantial part in human history. Fanaticism, superstition, pedantry—these and qualities such as these are always with us, and Scott handles them again and again. But he handles them always from the point of view of the ordinary sensitive man looking on, not from their *own* point of view. We see Balfour of Burley through Morton's eyes, and Redgauntlet through Darsie Latimer's. We feel for them, understand them even, but never live with them. That is what I mean when I talk of Scott's *central* vision: his characters and situations are always observed by some one standing in a middle-of-the-road position. That position is the position of the humane, tolerant, informed and essentially happy man. It is fundamentally the position of a sane man. Scott was never the obsessed artist, but the happy writer.

Scott's abundant experience of law courts, both in Edinburgh and in his own sheriffdom, gave him a fund of knowledge of ordinary human psychology, and he had besides both historical knowledge and imagination. His eccentrics are never as fundamentally odd as Dicken's eccentrics: they are essentially ordinary people, people he had known in one form or another. Most important of all, Scott *enjoyed* people, in the way that Shakespeare must have done. They live and move in his novels with a Falstaffian gusto. There is indeed something of Shakespeare in Scott—not the Shakespeare of *Hamlet* or *Othello*, but the Shakespeare of *Henry IV* or *Twelfth Night*, and perhaps also of *Macbeth*. His gift for dialogue was tremendous, and his use of Scottish dialect to give it authenticity and conviction is unequalled by any other Scottish novelist except very occasionally John Galt, Stevenson in *Weir of Hermiston*, and perhaps Lewis Grassic Gibbon in our own century. In spite of all the tragic undertones in so many of his novels, most of them are redeemed into affirmations of life through the sheer

A painting by Eugène Delacroix of Ravenswood and Lucy at the Mermaidens' fountain in The Bride of Lammermoor.

vitality of the characters as they talk to each other. Scott's gallery of memorable characters—characters who live in the mind with their own individual idiom—cannot be beaten by any other British novelist, even if we restrict the selection to some eight of Scott's novels and ignore all the rest. But they are not merely characters in a pageant: they play their parts in an interpretation of modern life. I say of 'modern life' to emphasize the paradox: Scott, the historical novelist, was at his best when he wrote either about his own time or about the recent past which had produced those aspects of his own time about which he was chiefly concerned.

Of course Scott was often careless. He wrote fast, and employed broad brush strokes. Sometimes we feel that he wholly lacked an artistic conscience, for he could do the most preposterous things to fill up space or tie up a plot. His method of drawing up the curtain is often clumsy, but once the curtain is up, the life that is revealed is (in his best novels) abundant and true. Scott can be pompous in his own way when his inspiration flags, but he never fools himself into mistaking his pomposity for anything else. Above all, though he is concerned about life he is never worried about it. We read his best novels, therefore, with a feeling of immense ease and satisfaction. We may be moved or amused or excited, but we are never worried by them. His best novels are always anchored in earth, and when we think of Helen Macgregor standing dramatically on the top of a cliff we cannot help thinking at the same time of the worthy Bailie, garrulous and kindly and self-important; Counsellor Pleydell is the perfect antidote to Meg Merrilies, and even Redgauntlet must give way before Wandering Willie and Provost Crosbie. The ordinary folk win in the end, and—

paradox again—the Wizard of the North finally emerges as a novelist of manners.. (pp. 119-21)

David Daiches, "Scott's Achievement as a Novelist," in his Literary Essays, 1956. Reprint by Philosophical Library Publishers, 1957, pp. 88-121.

ALEXANDER WELSH   (essay date 1963)

[*Welsh outlines the artistic function and key personality traits of the heroes of the* Waverley Novels.]

A soliloquy from *The Fortunes of Nigel* supplies the best introduction to the hero of the *Waverley Novels*. This romance is set in the London of James I and is imbued with the spirit of the public stage of that era: in the antics of his apprentices and in the spirited behavior of his middle-class heroine Scott gives free play to his fondness for the drama. Before introducing the reflections of his hero, imprisoned in Whitefriars, he therefore digresses on the nature of soliloquy. Though the device is more essential to drama than to narrative, Scott argues, the soliloquy still offers "a more concise and spirited mode" of conveying the thoughts of the hero.... Scott frequently resorts to this dramatic convention in his prose romance—one habit that undoubtedly estranges modern readers of the *Waverley Novels*. The device, in fact, represents more than a technical convenience. Soliloquies are appropriate to the Scott hero because he is always more eloquent in resolution than in action. The players in *Wilhelm Meister's Apprenticeship* agreed that *Hamlet*, of all plays, was in this respect closest to a novel, the species of fiction in which the hero "must be suffering."

In a fit of angry discovery Nigel draws his sword, in the king's park, against the villainous Lord Dalgarno. He flees to Whitefriars for sanctuary. Having arrived in the dreary hosue of old Trapbois, he is unable to find a servant to lay his fire or to help him dress. Mistress Martha Trapbois informs him that she has no servant and advises Nigel to be more independent. "Unable as yet to reconcile himself to the thoughts of becoming his own fire-maker," the hero paces to and fro while composing the following "reflections and resolutions." Here is the soliloquy:

> She is right, and has taught me a lesson I will profit by. I have been, through my whole life, one who leant upon others for that assistance which it is more truly noble to derive from my own exertions. I am ashamed of feeling the paltry inconvenience which long habit has led me to annex to the want of a servant's assistance—I am ashamed of that; but far, far more, am I ashamed to have suffered the same habit of throwing my burden on others, to render me, since I came to this city, a mere victim of those events, which I have never even attempted to influence—a thing never acting but perpetually acted upon—protected by one friend, deceived by another; but in the advantage which I have received from the one, and the evil I have sustained from the other, as passive and helpless as a boat that drifts without oar or rudder at the mercy of the winds and waves. I became a courtier because Heriot so advised it—a gamester because Dalgarno so contrived it—an Alsatian because Lowestoffe so willed it. Whatever of good or bad hath befallen me, hath arisen out of the agency of others, not from my own. My father's son must no longer hold this facile

and puerile course. Live or die, sink or swim, Nigel Olifaunt, from this moment, shall owe his safety, success, and honour, to his own exertions, or shall fall with the credit of having at least exerted his own free agency. I will write it down in my tablets, in her very words,— "The wise man is his own best assistant." ...

Nigel is actually one of the most complex of Scott heroes. His rigid moral resistance and puritanic fear of gambling are transformed, with psychological justice, into a niggling and cautious consent to play—by which he calculates always to win, and never risks even odds. Scott stands sufficiently outside his hero to make the sequence interesting. But when Nigel moves, in this soliloquy, from self-chastisement of his immediate folly to a sweeping condemnation of his total situation, he speaks generically for all the heroes of the *Waverley Novels*. Suddenly Nigel indicts not so much his own character as the entire fiction within which he finds himself. As we shall see, Scott himself reproached the inactivity of his heroes. Nigel's recriminations—"a victim of events"—"passive and helpless"—define the customary stance of the Scott hero; his circumstances and "the agency of others" are the stuff of the Scott romance.

The soliloquy suggests certain details of Nigel's predicament. As the title of the romance implies, his fortunes are in the balance. In the appropriate language of ups and downs, therefore, he speaks of what has "befallen" and how it has "arisen"; and again, that he shall rise or "fall." More precisely, since "safety" and "honour" flank "success," he shall either recover his just desserts or be cheated of them. He is not altogether hopeful and speaks twice in the language of drowning. He asserts his identity by addressing himself in the third person, but reinforces the obligation of his new resolutions by naming himself also "my father's son." He commits himself ultimately to an abstraction—"his own free agency." He fears he is not only a victim of events but in the hands of good and bad agents, who both protect and deceive him.

The previous events of the story justify Nigel's assault on his own dependence. More embarrassed than hungry in his destitution, Nigel fears to petition the king in person for the payments owed to his deceased father. George Heriot, the goldsmith whose kindness is entirely unmotivated by personal gain, seeks out the hero in his hiding place in London; and it is clear that Heriot is better acquainted with Nigel's state of affairs than is the hero himself.... When the goldsmith has advanced him one hundred pounds, unasked, and tidied him up for presentation at court, the door to the presence chamber is barred by the deputy chamberlain—one of those instinctive enemies who invariably discountenance the merits of heroes. The way is opened by the Earl of Huntinglen, who recognizes Nigel by his resemblance to his father; and the Earl generously exchanges his annual royal boon for Nigel's favor with the king.... Just as Master Heriot knows more of Nigel's business than the hero himself, so Margaret Ramsay has mysterious intelligence of the plots against him. She enumerates the motives of his enemies as "avarice" and "vindictive ambition," but inspired by an "absolute and concentrated spirit of malice"—the last suggesting that the hero's enemies are as unselfishly motivated as his friends.... As soon as Nigel becomes aware of Dalgarno's duplicity, an "impatient passion" involves him in the abortive duel in St. James's Park; but he stands there in risk of having his hand chopped off by the Star Chamber until "a decent-looking elderly man" urges him to run off. Luckily, he runs into a casual acquaintance, Lowestoffe, who knowledgeably arranges his admission to Whitefriars. . . . There we have discovered him, ''never acting but perpetually acted upon.''

The excellent resolutions represented by the soliloquy do not alter the tendency of these adventures in the least. By the end of the same chapter Nigel's decision to become an active hero takes a strange turn: he decides to surrender himself. He learns that Lowestoffe has been arrested for his timely assistance, and is thus confirmed in his purpose. However, ''he had, even before hearing of a reason which so peremptorily demanded that he should surrender himself, adopted the resolution to do so, as the manliest and most proper course which his ill-fortune and imprudence had left in his own power.'' . . . When forced to translate his vow of independence into a specific act, Nigel can think only of giving himself up. He is guided by what is ''manliest and most proper''—considerations that dictate his passive role. On the face of it his decision makes it more likely that he will die than live, sink than swim. Ordinarily when a character exclaims that he shall ''live or die, sink or swim,'' he expresses an overpowering determination to live. The hero of Scott expresses by these terms a stubborn allegiance to his society.

The hero of the **Waverley Novels** is seldom a leader of men. He is always a potential leader, because of his rank as a gentleman. He represents, however, a social ideal, and acts or refrains from acting according to the accepted morality of his public. Law and authority are the sine qua non of his being. Nigel is emotionally justified in drawing his sword in the park, but by doing so he has broken the law. Because he represents the individual acceptance of law and authority, he can only surrender himself. The hero of the **Waverley Novels** stands at the beginning of a tradition of which Sean O'Faolain celebrates the close in a book called *The Vanishing Hero.* Instead of a commander, this hero is an ideal *member* of society. By Mr. O'Faolain's account, the hero vanishes when society no longer defines him: ''the Hero is a purely social creation. He represents, that is to say, a socially approved norm, for representing which to the satisfaction of society he is decorated with a title.'' On the other hand, Mario Praz' study of Victorian fiction, commencing with Scott, is entitled *The Hero in Eclipse.* We are always in danger of a confusion of terms: it goes without saying that Mr. Praz' title refers to another person altogether, the romantic hero who is pitted *against* society. Such romantic characters figure large in the **Waverley Novels,** but the proper hero of Scott implicitly accepts his society. His nearly complete passivity is a function of his morality—the public and accepted morality of rational self-restraint.

Self-imposed respect for law and authority only partly explains the passive hero, however. His characteristic responses are more (or less) than moral. They have an interesting emotional content. This content may be demonstrated by an Alpine adventure in *Anne of Geierstein* . . . , an adventure that exaggerates the propensities of a typical hero by exposing him to very untypical surroundings.

The verse tags to the first two chapters of **Anne of Geierstein** are from *Manfred,* but the hero is not affected by the manners of his chief literary rival. Arthur Philipson and his father—the Earl of Oxford in disguise—have been led up a wrong and precarious path in the mountains. A storm is brewing, and the path suddenly disappears into a rock slide. Arthur proposes to make his way across the slide in order to seek help from a habitation that can be seen in the distance. The hero undertakes this dangerous effort in a significant fashion. He *reasons* his way past the abyss, by ''estimating the extent of his danger by the measure of sound sense and reality.'' The reader overhears his thoughts:

> ''This ledge of rock,'' he urged to himself, ''is but narrow, yet it has breadth enough to support me; these cliffs and crevices in the surface are small and distant, but the one affords as secure a resting place for my feet, the other as available a grasp to my hands, as if I stood on a platform of a cubit broad, and rested my arm on a balustrade of marble. My safety, therefore, depends on myself. If I move with decision, step firmly, and hold fast, what signifies how near I am to the mouth of an abyss?'' . . .

The moral expressed in this soliloquy is also general. As with most accounts of mountain climbing, the exercise is supposed to be symbolic. Unlike most climbers, Arthur does not pretend to enjoy the sport.

When Arthur has almost reached safety on the far side of the slide, a huge rock teeters under the climber's weight and smashes into the valley below—leaving the hero clinging to a tree. He is overcome by an attack of vertigo. The peril of his situation, and his consequent trembling fits, are spun out at great length in the narrative. Scott casts in peculiar language Arthur's determination to hang on: ''nothing, save the consciousness that such an idea was the suggestion of partial insanity, prevented him from throwing himself from the tree, as if to join the wild dance to which his disturbed brain had given motion.'' At this point a Swiss maiden appears out of the mist. She walks so close to the precipice that Arthur sinks back into his tree with a groan. It is Anne of Geierstein, and she points out to the hero that solid ground lies but one bold step from his perch. Arthur is ashamed of himself, and prepares to take the leap, but is again overcome by fear. In order ''to restore his confidence,'' Anne herself hops lightly from rock to tree and back again. She stretches out her hand to Arthur: '''My arm,' she said, 'is but a slight balustrade; yet do but step forward with resolution, and you will find it as secure as the battlement of Berne.''' Arthur has set out by imagining ''a balustrade of marble'' for his support; here he is offered one of real substance. He is sufficiently embarrassed—''shame now overcame terror so much''—that he leaps to safety without further assistance. In the following chapter the native Swiss chide the hero about this incident several times, though the writer continues to characterize him, without irony, as ''young and daring.''

Scott draws out this scene so as to leave no doubt of his hero's terror and its embarrassing associations. He stresses the hero's qualms much more than his prowess. The cause of ''sound sense and reality'' would seem better served if Arthur kept his head when the rock bounds into the abyss—or if he rescued Anne instead of the other way around. In **Anne of Geierstein** she comes to *his* rescue three times. Prudential morality might account for the fact that the hero can seldom be a savior, but it does not account for the mixed pleasure of being saved. The episode in **Anne of Geierstein** indicates that the passive hero only partially admits of a rational explanation. Romance, of course, is not a rational exercise. Nigel Olifaunt's decision to surrender cannot adequately be explained in moral terms; and Arthur Philipson's terror and embarrassment have reverberations throughout the **Waverley Novels.** (pp. 30-8)

We have a full account of the origin of the name **Waverley.** Scott explained that he skirted both chivalrous names like

"Howard, Mordaunt, Mortimer, or Stanley," and sentimental names like "Belmour, Belville, Belfield, and Belgrave," in favor of a name without associations. "I have, therefore, like a maiden knight with his white shield, assumed for my hero, WAVERLEY, an uncontaminated name, bearing with its sound little of good or evil, excepting what the reader shall hereafter be pleased to affix to it." . . . A similar account of the choice of *Ivanhoe* was given in the 1830 introduction to that romance. But who is not tempted to detect a subconscious premonition of Waverley's career in his very name? The word *waver* emerges in one very typical situation:

> The question indeed occurred, whither he was to direct his course when again at his own disposal. Two schemes seemed practicable, yet both attended with danger and difficulty . . . to go back to Glennaquoich, and join Fergus Mac-Ivor . . . [or] to take shipping for England. His mind wavered between these plans; and probably, if he had effected his escape in the manner he proposed, he would have been finally determined by the comparative facility by which either might have been executed. But his fortune had settled that he was not to be left to his option. . . .

The condition contrary to fact—"if he had effected his escape in the manner he proposed"—is an amusing commentary on the passive hero, who never engineers his own escape. Waverley actually has no escape plan, "the manner he proposed" having no antecedent in the text except as given above. Walter Bagehot found all Scott's heroes commonplace with the possible exception of Waverley, "whose very vacillation gives him a sort of character" [see excerpt dated 1858]. While acknowledging the uniformity of the heroes, the *Edinburgh Review* in 1832 applied the same word in a different judgment: "A strong fraternal likeness to the vacillating Waverley does not raise them in our esteem." The likeness holds throughout the long series of novels to which Waverley gave his name—unless one excepts, in the very last of the series, *Castle Dangerous*, an older hero, "Walton the Unwavering." . . .

The distinctive inactivity of the passive hero may be appreciated simply by contrasting him with the popular hero who succors the unfortunate, who makes his own fortune and wins the girl he loves, or who changes the course of history. That kind of heroism occurs to Scott himself, for example, as he sets forth the predicament of Adam Hartley in **"The Surgeon's Daughter."** Though the hero would willingly devote his entire life to Menie Gray, he can only lament his helplessness to save her:

> The consciousness of being in her vicinity added to the bitter pangs with which Hartley contemplated her situation, and reflected how little chance there appeared of his being able to rescue her from it by the mere force of reason and justice, which was all he could oppose to the selfish passions of a voluptuous tyrant. A lover of romance might have meditated some means of effecting her release by force or address; but Hartley, though a man of courage, had no spirit of adventure, and would have regarded as desperate any attempt of the kind. . . .

The hero eschews the use of "address" as well as the use of force; he must depend wholly upon reason and justice. The opposite course of action he would characterize as romantic and desperate. Yet reason and justice are here inadequate. The rescue is finally accomplished from outside by the native wisdom and absolute power of Hyder Ali Khan Behauder and the help of a ceremonial elephant to crush the life out of the villain.

The hero can best be defined by the words of Nigel Olifaunt—"a thing never acting but perpetually acted upon." But he is nevertheless the protagonist. He stands at the center of the struggle. He may not move, but his chances, his fortunes, are at stake. He is a victim, at the mercy of good and bad agents alike. He never aspires to property, nor actively courts the heroine. But he does not remain a victim, and he receives the heroine and the property in the end. The adventures of Nigel, outlined above, may be taken as typical. Instead of tediously tracing the inactivity of such heroes, however, it is easier to allow the exceptions to prove the rule. Even those protagonists of Scott whom one remembers as particularly bold and independent actors prove, on closer examination, to be cast in a passive role. Quentin Durward, for example, comes immediately to mind. The *Quarterly Review* considered him "not so passive as Waverley and Redgauntlet."

At the outset of **Quentin Durward** the hero, in a compassionate gesture, cuts down a corpse hung up by the king's provost, and he is forthwith attacked by friends of the deceased and by the executioners in rapid succession. With typical inadvertence he thus stumbles into a situation in which "life, death, time, and eternity, were swimming before his eyes"; and he is rescued only by the fortunate proximity of some Scottish Guards. . . . Quentin escapes from the consequences of this incident by reluctantly allowing himself to be pressed into service with the Guards. He has many qualms about service to Louis XI. "How did the youth know but he might be soon commanded on some offensive operation of the same kind?" . . . Next he sets out on a mission—to escort the Countess Isabelle and Lady Hameline to Liège—without knowing the country or the route, and evidently without instructions. Far from delivering orders to the expedition he commands, Quentin is informed in a whisper by one of his retinue "that their guide was to join them beyond Tours." Another man guides them out through the "pitfalls, snares, and similar contrivances" that surround the castle of Louis. . . .

When Quentin suspects treachery, however, he acts with exceptional alertness, following Hayraddin to a secret rendezvous at night, and overhearing the plot against the Countess. . . . Such information generally reaches the ears of the passive hero by accident, and then he will listen most unwillingly. The following chapter opens with Quentin carefully inspecting the shoes of the horses "with his own eyes"—an action symbolic of his unusual role. Subsequently he rescues Isabelle from the castle at Liège and restrains De la Marck, the Boar of the Ardennes, by holding a knife to the throat of his son. . . . So lively is Quentin by this point that the reader anticipates with gusto the slaughter of De la Marck in the last chapter—the stated reward for which deed is the hand of Isabelle of Croye. But just as Quentin is about to conquer the monster, Lady Hameline runs by in distress, and the hero has to nip out to save her from a French soldier. His uncle Ludovic Lesly, *alias* Le Balafré, finishes De la Marck, and refers his right to Isabelle to Quentin. "It is all that is left of a bit of work which my nephew shaped out, and nearly finished, and I put the last hand to." . . . This awkward contrivance, which saves Quentin the responsibility of killing someone outright, owes entirely to the rules of passive heroism. Quentin has "nearly finished" the villain; but even the foulest villains are safe from death at the hero's hand.

The prototype for Quentin Durward, in the *Waverley Novels,* is Captain Dalgetty of *A Legend of Montrose.* Significantly, this first soldier hero is not, strictly speaking, the protagonist of the romance. As danger increases Dalgetty becomes more and more outrageous. He overpowers the Marquis of Argyll and actually escapes from the dungeon with a bundle of military secrets in his pocket. Menteith, the proper hero of the romance, survives his part in the Civil Wars, as heroes are wont to, by contriving to be a party to both sides through his marriage. The survival of Dalgetty almost parodies this typical denouement. From two paragraphs at the end of the tale the reader hears that he is captured; that he refuses to change sides—an act that would violate his military enlistment; and that he is reprieved from death by friends, who point out that his enlistment will expire in two weeks. At the end of two weeks Dalgetty does change sides, and eventually he gains "his paternal estate of Drumthwacket" by marriage to the daughter of the Whig who has usurped it. . . .

Scott returned to a soldier hero for *Count Robert of Paris.* In that romance Hereward the Saxon displays a degree of initiative similar to Quentin Durward's and at a critical moment even employs deceit to protect the emperor. . . . Durward and Hereward act where the typical heroes of Scott would await events. Because these honest mercenaries fight for pay, it is as if their heroic role were also contractual. Their enterprise seems acceptable so long as the service they perform is formally owed to someone else. They are akin to certain of the ordinary heroes' retainers, who are often more alert to the main chance than their masters.

Edgar Ravenswood of *The Bride of Lammermoor* presents a special problem. He is the only hero of the several "tragic" romances who actually shares the unhappy fate of the heroine. Yet the Master of Ravenswood, as he is ironically called, suffers his fate passively, albeit passionately. Though the story takes place on his family estate, he often seems a complete stranger to the grounds. His one direct action, serving to introduce the principals of the romance, is to rescue Lucy Ashton and her father from a wild bull. . . . He leaves the possible recovery of his estate to the vague agency of the Marquis A——— and becomes the uneasy dependent of the Ashtons. At the climax of *The Bride of Lammermoor,* as the marriage deeds are signed, Ravenswood rushes into the room, sword in hand, pistol cocked, and threatening everyone in sight. . . . There is no comparable scene in the *Waverley Novels.* Yet his "fierce and free ideas" are never really enacted except in this scene, and here he does not go so far as to strike anyone. Nassau Senior, who thought Ravenswood exceptionally well drawn, found it "a blemish, that his faults are so remotely connected with his misfortunes. . . . His misfortunes spring from the enmity of Bucklaw and Lady Ashton; both arising from causes out of his own controul, and as likely to have arisen if he had been the meekest of mankind." His temperament is different, but his posture is fundamentally the same as that of the other heroes. Ravenswood himself tentatively recognizes the incompatibility in temperament between his dark passionate nature and the pale Lucy. "He felt that his own temper required a partner of a more independent spirit, who could set sail with him on his course of life, resolved as himself to dare indifferently the storm and the favouring breeze." . . . It is the temperament and want of deeds together that make Ravenswood distinctive, essentially unattractive, and therefore interesting.

The Fair Maid of Perth, finally, can boast the most active and energetic hero of the *Waverley Novels:* Henry Wynd, the armorer. The atmosphere of this romance, like that of *The Fortunes of Nigel,* derives from Elizabethan and Jacobean theater, though *The Fair Maid of Perth* takes place a century earlier in Scotland. Scott's title suggests Heywood; and Simon Glover, but for his different trade, recalls Dekker's Simon Eyre. There is a vigorous courtship in this romance, not merely an "affection" that achieves its fulfillment when events permit. Contrary to practice in the *Waverley Novels,* the hero kisses the heroine. It is the bride who must be won, not merely the permission to marry her. Simon Glover, Catharine's father, approves the match. In the two other romances in which the hero enjoys such wholehearted support from the heroine's father (*Kenilworth* and "The Surgeon's Daughter") the lady loves elsewhere. Unique among Scott heroes, Henry even possesses sexual experience: "a certain natural wildness of disposition had placed him under the influence of Venus, as well as that of Mars," before his love for Catharine "had withdrawn him entirely from such licentious pleasures." . . . In a climax of independent action Henry slaughters on Palm Sunday no less than five Highlanders in an extremely bloody (thirty against thirty) trial by combat. . . .

The extenuating circumstance for Henry's behavior is not far to seek. His social class is responsible: he is an artisan, whereas the proper hero is a gentleman. "A gentleman," according to Charles II in *Woodstock* . . . , "is a term which comprehends all ranks entitled to armorial bearings—A duke, a lord, a prince, is no more than a gentleman." But an armorer is not entitled to armorial bearings. Henry's role, like that of the soldier heroes, approaches the role of some of the retainers to proper heroes: a similar license both to kiss and to kill is granted only to Cuddie Headrigg in *Old Mortality* and to Joceline Joliffe in *Woodstock.* Henry Wynd is far too violent for an ordinary hero—though his spirited presence makes *The Fair Maid of Perth* one of the most enjoyable of Scott's inventions. (pp. 38-46)

In a highly interesting document Scott recorded his own opinion of his first prose heroes. In 1817 he opportunely reviewed the first series of *Tales of My Landlord* in the *Quarterly* [see excerpt dated 1817]. The anonymous review of his own work was favorable, but Scott charged the heroes as follows:

> Another leading fault in these novels is the total want of interest which the reader attaches to the character of the hero. Waverley, Brown, or Bertram in *Guy Mannering,* and Lovel in the *Antiquary,* are all brethren of a family; very amiable and very insipid sort of young men. . . . His chief characters are never actors, but always acted upon by the spur of circumstances, and have their fate uniformly determined by the agency of subordinate persons. . . . Every hero in poetry, in fictitious narrative, ought to come forth and do or say something or other which no other person could have done or said; make some sacrifice, surmount some difficulty, and become interesting to us otherwise than by his mere appearance on the scene, the passive tool of the other characters.

"Never actors, but always acted upon" are very nearly the words of Nigel Olifaunt's soliloquy. Elsewhere Scott criticized one of Clara Reeve's heroes in similar terms: "for if Fitzowen be considered the Old English Baron, we do not see wherefore a character, passive in himself from beginning to end, and only acted upon by others, should be selected to give a name to the story.'' This opinion had not deterred Scott from writing *Waverley,* nor had it affected the title in any way. Yet the author's opinion of Waverley as a hero seems to have been consistent from the beginning, since the well known letter to John Morrit in July, 1814, registered the same sentiment:

> The heroe is a sneaking piece of imbecility and if he had married Flora she would have set him up on the chimney-piece as Count Boralaski's wife used to do with him. I am a bad hand at depicting a heroe properly so calld and have an unfortunate propensity for the dubious characters of Borderers Buccaneers highland robbers and all others of a Robin Hood description. I do not know why it should be so [as] I am myself like Hamlet indifferent honest but I suppose the blood of the old cattle-drivers of Teviotdale continues to stir in my veins.

Scott's notion that he had a flair for a more romantic type of hero is recorded also in earlier letters on the metrical romances. He cherished the thought that some of his own ancestors led romantic and extralegal careers on the border. For our purposes, these several statements imply at least that ''a heroe properly so calld'' can be distinguished from the various romantic or historical personalities in the *Waverley Novels* who may be of heroic stature but are not the protagonists. Lovel is correctly designated by his author as the hero of *The Antiquary,* even though he is perhaps the least colorful character—he does not even possess a Christian name.

We are confronted, then, with an author who professes to scorn his unheroic hero and yet repeats the same creation in romance after romance. Scott offers an explanation—a somewhat halting and unconvincing explanation—in his review of *Tales of My Landlord.* The passive hero supplies a medium for introducing historical and topographical detail. He is a kind of representative of the reader at the scene of action. He is inactive because he shares the reader's unfamiliarity with the scene. Without such a hero the instructive or informative content of the fiction would seem dull. This much must be derived from two sentences of Scott: the passive role of the heroes

> arises from the author having usually represented them as foreigners to whom every thing in Scotland is strange,—a circumstance which serves as his apology for entering into many minute details which are reflectively, as it were, addressed to the reader through the medium of the hero. While he is going into explanations and details which, addressed directly to the reader, might appear tiresome and unnecessary, he gives interest to them by exhibiting the effect which they produce upon the principal person of his drama.

Secondly, and serving the same general end, a weak hero may be expeditiously dragged about by an author who is bent on immediate and temporary effects. For, Scott continues, the author ''hesitates not to sacrifice poor Waverley, and to represent him as a reed blown about at the pleasure of every breeze'' simply in order to get from one place to another. In sum, the virtues of a passive hero are that he may be a stranger and that he is at the mercy of his author. (pp. 49-52)

It is a mistake to dismiss the passive hero because he seems to initiate none of the action: he appears in every full-length romance except one; he is the only coherent focus in most of the plots; and he is therefore the best introduction to an understanding of the *Waverley Novels.* It is doubly a mistake to lose sight of the hero between the age of prudence and the age of violence, between the civil state and the state of nature. Whatever one may think of Scott's sympathies—I myself think that his ''romantic'' sympathies are those of a man confident of the superiority of modern civilization—his hero is not a neutral. He stands committed to prudence and the superiority of civil society. That commitment alone makes him a passive hero. Not only are his manners confined, in George Moberly's words, to the ''quiet and retiring character'' of modern virtues, but he represents the modern and conservative model of a member of civil society. The hero is not precisely Everyman, but every gentleman—not in some supercilious social sense, but in the profound conviction that society is a compact of independent owners of property. He is a passive hero because, in the words of Edmund Blake, a member of civil society surrenders the right ''to judge for himself, and to assert his own cause. He abdicates all right to be his own governor. He inclusively, in a great measure, abandons the right of self-defence, the first law of Nature.'' He abandons, in other words, all these various possibilities of action. Burke's next sentence is that ''man cannot enjoy the rights of an uncivil and of a civil state together.'' Scott surely concurs: but in fiction he can at least afford pleasurable glimpses of the uncivil state. In this sense his hero is an observer—even a vacationer—and so is the reader. He is committed to the civil state, and observes the uncivil. (pp. 56-7)

> *Alexander Welsh, "The Passive Hero," in his* The Hero of the Waverley Novels, *Yale University Press, 1963, pp. 30-57.*

An 1831 portrait of Scott by Sir William Allan.

BRIGID BROPHY, MICHAEL LEVEY, AND CHARLES OSBORNE (essay date 1967)

[*Brophy is an Anglo-Irish novelist, dramatist, and critic. As a literary critic, Brophy is known for her provocative and acerbic remarks, particularly the iconoclastic* Fifty Works of English and American Literature We Could Do Without, *in which she and coauthors Michael Levey and Charles Osborne attack such works as* Hamlet, Wuthering Heights, *and* Moby Dick. *In the following excerpt, the three critics ridicule Scott's* The Bride of Lammermoor, *faulting numerous aspects of the novel, including its style, structure, and dialog.*]

What can be made of a writer who at the most poignant and harrowing climax of his novel describes events only with the desperate phrase that they 'surpass description'? It is immediately obvious that we are dealing not with an artist but with Sir Walter Scott.

The non-artistry of Scott is not a matter *merely* of poverty of imagination, appalling style, insipid characterization and stunted emotional state. He is no artist by the standards not just of great novelists like Jane Austen or Henry James, but by the standards of any great writer—from Homer onwards. It is impossible to discover whether he was too lazy to try to be an artist—or whether he tried but could not succeed. His novels suggest the former; his poetry the latter. It is a double failure, largely concealed from the world by Scott's upright, honourable nature, his great fame in his lifetime, and his baronetcy. That this last was conferred for services to literature is to some people a compelling argument for believing he must have served literature; what he served it was in fact a bad turn. Only in the Kingdom of Philistia is Sir Walter Scott president of the Royal Academy of literature, but there he reigns, secure in the middle classes' affection for the non-literate writer, the one who is a great story teller with no affectations or artistic nonsense about him.

Because it is believed that Scott was a good narrative writer, he is still foisted on to children and mentioned at Christmas or in cold weather by some semi-literate journalist: still showing off his bluff, doggy face, that ghastly Abbotsford and his famous integrity. Everyone half recalls reading him as children; it's a good excuse for now not looking at his books but for retaining them in a vague limbo of nursery associations, only painfully—if at all—to be relinquished. Even E. M. Forster, who has said a few aptly harsh things about Scott, is found murmuring the old cliché: 'He had the primitive power of keeping the reader in suspense . . .' [see Additional Bibliography].

The Bride of Lammermoor has a plot in itself rich in suspense, horrific drama and genuine pathos. According to Scott it is basically a true story, so he need be given no credit for invention. What he has done is run the story under the cold tap of his immature mind, wring it free of anything resembling suspense or passion, and then iron it out with the full starch of his genteel, highfalutin and ever-creaking style. When Ravenswood broods beside the body of a dead woman who he thinks may have appeared to him as a vision, his reflections in part run thus: 'can strong and earnest wishes, formed during the last agony of nature, survive its catastrophe, surmount the awful bounds of the spiritual world, and place before us its inhabitants in the hues and colourings of life?' The man who can think like this may be a great loss to Parliament but has clearly nothing to do with literature. Scott's vocabulary betrays the un-thinking speech-writer who deliberately clogs the meaningless with clumps of useless adjectives and solemn-seeming commas. The style remains exactly the same in tone and pseudo-literacy when the author stoops to be funny or whimsical. Much of this is mercifully obscured by the useful device of unreadable dialect. But here is Scott assuming a would-be humorous character, actually no different from the way he writes when describing [*sic*] love and death: 'For when Dick, in his more advanced state of proficiency, became dubious of the propriety of so daring a deviation from the established rules of art, and was desirous to execute a picture of the publican himself in exchange for this juvenile production, the courteous offer was refused by his judicious employer, who had observed, it seems, that when his ale failed to do its duty in conciliating his guests, one glance at his sign was sure to put them in good humour.'

This is the style of the barely educated—preferring long Latin-style words to short ones. The prosaic inability of Scott to tell his story in terms more vivid than those of a police report effectively removes any feeling of suspense or interest. Bathos not pathos is the sole sentiment he can command. Fustian dialogue is followed by scarcely believable sentences of glossing (whether to eke out the book's length or to illustrate the author's own naivety, who shall say?). At the end of *The Bride* . . . (Scott having utterly failed in haste and repugnance to convey anything of the horrific dénouement) Bucklair proudly announces his refusal ever to reveal what happened on his wedding night. For the really stupid reader or for himself, Scott adds: 'A declaration so decisive admitted no commentary.'

Scott emasculated his work, presumably deliberately, to the point where it lacks not just sexual, but any, vitality. All the emotions which go to power characters in a work of art—the passions which are no less apparent in *Emma* than in the *Iliad*—have been dehydrated and reduced to formulae. His world view is pre-adolescent but post-infantile. He describes what he has never consciously experienced (and hence that significant frequent need of phrases like 'surpass description') and is incapable of imagining. He can do no justice to Lucy Ashton's love for Ravenswood, still less to the Juliet-style dilemma in which that loves places her. Instead, he surrounds the crux of the plot with irrelevant and in effect delaying incidents—delaying the author from having to deal with anything central or profound. Into the characters' mouths he puts dialogue that is essentially sham, more rhetorical than any situation would stimulate and more clumsy than could ever be spoken, even on the stage. It is all mouthing of emotions and descriptions of the indescribable. The result is a property cupboard of old costumes which the author *au fond* thinks are ridiculous but dons in condescending effort to entertain. He is a mountebank without a mountebank's courage, an actor who incongruously smiles at a tragic scene through his grease paint. He takes none of it seriously; as he is fond of insisting—it is all a story or history. He wants it to have happened long ago because that robs it of intensity, reality and passion: the enemies he most fears. He will waste pages on the commonplace chatter of subordinate characters and then sketch with ludicrous brevity a dramatic scene which should be given fully developed treatment.

Some people always take artists at other people's values, content to go along with the world's verdict. For them Italian opera composers are *a priori* silly, and Donizetti—over-prolific and tuneful—one of the silliest. Sir Walter Scott (also over-prolific, by the way and tuneless) is a gentleman-writer who made a lot of money and should be respected. Listen to *Lucia di Lammermoor* and then read the novel again. The Italian created a valid work of art, beside which Scott's book is revealed as the small heap of sawdust it always was. (pp. 35-8)

Brigid Brophy, Michael Levey, and Charles Osborne, "'The Bride of Lammermoor'," in their Fifty
Works of English and American Literature We Could
Do Without, 1967. Reprint by Stein and Day Publishers, 1968, pp. 35-8.

A. O. J. COCKSHUT (essay date 1969)

[*Cockshut explores some of the prevailing characteristics of Scott's
"secondary or inferior work," emphasizing the non-serious purpose and associated deficiencies of his novels with mediaeval
settings. The critic's commentary centers on* Quentin Durward,
The Betrothed, Ivanhoe, *and* Count Robert of Paris.]

If Scott was a great artist, . . . it is obvious that he was many
other things too. Without any attempt at completeness this
[essay] is intended to sketch some of the main tendencies in
his secondary or inferior work. One of the reasons for the
prevailing uncertainty about his position in our literature is that
this secondary work is about two-thirds of the whole. In general, the books written after 1820 are inferior, and the books
describing life more than two centuries before his own time
are inferior, and these two categories tend to overlap. Clearly
there are exceptions, especially in the first category, and of
these **Redgauntlet** and **"The Highland Widow"** are notable.
At the same time several of the books dealing with early times
have passages of merit, or interesting ideas treated with partial
success. And yet the general impression of inferiority is unmistakable, and its causes are clear. Scott was tired, and he
was writing much too fast. Though a learned man in his own
way, he did not know enough to recreate the earlier centuries.
Moreover, he was writing for a public ready to be entertained
and bewitched by an unreal middle age, a public that had
emancipated itself from the stock Augustan prejudices about
mediaeval barbarism, and was now ready to adopt different
misconceptions, and to be deceived in new ways.

All this means that this [essay] is in some ways a melancholy
one for an admirer of Scott to write. But not altogether so.
Scott can be dull; he can be hasty and careless. He is never
cruel or self-pitying. He never fails in that fundamental respect
for human life in all its forms without which literature descends
to triviality. Scott at his worst is a great artist and a great man
making a botch; he is never causing us to doubt whether we
were mistaken after all, in reading his best books, in supposing
that he was a great artist and a great man.

The historical novel depends on a synthesis of likeness and
unlikeness between the time of writing and the time portrayed.
If the past is presented as the present in disguise, we get the
'costume novel', and this is probably the commonest kind of
failure in the tradition of historical fiction. If the past is shown
as absolutely unlike the present, so that the men of the past
seem to have become a different species from men as we know
them, we get the Gothic novel. But in this second case, since
an author can only in the end write out of his own humanity,
what really happens is that a certain suppressed or despised
area of the mind is allowed free play as a kind of holiday.
Romola may serve as an example of the first kind, and *The
Castle of Otranto* of the second. Scott often in his inferior
works veers towards the first error, though seldom for the whole
duration of a book. His inexhaustible human sympathy, his
honesty, his large acceptance of himself with all his impulses
and imperfections, prevented him from ever falling into the
second. He is capable of making a mediaeval Jewess talk like
an eighteenth century bluestocking. He is not capable, as Mrs.

Radcliffe was, of making anyone talk like an abstraction of
the fiendish or animal tendencies of the human mind.

There is no sense of escape in Scott's mediaevalism; and it is
this, above all, that distinguishes it from so much of the mediaevalism of his century, from Keats to Rossetti. Scott had
no desire to escape from anything; he had an inexhaustible
curiosity about human life in all times and places. Sometimes
he was well-informed and showed a profound understanding.
Sometimes as in *The Abbot* he had considerable knowledge,
but an imperfect understanding. Sometimes, as in dealing with
the Saracens in *The Talisman,* his knowledge was slight and
his attempt to understand perfunctory. But this is no more than
the inevitable unevenness of grasp of a man of extraordinary
breadth of interests and ferocious energy who composed with
great rapidity. He would have been wiser not to attempt the
subject of *The Talisman,* but he did himself no real discredit
by the attempt.

The absence of that desire to escape, so strong both in his
'Gothic' predecessors and his pre-Raphaelite successors has
some surprising consequences. There is a strong strain of worldly
shrewdness, for instance, in **Quentin Durward.** Dealing with
the fifteenth century, the book is able to show chivalric customs
in decline, and men repeating by force of habit principles that
are no longer the motive of conduct. Moreover the ingenuous
Scots hero is viewed with a satirical eye. He is unable to
distinguish clearly between appearance and reality. He is influenced by the trappings of power and the flounces of beauty.
Thus Quentin meets Louis XI before he knows who he is.
When the identity is revealed: "Those eyes, which, according
to Quentin's former impression, only twinkled with the love
of gain, had, now that they were known to be the property of
an able and powerful monarch, a piercing and majestic glance;
and those wrinkles on the brow, which he had supposed were
formed during a long series of petty schemes of commerce,
seemed now the furrows which sagacity had worn while toiling
in meditation upon the fate of nations." Needless to say, he
had been more nearly right the first time. His feeling for rank
affects his sense of feminine charm also: "Invested now with
all the mysterious dignity belonging to the nymph of the veil
and lute, and proved, besides, at least in Quentin's estimation,
to be the high-born heiress of a rich earldom, her beauty made
ten times the impression upon him which it had done when he
beheld in her one whom he deemed the daughter of a paltry
innkeeper, in attendance upon a rich burgher."

Uncertainties and self-deceptions like these make Quentin a
suitable hero for a story in which Scott is trying to present a
changing society, which has been unable to develop new theories to support its new practice, and consequently is not sure
itself how much or how fast it is changing. I leave out of
account altogether the relation of this to the actual truth about
the reign of Louis XI. But in fictional terms this uncertainty,
this feeling of decline from an earlier high point of honour and
courage provides a core of serious interest in a book marred,
like the others, by sensationalism and haste. (pp. 90-3)

Despite some melodramatic extras, . . . the central relationship
in the book, between Louis XI and the Duke of Burgundy, is
seriously conceived. The Duke knows that he is the stronger
party and in a position to dictate terms. But he cannot escape
altogether from the idea that the King of France is his superior
by right, irrespective of power. Thus he orders the King to
appear before him in tones which may not be disobeyed, but
grants him a throne higher than his own when the meeting takes
place. All this is well done; but it is just at points like this

where the true Scott, the profound intelligence that triumphed in *Waverley,* seems to be once again at work, that we are disappointed. The point made is too general. The deep insight required into the mind of the Duke, and into the nature of the changing society, is lacking. We are left on the one hand with a sketch of great possibilities, largely unused, on the other, with an exciting tale of little lasting significance. This would be a fair summary of several other novels, too. It would cover the antagonism between Norman and Saxon in *Ivanhoe,* and the potentially interesting political situation between Douglas and March in *The Fair Maid of Perth,* as well as the more perfunctorily treated struggle of the courtiers in *Kenilworth.*

But there are times when the anti-romantic tendency, already noted in the treatment of the hero of *Quentin Durward,* has consequences that mark Scott off very sharply from other mediaevalists. Wilkin, the Flemish weaver in *The Betrothed,* and his daughter Rose provide a striking case. In the passage that follows Rose is trying to dissuade her mistress from promising to marry the man who has led the defence of her castle against attack.

> "He is too great to be loved himself—too haughty to love you as you deserve. If you wed him, you wed gilded misery, and, it may be, dishonour as well as discontent."
>
> "Remember, damsel," answered Eveline Berenger, "his services towards us."
>
> "His services?" answered Rose. "He ventured his life for us, indeed, but so did every soldier in his host. And am I bound to wed any ruffling blade among them, because he fought when the trumpet sounded? I wonder what is the meaning of their *devoir,* as they call it, when it shames them not to claim the highest reward a woman can bestow, merely for discharging the duty of a gentleman, by a distressed creature. A gentleman, said I?—The coarsest boor in Flanders would hardly expect thanks for doing the duty of a man by women in such a case."

The speech of the characters here, as so often in Scott's mediaeval works, is a slack Wardour Street, full of dead clichés. This was almost inevitable, since he did not know how mediaeval people really spoke, and since no doubt his readers would have felt cheated if they had spoken in contemporary style. But if we overlook the unreality of the idiom, and look to the substance of what is being said, we are faced with something both intelligent and original. It is nothing less than a serious critique of the insincerities and ambiguities of the knightly code. It grasps firmly the selfish core within humble professions of service, the class arrogance that claims for a gentleman a power to love differently from others, the brute male strength which is unmentioned but really present in the chivalrous devotion. (pp. 93-5)

There are times . . . when the calm, unillusioned view of the author himself adds its weight to the words of the Flemings. Here is the scene that follows a battle:

> That the spoil thus acquired might not long encumber the soldier, or blunt his ardour for farther enterprise, the usual means of dissipating military spoils were already at hand. Courtezans, mimes, jugglers, minstrels and tale-tellers of every description, had accompanied the night-

march; and secure in the military reputation of the celebrated De Lacy, had rested fearlessly at some little distance until the battle was fought and won. These now approached, in many a joyous group, to congratulate the victors. Close to the parties which they formed for the dance, the song, or the tale, upon the yet bloody field, the countrymen, summoned in for the purpose, were opening large trenches for depositing the dead—leeches were seen tending the wounded—priests and monks confessing those in extremity—soldiers transporting from the field the bodies of the more honoured among the slain—peasants mourning over their trampled crops and plundered habitations—and widows and orphans searching for the bodies of husbands and parents . . .

This indeed is life, not escape. But again, it is a *general* statement. It is touching and true, but it is not illuminating about one time and place rather than another. It is really a sign of the failure of these books as novels that such broad, meditative passages, which could occur in an essay as appropriately as in a novel, are often the most memorable. Their presence may even increase our irritation at finding a man capable of this large, clear view of life as it is, engaged in puerilities. For puerility is hardly an unfair word for the 'Benedicite' language of his monks, or the fantastic resolutions required by some of the plots.

Here again we are confronted with the basic cause of failure. To write a historical novel of any importance an author needs to know a great deal about his period. He needs much more information than he will ever actually use. He needs in G. M. Young's words "to read until he can hear people talking" [see Renwick annotation in Additional Bibliography]. Scott possessed this sort of knowledge about as far back as the reign of Charles II, in which one of his greatest books, *Old Mortality,* and one of his partial successes, *Peveril of the Peak,* are laid. Beyond that he never had it, and his earlier periods tend to merge into one. The twelfth century of *Ivanhoe* is nearer to the sixteenth in *Kenilworth* than the latter is to the finely realized late seventeenth century Scotland of *Old Mortality.*

Usually, what takes the place of the absent historical insight is an uneasy kind of ventriloquism or historical substitution. Either the words of the character, monk or king or baron, are recognizably the words of Walter Scott, or else they are not his own words but the words of a much later form of civilization, thinly disguised. [An example] . . . from *Ivanhoe* should make this clear. (pp. 96-8)

The following is a [clear] case of the author almost forgetting who is suposed to be speaking:

> "Rebecca," said the Templar, "dost thou hear me?"
>
> "I have no portion in thee, cruel, hard-hearted man," said the unfortunate maiden.
>
> "Ay, but dost thou understand my words?" said the Templar; "for the sound of my own voice is frightful in mine own ears. I scarce know on what ground we stand, or for what purpose they have brought us hither. This listed space—that chair—these faggots—I know their purpose, and yet it appears to me like some-

thing unreal—the fearful picture of a vision, which appals my sense with hideous fantasies, but convinces not my reason.''

''My mind and senses keep touch and time,'' answered Rebecca, ''and tell me alike that these faggots are destined to consume my earthly body, and open a painful but a brief passage to a better world.''

''Dreams, Rebecca—dreams,'' answered the Templar—''idle visions, rejected by the wisdom of your own wiser Sadducees. Hear me Rebecca,'' he said, proceeding with animation; ''a better chance hast thou for life and liberty than yonder knaves and dotard dream of. Mount thee behind me on my steed—on Zamor, the gallant horse that never failed his rider.''

It is an interesting point in the history of taste that generations of boys appear to have read stuff like this with excitement and even ecstasy. But it is not only unreal; it is an amalgam of different kinds of unreality with transitions of the most abrupt kind. What is one to say of a twelfth century brute who talks like a self-conscious sea-captain in a boys' story, but turns aside for a moment to refer to an obscure Hebrew heresy of the first century A.D.? Speeches like this show Scott almost appearing to forget that he is a novelist and allotting the content of his well-stocked mind with impartial abandon to male and female, to lustful and chaste, villain and heroine.

Many other such passages could be produced. It would be wrong to dwell on them; any author is entitled to demand that we pay more attention to his best than his worst. But to fail to mention them at all would be to miss two important points. One is that Scott like several other great English writers was something of a somnambulist. A hasty writer, a busy man of the world, a man both modest about his own intellectual powers, and delighted by his great popular success, he seldom knew whether he was writing well or ill. It is likely that he overrated a passage like that just quoted as much as he underrated his finest achievements. In this insensitivity to his own literary merits and defects he resembles Byron in his own time and a number of Victorian writers, notably Dickens. It might be an interesting question for scholarship—one for which I have neither the space nor the learning—whether or not this is, in the main, a new and characteristic development of the nineteenth century, or whether it is perennial and springs from the familiar difficulty of 'the subject as object'. Whatever the right answer to this question, it is clear that Scott is a very extreme case of this ignorance of his own achievement and of his own failure.

The other important point has been briefly mentioned already. A passage like the above exchange between Rebecca and the Templar, coming as it does at the climax of one of Scott's most popular works, could well lead the most sensitive critic astray. Life is short, and books (especially in the nineteenth century) are many. There must be many, capable of enjoying what is best in Scott, who have read passages like this and absolved themselves from further enquiry. It is certainly strange, but I hope that it is by now intelligible, that the same man should have written this and (say) the account of the battle of Drumclog in *Old Mortality*.

The same carelessness can be seen in the use of sources in many of these late books. *Count Robert of Paris*, dealing with Byzantine history of which Scott had no special knowledge, relies heavily on Gibbon. In the first chapter we are told that the official adoption of Christianity in the fourth century was 'unspeakably to the advantage' of Byzantium, because, ''The world was now Christian, and, with the Pagan code, had got rid of its load of disgraceful superstition. Nor is there the least doubt, that the better faith produced its natural and desirable fruits in society, in gradually ameliorating the hearts and taming the passions of the people.'' In fact, on the question which is central to Gibbon's whole interpretation he says exactly the opposite of what Gibbon says. But, within a page or two, he is saying: ''Constantinople, therefore, when in 324 it first arose in imperial majesty out of the humble Byzantium, showed, even in its birth, and amid its adventitious splendour . . . some intimations of that speedy decay to which the whole civilized world, then limited within the Roman empire, was internally and imperceptibly tending.'' In fact, Scott agrees exactly with Gibbon's general view.

It seems extraordinary that a man so intelligent should have so little intellectual curiosity here. If Gibbon is exactly right, but the main reason he gives is exactly wrong, a most interesting set of questions arises. Scott does not ask himself any of them, but labours steadily on with the task of covering blank paper with ink.

In saying 'it seems extraordinary', I meant so long as we are looking only at the text of *Count Robert*. But if we turn to Scott's journal for May 8, 1831, the day after the publishers warned him the public would not like *Count Robert*, it will seem much more natural. He writes: ''I have suffered terribly, that is the truth, rather in body than in mind, and I often wish I could lie down and sleep without waking. But I will fight it out if I can. It would argue too great an attachment of consequence to my literary labours to sink under . . . After all, this but fear and faintness of heart, though of another kind from that which trembleth at a loaded pistol. My bodily strength is terribly gone; perhaps my mental too?''

Reading that, and knowing that the writer was not inclined by nature to dramatize himself, we shall hardly judge with severity the lack of real attention to Gibbon's argument.

It is not surprising after all this, to find that there are times when the very intention of writing historically seems to falter. The author's convenience is allowed to play havoc with chronology. Scott's note 31 to *Quentin Durward* is typical of a large number of cases of a curious deliberate and determined neglect of the nature of the task he had set himself. He writes:

> In assigning the present date to the murder of the Bishop of Liege, Louis de Bourbon, history has been violated. It is true that the bishop was made prisoner by the insurgents of that city. It is also true that the report of the insurrection came to Charles with a rumour that the bishop was slain, which excited his indignation against Louis, who was then in his power. But these things happened in 1467, and the bishop's murder did not take place till 1482 . . . The murder of the bishop has been fifteen years antedated in the text, for reasons which the reader of romances will easily appreciate.

That last sentence is very characteristic. One does not know whether to be irritated by the easy manner of the popular idol, who knows that his wares are quite good enough to sell, or to admire that genuine modesty, that casual attitude to his own genius that was one of the most marked traits in his nature, and in such striking contrast to the self-importance of his great contemporaries.

In either case, we must recognize that we are dealing here not just with a casual remark in a note, but with a settled attitude to the writing of mediaeval fiction. He states it most clearly in his essay on the novels of Clara Reeve, whose *Old English Baron* is full of obvious anachronisms. He defends her by saying:

> He that would please the modern world, yet present the exact impression of the middle ages, will repeatedly find that he will be obliged, in despite of his utmost exertions, to sacrifice the last to the first object, and eternally expose himself to the just censure of the rigid anti-quary, because he must, to interest the readers of the present time, invest his characters with language and sentiments unknown to the period assigned to his story; and thus his utmost efforts only attain a sort of composition between the true and the fictitious,—just as the dress of Lear, as performed on the stage, is neither that of a modern sovereign, nor the cerulean paint-ing and bear-hide with which the Britons, at the time when that monarch is supposed to have lived, tattooed their persons, and sheltered themselves from cold. All this inconsistency is avoided by adopting the style of our grand-fathers and great-grandfathers, sufficiently an-tiquated to accord with the antiquated character of the narrative, yet copious enough to express all that is necessary to its interest, and to supply that deficiency of colouring which the more ancient times do not afford.

Many comments could be made. We might say that such a plan was perhaps good enough for Clara Reeve, but not for the vastly greater creative energies of Walter Scott. We might complain that the word 'antiquaries' begs the question, for the crucial word 'sentiments' tacitly admits that it is not just su-perficial details but the whole stuff of history that is being violated. For 'sentiments' is for Scott a much more impressive word than it is for us. It involves the whole way men thought and felt about the world—everything, in fact, which makes history, and hence historical fiction, interesting. We might note that the mention of *King Lear* is something of a red herring, because the theatre can in any case hardly attempt the fully historical treatment which Scott achieved in his seventeenth- and eighteenth-century settings, and that Shakespeare in *King Lear* did not erect any of that laborious pseudo-historical struc-ture which exists in all Scott's mediaeval novels, and which he is here almost admitting to be a waste of time.

But perhaps the simplest and best thing to say is that Scott is here admitting, in effect, that his mediaeval novels were not meant very seriously. For what, after all, can be the serious point of a mediaeval novel without distinctive mediaeval fea-tures, but full of the detailed pretence of being mediaeval? Scott is really admitting that in a large part of his writing life he was playing a game with the public. If we accept this, and we do because it answers exactly to our experience of reading many of the books, then his status as a real historical novelist is actually enhanced. For we are enabled to make a clearer division between the best and the worst in Scott. Scott was good precisely when his method was truly historical. It could only be that when he knew enough and felt enough about the

A contemporary commentary on Scott's willpower and per-sistence in his labors despite his illness.

period with which he dealt to recreate the past with imaginative insight. He could only do this for times within about a hundred years of his own boyhood. 1679, the imagined date of *Old Mortality,* is about the furthest reach of a process which relied largely on oral tradition. Most characteristically, the process works with shorter periods than this, as in *Waverley* and *Red-gauntlet.* It would be difficult to overestimate the importance of the experience of actually listening to the reminiscences of the old man who became the model for Baron Bradwardine. So, when considering Scott the man we must take his mediaeval interests into account; when considering the actual influence of Scott on generations of readers up till about 1914, we must take it into account. But when we think of his great and en-during contribution to our literature, we can forget it with relief. (pp. 98-104)

> *A. O. J. Cockshut, in his* The Achievement of Walter Scott, *Collins, 1969, 216 p.*

ANGUS CALDER AND JENNI CALDER   (essay date 1969)

[*The Calders discuss various features of Scott's prose style.*]

We do not go to Scott for the subtle pleasures of a careful style, like Jane Austen's, nor for the virtuosity which we find in Dickens or D. H. Lawrence. Scott's style at its worst com-bines the formality of the 18th century with the sentimentality and prudery of the Victorians, and he is not easily forgiven for it. At its best, it is very readable, once we are used to the slow pace, but not very distinguished. 'Workmanlike' is the adjective which springs to mind, and it is not an epithet which Scott himself would have shunned.

But this tepid judgment must at once be qualified. Wherever Scott sets a man or a woman talking, especially if the speaker is a lower-class character or a Scotsman of any degree, his prose is likely to touch the heights. Each of his best characters speaks prose with its own individual rhythm and life, so that we cannot discuss the prose without talking about the character. It is often objected that the Scottish speech is hard for a modern English reader to understand. It is basically no harder than Shakespeare's prose, and it is often as rewarding. The best approach to it is not to flee to the glossary every time an odd word crops up, but to read it as quickly as possible; one soon finds that words like 'breeks' and 'fou' have become as familiar as 'trousers' and 'drunk'.

Scott's 'own' style, it may be said, is the rather drab wall which sets off his lively portraits. Or perhaps we should compare it to a heavily framed but serviceable window, for Scott's visual imagination and his powers of social observation are easily discerned through it. Often, on going back to examine a passage which seemed to provide inspired writing well above Scott's usual level, we find that the prose is the same heavy prose we expect from him; what made it seem great was the picture which it conjured up or the understanding which flashed through it.

Clumsiness is easily found, and bad grammar is not unknown. Scott wrote very fast and sent his novels quickly through the presses. Even if he had had the temperament of a fastidious stylist, he had no time to be one.

His ponderous euphemisms can be annoying or funny, depending on the reader's patience—as when he refers to the eunuchs in Saladin's court as 'those unhappy officials whom eastern jealousy places round the zenana'. Scott is particularly prone to call a spade 'a traditional agricultural implement of the region' in any case where sex is concerned. When Henry Gow, the blacksmith, leads a 'glee-woman' through the streets of Perth, Scott's attempt to explain his embarrassment reads as follows:

> Ere our stout son of Vulcan had fixed his worship on the Fair Maid of Peth, a certain natural wildness of disposition had placed him under the influence of Venus, as well as that of Mars: and it was only the effect of a sincere attachment which had withdrawn him entirely from such licentious pleasures. . . .

This, alas, is on a par with the pompous 19th-century provincial journalism which Dickens loved to make fun of; and it could be paralleled in any of the novels.

A fairer example of Scott's 'workmanship' would be this, from *Woodstock:*

> It was often noised about, that Cromwell, the deep and sagacious statesman, the calm and intrepid commander, he who had overcome such difficulties, and ascended to such heights, that he seemed already to bestride the land which he had conquered, had, like many other men of great genius, a constitutional taint of melancholy, which sometimes displayed itself both in words and actions, and had been first observed in that sudden and striking change, when, abandoning entirely the dissolute freaks of his youth, he embraced a very strict course of religious observances, which, upon some occa-

sions, he seemed to consider as bringing him into more near and close contact with the spiritual world. . . .

Is this good prose or bad? Saving the clumsiness of 'as bringing him into', it seems to be neither. The long sentence is typical of Scott, though this is an extreme example. It is slow, and the heavy punctuation (which was usual at the time) slows it down still further; yet it is well-managed. We absorb all the information which it gives without difficulty, and there is a lot of it, nothing less than a brief biography of Cromwell.

The colourless adjectives and the abstract nouns help to sketch the man economically. Words like 'sagacious', 'intrepid', 'genius', 'melancholy', 'dissolute', 'observances' have no 'smell' to them, no life in themselves. But they have the necessary dignity. Their meanings, while they are broad, are quite clear. If we substituted more lively ones—'clever' for 'sagacious', 'moodiness' for 'melancholy', we would immediately be leaving something out or distorting the picture. 'Clever' has pejorative undertones, and it lacks the extra meaning of 'wise' and 'statesmanlike' which 'sagacious' carries. In the same way, the word 'dissolute' covers several types of bad behaviour in one word. Scott's apparently cumbersome Latinisms, in fact, work like a shorthand. They rapidly give us an accurate general impression.

The same efficiency appears in the swifter passages where Scott is describing action. The language is always unobtrusive and predictable. Scott almost never surprises us with his choice of words, and is never sensational in his descriptions of war and danger. Take this moment of suspense in *Waverley,* just as the Battle of Prestonpans is beginning and the hero is about to fight for the first time:

> The clansmen on every side stript their plaids, prepared their arms, and there was an awful pause of about three minutes, during which the men, pulling off their bonnets, raised their faces to heaven, and uttered a short prayer; then pulled their bonnets over their brows and began to move forward at first slowly. Waverley felt his heart at that time throb as it would have burst from his bosom. It was not fear, it was not ardour,—it was a compound of both, a new and deeply energetic impulse, that with its first emotion chilled and astounded, then fevered and maddened his mind. The sounds around him combined to exalt his enthusiasm; the pipes played, and the clans rushed forward, each in its own dark column. As they advanced they mended their pace, and the muttering sounds of the men to each other began to swell into a wild cry.

(pp. 107-10)

The syntax of this passage is, of course, far looser; the phrases huddle on top of each other, as the actions follow together or in quick succession. There is something very appropriate to the moment in the grammatical oddness of the first sentence; the rhythms of Scott's prose are rarely as subtle as this. But this is not 'fine' writing. There is not one word which gives us pause, or which makes us think, 'how clever of Scott'. This is a virtue; we have nothing to lose by reading fast. Again, we notice the usefulness of Scott's Latinised vocabulary. '. . . ardour . . . energetic impulse . . . enthusiasm' . . . these words stand for typical emotions, not unusual ones, and we hurry over them quickly, with complete comprehension. The Anglo-Saxon words—fear, dark, muttering, wild—are equally plain, equally broad, and equally effective.

Two of Scott's commonest mannerisms emerge from the passages just quoted. 'It was not fear, it was not ardour' shows a habit of mind characteristic of Scott when he is analysing a man's appearance or his feelings or his character. He rejects one or more of the obvious and expected words or phrases in this way, then combines them or plumps for the one which is right. To take a simple comparison, here is Prior Aymer in *Ivanhoe:* 'In his seat he had nothing of the awkwardness of the convent, but displayed the easy and habitual grace of a well-trained horseman.' Scott, dealing with a man, is always concerned to point out whether he is or is not typical, and if so, of what. Waverley might have been expected to feel either fearful or ardent, but in fact felt both. The Prior, instead of representing the *type* of the clumsy monk, conforms to the *type* of the well-trained horseman. Because he is a monk, this at once makes him a moderately complex character instead of a simple one. This obviously goes along with the generalising nature of Scott's vocabulary.

A second trait of Scott's writing—a more puzzling one—is illustrated by the word 'seems' near the end of the passage about Cromwell. A novelist, surely, knows all about the characters he chooses to introduce? Two further examples, small matters in themselves, come one after the other in *The Heart of Midlothian.* We are told that Reuben Butler was orphaned '*about* the year 1704-5'. About a page later, we read that old Dumbiedikes used '*pretty nearly* the following words'.

Partly, this must be a habit, a bad one perhaps, of which Scott is unconscious. But we can see how it arose. In the case of Cromwell, he is writing about a real person and going by what his contemporaries said about him. This is the method of the historian, which Scott was bound to follow with his major historical figures. What is odd is that Scott should write in the same way about purely fictitious personages. Two important points emerge. The first is that Scott was thinking of his novels as 'true' history, and adopting the caution of a scholar. The second is that he sees his invented people from the outside, as their friends or even a casual observer might have seen them, rather than from the inside, like a modern 'psychological' novelist. When he does get 'inside' Edward Waverley, he uses generalised language, so that the character is typical rather than sharply individual.

Scott's prose is mainly impersonal; except when it is bad we usually forget about it, and so forget about its author. (One could never say this of Dickens, or Graham Greene, who constantly take us aback with their personal and surprising use of language.) But he carries on from the 18th century the tradition of the author's comment. He quite often steps in to remind us that the people he is describing, though born long ago, have their counterparts in the present day; that is, he moralises about his characters. (See, for instance, the beginning of Chapter 22 of *Kenilworth,* where he makes Amy Robsart's interest in clothes the excuse for poking ponderous fun at 'ladies of fashion of the present or any other period'.) He is never afraid to tell the reader why he has left something out, or to remind him of the situation of characters who have been out of sight for a while. How well 'our reader' takes this kind of thing depends on how much he likes Scott's personality and how many of Scott's elephantine witticisms he can stomach. But, like Scott's caution which has just been discussed, these 'asides' sometimes have the effect of reminding us that we are reading not what the author *chooses* to tell us, but what he *can* tell us. Scott is ready to remind us of the limits of his own knowledge of people and periods, or to apologise for the sometimes clumsy results of [his] free-wheeling narrative method. . . . (pp. 110-12)

In fact, he produces something like the famous 'alienation-effect' in Bertolt Brecht's plays, and for similar reasons. Just as Brecht wishes to prevent the audience from sympathising with his stage characters as if they were real people, so Scott is candidly anxious to instruct and entertain the reader, but not to lead him astray. The historical detail he will vouch for as fairly accurate (often directly, in a footnote), but the mechanics of his plot, which he hopes will amuse the reader, are not to be taken seriously. (p. 112)

> *Angus Calder and Jenni Calder, in their* Scott, *Evans Brothers Limited, 1969, 160 p.*

THOMAS CRAWFORD (essay date 1982)

[*Crawford provides a modern assessment of Scott's poetry that focuses on the ballad epics* The Lay of the Last Minstrel, Marmion, *and* The Lord of the Isles. *The critic discusses Scott's structural principles, narrative techniques, descriptive methods, and treatment of landscape.*]

When the young Scott attempted wholly original poetry in the ballad measure, he at first wrote nothing so good as his interpolations into traditional ballads, few though these were. Years later, in *The Antiquary,* he went back to the method and the mood of the interpolated stanzas of "Kinmont Willie." Using the traditional "Red Harlaw" as his starting point, he gave his own ballad on that topic to one of his impressive spey-wives, Elspeth of Craigburnfoot. Elspeth's ballad succeeds because it is in character, and deliberately fragmentary. The too explicit **"Eve of St. John"** and **"Glenfinlas"** have been replaced by a mysterious, irrational sequence; and Scott's poetry has gained enormously by his adoption of a *persona.*

Elspeth's ballad is one of a remarkable series of varied lyrics scattered through the novels and longer poems, which are at one and the same time the apotheosis of *pastiche* and the concentrated expression of Scott's own personality. Comparing Scott's lyrics with Burns's, Grierson claims that Scott is more impersonal than Burns: "Even Burns in his recast of folk-songs frequently charges them with more of his personal feelings. . . . Scott's revivals of older strains, aristocratic as often as folk-song, are in a purer style" [see Renwick annotation in Additional Bibliography]. But Grierson ignores the fact that Burns's best lyrics are often dramatic lyrics, implying a *persona* ("My luve she's but a lassie yet," "Tam Glen," "Thou hast left me ever, Jamie"), while Scott's are impregnated with the spirit of the works in which they appear, which in its turn is Scott's own. Take Lucy Ashton's song from Ch. III of *The Bride of Lammermoor:*

> Look not thou on beauty's charming,
> Sit thou still when kings are arming,
> Taste not when the wine-cup glistens,
> Speak not when the people listens,
>
> Stop thine ear against the singer,
> From the red gold keep thy finger,
> Vacant heart, and hand, and eye,
> Easy live and quiet die.

In its context it is related to the defect in Lucy's character that is part cause of the novel's catastrophe, and is thus the emanation of Lucy, not Scott. At the same time it is connected with preoccupations of the author's own, with the wistful contemplation of temptations. Beauty charmed Scott only in a "respectable" and gentlemanly manner, not in Burns's or Byron's fashion: he would have dearly liked to be a soldier, but his lameness prevented him from serving fully when the kings of Europe were arming. In days when the people required leadership, all he could give them—magnificent though it was—was a picture of their past; the red gold and the wine cup attracted him greatly; often it must have seemed to him that there was an emptiness at the centre of his being—"vacant heart," if not hand or eye; and Abbotsford, for all the bustle of its social life, for all the hunting and fishing and entertaining, was surely in essence a retreat: the direct opposite of political and military life, and a substitute for strenuous action in the real world. Thus I do not think it is fanciful to trace the elements of this beautiful dramatic lyric to Scott's own experience, and to suggest that its mainspring is the author's ironical self-criticism.

Unlike Burns, Scott did not generally have a tune in mind when writing a lyric—but, despite the assertion that he had no ear for music, he could sometimes almost rival Burns in this strain, as in **"Bonny Dundee"** and **"Donald Caird"**; and his handling of vernacular Scots in this last song has all the vitality of the Scots dialogue in the novels. The most characteristic moods in Scott's lyrics are robust action, elegiac sadness, extreme, even stark poignancy, and the monolithic sublime. For robust action we need go no further than Flora MacIvor's song, **"There is mist on the mountain"** from Ch. XXII of *Waverley;* for stark poignancy, Madge Wildfire's **"Proud Maisie"** in Ch. XL of *The Heart of Midlothian;* for elegiac sadness united to a magical strain of high poetry, **"Rosabelle"** in *The Lay of the Last Minstrel,* Canto VI; and for the monolithic sublime, Rebecca's hymn in Ch. XXXIX of *Ivanhoe,* which contains within itself all the grandeur of the Hebrew strain in Scottish Presbyterianism. There are literally scores of fine stanzas and lines scattered throughout Scott's numerous lyrics, and a handful of songs as perfect as any ever written in Scotland. . . . One can only marvel that the popular handbooks on English romantic poetry and the "romantic imagination" ignore such poems; often, there is not even a single entry for Scott in the index.

Scott's longer poems grew out of his ballad imitations; thus, *The Lay of the Last Minstrel* was originally conceived as a ballad but grew into a longer work under the influence of medieval English romances. He began it in the *Christabel* measure, but soon varied it either with straight octosyllabics, his favourite form, or with one derived from late medieval romances. This latter occurs much oftener in *Marmion,* where octosyllabic couplets are repeated two, three, or even more times, then interrupted by a six-syllabled line, followed by another group of eights, then a second six, rhyming with the first. The effect of the three-stressed line has been well compared to the breaking and falling of a wave.

By the time he wrote *The Lady of the Lake* and the later poems, Scott's lines of eight had developed a "massed and cumulative force" of their own, just like that of the old pentameter; as the line pattern became less broken, his poems exhibited a facile monotony that had been inherent in them from the beginning.

If Scott's versification builds up to parallel climaxes, so, too, does his syntax—a characteristic which Donald Davie has described, in a phrase borrowed from the linguist Roman Jakobson, as "the poetry of grammar." Scott's poetical rhetoric repeats identical constructions in order to produce syntactic augmentation, a "principle of organization" which he uses along with the other repetitive orderings of rhyme and metre. As Davie says:

> it is when the traditional principles of order are reinforced by grammatical patterning and parallels that we recognize a poetry thoroughly achieved, structured through and through; and elegant variation, the saying of one thing many ways, brings with it for Scott this additional source of order.

But the "many ways" change what is being said, and give us a poetry that is quite alien to modern English modes, where the short or medium-length lyric is the norm, concentration a virtue, and expansiveness a positive defect. The type of order which is created by all Scott's metrical and syntactic accumulation, by all the elegant variations, may perhaps be regarded as his personal adaptation of that "Celtic ornamentation of a surface" which has often been considered one of the abiding features of Scottish literature. And it exists alongside another principle of order—that of narrative structure, of the tale itself.

In *Marmion* and the later poems, we react in the first place as we do to any other narrative—to the total shape, which in its turn is concerned with the creation and resolution of suspense, with the spectacle of persons and things, with recognitions and reversals, with the contrast and interplay of the expected and the unexpected. Scott's ballad epics consist primarily of situations: rhythms, rhymes, images and "the poetry of grammar" are therefore means to an end. And, as so often in the *Waverley Novels* also, the most striking elements within these situations are description and dialogue. Any of the longer poems provides a typical example; the situations are both visually and dramatically conceived, just as in the most successful modern popular modes—the film, the TV play, and the comic strip—and, what is more important, just as in the best popular ballads in the *Minstrelsy.* Thus the union of sight and sound, of drama and picture, is part of the ballad's contribution to the *Lays,* as it is later part of the ballad's contribution to the novels. Not only are dialogue and narrative linked so that the one interpenetrates the other, as in the scene of Marmion's death, but both dialogue and description are often subordinated to the characters and indeed to their social typology.

Scott's situations are so intensely seen and heard that it seems almost certain they must have existed in the first instance as mental pictures and speech heard with the mind's ear. The creative process with Scott would thus seem to have comprised, firstly, the visualisation of a series of scenes, then secondly, their *translation* into his chosen medium of verse or prose. In the *Lays,* the subsidiary units of the medium itself were often not so much words and images that Scott had impregnated with his own personality after the fashion of a modern lyric poet, as standard currency, like Homeric diction or the stock phrases of ballads and popular poetry. His expressions are often lifted bodily from other poets, or from the *clichés* of everyday life:

> But Isabel, who long had seen
> Her pallid cheek and pensive mien,
> And well herself the cause might know,
> Though innocent, of Edith's woe,
> Joy'd, generous, that revolving time
> Gave means to expiate the crime.

Scott's originality consists partly in his disposition of the larger situations rather than in his language as such. Nevertheless when he is working at full stretch, his "translations" can be intensely and beautifully vivid, as in Canto II of *Marmion*, where two abbesses and a blind and aged abbot sit in judgment on the guilty nun, Constance Beverley, in surroundings of Gothic gloom and horror, or—in *The Lay of the Last Minstrel*—William of Deloraine's wild ride form Branksome to Melrose.

Early critics of Scott's poetry spoke much of his descriptive powers, and one of the most acute of these, Adolphus, pointed out that his descriptions were often conceived in terms of a framed and painted picture rather than as direct renderings of reality. Adolphus also noted Scott's "marked attention . . . to what is called in painting Chiaroscuro"; there are, he said, very few of his "poetical descriptions . . . which do not owe part of their beauty to the distribution of light and shade," and he is always concerned "to point out some remarkable appearance of illumination or obscurity" [see Additional Bibliography]. To this might be added his fondness for moving pictures or pageants, especially processions, and his addiction to the poetical equivalent of "glorious technicolor," like the description of Lord Ronald's fleet at the beginning of *The Lord of the Isles*. The pageantry and cinematic quality reach their highest expression in the battle scenes at the end of *Marmion* and *The Lord of the Isles*. In *The Lord of the Isles*, Bruce slays a murderer with a brand snatched from the fire:

> The spatter'd brain and bubbling blood
> Hiss'd on the half-extinguish'd wood,
>   The miscreant gasp'd and fell!

After Bruce's fight to liberate his ancestral castle from the English,

>   . . . on the board his sword he toss'd,
> Yet steaming hot; with Southern gore
> From hilt to point 'twas crimson'd o'er.

In passages like these, or in the incident at Bannockburn where the Lord of Colonsay manages to slay d'Argentine, the knight who has given him his own death-wound, Scott's intensely visual and literal imagination was able to fashion out of his almost juvenile fascination with the horrors of war an anti-poetry of action that is far superior to the more conventional heroics for which he is famous.

In discussing Scott's descriptive verse, Adolphus notes that he never separates nature from human society, and that

> There is, indeed, throughout the poetry of this author, even when he leads us to the remotest wildernesses, and the most desolate monuments of antiquity, a constant reference to the feelings of man in his social condition; others, as they draw closer to inanimate things, recede from human kind; to this writer even rocks and deserts bear record of active and impassioned life, nay sometimes appear themselves inspired with its sensations; the old forgotten chieftain groans in the lonely cavern, and with "tears of rage impels the rill"; the maid's pale ghost "from rose and hawthorn shakes the tear," and the "phantom knight" shrieks along the field of his battles.

Such an attitude to nature is not so much "Augustan" as "pre-Romantic," for the persons whom Scott finds inseparable from his lonely places—the chieftain, the maid of balladry, and the phantom knight—are not those that would most readily occur to Pope or Johnson. There is, however, one aspect of Scott's treatment of landscape which is undoubtedly new—the poetical fusion of landscape with the sentiment of nationality. In previous Scottish poetry there is much evocation of a characteristically northern landscape, but without the specific and obvious infusion of national as distinct from local feeling. One thinks of the introductions to the various books of Gavin Douglas's *Aeneid*, of Thomson's *Winter*, of Burns's occasional sketches of the Ayrshire pastoral landscape. But it was reserved for Scott to strike such a note as the depiction of James V's incursion into the Trossachs in Canto I of *The Lady of the Lake*, or of Loch Coriskin and the Coolins in *The Lord of the Isles*, or of the border and lowland scenery of past and present in *The Lay of the Last Minstrel* and *Marmion*. The union of nationality with the perception of landscape becomes embarrassingly explicit in the rhetorical apostrophe which follows the often quoted:

> Breathes there the man, with soul so dead,
> Who never to himself hath said,
> This is my own, my native land!

The succeeding stanza begins:

> O Caledonia! stern and wild,
> Meet nurse for a poetic child!
> Land of brown heath and shaggy wood,
> Land of the mountain and the flood,
> Land of my sires! what mortal hand
> Can e'er untie the filial band,
> That knits me to thy rugged strand!

These hackneyed and oratorical lines exhibit a response to landscape that seems typically Scott's and which he renders with greater subtlety in many other passages—as, for example, this one, also from *The Lay of the Last Minstrel*—

> From the sound of Teviot's tide,
> Chafing with the mountain's side,
> From the groan of the wind-swung oak,
> From the sullen echo of the rock,
> From the voice of the coming storm,
>   The Ladye knew it well!
> It was the Spirit of the Flood that spoke,
> And he call'd on the Spirit of the Fell.

(pp. 34-42)

[The] strain of melancholy so noticeable in Scott's . . . ballad imitations is developed in the *Lays* to the point where it becomes mourning for Scotland's vanished independence. When the "last minstrel" is asked by the company at Branksome:

> Why he, who touch'd the harp so well,
> Should thus, with ill-rewarded toil,
> Wander a poor and thankless soil,
> When the more generous Southern Land
> Would well requite his skilful hand,

his reply is the "Breathes there the man, with soul so dead" passage already quoted, which soon, however, modulates into the nostalgic

> Still, as I view each well-known scene,
> Think what is now, and what hath been,
> Seems as, to me, of all bereft,
> Sole friends thy woods and streams were left;
> And thus I love them better still,
> Even in extremity of ill.

Thus the romantic-nationalistic attitude to landscape is to some extent a compensation for the desolate state of Scotland in the present. A similar mood occurs in *Marmion,* when a Highland tune puts Scott in mind of Scottish emigrants to Canada and America, chanting

> the lament of men
> Who languish'd for their native glen . . .
> Where heart-sick exiles, in the strain,
> Recall'd fair Scotland's hills again!

This is as close as Scott ever comes to what David Craig calls doing justice "to both the inevitability" of contemporary developments "and the losses involved"; the trouble is that he does not come close enough, and that his awareness is projected back into the past.

In the introduction to Canto V of *Marmion,* Scott shows himself quite conscious of his escapist role. After a glance at the danger to Kingship from the democratic and anti-royalist movements of his time, he goes on:

> Truce to these thoughts!—for, as they rise,
> How gladly I avert mine eyes,
> Bodings, or true or false, to change,
> For Fiction's fair romantic range,
> Or for Tradition's dubious light,
> That hovers 'twixt the day and night:
> Dazzling alternately and dim,
> Her wavering lamp I'd rather trim,
> Knights, squires and lovely dames to see,
> Creation of my fantasy. . . .

But what he finally beholds in "Fiction's fair romantic range" is the national disaster of Flodden, and in the Spenserians which preface *The Lord of the Isles* he sees himself as

> a lonely gleaner I,
> Through fields time-wasted, on sad inquest bound,
> Where happier bards of yore have richer harvest found.

Scott's conscious motive, in these Scottish Lays, seems identical with his intention in *The Minstrelsy of the Scottish Border:*

> By such efforts, feeble as they are, I may contribute somewhat to the history of my native country; the peculiar features of whose manners and character are daily melting and dissolving into those of her sister and ally. And, trivial as may appear such an offering, to the manes of a kingdom, once proud and independent, I hang it upon her altar with a mixture of feelings, which I shall not attempt to describe.

After this, Scott quotes some lines from an anonymous poem, *Albania,* published in 1742, which end:

> Hail! dearest half of Albion, sea-wall'd!
> Hail! state unconquer'd by the fire of war,
> Red war, that twenty ages round thee blaz'd!
> To thee, for whom my purest raptures flow,
> Kneeling with filial homage, I devote
> My life, my strength, my first and latest song.

In the General Preface to the *Waverley Novels,* however, he tells us that the purpose of his own "latest song"—the prose romances—was to serve Scotland by interpreting her to the English. In this he was following Maria Edgeworth, who

> may be truly said to have done more towards completing the Union than perhaps all the leg-

Scott in his study at Abbotsford, painted by Sir William Allan in 1832. The Granger Collection, New York.

islative enactments by which it has been followed up.

> Without being so presumptuous as to hope to emulate the rich humour, pathetic tenderness, and admirable tact which pervade the works of my accomplished friend, I felt that something might be attempted for my own country, of the same kind with that which Miss Edgeworth so fortunately achieved for Ireland—something which might introduce her natives to those of the sister kingdom in a more favourable light than they had been placed hitherto, and tend to procure sympathy for their virtues and indulgence for their foibles.

Comparison of these extracts suggests a certain deterioration in Scott's attitude to his native country between the *Minstrelsy* and the *Waverley Novels:* the pessimistic antiquarian had turned into a loyal subject displaying his ancestors and their quaint dependants to the Conqueror. (pp. 46-9)

> *Thomas Crawford, in his* Scott, *revised edition, Scottish Academic Press, 1982, 132 p.*

JANE MILLGATE   (essay date 1984)

[*Millgate discusses the* Heart of Mid-Lothian, *examining the ways in which the work both differs from and expands on Scott's earlier novels. The critic devotes a large portion of her remarks to analyzing the character of Jeanie Deans.*]

In *The Heart of Midlothian,* . . . [Scott] took as his protagonist not an educated young man of good family [as he had in his previous novels] but a young woman of humble origin, and set her upon a journey that led not from England to Scotland but in the opposite direction. Jeanie Deans is marked off from the outset by the absence of any tinge of the romantic in either her appearance or her perspective; at the same time those figures possessed of any significant degree of romantic sensibility are pushed to the melodramatic fringes of the text. In George Staunton, indeed, the figure of the travelling Englishman eager for excitement and the indulgence of his romantic appetites has become an anarchic and destructive force, incapable of reassimilation into the fabric of society.

The evidence that Scott was employing, deliberately as well as instinctively, a repertoire of motifs built up in the course of his earlier novels is too ample to require much elaboration. By this point in his career he had become highly self-conscious about his ongoing dialogue with the reader of the *Waverley Novels.* The Gandercleuch framework of *The Heart of Midlothian* and the other series of *Tales of My Landlord* allowed him to express this dialogue overtly, but the creation of his own subgenre of the 'Scotch' novel also allowed the Author of *Waverley* to engage in a more subtle interaction with his audience, to take for granted a familiarity with certain forms of plot, types of character, categories of incident, subjects for description, and so on, that could be exploited in various ways, each instance sharpened in its significance by the echoing presence of the full repertoire as it existed in the novels taken as a loosely related sequence. When, for example, particular emphasis was placed on Jeanie's lack of the handsome appearance of the traditional heroine or hero, or on her want of familiarity with any literature beyond the Bible and a few religious tracts, or on her innocence of anything resembling a taste for the picturesque, the author could safely expect his audience to make the appropriate comparisons with Edward Waverley, Harry Bertram, or Frank Osbaldistone.

Jeanie Deans is the heroine of truth. She has no need [like the heroes of Scott's earlier novels] to search for a father or an identity—her paternity and her selfhood are never in doubt. She is not concerned to define and locate her own situation in terms of literary analogues: that is left to Madge Wildfire. She is never found in disguise or decked out in clothes that shadow forth a different identity; the stress on her adherence to her Scottish dress and to such symbolic elements in that dress as her plaid and her maiden snood constitutes something more than the telling detail of a brilliantly realistic portrait. It is Madge Wildfire, Staunton, and Effie who appear in different guises and whose inconstancy and lack of any stable core of being mark them off from Jeanie. The role-playing and costume-changing that were harmless episodes in the growth of Edward Waverley and some of Scott's other young heroes become in *The Heart of Midlothian* dangerous signs of instability of character and failure of moral integrity. Staunton and Effie are possessed of the kind of imaginative responsiveness that was a positive quality in Scott's earlier heroes and heroines, but it avails them nothing. This is, as the references to Milton, Bunyan, and *Measure for Measure* indicate, a puritan fable—one in which Scott denies the imagination the kind of pre-eminence he had assigned it hitherto.

Scott was now moving into new fictional territory, turning away from the personal saga of the man of imagination caught up in the strangeness of historical action and regional disparity and towards a more intensive concern with moral questions.

The allusions to earlier literary forms and texts remain for the reader to pick up, but whereas in *Waverley* literary allusion and romance patterning were employed to tell the story of a young man who was of romantic temperament and himself deeply read in the works invoked, in this novel they are employed to tell the story of a young woman who is not merely a stranger to imaginative projections but literal-minded to the point of comedy.

The ribbon of contrastive allusion that connects *The Heart of Midlothian* to its predecessors is not designed merely to afford delight to those initiated in the Waverley game; it is a matter of substance. The inversion of many of Scott's favourite patterns and motifs helps to underline the fact that, by the use of this new novel to carry Scotland into England, the matter of Scotland and her national identity is being brought into the forefront of the action. Like Henry Morton in the first series of *Tales,* Jeanie herself is compelled into a self-consciousness about her Scottishness quite distinct from the pride in her descent from honest and God-fearing folk that she has learned from her father. Her appearance and conduct must do credit to her native country as well as to herself. Scottishness is everywhere at issue—not merely among the dissatisfied citizens of Edinburgh, their national pride offended by the compounded insensitivity of the British court in dealing with the Porteous affair, but also on the road to London and in the capital itself. Jeanie is handed on from one Scot to another, finally arriving at the home of her kinswoman at the sign of the thistle. What seems to the Scots like the natural fellow-feeling of exiles is interpreted by the English as clannishness— Queen Caroline assumes that Jeanie must be not merely a Scotswoman but a Campbell, so warm is the Duke of Argyle in her cause. The suppressed hostility detectable in the murmurings of the inhabitants of Wilmingham against Jeanie and Madge Wildfire bursts out in the violence of Harabee that delights in the hanging of Meg Murdockson and costs Madge her life: 'Shame the country should be harried wi' Scotch witches and Scotch bitches this gate—but I say hang and drown.' In the face of such animosity even the powerful Mr Archibald, surrogate for his employer the Duke of Argyle, can do nothing.

In the early part of *The Heart of Midlothian* the detail of Scottish history is close to the narrative surface. Though on the scale of historical importance the Porteus riots cannot be said to equal, say, Sheriffmuir or Prestonpans, they assume a central position here, event dominating over character at certain points in a fashion very different from *Waverley*'s avoidance of the detail of major historical episodes. In this respect *The Heart of Midlothian* is closer to *Old Mortality* than to any of its other precursors. The characteristic Waverley method is to play out the protagonist's fictional story against the background of an historical action, and though historical characters may be briefly encountered and individual incidents, such as Waverley's rescue of Colonel Talbot, based on historical anecdotes, no extended use is made of the lives of actual men and women. In *The Heart of Midlothian* not only are the public events fully displayed—especially through the extensive treatment of the Porteous affair and the historically very astute portrayal of the situation of the Duke of Argyle as Scotland's spokesman at the court of George II—but Jeanie's story goes beyond even Henry Morton's in its historicity in that it is based on that of the real Helen Walker. The novel's factual origin may have helped to push Scott towards presenting Jeanie with an amplitude that gives the reader access to the inner workings of her mind and feelings. She is a distinctly new figure in Scott's fiction, and he lavishes on her presentation an attention denied to his earlier youthful protagonists. In the process the balance of characterization shifts from the typical to the individual, from the conventional to the realistic, in ways that help account for this novel's popularity with critics who have little sympathy for the emblematic rather than psychological characterization found in those Scott novels that place a more overt reliance on romance conventions.

To speak of Helen Walker is to engage with Scott's sources—an ancient and honourable activity, but one that rarely yields substantial critical rewards. The impulse to find an original for Tully Veolan or Dandy Dinmont gripped even his earliest readers, and Scott himself gave such enterprises a certain legitimacy by his January 1817 review of the first series of *Tales of My Landlord* and, from 1829 onwards, by his new introductions and notes for the *magnum opus* edition. But Scott's own annotations and commentaries are themselves deceptive: what look like historiographical often turn out to be rhetorical devices; the citing of sources and invocation of parallels becomes a special version of the trope of amplification. Even in *The Heart of Midlothian,* for which he himself identified (in the 1827 Introduction to *Chronicles of the Canongate*) the actual germ from which his narrative sprang, the relationship between the raw material and the workings of the historical imagination is very difficult to assess, and it is not even possible to trace the way in which two separate factual strands—the story of Helen Walker and the account of the Porteous riots—came together as essential elements in a complex narrative design. Mary Lascelles, in her examination of Scott as retriever of the past, has recently attempted to confront this problem by carefully scrutinizing both the letter from Mrs Goldie that supplied Scott with the Helen Walker story and the subsequent recensions of the story in which Mrs Goldie was involved, and it is not necessary to reconsider the material she has so perceptively treated—beyond, perhaps, reemphasizing the extent to which Scott's historical understanding and novelistic imagination have totally transformed the narrative kernel with which he began. What is clearly of primary importance is Scott's choice in this novel of an actual heroine of the people rather than a fictional hero of good birth and the accompanying increase in historical matter in both public and private plots.

In combining the Walker and Porteous elements Scott was committing himself to 1736 as the date of his narrative. This was almost thirty years after the Act of Union, and it was clearly of symbolic importance to him that two very different assertions of Scottish independence should have been brought together at a moment when a particular phase of Scottish history came to a climax. In a letter written during the composition of the novel he spoke of the desire to break the Union of 1707 as being 'for thirty years . . . the predominant wish of the Scottish nation.' . . . Though it would certainly be an oversimplification to allegorize the novel so as to read the Porteous riots as the emblem of Scotland's hostility to the Union and Jeanie's successful pleading with the Queen as the Union's vindication, an element of this pattern certainly inheres in *The Heart of Midlothian.* As a novel about violence and rebellion it is connected to *Old Mortality;* as a meditation on the Union it is linked to its successor *The Bride of Lammermoor.* The three series of *Tales of My Landlord* that appeared between 1816 and 1819 have, in fact, closer affinities than has generally been recognized, and they can be seen as a kind of national trilogy marked off from the rest of the *Waverley* sequence. Many of Scott's actions and writings—from the dedication of the *Minstrelsy,* through the building of Abbotsford, to the annotation of the *magnum opus* edition—took much of their im-

petus from his yearning to assert a continuity between the old Scotland and the new. But while his commitment to the Union settlement and his belief in the economic, social, even moral advantages accruing to Scotland are not in doubt, it remained impossible for him to exorcise completely the fear that the incorporating Union of 1707, as distinct from the 1603 Union of the Crowns, constituted an absorption of Scotland into the body politic of England. It is that fear which haunts the three series of *Tales of My Landlord.*

During the later months of 1817 and the first part of 1818, when *The Heart of Midlothian* was in progress, these issues were very much at the forefront of Scott's mind. He had been directly instrumental in persuading the Prince Regent to send down a commission for the opening of the crown room in Edinburgh Castle and the investigation of the locked chest in which the regalia of Scotland were supposed to have been deposited in March 1707, upon the adjournment of the Scottish parliament. (pp. 152-57)

Scott was himself a member of the commission that entered the crown room on 4 February 1817 and opened the chest to reveal the regalia present and intact. He seems, in fact, to have orchestrated the entire ritual, and his fascination with the regalia made him think of using them as the basis for one of the tales in his new work. 'As I maintain a correspondence with Mr. Jedediah Cleishbotham,' he told Lady Louisa Stuart on 16 January 1818, 'I intend to recommend to him a tale founded upon an earlier adventure of these same Regalia.' . . . (pp. 157-58)

It is not clear exactly why or when Scott abandoned his plans for a regalia story. . . . As late as the end of April 1818 the plan was still to have *The Heart of Midlothian* occupy only the first two and a half volumes or so, and, as Scott told Daniel Terry, to devote 'vol. 4, and part of 3d' to 'a different story.' . . . As that first tale developed, however, something more than a change of narrative scale took place. It had been described to Terry as 'a Bourgeoise tragedy' . . . , and in sending Ballantyne the final pages of volume II Scott commented: 'The whole story must be mournful. There is no way of changing the tone that I can discover for it is a mournful story.' . . . But while the ending for Effie in the novel as completed remains 'mournful,' that can hardly be said of Jeanie's story.

What seems to have occurred in the process of writing the novel is that Jeanie's journey expanded in the telling until the 'weight' of her personal moral achievement called for a more positive emphasis to be given to the conclusion as it affected her own future—and, by extension, that of Scotland. Critical dissatisfaction with the novel tends to dwell on the problem of volume IV, and readers familiar with the text only in later editions frequently assume that this volume consisted merely of the Knocktarlitie pastoral. It is necessary to remember, however, that at the end of volume II of the first edition Jeanie has still not left Scotland, that volume III ends with her interview with the Queen, and that the first third of volume IV is taken up with her return to Scotland, a sequence integral to the shape and meaning of her journey as a whole. It is only by recognizing that the process which transformed the shorter structure into the longer is one of expansion rather than addition that we can engage with the problem of the ending in historical and generic as well as structural terms. Scott could, after all, have easily 'filled out' a fourth volume by writing the regalia story in which he was so much interested.

It is highly unlikely thtat Scott could ever have contemplated finishing his story, as some modern readers would have preferred, at the end of Jeanie's successful pleading with the Queen. Journeys in his fiction rarely follow the unidirectional pattern of the simple picaresque. Coming home to the father or the place of the fathers is an essential element in his characteristic design; the meaning of the journey inheres not in arriving at any particular goal but in coming to terms with the experience of the voyage and carrying that understanding forward into the life that extends beyond the narrative climax. *Waverley* is not finished at that moment in the Lake District when Edward thinks the romance of his life is over; no more is *The Heart of Midlothian* complete when Jeanie's eloquence wins Effie's pardon from the Queen. London cannot provide a conclusion; it is after all a Vanity Fair rather than a Celestial City, and to take Jeanie's quest as a straightforward Bunyanesque pressing-on towards eternity involves in any case a misreading of the text. It is Madge Wildfire who develops the analogy between Jeanie and Christiana, and though the comparison works to enhance the moral seriousness of the journey, it also serves as a defining contrast. Jeanie's personal salvation is not at issue: the triple temptation in her father's house, in the prison with Effie, and in the courtroom is already behind her before she sets out. If anyone's soul is at stake it is Effie's, but she must save that for herself. All Jeanie can do is buy time. Her most urgent concern is therefore with this world rather than with eternity.

The journey out and back allows the Independent's daughter to come into full independence, but it is the very reverse of an exercise in self-assertion. Determined to vindicate her faith in authority and providence, Jeanie is distinguished from everyone else in the novel—including her father and Butler—by her lack of egotism and by the absence of any impulse to self-dramatization. She is no rebel and has nothing in common with Staunton, Effie, or the Porteous mob. Though she leaves without her father's permission, she is superstitiously careful to obtain a blessing from him; though she cannot win Butler's approval for her plan, she uses her farewell visit to secure his acquiescence; she even extracts from the reluctant Dumbiedikes a gesture of goodwill in the form of money for her journey. Yet in the very process of winning these partial acquiescences Jeanie does inevitably disturb the customary order of her own small world. The dominant male figures—including Ratcliffe—are reduced to ancillary roles. Even the Duke of Argyle's intervention extends only as far as her introduction to the Queen; after that her own words must do the work.

Formerly quiescent and dutiful, a listener rather than a talker, Jeanie frees herself by her radical action and dominates for a time over her masters. She is herself undaunted by the paradoxes involved in her journey; its aim is essentially restorative—to save Effie's life and bring her back within the circle of the family—but she does not shy away from the disruption necessarily involved. She seeks rather, through the totally unaccustomed act of writing, to impose a new order on the future—as she tells Staunton, she wants 'To prevent farder mischieves, whereof there hath been enough.' . . . Her letters are masterpieces of persuasive rhetoric, instinctively phrased so as to reinstate a hierarchy shaken by her own assertion of the right of independent action. 'This is eloquence' . . . says the Queen after listening to Jeanie's plea, and the same could be said of what she writes. She seeks to remove the winning of Effie's pardon from the realm of the extraordinary—the Queen is 'not muckle differing from other grand leddies'; the Duke of Argyle is 'ane native true-hearted Scotsman, and not pridefu.' . . . If the disruptive effects of Effie's defection from the ordered ways of St Leonard's are to be diminished rather than reinforced,

the heroic nature of her elder sister's efforts must be underplayed. The good fortune has been achieved 'under the Great Giver, to whom all are but instruments' . . . , and the talk of other providential blessings—the promised cattle, a school for Butler—is directed towards controlling through language the perception of recent events and projecting a future ordered, harmonious, and unremarkable. By refusing in her letters to take personal credit for what has occurred, Jeanie uses them to give back authority to those to whom it has traditionally belonged.

There is, however, no letter to Effie. Jeanie pleads with her father to be gentle with the recovered lost sheep, but she does not herself have the chance to try whether, spoken in time and face to face, her own words can draw Effie back into the circle of light. The return journey exposes Jeanie to an actual hanging such as Effie has escaped, and she watches helplessly at the bedside of the dying Madge Wildfire, Effie's half-crazed counterpart. But these victims cannot serve as scapegoats for Effie; in withdrawing from the family to regions where Jeanie's word can have no power she commits herself to wilfulness and isolation. Effie and Staunton reject authority in favour of the individual will and are thus pushed beyond community. Jeanie does not arrive too late for the pardon—itself associated with a sentence of exile—but Effie has already gone beyond the point at which the pardon could reclaim her. In their farewell meeting Effie insists that she is 'a banished outlawed body' and refuses to listen to her sister's plea: 'O Effie, dinna be wilfu'—be guided for anes—we will be sae happy a'thegither!' . . . She cannot 'Come hame to us, your ain dearest friends' . . . ; she is already married to Staunton, and a smugglers' vessel waits in the darkness to carry her off. Winning the pardon thus stands isolated as a vindication of Jeanie's faith that authority can comprehend justice and mercy. But for those who stand outside the community of belief of which Jeanie is the centre, her action can have no efficacy.

It would be easy to turn this novel into a kind of feminist tract by insisting on the importance of the act of sisterhood in which Jeanie engages. Her initial refusal to be false to herself by lying—read by Effie as rejection—is transformed by the heroic action of the journey into an affirmation of sisterhood that comprehends even the Queen. Such a reading would stress that royal authority is embodied in a woman and note that the worst danger and deepest anguish Jeanie must endure are occasioned by two women who are themselves almost quintessential victims of male oppression. But this would be to politicize sexually a text concerned with human values in a wider sense. That Jeanie is a woman makes her task more difficult, her actions more heroic, and her success in wresting justice from authority all the more significant. But she never for a moment considers that the necessity of responding to a higher duty liberates her from the ordinary obediences of everyday. Unlike Mrs Dolly Dutton, she is perfectly willing to conform to the mandates of the Duke of Argyle and his surrogate Mr Archibald on the journey homewards, and she is quite ready to accommodate herself to the Highland strangenesses of Knocktarlitie. It is precisely because Jeanie believes in the hierarchy she temporarily subverts that her action carries meaning, transcends the impulses of one individual, and has significance for the community. By requiring that authority be true to itself, that the King's face be given the opportunity to give grace, she affirms the conservative as opposed to the revolutionary vision.

In compelling London and the Court to fulfil their responsibility towards one particular Scottish subject and recognize her own and her sister's humanity, Jeanie vindicates in this one instance the power arrangements regarded with such hostility by the Edinburgh citizenry of 1736: the Court is obliged to register Scottish feelings and desist from treating the inhabitants of North Britain as alien barbarians requiring to be taught their lessons by bloodshed. The narrative clearly requires this kind of reading in respect of Jeanie and Effie, and Scott also saw it as capable of extension into a larger political meaning. By expanding the emphasis on Jeanie's Scottishness at various points in her journey he moves deliberately towards establishing her as a nationally emblematic figure and transforming her achievement into a general vindication of the Union of 1707.

In *The Heart of Midlothian* an action that begins in violence and defiance ends with the violent and defiant destroying each other while leaving the moderate and humane to survive and even flourish within a political order that promises continuing economic and social progress. As always in Scott, the nineteenth-century narrator shows himself in no doubt as to the advantages of the current state of Scotland over its earlier condition, and this novel dwells less on the charms of certain aspects of the old social order than do some of his other texts. At the same time there is a confidence expressed—most powerfully through the portrait of Jeanie—in the enduring strength of certain moral values associated with the old Scotland, as well as a determinedly positive attitude towards the increasing 'civilization' of Scottish life. Where Scott gets into difficulties is in his attempt to make a narrative of the 1730s and '40s image forth his political vision of the overall pattern of Scottish history during the whole of the second half of the eighteenth century. He seeks to bring off the transition from historical narrative to political emblem by a fully orchestrated shift of mode—by

Scott's tomb at Dryburgh Abbey.

projecting the Knocktarlitie episode as a pastoral expressive of Jeanie's attainment of a restored but transformed harmony and by associating that harmony with the idea of Union, especially of Union juxtaposed against the alternatives of extended feudalism, violent rebellion, or anarchy. But the specifically historical problems prove not to be readily susceptible of the technical solution provided by the move into pastoral.

The transition itself could not be more clearly signalled. Journey by land concludes with a crossing over water necessitated as much by symbolic as by actual geography. A quotation from Alexander Ross's *Helenore: or The Fortunate Shepherdess* is followed by the statement, 'They landed in this Highland Arcadia, at the mouth of the small stream which watered the delightful and peaceable valley.' . . . The same kind of signalling introduced the Charlieshope episode in *Guy Mannering*, but there the evocation of the texture of life at a precisely defined time and place gave historical substance to the deployment of pastoral interlude in the moral allegory of Harry Bertram's proving. In the Knocktarlitie episode, however, the stylization accompanying the generic shift combines with the introduction of a somewhat strenuously comic tone to make the episode conform more closely to the simple contrastive pattern of traditional pastoral than to the more complex strategies of the historicized pastoral Scott had himself originated. This implausible Arcadia, where cows, pasture, and even ministerial livings flow from the beneficent hands of the Duke of Argyle, is threatened not by the economic facts of agricultural life in eighteenth-century Scotland—so sharply evoked in the earlier presentation of Davie Deans's struggles to establish himself as a farmer—but by incursions of such traditional pastoral figures as alien robbers; the faint historical ripples that reach it carry no import for the Butlers. (pp. 158-63)

In order that the prosperity of the Butlers may stand for the overall tendency rather than the particulars of Scottish history in the second half of the eighteenth century, Scott chooses not to look too closely at the Highland world of the 1740s. He supplies no historical articulation of the conneciton between the Knocktarlitie Arcadia and the actual discontent and ferment of the Edinburgh of 1736. Jeanie's success in staying the bloody hand of punishment—and in making London recognize the humanity of the Scots—can only have emblematic significance if the bloodshed of 1745 and '46 is displaced and, in effect, ignored. In refusing to take the history of the 1740s seriously Scott shifts the emphasis away from his historical and on to his moral and political fable. The final stress falls on Jeanie's imperviousness to violence, so that she is reassimilated to those stylized literary counterparts from whom she had earlier been discriminated—Christiana and the Lady in *Comus*—and on the Union as a solution to centuries of national violence. Peace and prosperity are presented as the natural outcome of both the private and public plots, and rebellion is displaced by a revitalized authority.

George Levine has recently reminded us of the way in which Scott uses happy endings and other 'tricks . . . from the romancer's bag' to 'do the work of history itself,' thus ensuring that the protagonist, 'having found the right side in large historical conflicts, is rewarded personally with the success of the winning party.' Although these comments are not specifically applied to *The Heart of Midlothian*, they seem on the surface to capture something of what happens in that novel. But, . . . it would be uncharacteristic of Scott to make uniform or uncritical use of any formula, even his own. In *The Heart of Midlothian* it can, indeed, be argued that it is the private plot that endows the public with significance and value. It is not so much that Jeanie chooses the right side—the Union settlement—but that the virtues of her private actions are harnessed to the projection of a positive vision of that settlement. In the process the narrative shifts away from psychological and historical realism in the direction of stylization, validating the course of Scottish history in a way that is essentially ahistorical. What starts out as the most 'authentic' of Scott's fictions, clearly distinguished from the earlier **Waverley Novels** by its displacement or inversion of their characteristic devices, returns in the end to a reliance on the stylized convention of pastoral for the transformation of historical narrative into an act of historical interpretation. (pp. 166-67)

> *Jane Millgate, in her* Walter Scott: The Making of the Novelist, *University of Toronto Press, 1984, 223 p.*

ADDITIONAL BIBLIOGRAPHY

[Adolphus, John Leycester]. *Letters to Richard Heber, Esq., Containing Critical Remarks on the Series of Novels Beginning with "Waverley," and an Attempt to Ascertain Their Author.* Boston: Samuel H. Parker, 1822, 216 p.
> The first full-length study of Scott's works. Adolphus attempts to show, using the evidence provided by Scott's texts, that the unknown "Author of *Waverley*" and Walter Scott the poet are the same writer.

Anderson, W.E.K. "Scott." In *The English Novel: Select Bibliographical Guides,* edited by A. E. Dyson, pp. 128-44. London: Oxford University Press, 1974.
> An overview of important critical and biographical studies of Scott, including an introductory essay and bibliography.

Ball, Margaret. *Sir Walter Scott as a Critic of Literature.* Columbia University Studies in English, series II, vol. II, no. 1. New York: Columbia University Press, 1907, 188 p.
> Explores Scott's critical opinions and critical methodology.

Bell, Alan, ed. *Scott Bicentenary Essays: Selected Papers Read at the Sir Walter Scott Bicentenary Conference.* Edinburgh: Scottish Academic Press, 1973, 344 p.
> A collection of essays by David Daiches, Edgar Johnson, Robin Mayhead, David Craig, and other critics. The essays cover a broad range of topics, from close textual analyses of individual novels to studies of Scott's reputation in various European countries.

Bradley, Philip. *An Index to the "Waverley Novels."* Metuchen, N.J.: Scarecrow Press, 1975, 681 p.
> A guide to locating characters, places, phrases, objects, and other important elements in the texts of the *Waverley Novels.*

Brandes, George. "Historical Naturalism." In his *Main Currents in Nineteenth Century Literature.* Vol. IV, *Naturalism in England,* pp. 102-27. New York: Macmillan Co., 1905.
> A biographical and historical overview of Scott's development and achievement as an author.

Brown, David. *Walter Scott and the Historical Imagination.* London: Routledge & Kegan Paul, 1979, 239 p.
> Studies Scott's understanding of history and his portrayal of the historical process in the *Waverley Novels.*

Buchan, John. *Sir Walter Scott.* New York: Coward-McCann, 1932, 384 p.
> A biography that has been praised for its readability, accuracy, and conciseness.

Cecil, Lord David. *Sir Walter Scott.* London: Constable and Co., 1933, 60 p.
> A widely respected general introduction to Scott and his works.

Chandler, Alice. "Origins of Medievalism: Scott." In her *A Dream of Order: The Medieval Ideal in Nineteenth-Century English Literature,* pp. 12-51. London: Routledge & Kegan Paul, 1971.
> Examines Scott's role in introducing medievalism into nineteenth-century English literature.

Clark, Arthur Melville. *Sir Walter Scott: The Formative Years.* Edinburgh: William Blackwood, 1969, 322 p.
> A biography focusing on Scott's life prior to his literary success.

Corson, James Clarkson. *A Bibliography of Sir Walter Scott: A Classified and Annotated List of Books and Articles Relating to His Life and Works, 1797-1940.* Edinburgh: Oliver and Boyd, 1943, 428 p.
> An annotated guide to writings on Scott and his works published before 1941.

Croce, Benedetto. "Walter Scott." In his *European Literature in the Nineteenth Century,* translated by Douglas Ainslie, pp. 66-78. New York: Alfred A. Knopf, 1924.
> Discusses Scott within the context of nineteenth-century European literature. Croce analyzes the reasons for the decline in Scott's reputation and popularity.

Cusac, Marian H. *Narrative Structure in the Novels of Sir Walter Scott.* The Hague: Mouton, 1969, 128 p.
> A study of narrative technique and organization in the *Waverley Novels.*

Daiches, David. *Sir Walter Scott and His World.* A Studio Book. New York: Viking Press, 1971, 143 p.
> A pictorial overview of Scott and the environment in which he lived.

———. "Scott's *Waverley:* The Presence of the Author." In *Nineteenth-Century Scottish Fiction: Critical Essays,* edited by Ian Campbell, pp. 6-17. New York: Harper & Row Publishers, Barnes & Noble Books, 1979.
> Argues that Scott "projects himself in a vivid personal way" in *Waverley.* According to Daiches, the novel's narrative tone and Scott's handling of its scenes are a direct reflection of his personality.

Davie, Donald. *The Heyday of Sir Walter Scott.* London: Routledge & Kegan Paul, 1961, 168 p.
> Explores Scott's influence on Alexander Pushkin, James Fenimore Cooper, and other authors.

Devlin, D. D. *The Author of "Waverley": A Critical Study of Walter Scott.* London: Macmillan, 1971, 142 p.
> A detailed study of five Scott novels: *Waverley, A Legend of Montrose, Rob Roy, The Bride of Lammermoor,* and *Redgauntlet.* Devlin focuses on Scott's portrayal of the past and on the structural functions of his comic characters.

———, ed. *Walter Scott: Modern Judgements.* Modern Judgements, edited by P. N. Furbank. London: Macmillan, 1968, 190 p.
> Reprints twentieth-century essays on Scott by various critics, including Edwin Muir, Alexander Welsh, Donald Davie, and Robert C. Gordon.

Farrell, John P. "Scott: The Implicit Note of Tragedy." In his *Revolution as Tragedy: The Dilemma of the Moderate from Scott to Arnold,* pp. 69-129. Ithaca: Cornell University Press, 1980.
> Argues that the sense of tragedy common to the *Waverley Novels* reflects Scott's anxiety about the future of Scotland rather than a nostalgic regret that the past was gone.

Fiske, Christabel F. *Epic Suggestion in the Imagery of the "Waverley Novels."* New Haven: Yale University Press, 1940, 141 p.
> A study of Scott's use of epic imagery and symbolism in the *Waverley Novels.*

Forster, E. M. "The Story." In his *Aspects of the Novel*, pp. 25-42. 1927. Reprint. New York: Harcourt, Brace and Co., 1956.

A negative appraisal of Scott, emphasizing his limitations as a novelist.

Gordon, Robert C. *Under Which King?: A Study of the Scottish "Waverley Novels."* Edinburgh: Oliver & Boyd, 1969, 178 p.

Focuses on the "Scotch Novels." Gordon asserts that they "exhibit a rough pattern of development from *Waverley* to *Redgauntlet*."

Gordon, S. Stewart. "*Waverley* and the 'Unified Design'." *ELH* 18, No. 2 (June 1951): 107-22.

Argues that *Waverley* is a well-constructed novel possessing unity and artistic purpose.

Grierson, Sir Herbert J. C. *Sir Walter Scott, Bart*. 1938. Reprint. New York: Haskell House Publishers, 1969, 320 p.

A highly regarded biography that supplements and corrects inaccuracies in Lockhart's *Life* (see annotation below).

Hart, Francis R. *Scott's Novels: The Plotting of Historic Survival*. Charlottesville: University Press of Virginia, 1966, 371 p.

A detailed study of the *Waverley Novels*. Hart divides his overview of the novels into four sections: "The Quixotic Tragicomedy of Jacobitism," "Opposing Fanaticisms and the Search for Humanity," "The Historical Picturesque and the Survivals of Chivalry," and "The Falls and Survivals of Ancient Houses."

Hayden, John O., ed. *Scott: The Critical Heritage*. Critical Heritage Series, edited by B. C. Southam. New York: Barnes and Noble, 1970, 554 p.

Reprints selected nineteenth-century critical commentary on Scott and his works.

Hillhouse, James T. *The "Waverley Novels" and Their Critics*. 1936. Reprint. New York: Octagon Books, 1970, 357 p.

A broad survey of critical opinion on the *Waverley Novels*, covering the period from their original publication through the first third of the twentieth century.

——, and Welsh, Alexander. "Sir Walter Scott." In *The English Romantic Poets and Essayists: A Review of Research and Criticism*, rev. ed., edited by Carolyn Washburn Houtchens and Lawrence Huston Houtchens, pp. 115-54. New York: Modern Language Association of America, New York University Press, 1966.

An extended bibliographical essay that surveys critical and biographical writings on Scott.

Hutton, Richard H. *Sir Walter Scott*. English Men of Letters, edited by John Morley. 1878. Reprint. London: Macmillan and Co., 1907, 182 p.

A highly regarded early biography.

Jack, Ian. *Walter Scott*. 1958. Reprint. Writers and Their Work, no. 103. London: Longman Group, 1971, 38 p.

A general introduction to Scott and his writings.

——. "The *Waverley* Romances." In his *English Literature, 1815-1832*, pp. 185-212. The Oxford History of English Literature, edited by F. P. Wilson and Bonamy Dobrée, vol. X. Oxford: Clarendon Press, 1963.

A biographical and historical introduction to the *Waverley Novels*.

Jeffares, A. Norman, ed. *Scott's Mind and Art*. Essays Old and New, no. 6. New York: Barnes & Noble, 1970, 266 p.

A collection of important essays on Scott by various critics, including Walter Bagehot, Georg Lukács, and David Daiches.

Johnson, Edgar. *Sir Walter Scott: The Great Unknown*. 2 vols. New York: Macmillan, 1970.

The definitive modern biography.

Kerr, James. "Scott's Dreams of the Past: *The Bride of Lammermoor* as Political Fantasy." *Studies in the Novel* XVIII, No. 2 (Summer 1986): 125-42.

Argues that *The Bride of Lammermoor* served as a medium for expressing the political fantasies in Scott's unconscious.

Kettle, Arnold. "Scott: *The Heart of Midlothian*." In his *An Introduction to the English Novel*. Vol. I, *To George Eliot*, 2d ed., pp. 99-114. English Literature, edited by John Lawlor. London: Hutchinson University Library, 1969.

A general overview of *The Heart of Mid-Lothian*, focusing on Scott's place in the history of the English novel.

Kroeber, Karl. "The Narrative Pattern of Scott." In his *Romantic Narrative Art*, pp. 168-87. Madison: University of Wisconsin Press, 1960.

Explores Scott's narrative techniques.

Lauber, John. *Sir Walter Scott*. Twayne's English Authors Series, edited by Sylvia E. Bowman, no. 39. New York: Twayne Publishers, 1966, 166 p.

A concise introduction to Scott and his works.

Lockhart, John Gibson. *The Life of Sir Walter Scott, Bart*. 2d ed. 10 vols. Edinburgh: Robert Cadell, 1839.

An indispensable source of information about Scott's life and works, written by his son-in-law. Despite its inaccuracies, Lockhart's work is considered one of the greatest biographies of an English literary figure.

Mayhead, Robin. *Walter Scott*. Profiles in Literature Series, edited by B. C. Southam. London: Routledge & Kegan Paul, 1968, 116 p.

A collection of extracts from Scott's works accompanied by critical commentary and an overview of his career as a writer.

McMaster, Graham. *Scott and Society*. Cambridge: Cambridge University Press, 1981, 253 p.

A study of how Scott's attitudes toward society and politics are reflected in "patterns, metaphors, and symbols" contained in his novels.

Muir, Edwin. *Scott and Scotland: The Predicament of the Scottish Writer*. 1936. Reprint. Folcroft, Pa.: Folcroft Press, 1969, 181 p.

Examines Scott and his works within the context of Scottish literature and history.

Parsons, Coleman O. *Witchcraft and Demonology in Scott's Fiction: With Chapters on the Supernatural in Scottish Literature*. Edinburgh: Oliver & Boyd, 1964, 363 p.

Discusses Scott's use of supernatural elements in his poetry and prose.

Reed, James. *Sir Walter Scott: Landscape and Locality*. London: Athlone Press, 1980, 188 p.

Assesses the importance to Scott's works of his portrayal of natural scenery and specific locales.

Renwick, W. L., ed. *Sir Walter Scott Lectures, 1940-1948*. Edinburgh: Edinburgh University Press, 1950, 170 p.

A collection of widely admired lectures on Scott by Sir Herbert Grierson, Edwin Muir, G. M. Young, and S. C. Roberts.

Rubenstein, Jill. *Sir Walter Scott: A Reference Guide*. Reference Publications in Literature, edited by Marilyn Gaull. Boston: G. K. Hall & Co., 1978, 344 p.

An annotated bibliography of writings about Scott and his works published from 1932 to 1977.

Ruskin, John. "Of Modern Landscape." In his *Modern Painters*, Vol. 3, pp. 254-85. London: Smith, Elder and Co., 1856.

Discusses Scott's portrayal of landscape in his poems as well as his place in early nineteenth-century literature.

——. "Fiction—Fair and Foul." *The Nineteenth-Century* VII, No. XL (June 1880): 941-62.

An unfinished, wide-ranging article that contrasts the healthy atmosphere of the *Waverley Novels* with what Ruskin sees as the morbid character of fiction in his own day.

Shaw, Harry E. *The Forms of Historical Fiction: Sir Walter Scott and His Successors*. Ithaca: Cornell University Press, 1983, 257 p.
    Explores the development of the historical novel, emphasizing Scott's crucial contribution to the genre.

Van Ghent, Dorothy. ''*The Heart of Mid-Lothian*.'' In her *The English Novel: Form and Function*, pp. 113-24. New York: Holt, Rinehart and Winston, 1953.
    Argues that the incoherent organization of *The Heart of Mid-Lothian* resulted from Scott's similarly incoherent view of life.

Williams, Ioan, ed. *Sir Walter Scott on Novelists and Fiction*. London: Routledge & Kegan Paul, 1968, 503 p.
    An extended survey of Scott's critical opinions of other writers.

Wilson, A. N. *The Laird of Abbotsford: A View of Sir Walter Scott*. Oxford: Oxford University Press, 1980, 197 p.
    A laudatory study of Scott and his works, with chapters on his poetry and various aspects of the novels, including his religion, medievalism, and heroines.

Henry Wheeler Shaw

1818-1885

(Also wrote under pseudonyms of Josh Billings, Ephrem Billings, Si Sledlength, Uncle Esek, Mordecai David, and others) American essayist, aphorist, sketch writer, journalist, travel writer, and poet.

Shaw was a minor American humorist whose works were instrumental in popularizing rough-hewn wit during the latter half of the nineteenth century. His name has become synonymous with that of his fictional counterpart: as Josh Billings, Shaw entertained readers with philosophical aphorisms and anecdotes in *Josh Billings' Farmer's Allminax, Josh Billings, Hiz Sayings,* and other works; he also regaled the public with his unaffected wisdom from the platforms of countless lecture halls. Shaw's moral-edged humor was specifically designed to edify as well as amuse his audience. Yet despite the popularity he enjoyed during his own era, Shaw is little known today.

Born to a prosperous family in Lanesboro, Massachusetts, Shaw attended a district school there before enrolling in a college preparatory course at an academy in nearby Lenox. In 1833, he entered Hamilton College, a Presbyterian school in Utica, New York, where he neglected his studies for nature walks, activities with friends, and a host of boyish pranks that eventually earned him expulsion during his sophomore year. For the next ten years Shaw worked at odd jobs throughout the Midwest. At one point, while he and two friends were traveling along the Maumee River, they found themselves low on funds in Napoleon, Indiana. They gamely determined to earn money by offering the town a public performance that included a lecture on mesmerism delivered by Shaw. Public lectures and related entertainment were enormously popular, and the three were so successful that they continued their venture in other towns for several years. But by 1845, weary of such a rambling existence, Shaw returned to Massachusetts and married his childhood sweetheart, Zilpha Bradford. The couple remained there briefly, then moved about the East over the next few years while Shaw again worked at odd jobs. In 1854, now with two young daughters to support, he and his family settled in Poughkeepsie, New York, where he made his living for a number of years as an auctioneer and real-estate agent.

In addition to his work as a realtor and active community member, Shaw became interested in writing. Around 1859 he began expressing his keen observations on human nature in humorous sketches, then much in vogue. With the encouragement of friends, Shaw sent these pseudonymous sketches to newspapers throughout the East, but his submissions were received with indifference. When Charles Farrar Browne, alias Artemus Ward, wrote an overwhelmingly acclaimed essay on the mule, Shaw took his own essay on that subject and converted its standard English to the quaint phonetic spelling used by Browne and others. His "Essa on the Muel, bi Josh Billings" launched his literary career. Shaw's reputation was further enhanced in 1866 with the publication of *Josh Billings, Hiz Sayings,* a book-length collection of witty aphorisms and sketches. Around that time, Shaw and his family moved to New York City, where he resided for nearly the rest of his life and worked as a columnist for the *New York Weekly.* New York afforded Shaw professional opportunities as well as the

chance to observe a panorama of human nature. His popular column, which appeared variously under the headings "The Josh Billings' Papers," "Josh Billings' Spice Box," and "Josh Billings' Philosophy," ranged from characteristic aphorisms and sketches to narratives and travel accounts. Shaw's homespun humor and folksy wisdom, manifested in his succinct witticisms and brief essays, also filled the pages of *Josh Billings on Ice, and Other Things,* his second book, and continued, with the addition of some verse and satire, for ten volumes in *Josh Billings' Farmer's Allminax.*

During the 1860s, Shaw also became well known as a lecturer for his piquant and sometimes cryptic humor. He was engaged by the then-famous lecture circuit entrepreneur James Clark Redpath, under whose auspices his lecturing career flourished. Shaw's loosely structured talks encompassing a variety of subjects, his studied stage mannerisms, and his ungainly appearance were all calculated to create the persona of Josh Billings, a shrewd but affable rustic philosopher. In addition to lecturing enthusiastically throughout his last years, Shaw composed several more works, contributed to the *New York Weekly,* and also began writing for the *Century Magazine.* Ultimately, the strenuous regimen of writing and lecturing resulted in his ill health, and the family moved to Monterey, California, where Shaw died in 1885.

The aphorism—pithy, often delivered with a decided twist, and seemingly spontaneous (despite Shaw's chronic struggle "to get it just right")—was his mainstay. Aphorisms peppered the columns he wrote for the *Century Magazine* and *New York Weekly,* and groups of the sayings were interspersed throughout his full-length works, most notably *Josh Billings, Hiz Sayings* and *Josh Billings on Ice, and Other Things.* These adages were among the first and last of Shaw's literary efforts, providing him with a form that was immensely popular during his day and one for which he was eminently suited. Most critics have found Shaw's aphorisms to be delightful representations of the genre, proverbs which, according to Josh Billings's own exemplum, "ar like good kambrick needles—short, sharp, and shiny." Shaw has been compared to Aesop and Benjamin Franklin for both his original observations and his unique restatement of common expressions. Although Shaw's proverbs predominantly address a broad range of human passions and predicaments, he also commented on such topics as politics, religion, and feminist causes. But, whatever their particular scope and despite their surface merriment, all of Shaw's aphorisms were firmly weighted by his conspicuous allegiance to many traditional and Christian values.

As author of the comic "Essa on the Muel," Shaw discovered a literary form nearly as well adapted to his talents as the aphorism. His subjects ranged from the concrete to the abstract, and his approach—however deceptive the digressions, misspellings, and improper grammar—was methodical. Though his essays proved lucrative, Shaw was not entirely happy with the deliberate stylistic measures he employed to "countrify" his work as they often limited his creative expression. Shaw has been censured in varying degrees for these practices: some years after his death, Shaw's orthographic eccentricities were labeled contemptible, and more recently commentators have argued that they diminish the impact of his works. But, on the whole, Shaw's brief essays—from jocular to philosophical or skeptical—have been enjoyed by many readers and critics.

Though his aphorisms and essays were extremely popular, Shaw's almanacs were his most sustained and ambitious endeavors. Providing his readers with an annual fund of proverbs, sketches, and light verse for roughly a decade, Shaw was able not only to satisfy the public demand for amusing fare but also to individualize those comic and farmer's almanacs that had long been literary staples. Typical of his whimsical but pointed humor is a forecast for 1870 of "semiockasional eklipses ov the moon, kauzed bi brandy smashes getting between that virtewous and pale old woman, and the eyes ov sum ov our most promising young men." Shaw good-naturedly burlesqued such standard elements of the farmer's almanac as horoscopes, weather predictions, and agricultural hints. Intended as the mildest caricatures of their conventional counterparts, the almanacs were collectively hailed by Mark Twain as "a pleasant conceit and happily executed." Some modern critics find Shaw's almanacs entertaining and historically significant for the colorful glimpse they provide into America's rural past. Yet because of evolving literary taste, the entirety of Shaw's work, though well known and appreciated in his time, has been all but forgotten today.

(See also *Dictionary of Literary Biography,* Vol. 11: *American Humorists, 1800-1950.*)

PRINCIPAL WORKS

*"Essa on the Muel, bi Josh Billings" (essay) 1864
Josh Billings, Hiz Sayings (essays, sketches, and
     aphorisms) 1866

Josh Billings on Ice, and Other Things (essays, sketches,
     and aphorisms) 1868
Josh Billings' Farmer's Allminax. 10 vols. (essays,
     sketches, aphorisms, and poetry) 1870-79
*Everybody's Friend; or, Josh Billings' Encyclopedia and
     Proverbial Philosophy of Wit and Humor* (essays,
     sketches, aphorisms, letters, and fictional letters) 1874
Josh Billings Struggling with Things (aphorisms) 1881
Josh Billings: His Works, Complete (essays, sketches,
     aphorisms, poetry, letters, and fictional letters) 1888
Josh Billings' Old Farmer's Allminax, 1870-1879 (essays,
     sketches, aphorisms, and poetry) 1902

*This essay was published almost simultaneously in the periodicals *Nick Nacks, Yankee Notions,* and *Budget of Phun.*

GEORGE WASHINGTON CABLE   (essay date 1870)

[*Cable contrasts Shaw and Mark Twain as humorists. Cable's remarks originally appeared in the* Daily Picayune *in 1870.*]

[Josh Billings] belongs to another day—the day when clowns were wondrous wise, and seasoned all their drolleries with the salt of truth and flavored [them] with the wine of wisdom. He is the true, old-fashioned fool; i.e., faithful at once to Comus and Minerva—a very Yorick; and no place in our minds so fit for him as that high niche where time too old for memory rests. [On the other hand, Mark Twain is] a man of the living today. . . . [There is in him] such practical sympathy with the themes and actions of the present, that his jesting betrays something of the tradesman's (for the world is one big tradesman now) restraint and method, and his humor must run a long way before it makes a summersault. (pp. 156-57)

If you would laugh at Mark you must first hear him through; but good old Josh is fun from first to last, and was born with the art of being wise and silly in a breath. Mark moves always with the laughing point in view as a goal, but Josh carries a thousand laughs with him, loaded like a Santa Claus. . . .

In point of moral tone, 'sly old J. B.' is certainly in advance, for while all that can be said of Mark Twain is that he writes little that has harm in it, his fellow joker is as full of goodness as a bunch of berries. His quaint saws and misspelt proverbs are better than poor Richard.

While we have that misspelling in hand, let us say there is very little credit in it. However, others try and fail, and people will laugh as long as Josh Billings does it, though there's no more real wit in it than in a grimace; yet it is the vehicle of that quality of playfulness so necessary to a humorist; and this indeed is what is most notably lacking in Mark Twain.

If we had to part with one of them, it would not be easy to choose. As for us give us Josh Billings. Mark spins a good yarn, but Josh is such a blessed old fool. (p. 157)

> *George Washington Cable, in a footnote to "Josh Billings' Notions on Humor," in* Studies in English, *The University of Texas Press, 1943, pp. 156-57.*

EDMUND CLARENCE STEDMAN   (letter date 1873)

[*A major nineteenth-century American critic and anthologist, Stedman gained wide critical influence as the author of* Victorian

Poets *and* Poets of America. *In conjunction with his popular American Anthology, the latter work helped to establish a greater interest in and appreciation for American literature. In the following excerpt from a letter to the American author Bayard Taylor, Stedman blames Shaw and others for causing the degeneration of American literary taste.*]

Cultured as are Hay and Harte, they are almost equally responsible with ''Josh Billings'' and the ''Danbury News'' man for the present *horrible* degeneracy of the public taste—that is, the taste of the newest generation of book-buyers. The whole country, owing to the *contagion* of our American newspaper ''exchange'' system, is flooded, deluged, swamped, beneath a muddy tide of slang, vulgarity, inartistic bathers, impertinence and buffoonery that is not wit. (p. 477)

> *Edmund Clarence Stedman, in a letter to Bayard Taylor on September 16, 1873, in* Life and Letters of Edmund Clarence Stedman, Vol. I *by Laura Stedman and George M. Gould, Moffat, Yard and Company, 1910, pp. 477-79.*

S. S. COX   (essay date 1875)

[*Cox delights in Shaw's humor, but claims it ''does not rise to the dignity of literature.''*]

There is much of Franklin's shrewd, practical humor disguised under the mask of Josh Billings's sayings. With a Puritan face all severe and sour; without a hearty open laugh to welcome the coming or speed the parting joke; with nothing but an odd pucker of the mouth and an elfish twinkle of the eye; with an inward chuckle which has no outward sign—Billings (aside from the small fun of bad orthography) hits the target of humor in the white when he says that with some people who brag of ancestry their great trouble is their great descent; or when he thanks God for allowing fools to live that wise men may get a living out of them; when he says that wealth won't make a man virtuous, but that there ain't any body who wants to be poor just for the purpose of being good; when he says that when a fellow gets to going down hill, it seems as if every thing was greased for the occasion; or when he gives us his way of keeping a mule in a pasture, by turning it into a meadow adjacent and letting it jump out; or when he has known mules, like men, keep good for six months just to get a good kick at somebody—he makes a species of drollery which even our English reviewers have begun to appreciate, and which does not require the drawl of bad grammar and spelling. I once had occasion, in a deliberative body, to use Billings's illustration that one hornet, if he felt well, could break up a camp-meeting. The effect amazed me. The application was made; and Billings himself afterward said, ''My name will go down to the fewter coupled with the hornet; we will be twins in posterity.'' The description of the nature of the insect, especially the use it makes of its ''business end,'' of the way it avoids the thousand attempts to ''shoo'' it and to fight it, and the consequent consternation of a pious body, has in it exaggeration of the raciest kind.

But this kind of humor, like that of Nasby, does not rise to the dignity of literature. It can not compare with Washington Irving, who, in his *Knickerbocker* and other works, has given us the very choicest brand, all sparkling and stimulating. But Irving is too refined, sweet, and shy for general appreciation. Besides, Irving is not an American humorist. He is more English than American, more cosmopolitan than either. Paulding, Hawthorne—alas for our literature! Oh, for one man for Amer-

ica what Richter is to Germany, or Dickens is to England! (pp. 698-99)

> *S. S. Cox, ''American Humor,'' in* Harper's New Monthly Magazine, *Vol. L, No. CCXCIX, April, 1875, pp. 690-701.*

JOHN NICHOL   (essay date 1882)

[*Nichol terms Shaw's observations essentially vulgar.*]

The objects of Mr. Billings' satire, . . . though generally of a minor description (as quack advertisements, sham sentiment, absurd caucuses, etc.), are worth attacking by those who have no higher game. . . . (p. 424)

We will not say of Mr. Billings' [work] . . . that it ''is like Pandora's box—the more you stir it the worse it smells.'' Some of his remarks are shrewd, and many ludicrous; but the majority are vulgar. . . . (p. 425)

> *John Nichol, ''American Humorists,'' in his* American Literature: An Historical Sketch, 1620-1880, *Adam and Charles Black, 1882, pp. 402-48.*

JAMES M. BUCKLEY   (essay date 1885)

[*Buckley considers Shaw unsurpassed as an American philosophical humorist. This essay marking Shaw's death was first published in the* Christian Advocate *in 1885.*]

The death of Henry W. Shaw (''Josh Billings'') has been cabled round the world, as it deserved to be. *The London Standard,* one of the most conservative and refined of the London papers, says that ''his death will be mourned in various circles more than that of more eminent instructors of the people.'' We hold this man up to commendation as a matter of cool judgment. Mr. Shaw was a man with a mission. He was the most philosophical humorist that has appeared in this country. Many of his sayings—moral, social, philosophical, and religious—were as original and valuable as anything in Shakespeare, Bacon, or Matthew Hale. An eminent minister, one noted for piety, force, and sententiousness, says that he owes seed thoughts of many of his most effective sermons to some of Shaw's aphoristic sayings. Shaw had an ambition to be the Aesop of the nineteenth century, and to teach the common people morality and faith in Christianity through the medium of humor.

None of his sayings promoted immorality or irreligion, but the homely virtues of which Franklin wrote are quaintly recommended, and the follies and excesses of society satirized. Some of the best short arguments against infidelity are from his pen. He was sometimes coarse, but not so much so as Peter Cartwright or Sam Jones, and never obscene or irreverent.

He told the writer that he thought out his proverbs in the best language he could command, spending hours on one sometimes, then translated them into ungrammatical forms and bad spelling, for the people will not take wisdom as wisdom. We think that a man who teaches common sense and all the social and domestic virtues and defends religion, and can make his sayings go with all classes, has genius, and deserves well of his country and of posterity. If we had to write a hundred sayings from humorists and sages of all times and countries to give to a boy we know of several from this man's pen that we should place among the hundred.

James M. Buckley, in an extract from ''A Philo-sophical Humorist,'' in The Methodist Review, *Vol. CI, March-April, 1918, p. 207.*

ANDREW LANG   (essay date 1889)

[*Lang was one of England's most powerful men of letters during the closing decades of the nineteenth century and is remembered today as the editor of the ''color fairy books,'' a twelve-volume series of fairy tales. In the following excerpt, he offers a reserved appraisal of Shaw's work.*]

The death of Mr. ''Josh Billings'' may have diminished the stock of harmless pleasures, but can hardly be said to have eclipsed the gaiety of nations. In this country, at least, however it may have been in the States, Josh Billings was by no means the favourite or leading American humorist. If phonetic spelling were universal, much of his fun would disappear. His place was nearer that of Orpheus C. Kerr than of Artemus Ward, or of Mark Twain. (p. 181)

Andrew Lang, ''Western Dolls,'' in his Lost Leaders, *Longmans, Green, and Co., 1889, pp. 181-88.*

ROBERT FORD   (essay date 1897)

[*Ford commends Shaw as a comic essayist rather than as a storyteller.*]

Take a little of Martin Farquhar Tupper and a little of Artemus Ward, knead them together, and you may make something which ap-proaches to a Josh Billings.

So says the showman's showman, Mr. E. P. Hingston, and the definition is not at all inapt; for Josh is a philosopher as well as a humourist—a Jaques and a Touchstone in one and the same person. His philosophy is always sound, too, and never wearisome, which, by-the-bye, is more than might be said of Martin Tupper. And he differs from Artemus Ward in this, that he is a comic essayist rather than a comic story writer.

Story! bless you, like the needy knife-grinder, he has none to tell. He could not tell it well if he had; his genius does not spread out in that fashion. He is a writer of comic aphorisms— a Solomon in cap and bells. What a success he would have been as a circus clown we can only fancy; what an improvement on the ordinary ring comedian we can easily imagine. The average age of a circus clown has been computed at about forty years, but the average age of a circus joke—it is immeasur-able—it had no beginning, and apparently will have no end. With Josh Billings in the ring something new—and not only new but good—would have appeared every night—sayings over which the gods might have laughed their fill and not exhausted the usefulness of, since the humorous rind of them having served the turn of the circus, the kernels could be carried away and provide food for reflection at home. For herein lies the peculiar value of nearly everything that Josh Billings has writ-ten. Immensely funny as it all is, there is invariably a higher purpose peeping out from among his quaint fancies and odd expressions. (pp. 61-2)

It was by short, sharp, shiny remarks . . . , printed in the corners of American newspapers, with the author's pen-name attached, that Josh Billings first became popular. First of all, I think, his hand was seen in the columns of the *Philadelphia Sunday Dispatch,* from whence his quaint sayings were copied into every paper in the States, and, in course of time, found their

way to Britain, and reappeared in nearly all the home journals. It is a curious fact, too—I might almost say a lamentable one— that his wittiest and wisest sayings passed almost unheeded until, following Artemus Ward's example, he began a system-atic course of phonetic and eccentric spelling. A contemptible sort of trick, though, no doubt, justified to some extent . . . by its success. (p. 64)

[Josh Billings] had a big soul in his body—was a man, as we may say, who could be safely entrusted with a generous gift of humour and satire, and be relied on to consecrate his genius to the purpose of making the world happier and better, which, verily, is the true vocation of the comic author. (pp. 71-2)

Robert Ford, ''Josh Billings,'' in his American Hu-mourists: Recent and Living, *Alexander Gardner, 1897, pp. 61-76.*

EDITH PARKER THOMSON   (essay date 1899)

[*Thomson comments that Shaw's humor is typically Yankee in character.*]

The fashion of a people's jests changes, as well as the fashion in dress. Josh Billings, like many another comic writer whose name was on every one's lips some years ago, is seldom quoted now; yet to the student of New England he will always possess significance, for he represents in a remarkable degree the pe-culiar element of humor that exists in the typical Yankee char-acter. Who but one imbued with the deeply religious spirit of his Puritan fathers, who made a solemn thing even of a jest, could turn his mirth to such good account in pointing a moral as Josh Billings? (p. 696)

Mr. Shaw's humor does not perhaps provoke a downright laugh so often as the humor of some others; it rather makes us laugh to ourselves. He was himself a quiet, unassuming man; and one who had known him for years testifies that he never saw him smile when saying even the wittiest things. This very fact enabled him to express so well the fun which an old-time New England countryman most enjoyed. The true Yankee knows well how to ''laugh inside'' and to crack jokes with a sober face. We can easily imagine the amused chuckle with which some farmer would greet these sayings,—how his keen eyes would twinkle and the corners of his mouth faintly twitch in spite of himself as he revelled in their quaint drollery and shrewd common sense. (pp. 697-98)

Applying to Josh Billings the test of his own definition, that humor implies ''a thing that is ludicrous and at the same time true,'' he was indeed a genuine humorist. He could put forth literary power on occasion, as many of his articles and bits of verse prove; but his genius lay in pure humor without additional literary qualities to recommend it. Hence the wonderful pop-ularity with which his writings burst upon the public has not endured. The quaint spelling, on which both he and Artemus Ward so much relied, was but a weak prop, and could not stand the stress of time. (pp. 698-99)

Edith Parker Thomson, ''The Home of Josh Bill-ings,'' in The New England Magazine, *Vol. XIX, No. 6, February, 1899, pp. 696-703.*

W. P. TRENT   (essay date 1901)

[*An American educator and literary critic, Trent was the founder and editor of the* Sewanee Review, *which was formed to provide the South with a much-needed literary organ. Throughout his* career, Trent specialized in histories and criticism of American literature, his most notable work being the Cambridge History of American Literature. In the following excerpt, he compares Shaw to Oliver Wendell Holmes in his accommodation to changing American taste.]

Set over against Dr. Holmes, physician, professor, and man of letters in cultured Boston, Henry Wheeler Shaw . . . , who left the East to work on Ohio steamboats, then became a farmer, and finally an auctioneer, before he ever published an article or an almanac, or delivered, with affected awkwardness, a lecture full of pithy humor. In the contrast between these two men's lives we have a key to the contrast between their writings. If, when Dr. Holmes, after the lapse of years, resumed his *Autocrat* papers, he had found himself addressing an obdurate public, is it likely that he would have accommodated himself as Josh Billings did to similar circumstances, changed his spelling, and won popularity? That was the trick of a typical American determined to make his wares sell, just as his phenomenally successful *Farmer's Allminax* was a joint product of his humor and his "hoss-sense." Yet none the less was the critic right who declared that Josh Billings's bad spelling hid but did not obliterate his kinship with La Rochefoucauld. "Cunning, at best, only does the dirty work ov wisdom; tharfore I dispize it," is a saying worthy of any moralist. On the other hand, the following advertisement is worthy only of the "enterprising" American that wrote it: "Kan the leopard change his spots? i answer it kan, bi using Job Sargent's only klensing sope. Job Sargent never told a lie—so did George Washington." (p. 50)

W. P. Trent, "A Retrospect of American Humor," in The Century, Vol. LXIII, No. 1, November, 1901, pp. 45-64.

JAMES MUDGE (essay date 1918)

[In this excerpt celebrating the centennial of Shaw's birth, Mudge maintains that for depicting human vagaries tempered with moral instruction, Josh Billings "has few if any superiors."]

[When Shaw died,] I had for some time been making a collection of the Josh Billings aphorisms freed from the orthographic eccentricities, idiosyncrasies, and disfigurements which repelled many, although they were a source of attraction to others. I have lately increased this collection by an examination of all that the humorist wrote, and it seems to me a duty to share . . . the riches there uncovered. The queer spelling is certainly a drawback where he treats the serious aspects of life, but it is easy to eliminate this excrescence, these fantastic habiliments, and let the solid truth stand forth in its naked majesty. For truth there is here in large abundance, truth expressed with a vigor, a sharpness, and an originality that compel attention. He did not write simply to amuse, although he was often amusing. There was frequently a higher purpose peeping out from among his quaint fancies and odd conceits. He directed his shafts against humbug, pretension, and falsity. He burlesqued the salient weaknesses of the people in a way to set them to thinking, and to doing better. His diagnosis of human nature was an exceedingly shrewd one. He punctured the follies and imbecilities of the multitude with a very keen rapier. He is especially copious in his discussion of fools of all sorts and shapes and sizes. He makes out the two main species under this genus to be natural fools and condemn fools.

There is, of course, much exaggeration in his writings, for American humor would hardly be recognized without this ear-

mark. There is quite naturally a good deal of repetition, and much that one more or less distinctly recalls as having been said substantially before. For he claimed the privilege, as do most writers, of laying hold freely, everywhere, of that which suited him, and putting the stamp of his own mind upon it by some unimportant changes or adaptation to his purpose. He had a cynical streak, and enjoyed showing up the seamy side of humanity, of which he had seen very much, but his sarcasms were well directed and struck the center nearly every time. Occasionally he says that which is not so, that which will not stand examination, but as a rule he hits the nail very squarely on the head. He is to be read with discrimination most certainly, for he was not wholly sound on all subjects, but in the great majority of his advices his opinion is extremely wholesome. (pp. 207-08)

The American public has luxuriated in the past thirty years in a vast variety of humorous writers, each with his own peculiar gift, each flourishing for a season and then giving way to a successor with a slightly different quality. Most of us can recall Artemus Ward (if not Sam Slick, Doesticks, John Phenix, and Major Downing), Orpheus C. Kerr, and Petroleum V. Nasby, whom President Lincoln so greatly enjoyed. Mark Twain, Bob Burdette, and Mr. Dooley are but of yesterday and have hosts of friends. But among these many Josh Billings has a niche all his own. For thorough knowledge of human nature, keenness of observation and philosophic insight into character, combined with purity of purpose and soundness of moral teaching, he has few if any superiors. The real beauty and worth of many of the sayings of this sage have been lost to sight in the multitude of those considerably inferior, and because of the comic dress which he felt obliged to throw around them. But relieved from this encumbrance, . . . we think they will commend themselves . . . as well worthy careful thought and frequent quotation. (p. 211)

James Mudge, "A Philosophical Humorist," in The Methodist Review, Vol. CI, March-April, 1918, pp. 207-15.

JENNETTE TANDY (essay date 1925)

[Tandy links Josh Billings to Charles Farrar Browne's Artemus Ward in his approach to common people.]

The ways of the professional humorist were lively in the middle nineteenth century. Joke columns were an extremely popular feature of newspapers and periodicals. There was a large crew of fun-makers to be read and enjoyed in the years between 1850 and 1880. George Harris, William T. Thompson, Mr. Bagby, and C. H. Smith entertained their Southern audiences. George D. Prentice, John Phoenix, Nasby, Mrs. Partington, Samantha Allen, The Widow Bedott, Private Miles O'Reilly, Hans Breitman, The Danbury News Man, and many others sent gales of merriment over the North and West. The Americans were digging for gold, they were staking out the Great Plains, they were quarrelling and fighting, they were building transcontinental railways, laying down the Atlantic Cable, swarming into cities, erecting huge industrial plants, and changing almost overnight from an aggregation of farmers and villagers into a nation of city dwellers and factory workers. And through it all they toiled and speculated and boodled and laughed,—great horse laughs, sardonic grunts, silly giggles, open-mouthed guffaws, sly chuckles.

Of the many men who kept them grinning, C. F. Browne and Henry Wheeler Shaw are best remembered. Both were fun-makers of a rare sort. They cracked jokes, sometimes inane, and sometimes vulgar. More than this, they breathed through their drolleries the exhalations of inborn and original personality. They made along with their witticisms an interpretation of human nature as they saw it, and an arraignment of the foibles of man and the imperfections of the social order. And in Artemus Ward and Josh Billings, their assumed characters, they created literary personalities of undeniable virility. Long life to them! (pp. 132-33)

[Shaw's] aphorisms, his most abundant contributions, may be studied in all his volumes. They range from punning and banality to homely wit and philosophy. In some the spelling is the only novelty. . . . (p. 152)

The effect of Billings's pithy lines is gained partly by the homely sophistication, partly by the ludicrous spelling, partly by bits of coarseness which heighten the color of lowly life. "Amerikans," as he said himself, "love caustick things: they would prefer turpentine tew colone-water, if they had tew drink either" (a trifle prophetic, that). "So with their relish of humor; they must hav it on the half-shell with cayenne."

The contradictions visible to his wordly perspicacity are easily translated into anti-climaxes and paradoxes. He is very skilled in reanimating a familiar platitude by turning it into the vernacular. Bill Arp [actually Charles Henry Smith] has remarked upon this gift:

> It is curious how we are attracted by the wise, pithy sayings of an unlettered man. It is the contrast between his mind and his culture. We like contrasts and we like metaphors and striking comparisons. The more they are according to nature and everyday life, the better they please the masses. The cultured scholar will try to impress us by saying *facilis descensus averni*, but Billings brings the same idea nearer home, when he says, "When a man starts down hill, it looks like everything is greased for the occasion." We can almost see the fellow sliding down. It is an old thought that has been dressed up fine for centuries, and suddenly appears in everyday clothes.

Americans love platitudes. Their favorite teachers, from Franklin to Harding, have fed them plenty of them. They love to be led along against wild courses. Whatever their secret transgressions, outwardly they accept the middle course with resignation, and console themselves with maxims, though they know, as does the whimsical Josh, that, "All the philosophy in the world, wont make a hard trotting horse ride eazy."

It must be some vestige of this preference for sage advice which makes a present-day critic commend the moral and advisory tone of Ward and Billings above their sly cynicism and genius for social satire:

> It is as moralists, however, that Ward and Billings serve us best. They had the Platonist and Christian instinct for a measureless leniency with persons, combined with a critical severity towards actions and policies.

Whatever their excelling grace may be, the two funny men gave a national presentation and a philosophical interpretation of the common man. They saw the unlettered man of the people on a grander scale than any of his sectional interpreters had ever seen him. And while preserving all his provincial charm

and whimsical individuality, they were able to make him, in person and in reputation, a national hero. (pp. 155-57)

> *Jennette Tandy, "The Funny Men: Artemus Ward and Josh Billings," in her* Crackerbox Philosophers *in American Humor and Satire, 1925. Reprint by Kennikat Press, Inc., 1964, pp. 132-57.*

CYRIL CLEMENS (essay date 1932)

[*In this excerpt from the conclusion to his biography of Shaw, Clemens demonstrates Shaw's importance in the evolution of American humor.*]

Josh Billings is a link and an important link in the chain of American humor, which has ever been a humor of shrewdness and of epigram, akin to the wisdom found in the proverbs of every nation. This is why he can be translated with such effectiveness, and enjoyed far beyond the confines of his continent. While his countrymen were laying railroads from ocean to ocean, bridging rivers, and settling vast stretches of wilderness, they found solace and refreshment in the philosophy of the man who held that, "best medisin I kno ov for the rumatism, iz to thank the Lord—that it ain't the gout."

"As a lecturer and witty philosopher he was not surpassed in his day," says [Will D. Howe in] the *Cambridge History of American Literature*. "He is the comic essayist of America rather than her comic story-teller" [see Additional Bibliography].

This is truly said. Shaw was not capable of such sustained narrative as his contemporaries Artemus Ward and Mark Twain. He did not take kindly to the story, but to the essay. Like Emerson's, his essays consist of random reflections upon one subject collected under a single title. In the work of both men, the sentence by reason of its own brilliance, enjoyed an independence not observable in most writers.

"With me," Billings once said, "everything must be put in two or three lines." As the narrow confines of a sonnet spur a poet on to excellence, so Josh, allowing himself only a few sentences achieves more than most writers do in many pages—and this in a poetical and unforgettable fashion. (pp. 165-66)

Josh Billings is an essential link in the chain of American humor that starts with Benjamin Franklin's *Poor Richard's Almanac*. The shrewd and droll sayings of Billings' *Farmer's Allminax* have much in common with the earlier book. (p. 167)

Franklin and Shaw are surprisingly alike in their outlook upon life: at once shrewd, philosophic, and humorous. Many sayings were not original with them, but they were always greatly bettered by their rugged wit. Some critic quaintly remarked that Josh Billings found many maxims in evening attire but left them in plain ordinary everyday clothes so that the man in the street would not be afraid to associate with them. (p. 168)

Up to the time of Josh Billings, most American authors had written for the educated and cultural classes. Josh's appeal was not only to these, but also to the average man. To him he brought a message of hope and encouragement. He taught in his inimitable way that the status of a gentleman was not dependent upon a large bank account or even upon an acquaintanceship with Homer and Vergil, but upon the right innate feeling:

The man who is as kind and courteous to his office boy as he is to a millionaire, is a gentleman.

It has been said with considerable truth that Josh Billings gives "a national presentation and a philosophical interpretation of the common man," and that he saw the unlettered man of the people on a grander scale than any of his sectional interpreters had ever seen him [see excerpt by Jennette Tandy dated 1925]. He had an utter scorn for artificial class distinctions, and believed that the honest intelligent God-fearing man of any rank of life was worthy of respect, and he alone. (pp. 176-77)

In Josh Billings' time the characteristic feature of our literature was optimism or, as the late V. L. Parrington would call it, "romantic optimism." Mr. V. F. Calverton brings this point out clearly in his *Liberation of American Literature,* when he states that not only were the humorists optimistic but also the serious writers and poets such as Longfellow, Whittier, Lowell and Holmes. It was the last mentioned who epitomized the philosophy of the day by declaring that "the more smiling aspects of life are the more American."

Since the turn of the century, however, American Literature has undergone a sea-change in becoming more and more pessimistic, until pessimism has reached its climax in men like Dreiser, Anderson, Lewis, O'Neill, and Hemingway. And even worse than their pessimism is their total lack of all guiding principles. The best antidote for such gloomy fellows is the humor of Josh Billings that links us to a deep and searching understanding of the national character. Perhaps some peoples are cut out for a pessimistic view of life, but in the author's opinion the Americans most certainly are not, and we will find no rest for our national spirit until we are again able to enjoy such humor spontaneously.

Josh Billings is as American as apple pie or the corncob pipe. No one could possibly mistake either his life or his work as emanating from any other country. Yankee of the Yankees, he smacks of his region just as much as did the old clippers that put out from Nantucket and Gloucester for all parts of the world.

With the times so out of joint and our literature so generally ill at ease, we need more than ever before the "Yankee Solomon" who can preach:

> Genuine laffing iz the mouth ov the soul, the nostrils ov the heart, and iz just az necessary for health and happiness as spring water iz for a trout.

(pp. 177-78)

Cyril Clemens, in his Josh Billings, Yankee Humorist, *International Mark Twain Society, 1932, 197 p.*

MAX EASTMAN (essay date 1936)

[*An American essayist, poet, and editor, Eastman was a leftist commentator on American life and literature who greatly influenced American criticism after the First World War. In 1911 and 1917, respectively, he helped found two notable Marxist periodicals, the* Masses *and the* Liberator, *which he edited and which were subjected to government censorship on charges of sedition. At one time a member of the Communist party, Eastman eventually rejected communism after witnessing firsthand the realities of Stalinist Russia, becoming an outspoken opponent of Marxist-Leninism. As a literary scholar, he is best known for his critical*

text The Enjoyment of Poetry. *In the following excerpt, Eastman extols Shaw's descriptive abilities.*]

It is the blending of . . . two strains—the primitive vigor of imagination and the mature enjoyment of nonsense—that gives its distinct flavor to American humor. Both Mark Twain and Josh Billings were aware of this flavor, and tried to identify it by isolating the word "humor" for the purpose. Mark Twain said that the art of telling a "humorous," as opposed to a "comic," or a "witty" story, "was created in America and has remained at home." And Josh Billings apologized for the failings of this art by explaining that "Americans haven't had time yet to bile down their humor and git the wit out ov it."

Josh Billings was a crude character in comparison to Mark Twain—a "cracker-box philosopher," and on some subjects rather more of a cracker box than a philosopher. But he possessed these two gifts, the comic vision and the liberated taste for foolishness, in a degree that enabled him to create a new artistic form. He would appear in our brief and reckless history as the father of imagism. For he was the first man in English literature to set down on his page, quite like a French painter reared in the tradition of art for art's sake, a series of tiny, highly polished verbal pictures, and leave them there for what they might be worth. (pp. 174-75)

> The gote iz a koarse wollen sheep.
> They have a good appetite, and a sanguine digestion.
> A maskuline gote will fite ennything, from an elephant down to his shadder on a ded wall.
> They strike from their but-end, insted ov the shoulder, and are az likely tew hit, az a hammer iz a nail hed.
> They kan klime ennything but a greast pole, and know the way up a rock, az natral az a wood-bine. . . .

There is little in New England poetry up to that date as graphic as some of this Poughkeepsie auctioneer's metaphors—nothing quite comparable to his statement that goats "know the way up a rock as natural as a woodbine," which is Homeric. Our history would make much of the originality of Josh Billings, and also of his crudity—for our whole history would be of something crude. (p. 175)

Max Eastman, "The American Blend of Humor—A Digression," in his Enjoyment of Laughter, *Simon and Schuster, 1936, pp. 163-78.*

WALTER BLAIR (essay date 1942)

[*Blair is an American educator and literary historian who has concentrated largely on American humor and folk themes. In the following excerpt, he observes that the personality of Josh Billings lends continuity to Shaw's varied subjects.*]

The humor which [Henry Wheeler Shaw] turned out and which sold so widely was shaped in several ways by the humor which was fashionable at the time he started to write it. The poor spelling, of course, and queer phrasing to which he was forced to turn were early tricks of the school of the latter half of the nineteenth century. Like most other writers of the time, Shaw steered clear of violent party attitudes in politics.

But long after misshapen words and sentences had gone out of fashion in most humor, Shaw kept using them in the greater part of his work (though he did produce a four-year series of pieces headed ''Uncle Ezek's Wisdom,'' properly spelled and grammatically phrased, for the *Century*). And he was a throwback in another way—a way suggested when he wrote for a friend a recipe for success as a lecturer. He said the author ought to give his listeners the characters they had enjoyed when they had read his books; Shaw himself had done this: ''What little success I have gained, I think has been got by sticking close to Billings, not leaving him long, and always believing him to be my best friend.'' The point was that Josh was a character—that, unlike many humorous writers of the day, Shaw saw to it that his spokesman was not thrust out of the limelight.

Josh Billings, to be sure, was not so localized or so individualized as a Downing, say, or a Major Jones. But like his creator, he was clearly from Way Down East—a Yankee farmer. He had a family almost as large and about as queer as a modern radio comedian, Bob Burns, has invented for himself—Jehossaphatt Billings, ''a very close man who died at the age of 63 . . . from an overdose of clam chowder drank at a free lunch''; Jamaika Billings, ''the laziest man that ever visited this world''; Zephemiah Billings, ''a fiddler by birth and perswashun''; Adam Billings, the first of the family, ''born, as near as I can figure, about the year 1200, more or less''; and others. However, these were not people who wandered in and out of stories, as the members of the Downing clan had earlier in the century. As a matter of fact, Billings wrote very few narrative passages except in the brief histories of his kinfolk.

For Billings was primarily an essayist, in the Addison-Steele-Goldsmith tradition, writing about all sorts of subjects in a fashion which was formal except in two respects: he did not follow grammatical rules, and the letters he used to form his words were not those generally in use. (pp. 221-22)

A book by Billings or an almanac or a lecture would be a gathering-together of many essays. . . . He would write on the virtues (''**Love,**'' ''**Fear,**'' ''**Beauty**''), on various fauna (''**The Mouse,**'' ''**The Poll Cat,**'' ''**The Striped Snaik**''), on kinds of men (''**The Honest Man,**'' ''**The Kondem Phool,**'' ''**The Model Man**''), on carrying out important tasks (''**How To Pick Out a Dog,**'' ''**On Courting,**'' ''**How To Pick Out a Horse**''), on miscellaneous subjects (''**The Fust Baby,**'' ''**Billiards,**'' ''**Habits of Grate Men,**'' ''**Spring and Boils,**'' ''**Tight Boots**'').

A lecture by Josh Billings would be a series of such bits following on the heels of one another. The synopsis of his last lecture, as he gave it out, shows how it leaped from one topic to another:

1. Remarks on Lecturing— 8. What I Know about
   General Overture   Hotels
2. The Best Thing on Milk 9. The Bumble-Bee
3. The Summer Resort   10. The Hornet
4. Josh on Marriage   11. The Quire Singer
5. Josh on the Mule   12. Josh on Flirting
6. The Handsome Man: A   13. Courtin'
   Failure
7. The Dude: A Failure

He introduced a lecture by saying:

> I don't propose this evening to speak of the ''Lost Arts'' nor the ''Rise and Fall of the Roman Empire'' . . . nor touch on the Darwinian Theory—nor the probable purchase of Great Britain by Secretary Blaine—Nor allude in any way to the Third Term Question—But rather

to deal with the Probabilities of Life, wrought out in Short Essays—monographs—Bits of Natural History, Answers to correspondents, and Proverbial philosophy.

Back of his books or lectures would be a personality which gave these wide-ranging compositions whatever unity they had. The personality was not notable for anything so much as its averageness in outlook, its sense of humor, and, finally, its pointed way of putting things. His closest approach to social reform was a hit now and then at feminism and a number of hits at intemperance (''Rum is good in its place,'' he said, ''and hell is the place for it''). For the most part, though, when he wrote about the problems men had to solve, he was satisfied to put into his queer language sentences which spoke well of old-fashioned virtues and the joy they brought—a good home life, an honest (though shrewd) business career, and simple but strong religion. These passages—and those which simply explained the characters of men and women of different sorts—showed his knowledge of human nature and his thorough acceptance of old ideas about it. Perhaps his greatest individual quirk was his fascination with animal life of many sorts—a fascination which showed itself in essay after essay about insects and snakes and animals of all kinds. In these essays Josh was interested in turning over in his mind the strange facts about animal life, phrasing his findings in a humorous way,

Josh Billings in a characteristic pose while lecturing. The Granger Collection, New York.

and decorating his remarks every now and then with a moral the discourse had suggested to him. (pp. 223-26)

Always, whatever the subject, Josh Billings showed a great gift for squeezing much lore into a few words. Shaw did not take pains to give Josh Billings a home or much of a family circle; he did not give him adventures. Instead, he gave much time to his way of boiling down thoughts. (pp. 226-27)

An English critic said of Shaw: "He is a writer of comic aphorisms—a Solomon in cap and bells" [see excerpt by Robert Ford dated 1897]. "He," said the creator of Bill Arp, "was Aesop and Ben Franklin, condensed and abridged." Turn anywhere in the writings of Josh, and you will find, every few lines, single sentences as good to quote as you will find anywhere in American literature. The long run of Billings is pretty tiring, but the short sentences are sparkling gems of bright expression. (p. 227)

It would be hard to say just what—aside from the spelling . . .— makes these aphorisms differ from the general run of such sentences. Mr. Max Eastman, looking at Billings' writings, makes much of the way he would "set down on his page . . . a series of verbal pictures, and leave them to stand for what they might be worth" [see excerpt dated 1936]. It may be true that, more than other creators of proverbs—the literary ones, at any rate—Josh had a habit of getting his ideas into picture form. . . . But, aside from this talent for vividness, aside from a few quirks of opinion and a comic way of abusing rules of spelling and grammar, this maker of almanacs in the last half of the nineteenth century was a sort of a throwback to the days of Poor Richard, many decades earlier. (pp. 228-29)

> Walter Blair, "Josh and Samantha," in his Horse Sense in American Humor from Benjamin Franklin to Ogden Nash, *University of Chicago Press, 1942, pp. 218-39.*

JOSEPH JONES (essay date 1943)

[*Jones examines the persona of Josh Billings and several of his humor techniques.*]

If the Lord High Executioner had prolonged his little list of "social offenders who might well be underground, and who never would be missed," I think he might soon have gleefully added some of the individuals who invent complicated theories to settle the baffling problem of what humor is. Let me hasten to claim for Josh Billings an exemption from such a blacklist. All we can attribute to him is a rather surprising number of interesting notions on the workings of his craft, scattered haphazardly throughout his works. My task has been that of assembling these notions into something which in arrangement, but in arrangement only, resembles a thing which Josh would have hastily disclaimed—a theory of humor.

Josh Billings has, I fear, been largely forgotten. But if this neglect is regrettable, as I believe it is, there are sufficient reasons for it. Humor, which seems so effortless when done well, is really very arduous, and the mortality rate among humorists is unusually high. A literature boasting a single great humorist is lucky; many are denied even one. Again, much humor is purely topical, and necessarily evanescent. But the fundamental reason for the ephemeral life of most humorous writings is, I feel sure, the inherent difficulty of the art. Somehow, it is easier to be sad than it is to be funny—perhaps because the race has had so much more practice at it. (p. 148)

[Josh Billings] worked principally in a single form—the short, rather vagrant essay ("loose bilt," as he called it). This served equally well in the columns of periodicals, in his ten-year series of comic almanacs, or on the lecture platform. It is, on the whole, an attractive medium; the total effect is pleasantly meditative, suggestive of thinking aloud, with just enough continuity to lend coherence and just enough looseness to allow unusual turns of phraseology to bob up in the most unexpected quarters. The form still has considerable virility. . . .

If one digs very deeply into the literature of humor, he will quickly encounter disagreements of all kinds. Humor appears to be an infection easy enough to diagnose, but the germ defies all attempts at isolation; consequently, the doctors are at loggerheads. (p. 149)

Josh Billings is quite certain that there are very few good judges of humor and that he is not among them. Any success the humorist may have, he thinks, generally comes through painful trial and error. (p. 150)

Just as the judges of good humor are few, so the supply of the real article itself is smaller than is commonly supposed. . . . Originality is practically unattainable; ". . . the very best that enny man kan do, iz tew steal with good judgement, and then own it like a man." . . . The humorous content of any given individual is likely to be limited: "Thare is about az mutch real humor in the best ov geniuses az thare iz juise in a lemmon: one good squeeze takes it out, and thare iz nothing but seeds and skin left." . . . His own limit Josh sets at one hour and a half, and even that "wants greasing towards the end." . . . (pp. 150-51)

If all this is true, one reflects, the humorist comes to bat with two strikes already called on him. This Josh is ready to concede; in fact, he deplores it many times. Clowning, he says, is "almost az dredful az the counterfiting bizzness," . . . and "more unsarting than the rat ketching bizzness az a means ov grace, or az a means ov livelyhood." . . . The chief difficulty seems to be that experience is no good; the only thing to do is to try out your new joke and take the consequences. . . . By way of explaining the uncertainties of this heartbreaking trade, Josh says, "Mi private opinyun iz—that humorous lektures kan never be a suckcess, for two reasons—one iz, bekauze most people look upon the men who makes them laff az vastly inferior to them, and the other iz, bekauze a writer in the *Atlantik Monthly* sez so." . . .

Since Josh fails to footnote his reference to the *Atlantic*, we shall be obliged to disregard the opinion of this authority and pass on to look briefly at the humorist's audience through his eyes. A number of interesting observations appear. First of all, the audience is the judge, sole and supreme. . . . (p. 151)

[The audience must be] conquered, and the conquest is no easy one. "Thare iz sum," says Josh, "who laff az eazy and az natral az the birds do, but most ov mankind laff like a hand organ—if yu expect tew git a lively tune out ov it yu hav got tew grind for it." Moreover, "It is dredful arbitrary tew ask a man tew laff who don't feel the itch ov it. One ov the meanest things in the comik lektring employment that a man haz to do, iz tew try and make that large class ov his aujience laff whom the Lord never intended should laff." Most audiences, he believes, need their bellwethers to lead the flock, and are likely to remain sullen without them. . . . (p. 152)

When we come to consider the means of producing laughter, we discover that Josh is less talkative. All he will hazard is a few hints that may aid in its production but which certainly cannot be taken as a recipe for it.

First, there is what comedians call the "dead-pan" technique. For best results, many of them believe, one must not laugh at his own foolery. Josh believes that "the men who kan make others laff the most, are generally light laffers themselfs," . . . and advises comic lecturers ". . . when they lay a warm joke, not tew akt az a hen doth when she haz uttered an egg, but look sorry, and let sum one else do the cackling." . . . Rigidly controlled gravity, then, is a first principle.

The second virtue of the successful humorist is simplicity. "I take hold ov things by the butt end," says Josh, "and if i kant raize them at that holt i leave them for the next fellow." . . . One always does well, he feels, to stay close to earth. . . . (pp. 153-54)

The companion virtue of simplicity is brevity. "Brevity iz the child of silence, and iz a great credit tew the old man." . . . "Maxims," Josh declares, "tew be good should be az sharp az vinegar, as short az pi krust, and az trew az a pair ov steelyards." . . . The same principle enters into his distinction between wit and humor—as satisfying a one as can be found with a great deal of searching: "Humor iz wit with a roosters tail feathers stuck in its cap, and wit iz wisdom in tight harness." . . . Josh's was the Blitzkrieg method—to hit hard and quick. This, he thinks, is especially characteristic of American humor. (p. 154)

Finally comes depth, which would seem also to embrace sincerity. Although Josh produced a few passages of pure falderal, most of his work is devoted to his principle that "the kream ov a joke dont never lay on the top, but alwus at the bottom." . . . He is very insistent upon the content of a jest. Wit without wisdom is "a song without sense," . . . "a razor without a handle." . . . We should not mistake mere vivacity for wit . . . ; "no man kan be a helthy phool unless he haz nussed at the brest ov wisdom." . . . For tricks such as punning he has no use, and the mere "funny man" is the object of his frequent scorn. . . .

A composite picture of Josh's ideal humorist, then, would be something like the following: He will be first of all a man who is skeptical of anything but hard experience, and will not place too much reliance upon even that. To understand his audience and to model his humor accordingly will be his principal concerns. He will make sure that what he has to say has a depth and sincerity despite its humorous integument, and will then present it as simply and briefly as he can, remembering to step out of the picture himself and let the audience do the laughing while he looks on with apparent indifference. But if nature has not already designed him as a clown, all his labors will bear no fruit.

In assessing the worth of Josh Billings as a humorist, we shall do well to remember his canons of wit. They reveal him, it seems to me, as a rather severely self-disciplined artist, just as every superior humorist is disciplined by the exacting regulations of the craft. While they restrict his range, they serve well to make him preëminent within that range. He is a great deal more than just a stage Yankee or a crackerbox philosopher: among the forerunners of Mark Twain he stands very close to the master. What he lacked was the gift of narrative; other gifts he had in abundance. He has been called a "poetical humorist" by Max Eastman, who even goes so far as to make him out to be the first American imagist [see excerpt dated 1936]. (One suspects that Josh might have been a bit ill at ease among his

descendants.) Certainly there must be something poetically humorous about a man who, looking at a conventional almanac cover bearing the familiar picture of the zodiac-anatomy, describes it thus: "The undersighned iz an Amerikan brave, in hiz grate tragick akt ov being attacked bi the twelve constellashuns.—*(May the best man win.)*"

Naturally, he shows many similarities to his fellows. One notices an occasional tall tale, some burlesque of descriptive purple passages and florid advertisements (not to mention "society" news), mock prayers, conundrums, beast fables, and the like. In some longer passages he is reminiscent of the character writers of the seventeenth century. All these, however, are but quavers and cadenzas in his normal tune, which is keyed to the comic definition and the epigram within the rambling essay.

Comparatively speaking, Josh is an ascetic in his repudiation of most of the stock comic devices of his day. While he never allows us to forget his designedly illiterate spelling, we must remember that he adopted it somewhat against his will and that he scolded his audience for preferring method to matter. We note further that his humor contains almost no caricature of politicians and other dignitaries, and indeed very little specific characterization of any sort. His model for caricature is Man, of whom he has, as he says, "a lonesum opinion." He contrives to make himself a character with a minimum of effort spent upon deliberate process, preferring to stand upon the merit of what he says rather than upon any painfully manufactured version of himself. It is this impersonal quality—occasionally marred, but sometimes approaching the awful impersonality of Swift—that makes him different from most of his contemporaries and at the same time links him with Mark Twain. (pp. 155-58)

One of the principal things which should recommend Josh Billings to later readers is that he is not submerged in a dialect long since gone stale. To be sure, the bad spelling and occasional perversities of grammar do give his writing a backwoodsy tang, but they are not essential to the final effect. While he is not greatly improved by transliteration, the surprising thing is that he is not destroyed by it. One of his biographers says that his composition involved translation from "the best language he could command" into poor grammar and spelling [see excerpt by James M. Buckley dated 1885]; and that is not hard to believe. His thoughts, by themselves, can bear their own weight; they are not legerdemain, but humor. Josh knew this, but he also knew that the sixties and seventies doted on slippery orthography just as they doted on spelling bees. And like Shakespeare, of whom he was extremely fond, he had an instinct for business.

One notices also that Josh does not give himself any particular locale. There are a few references, mostly in the almanacs, to Podunk ("Pordunk") village and its inhabitants, including a remarkable set of ancestors, but for the most part he seems quite unattached, and wisely so. The advantages enjoyed by the humorist-at-large need hardly be dwelt upon. The fact, too, that he covered most sections of the country on his lecture tours and with his comic almanacs probably helped to keep him from provincialism. "A sense of locality—," says Walter Blair, "except of the general American scene—was not important in the works of a majority of these writers [of the later nineteenth century]" [see Additional Bibliography]. Blair seems further to feel that in neglecting to maintain this sense of locality they somehow robbed themselves of "the most enduring stuff of American humor." I cannot agree that this is true of Josh

Billings. What little localization he attempts seems to me to be distinctly less successful than his comments on those aspects of life which have no geographical boundaries. If he endures at all, it may well be because he was not local.

One could hardly be very eager to thrust greatness upon the humble Josh by linking him with the Transcendentalists, but it may be worth noting that he is in some respects the humorous counterpart of certain ones among them. He praises the simple life with all of the insistence of Thoreau; he relies upon intuition as fully as does Emerson, and is determined to think for himself at all costs. "What little i know about things," he says, "haz bin whispered to me by the spirits, or some other romping critters, and is az distinkt and butiful, sumtimes to me, as a dream on an empty stummuk; it may be all wrong but it never iz viscious, and thus i konclude it iz edukashun." . . . He believes that the cosmos, as originally planned, is basically a good one. He does not, however, harp upon his dignity and worth as a human being; in fact, he considers it no particular honor to be a member of the human race (as what humorist ever has?). Josh cheerfully agrees with *The New England Primer* that "In Adam's fall we sinnéd all," and refers to the unfortunate event quite frequently; but hear him further: "I sumtimes, in mi sad, wet days, when i do mi sollum thinking, hav wondered, if it wouldn't hav been just az well, when Adam waz falling, if he had fell out ov sight." . . . (pp. 159-60)

Josh's occasional portraits of himself in awkward social situations or uncongenial surroundings are on the whole, I think, a good deal less boisterous than those of most nineteenth-century humorists. One may see in such sketches as **"Long Branch, Saratoga, and Lake George"** . . . or **"Josh Billings Insures His Life"** . . . a prototype of the humorous despair of Chaplin, Benchley, and Thurber, which so subtly and excellently blends the ludicrous with the pathetic. All this amounts, I suppose, to a reënforcement of what I have already asserted—that Josh Billings, among our earlier humorists, stands closest to Mark Twain in his ability to play the simpleton and the philosopher at once. His is the same blood that flows in the veins of Huckleberry Finn, that one peerless creation among a very populous tribe.

Josh's way of viewing life is that of the perennial vagabond—the Spectator, the Idler or what have you—who sees or pretends to see life from the loafer's point of view. (Will Rogers's "All I know is just what I see in the papers" and Ogden Nash's magnificent title *I'm a Stranger Here Myself* are familiar echoes of the humorist's perpetual insouciance, of which we all are perhaps a little envious.) Josh's writings in bulk reveal him as a Yankee Ecclesiastes, master of a brand of wit that "tickles as it hurts," and at the same time as a homely character who is honest, gentle, modest, and sometimes—as becomes a true humorist—a little wistful. "The route that i travel," he says . . . , "iz cirkuitus and blind sometimes, it haz now and then a vista, or a landscape in it, that iz worth, tew me, more than a farm ov tillable land, but you kant raize good white beans on a landskape." (pp. 160-61)

> *Joseph Jones, "Josh Billings: Some Yankee Notions on Humor," in Studies in English, The University of Texas Press, 1943, pp. 148-61.*

DAVID B. KESTERSON (essay date 1972)

[Kesterson explores such elements as mock astrological predictions and comic weather forecasts in Shaw's Allminax.]

Shaw did not realize it at the time, but in writing the **Allminax** he had launched what was to become his most popular work—the enterprise that would bring him more fame than any other. Selling well over one hundred thousand copies each of the first four years, the little book never dropped below fifty thousand in sales during each of its remaining six years. The success of the book is not surprising, for Shaw was not only an effective writer and humorist, but also an alert businessman. And in the latter regard he recognized in the development of the almanac in America a chance to capitalize on its two most popular trends while producing something characteristically his own.

These two trends, among the many diverse directions American almanacs had taken by the 1860's, were the comic almanac and the farmer's. Shaw's **Allminax** was to embody many techniques of the former and originate, of course, as a burlesque of the latter. The comic almanac in America, which, as Constance Rourke has said, shows more than any other source "the wide diffusion of a native comic lore," got its start in the eighteenth century, but really came to fruition in the nineteenth. More than thirty varieties of comic almanacs originated in Massachusetts alone between 1830 and 1860. Contents of these comic annuals usually consisted of jokes, humorous stories and poems, and ludicrous illustrations.

Farmer's almanacs in America likewise sustained multiple varieties of publications in the eighteenth and nineteenth centuries. But by far the best and most popular almanac, and the one to assert direct influence on Shaw's, was Robert Bailey Thomas's *(Old) Farmer's Almanac,* first printed for the year 1793 and still active. This almanac, usually of about forty-eight pages, contained calendar pages, astronomical calculations, weather predictions, hints and suggestions to farmers about farm routines. In addition there were numerous pages containing such matters as tables of American Presidents, eclipses and astronomical charts, lists of colleges, sections of literary interest with poetry, anecdotes, moral tags, and conundrums, and miscellaneous items about birds and insects, game laws, tide tables, and postal regulations. Thomas also included humorous character sketches for variety and entertainment.

In his **Allminax** Shaw brought to these traditions of the comic and farmer's almanacs his own flair for humor and satire and his own well developed forms of comic expression. Headings of calendar pages, for example, carry humorous verses and conundrums much like those in his jest book **Josh Billings' Spice Box**. The farmer's calendar column itself, which R. B. Thomas used for hints on crop planting and care of equipment, Shaw transforms into a column of humorous aphorisms similar to those appearing in his other works. . . . (pp. 7-8)

Short comic monographs appear on pages opposite calendar pages, the subjects—when not directly parodying almanac elements—ranging from catalogs of animals and insects to a comic genealogy of the Billings family. In addition, there is humorous advertising, a frequent ploy of Shaw's, much of it plugging issues of the **Allminax**. On one of these pages, entitled "How They Do Talk About **Josh Billings' Farmer's Allminax**," Shaw gives comments by readers (remarks actually of his own invention) lauding the enterprise. Acclaims one enthusiastic reader, "'Giv me liberty, or giv me deth, but if i kant hav either, giv me Josh Billings' allminax for 1870.'" Another man attests, "'It kured mi wife ov wanting to die.'" All of the above fare—from aphorisms to advertisements—is presented in Shaw's outrageous misspellings and syntactical chicanery. To put the finishing touches on the humorous complexion of the **Allminax**, Shaw included comic illustrations (by Livingston Hopkins) and also amusing miscellaneous filler items. Thus, there was enough of Shaw's typical humorous material in the ten issues of the *Allminax* to prevent it from being solely a burlesque of the farmer's almanac. Audiences could enjoy it as a jest book as well.

Still, the *Allminax* was essentially an attack on a tradition; thus the burlesque elements are of primary importance. Shaw's approach is fresh, the humor and satire characteristically pointed but not painfully sharp. After all, he wanted to amuse devotees of the almanac and perhaps cause them to take a second look at their devotion; he did not want to alienate them. The design of this satire—like that of all Shaw's satire—was not to be incongruous then, with his general philosophy of humor: "I pin all my faith, hope, and charity upon this one impulse of my nature, and that is, if I could have my way, there would be a smile continually on the face of every human being on God's footstool, and this smile should ever and anon widen into a broad grin."

The burlesque elements in *Josh Billings' Farmer's Allminax* cover everything commonly found in farmer's almanacs: the Man of the Signs, monthly astrological predictions and horoscopes, the farmer's calendar, weather predictions, supplementary stellar data such as dates of eclipses, and miscellaneous information such as civil laws, hints to farmers, and various agency regulations.

The Man of the Signs emblem is the butt of much ridicule in the *Allminax*. A chart of the *Homo Signorum* (a human figure surrounded by signs of the Zodiac which influence various parts of the body) with a humorous explanation of the chart stands as the first page in each of the ten issues. Shaw introduced some ingenious comic alterations of what customarily appears on such charts. (pp. 9-10)

Other burlesque astrological elements appear at random throughout the issues. A table of "extra eklipses" appears in 1870 with such notes as "Thare will be semiockasional eklipses ov the moon, kauzed bi brandy smashes gitting between that virtewous and pale old woman, and the eyes ov sum ov our most promising young men." A list of "Kalkulashuns ov a Prognostix Natur" in 1871 ridicules the penchant for interpreting signs; for example, "Whenever yu see a flok ov geese all standing on one leg, except the old gander, and he chawing hiz cud, look out for a south-west wind tewmorow, or the next day, or the day after, or a sum fewter time." New England weather watchers are the target in a mock weather synopsis appearing in 1873 "The byrometer will rize very sudden this morning at Pordunk, 3 foot, and fall the like amount at Sakramento City. The diffikulty in the weather for the last 2 days, which haz predominated at Boston and around New Orleans, waz owing tew the byrometer at Pordunk being took down and sent tew the blacksmiths shop for repairs."

Shaw's satiric eye did not overlook the miscellaneous entries tucked away in the pages of farmer's almanacs. To mock the lists of rules and regulations of various sorts frequently printed, his 1871 issue carries a list of "Rules, By-Laws, and Regulations" for the "Pordunk Valley Rail Road." In such burlesque rules as "Konduktors are positively forbid trieing tew pass each other on a single track" Shaw attacks the frequent irrelevance and vagueness of official regulations. Much the same spirit is found in his slate of "Konnektikut Blew Laws" in the 1871 *Allminax*: "No man must chu enny tobbacko on the sabbath day unless he goes down cellar and duz it." Then there are the numerous hints to farmers scattered throughout

the *Allminax*. Shaw's are humorous and satiric. The farmers should keep a cow so that the milk will have to be watered only once. To make a hoe cake, boil a hoe until it jells and then let it cake. To break a mule, "commence at his head," only one of Shaw's many remarks about mules (we recall his famous "**Essa on the Muel**"). Concerning crops, "Turnips should be planted near the top ov the ground, if yu want them tew turn up good" (punning is not unusual in Shaw), and "Egg plants iz good, but eggs sot under a stiddy hen will produce more chickens than they will tew plant them." The advice goes on and on. (pp. 11-12)

[The *Allminax* was] a favorite with thousands of readers. One reviewer, in praising especially the aphorisms in it, said that they "often rival in wisdom those of 'Poor Richard' himself; while they are exquisitely cool and humorous." Street and Smith lauded it perennially in the *New York Weekly,* their hyperboles echoing in part, of course, their own vested interest in Shaw's success. Their ad for the 1874 issue proclaims that the *Allminax* for that year "is about the richest and raciest little work that has ever been published." And for 1875 they proclaim, "The enormous advance demand for this famous comic almanac, and the immense sale all over the country, render its appearance one of the events of the publishing year."

Perhaps the best clincher of the strength and appeal of the work is Mark Twain's praiseful comment that the *Allminax* "is a pleasant conceit and happily executed." Whether readers today peruse almanacs and dabble in newspaper horoscopes, they can still delight in Shaw's abundant burlesque of astrology. The monographs are witty and pleasant to read; the aphorisms characteristically poignant. The work simultaneously entertains the modern reader and causes him to reflect on the interests and customs of an older, rural America relying on monthlies and annuals for entertainment and information. (pp. 12-13)

David B. Kesterson, "Josh Billings and His Burlesque 'Allminax'," in Illinois Quarterly, *Vol. 35, No. 1, November, 1972, pp. 6-14.*

DAVID B. KESTERSON   (essay date 1973)

[Kesterson examines Shaw's craftsmanship in various genres, among them the aphorism, essay, and jest book, and concludes with an appraisal of his accomplishments as a humorist.]

Because Shaw had the kind of mind that worked incisively and compactly, he felt most at ease in the literary form of the aphorism. Short sayings couching general truths were among the first of his literary productions (*Sayings* consisting of about half aphorisms), and they were the last pieces he contributed for publication in the "Uncle Esek's Wisdom" column for the *Century* and in his *New York Weekly* column.

Shaw's sayings are so natural that they give an air of ease and spontaneity of creation. Actually, however, they were often the result of hours of work on his part. Shaw's friend Melville Landon (Eli Perkins) wrote of finding Shaw composing aphorisms on a Madison Avenue streetcar:

> That morning, when the old man espied me, he was so busy with his thoughts that he did not even say good morning. He simply raised one hand, looked over his glasses and said, quickly, as if he had made a great discovery:
>
> "I've got it, Eli!"
>
> "Got what?"

"Got a good one—lem me read it," and then he read from a crumpled envelope this epigram that he had just jotted down:

"When a man tries to make himself look beautiful, he steals—he steals a woman's patent right—how's that?"

"Splendid," I said. "How long have you been at work on it?"

"Three hours," he said, "to get it just right."

Landon adds, "Mr. Shaw always worked long and patiently over these little paragraphs. . . . When he got five or six written, he stuck them into his hat and went down and read them to G. W. Carleton . . . who was an excellent judge of wit, and he and Josh would laugh over them."

Besides being compatible with Shaw, the aphorism appealed broadly to a reading populace bred in the American traditions of honesty, frugality, and general moral righteousness. Shaw knew this heritage, of course; and he remembered the influence that Poor Richard's sayings had asserted on an eighteenth-century audience, was aware of the attraction of sententious sayings in popular almanacs of the day, and appreciated the clever utterances of contemporary wits and phrase makers. The aphorism was both a comfortable and profitable mode to work in, and thus Shaw devoted serious attention to it. As Walter Blair has said, in discussing Shaw's dedication to pithy language, "He gave much time to his way of boiling down thoughts" [see excerpt dated 1942]. (pp. 34-5)

Aside from pithiness, there are several special characteristics of Shaw's aphorisms, and many of these traits are also applicable to his other writings. The most obvious is misspelling, a device Shaw employed in all his sayings except for those in the "Uncle Esek's Wisdom" column. Although his method of spelling is basically phonetic, it lacks consistency. (pp. 35-6)

In adopting this fad of the time, Shaw was not wholly pleased; for his first literary efforts had been written in correct spelling. And he personally considered cacography an unfortunate technique and one that in itself provides little humor. But, after first using it to gain success, he felt stuck with it, remarking, "When a man once puts on the cap and bells, no matter whether they bekum him or not, the world will insist upon hiz wearing them, however they pretend tew regret it." . . . He also sensed, however, the psychological advantage of using misspellings and ungrammatical syntax. He knew that by dressing truth in these folksy, funny clothes it would be accepted. People, he believed, "will not take wisdom as wisdom." He would see that they received it in appropriate dress. (pp. 36-7)

Incorrect grammar and occasional distorted syntax for comic effect are other characteristics of Shaw's aphorisms. Pointing to specific forms, Henry Lewis Mencken made the interesting, if somewhat clinical, observation that Shaw "seems to have been the first humorist to employ *saw* for *seen*, as well as *did* for *done*, extensively." It was common for Shaw to substitute the preterite for the past participle. Other examples of incorrect grammar are those usually found in dialectical humor, such as *hain't, ain't, hisself,* and *was* in place of *were* as the plural past tense of the verb *to be*. Actually, Shaw relied little on distorted syntax. He preferred clever wording and misspellings to loosely constructed sentences.

Other characteristics of the aphorisms lie outside the provinces of misspelling, slang, and malformed sentences. There are

anticlimactic sentences ("Buty iz power; but the most treacherous one i kno ov" . . .), uses of understatement ("found the ice in a slippery condition" . . .), and occasional puns and malapropisms. Shaw remarked that "a pun, tew be irresistable, don't ought to flavor ov malis aforethought; but wants tew cum sudden and apt, like a rat out ov his hole." . . . Of too much punning he was wary, feeling that the pun is "a sort ov literary prostitushun in which futur happynesz iz swopped oph for the plezzure ov the moment." . . .

Extraordinary or mixed figurative language—a trait which Walter Blair points out as characterizing all the literary comedians [see Additional Bibliography]—is also present in Shaw. (p. 37)

In common with other humorists of his day, Shaw practiced various comic techniques that, as Blair says, created a humor "of phraseology rather than of character." But in one major characteristic he differed considerably from the other humorists—in his imagery. Shaw had the rare poetical ability to convey his thoughts in sharp verbal pictures, surpassing the often trite, hyperbolic images of his contemporaries. Max Eastman, pioneer in recognizing Shaw's unusual way with imagery, labels Shaw a "poetic humorist," meaning that he is doing the same thing lightly that a poet does seriously: "using words in such a way as to give us visions, and even if he can, hallucinations." Moreover, Eastman continues, visual imagery does not adequately characterize Shaw's writing because "poetry and poetic humor appeal to every sense." (p. 39)

Finally, Eastman dubs Shaw the "father of imagism," saying that Shaw was "the first man in English literature to set down on his page, quite like a French painter reared in the tradition of art for art's sake, a series of tiny, highly polished verbal pictures, and leave them there for what they might be worth." Eastman even concludes that there is little in New England poetry up to Shaw's date "as graphic as some of this Poughkeepsie auctioneer's metaphors" [see excerpt dated 1936].

These observations are highly apropos, for there is an originality in Shaw's language that transcends that of his close rivals—Ward, Nasby, and Phoenix. These others were more adept at creating dramatic and narrative situations; Shaw mastered the language and found success in penning terse, fresh expressions and vivid, highly effective images.

In the tradition of the Yankee crackerbox philosopher, who appeared to be knowledgeable on all subjects, Shaw had a thought and comment about almost everything. Though he did not discuss politics as much as Nasby nor enter into social satire as often as Ward and Phoenix, Shaw's sayings do run a remarkably broad gamut. Virtues, vices, love, literature, religion, marriage, business matters, and quirks of human nature appear as subjects of his aphorisms. Also included are philosophy, advice, and random views of certain universal subjects and problems. (p. 40)

There is an undeniable strain of skepticism and pessimism running through Shaw's humor—a trait that existed in a large portion of American humor during and immediately after the Civil War. In a period distorted by war, Reconstruction, and the emergence of the Gilded Age, with its rise of big business and social evils, the comedian's role was anything but a glib one. Struck by the serio-comic incongruities of the new American way of life, Shaw composed a type of humor that, as Jesse Bier has observed, included the ingredients of "sad comprehension, disillusion, pessimism, and cynical amorality" [see Additional Bibliography].

On the subject of man—the human condition and human progress—Shaw's sayings express this strain of skepticism. (p. 43)

The same critical, skeptical attitude is found in the aphorisms that treat such specific topics as politics, religion, women, and the feminist cause. Showing both his amusement and perturbation over politics and politicians, Shaw remarked, "Az a gineral thing, if yu want tew git at the truth ov a perlitikal argyment, hear both sides and beleave neither." ... And "A man running for offiss puts me in minde ov a dog that's lost— he smells ov everybody he meets, and wags hisself all over." ... Religion attracted its share of Shaw's cynicism. Shaw was not really antireligious; he was simply critical of religious hypocrisy and man's misinterpretation and mismanagement of religious principles. He found little of the genuineness in religion that he felt necessary for a sound faith. (p. 44)

When various feminist groups such as the suffragettes rose to eminence in the last half of the nineteenth century, Shaw grew quite critical of woman and her role. He was definitely conservative on the matter of femininity. And he felt fully qualified—living with three women in his own family—to speak out on the qualities and shortcomings of the opposite sex. Of women in general he wrote:

> Wimmin quite often possess superior tallents, but their genius lays in their pashuns. . . .
>
> Woman haz no friendships. She either loves, despises, or hates. . . .
>
> Wimmin are like flowers, a little dust ov squeezing makes them the more fragrant. . . .
>
> I like a woman, (handsum if it iz convenient,) with more wisdom than larning, chaste, but not frozen, soft, but not silly, and fond, but not fussy, sich wimmin are skase, and are going tew be skaser. . . .
>
> (p. 45)

In spite of his occasional tone of skepticism and his penchant for criticism, Shaw's sayings, on the whole, affirm that life is worth living even if, as in a game of cards, "we must play what is dealt tew us, and the glory consists, not so mutch in winning, as in playing a poor hand well." ... No Puritan either, Shaw felt that man must live vigorously and feel free to express his nature: "I don't belief in total abstinence, enny more than I belief in total blindness, but I do belief in the reasonable gratification ov awl the desires that God haz given us." ... A strong undercurrent running through the aphorisms implies that, although there are many faults in man, his institutions, and his actions, thoughts, and words, man must try to reap from life as abundant a harvest as possible. Shaw's view is that of the idealistic reformer and satirist: he loves at heart the subject he attacks, and he attacks it in order to make it better.

It is obvious, to conclude, that Shaw mastered the form of the aphorism and used it to comment on innumerable aspects of life. Crisp, pithy, witty, and original (in expression, if not always in source), his sayings pleased readers and lecture audiences alike. (p. 46)

Since Shaw's initial fame as a man of letters was made as an essayist with his **"Essa on the Muel,"** he devoted a substantial part of his talent to the essay and the sketch. Walter Blair, in fact, calls him "primarily an essayist" of the "Addison-Steele-Goldsmith tradition" [see excerpt dated 1942], for Shaw wrote

"about all sorts of subjects in a fashion which was formal" (except in matters of spelling and grammar). Shaw's essays and sketches are all brief; they rarely total more than five hundred words and many amount to a third of that. Although they generally pertain to a single main topic, they are somewhat loosely structured and often appear, on a cursory glance, to be little more than a series of related aphorisms. In that the single sentence bears so much burden, Shaw's essays resemble Emerson's in style. Constructed in this manner, they provide an air of ease and leisure in a familiar tone.

Shaw's method, as Joseph Jones has observed, is "an attractive medium; the total effect is pleasantly meditative, suggestive of thinking aloud, with just enough continuity to lend coherence and just enough looseness to allow unusual turns of phraseology to bob up in the most unexpected quarters" [see excerpt dated 1943]. The more extensively the essays are examined, the more evident is their true artistry. Most of them, upon close scrutiny, emerge as finely sculptured little pieces with definite unity and stylistic charm.

Unlike Nasby, Shaw usually refrained from centering his writings on the major economic, political, and social problems of his era. Essays such as the one on **"Manifest Destiny"** . . . are rare exceptions in the Shaw canon, for most of his attention was devoted to lesser social concerns or to subjects of general human interest. In choosing subjects to satirize, for example, he was more inclined to single out the jargon of insurance-company questionnaires, the folly of letter-answer columns in newspapers written by supposed authorities on all subjects from love to horses, the activities of a woman's liberation group, or the ridiculous aspect of a dandy man than he was to address himself to the growing evils of the Gilded Age (pp. 47-8)

Shaw the moralist is never very distant in his essays. In an essay by the same title as one of his lectures, **"The Devil's Putty and Varnish"** . . . , he criticizes the trend of smoothing over scandalous and injurious deeds and practices. An unnecessary duel resulting in an "elegant murder" is called "an affair ov honnor"; if a man embezzles, the act is referred to by the examining committee as "a diskrepansy in hiz akounts"; when two young drunken, horse-and-buggy drivers are killed because of their ineptitude, the affair is reported as a "Fatal acksident"; and, when two trains collide because of the recklessness of the drunken crew, the wreck is dubbed "an unavoidable katastrophe." Shaw concludes by warning, "The Devil furnishes putty and varnish, free ov expense, tew hide the frauds and guilt ov men." ... (p. 50)

Thus from female education to problems of slack morality, Shaw was concerned with the subjects of the day and devoted many of his essays to them. A major aspect of his popularity and effectiveness with his audience lay in his being able to comment on particular instances as well as universal conditions. When his readers wanted to know what "Josh" had to say on a matter, they were never left wondering long.

However serious a moralist and philosopher Shaw was, he was at the same time a highly successful literary funny man. One reason for his success in the realm of humor is that he thought extensively about the nature and roles of wit and humor and about the value and effects of laughter. He and Bret Harte have even been called "our first tentative comic theoreticians." In several essays devoted specifically to humor, as well as in random passages in other essays, Shaw expressed his incisive views about the comic art.

In one of his several excellent essays on laughter . . . , Shaw points out that laughter is the special property of man (since the other animals cannot laugh) and is a vital sign of life, beneficial alike to mind and body. The power to laugh "is the power to be happy." The laugh is "an index ov karackter." Laughter accomplishes many things and has numerous virtues:

> Laffing keeps oph sickness, and haz conquered az menny diseases az ever pills have, and at mutch less expense.—It makes flesh, and keeps it in its place.—It drives away weariness and brings a dream ov sweetness tew the sleeper.— It never iz covetous.—It ackompanys charity, and iz the handmaid ov honesty.—It disarms revenge, humbles pride, and iz the talisman ov kontentment.—Sum have kalled it a weakness—a substitute for thought, but really it strengthens wit, and adorns wisdom, invigorates the mind, gives language ease, and expreshun elegance.—It holds the mirror up tew beauty; it strengthens modesty, and makes virtue heavenly. It iz the light ov life; without it we should be but animated ghosts. It challenges fear, hides sorrow, weakens despair, and carries haff ov poverty's bundles.—It costs nothing, comes at the call, and leaves a brite spot behind.—It iz the only index ov gladness, and the only buty that time kannot effase.—It never grows old; it reaches from the cradle tew the grave. Without it, love would be no pashun, and fruition would show no joy.—It iz the fust and the last sunshine that visits the heart; it was the warm welkum ov Eden's lovers, and was the only capital that sin left them tew begin bizzness with outside the Garden ov Pardise.
>
> (pp. 50-1)

Switching attention from laughter to its cause, humor, Shaw tries to arrive at a satisfactory definition of wit and humor. Though he feels his effort is ultimately unsuccessful, he makes some meaningful distinctions. Wit, he feels, "may be the bringing together two ideas, apparently unlike, and hav them prove tew be a cluss match." He explains and exemplifies: "I don't serpose that there would be enny grate quantity ov wit in yure telling sumboddy that yure gal was as hansum as a rose, but thare might possibly be sum wit into it if yu should go on and say that she was as frail, and as thorny, too." . . .

Humor, as opposed to wit, is gentler. Shaw compares it to heat lightning: it is "not the original artikle that gashes the heavens with a flaming sword and makes a fellow's hair get up on end and ake with astonishment. Humor don't dazzle, don't knock a man down with a sparkle; it is more a soothing syrup, sumthing tew tickle, without enny danger ov throwing the patient into fits." . . . Ultimately feeling his definitions of each subject inadequate, Shaw compares wit and humor with the intangible pleasure in kissing: "Thare is a peculiar kind ov bewitchment in awl three ov them, that evryboddy can acknowledge better than they can pictur out." . . . (p. 52)

As an essayist, then, Shaw was familiar, succinct, humorous, and diverse. Without indulging in major reform diatribes, he was very much interested in contemporary topics and in human improvement. . . . Predominant in his essays is the strain of optimism and good humor that overshadows the occasional notes of criticism. Considering the range and nature of his

utterances, Bill Arp's appraisal of Shaw as being "Aesop and Ben Franklin, condensed and abridged" is most apropos. (p. 63)

Besides his regular hardbound volumes, Henry Wheeler Shaw published several paperbound jest books. The jest book—a form that emerged in England during the Renaissance, became especially popular there in the eighteenth century and proliferated in America in the nineteenth—is, as Harry B. Weiss defines the genre, "the cheap, paper-covered, joke books that were, and still are, printed in large editions for sale to the general public, usually for comparatively small sums of money" [see Additional Bibliography]. The term *jest book* carries with it no particular specifications as far as contents are concerned; "jests" can be literally jokes, or epigrams, anecdotes, humorous almanac entries, ludicrous illustrations, and repartee (with frequent puns). Though not a requirement, the humor can be enhanced by any number of devices such as misspellings, exaggerations, incorrect grammar, and anticlimax. In short, as long as a work was a brief, inexpensive paperback containing an assortment of humorous material, it could be classified as a jest book.

The popularity of jest books during Shaw's day was augmented by the rise of comic periodicals and by the increasing number of humorous newspaper and magazine columns during the last half of the nineteenth century. This flourish of humorous journalism played into Shaw's hands as he mulled over the type of material most suitable for jest book form. (p. 83)

The lengthiest and most diverse of Shaw's jest books were the volumes he edited under the series title *Josh Billings' Spice Box* (1874 and following), a title Shaw borrowed from his *New York Weekly* column. Printed with sometimes as many as fifty large double-column pages and occasionally selling for as high as twenty-five cents, each of these volumes offers as much material as his other jest books combined. They are veritable potpourris of illustrations, cartoons, jokes, poems, anecdotes, narratives, letters, and other short pieces—works designed primarily for browsing. A major difference between *Spice Box* and Shaw's other jest books is that much of its material is only collected and edited by Shaw, not written by him. (p. 86)

Spice Box volumes are probably Shaw's most genuinely entertaining jest books. Unlike some of the others, their pages are uncluttered by prolific advertising, having only the customary publishing-house promotion pages. Every one of the sizable pages offers a sparkling variety of humorous odds and ends. Presented mostly in normal spelling, grammar, and syntax, these books are the most likely of all Shaw's jest books to provide an evening's curious entertainment for the modern reader. (p. 87)

It should be obvious at this point that Henry Wheeler Shaw both fulfilled the role of literary comedian and transcended it. Influenced by Artemus Ward with his quaint spelling, stage techniques, and general literary approach, Shaw was at home in the whole tradition of dry wit characterized by Ward, Nasby, Phoenix, and Twain—a tradition that led to twentieth-century counterpart Will Rogers, among others, who carried on Shaw's manner of having a ready, witty comment about almost any subject. In this comic tradition, Shaw appealed to everyone with homespun tastes from Lincoln to New England farmers.

But there is a side of Shaw that is distinctly separate from this tradition of the literary comedians. Unlike Brown and Locke, . . . he did not project an image of the persona to an extent that Josh Billings became a personality separate from Shaw. And he differed from Twain and others by remaining in the realm

An entry from Shaw's almanac for 1870.

of the essay and epigram instead of turning to comic narration or political commentary. Indeed, something of an older, more classical tradition stands behind Shaw's writings. Throughout his essays, he alludes to many of the standard great writers of Western literary tradition, quoting favorite or appropriate passages to corroborate his points, or commenting on some facet of the art or literary success of renowned authors. His favorite writers, judging from the number of times they or their works are mentioned, were Shakespeare, Dickens, Burns, and Bryant. (p. 129)

Shaw's conception of humor was broader and more classical than the type of folksy, exaggerated comedy usually associated with the literary comedians. Humor reflected his basic philosophy of life: he saw life as essentially pleasurable, and he wanted everyone to experience the pleasure and satisfaction for himself. As he phrased it, "I pin all my faith, hope, and charity upon this one impulse of my nature, and that is, if I could have my way, there would be a smile continually on the face of every human being on God's footstool, and this smile should ever and anon widen into a broad grin."

Humor should, above all, please; it should never discourage or confound. But it is also functional in correcting and informing mankind, and herein lies Shaw's belief in satire. Temperate in his attacks, Shaw accepted the Addison-Steele position that wit aids the presentation of morality: it softens the lesson and

amuses the beholder, while at the same time it couches unavoidable truths that hopefully lead to reform. Shaw's enthusiasm for life urged him to preach for reform—reform, that is, of an individual variety (he was skeptical of reform movements). He embraced all life: the animal and insect kingdoms were as fascinating to him as man. He never tired of dwelling on their species and characteristics and observing the very nature of human life reflected there. He was Chaucerian in his love of people, their habits of mind, their customs; just as he was Chaucerian in his keen perception of how man often seriously errs and destroys self and others. He readily excused, even found amusement in, the foibles of mankind; he was chagrined at major flaws that harmed humanity, and he spoke out against them.

Shaw had no codified, systematic philosophy of life.... His views were often as unrelated to any dominant, pervading philosophy of life as were his aphorisms foreign to a tightly structured paragraph. But he did, nevertheless, tend to view life with a basic optimism, a Yankee faith in the capability and perseverance of man, and a humane tolerance of man's blunders along the way to improvement. He approached all of life with eagerness and openness and then reflected on it with honest originality. At times he was skeptical, even occasionally pessimistic: he thought deeply enough to realize that Creation is not working as smoothly as it should. But he normally managed to eclipse gloom with an infectious lightness of heart and a witty remark that convinced his audience or reader that life was worth it after all. His New England heritage reminded him that the main function of man on earth is to see to the business of life; Shaw felt it his duty to show man the more propitious aspects of that function. (pp. 130-31)

Unfortunately, considering Shaw's qualities, contributions, and Realistic tendencies, he is currently too much ignored and is considered a literary curiosity. His spelling *is* a curiosity today, of course, and certainly it is a major drawback to his winning wide appeal. But his accomplishments as humorist, satirist, and knowledgeable stylist are significant and should receive more attention than they have. Jesse Bier [see Additional Bibliography], in a new, fresh discussion of Shaw and the literary comedians, appraises their achievement as being "a rapid maturity of gift on every side"; and he characterizes their work as being "national in scope" and as astonishing to the modern reader "in its comic energies." Bier's final assessment is that "in the bulk of its work it remains significantly and durably modern." Shaw, in his total contribution, lives up to Bier's appraisal.

Though Shaw dedicated himself as a man of letters to an upstart tradition that inevitably could not continue to arrest the attentions of the majority of readers in a rapidly growing, dynamic country, he was an artist who succeeded to a degree generally unrealized by literary posterity. The achievement of his humor alone is remarkable. Charles Dawson Shanly, a contemporary of Shaw's, points out the discipline and genius necessary to produce successful humor: "Great assiduity is a thing almost incompatible with humorous writing. The strain of always trying to be witty and epigrammatic on the surface, without losing grasp for a moment of the weightier considerations involved, is one against which few minds could contend successfully for long, continuous periods. . . ." Henry Wheeler Shaw's was one of those few minds. (pp. 132-33)

> *David B. Kesterson, in his* Josh Billings (Henry Wheeler Shaw), *Twayne Publishers, Inc., 1973, 157 p.*

ADDITIONAL BIBLIOGRAPHY

Benton, Joel. "Some American Humorists." In his *Persons and Places,* pp. 109-11. New York: Broadway Publishing Co., 1905.
    A vignette of Shaw's character and career.

Bier, Jesse. "'Literary Comedians': The Civil War and Reconstruction." In his *The Rise and Fall of American Humor,* pp. 77-116. New York: Holt, Rinehart and Winston, 1968.
    Highlights the shifting emphasis in popular humor after the Civil War, citing Shaw's work as indicative of the new trend.

Blair, Walter. *Native American Humor (1800-1900),* pp. 103ff. New York: American Book Co., 1937.

Includes scattered references to Shaw in an exposition of evolving American humor techniques and changing attitudes towards comedic material.

Clemens, Will M. "Henry W. Shaw ('Josh Billings')." In his *Famous Funny Fellows: Brief Biographical Sketches of American Humorists,* pp. 49-57. New York: John W. Lovell Co., 1882.
    Outlines Shaw's life and career, largely in the author's own words.

Cox, S. S. "American Humor: Part II." *Harper's New Monthly Magazine* CCC, No. L (May 1875): 847-59.
    A review of characteristic qualities of American humor that faults the "bad orthography and worse grammar" in the work of Shaw and others.

Dudden, Arthur Power. "The Record of Political Humor." *American Quarterly* 37, No. 1 (Spring 1985): 50-70.
    Addresses politically oriented humor over the last two centuries, naming Shaw among some of his well-known contemporaries.

Grimes, Geoffrey Allan. "'Muels,' 'Owls,' and Other Things: Folk Material in the Tobacco Philosophy of Josh Billings." *New York Folklore Quarterly* XXVI (March 1970): 283-96.
    Illustrates Shaw's distinctive use of collective folk objects and types.

Howe, Will D. "Early Humorists." In *The Cambridge History of American Literature,* Vol. II, edited by William Peterfield Trent and others, pp. 148-59. New York: G. P. Putnam's Sons, 1918.
    Contains a brief reference to Shaw.

Kesterson, David B. "Josh Billings on Lecturing and Humor: Some Recently Discovered Letters." *Studies in American Humor* I, No. 1 (April 1974): 23-7.
    Discloses some of Shaw's personal observations on humor and the nineteenth-century lecture circuit by examining previously unpublished correspondence.

Lukens, Henry Clay. "American Literary Comedians." *Harper's New Monthly Magazine* LXXX, No. CCCCLXXIX (April 1890): 783-97.
    A survey of American humorists since colonial times. Lukens styles Shaw a "heart-searching philosopher."

Matthews, Brander. "American Humor." In his *The American of the Future and Other Essays,* pp. 161-76. New York: Charles Scribner's Sons, 1909.
    Mentions Shaw in distinguishing American humor from that of other nations.

Pattee, Fred Lewis. "The Laughter of the West." In his *A History of American Literature since 1870,* pp. 25-44. 1915. Reprint. New York: Cooper Square Publishers, 1968.
    Admires the liveliness of Shaw's aphorisms but finds his more sustained work essentially flat.

[Thompson, Harold W.] "Humor." In *Literary History of the United States: History,* 4th ed., edited by Robert E. Spiller and others, pp. 728-57. New York: Macmillan Publishing Co., 1974.
    A short synopsis of Shaw's life and literary career.

Weiss, Harry B. "A Brief History of American Jest Books." *Bulletin of the New York Public Library* XLVII (April 1943): 273-89.
    Briefly mentions Shaw's work in tracing the evolution and popularity of the American jest book.

Juliusz Słowacki

1809-1849

(Also transliterated as Julius, Juljusz; also Slowacki) Polish dramatist and poet.

Słowacki is regarded as one of the greatest Polish romantic poets and dramatists. In his best-known works, the poems *Anhelli* and *Król Duch* and the dramas *Balladyna, Kordian,* and *Lilla Weneda,* Słowacki explored the course of Polish history, particularly the nation's subjugation and partition by other European nations. Intended to offer solutions to Poland's political problems, Słowacki's works convey his belief that independence could be won only through the cooperation of the Polish people and their spiritual purity. Słowacki successfully incorporated the influences of other writers in his works and, because he experimented with language and structure, he is now recognized as an innovative poet and as one of the founders of modern Polish drama.

Born in Krzemieniec in eastern Poland to middle-class intellectuals, Słowacki studied law at the university in Wilno, preparing for a civil service career. He was employed in Warsaw at the treasury department as a diplomatic courier when the 1830 November Rising occurred. Aimed against Russia, which had become the dominant political force in Poland, the movement failed the following year, and Słowacki, dispatched by the revolutionaries to London, found himself in exile. Residing first in Switzerland and later in Paris, Słowacki was supported by his mother and was therefore able to devote himself to writing and traveling. In addition to composing poetry and drama, he carried on an extensive correspondence with his mother, which critics now praise as some of the finest prose in Polish literature. During his years in exile, Słowacki became a friend and admirer of two other Polish émigré authors, Adam Mickiewicz and Zygmunt Krasiński, from whom he eventually became estranged because of philosophical differences concerning the restoration and character of a sovereign Poland. Few of Słowacki's works were published during his lifetime, and when he died, he was almost unknown beyond a small circle of friends and acquaintances.

Słowacki's works are frequently divided by critics into three groups: the early poetry, the middle dramas, and the late, messianic poetry. In his early poetry, which he wrote almost entirely after leaving Poland, Słowacki expresses his concern for his homeland and attempts to show the influence of its past on its contemporary problems; indeed, his strong desire for liberty is considered one of the hallmarks of his romantic style. His early poem *Lambro,* originally included in the collection *Poezye,* pessimistically depicts the story of a Greek leader who dies of a drug overdose, unable to help his people win independence. *Anhelli,* a symbolic poem about a group of exiles in Siberia, exemplifies his apprehension about the squabbles that jeopardized the unity of Polish émigrés. In this poem, Słowacki proposes that the sacrifice of a young man who is pure of spirit may lead to Poland's redemption; critics have viewed this aspect of *Anhelli* as evidence of Słowacki's belief that such elements of the Polish character as self-interest and an inability to act quickly contributed to the disintegration of Poland as a sovereign nation. *Beniowski,* one of Słowacki's most critically acclaimed poems, is a satiric look at romanticism.

He later began work on a dramatic version of *Beniowski* that remains a fragment. Inspired by Lord Byron's *Don Juan,* the poem ridicules the émigrés' ideas and plans to free Poland. Since their publication, Słowacki's poems have provoked extensive critical interest. In addition to noting the many influences that inform these works, including those of Byron, François René de Chateaubriand, Dante Alighieri, William Shakespeare, and Pedro Calderón de la Barca, critics have unanimously praised Słowacki's superb lyrical ability and his sensitive handling of the themes of loss and hope.

Słowacki's dramas are even more highly regarded than his poetry. Many critics consider him the founder of modern Polish drama, citing his *Marja Stuart (Mary Stuart)* as an important transitional piece. According to some commentators, in this work Słowacki broke from the neoclassical tradition and turned to romantic drama by emphasizing this historical character's psychological makeup. Several of his subsequent plays exhibit the same concern over Poland's future that is displayed in his early poetry. In *Balladyna,* a fairy-tale-like drama in which he skillfully combined tragedy and farce, he again sought to explain the fate of a nation. The tone of *Balladyna* is pessimistic and ironic, with destiny overturning human plans. Critics frequently note Shakespeare's influence in this play, which combines plot elements from *King Lear* and *A Midsummer Night's Dream.* Commentators view *Kordian,* which Słowacki intended to form part of a trilogy that he never completed, as his admonition to émigrés not to look for a particular leader to reclaim Poland for them. A psychological character study that centers around the Hamlet-like Kordian, this drama depicts a man paralyzed at a moment—the planned assassination of Czar Nicholas I—that demands quick action. Critics note that although the theme of *Kordian* is a warning against relying on a hero, the play's action centers around the evolution of the hero. In *Lilla Weneda,* Słowacki looked back to prehistoric Poland, treating the theme of a superior race's subjugation by an inferior, warlike tribe. Commentators contend that *Lilla Weneda,* with its affirmation of the survival of a culture, represents Słowacki's hope that Poland would triumph over its history of invasions and defeats. In assessing his dramatic works, critics commend Słowacki's innovations in point of view, his search for new dramatic structures, and his use of lyrical language.

Słowacki's last works display his new interest in mysticism, sparked by his short-lived association with the followers of the mystic Andrzej Towiański. In the transcendentalist poem *Genezis z ducha (The Genesis of the Spirit),* Słowacki set out the basic thesis of his projected epic *Król Duch,* in which he intended to present his philosophy of history and evolution. Although the whole epic cycle remains unfinished, some critics liken the work to Dante's *Divine Comedy* and judge it Słowacki's masterpiece.

Critical response to Słowacki's works has been largely laudatory. Scholars praise his poetic ability and his extraordinary control of language. Indeed, Słowacki's use of language is considered his greatest achievement: *Anhelli,* according to Francis J. Whitfield, was as central to the development of the Polish language as the King James Bible was to English. Focusing most frequently on *Anhelli* and *Król Duch,* commentators also note his ability to combine epic subjects, tragedy and comedy, realism, satire, mysticism, and psychological insight in his works. In addition, scholars point out that Słowacki's imaginative and innovative use of imagery, poetic symbolism, and fantasy anticipated the poetry of the French Symbolists and influenced the Young Poland authors, a neoromantic group of the mid-nineteenth century who championed Słowacki's works. His dramatic talent is widely praised, yet some critics contend that he weakened his dramas by imitating other writers or by subjugating character and plot to political concerns. Although only one was produced during his lifetime, many commentators insist that his plays are his greatest contribution to Polish romantic literature, and they are found in the repertoire of many modern Polish theater companies.

Today, Słowacki, together with Mickiewicz and Krasiński, figures as one of the most important poets and dramatists of Polish romantic literature. As the critic Julian Krzyżanowski writes, Słowacki is the "pure essence of Romanticism."

PRINCIPAL WORKS

Poezye. 3 vols. (poetry) 1832-33
Anhelli (prose poem) 1838
  [*Anhelli,* 1930]
Trzy poemata (poetry) 1839
Beniowski (poetry) 1841
Genezis z ducha (prose poem) 1844
  [*The Genesis of the Spirit,* 1966]
Król Duch (poetry) 1847

Mazepa (drama) 1851
  [*Mazeppa,* 1929]
W Szwajcarii (poetry) 1861
  [*In Switzerland,* 1953]
Balladyna (drama) 1862
Marja Stuart (drama) 1862
  [*Mary Stuart,* 1937]
Podróż na Wschód (Podróż do Ziemi Swietej z Neopolu) (poetry) 1866
Fantazy (drama) 1867
Lilla Weneda (drama) 1869
Mindowe (drama) 1869
Beatryks Cenci (drama) 1872
Horsztyński (drama) 1879
J. Slowackiego Ojciec zadżumionych (poetry) 1884
  [*The Father of the Plague-Stricken at El-Arish,* 1930?]
Kordian (drama) 1899
Złota czaszka (drama) 1899
Ksiądz Marek (drama) 1900
Sen srebrny Salomei (drama) 1900
Korespondencya: To jest Listy do matki i wszyskie inne (letters) 1910
Samuel Zborowski (drama) 1927
Dziela. 14 vols. (poetry and dramas) 1930
The Letters of Juliusz Słowacki to His Mother in the Years 1830-1842 (letters) 1965
Dramaty: wybór. 2 vols. (dramas) 1972
Dziela wybrane. 5 vols. (poetry and dramas) 1974

JULJUSZ SŁOWACKI (essay date 1836-37)

[*In his introduction to* The Father of the Plague-Stricken at El-Arish, *Słowacki described his stay at a quarantine area in the Sinai Desert, where he learned the tale that forms the basis for his poem. Słowacki's commentary was written in 1836-37.*]

In explanation of the following poem, I must needs say a few words of the quarantine in the desert between Egypt and Palestine, near the village of El Arish. Through some strange caprice Mohammed Ali has marked on the shifting sand an imaginary boundary between his two states; here he has forced the free Bedouins, under pain of death, to pitch their tents and to live for a fortnight under the oversight of watchmen and a doctor; otherwise they are forbidden to pass from Egypt to Syria. When travelling by camel I was forced to submit to the same fate. After a trip of eight days from Cairo I arrived at a gloomy, sandy valley, where I was doomed to tarry for twelve days. At first I could not comprehend how a desolate spot, strewn with shifting sand, without a single house, could be subject to human law; but the sword of the Pasha seemed to hang in the blue sky above the heads of my Arab guides, for when they came to the valley of the quarantine they at once made the camels kneel, and their dark faces expressed the deep submission of free men to the law of a dreaded ruler. A doctor arrived from the village of El Arish; that village was the first of which I had caught even a distant glimpse since leaving Cairo, and the doctor was the first man whom I had met. This physician was an Italian emigrant named Steble, and he had recently married a lady named Malagamba, a famous oriental beauty of whom Lamartine speaks with enthusiasm. He at once did his best to make comfortable my stay under the open sky. He provided several tents for our troupe; and, as I learned later, his wife's hands were buried in white and silvery flour in order that I might not lack European bread.

Settling myself within the tent, I gradually became accustomed to the gloomy scene that surrounded me. At some distance from me a brook, almost entirely dry, traversed the sandy valley on its way to the sea; beyond it was a grey fringe of palm trees; to the north the blue ribbon of the Mediterranean broke upon the sand and filled the quiet air above the desert with the dull murmur of its waves. And above the sea, on a pyramidal tumulus of sand, shone the white dome of the Tomb of the Sheik, which inspired terror, for in its vaults were laid the victims of the pestilence; its architecture and its yellowish white colour reminded one of a skeleton. In other directions rose sandy mounds, crowned with the tents of the garrison; from them guardsmen in gay oriental costumes kept watch over the quarantine. The centre of the valley was marked by a hillock that reminded one of a haystack, from which the muezzin in a piercing voice proclaimed the greatness of God each morn, evening, and night. All these pictures the reader will find reproduced in the following tale, and they will appear in their true light, for he will see them through human eyes. As for me, I grew wonted to my tent and enjoyed the quiet of the sandy plain and the roar of the sea, to the shore of which I was allowed to walk, if I took with me one of the quarantine watchmen.

On Christmas Eve . . . , when my thoughts had fled from this quiet desert to my distant country, and to the days of old that I had spent feasting amid my family, a terrific thunderstorm, blown from the Red Sea to the Mediterranean, burst by night and deluged with rain my isolated tent. My gloomy spirit, musing upon its own land, gradually became filled with terror. My tent, flapping in the wind and beaten by the rain, tottered above me; reddened by the lightning flashes, it seemed a fiery cherubin watching over a sleepless couch. The tempest had put out my light, and the damp wick could not be rekindled. Description is impossible, for this storm in the desert was of biblical majesty. I thought that the tempest had come which should waft me from the earth and bear me to the land of calm. Yet this sleepless night of dread passed by, and when at dawn I emerged from my tent, iron-grey clouds covered the sky and a fine rain darkened the air. But further fears were in store for me; the cries of the Arabs warned me of a new danger. The brook, which yesterday had been a mere thread of water trickling along its sandy bed, had become a roaring torrent, and with its silvery fins was fairly rushing to engulf the valley on which stood our tents. There were but a few moments to spare. With the help of the Arabs we carried our tents to the nearest sand mound, and immediately after our departure the water came and filled those circles of sand that remained in the valley as traces of the dwellings that we had torn up. Chilled and downcast, I gazed from on high at the triumph of that poor little brook, and while gazing I experienced a strange sensation. I was without roof, without fire, without food; I had suffered what amounted to a shipwreck on land; yet I could not betake myself to the village near by, where men were living, and ask them to give me the shelter of a roof or a seat by a hospitable hearth. And still more horrible storms might occur; the sea might come and swallow up the mound on which I was standing: and all this I must endure as best I could; I must survive or perish under the eyes of men who could not and dared not touch either me or my belongings.

Finally the sky cleared, and, taught by experience, I pitched my tent once more, not in the valley, but on the highest mound;

and upon the desert descended calm, serene days, which passed quietly by. My interpreter Sulaiman, famous and boastful because he had once been in the service of Champollion, Rosellini, Fresnel, and many others, told me various small details of the travels of his former masters, and probably gathered from me a store of petty observations with which he would divert future wanderers. In the evening this handsome, long-bearded Arab, seated on the ground at the entrance of the tent and illumined by the moonbeams that poured in between the flaps, would sing me strophes of Arabic poems, whose unintelligible sounds and mournful melody lulled me to sleep. And then—perchance the angel of sleep covered me with the cloak of a Crusader, and marked a red cross on my bosom, and transformed the Arab into a squire singing mournful ballads of his native land.

But enough of this mysterious dream of my life, of that golden plain, and of that tent where I had moments of calm; where, when I awoke, my eyes beheld between the opened flaps of cloth the constellation of Orion, so like a starry lute, hung by God over the poor tent of a wandering Pole. Enough of that quiet week of my life—it passed by. Again my camels kneeled before me and rose beneath the musing pilgrim, stretching out their long, snake-like necks towards the sepulchre of Christ. And when I was already an hour's journey towards the east, I turned in my saddle and gazed once more at my green tent; I beheld it on the mound and fancied that of its own will it had ascended a high place in order to bid me farewell. And whether it was merely the act of men packing their goods, or whether the tent itself, feeling that it no longer sheltered a traveller, pulled some stakes from the ground and waved its folds towards me, disclosing its black and desolate interior— I turned aside from that thing of which the heart was broken on my departure. Soon white lilies began to appear on the sand, announcing that I was approaching a more fertile region; and I reflected that, glancing at those very flowers, Christ had said to his disciples that they should take no thought for the morrow nor for the things of this world, but should consider the lilies, which God himself clothes.

Such is the description of the quarantine through which I passed in the desert; far worse was that endured by the old man who relates his misfortunes in the following poem. The story of his sufferings is not entirely imaginary; it was told me by Dr. Steble, to whom I would here record my thanks both for his tale and for his bread and for the courtesy that he showed me, if I were sure that these few words would find him in the desert. But what would he care for a memorial in an unintelligible language, uttered by a voice that hardly spreads as far as the circles raised by a stone cast in the water? (pp. v-viii)

> *Juljusz Słowacki, in an introduction to his* The Father of the Plague-Stricken at El Arish, *translated by Marjorie Beatrice Peacock and George Rapall Noyes, Eyre and Spottiswoode Limited, 1930?, pp. v-viii.*

PAUL SOBOLESKI (essay date 1881)

[Soboleski surveys Słowacki's works, assessing them favorably and claiming that no other Polish author had a ''greater power of fantasy.'' Soboleski's remarks were first published in 1881.]

Julius Słowacki tried his strength at all kinds of poetry. There are beautiful lyrics of his; others again are epics, and also dramas. In each and every one of these his creative mind shines with a resplendent luster. Everywhere he is new, fresh, and poetic; always exhibiting extraordinary strength, always soaring high.

For a long time Słowacki was not understood, although he was a poet belonging to all humanity; but some of his poems were not understood, and others did not come into general use. Almost thirty years had elapsed before the people could look into them and fully comprehend them. But as everything of the highest order will ultimately find its vindication with the people, so it was with Słowacki's writings; they at last found their deserved acknowledgment and justification.

Of all the poets from Krasicki to Krasiński, no one possessed greater power of fantasy than Słowacki. This was shown in a volume of poems written at the time of the Polish Revolution . . . , and since its fall. Another poem, *Zmija (The Viper)*, is also a fantastic production. But there is much higher and truer poetic merit in his *John Bielecki*. The subject is taken from the Polish Chronicles, partly oral, of a certain occurrence having taken place in eastern Galicia. Here the portraitures of the Polish nobility are striking, and scattered throughout the poem very happily, showing the greatest force, and with it the characteristics of his own individuality as a man of uncommon genius. [*The Father of the Plague-Stricken at El-Arish (Ojciec zadzumionych)*)] contains in it a power likening to the suffering of the Laocoon not carved in wood nor chiseled in marble, but in the painting of poetic genius. Among all the creations of Słowacki, nor in the whole Polish literature, is there anything that could equal it in finish, conciseness, power and truth, and finally the incomparable mastery in the diversification of the particulars of this awe-inspiring poem. What the statue of Laocoon or the groups of Niobe is in sculpture, *The Father of the Plague-Stricken* is in Słowacki's poetry. If it concerned the vivid representation of accumulated strokes of misfortune heaping thunderbolts upon the head of a doomed human being, weeping till its tears are dry, and moaning under the weight of misery until the last vestige of human feeling is gone; when it becomes a lifeless statue, unable to weep or feel more—to reflect over its unutterable misery—then surely Słowacki's design is fully accomplished.

Then comes "Hugo," tales of the Crusades, followed by *Balladyna*, and *Lilla Weneda*. The first one a beautiful epopee, not exactly in the Homeric style, but somewhat in the manner of Ariosto; prehistoric account of Poland is the subject. *In Switzerland* is a charming idyllic intermixed with tragic incidents, so abstruse and yet so truthful that it is not possible to find any such love-dream in any foreign tongue. Truth and fiction, reality and poetry, man's love and genius of the artist, all here strike hands to produce a poetic creation, and one knows not which to admire the most. In *Wacław* is a full confession of beautiful motives, such as are seldom to be found. This poem is equal to any of Lord Byron's in the masterly carving out of each particular. "The Arab" and "The Monk" are also wrought in an artistic manner. *The Silver Dream of Salomea [Sen srebrny Salomei]* seems to be only a dramatized tale concerning two different pairs of married people, who, in order to accomplish the desired end of being united in marriage, have to wade through a sea of misfortunes and fears caused by national troubles, which so ruthlessly passed over their devoted heads. It is for that reason that the poet called it "The Romantic Drama." The tragedy *Mindowe* is one of the latest of the poet's productions. In this tragedy the incidents relate to the times when Lithuania had not yet the light of christianity. It represents the renegacy and the return to the faith of his sires of Prince Mendog. The tragedy *Mazeppa* is full of tragic in-

cidents, and of vivid and passionate poetry; where the most delicate shades of human nature are wrought up to perfection. The background of *Kordyan* is the age, which, from the very beginning, the poet reproaches and chastises for its dwarfishness, condemned to pass away as unworthy of mention. The poet here creates a character which is too exalted, and outgrew the littleness of the spirit of the present generation. He feels keenly the misery of this life, and desires to fill it with something more noble, and hence throws himself about, here and there, to attain the desired object. Słowacki's *Kordyan* unites almost all the characteristics of greatness and the contempt of life—ready for all sacrifices, desire for fame, bravery and noble pride.

In the historical drama *Maria Stuart* the frame of the picture is tolerably narrow. It was not the intention of Słowacki, as it was of Schiller, in the tragedy of the same name, to draw within the confines of it the whole history of the given epoch, but for all that there are in it splendid passages that enchant the reader. The verse is flowery and masterly, and his language sparkles with diamonds of the first water. The epopee *Lambro* proves Słowacki's great power of fancy and a great gift of poetical invention. The subject is taken from Greek history, that is to say from the last part of it of last century. He tries to represent a hero endowed with every necessary condition, and to excite for him the wonder and admiration of the reader, whereas it is discovered that from under these artificial coverings appears a man full of moral corruption—the more unpleasant to the eye since it is plainly seen that he comes out with gigantic pretentions which nothing can justify.

It being impossible for our poet to travel all the time in the realms of poetic fantasy of the past, and hearing the subterranean moanings and weeping of the people, he created, with a power at once charming and genial, *Anhellim,* where the infernal regions of Siberia take a shape of strange illusion which makes it beautiful and fearful, dismal and at the same time enticing. In this production the poet gives a portraiture of the fate of the whole people, and a review of their relations which we suffer for the guilt of others, as also of transgression of which we ourselves are guilty. It was the poet's fancy to call a Siberia the whole of our social condition. The doctrine advanced in *Anhellim* is turbid and fantastic,—it loses itself in the unfathomable depth of mysticism, and is written in biblical style. In *Bieniowski* one is reminded from its construction of Byron's *Don Juan,* but in spirit it resembles the creations of Ariosto. The poem uncovers to the reader the bloody wars toward the end of the last century, in which Poland has manifested her patriotism, which are shown by various drifts in the poem. Here, in imitation of an English bard, Słowacki marks strongly his own individuality. Besides the strophes marked by deep moral feeling, colored mostly by the poet's fancy, we find others in which is seen a most extraordinary power of language in form, and unlimited bitterness of feeling. This powerful poem by turns causes tears to flow, astonishes, cheers up the public, and moves their passions. Being deeply engaged in the investigation of questions beyond the comprehension of human understanding, brought about by Towiański (a votary of whose doctrines Słowacki became), it engrossed his mind to such a degree that in his last composition their influence is obvious. It is plainly seen in his *Priest-Mark [Ksiądz Marek],* a drama in which the character and stamping of the Jewess Judith answers exactly the conception of Towiański's sect as regards the mission of the Jewish people. From the plot and characters introduced it is evident that the poet was intent upon the conquering of the evils of the world, and the erecting upon their ruins of a great epoch of the future for the people and for humanity itself.

The Spirit King [*Król Duch*] was the first great national epopee in song wherein the author puts aside the veil and presents to view his grand philosophical thoughts in regard to his country; and in order to legitimize it the author gives us to understand that he thoroughly comprehends the long sufferings of his nation; and we further infer that the poet knew the way to solve the problem of the nation's future destiny. The author makes this production an offering upon the altar of art for humanity, but not for the real interest of a perishable generation. *The Spirit King* displaces but does not divide the vital parts of his country. His plan comprehends the eternal future, history corroborates it; the present bears witness to it, and the future will demonstrate its truth. All of Słowacki's works possess a powerful feeling, exalted thoughts, and stormy passions. Oftentimes he pours out to the world the bitterness of his heart; but above all his fancy is so active that his mind and feeling can hardly keep pace with it.

It is not to be wondered at then, that he reaches with so much tenderness the hearts of the Polish youth. He was their songster and their spiritual leader. The spirit of youth, like the gentle breezes of spring, breathes from every one of his songs. The age of dreams, the inward emotions of the soul, and sudden but noble impulses, permeate each of his creations. (pp. 273-78)

> Paul Soboleski, ''Słowacki,'' in Poets and Poetry of Poland: A Collection of Polish Verse, *edited by Paul Soboleski, second edition, Knight & Leonard, Printers, 1883, pp. 272-80.*

JOHN W. CUNLIFFE AND ASHLEY H. THORNDIKE (essay date 1896)

[*In reviewing the poems and plays of Słowacki, Cunliffe and Thorndike assert that while the author was more pessimistic than his contemporaries, he surpassed them in imagination and in the richness of his language.*]

During the period of his official bondage in Warsaw [Słowacki] produced his early Byronic tales in verse: ''Hugo,'' a romance of the Crusades, ''Mnich,'' (''The Monk''), *Jan Bielecki*, ''The Arab,'' etc. They are distinguished by boldness of fancy and great beauty of diction; but their gloomy pessimistic tone ran counter to the prevailing taste of that still hopeful time, and the day of their popularity was deferred until renewed misfortunes had chastened the public heart. Two dramas belong to the same period,—*Mindowe* and *Mary Stuart*. The scene of the former is laid in the ancient days before Christianity had been established in Lithuania; the latter challenges comparison with Schiller's play, and surpasses it in dramatic vigor. It is still a favorite in the repertoire of the Polish theatres.

Słowacki delighted in powerful overmastering natures: it was the demonic in man that most appealed to him; and that element in his own nature during the turbulent days of 1830 and 1831 burst forth into revolutionary song. His fine ''Ode to Freedom,'' the fervid ''Hymn to the Mother of God,'' and the ringing martial spirit of his ''Song of the Lithuanian Legion,'' stirred all hearts, and raised Słowacki at once to the front rank among the poetic exponents of the Polish national idea.

When in 1832 Słowacki settled in Geneva, a new period in his literary career began: he emerged from the shadow of Byron, and his treatment of life became more robust and earnest. Unconsciously his Kordjan came to resemble Conrad in the

third part of Mickiewicz's *Dziady* (*In Honor of our Ancestors*). The first two acts of this powerful drama are still somewhat in the Byronic manner, but the last three acts are among the finest in the whole range of Polish dramatic literature. The theme is patriotic: the hero plunges into a conspiracy at Warsaw to overthrow the Czar; but at the critical moment the man is found wanting, and because he puts forth no adequate effort he miserably fails. This dramatically impressive but morally impotent conclusion reveals the ineradicable pessimism of the poet's mind. Kordjan is of that irresolute Slavic type which Sienkiewicz has so mercilessly analyzed in *Without Dogma*. To this same period of Słowacki's greatest productivity belong the two splendid tragedies *Mazepa* and *Balladyna*. In *Mazepa* is all the fresh vigor of the wind-swept plains; it has a dramatic quality that reminds of Calderon, and maintains itself with unabated popularity upon the Polish stage. *Balladyna* is the most original of all the poet's creations. Shakespeare superseded Byron; but the master now inspired and no longer dominated. *Lilla Weneda*, of later date, was the second part of an unfinished trilogy, of which *Balladyna* was the first; the design of the whole was to recreate the mythical traditions of Poland. On this ancient background is portrayed the conflict of two peoples; and it is characteristic of the poet that he allows the nobler race to succumb to the ruder.

It was during Słowacki's Swiss sojourn also that he wrote one of the finest lyric gems of Polish poetry, *In Switzerland*. In it he immortalized the Polish maiden who for too short a time ruled his wayward nature in a brief but beautiful dream of love. In Rome in 1836 he met Krasinski, to whose lofty inspiration his own soul responded. During a trip in the Orient he wrote his deeply pathetic poem *Ojciec Zadzumionych* (*The Father of the Plague-Stricken*). Upon this doomed man, as upon Job, is heaped misfortune on misfortune until human capacity for suffering is exhausted, and the man becomes a stony monument of misery. There is an overwhelming directness of presentation in this poem that suggests the agony of the marble Laocoön. It surpasses Bryon at his best.

In 1837 Słowacki rejoined Krasinski in Florence, and under his influence wrote in Biblical style the allegory of *Anhelli*. It is a song of sorrow for the sufferings of Poland and her exiled patriots; but it loses itself at last in the marsh of mystic Messianism into which the masterful but vulgar Towianski lured many of the nobler spirits of Poland, including Mickiewicz. Krasinski resisted, and the two friends were separated. Słowacki and his greater rival were stranded on the shoal of Towianism. The works which he had written in Switzerland he began to publish in Paris in 1838; but *Beniowski* was the only work of art that he wrote after that time. This is a lyric-epic of self-criticism. His works thenceforth were water-logged with mysticism, and do not belong to the domain of art. In *Król Duch* (*King Mind*) this madness reaches its height. (pp. 13509-10)

Słowacki surpassed all his contemporaries in the magnificent flights of his imagination, and in the glowing richness of his language and imagery. His dramas are among the chief ornaments of Polish literature; and his beautiful letters to his mother should be mentioned as perfect gems of epistolary style. His contempt for details of form and composition seems sometimes like a conscious defiance of the recognized requirements of art; but the splendid exuberance of his thought and fancy ranks him among the great poets of the nineteenth century. He was keenly alive to the faults and failings of his countrymen, as is shown in his *Incorrigibles* [*Fantazy*]; but in the temple of Polish fame his place is secure at the left of Mickiewicz, at whose right stands Krasinski with the 'Psalm of Sorrow' in his hand. (p. 13510)

John W. Cunliffe and Ashley H. Thorndike, "Julius Slowacki, 1809-1849: Critical Essay," in The World's Best Literature, Vol. 22, Charles Dudley Warner, John W. Cunliffe, Ashley H. Thorndike, eds., 1896. Reprint by The Warner Library Company, 1917, pp. 13508-10.

GEORGE BRANDES   (essay date 1903)

[Brandes, a Danish literary critic and biographer, believed that literature reflects the spirit and problems of its time and that it must be understood within its social and aesthetic context. Brandes's major critical work, Hovedstrømninger i det 19de aarhundredes litteratur, won him admiration for his ability to view literary movements within the broader context of all European literature. In the following excerpt, Brandes praises Słowacki's "great gift of language," but contends that the imitative quality of his work dilutes its impact.]

[Slowacki's] strong imagination was, in its essence, not so much creative as musical, picturesque, and decorative. In fact, his talent was a great gift of language. He impresses by the melody of his verse and his wealth of imagery. (p. 254)

In the first as in the later poems which he publishes, his poetry shows a basis of agony, a frame of mind apparently induced by a vision of annihilation.

Naturally, with him as with other poets his mood depends mainly upon the harmony which exists between an artist and his public. Wherever such a sombre seriousness has mastered all minds as that which fell upon the Poles after the unsuccessful revolution, a poet simply to be heard, in order not to be pushed aside as a buffoon who misunderstands the common temper, must necessarily in his art reflect suffering, discontent, wrath at terrestrial or celestial injustice, and depict numberless unsuccessful attempts to prevent wrong, or at least to avenge outraged right. He does it because generally he is subject to the same influences as his people, receiving all impressions far more keenly and sympathetically.

This disposition appears in its most abstract form in such works as Slowacki's *The Plague in the Desert* [*Ojciec zadżumionych*], which is justly celebrated as a tragic description of a calamity recalling that of Niobe. . . . This narrative, which, in contrast to several others by the author, has not a line too many, but is characterised by an antique severity and Biblical grandeur, has obtained such high recognition, not only because of its artistic excellence, but because of its harmony with the melancholy of its readers. More than one found the picture of his own trials and losses in the poem. With a vague feeling that there was a certain bond, a certain point of union between the subject and the reader, commentators have endeavoured to give a symbolical explanation of the episode, seeing allusions to the loss of their fatherland, and their grief thereat, only to be arrived at by the most far-fetched interpretations. The truth is that without any symbolism whatever, the reader might well see, in the family visited by the plague, a group of beings whose fate was akin to his own.

Slowacki's "Arab" is a poem of the same character. It depicts the abstract mania for annihilation, the Satanic desire to spread death and destruction, and destroy the joy of life, wherever it is found. The being, who from an ambush shot the arrows of the plague against the unfortunate Arab father and his children, might be supposed to have such thoughts.

Nevertheless there is more here than the mere poetry of suffering. The poetry of cruelty is combined with it, a theme which recurs again and again. Slowacki especially revels in the description of horrible cruelty. It came near home. For these poets had experienced great cruelty in their lives, and fancy is receptive above all things; it gives out the pictures with which it has been filled. The cruelties with which all Slowacki's dramas and most of his narratives swarm, betray how deep an impression the tortures he experienced in his life, or had heard or read about, made upon his mind. Several of the fiercest traits of cruelty in his poems are founded on actual historical incidents. Ivan the Terrible, like the leading character in *Król Duch,* on one occasion nailed the foot of a messenger to the ground with his sword, without diverting him from the delivery of his message, just as happened with the old bard in the poem. And the prototype of many such traits in Slowacki must be sought for in contemporary events, which made his blood boil and inflamed his fancy. (pp. 255-57)

The Hamlet nature plays a . . . rôle in the character of Slowacki. He was wild and gentle, unruly and ivy-like, in life clung to his friends, in art to predecessors, lived not with his whole person, but with his head, in his ideas and his fancy. His imagination is richly coloured and melodious, decorative and sonorous, but he is wholly lacking in the plastic sense. It is on this account that Krasinski's advice to him is so excellent: "Put granite under your rainbows."

Practically, he was greatly influenced by his consciousness of rivalry with Mickiewicz. His poetical writings are mainly governed by this. In the history of the Middle Ages we read of anti-popes. Slowacki belongs to the race of anti-popes. His real originality is that of form. So far as characters and fundamental themes are conerned he is almost wholly limited by the models he imitates, and the rivals he strives to outstrip or contradict. Thus we can trace all the more plainly the general tendencies of Polish literature in his receptive nature. (p. 272)

It is neither their robustness nor their independence that will enable Slowacki's productions to defy time. It is true that, in religious respects, he is more liberal, in political, more audacious, than his great rivals, but he is so as much from a spirit of contradiction as from conviction. No one is more brilliant than he. He has the genuine Polish love for show and colour, he for whom the divine was symbolised by the plume in the helmet. But if he has the Polish love for pomp, he has, above everything else, the common Slavic faculty for imitation. In almost every one of his works we are distracted in our enjoyment by the recollection of a very definite exemplar.

The manner in which he appropriates Shakespeare is slavish; his *Balladyna,* a blending of *Midsummer Night's Dream, King Lear,* and *Macbeth,* in which beautiful single passages and profound scenes are to be found, but in which the elements are inharmoniously adjusted to each other, leaves a painful impression as a whole, in spite of the boldness of certain conceptions. He has utterly ruined his treatment of the tragedy of *Beatrice Cenci* [*Beatryks Cenci*], supplanting the study of the human soul by a long drawn-out romantic dance of witches, a mere dilution of the witch theme, treated with the judicious reserve of the master in *Macbeth.* His *Cenci* is far behind Shelley's much earlier and more admirable version of the same theme, with which Slowacki was evidently not acquainted, otherwise he would have imitated it. His *Mary Stuart* is more independent and characteristic. It follows, almost act for act, the same portion of the life of the Scottish Queen, afterwards treated by Björnson and Slowacki's Mary, as a character, is more interesting and more important than Björnson's, while the treatment as a whole is more lyrical.

Slowacki was perhaps too much taken up by himself to become properly absorbed in humanity before he described men. He studied human life less than the works of Byron, Shakespeare, Mickiewicz, Krasinski, and finally Calderon. So he drew figures half living, half dream-like; characters of which some fragments are true, others incorrect, and concealed the weakness of the drawing by throwing the rainbow glow of his diction over it. His style is bold and eloquent but seldom closely knit. Its strength and weakness is its overwhelming richness of colour.

There is no bird which in strength of wing and power of flight can rival the eagle. Fitly is it called the king of birds. There is no bird which, in unblemished whiteness and quiet dignity of movement can rival the swan. Fitly is it called the symbol of noble purity. The peacock cannot fly like the eagle, nor sail like the swan, but neither of them can come near it in the incomparable splendour of its plumage.

Mickiewicz is the eagel, Krasinski the swan, Slowacki the peacock among the winged spirits of Poland. (pp. 280-81)

> *George Brandes, "The Romantic Literature of Poland in the Nineteenth Century (1886): Points of Contact in Polish and Danish Literature," in his* Poland: A Study of the Land, People, and Literature, *William Heinemann, 1903, pp. 192-310.*

ROMAN DYBOSKI (lecture date 1924)

[*Surveying Słowacki's dramas, Dyboski argues that his interest in Polish political history became dominant over his interest in character and plot. Dyboski also discusses the influence of Shakespeare, Calderón, and Mickiewicz on Słowacki's style, noting his great lyrical power and ability to combine tragedy and fantasy.*]

Modern Polish comedy rose, in the work of Fredro, to a height never attained before and not equalled since. (p. 83)

No such absolute perfection can be said to have been reached by Polish serious drama in the works of any of its masters. Efforts in this domain have been more numerous and more varied, ambitions higher and more intense than in the field of comedy. But most of the efforts are too closely connected with the literary tendencies of a particular group and period to produce anything of lasting value, and high ambitions rarely go together with exceptional creative gifts. The long array of nineteenth-century dramatists shows some figures respectable enough as writers, but devoid of dramatic power, some popular enough in their day on the stage, but ephemeral in their literary quality. And one feature is present almost throughout—a strange unfamiliarity with the elements of stage-craft. This is partly to be ascribed to the abnormal political condition of Poland, which made constant contact with the theatre impossible for many writers, but partly also to the national tradition of an agricultural country, whose educated class were country gentlemen living in scattered manors and rarely gathering in towns. The absence of a highly developed town civilization, such as France has had ever since the late Middle Ages and Poland lost before their close, accounts, perhaps more completely than any other circumstance, for the fundamental weakness of Polish drama.

Finally, one more factor must be considered. The moments of high dramatic emotion in nineteenth-century Polish life, such as may inspire a playwright, have in general been associated with the dramatic fate and history of the nation itself; and events

in which a community as a whole is the agent or the sufferer hardly lend themselves to effective treatment in dramatic form. Their magnitude makes them rather fit for epic poetry or for prose, the strength of the collective feeling accompanying them induces lyrical eloquence rather than dramatic restraint. Hence it happens that much of the best dramatic work of Poland in the nineteenth century, strongly national as it necessarily is, shows epic rather than dramatic structure, and is all of it highly lyrical in expression.

The Polish drama of a hundred years culminates in two poets—Słowacki at the beginning and Wyspiański at the end of the era—and it is a disputed point of criticism whether both are not lofty singers rather than great dramatists. At any rate, the irresistible appeal which their works make, even on the stage, is the musical and imaginative appeal of splendid verse, addressed to emotions wherein the individual soul is absorbed and effaced, rather than the personal and human interest of pity and terror. And where that is stirred by spectacles of personal conflicts, trials, and sufferings, the thought of the great background of national history again and again diverts the poet from the portrayal of his individual figures, and the voices of the weavers are drowned in the roar of the great loom of Time.

The above description certainly applies to most of the mature work of Julius Słowacki, and gives the clue both to his grandeur as a poetic prophet and to his deficiencies as a theatrical writer. It was, indeed, a purely personal drama, though in political guise, which he had in his mind's eye when he wrote a tragedy on Queen Mary Stuart; but the childish characterization and primitive dramatic technique of this beautiful, inspired, and promising, but very youthful attempt absolve us from dwelling on it. Again, when in his later years, he turned to another foreign theme and wrote a tragedy on the Shelleyan subject of **Beatrix Cenci** [**Beatryks Cenci**], he had fallen too much under the spell of the highly-coloured and rhetorical style of Victor Hugo. Under that author's influence he strives to pile up horrors and to rack the nerves too much for high and pure artistic effect. Of the works produced in the heyday of Słowacki's dramatic genius, between his early inexperience and later exaggeration, there is one only which can be said to attain anything like unmixed dramatic perfection, and which does so largely in consequence of the utter dissociation of a personal and domestic theme from the broader aspects of national history. This is the tragedy of **Mazeppa**, recognized by the verdict of generations of the Polish public as supreme in dramatic excellence among the productions of Słowacki, quite as *Macbeth* stands in this particular respect supreme among those of Shakespeare. **Mazeppa** is a tragedy of the causeless but unappeasable jealousy of a young wife's old husband, and of the unhappy love of stepmother and stepson. Although the scene is laid in the Polish seventeenth century and a king is an important character in the story, **Mazeppa** is as free from emphasis on political events as *Othello* from association with the wars and policy of the Venetian republic; in this and other points it resembles *Othello* by its severe artistic economy, directed wholly and exclusively to dramatic effect. There is the same paucity of characters, and these are placed in the same strong relief; the real innocence of the chief actors and victims is as complete, and human characters, seemingly sane and free, are compelled to their actions by the fascination of the same relentless fate. There is in both an overpowering pathos in the ruin of noble creatures trapped by circumstance; and the figure of the king in **Mazeppa,** though less villainous than that of Iago, exhibits the same mixture of normal human motives with the inexplicable promptings of evil.

In his later years, the poet repeated the theme of an old husband's jealousy in another powerful play, *Horsztyński,* where its pathos is heightened by the old man's blindness. But by this time his interest had become so absorbed by the great events of national history, that in this second treatment the personal drama is intertwined with an affair of State—the high treason of one of Poland's great nobles at the time of the partitions. The blending of a private theme with public history is perhaps more successful in this than in any other drama by Słowacki. Altogether, the play is one of his grandest conceptions, and it is much to be regretted that it remained unfinished. It is in prose, and therefore more natural in its dramatic realism, but by no means devoid of both loftiness of idea and tender poetic charm. Its only blemish lies in some rhetorical conceits and melodramatic effects after the manner of Victor Hugo.

Next in popularity on the stage to *Mazeppa* there stand two poetic plays by Słowacki, which do not share its austerity of dramatic outline and economy of speech, but, on the contrary, abound in lyric ornament, variety of episode, complication of dramatic action, intricacy of characters, and wealth of imaginative detail. They are the two which were completed of a series of six, planned to illustrate the legendary history of earliest Poland. The conception was suggested by Shakespeare's plays from ancient British history and fable—*King Lear, Macbeth, Cymbeline;* and the two tragedies of Słowacki, named after their heroines, are almost overloaded with Shakespearian detail, which sometimes, however magnificently poetic its Polish garb, calls forth a smile of recognition from the lover of Shakespeare. The first play, *Balladina,* the tragedy of a criminal and ambitious Queen, is essentially a Polish *Macbeth;* the second, *Lilla Veneda,* the tragedy of the devoted daughter of an unhappy deposed old king, may be called a Polish *King Lear.* But besides fundamental resemblances to these two great Shakespearian models, both dramas are full of echoes from the fantastic world of the *Midsummer Night's Dream* and *The Tempest.* There is in one of them a fairy queen, like Shakespeare's Titania, haunting the shores of a romantic lake, attended by twin elfin spirits like Puck or Ariel, and falling in love with a 'hempen homespun', a coarse and ordinary mortal, like the Shakespearian Bottom. The tragedy of *Balladina,* with its heroine modelled both on Lady Macbeth and on Regan and Goneril, is dominated by personal passions and has little political background; it is therefore nearer in dramatic force to *Mazeppa,* and the part of its heroine is as much a goal for the ambition of the tragic actresses of Poland as that of Lady Macbeth herself. The second play, *Lilla Veneda,* with a heroine who is a worthy sister of Shakespeare's Cordelia, is less of a personal drama: it is full of the catastrophe of a nation conquered by invaders; the old unfortunate king is at the same time a harper, like the nebulous figures of the old Celtic kings in Ossianic poems, and the fate of the falling nation is bound up mystically with the harp played by the king. With this national theme and its poetic symbolism, lyrical emotion intrudes irresistibly into the dramatic structure, and the poet's melodies attain their greatest power in the declamations of the chorus. These explain the allegory and convey to the audience that the wonder-working harp is the life-giving poetry itself of enslaved Poland, the poetry of Słowacki and his two great brethren Mickiewicz and Krasiński.

If Słowacki was under the spell of Shakespeare in his earlier poetic plays, he came, in his later work, under the no less

potent spell of another great magician of the drama—the Spaniard Calderon. It was the growing religious mysticism which marked the later days of all the great Polish Romantic poets that brought Słowacki under the influence of this greatest worshipper of Spain's grand Catholic tradition and led him to rival the chivalrous exaltation and torrential flow of the Spaniard's four-stressed verse. The Polish poet translated, or rather paraphrased with noble inspiration, one of Calderon's masterpieces, the tragedy of *The Constant Prince,* who returns to die in Moorish captivity, as Regulus returned to Carthage, because he had pledged his word to do so. Henceforth, the diction of Słowacki's plays framed itself in the rushing, unceasing flow of Calderon's trochaics, and mystic raptures and miraculous events were freely interspersed among authentic facts in dramas taken from eighteenth-century Polish history. The armed rising against Russia which preceded the first partition—the heroic partisan warfare of the 'Confederates of Bar'—became the poet's favourite subject both for drama and epic; these men had defended the Roman Catholicism of their country against invaders of another faith, and the poet, a democratic Radical himself, found their simple piety one of the chief attractions of their exploits. Here was indeed a theme to call forth all his new-found spiritual enthusiasm, and two of his verse plays are aglow with it. One [*Father Mark (Ksiądz Marek)*] has for its hero Father Mark, the great preacher of the Polish Confederate Army: his sermons are rendered in magnificent cascades of verse, and miracles attest the spiritual strength of his cause. In a second, *The Silver Dream of Salomea* [*Sen srebrny Salomei*], it is the heroine, an exalted visionary and seer, who becomes the vessel, or rather the lyre, of the poet's own mystic ecstasy. The drama centres round the terrible massacre of Polish gentry by Ukrainian peasants shortly before the first partition, and, as is not infrequent with Słowacki's plays, it is steeped in the horrors of its theme; but the stream of his trochaic cadences carries even physical horrors into a realm of beauty, and the noble figure of the Ukrainian Cossack, Sava, who faithfully stands by the old Polish civilization of his country, fascinates by its sublime idealism.

For a third time Słowacki drew from this favourite sphere a play, *The Golden Skull* [*Złota czaszka*], which has unfortunately survived only in fragments. It charms us by the central figure of a Polish knight, without fear and without reproach, by Christmas scenes from a devout old Polish home, and by a delightfully naïve Christmas carol in old-fashioned, half-Latin rhymes. Here again, in all likelihood, as in *Lilla Veneda* among the plays from pre-historic Poland, it is the poet's ever-throbbing lyrical vein which would have predominated, had the play been finished, rather than that of dramatic movement.

The excellences of a fourth play from the same sphere—happily complete—are again emphatically of a lyrical order. The *New Deianeira,* or *The Incorrigible Ones* [*Fantazy*], has held many a Polish audience spellbound. . . . [Its charm] is breathed by two most poetical, though slightly ironic characters—Count Phantasus and Lady Idalia—who weave the gossamer of their imagination round melancholy dreams and delicate tendernesses. To see them impersonated by an actor and an actress endowed with the subtle spirit of poetry is to fall in love for ever with these two embodiments of Romantic sentiment.

Poetic acting also brings out the theatrical possibilities of an earlier verse drama by Słowacki, mention of which has been deferred to the last because its literary character places it outside the roll of his other masterpieces. This is *Cordian,* announced as the first of a cycle of three plays, and written by Słowacki in jealous emulation of *The Feast of the Ancestors,* the mystical and patriotic poem of the greater Mickiewicz. Słowacki shows his superior capacity for true drama by choosing for the central theme of his play, not as Mickiewicz did, a symbolic popular ceremony, but a very real political conspiracy of 1829. The work is, however, less a dramatic structure than the story, in the form of a string of changing scenes, of the hero's psychological evolution. It carries us with this Byronic youth first abroad, to Italy and London and the summit of Mont Blanc; it then shows him, awakened to a sense of his life's mission, organizing a conspiracy against the Tsar, who is to be crowned King of Poland in Warsaw; and finally shrinking from crime and breaking down on the very threshold of the deed. We are left in uncertainty whether this Polish Hamlet dies or is reprieved; and what we have are isolated scenes, many of them masterly in the sword-play of pointed dialogue, in the fire of powerful speeches, and in the rendering of the impulses and confusion of blindly-moving crowds.

Here once more, as in so many other dramatic works of Słowacki, poetic excellence and powerful effect are focused in jewels of lyrical expression, such as the short and passionate song of a nameless conspirator whose allusive promptings stir the crowd on coronation day. Similar gems add lustre to many of the dramatic fragments which in profusion strew the field of his poetic work, and are too numerous and disjointed to be recorded systematically by any but a devoted bibliographer. Some of these unfinished or lost dramas, like two of the finished masterpieces, were drawn from early Polish legend; one had the Scottish hero William Wallace for its subject; another, the two ancient kings of Sparta, Agis and Agesilaos. In most of them, even in one taken from Polish legend (*Krakus*), the influence of Shakespeare has been traced: the king of dramatists never ceased to exercise his fascination over the Prince of the Polish Stage, although this fascination became latent in the period of Słowacki's mystic fervour.

We have beheld in Słowacki something akin to the meteoric figure of Shakespeare's great predecessor Christopher Marlowe: a dramatic poet of Titanic passion and force, but having in him a source of lyrical melody which pours its stream of music through nearly all his dramatic fabric. We have also seen how the power of national feeling, which throughout his career preys on his very being like a fever, struggles victoriously for the mastery with the born dramatist's interest in individual character and personal story. (pp. 84-91)

> Roman Dyboski, *"Modern Polish Dramatic Literature,"* in his Modern Polish Literature: A Course of Lectures Delivered in the School of Slavonic Studies, King's College, University of London, *Oxford University Press, London, 1924, pp. 67-103.*

M. SZYJKOWSKI (essay date 1926)

[*Szyjkowski explores the historical and literary influences on Słowacki's work.*]

[Słowacki] wrote two historical tragedies, one of them *Mindowe,* consecrated to a subject taken from the history of Lithuania; the other to the youth of Mary Stuart, the queen already immortalised by Schiller and Alfieri. These two pieces already show the great dramatic talent of their author, assuredly the greatest dramatic talent Polish tragedy has ever known. Above all *Maria Stuart,* written in Shakespearian mood, contains scenes which exhibit a passion as high as it is sincere. (pp. 392-93)

Słowacki possessed a nervous, sensitive, frail organism, he was devoured by measureless ambition and social questions left him indifferent. His inner tendency to "Hamletism" was mingled in him with a certain disposition to melancholy. As an ardent patriot, he was full of desire to work for his country. As a poet, he possessed to a high degree the subtle sense of poetical form, a wonderful impressionability which he translated into picturesque words, full of colour, of music, of harmony.

Such are the characteristics of the creative genius of this great solitary.

His ardent craving for glory was only realised after death: posterity granted him a place among the greatest poets of the nation. Realising the words of a friend (Krasiński), he really shines as an eternal rainbow over Mickiewicz's granite statue! He really represents the necessary complement to the full expression of the Polish national genius.

Słowacki's talent shines with all its radiance, when, after having left Paris, he lived for many years in Switzerland on the borders of the lake of Geneva. It is there that he wrote his most beautiful lyrical poems, there, that under the spell of the beauties of the Swiss scenery, he conceived many artistic ideas, which he later expressed, such as the masterpiece: *In Switzerland.* On the wonderfully harmonious background of lake and mountains, the golden thread of a love tale unrolls itself. He does not forsake dramatic works. This Polish Shakespeare worked in the most unfavourable conditions, far from his country, never seeing any of his works on the stage. But his conceptions were gigantic. Only an exceptional theatrical intuition could create works, which, to-day still live on the Polish stage, full of most palpitating interest. Excited by the reading of *Konrad Wallenrod* and of the *Ancestors,* Słowacki began an autobiographical trilogy but only finished the first part: this dramatic poem called: *Kordian,* notwithstanding many weaknesses, contains scenes of absolute beauty. Shakespeare's work tempted him to write a dramatic cycle, whose subject was inspired by the legends of Poland. He left two tragedies of this kind: *Balladyna* and the *Lilla Veneda.* He did not trouble much about historical truth, not even about the logical unfolding of facts, as he himself avowed. In writing his "dramatical chronicles" he relies on his own literary recollections and on the inexhaustible wealth of his fancy.

Master of the spoken word, and a born dramatist, he builds scenes full of genius, sounding, at will, the pathetic note, hastening or slackening the tone of the dialogue. In *Balladyna* appears a whole fairy-world, so subtle and ethereal that, even compared to the *Midsummer Night's Dream* it loses nothing. In the *Lilla Veneda* he revives the choruses and, in a most subtle way, introduces a lyrical element, personified by the magic harp, and brought to its apotheosis in the character of his heroine. The Polish "Antigone", at the same time priestess and victim, is one of the most beautiful women-characters in all literature.

During his stay in Switzerland, Słowacki undertook many other dramatic works; he only completed a few and left the others unfinished. Let us, first of all, mention: *Mazeppa.* The historical period to which Mazeppa belongs does not appear clearly, though the characters of this tragedy belong to the history of Poland in the XVIIth century. The whole tragedy rests on complex love-problems, the character of the heroine reminds one of Desdemona. (pp. 393-94)

[It] is, above all, thanks to his journeys to Greece, Egypt and Palestine, that Słowacki's spiritual life grows and expands. (p. 394)

He brings back with him poems of unique beauty, amongst which a description of his journeys, under the form of a poem in "octaves".

Never before had this poetical form been used in Poland with such gorgeousness. We must also mention the masterpiece of elegiac poetry named: *The Father of the Plague-Stricken* and other poems, to say nothing of sketches of vaster works.

These manifold conceptions gave birth to an important work, different from all the poet had yet produced. It was the outcome of long meditations in the solitary hermitage on Lebanon, meditations, thanks to which, the poet ripened inwardly and deeply examined what had up to that time, been his attitude towards national work.

It was for him of first rate importance to justify his attitude towards the nation. What benefits could the nation receive from the solitary efforts of his artistic creation? The nation needed action. Słowacki was not, like Mickiewicz, born for political action. He well understood that his work enriched the national treasure of Beauty—but this assurance no longer satisfied him. Like all great romantic writers, Słowacki was inclined towards mysticism, when still very young, he studied Swedenborg's theories and his books. He believed in presentiments and in premonitory dreams. Meditating on the road he had followed in his life, he discovered there a deep sense: silent and passive sacrifice for the good of his country. Sincerely and deeply he believed it, believed that such a sacrifice could be effective.

He expressed this idea in the form of a biblical poem, recalling, as to form, the *Books* of Mickiewicz. The subject of the poem, called: *Anhelli* has for its frame the ice-land of Siberia, where the banished Polish exiles live. In this land of cold and darkness, lighted only by the sinister dimness of the aurora borealis, Słowacki showed the sufferings and the dissensions of Polish emigrants. Each picture breathes of deep sadness, as do all the incidents in the lives of this handful of unhappy men.

The prose, in which this story is told, is wonderful. Never could its rhythm and the strength of its descriptions be sufficiently admired. Such melancholy is also found in some pages of the work of Dante. Even the final prophecy of delivery cannot attenuate this sadness, which shrouds in black veils the Siberian poem.

At the end of the year 1836, Słowacki establishes himself definitively in Paris. He begins then the rich literary production of recent years, which included not only the works of which we have just spoken, but shorter poems and less perfect works. At that time his fecundity was remarkable.

Unceasingly, he composed new dramatic works and poems, which, generally, he does not complete. These fragments mostly published after his death, make one think of the heads of the statues of Phidias and are to be admired for the daring boldness of the chisel and the immaculate purity of the colouring. The unfinished poem *Beniowski* (the Polish *Don Juan*) shows a masterly artistic technique. Fragments of dramas such as *The Incorrigibles* [*Fantazy*] and the *Golden Skull* [*Złota czaszka*] show new characteristics in the dramatic talent of Słowacki. He read much in different languages. When at Florence, he was interested by the talent of Calderon, especially by the *El Principe Constante*. He reproduced this Spanish tragedy in wonderful poetry and transformed the subject according to his

will. This transformation of a Spanish drama of the XVIIth century into a romantic Polish tragedy is really a unique work of its kind.

The author of *Anhelli,* the transformer of the *Indomitable Prince* could not escape Towiański's influence. He gets connected with the new teaching as closely as Mickiewicz.

He undergoes inner transformation, forsakes earthly ambition and gets reconciled with Mickiewicz. But he did not follow blindly the teaching of the "Master". He accepted what already existed potentially in the sphere of his own belief and of his own feelings. But he adds much, not being in sympathy with the methods of activity of the "Towianists". (pp. 394-95)

Under the unceasing strain of all his mental faculties, he wrote dramas, sketched new poems, and undertook the execution of gigantic conceptions. He was dying, but pen in hand, leaving fragments of a grand unfinished epic, called: *The King-Spirit* [*Król Duch*]. The subject is gigantic. It would be difficult to find one akin to it, in the whole of universal literature. It was based on the idea of Re-incarnation and described the successive incarnations of the Creative Spirit, the Leader of the Polish nation. He hoped to show in this poem the historiosophical mission of Poland. The poet was allowed to finish only the narration of the first incarnations. They are fragments of untold power, marvellous paintings, expressed in octave stanzas of wonderful perfection.

He died before reaching his fortieth year. Like Mickiewicz he sacrificed himself to the Polish cause; like his great colleague, he confounded this cause with that of humanity. He died early, broken by the ungrateful struggle to establish the Kingdom of God on earth. He was as he beautifully expressed it: "the pilot of a boat laden with spirits".

Particularities of his genius account for the fact, that, to-day, for modern Polish poets, it is Słowacki and not Mickiewicz, who is the adored Master and Model. But history, the "corrector of life", does not establish any comparison between these two lofty beings. It will set them both on the same level as two different expressions of Poland's national genius. And it will say of Słowacki, that he was, in the world's literature, one of the great Masters of the Word. (p. 396)

> *M. Szyjkowski, "Romanticism and Contemporary Literature," in* Polish Encyclopaedia: The Polish Language, History of Literature, History of Poland, Vol. I, *edited by The Editorial Committee of the Polish Encyclopaedia, Edition Atar, 1926, pp. 371-480.*

Z. SZMYDTOWA   (essay date 1929)

> [*Szmydtowa notes Dante's influence on Słowacki's work, asserting that Słowacki assimilated Dante's idea of love but modified his concept of hell.*]

There were several excellent reasons why the fascination of Dante should not be lost upon Polish Romanticism. To exiles he appealed as an exile, to patriots as a patriot; hearts inclined to mysticism acclaimed in him the visionary; minds steeped in the Catholic traditions felt his attraction as the great Catholic poet. The exaltation of Woman, by Dante, had its counterpart in the Romantic cult of love. (p. 292)

[The] influence of Dante was reflected in the love-poem: *In Switzerland,* by Julius Słowacki. Here an exquisite paraphrase of the episode of Paolo and Francesca, ending however on the

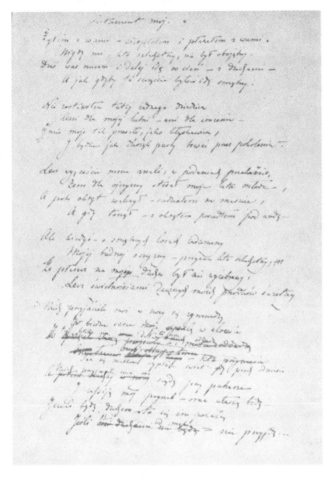

A page from the manuscript of Słowacki's "My Testament."

idyllic note, is a conscious adaptation of that fragment of the *Divine Comedy* and possibly of Byron's translation of it.

The love story develops on the lines of the theory of love laid down by Dante in the *Vita Nuova.* The beloved of the poet, as visualised by him, seems to be scarcely a creature of this world; it is as if she were an ethereal being walking the earth only for a while before she returns to her heavenly home. Like Beatrice, she is modest, angelic, a saved soul. She possesses a charm to which man and nature are sensible. Love suddenly overcomes the poet. At first it is rapture and contemplation, and then adoration and prayer. His bliss makes him almost lose consciousness. An emotion so absorbing and rare has for its ever-prsent shadow the fear of some catastrophe overtaking the lovers—such a fear as haunts the couple in the *Vita Nuova.* And in both poems the catastrophe actually comes, though we are not told of the fact, but it is revealed by the bitter sorrow into which the lovers are plunged, lamenting their dead loves. The pain of that loss is expressed, as in Dante's poem, by tears, by a clinging to despair and a yearning for solitude and death. There is, moreover, a similarity in composition between *Vita Nuova* and the Polish poem, which consists of twenty-one fragments resembling canzones or sonnets.

The spell of Dante's poem has not however affected the originality of Słowacki's own poetic conception, carried out through a wonderful series of love episodes, ranging from pure transports to sensual ecstasies, and projected against the background of the Swiss mountain scenery. In the sensual element lay the

cause of the catastrophe. The problem was, therefore, different from that presented in the *Vita Nuova;* and it was given a different artistic solution. What was of Dante in this poem was its emotional key and the adoption of the Dantean theory of love by the Polish author. (pp. 293-94)

The idea of earthly Hell and Purgatory has inspired two works by Julius Słowacki. One of them, **"Posielenie"** (**"The Settlement"**) has remained a mere fragment, the other, *Anhelli,* is a prose poem of Siberia, the land of exile.

In **"Posielenie"** the poet planned to introduce the figure of Dante as a guide through the earthly Hell and the Hell beyond. In the first he was to depict the sufferings of the Poles, in the second—the punishment meted out to their Russian oppressors. Finally, however, he gave up the idea, and beyond sketching a detailed plan for the work, wrote nothing except two fragments in *terze rime,* stating his relation to Dante and announcing that he was to describe wanderings though regions beyond the world.

More fully the idea of an earthly Hell was developed by him in *Anhelli.* The title gives the name of the youth who, under guidance of one Szaman, king of the Siberian people, passes through the land of the exiles, sharing their lot until he dies, a pure sacrifice for the nation's future. Szaman shows him more sympathy and friendliness than Virgil bestowed upon Dante, for Anhelli is a truly angelic soul, anxious to suffer with the sufferers without any fault of his own. The dire, strength-consuming labours of the Polish exile; the agony of the father who, like Ugolino, had lived upon his sons' bodies when pressed by a loose boulder to the rock in a mine; the dead who asked about the living and vanished into their graves again upon hearing heart-breaking news—these themes are decidedly in keeping with the tradition of the Dantean Hell.

In keeping with it, too, is the colour scheme of the Siberian mines. Grey, black and flaming red are dominant. The mellow and soothing star-influence is another transposition of a motive borrowed from the *Divine Comedy,* though the colour-scheme is here much enriched in the process. Despite analogies in scenes of suffering and the tendency to transpose the Dantean Hell into earthly surroundings, the prevailing note is gentle— a gentle sadness; and white is the dominating colour effect throughout—an effect characteristic of the Siberian plains and also suggestive of Anhelli's purity of soul. The land of exile being conceived symbolically, there is hardly an air of reality about it; it is the idealogical aspect that is stressed throughout.

Life changes into a Hell for Wacław (Wenceslas), the personage from whom another poem by Słowacki has been named. It is, however, one of Słowacki's less important works. Wacław, the traitor to the national cause, is a victim to abominable sufferings, and yet manages to preserve some qualities of greatness—like some mighty sinners among the damned of the Dantean Hell.

Suffering, which in the conception of a Hell on earth bears no relation to guilt, has been the dominant motive in many of Słowacki's works. The tragic gruesomeness of such themes as the extinction of a whole family or of a whole nation, Słowacki himself associated with the Dantean conception of Hell; but in their treatment he was entirely independent of the Italian master, and these works of his show no reminiscences of the *Divine Comedy.* (pp. 296-97)

[Słowacki's] poem *Poema Piasta Dantyszka o piekle (Piast Dantiscus's Poem of Hell)* . . . was a deliberate attempt at a grotesque. Dantyszek, an average representative of the mass of Polish gentry, is held up to satire. He is an object both of sympathy and irony on the part of the author, who occasionally puts into his mouth some of his own reflections and remarks. This incongruity appreciably contributes to the grotesque effect of the work. Słowacki's plan was to lend a Dantesque air to a fantastic satire on the Tsarist Russia. The torments to which the Tsars are subjected in hell remind one of the *Inferno,* though bathos is frequently achieved owing to the irreverent outbursts of Dantyszek. He slashes at enemies of his country with his sabre, and flings before him the heads of his dead sons, to ensure himself free passage. His impatient, violent nature prevents him from finishing his journey at God's throne. There is a lack of reticence in this poem which makes the scenes of sufferings abominable reading, and a complete disregard of all probability. The effects have been exaggerated. The work is in places absolutely repulsive; in others it contrives to make a powerful patriotic appeal.

Once more did Słowacki invite comparison with Dante, but this time it was when his own genius rose to the supreme heights of poetical power in the poem, gigantic in every sense of the word, *Król-Duch (King Spirit).* In this mystical biography of the King Spirit of Poland, capable of incarnation in the leaders of the nation, Słowacki discarded the idea of a trichotomous structure of the world beyond. Sufficient to him then to believe in the purifying power of suffering. He rejected the dogma of the existence of Hell. Consequently, there is no eternal punishment for the heroes of his poem, though every guilt has to be redeemed with suffering. It is not physical pain that is inflicted as it was in the *Divine Comedy*—the torments are spiritual; it is the loss of all energy and capacity for action coupled with a keen perception of the effects of the wrong done. A few slight traces of the Dantean influence are to be noticed in the imagery of the poem.

To sum up, the influence Dante exercised on Polish Romanticism was reflected in several tendencies. There was the conception of a terrestrial Hell and Purgatory, where Poland's sufferings were in the nature of expiation. This was the most popular idea. Further there arose the longing for a terrestrial paradise, which sought expression in visions of the days to come. Prayers were written in which meditations on truths, religious and patriotic, were an important feature. Nearest by their subjects to the Italian model came two poems: the one about Dantyszek in hell, and the other about the three regions of the world beyond, as seen through peasant eyes. Complementary to the Dantean poem was a series of Norwid's works, treating of Earth and Man. The really worthy counterpart of the *Divine Comedy,* in Polish Romantic literature, was Słowacki's poem: *King Spirit,* otherwise but slightly related to Dante's work through minor resemblances of artistic detail. (pp. 303-04)

> Z. Szmydtowa, "Dante and Polish Romanticism," in The Slavonic Review, Vol. VIII, No. 23, December, 1929, pp. 292-304.

GEORGE RAPALL NOYES (essay date 1930)

[*In this excerpt from his introduction to the first English translation of* Anhelli, *Noyes asserts that Słowacki deliberately wrote a symbolic interpretation rather than a realistic depiction of Polish political struggles. Noyes also traces the various literary influences on the work.*]

In *Anhelli* . . . Słowacki pictures with tender sympathy the sufferings and miseries of the Poles, but at the same time he

scourges their weakness, their folly, and their disunion. The present generation must pass away before Poland can be restored. After that he sees a chance of relief only in a democratic revolution thoughout Europe. Unlike Mickiewicz, Słowacki gives little direct moral counsel. Yet he proffers the hope that *possibly* the sacrifice of a sinless victim, even the poet Słowacki himself, represented by Anhelli, may be a means for the redemption of Poland.

Such is the fundamental idea of *Anhelli,* an idea congenial to the romantic school of poetry, and to the nervous, self-centred character of Słowacki himself. The conception is, of course, of Biblical origin: Anhelli, though unconscious of his high destiny, is to die that Poland may be redeemed, just as Christ died that He might bring salvation to mankind. In the words of Caiaphas: "Consider that it is expedient for us that one man should die for the people, and that the whole nation perish not" (John xi. 50). But we need not assume that Słowacki arrogantly compared himself to Christ. He was probably more directly inspired by a passage in [Chateaubriand's *Les Natchez*]. . . . [As] in *Anhelli,* great emphasis is laid on the personal purity of the victim.

The interest and charm of *Anhelli,* however, lie not so much in the intellectual opinions and theories held by Słowacki as in the poetical imagery with which he clothes them, or rather which he allows to flutter about and conceal them. Słowacki's poetry was the culmination of the romantic spirit in Polish literature. Though Słowacki was profoundly influenced by Byron, of whom he is the chief disciple in Poland, he was by temperament far more akin to Shelley. In *Anhelli,* as in *Prometheus Unbound,* there is a firm underlying idea, and this poem, like Shelley's, would be of far less worth if it lacked its intellectual substructure; but in each case the idea is hidden rather than illustrated by the wealth of ornament heaped about it. To trace the idea in plain prose may for some readers even spoil the impression of the poem. So Shelley's *Cloud,* to make our illustration almost grotesque, contains reasonably exact meteorological information, but it would be absurd to call it didactic poetry; its imagery, "of imagination all compact", gives it poetic beauty. *Anhelli* deals with the destinies of Poland, but as an imaginative fantasy it should appeal even to readers who know little of Poland and have only a distant interest in its destiny. Its atmosphere is symbolic rather than allegorical; Słowacki's method was not so much to formulate a moral and historical theory and then devise a story that should illustrate it, as to create poetic images that prove capable of symbolic interpretation, sometimes definite, sometimes vague and indistinct.

The scene of *Anhelli* is laid among Polish exiles in Siberia. For his description of Siberia and its inhabitants Słowacki, who had never been in the country, drew somewhat on literary sources, but his picture has few traits of reality. His Siberia is a snowy waste, suggested to him mainly by the view of Mont Blanc from the window of his boarding-house in Geneva. The action of the poem takes place mostly under a sky lighted only by the stars or by the flickering aurora borealis. This Siberia is but a symbol of the state of the Polish people, and above all of the Polish exiles, whether they be in Siberia or in France. It is noteworthy that only three Polish names occur in the poem, and these (Kimbar, Lach, and Piast, all in minor positions) are such as do not clash with the fanciful names of the main characters, Anhelli, Eloe, and Ellenai, which may have been modelled on the equally fanciful name of Elsinoe, the heroine of the drama *Iridion,* by Słowacki's friend Krasiński. Thus Słowacki throughout his work carefully avoids any pretence at realism. (pp. 12-15)

Literary influences are prominent in *Anhelli*, as they are in all Słowacki's poems. As might be expected from a work written in the Holy Land, and after earnest reading of the Bible, a Biblical atmosphere prevails. The idea of *priest* (Shaman) and *victim* (Anhelli) is of the Old Testament; that of *teacher* (Shaman) and *disciple* (Anhelli), of the New Testament. The Shaman is a distant reflection of Moses; Anhelli, of Christ Himself.

The influence of Dante is also important. Słowacki had once planned and begun to write a poem to be composed in *terza rima*, like *The Divine Comedy*, in which Dante should guide him through the Polish Hell. The fundamental conception of *Anhelli* is the same, though the form of the work is altered. Certain details are also borrowed from Dante.

Eloe, the angel of pity, is taken from the poem *Eloa* of Alfred de Vigny, though she also represents in certain ways Ludwika Sniadecka, whom Słowacki had loved in his early years. The conception of Anhelli as a poet victim may also be inspired by Vigny. To quote Kleiner:

> The sacrifice of Anhelli is of a somewhat different sort from the typical religious sacrifice. It is no ordinary martyrdom. It is a boundless absorption of his own woes and those of others, then an isolation not brightened even by hope, and finally a death before the day on which his ideals shall begin to be realized and the worth of his life shall be made plain.

> This is a special sacrifice, the tragedy of the poet, of whom Alfred de Vigny has said that he must be solitary and unfortunate, that he has a curse on his life and a blessing only on his name, that he must cherish no hope during his lifetime.
>
> (pp. 16-17)

For the suggestion of the episode of Ellenai, Słowacki seems to have been indebted to *Le mie prigioni (My Prisons)*, by Silvio Pellico, rather than—as has hitherto been supposed—to the story of Mary Magdalen in the Gospels. In his prison at Milan, Pellico was cheered by the singing of his neighbour Maddalena, a woman whom he regards as a penitent sinner; later, in his prison at Venice, he was comforted by the compassionate girl Zanze, daughter of his jailer. Verbal resemblances are sufficient to show that Słowacki had read Pellico's book with attention. Yet Ellenai may also owe something to Eglantine Pattey, ''the daughter of the keeper of the boarding-house in which Słowacki lived in Geneva. She loved the poet with the same quiet, shrinking love with which Ellenai loves Anhelli, and this love consoled the poet in his longing for his native land, just as the love of Ellenai consoled Anhelli'' (Ujejski). Thus in Ellenai, as in Eloe, Słowacki may have blended his reading with his personal experience. (p. 17)

In 1839, writing to his friend Gaszyński concerning a projected French translation of *Anhelli*, Słowacki explains that such a version would require an introduction and extensive notes:

> The notes should be an interpretation of the work. *Anhelli*, like Dante, requires a commentary, for I purposely wrote it with concision and with great economy of detail. Therefore if the reader does not work with his imagination on every phrase of *Anhelli*, everything in it will

be pale; for the literature of the present day is defective through its extreme fondness for enlarging on every point and bestrewing everything with false diamonds. Hence the imaginations of readers have gone lame, and are lazy.

The poet then explains certain historical and personal references in the poem, but admits that some of them are by no means exact.

Anhelli, however, is far from being a mosaic of suggestions from other writers, and of cryptic allusions. Like Shakespeare and many other great poets, Słowacki borrowed from his reading whatever pleased him. Like all great poets, he transformed by his own individuality whatever he borrowed, and fused all the elements of his work into an harmonious whole. Słowacki's friend and brother poet Krasiński, on hearing of his death, wrote that his grave should be marked with the inscription, *To the Author of 'Anhelli'*: ''This alone will suffice to secure his fame to future generations.'' And in truth, despite its obscurity, *Anhelli* has already charmed three generations of Poles by its imaginative suggestiveness. Some portion of its beauty may remain even in a translation. (pp. 17-18)

> *George Rapall Noyes, in an introduction to* Anhelli *by Juljusz Słowacki, edited by George Rapall Noyes, translated by Dorothea Prall Radin, George Allen & Unwin Ltd., 1930, pp. 11-18.*

JULIAN KRZYZANOWSKI   (essay date 1930)

[*Krzyzanowski details the author's philosophical development and its impact on his work, asserting that Słowacki exchanged his youthful pessimism for his later belief that the spiritual is embodied in all creatures. In addition, Krzyzanowski analyzes Słowacki's interpretation of history and assesses* Król Duch *as "the best and finest expression [of] the idealistic aspirations which animated [his] contemporaries." For additional commentary by Krzyzanowski, see excerpt dated 1969.*]

[Słowacki] began his literary career at the moment when Romanticism in Poland was already established, *i.e.* six years after Mickiewicz had published his fundamental *Ballads and Romances*, and at the very moment when *Conrad Wallenrod* was in the press. Thus, it is no wonder that the young adept of poetry entered the field of literature with the Romantic flag in his hand. It was typically Romantic material that arrested his attention and stirred up his imagination; and he began with tales concerning, sometimes the battles of Lithuania and the Knights of the Cross, and sometimes Oriental adventures. The first inspiration he owed to Mickiewicz, the second to Lord Byron. Taken as a whole, the juvenile works of Słowacki were, and really may be considered as curious instances of Byron's influence on Polish literature, and even the Polish mentality of the younger generation of those days. It is clearly evident in Słowacki's characters, clearly reproduced in his tales. They all are rebels fighting against their Fate and making war on Society, mysterious criminals who find no other alternative than to persecute their fellow creatures because they themselves never met with anything but persecution. (pp. 115-16)

Already in the period spoken of, *i.e.* in his first literary works, Słowacki, starting from this pessimistic point of view, had successfully tried to consider its consequences with regard to his own epoch and contemporaries. In this way he broke the narrow boundaries of problems which were of rather an egotistical nature, and gave voice to his relation to social and national problems. The bridge between these two groups of problems is represented by his Greek verse story called **Lambro.** In it he dealt with contemporary history, that of Greece's fight for independence. The main character of this story [is] Lambro, a Greek chieftain, fought against the Turks the oppressors of his country, until, disappointed with the pettiness of his contemporaries, he shut himself up in the mountains. Although he was considered the heroic leader of his nation, he could not find in himself the strength needed for the conditions of life, and he died prematurely, intoxicated with hashish. Słowacki considered his story an illustration of the average mentality of his age. In his opinion the curse of individualism hung over his contemporaries, it bade them waste their spiritual strength in dreams, and forbade them victory in their fight against the evil hidden in their life. This particular case, as expressed in **Lambro,** explains better the roots of the young poet's pessimism. It was the consequence of his overgrown imagination, regulating his attitude both as an artist and a man towards his life and everything he met with. His fantasy compelled him to seek after wonders which were not to be found in everyday life, and this resulted in continual disappointments, which he felt the more painfully because his imagination again bade him see in these very disappointments a new source of further sufferings. (pp. 117-18)

[In] his works published after his return from the East, one finds something unexpected, real men and real life, though veiled in the fantastic atmosphere of wonder. This is evident in a large group of poems published in the years 1838-41, such as **Three Poems (Trzy Poemata), Piast Dantyszek's Poem on Hell (Poema Piasta Dantyszka o Piekle), Anhelli** and **Beniowski.**

Słowacki, who in his earlier works had remained under the strong influence of contemporary writers such as Chateaubriand and Byron, who confirmed him in his pessimistic views, found in course of time another master and guide whose importance was to him considerably greater, and who taught the Polish poet to combine both the natural and the supernatural into a perfect whole. It was Dante—and Słowacki never concealed his gratitude to his mediaeval patron whose *Divine Comedy* became his beloved book, a sublime source of contemplation and even inspiration. Dante's art, consisting of the masterly combination of both elements, the earthly and heavenly, his skill in depicting real men with their passions, their everyday aspirations, their crimes and, at the same time, in showing their relations to the unseen powers from on high, corresponded with Słowacki's own artistic ideals, and therefore taught him to seek for human motives even in the supernatural.

The beneficent results of this reconciliation with reality, caused by both these factors, the poet's Eastern journey and Dante's influence, can be noticed in Słowacki's later poems. It is evident not only in his **Piast Dantyszek,** in the very title of which (Dantyszek meaning Dantiscus, an offspring of Dante) already Słowacki expressed his attitude to the great Italian poet, but even in his **Three Poems.** These form a cycle, though their subjects have nothing in common with each other. The poet's previous pessimism had turned into a wonderful mist of melancholy, veiling men and their adventures. The first of them, one of the masterpieces of Polish poetry, called **In Switzerland,** is a love-story. The contents of it cannot be reproduced; one may even say, there are no concrete contents in it at all. In stanzas full of charming melody the poet narrates the plain story of two human beings who have fallen in love with each other, beginning with the moment when they first meet up to the sad hour when the lover is compelled to leave Switzerland and his bride's grave. There are no names in the poem, and

yet the characters and their background, Nature, are clear and exact, and—above all—clear and exact is the melancholy history of two unfortunate hearts. One is used to compare Słowacki's idyllic poem with works like Shelley's *Epipsychidion,* for the method of the writers is analogous; it is pure music, appealing not to the reader's imagination but to his feelings, bidding him share the lovers' fortunes and misfortunes.

The Romantic writers loved Nature and delighted in reproducing its beauty and its charms; the best evidence of which may be found in *Pan Tadeusz,* with its pictures of Lithuanian fields and forests. But in Słowacki's idyll there is no picturesqueness; he is no painter, he does not care about rich colours, and yet one feels, when reading **In Switzerland,** the unique beauty of the Alps. He represents them as if he saw them in a dream; they are near and real, and yet unreal, like a dreamer's vision. The union of both these elements, of the truth of the human heart and the beauty of Nature, is, perhaps, the most striking feature of Słowacki's poem and its highest artistic value.

It must be added that there are very few poems in European poetry which are so difficult to translate into other languages, because of their perfect and unique literary form, as this **In Switzerland.** A prose translation of it is unthinkable; it would lose its original character; and an equivalent translation could be made only by a poet of the first rank, able to render all the soft charms with which Słowacki endowed his work. That is the reason why **In Switzerland** has been, is and probably will always be unknown outside Poland.

The idyll **In Switzerland,** in one of its episodes, contains a distant reminiscence of a story in the *Divine Comedy,* that of Francesca da Rimini; the subject of the next part of the **Three Poems,** called **The Father of the Plague-stricken (Ojciec zadżumionych),** may be compared with the famous canto on the disasters of Ugolino. Słowacki created here a modern Laocoon, an unfortunate Arab who has lost his numerous family in a pestilence; one after another his sons and daughters have died before his eyes, and he is compelled to endure his misery to its full extent. The story, related by him, contains a series of sad pictures, based on the same theme, that of death. The poet evidently was in danger of repeating the same, or at least analogous events; yet, following the same principles which he used in his **Switzerland,** he softened the realistic picture by means of the special pathos with which he coloured his poem. It is a sorrowful father who tells us of his plague-stricken children; a certain length of time between him and his misfortune permits him to overcome his sufferings; his resignation gives a peculiar softened effect to all his memories; they are the lyric tunes that allow him—and also the reader—to accept his story, which—at the same time—loses all the cruelty of actuality, so impressive in Dante's narration of the tragedy of Ugolino d' Arezzo. All these high artistic qualities are absent in the third and last of the **Three Poems,** called **Waclaw.** Its subject Słowacki found in Poland's history and poetry; it deals with the dreadful death of a Ukrainian magnate, a traitor haunted by remorse of conscience, a desperate criminal who can find release neither in life nor after death. The naturalistic method of dealing with this subject, obviously learned from Dante's *Inferno,* proves rather disadvantageous both in **Waclaw** and in the parody of Dante, **Dantyszek's Poem on Hell.** Harsh naturalism was thoroughly foreign to the elfish imagination of Słowacki. It had to be mixed with idealistic and fantastic elements to be able to express the poet's true attitude towards the world. And it is **Anhelli,** a poem in prose, that bears evidence of the importance of the unity of both these elements.

So far Słowacki's poems are of a universal nature, *i.e.* their relation to the Polish national life of the period is vague; they contain (except *Dantyszek*) no political elements, though these elements found their expression in Słowacki's dramas written contemporaneously. His further two poems, however, are of quite a different nature; they are as closely connected with the emigrant life as were the works of Mickiewicz; for both *Anhelli* and *Beniowski* owed their existence to the fact that Słowacki tried to solve the problems which each Polish emigrant was compelled to solve, concerning the more important questions of to-day and of to-morrow. (pp. 118-22)

Mickiewicz, who warned his countrymen against vain expectations of foreign help, bade them rely upon themselves and develop heroism in their souls, for it was heroism which he considered a guarantee of the deliverance and greatness of his free country. Słowacki did not share these views, for he could not. Everywhere he saw weakness and pettiness among his contemporaries, and he decided to tell them the truth about themselves. *Anhelli* was to express this hard and pitiless truth. But he did not wish to produce a political pamphlet of the kind represented in Mickiewicz's *Books;* his schemes were greater and, from the artistic point of view, higher. He chose the form of a vision like Dante's *Divine Comedy.* He introduced Siberia, that vale of tears to Poles, into his poem. (pp. 122-23)

We are to understand that Siberia means the contemporary Europe; the dark places of torture may be considered to represent Russia and her prisons; but if so, the views of Słowacki concerning the future of his nation would seem quite sad and hopeless; *Anhelli* would represent the utmost degree of the author's pessimistic outlook. This conclusion, however, is untrue. Słowacki's pessimism, which he could never fully abandon, had been partly cured during the poet's Eastern journey; he had spent a night at Christ's grave in Jerusalem, contemplating the merits of Our Lord's life and death, and had learned to appreciate the mysterious value of sacrifice; these new opinions allowed him to find deliverance, to get rid of despair in his views upon the future of his nation.

Thus the exiles in his fictitious Siberia pérish; there perishes even the best amongst them, Anhelli, though his soul is untouched by the crimes of his countrymen. But there is something that remains. It is Anhelli's chastity, the beauty of his character, his love of his country, his self-immolation for the cause of his brethren, which he leaves behind and which is to become a guiding star for the coming generation. The ideology formed by the exiles is right, and is to prove victorious, though owing to their weakness they are unable to live to see the moment of its realization; even Anhelli, the best representative of their group, dies before the moment of victory; and yet— the poet maintains—the victory is inevitable. In this way the solution of earthly and everyday problems is transferred to the realm of ideas. (pp. 124-25)

[The] highest merit of *Anhelli* consists in its symbolical form; written in Biblical prose, it is based—like *In Switzerland*—on elements musical rather than picturesque. The poet's method of employing symbols instead of reproducing real life rendered good service to his work. To a person who possesses the key which enables him to penetrate the "political" meaning of some episode or other, *Anhelli* appears as a reflection of life at a certain period of Poland's history; to a lover of poetry seeking for the poetical it represents a masterpiece of pure poetical inspiration—like Dante's *Divine Comedy,* the readers of which, even if they are not experts in the mediaeval history of Italy, can enjoy its permanent beauty.

The last of the poems published shortly before the mystical period in Słowacki's life and poetry, called *Beniowski,* though quite different from *Anhelli,* for it is a masterpiece of realism, is much more difficult to understand. It needs comment and explanation in conformity with the very nature of the poem. Its plot is thin and does not bear inspection. (pp. 125-26)

Still, the plot forms only a bare skeleton of Słowacki's epic, and is its least important element. For, like Byron in his *Don Juan,* Słowacki produced in *Beniowski* a peculiar kind of epic poetry combining different elements—epic and lyric, general and personal, tragic and comic. (pp. 126-27)

[The] example created by Ariosto's *Orlando Furioso* and by Byron's *Don Juan* seemed sufficient to justify the blending of the epic subject with lyric excursions, the more that such a medley allowed the Polish poet in a wonderful manner to give vent to his indomitable fantasy and, at the same time, to settle accounts with his numerous antagonists. The latter point was, perhaps, the most important, and hence the satirical elements that entered largely into the exquisite stanzas of *Beniowski* changed the poem into a gallery of literary and political caricatures of the poet's contemporaries. (p. 127)

However, [Słowacki's] satire, though apparently personal throughout—that is the reason why *Beniowski* requires so many commentaries to-day—was actually impersonal; that is, it hurt, not individual people, but the ideas represented by them, or rather the permanent human folly which found expression in them. (p. 128)

Broadly speaking, *Beniowski* became the very mirror of the poet's personality, showing it both in its attitude to the external world and in its most intimate interior life, and must be read by everyone who wishes to penetrate to the very core of both the man and the writer. (p. 129)

The painstaking and untiring literary activity, so profoundly characteristic of the last years of Słowacki's life, produced two works in which the poet set out his views on God, the World and Man in his peculiar and unique manner. They are so important, so many-sided and far-reaching, that they form the climax not only in Słowacki's production, but also in that of the Romantic generation in Poland; accordingly, they deserve a more detailed investigation than the earlier works of the poet. (p. 151)

Słowacki, who in his young years was an agnostic, saw the main principle governing the world in some blind and irrational power which aimed at destroying human happiness, both in individual and in social life. His outlook was hopelessly pessimistic, and its tendency is easy to detect in the greater number of his works. One must remember, however, that in time Słowacki endeavoured to release himself from the spell of pessimism, and he succeeded. He found a strong support in his new experiences gained during his Eastern voyage, which taught him to appreciate the real in the world surrounding him, and at the same time awakened in his soul the lively desire for religion. The solitary life of an exile and the influence of Towianski's religious personality helped Słowacki to create his own world of religious ideas, which was to become the groundwork of all his later poems.

The poet's independent and revolutionary mind could not be satisfied with second-hand opinions, borrowed from his friends or from the books which he came across; his mentality pushed him to form his own system in which he could entirely express his attitude to the Universe, to Humanity, to his Nation and to himself. His thought and imagination, once set in motion, accomplished a difficult task in arranging the construction of ideas, by means of which he finally arrived at the goal he wished to reach. His numerous posthumous papers, filled with drafts, feverishly cast, cancelled, changed and worked out again and again, bear the best evidence of the poet's endeavours to find a convincing manner in which to accomplish that which he considered a revelation and a final result of his life-work. The difficulties, bound up with the achievement, were of a double nature, corresponding to the poet's state of mind. He tried to be plain, for plain—to him at least—were the truths which he was revealing, and yet the involved system of his beliefs seemed to him sometimes not convincing enough; on the other hand, it was based not only on his thoughts and elaborated doctrines, but also on his emotional powers, which bade him consider some ideas as being conceived in moments of ecstatic inspiration, in his mystic conversations with God. (pp. 152-53)

But finally he reached the moment when all contradictions were put aside and his system was ready, in a broad outline; then the poet could make it the solid basis of . . . *The Genesis of the Spirit (Genezis z Ducha)* and the *King Spirit (Krol Duch),* their very headings showing the direction in which the author was going.

The themes of both Słowacki's works were the same; it was the theory of evolution, applied to the making of the Universe and to the history of his native country; accordingly, the *Genesis* represented the poet's cosmogony, the *King Spirit* his philosophy of history.

The word "evolution" has had a precisely defined meaning since Darwin, whose theory was to form the groundwork of the contemporary scientific outlook. The difference between Słowacki and Darwin is in some respects very great and in others very small. Darwin's outlook is materialistic, that of Słowacki spiritual, but the tendencies of each of them are analogous. For, like the English scientist, the Polish poet considers the Universe and the history of mankind as a long march of progress, a chain of forms, bound up with each other, the first phase being one which implies the potential possibility of the following one; consequently, there is nothing ready-made, all the phenomena are in constant motion, Nature and Life are the moving and living "fabric of Spirit" which develops and longs for new and more perfect forms.

The starting-point for his views Słowacki found in Greek philosophy, in the system of Plato, whose fundamental doctrine of the migration of souls he made a corner-stone of his own teaching. Human life does not end at the moment of death; the spiritual elements of man's individuality survive and reappear in new bodies; consequently, every man has had his long history of incarnations. Moreover, in some exceptional moments of ecstatic inspiration he is able to discover his own Past; he can read it within his own soul, through the anamnesis, the inner and mysterious memory, that is the very basis of all historical research. In this way. Słowacki created his system of the philosophy of history on which, as we know, his mystic plays, such as *Father Mark [Ksiądz Marek]* or *Samuel Zborowski,* rested.

But the poet did not limit himself to the huge field of history. His imagination and his mind hankered for something greater; they wanted to find a universal outlook which would allow him to link up man with the Universe and with its great Maker. The philosophy of History needed a larger and more solid

foundation to rest on; it was found in the philosophy of Nature; both these concentric circles formed the system within which the poet was able to answer the eternal questions.

Like the mystic philosophers of the early periods of Christianity, the Gnostics, Słowacki was of the opinion that God created the Universe not immediately but by means of Spirits which left God, their source, and became makers of the visible. They produced the celestial orbs, among them also the Earth; they established organic life on earth; they finally appeared in human shape. The most important and striking idea of Słowacki was his view on the relation between the maker-spirits and their creations. The Spirits were not outside their creatures, like God in the Biblical narration, but they formed the spiritual, inner grain of the created shapes, these shapes being their external expression, their form. Consequently the spirit who in the nineteenth century assumed the body of a mighty warrior, a powerful thinker or an inspired poet might have appeared, in his earlier periods, as a powerful antediluvian monster, a gigantic plant or a huge rock. From this point of view Nature seemed to the poet's eyes a long and many-shaped "ladder of lives", its bottom resting on the dark ages of the Past, its top reaching into the "final aims" of further Evolution.

The key enabling man to decipher the Past, as was mentioned above, has been hidden in his own consciousness; he can reproduce in his memory his own history both in its human and pre-human forms.

It is easy to estimate the meaning and the importance of this philosophic system for the poet himself. It may seem eccentric and insufficient to a person who does not share Słowacki's views; but the poet, who had based his views not only on his own ideas, but whose arguments had been often irrational, resting on his beliefs, could now consider the Universe and Man as a perfect whole. The terrible problems and doubts that torture the human mind did not exist for him any more; they were answered within him and by means of his system. No wonder, then, that he was able to extricate himself from the anxieties which had been so profoundly characteristic of his earlier pessimistic works. Nevertheless, his newly acquired views included some dangers which were inevitable.

The philosophic system of Słowacki covered the large field of facts in the history of the Universe and Mankind; therefore it demanded the most careful investigation of these facts in order to produce unity of design. It was, then, a task surpassing even the powers of a great philosopher. Słowacki was a poet gifted with immense imagination, and a mystic who believed in the value of his ideas as revelation. This circumstance facilitated his work on the whole, but in some respects it made it more difficult. In some cases where the facts he wished to explain were so involved that any explanation was impossible he could cover their obvious incongruity by means of marvellously fine pictures, suggested both by his imagination and by his creed. At the same time, however, he was conscious that things which seemed to him quite clear and plain, when looked at from outside, might be misunderstood or wrongly interpreted. This fear bade him seek for formulae appealing to his readers; he revised his manuscripts and changed them, sometimes achieving thereby just the opposite to that which he wished to achieve. Moreover, he delayed the publishing of his works, the greater number of which, indeed, were found among his posthumous papers.

There is something sad and even tragic in the sight of the Polish mystic, weaving his rich ideas for himself and for future generations, aware that his contemporaries would be quite indifferent to what he considered "an Alpha and Omega" of the true and unique wisdom, revealing the most profound mysteries of the Universe, its Past, Present and Future.

His fears with regard to his contemporaries were justified. They were unable, in fact, to penetrate to the core of the poet's spirit. For, it must be repeated, Słowacki was more a poet than a philosopher, and therefore he often preferred to use poetic figures and symbols in place of definite and concrete ideas. Consequently a reader of his work must get used to the manner in which Słowacki expressed his views. In other words, his poetry and philosophy, being esoteric and addressed to the small group of the initiated, the poet could not have expected to be understood and appreciated in his time.

And it was only after some decades had elapsed that his mystic works found willing readers and won comparative popularity. Thanks to the comments and researches of many scholars, . . . the modern reader can easily find his way in the labyrinth of Słowacki's mystic legacy. (pp. 153-57)

Its main thesis has been set out in a short treatise in prose, *The Genesis of the Spirit*. It resembles the Gospels as to its form and spirit. It is a sublime prayer, a conversation of the poet with his Creator, its theme being the history of the Universe. The poet stands on the rocky seacoast and hearkens to the sound of the waves. He clearly understands them because the Ocean is nothing but an earlier and discarded form of the Spirit now enlivening the poet's frame. As yet in chaos, it is working out its future and more perfect form. The presence of Nature in its various aspects bids the poet dive into his memory and recall the history of his spirit, which will be, at the same time, the history of the material forms created by his spirit along its way of evolution, consequently the history of the Earth. (p. 157)

From the literary point of view, . . . one can call *The Genesis of the Spirit* one of the greatest philosophic poems produced by human inspiration.

The difficulties implied by the subject of the work did not allow the poet to express his views on all points, but the main lines of his ideas were clear enough to lead him to his goal; he pauses to decipher the history of creation, in his work, at the very moment when Nature was preparing to welcome the last stage of its development, the appearance of man. The poet finishes his "revelational" prayer with the statement that Nature demanded of God the creation of Man. Man, consequently, must run the same course as has been passed by his predecessors, and experience the same difficulties which were overcome by the Spirit in his earlier manifestations, falling into the sin of sloth and being forced by his creator to further endeavours until he is able to arrive at the final stage, that of universal happiness, in the period of God's Kingdom on Earth.

In this way the poet made a bridge between his philosophy of Nature and his philosophy of history; by it he passed from his cosmogony and biology to historiosophy.

His ideas on this subject he expressed in his grand epic, the *King Spirit*, the first rhapsody of which he published in 1846; the rest of the work, embracing three further rhapsodies and a bulky mass of innumerable fragments, was left in his papers. This his last poem was based on the early history of Poland, in accordance with the poet's interests as manifested in his plays. Moreover, he stressed the connection between his preceding works and the *King Spirit* by means of a strange relationship between the hero of his epic and one of the characters

of his tragedy *Lilla Weneda*—that of the sad priestess and prophetess Roza Weneda, whom, impregnated with the ashes of her slain brother-heroes, he supposed to have given birth to the future builder of Poland's power. Weird as it is, this idea was acceptable from the mystical point of view of the poet. He composed his tragedy, he declared, in an inspired state, under the influence of invisible spiritual powers which revealed to his eyes truths unknown to the rest of his countrymen; consequently his poetic ideas were revelations of truths lost in the chasm of Time.

The essence of the poem was expressed in its title. It was to deal with history, but history looked at from its essential, spiritual and inward side. A son of the Romantic period which appreciated the individual and worshipped heroism as the highest human virtue, Słowacki considered history as a long chain of great man-spirits whose activity shapes the life of whole epochs; the ship of historical life aims at the goal to which it has been directed by the mighty oar of its captain. In this way what a contemporary historian or thinker could call "the dominant ideas" of a period presented themselves to Słowacki's eye as the result of the activity of a great personage who, reincarnated, watched the fulfilment of the work which he had begun in his earlier incarnations. (pp. 160-62)

To appreciate duly [the epic] one must find an analogy to it; it may be easily compared with Dante's great achievement, *The Divine Comedy*. Both of them deal with the spiritual in mankind, considering it to be of a higher value than the material; both of them take the form of a vision penetrating the supernatural region of belief rather than life on earth; both show man in his attitude to God and to the Universe. Yet there is a great difference between the Italian epic and the Polish. The mediaeval poet, thanks to his Latin sense of reality, remained realistic even when dealing with the heavenly world of ideas; the Polish Romantic is idealistic even when he deals with real man and real facts. Dante's pilgrimage to the other world is related by a living man who, in flesh and blood, visited the realms of souls; Słowacki's account, based seemingly on history, is told by a royal spirit who remembers the events of his earlier lives. But by this manner of spiritualizing all things which he introduced into his poem, Słowacki created a work which is unique in its method and in its subject.

Like Dante's *Divina Commedia*, the Polish epic too needs comments; it is difficult to understand, but the reader who will undertake the task of breaking the back of the first difficulties will be rewarded abundantly. Słowacki created his own style, a style able to express all that he wanted to express. . . . Both the stern, knightly sounds of battles and the soft womanly tones of a folk-song are to be found in Słowacki's stanzas. With the same marvellous ease he expressed there the exceptional, mystic states of ecstasy, and human griefs and joys caused by daily events.

Especially noteworthy is his method of using colours and sounds to render the inner and secret life of man. His colours are limited; he is no painter of real life; but brilliantly they correspond to the poet's wishes. They have their special meaning, and aim at appealing to the reader's emotional powers, to his ability of associating rare sights, sounds and scents, not only to his imagination. The artistic methods used by Słowacki in his epic, anticipating those of such schools as the Symbolists and the Pre-Raphaelites, were not to appear in European literature until many years after the poet's death. They proved that in his innovations he was a forerunner of the new artistic tendencies, a bold herald of coming artistic views.

This fact largely explains the indifference of his contemporaries, who were unable to appreciate Słowacki's greatness; one is the more inclined to admire the poet's spiritual power, which bade him proceed despite all the hindrances he met on his way.

Description of the *King Spirit* as a masterpiece does not contain any exaggeration as regards either the poet or the generation to which he belonged. As to the poet, it best showed the marvellous progress in his life and literary activity, both of which started from discontent with common life and ended in reconciliation with God and Man in the lofty regions where religion, philosophy and poetry were blended into unity. For that period and generation, the *King Spirit* gave the best and finest expression to the idealistic aspirations which animated the contemporaries of Słowacki in Poland as well as everywhere else in Europe at that time. (pp. 167-69)

> *Julian Krzyzanowski, "Julius Słowacki," in his* Polish Romantic Literature, *1930. Reprint by E. P. Dutton and Company Inc., 1931, pp. 107-69.*

ARTHUR PRUDDEN COLEMAN AND MARION MOORE COLEMAN (essay date 1937)

[*In this excerpt from their introduction to* Mary Stuart, *the Colemans argue that Słowacki's main interest in the drama was psychological rather than historical.*]

It was undoubtedly a conjunction of forces and of circumstances that gave Słowacki Mary Stuart for the heroine of his second drama. He was interested, in the first place, in personalities upon whom the dark shadow of disloyalty, even of treason, had fallen. (p. 6)

Even the most superficial reading of *Marya Stuart* is sufficient to establish the impression that this is psychological rather than historical drama. It is the charting in dramatic form of the course pursued by a woman whom forces both outside herself and within eventually drive to deeds of violence in order that she may achieve the end her passions bind her to desire. Neither the central conflict of the 16th century nor the significant movements of that age have anything to do with this Polish *Mary Stuart*.

Contrarily enough, in its chill opening scene *Marya Stuart* starts out to be historical drama. A central conflict, the war of the faiths, threatens. Mary's devoted Page runs in to his mistress with news of what he has seen and heard on the High Street of Edinburgh: the gaunt, pale-cheeked Knox has been exhorting the carnival-makers, urging them to treason against their Queen; the mob, roused to a frenzy by his words, has ransacked Mary's own chapel. The epoch, Scotland in the century of its bitterest religious wars, gets into the drama. (pp. 7-8)

From the action reported in the opening scene of *Marya Stuart* it would . . . appear that a great historic drama was about to unfold, that a final conflict between Mary's Roman Church and Knox' Scottish was about to be plotted. But as a glance at the cast of characters will reveal, Słowacki shied deliberately away from persons whose use would have forced him to make his work historical drama: from Moray, Mary's half brother; from Maitland of Leithington, Mary's Secretary of State; from Elizabeth and Burleigh and Knox himself. With the close of the first scene the conflict of the faiths ceases to be an issue in *Marya Stuart*. Only Mary herself matters.

The Mary Stuart whom Słowacki inherited from Schiller was the classic Mary of the final deadly years of imprisonment, the proud, tearful victim of her cousin Elizabeth. The Mary whom he inherited from Alfieri was a woman of passive personality whose destiny it was to be the pawn of persons and nations with powerful convictions. The Mary he knew from his reading of Scott was such a one as Adam Woodcock describes when he retorts, "Well, they may say what they will, many a true heart will be sad for Mary Stuart, e'en if all be true men say of her; for look you, Master Roland, she was the loveliest creature to look upon that I ever saw with eye, and no lady in the land liked better the fair flight of falcon." She was a lovely lady and a regal one, but never quite lifelike, always a little too good to be true, and invariably more sinned against than sinful.

Słowacki's Mary turns out to be mostly his own. In the depiction of minor characters in the play he piled up large debts to his predecessors. But Mary is Słowacki's own. She is a living woman, sometimes tender, often ruthless, a woman with positive passions that are alternately noble and evil. But always a woman, never a flat, stylized, bloodless figure in a play.

Słowacki's Queen of Scots starts out to be the conventional Mary, the sad and lovely lady whom diabolical forces are conspiring to crush and whom she resists only with tears. But before the first scene is more than half advanced Mary has pulled herself together and is girding herself for battle. . . . In the bosom of the "burned-out lamp," which Rizzio has called her, a bright new flame begins to "glitter and consume." (pp. 8-10)

As woman no less than as Queen, Mary is lifelike and varied. When she dreams above her dressing-table of Bothwell, the black, gloomy-browed Bothwell, she is the maiden swept off her feet by a sudden virginal passion. When Rizzio's romantic ardor embarrasses her she is the woman who knows how effective a weapon ridicule is against overheated passions. When she is sewing at her embroidery frame, she is a simple village girl, making flowers grow on the linen beneath her hand. When she orders the would-be murderers of Rizzio to beware lest the scaffold find them out, she is the lioness holding the wolves at bay lest they devour her cubs. When she broods over her dying Page she is the tender woman whose heart is touched by suffering. When she administers poison to her husband she is the cold, sly avenger.

Słowacki does not sidestep the darker side of Mary's character. He deliberately makes his biggest scene illuminate that darker side's most damning manifestation. He makes her blackly guilty of Darnley's murder, guilty the more because it is in her brain, not Bothwell's, that the idea is born that Darnley must pay with his own death for Rizzio's. Her mind and her soul are guilty whether her hand is or not. (p. 10)

Here is the Romanticist's Mary: a guilty, passionate woman who could with truly Tudor facility put the fairest face on the foulest conduct. She is no pretty figure but she is real. And when all the faults of technique in *Marya Stuart* have been written down against its young author, the truth will still remain that to have created this Mary in an age whose drama was still dominated by the pseudo-classicist Feliński's *Barbara Radziwiłłówna* was something of an achievement.

Słowacki's minor characters in *Marya Stuart* are type figures, derived, for the most part, from characters whom the poet had met in his reading of Hugo, of Dumas, of Alfieri and of Scott. . . . Mary is Słowacki's single contribution to dramatic portraiture in this play that has claim to originality. . . . (pp. 11-12)

A watercolor of Słowacki by an unknown contemporary artist.

On [Słowacki's] tombstone might with justice have been graven the Stuart epitaph, "In my end is my beginning." Neglected more or less in his lifetime, he has come to be regarded as the founder of Polish dramatic literature, Poland's Shakespeare an Molière in one. In the ladder of the poet's renown as dramatist, *Marya Stuart* is the second rung. (p. 12)

> *Arthur Prudden Coleman and Marion Moore Coleman, in an introduction to* Mary Stuart: A Romantic Drama *by Juljusz Słowacki, translated by Arthur Prudden Coleman and Marion Moore Coleman, Electric City Press, Inc., 1937, pp. 5-12.*

GIOVANNI MAVER   (essay date 1949)

[*Chronicling the growth of Słowacki's literary skills, Maver assesses the influence of various events, individuals, ideas, and writings on the author's life and works. According to Maver, none of Słowacki's individual pieces is a masterpiece; instead, his greatest achievement was the "symphonic unity" of his works, which together form "one sublime masterpiece."*]

In his third volume of poetry, . . . Słowacki published, besides several lyrics and *Lambro*, a story in verse, a singular poetical composition entitled *Godzina Myśli (An Hour of Thought)*. Apparently a brief romance, it is in reality a poetical evocation of those aspects of his own childhood and adolescence which contributed to a greater extent in the formation of his character and work. Saddened and disillusioned by the cold and partly hostile reception of his first two volumes of poetry, he reveals in it the motives for his deep melancholy and lack of faith; he

outlines, with singular introspective perspicacity, the origin of his poetry, and he fixes its essential lines almost prophetically. Słowacki said with reference to his own childhood—"He gave winged thoughts to his inspirations, and with so much happening in his thoughts he lived in a seventh heaven. He reclothed his dreams in magic raiment: then with a strong will he projected them ahead, so that they rose straight up before him, and he saw in front of him images from which he detached himself by cold reasoning." He fled with a romantically tender sensibility from concrete reality; if he grasped reality it was only by chance; and he looked only for its most evanescent aspects: "annoyed by the confused, multiple perfumes of flowers, he discovered the perfume of sorrow—savage and fleeting: it was the perfume of water swept by the willows and which, arising every night from the silent wave, spread a mysterious freshness in the air."

The future poet and his young friend [Ludwig Spitznagel] became enthusiasts of Swedenborg's writings, and from adolescence he intuitively perceived the bonds between animate and inanimate nature—("The soul created by the Divine spark is in flowers the essence of their perfume and the substance of their colouring, while in men it is their thoughts and in Angels it becomes light")—and between the past, present and future ("The youthful memory of both, an immense memory made up of thoughts entwined by chains, bore witness to the pre-existence of the spirit"). On this double unit will later rest, not only one of the principal characteristics of his poetry, in which not seldom everything appears suffused by a single colour, but also, in the mystic period, the great structure of his conception of life and the World. Thus in *An Hour of Thought* the limits between concrete and abstract, past and future, disappear; memories become fore-warnings, and so much characterise the temperament of the young dreamer as to become the substance of his future art.

Now, in 1833, Słowacki was only twenty-four years old; in his poetry imagination ruled supreme; to this, with fantastic facility, the word, the rhythm and the rhyme were added. However, more than from experience of life, his imagination was nourished from literary sources, and the result is more artifice than art. In the poetical stories of his first volume of *Poems,*. . . the reminiscences of Byron and the two Polish poets, Mickiewicz and Malczeski, who were ahead of him in affirming romanticism in Poland, were so numerous and so open that, without being too severe with the young poet, we may call these first works of his a succession of variations on the theme and motives of others, even if they were full of suggestive virtuosity. Independence of literary sources was greater in the two dramas which make up the second volume; specially in *Mary Stuart,* in which it is to be noted that besides the indisputable drama of the action and dialogue there is also expert characterisation of some of the actors. However, both his dramas and poetic stories lacked finish, except for the poet's too facile and too fluent discursive vein; nor did he employ those more substantial artistic qualities which *An Hour of Thought* was to reveal a little later. In his heart Słowacki was aware of all this. So much is true since, although he hoped his first works would be successful, he was not at all surprised when he knew that Mickiewicz had judged his poetry to be like "a beautiful temple without a God."

Not only God, but also the Fatherland was absent from the youthful works of Słowacki; and in the eyes of the Polish émigrés living in Paris after the sad failure of the insurrection of 1831 this second absence was even more serious than the lack of a real religious faith. Słowacki at once made reparation, and in the poem *Lambro* he confronted the patriotic problem, shading it under the transparent veil of the fight of the Greeks for liberty. According to him defeat in 1831 was due to the insufficient spirit of sacrifice of the Poles. Many of them had preferred the road to exile to that flame of vengeance which destroys all. What remained to be done was to preserve the spirit from dissolving further, and to pass it on pure to future generations so that they could redeem the fault.

Blameworthy himself among the others, Słowacki realised his heroic conception of life in his poetry. The discord was serious and it filled him with sadness, with scepticism, and with a continual restlessness which he himself defines as "the restlessness of swallows." It was several years before he could see his own and his country's problems in the perspective of the much vaster problem of the Cosmos, and succeeded in finding peace and that superior harmony of which he had caught a glimpse in *An Hour of Thought.* For the moment his own dissatisfaction, and, still more, rivalry in the field of thought and poetry with Mickiewicz, encouraged him to continue to persist along his chosen road. His new work, the drama *Kordjan,* was in fact a renewal of the themes alluded to in *Lambro,* but with much greater ideological and artistic obligations. On an ample background, on which are placed in relief the defects of the leaders and the apathy of the masses, is outlined the moral state of Poland at the dawn of the 19th century,—the victim of "mal du siècle" which paralyses both her will and also that of young Kordjan who, having tried in vain to escape from his own boredom, at last wishes to redeem himself and his contemporaries by an act of great heroism and sacrifice— an attempt against the Czar—but at the last moment withdraws, dismayed by bravery which surpasses his moral forces. The avenger becomes the victim—of his own time and his own temperament. Of the unrealised gesture there remains nothing but the inflamed word, the memory and the expiation.

Thus the new drama dissolved in shipwreck; but it was a shipwreck which confirmed again the absolute sincerity of Słowacki in the circles of poetry. This sincerity, moving even in its grandiloquence, together with a few scenes of great dramatic power, redeems the defects in clearness, in interior coherence and also in the structure of this drama of purely Shakespearean type.

In art and in life Słowacki appeared condemned to isolation and solitude. His flight from Paris and retirement within the intimacies of a Geneva boarding-house had been a warning of this. His nervous and eclectic search for a contact with the public that would satisfy his greatest literary ambitions was its most disconcerting symptom. Thus was formed *Mazeppa,* a drama of a worldly type. This, however, left him dissatisfied and he destroyed it, to take it up again a few years later. There came next the fable-like drama *Balladyna,* in which, leaving free play to fantasy, he proposed to re-create the mythical past of Poland, but which instead resolved itself into a kind of exaltation of the fatal irrationality of every human destiny; and also the drama *Horsztyński,* in which the theme of Hamlet is reproduced in a Polish setting.

Shakespeare's influence was evident in all these attempts; often, however, combined with a certain sympathy for the technicalities of French romantic drama. But apart from a few scenes of *Balladyna* which are full of delicate poetry, these works do not show any effective progress compared with his preceding ones. Rather than realisations they are essays, searchings for new ways and more suitable means of reaching them.

Yet the way best conforming to the character and poetical talent of Słowacki had already been indicated in *An Hour of Thought:* the sublimation of reality in dreamed visions, in which the contrasts that made the mind of the poet so restless were composed in a higher unit of thought and poetry.

An attainment of this goal, within the limits of poetic style, is represented by the idyll *In Switzerland;* conversely, in the great religious and patriotic parable *Anhelli,* it is fulfilled in the harmonious fusion of poetry and thought. The idyll is the description, written several years afterwards, and therefore shrouded in a veil of sweet memory, of an excursion made from Geneva to the waterfalls at Aar. On this excursion Słowacki had for companion, as well as other compatriots, the Maria Wodzinska who later played such a great part in the life of Frederick Chopin. The poet's falling in love with Maria, against the background of the Swiss countryside, forms the subject of *In Switzerland.* In it words seem to have been transferred to a sphere of the lightest colours and of melodious musical recitation; in it the countryside is lived over again as in a dream, which makes it almost immaterial; the narrative of love assumes those tones proper to the 12th century *dolce stil nuovo.* (pp. 60-3)

It is difficult to say exactly whether, and up to what point, his stay in Italy may have influenced his art. His contact with the countryside and its ancient and Italian culture was somewhat superficial; the Roman monuments left him rather indifferent; of the art of the Renaissance only painting (he himself delighted in painting) aroused a productive echo in his mind; of Italian literature, only Dante had a real influence on his poetry. However, this was rather of secondary importance in the face of the much greater influence, because exercised by more congenial poets—of Byron in his youthful period (and not only then) and of Calderon in his mystic period. It was for Słowacki more a question of his capacity for assimilating the art of Dante, of repeated attempts, for the most part of failures, at approaching it and adapting it to his own poetic character. If it is not an exaggeration to say that the spirit of Dante hovers over the brief composition *The Father of the Plague-stricken* . . . , it is also not just to attribute to Dante the classical perfection of this poem, nor the hieratical atmosphere in which it is wrapped— something that is rather the reflection of an oriental country.

Dante and the Orient; the Holy Scriptures and the biblical style used by Mickiewicz in his *Books of the Nation and of the Polish Pilgrims;* the personal and national problems and the religious sublimation of the one to the other—these are the elements needed for the analysing of his principal work of this period, e.g. *Anhelli,* even though in this work he may not have fully attained that harmony for which he had been searching so long. The whiteness of the Siberian snows spreads over each chapter of this parable in which is related the fate of exiles, stricken through their own faults and those of others; in which the Shaman, a new Virgil, chooses the most pure, young Anhelli, leaving to him, by limitless expiation, the task of foreseeing the dawn of future redemption. That sacrifice, made in absolute purity of heart, will redeem the faults of the generation contemporary with the poet; who with this work, under the veil of a fantastic narrative done in the style of biblical verses, wished to represent the past, present and future destinies of Poland.

New experiences of life and art, the growing certainty of having a great mission to fulfil and of being able to realise it by means of his poetry, put the sadness of his mind to flight at least for a short time, and changed the dreamer into a fencing-master.

The drama *Lilla Weneda* belongs to the period of transition between this new attitude and the uncertainties of the past; it portrays the genesis of the Polish nation (but with clear references to the present) and resumes, continuing it, the theme of *Balladyna*. This drama, in which Słowacki, going back to its origin, insists on the duplicity of the Polish soul, angelic and rude at the same time, is distinguished by the striking quality of the contrasts in which such duplicity is made an outward show, by the sublime nobility of the protagonist, a female incarnation of Anhelli, and by the great richness of the images, sustained by a suggestion of stylistic tension. Nevertheless, it cannot be considered Słowacki's masterpiece, as some authoritative Polish critics would wish, because of the too many unrelated elements which are mixed up in it. Here, in contrast with *Lilla Weneda,* in which his wavering is still evident, Słowacki appears more sure of himself, whether in *The Tomb of Agamemnon* [*Grób Agamemnona*], published in an appendix to the drama itself, where with vehement impetuosity he sets himself up as an infallible judge of the Polish past, or in the final exhortation of **"My Testament,"** "I entreat the living not to lose hope . . . even when it is necessary to go to death one after the other, like the stones thrown by God into the trench."

But it is only in *Beniowski* that the battle-cry of the poet breaks out in full. The plot of the poem is a pretext (modelled in fact on *Don Juan* and *The Pilgrimage of Childe-Harold,* but also, and especially for the formal part—the eighth rhyme used with great skill—on *Orlando Furioso*): what counts are the episodes, digressions, lyrical flights, the constant injection of the personal element, sometimes boldly and sometimes in sorrow. Above all Słowacki boasts his absolute mastery of poetic language:

> . . . to verse, in my judgement, I have the right:
> Rhyme bows to me of itself, tenderly;
> The octave caresses me, the sextain loves me.
> Someone has said that, if words could
> Suddenly change themselves into individuals,
> If the fatherland were discourse and speech,
> My statue would be erected, created by sounds,
> With the inscription: *Patri patriae. . . .*

[Almost] at the same period in which he was intoxicated with his own select triumphs, he was overcoming emphasis and romantic grandiloquence in order to substitute for it a preference for what is humble, simple and everyday. Not that he had despised this in the preceding years; even in *Kordjan, Balladyna* and *Lilla Weneda* he had always reserved a small place for the good sense and the good heart of the people. Only now, however, in the figure of an old Russian major (in the drama *Fantasy* in which the character is represented under a lightly caricatured form as the poet Krasiński, for many years his great friend), was he able to render homage, full of poetic realism, to modesty.

At this point there came about a decisive happening in his life and art: his meeting with Andrzej Towiański on 12 July 1842. It was the hour of greatest prestige for this strange apostle of exiled Poland. He had gathered, more by the fascination of his ascendant personality than by his doctrine, a small but very devoted band of followers about him, captained by Mickiewicz. The very next day after this fatal and almost predestined meeting, Słowacki wrote in outline, in an impetuous and ingenious dash, the poem **"So Help me, Thou, O Lord!"** In it every hint of the doctrine of the master is absent. However, from its disconcerting emphasis on humility and haughtiness it clearly

emerges that the words of Towiański had done nothing but unseal, in him and for him, the truth, allowing him to accomplish the great discovery of which he had been for some time the trustee and the herald:

> The clear idea of a new faith
> Has arisen in me, in a flash,
> Entire, ready for action and holy. . . .
>
> When I shall arise my voice shall be that of the Lord;
> My cry shall be the cry of the whole fatherland;
> My spirit shall be the angel whom nothing resists.
> So help me, Thou Christ, Lord God!

Thus closed for him, now and for ever, the period of that "restlessness of swallows" which he had diagnosed in himself ten years previously, and which from then onwards had been his torment. Not, however, without the secret hope that the possession of the truth would one day turn into a calm and fruitful certainty. Towiański had only been an instrument of the investiture received from above. Słowacki had but to proceed along the designated way, with no reference to Towiański's doctrine (a great difference in this respect between him and Towiański's disciple, Mickiewicz!) in order to construct his own cosmogonic edifice; even if only in the wake of the investiture itself, in which is eliminated every breach between individuals, societies, nations and universe, and where all together, in full liberty of spirit, tend towards the realisation of their ultimate goals.

Considered thus, the meeting between Słowacki and Towiański signifies nothing in the life and art of Słowacki, except the milestone where the ways followed up to then meet, and the departure point of the road which remained to be travelled. In fact the last seven years of his life were all dedicated, with feverish activity, to the realisation in thought and in poetry of his own doctrine. Spiritually they were the richest years of his life, and in spite of uncertainties and deviations he never halted. From the dramas in the style of Calderon (and here we should at least note *Father Marek* [*Ksiądz Marek*], which with all its verbosity and prolixity is the most compact and the richest in spiritual content of all Słowacki's works) to the liberal dramatic compositions (best among these is the ponderous transposition in heaven of the case in favour of the rebel *Samuel Żborowski*); from the beautiful, and not sufficiently appreciated, lyrics to religious philosophical treatises in prose and verse, and also the great unfinished poem *King-Spirit* [*Król Duch*], a large part of the production of these years was uncompleted. *King-Spirit* is a continual subjugation of expression to a labour which forces itself to clarify the incessant process of a thought that embraces everything, from primeval rocks to man; and everything revives with the flatus of poetry and of faith, in a portentous pilgrimage towards the pure light of the spirit.

It would be an exaggeration to state that Słowacki had succeeded to the full in this labour, which is in any case too vast for human efforts. Confronted with death, which at an early age approached nearer and nearer, he himself had to recognise his own impotence to finish the work he had undertaken; but he did so with faith that it would not remain uncompleted:

> This hymn is left to the centuries
> Which have powerful hands and voices;
> So that they may complete the song in Heaven with a
>   more robust voice
> Than have I, who terminate here my sorrowful
>   destinies.

The fundamental point of Słowacki's thought is that "all is created by the spirit and for the spirit and that nothing exists for material ends." The history of the spirit begins in the hard rock and finishes in the deification of humanity. To reconstruct the progressive phases of the spirit, which create for themselves the forms most corresponding to their needs, means to remember them, since all of us have passed through these stages while waiting to make further steps.

It is thus that the principal work on the "doctrine of origins"—*The Genesis of the Spirit*—begins with this majestic arrangement: "Thou hast placed me, O God, on the rocks of the ocean, that I may recall the age-long history of my spirit; and in the past I suddenly felt immortal, a Son of God, a Creator of the visible, and one of those who of my own accord offer Thee love on golden suns and garlands of stars." Here we are present at a singular union between mysticism and the elaborate evolutionary doctrine of the beginning of the century. Progress is inherent in the nature of the spirit and, given the sorrowful labour with which it fulfils itself, it has a character purely revolutionary—in fact Słowacki calls it the "eternal revolutionary." Each halt, each slackening towards laziness, each declining of the sacrifices which progress requires is a sin against the spirit; while every advance of the spirit, "even if it is not free from blemish and imperfection, is noted in the book of life." In this original pilgrimage there are some spirits who precede others, who serve as models to the columns of kindred spirits and help their ascent. These pilot spirits to a certain extent find their most perfect expression among the poets ("the great grave-openers of the words of the spirits— who make suggestions to them and use rhyme and have a great revealing power") and are called King-Spirits. When the spirits reach the historical phase, we follow their progress in the history of humanity. Liberty, love, striving towards perfection, the spirit of sacrifice and solidarity—these are the forces that push humanity along the road to perfection. The solidarity of the spirits carries with it the regrouping of those who have the same fundamental aspirations, and these settle down, in the last analysis, into each separate nation. Each nation has its own King-Spirits who guide it, fix its directing idea, and by the same means act on the whole of humanity.

The great poem *King-Spirit* is the most perfect poetical expression of the stage of genesis which leads us from the dawn of Polish history to its early beginnings. In it Słowacki relives, almost contemplates over again, his own life on earth, all its aberrations, aspirations and realisations, in previous incarnations in the principal figures of the early years of Polish history. His own autobiographic character *King-Spirit* appears at once wrapped in an aura of most singular poesy, reinforced also by the fact that Słowacki, when dealing with his own past incarnations, uses the first person with sympathetic coherence. On the other hand the same doctrine of genesis resolves itself as a rule more into an incentive than into a respite for fantasy; in some scenes this allows the poet to attain overwhelming poetic impetus. (pp. 64-9)

Misunderstood and ignored during the twenty years of his fervid literary activity, Słowacki really enters the history of Polish literature only fifty years after his death. However, from then on he has occupied one of its very first places, by the side of Mickiewicz, to whom he had always been hostile owing to a strange personal aversion. Modern Polish poetry cannot be conceived without the great influence which Słowacki exercised on it. His dramas represent the most conspicuous part of the national repertory. Even Polish prose is not without his influence.

Nevertheless Słowacki is still unknown outside Poland. Is there any chance of his discovery by the West? Since prophecy is not in order, a reply cannot be given to this question; but an indication of the reasons which hinder a just valuation of his poetical work outside Poland can be permitted.

Since the poet wrote in a language accessible only to a few, the appreciation of his work necessarily depends on its translation. Now all poets are either translatable or untranslatable, and Słowacki is certainly one of the least translatable.

This appreciation is in fact not only intimately dependent on the expressive possibilities of the Polish language but, to use a paradox, one can say of this "grave-opener of the word" that the thought springs from the language, and not the language from the thought. No translator's skill can adequately render this process in another language. But beyond this initial difficulty there is another, equally great, which hinders the diffusion and comprehension of Słowacki's work abroad: the fact that this great poet has not written a single work which, taken as a whole, can be considered among the poetic masterpieces of humanity. Słowacki's greatness lies, on one hand, in the episodes, in what might be defined in film terminology "the sequence," considered by itself, independently of the work in which, although incorporated, it is a thing apart: and on the other hand in the admirable symphonic unity which binds one work to the others, forming them all together into one sublime masterpiece. Defect and value have really the same origin: Słowacki's incapacity to stop himself and control the excessive facility with which the word clings to his imagination.

Taken separately, each of his works has some imperfection of construction, of coherence or of insufficient finish; and naturally this defect becomes the more evident the longer and more complex each single work may be. From it derives the great value of some of his lyrics, especially in his later period. Nevertheless, except for some roughness noticed by Słowacki himself, incongruencies and contradictions appear and disappear in the progressive purification of his visions, upheld by a single goal: the light. This light revealed by him, certainly deserves to be known. (pp. 70-1)

> Giovanni Maver, "Juljusz Słowacki: 1809-1849,"
> translated by Louis Varipati, in The Slavonic and
> East European Review, *Vol. XXVIII, No. 70, No-*
> *vember, 1949, pp. 60-71.*

FRANCIS J. WHITFIELD (essay date 1949)

[*In this analysis of* Anhelli, *Whitfield explores the dual influences of the Bible and Dante and examines Słowacki's concept of patriotism.*]

Of all Słowacki's works, *Anhelli* is perhaps the most easily accessible to us—more understandable now, even, than it could have been when it was first published, one hundred and eleven years ago.

It was . . . Krasiński who remarked that Słowacki possessed the Polish language as one possesses a lover, and he thereby indicated what is at once Słowacki's glory and, so far as foreign audiences are concerned, his great disadvantage. A language is the most jealous of mistresses, and it is just because Słowacki's poetry is so intimately involved with the spirit of the Polish language that so little of it can be satisfactorily carried over into a foreign language. In *Anhelli,* however, Słowacki deliberately restrained his muse and chose a form which, as it happens, brings with it a special feeling of familiarity for the

English reader. At the same time, the Biblical style in which *Anhelli* is written is as central in the development of the Polish language as in that of our own, and Słowacki was never more faithful to his chosen mistress than when he used it. One need think only of the influential sixteenth-century verse translations of the Psalms by one of Słowacki's favorite poets, Jan Kochanowski, or the majestic Biblical prose of Piotr Skarga's *Parliamentary Sermons* to recall the part that Biblical literature has played in the refinement of the Polish language. Wespazjan Kochowski, in the seventeenth century, confirmed the tradition with his *Polish Psalmody,* and it was natural for Mickiewicz to turn to the form in his *Books of the Polish Nation and Polish Pilgrimage.*

One could imagine a poem in Biblical prose—especially one written by a romantic poet—that would be tediously diffuse and prolix (and we may recall that the influence of the King James Version has not been an unmixed blessing for our own literary language), but *Anhelli* is at an opposite stylistic pole—concise, even terse, and bare of ornamentation. And behind these qualities may be sensed the language and style of Dante, for the influence of the *Divine Comedy* on the form of *Anhelli* is at least as great as is that of the Bible. . . . [It] is certain that Słowacki . . . enjoyed a special gift for learning from other poets. An omnivorous reader from earliest youth, he made use of what he read as other writers make use of the matter of direct experience, and much of his work—particularly his dramas, where he feeds on Shakespeare as no one before or since has ever done—is like a second distillation of poetry, not a reworking, but a transmutation of the common heritage of Western European culture.

The story of *Anhelli* is essentially a very simple one, in harmony with the simplicity of the whole work. (pp. 317-18)

The chapters in which Anhelli receives [his] terrible instruction are the most immediately impressive of the entire poem. Perhaps only now, with our experience of the modern concentration camp, is it possible to appreciate the depth of poetic vision in these pictures of the Siberian hell. For Słowacki sees and depicts more than the bodily torments inflicted by the Russians. As in Dante, the physical suffering is almost incidental, a necessary concomitant of the spiritual suffering and degradation, but immeasurably inferior to it in importance. (p. 319)

From his letter of May 22, 1839, to Konstanty Gaszyński, concerning a projected French translation of *Anhelli,* we know that Słowacki himself—although he demanded that the reader "work with his imagination on every phrase" of the poem—refrained from offering exact interpretations of several allegorical passages. This is not to assert that the allegory in *Anhelli* is everywhere and always a mere poetic device, an echo of the *Divine Comedy,* but the basic simplicity of the poem remains undisturbed by such incidental problems. . . . [The elements that strike with the greatest force are] the Dantesque descriptions in the middle chapters. If one reads the poem as Słowacki warned it should *not* be read, with insufficient attention and a lagging imagination, and if one does not return to the poem, these are the episodes that will remain, and one will remember *Anhelli* simply as a powerful protest against the enslavement of Poland by the tyranny of Nicholas I. But if only this could be found in *Anhelli,* however powerfully it were expressed and with whatever particular force it struck us now for reasons not directly connected with the poem itself, it would hardly justify the esteem in which the poem is deservedly held. Even granted that the Poles today might conceivably be moved by this miniature epic of their ancestors' sufferings, a work which was no

more than that could hardly present the claim to being a piece of living world literature. (p. 320)

There is more concrete evidence, from the poem itself, that *Anhelli* cannot be read simply as a patriotic tract. For one thing, the Siberia depicted in *Anhelli* is, for the most part, hardly an actual Siberia. While the terrible episodes of the middle chapters do represent the very real tortures inflicted on the Poles by the Russians, it is clear that in the major portions of the poem the snow-swept waste that Słowacki calls Siberia is not intended to be a realistic picture of that part of the Russian Empire. The literary reminiscences alone in these descriptions—reminiscences of Chateaubriand's America, the Lake of Genesareth in the New Testament and the waters of Babylon in the Old, reminiscences of Dante's Italy and of other places—would only be a distraction in a realistically intended poem. For the reader who is aware of these reminiscences, as the poet obviously wished him to be, they must inevitably raise the poem and its setting to a higher, more symbolic level. Already here the poet is breaking the bonds of a single place in order to follow better his program of expressing something more inclusive, the time in which he lives.

The actions of the exiles confirm this interpretation. As soon as the Shaman and Anhelli have left them, they become divided into three groups, each dreaming of the deliverance of the fatherland and each convinced that such deliverance can be accomplished only in the way that it recommends. But these aristocrats who wear the *kontusz* and put their faith in the rights of ancient blood; these demagogues who cry for equality, by which they mean equality in degradation; and these fanatics who call men to a corrupted religion of self-glorification—these "political parties," which dare to think that they are acting for the good of the fatherland and are, in fact, digging the grave of Poland by destroying themselves and their fellow men—these are no Polish exiles in Siberia, but quite clearly the exiles of another place, the great Polish Emigration in Paris. (pp. 321-22)

[There] is one scene above all that illustrates this harsh severity of Słowacki's judgments. This is the scene of the ordeal, where each of the three parties offers a champion to test the truth of its doctrines:

> And [the] counsellor said to them: "Lo, let us set up three crosses in imitation of the agony of our Lord, and on each of these three trees we will nail one of the mightiest knights in each group; and he who liveth longest, with him shall be the victory."

There is something here of Krasiński's apocalyptic vision in the last scenes of the *Undivine Comedy,* and it is in passages such as these that we see most clearly why Krasiński should have felt so deeply the power of *Anhelli.* Here, added to everything else, is the final horror of blasphemy. The very wretches who have sunk farthest from the ideals of Christian charity and humility have dared to stage a parody of Golgotha.

Słowacki's meaning is far from obscure, and his allusions could not fail to be recognized by his contemporaries. There was one poet above all with whom these ideas would be associated—one who had compared Suvorov's massacre of Praga to Christ's first day in the tomb, and Paškevič's capture of Warsaw, which marked the end of the November Uprising, to Christ's second day in the tomb, and who had predicted that "on the third day the soul shall return to the body, and the Nation shall arise and free all the peoples of Europe from slavery." It is true that Mickiewicz himself had warned against the heresy into which his teachings might be transmuted. Although national Messianism, in its simplest form, is only an extension of orthodox Christian teachings on the imitation of Christ, it may easily confuse "imitation" of Christ with "resemblance" to Him. Mickiewicz had cautioned his followers: ". . . the Polish Nation is not a divinity like Christ, therefore its soul on pilgrimage over the abyss may go astray, and its return to the body and the resurrection may be deferred."

But if Mickiewicz had contented himself with this reminder of man's imperfection, Słowacki was not satisfied. In the scene of the triple crucifixion, martyrdom for the wrong reasons and with the wrong intentions is pitilessly exposed as pure blasphemy. The same criticism is expressed even more directly in the famous words of Słowacki's open letter to the Polish Emigration: "Woe to you! Woe to you who say to yourselves that in your cross you are like unto Christ. For you forget that it was in His innocence, and with submission of His will to the will of the Father, that Christ suffered on the cross for mankind."

Słowacki will not allow the Poles to forget, even in their darkest moments, that they can hardly be reckoned an immaculate victim, that their own sins are in large measure responsible for their downfall, and that only culpable madness could compare the will of God the Father to the will of Catherine II. In *Anhelli*, the two angels who come to warn the hero of his approaching death are symbolic of the same message. They are the angels who, according to Polish legend, visited the wheelwright Piast at the beginning of Polish history, made him the founder of the first Polish dynasty, and promised that God would protect Poland so long as she maintained her ancient virtues. Their mission to Anhelli is quite different. The Polish nation has broken the covenant—here the Old Testament elements in the poem break out in full splendor, as they do in Skarga's *Parliamentary Sermons*—and the angels no longer have any message of comfort or prophecy of future greatness. Anhelli himself, the last survivor of the exiles, who has tried to purify his heart through sacrifice and suffering, is nevertheless found wanting and must die without knowing the results of his labors.

If such elements of the poem are given the attention they deserve, it becomes clear that *Anhelli* is far from being the poem of patriotic pathos that it might seem on first reading. It is rather a criticism and indictment of mere patriotism, and not only of the Polish patriotism that Słowacki observed around him, but of any mystique of nation, blood, class, or religion that threatens to diminish the dignity and freedom of man. The angel-like hero of the poem is borne through his sufferings by the hope that they will teach him where true patriotism lies. But if *we* are granted the vision of the fiery knight, Anhelli is not. The moral regeneration of the individual man, without which the claims of nations, parties, and creeds will have been in vain, has not come about, and Anhelli sleeps on. On this deeper level of meaning, the scope of the poem is broadened beyond the mines of Siberia, beyond the quarrels of the Great Emigration, and even beyond the confines of the nineteenth century. As Krasiński predicted, *Anhelli* and its author can speak to us today. (pp. 323-25)

I have perforce centered attention on the interpretation of only one poem, but it should not be concluded that *Anhelli* is unique among Słowacki's works in that critical transcendence of patriotism which it expresses. Even in the patriotic odes which he composed during the early days of the November Uprising, his fervor is not confined to the Polish cause, and he expresses

hope that the "song of revolution will echo in Moscow and Petersburg," bringing freedom to the Russians as well as the Poles. This democratic pan-Slavism, with its friendly regard for the Slavic peoples of the East, is typical of Słowacki. If he could ridicule the Czech pan-Slavists of his day, as he does incidentally in his sparkling satirical poem *Beniowski*, he was still jealous for the honor and prestige of the Slavic peoples as a whole. The earliest poem of his to be preserved is entitled **"Ukrainian Duma,"** and in his unfinished French romance *à la* Walter Scott, *Le Roi de Ladawa,* he says that the poetry of the Ukrainian folk holds a comparable position in Polish literature to that of the troubadours in French or that of the Minnesinger in German. He even expects it to be the basis of the new, romantic Polish literature of the future. Later, it is true, he modified these views, finding that a healthy national literature must be founded on something more than a superficial assimilation of folk themes, but he never repudiated the special affection in which he held Ukrainian folklore.

In the sphere of the spirit, where he placed the real action of history, it was for all the Slavs, and not for the Poles alone, that he reserved a role of honor for the future. In that curious document, his memorandum to Prince Adam Czartoryski, he writes:

> The Slavic race is one of the last to make its appearance . . . prepared by God for the future. The Slavs are the workers of the freedom of the spirit. Already long ago the Grand Dukes of Muscovy set out to banish this characteristic freedom of the Slavs from the face of the earth. But in the earliest times of Slavdom Poland appears as a great sunlike sea of freedom—*jako wielkie słoneczne Wolności Morze*—and two stars of that freedom (of the same color, as it were, but perhaps of more beautiful brightness . . . because they are advancing to the regions of darkness) Novgorod and Pskov gleam in the North—*Nowogród i Psków świeca na Północy.*

We need not concern ourselves here with the history, or the philosophy of history, that Słowacki is expressing, nor need we stop to compare other texts of his on similar subjects. We do not, if we are wise, adapt our practical politics to the immediate application of poets' fancies. We do not dispose of Constantinople *à la* Dostoevskij; we do not sing with Nekrasov the praises of a Murav'ëv or with Blok the onrush of the Scythians; and we even part company with Puškin when he dares to cloak tyranny under the guise of family quarrel. No more do we have to feel that Słowacki's reputation must rise or fall with our judgment of his purely political views. My purpose has been only to show with another example how generously Słowacki associated the Slavic peoples of the East with everything that he considered most precious in his own Polish and European traditions. The outstanding example of this generosity is, of course, the character of the Russian major in Słowacki's play *Fantazy,* a creation in the same order of magnitude as Captain Mironov and Maksim Maksimyč, and the most attractive and sympathetic portrait of a Russian to be found in non-Russian literature. But I am less concerned here with Słowacki's attitude towards the Russians than with what that attitude implies in his understanding of patriotism. It seems to me that here again we find support for the kind of reading of *Anhelli* that I have suggested.

If such a reading be accepted, it may suggest an answer to another problem, a problem that exceeds in scope both *Anhelli* and its author. That is the problem of the value for us of Polish romantic poetry in general, especially of those works like *Anhelli* which are intimately involved in the history of the Polish nation. It is a problem the answer to which is not immediately apparent. If there is a direct appeal for most of us in such a masterpiece as *Pan Tadeusz*, that poem is surely exceptional, even among Mickiewicz's works, in the ease with which it is understood and valued by foreign readers. With most of the other great works of the Polish romantics such is not the case. We may know that they have provided a sustaining heritage for the Polish people through the darkest days of their nation's existence. We may admit that each succeeding period in Polish intellectual history has found in them something new, something worthy of fresh study. Yet, when it comes to a question of our own appreciation and of the meaning that this literature can have for us, we may still hesitate in our answer. Is there, after all, a "not-for-export" sign on these works? Is it one of the sacrifices that the Polish poet has had to make, that he has had to put his art exclusively in the service of his country and has thereby lost the opportunity of speaking to other peoples?

If Słowacki may stand as an example, I think we cannot admit the charge of parochialism against the Polish romantic school. It is rather his glory—as it is the glory of Polish literature—that at a time when the nation needed their inspiration and when men of smaller stamp would have been content to fire the patriotism of their countrymen, Słowacki and his poet-contemporaries subjected the very concept of patriotism to searching moral analysis. It is this above all that has made them more than the poets of a day and that enables them to speak to us, across an ocean and a century. (pp. 325-27)

Francis J. Whitfield, "The Author of 'Anhelli' (1809-1849)," in The American Slavic and East European Review, *Vol. 8, December, 1949, pp. 317-27.*

CLAUDE BACKVIS (essay date 1950)

[*Praising Słowacki's experimental efforts as crucial to the development of an original Polish drama, Backvis contends that it was the poet in Słowacki who led the dramatist to his most important accomplishments.*]

By his intimately sensitive nature, Słowacki has emerged as the personification of the poet, even as Plato portrayed him in *Ion*—a winged being which flies above the asperities of earth, intoxicated by light and heaven. And among those who were his immediate predecessors in time we recognise at a glance the artist with whom it is convenient to compare him. This "older brother" of Słowacki is undoubtedly Shelley. But, somehow or other, it happened—almost without any divining of this by their contemporaries—that these great and pure lyricists were *also* the dramatists of their generation—most effective and most enduring. (p. 361)

[But] there was no common measure between the task faced by Słowacki and that of Shelley from the time when, kindred geniuses at bottom, they resolved to endow literature with dramatic works which rose above the level of anecdote. Shelley, Manzoni and Musset created or applied a mutation of literary techniques to a dramatic tradition that was already ancient, illustrious and firmly rooted. Notably for Shelley this effort was the more natural since in fact he was only concerned to re-establish in its rights the only one of the older dramatic forms which towards 1820 had showed itself still vigorous and

life-giving—that of Shakespeare. Conversely, Słowacki, wishing to accomplish something else than empty exercises of a writer, *found himself in 1830 in the same situation* as once, in their respective *milieus,* were Trissin, Robert Garnier or Marlowe.

It is the real merit of Słowacki as a dramatist that he was aware of the dimensions and the novelty of this task, and that he knew how to put forth with patience and courage the Titanic effort entailed by the fact of its acceptance and achievement. (p. 364)

In *Mindowe* [Słowacki] applies the formula of the 18th-century political drama, in which the characters and their conflicts set out the problems and complex conditions of societies whose people are in a way eponymous. It was a hybrid formula but rich in possibilities. The result is a work extremely intelligent and interesting, but marred by a few gross naiveties. This is the habit of beginners destined to succeed in something difficult, but to be guilty of oversight in things that belong to the childhood of art. In *Maria Stuart* he set about writing a drama of psychological analysis, perfectly built, and this time the result was above all praise. He succeeded in revealing with cruel insight the petty character of the Queen, without touching anything of her charm or poetry; and, alongside her, he illumined in a plausibly just way the sacrificed personality of Darnley. Even though it is never said, it seems beyond doubt that this drama of a twenty-one-year-old can stand comparison with the works of Alfieri or Schiller.

Here is the proof of this: had it not been for his boundless ambition Słowacki could have been content to go on as he had begun and compose a whole library of interesting dramas—clever and perfectly useless.

Yet, on the contrary, he soon passes at once to a third experiment. In *Kordian* . . . he sets himself to transmit ideas, and from this point of view the work is not without interest. But as regards the dramatic formula, which is what interests us here, we find ourselves in admitted retreat from *Maria Stuart*. Partly no doubt under the power of a dual protective camouflage imposed on Słowacki by his nervous and aggressive nature (*Kordian,* being set up as answer to Mickiewicz's *Dziady*, Part III, and in a deeper way to Byron's *Manfred,* ought to have been moulded on these two texts) the author chose here a form at that time the most fashionable and the most ambitious, but also the most debatable. This was the brand of "romantic drama" in which one sole character is seen in depth illumined from all sides but especially within (by a sorry intrusion of lyrical oratory and an abuse of the soliloquy)—whereas all other characters appear only in *bas relief*.

The two first parts of *Kordian* are worth neither more nor less than the more famous samples of *genre,* i.e. they are dramatically insipid. But here perhaps the true vocation of the dramatist breaks out in that even in this framework, doomed in advance, Słowacki knew how to insert discoveries truly dramatic and of the first order. The crowd scenes with which Part III opens, and the oath-taking by Tsar Nicholas I, unloose an impression of terrifying unusualness by the simplest of treatments, by the unreal swiftness of the rhythm of events, and by a bold and revealing use of the pantomime. Further, the way in which the psychic disorder of Kordian at the time of the abortive attempt at assassination is staged in a monologue artificially spoken by two "actors"—an *agonia* of the highest quality—constitutes a striking success. Thus, even in this tribute paid unhappily to the tastes of the era, the author knew how to try out new methods—which were soon to be of wondrous use to him in the day when he would find his true formula.

However, in the long run, this was a dead end, and the poet was aware of it in time. The promised trilogy remained only a portico. Wisely refusing for a time to confer an ideological meaning on his work, he turned to experiment with the form in which one day he would be able to express what he had to say, and wrote *Balladyna.* . . . I emphasise the character of literary experiment which this drama affects, an experiment this time conclusive. The features which in future will mark Słowacki's work—its mythical character, the fact that the poetic atmosphere has here more range than the mentality of the *dramatis personae,* the use of highly contrasted settings to bring out the complexity of human situations, are shown here in a state chemically pure, and without external justification. Moreover the achieving of the planned result would represent the main difficulty to be faced. We have indeed to do with a test case: if the form were to give this time the desired result, it would be possible to use it henceforth with the same mastery which is grounded from the start in technical ingenuity.

Indeed, what could be riskier than to place side by side characters taken from different ages and literary registers, coming from the popular romantic ballad, the idyll, the romance comedies of Shakespeare (*Midsummer Night's Dream* and *As You Like It*), from *Macbeth* and *King Lear;* to put them all into a prehistoric Poland, which from the outset is not taken either tragically or even seriously; to sprinkle the whole with literary *pastiches*—but expect all the same to make of this mixture a spectacle which in conformity with the antique releases at once both pity and horror!

Since the days of symbolism we have known more than one experiment characterised by a gratuitous overweighting of po-

etic values. Precisely the check which they have met with in the properly dramatic field, shows up how exceptional and deserving was Słowacki's success.

It seems possible to set out some at least of the reasons for this success. First then, as always when hazardous battles end in victory, the enterprise which was foolishly ambitious in its ends was handled with the wisdom of a serpent in regard to means. These unreal and diverse characters are presented by the author from the start in their appropriate surroundings, methodically using nuances and contrasts to link them together. It is only when this alchemy has produced a whole series of partial effects, safely measured out, that at the beginning of Act IV he ventures to unite them. At this moment the game is won; and it is not without reason that then and only then the dramatic element takes precedence over the fairy-tale—the latter only surviving in so far as it is necessary to give to the action a symbolism of "morality." Besides, one must note that, even if the psychology of the characters is reduced to the simplest features (with more complications and nuances it would with a disproportionate weight crush those characters like soap-bubbles) it remains more or less constant and consistent. The author has seen that whims can play a part in the assembling of a drama, but not in its fundamental character. Finally, I should particularly emphasise the outstanding rôle which, through the early parts of the play, i.e. those where the success of the *tour de force* is still at stake, is assigned to the main *décor*—the great green forest of idylls and operas where it is a daily thing to meet hermits and poetical shepherds, and where enchantments can be unleashed and tales of wonder unfolded. It is by mobilising to the limit the power of envelopment, which conceals this *genius loci,* that the cohesion of elements, so astonished at finding themselves together, is finally attained.

Słowacki's sketch of a monastery on the Nile.

For the author this was "a possession forever," in the sense that if in the sequel the ingredients of these exciting literary "cocktails" differed almost every time in genus or even in species, and if these methods of the alchemist served later to communicate something which to the author meant dynamic ideas, the general formula was unchanged: fantasy, symbolism and even revelation super-imposed on everyday psychological truth; the grandeur of the saga or theogony shot through with grotesque triviality—and everything dominated by a powerful emotive atmosphere designed to suggest the situation to be faced by the social group.

True it is that to this lofty and fine aesthetic Słowacki was at times unfaithful. As noted above, the weaknesses of his mental make-up, his love of success (so cruelly and almost invariably disappointed while he lived), and the capriciousness which was no longer daringly imaginative but even incapable of submitting to any rules (even its own), explain the zig-zags which mark a superb record of effort and of depth of thought. Thus *Horsztyński*. . ., in which he tried to revive *Hamlet* (the sort of thing that was most certain to lead to disaster), is set in Lithuania at the time of the Rising of Bar but is paradoxically dated 1794. Thus **Beatrice Cenci [Beatryks Cenci]** . . . , where he succumbs to the vulgar blandishments of the French dramatic romance, with its Renaissance duelling and devilish priests richly provided with bastards and with purely physical *coups de théatre;* and thus even **Mazeppa.**

Yet apart from these uncertainties, the grand line is followed in **Lilla Weneda** . . ., in **Ksiądz Marek,** and in **Sen śrebrny Salomei,** as well as in the splendid fragments **Beniowski** and **Krak.** . . . And this line is neither more nor less than in the tradition which begins with an authentic *Polish drama* to be placed alongside the Elizabethan, the comedy of Castille and French tragedy.

The time has now come finally to sum up the features that mark it. These dramas are always collective. Each time there is at stake the destiny of a whole people, committed to a choice that involves its whole future. The significance of the crucial moment is symbolised in the fate of an exceptional personality: saint, martyr, political and social reformer or sage, in whom culminate the confused longings and lofty aspirations of a social mass, as well as its determination to bear disaster with dignity. Apart from King Agesilaus of Sparta, the features of these "leaders of the people" such as the Druid King Derwid, Father Marek, the Ukrainian sage Wernyhora, the adventurer Beniowski, the Polish Parsifal-Zawisza Czarny, the herald of individualism Samuel Zborowski, have not a trace of the historical, in the sense that they are either wholly imagined or their portraits have been highly magnified or distorted.

It is indeed significant that precisely this exception of the realism in **Agesilaus** . . . is paid for by a check-mate. Słowacki is only at his ease when he can confer on these "people-symbols" the dimensions and mythical character which alone can raise them to the functional rôle they are to play. What is more, these pictures of historical crises, so perfectly set in an atmosphere of exactness that is often striking; traversing the ages from pre-history to the end of the 18th century (or even farther if one includes Kordian), have nothing in them of archaeology: never is it their aim, whether nearer or remoter, to play with the exotic in time, with this purely aesthetic transposition into other ages to which Romanticism attached so much of its effort and hopes. With Słowacki, contrariwise, the conflicts of values of the Venedic age, or of that of Bar (1768), not only do not remove the reader (or the alas! imaginary

spectator!) from the year 1840 and from the basic problems the author had to set himself whether as thinker or citizen. They lead him to a profounder appreciation than if they had been stated in the language of 1840—a speech encumbered with wrappings which belonged only in fleeting fashion or by accident belonging to the spiritual dramas of the epoch.

This effect is in no way achieved by the method of allusion, which consists in falsifying the portrait of a moment of the past to draw from it specious lessons affecting the present. As a consequence the dramatist has chosen, or more often pictured in the limits of what is historically plausible, crises which retain a quite fresh eloquence for the people of 1840. Something is achieved far removed from what on the continent in the 19th century was called "Shakespearean drama," amounting to an excursion of slight meaning into the domain of amusing archaeology, where the authority of Shakespeare only served to excuse the use of easy technical construction. But, conversely, there is something much nearer to the real Shakespeare, since instead of being always occupied with the nature of the 9th or of the 18th century the characters are essentially people of all ages.

Before leaving this important point, I should like to detain the reader's attention for a moment on a detail which seems to mark best this aspect of Słowacki's drama, i.e. the use, unknown in the 19th century, of the antique chorus in **Beniowski, Złota Czaszka** and **Zawisza Czarny.** True, it would not be fair to envisage this literary artifice only in respect of the problem of historicity which concerns us here. One should also see here in the first instance the characteristic of prowess and virtuosity, which influences all Słowacki's work—both drama and lyric— in that both these are functionally baroque. In regard to drama the whole power consisted in forcing on the reader the plausibility of an action that always had in it something unreal. *For this very reason* it is in this unusually dangerous region that the artist ventured to create additional difficulties: at the moment in the play, when the desired result seemed to be reached, when the spectator was compelled to believe in these characters however weird, and in the situations however fantastic, the author with a calm gesture steps in, dismisses the scenery, the costumes and even the actors, in order himself to get on the stage and proclaim to the public a poetical commentary on his work. The charm is thus broken, the illusion shattered, and they have to be revived afresh later.

If, however, it is by these considerations of virtuosity that one must explain the genesis of Słowacki's chorus, it is certainly permissible to see it also as an extreme and emphasised proof of the poet's predilection for treating history not from the angle of anecdote or the picturesque, but from that of values and eternal conflicts. . . . [In] **Samuel Zborowski** . . . he sought no longer to throw into relief what was piquant or odd but what, in the catastrophe of this reign, seemed to him to conceal an eternal lesson on the problem of individual rights as opposed to those of the community. One can easily see that the chorus was best suited to induce the reader to free himself for a moment from the spectacle of the age, the people, the plot which the play sets before him, to return to the present and to get the necessary perspective for watching that which has just aroused his interest and emotions. In **Zawisza Czarny,** in order to determine how far the feudalism of the magnate and hero Jagiełło, which the poet believed he knew well through a historical tradition inevitably trivialised (as all traditions are), the author created in fancy a stage of culture quite comparable to the Greece of heroic times, whose image equally conventional slumbered in the depth of his memory. Their unforeseen meeting conferred on them not only a quite new freshness but also a gripping significance.

One has, in this fashion, the effect of super-imposition, as the phrase has it in the modern film, which sets things all at once in an unaccustomed dimension where stereotyped perspectives are confused, and which helps us the better to comprehend as well the exact meaning of the thing pictured as its prolongations in both directions of time.

A second major feature of [Polish] drama, a bit contradictory of what has just been said—though it is the union of its two contraries that makes Słowacki's work such an achievement— is the following. Placed on the precise borderline of the fantastic and the real, it knew how to remain faithful to the facts of everyday life. This is true both of the characters and of the sequence of their deeds.

So then Father Marek is a "holy soul," a hero and a miracle-worker, and in that way he takes us far from the 18th century into the open climate of oriental religiosity of the most powerful and magical sort. Yet recurring details of style or speech, or a character trait, remind us all the same that he does not cease to be also a jovial, round and partriarchal monk, a full-blooded impulsive warrior—in short a Sarmatian nobleman, very imperfectly disguised as a churchman. That this man, so well rooted in the soil that feeds him, so like the rest of his fellows of the "Saxon" age, should even be an instrument of God, and by natural impulse reach heights of sacrifice and devotion—all this, so presented, gives us the powerful impression of a miracle and makes us believe in it, at least in the realm of art.

What is valid for the picture of Father Marek goes also for those about him, and for the society out of which he springs. And if these creatures of flesh and light are plunged into a criminal adventure, strongly and mysteriously lit up by divine signs, the motivation of the incidents in which they are involved and where their passions find expression is also undeniably logical. (pp. 364-71)

The third element of the dramatic art, that which assures the intimate cohesion of the other two, is clearly . . . the continued flowering of poetry in its grandest and most generous form. It is because the characters and their deeds are carried from beginning to end by this stream of lava with its ceaselessly seething eruption of blazing, baroque pictures, and because the senses of the reader succumb to this inspired and crazy din which stuns and stimulates, that the events he witnesses are able to take on the character of a quasi-religious revelation.

From whatever angle one looks at this dramatic art, no doubt is left that it aims at reaching, and will achieve a quality of conviction which is at the opposite pole from the classical art of Europe. In place of a construction which seduces the intelligence, and of which the mechanism operates quite openly, one has here a mountain of vehement passion which seizes and carries one away. But it would be naïve not to see how much choice and skill is at the base of this outbreak of power. Perhaps a good part of this facility had become unconscious and was nothing more than the application of technical mastery—this does not matter. What does count is that we find ourselves face to face with a great work of art, with the fruit of a lofty and refined civilisation.

That this demands the union of rare qualities and favourable conditions, is proved moreover by the final phase in the career

of the master dramatist. It seems to me beyond question that *Zawisza Czarny* . . . and *Samuel Zborowski* . . . mark a perceptible decline. Here the diverse elements remain in a state of discord, and one has, in fact, great fragments of poetry that amaze but do not convince. The dramatic emotion is no longer attained. In fact the ways of the dramatist and the poet have again parted.

Perhaps the reason is that [Słowacki's] organism, as it became more and more destroyed by the ravages of disease, did not provide the amount of vital energy required for conceiving such dramas and making them a success. One thing which makes us think so is that in these final years this man who, though a pure lyricist, had by a curious paradox expressed his thoughts hitherto in the plastic forms of narrative poems or of drama, now gives his best in tiny bits of spontaneous lyric which he scribbled for his own use in *Raptularz*. It seems, indeed, that he had no longer sufficient confidence in a doubtful to-morrow to attempt works that demanded time and perspective.

But it is also possible that we have here a moving example of the law which Professor Toynbee calls that of "diminishing returns." The psychological challenge that is seen in the fact of having to compose dramas, without hope of seeing them produced, had at first provoked an enriching response. Indeed, if one considers the material means at the disposal of the stage in those days, one realises that it was because Słowacki's plays had no chance of being produced that he had been in process of breaking completely with the tradition of "a conversation in front of a mirror," continued in "period" *décor*. But in the long run the challenge proved excessive and after the culminating period of 1842-1843, as a result of having no contact with the boards of a real theatre, he lost year by year his feeling for drama and finally even his desire to write plays.

Nevertheless these fourteen years of pioneer work had marked a stage of supreme importance in the birth of an original type of Polish drama. (pp. 373-74)

At the moment when he was finishing *Balladyna*, Słowacki wrote to his mother (18 December 1834) with the timid pride which can be revealed only to those who are near and dear:

> Of all the things which up to now my brain has
> brought forth, this tragedy is the best; above
> all because it has opened for me a new road,
> a new land of poetry which has not yet been
> trodden by the foot of man. . . . I cannot give
> you here, dear mother, a more precise picture
> of the kind of drama my tragedy represents. If
> it bears any family resemblance to any known
> work, it should be to *King Lear* by Shakespeare. Oh, if it could only one day be placed
> alongside King Lear!

Posterity should, with all justice, confirm this hope. Certain it is that Słowacki is not the equal of Shakespeare. Perhaps that will always be something impossible; perhaps it will never again happen that the greatest dramatist and the greatest poet will be found in one man. In Słowacki's case the poet is greater than the dramatist, and that is why at vital moments the poet has taken the dramatist by the hand and led him to the most ambitious goals. But the fact remains that this weakly and nervous man was a natural force, that this Ariel of poetry divined with the intuition of genius the passions of man and the problems of society, that this lover of baroque, of preciosity, this disciple of formal beauty was willing and able to create myths which, on a par with the grand figures of the international field, will remain dynamic images which each generation invests with a meaning every time different. The fact remains that this exile, this solitary poet, has built in silence a communal drama which even to-day is an earnest of the future. (pp. 374-75)

Claude Backvis, "*Słowacki's Place in Polish Drama,*" in The Slavonic and East European Review, *Vol. XXVIII, No. 71, April, 1950, pp. 359-76.*

MANFRED KRIDL (essay date 1956)

[*In his examination of Słowacki's career, Kridl focuses on the author's treatment of Polish history and concludes that Słowacki's influence on Polish literature will endure because of his extraordinary lyrical and linguistic skills.*]

Even in [his] early works a certain characteristic trait of Słowacki's may be seen, namely, that he draws his impulse to write from literature—Polish and foreign literary works. This is not simple imitation, however, but a distinct and perhaps conscious working over of literary motifs which are known from elsewhere. We have in [the] first volumes of Słowacki a kind of anthology of the contemporary romantic motifs taken from Malczewski, Mickiewicz, partly also from Zaleski and Goszczyński, and all conceived in a morbid Byronic tone. Next to *Konrad Wallenrod*, these are the most Byronic verses in Polish literature. However, an extraordinary nascent talent is visible even here. The short poem, **"Godzina myśli"** (**"An Hour of Meditation"**), is full of subtle, soft tones, dimmed colors, delicate feelings and the profound problems of the romantic psyche. . . . His tragedy *Mindowe* maintains on the whole a classical form, but in *Marja Stuart* the author is seen to begin breaking away from that form to a search for his own type of structure and dramatic technique.

The next larger work of Słowacki is *Kordian* . . ., intended as the first part of a dramatic trilogy, which, however, was never written. This work is evidence that the poet had begun to turn away from experimentation with the romantic motifs, which he had practiced until that time, toward the national-psychological problems of the day. But at the root of its genesis lies a literary work, namely, Part III of [Mickiewicz's] *Forefathers' Eve*. Of course, the aim was not—as older literary historians used to believe with excessive simplicity and ease—to place a new figure, Kordian, 'a hero of action,' against the Konrad of *Forefathers' Eve,* that 'hero of feeling,' an aim which Słowacki apparently did not achieve. What he did was to take up, to pose and interpret in a basically novel way, the question of the contemporary Polish generation, its psychology, its attitude toward national problems and its ability to act. This question was connected with that of the recent insurrection, which occupied all the minds at the time. But it was set against a broader background, and the manner in which it was posed and solved concealed a polemic with the attitude of Mickiewicz as expressed in the latter's last dramatic work. *Kordian* was, therefore, not an 'imitation' of Mickiewicz, but an original work of a subtle and critical mind which could not agree with the apotheosis of Poland exposed in *Forefathers' Eve*. In the symbolic figure of Kordian, Słowacki presents other psychological facets of the contemporary Polish generation, important and basic ones, according to him, namely, the spiritual dichotomy, a lack of strong will and decision, a sickly imagination, sudden impulses and equally sudden discouragement and apathy, a search for truth and aim in life, accompanied by an innate skepticism in relation to everything, a momentary passion for

some idea without the internal faith in it, the desperate sacrifice for a cause without inner conviction, and the search for death as the liberator from internal torture. Those are the characteristic stigmas of a generation forced by fate to play an active and heroic part but devoid of the ability to do it. Słowacki's drama contains, furthermore, a sharp and venomous criticism of the leaders of the Insurrection as well as a negative characterization of the insurgents and of the stupid Warsaw mob. The messianic idea of *Forefathers' Eve,* the idea of leadership and salvation of the nation by an individual, is satirized in the prologue. Moreover, Słowacki opposes to the Catholicism of Mickiewicz's poem a sharp criticism of the Pope's policy toward the November Insurrection (in the Vatican scene).

The structure of *Kordian* is reminiscent of the contemporary romantic dramas. The three acts are composed of fairly loose scenes designed to portray the spiritual development of the hero through relations with various persons, the observation of various matters of this world, and the search for an 'aim.' The scenery necessarily changes very frequently, while the individual scenes and characters are treated sketchily. 'Action' proper takes place within the soul of the hero. Some scenes are presented with great power of dramatic expression, for instance, Kordian's intended murder of the tzar, where personalized Fear and Imagination take hold of Kordian's sickly mind and prevent him from carrying out the deed.

The words of the third person in the prologue forecast, as it were, Słowacki's new poetic program. This person chases from the stage not only the prophet and the messianist but his opponent as well, stating that he himself will reach into the past, to the essence of the national tradition after previously cleansing it of the 'rotten mortal shrouds', and will pull the true Polish idea out of the past. These words throw a certain light on almost all of Słowacki's subsequent production, which was indeed devoted to the past and to the search in the past for positive and durable values and, at the same time, to a sharp and acute criticism of the present. (pp. 269-71)

The idea for [*Lilla Weneda*] was drawn from two sources; the first is Byron's note in *Childe Harold* about Julia Alpinula, who tried vainly to save her father from imprisonment; the second was a contemporary historical theory which maintained that the Polish state was created by way of invasion of a settled Slavic tribe by foreign knights, who, having conquered the land and created a political organization, gave rise to the Polish gentry. This theory supposedly proved that the gentry was of different origin from the native Polish people. It is from these two sources that the double plot of the tragedy arises: one is the story of Lilla Weneda (the Julia Alpinula of Słowacki's version) and her father, Derwid; the second is the story of the fight of the Wenedi with the invaders, the Lechites. These two plots are related through Derwid, who is the leader of the Wenedi and is captured by the Lechites. Lilla tries to liberate him, for the Wenedi depend on his playing of the harp to spur them to victory. In this way the 'family' motifs join with the 'national' ones. What grows out of them is the basic subject of *Lilla Weneda:* the tragedy of a perishing nation. In Słowacki's interpretation it becomes true tragedy, for the fate of the Wenedi is unavoidable and irrevocable, and at the same time a great value perishes. This nation is meek, kind, cultured, poetical (symbolized in the harp players who encourage the knights in battle); it is defeated by invaders who are on a much lower level in every respect, and are endowed with many traits of the future Polish gentry. Among these traits the poet mentions 'a liking for shouting, dill pickles, and coats of arms.' In this way a distinction is also made between the Polish people and the gentry who rule them.

The structure of this tragedy is in the realm of the new and experimental for Słowacki. He employs some classical forms—prologue, chorus, and the concept of inevitable doom which hangs over the heroes. On the other hand, however, he has modernized the classical structure considerably; he has dispensed with the unity of action and time and has introduced 'Shakespearian' motifs (the comical characters of Gwalbert and Ślaz; the figure of Derwid who resembles King Lear at times, and of Gwinona who is reminiscent of Margaret in *Henry VI*), and up-to-date allusions which touch upon conditions in Poland after the Insurrection. The chorus of harp players fills the play with tones of deadly fear for the fate of the nation, and the whole conception of the tragedy is imbued with dark foreboding about the future of Poland. Once more in this work, as in previous ones, a voice of warning and despair falls in the midst of the émigrés who are intoxicated with faith and hope—a menacing memento for the compatriots who so easily let themselves be swayed by their own illusions. (pp. 277-78)

In *Beniowski,* Słowacki offered Polish poetry something new—a poem after the manner of Byron's *Don Juan. The Journey to the Holy Land* [*Podróz na Wschód (Podróz do Ziemi Swietej z Neopolu)*] had already been conceived in this form, but *Beniowski* became a new reincarnation, artistically far more mature. The previous poem had been a description of a trip by boat to Greece and across Greece and, as such, was well suited to numerous digressions, expressions of opinions about people and problems, interruption of the description to take up a timely problem—be it a matter related to the émigrés, rumors, or even gossip—and disclosure of impressions, ideas, and projects. In *Beniowski* there is a different aspect. Formally it has a main 'subject': the history of Maurycy Beniowski, a Hungarian nobleman, soldier, traveler, adventurer, and other characters connected with him. It was difficult to interpolate into this kind of tale all sorts of 'parentheses' and to place within them digressions which had no connection with the main plot. But, if one could not do these things, what would then be the use of the law of romantic freedom which imposes no rules, which follows inspiration alone, and which lets itself be drawn wherever 'the spirit moves'? Słowacki, therefore, did not hesitate to break structural laws; he indeed made the breaking of all laws of structure his own structural principle for the new poem, just as Byron had done in *Don Juan.* Thus was written a work in which—as Norwid later expressed it—'the parentheses are the principal aim,' while the epic narrative plays a secondary role. As he progresses into the poem, the reader gradually relinquishes his interest in the adventures of Beniowski and his acquaintances; not because it is difficult to keep them straight or to maintain the continuity throughout the constant breaking of the thread of action, but in order to abandon himself with delight to the poet's unusually agile thought and vivid fantasy which constantly cause surprise. The reader is hurled from object to object, amidst cascades of poetic images, moving confessions and statements, sharp, satirical invectives against everybody and everything, extremely ingenious characterizations of people and timely problems, outbursts of the most varied feelings that can fill a human being, and high comedy juxtaposed with a profound conception of the basic problems of life. In one word, the poem sparkles with an unheard of wealth of elements, motifs, matters, and problems the like of which cannot be found in any other single Polish work. The language and verse match this wealth. For sheer virtuosity of language, rhythm, and rhyme, *Beniowski* is probably surpassed

only by *King Spirit* [*Król Duch*], Słowacki's last work. But in *Beniowski* too the poet achieves the summit of what can be done with the poetic language, the maximum of absolute control over it which permits him to make experiments at times bordering on virtuoso feats. (pp. 279-80)

One can observe in Słowacki's manuscripts of [the early 1840s] the tortures of the intellect, as it tries to explain the riddle of existence and universe and to put reasoning in a concise and logical form. One may also see a very painful thing, namely the complete sterility and hopelessness of these efforts, based only on imagination and dreams. It is difficult to suppose that, with his keen intelligence, Słowacki did not, at least in part, perceive this hopelessness and experience moments of terrible, painful doubt. (pp. 282-83)

[Słowacki's] leading theory is based on the principle that 'everything is created by the spirit and for the spirit, nothing exists for physical aims.' It is on this absolutely spiritualistic basis that Słowacki explains the creation of the universe in his most finished work in this domain: *The Genesis from the Spirit.* In it he also traces the evolution of shapes and forms from inorganic matter to man, stipulating that the evolution cannot finish with man, for its aim is 'the spiritual force of Christ's nature' and the approach of man to Christ. In connection with his theory of evolution the poet advocates the idea of metempsychosis, that is, a reincarnation of the same spirit in gradually higher (or lower) bodily forms. In this work of growth humanity needs leaders, whom the poet calls 'king spirits.' Sometimes such spiritual leadership is bestowed upon whole nations rather than on individuals. This leadership is now given to Poland, who, purified by suffering and tortures, is to advocate and realize the 'new Gospel' on earth and lead the world to the Heavenly Kingdom, that is, to 'global angelhood.'

Słowacki's most important poetic work of this period is the long poem, entitled *King Spirit,* the first 'rhapsody' of which appeared in 1847, while the much longer remainder was published after the poet's death. The basic concept of the poem is the reincarnation of a powerful, 'kingly' spirit in prehistoric and historic characters who personify Poland and carry out its 'genetic work.' (pp. 284-85)

[If] we treat *King Spirit* as a fantastic tale about the history of Poland rather than as a revelation of new genetic truths, we shall not encounter excessive difficulty in understanding it. Of course, mysterious things occur in the poem, and allusions to obscure theories are frequent. But such things at times occur even in poems which have no complicated philosophy to propound. The obscurity and confusion of Słowacki's poem are amply compensated with outstanding beauty and power such as Polish poetry seldom possesses during its whole existence. This poem clearly demonstrates that even the most abstract and strange theory may become a vital force in poetry if it is applied in a truly poetic manner by a great poet. This is definitely the case of *King Spirit.* One of its completely original and highly suggestive characteristics is the thorough, perfectly organic union between the earthly and supernatural worlds; the union is even more integral than in Part III of *Forefathers' Eve.* This results from the theory of 'spirits,' which all mystics hold in common; it may even originate in 'the columns of spirits,' about which Towiański said 'they press on man from all sides.' In Słowacki's poem, however, this theory was transformed into a powerful poetic tool. The inner life and deeds of each character, the events which occur in the poem, and even the phenomena of nature are thus tied, by means of invisible but strong threads, to the supernatural world, to eternal matters, and to the fate of the nation molded in its historical develop-ment. The action of *King Spirit* thus achieves a distant, heav-enly, 'global' perspective, permeated by a breeze of infinity, because the genetic evolution of the nation does not end until it reaches the distant horizons of God's Kingdom on earth. In Polish poetry there is no work of such character, while among foreign works *King Spirit* may be compared, in this respect, only with some parts of Dante's *Divine Comedy*.

We have said that the language of *Beniowski* reaches the summit of poetic virtuosity. About the language and verse of *King Spirit* one would be tempted to say that they have been freed (as far as is possible) from all earthly ties and from physical-material traits to become spiritualized to the highest possible degree. In accordance with the general symbolic-supernatural character of the poem, the individual words, designations, phrases, images, and descriptions, generally do not stand for any physical, material objects but are symbols of distant and eternal things. Not only the characters' feelings and experi-ences, which by nature must be of such a character, but nearly every description, apparently purely epic, is imbued with this symbolic light of the hereafter. *King Spirit* was the first 'epic poem' of this kind in Polish poetry, and it may not be compared with anything in foreign literatures. It is a unique kind of lyric epos—an epic about the history of a nation, presented as the experience of a spirit who is incarnated into that history con-ceived as phases of his evolution, as he marches toward infin-ity.

We speak here of *King Spirit* as it reached us in his published first rhapsody and a number of manuscripts which were later arranged by editors into further rhapsodies, without certain knowledge of the poet's intentions. Thus we speak of a work unfinished by the poet himself, a work which he perhaps might never have finished, so gigantic was his conception for human capacity. Our judgment cannot therefore apply to the whole, which does not exist, but rather to fragments. But what was left represents a magnificent, gigantic torso, as those splendid torsos of ancient Greek sculpture which, though mutilated and disfigured, reveal genius in all their fragments.

Such beautiful 'torsos'—such parts and fragments of splendid conceptions—are frequent in the last period of Słowacki's cre-ativity. One of the most finished is the play, *Samuel Zborowski*. The problem of this sixteenth-century rebel, decapitated at the time of Jan Zamoyski's chancellorship, is here—like the prob-lem of *King Spirit*—transported onto the ground of eternity—to heaven and before Christ's court. And again the poem is not concerned with historical truth, as the action is played in cosmic rather than in earthly dimensions. . . . The whole genetic-messianic ideology of the play is . . . without any basic sig-nificance. It represents Zborowski as a spirit who raised Poland and suggests that his decapitation also signified the 'decapi-tation of Poland,' as it arrested the country's ascension towards the Kingdom of Heaven. After the elimination of these ele-ments the drama about Samuel Zborowski—just as *King Spirit*—will appear as a dramatically daring and theatrically advanced concept of the transposition of historical and earthly matters to a cosmic level. The historical Zborowski and his problem disappear, leaving room for the eternal problem of crime and punishment, which is here presented in an entirely novel way; what is left also is the problem of the strength of the human spirit, whose growth may take place through falls and crimes. The question of man's right to arrest this growth, about whose individual phases and ultimate destination man knows nothing, also emerges. These are some of the perspectives opened by

the drama, a play conceived in the spirit of romanticism and mysticism, but surpassing both these trends artistically. It opens new possibilities for dramatic and theatrical art, going beyond the devices of subsequent realism and even symbolism. (pp. 285-87)

According to Krasiński's brilliant characterization in his article "Kilka słów of Juljuszu Słowackim" ("A Few Words About Julius Słowacki"), Słowacki's works are at once a contrast and complementary to the works of Mickiewicz. They provide contrast in the sense that Mickiewicz's genius is expressed as a 'centripetal' force which creates a base and foundation and builds on them solid, homogeneous edifices, concentrating the individual elements with tremendous synthetic power, while Słowacki's imagination is revealed in a 'centrifugal' ten-dency—a force which, instead of acting from the outside to-ward the center, acts from the center (or from several changing centers) toward the outside. This is a dispersing rather than a concentrating tendency, which attempts to comprise the largest domain possible, to reach the farthest horizons, and to try the most varied methods and means of conceiving phenomena and molding them into artistic forms. It is in this trait of Słowacki's imagination rather than in 'imitation,' as was formerly thought, that the unusual variety of his production lies—those infinite poetic genres and forms, changing as in a kaleidoscope. This variety poses difficulties and even riddles, as in the apparent chaos the critic tries to find a solid basis, a fundamental di-rection, or at least a trace of a line of evolution. Many attempts in this field have been made, but none has yielded satisfactory results. Therefore—following Krasiński—we must accept that centrifugal force as the leading 'principle' of Słowacki's cre-ation. It helps us to see our way in this maze, frees us from the arid search for a 'leading idea' (which is disappointing in the case of many poets), because the 'radiation' of Słowacki's production in various directions naturally produces a series of 'ideas' and 'centers.' (p. 289)

As it encompasses the natural and supernatural worlds, Słowacki's poetry sparkles with all the colors of the rainbow; it embraces a world of national and universal feelings and thoughts in its elevation of the national cause to a universal level; it takes that cause to the gates of heaven and with *beauty* tries to revive the dead fatherland. Słowacki believed pro-foundly in the power of beauty to create and to transform. Throughout his life he fought for the recognition of this truth by a society which still held the view that poetry was either entertainment or teaching; he fought also for the recognition of his freedom as an artist, his right to that freedom and to his role and significance in society. He gave to Poland a new type of artist, conscious of his vocation and means and deserving of recognition. Conditions and circumstances led this great and independent artist, who followed his inspiration and imagi-nation wherever they led him, to embrace the national cause of his own free will. The majority of his works were devoted to the national past, according to the program expressed in *Kordian*. In this past he saw two sides of the national character: the angelic soul and the coarse skull. It is in this angelic soul that he sought the 'Polish idea,' sharing the lofty illusion of many contemporary Poles that his own noble dreams and fan-tasies corresponded to reality. (p. 290)

In his poems and plays Poland was resurrected in all the beauty of her land and people, but also in the sins of her sons. Indeed, she was immortalized and revived in song, though her body remained in the grave.

The characteristic differences between the poetry of Mickiewicz and that of Słowacki are best seen in their language and
verse. Mickiewicz was a master in his simplicity, precision,
and clarity of style. Taken separately, his words are simple,
common, current, and understandable to all. Only the proximity of other words, their distribution, succession, rhythm
and rhyme combinations lend them poetic expression, making
them unusual, giving them a new sparkle, and revealing them
in a new, startling form. Słowacki is different. His vocabulary
is in itself unusual, poetical by birth, as it were, and often
difficult and 'artificial'; it abounds in neologisms, created with
brilliant linguistic intuition, and changes in structure, declension, and syntax. The later his production, the more distinct
and intense this trait becomes; it reached its summit in the
period of Słowacki's mysticism, when his works required a
special language all the more. In those works his linguistic
inventiveness and creativeness surpassed everything that has
ever been done in Polish poetry. All the known means of poetic
expression—the poetic image, description, symbol, metaphor,
simile, to mention only the principal ones—assume a new
shape. The metaphor joins very distant clauses, symbolism
penetrates every description and image, colors operate in the
most unusual combinations, and the world of sound intensifies
the voices of nature, making them unusual.

The poet's exclamation in *Beniowski*—'And mine will be victory beyond the grave!'—was fulfilled in the third generation
of Polish poets. 'Young Poland,' at the end of the nineteenth
century, acknowledged him as its master, placing him at the
very pinnacle of Polish poetry. His influence was strongest in
that epoch, but even the one which followed was not independent of the fertile force of his poetry. It had entered the
blood of creative Poland, and lives on; it will continue to live
as long as poets are born on Polish soil. (pp. 290-91)

> *Manfred Kridl, "Polish Romanticism after 1831,"*
> *in his* A Survey of Polish Literature and Culture,
> *translated by Olga Scherer-Virski, Mouton, 1956,*
> *pp. 241-321.*

ZBIGNIEW FOLEJEWSKI   (essay date 1962)

[*Folejewski discusses Słowacki's development of the theme of
crime and punishment in several of his works, noting that for the
author crime is necessary to affirm the existence of justice and
punishment is needed "to establish the proper relationship between good and evil."*]

Słowacki . . . is a writer who from his early period to the very
end of his creative work occupied himself with the problem of
the tragic unity of crime and punishment. One could almost
venture the statement that along with Shakespeare, Słowacki
is the writer who gave the fullest treatment of this problem in
his artistic creations, especially in his visionary drama *Samuel
Zborowski*.

In practically all of Słowacki's works the problem of crime
and punishment occupies an important place, either separated
as a central point (*Balladyna*), or presented as an organic part
of the wider issue of the eternal struggle between good and
evil in the souls of individuals and in the history of nations
and of entire mankind. National aspects, of course, absorbed
the Polish poet most of all, and he obviously could not but
approach them from the point of view of his particular situation
as an exile tortured by a complex of guilt, unable to be completely objective; but, at the same time, as an exile the poet
was able to see the problems of his people from certain per-

spective, not dimmed by the usual trivial worries of everyday
life.

Of course, there are in Słowacki certain metamorphoses. The
problem of crime and punishment, which absorbed him at first
mostly as a literary and psychological motif, later became one
of the central points of his creations in which, through a stage
of personal involvement, he gradually moved to more detached
philosophical and historiosophical speculations. However, from
the very beginning—in spite of the fact that he himself later
deplores his all too literary attitude—the poet shows a surprising consistency in his basic concept of the problem. One
of the main features of this concept is the fact that Słowacki
never presents the ideas of crime and punishment as a chronological sequence. For him the problem is ever one of integral
unity. This is so in his early *Lambro* and in his *Kordian*, and
the same concept dominates Słowacki's final creation, *King
Spirit* [*Król Duch*]. It is not without reason that Słowacki himself mentions two specific works as the ones which were for
him "a matter of conscience". They were *Agmemnon's Tomb*
[*Grób Agamemnona*] and *Samuel Zborowski*, works in which
Słowacki in a daring and passionate way and yet with impressive philosphical foundation, struggles with the problem of
guilt and suffering of his people—the guilt of his contemporaries, of "the half of the warriors" who, like himself, stay
alive in the midst of a national disaster—and with the guilt of
the Zborowskis and of the Zamoyskis, a guilt which Słowacki
rationalized to a degree (if one can call his concept of history
rationalization) but which he did not idealize or falsify.

We know that in his critical analysis of his people, Słowacki
never put himself in the role of a Cato; the awareness of his
own responsibility adds to the general authenticity of his presentation. But the negative aspect, the element of guilt, is only
a part of his poetic concept of the problems; the demand of
punishment is conceived by Słowacki in a more constructive
way, not as passive suffering, but as a struggle through expiation to a higher form of life.

Mickiewicz started with a proud individualistic revolt of a
romantic poet who challenges the whole world, for he feels
entitled to fight for his entire people. In his subsequent ideological development he came to the humble, Franciscan attitude
of Father Robak, the actual hero of his epic *Pan Tadeusz*. It
was a natural and logical development and even in his poetic
rivalry Słowacki had to admit that this *was* the road leading to
God.

But this road of meek self-denial, of martyrs and humble saints
was not the road of the people whose history Słowacki undertook to present to the world. The riotous, revolutionary Satanic
spirit could not be thrown out of the Polish past, Słowacki felt.
A truly romantic poet, he could not see a simple biblical pattern
of Christian suffering as a solution of Polish history. For him,
as for Mickiewicz, the political catastrophe was punishment
for past crimes. And he was the one to see and condemn these
crimes much more severely than did Mickiewicz or did Krasiński, who glorified the past in exaggerated stanzas of his
Psalms. But to Słowacki, both the angelic, peaceful, peasant
element of the Polish past and the Satanic elements of the
constant rebellious struggle of the guilty gentry was an organic
part of the Polish road in history.

From Oriental, Indian philosophy, Słowacki acquired the sympathetic outlook on the struggle of Aryman against Ormuzd.
He saw it in the struggle between the rough "golden skull"
of the gentry and the angelic soul of his people incorporated

in the peaceful peasantry. The spirit of Polish history had to contain both these elements in the same way as the spirit of Christianity could not exist without the dynamic concept of a constant struggle against Satan. It may seem rather sophisticated, but it is closer to reality than is the one-sided justification of the past in Krasiński and even in the maximalistic formula of complete Christian purification in Mickiewicz.

Słowacki's concept of the indivisibility of crime and punishment in any process of individual and collective development, a concept combining ancient principles with modern Hegelian formulae of dialectic oppositions, is reflected in a series of poetic works in which the Polish poet with unique force and suggestivity strives at a synthesis between the angelic and the satanic elements in the history of mankind.

The fullest dramatic interpretation of these ideas can be found in *Samuel Zborowski,* one of the most daring visionary dramas in world literature. Słowacki reviews here the entire Polish history, epitomized in a court case where the poet himself appears as advocate of the accused criminal, before the highest judge—God. What here is crime and what is punishment? What is good and what is evil? The reader really has to "struggle" with the poet's spirit in order to penetrate beyond the apparent chaos of visions and ideas. This work of literature is one of the most baffling and difficult to analyze, especially since it remained unfinished. But the main line of reasoning is in agreement with Słowacki's chief idea of history and human progress, as represented in a number of his other works.

Samuel Zborowski was punished by the Chancellor for his undeniable crimes. Zborowski was an admitted rebel, he obstructed the lawful process of governing the country. This was an obvious crime, a crime which personified the guilt of the entire dominating class—the gentry. But in historical perspective Zborowski the criminal and Zamoyski the guardian of the law are two inseparable elements of one organism. Zborowski's crime was inseparable from the concept of perpetual rebellion as an element of progress; on the other hand Zamoyski's ruthless verdict was also a crime from the point of view of absolute moral values necessary for human progress. The punishment executed by Zamoyski was at the same time self-punishment, Zborowski's execution was Zamoyski's moral suicide. We have a pattern of classic tragedy in which this or that decision does not change the final catastrophe. No longer is it a clear Christian opposition of sin and virtue or the Hegelian thesis and antithesis. Zborowski's crime is an element of progress to the same extent that Zamoyski's justice is a crime since it obstructs progress. The two opposite forces form the axle of historical process, and the final scene, in which the Chancellor repents, begging the criminal's forgiveness and asking him to shake his hand, constitutes a poetic synthesis. Perhaps, speaking in Hegelian terms, it could be called "unity in contradiction."

Here Słowacki deepens the concept of crime and punishment, pointing to the element of expiation as constructive in individual and historical struggle between good and evil. The Polish Romantic is in this respect more optimistic than the great Russian who leaves even his most "angelic" heroes, Alyosha and Myshkin in disappointment and resignation.

One can, of course, say that Słowacki's optimistic goal is unattainable, that his conception is a Utopia. The poet himself was aware of this, showing—especially in his last poetic work, *King Spirit*—how this idealistic striving toward an unattainable absolute degenerates into crime. But even this for Słowacki is an organic part of the dynamic process of human progress,

since in the final analysis and in the light of the unavoidable punishment crime must become an ultimate test of the existence of justice. In this way the fantastic scenes in *King Spirit* present the Polish past in a curiously suggestive light.

We see in *King Spirit* a long gallery of historic figures and scenes, from the nebulous old Slavic patriarchal community through the first individual attempt at organizing a larger social and political unit up to the higher level of collective progress interwoven by stages of individual struggle. In the first symbolic vision in the work, a vision anticipating future history, we see a heroine holding the sun above her head and with the moon under her feet. In this vision this is the symbol of the ideal to which the Polish people were to strive in a series of individual and collective victories and defeats. The long line of leaders incorporates the satanic element of constant turbulent opposition and the angelic element of peaceful progress. They symbolize a test of the ultimate law of human history.

Here, too, the problem of crime and punishment is an organic part of development: through crime the existence of divine justice is tested and it appears as the natural human lot to challenge fate, to call for punishment, in order to establish the proper relationship between good and evil.

The best illustration to this can be found in the battle between the satanic spirit of Rettiger-Popiel and the angelic Zorian. It reminds one of Rogozhin-Myshkin's struggle in Dostoevsky's *Idiot* (and also, to a certain degree, the struggle for Raskolnikov's soul between Svidrigaylov and Sonya in *Crime and Punishment*): However, while Dostoevsky with a fatalistic feeling of helplessness leaves Myshkin lost in the world in a state of surprised resignation, Zorian's spirit in Słowacki's creation triumphs in a posthumous victory. The main difference here is the level on which the conflict between good and evil is being decided. The duality, which the Russian writer so suggestively presents within the frame of reference of the individual human dilemma, is conceived by Słowacki as an element of collective striving with optimistic faith in human progress. (pp. 163-66)

Zbigniew Folejewski, "The Theme of Crime and Punishment in Słowacki's Poetry," in Studies in Russian and Polish Literature in Honor of Wacław Lednicki, edited by Zbigniew Folejewski and Others, Mouton & Co., 1962, pp. 160-67.

JULIAN KRZYŻANOWSKI (essay date 1969)

[*Krzyżanowski describes Słowacki as the "founder of modern Polish drama" and examines his skillful handling of action, characterization, structure, and language. These remarks were first published in 1969. For additional commentary by Krzyżanowski, see excerpt dated 1930.*]

Słowacki was the founder of the modern Polish drama. This very prosaic statement may seem extraordinary, for it cannot be backed by any monumental scientific work on Słowacki as a playwright, for no such work has been written. So the gap must be filled by three series of arguments, shall we say: historic and literary, beginning with bibliographic information up to the reception of the works of Słowacki in the theatrical life of Poland.

The bibliographic information shows that out of the fourteen volumes of Słowacki's works, five contain his plays, totalling twenty six works. They include both long, five-act tragedies and small pieces of various length from several dozen to several thousand lines. The eloquence of these figures is all the greater if we look at Słowacki's plays against the background of his purely poetic works written in verse which fill seven published volumes. It will then be found that Słowacki's dramatic works account for more than half of his poetic legacy. (p. 279)

The period of Słowacki's most intensive activity as a playwright was at the time when writers both in Poland and in exile were all full of enthusiasm about the Confederation of Bar. Słowacki was also very interested in this subject, and apart from the long epic poem *Beniowski,* which did not exhaust his knowledge of the epoch, he wrote three plays. The first of them, of which only two acts were written, bears the same title as his own poem *Beniowski;* the two others published by Słowacki himself, *Father Mark (Ksiądz Marek)* and *The Silver Dream of Salomea (Sen Srebrny Salomei)* form a kind of whole, for the first is about the Confederation and its significance in the history of the struggles to regain independence, while the second deals with events accompanying the Confederation, the scene being set in the Humań region at the time of the peasants' rebellion, where the terrible results of the severance of peaceful relations between the Polish and Ukrainian people was demonstrated in the stories of the lyre-player Wernyhora and his foster-child Sawa.

The struggle for independence, from Kościuszko's Insurrection to the November Rising was also the subject of *Horsztyński, Kordian* and . . . *Lilla Weneda.* The mention here of this tragedy, previously referred to as depicting the birth of the Polish state, has its special eloquence; for it spans and links in a specific way the whole of the dramatic production of Słowacki, the creator of Polish historical drama. Although the action of *Lilla Weneda* takes place at the dawning of Poland's history, its ideological problems are presented so as to bring out and throw light on the meaning of Poland's past as understood by the generation who lived through the tragedy of the Rising. If we add to these plays, *Fantasius (Fantazy)*—depicting the conditions following the Rising, the nation petrified by the knout of Tsar Nicholas I, a period of political oppression and economic ruin, this will complete the immense cycle of dramatic pictures from the history of Poland.

It should be supplemented with three or four excursions into the history of other countries. Omitting *Prince Michael Twerski,* they are: *Agesilaos (Agezylausz),* about ancient Greece, the Renaissance tragedies *Maria Stuart,* and *Beatrice Cenci (Beatrix Cenci)* [*Beatryks Cenci*] fully edited in Polish and partly in French. To be accurate as far as bibliography is concerned, mention should also be made of two translations, a small part of *Macbeth* and Calderon's *El Principe Constante,* the translation of the latter tragedy being considered one of true genius.

Having before one's eyes the vast panorama of tragedies of this Polish playwright, written in the course of less than twenty years and forming the framework of modern Polish drama, one cannot refrain from asking several questions which involuntarily come to mind, namely, concerning the character and artistic value of Słowacki's works. The most general question would be: to what should we attribute the fact that these works, having once been included in the theatrical repertoire, have become permanent items in the Polish theatre programmes.

Fifty years ago the answer to this question would have been that this was due, first of all to considerations of an ideological nature, the "divining powers" of the bard, although even this was not true, for it would be difficult to find such elements in *Maria Stuart, Mazeppa* or *Balladyna,* and these plays were the

most popular then. The right answer is a different one, namely that Słowacki's position in the history of Polish drama was due to the artistic value of his works and it is for this reason that Słowacki's works are read and staged today. There are several factors responsible for this.

The first of them, already referred to here in discussing the subjects of Słowacki's historical tragedies, is his undisputed ability to choose subjects making a strong appeal to the imagination of his readers and audiences and holding their attention with the great dynamic force of his works. The life and death struggle of two nations, the antagonism of two generations, compelled by fate to play for the highest political stakes, the conflict created by a son's duty to his father and his duty as a patriot, the tragic inner struggles caused by conflicting emotions like passionate love and hate, like dreams of great deeds and Hamlet-like inability to carry them out, the problem of leadership and the ethic complications inseparably connected with it—these are just a handful of the typical motifs and ideas to be found in the dramas of Słowacki. They are all tragic motifs, for they are the fundamental components of highly individual characters, both heroes and heroines, who live and suffer and evoke the strong sympathy of the theatre-goer or reader. In the great multitude of human characters born in Słowacki's imagination, some stand out distinctly as figures that Mickiewicz described as "heroes and saints". And they are found not only in such plays as *Father Mark,* that is, works written towards the end of his creative life, but appear in his earlier works too. The male characters are accompanied by a whole gallery of heroines, a collection so rich that young Michał Bałucki, enchanted by its beauty, devoted a whole book to them as early as 1867, *The Heroines of Słowacki's Dramas (Kobiety dramatów Słowackiego).* Suffice it to mention Amelia and Diana, Balladyna and Gwinona, Lilla Weneda and The Princess, to realize what a wealth and variety of female characters Słowacki created, how finely he drew their inner spiritual and emotional life against the background of happenings that make one's blood run cold with horror.

The playwright skillfully guides the action, combining and opposing these events, accumulating and building them up with absolute certainty, not hesitating to produce glaring and even, at some moments, really monstrous effects. This liking for effects of this kind, understandable in a writer who looked to Shakespeare as his master, and whose cultural outlook was shaped to quite an extent by the French popular drama of those times, the plays he saw in the Paris theatres, is severely judged by some, who charge Słowacki with being melodramatic. And indeed, in some of his tragedies there are many melodramatic moments and what is more, in *Mazeppa,* and particularly in *Beatrice Cenci,* their function is not that of incidental episodes or ornamentation, but of basic, constitutive components, deliberately included and written with careful consideration for the desired effect. What was their function? The melodramatic effects in both cases are an instrument calculated to reveal life in all its atrocity, stifling the most noble elements of the human spirit, such as deep love and friendship in *Mazeppa,* the overpowering passion of love in *Beatrice Cenci.* The playwright used these elements to achieve effects heightened to such an extent that they become superhuman, bringing their role into prominence and contrasting them with the cumulation of crime and thus producing the impression of exaggeration typical of melodrama. In other words, by using melodramatic effects, Słowacki was experimenting with them, his aim being to achieve or concentrate tragic impact. So here we have a device which is an analogy of another, seen above all, in *Balladyna* and *Lilla*

Jan and Idalia meet in Act II, scene iii of the 1967 Cracow production of Fantazy. *Photograph by Wojciech Plewinski.*

Weneda, namely contrasting the tragic and the comic, in a typical Shakespearean way as in the traditions of mediaeval drama which lived on in his works.

Another fact linking problems of public life, psychological conflicts, uncommon characters which often assumed super-human dimensions, with events painted in colours of the tragic in all its aspects, is Słowacki's specific and excellent mastery of the art of constructing a dramatic work. The poet, whom fate in all its irony destined to write only for the "new theatre", depicted as "a distributor of small riches traversing the world" or in other words a poet who was never to see any of his plays performed in the theatre . . . , was a born man of the theatre, who knew down to the last detail all the specific requirements of the stage. He was a seeker of new forms, a great theatrical experimenter. And this explains the great variety of types of plays he wrote, including some in the Shakespearean style, and that of Calderon, or the refined form of the melodrama that was reigning triumphant in the Paris theatres of his times. This wealth and variety of mood in his dramas, from dramatic poems of all kinds to works of extemely compact structure, all meet the most rigorous requirements of dramatic art. To give an idea of Słowacki's great mastery of structure, suffice it to point to four scenes from *Kordian,* one of his earlier works, although it was to mark the beginning of a series of great works. In *Kordian,* we have the shortest scene, known to world lit-

erature not only because it is composed of only one "line" but simply of one word, in which the Tsar swears by the Constitution. The meaning of this scene is clear. If the Tsar had not taken the oath, he would not have become the Polish king and the central conflict of the play, between the loyalists and the revolutionaries, would have no dramatic justification. Another scene from the play is Kordian's monologue before the door of the Tsar's bedchamber. This scene, written by Racine or even Shakespeare, would have been just the monologue of a young soldier, whereas Słowacki creates an exceptionally expressive and picturesque scene of the hero's delusions when Kordian speaks with hypostases, with personified psychic conditions. Then there is the monumental scene showing a quarrel between Tsar Nicholas I and his brother the Grand Duke Constantine, which is a real masterpiece of psychological realism and which is unique both because it brings into the play a living and universally known personage, the Tsar of all Russia, and because of the mastery with which the dramatic dialogue is written, equalled only by a few such scenes in modern European drama. And finally, the scene of only a few lines which ends the play—the execution scene—of which Wiktor Gomulicki once said "it is a drama in itself".

And while we are on the subject, this seems the place to add that two of the scenes mentioned are of a decidedly precursory nature, for they introduce ideas which were only to be acclaimed in neo-Romantic drama fifty years after the death of the author of *Kordian*. The idea of Kordian's monologue in which he sees apparitions, is found in the works of Wyspiański, among others in *The Wedding (Wesele)*, where the conversations of real persons with spectres is the core of the drama of Bronowice. A counterpart of the execution scene is found in the suggestive atmosphere of the dramatic images that brought fame to Maeterlinck for his plays based on the same principles, the ominous time of waiting, created by Słowacki in *Kordian*.

And finally, Słowacki's strange and unique language, just as brilliant in the prose of *Horsztyński* as in *Kordian, Balladyna, Zawisza the Black* [*Zawisza czarny*] and *The Silver Dream of Salomea*, written in verse. All that the poet himself said of what was to be accomplished by his "pliable language", already evident in his lyrics and epic poems, was perhaps brought to even greater perfection in his dramas. For every character spoke in his own way. Declarations of love, heroic speeches, philosophical reflections, mockery of self and the world, ardent manifestoes and whispered confessions introduced thousands of tones, so varied that, to use the words of Mickiewicz, they run right through the poetic scale from the song to the epopée. The scale of artistic possibilities of such a virtuoso of the written word as Słowacki was as vast as his programme was exceptional, for he was a writer who could express in his native speech "a prayer that weeps and lightning that flashes" and who wrote with equal ease "simply, voice raised in a shout" and weaving his very entertaining comic grotesques.

And these are the artistic values typical of Słowacki's dramas; in the opinions formulated fifty years ago they were overshadowed by values of a different kind, namely, ideological, though they are not what gave the works of the author of *Lilla Weneda* universal general human importance going beyond the bounds of Poland. All of Słowacki's dramatic works are strongly bound up with the life of the nation, its past, present and future. The nation, in keeping with the programme of the playwright, is an element constantly present in all his works, the nation depicted in moments of triumph and the hour of defeat, fighting for its greatness, striving to achieve noble aims, shining like a beacon for all mankind on the paths of its life. This poet, who was particularly sensitive to the problems of national life because of the historic events he experienced in his lifetime, never forgot them, though he was not prone to exaggeration, and never went to the extremes which we know as nationalism, to say nothing of chauvinism. A republican, consistent in his beliefs, seeing himself as "the spirit of the eternal revolutionary", a spokesman of progress, he expressed his views through the characters of his plays, which breathed forth the clear air of the heights, and this is undoubtedly what has raised these works to the high position they occupy in the Polish theatre and, it may be assumed, will give Słowacki a place in world drama. (pp. 283-87)

Julian Krzyżanowski, "Polish Romantic Literature," in his A History of Polish Literature, *translated by Doris Ronowicz, PWN-Polish Scientific Publishers, 1978, pp. 220-353.*

BARBARA KEJNA SHARRATT   (essay date 1973)

[*Sharratt analyzes* Fantazy *and contends that its psychological portraits, realism, and irony illuminate Słowacki's break with romanticism.*]

[*Fantazy*] belongs to the most popular and most frequently staged works of the poet. Since its first performance in 1867 at the Town Theatre in Krakow, *Fantazy* has occupied a permanent position in the repertoires of Polish theatres....

The reason for this extraordinary popularity of the play could lie in the convincing psychological portrayal of its protagonists as well as in the peculiar "contemporaneity" of *Fantazy*. It is the sole drama of Słowacki in which he depicts his contemporaries; the action of *Fantazy* takes place in 1841. The elements of fantasy, so prominent in other dramas of this poet, are toned down here and replaced by psychological realism. In a way, *Fantazy* could be called the most realistic drama of Słowacki. (p. 117)

To him, as to many of his contemporaries, the byronic vogue was a *dernier cri*. He was prepared to accept romanticism wholeheartedly and unquestioningly, its virtues as well as its follies. The fantastic apparel which he wore during the excursion into the Alps, his flowery vest described with such gusto in letters to his mother, romantic gestures accompanying his platonic love affairs, and the aura of all-pervading poetry all belong to the sphere of romantic modes and manners. Słowacki has sometimes been called the most romantic among Polish romantic poets. However chary we may be of such sweeping generalizations the fact remains that he is a veritable *enfant du siècle*, whose works are saturated with romanticism. In him the distinction between romanticism as a literary trend and romanticism as a mode of life often tends to become obscured.

An adopted pose, a mask eventually become an inherent part of the bearer and to tear them off is an almost impossible task. On the other hand men grow out of masks and have either to reject them or to remain forever immature, stunted in their development. If they are truthful to themselves they can see the disparity between the pose and the real self. Słowacki reached this age in the early 1840's.

It is strange that no comprehensive study of this important stage in the poet's life has been made so far. Critics, dazzled by the originality of *Beniowski*, and the realistic elements in *Fantazy* jointly admit that Słowacki has entered a new phase of poetic simplicity, clarity, and—as some tentatively suggest—critical realism.

A critical attitude to life has always been one hallmark of Słowacki's writing, and romanticism by no means excludes a certain amount of realism. What differentiates *Beniowski* and *Fantazy* from the earlier works of Słowacki is a new outlook on life—ironic and detached, and a reevaluation of his youthful attitudes. He finally accepts life as it is, even though it falls short of his dreams and expectations:

> I used to like such souls—not unpunished—
> Dreaming capriciously of black coloured roses.
> Now, half-cured, I like roses to be pretty and fragile,
> As God created them....

Having rejected the romantic pose, Słowacki sets out to ridicule it, and to show the superiority of virtuous simplicity over empty aestheticism. Significantly, his judgment is based on ethical, not on aesthetic criteria.

Fantazy belongs to the most popular and at the same time most controversial dramas of Słowacki. It has been evaluated and reevaluated, criticised for its shortcomings, and glorified these very same "imperfections," explained and given a multitude of interpretations. A truly romantic work, it refused to be classified and labelled, and has always baffled the critics and the readers alike by its uncanny mixture of the sublime and the grotesque, the realistic and the fantastic. (pp. 118-19)

Fantazy [has been called] a drama about love. There are two loving couples in the play, and their different attitudes to love and life provide the desired counter-point. All the four protagonists believe in romantic love (even though Fantazy seems to be somewhat sceptical) which does away with conventions such as marriage based on money, but while the feelings of Jan and Dianna are deep, simple, sincere, Idalia and Fantazy have been contaminated by the spirit of the age and covered with the "byronic lacquer." Rather than accept life, they try to make it match their dreams, and are consequently disappointed with their lot. Similar parallelism for the sake of contrast appears in the two death scenes of *Fantazy:* the meeting at the cemetery and the death of the Major. There the pose is set against genuine heroism. There is another parallel in the play. Although traditionally Fantazy is regarded as the hero of the drama, it is interesting to note a precarious balance of power between him and Idalia, which continues throughout the play. Other characters are placed on the orbit of these two as the necessary foil and the Major emerges as a key figure only in the last scene.

Among other achievements of Słowacki's dramatic technique the character of Stella deserves mention: she is the Puck of *Fantazy,* carrying out errands, listening to emotional outpourings and supplying the audience with extra information which throws a new light upon a situation and explains hidden motives of behavior (for example, she recounts the financial ruin of her parents, she describes the scene in which her parents forced Dianna to agree to the hateful marriage, and reminisces about the family's stay in Siberia).

It is evident from some early drafts that originally Słowacki intended to write a drama of national life containing a much harsher judgement of Polish aristocracy. For reasons unknown he abandoned the project and created instead a psychological drama which, however, is not devoid of satirical touches. As in *Beniowski,* Słowacki depicts here a "nest of gentlefolk" and its inhabitants, stressing the difference between the appearances and reality, the overt pomposity and hidden poverty. Applying the whip of his satire, the poet seldom reverts to caricature, with the exception of Mrs. Rzecznicka who, significantly, never appears on stage. He views his characters with an ironic benevolence, showing their virtues and foibles, and ridiculing without condemnation. Consequently, even the ruthless Respekts and base Rzecznicki do not appear entirely antipathetic. (pp. 120-21)

Regarded as a psychological drama, *Fantazy* is strikingly static. Its characters do not show any development but merely reveal themselves, the most unexpected revelation being that of the Major. It is a mirror-image study of the romantic soul in its various representations, but primarily a study of romantic *malaise.*

Idalia and Fantazy provide a dual insight into the nature of this disease of the spirit, they complement each other. Like a typical woman, Idalia gives full reign to her feelings, her reactions are purely emotional, and so is her logic, while Fantazy suffers from over-intellectualizing, from too analytic a brain. Both reveal a self-centredness which in Fantazy has become egotism. As a human being Idalia is the better of the two: she is capable of a great all-consuming love and is prepared to give her life for it. When Fantazy suggests that they should die together, Idalia does not hesitate. For her, life without her beloved is meaningless. Idalia's attitude to the Respekts, who are taking Fantazy away from her, is also noble. She does not seek revenge: "Although my heart is wounded, I bring no poi-

son. . . ". She forgives easily, and is only too happy to have Fantazy back. Idalia is a woman who has violated social conventions, to whom love is the thing most sacred. In the name of her passion she ignores public opinion, exposes herself to criticism by running after her lover, sacrifices her pride. After feeling, imagination plays the most important part in the soul of Idalia and it is the romantic exulted imagination which makes her see herself as a heroine of a drama. (p. 122)

If Idalia suffers from a surfeit of feeling, Fantazy is painfully cerebral. His emotions are no longer spontaneous (one may assume that his love for Idalia was) but sifted through the sieve of intellect. Like Idalia, he has a craving for truth and beauty which he covers with a veil of cynicism. His egoism does not allow him to love as deeply as his mistress, whom he both needs and slightly despises. Noble birth, money, talent have brought him success and popularity, but he is still unhappy, disappointed and still searching. The byronic pose taken on in his youth is beginning to oppress Fantazy, he craves a change. (p. 123)

His salvation, the saving of face which he considers so important, lies in death. In the end he is deprived of this last consolation and, witnessing the sacrifice of the Major, has to admit to Idalia: "Our taking of poison was ridiculous." A romantic pose did not survive a confrontation with genuine love and true sacrifice. Fantazy realizes that he has wasted his life:

> If I could come back
> From the grave, I would start my life differently,
> In a simpler way.

The death of the Major, the true romantic, shatters Fantazy and at the same time produces a catharsis:

> I have been christened: man
> Through this dark and bloody death! . . .

It is doubtful, however, whether the transformation will prove lasting. Even that final statement, giving credit to Fantazy's basic honesty and self-criticism, has a slightly theatrical flavor. After all it is only "words, words, words" and "lakier byroński szatana" [satan's byronic lacquer] has great adhesive powers.

Słowacki, not free from it himself, must have felt some sympathy for his protagonists. After all, Idalia and Fantazy, compared to the Respekts and the Rzecznickis are better and infinitely more interesting people. Their charm, their appreciation of beauty and a genuine feeling for poetry compensate amply for their deficiencies. Słowacki admits Fantazy is a great poet, a kindred soul, and often makes him his mouthpiece. When Fantazy says:

> . . . some lights
> Pass through my mind as they do in children.
> Green, light, red—like saints' figures
> Set against golden backgrounds
> By a Venetian . . . various strange tones . . .

it can be regarded as a confession by Słowacki himself. Fighting the romantic pose, he is at the same time attracted by it: he relishes extravagant situations, falls prey to moods, abhors the vulgar and the ridiculous. (pp. 124-25)

Irony in *Fantazy* is complex: besides Sophoclean irony inherent in any good drama, there is the specifically romantic, byronic variety (originated in *Don Juan*), irony of situations, irony of names. The very title *Nowa Dejanira,* reminiscent of *La Nouvelle Heloise* by Rousseau, is a joke. Placing a mythological topic in a rural Polish setting inevitably results in incongruousness, especially when Dejanira turns out to be the epitome of vulgarity, Mrs. Rzecznicka. The choice of names for the main protagonists is also ironic: "Fantazy," a fit name for a poet, implies that imagination and fancy are the dominating qualities of its owner, Dafnicki (Fantazy's surname) links it with the Daphne myth. "Idalia" has a slightly ancient flavor, bringing associations with the Ides of March of Caesar, the motif played on by Fantazy. Sophoclean irony becomes most prominent in the scene between Idalia and Rzecznicki when he is trying to tease Idalia, unaware that his own wife has been abducted. The most militant satire is displayed by Fantazy, especially in his description of the Polish colony in Rome. His unkindly portrayal of Idalia in front of the Respekt ladies is another example of malicious irony.

The play is built on contrasts and its effect depends on sudden transitions from the lofty to the vulgar. Contrasts are apparent already in act I. As the Respekts are in a financial crisis, signs of disrepair are becoming visible. The garden has not been tended for some time. Trying to disguise this shortcoming Countess Respekt plans a little deception, which is fully in accordance with her sentimental taste—a pastoral scene à la Versailles. She is going to have the cattle driven into the meadow, the old servant Anton fishing under a tree, boys basket weaving on the shore. Harvesters will sing, Anna will tend the goats on the rocks and, to complete the picture, the cascade must be put in motion. It would also add a pleasant touch if Dubyna would stand close by singing a Ukrainian *dumka*. Unfortunately, her instructions cannot be carried out fully for very prosaic reasons: the cascade has been ruined by rain, Dubyna is gone to town to buy sugar and arak, and the wheat has been reaped already. Creating theatrical effects has become a mode of life for the Respekts: everything is calculated to this end. Disparity between life and illusion comes out most strikingly in the famous cemetery scene where the deflation of pathos reaches its zenith. Fantazy's demonic laughter is the result of this brutal awakening; all of a sudden he sees his actions in the right perspective. Very often, and this is characteristic of Słowacki, the irony remains totally in the sphere of words. . . . (pp. 125-26)

Irony in *Fantazy* is applied to most characters: only the dramatic (i.e. tragic) heroes Jan, Dianna and the Major are spared. The three represent true romanticism, romanticism of action, simplicity and genuine feeling, capability to sacrifice one's own happiness for a greater good. And this seems to be the moral lesson of *Fantazy*. Idalia and Fantazy's individualism, originality, lofty sentiments do not stand confrontation with life. In their search of a personal goal, of their own happiness, they appear petty when placed side by side with the Major. But the fact that Słowacki deliberately suspends his judgement and does not condemn the artistic pair seems to indicate that his sympathies were not equivocal. The author of this splendid "koncert śmiechu i słowików" [a concert of laughter and nightingales] must have felt some affinity with his protagonists. He had encountered disappointment in his own life and felt acutely the rift between dream and reality. Although by disposition Słowacki preferred dream, in *Fantazy,* contrary to himself, he declared war against self-centered individualism. By promoting the central ideas of romanticism, he ridiculed the outmoded pose. (pp. 126-27)

> *Barbara Kejna Sharratt, "A Critique of Romanticism in 'Fantazy'," in* Slavic and East-European Studies, *Vol. XVIII, 1973, pp. 117-27.*

ADDITIONAL BIBLIOGRAPHY

"The Lily-Maid of the Venedi: The Genesis of Słowacki's *Lilla Weneda* and a Word on Its Symbolism." *Alliance Journal* (June 1951): 45-8.
  Interprets the plot of Słowacki's drama *Lilla Weneda* as an attempt by the author to understand and resolve Poland's tragic political problems.

Calina, Josephine. *Shakespeare in Poland*. Shakespeare Survey, edited by Sir I. Gollancz, vol. I. London: Oxford University Press, 1923, 76 p.
  Includes a discussion of Shakespeare's influence on Słowacki's dramas.

Coleman, Arthur Prudden and Coleman, Marion Moore. "Juliusz Słowacki: Poland's Bard of the 'Golden Harp.'" In *Great Men and Women of Poland*, edited by Stephen P. Mizwa, pp. 205-17. New York: Macmillan Company, 1943.
  Examines Słowacki's development as an author and his attempts to both preserve and advance Polish culture through his works.

Dyboski, Roman. "The Evolution of Polish Romanticism." In his *Periods of Polish Literary History: Being the Ilchester Lectures for the Year 1923*, pp. 85-113. London: Oxford University Press, 1923.
  A study of mysticism in Słowacki's works. According to Dyboski, Słowacki's concern for Poland's uncertain political situation underlies all of his work.

Kolbuszewski, Stanisław. "The November 1830 Insurrection in the Work of Juliusz Słowacki." *The Polish Review* VII, No. 1 (Winter 1962): 59-66.
  Explores the development of Słowacki's solutions to Poland's political situation as evidenced in his writings.

Kridl, Manfred. *The Lyric Poems of Julius Słowacki*. Musagetes: Contributions to the History of Slavic Literature and Culture, edited by Dmitrij Čiževskij, vol. VI. The Hague: Mouton & Co., 1958, 77 p.
  A study of Słowacki's style and influences and the thematic connections between his various works.

Michael, M. A. Introduction to *A Polish Anthology*, edited by T. M. Filip, translated by M. A. Michael, pp. 5-31. London: Duckworth, 1944.
  Contains a brief biographical and critical section on Słowacki.

Miłosz, Czesław. "Romanticism." In his *The History of Polish Literature*, pp. 195-280. London: Collier-Macmillan, 1969.
  Describes Słowacki's artistic development and concludes that although his work is uneven, Słowacki "attains the highest perfection of his art" in his mystical poems.

Morelowski, Jan. "Elements of Law in the Works of Poland's Greatest Poets." *The Polish Review* XIX, Nos. 3, 4 (1974): 151-56.
  Traces the influence of Słowacki's law studies on his work.

Sawczak, George. "Shelley and Słowacki: Two Dramas on the Beatrice Cenci Theme." *Alliance Journal* (June 1951): 4-5.
  Compares Słowacki's treatment of the Cenci legend to that of Percy Bysshe Shelley.

Segel, Harold B. "Słowacki's 'Arabic' Poems, 1828-1830." *The Polish Review* VIII, No. 2 (Spring 1963): 38-54.
  Examines Słowacki's adaptation of the vengeance theme from the Arabic poem *Szanfary* and the use he made of the work's Polish translation.

———. Introduction to *Polish Romantic Drama: Three Plays in English Translation*, by Adam Mickiewicz, Zygmunt Krasiński, and Juliusz Słowacki, edited by Harold B. Segel, pp. 21-71. Ithaca: Cornell University Press, 1977.

Provides the political background essential to understanding Słowacki's dramas.

Steele, Eugene and Welsh, David J. "'Men of Letters'—Słowacki and Byron." *Antemurale* XXIII (1979): 153-60.
　　Explores the similarities between the lives and works of Słowacki and Lord Byron.

Treugutt, Stefan. *Juliusz Słowacki: Romantic Poet*. Warsaw: Polonia Publishing House, 1959, 133 p.
　　An illustrated biography that includes some drawings by Słowacki.

———. "Byron and Napoleon in Polish Romantic Myth." In *Lord Byron and His Contemporaries: Essays from the Sixth International Byron Seminar*, edited by Charles E. Robinson, pp. 130-43. Newark: University of Delaware Press, 1982.
　　A brief discussion of Byron's influence on Słowacki's work.

Dionysios Solomos

1798-1857

(Also transliterated as Dionysius, Dhionýsios, Dionysiou, and Dionisio; also Solomós, Salomone, Salamon, Salomon, Solomon, and Solomou) Greek poet.

Solomos is widely regarded as the father of modern Greek poetry. In his small body of work, he broke with the scholarly, classical diction used by all Greek poets until the nineteenth century and adopted the spoken idiom of the common people. Though Solomos's patriotic poem "Hymnos eis ten Eleutherian" ("Hymn to Liberty") was extremely popular in his lifetime, Greek critics were initially unappreciative of his works, and it was not until the twentieth century that his contribution to Greek literature was recognized and acclaimed.

Born the illegitimate son of the Greco-Italian Count Nicholas Solomos and his young Greek servant, Angelica Nikli, Dionysios became a legitimate heir in 1807 when the count married Angelica hours before he died. At the age of ten, Solomos was sent from his native island, Zante, also known as Zakynthos, to be educated in Italy. After studying law, Solomos returned to Zante in 1818. There, he was celebrated in social circles for his witty, impromptu Italian verses, and in 1822, a collection of these poems was published, apparently without his knowledge, as *Rime improvvisate*. The volume came to the attention of Spiridion Tricúpi, a Greek patriot, historian, and diplomat who encouraged him to become the voice of Greek nationalism. Solomos agreed, yet he first had to learn Greek, for, like most aristocrats in the Heptanese Islands, he spoke Italian and understood little conversational Greek. Under Tricúpi's tutelage, Solomos progressed quickly in his study of the Greek language and folk literature and soon composed "Xanthoula" ("The Little Blonde Girl"), a simple lyric poem in the common dialect. Shortly after, Solomos wrote his most famous work, "Hymn to Liberty." The fervidly nationalistic poem became the rallying song of the Greek revolutionaries who fought against Turkish rule, and "Hymn to Liberty" was widely known even before its publication in 1825.

Following the immediate success of the "Hymn," Solomos began several works, but failed to complete any of them. In his "Dialogos" ("Dialogue"), an imaginary conversation in prose, he discussed the controversial issue of literary use of the vernacular as opposed to the classic, "pure" language, while in his lengthy poem "O Lambros," he dealt with death, incest, and fate. In 1824 Solomos abandoned both of these works and began a eulogy on the death of Lord Byron, "Poiema lyriko eis ton thanato tou Lord Byron," often referred to as the "Lyrical Poem on the Death of Lord Byron." Although similar in form to the "Hymn," the "Lyrical Poem on the Death of Lord Byron" is generally considered inferior. In 1828, Solomos settled in Corfu, where, except for occasional visits to Zante, he lived for the remainder of his life. In Corfu, Solomos commenced work on his bitter portrait of evil, "I gynaika tis Zakynthos" ("The Woman of Zakynthos"); at the same time, he wrote "O Kritikos" ("The Cretan"), a tragic, mystical romance, and other minor poems. While in Corfu, Solomos also composed "Oi eleftheroi poliorkimenoi" ("The Free Besieged"), which scholars generally agree is his most ambitious and sustained work. Though he revised this patriotic

poem inspired by the siege of Missolonghi three times, it was never completed. "O pórphyras" ("The Shark"), written in 1847 following the attack of a young British soldier by a shark, was Solomos's last significant composition in Greek. His final poems, including "La navicella greca," a commentary on the British blockade of Greece, were written in Italian. Solomos's later years were marked by a steady decline in health and productivity, and his Italian poems have received little critical attention.

After Solomos's death in 1857, scholars anticipated the discovery of important early manuscripts. However, they were universally disappointed by the disjointed fragments he left, and some study has been devoted to determining his reasons for not completing his works. Critics suggest that his quest for perfection in form, inspired by the works of the German philosopher Johann Christoph Friedrich von Schiller, and the difficulties of writing in Greek resulted in his dissatisfaction with each effort, which he subsequently abandoned in favor of a new form. Some scholars believe that his inheritance disputes with his half brothers, his alcoholic tendencies, and his melancholy personality were also factors.

Despite the fragmentary state of nearly all his works, Solomos is considered a major figure of modern Greek literature for his patriotism, linguistic innovations, and synthesis of Western and Greek cultures. Yet his importance to Greek literature is not reflected in English-language criticism: while extensive studies and collections of his works have been published in Greek, little is available in English, due, in part, to the difficulty most scholars find in translating his works. However, for many Greek readers of Solomos's works, his poems are the ultimate expression of Greek nationalism and patriotic enthusiasm for independence. Indeed, King George I established several stanzas of "Hymn to Liberty," set to music by Nicholas Mantzaros, as the national anthem of Greece in 1865. Critics have also evaluated Solomos's contribution to modern Greek culture, citing in particular his influence in substituting the demotic, or spoken dialect, for the ancient classical language as the poetic idiom. Finally, some scholars have focused on his place in literary history; they have commented that Solomos synthesized his Italian education and knowledge of German and English literature with his Greek heritage.

As the first to use the spoken Greek idiom as a literary language, Solomos is considered the founding poet of modern Greece. His "Hymn to Liberty," still sung as the national anthem, and his profound influence on later Greek poets have earned Solomos a prominent place in the history of modern Greek literature.

*PRINCIPAL WORKS

Rime improvvisate (poetry) 1822
"Hymnos eis ten Eleutherian" (poetry) 1825
   ["Hymn to Liberty" in *The Songs of Greece from the Romaic Text*, 1825; also published as "The Greek National Anthem" in *A Choice of Kipling's Verse* (partial translation), 1945]
Ta euriskomena (poetry and prose) 1859
Hapanta (poetry) 1880
Hapanta ta euriskomena (poetry, prose, and fragments) 1901
Anekdota erga (poetry and prose) 1927
Hapanta. 2 vols. (poetry and prose) 1948-60
Hapanta ta hellinika erga: Dionysiou Solomou (poetry and prose) 1972

*The principal source of information for this list is M. Byron Raizis's bibliography in *Dionysios Solomos*.

Selections of Solomos's poetry in English translation have appeared in the following publications: *Modern Greek Poetry, Dionysius Solomós* (Jenkins), and *Modern Greek Literary Gems*.

DIONYSIOS SOLOMOS (essay date 1827)

[*In the following excerpt from his obituary for the poet Ugo Foscolo, written in 1827, Solomos defines poetic style. For a discussion of this passage, see the excerpt by Lorenzatos dated 1965.*]

Ugo's mind proceeded from the conception of his art to those outer forms of thought through which we usually express ourselves; thus these forms came into being and developed in a natural conjunction with that conception. In contrast, the mind of his imitators used those external forms as stepping-stones in the hope of reaching, by these alone, the intellectual powers of another artist, the external imprint of which is called, in the art of writing, style. (p. 71)

We are talking here only of imitation of another person's style in prose, and of the limited possibility of such imitation. But in poetry imitation becomes an impossibility, for there it is necessary to seize the truth by means of powerful combinations, stripping away all the false parts, so that the truth becomes impregnable in the other person's mind (which process is known as thought); it is also necessary to condense the truth, while amplifying it and animating it by means of suitable forms (and this is known as imagination), to make the heart receptive to the impressions made by these things (and this is feeling), and finally to transfuse all this into the other person by means of language. This is also the case in long prose pieces. (p. 72)

> *Dionysios Solomos, in a footnote, in* The Lost Center and Other Essays in Greek Poetry *by Zissimos Lorenzatos, translated by Kay Cicellis, Princeton University Press, 1980, pp. 71-2.*

ALEXANDER SOUTSOS (poem date 1833)

[*Soutsos was a critically acclaimed Greek poet of the nineteenth century who wrote in the puristic, neoclassical idiom. His disdain for Solomos's work, evidenced in the following epigram, typifies contemporary critical reaction. This piece was originally published in* Panorama tes Hellados *in 1833.*]

Kalvos and Solomos, great makers of many an ode,
Both of them have violated our linguistic code.
Lofty ideas, however, expressed in poor diction,
Are not destined to stay long in the literary tradition.

> *Alexander Soutsos, in an extract from "The Aftermath: The Legacy of Solomos," in* Dionysios Solomos *by M. Byron Raizis, Twayne Publishers, Inc., 1972, p. 127.*

SPIRIDION TRICÚPI (essay date 1873?)

[*A Greek orator, diplomat, and historian, Tricúpi is widely credited with inspiring Solomos to become the "Greek national poet." In this excerpt, he describes his first meeting with Solomos. As the date of Tricúpi's composition is unknown, the year of his death has been used to date this excerpt.*]

A friend of mine, to whom I had communicated my desire to make the acquaintance of so remarkable a character, advised me, if I should be fortunate enough to be received, to speak to him only about poetry. Accompanied by Mr Lekatsá, I went to his country-house, where I gained admittance, and we conversed about English poets, whom he admired no less than I, and understood a great deal better. On the following day he made a special visit to the town in order to return my call. During our conversation, he recited to me, in Italian, an ode **"Per prima Messa."** I do not know if this ode, to which he at that time attached great importance, has since been published. Solomós, observing that after his recitation I had remained thoughtful and silent, at length asked me my opinion. 'Your poetical talent,' I replied, 'assures you a distinguished place on the Italian Parnassus. But the highest positions there are occupied already. The Greek Parnassus has not yet found its Dante.' At his request I then gave him a sketch of the position of our language and literature. 'I don't know Greek,' he said, 'how could I write well in Greek?' And in fact he knew the spoken tongue very imperfectly. I said, 'The language which you imbibed with your mother's milk is Greek. So you can easily bring it back to your memory, particularly if you will consent to my giving you all the assistance I can during my stay in Zante, which will be prolonged. I do not speak of the tiresome "literary dialect," or of the ridiculous jargon of macaronism; but of the living, mother tongue of our race.' I saw that I had fired his ambition. The same day I procured him a copy of the Poems of Christópulo. On the morrow we began our study and for many days to come our whole time was given to the study of Greek. Hardly a week had elapsed since our first conversation when I was astonished to hear him reciting a poem in Greek:

> At eventide I saw her
> The little maid fair-tressed
> As swift the white sail bore her
> To exile in the west.

It was his first Greek composition. No sooner did the poem become known than all Zante was singing it beneath his windows. This touched him deeply. A few days later he began his **"Hymn to Liberty"** [**"Hymnos eis ten Eleutherian"**] which he completed after a short interval. He was not one of those who have recourse to grammars and lexicons. He did not hunt up words, but with the few at his command he would express in Greek ideas which he had conceived in Italian. (pp. 54-5)

> *Spiridion Tricúpi, in an extract from* Dionysius Solomós, *by Romilly Jenkins, Cambridge at the University Press, 1940, pp. 54-5.*

DANIEL QUINN   (essay date 1902)

[Taken from a report of the celebrations in Zakynthos commemorating Solomos as the national poet of Greece, this excerpt includes commentary on Solomos's most noted patriotic work, the "Hymn to Liberty." Quinn's essay was written in 1902.]

On Saturday, the 15th of June, was ended in the pretty island of Zakynthos a proud and glorious triduum of feasts commemorating Dionysios Solomós, the national poet of Greece. (p. 50)

While yet a student in Italy [Solomos] had begun to compose in Italian verse, and these first short poems of his were so sweet and artistic that one of his friends and teachers, the learned priest Santo Rossi, who, like many other Italians of that time, regarded Monti as the favorite poet of Italy, used, in his enthusiastic admiration for the young poet from Zakynthos, frequently to exclaim: "Greco, tu farai dimenticare il nostro Monti." If, following the example of his townman Ugo Foscolo, our poet had permanently established himself in Italy, the enthusiastic hopes of Rossi and his other friends might possibly have come true.

After his return home he continued to compose successfully in Italian. These poems, just like many of those which he wrote in his later years, were not primarily intended for publication, and a good number of them have been lost. But, in spite of the beauty of his Italian compositions, his fame rests entirely on what he wrote in Greek. In the year 1822 Spiridion Trikoupes, the noted historian and patriot, on the occasion of a visit to Zakynthos, heard Solomós read one of his Italian poems, **"La Prima Messa"** [see excerpt dated 1873]. Trikoupes warmly exhorted him to cultivate his native language and to write in Greek, and thereby to assist in encouraging and inspiring the men who were engaged in the desperate fight for freedom. The

poet accepted the patriot's advice, and began to study the Greek language. But he never thoroughly mastered it, and one of the peculiarities of his Greek poems, if not also one of their attractions, is a certain precipitous inaccuracy of expression. He had no correct knowledge of ancient Greek, for he had studied the classical writers not in their original tongue but in Italian translations. He fell in love with the popular ballads and klephtic songs of the people, and became persuaded that the language in which these unpretentious compositions were clothed was the best linguistic medium for the Greeks of his day.

In Greek, his first poem of note was his paean to Liberty. Whatever virtues his other poems may possess, it is this hymn which created his fame and sustains it. . . . The **"Hymn to Liberty,"** as soon as published, became widely known. Attempts have been made to translate it into most of the languages of Europe, but always with ill success. Many of the strophes are absolutely untranslatable on account of their strange language and strange thought. (pp. 50-1)

Besides other poems of a patriotic nature, such as the **"Death of Byron,"** fragments of a hymn to Marco Bozzaris, **"Missolonghi, or the Freemen Besieged,"** the **"Destruction of Psara,"** he wrote a number of short poems, most of them beautiful and touching—some of them, like his **"Lampros,"** too weird for art; many of them merely disjointed members of some unfinished masterpiece. (p. 51)

Literary men in Greece are divided into two antagonistic schools as regards the phase of language which ought to be employed by writers. Some prefer the archaistic "katharevousa," which bears a remarkable outward resemblance to the language of ancient Greek prose of the later period, while others, known as the demoticists, prefer the types of language which are common among the uneducated classes. But both schools unite in admiration of the poems of Solomós. The demoticists have full reason for doing so, because Solomós always composed his Greek poems in a language similar to the demotic, and often uttered bitter words against those who preferred the older forms. On the other hand, the purists make a very proper distinction between literature and language, and love Solomós for his thoughts and patriotism and poetry, in spite of his language. (p. 52)

> *Daniel Quinn, "The National Poet of Greece," in* The Nation, *Vol. 75, No. 1933, July 17, 1902, pp. 50-2.*

ROMILLY JENKINS   (essay date 1940)

[The following excerpt from Jenkins's biography of Solomos traces his literary reputation and focuses on the importance of folk culture and the koinè, or common Greek dialect, in his "Hymn to Liberty," several shorter poems, "Dialogue," and the "Lyrical Poem on the Death of Lord Byron."]

The **"Hymn to Liberty"** [**"Hymnos eis ten Eleutherian"**] made Solomós' reputation as a poet. It was indeed many years before the literary critics of his own country, besotted with the influence of Byzantine purism, recognized its merit or indeed regarded it as poetry at all, and only in 1863, after the dethronement of Otho, was it canonized as the national hymn and its first two stanzas, sung to Mánzaro's jigging air, adopted as the anthem of Greece. But the effect on the common people of Greece was electrical. 'From the Heptanese,' wrote the poet Zalokósta, 'the dithyramb of Solomós flew like lightning to the comrades in Greece. In every mouth were his patriotic phrases, which fanned the flames of the fire lit in every heart.' Solomós was instantly the national poet. But he was more. His reputation in Europe was of simultaneous growth. The second edition of the **"Hymn"** was printed in Paris in 1824, and thence it spread far and wide even to the Russian steppes. It was indeed *felix opportunitate ortus*. In its simple fervent joy at the idea of liberty, in its unrestrained assault on the dark powers of the 'Holy' Alliance, in its exhortation to a brave people to cast off a cruel yoke, it was a second "Marseillaise," and it communicated to the oppressed of Europe something of the exhilaration of the outspoken tirades of *Don Juan*. Hugo, Lamartine and Chateaubriand hailed it with delight. Manzoni applauded and spread the fame of his pupil in Italy. Goethe christened the poet the 'Byron of the East.' Canning is said to have come to the signing of the Treaty of London fresh from a perusal of the concluding stanzas, addressed to the Monarchs of Europe:

> Instruments of God most High,
> See ye not her agonies?
> Never silent is her cry
> Down the endless centuries.
>
> How then? Can ye leave alone
> Those who strive for Liberty
> Or destroy it when 'tis won,
> From the needs of policy?
>
> Ah not so! for turn your eyes
> Where the Christian banners swell!
> Rise, ye Christian monarchs, rise,
> Arm and strike the Infidel!

and in one of his speeches he refers gracefully to the line 'Rise from the tomb where heroes lie.'

But one voice was silent, whose praise would have been worth all the rest to the poet. Tricúpi seized a manuscript copy of the **"Hymn"** and hastened with it to Missolonghi to present it to Byron. He arrived too late. Daphnis had gone the stream: the eddy had closed above the youth dear to the Muses, to the Maidens not hateful.

Since the **"Hymn to Liberty"** is by far the most famous poem of Solomós, we must give some analysis of it here, and then venture on a few critical remarks.

The poem consists of 158 four-line stanzas of alternately rhyming trochaic dimeters. The trochaic metre [was] traditionally that of the patriotic or marching song. . . . Stanzas 1-16 describe the rising of Liberty from the tomb where she has lain so long with the bones of her champions of old, waiting for one brave voice to summon her once more to earth; but she hears only the clank of chains and the weeping of the slave. At length she is stirred by the blood shed in her defence by the Greeks, and she rises and tries to win support for them; but one only weeps on her breast, another deceitfully promises aid, and others openly deride her. She returns to Greece like the beggar who knocks in vain at the doors of the rich; and here at least, she finds those who will conquer or die in her name. Stanzas 17-34 tell of the effect of her appearance on the world: the people are glad; the Ionians, for all that England holds them in the artful bonds of a free-seeming servitude, join with America and Spain to hail her. England, Russia and the bloody Eagle of Austria are filled with rage and spite. But she is like a rock on which the waves cast their dirty foam, and hail and tempest lash her in vain; woe to those who would do her a mischief. She is like the lioness robbed of her young,

she roams far and wide, spreading destruction and ruin. Stanzas 35-74 illustrate this by giving an account of the horrible storming and sack of Tripolitzá by Kolokotróni in 1821. The battle of Valtétzi is touched on, and after it the Turks fly and shut themselves in the citadel. The assault begins by night; and is very graphically described; as a counterweight to the merciless savagery of the Greeks (and indeed the horrors of that sack were not inferior to those which distinguished the massacre of Chios), the ghosts of all whom Turkish rage and lust has dishonoured or slain in the past are made to rise and dance and sway among the excited troops. Thereafter the slaughter knows no bounds; as the butchery proceeds, even the poet is moved to enquire 'how long?' At length the war cry of Allah dies away; the fourth day dawns and shows the innocent grass watered with blood for dew, and the cool morning wind blowing at length on the standard of the Cross.

Stanzas 75-87 touch on the siege of Corinth (1823): its plain is transformed from rustic peace to martial turmoil. There follows the famous reply to Byron's lament that fair Greek girls should be the mothers of slaves: the poet pictures the girls who are dancing in the shade, and rejoices to think that their breasts shall afford the milk of courage and freedom.

In stanzas 88-122 the scene changes to Western Greece; here, at Missolonghi, Freedom is embraced by Religion, and goes forth transfigured to repulse the besiegers and to win the battle of the Achelous, fought at Christmas 1822. The Turks are hunted by scores, horse and man, into the turbulent river, and after desperate struggles the waters finally close over them. The poet wishes for the voice of Moses to rejoice over Egyptians overwhelmed once more in the Red Sea.

Stanzas 123-138 observe that Liberty is triumphant on sea no less than land; the exploits of Kanári are hinted at, and the shade of the murdered Patriarch Gregory is bidden to rejoice at so many drowned captains of the Infidel. The curse of God is upon the Turks for this outrage—but soft! Liberty herself here restrains the poet, and in stanzas 139-158 administers some salutary advice to the Greeks not to let disunion and internecine feuds ruin their cause: not merely will division in their ranks aid the Turks, but the nations of Europe will say that Greece is unworthy to be free. She pleads that common Faith may unite them against the oppressor, and ends with an appeal to the Powers of Europe to strike with them for the Cross.

When we come to criticize this poem, we have to make plain on what grounds we are to survey it. There are many people who still regard it as Solomós' masterpiece, and from many points of view it deserves all praise. But we should do violence to our own judgment and to Solomós' reputation, if, in criticizing it as pure poetry, we gave it the highest or near the highest place among his works; nor will this be surprising if we consider his youth, his inexperience in manipulating the language, and the speed at which he composed the **"Hymn."** The matter of the poem shows little originality. Critics have discerned in it more or less flagrant borrowings from Dante, Monti, Manzoni, Ariosto, Parini, Byron and Foscolo. The first two stanzas, the best known of all,

> Yea I know thee by the playing
> Of that terrible keen blade,
> By that glance, the world surveying,
> Stern, triumphant, unafraid—
>
> Glorious captive! for thy prison
> Was the tomb where heroes lie;
> Now at length in might arisen,
> Hail, thrice hail, O Liberty!

were directly inspired by Rhíga and Marteláos. The credit for the lovely stanza 48, where the horde of ghostly victims arises to tarre on the avenging Greeks,

> See! a myriad naked shades
> Rise from out their earthy rest;
> Old men, youths and tender maids,
> Tiny babies at the breast,

is Vergil's, who is himself borrowing from Homer. Again, stanza 51

> Thick as fall before the reaping-
> Hook the swathes at harvest-tide. . . .

echoes [Homer]. . . . Borrowing from or echoing previous masterpieces is of course in itself no argument against a poem if the vibration it produces be smoothly and subconsciously set in motion, but here the borrowing is wholesale, indiscriminate, ill-digested, and ill-supported by the rest of the poem. To take a single instance—stanza 51, of which we give the first two lines above, ends

> So those phantom hordes were creeping
> Up on nearly every side.

Lapses such as this are indeed rare in the poem, but too often the narrative which owes nothing to outside inspiration is bald and prosy, dull foil wherein to set the priceless jewels collected from others, though these latter are often most happily re-cut.

The fact is that the composition shows too many signs of over-haste, as Solomós recognized himself in his later years, and this brings us to our second criticism. The poem, 'like so much of Byron's work,' owes more to passion than to inspiration. The poem, was, as Solomós said, the 'overflow of his soul,' a phrase which recalls Wordsworth's 'spontaneous overflow of powerful feelings.' The powerful feelings were indeed there; they were dominant and continuous. . . . His passion was at fever-heat; even while he wrote, the pounding of the artillery at Missolonghi was in his ears. But the ground had not been adequately prepared: the seed was plenteously sown, but the furrows were not deeply excavated, and hence the crop is patchy and uneven. Solomós was indeed trying to do the impossible—to write at white heat in an idiom which required great care and thought and cultivation before it could yield a mature harvest, and hence the poem. . . . is addressed to the passions, not, as the finest poems are, to the spirit.

But when all this is said—and we say it in no detracting spirit—the achievement of such a poem was immense. The faults themselves were, in view of the peculiar circumstances of the medium, very near to virtues. The overweight of borrowing from abroad, while it might spoil the poem as an individual masterpiece, was exactly what was required for the 'cultivation' (the expression is Solomós') of the tongue; and the ingenuity and taste required to translate into Greek the nobler poetical ideas expressed in the cultivated languages of Europe were the most salutary faculties which could have been brought into play. Again, the ardour with which the poem is informed, while it causes occasional oversights, uglinesses and lapses of taste, sustains the pitch and unites the whole in a way which no amount of tedious researching, word-weighing and lexicon-hunting could have done. And with this aspect we must connect the extreme vividness of many of the passages. Greek vernacular prose . . . is distinguished by its qualities of graphic description, but to possess the technical facility (after so very short an apprenticeship) to use these qualities to the full in verse shows no common talent. The rhythm here assists; the

niggling critics of the Byzantine or 'Phanariot' school chose to condemn the poem because every syllable was not given its full value in the metrical scheme, as in the prosody of ancient Greek verse. To answer this argument, which would exclude many of the finest verses of all modern poets from Dante downwards, we have only to point to the vivid life and feeling which the freedom of rhythm communicates. . . . (pp. 67-75)

But, if we continue to view the "Hymn" merely as a work of literature, its chief quality, that which chiefly arouses the admiration and the astonishment of the reader, is the size and weight of the contribution it makes towards the formation of a literary koinè in Modern Greek. In a poem of 632 lines, possessing a wider range than any Greek demotic poem written since the seventeenth century, there is scarcely a form which is not familiar in everyone's mouth, and yet scarcely a passage where the language is unequal to the thought. And this was the work of a man of twenty-five who until his twenty-fourth year had known only the Italianate patois of one island in the Heptanese, and that imperfectly.

The poem to be sure was not judged on such grounds as these, either in Greece or outside it. Solomós, like Byron, 'woke and found himself famous' on the strength of a piece of work by no means worthy of his genius, but wildly popular because the sentiments it expressed were exactly in accord with those universally felt at just that time. . . . The commanding reputation which the "Hymn" secured for him in his lifetime caused a corresponding disappointment and disillusionment in his admirers after his death, when it was discovered that his unpublished manuscripts were only fragments, abominably confused and cryptogrammatic. The result was that little or no attention was paid to passages which can hold their own with the best lyric poetry of the day. The Greeks, indeed, had more excuse than most in their blind adulation of the poet. He was their first national poet, who spoke to them in their own tongue, and was making that tongue an organ through which they could communicate with the civilized world. He had written a poem which expressed their aspirations in a life-and-death struggle, and disseminated them through Europe. Nor had they the criteria which critics of countries with a long unbroken literary history were able to command. Patriotism is perhaps the most dangerous of literary touchstones, and patriotism was the only touchstone they possessed. A nation which could exalt, for however short a time, a writer of the calibre of Valaoríti to the first place among its poets, largely, it would appear, on the strength of his admittedly single-minded and disinterested desire to free his native islands from the English yoke, might well have overestimated the literary value of a work by Dionysius Solomós.

Upon the poet himself this adulation had both good and bad effects. The evil effects were quickly seen in his "Lyrical Poem on the Death of Lord Byron," beyond doubt the worst poem he ever wrote. But it was good that he should have been taken seriously, that his confidence . . . should be thus fortified by the success of his initial efforts. He would do still better: if he could capture Europe with such poor resources, what ought he not to achieve when he was master of a tractable and copious medium? He set to work with daemonic energy. . . . He eagerly devoured the Cretan demotic literature, the "Erotokritos," the "Erophile," "The Fair Shepherdess," and from the first two he learned not merely the richness of the Greek vernacular but the potentialities of the native 'rhyming political' or quindeca-syllablic verse, which we may call the 'Cretan' metre par excellence. Hitherto he had thought only in terms of European metres; now for the first time he became acquainted with a rhythm intimately connected with the Greek idea of poetry and music for more than a thousand years. Many years were to elapse before he reached the conclusion that native metre must join with native tongue to form the instruments of the highest Greek poetry. But he tried the Cretan metre in small pieces, such as the so-called "**Death of the Orphan,**" the "**Death of the Shepherd,**" and the "**Eurycome.**" They are all slight. The "**Death of the Shepherd**" is the best, with its pretty lament of a mourning Shepherdess for her lost love, borne on four stout shoulders to the grave, while the cracked voice of the priest intoned and the wooden bier creaked again.

But while the metrical inspiration of these *juvenilia* was Cretan, the ideas were generally suggested by the second source of his study—the great body of folk-poetry. (pp. 75-8)

Perhaps his debt to folk-poetry in these earlier years emerges most clearly in two songs put into the mouth of the unhappy Maria, the heroine of his elaborate narrative poem "**Lambros,**" which he began at this time to sketch out. The songs are "**The Brother and Sister,**" which has found its way into Passow's *Carmina popularia Graeciae recentioris* as a typical Greek folk-song; and "**The Mad Mother,**" which is inspired by a lovely dirge, "The Death of Irene," preserved to us by Count Marcellus, who heard it from a Corfiot seaman. . . . (p. 79)

If the "**Death of the Shepherd**" and "**The Mad Mother**" illustrate two influences, the Cretan and the folk-poetical, at work in the early training of Solomós, the "**Dialogue,**" written also in 1824, illustrates a third. The "**Dialogue,**" the only prose work of Solomós in Greek that survives, is, like many of his compositions, no more than a fragment. . . . It is a reasoned defence of the demotic tongue as a national idiom, and a telling onslaught on 'Purism,' put into the form of a conversation between a Poet (who is Solomós himself), his friend (perhaps Tertzéti), and a Pedant (who is drawn from Anastasius Karavía, a local exponent and defender of the purist idiom). The general thesis is that the demotic idiom is the true and natural means of expression; that efforts to supplant it—nay, even to 'correct' it, as Coray had tried to do—by introducing a collection of old mummified junk, as lifeless and as poisonous as the exhibits in the shop of Romeo's apothecary, are crimes against enlightenment and consequently against Liberty herself; and that the expressions 'common' or 'vulgar' when applied to a language or a vocabulary have no objective validity—the 'nobility' of words depends on who uses them and how: the Tuscan was a 'vulgar' idiom until the *Divine Comedy* appeared; could anyone call it so now? The piece is beautifully written, and it is certainly a no less remarkable achievement in the mastery and 'cultivation' of the Greek vernacular than the "**Hymn to Liberty**" itself. It is, in fact, a living proof of the arguments it maintains. Moreover, the erudition displayed is considerable, and authors such as Shakespeare, Condillac, Locke and Bacon are quoted with telling effect. . . . There is, indeed, little or no originality in the ideas of the "**Dialogue**": these are drawn from the *de Vulgari Eloquio* of his beloved Dante, and even more from the *Romaic Tongue* and other philological writings of Vilará, whom in several passages he quotes nearly word for word, though without acknowledgment. But what makes the "**Dialogue**" of far greater power and pressure than the work of Vilará is the intense emotion with which it is written, and the undisguised identification of the demotic thesis with political and spiritual freedom. 'I think of nothing,' says the Poet, 'but liberty and language'; and again (to the Pedant):

You to speak of Liberty? *You,* who have chained our minds with your circumflex accents and your discoveries of 'correct writing'—*you* talk of Liberty? We have seen the contribution you have made to the Greek Revolution with your enlightenment; we have heard your piddling poetasters, who would immortalize its Heroes, while the Heroes they eulogize understand not one word they write. . . . But I tell you that your rule over Greece has ended with the rule of the Turks. It has ended, and you may live to curse the hour of the Greek Revolt!

'My soul is sick,' says the Poet at the end; 'our countrymen are spilling their blood beneath the standard of the Cross to make us free, and this Pedant and his like are striving to make them inarticulate for their reward.' (pp. 82-4)

But perhaps the feature of the "**Dialogue**" which makes it most interesting to us is the light it throws on the character and personality of Solomós himself. As the Poet he simply states his own arguments in the words and with the emotions which he would have used and suffered in real life. There is no attempt at objectivity, and hence the personal details which the Poet gives of himself acquire a peculiar interest. 'Do you like the sea better when it is calm or rough?' asks the Friend.

> I must confess (replies the Poet) that I always used to prefer a calm, when the sea lies most transparent; I used to compare it to a man who withdraws himself from the turbulence of the world and frankly reveals all that he has within him. . . . But since our ships have passed on the way to Missolonghi, I like a rough sea better. They appeared two by two, three by three, and you could see their rigging white from the wind-filled sails, white too from the scattered foam of the billows, which with a roar of joy rolled exulting into the Ionian Sea, and broke on the shore of Zante.

The delight of the poet in a calm sea recurs over and over again in his writing, and the moment about seven o'clock in the evening, when the clear mirror was suddenly clouded by the breeze that arises at sunset, particularly caught his imagination. We catch a glimpse, too, of the ungovernable rages into which Solomós would fly—he never learnt to control his temper—in the passage which ends the "**Dialogue.**"

> [Friend]. Remember the words of Holy Scripture—Let not the sun go down on thy wrath.
>
> [Poet]. Most sacred words! And I try to keep them in mind so far as I can. But whenever I argue with Pedants who are trying to blind our race, such injunctions pass quite out of my mind.
>
> [Friend]. Your eyes are fastened on the coast (*i.e. the Morea*)—Your face is glowing and your limbs a-tremble.

. . . . .

These examples drawn from the prolific year 1824 must suffice to illustrate the educational 'tripod' of Solomós: Crete, Folk-poetry, Vilará on the theory of language. The ardour with which Solomós threw himself into these pursuits was largely inspired by the success of the "**Hymn to Liberty,**" and to that extent success was beneficial. Its evil effects were seen to the full in the **"Lyrical Poem on the Death of Lord Byron."** (pp. 85-6)

We do no wrong to Solomós' memory when we say that this poem is a failure, since he was well aware of the fact himself. Its faults are indeed glaring and obvious. Firstly, it is far too long and involved, and entirely lacks cohesion. The poet jumps from one subject to another, purely as his capricious fancy directs, until the reader is in a constant uncertainty as to who is being addressed or what incidents described. The sections into which the **"Hymn to Liberty"** is divided are self-contained, clearly divided, and logically connected; here, all is confusion. The incidents themselves, whether real or imaginary, are characterized by a drawling narrative and a wealth of insipid and stereotyped epithet which remind us of journalese. Moreover, the political homilies are over-emphasized: the exhortations against disunity, which occur naturally in the **"Hymn to Liberty,"** are out of place in a memorial ode, even though Byron himself strongly represented to the Greeks the folly of their internecine feuds. Finally, the poem is, in many passages, simply a feeble copy of the **"Hymn to Liberty"**; this is particularly noticeable in the sections descriptive of the siege of Missolonghi, the rise of Liberty, the malevolent policy of the European Powers, and the condemnation of Disunity.

Some good passages there undoubtedly are, notably the vision of Alcaeus, the pictorial imagery of the cluster of heroical spirits surrounding the Patriarch as they hover above the fray, the description of the eagle flying into the sun, Ada's prayer to her father, and best of all, the shadow of Byron falling across Bótzari's tomb. Here the versification, which is uniformly adequate, combines with the thought to produce images of considerable merit. Again, there are in some stanzas hints of ideas which the later Solomós was to elaborate and to immortalize; so in stanza 127, the thoughts of Byron turn homewards as those of the young soldier in that acute psychological study the **"Pórphyras."** . . . But such meritorious or interesting elements are, considering the length of the poem, rare, and they occur so unexpectedly that we have often to go back and re-read several stanzas in order to set them in their true context. It would seem that for the faults of the poem we are justified in putting the chief blame on the enormous success of the **"Hymn to Liberty."** This phenomenon gave Solomós the temporary illusion that whatever he wrote was bound to be good. The **"Hymn"** was written all at once, in a sustained ardour, and it is probable that large sections of the **"Lyrical Poem"** were similarly produced; but the ardour which gives birth to a readable patriotic poem is different from the inspiration required for a moving elegy on an individual. The one is a passion, the other should be a feeling. The patriotic outbursts which disfigure the **"Lyrical Poem"** detract from the interest of the central figure, and we get the impression that one particular of Byron's character—his liberalism—has been isolated and used as a peg on which to hang a patched and amorphous replica of the **"Hymn to Liberty."** Moreover, the very just sense that Solomós had acquired of his duty and capacity as a national teacher led him to suppose it incumbent on him to instruct, and it is hard to combine the didactic with the lyrical. (pp. 92-4)

* * * * *

[It] cannot be denied that, when in 1859 the **Found Remains** [*Ta euriskomena*] (as they were tactfully called) of Dionysius Solomós were published with Polylá's delightfully written preface [see Additional Bibliography], the disappointment throughout Greece was very great. His poetry had hardly been heard

of in Athens till 1849, and only in 1853 did he find any sort of following in Greece. Until 1850 he was much better known in Italy and France than in Greece proper. The curse of purism and pedantry lay like a winter on the land. Solomós did not write like a schoolmaster, and that was all one needed to know. 'With all his innumerable errors in speech and rhythm,' wrote the ineffable Soútzo in 1833, 'which mar every one of his compositions'; and the dictum of an usher named Chrysovérgi that 'the tongue, metre and form of Solomós' poetry are of no value whatsoever' was generally felt to be just. . . . His friends Regaldi and Zalokósta were the first to turn Greek literary opinion in favour of Solomós in the early 'fifties, and though every step made toward establishing him was stubbornly contested by the pedants, until during the years 1853-1855 Athenian literary circles were rent in twain over the question, so much ground had been made by 1857 that Solomós before he died was able to read in the Athenian periodical *Euterpe* that 'he was a poet most studious of and beloved by the people, a poet of golden phrases and verses many of which were alive on the lips of his countrymen all over Greece': they were beginning to take him seriously. The publication of the **Found Remains** put a stop to all this. It was very understandable. How could a set of prejudiced and ill-educated critics, who might have stomached another **"Hymn to Liberty"** to swell the patriotic breast, grasp the significance and the value of those scattered, mystical, seemingly meaningless fragments, which told of the soul's adventures and shone with the intangible, iridescent beauty of the rainbow? 'The nation must regard everything truthful as truly national,' Solomós had said. But where was truth to be found in these *disjecta membra*? The prevailing, the only too easily gathered impression that Solomós was an over-rated poet, an idle, dissolute creature who counted for very little, was artfully fostered by the shrewd criticisms of ''Idiot-Zambelio,' and strongly rammed home by the assertiveness of Valaoríti. Solomós' fame slumbered and slept for years, until at the end of the century the champions of the demotic speech arose with power, and Roídi . . . and Palamá brought Solomós to the fore again. Only in recent years, with the scientific study of the demotic, has the extraordinary contribution of Solomós' genius to the Greek tongue been appreciated. He took the degraded, ravaged demotic of 1822 and advanced it so far on the road with so gigantic a shove that writers of the demotic have hardly caught up with him yet. But this was by the way. Solomós was a poet, and as a poet we can now judge him, when the mists of prejudice and ignorance have very largely cleared.

In the Heptanese he continued to have a considerable following. Tipaldo, Gerasimo Marcorán, Valaoríti, Polylá, and greatest of all Lawrence Mavilli, were all strongly influenced by him, and the best poetry of the later nineteenth century was in consequence written in Corfu. But none of these had Solomós' genius.

> Fairest of stars, last in the train of night
> If rather thou belong not to the dawn

—it might well have appeared doubtful. Solomós should have been from the first the morning star of Modern Greek poetry. Once the envious clouds of purism, which he, like the blushing, discontented sun, perceived were set to stain the track of his bright passage, have been dispersed, his influence will continue to shine and to fertilize future generations of Greek literature, but it was a tragedy for his country's literature that that influence should for so long have been obscured by prejudice and lack of understanding. (pp. 201-04)

Romilly Jenkins, in his Dionysius Solomós, *Cambridge at the University Press, 1940, 225 p.*

DEMETRIOS CAPETANAKIS (essay date 1944)

[*Here, Capetanakis points out aspects in which Solomos's poetry transcends mere Greek patriotic verse.*]

Dionysios Solomos is considered the national poet of modern Greece. The words of the Greek national anthem are his; he lived during the war of Greek Independence and his poetry is burning with patriotism and the love of freedom; but, in spite of that, Solomos was not only a patriotic poet, and his poetry is significant not only for the Greeks. . . . Solomos' poetry has a freshness—and at the same time a depth—which make him one of the most interesting poets of the nineteenth century. His poetry has such a freshness because when he started writing it was before the liberation of Greece, and the modern Greek language was something fresh, which had not been much used by deliberate poetry. Solomos could use in his poetry the simplest and most ordinary words such as 'kalos' = good, 'omorfos' = beautiful, 'glykos' = sweet, words which the poets of a worn-out language rather avoid, and he could make poetry, a poetry full of freshness, out of them. There are some admirable lines, . . . which I have translated as follows:

> Blond April dances with the God
> Of Love, and Nature's happy.
> And in the growing shade which hides
> Riches of fragrant coolness,
> One hears unheard-of, fainting songs
> Of birds. Clear, lovely waters
> Run into scented depths of earth,
> And rob them of their perfumes,
> And showing all the treasures of
> Their sources to the sun,
> They run hither and thither, mad,
> And sing like nightingales.
> A butterfly which scented her
> Sleep in the heart of lilies,
> Played on the silent surface of
> The lake with a small shadow.
> —You who can see the spirits move,
> What did you see to-night?
> —The night was full of miracles,
> The night was full of spells.

This lovely passage, full of the freshness of nature described in a new, fresh language, is not only a charming description. It is much more than that. This passage belongs to a long, unfinished poem called **"The Free Besieged"** [**"Oi eleftheroi poliorkimenoi"**], inspired by one of the most stirring incidents of the Greek War of Independence, the Siege of Missolonghi. Missolonghi, the Greek town where Byron died, had been besieged by enemy forces so overwhelming that there was no doubt about the issue of the struggle. In spite of that the Greeks were not giving in. Mr. Jenkins in his book on Solomos, says about the poem:

> The scene is Missolonghi, but Missolonghi now stands for the world of men. The protagonists are Greek heroes, but their adventures are those of the human soul. We have passed from historical and political poetry to Greek tragedy. The conflict of the rational soul in opposition to the brute forces of matter, the weakness of the flesh, and the temptations of the senses, are

now the theme. The Besieged are led into temptation, in order that they may overcome it and win the crown that shall not be taken away from them. Brutality and cruelty strive to intimidate them; their starving bodies are tempted at the sight of the vigorous enemy, strong in the plenty of unhampered supplies; the women must survive their children's slow death; the men must endure a final, heart-rending failure of nerve on the part of the women, as the hour of dawn draws nigh when the sortie is to be made; hopes of relief are raised only to be dashed when it is seen that the approaching squadron is not Greek. And last and most powerful of all, nature and spring time conspire to defeat their resolution by appearing all round them in their most alluring manifestations. In vain: they have the courage never to submit or yield—reason is triumphant, and the Besieged by their indomitable endurance become finally and absolutely free.

This absolute freedom of man in life, a freedom which is there as an attitude in spite of the facts of bondage, of failure and death, pictured in a wonderful way by the Greek ballads in which man does not surrender to death, but wrestles with him on iron threshing floors—this absolute freedom, which means everything to the Greek of to-day, is also the theme of our national poet's most important work, **"The Free Besieged."** An attitude of absolute freedom similar to the one we find in modern Greek literature, we find in some works of Russian literature, in Dostoevsky's *Letters from the Underworld*, for instance. The hero of *Letters from the Underworld* speaks of the limitations of man, which make absolute freedom impossible. He describes them as a stone wall and says: 'Of course, I am not going to beat my head against a wall if I have not the necessary strength to do so; yet I am *not* going to *accept* that wall merely because I have run up against it, and have no means to knock it down.' Yet, Dostoevsky's attitude of absolute freedom is expressed with too much passion while Solomos' attitude of absolute freedom has no bitterness in it—it is full of dignity and pride. (pp. 66-8)

> *Demetrios Capetanakis, "An Introduction to Modern Greek Poetry," in* New Writing and Daylight, *No. 5, Autumn, 1944, pp. 64-72.*

C. A. TRYPANIS (essay date 1951)

[*Trypanis offers a brief overview of Solomos's career and identifies the significant elements in his works.*]

The originator and greatest representative of the Ionian school of poetry is the Greek national poet Dionysius Solomos. . . . Like so many others of the Ionian aristocracy of those days, he was practically bilingual, and having received most of his education in Italy, he wrote his first poems in Italian. It was in contact with Italian classical and classicist poetry that his early taste was cultivated. He soon, however, was converted to Greek, and avidly read all the Greek poetry that he could lay his hands on; he was greatly charmed by the living folk-songs. His first Greek creations were sentimental lyrics . . . , but from the outbreak of the Greek War of Independence his art took on a definite tinge of heroic and lyrical patriotism . . . , which developed as the years passed on into a deep philosophic approach to life and art, expressing itself in verse of unique delicacy and balance unsurpassed to this day in modern Greek. . . . (pp. li-lii)

In the struggle that continued from Byzantine days between the *katharevousa* and the demotic, Solomos marks the turning-point; for by choosing the latter as the language of his poems he opened the way for all real subsequent Greek poetry. Solomos differs from his poet-contemporaries in that while acknowledging his debt to romanticism—and Lord Byron exercised no small charm upon him . . .—he is not content to limit himself to its forms, but rather uses it as a starting-point, adapting and assimilating it. In the new paths he followed, German philosophy and in particular Schiller's aesthetics influenced him. He is a figure outstanding in the whole of European literature because he finally succeeded in combining harmoniously the classical and romantic spirits. His creations attained greater perfection with every year as he mastered his tools of language and moulded his imagination by the rules of great art. From his **"Hymn to Liberty"** (the first stanzas of which became the Greek national anthem) to his **"Free Besieged,"** which was to sing the heroic resistance and sally of Missolonghi, we see gradations continually ascending. Understanding of nature, love for his country, a sense of duty, a deep religious feeling, moral excellence combined with perfection of form—these are the quintessence of his mature work, which unfortunately we know mostly from fragments, as the instability of his disposition prevented him from finishing many of his major writings.

Solomos' reputation and success helped to establish in Greek poetry a number of things which had previously been used only occasionally and without great confidence: among them, the demotic language; certain Western metres, such as the sestina, the terza, and ottava rima; and finally, the strophic element (borrowed from Italian literature), which freed it from the unvarying monotony imposed by the unrelieved political verse during the long years of servitude to the Turks. (pp. lii-liii)

> *C. A. Trypanis, in an introduction to his* Medieval and Modern Greek Poetry: An Anthology, *Oxford at the Clarendon Press, Oxford, 1951, pp. ix-lxiii.*

ARNOLD J. TOYNBEE   (essay date 1954)

[*An English historian and professor of Byzantine and modern Greek language, literature, and history before his death, Toynbee is best known for his ten-volume* A Study of History, *in which he traces cycles of productivity and decay in major world civilizations. Here, Toynbee suggests factors in Solomos's character and experiences that may have shaped his work.*]

The career of the conventional Italian poet Dionisio Salomone, who became the original Greek poet Dhionýsios Solomòs, is one of the curiosities of the history of the transmission of culture. His genius found its opportunity for making its literary fortune thanks to the lucky accident of his being the bastard son, by a Zantiot Greek servant-girl, of a Zantiot landowner—Venetian in culture and origin, though Orthodox in religion—who, on his death-bed, married Dionisio's mother and left Dionisio and his brother handsome shares of his estate. At the age of ten, Dionisio was sent by his guardian to Italy for his education, and he remained there for ten years on end . . . , first at Venice, then at Cremona, and finally at the Venetian university of Padua. During these years in Italy he received a thorough schooling in Italian and Latin literature; made friends with Monti, Manzoni, and other Italian men of letters; and became a disciple of the Western Romantic movement. After his return to Zante he joined an aristocratic Italianate literary

circle there whose parlour-game was the extemporization of sonnets in Italian on some given subject or given set of line-endings; and there seemed no reason why he should not end his days in this conventionally cultivated obscurity.

Solomòs found his true *métier* when, after the outbreak of the Ottoman Greek insurrection in A.D. 1821, a Mesolonghiot patriot-publicist, Spiridhiòn Trikoúpis, visited him in Zante at his country villa . . . and invited him to become the Dante of a Greek Parnassus [see excerpt by Tricúpi dated 1873]. 'I don't know Greek,' Solomòs replied, meaning that he had never been taught the Byzantine ecclesiastical Attic *koinê*. 'The language which you imbibed with your mother's milk is Greek,' Trikoúpis retorted, meaning that Solomòs could have communicated with his low-born mother in no other tongue than her Zantiot Romaïc Greek patois. Thereupon Solomòs sprang into fame by composing in this mother tongue of his, in Italian metres, Western poetry, first in Byron's vein and later in Schiller's. Thanks to his being a Heptanesian aristocrat, Solomòs was a highly cultivated man who did speak one of the dialects of living Greek as his mother tongue without knowing the dead language. In the early nineteenth century the Ionian Islands were perhaps the only place in Greek Orthodox Christendom where this could have happened, and the composition of Western poetry in living Greek—without murdering the language by trying to transform it into a resurrected Attic—was Solomòs' inestimably valuable service to a new Greek nation that was seeking to enter the Western comity.

Solomòs work suffered, nevertheless, from another form of pedantry that was likewise inimical to poetry. His method of composing a Romaïc Greek poem was to take Italian notes, expand these into Greek prose, and then hammer this prose into verse! And in his latter years, when his mental vigour was on the decline, he relapsed into writing his poetry in the Italian which, in spite of his Romaïc Greek *tours de force*, was, from first to last, his natural medium of literary expression. Moreover, his invincible native Westernism, which made him so effective a psychopompus for Greek souls seeking initiation into the Western culture, also inhibited him from going out to meet his Ottoman fellow Greek Orthodox Christians in deed as well as in word. When, on the eve of the fall of Mesolónghi, just across the water, the cannonade bombarded his ears in his peaceful villa on Zante, he suffered anguish but did not seek relief by going to the front in defiance of British regulations; and, though he lived on for a quarter of a century after a fragment of the Ottoman Empire had been transformed into a sovereign independent Kingdom of Greece with its capital at Athens, he preferred to end his days at Corfù under a British régime. (pp. 679-80)

> *Arnold J. Toynbee, "The Conflict of Cultures in the Soul of Solomós,"* in his A Study of History, Vol. VIII, *Oxford University Press, 1954, pp. 679-80.*

PHILIP SHERRARD   (essay date 1956)

[*Sherrard surveys Solomos's treatment of good and evil, triumph and defeat, and the natural and supernatural worlds as depicted in first his early lyrics, including "Woman of Zakynthos" and "Lambros," in the more mature "The Cretan," and finally in his most ambitious poems, "The Free Besieged" and "The Shark."*]

Solomos' parentage betokens his future poetry, that fusion, as the poetry of Dante to which he was so greatly devoted, of an aristocratic spirit with the simplicity and freshness of his mother tongue, the demotic Greek language; and, although it is a theme which lies outside the scope of this study, it is worth while to remark in passing that Solomos' choice of the people's language for his poetry was to have a significance for modern Greek poetry comparable to that which a similar choice by Dante had for Italian poetry. (p. 1)

[The great part of Solomos'] early poetry is made up of a series of short lyrics. It must at once be confessed that these lyrics are not altogether encouraging. They are in the main devoted to singing, in a conventional and sentimental way, the praises of virgins, of virginity, and of those who die young and innocent. Among the first lines that he wrote in Greek, for instance, is a song addressed to a girl brought up in a convent:

> My beautiful convent girl, I am here and I wait;
> Come to the grill to see how I am singing.
> For you my verse goes sweetly from my heart:
> May the wall let it pass and not be jealous.
> Try to flee if you can; come, so I may kiss you.
> Only with a kiss shall I put out my flame.
> My beautiful convent girl, come here, and think
> That I will not, my innocent one, deflower you. . . .

The theme is slightly varied in another early poem, **"The Dream."** The poet dreams that one night he was with his beloved. He asks the stars if ever they saw anything so beautiful:

> Say if you ever saw
> On another such lovely hair,
> Such a hand, or such a foot,
> Such an angelic look. . . .

As he speaks to the stars, other women appear, adorned with the moon's light. They dance hand in hand round the dreamer and try to capture his heart. One may assume that these are ordinary common ladies. His beloved asks him how he likes them. He replies that they are very ugly. The poem continues with the dreamer embracing his beloved, whom he sees as a rose and whose every kiss is the planting of a new rose, and the whole thing ends:

> This is the dream, beloved;
> Now it depends on you
> To turn it into truth
> And to remember me. . . .

In another of these early lyrics, **"The Poisoned Girl"** . . . , Solomos comes to the defence of a young girl who has committed suicide. Rumour had it that the reason for her suicide was her disappointment in a love-affair in which she had been "dishonoured." In Solomos' poem, the girl comes before her Maker on the Day of Judgment, and calls upon Him to witness to her innocence. Finally, written a little later, but belonging to this group, is a poem in which these sentiments are expressed more directly and with more emphasis. The poem is called **"To a Nun."** It was written on the occasion of a young girl's entry into a convent. As she goes into the church, angels descend to see who approaches. On discovering that it is one who is about to take the veil and become the bride of Christ, they sing to her, contrasting the world she is now entering with the storm and turmoil of that she is leaving behind:

> Sweet it is to meditate
> Paradise's beauty;
> Bitter is the terrible
> Whirlwind of the world;
> Only the echo comes here,
> The tempest does not come.

> Here does Christ descend
> Down to you in dreams;
> There arms shake
> And blood-stained thrones;
> Here is joy and triumph,
> There is wretchedness.
>
>   (pp. 2-4)

The reason for quoting from these early lyrics, which in themselves have little value, is that in them is beginning to appear, in however fragile and sentimental a way, the outline of a contrast between a state of goodness and innocence on the one hand, and a world of evil and corruption on the other; and this contrast is something which continues, with modifications, through all Solomos' work. In two other early pieces, **"The Woman of Zakynthos"** [**"I gynaika tis Zakynthos"**], a prose satire, and **"Lambros,"** a Byronic melodrama, one aspect of this contrast, the sense of evil and corruption in the world, and of the disgust that goes with it, is more forcibly uttered. **"The Woman of Zakynthos"** is the portrait of a woman who seems entirely vicious and evil, the personification of all the vile and hideous aspects of human nature. The poet describes her:

> Well, the body of the woman was small and misshapen, and her chest almost always marked by the leeches which she stuck on it to suck the phthisis; and lower down hung two breasts like tobacco pouches. And this small body walked very quickly and its joints appeared dislocated. Her face had the shape of a shoe-last, and you could see, if you looked from the bottom of the chin to the top of the head, on which was a round twisted plait and, above, an enormous comb, that it was of great length. And whoever tried to measure the woman with a foot-rule would find a quarter of the body in the head. And her cheek broke out in eczema, which sometimes was liquid pus and sometimes was dried up and withered. And she opened every so often a big mouth to mock at others, and she showed her lower teeth, the front teeth, small and rotten, which met the upper teeth, which were very white and long. And although she was young, her temples and her forehead and her eyebrows and the snot of her nose were senile, always senile, but especially when she leant her head on her right fist, meditating her wickedness; and this senile head was enlivened by two shining and jet-black eyes, and one of them squinted slightly. And they circled hither and thither, seeking evil. And they found it even where it did not exist; and in her eyes flashed a certain something, which made you think that madness either had just left her or was on the point of possessing her. And that was the dwelling place of her wicked and sinful soul. And it revealed its wickedness both in speech and in silence. And when she spoke secretly in order to defile someone's reputation, her voice seemed like the rustling of the straw, trodden by the foot of the thief. And when she spoke aloud, her voice was like that which people use to mock at others. And in spite of that, when she was alone, she would go to the looking-glass, and, gazing, would laugh and weep, and she thought she was the most beautiful of

all those in the Seven Isles. And her work was to separate husband from wife, and brother from sister, craftily, like Death. And when in sleep she saw the beautiful body of her sister, she awoke terrified. Envy, hatred, suspicion, falsehood, tugged continually at her bowels, in the same way as you see local urchins, ragged and dirty, ring the bells on the day of festival, driving everyone insane.

Much ingenuity has been spent on trying to identify the female whom Solomos here describes; she has been linked with actual historical characters in contemporary Zante, and even with the British rule of the Seven Isles. But such attempts at identification are not important, and it is enough to consider the Woman simply as a type of harridan, loose, evil-tongued, overbearing, the terror of her husband and her home. She is the equivalent of the French Margot and the English Meg, those mediaeval viragos who, at their delight in evil, challenged even the most formidable power on earth, the Devil himself. The Elder Bruegel has given us a portrait of a similar woman in his "Dulle Griet."

This study in evil and corruption is further elaborated in "**Lambros.**" Lambros seduced and deceived a fifteen-year-old girl, Maria. By her he had four children, all of whom he sent into an orphanage. Now Maria has lived for fifteen years unmarried in Lambros' house. The thought of her dishonour and of the unknown fate of her children weigh heavily on her; her days are full of lament and her nights of black dream:

> It seems that I am voyaging
> In dream on the ocean's waste;
> Alone with wave and wind
> I fight, you not being near me;
> Nothing in my danger do I see
> But the sky wherever I look;
> I gaze at the sky: "Help," I call,
> "Sailless, rudderless, out at sea I drift."

> And thus as with courage I call
> My three young lads spring up;
> The boat's planks from their weight
> Creak as though they splinter;
> Then inescapable death appears;
> Huddled, together they whisper,
> And having in secret spoken
> Row on with broken oars.

> With bitter smile on her mouth
> My girl approaches me;
> A shroud enfolds her body
> Blown out white by the wind;
> But more pale is the hand
> She raises up before me,
> Which trembles, as the reed trembles,
> Revealing the cross in the palm.

(pp. 4-6)

This cross Maria had made with a knife on the palm of her daughter's hand when Lambros had forced her to yield the child up for him to take to the orphanage. At the same time she had put a necklet round the child's neck.

Meanwhile, Lambros has joined the Greek revolutionaries fighting the Turks, inspired by the justice of the Greek cause and by the desire to revenge the death of a holy monk, brother to Maria, whom Ali Pasha had burnt alive. In the army camp

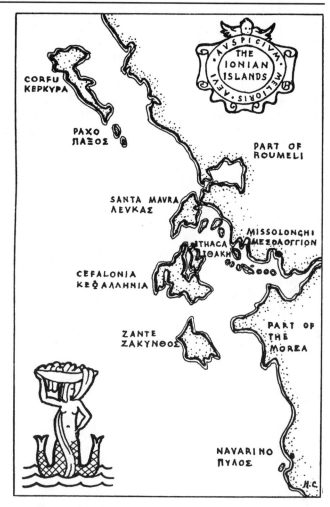

Zante and Corfu in the Ionian Islands, where Solomos lived. From Dionysius Solomos, *by Romilly Jenkins. Cambridge University Press, 1940. Copyright by Cambridge University Press. Reprinted with the permission of the publisher.*

where Lambros is encouraging the men to battle, a young Turk appears, who warns the Greeks that the Turks are preparing an ambush for them. The young Turk then, struck by Lambros' kindness and moved by his protection, confides in him that she is really a girl who has left the Turks after witnessing the sacrifice of another girl, her friend; she had watched the calm with which this girl, a Christian, had gone to her death, and she had then and there decided that she also would become a Christian. She now asks Lambros to baptise her. He, stirred by the girl's beauty and her sensitivity, falls in love with her, and eventually seduces her. He has never before experienced such passion with a woman. And it is only after the seduction that he notices on the girl's hand the cross which Maria had cut on the hand of her—and his—daughter, and round her throat the well-remembered necklet.

In the next scene, Lambros with his daughter, to whom he has confessed the whole ghastly story, is rowing on a lake one moonlit night. The daughter, sitting in the prow of the boat, unplaits her hair and lets it fall before her, so the rising moon does not behold her. Then, as Lambros is rowing, he suddenly hears a splash, and, turning, sees that his daughter has thrown herself into the lake. For a moment he hesitates: Shall he save her? Then he rows on as fast as he can for the shore of the lake, imagining that every impediment his oar meets is the body of his drowned daughter.

Guilt-stricken, Lambros now returns to his house. His appearance terrifies the already distraught Maria. At her insistence, he tells her what has happened. It is now the night of Easter Day. Lambros rushes into the church which that same morning had been the scene of rejoicing at the renewed miracle of the Resurrection and at the return of spring to earth. But for Lambros there is no Resurrection and no return of spring. The saints are as dumb and as motionless as tombs. Lambros' despair turns to defiance. Man, he cries, let fate do what she will, is his own God. And he turns to leave the church. But at the first door from which he seeks to go out a voice gives him the Easter greeting: "Christ is risen." He turns to the second door. A similar voice greets him with the same words. At the third door the same. The three voices are those of his three young sons risen from the grave. They pursue Lambros through the church as he tries to flee them. They compel him to kiss their dead lips. Lambros' crimes have created his own Hell and now that Hell has risen up around him and has made him its prisoner. There is no escape except, as Lambros thinks, in death; and at dawn, when the visiting avengers return to the grave, he rushes from the church and throws himself into the same lake in which his daughter had drowned herself. And the poem concludes:

> And Lambros died with open mouth, not in the peace of God. But who will close his eyes? Where is Maria, the unfortunate Maria? She has been missing since dawn. She has been wandering over the fields by herself, and the sun's rays, which, rising, call on mortals to enjoy life, sparkle on all the still waters of the wilderness. Motionless was the centre of the lake, like the blue pupil of an eye untroubled by future cares. But at the lake's edge the scattered encircling trees were reflected faithfully in the eye. Forlorn Maria, when she had circled round about, approached the lake and seeing there the objects reflected, thought in her distraction that that was another world. She stopped short, and, raising her arms on high and smiling the smile of madness, she murmured: 'That surely will be a better world than this, and I will make ready to go thither. I shall see, maybe I shall see whether there no merciful hand reaches out to me. For on this earth I have walked so long frightened among strange people, as if I had appeared before them for the first time. Now I shall go yonder. Let me therefore adorn myself as best I can, lest new strangers there despise me.'

> So saying she stretched her thin fingers towards some wild grasses growing in the waste. Then she wove a wreath for her disconsolate head, she put round her throat the so lamented necklet,

> And into the water, which she as a mirror sees,
> She gazes again, and smiles, and downward falls.
> (pp. 6-8)

This Ophelia-like death of Maria, the seduced demented girl, together with Solomos' early lyrics in praise and defence of maiden innocence and chastity and with his portrait of the obscene abandoned Woman of Zakynthos, give the impression that the poet is a kind of Hamlet-figure caught between dreams of virgin purity and disgust at that corruption of which the sexual passions seem to him the evidence, if not indeed the root. On the one hand, there is the admonition to the innocent girl:

> Get thee to a nunnery . . .

On the other hand, there is the embittered venom spat at the carnal woman:

> Nay, but to live
> In the rank sweat of an enseamed bed
> Stew'd in corruption, honeying and making love
> Over the nasty sty . . .

In a note to his **"Ode on the Death of Lord Byron"** [**"Poiema lyriko eis ton thanato tou Lord Byron"**], Solomos, with considerable perspicacity, points out in how many ways Byron resembles Milton. In particular, "the antithesis (in 'Paradise Lost') between the first-formed beauties of Creation and the terrors of Hell made a great impression on the mind of Byron." . . . One wonders whether it did not perhaps make a great impression also on the mind of Solomos, for, as we have seen, already in these early poems can be discerned the shadow of a myth that in many ways reflects that of Milton, not only in the antithesis it presents between the beauties of Paradise and the terrors of Hell, but also in its implied denigration of the sexual passions, of which woman is the provoker, as evil. Solomos was in addition saturated in the poetry of Dante, where, although the antithesis between Heaven and Hell is as strong as that in Milton's myth, the woman is not the temptress but is on the contrary a kind of redeemer, and it may be that the figure of Beatrice is the original of which Solomos' images of virgin purity are the somewhat etiolated copies. This contrast of the Beatrice-figure with the figure of the carnal temptress and instrument of human overthrow, the Miltonic Eve, may explain the dual aspect woman has in Solomos' early poetry. At all events, Solomos seems to have felt that underlying the appearance of things, forces of evil are at work which have the power to destroy all that is noble in man's nature. Lambros, for example, is not a man without any redeeming features. He is able in a spirit of self-sacrifice and disinterested love to devote himself to and risk his life in the struggle for Greek freedom. And he is a man of action who can command respect and loyalty. But the blind destructive passions which flesh is heir to, drive him to inhuman and bestial crime. And, what is more, such is the damnable cunning of evil in this world, man may commit his worst offences altogether unwittingly: Lambros may have been responsible for his sin in seducing the young girl whose confidence he had won; but it was hardly his fault that this young girl should have been his daughter. Solomos seems to have felt that in this "kingdom of Satan," man, if he is the doer of evil, is just as much the victim of evil. He is simply and hopelessly involved in a blind fate-driven world whose essential character is evil. And from this point of view, Maria also, that afflicted woman, is a portrait of the human soul caught up in the corrupt world of generation and death, and suffering the consequences of such entanglement. The young Solomos seems to have had some experience like that of the young Keats when he peered beneath the surface of nature and beheld her hidden workings:

> But I saw
> Too far into the sea, where every maw
> The greater on the less feeds evermore.
> But I saw too distinct into the core
> Of an eternal fierce destruction,
> And so from happiness I far was gone . . .

Solomos too had seen this fierce destructive element and like Keats he was gone far from happiness.

But there is another note in these early poems which is more elusive. To describe it as an intimation of a mystical experience may be to beg the question, yet it is difficult to know what else to call it, especially in view of certain aspects of Solomos' later development. For now and again in these early poems occur lines which seem to refer to a kind of ecstasy, to a sudden suspension of distress and pain at the touch of an invisible hand. Sometimes this suspension of normal consciousness is indicated by the awakening of a delicate wind. This is the case in the poem "The Brother and Sister" and in the poem "The Mad Mother." Both these poems are songs which the disconsolate Maria sings in the longer poem "Lambros." In the first of these two poems, a young boy goes out at evening to look for his sister whom he has lost. He cannot find her anywhere. At length he reaches a cemetery, and there, on a tomb, he sees the girl. She is dead. The poet describes how, as she lay on the tomb, this sudden wind rose:

> Innocent butterfly,
> In the burning heat
> She seeks a breeze
> To cool herself.
>
> And there by chance
> On a tomb she lay,
> And suddenly blew
> A sweet breeze.
>
> She felt the breath
> Which the air sent
> And she did not know
> Where she was, where.

> (pp. 9-11)

The second song of Maria, "The Mad Mother," is about a woman whose two children have been killed by lightning. One night she comes to the cemetery where they are buried. She circles round the wall of the cemetery in the darkness, groping with her hands. Then she enters the moonlit bell-tower. The black patches of night in the ravines seem to her like the torn clothes of her dead children. In her distraction she tugs on the bell-ropes. The sound of the bells clangs out over the surrounding wilderness, while the mother weeps for her loss. Suddenly, at the depths of her despair:

> Suddenly a cooling
> Breeze awakens;
> Whispering it comes
> Laden with sweet
> Scents of the dawn,
>
> Into the mother's
> Heart-depths it passes
> Like the movements
> Of imagination
> That paint happiness. . . .

It is significant that the scene of both these episodes is the graveyard, for the graveyard is the traditional image of the place where body and soul fall apart, of the place at which the old life ends and the new life begins.

In "The Woman of Zakynthos," however, is a passage which describes an unmistakable visionary experience. The narrator of "The Woman of Zakynthos" is a monk, Dionysios (Solomos' own name). After describing, in a passage already quoted, the appearance of the Woman, he goes on to speak of the women of Missolonghi: . . .

> I saw behind the church an old woman, who had set up small candles in the grass, and she was burning incense, and the small candles shone in the greenness and the incense went up. And she raised her bony hands, passing them through the incense and weeping. And opening and closing her toothless mouth she prayed. And I felt within me a great disturbance and I was carried away in spirit to Missolonghi. And I saw neither the castle, nor the camp, nor the lake, nor the sea, nor the earth I trod, nor the sky; a pitch-black darkness covered the besieged and the besiegers and all their works and everything that there was. And I raised eyes and hands towards heaven in order to pray with all the fervour of my soul; and I saw, lit up in the incessant flashing, a woman with a lyre in her hand, who stood in the air among the smoke. And I had just time to marvel at her dress, which was black like the blood of the hare, and her eyes . . . when she stopped, the woman, among the smoke, and she looked at the battle; and the thousand sparks which flew into the sky touched her dress and went out. She spread her fingers on the lyre and I heard her chant:
>
> > At the dawn I took
> > The road of the sun
> > Hanging the just
> > Lyre from the shoulder;
> > And from where it dawns
> > Until where it sets . . .
>
> And scarcely had the goddess finished her words when she vanished, and our people shouted furiously because of the victory, and they and everything else disappeared from me, and my bowels again shook terribly, and it seemed that I had become deaf and blind. And soon I saw in front of me the old woman, who said to me: 'God be praised, Hermit, I thought that something had happened to you. I called you, I shook you, and you heard nothing and your eyes were fixed on the sky, while the earth leapt like bubbles in seething water. Now it is over, and the small candles and incense are exhausted. Would you say that our people have triumphed?' And I began to go, with Death in my heart; and the old woman kissed my hand, and, kneeling down, she said: 'How frozen your hand is!'"

"The Woman of Zakynthos" was probably written in 1827. In 1828 Solomos left Zante and went to live in Corfu. Looking at the work which he produced during those ten years on Zante after his return from Italy, one can begin to make out, beneath the effusion of his patriotic poems, beneath the sentimentality of his lyrics to young maidens and the Byronising of his "Lambros," the lineaments of a more solemn drama. Briefly, this drama seems to hinge on a contradiction that Solomos felt in life. On the one hand, he seems to have felt that human beings are the victims of a blind, evil, destructive force which drives them to commit acts of brutality and beastliness and sometimes corrupts their nature altogether. On the other hand, noble traits in human nature do sometimes reveal themselves and permit man or woman to triumph over the forces of corruption and to achieve a certain release by contact with some invisible power. Often this contact is only achieved at moments of great despair or of near madness, when the senses and human reason are deranged, unseated, and overthrown, and there is a kind of death. At such moments, man may feel relieved of the weight of mortality and even be granted insight into another world. The growing disgust for the "natural" world, and the definition of this disgust in such works as **"The Woman of Zakynthos"** and **"Lambros,"** and at the same time, one must believe, a growing conviction that man's true life was not to be realised in this world, but in the attainment of a level of reality of which this world was the negation, seem to have compelled Solomos to make a change in his life and also a change in his work. His move to Corfu in 1828 is a fitting mark of both these changes.

As far as the change in his life was concerned, this move seems to have represented an advance to greater solitude and meditation. . . . But it is not so much the change in his life that concerns us, as the kind of work with which Solomos was to occupy himself in the coming years; and it is about this that something must now be said.

In an introduction to an edition of Solomos' work published shortly after his death, Polylas, friend and biographer of the poet, writes: "His work in Art, as well as in conversation, was a spontaneous uninterrupted endeavour to extinguish his individuality in absolute truth"—giving effect, he adds, to the axiom of Heracleitos: "Although possessing a common Word, the majority live as though they have a wisdom of their own." Side by side with this estimation, and supporting it, are several of Solomos' own remarks. While still a young man in Italy, he was present at some discussion during which Monti, the Italian poet and critic, is reported to have said: "One must not think so much, one must feel, one must feel." Solomos thereupon replied: "First the mind must conceive strongly and then the heart must feel warmly what the mind has conceived." Again, in a note to his **"Ode on the Death of Lord Byron"** from which I have already quoted, Solomos writes: "The difficulty which an artist experiences (I speak of great artists) does not consist in showing imagination and passion, but in subordinating these two things, with time and with labour, to the intelligible meaning of Art." . . . [In] some notes that Solomos made in connection with the writing of what was to be his major poetic endeavour ["The Free Besieged"], he gives a more complete statement of his view of the poet's task and of the nature of poetry:

> Apply to the spiritual form the development of the plant, which begins with the seed and turns back to the seed, after it has been through, as stages of evolution, all natural forms, *i.e.*, root, stem, leaves, flowers, and fruit. Apply it and reflect deeply upon the nature of the subject and the form of art. See that this work is performed without interruption.

> A ripe and beautiful democracy of ideas, that will present substantially the Monarch invisible to the senses. Then it is a true poem. The Monarch, who is hidden to the senses and is known only by the spirit, within which it was born, is outside the area of Time; but a democracy of ideas acts sensibly within the limits of Time.

> Reflect deeply and firmly (once and for all) upon the nature of the Idea before you realise the poem.

> Let the whole poem express the Intelligible Meaning as a self-existent world, graded mathematically, rich and deep. Only in this way is it possible to produce, with various and successive inventions, the biggest and most terrible effects. This has never been done well enough. Those who have tried to do it (like Euripides, and with him most of the moderns who are his children), have remained outside the Idea, and this is intolerable for anyone with intelligence.

> Grasp and concentrate a spiritual power, and divide it among various characters, men and women, in whom everything will correspond. Reflect well whether this will be romantic, or, if possible, classic, or a mixed but legitimate type. The highest example of the second type is Homer; of the first Shakespeare; of the third I do not know.

> Let the poem possess a bodiless soul, which emanates from God, and which is then embodied in the organs of time, of place, of nationality, of language, with different thoughts, feelings, inclinations, etc. (let a small bodily world be adequate to reveal it); finally, the soul returns to God. . . .

(pp. 11-16)

Some of these last notes, it has been remarked, reflect in many ways the ideas of various German philosophers, from Kant to Hegel, whose works Solomos is known to have studied after his move to Corfu. This may well be so, but in case it should be thought that thereby the ideas are of less import, it should be pointed out not only that they are implicit in those earlier remarks of Solomos on the same theme . . . which were made before Solomos became acquainted with the German philosophers, but also that there is no connection between profundity and novelty, and as long as an artist has made an idea his own it does not matter whether it first occurred yesterday or before the dawn of history.

As a matter of fact, many of these ideas which Solomos held concerning his art do come, if not from before the dawn of history, at least from an early age, for they are implicit in the art forms of many cultures, above all of those based on principles enshrined and preserved in a living religious tradition and which may therefore be called traditional. . . . (pp. 16-17)

What, then, is [the] understanding which Solomos so persistently sought to communicate in his later work? We have already discerned the outlines of it in his earlier work, though because of the inadequacy of the expression it never becomes very convincing. We saw that this early work seems to point to a certain antithesis in life between an evil destructive force and a level of reality beyond the reach of such a force. We also saw that this destructive element seems to be identified with the natural world and with the passions, and that the poet seems to have regarded this world and life in it as evil. We saw finally that this other level of reality is realised at times of great distress, when the normal conditions of life are overthrown, and that this overthrow Solomos presents as a kind of death. In the passage which describes the vision in **"The Woman of Zakynthos"** and from which I cited, the other level of reality is revealed as a presence of deep darkness, a kind of superlunary power, and it is as such that it is again revealed in the first of Solomos' mature poems, "**The Cretan.**" . . . The poem opens at the eighteenth section. The first seventeen sections are missing and were probably never written. As it now stands, the poem opens as a Cretan is escaping from Crete, after the Turkish conquest of the island. He is out on the open sea, in a small boat, and with him is his beloved, all he has been able to save from the disaster. There is a storm. Lightning flashes and it thunders. But suddenly the sea becomes quiet, a perfect mirror in which the stars are reflected. Some mysterious power constrains nature. The wind drops, and wound in the moonlight the dark presence rises, a dazzling darkness that fills creation with light. She—for this presence is for Solomos a feminine, a maternal power—stops before the Cretan and gazes at him. She reminds him of someone he has once known, of some Madonna painted in a church, of something that his loving mind has fashioned, some dream dreamt when taking his mother's milk, an ancient pre-conscious memory. In the tears he sheds at the sight of her, his eyes are confused and he cannot see her, only he feels her eyes deep within him, for she is one of the divine powers who "dwell where they see into the abyss and into the heart of man; and I felt that she read my mind better than if I spoke sadly with my own lips." . . . But now she vanishes, and in her place a still music sounds. "It was," the poet notes, "an inexpressible impression, which perhaps no one has known unless the first man, when he first drew breath, and the sky, the earth, and the sea, formed for him, still in all their perfection, rejoiced within his soul, until in the drunkenness of his mind and heart, sleep, image of death, seized him." . . . And he seeks in the poem to express this inexpressible, to communicate the living nature of this all but incommunicable experience:

No girl's voice it was from the green woods,
Singing, as eve-star rises and the waters cloud,
Her secret love to tree and budding flower;
No Cretan nightingale, high on the wild rocks,
Beside his nest, spilling the night-long over
Far off plain and sea, his music till,
Melting starlight, dawn breaks, and drops
Roses from her hand in listening wonder;
Nor shepherd's pipe it was, as once I heard
Alone on Ida, when sorrow drew me thence,
And, the sun mid-heaven, I saw
Mountain, field, sea, smile in the brightness;
Then did hope of freedom stir within my breast;
Weeping, reaching out my hands, I cried:
"O my country, my country soaked in blood"—
Proud of her dark stone and of her barren grass.
No, no sound, bird or voice, was like this sound—
Perhaps nothing on earth is like it,
Wordless, so delicate, without echo even.
Whether from far or near it came I did not know,
Only as May-time scents it filled the air,
Utterly sweet, unspeakable . . .
Love and death themselves have not such power.
It seized upon my soul: sky, the sea and shore,
The girl—nothing of these did I remember;
It seized upon me, it made me even seek
To leave my flesh behind, that I might follow it.
Then at last it ceased, withdrawing from nature and my
  soul,
Which sighed and at once recalled my loved-one—. . . .

Or, as Solomos put it in his note, "sleep, image of death, seized him," and he returned, as the initiate when the epiphany

ends, back to his ordinary and habitual self, but only to find, as he reaches the shore with his beloved, that she is dead.

There is here, in ["**The Cretan**"], an attempt to express an original experience of considerable complexity, and we shall do it scant justice if we try to explain away the supernatural element by calling it a sublimation of nature or a hallucinated vision. It is something more than this. The experience is not first of all a natural experience: nature is eclipsed while it endures, and the young girl, the natural creature, is found dead after it. . . . [For] Solomos, who seeks to leave his flesh behind that he might follow the wordless music, the return to the natural world is a return to darkness and death. It would seem that for Solomos . . . the world is a prison-house of wrath and it is only through great struggle involving the sacrifice of all that is natural that man can attain happiness; by shattering all nature's forms he experiences a supernatural Nature, what I called a Mother Nature, Creatrix, Natura naturans. Boehme describes an understanding similar to that which would seem to lie behind "**The Cretan**":

> For man's happiness consists in this, that he has in him a true desire after God, for out of the desire springs forth the love; that is, when the desire receives the meekness of God into itself, then the desire immerses itself in the meekness, and becomes essential; and this is the heavenly or divine essentiality, or corporality: and therein the soul's spirit (which lay shut up in the anger, *viz.*, in death) does again arise in the love of God; for the love tinctures the death and darkness, that it is again capable of the divine sunshine.

The attainment of this happiness, in which, by a breaking through of all attachments to the world of time and place, "the love tinctures the death and darkness, that it is again capable of the divine sunshine," is the consummation of human life.

It was in what is perhaps his major poetic endeavour, "**The Free Besieged**" ["**Oi eleftheroi poliorkimenoi**"], that Solomos tried to symbolise the drama of the human soul as she seeks to break through all the attachments and entanglements of the world of time and place and to realise her divine nature. I have already cited some of the notes which the poet made in connection with the writing of this poem and which indicate his intention clearly enough. He wanted to present this drama of the human soul in images of which each individual could, according to his or her capacity, partake, and which would thus serve as supports by means of which each individual could slowly raise his or her consciousness to that level at which the Great Realities, the Monarch invisible to the senses . . . , the divine nature, became the liberated and determining forces of his or her life. He therefore chose as the scene for his symbolic drama the now famous Missolonghi, and sought to unfold the drama in terms of that contemporary historical event which had made it famous, its besieging by the Turks and the final desperate attempt of the besieged to break out to freedom. Such a representation, fixed by the attention, would slowly induce in the reader a transforming process whereby he would become aware of the reality to which the symbolism corresponded and would thus be initiated into the way through which his own liberation from "darkness and death" might be attained. It would have the function, that is, of a myth or a ritual drama. . . . In "**The Free Besieged**" Solomos sought to create such a symbolic representation—"la Grecia (o altra cosa)"—which "closed in the soul" would conduct towards happiness. He sought to create that "imitation" which would remind the reader of its original and supersensual model. In the poem **"Duty"** (this was the title he first gave to **"The Free Besieged"**) he writes: . . .

> In the poem **"Duty"** long must the terrible struggle among misfortune and suffering last, for in this struggle is revealed, immaculate and holy, the intellectual and moral Paradise.

Or again:

> Realise this Idea: all human ties—of father—of brother—of wife—rooted in the earth, and with them the desire for glory:—the earth seizes upon them, and in this way they are forced to uncover in all its depth the holiness of their soul. At the base of the representation always Greece and her future. From start to finish they pass from suffering to suffering; then 'the sea ran,' and their soul floated in bitterness and they staggered like drunkards. Then the enemy asks them to change their faith. St. Augustine says that the Cross is the seat of true wisdom, because all that Jesus taught in three years with the Gospel, he recapitulated in three hours upon the Cross.

Or again:

> Arrange it so that the small Circle, in which the besieged town moves, makes clear within its encompassment the greatest interests of Greece, where the material state is concerned—worth as much to those who seek to retain it as to those who seek to capture it—and, where the moral state is concerned, the greatest interests of Humanity. In this way the situation is linked to the universal pattern. Look at Prometheus and in general at the works of Aeschylus. Let the smallness of the place be obvious, as well as the iron and unbroken circle that has enclosed it. In this way, from the smallness of the place which battles with huge contrary powers, will come forth the Great Realities. . . .
>
> (pp. 21-6)

In other words, the poem, through its presentation of Missolonghi and the events which took place there, was to act as a kind of mirror in which the reader might see reflected the developing drama of man's inner life in its struggle for freedom through the realisation of its divine potentialities. At the same time, his contemplation of the poem, by inducing in him an awareness of that drama to which its symbolism corresponded, might reveal to the reader a knowledge of his own proper destiny and fulfilment. (pp. 26-7)

Solomos, in his effort to communicate that understanding of which all his later poetry is the outcome, never again attempted anything so ambitious as **"The Free Besieged."** But he did not cease to meditate his problem, which was always one and the same: how to create an adequate symbolisation of the struggle of Heaven and Hell in which man, the protagonist against the relentless violence of the world's flow, emerges, even at the moment of self-annihilation and death, triumphant. As Dante said with reference to the Commedia, Solomos might have said with reference to all his later poetry: "the whole work was undertaken not for a speculative but a practical end. . . . The

purpose of the whole is to remove those who are living in this life from the state of wretchedness and to lead them to a state of blessedness." He seems to have felt that this life, the natural life, and the very existence of the natural world, were, as the product and sphere of Fate, incompatible with man's true happiness, and that such "happiness" as man achieved in them was the result of his own forgetfulness and selfishness. Solomos stands at the opposite pole to the Wordsworth who could write [in his preface to the 1814 edition of *The Excursion*]:

> How exquisitely the individual Mind
> . . . . to the external World
> Is fitted:—and how exquisitely, too—
> Theme this but little heard of among Men—
> The external World is fitted to the Mind?

Such complacent adaptability could only, from Solomos' point of view, be the consequence of spiritual death. For, to Solomos, the external world, far from fitting the "individual Mind," was man's most bitter and irreconcilable enemy. The world in its natural state is a kind of Hell, life in it is death, and only within, by a break through into another state of existence, can "the pure world with its lilies flower." . . . In the only poem he wrote after **"The Free Besieged"** that came anywhere near to receiving a definite form, **"The Shark"** . . . , Solomos sought to bring together his recognition of the world of nature as the sphere of Fate and his sense that the moment of self-annihilation is the moment of self-realisation into a single and sudden clash, so that the resolution of the conflicting opposites might appear the impossible miracle it is.

The actual occasion for the poem was the killing by a shark of a young English soldier while he was swimming in a bay off Corfu. The day after his death, what was left of his body was washed up on to the shore of the island. The poem opens with what one might call a "Prologue in Heaven": Hell surrounds man on all sides, but has no power over him except when he is far off from the Paradise of which his nature partakes. The young soldier is then presented: he is in the full bloom of youth and beauty; he is the crown and perfection, the outcome and end of the natural loveliness about him; he is the embodiment and highest expression of the ravishing world which greets him as he comes down to bathe and which seems to have flowered solely for his delight and happiness, as if in recognition of his sovereign presence. In him the partial beauty of flower, sky, sea, rock, and birdsong is fully achieved and consummated. Like a classical statue of a god, he is the harmonious perfection of the universe around him, the idealisation of nature, blessed by every natural grace. But as this human creature on whom nature has lavished all her care and all her gifts enters the water, the force of fierce destruction which she hides beneath her dazzling surface strikes him: the shark, the "tiger of the sea," rises from the depths and in a few seconds rips all that physical perfection to shreds. Solomos, in a note . . . which refers to the poem, expresses his intention:

> In him were rifle and sword, in him the strength of assembled regiments. The struggle was short, but unrelenting and immense the courage. This ceased only with life, and the irrational monstrous force did not know what world of grandeur it had destroyed. If secret worlds had opened around in order to shower crowns upon him, they would have found him indifferent, like the thought whose operation no one will ever know. Immaculate and holy is often the inspiration of

man. A Paradise of happiness must have filled his great-hearted breath before it ceased. At the moment at which he felt like lightning his arm shattered:

Light flashed and the young man knew himself. . . .

As in **"The Free Besieged,"** the opposites of life and death are fused and transcended: death is life, the moment of self-annihilation the moment of self-realisation; as man frees himself from the embrace of the world of the five senses, from the mortal world, he awakes to a true knowledge of himself and experiences the touch of divinity, for then the gate of Paradise, which remains closed to all who have not overcome the sphere of Fate, is opened, and Nature, all her forms broken, stands at last revealed.

These, then, are the main works in which Solomos sought to give expression to his understanding of life. From a formal point of view, they are easy to criticise. To begin with, not one of them is more than a collection of fragments. Then, often, the form seems ill-chosen. Was Solomos, for instance, in writing **"The Free Besieged"** trying to write a drama? In which case, the insufficiency of his protagonists, of his dialogue, and, more important, his inability to subordinate the various parts of the poem to a continuous and developing line of action, condemn it straight away. Or was he trying to write an epic? Then, there is no successive narrative, only a series of static incidents not linked in any organic way. On this line of analysis, one is bound to confess that Solomos' poetry possesses one or two beautiful lyric passages, one or two lines of concentrated insight and meaning—"At the root of the child's mind is the eye of the Mother of God" or "Light flashed and the young man knew himself," for instance—, but that it possesses little more; and that as an attempt to hold up before the reader a pattern of the inner purpose that he should confer upon his own life, it is too tattered a fabric to permit of serious judgment.

Or one can criticise the understanding itself. This I shall not attempt to do fully here, and will only indicate what seems to me its main weakness. Solomos seems to have thought that man's life reaches its ultimate end when all functions of body and mind are suspended, and realisation takes place in one single moment of the present in which a state of eternity-in-one-moment is attained, a state of absolute transcendence at the still centre of the turning world. It is an attitude that recognises a duality in life, a duality in reality. On the one hand there is the world of the spirit, which is good, and on the other hand there is the world of the flesh, which is evil. Such an attitude not only ignores the bonds that link these two aspects of reality, but also, and as a consequence, threatens the very heart of life itself.

But when one has said all that, and a lot more besides, one is still faced with the deep power which Solomos' poetry does nevertheless contain. It is not simply that a rare and complex vision of man's part in the great universal drama is, however spasmodically, allied to a concentrated simplicity of expression, to a language in which music and imagery are wrought to a degree of perfection seldom attained—and which disappears of course entirely in translation. It is that the few fragments themselves—a passage here, a line there, another passage, a few words, a note in the margin, a blank space—all without any realised external coherence, are yet held together by an internal unity which becomes, as one contemplates the poetry, suddenly visible and convincing, just as the spiritual

power which lies behind the form of some ancient temple of which perhaps but a few columns remain standing, will reveal itself to whoever has the creative capacity to look penetratingly and deep. A poetry like that of Solomos, which seeks to be the faithful servant of the Great Realities, does not ask merely to be enjoyed; it summons to an understanding; it makes demands upon the reader equal to those made upon the poet himself, no less than that he should endeavour "to extinguish his individuality in absolute truth." And, where Solomos' poetry itself is concerned, its broken fragments testify both to the strictness of that endeavour and to the beauty of the truth which the poet sought to express. (pp. 34-7)

> *Philip Sherrard, "Dionysios Solomos," in his* The Marble Threshing Floor: Studies in Modern Greek Poetry, *Vallentine, Mitchell & Co. Ltd., 1956, pp. 1-37.*

ZISSIMOS LORENZATOS   (essay date 1965)

[*In this excerpt from an essay written in 1965, Lorenzatos draws his understanding of Solomos's concept of style—form and content merged as a whole in which the personality of the author is obliterated—from the analysis of a footnote in an obituary Solomos wrote for his compatriot, the poet Ugo Foscolo (see excerpt dated 1827). For additional criticism by Lorenzatos, see the excerpt dated 1972.*]

Some years ago, during an evening at a friend's house in Kifissia, the archeologist Christos Karouzos drew our attention to a deleted passage by Solomos, which later became a footnote in the obituary he wrote for Ugo Foscolo. . . . The note comes . . . underneath a definition of style given by Solomos in the obituary, despite the fact that it really belongs to the text proper. . . . The passage was finally omitted from the hurriedly written obituary when Solomos read it in the Catholic Cathedral of St. Mark, Zante, in 1827. (p. 70)

The fact remains that the passage has finally reached us. It is undoubtedly a Solomic text, in other words, invaluable. Besides, the best works of Solomos have come down to us more or less in the same form: extracts, fragments, deleted passages. Ever since I came across the footnote in that Kifissia house, long ago, I have brought it to mind many times and used it as a kind of touchstone. It has remained with me almost in the manner of a chronic fever. (pp. 70-1)

I shall limit myself . . . to the first section of the passage and to the deleted footnote, which deal with matters pertaining to the imitation of style in prose and poetry, and fuse the two together in order to approach as best I can what Solomos had in mind when he wrote the passage. . . . I shall now make my own paraphrase, or analytical "epanodos" (recapitulation), of the original text. (p. 74)

My paraphrase: "Using his conception of art as a starting-point, Foscolo's mind proceeded to those external aspects and forms of thought with which we customarily express ourselves. As a result, these forms of thought came into being and developed in a close and natural conjunction with his conception of art: form and content merged together into an indivisible whole. No chasm, no scrambling in the void. In contrast, Foscolo's imitators used his external forms as stepping-stones in the hope of reaching, by these alone, the intellectual powers of another artist. The external imprint (*esterna impronta*) of these intellectual powers is called, in the art of writing, style (*stile*). We are speaking here of the imitation of style in prose, which may only be achieved in a short piece of writing, but not in a more extensive piece. Now why do we so readily agree that imitation in poetry is an impossibility? Because in poetry (a) we seek to seize the truth (*afferrare il vero*) by means of powerful, or effective, combinations, stripping away any false parts (or elements) so that the truth may remain impregnable (*inoppugnabile*) within the minds of others (and this is where thought comes in); (b) we seek to condense the truth and at the same time to amplify it and bring it to life by means of suitable forms (and this is the role of imagination); (c) we ask the heart to be receptive and consenting to the impressions made by the objects that are conveyed through those suitable forms (and this is called feeling); and, finally, (d) we seek to transfuse all these things into the other person (or reader) by means of speech, language (*parola*). For all these reasons, then, imitation in poetry remains an impossibility."

After this "epanodos" on the Italian text, I shall now attempt a few comments. What is Solomos telling us in the passage? First of all, we must not limit ourselves to Foscolo, but generalize the particular. Foscolo is only the incidental excuse, the stimulus. We know that Solomos was not interested in the incidental, the exclusive, the particular, but in the general, the unlimited, the universal. In the mind of our contemporaries, poetry (and art in general) is an expression of personality. For Solomos, however, "Poetry is . . . not the expression of personality, but an escape from personality" [to use the words of T. S. Eliot]. . . . Moreover, Polylas calls Solomos' work "a spontaneous and continuous attempt to obliterate personality in absolute truth." And Solomos, let it be remembered, made this attempt in situations that were crucial, and from which man is still vainly struggling to escape. This is what he teaches us in phrases like: "Chiudi nella tua anima la Grecia (o altra cosa) . . ." [Enclose within your soul Greece (or any other thing)], or his other relevant injunction that we must consider "national whatever is true."

The central theme, then, begins with Foscolo, but it soon breaks away from the concrete and ends up in the abstract and the general. The passage formulates thoughts and general rules on the art of writing. What Solomos is saying here is that true style, not the imitation of style, is born and grows naturally in man out of his own thought in conjunction with his intellectual powers (*potenze intellettive*) and the conception he has formed of his art. The personal conception of art and the intellectual powers of a writer are manifested in external forms, in the written surfaces which bear the unmistakable imprint of that particular writer's thought and intellect, not only as a writer, but as a whole man; that imprint is what we call style. "Let style est l'homme même," said Buffon: style is man himself, and not "Le style, c'est l'homme," as it is usually misquoted. Solomos' definition means that every writer's external imprint (*esterna impronta*) is unique and peculiar to himself, like his finger-print; it is the man himself. It is through this external imprint, known as style, that each writer finally reveals himself; style betrays him, and it also betrays the imitator. For this reason the imitation of style is impossible, except perhaps in a short piece of prose. But it is never possible in poetry or in extensive pieces of prose. Solomos is explicit; he is making an axiomatic statement. This is unusual in him; but he makes an exception for poetry, which was always his deepest concern, his life-work, and tries to explain, in a rather abstract and schematic manner, it is true, the nature of the articulations through which the living wealth of a poem slowly and organically reaches its final crystallization in the poet's being, the nature of the irreducible metabolism of poetry. It is because this metabolism is irreducible and irreversible, ana-

lytically, that imitation is impossible in poetry as opposed to other intellectual functions, of which the limit, at the very most, is a short piece of prose. In the case of short pieces of prose, the articulations slacken, give way for a brief moment (*per poco*), whereas in poetry the elements are tightly bound together (*strette legate*). Polylas says in his *Prolegomena* that in poetry, "the most graceful images mingle effortlessly with the most fearful"; this is the secret of poetry, the thing that touches us so mysteriously. In a marvellous passage from Draft B of **"The Free Besieged,"** Solomos sums up this secret in a characteristic injunction: "Tieni fermo: tra le cose strette legate terribili o meste o altro un tocco semplicissimo e breve ridente (o vice versa) come l'imagine del piccolo rovo verde negli immensi sabbioni dell' Africa" [Hold fast to this: amongst things fearful or sad or whatever, all tightly bound together, put in a brush stroke, the simplest, briefest touch of laughter (or vice-versa), as for instance the image of a small green bush in the immense sandy stretches of Africa]. In order to be transfused into another person and remain impregnable within that other person, poetic truth needs thought, imagination, feeling, and language, all subjected to a multiple process of interrelationships and transformations—in other words, the irreducible metabolism of poetry—which finally renders vain and chimerical any attempt at imitation in poetry. We might say that Solomos' schema presents us with a four-dimensional poetical continuum. Solomos wishes to give us a succinct outline, a mathematical formula for the diversified process we have just described, though he knew very well that no formula or statistical, objective "truth" can ever capture the essence, the living being (and hence the inconceivable mystery), of things. In short, Solomos wants to define poetic style, the essential mystery of poetry, by means of a brief descriptive device, in the same way that Einstein wanted to express the quantitative function of the universe in his Unified Field Theory, using only three or four mathematical formulae, for he *believed* in the unity of the universe or in what the ancient Greeks called [harmony]. . . . Solomos attempts to describe the living mystery which is poetic style with that critical skill which always attends the creative skill in great artists, thus making him the perfect example for T. S. Eliot's inviolable rule:

> Probably, indeed, the larger part of the labour of an author in composing his work is critical labour; the labour of sifting, combining, constructing, expunging, correcting, testing: this frightful toil is as much critical as creative. I maintain even that the criticism employed by a trained and skilled writer on his own work is the most vital, the highest kind of criticism; and (as I think I have said before) that some creative writers are superior to others solely because their critical faculty is superior. . . . The critical activity finds its highest, its true fulfilment in a kind of union with creation in the labour of the artist.

Solomos is ambidextrous. The concise critical summary of the irreducible element in poetry which he is attempting to make shows once more how truly "fearful" can be the "sharp edge of the sword" which he holds in his hands, that two-edged tool which is both critical and creative. And so the material encountered in the passage in question comprises both the procedure Solomos followed in writing his works and the critical method which enables us to judge his poetry according to his own criteria.

Though he knew from the start that in poetry the mind cannot capture the prey alive, Solomos performed on the immobilized body of poetry a kind of "lesson in anatomy." What is the thinker-anatomist trying to do, exactly? With the instruments available to the mind, he attempts to cut, slice off, separate, some of the basic components of the organism under examination; he then tries to demonstrate that the study of these parts can constitute a useful approach to the truth. But, ultimately, any possible arrangement, any assemblage or *a posteriori* combination of the body's parts and organs, will always lack that simple thing—"we live, and move"—which defines all things, yet cannot be defined by any one thing: life. In the same way, poetry will always be absent from any description of the poetic function. This is why Solomos believed that the imitation of poetry, of poetic style, is an impossibility. Any attempt to dismantle or replace creation ends in the test-tube *homunculus* of the Faustian experiment: a typical orientation, a brain-child of modern Western curiosity.... Solomos analyzes, solves; he never dissolves. He takes the basic presupposition of poetry, which he believes to be the conquest of truth (*afferrare il vero*), a conquest, however, achieved only by means of powerful combinations (*per mezzo di forti combinazioni*), combinations different for each writer, without established laws or preliminary collective procedures such as are used in mathematics. With the adjective "powerful," Solomos points out the dangerous breaches which may be opened in the citadel of truth by the false elements which initially accompany most poetic combinations or formulae. Only after the false elements (*le parti false*) have been mercilessly cut away from these combinations can the truth remain impregnable within the minds of others (*nell'altrui mente inoppugnabile*).... Like God, poetry is approached through the heart: "C'est le coeur qui sent Dieu, et non la raison" [according to Pascal]. Once we complete this third quarter of the whole poetic circle as Solomos designed it (*pensare, imaginare, sentire*), we finally seek to transfuse it all intact into the mind of the reader by means of language: "e transfonder poi colla parola tutto questo in altrui." How then can we talk of imitation in poetry?

The conquest of truth, which was for Solomos the basic pursuit of the poet, and the necessary pruning of false elements from those "combinazioni" with which we initially dare to seize truth in order to make it impregnable for others as well as for ourselves, may be said to belong generally to the sphere of thought (*pensare*). Spreading the truth and bringing it to life in suitable forms belong to the sphere of the imagination (*imaginare*). Our heart's consent and concordance with the impressions made by the various and varying objects projected by these forms, the marriage of the moving interior with the unmoving surface, belong generally to the sphere of feeling (*sentire*). By means of language, written or spoken, we then need to transfuse into others this complex nebula of thought, imagination, and feeling. We have to give voice to the unvoiced interchanges of poetic matter, carefully balancing and mixing the fourth element, language (*la parola*), with the three others in an unbroken, personal, particular (yet universal) unity. The poet is a particular *sui generis* individual, but he is also a member of the community, or *demos*. In other words, he works ... for the *demos*.... The significance of the fourth element, language, for the poet Solomos becomes clear when we consider the fact that he couples it with freedom, a word most sacred to the Greeks of 1821, in his **"Dialogos:"** "I have nothing else in my mind beside freedom and language." It should be remembered here that the Greeks of the Ionian Islands were quite free of pedantry and scholarly affectations, as opposed to the mainland Greeks of that period. Solomos is a good

example of this; his language was untouched and innocent of the "learned tradition." ... (pp. 74-81)

There exist poets and writers with whom one spends a lifetime. There are others with whom one spends only certain periods or decisive phases of one's life. Finally, there is the large majority of writers whom one encounters fleetingly once or twice in one's life; they are mostly the *minores*.... [With] the first group, we live out our entire lives; we even die with them—supposing we have first managed to live—slowly learning through their work the terrifying compliance of death.

Of all the Greek poets who have appeared until now, it is only with Solomos that one can spend a whole lifetime. (pp. 83-4)

Zissimos Lorenzatos, "A Definition of Style by Solomos," in his The Lost Center and Other Essays in Greek Poetry, *translated by Kay Cicellis, Princeton University Press, 1980, pp. 70-84.*

M. BYRON RAIZIS (essay date 1972)

[*In this extract from his book-length survey of Solomos's life and works, Raizis demonstrates the impact of "Hymn to Liberty" on Greek literature and traces the sources that influenced the poet.*]

One can imagine with what interest, burning anxiety, and strong sentiments the young Greek poet followed the dramatic events of the Revolution of 1821. Would it prove to be, like so many others before it, just a spontaneous but short-lived uprising against the all-powerful oppressor, which would be stamped out and forgotten as rapidly and easily as it had started? Or would it develop into an all-out and decisive war to secure freedom, human dignity, and a national identity, a now-or-never liberation movement? Events soon proved that the latter was the case this time.

While Solomos eagerly awaited the news from the motherland, the hitherto wretched and uncouth Greek peasant-warriors, mountaineers, and formerly peaceful merchants with their small ships, were now proving themselves worthy descendents of the historical figures of the Greek past.

The poorly equipped, undersized, and irregular bands of shepherds, farmers, and sailors had begun to shake the edifice of a mighty empire and to defeat its great armies and fleets again and again, with unprecedented determination and courage. Yes, it was a now-or-never war; it was a holy cause.

What was the duty of a twenty-five-year-old Greek under the circumstances? To join the fight, of course. And that is what Solomos did. As a poet, he chose to fight with his pen, not with pistols and swords which he had never touched before. The purely military contributions Solomos could make to the cause of Greek independence would be ridiculously insignificant. The immediate consequences to his beloved ones and himself were easily predictable. But as a writer he could wield the most powerful of all weapons, his talent, and achieve much more in the long run.

If Solomos were to propagate the sacred ideas of this war to friendly fellow Christians in the West, if he were to inspire more enthusiasm and faith and preach unity and unselfish cooperation to the unruly but stubborn warriors, he would then do something no one else had done. Reghas Pheraios and the other prophetic versifiers of Greek freedom were long dead. But Liberty needed a Bard to proclaim her to Greece and to the whole world. This Bard would be the hitherto composer of Italian sonnets, Greek idylls and requiems, and "Society verse,'' Dionysios Solomos, the peace-loving intellectual and esthete son of ''Old Tobacco.''

Solomos composed over one hundred and sixty quatrains of trochaic tetrameters alternating with seven-syllable lines. Some sources have it that he was writing under the influence of Italian Romanticism, in general, and Manzoni and his or others' techniques in particular. It is true that many of the ideals of Italian and Western Romanticism are in the background (the quest for national identity, independence, popular culture, and the like), but most of Solomos's immediate and available models were genuinely Greek. One does not have to turn to Manzoni, whose ''Triumph of Liberty'' (c. 1801) was suppressed and never published before Solomos's death, to find a source. Nor did Dionysios imitate the *terza rima* of the Italian poem, or its divisions into cantos, or its generally discursive recitation. On the other hand, details in imagery, especially related to the allegorical depiction of Liberty, temptingly echo Manzoni's, as does Solomos's style of notes appended to the poem. But that was a more or less general practice at that time, for Byron, Shelley, and others, added notes to, or prefaced, their long works with ''arguments.''

There is no doubt that Solomos was inspired by Greek literary sources to write this long lyric, in addition, of course, to the dramatic developments of the war itself and to his psychological identification with the Greeks.

The opening of the **''Hymn to Liberty''** [**''Hymnos eis ten Eleutherian''**] utilizes the imagery borrowed from Anthony Martelaos's patriotic hymn to France, to Napoleon, and the like, whom the Zantiot radical had considered a would-be liberator of Greece. Solomos also echoes Reghas Pheraios's ''War-Song'' and other revolutionary lyrics, as well as Thomas Danelakis, who had imitated both Martelaos and Reghas in exactly the same verse form. The original model and source of all these, and other Greek political versifiers, was the French ''Marseillaise'' by Leconte de Lisle. This revolutionary anthem had been very popular in Zante and elsewhere since shortly before the turn of the century, and many of its numerous Greek imitations were sung to its tune. The pristine source of inspiration for all these literary effusions was, of course, man's love for freedom and self-dignity, which had been dramatically reiterated by the Enlightenment. (pp. 77-9)

[No] major poem on freedom can be based merely on abstractions, praise, and wishful thinking. Solomos, as an intellectual product of the Enlightenment, was trained in logical argumentation and realistic attitudes. As he was living outside Greece proper, he could observe all happenings from a certain perspective that afforded him the opportunity to be objective. The **''Hymn''** could not be a sustained and grandiose exercise in ambitious poetics alone. It would have to be a document, a gospel, a manifesto, a loud and irrevocable declaration to friend and foe. And this it was.

The success of the **''Hymn''** was immediate. Copies were sent overseas. (p. 82)

By 1825 the **''Hymn to Liberty''** had been published in Greek, French, English, and Italian. Many Greeks and non-Greeks read or heard it, or practiced their Greek on it, in Europe and even in America; and the reaction was always one of deep satisfaction, pride, and enthusiasm.

Chateaubriand and Lamartine applauded it with delight. Manzoni hailed it with pride and spread Solomos's fame in Italy. Victor Hugo remarked with touching sympathy: ''The young

poetry singing the young freedom.'' It is even reported, but not verified, that the great Goethe read his copy and proclaimed Solomos the ''Byron of the East.''

The Greek and European press announced its publication, or reviewed it most favorably, often thanks to the energies of men like Fauriel and Trikoupis. Even in America the Hellenist Cornelius Felton praised the **''Hymn''** as a masterpiece and compared Solomos to the ancient martial and patriotic poets Simonides and Alkaios. Equally favorable were the comments of New York University Professor Corby, who proclaimed Solomos the Pindar of modern Greece. (p. 83)

It is not possible to estimate the contribution of this hymn to the Greek cause. Suffice it to mention here that Sir George Canning had read Solomos's poem and quoted the lines, ''Sprung from Grecian bones scattered . . . ,'' in a speech. The same source has it that the British prime minister had read the **''Hymn''** the day he signed the protocol of London, which guaranteed Greek independence.

From the purely artistic side, its success was not less. The **''Hymn''** was the greatest and most ambitious poem written in modern Greek for centuries. Its vocabulary and metrics were not always perfect, but they were considerably better than anything else in that genre. The signs of hasty composition were certainly there. But since this one time Solomos had allowed his emotions to be recollected, not in tranquillity, but when he was overwhelmed by his passion for freedom, the result was spontaneous, vigorous, spirited, and easily flowing numerous lines.

In a poem of so many stanzas not all of them can be of equal quality, not all expressions equally felicitous. Some connecting passages, rhetorical outbursts, a few images in poor taste, some unfortunate linguistic liberties, the organization of the material, and even some echoes or borrowings from other poets, Greek and foreign, have been cited by erudite philologists either as minor weaknesses or as serious flaws.

The truth is that Solomos had produced a series of pictorial stanzas whose audiovisual imagery was of the highest caliber, even though in 1823 he was still in his period of apprenticeship. After the completion of the **''Hymn''**—a major work in most respects—Solomos had to move on to achievements of a higher level. The echoing directly or indirectly of Manzoni, Monti, Ariosto, Parini, Foscolo, Dante, Milton, Byron, Homer, Virgil, and other ''moderns and ancients'' should not be taken as a weakness at all. On the contrary, Solomos in so doing experimented with the verbal expressions and images of these masters to see how they sounded in Greek. It is not artistic paucity that made, on the other hand, Solomos echo the stilted but patriotic lines of Reghas and Martelaos. By doing so the young poet joined the invisible chain of cultural tradition, so to speak, and inherited the lighted torch. No poet can exist and function outside the literary tradition of his culture, as T. S. Eliot implies in ''Tradition and the Individual Talent.'' And in this way Solomos joined the Hellenic tradition and continued it. The result was both impressive and encouraging: modern Greek, Solomos's own language, was capable of emulating the language of the great masters. But there was need for improvement, both quantitative and qualitative.

Jenkins [see excerpt dated 1940], has correctly summarized the role of the borrowed element in the **''Hymn''**:

> The overweight of borrowing from abroad, while
> it might spoil the poem as an individual mas-

terpiece, was exactly what was required for the "cultivation" (the expression is Solomos') of the tongue; *and the ingenuity and taste required to translate into Greek the nobler political ideas expressed in the cultivated languages of Europe* were the most salutary faculties that could have been brought into play [italics mine].

Perhaps the one negative legacy that this poem left to Solomos himself, who now virtually woke up to find himself famous, was the idea that poetic greatness had to, and could, be achieved only in conjunction with the expression of patriotic and religious fervor. For if that was the case, Solomos was unconsciously imposing undue limitations on his artistic range and particular talent. (pp. 83-5)

> *M. Byron Raizis, in his* Dionysios Solomos, *Twayne Publishers, Inc., 1972, 158 p.*

ZISSIMOS LORENZATOS   (essay date 1972)

[*In this excerpt from an essay written in 1972, Lorenzatos calls Solomos the Greek "voice," for he identified completely with the people while experiencing a spiritual ascension through his poetry. For additional criticism by Lorenzatos, see the excerpt dated 1965.*]

Anyone progressing along the road of faith, which is also the road of great art and the road of truth (beyond a certain point, there is a common center toward which all roads converge), knows that "it is not ye that speak, but the Spirit of your Father which speaketh in you" [Matt. 10:20]. There comes an end to empty boasting and a loss of physical identity. "A poet has no identity . . . no nature," wrote John Keats in a letter dated October 27th, 1818. Once a person reaches this point, he partakes of the spirit.

Solomos knew that his voice belonged to another. In return for the grace of having been chosen, he celebrated the gift, regardless of whether he finally became worthy of it through the slow process of "time and toil":

> And glory and wealth to you,
> Good Spirit, that it pleased you to give me a voice.

The spirit gave him a voice with a perfectly free will, because it thus pleased it. It is the divine prerogative to freely create the world *ex nihilo,* in the Christian tradition of Solomos; it is the cosmic play of the divinity, the *līlā,* in the Hindu tradition. The verb "pleased" expresses the total freedom of God and his pleasure in his works. Solomos used that verb and no other. He had his own deep motive in doing so. As opposed to lesser voices that usually fall short of the mark, he had to utter the truth directly; he spoke literally.

What voice would be ours today, if he had not spoken then? Solomos is our voice.

The gift he received he had to pass on to others in turn, according to the command: "Freely ye have received, freely give" [Matt. 8:10]. And now let us stand before his great invocation, spoken in that ancestral voice that can never be attained again, not in a thousand years, because it was a God-given Greek voice:

Mother, magnificent in suffering and in glory,
even if your children always live—with thought, with dream—
embraced by your secret mystery, what joy have these eyes,
my eyes, to see you in the desolate wood
which—look—has suddenly scattered around your feet
leaves of Easter, Palm Sunday leaves.
Calm as you are, like the sky with all its beauty
half hidden, half disclosed,
I have not seen, not known, your divine step.
But, Goddess, am I not to hear your voice
and to bestow it at once on the world of Greece?
Her dark rock is full of glory, and her dry grass.

What joy, indeed, falls upon mortal eyes when they behold a transcendental vision containing the promise of a double Resurrection; resurrection of the world (springtime) *o altra cosa* for the Greeks, and resurrection of the spirit (Eastertide). Solomos may not have heard or seen the divine footstep within the forest, but at least he sought to hear the voice of the Goddess in order to bestow it forthwith as a gift upon the Greek world. Need we add that he did hear the voice, and handed it as a gift to us in the form of that very invocation, particularly that final line with its fifteen syllables that evoke not only the radiant land, but the soul of that small place which is the world of the Greeks: "Her dark rock is full of glory, and her dry grass."

A "secret mystery" governs the life of man. Solomos refers to it in **"The Cretan,"** saying that it "hems in nature"; the passage echoes the teaching of Paul about "the earnest expectation of the creature for the manifestation of the sons of God" [Romans 8:19]. Within that mystery, there are always two roads leading out of the desolate wood of Solomos' invocation: thought and dream; we find them once more coupled together when the Cretan recalls the moon-dressed girl, and he cannot tell whether it was his waking thought that "created her" or a dream he had when he was still at his mother's breast. With thought and with dream, with these two fundamental resources, man must go forth within the secret mystery of life until the day he is set free.

The voice that Solomos bestowed as a gift upon the Greek world was that world's own voice, miraculously preserved, together with its faith, through the "menace" and the "slavery" of centuries, filtered through the treasure-house of Solomos' mind, ever rooted in oral tradition, in the language of the folk songs ("la lingua clefta"), yet not ending there, but raised perpendicularly: "è bene sì, piantarsi su quelle orme, ma non è bene fermarvisi: conviene alzarsi perpendicolarmente" [it is indeed good to tread upon those footprints, but it is not good to stop there; one must raise oneself perpendicularly]. Solomos served his apprenticeship among the people—in order to learn from them, not to teach them or tamper with their speech and faith. . . . This is "the secret of my art," as he says in his "Notes to the **'Hymn to Liberty'**." The whole passage reads: "Who told me this? The secret of my art and the example of the great masters." Himself a master, he faithfully followed the example of the masters—who else was he to follow? Dante was his constant teacher, but there were others as well, according to this other sentence from the "Notes": "I find art wherever art is to be found." This is the double school that Solomos refers to in the Italian phrase quoted above: the people and, out of the root of the people, *alzarsi perpendicolarmente,* always concentrating on the great exemplars.

The secret of Solomos' art is his identification with the people and his "perpendicular" rising *out* of the people. As I said, he served his apprenticeship with the people, but not in order to teach them or remove them from "the unhappy ages of barbarism" and "the sleep of ignorance." (pp. 181-85)

"Our people are shedding their blood under the Cross to make us free," says Solomos in his **"Dialogos."** After all, the literati, whether enlightened or unenlightened, were not the ones who liberated the enslaved Greeks. It was the enslaved who set free the literati, together with the rest of the Greeks. (p. 185)

Solomos . . . identified himself utterly with the people. The bond which connects him to the totality of the people is spiritual: community of faith and language; the spirit, not only the letter, of faith and language. The letter, at least, can be taught or defined or even directed; the spirit remains unfathomable. "The wind bloweth where it listeth" [John 3:8]. Solomos sought them both at their inexhaustible common spring, in the place where faith still flowed and language still breathed. Solomos had no reservations or preconceived ideas about altering our faith or weeding our speech. Constant service, humble apprenticeship in the spirit of the community alone can lend authority to individual contributions. There must be obliteration of individuality in the cleansing waters of the community, a loss of the "I" in the "we," as Makriyiannis said. There must be unconditional surrender and submission to the faith and language of a people, the realm which embraces and consecrates the Saint and the Poet. In faith there is humility before the One, in language humility before the many. And where there is humility, there is also elevation, as the Gospels say and as Solomos echoes back; where there is loss of the soul, there lies the discovery of the soul.

No man can evade his mother tongue. There is no such thing as linguistic emigration. . . . If we may say of the great masters of literature that in their struggle for expression they touched either the skin or the flesh or the bone of their language, according to their gifts, then about Solomos we can only say that he reached the very marrow of the modern Greek language. Apart from the anonymous popular poets, he is the only one who was graced with this gift. Our logic may not grasp why and how this was so, but we can feel it in our flesh. This explains why his poetry is so hard to translate. I might add that if one is to be allowed to watch the **"Navicella Greca"** sail past in "the proud full sail of his great verse," to use the words of Shakespeare, it is not enough to have studied or read the language of Solomos; one must have been born to it. Solomos' utterance is part of the soul of this small place, this world. They are one and the same thing; they are born of this soil. And that is a rare thing. (pp. 187-88)

Quite early in Solomos' writing, in the poem **"Lambros"** (Fragments), we witness an astonishing welding of the verse, which consists, at times, almost exclusively of verbs and nouns. Never before Solomos do we find so many verbs and nouns in so small a space: verbs crowding on top of each other, condensing the action or stretching the sinew of the line; nouns shaking off the adjectives, pushing aside every element of platitude or vain ornamentation. With the few examples that follow, I do not hope to show the final poetic result—that should be sought in Solomos' mature period—so much as his method of working:

> I look at him, help, I tell him, I have
> no sail, no tiller, and I am sailing the sea.

Here is another:

> And she sings, and as she sings, she weeps,
> And he: "Don't weep, don't sing," he tells her.

The third example has a piece of prose accompanying the verse:

> As she spoke, she spread out her slender fingers
> to the wild weeds growing in that solitary place,
> she wove them into a crown for her most
> wretched head, put around her neck the braid
> made of sighs

> and into the waves, which are like a mirror to her,
> she looks again, smiles, and falls.

Certain of these qualities Solomos may have received from Dante. Perhaps he owed his method to Dante or to the "example of the masters." But the basis—"the secret of my art"—and a great many of its later applications, do not belong to any one person; they belong to the people. For there he served his apprenticeship.

First of all Solomos had to utter the truth. Where did he learn the truth? This is where [in lines from a Greek folksong]:

> Down by the white stone and the cold water,
> There lies Yannos, the son of Andronicos,
> Hacked and slaughtered and unrecognizable.

What is the secret of art, any art, any piece of work that is well and rightly done—in this case, what is the secret of poetry, infinitely simplified and free of philosophical verbosities? *Telling the truth.* (pp. 188-89)

We read those three lines once again: the stone is white, the water is cold. No concession, no slipping away into some other, irrelevant direction. Absolute literal accuracy. A man appears before us, fatally wounded in the wilderness. Three lines. A whole world. Nothing is missing.

Next, Solomos had to utter the truth directly. The direct approach he also learned at the same source: the folksong, where immediacy of language is such that there is no room for anything else between the words; they drive straight to reality, and reality drives straight into the words. "With time and toil," language becomes nature. All is washed in light. No obscurity, no awkwardness, no vagueness or hesitation, no fear that the finished result may not conform to the formula of some disfigured, fictitious world taunting us from the opposite shore. (pp. 189-90)

The folksong is sturdily built; each word is hewn and fitted perfectly to the one that follows it; there are no gaps, no filling. The words are secured into place once and for all, powerful means serving a concise purpose, safely in the care of the anonymous, omniscient people who speak them, like the stones in a Cyclopean wall, like mountain-paths, like Byzantine kourasani, like a rubble fence. This is where Solomos learned the "secret mystery" which is to be found in all these imperishable popular texts, not recorded on paper but fashioned out of the very heart-beat of life. (pp. 190-91)

If only we could listen more attentively to the message, the "secret mystery" which "hems in nature" (**"The Cretan"**) and shelters the children of the Mother Goddess (**"The Free Besieged"**)! Within this mystery Solomos searched for his true self from his earliest youth; there is a clear hint of this in the line:

> Light flashed and the boy knew his true self . . .

Out of this mystery Solomos proceeded to make his "perpendicular" ascent. In the language of the people, and in the faith of the people, he successively discovered both the letter and the spirit of his prophetic mission.

Thus Solomos passed from his everyday self, in the narrow sense of the word, to his true Self; from *personal thought* to *common logos.* In order to go forward, he receded; in order to be raised, he humbled himself. A two-way movement: in language (the letter) he moved from common logos to personal thought; in faith (the spirit) he moved from personal thought to common logos. If he became worthy of hearing the voice of the Mother Goddess and bestowing it as a gift upon the Greek world, it was the result of "time and toil." . . . (pp. 191-92)

Solomos' spirit lives on among us, not owing to the work of literary historians and critics, but thanks to those true craftsmen who quietly make sure that whenever a major or even a minor poet falls silent in this country, the ageless poetry of Greece will unfalteringly take the next step along the course it has been following almost without break from Homer to our time. (pp. 193-94)

> *Zissimos Lorenzatos, "'Ultima Verba': Solomos," in his* The Lost Center and Other Essays in Greek Poetry, *translated by Kay Cicellis, Princeton University Press, 1980, pp. 181-94.*

ADDITIONAL BIBLIOGRAPHY

Lorenzatos, Zissimos. "Solomos' 'Dialogos': A Survey." In *Modern Greek Writers,* edited by Edmund Keeley and Peter Bien, pp. 23-65. Princeton Essays in European and Creative Literature, no. 7. Princeton: Princeton University Press, 1972.
> Draws parallels between Solomos's "Dialogue" and Dante's *De vulgari eloquentia.* This study includes a historical survey of the controversy over classic versus demotic language in Greek literature.

———. "Solomos." In his *The Lost Center and Other Essays in Greek Poetry,* translated by Kay Cicellis, pp. 3-69. Princeton Essays in Literature. Princeton: Princeton University Press, 1980.
> A record of Lorenzatos's "thoughts and emotions roused by the reading of Solomos."

Michalaros, Demetrios A. "Solomos the Poet." *Athene* V, No. 2 (June 1944): 3-6.
> Asserts that Solomos's "Hymn to Liberty" is unique for its poetic genius, craftsmanship, and linguistic innovation.

Polylas, J. "Prolegomena." In *Hapanta,* Vol. 1, 2d ed., by Dionysios Solomos, edited by Linos Polites, p. 10. Athens: Ikaros, 1961.
> A frequently cited Greek-language criticism originally published as the prologue to J. Polylas and P. Quartano's 1859 edition of Solomos's *Ta euriskomena,* also known as *Found Remains.*

Raizis, M. Byron. "The Greek Poets Praise the 'Britannic Muse.'" *Balkan Studies* 20, No. 2 (1979): 275-307.
> Comments on Solomos's eulogy on the death of Byron.

Hippolyte Adolphe Taine

1828-1893

French critic, historian, philosopher, essayist, and travel sketch writer.

One of the most accomplished, original, and versatile French scholars of the second half of the nineteenth century, Taine greatly influenced the development of criticism. Insisting that criticism should be based on scientific principles in order to ensure impartiality, certainty, and depth of analysis, Taine incorporated techniques from the fields of sociology, psychology, and biology into his writings. His numerous works on literature, history, art, and scientific subjects set the standard for analytical inquiry in his era and helped to popularize the newly emerging cult of science. Although Taine's precepts met with much resistance and continue to be disputed today, commentators acknowledge his pivotal role in the history of ideas.

Taine was born in Vouziers, France, into the family of a locally prominent attorney. Though the family was not wealthy, Taine received an excellent education, beginning with lessons at home when he was eleven years old. Upon his father's death in 1840, Taine was sent to Paris, where he studied at the Lycée Bourbon and at a private school. An exemplary student, he entered the École normale supérieure in 1848 to prepare for a career in education. But after winning an appointment as a substitute philosophy teacher in Nevers in 1851, Taine began to encounter political difficulties stemming from his refusal to sign a pledge of loyalty to Louis Napoleon. Twice transferred during the next two years, each time to an inferior post, he soon asked for a leave of absence from teaching and returned to Paris to resume his studies. Taine received a doctorate of letters from the Sorbonne in 1853 for his *Essai sur les fables de La Fontaine* and continued to study physiology, psychology, and mathematics on his own. Suffering from physical and mental overexertion, he fell ill and on a doctor's recommendation traveled through the Pyrenees to regain his health. Soon afterwards, he began writing a series of articles vehemently criticizing contemporary French philosophers. These were later published as *Les philosophes français du XIXme siècle*, a highly controversial work that instantly brought Taine to the attention of the public. Professional recognition came, too, when the Académie française awarded a prize to his *Essai sur Tite-Live* in 1855.

Between 1855 and 1863 Taine traveled widely, published several collections of essays and travel sketches, and began his most famous work, *Histoire de la littérature anglaise* (*History of English Literature*). In 1864 he obtained two appointments—as admissions examiner at the military academy at Saint-Cyr and as professor of aesthetics and art history at the École des beaux arts in Paris—that assured his financial security and allowed him to devote more time to writing. Taine subsequently lectured in France and England, wrote voluminously, and contributed regularly to the *Revue des deux mondes* and the *Revue de l'instruction publique*. Respected in Parisian intellectual circles, he enjoyed friendships with Joseph Ernest Renan, Charles Augustin Sainte-Beuve, Gustave Flaubert, and Jules and Edmond de Goncourt. Though faulted for his atheism, political conservatism, and scientific methods, Taine received an honorary degree from Oxford University in 1871 and gained admission to the Académie française in 1878. He had begun an

ambitious six-volume history, *Les origines de la France contemporaine* (*The Origins of Contemporary France*), in 1872, and he retired from teaching in 1884 to work on that project. Taine published five volumes of *The Origins of Contemporary France* but died in 1893 before the last was completed.

Almost all of Taine's writings derive from his theory of "la race, le milieu et le moment," or race, environment, and time, and his ultimate belief that the personality of an individual and the literature and art of a people are determined by forces that can be scientifically ascertained and analyzed. In his criticism, Taine examined first how writers and artists were influenced by heredity ("race"); second, by physical environment ("milieu"); and third, by historical, social, and political circumstances ("moment"). His notorious proclamation in *History of English Literature* that "vice and virtue are products, like vitriol and sugar" underlies his claim that methods borrowed from science could yield certain results. Taine's three-part system, first formulated in that work, had its roots in his study of the philosophers Baruch Spinoza, John Locke, David Hume, Étienne Bonnot de Condillac, and Georg Wilhelm Friedrich Hegel. Closely linked to eighteenth-century thought, Taine's doctrine was anti-Romantic and, like August Comte's Positivism and John Stuart Mill's Utilitarianism, was grounded in sociology and empiricism. Certainly, Taine's best-known work employing this doctrine is *History of English Literature*, but he also applied it in *Les philosophes français du XIXme siècle,* as well as in such essays on individual authors as *Essai sur les fables de La Fontaine, Essai sur Tite-Live,* and *Le positivisme anglais: Étude sur Stuart Mill (English Positivism: A Study of J. S. Mill).* Just as he probed the relevance of race, environment, and time for literature, Taine inquired into their implications for art in *Philosophie de l'art (The Philosophy of Art)* and *De l'idéal dans l'art (The Ideal in Art).* Considered a perceptive fine-art critic, he particularly garnered praise for his lectures on the art of Italy, Greece, and the Netherlands, later translated in *Lectures on Art.* As an adjunct of his overall theory, Taine also formulated the idea of the ''master faculty.'' Employing this concept most successfully in his essay on Honoré de Balzac, he speculated that an author's career could be mapped out once his or her chief talent was determined. Taine expanded this notion even further in *De l'intelligence (On Intelligence),* in which he argued that since psychological and physical development are parallel, it is possible to explain and even predict the course of human personality based on a few key psychological facts and on the individual's physical growth.

Although less theoretical than his academic writings, Taine's travel sketches and historical works also attest to his interest in the effect of heredity and environment on individuals and society. In *Voyage aux eaux des Pyrénées (A Tour through the Pyrenees), Carnets de voyage (Journeys through France),* and *Voyage en Italie (Italy),* Taine explored the interrelationships between geography, culture, and national temperament while providing wry observations gleaned from his travels. Basing his commentary on his own impressions, Taine described English life in *Notes sur l'Angleterre (Notes on England)* and offered a witty critique of Parisian society in *Notes sur Paris (Notes on Paris).* His last project, *The Origins of Contemporary France,* traces the events that occurred in France before, during, and after the Revolution. Adopting a medical approach, Taine intended to study the social and genetic factors that led up to the weakening of contemporary France, to describe the symptoms of her ''disease,'' and to suggest a course of treatment. Starting with *L'ancien régime (The Ancient Regime),* Taine examined the structure of the pre-Revolutionary government, concluding that its chief weakness was excessive centralization. An increase in centralization during the Revolutionary period, coupled with the French people's predisposition to bestial behavior and their susceptibility to mob rule, he wrote in *La révolution (The French Revolution),* caused even more instability in the French government. Finally, in *Le régime moderne (The Modern Regime),* Taine attempted to predict, aided by past and present indications, the future political development of France.

The wide range of Taine's writings, his innovative theories, and his espousal of the scientific method drew mixed reactions from contemporary critics. Responding to *History of English Literature,* the publication that solidified his fame, reviewers acknowledged the astuteness of Taine's reasoning while judging his race, environment, and time criteria reductionistic and his goal of objectivity in criticism unrealistic. Unlike many nineteenth-century commentators, Sainte-Beuve recognized that Taine's rational, systematic approach to literature and art criticism was an important contribution to a field that had previously been characterized by personal opinion and sentiment. Yet to other contemporaries, Taine's writings were merely abstract and dehumanizing. As the Swiss author Henri Frédéric Amiel wrote, ''I feel a painful sensation with this writer, as of the odour of a laboratory, a grating of pulleys, a clicking of machinery.'' Though Taine's style struck some reviewers

as engrossing and charming, many condemned his critical methods as too narrow and stressed that race, environment, and time could never account for the spontaneous flowering of genius. To some readers, Taine's scientific orientation appeared subversive because methodological considerations took precedence over traditional humanistic values. Even critics who were favorably inclined toward Taine's ideas pointed out that he was perhaps too eager to draw general conclusions and that his method may have led him to rather superficial criticism. Taine's theories about the influence of biology and geography on literature and art have fallen into disrepute in the twentieth century, but he is still recognized for his role in the development of social criticism.

While critical response to *History of English Literature* has changed over the years, reaction to *The Origins of Contemporary France* has fluctuated little. Citing its influence on French historiography, most commentators have judged *The Origins of Contemporary France* an imposing piece of scholarship. Critics have also praised Taine's vivid reconstruction of historical events, but they have added that his conservative and elitist tendencies distorted his perceptions and led to inherent contradictions in his narrative. In addition, scholars have reacted negatively to the second part of the work, *The French Revolution,* because of Taine's melodramatic depiction of mob violence, societal chaos, and wanton destruction of property. Some critics have suggested that Taine's peculiarly negative and pessimistic view of the Revolution was the result of a preoccupation with mob psychology. Although Taine's interpretation of French history, as well as his doctrine of race, environment, and time, is widely challenged today, his works continue to attract the attention of critics, who underscore his important contribution to the history of ideas. Recent studies have focused on such topics as Taine's attitude toward Romanticism and Classicism, his aesthetic principles, and his influence on Naturalism, Marxism, and Structuralism.

Despite the limitations and outmoded presuppositions of Taine's theories, he is regarded as a historically important figure because he helped to delineate and systematize the methodology of criticism at a time when it was just emerging as a distinct discipline. Summing up Taine's achievement, Flaubert remarked that *History of English Literature* ''got rid of the uncritical notion that books dropped like meteorites from the sky.'' In urging a scientifically objective, interdisciplinary approach, Taine significantly broadened the scope of criticism.

PRINCIPAL WORKS

Essai sur les fables de La Fontaine (essay) 1853; also published in revised form as *La Fontaine et ses fables,* 1861
Voyage aux eaux des Pyrénées (travel sketches) 1855 [*A Tour through the Pyrenees,* 1874]
Essai sur Tite-Live (essay) 1856
Les philosophes français du XIXme siècle (essays) 1857; also published in revised form as *Les philosophes classiques du XIXme siècle,* 1868
Essais de critique et d'histoire (essays) 1858
Histoire de la littérature anglaise. 4 vols. (essays) 1863-64 [*History of English Literature.* 2 vols., 1871]
Le positivisme anglais: Étude sur Stuart Mill (essay) 1864 [*English Positivism: A Study of J. S. Mill,* 1870]

"Balzac" (essay) 1865; published in *Nouveaux essais de critique et d'histoire*
  [*Balzac: A Critical Study,* 1906]
Nouveaux essais de critique et d'histoire (essays) 1865
Philosophie de l'art (lectures) 1865
  [*The Philosophy of Art,* 1865]
Philosophie de l'art en Italie (lectures) 1866
  [*The Philosophy of Art in Italy* published in *Lectures on Art,* 1875]
Voyage en Italie. 2 vols. (travel sketches) 1866
  [Published in two volumes: *Italy: Naples and Rome,* 1867; *Italy: Florence and Venice,* 1869]
De l'idéal dans l'art (lectures) 1867
  [*The Ideal in Art,* 1870]
Notes sur Paris: Vie et opinions de M. Frédéric-Thomas Graindorge (sketches) 1867
  [*Notes on Paris,* 1875]
Philosophie de l'art dans les Pays-Bas (lectures) 1868
  [*Art in the Netherlands,* 1871]
Philosophie de l'art en Grèce (lectures) 1869
  [*Art in Greece,* 1871]
De l'intelligence (essay) 1870
  [*Taine's On Intelligence,* 1871]
Notes sur l'Angleterre (travel sketches) 1872
  [*Notes on England,* 1872]
Lectures on Art (lectures) 1875
L'ancien régime (history) 1876; published in *Les origines de la France contemporaine*
  [*The Ancient Regime,* 1881]
Les origines de la France contemporaine. 6 vols. (history) 1876-94
  [*The Origins of Contemporary France.* 6 vols., 1876-94]
La révolution. 3 vols. (history) 1878-84; published in *Les origines de la France contemporaine*
  [*The French Revolution.* 3 vols., 1878-85]
La régime moderne. 2 vols. (history) 1891-93; published in *Les origines de la France contemporaine*
  [*The Modern Regime.* 2 vols., 1890-94]
Derniers essais de critique et d'histoire (essays) 1894
Carnets de voyage: Notes sur la province, 1863-1865 (travel sketches) 1897
  [*Journeys through France, Being Impressions of the Provinces,* 1897]
H. Taine: Sa vie et sa correspondance. 4 vols. (letters) 1902-07
  [*Life and Letters of H. Taine.* 3 vols., 1902-08]
*Étienne Mayran (unfinished novel) 1910

*This work was written in 1861.

THE NORTH AMERICAN REVIEW (essay date 1861)

[*Discussing several of Taine's early works, this anonymous critic praises Taine's learned and witty style but expresses disagreement with his "bold, subversive, and revolutionary" theories.*]

The excellences of [M. Hippolyte Taine] consist in his style and method;—the one clear, forcible, and concise; the other analytical in form, though somewhat hypothetic in fact, bold, novel, and striking. (p. 101)

Applied to particulars, [his] ambitious doctrine [in *Les philosophes français du XIXme siècle*] gives rise to questions which

have not yet been solved. Can we sum up all individualities, all talents, all capacities, within a mere formula? Can we use exact methods in our appreciation and criticism? Do the faculties of a man, like the several organs of a plant, really depend on one another, and were they created by a law sole and universal? Granted that there is such a law, can we calculate its force and vitality, or foresee its good and evil effects? Do we possess a ruling faculty, the uniform action of which imparts a necessary system of motions which philosophy may foretell and analyze?

To all these questions M. Taine unhesitatingly answers in the affirmative. Many opponents of note give a negative reply. We can only hope that time, thought, and experience may sustain every one of our author's assertions. But, in the present state of our knowledge, we do not feel disposed to indorse doctrines so bold, subversive, and revolutionary. Our reasons are as follows.

The mutual dependence and close connection which form the basis of M. Taine's system undoubtedly exist in the physical world, and every discovery in science adds new evidences of necessary relations. But when endeavoring to carry the analogy into a new field, and to apply similar rules to the mysterious workings of the intellect, aspirations, and destiny of man, we find that they yield no such satisfactory results. There is too much individuality, the dissimilarity of primitive types is too great, the consequences are too various and uncertain, even with original conditions wholly similar, to admit of the application of dogmatic formulas to the inner workings and decisive actions of men. We fail to perceive in the individual history of a poet, artist, or statesman rules and ultimate effects which are entirely and necessarily reproduced or reflected in the workings of the state, and *vice versa*. No analytical historian, no critic, has yet succeeded in giving absolute rules, deduced from positive examples, which could enable us to unlock and unfold the necessary principles of action of any representative man or era in their universality, Vico, Herder, and Hegel not excepted. It is no argument to say that in such matters the proofs cannot be of such a positive and absolute nature as to exact the assent or conviction of all. If you adopt mathematical reasonings, give mathematical conclusions. There are facts in the domain of abstract truth which no one can deny; and it is no unreasonable presumption to require evidences adequate to the subject, and possessing the same degree of clearness which we find in matters equally abstruse and difficult. Nor should we forget that M. Taine claims to have discovered a method wholly algebraical, and a sort of philosophical geometry, of which the high-sounding principles, severally named *abstraction, hypothesis,* and *verification,* form the magic key.

Yet, if we believe in the science of history as now taught and expounded,—in that science which aims at unfolding the laws of the social and political world, exhibiting, through the medium of historical similitudes, a progressive march toward a necessary end, as yet unknown to us, but believed to be within our reach,—we cannot entirely disprove in men what so many concede to states, however large or however insignificant. But can we admit with M. Taine—and it is not the most serious objection—that "the forces which govern men are similar to those which govern nature," without granting likewise that a succession of necessities governs both the moral and physical worlds? Can we repeat with our author, after Condillac, that the nature of a being consists only in a group of distinct abstractions, embodied in systematic combinations and relations of facts, without destroying a belief, universal and overwhelming, in the substantial reality of all beings?

M. Taine's repeated efforts in the field of British literature [in *Essais de critique et d'histoire*] claim at our hands a slight digression from his metaphysics to literary criticism. It is rarely given to French critics to review the works of an English author with skill and impartiality. Whatever they may say to the contrary, it is evident that a large majority of them can never be made to feel the force of the Anglo-Saxon, and perceive all the excellences of the British writers. (pp. 102-04)

M. Taine, who is evidently drifting toward a specialty, has been . . . successful in his attempts at describing . . . the characteristics of our first novelists and historians. English literature seems to him a rich and promising mine, as yet unworked. Eager to carve out for himself a reputation based upon original researches, he evinces in his later articles marks of close study and of a certain insight into the peculiarities of men and manners in England. That he analyzes the modern authors, as yet, with more enthusiasm than accuracy, and favors Dickens and Thackeray with classifications, divisions, subdivisions, and finicalities of which they never dreamed, does not admit of a doubt. He may also be charged with giving vent to an admiration so continuous and so overwhelming, when commenting upon writers who are merely clever and interesting, that the reader is often tempted to ask where our critic will find adequate words and exclamations when obliged to speak of Shakespeare and Milton. This unlimited disposition to praise and admire is often the result of a first acquaintance with foreign authors. (p. 105)

We do not know what advantages M. Taine may have enjoyed in studying Carlyle and Macaulay; but candor prompts us to say that his reviews of those two authors are not calculated to alter the opinion already formed by most English readers. The racy style, striking form, and grandiloquent encomiums which are the leading features in his essays may please, but fail to instruct. An entire History of English Literature, which we understand our critic is engaged in preparing for the press, should be so written as to prove useful not only to French readers, but also to the English, who are after all the best judges of such matters. Now, how few of the foreign comments on *Hamlet* or *Cymbeline*, *Hudibras* or the "Rape of the Lock," can bear a translation!

In his last article on Mill's *Logic* . . . we discern a decided improvement, which may be attributed to the subject,—Logic, M. Taine's constant study, the object of his love and admiration, the ideal which he sees or inserts in all things. There, in the midst of those attenuated processes of reasoning, he breathes freely, feels his strength, expounds and teaches with zest and success. It is really interesting to see how faithfully he dissects the work of the great English logician, and with what consummate skill he simplifies and abridges the most fugitive thoughts to be found in the whole range of human abstractions. The dialogue form, that faint echo of the thorough analyses of Plato, for which the Paris Normal School has always been noted, is made to play an important part in this, as well as in most of M. Taine's later essays. No reader can forget the striking, lively, though one-sided dialogues between Peter and Paul, in his exposition of the modern French philosophers. Yet it is not every subject which admits of such a rapid succession of questions and replies; and when too often repeated, it never fails to impart a certain sameness which justly fatigues the reader.

It is due to M. Taine to say, that he is not only an imaginative, although analytical writer, but a critic of great scientific attainments and erudition. He exhibits at all times a knowledge of history in its philosophy, and of philosophy in its history, which can be the growth only of deep and extensive research. Whether he defines the salient characteristics of Livy or Machiavelli, Cousin or Jouffroy, the reader perceives that page after page teems with sound inferences, and with criticisms terse and true. His comprehensive surveys and deductions manifest intellectual power of the highest order, fully evolved and methodically trained. Disdaining the details of a precise or technical erudition, he is ever in search of ruling and universal principles, susceptible of scientific verification. He may occasionally mistake preconceived notions for the logical results of a careful investigation; his hypotheses sometimes dictate the expected consequences; but his earnestness is so great that, even when sporting with logical forms, every word tells, every assertion leaves an indelible mark. His forms are sometimes abrupt, his assertions always dogmatical, his illustrations familiar. He cannot be said to aim at producing rhetorical effects, and yet one may easily detect evidences of a close attention to the rounding of his periods. Familiar as he is with the methods of logic, fond of analysis, eager to introduce at all times formulas, axioms, postulates, and corollaries, some of his pages bristle with geometrical forms which startle without convincing the reader.

He is eminently witty and ironical, and his style of sarcastic argumentation has rarely been surpassed. (pp. 105-07)

In fine, M. Taine must be considered as an author of uncommon literary excellence, unquestionable originality, and surpassing energy and promise. His style is peculiar, at times eloquent, always correct, firm, and forcible. And when we recollect his strength as a writer, his ingenuity as a logician, and his success as an acute reasoner, we feel tempted to apply to him the measure which he has so felicitously applied to others. Livy, he says, is *orator in historia*, Cousin, *orator in philosophia*. What shall we say of M. Taine? *Orator in dialectica*. (p. 107)

> *"French Critics and Criticism,—M. Taine,"* in The North American Review, *Vol. XCIII, No. CXCII, July, 1861, pp. 99-107.*

[W. F. RAE] (essay date 1861)

[*Rae discusses Taine's system as he employs it in regard to poetry, descriptions of nature, history, and philosophical doctrine. In addition, Rae faults Taine's over-reliance on a system, his aspiration to certainty, and the inconsistencies inherent in his method. For additional commentary by Rae, see excerpts dated 1864 and 1876.*]

[M. Taine] writes forcibly and pleasantly, and can weave incidents into an effective narrative. But these are secondary qualifications with him. His attainments as a scholar are exceptionally vast. With ancient and modern literature he is intimately acquainted, and few Frenchmen are equally well versed in the literature of [England], and equally capable of appreciating its excellences. (p. 57)

The author has erred, in our opinion, by attempting to prove too much [in his *Essai sur les fables de La Fontaine*]. Considering every "poetical fabulist a systematizer," he asserts that these fables were composed in accordance with a system, and upholds this opinion by applying to them a system of his own. In so doing he has laid himself open to the reproach levelled by Rousseau in his *Emile* against the would-be philosophers of his day, "who were all so smitten with the rage for system, that none of them tried to consider things as they were, but as they accorded with each one's pet system."

If it were possible for La Fontaine to peruse this commentary, he would be exceedingly puzzled and amazed. He would learn, probably for the first time, the real ends he had in view when he composed his verses; how under the guise of animals he had portrayed his contemporaries, and how writings which were meant to amuse became to be regarded as of priceless historical value. Moreover, he would be made aware of the little personal merit he could lay claim to for what he had achieved, seeing that the accidental circumstances of his possessing a purely Gaulish temperament, and having been born and bred among a Gaulish race, combined with his having had the good luck to be admitted to the Court of Louis XIV., irresistibly biassed him in the method of treatment he adopted and the topics he chose. He was sufficiently vain of his talents not to feel flattered by reading that he was a man of striking originality and rare genius; but how bitterly would he be disappointed to discover that the possession of genius is of little importance, ''because genius is nothing more than a developed force; a force which cannot be developed except in the country wherein it is natural and common, where it is nourished by education, strengthened by example, sustained by character, and elicited by the public taste.'' These assertions would unquestionably dissipate many of his old delusions regarding his exceptional powers and individual greatness. In reply, he might adopt the words of one of his epistles, and say that he was merely a butterfly of Parnassus, resembling a bee in skimming every flower, and roving from object to object, mingling a little glory with many pleasures; that possibly he might have attained a higher niche in the temple of Memory had he devoted himself to one kind of work, but that in verse, as in conduct, he was volatile, ever following the bent of his inclination, solicitous above all things to enjoy himself and amuse his fellows. Nevertheless, he would add, though his aims were not lofty and his achievements comparatively trifling, what he had performed was to be ascribed to his capacity for the work he undertook and his determination to excel. So far from being altogether indebted to the accidents of birth and position, he alone of those born with like temperaments and reared under analogous circumstances, succeeded in composing fables of such celebrity and merit as to appear in the eyes of M. Taine worthy of this laboured commentary and paradoxical explanation. Nay more, supposing La Fontaine versed in literary history, he might refute M. Taine's definition of genius by asking him whether the poetical genius of Dante, Burns, or Schiller, was merely a force developed by surrounding circumstances, or whether, on the contrary, it was not a mysterious faculty which enabled them, in spite of unpropitious training, adverse fates, and uncongenial situations, to produce poems which are at once inimitable and immortal? (pp. 59-61)

He might add that whatever honour he had obtained was due to his having ''sung as the bird sings,'' spontaneously and unmindful of system—that influence and reward such as his, a poet of any other cast could not hope to acquire and would not deserve.

Yet, after having raised several objections, and pointed out some important defects, La Fontaine would not be slow to admit the exceeding merits of this book. He would recognise in M. Taine both a native of the same province, and a man whose tastes and sympathies qualified him for having laboured at the same time as himself. The writers of the seventeenth century would undoubtedly have hailed in him a congenial associate. His fondness for paradox, and the cheerfulness with which he immolates himself on the altar of system, would have attracted much notice, and secured for him a wide reputation

among the leading men of that age. The happy illustrations with which this commentary is adorned, and the extreme gracefulness of its style, would assuredly draw forth from La Fontaine very high commendation, and would almost atone, in his opinion, for the double blunder of its having been written to advance a theory alike extravagant and untenable, and to enunciate a conclusion which is a truism.

M. Taine's next work was a *Journey to the Pyrenees*. It is a rare thing for a book of travels to denote the possession of uncommon talents. (pp. 61-2)

He regards everything with the eyes of a lettered critic, and delights in comparing the present which we know with the past of which we read. The chronicles of olden times afford him great pleasure, and he diversifies his narrative by citing a tale illustrative of the manners and people of bygone days. His critical tastes are curiously exemplified in descriptions of scenery. Not satisfied with reproducing, as he can do most effectively, the salient features of a landscape, he analyses the component parts of it, and points out why these produce an impression of beauty. He goes still further, and does not scruple to find fault with Nature for being in some cases a bad landscape-maker. This censure is not pronounced by him in person. A M. Paul is introduced, with whom he discusses various matters, and whose extreme opinions he generally combats, but in such a way as to allow him to have the best of the argument. In this manner, views which he does not choose to advance himself, are put into the mouth of M. Paul, and upheld by him. (p. 63)

In describing the varied beauties of the Pyrenees, M. Taine displays unusual powers as a writer, combined with an intimate knowledge of what is most striking in natural scenery. His descriptions, though minute, are not mere pieces of word-painting; an art which has become so common, and which, when practised for its own sake, is so contemptible. He evidently feels the beauties he depicts, and admirably succeeds in embodying his feelings in words. The most difficult of his undertakings was to describe the circle of Gavarnie; a spectacle than which anything more sublime is not to be found in Europe. The effect it produces is chiefly owing to its vastness and simplicity. It is a semicircular mass of naked rock, rising perpendicularly to the height of fifteen hundred feet, crowned with glaciers, and furrowed by tiny cascades. Painters have repeatedly tried to reproduce it on canvas, and innumerable writers have vainly essayed to convey an adequate notion of it. Of the latter attempts, this one is the most successful; still, the reality must be seen to be comprehended.

Not satisfied with recounting what he has witnessed, M. Taine must needs explain every appearance, and assign to everything its cause. He describes the origin of the Pyrenean chain, and notes the transformation it has been made to undergo. The soil, the aspects of the mountains, the beasts which inhabit and the plants which cover them, are shown to be in harmony, and to be linked together by necessary relations. Sometimes he generalizes, and then he expresses his views in lofty and sonorous language. (pp. 66-7)

This book is by no means a commonplace one. It has its faults. Nearly every paragraph is intended to elucidate or support some opinion which the author entertains. The hand of the critic is everywhere perceptible; of the young, ardent, and ambitious critic, who would reopen every question, and judge every cause on its merits. Although we dissent from some of the doctrines which the author is at great pains to inculcate, yet we must allow his views to be acute, comprehensive, and worthy of consideration. By introducing M. Paul he contrives to discuss many extraneous topics without wandering too wide from the subject in hand, or lapsing into tiresome dissertation. The style is never monotonous, and varies with the subject. Most Frenchmen of good education write neatly and clearly; but M. Taine writes exceptionally well for a Frenchman. He thinks more profoundly than the majority of his countrymen, is extremely sensitive to external impressions, and thus, with his mastery over language, he becomes truly eloquent where others would simply sink into bombast. We shall find these excellences still more conspicuously displayed, and his distinguishing peculiarities still more marked, in his next work, [*Essai sur Tite-Live*]. (pp. 67-8)

In the first place, . . . we detect him in an inconsistency. He charges Livy with being a bad philosopher because he neglects to group his facts, disregards the proper order of ideas, and writes merely that he may give a striking picture, and produce a pleasing tale. What confirms this view is his omitting to put characteristic expressions into the mouths of his personages, and, when describing barbarous times, making no use of those telling barbarisms which, however they may grate on the fastidious ear, serve so well to stamp an era. His deficiencies in these particulars lay him open to the designation of an oratorical historian, thereby distinguishing him from the philosophical Thucydides and the practical Tacitus. But if the failings we have cited prove Livy to be an orator, they prove the latter historians to be orators also, seeing that both of them are equally chargeable with them. To make any distinction in this matter is to employ two weights and two measures. It is indisputable that Thucydides made of Pericles an orator after his own image, as much as Livy softened and polished the rude speech of Cato. Nor is it less certain that the uniform grandeur and forced conciseness of Tacitus equally denote an oratorical historian, as the sustained and long-drawn-out harmony of Livy's periods. Had not M. Taine been too anxious to prove his theory, he would not have rashly attempted to make facts square with his system. What he says of Niebuhr might be applied to himself. "According to the custom of innovators, he strains truth till it becomes error; to exaggerate is the law and misfortune of the human mind; the goal must be passed in order to be reached." We may add that in the above instance M. Taine has bolted from the course, and can never approach the winning-post.

The circumstance of Livy having disregarded original documents does not prove him to be an orator; but that he was indolent. (pp. 71-2)

While considering this author mistaken in his criticism, we hold that he is absurd in his requirements. A work so comprehensive and complete as that which he requires from Livy is beyond human capacity. We are surprised, indeed, to find a man of his discernment countenancing the vulgar error that any history can be faultless and perfect. The work he has criticised is emphatically Livy's *History of Rome*. It is not *the* history of Rome, any more than M. Taine's is *the* essay on Livy. The man who should do more would be supernaturally gifted, and be unaffected by human sympathies and passions. But as such a historian is an impossibility, we may regard such a history as a chimera. (p. 73)

We have considered M. Taine's system as applied to poetry, natural scenery, and history, and have next to consider it as applied to philosophical doctrines. (p. 75)

[*Les philosophes français du XIXme siècle*], though clever, is very unsatisfactory. It is written with too much levity. The author neglects no artifice to make his opponents ridiculous, and thereby lower the value of their systems and render his account of them entertaining. Far be it from us to maintain that philosophical discussions should be rendered as repulsive as possible by overcharging them with technical terms, and by using a jargon which only the initiated pretend to be intelligible; a pretension which is usually held to be evidence of their being ashamed to confess their inability to comprehend what others cannot understand. We do not wish any one to fall into Kant's error, who wrote books in a language which seemed to be German, but which could not be read by Germans until a lexicon had been compiled for their use. But the contrary mistake should be equally avoided. By dramatizing his personages, M. Taine has given a degree of liveliness to his book, at the same time making it seem rather childish, and bear an unpleasant resemblance to Mrs. Marcet's dialogues. It is philosophy made easy. We regret this the more, seeing that the author's clear and effective style would have sufficed to give piquancy to his censures and attract attention to them.

The only one whom he praises is Laromiguière, and he does this more from admiration of his style than approval of his doctrines. (pp. 75-6)

The criticism on Maine de Biran is perhaps the most unfair in the volume. His opinions are laughed at both on account of their extravagance, and also because they are fallacies expressed in obscure and lumbering phrases. We share M. Taine's antipathy to the spiritualistic philosophy of that writer. Much of his censure is well expressed and deserved. But we cannot admire or unite with him in heaping sarcasm, without making allowance for one who was an honest though very mistaken thinker. (pp. 76-7)

[In the case of M. Cousin], as in the other cases, [M. Taine's] system has miscarried, and his application of it is unfair. J. S. Mill has justly remarked that "a doctrine is not judged at all until it is judged in its best form." This wise course has not been followed by M. Taine, who seems to have set out with the intention of refuting M. Cousin on every point, and has tried to accomplish this by ridiculing him. The truth is not eliminated by his system: the system is employed to bolster up a foregone conclusion. After having discovered by intuition that M. Cousin is an orator, he demonstrates by selected quotations and unsupported assertions, that hence he is a bad philosopher, a bad historian, and a bad biographer. These things may be true, but the reasons he has assigned do not put them beyond cavil. Standing apart, as we do, from the scene of controversy, uninfluenced, as we are, by prepossessions of any sort, we cannot be so unjust to M. Cousin as to affirm of him, or coincide in the opinion, that he is nothing better than an adroit and popular mountebank who can turn out fine periods. Whatever may be his demerits as a philosopher, his services to the cause of education and of free discussion should be frankly recognised. (p. 81)

Throughout all his criticism [M. Taine] proceeds on the assumption that "man is a walking theorem," that "the critic is the natural historian of the mind;" in short, "that the forces which govern man resemble those which regulate natural objects; that the necessities which regulate the successive states of his thought are equivalent to those which regulate successive states of temperature, and that criticism imitates physical science in having no other object than defining and measuring them." He starts with and acts on the assumptions contained in these sentences as if they were indisputable propositions; thereby taking for granted what he ought to prove. We do not deny the possibility of doing so, though we greatly doubt its feasibility. We speak of the faculties of the mind as of the members of our bodies; this we do merely because of our inability to conceive it otherwise than as a corporate existence. In like manner we explain why a poet or a painter is great by saying that he possesses genius; that one less remarkable possesses talent, and that an ordinary individual is destitute of both. These phrases are simply formulas which serve to express our meaning; but when it is asked what is mind, what are genius and talent, how are they compounded, whence are they derived, we are obliged to acknowledge our ignorance and lament it. This M. Taine will not do. For him there are no mysteries or difficulties; he has a key to unlock every enigma, and a clue to guide him along the windings of every labyrinth. He composes a formula to the effect that the mind is ruled by forces like natural objects, and that one force dominates over the others and renders them subordinate to it. He then says of a writer that the dominating principle of his mind is eloquence, that this necessitates the minor forces acting so as to make him compose his works in a certain way, choose particular subjects, exhibit various peculiarities of style, and thus demonstrate unconsciously and unavoidably that he is an orator. Facts are not lacking to make out a plausible case. Indeed, M. Taine has the power of marshalling facts with great subtlety and skill; of directing them against any given point, and obtaining to all appearance an easy and decisive victory. However, as he has well remarked, "Nothing is so pliable as facts; nothing is more convenient than a system." He has fabricated a system which serves to cut the knots he cannot untie. (pp. 83-4)

It might be asked why we have discussed this author's works at such length, seeing that we disagree with him so fundamentally? Our answer and defence are that, although we are unable to accept his conclusions, we greatly admire the ability with which he forms and inculcates them, and can most heartily praise the earnestness of purpose he exhibits, and his desire to separate the true from the false. We value the man more highly than his system. That he possesses no ordinary capacity and considerable originality is evident, we think, from our account of his writings and opinions. (p. 85)

Among the Essays not yet collected are many on English authors. Shakespeare, Milton, Dryden, Swift, Addison, the Comedy of the Restoration, the writings of Mr. Carlyle, Mr. Mill, and Mr. Tennyson, are all treated of by M. Taine and judged in accordance with his own system. We shall not specify his conclusions with regard to each of them, but recommend them for consideration. In many respects the three last essays are the most remarkable ones he has written. It is always difficult for a foreigner to judge English authors with equity and discernment, but the difficulty is vastly increased when these authors are his contemporaries. A Frenchman who takes up the works of Shakespeare or Milton for the purpose of writing a criticism on them, has the advantage of being able to learn how they have been judged by his countrymen, and, if he place confidence in them, he may allow their views to influence his own. M. Taine has no such advantage when he undertakes an estimate of the powers of Carlyle, J. S. Mill, or Tennyson. Nor does he require it. Beyond all question, he can cope with all of them single-handed, and acquit himself with wonderful success. We do not hesitate to say that a better exposition and vindication of the philosophy of Mr. Mill has never appeared than the one by M. Taine. Perhaps his article on Mr. Tennyson is even more deserving of praise, seeing that the difficulties of the task are enormously greater. Certainly, he has communicated to his countrymen that a great poet is now living in

England, who is in many things equal to the greatest of his predecessors, while differing essentially from all of them. (pp. 85-6)

Whether or not M. Taine's future career will fulfil the promise of its opening, is of course uncertain. That he may accomplish great things is probable. He is young, and his powers are still in embryo. We not shall treat him as he has treated others, and affirm that the dominating principle of his mind is criticism, that he beholds everything through a critic's spectacles, and can never rise to the dignity of a creator. Believing, as we do, that every man of genuine and large capacity has many veins in him unknown to himself, and unsuspected by others, we think that he may yet open up a new one, and extract from it far richer ore—gold having the true ring, and resisting every test.

Desiring to attain certainty, he has adopted the demonstrative method and applied it to criticism. After all, we must retain the opinion expressed at the outset, to the effect that critical conclusions are mere matters of opinion, which are liable to be questioned and reversed. Every critic views objects by the light of his own mind—a light which is peculiar to himself in hue and brilliancy, and which tinges his opinions with its own colour. What M. Taine has attempted, has been often essayed before, but always miscarried. . . . It is not enough to intersperse *because* and *therefore* in a paragraph to bestow on it the certainty of a mathematical demonstration. These words will effect this when used aright and in the proper place, and that place is the pages of Euclid. We earnestly hope that M. Taine may live to correct his mistakes and eclipse them by the splendour of his future success. As it is, he has acquired notoriety, the praise of some contemporaries, and the censure of others. We trust that he may aim higher, and have his name inscribed in that Golden Book wherein are registered all those who have been ennobled for ever by the voice of fame. (p. 90)

[W. F. Rae], "The Critical Theory and Writings of M. Taine," in The Westminster Review, n.s. Vol. XX, No. 1, July 1, 1861, pp. 55-90.

H. A. TAINE (essay date 1863)

[*In the following excerpt from his notorious introduction to* History of English Literature, *first published in 1863, Taine proclaims his intent to treat history in a purely scientific fashion because "history in its elements is a psychological problem." In addition, Taine here makes his famous assertion that "vice and virtue are products, like vitriol and sugar." For additional commentary by Taine, see excerpts dated 1870 and 1875.*]

When you have observed and noted in man one, two, three, then a multitude of sensations, does this suffice, or does your knowledge appear complete? Is Psychology only a series of observations? No; here as elsewhere we must search out the causes after we have collected the facts. No matter if the facts be physical or moral, they all have their causes; there is a cause for ambition, for courage, for truth, as there is for digestion, for muscular movement, for animal heat. Vice and virtue are products, like vitriol and sugar; and every complex phenomenon arises from other more simple phenomena on which it hangs. (pp. 10-11)

There is, then, a system in human sentiments and ideas: and this system has for its motive power certain general traits, certain characteristics of the intellect and the heart common to men of one race, age, or country. As in mineralogy the crystals, however diverse, spring from certain simple physical forms, so in history, civilisations, however diverse, are derived from certain simple spiritual forms. The one are explained by a primitive geometrical element, as the others are by a primitive psychological element. In order to master the classification of mineralogical systems, we must first consider a regular and general solid, its sides and angles, and observe in this the numberless transformations of which it is capable. So, if you would realise the system of historical varieties, consider first a human soul generally, with its two or three fundamental faculties, and in this compendium you will perceive the principal forms which it can present. After all, this kind of ideal picture, geometrical as well as psychological, is not very complex, and we speedily see the limits of the outline in which civilisations, like crystals, are constrained to exist. (p. 13)

History now attempts, or rather is very near attempting [the psychological] method of research. The question propounded now-a-days is of this kind. Given a literature, philosophy, society, art, group of arts, what is the moral condition which produced it? what the conditions of race, epoch, circumstance, the most fitted to produce this moral condition? There is a distinct moral condition for each of these formations, and for each of their branches; one for art in general, one for each kind of art—for architecture, painting, sculpture, music, poetry; each has its special germ in the wide field of human psychology; each has its law, and it is by virtue of this law that we see it raised, by chance, as it seems, wholly alone, amid the miscarriage of its neighbours, like painting in Flanders and Holland in the seventeenth century, poetry in England in the sixteenth, music in Germany in the eighteenth. At this moment, and in these countries, the conditions have been fulfilled for one art, not for others, and a single branch has budded in the general barrenness. History must search now-a-days for these rules of human growth; with the special psychology of each special formation it must occupy itself; the finished picture of these characteristic conditions it must now labour to compose. No task is more delicate or more difficult; Montesquieu tried it, but in his time history was too new to admit of his success; they had not yet even a suspicion of the road necessary to be travelled, and hardly now do we begin to catch sight of it. Just as in its elements astronomy is a mechanical and physiology a chemical problem, so history in its elements is a psychological problem. There is a particular system of inner impressions and operations which makes an artist, a believer, a musician, a painter, a man in a nomadic or social state; and of each the birth and growth, the energy, the connection of ideas and emotions, are different: each has his moral history and his special structure, with some governing disposition and some dominant feature. To explain each, it would be necessary to write a chapter of psychological analysis, and barely yet has such a method been rudely sketched. One man alone, Stendhal, with a peculiar bent of mind and a strange education, has undertaken it, and to this day the majority of readers find his books paradoxical and obscure: his talent and his ideas were premature; his admirable divinations were not understood, any more than his profound sayings thrown out cursorily, or the astonishing precision of his system and of his logic.... In his writings, in Sainte-Beuve, in the German critics, the reader will see all the wealth that may be drawn from a literary work: when the work is rich, and people know how to interpret it, we find there the psychology of a soul, frequently of an age, now and then of a race. In this light, a great poem, a fine novel, the confessions of a superior man, are more instructive than a heap of historians with their histories. I would give fifty volumes of charters and a hundred volumes of state papers for the memoirs of Cellini, the epistles of St. Paul, the Table-talk of Luther,

or the comedies of Aristophanes. In this consists the importance of literary works: they are instructive because they are beautiful; their utility grows with their perfection; and if they furnish documents it is because they are monuments. The more a book brings sentiments into light, the more it is a work of literature; for the proper office of literature is to make sentiments visible. The more a book represents important sentiments, the higher is its place in literature; for it is by representing the mode of being of a whole nation and a whole age, that a writer rallies round him the sympathies of an entire age and an entire nation. This is why, amid the writings which set before our eyes the sentiments of preceding generations, a literature, and notably a grand literature, is incomparably the best. It resembles those admirable apparatus of extraordinary sensibility, by which physicians disentangle and measure the most recondite and delicate changes of a body. Constitutions, religions, do not approach it in importance; the articles of a code of laws and of a creed only show us the spirit roughly and without delicacy. If there are any writings in which politics and dogma are full of life, it is in the eloquent discourses of the pulpit and the tribune, memoirs, unrestrained confessions; and all this belongs to literature: so that, in addition to itself, it has all the advantage of other works. It is then chiefly by the study of literatures that one may construct a moral history, and advance toward the knowledge of psychological laws, from which events spring. (pp. 32-5)

H. A. Taine, in his History of English Literature, *Vol. I, translated by H. Van Laun, Henry Holt and Company, 1900, 433 p.*

[W. F. RAE]   (essay date 1864)

[*Though he censures the narrowness of Taine's doctrine of race, Rae deems* History of English Literature *one of the best studies of its kind to date. For additional commentary by Rae, see excerpts dated 1861 and 1876.*]

[M. Taine] has produced the most elaborate and valuable history that now exists of the copious and splendid literature of England. (p. 473)

Whatever exceptions may be taken to some of M. Taine's doctrines [in his *Histoire de la littérature anglaise*], it is unquestionable that he has mapped out the epochs of English literature with singular originality and precision, that he has analysed the works of the greatest English writers with acuteness, has stated the results of his investigations with a fulness and grasp of thought which denote an acquaintance with that literature at once minute and comprehensive, and an admiration for whatever is noble in it, as genuine as rare. His doctrines . . . appear to disadvantage; they lack those accessories of illustration and argument which in the work itself illumine and enforce them. The doctrine which underlies all his speculations, that of the influence of race, has never yet been applied to our whole literature by any other writer. Of its importance we are fully aware. That even M. Taine has not applied it with perfect success we attribute to the imperfection of his generalization. The Saxon race is undoubtedly the backbone of the English people; but other races have had an influence on their history and progress. No one who carefully considers the peculiar talents displayed by such very dissimilar yet very national writers as Edmund Burke, Richard Brinsley Sheridan, and Thomas Moore can contend that these men displayed much in common with the Saxon temperament and talent. That Celtic influence has largely modified the Saxon character is rightly, though rather too unreservedly, maintained by Mr. Morley. According to him, ''but for early, frequent, and various contact with the race that in its half-barbarous days invented Oisin's dialogues with St. Patrick, and that quickened afterwards the Northmen's blood in France, Germanic England would not have produced a Shakespeare.'' ''It may be said that there is in the unmixed Anglo-Saxon an imagination with deep roots and little flower— solid stem and no luxuriance of foliage. The gay wit of the Celt would pour into the song of a few minutes more phrases of ornament than are to be found in the whole poem of Beowulf.'' The admission that there has been a Celtic influence at work in English literature would not destroy the value of M. Taine's speculations, it would merely necessitate the reconsideration and enlargement of his doctrine. It is the narrowness, not the tendency, of his doctrine which dissatisfies us.

The absence of a detailed account of the origin, progress, and character of English journalism is a great blemish in a work purporting to be a history of English Literature. This omission may be remedied in a future edition, as well as several trifling errors of detail, which on a careful revisal of the work must become apparent to its author. When reviewing a work so valuable and masterly as this one, we gladly exchange what Chateaubriand styled the paltry and meagre criticism of faults, for the large and prolific criticism of beauties. The beauties predominate. As a piece of historical composition, this history has few equals in our day. As a gallery of pictures, it rivals the matchless work of Macaulay; as a statement of philosophical views, it more than rivals the pregnant disquisitions of the late Mr. Buckle.

No other history of our literature can match M. Taine's in comprehensive grasp of thought, brilliancy of style, and trustworthiness of statement. It deserves a conspicuous place in every library filled with the immortal works of which it narrates the history, explains the character, and magnifies the excellence. . . . Until superseded by a better history than any yet produced, M. Taine's masterly volumes will supply the best and most finished picture that can be found of the noble literature of England. (pp. 510-12)

> [W. F. Rae], *''Taine's History of English Literature,''* in The Westminster Review, *n.s. Vol. XXV, No. II, April 1, 1864, pp. 473-512.*

CHARLES AUGUSTIN SAINTE-BEUVE (essay date 1864)

[*Sainte-Beuve is considered the foremost French literary critic of the nineteenth century. Of his extensive body of critical writings, the best known are his ''lundis''—weekly newspaper articles that appeared every Monday morning over a period of several decades, in which he displayed his knowledge of literature and history. While Sainte-Beuve began his career as a champion of Romanticism, he eventually formulated a psychological method of criticism. Asserting that the critic cannot separate a work of literature from the artist and from the artist's historical milieu, Sainte-Beuve considered an author's life and character integral to the comprehension of his work. In reviewing* History of English Literature, *Sainte-Beuve hails Taine's originality and perceptiveness and posits that Taine has made a significant contribution to the field of literary analysis. Sainte-Beuve's comments were first published in his* Nouveaux lundis *in 1864.*]

[M. Taine's *History of English Literature*] is, all said and done, a great book; had it attained only a fourth part of its purpose it would have advanced the subject, and would not have left it as it was before. The attempt is the boldest yet made in that particular style of literary history, and it is not astonishing that in prejudiced minds, accustomed to the older ways of thought, it should have raised so much opposition and resistance. Old habits and old methods are not changed in a day. The author might perhaps have diminished the number of his opponents if he had given the book its true title: ''History of the English Race and Civilisation through its Literature.'' Then impartial readers would have had only to approve, and for the most part to admire, the force and skill of the demonstration. (p. 228)

M. Taine attempted to study methodically the profound differences that race, surroundings, and epochs bring to the composition of minds, to the forming and directing of talent. But it will be objected that he has not sufficiently succeeded. In vain has he described to perfection the general characteristics and fundamental lines of race; in vain has he, in his vigorous pictures, characterised and brought into relief the revolutions of the times and the moral atmosphere which obtains at certain historical periods; in vain has he skilfully explained the complication of events, and the particular circumstances in which the life of an individual is involved and cogged, as it were; something more is wanting: I mean the living soul of the man, the reason why among twenty or a hundred or a thousand men apparently subjected to the same intrinsic or outward conditions, no two should be alike, and why one alone of all of them should excel in originality. Thus he has not recognised the essential importance of the spark of genius, nor does he show it in his analysis; he only put before us and deduced, blade by blade, fibre by fibre, cellule by cellule, the material, the organism, the parenchyma, if we may so call it, in which the soul, life, spark, once within, displays itself, is freely or almost freely diversified, and triumphs. Have I not well stated the objection, and do you recognise in it the argument of his most learned opponents? Well, what does it prove? That the problem is difficult, that in its entirety it cannot perhaps be solved. But in my turn I ask, is it nothing to state the problem as the author has done, to embrace it so closely, to surround all its parts, to reduce it to its simplest final expression, to cause all its data to be better weighed and considered? After making every allowance for general or particular elements and for circumstances, there still remains room and space enough round men of talent for freedom of movement and change of place. Besides, however circumscribed the line round each, every man of talent and genius, because in some degree an enchanter and a magician, possesses a secret, which is his alone, for producing marvels in that space, and for bringing wonders to light. I do not see that M. Taine, if he seems to neglect it, combats and absolutely denies that power: he limits it, and in limiting it, assists us in many cases to define it better than has hitherto been done. Indeed, whatever those who were content with the old vague conditions may say, M. Taine has done much to advance literary analysis; those who now study a great foreign writer will no longer set to work in the old way nor so lightly as before the publication of M. Taine's book. (pp. 229-30)

The *History of English Literature* is a book possessing unity from beginning to end: it was conceived, constructed, and executed at one time; the first and the last chapters correspond. Barbarism and Saxon semi-civilisation, crossed with Norman skill and refinement, the whole confined, rammed down in its island, wrought, finely ground, kneaded, and matured through the ages, is, as the author well demonstrates, to be seen again in the conclusion, in the condition of the most rigorous, solid, sensible, esteemed, well-balanced, positive and poetic of free nations. (pp. 240-41)

Until after the period of the Norman Conquest and of the formation of the new language, only slight and fragmentary evidence exists. The conquest of England by the Normans is the last in date of the great territorial invasions that everywhere preceded the middle ages. When it took place, mediaeval times had already commenced in other countries; the English language, and consequently the literature that was to be written in it, was behind other continental literatures, especially the French: it was inspired and impregnated by French forms, and only acquired with time its real temperament, its own quality. . . . What is chiefly to be remarked in the oldest productions of English literature is how the Saxon character kept its ground, and yielded in language and literature no more than in politics; under brilliant superficial coatings it preserved its taste, traditions, accent, and vocabulary. Comparing the ballads of Robin Hood with the French fabliaux, and in contrasting them with what is of French origin, M. Taine clearly hits on the difference of the two minds, of the two races, a difference that the Norman conquest in no way destroyed. (p. 241)

A feeling for what is robust, solid, spirited, gay, succulent, loyal, and honest in the English character, even as far as violence and excess of strength, breathes through M. Taine's book. (p. 242)

From its arrangement his book possesses the advantage of bringing into relief the most difficult and arduous parts, the great early epochs of English literature. The Renaissance is admirably treated. It did not work in England as in France; it did not put a sudden end to the middle ages; it did not produce *topsy-turvydom* or a destructive inundation in art, poetry, and the drama; it found a rich, solid basis resisting as always; it covered it in some places and mingled with it in others. By the enthusiasm and ardour of his writing, M. Taine makes us understand and almost love the chief actors and heroes of the English literary Renaissance: in prose, Sir Philip Sidney, a d'Urfé anterior to the French; in poetry Spenser, the lover of fairyland, whom he admires more than all the rest. When describing and painting him, he seems to swim in the open lake, to float in his element like a swan. He likes strength even in grace, and does object to extravagance and excess. He might astonish the English themselves by that animated impression which absolutely depends on his own way of reading. M. Taine has the courage of his opinions. He evades nothing, he cares for nothing but his purpose. He approaches the author he is reading directly and with all his vigour of mind; he receives a clear impression at first hand and first sight *facie ad faciem;* his conclusion springs naturally from the source, bubbles up, and overflows. In some cases this leads him to go beyond received opinions, to shatter those that are established, and to introduce new ones even at the risk of surprising and wounding. Little matters it to him! He goes straight on his way and takes no heed. He underrates or overrates just as he is impressed: he despises Butler for his much-praised *Hudibras,* and extols the fanatic Bunyan's *Pilgrim's Progress.* When I say he praises him I exaggerate: he describes the man and his work, but with such art that his words conjure up a picture that produces a life-like impression.

The concise, compressed style, taking its way by series, lines, and sequences, by frequent and repeated strokes, by phrases and as it were small, deep-cut hatchings, of his picturesque descriptions and analyses, made a critic of the old school say that he seemed to hear the rough, sharp hail falling and jumping on the roofs—

   Tam multa in tectis crepitans salit horrida grando.

In the long run the style produces a fixed, inevitable impression on the mind, which occasionally acts on the nerves. It is there that the man of science and the man of vigour must be careful not to weary the man of taste.

I know that at the present time the doctrine of too much, of so-called legitimate exaggeration, even of monstrosity is regarded as a mark of genius, but I ask to go as far as that only with many reservations. I prefer to dwell on this side, and have retained of my old literary habits the necessity of not fatiguing myself, and the desire of taking pleasure in what I admire.

Force and majesty suit M. Taine, and he holds to them with visible delight. He surpasses himself in describing the tumultuous medley of the English drama of the sixteenth century, the stage and audience made for each other, the constellation of powerful dramatists, including Marlowe, Massinger, Ford, Webster, and others, of whom Shakespeare was only the greatest. They have of late, with praiseworthy rivalry, been studied in France, but no one has so forcibly interpreted and described them as M. Taine: he puts them before us as if they were living and moving. The translations embodied in the text are the very essence of the originals, the flesh and blood of the English drama.

I leave to Shakespearian scholars M. Taine's particular interpretation of the poet's genius and ruling faculty, "imagination and pure passion." I confess that in my view the method of interpreting a great genius as an absolute type and symbol for the future seems necessarily conjectural: he is not exactly overrated, but too much generalised, and, as it were, raised in imagination above his work, no matter how strong and great it may already be in itself. It is an eternal problem remaining for competition. From time to time we like to try our strength: each in turn breaks a lance for it. It is, nevertheless, right that every critic who assiduously applies himself to one of the master geniuses, and aspires to understand him, should frankly state his opinion, should while criticising be himself criticised, and that all interpretations should be given forth and should be spread abroad. To speak the truth, they are less interpretations than experiments: and it thus makes an everlasting combat over master spirits the noblest and most generous dispute for future races. (pp. 243-45)

Milton, England's most splendid and most complex poetical genius, is appreciated and expounded by M. Taine in a fashion, as far as my knowledge goes, never before accomplished. He appears just at the right moment, after a characteristic picture of the Christian Renaissance, of which he is the gentle and tender blossom, the sublime, although slightly fantastical crown. His moral complexity, his unity, the contradictions he combines and arranges in himself, his stability of mind and genius, is all described, analysed, reproduced in more than a hundred pages, as beautiful in thought as in expression, and quite on a level with the subject. . . . (pp. 245-46)

After Milton, the variable, fertile, flexible, unequal Dryden, man of change and uncertainty, in point of date the first classical author, though at the same time broad-minded and powerful, does not give M. Taine much cause for complaint. The critic sets clearly before us the versatile, needy life, and the genius which like life goes somewhat by chance, yet is broad, abundant, imaginative, vivified by a vigorous sap, and nourished and watered by a copious vein of poetry.

It is rather the great poet of the following age, the classical writer in his perfection and concise elegance, it is Pope whom M. Taine does *not* praise; and since, for fear of monotony, it is well to vary praise by a little blame, I disagree with him on that point.

It cannot be the elegance and politeness in Pope's genius and person that displeases M. Taine; for no one better appreciates Addison, the earliest type of English urbanity in so far as there is urbanity. He criticises Addison and his temperate, discreet, moral, and decorous style capitally, the *quod decet* he was the first to teach his fellow-countrymen: he gives due justice to the characters of an entirely English physiognomy so exquisitely sketched in the *Spectator*. But in regard to Pope, M. Taine does not make the effort, necessary to every literary historian, of putting at need restraint on himself and against himself, and consequently his picture of the poet, long regarded as the most perfect of his nation, and so greeted by Byron, is full of marked disfavour and displeasure. (p. 249)

It must be well understood that while designedly and by way of example insisting on Pope's merits, I only indirectly find fault with M. Taine's work. He, in fact, recognises the merits and distinctive traits of Pope's splendid genius, and we might even borrow his phrases for defining them. But he does not treat him like the other great poets, and does not care to put him in his fitting place; on the whole, he rather disparages and lowers him, and when obliged to recognise a fine quality, only does so grudgingly.

[Modern] English literature of the nineteenth century does not altogether occupy the place in the book it has a right to exact. Some parts of the eighteenth century also might be more fully developed. Perfectly just in what he says of the chief poets he comes across, the critic, filled with the unity of his plan, seems in too great a hurry to reach the end and to conclude. Too little prominence is given to the melancholy, refined, original Gray; there is no more likeness between Gray and Lamartine than between a pearl and a lake. Collins is mixed up with a dozen others: he is worthy of a place to himself. Goldsmith, as poet, deserves, for the sake of his village of Auburn, a brief visit in his own home. If the Scotch Robert Burns is clearly understood and worthily classified, William Cowper is not allowed, it seems to me, a sufficiently proportionate part in the renaissance of natural taste and of true poetic expression. Again, the Lake poets are not allotted space enough. Sir Walter Scott is harshly treated, and not in accordance with our memories. M. Taine does not give him the rank to which as a novelist he has a right. Speaking generally, the conclusion is wanting in proportion. The philosophical critic brought all his force to bear on the different parts and on the high tablelands; he descended the pleasant slopes, rich, however, in charming undulations and windings, too hastily; he disdains to stop, forgetting that they would be the most accessible for French readers, and would form an interesting series of halting-places on account of their likeness to French points of view. If the author pleases, that defect can be easily remedied. In any case, M. Taine's work, as presented to us in the unity and completeness of this first form, will remain one of the most original productions of our time. (p. 265)

> *Charles Augustin Sainte-Beuve, "Taine's 'History of English Literature'," in his* Essays, *translated by Elizabeth Lee, Walter Scott, Ltd., 1892, pp. 228-65.*

GUSTAVE FLAUBERT (letter date 1866)

[*Flaubert was a French novelist, short story writer, and dramatist. One of the most influential French novelists of the nineteenth century, he is remembered primarily for the stylistic pre-*

cision and dispassionate rendering of psychological detail found in his masterpiece, Madame Bovary. *In the following extract from a letter that Flaubert wrote to Taine in reaction to some harsh criticism of* Italy: Florence and Venice, *Flaubert reassures him about the quality of his prose style.*]

Let the blockheads talk away, cher ami—your style is neither "fatiguing" nor "unintelligible." The author of the brilliant passages which fill your [*Italy: Florence and Venice*] has mastered the art of expressing his thoughts in prose.

Only, travel writing as a genre is *per se* almost impossible. To eliminate all repetitions you would have had to refrain from telling what you saw. This is not the case in books devoted to descriptions of discoveries, where the author's personality is the focus of interest. But in the present instance the attentive reader may well find that there are too many ideas and insufficient facts, or too many facts and not enough ideas. I'm the first to regret that you don't describe more landscapes, to counterbalance—for the sake of the total effect—your numerous descriptions of pictures. But I have very definite ideas about travel books, having written one myself. (p. 96)

> *Gustave Flaubert, in a letter to Hippolyte Taine in November, 1866, in his* The Letters of Gustave Flaubert: 1857-1880, *edited and translated by Francis Steegmuller, Cambridge, Mass.: Harvard University Press, 1982, pp. 96-7.*

H. TAINE (essay date 1870)

[*In this excerpt from his preface to* On Intelligence, *published in 1870, Taine sets out the purpose and method of his study. For additional commentary by Taine, see excerpts dated 1863 and 1875.*]

If I am not mistaken, we mean nowadays by Intelligence, what was formerly called Understanding or Intellect—that is to say, the faculty of knowing; this, at least, is the sense in which I have taken the word.

At all events, I . . . intend to examine our knowledge, that is to say our cognitions, and nothing else. The words *faculty, capacity, power,* which have played so great a part in psychology, are only . . . convenient names by means of which we put together, in distinct compartments, all facts of a distinct kind; these names indicate a character common to all the facts under a distinct heading; they do not indicate a mysterious and profound essence, remaining constant and hidden under the flow of transient facts. This is why I have treated of cognitions only, and, if I have mentioned faculties, it has been to show that in themselves, and as distinct entities, they do not exist.

Such a precaution as this is very necessary. By means of it, psychology becomes a science of facts; for our cognitions are facts; we can speak with precision and detail of a sensation, of an idea, of a recollection, of a prevision, as well as of a vibration, or other physical movement; in the one case as in the other there is a fact in question; it may be reproduced, observed, described; it has its precedents, its accompaniments, its consequents. In little, well-selected, important, significant facts, stated with full details and minutely noted, we find at present the materials of every science; each of them is an instructive specimen, the head of a rank, a salient example, a clear type to which a whole row of analogous cases conform; our main business is to know its elements, how they arise, in what manner and under what conditions they combine, and what are the constant effects of combinations so produced.

Such is the method it has been attempted to follow in this work. In the first part, the elements of knowledge have been determined; by consecutive reductions we have arrived at the most simple elements, and have passed from these to the physiological changes which are the condition of their origin. In the second part, we have first described the mechanism and general effect of their combination; then, applying the law we have discovered, we have examined the elements, formation, certitude, and range of the principal kinds of our knowledge, from that of individual things to that of general things, from the most special perceptions, previsions, and recollections, up to the most universal judgments and axioms.

In these inquiries, Consciousness, our principal instrument, is not sufficient in its ordinary state; it is no more sufficient in psychological inquiries than the naked eye in optical inquiries. For its range is not great; its illusions are many and invincible; it is necessary continually to beware of it; to test and correct its evidence, nearly always to assist it, to present objects to it in a brighter light, to magnify them and construct for its use a kind of microscope or telescope; at all events, to arrange the surroundings of the object, to give it the necessary relief by means of contrasts, or to find beside it indications of its presence, indications plainer than it is, and indirectly pointing out its nature.

Here lies the principal difficulty of the analysis.—As far as pure ideas and their relations with names are concerned, the principal aid has been afforded by names of numbers, and, in general, by the notations of arithmetic and algebra; thus we have brought again into light a great truth guessed at by Condillac, and which has lain for a century dormant, buried, and as though lifeless, for want of satisfactory evidence.—As to images, their effacement, their revival, their antagonist reductives, the necessary magnifying is found in the singular and extreme cases observed by physiologists and medical men, in dreams, in somnambulism and hypnotism, in illusions and the hallucinations of sickness.—As to sensations, significant instances are found in the sensations of sight, and especially in those of hearing. By means of such evidence, and of the recent discoveries of physicists and physiologists, we have attempted to construct or sketch out the whole theory of elementary sensations, to advance beyond the ordinary bounds, up to the limits of the mental world, to indicate the functions of the principal parts of the brain, to conceive the connection of molecular nervous changes with thought.—Other abnormal cases, borrowed both from students of insanity, and from physiologists, have enabled us to explain the general process of illusion and rectification, whose successive stages constitute our various kinds of knowledge.—After this, to elucidate our knowledge of bodies, and of ourselves, valuable indications have been found in the profound and closely reasoned analysis of Bain, Herbert Spencer, and Stuart Mill, in the illusions of persons who have lost limbs, in all the different illusions of the senses, in the education of the eye in persons born blind who have recovered their sight by operations, in the singular alterations which the idea of self undergoes during sleep, hypnotism, and madness.—We have then been able to enter upon the examination of the ideas and general propositions which make up the sciences, properly so called, to profit by Mr. Mill's acute and accurate inquiries respecting Induction, to establish against Kant and Mill a new theory of necessary propositions, to study by a series of examples what is termed the explanatory reason of a law, and to conclude with general views on science and nature, while pausing before the metaphysical problem which is the first and last of all.

Between psychology thus conceived and history as it is now written, the relationship is very close. For history is applied psychology, psychology applied to more complex cases. The historian notes and traces the total transformations presented by a particular human molecule, or group of human molecules; and, to explain these transformations, writes the psychology of the molecule or group; Carlyle has written that of Cromwell; Sainte-Beuve that of Port Royal; Stendhal has made twenty attempts on that of the Italians; M. Renan has given us that of the Semitic race. Every perspicacious and philosophical historian labors at that of a man, an epoch, a people, or a race; the researches of linguists, mythologists, and ethnographers have no other aim; the task is invariably the description of a human mind, or of the characteristics common to a group of human minds; and, what historians do with respect to the past, the great novelists and dramatists do with the present. For fifteen years I have contributed to these special and concrete psychologies; I now attempt general and abstract psychology. To comprise it exhaustively, there would be required a theory of the Will in addition to the theory of the Intelligence; if I may judge of the work I do not venture to undertake by that which I have attempted to accomplish, my strength is not equal to this; all that I venture to hope is that the reader will grant me his indulgence, in consideration of the difficulty of the task and the length of the effort. (pp. vii-x)

> *H. Taine, in a preface to his* On Intelligence, *translated by T. D. Haye, revised edition, Holt & Williams, 1872, pp. vii-x.*

HENRI FRÉDÉRIC AMIEL   (journal date 1871)

[*A nineteenth-century Swiss diarist, critic, and poet, Amiel is best known for his diary,* Journal intime, *which is considered an outstanding example of introspective literature. In the following excerpt from that work, Amiel criticizes* History of English Literature *for being too scientific and impersonal. For additional commentary by Amiel, see excerpt dated 1880.*]

Reading: a few lusty, hoarse chapters of Taine (***Histoire de la littérature anglaise***). I feel a painful sensation with this writer, as of the odour of a laboratory, a grating of pulleys, a clicking of machinery. This style suggests chemistry and technology. The science in it seems inexorable. Moreover, one feels in it only clearsightedness, no delicacy, no sympathy. It is rigorous and dry, penetrating and hard, strong and rough; but it is altogether lacking in humanity, nobility, grace. This sensation as of verdigris, painful to tooth, ear, eye and heart, that is, wounding one's taste in every way, probably springs from two things, the moral philosophy of the author and his literary principles. The profound contempt for humanity that characterizes the physiological school, and the intrusion of technology into literature, undertaken by Balzac and Stendhal, explain the inner aridity that makes itself felt in these pages and that catches at one's throat like the unhealthy exhalations of a factory of mineral products. This reading is instructive in a very high degree, but it is anti-vivifying; it is withering, corrosive, saddening. It is no more inspiring than the sight of a pharmacy, an osteological museum or a herbarium; it only adds to one's knowledge. I imagine that this will be the literature of the future, in the American style, a profound contrast to the art of the Greeks: algebra instead of life, the formula instead of the image, the effluvia of the alembic instead of the intoxication of Apollo, cold vision instead of the joys of thought, in short, the death of poetry, flayed and anatomatized by science.

This criticism savours of the anatomical chart, of chlorine and reagents, and one is hardly grateful to it for the glimpses it opens up, because it drains away at the same time the source of our illusions and creations. It stupefies one like an anaesthetic, it is as cheerful as a morgue. What it lacks is not depth, perspicacity, information, but love and the power to inspire love.

> *Henri Frédéric Amiel, in a journal entry of February 10, 1871, in his* The Private Journal of Henri Frédéric Amiel, *translated by Van Wyck Brooks and Charles Van Wyck Brooks, revised edition, Macmillan Publishing Company, 1935, p. 334.*

[WILLIAM DEAN HOWELLS]   (essay date 1872)

[*Howells was the chief progenitor of American realism and the most influential American literary critic during the late nineteenth century. He is recognized as one of the major literary figures of his era: he successfully weaned American literature away from the sentimental romanticism of its infancy, earning the popular sobriquet "the Dean of American Letters." Here, Howells discusses Taine's* History of English Literature *and* Art in Greece *and notes that his method, while valuable, is incomplete because it does not account for the individuality of the artist.*]

No doubt troubles M. Taine [in his *History of English Literature*], who flashes his jack-a-lantern over the boggy ups and downs of English life, and upon the pages of the great romancer [Dickens] and the great satirist [Thackeray], with a lively belief in its solar power. We speak slightly now of only a small part of a large work, which may have more value than we have been led to hope by what we have read in it. If the suspicion which our partial acquaintance has cast upon the whole proves unjust, we shall be prepared to make full amends hereafter; but in the mean time we own our misgiving. In treating of the remoter literary epochs, M. Taine has us more on his own ground, for our ancestors are a kind of foreigners to us; yet if we may guess from his criticism on Dryden, which we have read, we must still prefer a critic who has not had to judge his author with all his finest and his sweetest left out. It is not so much that he is mainly mistaken; Dryden is rather too plain a case; but if any one will read Mr. Lowell's essay on Dryden after M. Taine's, he will have our meaning, and will perceive the difference between interpreting a poet by every delicate faculty, and feeling for him with the thumb. Still, one has to admire M. Taine's zeal and industry, and the strictly historical portions of his work. He succeeds better, we think, in relating the history of a foreign people to its art, as in his *Art in Greece*, than to its literature; but his success there may be chiefly in our necessary modern ignorance of antiquity, and, if they could, those poor ancients might cry out in indignant protest. It is certain that it is safer to infer Greek art from Greek life, as M. Taine does, than to infer Greek character from Greek art, as Mr. Ruskin would prefer to do. His method of showing the influences of daily life upon art is admirably brilliant and effective, but the reader will do well to guard himself against the author's too inflexible and exclusive application of his theory. Stated in rather an extreme form, it is this: given the time and climate of a people, their art can be accurately deduced therefrom, without reference to their artistic productions,—just as Agassiz can sketch you off a portrait of our affectionate forefathers the ichthyosaurus or the pterodactyl, after glancing at their fossilized foot-tracks. M. Taine's method does not take into sufficient account the element of individuality in the artist. Rigorously applied, it would make us expect to find all the artists of a given people at a given time cast in one mould,

good or bad as the case might be. In the history of art it should be borne in mind that, beside the study of works of art proper, not only the general circumstances of the time and people are to be considered, but the personal circumstances of each great artist,—his obstacles and aids, his failures and triumphs, which modify the character of his works. Each study should supplement the other two. By following these three paths *seriatim*, among every people in every period, and comparing the results, we arrive at a comprehensive knowledge of the world's art. In respect to Greece, the study of biography and of art-products is, of course, mainly out of the question, from the absence of material. But in the study of modern art, it should always be remembered that M. Taine's method is only one side of a complete view. Much gratitude, however, is due him for his valuable contributions to one portion of the science of art-history.

> *[William Dean Howells], in a review of "History of English Literature," in* The Atlantic Monthly, *Vol. XXIX, No. CLXXII, February, 1872, p. 241.*

LESLIE STEPHEN   (essay date 1873)

[*Many scholars consider Stephen the most important literary critic of the Victorian age after Matthew Arnold. He has been praised for his moral insight and judgment, as well as for his intellectual vigor. However, many others, who consider him less influential than and certainly inferior to Arnold in his contribution to English literature, argue that his work was deficient in aesthetic and formal analysis and that he failed to reconcile his moral and historical philosophies. In the following excerpt from his review of* History of English Literature, *Stephen discusses many of Taine's opinions on English writers. Though he credits Taine with applying "a genuine comparative method" in his criticism, Stephen argues that Taine's theories, with their reliance on generalization and a priori conclusions, sometimes lead him to make "superficial" judgments. Stephen's comments first appeared in the* Fortnightly Review *in December 1873.*]

M. Taine's [*History of English Literature*] has attained a degree of popularity which is in some sense a sufficient proof of its merits. M. Taine's critical judgments are at times irritating; his philosophy may be questionable; and his leading principles are sometimes overlaid with such a mass of epigrammatic illustration that we have some difficulty in distinctly grasping their meanings. To protest against some of these faults is indeed the purpose of this paper. And yet, whatever his faults, it is impossible not to be grateful to him. He has done for us what no native author had done, or, it may be, was able to do. Most of our home-bred critics, however keen their insight, failed to supplement their microscopic acuteness of vision by the application of a genuine comparative method. We still frequently discuss Shakespeare as we discuss the Bible; we regard him, that is, as an isolated phenomenon unrelated to the general movement of European, or even of English thought. M. Taine has done much to inculcate a sounder method, and to widen our intellectual horizon. He has the force which belongs to the apostle of a new theory, who preaches it in season and out of season, and inevitably rather exaggerates its value. Our thick English heads are all the better for incessant hammering upon a single point. With admirable persistence, one of our historians has managed to drill us into a faint belief in the truth that there were Englishmen before William the Conqueror; and M. Taine is rendering an analogous service in proving to us that as our history is continuous, so our great writers are the natural expressions of its dominant ideas. Let us add that he has that special felicity, characteristic of Frenchmen generally, that in spite of all his reiterations of a single doctrine, he is quite incapable of becoming a bore. Once taken up, it is always hard to lay him down.

That his fundamental doctrine is substantially true may be at once assumed. We ought to study the organism in connection with the medium. Botany becomes more fruitful as we investigate the relations between a given flora and the various conditions of its growth. In the same way a Dante, a Shakespeare, or a Goethe is a flower of literature in no merely fanciful metaphor. We first understand the full significance of their writings when we have made ourselves familiar with the intellectual soil from which they spring. There is, however, one obvious limitation upon the value of this truth. Briefly stated, it is that even Frenchmen are not omniscient and infallible. An angel might possibly predict the occurrence of a Shakespeare in the world as certainly as a chemist can foretell the appearance of a crystal in his crucible under given conditions. We, however, are a long way below the angels. We have not analysed human nature into its primary constituent elements; and still less can we say how they are affected by surrounding circumstances. Granting that a science of history is conceivable, its bases are scarcely laid. Trying to describe the peculiarities of a race or climate, we feel at once the absence of anything like a scientific nomenclature. Our words express mere rough popular generalisations, and at every step we say too little or too much. Far from having arrived at the stage of prediction, we have not yet arrived at the stage of trustworthy observation. We are limited to mere empirical statements, and are reduced to the unsatisfactory method of *ex post facto* explanations. We cannot predict a Shakespeare, though when he has actually come, we can give some ostensible proof that he must have appeared in this shape and no other. Indeed, the process is only too easy. An uncomfortable misgiving besets us when we read M. Taine's lucid explanations. Are they not too lucid? Is he not accounting for the planetary orbits before he has discovered the theory of gravitation? Suppose, to make a wild hypothesis, that he had somehow been under the delusion that Balzac, Pascal, and Montaigne were Englishmen, and that Byron, Pope, and Hobbes were Frenchmen, would not his ingenuity have been equal to the task of reconciling the phenomenon to his theories? His theories, in short, may be admirable, but they are of necessity liable to the objection that, having been made after the facts, they are not susceptible of independent verification.

The difficulty grows as we examine M. Taine's arguments in greater detail. The national character, he tells us, is determined by three causes—the race, the *milieu*, the epoch. Giving a sufficiently wide interpretation to these words, there can be no doubt of it. If you understand the nature of a plum-pudding (Englishmen, M. Taine tells us, like homely illustrations), the temperature of the water in which it is placed, and the stage of cooking at which it has arrived, you can tell pretty well how it will taste. But when for a plum-pudding you substitute the more complex phenomenon of a race, and the cooking process is represented by the infinitely complex forces which mould human character, the problem becomes something of the hardest. By the *milieu* M. Taine seems generally to understand the climate. The influence of climate upon constitution is itself a problem of vast perplexity; even such a simple generalisation as the connection between drunkenness and fogs, of which M. Taine elsewhere assumes the truth, would require to be tested by a whole series of observations, never yet made. Climate, again, is but one condition amongst many. How many peculiarities of the English political and social constitution, and therefore indirectly of our modes of thought and literature,

result from our insularity and from the geological conditions of our soil? It is easy to trace the reflection of English scenery in the descriptive passages of Spenser, Thomson, and Wordsworth; but this is at most a superficial influence, and is far removed indeed from supplying a base for scientific theories. M. Taine carries his remarks rather further than Voltaire's crude statement that there are certain days of east wind in London when it is customary for people to hang themselves; but his criticism does not always go much deeper. M. Taine, indeed, does not really trouble himself to trace back English peculiarities to the source which he indicates. He is content in practice to start from a lower point; and to regard the race as already acclimatised. He assumes our idiosyncrasy to be sufficiently well known, and only suggests vaguely the general conditions by which it may have been developed.

Is this idiosyncrasy sufficiently known? Can we really say with any precision in what respects an Englishman differs from a Frenchman? Is our knowledge of the subject really entitled to be called in any sense scientific, or does it merely consist of those rough, empirical approximations, which may give some practical guidance, but fail to supply sufficient rules for satisfactory theorising? M. Taine's main distinction is certainly vague enough. He habitually contrasts the northern with what he sometimes calls the classical races, and seems to assume that each race conforms to a well-ascertained type. Can there, we are prompted to ask, be much value in so rough a division? On the one side we have the English races considered as a single unit. Yet it is plain that in spite of all the levelling influences of civilisation, the inhabitants of the British Islands are as far as possible from being homogeneous. The Englishman differs from the Irishman as widely as he differs from the Frenchman. Climate has not extinguished all contrasts between the Celtic and the Teutonic imaginations. M. Taine does not condescend to take account of these minutiae. . . . [His] modes of reasoning suggest that after all M. Taine is, like the rest of us, in the days of superficial classification. A physicist who has only got so far as to divide the material world into four elements, is not yet capable of making a really scientific statement. We are still in the analogous position in regard to races of men. That even with such rough generalities, a man may make very instructive remarks is possible enough. I only observe that it is altogether premature to give ourselves the airs of scientific accuracy. Our efforts to make faithful portraits are too much like trying to paint miniatures with a mop. Endless confusion is produced, and the apparently precise statements crumble in our hands. M. Taine is better than his philosophy; but it is because his showy generalities generally cover clever remarks about the difference between Englishmen and Frenchmen; and here, if not scientific, he can be picturesque and approximately accurate.

Before examining his account of the English character, however, it is necessary to say a word or two upon his third condition. The epoch, it is undeniable, must be taken into account in discussing the psychology of a people. What, then, is the epoch? M. Taine speaks of the mediaeval period, the renaissance, the classical and the modern periods. To each of those periods belongs an appropriate philosophy, an appropriate social organisation, and, as the result of both, an appropriate tone of sentiment which expresses itself in the contemporary literature. For the most part, M. Taine is content to give rather a picturesque description than a philosophical analysis of the peculiarities of the time. He accumulates a number of vivid details and acute critical remarks which show how the English nobleman in a wig is the old feudal baron in disguise; how

Puritanism was already latent in our mediaeval religion; and how Byron was but a new avatar of the old Berserker spirit. One mode of characterisation is comparatively neglected. As he was not writing a history of thought, but of literature, it is of course natural that he should dwell rather upon the general temper of the period than upon the particular dogmas which were current. He has therefore occupied himself more with our poets and novelists than with our theologians and philosophers. Hobbes and Locke interest him as illustrations of character rather than as landmarks for the history of speculation. The plan of his book imposed this restriction upon him; but at times it seems to lead him into a certain injustice, or, at least, incompleteness of view. The epoch cannot be fairly understood without taking into account the speculative stage which has been reached. As M. Taine truly says, "beneath every literature there is a philosophy"; and, if you put the philosophy out of sight, you are apt to misunderstand the literature. (pp. 81-7)

Much that he says is but the reproduction, in a more pretentious form, of the good old theory symbolised by the figure of John Bull. Hogarth, in one of his pictures, represents the jovial Englishman confronted by the wretched frog-eaters at Calais; and M. Taine gives us the frog-eaters' view of the contrast. We are large, overfed, beer, port wine, and gin swilling animals; coarse, burly, and pachydermatous, with little external sensibility, and no love for things of the intellect; but yet with strong passions which sometimes express themselves in broad humour, and sometimes give birth to a rich but overcharged poetry. All this, however, which sometimes verges upon caricature, is no more than we have heard before. It does not require a philosopher, with theories about race, climate, and epoch, to tell us as much. The first drawing in *Charivari* of a British Goddam gives the same theory in a coarser shape; and it has certainly been familiar since the days of Froissart. That there is a great deal of truth in the doctrine is indeed undeniable. Vague as are most international judgments, there are yet some contrasts too striking not to be perceived. A man must be extremely inferior to M. Taine who could not roughly indicate the difference between Shakespeare and Corneille, or between Voltaire and Dr. Johnson. On the other hand, such general remarks do not take us very far. When M. Taine has pointed out that an English writer is more harsh and positive than the analogous Frenchman, he has gone but a little way towards defining his real character. Beneath the qualities which make a man English there lie the qualities which make him a man; and if you stop short at the specific differences you do not reach the essence. M. Taine's criticism is thus apt to become superficial. A French critic of the old school was satisfied to point out that in the English drama murders were committed on the stage, and ribaldry mixed with the most solemn sentiments; and then summarily condemned us as hopeless barbarians. M. Taine is too scientific in spirit and too generous in feeling to agree in these rash judgments; and yet he is often content to stop at the same point. The want of classical taste is the one fact which occurs to him about many of our writers, and that failing, though it does not make him deliberately unjust, prevents him from really sympathising with their spirit. Too often we see the old Frenchman under the mask of the modern psychologist, and we feel that, with all his philosophy, he can only hold up his hands in amazement at our grotesque modes of thought. . . . M. Taine has laboured conscientiously and sometimes with remarkable success to train himself in the English taste; but we are frequently conscious that an innate insensibility to our specific methods renders him an incompetent judge of the finer literary essences. His judgment of our poets often implies a misconception—such at least it appears

to me—of the relative positions which they really occupy in the opinion of competent judges. Mr. Tennyson's *In Memoriam* appears to him to be the cold and monotonous lamentation of a "correct gentleman, with brand new gloves," who wipes away his tears at a funeral with a cambric handkerchief; whilst he speaks of the idylls with rather an exaggerated enthusiasm. This opinion, as I fancy, follows rather from a theory as to what Mr. Tennyson ought to be, than from a perception of what he really is. (pp. 91-2)

[However], M. Taine has certain theories which, though not systematically expounded, are frequently indicated with more or less clearness. The Englishman, so far as I can venture to state his doctrine, is a combination of two distinct characters. Sometimes, he tells us, we give up everything to liberty, sometimes we enslave everything to rule. Our frames are too vigorous and too unyielding. Some of us, "alarmed by the fire of an overfed temperament and by the energy of unsocial passions," regard nature as dangerous, and place her in a straitwaistcoat of propriety, morality, and religion. The restraint gradually becomes too severe; and then nature breaks her fetters and gives herself up to excesses. Shakespeare, we are told, led to the reaction of the Puritans, Milton produced Wycherley, Congreve Defoe, and Wilberforce Lord Byron. This struggle is represented in the period of which he is speaking by Fielding and Richardson. An Englishman is always oscillating vehemently between these two extremes. He is a Berserker (M. Taine is fond of the Berserkers) in a black coat and white tie. He behaves for a long time with an overstrained decorum, which makes him rather ridiculous and very tiresome to his neighbours; and then suddenly the old madness fires his blood, and, like a half-reclaimed savage, he throws off his decent apparel and furiously runs amuck, hewing down every impediment that comes in his way. The theory has certainly some conveniences. At first sight it seems to be so wide as to include almost every conceivable case. Every Englishman, and indeed every human being, must be somewhere between the extremes of obedience to law and revolt from law, and it is easy enough to recognise in every writer an admixture of these two different elements. M. Taine, however, means to express something more than this. He means to say that the characteristic of English writers is an incapacity for obeying the dictates of that moderate good sense which gives laws to French literature. If the Puritan element predominates in him he becomes a bore, and preaches eternal sermons of flat morality. If he has a dash of Berserker blood, he takes leave of all decency, and plunges into artistic as well as moral extravagances. He is like an overfed horse, who can be forced to walk by a strong hand, but, if allowed the least liberty, will break into a mad gallop. And therefore he is incapable of that regulated energy which is characteristic of the classical school. His merit is in his outbursts of demoniac power; and he is wanting in a sense of harmony and proportion. It would be curious to inquire how far this theory is confirmed by our political history, and whether, as it would seem to imply, Englishmen have been more remarkable than their neighbours for vehement alternations between tyranny and licence. Nothing, as we are frequently told, is more characteristic of Englishmen than their love of compromise. How is this tendency to be reconciled with a theory which should make them conspicuous for a love of extremes? The theory is picturesque rather than scientific, and though it enables M. Taine to describe certain aspects of English literature with great vividness, it breaks down when we try to interpret it too strictly. The thesis suggested seems to be in one respect fundamentally erroneous. If by the Berserker element in the English race he means their capacity for deep emotion and gloomy imagination, this capacity does not really involve an unwillingness to obey laws, but only to obey a particular kind of laws. M. Taine sometimes seems to mistake for mere licence conformity to a type differing from his own ideal. (pp. 95-7)

M. Taine's incapacity for appreciating English humour often hinders his perception of the guiding principle of our best writers. Gothic architecture has its rules, as well as Classical; though it may be that they are not so easily reducible to a simple code. A critic who fancies that it is purely arbitrary because it allows certain liberties which he condemns, has merely abandoned the problem on account of its complexity. Humour condemns certain faults as rigorously as the "classical" taste condemns others. If our realism, our tolerance of harsh contrasts, and our occasional buffoonery is disagreeable to M. Taine, so the frigid conventionalities, the empty generalities, and the irreverent intrusions of epigram of some French writers are disagreeable to us. Our sense of humour makes us laugh at the pompous declamation of a French tragedy, as his sense of proportion makes him laugh at our more highly coloured extravagances. With all his laudable anxiety to enter into the spirit of English writing, M. Taine can never really believe that our daring disregard of foreign conventionalities can be anything but wanton caprice. "Burke," he says, in his summary fashion, "has no taste, nor have his compeers." Burke certainly has not the French taste; but if M. Taine really believes that the grand rhetoric of Burke, of Jeremy Taylor, or Milton, or Sir Thomas Browne is produced by a kind of strange accident; that it is the result of a writer simply throwing the reins upon the neck of his imagination, and letting it carry him whither it will, he might believe that Westminster Abbey was built by mere wild fancy confined by an artistic principle. The theory of this literary style has been admirably expounded by De Quincey, himself no mean master of the art, but, unfortunately, far blinder than M. Taine to the merits of styles differing from his own. De Quincey is as unable to see the art of Swift as M. Taine to perceive the art of Burke. To have a fair account of English literature we should combine the two modes of judgment. To the writers of whom Swift is the most eminent type, M. Taine really does justice. Though we may differ from some of his opinions about Swift, Burns, and Byron, we must admit that his essay upon each of them is instructive and appreciative. They possess in common a quality which, though emphatically English, belongs to that side of English character with which a Frenchman can sympathise. That masculine vigour confined by sturdy common sense, which animates the style of Hobbes and Chillingworth in the seventeenth century, of Swift and Defoe in Queen Anne's days, and which was transmitted through Cobbett to some of our best modern periodical writing, is thoroughly English, and yet has an analogy to the French sparkle and clearness. A critic to whom Voltaire is the type of literary excellence, can admire the more clumsy, less brilliant, but richer and more impassioned style of Swift. The Berserker energy fires a mind, not indeed bound by rigid rules, but concentrated by its own passion upon a distinct purpose. The eloquence pours along a narrow channel, instead of spreading itself like a deluge over a wide surface. The imagination is not indulged in the apparently arbitrary freaks of the lawless Berserker, because it is in the service of a masterful emotion. And under such conditions, M. Taine can heartily admit its force without being shocked by its capriciousness. This is what he really admires in Byron, whose love of the classical school expressed, as M. Taine truly says, a genuine tendency of his nature. The glowing and concentrated passion atones for his occasional affectations and his wayward humour. Though not polished after the French model,

his vigour spontaneously produces the unity of effect which is wanting in less passionate natures. (pp. 105-07)

Stripping M. Taine's remarks [on Shakespeare] of their epigrammatic surroundings, his criticism may be summed up by saying that Shakespeare . . . was a madman. It was in no mere figure of speech that his eye rolled in poetic frenzy, whilst his pen swarmed with images from heaven and earth, heaped together with incongruous profusion. His style is a "compound of furious expressions." "Raving exaggerations . . . the whole fury of the ode, inversion of ideas, accumulation of images, the horrible and the divine, are jumbled into one line." He "never writes a word without shouting it." Hamlet talks in "the style of frenzy." His vehemence will be explained by the fact that he was half-mad; but the truth is that he was Shakespeare. Now Shakespeare "never sees things tranquilly"; his "convulsive metaphors" seem to "have been written by a fevered hand in a night's delirium," and so on through pages in which the same criticism is presented to us in a hundred different forms. . . . [He] has no sense of social proprieties, for his nobles, such as Coriolanus, use the language of modern coalheavers; he cares nothing for virtue, for he sympathises with the ribaldry of Falstaff and the cynicism of Iago. The purity of his women is a mere matter of organisation, not of principle. He has no sense of religion, for to him the future life is merely a scene where the gloomy forebodings of Claudio will be fulfilled, or at best the sleep which perchance may be broken by fearful dreams. (pp. 107-08)

I do not wish to argue for a moment that Shakespeare was much given to preaching moral truths. M. Taine's judgment, though exaggerated, gives one side of the truth. Shakespeare's characters do as a rule act by overpowering impulses, and are not calculating utilitarians. What morality he actually preaches does not take the form of concrete maxims, but is diffused through the general spirit of his writing. He is a moral writer in this sense, that he was (as I venture to say in spite of M. Taine's theories) one of the sanest and healthiest of men. He produces a moral effect, not because he lectures us, but because in reading him we feel that we are in contact with a mind erring in tolerance rather than rigidity, sensuous rather than ascetic, but still blessed with superabundant health. Nothing is more characteristic of him than that intense delight in all natural beauty which appears in so many of the most exquisitely poetic passages in his writing and in our language. To consider his love of the "meanest flower that blows," of the moonlight forest, and the enchanted island, as a mere reaction from overstrained excitement, is to distort his whole character. This marvellous tenderness is part of the very groundwork of his nature, and could exist only in a mind unpoisoned by the vices which he contemplates. What we know of Shakespeare's life (putting aside strained inferences from uncertain interpretations of the sonnets) is clearly in harmony with this view. M. Taine makes it a kind of miracle that Shakespeare, unlike so many of his brother dramatists, made money like a good man of business, and retired to enjoy a country life. The miracle is only that it contradicts M. Taine's theories. . . . Shakespeare, according to M. Taine, is irreligious, because he holds that our little lives are rounded with a sleep. Shakespeare, no doubt, was potentially a Prospero and a Hamlet, and could feel their despair and the awe with which they looked upon the gloom of the surrounding universe. But Shakespeare was of necessity something more than any one of his characters. He was not essentially gloomy because he could feel that mysterious awe which comes upon every noble and imaginative nature looking out upon this little island in the infinite. As M. Taine remarks, Mr. Carlyle shares the awe and is fond of repeating that our lives are such stuff as dreams are made of. The fact is sufficient to prove that the sentiment is not incompatible with a deep religious feeling. That Shakespeare was not a professed theologian is true enough, but I think that M. Taine, of all people, should scarcely cast it in his teeth, and infer that he is speaking in his own character, when for dramatic purposes he makes a coward express a slavish fear of hell. The temper expressed in such utterances as those which Mr. Carlyle delights to repeat, is indicative, not of mere gloom or sordid cowardice, but of the solemn sense of the visionary and transitory nature of the world which must be in the background of every grand imagination. And therefore I venture to conclude that here, too, M. Taine's confidence in certain *a priori* theories about Berserkers, and other types of national character, has led him to overcharge one side of his portrait so strongly that we cannot accept it for a faithful representation of our greatest literary celebrity. (pp. 109-11)

> Leslie Stephen, *"Taine's 'History of English Literature',"* in his Men, Books, and Mountains: Essays, *edited by S.O.A. Ullmann, University of Minnesota Press, 1956, pp. 81-111.*

HIPPOLYTE ADOLPHE TAINE   (essay date 1875)

[*In this excerpt from his 1875 preface to* The Ancient Regime, *the first volume of his* The Origins of Contemporary France, *Taine outlines his purpose in undertaking a study of French history and briefly discusses his methodology. For additional commentary by Taine, see excerpts dated 1863 and 1870.*]

In 1849, being twenty-one years of age, and an elector, I was very much puzzled, for I had to vote for fifteen or twenty deputies, and, moreover, according to French custom, I had not only to determine what candidate I would vote for, but what theory I should adopt. I had to choose between a royalist or a republican, a democrat or a conservative, a socialist or a bonapartist; as I was neither one nor the other, nor even anything, I often envied those around me who were so fortunate as to have arrived at definite conclusions. After listening to various doctrines, it seemed to me that I was laboring under some mental defect. The motives that influenced others did not influence me. I could not comprehend how, in political matters, a man should be governed by his preferences. My affirmative friends planned a constitution the same as a house, according to the latest, simplest, and most complete notion of it, and many were offered for acceptance—the mansion of a marquis, the house of a common citizen, the tenement of a laborer, the barracks of a soldier, the philanstery of a socialist, and even the camp of savages. Each claimed that his was "the true habitation for man, the only one in which a sensible person could live." I was not satisfied with such reasons, for I did not regard personal tastes as authoritative. It seemed to me that a house should not be built for the architect alone, nor for itself, but for the owner who was to occupy it.—Referring to the owner for his advice, submitting to the French people the plans of its future habitation, would evidently be either for show or to deceive them; such a question, in such a case, answers itself, and, besides, were the answer allowable, France was scarcely better prepared for it than myself; the combined ignorance of ten millions is not the equivalent of one man's wisdom. A people may be consulted and, in an extreme case, may declare what form of government it would like best, but not that which it most needs. Nothing but experience can determine this; it must have time to ascertain whether the political

structure is convenient, substantial, able to withstand inclemencies, and adapted to customs, habits, occupations, characters, peculiarities and caprices. For example, the one we have tried has never satisfied us; we have demolished it thirteen times in twenty years that we might set it up anew, and always in vain, for never have we found one that suited us. If other people have been more fortunate, or if various political structures abroad have proved stable and enduring, it is because these have been erected in a special way, around some primitive, massive pile, supported by an old central edifice, often restored but always preserved, gradually enlarged, and, after numerous trials and additions, adapted to the wants of its occupants. Never has one been put up instantaneously, after an entirely new design, and according to the measurements of pure reason. It is well to admit, perhaps, that there is no other way of erecting a permanent building, and that the sudden contrivance of a new, suitable, and enduring constitution is an enterprise beyond the forces of the human mind.

In any event, I concluded for myself that, if we ever discover the one we want, it will not be through the processes now in vogue. In effect, the point is, to *discover* it, whether it exists, and not to submit it to a vote. Our preferences, in this respect, would be vain; nature and history have elected for us in advance; we must accommodate ourselves to them as it is certain that they will not accommodate themselves to us. The social and political forms into which a people may enter and *remain* are not open to arbitration, but are determined by its character and its past. All, even down to the minutest details, should be moulded on the living features for which they are designed; otherwise, they will break and fall to pieces. Hence it is that, if we succeed in finding our constitution, it will come to us only through a study of ourselves, and the more thoroughly we know ourselves, the greater our certainty in finding the one that suits us. We must, accordingly, set aside the usual methods and have a clear conception of the nation before drawing up its constitution. The former is, undoubtedly, a more serious and more difficult task than the latter. What time, what study, what observations correcting each other, what researches into the past and the present, in all the domains of thought and of action, what manifold, secular efforts are necessary for acquiring a full and precise idea of a great people, which has already lived to a great age, and which still lives on! Only in this way, however, can what is sound be established after having resorted to empty theories, and I resolved, for my own part, at least, that, should I ever attempt to form a political opinion, it would be only after studying France.

What is contemporary France? To answer this question, requires a knowledge of how France was formed, or, what is much better, being present at her formation, as if a spectator. At the close of the last century she undergoes a transformation, like that of an insect shedding its coat. Her ancient organization breaks up; she herself rends the most precious tissues and falls into convulsions which seem mortal. And then, there is recovery, after multiplied throes and a painful lethargy. But her organization is no longer what it was; a new being, after terrible internal travail, is substituted for the old one. In 1808, all her leading features are definitely established: departments, *arrondissements,* cantons and communes—no change has since taken place in her outward divisions and adjunctions; the Concordat, the Code, the tribunals, the University, the Institute, the prefects, the Council of State, the imposts, the tax-collectors, the Cour des Comptes, with a centralized and uniform administration—its principal organs remain the same; henceforth, every class, the nobles, the commonalty, the laboring class, and the peasants—each has the place, interests, sentiments and traditions that we now observe at the present day. Thus, the new organism is at once stable and complete. Its structure, its instincts, and its faculties indicate beforehand the circle within which its thought or action will be exercised. Surrounding nations, some precocious, others backward, all with greater caution, and many with more success, effect the same transformation in passing from the feudal to the modern State; the parturition is universal and nearly simultaneous. But in the new, as well as under the old form, the weak are always the prey of the strong. Woe to those whose too tardy evolution has subjected them to the neighbor suddenly emerged from his chrysalis state fully armed! Woe likewise to him whose too violent and too brusque evolution has disturbed the balance of internal economy, and who, exaggerating his governing means, radically changing fundamental organs, impoverishing by degrees his vital substance, is condemned to rash undertakings, to debility and to impotence, surrounded by better proportioned and healthier neighbors! In the organization effected by France at the beginning of the century all the main lines of her contemporaneous history are traceable,—political revolutions, social utopias, the divisions of classes, the rôle of the Church, the conduct of the nobles, of the bourgeoisie and of the people, and the development, direction or deviation of philosophy, literature and science. Hence it is that, in striving to comprehend our actual situation, we constantly revert back to the terrible and fruitful crisis by which the Ancient Régime produced the Revolution, and the Revolution the Modern Régime.

The Ancient Régime, the Revolution, the Modern Régime, are the three conditions of things which I shall strive to describe with exactitude [in *The Origins of Contemporary France*]. I have no hesitation in stating that this is my sole object. A historian may be allowed the privilege of a naturalist; I have regarded my subject the same as the metamorphosis of an insect. The event, furthermore, is so interesting as to render it worthy of study for itself alone; no effort is necessary to exclude mental reservations. Without taking any side, curiosity becomes scientific and centres on the secret forces which direct the wonderful process. These forces consist of the situation, the passions, the ideas, and the wills of each group of actors, and which can be defined and almost measured. They are in full view; we need not resort to conjecture about them, to doubtful surmises, to vague indications. We enjoy the singular good fortune of seeing the men themselves, their exterior and their interior. The Frenchmen of the ancient régime are still within visual range. All of us, in our youth, have encountered one or more of the survivors of this vanished society. Many of their dwellings, with the furniture, still remain intact. Their pictures and engravings enable us to take part in their domestic life, see how they dress, observe their attitudes and follow their movements. Through their literature, philosophy, scientific pursuits, gazettes, and correspondence, we can reproduce their feeling and thought, and even enjoy their familiar conversation. The multitude of memoirs, issuing during the past thirty years from public and private archives, lead us from one drawing-room to another, as if we bore with us so many letters of introduction. The independent descriptions by foreign travellers, in their journals and correspondence, correct and complete the portraits which this society has traced of itself. Everything that it could state has been stated, except what was commonplace and well-known to contemporaries, whatever seemed technical, tedious and vulgar, whatever related to the provinces, to the bourgeoisie, to the peasant, to the laboring man, to the government, and to the household. It has been my aim to supply these omissions, and make France known to others

outside the small circle of the literary and the cultivated. . . . I have been able to examine a mass of manuscript documents, consisting of the correspondence of numerous intendants, customs-directors, farmers-general, magistrates, employees and private individuals, of every kind and degree, during the last thirty years of the ancient regime, including reports and memorials belonging to the various departments of the royal household, the *procès-verbaux* and *cahiers* of the States-General, contained in one hundred and seventy-six volumes, the despatches of military officers in 1789 and 1790, the letters, memoirs and detailed statistics, preserved in the one hundred boxes of the ecclesiastical committee, the correspondence, in ninety-four files, of the department and municipal authorities, with the ministries from 1790 to 1799, the reports of the Councillors of State on mission at the end of 1801, the reports of prefects under the Consulate, the Empire, and the Restoration down to 1823, and such a quantity of unknown and instructive documents besides these that the history of the Revolution seems, indeed, to be still unwritten. In any event, it is only such documents which can portray to us all these animated figures, the lesser nobles, the curates, the monks, the nuns of the provinces, the aldermen and bourgeoisie of the towns, the attorneys and syndics of the country villages, the laborers and artisans, the officers and the soldiers. These alone enable us to contemplate and appreciate in detail the various conditions of humanity, the interior of a parsonage, of a convent, of a town-council, the wages of a workman, the produce of a farm, the taxes levied on a peasant, the duties of a tax-collector, the expenditure of a noble or prelate, the budget, retinue and ceremonial of a court. Thanks to such resources, we are able to give precise figures, to know hour by hour the occupations of a day and, better still, read off the bill of fare of a grand dinner, and recompose all parts of a full-dress costume. We have again, on the one hand, samples of the materials of the dresses worn by Marie Antoinette, pinned on paper and classified by dates, and, on the other, we can tell what clothes were worn by the peasant, describe the bread he ate, specify the flour it was made of, and state the cost of a pound of it in *sous* and *deniers*. With such resources one becomes almost contemporary with the men whose history one writes and, more than once, in the Archives, I have found myself speaking almost aloud with them while tracing their old handwriting on the time-stained paper before me. (pp. 3-8)

> *Hippolyte Adolphe Taine, in a preface to his* The Origins of Contemporary France, *edited by Edward T. Gargan, translated by John Durand, The University of Chicago Press, 1974, pp. 3-8.*

HENRY JAMES   (essay date 1875)

[*In this excerpt from a review originally published in the* Nation *in May 1875, James evaluates Taine's* Notes on Paris *as a "brilliant failure."*]

[*Notes on Paris*] is a very clever work, but it is by no means one of the author's most successful. Indeed, though a brilliant failure, no one, we believe, has ever pretended that it was anything but a failure. The author has tried a *tour de force,* and missed his effect. He has attempted to force his talent, but his talent has resisted and proved fatally inflexible. He has wished to be light and graceful, but he has succeeded only in being most elaborately and magnificently grave. For M. Taine to attempt lightness was, it seems to us, a most ill-advised undertaking. It is true that he has been charged, as the historian of English literature, with a certain presumptuous levity of judgment; but in form, at least, he is always solid, weighty, and majestic. There are few writers whom, as simple writers, we prefer; his style is full of color and muscle and savor; but we never suppose ourselves, in reading it, to be dabbling in light literature, and we rarely take it but in moderate quantities at a sitting. If M. Taine treats a subject at all, he bears heavily; the touch-and-go manner is a closed book to him. Here he has tried the touch-and-go manner, and the effect is very much like hearing a man with a deep bass voice trying to sing an air written for a thin tenor. There is such a thing as being too serious to succeed in a *jeu d'esprit,* and this has been M. Taine's trouble. A writer of half the value would have done much better with the same material. . . . Yet one reads the book, as a failure if not as a success, and, all abatements made, we feel ourselves to be dealing with a man of extraordinary talent. (p. 68)

Exactly what M. Taine desired to do we hardly know; what he has done is to produce a singular compound of Stendhal and Théophile Gautier. Stendhal, as all readers of our author know, is the divinity of whom M. Taine is the prophet. Stendhal invented a method of observation which, in M. Taine's opinion, renewed the whole science of literary and social criticism. This method M. Taine has constantly applied—first to authors and books, then to works of art, and at last, in this case, to men and women, to a society. . . . M. Taine has proposed to do for Paris what Stendhal did for Milan; but he has come fifty years later, and he is consequently much more complex and needs a great deal more machinery. He is picturesque, for instance, both by necessity and by style, which Stendhal was not at all, in intention; his book overflows with the description of material objects—of face and hair, shoulders and arms, jewels, dresses, and furniture—and it is evident in all this description that, although M. Taine is a man of too individual a temperament to be an imitator, he has read Théophile Gautier, the master in this line, with great relish and profit. He is shooting in Gautier's premises, and when he brings down a bird we cannot help regarding it as Gautier's property.

M. Taine has endeavored to imagine a perfect observer, and he has given this gentleman's personality as a setting to his own extremely characteristic lucubrations. His observer is M. Frederic-Thomas Graindorge, a Frenchman, a bachelor, a man of fifty, who has made a fortune by hog-packing in Cincinnati, and returns to Paris in the afternoon of his days to take his ease, see the polite world in epitome, and systematize a little his store of observations. He has gone through the mill and been ground very fine; he was at school at Eton, as a boy; he was afterwards at the University of Jena; he has passed twenty years in our own great West, where his adventures have been of the most remarkable description. In his local color, as to this phase of his hero's antecedents, M. Taine is very much at fault; and this is the greater pity, as he has never failed to profess that one should speak only of that which one directly and personally knows. He knows the manners and customs of our Western States in a very roundabout and theoretical fashion; he seems to be under the impression, for instance, that the picturesque art of hog-packing (up to the time of our late war) was carried on in Cincinnati by slave-labor. "I desire only to listen and to look," says M. Graindorge; "I listen and I look; no woman is displeased at being looked at; nor any man at being listened to. Sometimes, as I button up my overcoat, an idea comes to me: I write it down when I go home; hence my notes. You see that this is not a literary matter." It is much more literary than M. Graindorge admits; and his notes have been for M. Taine quite as much an exercise of style as an

expression of opinion. He writes admirably; he writes too well; he is simply the very transparent mask of the real author. He is, therefore, as a person, a decidedly ineffective creation, and it was hardly worth while to be at so much labor to construct him. But the point was that M. Taine desired full license to be sceptical and cynical, to prove that he had no prejudices; that he judged things not sentimentally but rationally; that he saw the workings of the *machine humaine* completely *à nu,* and he could do all this under cover of a fictitious M. Graindorge more gracefully than in his own person. M. Graindorge is the most brutal of materialists, and the more he watches the great Parisian spectacle, the greater folly it seems to him to be otherwise. He finds it all excessively ugly, except in so far as it is redeemed by a certain number of pretty women in beautiful dresses, cut very low. But though it is ugly, it is not depressing; exaltation and depression have nothing to do with it; the thing is to see—to see minutely, closely, with your own eyes, not to be a dupe, to find it very convenient that others are, to treat life and your fellow-mortals as a spectacle, to relish a good dinner, and keep yourself in as luxurious a physical good-humor as possible until the "machine" stops working. That of M. Graindorge ceases to operate in the course of the present volume, and the book closes with a statement of his "intimate" personal habits by his secretary, in lieu of a funeral oration. (pp. 69-71)

> *Henry James, "Taine's Notes on Paris," in his* Literary Reviews and Essays on American, English, and French Literature, *edited by Albert Mordell, Vista House Publishers, 1957, pp. 68-71.*

THE NATION (essay date 1876)

[*Praising Taine's accurate portrayal of pre-Revolutionary France, this reviewer compares his* L'ancien régime *with Alexis de Tocqueville's earlier work with the same title.*]

[In **L'ancien régime**], Taine is not an original thinker or a brilliant writer. He is an intelligent and industrious disciple of De Tocqueville. He has thoroughly mastered the principles of his teacher, and though he has added to them no original conclusions of his own, he has brought together an immense mass of facts in support of the views laid down by De Tocqueville in *his Ancien Régime.* Taine's book might, in fact, be considered with justice an appendix to De Tocqueville's treatise, containing a mass of citations and extracts in confirmation of the theories contained in the body of the book. As far as Taine's general views of French history are concerned, he has the merits and also displays the deficiencies of his teacher. Wherever De Tocqueville is strong, there Taine is strong also. Where De Tocqueville failed to grasp any aspect of his subject Taine's insight also fails him. De Tocqueville, for example, certainly failed fully to appreciate the permanent injury done to France by the ruin of French Protestantism. He failed, also, as compared with a writer like Quinet, fully to understand what may be termed the spiritual side of the Revolutionary movement. Precisely the same shortcomings can be discerned in Taine. He alludes very cursorily to the persecution of the Protestants, and, curiously enough, never seems to trace the connection between the triumph of Catholicism and the increase of centralization, to which he, in common with all writers of his school, ascribes the ruin of the *ancien régime.* . . .

But to state that the first volume of **Les Origines de la France contemporaine** will not entitle its author to take his place among historians of the first rank, is quite a different thing from denying that the book has noticeable merits. It is a successful attempt to collect together a body of actual facts about the state of France towards the end of the last century. When we reflect how much obscurity has been thrown over the history of the Revolution by its having been made the theme of rhetoric, of imagination, of invective, or of eulogy, we can scarcely feel too grateful to a man who makes it his business to dismiss as far as possible all vague generalizations, and put before the world trustworthy information as to the actual condition of France before and during the great change which transformed the France of Louis the Sixteenth into the France of Napoleon. Taine has attempted honestly to ground every statement he makes upon an elaborate investigation of authorities on whom reliance can be placed. No one who has not a far greater knowledge of French history than scarcely one educated man in ten thousand can pretend to, is in a position to determine whether so careful a student as Taine has or has not fallen into errors; but the candid reader will not fail to be convinced that the work is one which deserves careful attention, and which has at least two very considerable merits.

The first merit is that the facts which it contains give reality and substance to many general notions the truth of which every English or American reader would admit without fully appreciating their real bearing or force. Thus most of our readers will easily concede that the French *noblesse* excited popular ill-will through the possession of unjust privileges, but it is easy enough to make this admission and yet at the same time entertain very vague and indefinite conceptions as to the nature of these privileges, the persons by whom they were possessed, and the causes which rendered the privileges and their possessors odious to the French nation. Nothing will more certainly dissipate all such vagueness and haziness than a perusal of Taine's first volume. In place of the general outlines supplied by De Tocqueville you have put before you a minute picture of the condition of French society. As you read page after page of petty details and trifling anecdotes of small importance in themselves, each adds a new touch to the drawing, till you may be said, almost without exaggeration, to see the nobility as they actually existed immediately before 1789. (p. 292)

The second merit of Taine's treatise is that his vast accumulation of facts constantly suggests conclusions which are not directly drawn by the author himself. Englishmen, for example, are constantly perplexed to account for the French passion for equality. A study of life under the *ancien régime* fully accounts for the origin at any rate of this sentiment. Inequality, or in other words privilege, was, down to the Revolution, the actual source of half the evils under which France suffered. The evils which it caused were felt in all the transactions of daily life, and these evils the Revolution in fact removed. If any one reflects for how great a length of time a sentiment will often survive the state of things which gave rise to it, he will see little cause for wonder that in 1876 Frenchmen should prize above all things the equality which not a century ago was in reality the great need of the country. Another phenomenon of modern French society is, it may be suggested, in part at least attributable to this same source. The desire for Government employment which certainly distinguishes modern Frenchmen is almost certainly, like so many other features in French society, a legacy of the monarchy. In the eighteenth century Government employment had two great recommendations: to the ordinary man it offered an escape from many burdens; to the man of energy or benevolence it offered the one sphere for display either of political ability or public spirit. The attraction in this case has also survived the state of society which made

Government employment specially attractive. In nothing, however, does the suggestiveness of Taine's facts appear in a stronger light than in that occasional tendency to force upon the mind of the reader an inference to which Taine himself does not, as we have already pointed out, appear to attach as much importance as it deserves. The conclusion that the fall of Protestantism gave, if not a deadly, yet certainly a most serious blow to the prosperity of France, is one which the Catholic sympathies of De Tocqueville disinclined him to draw. Here as elsewhere Taine is silent where his teacher has not spoken, but the facts he collects tell their own tale. (p. 293)

"Taine's Ancien Régime," in The Nation, *Vol. XXII, No. 566, May 4, 1876, pp. 292-93.*

W. F. RAE   (essay date 1876)

[*In this excerpt from his introduction to* Notes on England, *Rae faults Taine's methodology for being too systematized, but praises the artistry of his travel sketches. For additional commentary by Rae, see excerpts dated 1861 and 1864.*]

A critic is commonly supposed to be a man who, having carefully studied certain subjects, is specially qualified for giving an opinion upon the way in which these subjects have been treated by an author, a painter, an architect, an orator. The critic may either announce his decision after having applied to the matter in hand certain fixed rules or canons, or else he may enumerate his own rules and express an independent judgment. In any case the critique is a reasoned or arbitrary opinion, and nothing more. It may be disputed, if the standard to which the critic appeals has not been fairly and adequately applied. It may be disregarded, if the personal opinion appears to be merely an individual crotchet. To expect that the result could ever be accepted as universally and implicitly as the demonstrations of an authority in the natural sciences, of a botanist and a zoologist, is what no critic of eminence, with one conspicuous exception, has hitherto ventured to do.

That exception is M. Taine. He believes that he has succeeded in removing all ambiguity and fluctuation from critical judg-

An illustration from Notes on Paris.

ments by following a particular method of procedure. He professes to have eliminated chance from ethical products, to have found a clue to the labyrinth of the mind. The ordinary saying that man is a creature of circumstances, he employs as a philosophical formula. The purport of his main contention and fundamental proposition is that man is the unconscious agent and manifestation of unseen forces. In his opinion, these forces may be measured, though they cannot be grasped; may be classified, though they cannot be directly controlled. He considers it practicable, by duly estimating and carefully determining their nature and effect, to explain why an author, artist, or architect produced a particular book, painting, or edifice; why an age was distinguished for a particular form of literature, art, or architecture; what was the mental history of past generations as exhibited in the writings or doings of individuals. In short, M. Taine deciphers the man in the age, and the age in the man, and becomes the historian of the human mind in depicting the events of a particular generation, and in exhibiting the share which the finished work of one era or race has had in moulding the work of the era which has succeeded, or the race which has displaced it. (pp. xxx-xxxi)

These are lofty pretensions. It is because all his writings have been designed to maintain and advocate them, that they have all merited special attention. (p. xxxii)

[My objection to M. Taine's method in his *Notes on England*] appears to me so serious as to be almost fatal. It relates to the fundamental difference between the positions occupied by the botanist and zoologist, and the critic and historian. The former have no personal and national bias in favour of the results of their observations. They may prefer, as a matter of taste, one plant or one animal to another, but this does not interfere in the slightest degree with the manner in which they classify and explain either. They do not care whether a group of plants, or of animals, exists in a particular country and under particular conditions. When a Frenchman examines a flower or dissects a bat, he thinks nothing about the spot on which the flower grew or the bat was produced. But when a Frenchman deals with an author or artist of a foreign nation, he does not forget, nor will he forget until the millennium shall arrive and human nature shall be transmogrified, that he is a Frenchman, and that the author or artist is a foreigner. Intentionally or unconsciously, he judges the eloquence, the style, the diction, the talent, and the works of the foreigner by a French standard and from a French point of view. M. Taine himself is a proof of this. No foreigner has written more acutely and instructively about England and the English than he has done, yet, while the result is admired, the remark is made, either aloud or in a whisper: "Very wonderful, certainly, considering that M. Taine is a Frenchman." Language, that living expression of a nation's mind, is in its essence a sealed book to him who is not one of the nation. There is a flavour in words which a native of the land wherein they are current can alone detect and enjoy. (pp. xlviii-xlix)

After examining the results of M. Taine's method, as applied by him to men of note in the world of art and letters, I do not find that these are so conclusive as to reflect glory upon the method itself. . . . For his particular method . . . , M. Taine exhibits what appears to be a disproportionate affection. He acts with regard to it as Shelley said authors frequently do, resembling mothers in preferring "the children who have given them most trouble." Yet he is noteworthy as a writer not in consequence, but in spite, of his method. Strip off everything relating to it in his several works, and the works themselves

will continue to attract and impress; they will still reflect the beauties of his own mind, and be radiant with the splendours of his brilliant style. Of the method itself, I may say what Condillac said of rules; like the parapet of a bridge, it may hinder a person from falling into the river, but will not help him on his way. M. Taine no more requires it to sustain him than Byron required bladders or corks, to buoy him up when he entered the water, after he had demonstrated his powers by swimming across the Hellespont.

The expectation which he has of ultimately using history for the purpose of framing laws, and so giving to it a place among the natural sciences, is an expectation which no one can entertain who disagrees with him as to first principles, who contemplates the universe in a different fashion, who puts a different interpretation upon the word cause. According to him a cause is a fact; in my opinion it is a figure of speech. He thinks that a fact can be found of such a kind that from it may be deduced the nature, the relations, and changes of the other facts, and that this dominant and generative fact is the cause of the others; I regard the relations of cause and effect simply as sequences. All that we can know or note is that the one follows the other, and to call the one the cause of the other is merely another way of expressing this succession of continuity. Where he detects "dependencies and conditions," I merely perceive successions and appearances. Where he discerns laws, I perceive nothing but explanations, and explanations, too, of the case as put by him. With him I agree in thinking that the result of a closer observation and more careful estimate of facts will be to render both criticism and history more exact and trustworthy. But, after all, the individual critic and historian will announce his individual opinion. He will have no right to demand a hearing on any other ground than mastery of the subject and freedom from obvious and undue bias. He will, if endowed with M. Taine's industry, learning, skill in grouping facts, power in stating opinions, talent in manipulating words, be regarded, as M. Taine is deservedly regarded, as a master of his craft, as an authority in his sphere.

Yet, even if his philosophical views should be established beyond dispute, an insuperable difficulty will remain. To interpret the individual, or a course of historical events, after his fashion would require an investigator so entirely impersonal as to be almost superhuman. A man who had no national leanings or private sympathies might possibly deal with human beings and their literary, artistic, or historical concerns in the same scientific fashion that a physiologist deals with human crania, and a botanist with plants and flowers. So long, however, as it remains true that "there is a great deal of human nature in man," so long will the efforts of the profoundest thinkers and most brilliant writers fail to elevate and alter history and criticism to such an extent and in such a way as to make of them sciences fitted to rank in precision and universality with the recognised natural sciences.

Inability to advocate all M. Taine's pretensions does not imply a want of admiration for what he has performed. He is greater than his method. His own personality is too marked to be concealed under any formula, however abstract; his powers are too rare to fail to extort the admiration of those who may differ the most from him on purely speculative points. His characteristic is a passion for facts; his excellence consists in the skill with which he can turn his facts to the best account. He has a keen appreciation of beauty in every form; he can convey his impressions to a reader in language of singular felicity. He requires the aid of no method to enunciate conclusions which are very plausible and often very just. His judgments are formed on so complete an array of evidence, and with such an unquestionable desire to be impartial, that they deserve to be treated with respect, even when they cannot be implicitly accepted.

In his *Notes on England,* as in all his works, there is no lack of theories which may be called in question, of explanations which are sometimes partial and one-sided, of general views based upon insufficient data. (pp. li-lv)

Generally, however, when M. Taine records his own observations, he is alike acute and correct. Information given him by inexcusably ignorant persons appears to have misled him when he errs the most notably. Thus his informant who told him . . . that medical men are not created peers because "no man who has held out his hands for guineas could take his place among peers of the realm," must have been strangely unacquainted with the fact known to every schoolboy that barristers not only take guineas, but accept them willingly, and that the more guineas they receive, owing to the increase of their practice, the better are their prospects of a seat on the woolsack and elevation to the peerage. Moreover, at least one member of the House of Lords entered it not many years ago solely because, as a banker, he had handled the money of his customers so judiciously as to have accumulated an enormous fortune. After all, however, these slips, and others which the well-informed reader will readily detect, are comparatively trivial blemishes. In estimating the work as a whole, it would be well to exchange, what Chateaubriand called the petty and meagre criticism of defects, for the comprehensive and prolific criticism of beauties. These *Notes on England* are really of first-rate quality; they form an admirable picture of what is truly distinctive and noteworthy. M. Taine approaches so closely to the ideal intelligent foreigner whose advent is so often proclaimed, but whose presence in the flesh we never enjoy; his general tone is so excellent and his endeavour to be fair so conspicuous; his qualifications are so exceptional and his actual achievements give him so clear a title to our esteem; he is so singularly free from the sins which beset his countrymen who retail their experience after having sojourned in this country; he is so sympathetic without stooping to flattery, and so candid without lapsing into discourtesy; he is, in short, such a model traveller, such an acute observer, such a graphic and an artistic narrator, that he merits, what he will doubtless receive, a cordial welcome from all who enjoy reading the opinions of a genial and capable foreign writer upon the social life, the domestic arrangements, the religious sentiments, and the political constitution of this country. (pp. lvii-lix)

W. F. Rae, in an introduction to Notes on England *by H. Taine, translated by W. F. Rae, Henry Holt and Company, 1876, pp. vii-lix.*

JAS. COTTER MORISON (essay date 1878)

[*In discussing Taine's view of history as presented in* The French Revolution, *Morison posits that his seemingly objective stance veils his antirevolutionary sentiments.*]

M. Taine is by far the most conspicuous writer who has taken up the task of criticising the Revolution, and some evidence that he has discharged his task only imperfectly may perhaps be found in the fact that, while he has mortally offended one set of partisans, he has filled another set with delight. The Republicans in France have regarded his [*La révolution*] as nothing short of a scandal, but their Conservative opponents have found it so much to their liking that they have forgiven on the spot a long literary career, which up to this time they have condemned loudly. At the same time M. Taine may justly plead that if he has not offended both parties at the same time, he has offended them alternately, and so far has experienced the usual fate of the critic. His recent work on the *Ancien Régime* was as distasteful to the Conservatives as the present one on the Revolution is to the Liberals. He in the first unsparingly criticised the old Monarchy: in this he unsparingly criticises the Revolution. Neither work is marked by lofty impartiality and sobriety of tone, and each resembles the vehement impeachment of an advocate rather than the calm equity of a judge. Still, as it is difficult to depreciate the old Monarchy without, in a measure, excusing or justifying the Revolution which abolished it; or to depreciate the Revolution without seeming to say a good word for the Monarchy, a sort of balance is established, and a sort of justice is meted out to both, though not in the worthiest form such a great subject deserved. Two blacks do not make one white, and two opposite invectives do not make a thoughtful political work. (p. 236)

Without any great novelty of research, or depth of thought, or charm of style, M. Taine must be admitted to have very seriously damaged the popular views of the Revolution which have been propagated by eminent Republican writers, and obtained general credence. (p. 237)

He proves by accumulated instances of cruelty, outrage, and murder, that the Revolution was from the very first what all unprejudiced persons knew it to be, a fierce uprising of vindictive revenge, and that the pretence that it was made cruel and sanguinary only through the conduct of its natural enemies, the nobles and priests, is one of the most unfounded ever maintained. The pretension is as untrue, as much against the evidence, as the pretension of Roman Catholic divines that the Church has never persecuted, never shed blood, never been cruel and unjust. The evidence which M. Taine adduces to prove his point is by its nature difficult to set forth in a review of this kind. Long extracts from MS, authorities, instructive but somewhat wearisome repetitions of monotonous crimes, of disgusting brutality and violence, fill some hundreds of pages of his volume. One can understand how, writing for the public he addresses, the exhibition *in extenso* of the evidence which supports his case was a wise proceeding. Those who would refute him must prove that his authorities are untrustworthy, or incorrectly cited. As most of them seem to be taken from official records, the task is not likely to be an easy one. In any case it is the business of native critics to control his excerpts from the *Archives Nationales.* That he will be tripped up here and there is highly probable. But that the bulk of his indictment will be rebutted is extremely unlikely. (p. 238)

M. Taine deals with the Republican legend in the way that modern criticism habitually deals with mythical story, by appeal to ascertainable facts. The facts he adduces are certainly not all new—many of them are probably not true—and in any case an impression of one-sidedness and partiality is conveyed by a writer who carefully culls all the damaging charges which can be alleged against one party, and is silent upon everything of an opposite character. But it must still be admitted that M. Taine is an able polemic, and is a master in the art of dropping a cold, penetrating fact, drawn from contemporary authority, into the effervescent theories of his opponents. He shrewdly abstains from personal controversy, in which he shows tactical skill. His book in consequence appears far less controversial than it really is. He seems to be quietly stating his own case, whereas he is replying with veiled vehemence to well-known writers. It is easy to see how one story is told in order to discomfort Michelet, how another is related to damage Louis Blanc; and there is no denying that the small and un-influential class of persons who care seriously for the truth of history have much to gain by this collision of sturdy partisans. The multitude who sympathise with one or the other side, and applaud or execrate as the hits tell for or against them—will, it is needless to say, derive no instruction from M. Taine's labours. But controversy has ever been a bad school for the cultivation of equity, though in the long run it is a necessary stage on the road to impartial conclusions.

M. Taine empties his cornucopia of crimes with such evident and grim satisfaction—he so abounds in ghastly narratives, revolting outrages, and disgusting cruelties, that it is difficult to give a notion of the frightful repast he has prepared for us. We are embarrassed with horrors. . . . (p. 240)

An important section is properly devoted to a less repulsive subject, the trade in corn. Every one is aware that from the date of the famous hailstorm which destroyed the crops in 1788, the question of an adequate supply of corn was constantly discussed. Even when in subsequent years the harvests were fairly good matters did not mend much, and riots all over the country were provoked by the dearness or the insufficiency of bread. M. Taine shows with much force that it was really the mad panics and violence of the people that caused the greater part of their sufferings. . . . On the other hand, M. Taine has neglected to point out, as he was clearly bound to do, that many of the errors of the people in reference to the corn trade had been shared, at least apparently, by their rulers, and that Necker himself had given the signal for alarm by his unwise measures in 1788. And further, although there was monstrous exaggeration abroad in reference to the forestalling of corn, yet the terrible facts which had transpired not many years before in connection with the so-called "Pact of Famine"—when the odious Louis XV. coerced the corn trade to his own profit—were enough to goad a cooler people than the French to madness. Such breaches of historic equity detract much from the value of M. Taine's book, and tend to degrade it to the level of a party pamphlet.

M. Taine touches on several other interesting subjects. . . . For instance, the undoubted and somewhat pathetic fact that although the nobles were the objects of such ferocious hatred on the part of the people, at no time had the upper classes in France been so benevolently inclined to their inferiors. (pp. 243-44)

M. Taine also makes some good remarks on the functions of an aristocracy in a civilised state. It is almost the only occasion on which he allows himself to indulge in a vein of philosophic reflection, for his book, taken as a whole, is one of facts and not of ideas. (p. 244)

Regarded as a contribution to science and serious literature, the work offers occasion, in many ways, to grave objection; but, regarded as the ephemeral production of an able man of letters, one may feel surprise at the tempest of anger which it has called forth on the part of those who hold liberal opinions. . . . If he is free to write and publish what he thinks proper, which surely no sensible person can regret, the reason is that the last French Republic, which has the good will of all civilized men, differs nearly in every particular from its terrible predecessor. (p. 245)

Jas. Cotter Morison, "La Révolution," in Macmillan's Magazine, *Vol. XXXVIII, No. 225, July, 1878, pp. 235-45.*

HENRI FRÉDÉRIC AMIEL   (journal date 1880)

[*In this entry from his journal, Amiel lambastes Taine and the materialist school of writers for their cynicism and degrading view of humankind. For additional commentary by Amiel, see excerpt dated 1871.*]

Stendhal is the novelist after Taine's heart, the faithful painter who is neither moved nor indignant, who is amused by everything, the rascal and the slut as well as the good man and the decent woman, but who has neither belief, nor preference, nor ideal. Literature here is subordinated to natural history, to science; it is no longer one of the *humanities,* it no longer honours man with a rank apart; it ranges him in with the ants, the beavers and the monkeys. This indifferent non-morality encourages a taste for immorality, for the base has more savour than virtue. Vitriol is more singular than sugar, and poisoning presents more phenomena than simple nourishment.

The vice of this whole school is cynicism, contempt for man, who is degraded to the rank of the brute; it is the cult of force, indifference to the soul, a lack of generosity, respect, nobility, which is visible despite all protestations to the contrary, in other words, inhumanity. One cannot be a materialist with impunity; refined as one's culture may be, one is gross, nevertheless. A free mind is a great thing, surely, but elevation of heart, belief in the good, the capacity for enthusiasm and devotion, the thirst for perfection and sanctity is a still finer thing. (p. 599)

Henri Frédéric Amiel, in a journal entry of June 1, 1880, in his The Private Journal of Henri Frédéric Amiel, *translated by Van Wyck Brooks and Charles Van Wyck Brooks, revised edition, Macmillan Publishing Company, 1935, pp. 598-99.*

W. F. ALLEN   (essay date 1881)

[*Analyzing Taine's style as a historian in* The French Revolution, *Allen objects to his method of organizing and presenting the material, partisan tone, and insufficient investigation of causes and effects.*]

[In *The Origins of Contemporary France,* M. Taine's] task is to analyze the several elements out of which contemporary France has been developed. The first of these elements was the Ancient Régime—society and government before the Revolution; this was treated in an analytic and descriptive manner, as befitted the subject. The second element is the Revolution, the great and sudden changes which this society experienced in the course of a very few years. If the first element was a state of society stationary, or nearly so, the second is a movement of society, rapid and violent. This subject, therefore, is not capable of the purely analytic method of the first, but must be treated historically; not description, but narration, must preponderate.

Nevertheless the reader must constantly bear in mind that [in *The French Revolution*] the object of the author is not to write a history of the French Revolution as a great event, but to describe and analyze it as one of the elements out of which the France of the present day has been developed. The chronological order is necessarily followed, and the successive books depict the successive steps in the great movement; but the method is throughout that of the disquisition, and the tone and spirit are philosophical rather than narrative.

There result from this two characteristics, which are proper enough from the point of view of the writer, but at which the reader is disposed to take exception. In the first place, the story is not told in a direct and straightforward manner, but is brought in as it were incidentally to illustrate the theories presented. It is very hard to trace the succession of events, scattered as these are in different chapters; it is even harder to tell when an event happened, because the dates are few and imperfect: even the table of contents is of very little assistance. We cannot all be expected to have at our fingers' ends the whole history of the French Revolution; but M. Taine has little mercy for those who have not. . . . Everything is refined down to theories and ideas, and concrete facts are left to take care of themselves.

A second characteristic of the work is its partisan tone. With certain reservations, this is well enough from M. Taine's point of view. He has by careful study made up his mind as to the influence that the Revolution has had upon modern France, and his conclusion is that this influence was wholly bad, and inexcusably so. To the reader of the same author's *Ancient Régime* it may appear that a condition of things so rotten and oppressive as that depicted in that volume needed to be swept away, even if it must be by so violent a storm. Without justifying evil passions and carnage, it may nevertheless appear that there were good effects wrought by this event which will partly balance the horrors by which the work was accompanied. To M. Taine it seems otherwise, and his work is simply to present the case as it appears to his own mind.

And yet the effect upon the reader would be vastly greater if he had done this in a more temperate tone—if he had admitted the possibility of some good motives on the one side, and of some wrongs and outrages on the other. . . . M. Taine's volumes are crowded with horrors and outrages committed by the revolutionists even before the Terror. They are fearful enough; but turn to his own account of the misgovernment and abuses of the Ancient Régime, and it will appear that there were abuses on the other side, too. (pp. 91-2)

The Jacobin conquest is analyzed and narrated in a masterly manner, and few would undertake to defend or extenuate the conduct of the revolutionists after the summer of 1792. At this time the balance had fairly turned, and revolution was triumphant. In judging events, however, there are two points of view that the historian should keep distinct. Motives—the right and wrong of actions—he is not able to see, but can only infer. The revolutionary leaders asserted for themselves the most absolute purity and disinterestedness; their claim was that the end (the salvation of society) justified the means (murder). From whom did they learn this principle of action but from the church and the state which had held them in subjection so many generations? The massacre of St. Bartholomew, the dragonnades of Louis XIV, the arbitrary imprisonments and punishments of the old régime: these were the models that Danton, Murat, and Robespierre took—and they did not improve upon their models.

Motives, therefore, are a dangerous subject to meddle with; the other point of view is that of cause and effect, and to trace these is the true task of the historian. It is the great merit of the second volume that the causes and method of the Jacobin conquest are developed with such clearness and accuracy. But the analysis of cause and effect is not carried far enough. We

need to be told not only what Jacobinism is, and how and why it got the upper hand in France, but why, when it got the upper hand, it instituted a reign of terror. "Jacobinism," as M. Taine defines it . . . , is not a phenomenon peculiar to France, but has made its appearance in every revolution—in every popular movement; but only this once has its history been written in blood. Precisely the same succession of parties exercised control in the great English revolution of the seventeenth century as that which appears in this volume. Hyde and Falkland correspond to Mirabeau and Lafayette; Pym and Hampden to the Girondists; Cromwell and the Fifth Monarchy men to Robespierre and his crew. Indeed, one can trace in American history, in a mild form, every characteristic and almost every doctrine described in the chapter in question; the mastery of society which French Jacobinism achieved in three years occupied more than ten in England, and more than two generations in the peaceful developments of American politics. To answer the question why the French revolution was attended with a reign of terror, from which the English and American revolutions were free, would require a volume; but does not M. Taine partly answer it himself in his *Ancient Régime*? (pp. 92-3)

W. F. Allen, "M. Taine as an Historian," in The Dial, *Vol. II, No. 17, September, 1881, pp. 91-3.*

LEOPOLD KATSCHER   (essay date 1886)

[In this excerpt from a survey of Taine's works, Katscher focuses on his critical method, arguing that its faults are balanced by Taine's eloquent style.]

That every human being is born with certain tendencies peculiar to his race, which guide his thought and actions; that all his ideas and his deeds, whether good or evil, are to be traced to these innate tendencies, as a river to its sources,—these are the views which Taine, since his [*Essai sur les fables de La Fontaine*], has ever and everywhere asserted, maintained, and, according to his own conviction, established.

Established! yes, that is the crucial point. As a rule it is admitted that the critic can do no more than express his own opinion. He fulfils his duty when he carefully studies his subject and deals with it dispassionately and as impartially as possible. More is not, and cannot be, demanded from him. Every critic judges according to his circumstances, his experiences, his degree of culture, his fancy, his prejudices, expectations, and sympathies; hence each single criticism remains in every respect an expression of individual opinion. If a criticism commends itself to a majority of men as true and just, it is adopted; but it is not *necessarily* competent to establish the real worth or worthlessness of the subject under discussion. Quite different are Taine's views of criticism. He deems it possible to bring *certainty* into criticism; he insists upon endowing criticism, like physics and mathematics, with the fixedness of scientific formulae, hedging it round with irrefragable dogmas. His point of view is that criticism must no longer be unreliable, its results no longer fluctuating. At the age of five-and-twenty he springs, a modern Pallas, into literature, ready armed at all points with a critical system, a philosophy, and last, not least, a style of his own. All that he has more minutely developed in the course of several decades is already to be found in his maiden work on Lafontaine. (p. 55)

[In his *Essai sur Tite-Live*] Taine contends that the birthplace and mode of life of Livy, the time in which he lived, the events of which he was witness, the direction of his taste and of his studies—that all these co-operated to make him an 'oratorical historian.' The want of method in the arrangement of his great work, the sentiments expressed in it, the prevailing tone and style, the frequency of the speeches occuring in it—all these things are adduced by Taine in support of his hypothesis, and he goes so far as to assert this to be incontestable certainty. Now everyone will allow that the 'surrounding circumstances,' which Taine makes the foundation of his deductions respecting Lafontaine, Livy, and others—time, place, conditions of life, &c.—are valuable and weighty factors in forming a decision about individuals and peoples; but nobody can allow them to constitute infallible certainty in questions of criticism, least of all when we are discussing persons and races long gone by, and whose 'surrounding circumstances' we have not before our eyes, but are obliged to *construct* in a great measure; such a necessarily inductive criticism must ever remain hypothetical. It does not follow that it must be erroneous; it may quite as possibly be correct; but Taine's conclusions with regard to Livy are not only hypothetical and fallible, but actually false. His argument is that Livy was rather a great orator than a great historian. He holds him not to be a good historian because he wields the pen as an orator; he calls him an 'oratorical historian,' and attributes the beauties as well as the defects of his historical style to the preponderantly rhetorical character of his mind. The principle on which he bases this estimate of Livy is evidently erroneous, for Montesquieu, Macaulay, Gibbon, and others were no contemptible historians, notwithstanding their very eminent oratorical power. The same method by which Taine stamps Livy as an 'oratorical' historian might lead to the conclusion, equally hypothetical, that Livy was capable of writing the *History of Rome* only because he was endowed with the genius of a painter or poet. The logical premisses which Taine holds to be unassailable are by no means so. He tries to prove too much, and in his impatience to reach his conclusion, overlooks many things which make against his point of view. The fact that Livy—in contradistinction to the philosophical Thucydides and the practical Tacitus—neglects the grouping of incidents, the consultation of original authorities, and places characteristic expressions in the mouths of his personages, proves, not that he was an 'oratorical' historian, but that he was a careless writer. Facts are in direct opposition to Taine's hypothesis; he has only *maintained,* but not *proved,* that the absence of philosophical generalisations and of diligent research is the characteristic of an orator, and that therefore Livy deserves to be called an 'oratorical historian.' Many great orators, as we have said, have been admirable historians, and have exhibited remarkable powers of research. Taine seems to demand from Livy what is simply an impossibility: faultless, absolutely perfect writing of history.

Much more might be alleged against the propositions maintained in the *Essai sur Tite-Live;* suffice it to emphasise once more that the effort to constitute criticism an exact science has been as unsuccessful here as in the book on Lafontaine. In spite of diligent and careful application of the demonstrative method, criticism remains fallible and individual. By the repetition of 'because' and 'therefore' a case may be made clearer and less unreliable, but that is not equivalent to proof. As a result of Taine's process we have only a series of paradoxes and generalisations, which, indeed, are always most ingeniously carried out, testify to earnestness and ardent pursuit of truth, and are worthy of the highest recognition, but unfortunately are not always infallible. While this clever mode of generalisation in Taine's hands served to enhance the poetic inspiration of Lafontaine, it served also to depreciate the historical endowment of Livy. (pp. 56-7)

[*Voyage aux eaux des Pyrénées*] showed Taine in a new light: as a descriptive writer of the first order. Hitherto he had been known as an acute critic and an original philosopher; but now it was discovered that in him lay also a fanciful poet, a profound observer of men and manners, a genial and amusing *raconteur,* a close observer and interpreter of Nature. Books of travel may be divided generally into two classes: the first pretentious, in which the author decides dogmatically upon all that comes across him, without possessing the necessary information and capabilities; these books overflow with stupidity, vanity, and shallowness. The second class are less pretentious, but equally valueless; the author contents himself with transcribing from his guide-books descriptions of what he has seen, with some slight modifications, and giving a tolerably accurate list of the hotels in which the best beds, the cheapest dinners, and the lowest fees are to be secured. The only travels worthy of notice are included in neither of these two classes; among these Taine's works on the Pyrenees and Italy take a foremost place. He looks not so much on the external aspect of things as on their inner, their psychology; he only occupies himself with the outward so far as is necessary to draw from it arguments for the demonstrations and ratiocinations which he applies to all that he sees and observes. If he describes a landscape—and he does it in the most effective and picturesque manner—he at the same time analyses its separate constituents, and makes it clear how and why their combination produces the impression of beauty. He seeks to explain why many things appear beautiful to us to-day which formerly passed for ugly, and *vice versâ.* He inquires into the influence of civilisation on the inhabitants of a region, and the changes which take place in the course of time in the condition of these inhabitants, as well as in their physical and moral constitution. He traces all things up to their causes, and endeavours to investigate all, even the geological, botanical, and climatic conditions of the Pyrenees, but he dwells only so long upon them as to instruct the general reader without boring the initiated. He draws delicate pictures of the customs of the people and the tourist life. No doubt there may be errors and mis-statements in his travelling descriptions, as they are made subordinate to the illustration of his theories. But on the whole they are of considerable merit and the reverse of superficial.

His next publication was [*Les philosophes français du XIXme siècle*] . . . , a witty, telling, acute analysis of 'official philosophy,' a positivist irruption into the reigning school of the Eclectics, an attack upon that rhetorical spiritualism which, in the eyes of the authorities had the advantage of giving no umbrage to the clergy, in the eyes of the thinkers disadvantage of tripping airily over the difficulties which it undertook to clear up and do away with, or else of evading them altogether. Taine slays the tenets of five men with the superficial knife of ridicule on the altar of sound human reason. Here also he excels in treating a dry subject in an amusing manner. Thanks to his clearness and his *espri* the public found itself surprised into taking interest in a scientific tournament. Why did Taine select Cousin, Laromiguière, Royer-Collard, Maine de Biran, and Jouffroy for his target? Apparently because he found most to censure in them. However, we are far from being ready to endorse the whole contents of the book. Victor Cousin, the high priest of the Eclectics, is the most fiercely handled of all; Taine denounces him as a charlatan, and satirises him vigorously in five long chapters. This specimen of Taine's polemics excited great attention. (pp. 58-60)

[*Notes sur l'Angleterre*] would be his best book of travels had he not so often allowed himself to be misled by his inductive process into superficial and inaccurate conclusions. He methodically and with exaggerated acumen ascribes influences to 'surrounding circumstances,' which anyone acquainted with England, and unbiassed by foregone conclusions, sees to be purely imaginary. Numerous are the erroneous generalisations founded on superficial and imperfect comprehension of facts. We are sometimes reminded of the traditional traveller, who, finding a red-haired chambermaid at an inn in Alsace, recorded in his journal 'Alsatian women have all red hair,' or the other who saw some wandering gipsies making nails by the roadside, and drew the inference that the inhabitants of the country led a nomad life and subsisted by manufacturing *quincaillerie*. But such slips are too trifling to militate against the reputation of the author as an exceptional traveller, delicate observer, and master of descriptive style. He is the ideal of the 'intelligent foreigner.' (pp. 60-1)

[In his art criticism, we] recognise all through the learned, delicate, animated critic. Every sentence bears the stamp of originality and is full of suggestive meaning. Taine does not need to repeat what others have said before him, he thinks for himself. He never writes without a special purpose. He always says what he believes to be true, and not what people like to hear—and that means something in France. . . .

[Taine's *History of English Literature*] contains monographs of Macaulay, Dickens, Carlyle, Mill, Thackeray, and Tennyson, in which he takes six of the greatest authors of the time as representative types of their different classes of literature, and in the most skilful manner uses them as illustrations of his subject. This history is the best which a foreigner has yet written on English Literature. (p. 61)

Exceptions, numerous and justifiable, may be taken to the *History of English Literature*, but its importance can never be denied. The fact is, Taine builds up his system with such a loyal striving for accuracy, that it is impossible to refuse our attention to it, even though we may consider that the desired accuracy has not been attained. Emile Zola designates the *History of English Literature* 'a delicately and finely constructed valuable work of art.' Any reader who takes up the work with the expectation of finding a methodical *history* of literature will be disappointed, but not disagreeably so, for instead of a history he will be introduced to a series of portraits on a large scale. He will miss much which appertains to an actual history of literature; many an estimable work and many an author of eminence is barely named or even altogether omitted; hardly any regard is paid to chronology, all literature since Byron, with the exception of the six great portraits above mentioned, is passed over in silence, or only acknowledged by a stray mention of isolated names; nor is there the slightest allusion to the periodical literature which plays so conspicuous a part in the modern life of England. With all these omissions, however, what remains is sufficient to bring clearly before our eyes the rich treasures to be found in the field of British authorship. The main reason, however, why this masterpiece of Taine's fails to deserve the title of *History of Literature* lies in the prominence which it gives to the treatment of the *psychology* of England. He uses literature only as a delicate, sensitive apparatus, with the aid of which he measures the gradations and variations of a civilisation, seizes all the characteristics, peculiarities, and *nuances* of the soul of a people. In short, he applies his 'method'—an ingenious conglomerate of the Hegel-Condillac-Taine inductive philosophy—to the literature of a nation as a whole, as he has hitherto applied it to individual men, to individual works, to art and to observations by the

way. The book has met with universal appreciation, but even its admirers cannot overlook its faults. It would no doubt have been easier to disarm opposition, if Taine had given to the work a title more corresponding to its contents, such as 'Psychology of the History of English Culture illustrated by Portraits from Literature;' or, as a somewhat less long-winded title, 'Psychology of English Literature;' Sainte-Beuve suggested 'Histoire de la race et de la civilisation anglaises par la littérature' [see excerpt dated 1864].

Here as elsewhere Taine shows himself to be an acute critic, and even his errors reveal the subtle thinker. But he is something besides that—he is also a true artist. He wields, indeed, not the brush, nor the chisel, nor a musical instrument, nor does he write verses or novels; his art is that of treating learned and scientific subjects attractively and beautifully, of raising them to a high level, especially in the *History of English Literature*. As a rule, those who have to deal with a dry theme, think they have done quite enough if they have expressed their ideas and views with perspicuity and in appropriate language, and how frequently they do not even succeed in that! The possibility of working up the material and arranging it so as to produce the greatest possible effect did not enter the mind of many writers before Taine. He understands better than most how to impart not only instruction but literary enjoyment at the same time. If only for this reason, his *English Literature*, as we have said, remains, in spite of all deficiencies, a remarkable and unique work. (pp. 62-3)

[*Les origines de la France contemporaine*] certainly bristles with all Taine's peculiarities, but with this difference, which we gladly acknowledge, that in this case he applies his method with much greater caution and moderation than hitherto, and consequently stumbles into fewer hasty and illogical paradoxes and generalisations than on former occasions. This is a great advantage, and adds to the charm which we find in the book. (p. 64)

It may be said generally that in this work Taine allows himself to be guided chiefly by an accurate study of facts. He plods with incredible patience through archives and libraries, deeds, reports, correspondences, and memoirs. His work is strong, solid and trustworthy, so far as the term is applicable in speaking of the historical research, because it is eminently conscientious and founded on well-authenticated contemporary records. As soon as we open the first volume [*L'ancien régime*] we observe at the first glance what a difference lies between the manner in which Taine regards and handles these themes, and the way in which they have been treated by Carlyle, Thiers, Mignet, Louis Blanc, Michelet, and others. The most striking circumstance is that Taine has no political sympathies or antipathies whatever. Facts are more important to him than theories. Instead of attaching himself to a party, his chief concern is to fathom the causes of events, to inquire into their connection with other events, and to reveal the results arising out of them.

A. de Tocqueville in his valuable work *L'ancien régime et la Révolution* has treated the very same subject as Taine. But there is no kind of similarity between the methods of treatment followed by the two authors, although both occasionally arrive at the same conclusions. Taine cannot be denied the merit of being more original than most other modern authors. His style here is as brilliant and pithy as in any of his works. Tocqueville's dry facts become in his hands living and real. In the arrangement of his material Taine is immeasurably superior to his famous predecessor, whom, however, he highly esteems and frequently quotes. In contradistinction to Tocqueville, Taine divides his subject-matter into compact, well marked-off sections, thus securing an exactitude and clearness which afford great help to the reader. On the other hand, he is inferior to Tocqueville in the point of discretion in the choice of citations and in loftiness of reflection. He often loses freedom of vision in his attention to detail, and thus fails to command a large horizon and large fields of view. He forgets Michelet's warning that the microscope may become a snare to the writer of history—'It is only too easy to mistake low mosses and fungi for high woods, or insects for giants.' (p. 65)

Taine judges and illustrates the spirit of the eighteenth century in a masterly manner; he develops clearly and criticises ably the theories of Rousseau and Voltaire. The most remarkable chapters are those on the condition of the people towards the close of the *ancien régime;* this portion of the book is at once the saddest and the most interestingly written. (p. 67)

The delineation of this violence and rage of the Revolution forms the subject of the three volumes of the second section. From a purely literary point of view this differs considerably from the first. Whereas *L'ancien régime* contains many artistic brilliant descriptions of the Salon life, of the Court, of the so-called French 'classicism,' of the customs of the time, &c., which, apart from the psychological and historical interest of the book, afford most interesting and stimulating reading, all this is absent in *La Révolution;* this section is veritably dry—*i.e.* purely scientific and analytical; bare facts are recorded in it and knit together by philosophico-psychological comments strictly pertinent to the subject in hand. We do not miss the long spun-out metaphors and the like which stamp Taine's literary style with so unique a character; but not much actual description is to be found; on the contrary, the author often oppresses us with the weight of his evidence; the excessive multiplication of minute details—however valuable they may be for his purpose—becomes wearisome at last. His study of original sources is here more thorough, more careful, and more comprehensive than ever. His judgments betoken such practical wisdom and sound common sense as is rarely found in abstract thinkers like Taine—more especially in those who, like Taine, have never taken an active share in politics.

It is almost impossible for one who has not lived in France, and does not know what an enthusiastic veneration most Frenchmen—above all most French writers—cherish for the Revolution of 1789, to realise what courage it requires to raise one's voice against it; and this is what Taine does. He dares to confess that he has arrived at the same conclusion as Burke; he dares, through many stout volumes, to give in his adhesion to Burke's views on the great Revolution; he dares to pronounce Burke's *Reflections,* which Michelet called a 'miserable piece of declamation,' 'a masterpiece and a prophecy.' What daring! Who could have expected it from an author avowedly liberal, equally denounced by the reactionary party and the clericals? Only one who has kept himself immaculate, who enjoys such a reputation for political impartiality, scientific accuracy, and literary conscientiousness, only one who stands so absolutely independent as a man, a thinker, and an investigator as Taine does, can venture to permit himself such heresy without incurring grave suspicion on the part of liberally minded people. (pp. 67-8)

In short, he shatters the ideal of his compatriots in the most cruel and reckless fashion, and does not leave the Revolution a leg to stand on.

That Taine, despite his well-known antecedents, could come to such conclusions, can only be explained by what we may call his boundless impartiality. He is so free from bias, and forgets himself so completely in the handling of his subject, that many a reader, taking up *La Révolution,* without any previous acquaintance with his method and his earlier writings, would take him for a Conservative; while there are some passages which, severed from the context, might mislead a superficial reader of reviews into the supposition that he was even a reactionary. In truth there can be no question here of tendency in one direction or another. Taine is, as he always has been, without political bias, but he is sufficiently free from prejudice to desire a *good* government for his country; and as his investigations have convinced him—not in accordance with his inclinations, but in defiance of them—that France was *ill* governed under the Revolution, he makes no secret of his conviction. He quite sees how desirable it was that the miserable state of things under the *ancien régime* should be improved to the advantage of the people, but he fails to see this desirable improvement in the changes introduced in 1789; he even considers that they made things worse. He looks upon the *contrat social* as a very beautiful ideal, but sees the impossibility of its being carried out in practical life, so long as men remain what they always have been and still are. He proves himself through the whole course of his attack upon the constitution of 1791 to be thoroughly acquainted with human nature. To say that Taine wrote against the Revolution in order to ensure his election to the Academy . . . is nonsense. (p. 69)

Taine insists on justice above all and in all things, and it is all the same to him whether it is violated towards the people or the king, towards one rank or party or another. This standpoint is certainly a noble, a truly liberal one, and hence it is that he, the free-thinker, enters the list for the clergy and the Church, for the king and the nobility, wherever justice is dealt out to any of these powers. In the first volume he sets forth the encroachments of the higher classes and the sufferings of the people. Why should he be forbidden in the second to describe the encroachments of the people and the injuries inflicted on the upper classes? Doubtless his speculations will be distasteful to theorists, and politicians will condemn him for having no political views on points which usually call forth party strife; doubtless he refuses to allow either to monarchs or to philosophers the right to rule despotically, to model the world according to their respective fancies, and his impartiality may be censured as lukewarmness by partisans, but it is precisely for these very reasons that his book will awaken the interest and secure the confidence of unprejudiced readers. . . .

While discussing Taine's works individually, we have taken occasion to explain his critical method; let us now attempt a general survey of this method as running through them all. (p. 70)

Were Taine's method really perfect, objective, and infallible, it would necessarily yield the same results in the hands of others as in his own; as in the case of the exact sciences, all difference of opinion would be at an end. But in reality another, armed with Taine's capability of analysis, his keen critical faculty, his comprehensive knowledge, and his charming and effective style, might with the very same method consistently obtain quite opposite results. Taine frequently delights to compare himself to the anatomist wielding the scalpel, to the botanist, or to the zoologist. But in the first place these men of science, when they institute their researches, lay aside all human passions, personal predilections, national prejudices, and individual feelings, whereas the critic who can divest himself of all these things in pronouncing judgment is not yet born, and is not likely ever to be born, so long as men remain only human. And, secondly, the anatomist, the zoologist, the botanist can actually make good what he demonstrates in concrete form, for he has the objects bodily before him, while the critic who has to deal with abstract conceptions—such as beauty, goodness, &c.—can only conjecture or surmise, as conceptions are almost always open to various interpretations. Taine's critical method is then not a science, his conclusions are not proofs, they are, on the contrary, often fallacious. Nevertheless his process has . . . the advantage of enhancing the reliability of criticism by continuous grouping of facts and constant endeavour to obtain certainty.

On the other hand, this virtue is apt to degenerate into a fault. The effort to prove too much frequently misleads Taine to wander into false paths. He eagerly sweeps along all that serves his purposes, and thus not infrequently falls into self-contradiction. It happens sometimes that he brings forward the same evidence to confirm one assertion, at another time a quite opposite one. By high-sounding generalisations he magnifies phenomena and occurrences, which appear to anyone else quite harmless or unimportant, into weighty and portentous records. He ascribes much too great and wide-reaching an influence to his three forces or 'surrounding circumstances.' However much, as everyone must admit, this influence of race, of sphere, and of the spirit of the age may operate on the life and the activity of the man, we cannot go so far as to assume that it alone moulds individuality. If so, how does it happen that brothers and sisters can be so unlike one another? Taine is too inductive by half. He appears to set about his reading with all his preconceived theories and foregone conclusions mustered before him, and to note all that seems to him to confirm them, while he ignores all that tells against them. But this is the direct opposite of objectivity, which can only be approached by the deductive process.

But however far we may be from finding ourselves on the whole in harmony with Taine the philosopher, or rather the anatomist, we must adjudge the highest praise to Taine the writer, the artist. In the former capacity he is, as Zola aptly remarks, a 'thought-mathematician,' systematician, a slave to the consistent application of his own theories; and the reading of his works often conveys the impression that we are attending the lectures of a professor of geometry. This side of his nature is the result of his erudition, it is not the side from which we can fairly judge our author. The real Taine must be sought in the other direction—in his style, his pictures, his descriptions, his narrations. The merits which he unfolds here are his own, and are not due to study. The poet Taine, the man of flesh and blood, is far preferable to the cold mechanical Taine. Stripped of the 'method,' his writings would be all the more beautiful; indeed, this method would play but a miserable part in the hands of a less skilful and gifted writer; it is only Taine's style that holds it above water. In this clear, trenchant, vivid, glowing, luxuriant style stands revealed, as Zola says in *Mes Haines,* 'the prodigality and love of splendour which characterise a fine gentleman.' This style is deliberately unequal and unpolished, in order to produce the more powerful effect. We see that nothing is undesigned, that the author has his pen well in hand. It possesses all the glow and inspiration of fancy, though fettered by a 'method' which directly tends to the suppression of fancy. His highly finished diction always accommodates itself to the subject under discussion. Apart from the too frequent heaping up of epithets and metaphors *a la* Shakespeare, Spen-

ser, Milton, and Bunyan, we are as much surprised by their suitability as by the ease with which they flow from his pen. This is attributable in great measure to the amount of reading, in which he rivals Macaulay, and the assimilatory power of his memory, akin to that of Buckle. His method is mechanical, analytical; his literary individuality, on the other hand, synthetic in its character. Karl Hillebrand says very gracefully in his *Profiles*—'In Taine philosophy is only the frame in which the . . . always lifelike pictures of times and men are set. It is a pity that in the artist's eyes the frame is more important than the picture, that the latter seems to exist only for the sake of the frame.' It is no exaggeration to call Taine an artist in style. (pp. 72-3)

> *Leopold Katscher, "Taine: A Literary Portrait," in The Nineteenth Century, Vol. XX, No. 113, July, 1886, pp. 51-73.*

IRVING BABBITT   (essay date 1898)

[*With Paul Elmer More, Babbitt was one of the founders of the New Humanism (or neo-humanism) movement, which arose during the twentieth century's second decade. The New Humanists were strict moralists who adhered to traditional conservative values in reaction to an age of scientific and artistic self-expression. In regard to literature, they believed that the aesthetic qualities of a work of art should be subordinate to its moral and ethical purpose. Here, Babbitt briefly discusses Taine's critical theory in relation to Naturalism and speculates on the impending demise of the "era of scientific positivism."*]

[One] thought—the application of scientific method to the soul—runs through all the writings of Taine, and gives them their extraordinary unity. He has ranged through ancient and modern history, literature, and art in search of illustrations for this his main thesis. A book or picture interests him chiefly as a "sign" or "document" giving evidence of some phase of the human spirit in the past. This general character visible in a work of art is due, not to the free choice of the artist, but to the fact that he acted under the impulse of a "master faculty"; and the nature of this "master faculty" is determined in turn by the artist's "race" and heredity, by the climate and "environment" which has made his race what it is, and by the "moment" in the historical development of his race at which his life has happened to fall. Under this accumulation of outer influences the free agency of the individual tends entirely to disappear. For it would not be possible to prove that "vice and virtue are products like sugar and vitriol" [see excerpt by Taine dated 1863], if a single act of the individual will intervene to break the chain of natural causes and thus baffle all the previsions of the analyst. This determinism or scientific fatalism, though nowhere expressly formulated by Taine, is a necessary corollary of his doctrine.

Taine is also led logically by his method to deny the existence of the soul in the sense of a permanent ego behind the flux of phenomena. Thus understood, the soul is only the last and most troublesome of the mediaeval "entities" of which the positivist is trying to purge science. The ego in the eyes of Taine is only a resultant—the point of convergence of certain natural forces, and having no reality apart from these forces, or from what he calls the "succession of its events." "Beings, whether physical or moral," seen from this point of view, resemble "an infinite number of rockets . . . forever and unceasingly rising and falling in the blackness of the void." Man, thus bereft of all principle of superiority over nature, is tossed helplessly in the vast ebb and flow of natural forces:

O we poor orphans of nothing—alone on that lonely
   shore—
Born of the brainless nature who knew not that which
   she bore!

In a celebrated image Taine compares the position of the human
family in the midst of the blind and indifferent powers of nature
to that of a lot of field-mice exposed to the tramplings of a
herd of elephants; and he concludes that "the best fruit of our
science is cold resignation which, pacifying and preparing the
spirit, reduces suffering to bodily pain." Bourget has traced
the relation between this philosophy of Taine and the pessimism
and discouragement so rife in France during the last generation
[see Additional Bibliography]. All the nobler aspirations of
man, all his notions of conduct, had clustered around the old-
time conception of the soul, and that of the struggle between
a higher and lower self. The weakening of the traditional belief
has been followed by such an unsettling of all fixed standards,
by such intellectual and moral chaos, that we are inclined to
ask whether the modern man has not lost in force of will and
character more than an equivalent of what he has gained in
scientific knowledge of life. Do we not miss in Goethe himself,
that high-priest of the modern spirit, a certain elevation and
purity which we find, for example, in Pascal, one of the last
great representatives of the mediaeval idealism? The triumph
of naturalism has been followed by a serious falling off, for
the moment at least, in the more purely spiritual activities of
man. Taine is said to have resented the claims of writers like
Zola of the naturalistic school to be his disciples. Yet there is
a real relation between the doctrines of Taine and those of Zola
and the other promoters of what has been termed *la littérature
brutale*—the literature which exalts the power of the animal
passions, proclaims the tyranny of temperament, and seeks the
determining factors of conduct in the blood and nerves. Taine
himself in his *English Literature* has multiplied epithets describing the irresistible pressure of natural causes upon man—
the fatality of the primary instincts.

The main fault to find with Taine and his followers is that in
their eagerness to apply natural methods to psychology, they
have failed to respect sufficiently the mystery of personality.
Sainte-Beuve, anxious though he was to write "l'histoire *na-
turelle* des esprits," the history of the human spirit as determined by nature, showed greater prudence when he confessed:
"We shall doubtless never be able to treat man in exactly the
same way as plants or animals." The contrary supposition has
found fitting expression in a certain school of experimental
psychology. Emerson perceived this drift toward scientific materialism and raised a cry of warning:

> I see not, if one be once caught in this trap of
> so-called sciences, any escape for the man from
> the links of the chain of physical necessity.
> Given such an embryo, such a history must
> follow. On this platform one lives in a sty of
> sensualism, and would soon come to suicide.
> But it is impossible that the creative power should
> exclude itself. Into every intelligence there is
> a door which is never closed, through which
> the creator passes. The intellect, seeker of ab-
> solute truth, or the heart, lover of absolute good,
> intervenes for our succor, and at one whisper
> of these high powers we awake from ineffectual
> struggles with this nightmare. We hurl it into
> its own hell, and cannot again contract our-
> selves to so base a state.

We may add that in the most commonplace personality there
is a fraction, however infinitesimal, which eludes all attempts
at analysis; and this indefinable fraction, this residuum of pure
and abstract liberty, not to be expressed in terms of time and
space, increases in strict ratio to the man's originality; and
what is true of an individual applies equally to a race or historic
period. The bushmen of Australia fall more readily into the
categories of Taine than the Greeks of the age of Pericles.

Taine has succeeded admirably in his *English Literature* in
marking the main characteristics of an epoch, in following out
the great streams of tendency, in noting interactions and interdependencies. He has been less successful in rendering the
peculiar originality of single writers. It is but natural that he
should have failed most signally in trying to apply his method
to the supreme originality of Shakespere. We may object to
Taine's attempt to confine the genius of Shakespere in a formula as he would a chemical gas, even though we may not,
like Matthew Arnold, see in Shakespere one who "out-tops
knowledge," even as a mountain, which

> Making the heaven of heavens his dwelling-place,
> Spares but the cloudy border of his base
> To the foil'd searching of mortality.

The era of scientific positivism, of which Taine is one of the
chief representatives, seems at present to be drawing to a close.
The protest against quantitative psychology which was made
half a century ago by a few idealists like Emerson, is being
echoed at present by the more thoughtful of the experimental
psychologists themselves. "There is no measurement of psychical facts," says Professor Münsterberg in a recent article, and
he adds that "the real psychical facts cannot be anything else
than a world of qualities." The way is thus prepared for a
return to methods in psychology which the positivist has scorned
as mediaeval—in any case for a reaction against the theory
which would reduce everything to a "problem of mechanics."

However, our impatience at the exaggerated determinism of
Taine and his disciples should be tempered by the reflection
that it was perhaps only a necessary recoil from an equal exaggeration in the opposite direction. Mediaeval religion tended
to isolate man entirely from nature and from his fellows, to
raise him above time and space, and to regard him as entirely
dependent upon divine grace and his own free will. The saint
strove to attain perfection by the repression of all the natural
instincts. The extravagances of the romances of chivalry which
Cervantes satirized are only another expression of this cult of
the heroic personality in defiance of all the limitations of the
real. Taine, on the contrary, has devoted extraordinary powers
of analysis to showing the manifold ways in which the individual will is limited and conditioned by natural law, and to
demonstrating how "every living thing is held in the iron grasp
of necessity." He also undertakes to prove that man is circumscribed in his institutions no less than as an individual by
this natural necessity; these, too, are historical products, largely
related to their surroundings, and to be modified, if at all, only
by slow process of evolution. He is, therefore, perfectly logical
in his attack upon the French Revolution; for at bottom the
revolutionary spirit is only a transformation of the old idealism
and its misapplication to politics. The Jacobin like the mediaeval doctor substitutes an ideal entity for living, breathing
men, lets formulae come between himself and direct contact
with reality, and believes of human institutions as his mediaeval
predecessor had believed of individuals, that they may be recreated with reference to an abstract model by a mere fiat of

the will. To the psychologist Robespierre is hardly less me-diaeval in his mental habit than Joseph de Maistre.

Naturalism has thus worked a far-reaching transformation in all departments of thought by its twofold instrument of his-torical sympathy and scientific analysis. In literary criticism, for instance, it will hardly be possible after Sainte-Beuve and Taine to return to the point of view of Boileau—to treat a book as though it had "fallen like a meteorite from the sky," and judge it by comparison with an aesthetic code, itself constructed on *a priori* grounds like a mediaeval creed. In general, as a result of the labors of the naturalists, it will not be easy for men to neglect as they once did the element of change and relativity—to fancy as in the middle ages that they are living in a stationary universe, and that absolute truth can be caught and fixed in a set of formulae. They are not likely to revert to the crude dualism, the mechanical opposition of the soul and body, the ascetic distrust of nature that marked the mediaeval period. In short, the great naturalistic movement which extends from the first thinkers of the Renaissance to Taine will be seen in the retrospect to have been a necessary reaction against the excesses of the idealism of the past, a necessary preparation for a saner idealism in the future. It will have served its purpose if it has helped men to realize with Goethe that the ideal be-comes valuable in proportion as it is founded firmly upon the real, that the highest type of idealist is he who borrows the means by which he transcends nature from nature herself. . . . (pp. v-x)

> Irving Babbitt, "The Method of Taine," in Intro-duction à l'histoire de la littérature anglaise *by H. Taine, edited by Irving Babbitt, D. C. Heath & Co., Publishers, 1898, pp. iii-x.*

ÉMILE FAGUET (essay date 1899)

[*Faguet, a French literary historian and critic, was influential during the late nineteenth and early twentieth centuries. His crit-ical writings are recognized for their emphasis on the work itself and their understanding of the history and evolution of French poetry. Here, Faguet offers a detailed examination of Taine as a philosopher, critic, and historian, delineating his mental char-acteristics, evaluating his critical method, and summarizing his contribution to European intellectual history. Faguet's comments were written in 1899.*]

Taine's leading quality was probity. He had an upright soul. He had a horror, not only of any falsehood, but of charlatanism and anything approaching to charlatanism, such, for example, as inexactitude, and a certain ability to present it in an appar-ently honourable form; confusion, disorder, more or less poetic vagueness, dreaming, or, if not dreaming, complacency in giving expression to one's dreams, as though they could be considered as beliefs, or as though beliefs could be drawn from them. And oratory, too, is, or can easily become, included in this category of things.

All this repelled Taine. He had a passion for precision; he had a straightforward sort of mind. (p. 207)

He was first drawn by an invincible attraction to the fact. The fact, difficult to distinguish, to disentangle, to verify, to define, is, when once extracted, clear, luminous and essential: it im-poses itself upon our minds in a curiously authoritative way; it impels us; it defies us not to accept it. The mind finds a sort of austere pleasure in accepting it. Taine gave himself up pas-sionately to this pleasure. He read with eagerness, picked out, piled up and collected facts with energetic patience. He was

curious especially about little facts, details of customs, tiny features that are overlooked in rapid inquiries. It is to them that the probity of an inquisitive mind is naturally attracted. Such facts have not been handled by others, distorted, con-verted into ideas, stamped with the mark of a mind, false, perhaps, or uncertain. They are more themselves than any others. They come fresh from the ore, in a pure state. More-over, a big fact is complex; consequently it is, or seems to be, vague; a big fact is a fact, but it has the appearance of a general idea. Instinctively Taine prefers facts that are not big. (p. 208)

Taine's mind had a quality which is rare among systematic minds: it was modest. . . . The system which a systematic mind imposes upon facts is very often a general thought, drawn not from facts but from itself, not from without but from within itself, from inside suggestion, from a tendency of character, or even of temperamental disposition. Taine's conscience told him that he had nothing to fear in this respect. His modesty reassured him. He was sure that he would not yield to the need, which most of us experience, to impose an accident of our personality upon the universe, and to explain the world by what is scarcely more than an explanation of ourselves, or even merely an indication of what we are. He assured himself that "nature seen through a temperament" was the definition of an artist's talent, not of the system of a learned, patient, pain-staking and scrupulous philosopher. Perhaps he was wrong. But his good will and his modesty were so certain and so obvious to him that it was quite natural that he should have reassured himself by trusting to them.

And if his system was perhaps narrow that, too, was an effect of probity and modesty. He disliked rashness in the making of assertions which are, or even run the risk of being, beyond the powers of the human mind. Exaggeration of the sphere of human intelligence was for him one of our most common fan-cies. To him it was more or less conscious charlatanism to pretend that we can understand the entire scheme of things, or that we can even catch a glimpse of its meaning. (pp. 209-10)

[Taine's ideas were] those of the positivism already constituted by Auguste Comte when Taine arrived upon the scene of in-tellectual life. His ideas on Man are newer and more personal. They are very clearly pessimistic. Comte was content to say that Man is a "continuation of nature," a being made like the other "guests of the universe, called animals," only a little more complex. Taine made a more minute inquiry than Comte into humanity, and from this inquiry Man emerges practically abominable. (p. 219)

His earliest literary admirations are at the same time a proof and a confirmation of this mental attitude. From youth he was, as it were, smitten with Balzac and Stendhal, very bitter minds, more disposed to exaggerate men's failings than to mitigate them, who drew up in the form of novels a fairly harsh de-nunciation of humanity. Later, as was natural, the grey pes-simism of Maupassant was entirely to his taste.

The influence of Balzac and Stendhal is very marked in the only volume of direct observation made by Taine, [*Notes sur Paris: Vie et opinions de M. Frédéric-Thomas Graindorge*]. This book of youth is far from being youthful, and it is a singularly morose entertainment. The author is seen to be astounded and stupefied, irritated and exasperated, by the covetousness and brutality of men, and by the coquetry and frivolity of women, and he repeats his assertions on these matters with a gloomy insistence and a provoking obstinacy, which reveal, if I may say so, a spirit wounded to the quick; and, finally, he takes refuge, full of weariness and disgust, in artistic and contemplative life: "Play me some Beethoven." (p. 221)

I know that the *Notes on England* are less gloomy. I will not say that they are less sincere, but that they are more systematic. The *Notes on England* are secretly inspired by an aristocratic thought. The author wanted to prove that the existence of an upper class, the political and particularly the moral influence of this class on a nation, and the acceptance, more or less formal yet real, by the nation of this state of things, provide still the best conditions of stability and strength for a nation. This led him to consider with a certain complacency the character and customs both of this upper class and relatively of the nation as a whole.

But his general idea of humanity was not perceptibly modified in this way. It is very unfavourable. Taine sees always in Man "the ferocious and dismal gorilla," to whom it is supposed that our original ancestors must have borne a resemblance; "the carnivorous beast" who "has canine teeth like the dog and the fox, and who has, since his origin, dug them into the flesh of others." Thus he was, thus he is still, and he "cuts throats," as in prehistoric times, "for a bit of raw fish." There are only very slight differences in method. If you scrape off a little of the thin coating of varnish which social invention, civilization and religions have succeeded, after so much effort, in putting on any man you see, here is what you find. (pp. 221-22)

Such is Man in his general characteristics; though he does not seem to be like this, because, yoked, bound and repressed, he moves round fairly regularly and at regular periods in social intercourse, impelled by the necessity of gaining his livelihood. But he is such at bottom, and is so revealed as soon as an upheaval of the social organization leaves him free to go back to his true nature.

Taine not only has little liking for this Man, but is frightened of him. There is something slightly unhealthy in this fear which Taine experiences when he considers humanity. He, too, in some ways was imaginative, and knew these "amplifications," these exaggerations of inner thought, these "sad and heavy dreams," as Heine says, which tremendously increase our natural misery. He did not know thoughtlessness and its light and divine benefits. Continual meditation turned within him very easily into sadness, and his meditation was most often directed towards what was bad, defective and dangerous in human nature. He jeered most harshly at the optimistic dream of the eighteenth-century philosophers and of the Revolution in its initial stages. It seemed to him the most absurd and the most disastrous folly that ever intoxicated human brain. It seemed to him prodigious ignorance of human nature.

We do not need to point out once more that difference in dates partly explains difference in points of view, and that after the Revolution, the Empire, three invasions and the civil war of 1871 no philosopher in France could be as peacefully optimistic as an eighteenth-century philosopher. But, also, personal temperament is a leading element in such matters, of which the proof is that, in this same eighteenth century, and in the midst of wealth and surrounded by pomp, Voltaire wrote *Candide*. Taine had, like Voltaire, a dread of human folly, and all his life his writings bore a certain resemblance to *Candide*, from *Graindorge* to *The Origins of Contemporary France*.

When once the study of Man has taken hold of a person it cannot be got rid of. He comes back to it always, and even when he seems busy with something else it is still of this question that he is thinking, and on which he bases the particular work with which he is occupied, or seems to be occupied. When Taine, in wonderfully bold, colourful words, described the Pyrenees, he stopped to listen to the idle talk of his neighbours in inns, or to consider the appearance and nascent—already disturbing—coquetry of the little girls skipping on the pathways in the park. Taine did much criticism. He did not for a moment think of studying books; he considered the study of books only as a means of knowing the temperament of peoples. All his books of criticism are history-books, the books of a moral historian.

It is true that, previous to Taine, there was already much history mingled with criticism. But there was a difference. Before Taine, history in criticism was a framework whose function was to set off the picture. The object was to give better knowledge and a better picture of a literary personage by showing him in the time in which he lived and surrounded by his contemporaries. In order to portray Madame de Sévigné, for example, an outline of her time was sketched around and behind her.

Taine, as it were, reversed this picture. He will make the portrait of Mme de Sévigné in order to depict the seventeenth century. Literary personages will be for him first of all only *specimens*, then significant *products* of a certain epoch, and he will study them only in these two respects. The study of Man through history, history through literary history, literary history through the study of great writers, such might be the epigraph of all his books, and in this formula are contained all the originality and all the defects of Taine's criticism.

He set out with the idea, which was a sort of axiom in his day, that literature is the expression of social life. Consequently the best way to find out about any period of social life is to study its literature. In considering a great writer, we must persuade ourselves that he did not make himself; he is a product of a thousand different causes. If we restrict ourselves to the chief of these causes we find that he is the product, firstly, of his race, then of the world in which he lived, finally, of the circumstances which left their impress upon him at the time of his talent's formation. He is a product, and representative, of all these.

Therefore *race, environment, time*—these are the three things which must be considered before considering the man himself. (pp. 223-25)

The first part of this method is very ingenious, and is scientific in appearance, in manner and in procedure. It is an application of Comte's method, which consists in proceeding from the more general and simple to the more particular and complex. (p. 225)

It must be observed that this method is productive of much beauty. In regard to any great writer it offers great scope, and permits of descriptions of his race, his native province, the town in which his infancy was passed, the population of this town, and so on; and thus provides the author with an opportunity to make very fine, very brilliant, very extensive and very varied pictures. It is a method essentially *interesting*. Merely for this reason it would be liked, and one would wish that it were the method of any critic with the power to be a great historical painter; which in fact it is, for, whenever a critic is also a great historical painter, he will instinctively choose, if not this method, at least this procedure.

This method has therefore a great deal in its favour, and can attract the reader even as it attracted Taine himself: but it has only a very slight foundation in reason and truth, and almost at every step it lends itself to grave objections.

In the first place, the axiom on which it is based is very controvertible: "Literature is the expression of social life." It is necessary to know which literature is in question: for literature is not a homogenous mass, and at any given period there are three or four literatures side by side. We must admit that the literature of memoirs, of intimate correspondence, of little diaries and gazettes (those which were popular and very widespread, not those of a coterie or a section of a town), this lower literature, represents more or less the state of mind of a nation at a given period; but it is obviously less true—indeed, almost false, and scarcely at all proved—that the higher literature is representative of the popular or middle-class state of mind, of the average mind, at a particular date in the history of France or England. (pp. 225-26)

Thus literature is the expression of social life on condition that it is first deprived of all its greatness, of all the big literary monuments. It can be done when one looks only for the history in literature. But, and this is the point, Taine wanted to study the great writers, and, in fact, studied these only. So there was a sort of conflict between his method and his object. His object was precisely the one incompatible with his method. His method ought to have led him to study anything but what he took as the object of his study.

He refused to see the difference between criticism and history. The literary value of a monument is almost in inverse proportion to its historical value, and vice versa. History is connected with things of a general character: a great literary work is, above all, a document of individuality. Thus criticism and history can be considered side by side, but they cannot be united. The very title of [*Essais de critique et d'histoire*], which is very significant, contains an error.

As for the investigation of race, environment and time, just as it is interesting, so is it vain, because it is, as it were, external, and always remains external, to the real object of criticism. Certainly Corneille is a product of the French race, of Norman soil, of the Rouen middle classes and of the circumstances which surrounded him from 1604 to 1624. Only, these various things explain everything about Corneille except his superiority, and the business of criticism is to account for superiority. These things describe a Rouen bourgeois of 1625, but not the difference between an ordinary Rouen bourgeois and Pierre Corneille; and, since this difference is the important thing, it follows that such considerations better describe Corneille's neighbour than Corneille himself. Hence, of what use are they?

Further, considerations of this sort not only fail to explain superior men, but can eventually give a wrong impression of them. These studies help the critic to represent to himself more or less exactly *any man* of a certain race, a certain place and a certain date; when they are applied to, brought to bear upon, a superior man they bring to light, throw into relief, beneath the critic's eyes, those parts of this great man through which he resembles any other man of his race, place and time—that is to say, his common and popular parts; and these are the parts which the critic will be, as it were, led and invited to depict. A humble citizen, lively, witty, jesting, rather talkative, telling dirty and satirical stories aimed against all authorities, not very devout, of a very unsound morality—here, perhaps, is a portrait of a middle-class inhabitant of Champagne about 1650. Well, for Taine, it is La Fontaine. Undoubtedly La Fontaine had all these traits in his character; but, further, he was a great poet,

and it is the great poet who must be described to us. Taine does this: but all the rest, which is secondary, encroaches in the portrait upon the poetic genius, which is the essential, and hardly lets us catch a glimpse of it.

Actually, this idle and dangerous way of painting distinguished men is not even right for the painting of individualities *of any sort*. Properly speaking, it is "race psychology" applied to the psychology of individuals. Here, again, there is a confusion. The psychology of peoples is legitimate. There are certain very general characteristics which are common to nearly all the individuals among a people. There is nothing more reasonable, perhaps more useful, than the distinguishing and discovering of these traits, and inferring from them of conclusions as to the development and future of a nation. But there is no sense in depicting any man whatsoever by the general characteristics of his race. His personality—and, however slightly original, he has a personality—consists of the two or three particular tendencies which distinguish him on the common background. Every southern Frenchman is an orator. Yes, but it is precisely for this reason that, if you are content to paint Mr X by saying that he is an orator, you will not at all have made his portrait. Since he is an orator it is necessary, first of all, to say what sort, and then to explain what are his other faculties besides that of being able to talk. It is evident that individuals are composed of peculiarities, or at least it is by means of these that we recognize individuals, distinguish them from the mass and keep them in our memory as individuals. Race psychology applied to individual psychology has the effect of identifying individuals with the common crowd—that is to say, its effect is not to depict but to blot out individuals.

And, lastly, this method is vain because it claims to attack and reduce the infinite complexity of nature, and cannot possibly succeed. Any man is certainly the product of his race, environment and time generally—that is to say, vaguely speaking; but race, environment and time even are very general terms, which embrace hundreds of thousands of different influences, hundreds of thousands of generative elements; and of these elements only a small number, in comparison with the great mass, has contributed to the formation of this man. The rest is unimportant, or practically so, and relative to him. Therefore, to explain this man by his causes, it is necessary to recognize, among the thousands of possible causes, the twenty or thirty which, in his case, are the essential ones. (pp. 227-29)

[This] is why Taine's critical studies seem so often "prefaces" or "introductions," which do not lead to the subject to which they claim to lead. (p. 230)

But for us the most important thing at the moment is not to prove or affirm, with reasons, that the method in question is dangerous, unproductive and deceptive: it is important to indicate how far, in making use of it, Taine is loyal to himself, and how his method in criticism is an application of his philosophical system.

We have seen that for Taine everything is "determined" in the world, and there is no room in the universe for accident and unforeseen events. What is true of the world must be true of Man himself. The world is a moving theorem; Man must be a "walking theorem." *To prove this hypothesis* let us take precisely an exceptional, unexpected, accidental man, one who seems less than any other preordained, who seems more than any other to interrupt the rigorous series of causes and effects, or to avoid it, and let us show that *even he* is a natural and necessary product of a series and convergence of facts, that he is only the result of these and that anything which is in him was in them. Taine had a law of the world; he clung to it; he believed it to be exact; he believed it to be universal; he even challenged the exception that did not seem to fit into this law and tried to make it fit in. His critical method was at the service of his philosophic system and was invented only to serve it. But the trouble is that one is too conscious of the fact that it was invented for this reason, and that the philosophic system preceded the critical method.

Inversely, it seems almost certain that it is not the study of great authors that would have led Taine to a system of determinist philosophy; it is even difficult to believe that these two sets of ideas could have sprung up simultaneously, and fitted in with each other from the first, in the philosopher's mind. It is possible, but not probable. It seems almost certain that the philosophic system showed the way to the critic and even laid down his conclusions for him. (pp. 230-31)

[This] race-environment-time system was only part of Taine's method of criticism. He completed it by his consideration of the leading faculty. (p. 231)

This idea is also interesting as a revelation of Taine's ideas, both as a moralist and as a critic. In this case he is more loyal to his essential mental tendencies than to his system, properly speaking. In the matter of mental tendencies he is pre-eminently a simplifier. Man has only one means of knowing: sensation. The brain can operate in only one way: abstraction. We have seen the effects of Taine's simplifying tendency. He still obeys this tendency by wanting to see in each man, as it were, only one faculty, only one at least which counts, gathering into a unity the complex whirlwind of a human soul. (p. 232)

There is another possible reason for our author's doctrine. The normal man is an idiot, less an idiot than those who are officially described as lunatics, but his superiority to them is only a difference of degree. The clearest characteristic of a lunatic is a fixed idea. Normal man has no fixed idea, but he has undoubtedly the predominance of one instinct over all others, which at least encourages the fixed idea, and would lead to it if sufficient time were given for its attainment. The normal man is a so-called rational being who does not live long enough to become insane. And the same thing is even more true of the superior man, who is especially a man of a more intense cerebral activity. Such a man is naturally endowed with a faculty which profits more than others from the superabundance of cerebral activity. Popular opinion on the close connexion between genius and madness is false; but it is true in so far as that the brain of the superior man is, as it were, tending in a single direction, just as the lunatic's brain is concentrated on a single thought.

Finally, and more than anything, it was taste for abstraction which led Taine to the theory of a leading faculty. His conception of Man was the same as that for which the classical French writers have been so much reproached by various critics, including Taine himself. He saw in Man a passion invested with a body and served by organs. He depicted Man (often), not in his complexity, but as if he were only an abstraction called for a moment into life. (pp. 232-33)

He did as the classic authors and as his beloved Balzac. Only, as a philosopher, he generalized. He not only constituted his characters from a single passion; sometimes it was a passion and sometimes a faculty. Or rather he considered that ordinary men are composed of a dominating passion which groups and gathers around it all the forces of their being; but that men who lead especially an intellectual life are composed, not of a passion, but of a faculty, a gift, a dominant mental power which groups and gathers around it all their intellectual energies. The leading faculty is the monomania of the intelligent man.

Whatever may be the road by which Taine arrived at this idea, it belongs to that class of ideas which can neither be refuted nor completely accepted. Unprejudiced observation and unsystematic experience find it sometimes almost correct, sometimes very nearly false. (pp. 233-34)

[Taine] was carried away, if not by his system, at least by all his mental tendencies, to an invariable, inflexible and, it would seem, inexorable kind of criticism. He was dominated always by the scientific mind, and by the desire to transform the object of his study into a scientific affair. To multiply points of view in the study of mankind would have been, for him, to behave like an artist or even almost an amateur; and to forget that the laws of nature are simple and that the scientific mind has as one of its objects their further simplification by drawing them nearer and nearer to a unity.

It is true that nature's laws are simple, but Man's are much less so, and in this case scientific simplification risks turning into mutilation.

The theory of the leading faculty allowed Taine to see more clearly into some groups of artists but to see others in an incomplete fashion. It is unnecessary to add that when great minds are systematic, their being systematic does not prevent them from being great, and hence it results that they remain powerful even when they put aside their system, and never seem to be more powerful than when they do put it aside, because then they remain powerful but are also freer. Taine was an artist whom the scholar in him tried to discipline. But luckily the scholar was not completely successful. When the scholar had marked out the framework of the matter in question, imperiously indicated the starting-point, laid down the stages of advance and implacably fixed the terminus, the artist slipped in in the intervals and through the cracks in the system. Between two marks firmly planted by the surveyor, the artist was allowed a contemplation, for he was not so far obedient as to deny himself feeling, and then some pages would be made such as might have been written by a Gautier, more sensitive to different kinds of beauty, or a Sainte-Beuve, richer in language, more powerful in style and more vigorous in colouring. The study on La Fontaine, the articles on Balzac and Racine, the passages on Voltaire and Rousseau, in [*The Ancient Regime*], are full of such pages. They can be detached from the system; they are beautiful and true without it, perhaps in spite of it; they do not prove either its truth or its falsehood, because they are not derived from it; they only illustrate it in every sense of the word, being brilliant illustrations which have recommended it to fame. It is not the system which has given them being. Taine, as a purely sensitive and "impressionist" critic, as an artistic critic, had something of the "violent vision" of which he spoke in an allusion to Hugo. He saw an author, or the world created by an author, in incredible relief, and he knew how to put this vision on to paper as on to a canvas. Designs, expressive, full of colour, bold, vigorous—and always too vigorous—abounded beneath his pen, and the reader was left with an ineffaceable impression.

This was certainly a style of decadence. Undoubtedly, Taine, with his sense of the enormous accumulation of different ideas with which modern brains are overcrowded, was rather too inclined to think that it was necessary to strike very hard upon these tired and dull minds if a fairly durable impression were to be left upon them. However, it must be remembered first of all that he was not altogether wrong, and that his idea of the mental state of his readers has really some truth in it. Again it must be remembered that, whatever his desire, it is always of himself that the most impersonal and even the most systematic critic makes a portrait; he always paints himself, modified by something which he has just read, such as himself after a visit to Balzac, to Corneille or to Voltaire.

The portraits which Taine made in turn of himself were true, sincere and exact. This scholar who wanted to be cold was violently, strongly and deeply emotional. This was sufficiently demonstrated when he handled history. He showed, or betrayed without wanting to do so, as much nervousness as a Michelet or a Carlyle. As a critic he had already something of this quality. Exaggeration, the enlargement of contours, extreme prominence of forms and accentuation of colours, are therefore signs especially of his own mental condition. (pp. 235-37)

We have studied Taine as a philosopher and a critic; it remains for us to study him as an historian before we conclude.

The inquiry into Mankind which Taine made, not in books but in history, is also very interesting. In truth, he did not do enough general history, and applied himself too late to historical studies, to have become a real historian, to have acquired all the virtues and the qualities of the historian. But the effort was great, the labour enormous, the conscience, if not the impassibility, unquestionable, and the monument thus raised lasting.

Taine, when he began his *Origins of Contemporary France,* set himself one object, and had two. He set himself to inquire into present times, the present constitution of France, by tracing back to the nearest origins of this present condition, by studying the last years of what is called the old régime, the Revolution and the beginning of the nineteenth century; and on the other hand, without being fully conscious of it, he had a secret aim to study once more the human being by considering him in one of these crises, in one of these pathological conditions, at one of these moments, in which the basis of his nature, rudely awakened by a violent eruption, is displayed and opened out in broad daylight.

Hence he had two points of view in this long study, and two preoccupations, one of which gives place from time to time to the other, and also two very different *tones;* and, finally, two works, one of which is historical, the other philosophic, which have never a very close connexion with each other and which must be distinguished one from the other, better than he did it himself, if they are to be well understood. In general, critics and readers have seen only one or other of these points of view, and, according to the one they have adopted, have passed judgment on the work as a whole always incompletely, in a very particular way, and very differently from their neighbour, to such an extent that it was almost impossible to believe that the same work was under discussion. (p. 238)

The historical work, which must be sought especially in the first and the last two volumes, is a brilliant and original continuation of Tocqueville's work. (pp. 238-39)

The old, gloomy, bitter moralist, whom we have already considered, reappeared again when Taine had penetrated somewhat deeply into the history of the French Revolution. Loyal to his practice of studying organs in their pathological state, as he had observed intelligence among idiots, he observed the sensibility, passions, dreams and chimeras among the men associated with the French Revolution. In this he verified his pessimism and misanthropy. The primitive cannibal, the "gorilla," which he had always glimpsed or seen clearly beneath the surface of Mankind, showed up fully to him in this period of violent commotions and unbridled passions. It is not a "sectarian" who dwells with such complacency upon the horrors, miseries and scenes of savagery of the revolutionary epoch; it is the author of *Thomas Graindorge,* the La Rochefoucauld or the Chamfort of 1855, who was not displeased to recognize and to show how far true and well-founded were his original general opinions of Man.

Hence this passionate care to pick out in the "anarchies," either spontaneous or organized, in all the social troubles of this period, anything which shows the extent to which Man, bereft of the burden of secular constraints, is a blind, deluded, furious and cruel animal. Taine's secret preoccupation in writing these pages, which created so much sensation, was to study the human temper in one of Man's crises of ill-health.

The method is not bad, on condition that it is only complementary and supplementary. I believe that intelligence cannot be realized when foolishness is not known; I believe also that Man cannot be understood when he has not been seen in a revolutionary period; but, first, intelligence must be studied in its state of equilibrium, and man at a normal epoch. (p. 252)

Moreover, although it is true that it is especially the pessimistic philosopher who has written the really narrative pages of *The Origins of Contemporary France,* it must be added that the tone in which these pages are written sometimes betrays something in Taine which is not the calm of a philosopher, even a pessimistic one. Many passages savour of indignation, hate and anger, a fact which has caused some amusement to Taine's critics. "What!" they say. "You are a resolute determinist, and you can condemn or stigmatize! If there is no sort of free will in Man, the man who commits a crime is no more a cause for anger than the plant which secretes a poison! Here is a naturalist who studies men as a naturalist and believes that there is no other way of studying them, but, instead of pointing out the good and the evil they have done, with an equally indifferent curiosity, he ends up by declaiming against them as would a preacher:

"Vous êtes fataliste et vous vous emportez!"

This is true; but it serves to prove once again the fact that a system never takes such entire possession of a man as to abolish in him the innate instincts, which may be illusions, but are probably the very conditions of our existence and are the root, as it were, of our general feelings. The philosopher who does not believe in human liberty believes in his own liberty, or acts as if he believed in it, or as if he were only pretending not to believe in it. He confesses this, when he is sincere, by saying: "I am deceived by an illusion by which I must be deceived in order to be able to live, and I can rid myself of it only when I lead an intellectual life." Similarly, Taine does not believe in human liberty, yet cannot prevent himself from getting angry, as if he believed in it, when he contemplates acts which are crimes only if it exists. We are enveloped in the tissue of necessary beliefs in such a way that we can come again under their sway as soon as our sentiments interfere with our ideas. Taine allowed his sentiments to mix with his ideas in writing the history of the French Revolution; but there would have been something forced in an attempt to prevent this mixture from being or showing itself; he would have had to force himself to seem cold, when it was possible for the philosopher but impossible for the man to be so. And, in the end, if it is sincerity alone which is of importance, *The Origins of Contemporary France* gain something from the fact that the author's sincerity has not been smothered by a sort of philosophic constraint; and they are already systematic enough to give cause for rejoicing rather than for regrets when, from time to time, they forget to be systematic in order to be living. (pp. 253-54)

As for Man considered in society, and the way in which men should be organized on earth, Taine had no advice to give, either to his fellow-citizens or his fellows. His belief, which was expressed in the last words of his *Notes on England* and would no doubt have been expressed at the end of his *Origins of Contemporary France* if he had finished it, was that the history of each people was in keeping with its physiological organism, its essential tendencies, the inner forces and weaknesses in the depths of its temperament, and that, consequently, each people has, at each stage in its evolution, the political régime which is in keeping with the precedents and "momentum" of this evolution. A people no more makes its history than a man his life, and perhaps even less—supposing that in this matter there is any question of more or less. Hence, no advice can be given and there cannot be any didactic politics.

As for his preferences, Taine did not conceal them and they are already known. The best political constitutions, the best social organisms, are those which are consistent with Nature. [But] Nature has made Man essentially unequal. (pp. 259-60)

[Taine] expressed, with the assiduous probity which was the basis of his character, his opinion on the majority of questions in which modern humanity is interested. He expressed it loyally, scrupulously and sadly. He was sad. The reason for this is fairly easy to see. He did not believe in religion, and his only love was science, though he did not believe in it, or, it might be better to say, he only believed in science but had no expectation from it.

In that lay his originality. The men who were carried away by the admirable scientific movement of the nineteenth century were not merely carried away: they were enchanted by it. They put their hope in it. They all believed more or less, and only with the differences which greater or less temperamental ardour gives to the intensity of hopefulness, that the improvement, even moral, the progress, the uplifting, the "salvation," of humanity lay in science and depended on its conquests. In a word, science was their faith. They were all Condorcets, more or less enthusiastic, more or less candid, more or less reserved. Taine, perhaps alone, had reverence without faith, zeal without belief, in science.

Cousin had completely disgusted him with hasty acts of faith. As another had said, "I will not make hypotheses," he said, "I will not make any act of faith." Indeed, his probity would have held him back, if he had needed to be restrained, from descending to any such thing. He saw in any confidence or any abandonment to confidence something not far removed from a mild sort of charlatanism, which deceives others as well as oneself. Consequently he viewed everything with a cold eye, and was inquisitive without eagerness, diligent without excitement, obstinate without hope, and disillusioned beforehand.

His didactic and even peremptory tone must not be allowed to deceive his readers. It is not his thought but his method which is dogmatic. He believes his method is good and it is the only

thing in which he has confidence; but of science he believes nothing more than that perhaps it is true, limited, necessary and, on a final analysis, useless. Being true, it is a satisfaction to the mind; but when it loyally resigns itself to being *really true*, its sphere is so limited that it no longer satisfies the liveliest and eternal curiosities of the mind. It is necessary and Man cannot cease to utilize this instrument which has helped him to become what he is; but, since it does not improve him in his basic qualities, it has only apparent utility, and constitutes yet another of those illusions which Man destroys when he seeks beneath the surface of it.

Thus, Taine gave to humanity an example of a worker attached to work from which he expects no result. The impression of grave melancholy which is left when his works are read arises from this absence of any enthusiasm, of any confidence and of any hope. He inspires a pessimism which does not even smack of the tonic of bitterness. We move with him through a narrow world, whose distant avenues are forbidden our curiosities, which is neither beautiful nor good, and which will become neither more beautiful nor better. The eighteenth-century philosophers, some of them at least, had brought hope down from heaven to earth; Taine banished it from the earth without reinstalling it in heaven.

He had a very great influence. The taste for pessimism crops up periodically in humanity. We grow weary of everything, even of hope, as a very isolated verse of Lamartine's tells us. There are periods when men like, for a time, to cease being deluded and to remain motionless and thoughtful and experience "the gloomy pleasures of a melancholy heart." Sometimes this period lasts a number of years, if certain painful circumstances are joined to this need born of certain deceptions.

A depiction of Frédéric-Thomas Graindorge from Notes on Paris.

After the romantic period, when melancholy was hardly more than a pose, and when enthusiasm, artistic gaieties and beautiful intoxications were very plentiful, the French soul had already begun to grow gloomy when Taine started to write; it became more gloomy still after 1870; Taine was characteristic of the general mental condition. Also his influence crept even into contemporary literature; the novel, from 1870, and the theatre too, from 1880, had very marked pessimistic and misanthropic tendencies. Although he would not like to have the influence of his mind discovered in productions which he abhorred, it is very difficult not to find him in them.

As a matter of fact, he did have not only an influence in the direction we have just mentioned, but also one in quite an opposite direction. The reaction against positivism and pessimism, the attempt at spiritual renaissance which is going on at the present moment, must be attributed partly to him. (pp. 261-63)

Positivism—not the sort practised by Auguste Comte, which attacked itself, or, at least, enlarged itself to such an extent that unheeding minds forgot the sharpness of its original outlines; but Taine's sort, which was contracted and gathered together into itself and presented to men in all its precision and in the dryness of its close definitions—had to have its school and to create an opposing school; resolute disciples, quite sure of what they were defending; determined adversaries well aware of what they wanted to attack; and Taine was the father of the former and the grandfather of the latter.

So the intellectual movement of which Taine is the starting-point was very considerable, and occupies a large place in the history of European thought. The future will disclose its remote consequences to us. For the moment, it is sufficient glory for a man born in 1828 that the movement to which he gave rise should be in 1899 one of the preoccupations of the human mind. (pp. 263-64)

> *Émile Faguet, "Taine," in his* Politicians & Moralists of the Nineteenth Century, *translated by Dorothy Galton, Ernest Benn Limited, 1928, pp. 205-64.*

GEORGE SAINTSBURY (essay date 1904)

[*Saintsbury has been called the most influential English literary historian and critic of the late nineteenth and early twentieth centuries. His numerous literary histories and studies of European literature have established him as a leading critical authority. Arguing that Taine would have been a great literary critic if he had not relied too much on philosophy, Saintsbury focuses in this excerpt on* History of English Literature, *describing it as a "brilliantly written" work, but "positively and utterly worthless" as criticism.*]

Hippolyte Taine *was* a critic, though too often (not always) a "black horseman" of criticism. He was a great aesthetician, he was a brilliant literary historian—that is to say, what should be a critic on the greatest scale. He could do splendid justice to another critic of tendencies and predilections so different from his own as those of Paul de Saint-Victor. To question his competence in pure criticism may seem more than presumption, it may seem pure fatuity. But, though a poet is dispensed from having a conscience, a critic and a historian of criticism is not. (p. 440)

He did not understand the sublime—the "magnificent"—in literature, as no less a person than Sainte-Beuve told him . . . :

and he did not understand it, because, as no less a person than Gautier (consciously or unconsciously repeating Longinus) told him, he did not see that the secret of literature lies in the "mots rayonnants," the "mots de lumière." Or, rather, he *would* not understand: . . . he had the root of the matter in him, but would not let it grow.

Taine is, therefore, the capital example of the harm which may be done by what is called "philosophy" in criticism. If he had resisted this tendency, and had allowed himself simply to receive and assimilate the facts, he might have been one of the great critics of the world. That he *could* have done so is shown, I think, completely by the greatest work of his life, the ***Origines de la France Contemporaine***—in which, with a good grace, if not explicitly, swallowing all he had said in his earlier remarks on Carlyle's *French Revolution,* he allowed himself to yield to the other facts, and established the truth for ever, on and in an impregnable foundation and circumvallation of document. But he had no time to do everything: and in his literary perversity he had gone too far. He as quite a young man, but not young enough to be immature, in the famous studies on La Fontaine and Livy, by a philosophical crystallisation of the process which Sainte-Beuve had almost invented, but had always kept in a fluid and flexible condition—the process of inquiring into the "circumstances," the ancestry, country, surroundings, religion, tastes, friends, career, of the man of letters. As crystallised under the influence of a philosophical determinism, this process became one of inquiring into the racial origin, chronological period, and general environment (*milieu*) of the individual, the school, the literature, as a result of which these "had to be"—what they seemed to M. Taine. The man of letters, be he Shakespeare or Voltaire, Dante or Cervantes, was simply a made-up prescription.

It might not have been so disastrous as it was, if M. Taine had had the audacity—or from a different point of view the pusillanimity—to choose the literature of his own country as his sphere of principal operation. His theory would not have been so cramping as Nisard's, and he was better furnished with facilities of direct appreciation. That there would have been faults, gaps, oddities, in the survey is certain: but it would have been a great and an invaluable history of French Literature. Now his famous ***Histoire de la Littérature Anglaise***—one of the most brilliantly written of its class, one of the most interesting, perhaps *the* history of literature, which has most of literature itself—is only valuable for qualities which are not of its own essence, and in the qualities which are of its essence is very nearly valueless. To any one who knows "those who are there and those who are not"—the authors whom M. Taine discusses and the authors whom he skips—it is a stimulating and piquant, if not exactly an informing, book to read. Those who do not know them will be led hopelessly astray. To begin with, M. Taine himself did not know enough, though he knew creditably much. He had many distractions and avocations at the time, and did not plunge on the document with anything like the "brazen-bowelled" energy which he afterwards showed in the *Origines.* Whole periods—especially where language or dialect present difficulties—are jumped with the most perfect nonchalance, but unfortunately not always in silence. Those minor writers who give the key of a literature much more surely than the greater ones (for these are akin to all the world) receive very little attention. The native, automatic, irrational, sympathies and preferences, which keep a man right much oftener than they lead him wrong, are necessarily wanting. Nothing interferes to save the critic from the influence of his theory. He has constructed for himself, on that theory, an ideal Englishman with big feet (because the soil of our country is marshy and soft), with respect for authority (as is shown by English boys calling their father ''Governor''), Protestant, melancholy, with several other attributes. This ideal Englishman is further moulded, tooled, typed, by race, time, *milieu:* and he becomes Chaucer, Shakespeare, Pope, Byron. And the literature of Byron, Pope, Shakespeare, Chaucer has to deliver itself in a concatenation accordingly. (pp. 440-43)

[The] only adequate verdict that can be pronounced on Taine's **History of English Literature** is that, great as a book and as a creation, it is as criticism not faulty, not unequal, but positively and utterly worthless. It does not even supply the native with useful independent checks and views ''as others see,'' for the views are the views of a theory, not a man. It supplies the foreigner with a false and dangerous travesty.

But in reference to so famous, and in a way so engaging, a book, it might seem impertinent not to descend a little more to particulars. Let anybody contrast the handlings of Dryden and of Swift. The former is one, I do not hesitate to say, of the worst criticisms ever written by a great writer, the latter one of the best. And why? Because Swift—great, arch-great as he is—is very much of a piece: and Taine can adjust him to his theory. Dryden is not of a piece at all, except in regard to that purely literary craftsmanship which a foreigner can judge least well. He is scattered, eclectic, contradictory: and if you make any general theory about him, or even bring any general theory in contact with him, you get into difficulties at once. About Keats—a great person surely, and in casting shadows before him immense—Taine is null; about Shelley, ludicrous; I am not sure that he so much as mentions Browning, most of the best of whose work was done when he wrote. To take examples all over the history, on *Piers Plowman,* on the Caroline Poets, on Gray and Collins, he is at the mercy of any cub in criticism, and a thing to look at and pass for the more gracious and benign animals therein. Sometimes, . . . he tempts the horrid reflection, ''Had he really *read* the authors of whom he speaks?'' And always his neglect . . . of the minor figures throws his sketches of the major out of drawing, out of composition, out of proportion. That he started from Sainte-Beuve is certain; but he comes round to a point absolutely opposed to Sainte-Beuve's serene observatory. He speaks of what he has *not* seen. (pp. 443-44)

> *George Saintsbury, ''The Successors of Sainte-Beuve,'' in his* A History of Criticism and Literary Taste in Europe from the Earliest Texts to the Present Day: Modern Criticism, Vol. III, *third edition, William Blackwood and Sons, 1904, pp. 431-71.*

LORENZO O'ROURKE   (essay date 1906)

[*In this excerpt from his introduction to Taine's* Balzac: A Critical Study, *O'Rourke surveys his critical method, style, and influence on French society and predicts that his future reputation will rest on his* The Origins of Contemporary France.]

Taine is the type and embodiment of that form of materialist determinism which the definitive overthrow of the old ideas by historical criticism, comparative philology, and the modern conception of evolution, established to so large an extent in the learned world. His method exhibits a temperament in which science, wholly dominant, excludes the spiritual from the conception of life. In Taine the modern materialist type achieves completeness, while the spiritual has reached its nadir. He is the creative literary artist of the laboratory, the alchemist of

modern thought, whose ingenious and persistent search for truth rivalled the historic quest of the alchemists for gold. His prose has the glittering beauty of the flame blooms of the crucible. He is the anatomist of literature under whose jeweled scalpel modern thought is revealed in forms of striking originality.

Taine's achievement in history, philosophy and criticism may be said to match Zola's in the field of fiction, for the methods of the realist of romance and the realist of science were singularly alike. The characteristic traits, in fact, are identical: unrivalled power of analysis, a genius for detail, and a philosophy of stark materialism unrelieved by a ray of the ideal. The descriptive prose of Taine is suggestive of the realistic and graphic paintings of Meissonier, in which a blade of grass is as perfectly depicted as the silhouette of Napoleon. To this species of mind there is neither great nor small; an atom is equal to a world: hence infinite care for detail arriving almost at infallibility within its peculiar sphere. Taine approaches the problems of philosophy, equipped with microscope and alembic. The seer's vision is replaced by the methods and instruments of the anatomist and chemist. In the hands of Taine science becomes magic.

Master of an original and striking style, he advanced as with a stride to the forefront of French letters. Out of the opulent and multi-colored French language he fashioned an instrument of wondrous potency. Clear, exact, enriched with an abundance of illustration that has never been surpassed, his writings make an effective appeal to the modern mind. He is a multi-millionaire of ideas, the spoil of many literatures and sciences,—of philosophy, art, history, philology, biology. Probably with the exception of Balzac and Victor Hugo, no other writer succeeded in gaining so perfect a mastery over the French language, with its delicacy, its nuances, its infinite variety. Such a writer loses in translation, however faithful. It is impossible to transplant with entire success ideas sprung from so rich a soil.

This luminous intellect, capable of reflecting truth in its myriad phases, and ever striving to pierce to the heart of its mystery, had, it must be acknowledged, a serious defect. With all its brilliance and wealth of metaphor, his prose sometimes leaves the reader cold. Saintsbury has applied a peculiar epithet to his style. He calls it ''hard and brassy.'' One sometimes feels that the milk of human kindness has been dried up by the blaze of intellect, that the poet has been annihilated by the savant. Even his beautiful passages have at times the taint of the laboratory. The descriptions of natural beauty are often catalogs rather than canvases, heaped up with details painfully elaborated,—mosaics, which appeal to the mind, never to the heart. At times his pages remind us vividly of what we see in the kaleidoscope—of those pictures hard, glittering, and highly interesting, composed of the fortuitous contributions of a thousand colors and figures, ever changing, always revealing finished forms,—exact, sudden, brilliant, without inspiration, but compelling attention and admiration. This glorified kaleidoscope of thought is revealed in contrasts so dazzling, and is at times so elaborate, that it imposes upon us for beauty. Taine is a kind of surgical Victor Hugo armed with microscope, alembic and scalpel, but lacking the poet's Olympian imagination. At times his sentences are so striking, so poignant, that they suggest the possibility of his having studied with profit the greatest of modern Frenchmen. In Taine's most popular writing, as in Hugo's, the interest never flags. This is incomparable merit. The opulence of his illustrations and his display of learning tempt one to compare him with Rabelais. Certainly no modern is to be named with him in this respect, and his primacy in technical and general erudition has been freely acknowledged by his enemies.

His appetite for detail was insatiable. No modern writer ever massed such quantities around a fact. This is what invests his writings with so interesting a quality, notwithstanding his hard, uncompromising method and his lack of human sympathy. His prose has the same attraction as an intricate original piece of machinery. It extorts admiration by reason of the fine adjustment of its parts, and by its highly wrought and rigorous mechanism. But the human sympathies are seldom stirred. Taine, indeed, is not concerned about them. At times the hard, flint-like brilliance of his thought becomes almost painful; it sears like the glare of dry sun-rays from polished rocks. We can not resist the suspicion that this arid quality has had a large share in influencing his judgments of historical personages, and of the human drama which has formed the subject of his constant meditations. (pp. 12-17)

The definitive phase of Taine's philosophy is stark materialism. He became a partisan who gave no quarter. Holding to an inexorable determinism, he declared war upon the spiritual ideas, which, in 1845, began to dawn in France. These ideas positively maddened him. He proclaimed that knowledge was impossible except through sensations, transferred by means of abstraction into ideas. His final word was "Metaphysics does not exist." (pp. 35-6)

Conceptions in the higher regions of metaphysics are restricted to a certain order of minds. It is a fact of much interest that to many persons, by no means deficient in intellect, a metaphysical concept presents itself in the light of an absurdity. Very often men with a special aptitude for material science are incapable of comprehending the simplest metaphysical idea. Herbert Spencer, in his recently published autobiography makes the astonishing statement that Kant's doctrine of Time and Space remained for him an absurdity throughout his life. He admits his sheer inability to understand the *Critique of Pure Reason*. If a mind of Spencer's capacity betrayed a lack in this domain, is it not possible that Taine may have been equally deficient? The two men were singularly alike in their grasp of reality, and their systems of thought have many points of resemblance.

What Taine possessed was a constructive imagination. He was denied the rarest gift. This is the reason that his letters and his personality are rather uninteresting, while his scientific and literary productions vibrate with interest. The descriptions of natural scenery which abound in his works, and his descriptions in general, are often catalogs, and sometimes tiresome catalogs. They bear the same relation to real and poetical description that a photograph bears to a painting. The immense range of his learning had supplied him with a vocabulary of astonishing opulence, and this, used to advantage and coupled with a striking and bizarre manner of antithesis and poignant metaphors, give an original distinction to his style. This style, powerful at times, but often meretricious, has provoked severe criticism. Compared to the purity and clear beauty of the prose of Renan, it becomes unendurable. It is as tho we were to compare the Acropolis to a modern skyscraper.

His scenery is not nature; it is a herbarium lit by electricity. The magic, the sorcery of words, that indefinable, subtle, and inspiring essence which is the soul of poetry and which lies

beyond the reaches of chemistry, is non-existent in Taine. Hence a notable dryness characterizes some of his work.

In spite of his lack of the poetic faculty, however, he is able to astonish us at will by his brilliant paradox and wizardry of words. Certain passages remind us of a brightly uniformed army marching with streaming banners and glittering bayonets to the strains of martial music. We hear the blare of trumpets and watch with a certain admiration the glittering phalanxes moving in ordered files and exhibiting different maneuvers.

The unique and extraordinary influence which Taine acquired over the thought of contemporary Europe was, nevertheless, due to no factitious circumstance, to no tricks of style. It was the result of vast intellectual labors pursued with a Spartan severity from early youth onward through a long life. When hardly more than a boy he had solemnly "dedicated himself upon the altars of knowledge," and vowed to spend his life in the pursuit of truth. His devotion to science has somewhat the character of the medieval ascetic. It is a kind of holy enthusiasm far removed from passion and devoid of all trace of human tenderness. The divinity to whom he yields homage is the God of pure intellect.

This Trappist of science presents a striking contrast with his famous contemporary and friend, Renan. Poetic charm, human sympathy, spiritual imagination, the beauty and purity of style, the inimitable and subtle graces of creative literary art, which were the endowment of the most brilliant of the thinkers of modern France, were wholly lacking in Taine. They were even despised by him. His intellectual armament was of a wholly different caliber. (pp. 37-41)

Taine's famous theory that great men are the product of "race epoch and environment" [see excerpt dated 1863], applies with singular accuracy to himself. He is typical of his country and his race. In him the distinctive French traits attain complete development. Harmonious simplicity, an intuitive faculty almost equal to clairvoyance, an utter absence of mysticism, are now his dominant traits. Naturally he has the defects of his qualities, and his genius for comprehending facts and arranging them into coordinate systems, his unrivaled skill in generalizing, are at the cost of certain magnetic qualities which we expect in a writer.

The famous theory of the influence of climate and environment upon human character had been formulated by Montesquieu and Stendhal, but in Taine's hands it underwent such development, and was carried to such perfection, as to constitute an original creation. This theory of the influence of environment upon human character colors deeply the entire work of Taine. It is wrought out with much elaboration in his *History of English Literature,* and it plays the chief rôle in all his historical and literary studies.

Taine's philosophical system, he tells us, was largely influenced by Hegel, for whom, strangely enough, he had an intense admiration. He once declared that the principal task of contemporary philosophers is to "re-think" the ideas of the famous German metaphysician: "They (Hegel's ideas) may be reduced to a single one: development *(Entwickelung),* which consists in representing all the constituents of a group as solidary and complementary, in such fashion that each one necessitates the rest, and that when reunited they manifest by their successive series and contrasts the eternal quality which brings them together and produces them." This identical quality, which Hegel calls the *idea,* becomes for Taine the "dominating fact." The vague metaphysical formulas of the German metaphysician crystalize in the crucible of the Frenchman.

It is difficult to trace any real resemblance between the German somnambulist of thought and the keen and practical Frenchman whose final declaration was, as we have seen, "metaphysics does not exist;" but Taine has more than once insisted on his debt to Hegel, and it is at least probable that his talent for organization was aided by his study of that philosopher. (pp. 46-8)

Taine, himself, tells us that it was his ambition [in his *History of English Literature*] to write the history of a literature and to investigate the psychology of a people [see excerpt dated 1863]. In order to accomplish this task adequately it was necessary to select a complete literature. Latin literature is largely an imitation, German literature lacks continuity, the literature of Italy and Spain come to an end in the middle of the seventeenth century. There remained ancient Greece and modern France and England.

It was for weighty reasons that the historian fixed his choice upon England. The literature of that country, he declares, presents a continuous development, and its varied epochs teem with dramatic episodes full of interest for the critical investigator. This vast unexplored region, rich in life and color, was almost ideally adapted to the purposes of Taine, and he entered upon his task with the vigor and enthusiasm of a discoverer. The immense field which lay before him was almost virgin. A history of English literature in the modern sense did not exist. So-called histories had been attempted, but they were superficial and without value as criticism. Taine ignored them utterly and entered upon his work under wholly original auspices. The result of his immense labors is not merely a brilliant record of literary epochs, but a history of the English people and character possessing incomparable interest and value.

For Taine a literary work is not a mere product of the imagination, it is a transcript of contemporary manners and the symbol of a particular state of intelligence. Works of literature are, therefore, historical monuments and the truest of all records of the past. This truth, which had already dawned upon Montesquieu and Stendhal, arrived at its full development in the hands of Taine, and its effect has been completely to revolutionize historical methods. According to this view a literary document, an ancient manuscript or book, a poem, a code of laws, is simply a mold on a fossil shell. Beneath the shell there once existed an animal; behind the document there lived a man. As an idea of the animal may be had from the study of the shell, so the man may be comprehended from a study of the document. Both are dead fragments, whose chief value is that they enable us to reconstruct the living being. "True history," says Taine, "begins when the historian has discerned beyond the mists of ages the living, active man, endowed with passions, furnished with habits, special in voice, feature, gesture, and costume, distinctive and complete, like anybody that you have just encountered in the street." According to him a language, a law, a creed is never more than an abstraction. The real thing is to be sought in concrete form, in the living man. (pp. 49-52)

What gives Taine unique distinction among the learned men of his time, is the fact that his writings have exerted an important practical influence upon political events in France. What gives him an unrivaled place in a group of thinkers rarely equaled in a single generation, is the fact that his ideas have actually altered the current of French history. Taine's profound

studies in history, illuminated by the apparatus of modern scientific criticism which he invented, convinced him that the political malady of his country, culminating in the frightful crisis of 1870, was due to a false principle which had been assimilated by the nation. He believed that the great Italian whose supreme genius still obsessed the French people, had, in reality, done them mortal injury by seducing them into paths which led into the past instead of toward the future. In his view Napoleonic imperialism was a survival rather than progress, and he believed that until the taint of the Napoleonic virus was extirpated from the blood of Frenchmen, there could be no real advancement. This idea, which in time took complete possession of Taine, is the soul of the *Origins of Contemporary France*. The literary recluse, the dreamer of metaphysical dreams, had become an active political propagandist, and his motto was a portentous one: *"Écrasez l'infâme!"* (pp. 59-61)

Up to the time of Taine the name and memory of Napoleon had exerted a species of sorcery over France. The halo of splendor was rather enhanced than diminished by the bastard purple and sham empire of Louis Napoleon, and not even the shame and disgrace of 1870 could uproot from the hearts of Frenchmen the inherited idolatry of the great Emperor. The dizzy eminence of that fame had made criticism puerile. The spectacle of the antique Caesar become incarnate in France at the definitive epoch of human enlightenment, the apotheosis of the people in his person, the established humiliation of the royalty and aristocracy of Europe, the flood of splendor which the genius of this incomparable Italian had shed over France— all seemed to make his fame secure.

Up to the time of Taine that career had baffled criticism. Against the background of modern history loomed the figure of the Man of Destiny, original, dazzling, and incomparable. That personality, surrounded by national idolatry, had become almost august. Seen in the luminous haze of history, it had assumed gigantic proportions. It imposed upon history. Victor Hugo said of Napoleon: "He was a hindrance to God."

Taine found himself confronted with a problem of startling proportions. How was it brought about that an outcast foreigner, flung by fate into the whirlpool of the French Revolution, had arrived at the hegemony of Europe? (pp. 61-2)

Such was the problem, desperate enough seemingly, that Taine set himself to unriddle; and he began by inquiring into the racial origins of Napoleon. The antique beauty of that personality had not escaped the admiration of man. But the identification of Napoleon with the unique and masterful species enrooted originally in the soil of Italy, had been merely fanciful. In the original mind of Taine it assumed reality. It remained for this penetrating, critical intellect to perceive the astonishing, tho natural enough, fact that this son of Italian Corsica, who held Europe in his iron grip in the nineteenth century, was the lineal descendant of the Caesars, the Sforzas, and the Borgias, of the mighty condottieri of the Renaissance. There was nothing French in this idol of France. This mind and personality, cast in the antique mold, were entirely out of harmony with modern ideals. By heredity, by right and logically there descended to that head with the Roman profile, the diadem of the Caesars.

It was Taine with his scientific insight, and his marvelous apparatus of modern criticism, who penetrated to the heart of the mystery. Focussed in the reflecting telescope of Taine, the figure of the Titan emerges from its haze of legend, and stands revealed as one of the rarest types in Nature's laboratory, but a type entirely explicable by scientific criticism. We are brought face to face with the last scion of the mother of empires; we recognize the latest descendant of the Mistress of the World. As scene by scene is unfolded, we are enabled for the first time to study that unequalled career under the blaze of the searchlight of science. Suddenly there dawns for us a new conception of Napoleon, startling, disillusionizing, and terrible. (pp. 63-5)

Taine shows conclusively that in Napoleon we are confronted with a survival of that insatiable Italian egotism that throws so lurid a charm over the despots of the sixteenth century. He points out that the rare species had appeared before upon the stage of History, but that, hitherto, the theater had been inadequate. At last all was prepared, the man and the hour had arrived: and what the world then witnessed, and history has since stood aghast at, was simply the working out of natural laws when an intellect of supreme force and originality imposes itself upon a nation in the throes of political transformation. Taine has shown clearly and irrefutably that absolute egotism was the basis of Napoleon's character and that his unexampled triumph was at the cost of all that mankind holds dear. Personal glory, self aggrandizement, the gratification of a measureless ambition, are shown to be the mainspring of his acts. Taine exhibits him as the supreme artist of history, producing an unexampled masterpiece; only, instead of marble his chisel is at work upon the sensitive flesh of humanity. (pp. 66-7)

Taine spent twenty years of labor upon his master work, *The Origins of Contemporary France.* . . . This work will probably be the test of Taine's future fame. It is unlike all other histories, is wonderfully accurate in its facts, and whatever may be thought of the peculiar philosophical doctrines upon which its main thesis rests, it has been acclaimed as an important contribution to modern history. (p. 81)

Lorenzo O'Rourke, "An Appreciation of Taine," in Balzac: A Critical Study *by Hippolyte Adolphe Taine, translated by Lorenzo O'Rourke, 1906. Reprint by Haskell House Publishing Ltd., 1973, pp. 9-82.*

FRANCIS B. GUMMERE (essay date 1911)

[Gummere focuses on Taine's attitude toward individualism in the artist, stressing that his refusal to accept the poet "as an independent force" was his greatest error as a critic.]

[Taine became] a resolute foe of political democracy. He looked back upon the great revolution, as one of his countrymen remarks, through the smoke and the foul odours of the Commune. For him democracy meant unbridled license; it was a mad bull that "sees red," that tramples on all that is delicate, fragile, all that is august and sacred. And yet this hater of political democrats is the most resolute and extreme representative of . . . democracy in science and in the theory of art. . . . (p. 131)

Convention, that is to say the active function of the community, in very wide use of these words, was made by Taine sufficient explanation for poetry and for the other arts almost without reference to the individual mystery of creative power. If Whitman, exponent of democratic art, thought that he could produce poetry as the expression of all the people, the *en-masse,* voiced at will of the over-soul by his individual self, Taine, on the other hand, in an extreme democratic apotheosis of law, thought that he could explain poetry by convention, and could ground and found the everlasting science of it on the community alone. Here . . . is mystery, the mystery of law; and here too is the

will to explain all things by one principle, to build up your universe with one force, to let the two-celled heart work with only one cell. Taine is the conventional monist. It is through him that the ultimate democratic faith in science can best be felt; he undertook to find the explanation of every artistic fact in some inerrant and inevitable law. The romantic school has been derided often enough for its perversion of Herder's doctrine, for its absurdities about the heart of the people, about epics and ballads that sing themselves. No one would have joined more heartily in this derision than Taine, who, nevertheless, by the scientific path, came to conclusions about the making of poetry almost as extreme as those fancies of the romantic folk. His science, however, was not the old and shop-worn kind. He was a psychologist with new ideas. An amiable ignorance of Taine's real theory confounds it with that ancient doctrine of climatic influences, discussed in Greek philosophy, noted by Tacitus, on which almost every learned man of the eighteenth century, including even Dr. Johnson, had something to say, and which Landor summed up in certain charming Hellenics:—

We are what suns and winds and waters make us. . . .

Taine, of course, made this influence a part of his *milieu,* and in his books on Art had much to say of it; but it is only an old paragraph in his new chapter. His psychology was exact. It is not even true . . . that Taine laid no stress on excellence of poetic or other artistic work. He laid immense stress on this excellence, and in his own field was an admirable critic; but for Taine the artist who did the excellent work was simply an agent of the forces about him and in him, of the race, the moment, the *milieu* or environment, and counted only as a sign, a register of values. The poet or artist, by this reckoning, comes to be only a sort of bell-buoy sounding with the rise and fall of the waves, themselves obedient to a long and inevitable if complicated series of causes which rest in the last analysis upon invariable laws. In one sense, this theory does lead, if not to undervaluation of great work, at least to overvaluation of unimportant work; for all links in the chain are so many operative causes, and therefore important. Hence, I think, has come a little of that tendency in comparative literature to exaggerate the influence of the minor poet upon the great poet, and to restore reputations or, more often, to create them, by a doctor-thesis. But that is not Taine's real concern. Submission to the reign of inevitable law, ecstasy over evolution as the principle of the universe, and a stoic attitude towards the pressure of things, towards the sadness which all this new lore forced upon the individual,—these are the ideas of Taine which help to make clear his doctrine of poetry. De Goncourt has a remarkable passage in the *Journal* about the joyless youth, the mature seriousness of Taine, who took even his pleasures in a sort of scientific austerity. There is much of the stoic in him; he looked wide-eyed at the world, and, in George Eliot's phrase, took no opium. The individual, he held, must not exalt his individuality; it is a mere chemical combination, at the mercy of the forces plying always their inevitable tasks about us; the point is to observe facts, to resolve them into right relations, and to find their cause. "Let the facts be physical or moral," he says, "no matter; they always have causes; there is cause for ambition, for courage, for truthfulness, as for digestion, for muscular movement, for animal heat. Vice and virtue are products like vitriol and sugar" [see excerpt dated 1863]. It is very clear that for Taine there is to be no mystery of the genius of individual poets. He simply finds the cause of this genius in whatever combination of forces the law has brought about. In a letter to a friend, he once defined art as "the general in the particular." It is almost as if the player himself were made by the rules of the game. Defending his theory, protesting that literature is not the "record of ideas," but rather the history of the work of men of genius, he declares that his own method is to "generalize" and then to "fill in" with great men as the particulars. But the great man and the great man's work . . . are for Taine but "signs"; the law is the thing. And submission to this law is man's religion; in the end law must be right. Nowhere is the constructive idea of democracy, taken, of course, as abstraction and intention, not worked out as a theory of science or of art, so well glorified in latter days as in Taine's praise of justice.

> There is nothing more beautiful than justice. I love history because it makes me take part in the birth and progress of justice; I find it more beautiful yet because it seems to me the final development of nature. Everywhere, above and below us, is force. . . . This light of justice, of the right, it is for us to kindle and to carry across the wastes of nature and the violences of history. . . .

Nothing could be more characteristic; there is no democracy so noble as this. But one sees the mechanical, the fatal, the ultra-conventional tendency of Taine's doctrine. It is quite hostile to individual initiative; a confederacy of natural forces, animated by a single law, makes and unmakes with mechanical accuracy all the combinations which we call facts. Man must even carry justice to its triumphs by obeying these inexorable laws. Here is the fatal error which left genius and individual initiative out of the account, or rather reduced them to mere terms of convention; and the error is fatal because it foils a comprehensive triumph. Taine nearly solved the problem of art and so of poetry. Had he simply called his *milieu*, his place and time and race, conditions and not causes, had he seen the great dualism here, as one must see it in the universe, as play and interplay of centrifugal and centripetal forces, he would have achieved the whole instead of the half success.

Taine refused to accept the artist, the genius, as an independent force in poetry; and he would not concede what Sainte-Beuve in a memorable review declared to be the final point,—"as it were, a last citadel, never to be taken," *une dernière citadelle irréductible,* sacred from even the most searching analysis of the critic and the scholar, the one thing inexplicable, the inventive genius of the poet. And this refusal, this neglect, was Taine's fundamental error in poetics. (pp. 132-39)

> *Francis B. Gummere, "Whitman and Taine," in his* Democracy and Poetry, *Houghton Mifflin Company, 1911, pp. 96-148.*

G. P. GOOCH (essay date 1913)

[*Gooch analyzes Taine's* The French Revolution, *depicting it as an impassioned, amateurish work that often lacks objectivity and accuracy.*]

Taine's picture [of France in **The French Revolution**] is unfavourable without being hostile. He gives full credit to the monarchy, the *noblesse* and the clergy for building up the nation; but the utility of the Crown had been forgotten in its abuses, and the nobles had ceased to render the services which had once justified their privileges. The Church is censured for its intolerance, the unequal distribution of its vast wealth and its non-resident clergy; the merits of its humbler members are fully recognised. The condition of the peasant, crushed by taxation, is painted in dark colours. The grievances of the *tiers état,* on the other hand, were rather sentimental than practical. 'Already, before the final crash, France is in dissolution, because the privileged classes have forgotten their duties and responsibilities.' The determination to substitute a picture for a narrative is legitimate; but in attempting to portray a century he commits the fatal error of drawing traits from different generations, and presents a description which is not wholly true of any period. By the side of Tocqueville he is merely a brilliant amateur.

The novelty of the volume lies in its derivation of the revolutionary spirit. The thesis is that the philosophy of the eighteenth century was the product of 'the classic spirit,' which was invented by Descartes and the essence of which was to pursue the absolute and to worship uniformity. When the French mind turned to politics it proceeded to prescribe according to the dictates of pure reason. This neglect of the individual, the concrete, the real, was the mark alike of literature, of the *Philosophes* and of the Revolution, and its predominance was the main cause of the tragedies of modern France. But the tendency which he condemns should rather be called the deductive spirit. The classic tradition was boldly challenged by Rousseau, the chief inspiration, in Taine's view, of the revolutionary leaders, and Montesquieu was its open enemy. In the next place he forgets that the French political theories of the eighteenth century were borrowed from the thinkers of other lands. Thirdly, the deductive spirit was a reforming and fertilising as well as a destructive influence. The free play of the strongest minds of France led to the removal of much that was below the standard of the age, and to a notable advance in tolerance and justice. Large parts of their programme . . . were suggested not by deductive reasoning from abstract notions, but by observation of the society in which they lived. 'This vast and admirable effort of intelligence and speculation,' remarks Sorel with justice, 'was not fated to end in Utopias and Revolution.' It pointed to reform, not to anarchy. The comparison of France to a man, rather weak in constitution, who drinks greedily of a new liquor and suddenly falls to the ground, foaming at the mouth, is utterly delusive. To attribute the Revolution to Rousseau is as childish as to attribute it to Plutarch.

L'Ancien Régime was greeted with general admiration, though it completely satisfied no one. Royalists noted with satisfaction that the Revolution was attributed in such large measure to the *Philosophes;* Catholics welcomed the testimonial to the lower clergy; Republicans quoted his views as to the sufferings of the peasantry. When Taine reaches the Revolution itself the relatively balanced attitude disappears. In his **English Literature** he had sharply criticised Carlyle's disparaging verdict.

> These madmen, these hungry sans-culottes, fought on the frontier for humanitarian interests and abstract principles. Generosity and enthusiasm abounded here as with you. They pursued philosophy as your Puritans religion. Their goal was the salvation of all, as your Puritans sought the salvation of self. They combated evil in society as your Puritans in the soul. Like them, they possessed heroism, but of a propagandist kind which has reformed Europe, while yours only helped yourselves.

The Commune and further study completely altered his opinion. In a letter of 1878 he writes, 'Till I studied the documents

I took the same view of the Revolution as other Frenchmen. Since Thiers we have chosen to live in a world of illusion. Drama, poetry, a vague humanitarian philosophy have magnified all these people.' A work was needed, he declared, based solely on contemporary testimony and official acts, without reference to the controversies of a later generation. 'I have written as if my subject was the revolutions of Florence or Athens.'

When the Duc de la Rochefoucauld-Liancourt brought the news of the rising in Paris, Louis XVI remarked, 'It is a revolt.' The duke replied, 'Sire, it is a revolution.' As the duke corrected the King, the historian corrects the duke. 'It is not a revolution, but a dissolution.' With the fall of the central government disappeared the security of life and property. The distinction between the principles of '89 and '93 was contemptuously rejected. On being asked when the Terror began, Malouet had replied, 'On the fourteenth of July, 1789.' Taine shared his opinion. The 'golden dawn' never existed. Moderate men were never at the helm. Sound principles never prevailed. Bloodshed and rapine began at once, and the human tiger bounded forth from his lair. He gathered a good deal of valuable material in reference to the burning of châteaux, the maltreatment of nobles, and the influence of famine in the provinces. The Revolution, he declared, was in essence a transfer of property. 'That is its permanent force, its primary motive, its historical meaning.' No historian can now assert that the opening months were a period of peaceful reform, interrupted only by an occasional explosion like the march to Versailles. On the other hand, the label of 'spontaneous anarchy' is a gross exaggeration. There were thousands of villages in which the Ancien Régime fell without bloodshed or disturbance. The reader is told of no single act of virtue or wisdom. He hears only of evil men and the crimes and follies they commit. The attack on the Bastille is attributed to popular frenzy, and no reference is made to the belief that the troops summoned by the Court were to be employed for a *coup*. The Constituent Assembly is allowed to have planted some useful germs in the domain of private law; but in the sphere of political and social reorganisation it acted like an academy of Utopians. Like a blind operator it destroyed not only the tumours but the living organs. 'It had only one fault left to commit, and this it committed by resolving that none of its members should find a place in its successor.' The King was retained as an impotent mockery. The 'spontaneous anarchy' of 1789 had become the 'legal anarchy' of 1791. 'Such was France—exhausted by fasting under the Monarchy, intoxicated by the bad brandy of the "Contrat Social" and a score of other heady beverages. The period of joyous delirium is over, and the period of sombre delirium is about to begin.'

The work was received with plaudits by Royalists and Catholics, and with indignation by Republicans of every school. Shortly before it appeared Taine wrote to his mother, 'The Revolution seen at close quarters is quite different from what is generally believed. It is a religion, and people will rush at me as if I was a blasphemer.' The attribution of the violence of the leaders to their philosophy is a gigantic delusion. Many of the actions of the Constituent were unwise, and the Civil Constitution was a colossal blunder; but a definite reason can be assigned for every one of them independently of any philosophy. The Rights of Man were not only a declaration of abstract principle, but a protest against concrete abuses. The dominant personality of the Constituent was Mirabeau, one of the greatest of political realists; but Mirabeau is scarcely mentioned. Its mistakes were caused, not by the teaching of Rous-

seau, but by the inherent difficulty of regenerating France, complicated by its own inexperience.

The second and third volumes on the Revolution deal with the conquest of power by the Jacobins and with the use they made of it. Taine thought little of the Constituent, but he looks back to it with something like regret when he reaches the mediocrities of the Legislative and the pygmies of the National Assembly. In the Constituent there had been a handful of wise and sober men like Malouet and Mounier; but the later Assemblies were filled exclusively with theorists, whose dominating principle was the sovereignty of the people, by which they understood, not the majority of French citizens, but the mob of Paris. The Jacobins installed a power at once terrible and imbecile, 'a fierce and suspicious Sultan, who, having appointed his viziers, holds his sabre ready at any moment to cut their throats.' On the foundation of maxims of universal liberty they erected a despotism worthy of Dahomey, a tribunal like that of the Inquisition and human hecatombs like those of ancient Mexico. Visitors to the sanctuaries of ancient Egypt, on asking to see the statue of the god, were shown a crocodile lying on a purple carpet behind a richly embroidered veil. France possessed a similar theology, the tenets of which were formulated by Rousseau. 'In three years they conducted the crocodile into the sanctuary and installed him behind the golden veil on the purple carpet. The god naturally chose fat victims; but his voracity was so great that he also devoured the thin. Once or twice a year he devoured a fellow crocodile, or was himself devoured.'

Such in brief is Taine's celebrated picture of Jacobin psychology. It is the kernel of his work, the part to which he gave most attention and by which his reputation as an historian must stand or fall. But is the Jacobin unlike all other men before him? Are his actions explained by his adoption of the theories of Rousseau? No serious student can answer these questions affirmatively. The heated feeling and violence of language recall the fevered accents of the 'Reflections on the French Revolution' and the 'Regicide Peace.' He professed to be a naturalist; but naturalists do not abuse the objects which they investigate. [*The French Revolution*], declared Scherer in astonishment, 'has transformed the most abstract of our thinkers into an excited polemist.' In his anger he throws his determinism to the winds. We are dealing with a pessimist in a passion. He charges the Jacobins—the term is used generically—with regarding men as automata; but his own Jacobins are pure automata, strange monsters which never existed. He convicts them of blindness to the facts around them; but he is himself blind to the most important influences which guided their conduct. He depicts them springing fully armed from the brain of Rousseau, learning nothing, forgetting nothing, functioning in the void; whereas the real Jacobins, the members of the Jacobin Club, were monarchists during the early part of the Revolution. He warns his readers that he is not going to relate the history of diplomacy and war; yet he omits not only their history but their influence. He portrays the Representatives on Mission as wild beasts, of whom Carrier is the type, their actions governed by blood-mania. The Émigrés on the Rhine, the ceaseless intrigues of the Court with foreign Powers, the flight to Varennes, the hostile armies massed on the frontier a few days' march from the capital, the savage threats of the Brunswick manifesto, the rebellion in the West—these menacing facts, without which the domestic history is unintelligible, are left virtually unnoticed. The leaders were driven to madness, not by Rousseau, but by fear of losing the fruits of the Revolution. Taine confesses that he has only reached one

NINETEENTH-CENTURY LITERATURE CRITICISM, Vol. 15   TAINE

conclusion in politics, namely that society is very complicated. He forgot that man also is complicated, that his motives are manifold, and that it is the duty of an historian in judging men to understand the nature of the problems by which they are confronted.

His letters show that he had formed his judgment of the Revolution before he began the detailed study of its sources. Having formed it, he sought for confirmation. He trusts too much to memoirs, and surrenders himself unreservedly to the guidance of Gouverneur Morris and Mallet du Pan. He greedily swallows every scrap of hostile evidence. He condensed and translated a volume purporting to contain the experiences of an English lady in France during the Terror, but more probably the work of John Gifford, an extreme anti-Jacobin of low character. By following his footsteps in the archives Aulard has discovered how superficial was his research and how unscientific his method [see Additional Bibliography]. He dipped into the bundles to find confirmation for his views. He tears passages from their context. He only makes use of two newspapers, the *Moniteur*, the authority of which has been overthrown, and the *Mercure*, because Mallet du Pan wrote in it. Scherer remarked that he had plunged into the ocean of documents and been drowned. He collected a mass of details, many of them utterly insignificant, while omitting matters of vital importance. It is his method, not his verdict, which leads Aulard to declare that the work is virtually useless for the purposes of history. (pp. 241-46)

> G. P. Gooch, "The French Revolution," in his History and Historians in the Nineteenth Century, *1913. Reprint by Peter Smith, 1949, pp. 226-54.*

JULES LEMAÎTRE (essay date 1921)

[*A prominent French critic of the late nineteenth and early twentieth centuries, Lemaître is known for his highly subjective and impressionistic criticism. Discussing Taine's* History of English Literature *and his treatment of history, Lemaître analyzes some of the contradictions inherent in Taine's life and philosophy.*]

[Hippolyte Taine] is very great. His is perhaps the brain of this century which has stored away most facts and arranged them with most vigour. Each of his 'histories,' each of his 'descriptions'—description of a man, of a literature, of an art, of a society, of an epoch, of a country—resemble massive and serried constructions. Beneath the propositions that are linked together, the series of facts control one another—like the successive layers of a monument. Taine is a prodigious builder of pyramids.

No one has more sternly applied, nor to more varied objects, more narrowly determinist theories. But the experience of the most scholarly man being always very restricted, every explanation of any rather considerable mass of phenomena, inevitably becomes creation. The mind begins by accommodating itself to the portions of reality on which it has been able to seize, but as soon as a more extended reality or all reality is in question, it is this which we accommodate to our mind; it is our mind which completes the facts, and which moulds them, and which supposes relations to exist between them in order to justify certain laws. All philosophy is poetry.

And this is why no one, more often than Taine, has done something different from what he believed he was doing; no one has more felt and imagined, when he believed he was merely perceiving, observing, and classifying.

The theory which is reputed to be the buttress of *L'Histoire de la Littérature Anglaise* only accounts for the mediocre individuals; consequently it only throws light upon what interests us least. It hardly explains the great writers. Whilst Taine labours to see in them the products of the race, the environment, and the moment, he shows them to us, above all, as the producers of a certain sort of beauty to which we shall never know how much is contributed by the race, the environment, and the moment. *L'Histoire de la Littérature Anglaise* is a splendid book; but the best part of it would remain if the theory were taken away or reduced to some rather modest truisms.

Similarly, 'the mistress faculty' explains everything in an artist's work, except beauty. 'The mistress faculty' can, in fact, be met with as well in a 'glutton' as in a man of genius.

In history also, Taine is often a dupe. His determinist conception inevitably leads to gloomy results, whatever be the country or time that he studies. For he always goes back in his analysis to causes that are confused with animal instinct. This is why he has seen both the old system and the Revolution to be equally sad and hateful. Decomposed in the same manner, the Middle Ages and antiquity would none the less surely have appeared hideous to him. Even the beauty of the age of Pericles, if Taine had been able to rummage among the Athenian archives, would not have been able to withstand that operation. The whole destiny of humanity is summed up for him in the sombre picture which Thomas Graindorge paints for his nephew's instructions [in *Notes on Paris*]. (Little rabbits, big elephants—do you remember it?)

He deforms facts by this alone that he coordinates them without knowing them all. He is very little of an evolutionist, for his mechanical system claims to exclude mystery, and there is mystery in 'evolution.' He forgets the fluctuation, the vagueness, the want of precision, the flight and transformation of things. He immobilizes the real in order to observe it, so that what he observes is no longer the real. Assuredly Jacobin and Napoleonic institutions are artificial and oppressive; but have they in ninety years been able to modify the people whom they crush into their moulds, and have they given them another nature? Could we go back to the system of decentralization and small free associations?

Perhaps there is a secret relation between the contradictions in Taine's work and the contrasts which one divines in his mind and character.

This logician is a poet. This abstractor has the most concrete style you can see. No writer has more continuously expressed himself by metaphors that are more coloured, or developed with more minuteness, or that are more exact down to the least detail. This commonly extends even as far as symbols and parables. And thus one fears that, the correctness of the images conquering in his mind the underlying truth, this suspicious positivist may have sometimes allowed himself to be deceived by words.

This man of violent and carnal imagination (you remember his studies of the Renaissance and of Flemish painting) has lived the life of an ascetic and a Benedictine. This great apostle of observation has lived in great retirement, and has associated little, I believe, with men of any other class than his own; and this great collector of facts has sought them above all in books.

This determinist who regards history as a development of inevitable facts, and who has often artistically enjoyed the manifestations of force, has melted with compassion as soon as he saw blood and suffering near at hand. He would have been indulgent to Sulla and to Caesar: Robespierre and Napoleon found him inexorable.

This enemy of the classic spirit has, in his need for unity, subdued reality to the most imperious simplifications and generalizations. His philosophy is to be found, in dramatized form, in the naturalist novel; and we know that the naturalist novel horrified him.

Through having seen too much of human beastliness in history, he ended by being afraid of men. In his later years his sympathy was evident for doctrines of which his own were the radical negation, and even for virtues which his own philosophy was most calculated to discourage.

This man of such uncompromising audacity of thought had become an energetic 'conservative.' (Was he one for the same frightful reason as Hobbes? We do not know.) And not only did he refuse the civil burial which alone would have been sincere, but he did not allow himself to be buried simply according to the rites of the religion into which he was born, rites which would have had, under the circumstances, but slight significance; he demanded—or accepted—a Protestant funeral. I never felt a greater intellectual melancholy than at that lying ceremony.

But this has not abolished his written work. Hippolyte Taine was one of our masters. The positivist period of our literature—that which begins about 1855 and which we see ending—bears the profound traces of his imprint.

One only discovers new truths by means of great foregone conclusions which bring with them quite as many errors. What does it matter? The truths remain. Taine is the writer who has most strongly made us feel and understand the animal and the machine that man always is. Only that is a truth of which we have seen enough, and truths a little different are beginning to attract us more. And then it will happen with Taine as with other great inventors or rejuvenators of ideas; men will abandon him for thirty years—to return again to him. (pp. 219-25)

> Jules Lemaître, "Hippolyte Taine," in his Literary Impressions, *translated by A. W. Evans, Daniel O'Connor, 1921, pp. 219-25.*

N. McWILLIAM (essay date 1924)

[*McWilliam explores Taine's stance toward nature and concludes that although Taine sometimes feared its indifference to human affairs, he turned to nature for relaxation and relief from intellectual activity.*]

Much has been written of Hippolyte Taine as philosopher, historian, and critic, and these outstanding aspects of a great thinker have obscured a side which, though less prominent, is at least as intimate a part of his personality—the side which reveals him as the lover and poet of nature. French literature has not too much of that type to offer. The descriptions of nature which it contains are apt to leave the English reader cold. They appear to him beautiful pieces of artistic workmanship rather than the expression of deep, spontaneous feeling. In Taine we find the two combined. Nature affected him as profoundly as ever it did Wordsworth, and though he did not write of it in immortal verse, no poetry could thrill us with a sense of captured beauty more than do certain accents of his prose.

If it is true, as has been said, that Taine at bottom was only interested in the human soul it is equally true that his deepest joy was inspired by nature. (p. 116)

No masterpiece of Italian painter or Greek sculptor ever filled Taine with the complete joy he felt in the presence of natural beauty. He acknowledged this frankly when he set out on his journey to Italy, and it was proved to him by repeated experiences during his travels. (p. 117)

When he turned to nature, . . . Taine's immediate impression was one of relief and harmonious well being. Here he relaxed for a time the superhuman efforts of his intellect and his will, and lived through other faculties than that of reason. No one has better described that state in which "on rêve avec des sensations, non des idées. . . . cet état incertain entre le sommeil et le rêve, qui replonge l'âme dans la vie animale et qui étouffe la pensée sous les sourdes impressions des sens. . . . on trouve dans son être une harmonie qu'on n'y connaissait pas; on ne porte plus le poids de sa pensée ni de sa machine, on ne fait plus que sentir, on redevient animal, c'est-à-dire parfaitement heureux." He found in short that "la campagne est un opium pour les cerveaux tourmentés." For him, to think too often meant to suffer, either from his own excessive efforts to attain knowledge, or from his painful realisation of the woes of humanity. What he said of Shelley was true of himself. He too was one of "ces âmes trop finement sensibles pour trouver une distraction dans le spectacle et la peinture de passions humaines," and so he too turned to rocks and clouds—"des êtres vivants et divins qui reposent de l'homme." It is this that explains the strange combination of cynical comments on human nature and exquisite appreciation of natural beauty in the *Voyage aux Pyrénées* and the *Notes sur Paris*. When Graindorge has passed in review the various forms of the brutal struggle for life in the modern world, "Regarde autour de toi," he says finally to his nephew, the fashionable young Parisian, "voici une occupation moins animale: la contemplation. Cette large plaine fume et luit sous le généreux soleil qui l'échauffe; ces dentelures des bois reposent avec un bien-être délicieux sur l'azur lumineux qui les borde; ces pins odorants montent comme des encensoirs sur le tapis des bruyères rousses. Tu as passé une heure, et, pendant cette heure, chose étrange, tu n'as pas été une brute; je t'en félicite: tu peux presque te vanter d'avoir vécu." The vision of what "man has done to man" became at times so intolerable that it drove Taine to break through his characteristic reserve and cry out that there was indeed too much evil in the world and that the only way to endure life was to forget it. He sought forgetfulness in the presence of nature and under the spell of the "somnambule éternel" oblivion fell upon him. Thought was suppressed and with it suffering.

But the happiness he found in nature was many-sided, and if its instinctive and most direct form owed nothing to reason, it did not disappear when he examined it in the light of his philosophy. Nature appeared to him "a hundred times fairer" when he brought his thought to bear on her. Why, he asked, did secret weariness overtake him when he looked too long upon humanity, why did he feel impelled to turn to nature for rest and consolation? Was it not because man is indeed incomplete so long as he confines himself to man? He is only a part of universal life, one of the manifold forms of being, and cannot find satisfaction until he has re-united himself to the whole. How narrow, how one-sided is the existence of modern man, especially of the dweller in towns! "Nous vivons claquemurés au 2ᵉ étage et nous trouvons au sortir de nos cages la boue des rues, l'odeur du gaz, l'air étouffé des salons et des bureaux.'' If we are not absorbed by the petty cares of an artificial and prosaic existence, we are overwhelmed by the demands which civilization makes upon our intellects. Modern man is no longer able to bear the weight of accumulated knowledge. One small branch is more than he can master unless he is willing to sacrifice his development in other directions. When we compare such an existence with that of an ancient Greek, must we not ask if man has not strayed from the path of his true happiness? ''Pour s'affiner, il s'est détraqué; il a opposé le surnaturel au naturel, et l'épuration de la conscience humaine à l'animal humaine.'' Man is a child of the earth. His body is nourished by it, its climate determines his habitual sensations and ultimately his whole temperament. Little wonder then that the very essence of his being feels an affinity with its forms and colours, and recognises that here is its ''patrie primitive.'' To live completely, man must transport himself into other forms of being outside his narrow personality. He must deliberately divest himself of his logical nature and yield himself up to what his reason knows to be an illusion. In identifying himself with the life of the animal guided by the wisdom of instinct, he becomes aware of a simplicity, a relaxing of tension, in which his overtaxed faculties find relief. As he descends lower in the scale of creation this realisation of wider, simpler modes of being increases. The animal reveals to him life without reason, in the plant he finds it freed from thought. When he looks upon this tree whose buds form and swell, unfold and fall, steadily, unhurryingly year by year, his soul must partake of its tranquil, unthinking existence. Lower still he finds life in yet more elemental, unlimited forms. The line of a landscape, the sphere of the sky, the play of light and shade—these are but varying expressions of the all-pervading force or life of the universe.

The contrast between the apparently serene and effortless life of nature and the laborious life of man was felt so strongly by Taine that he was tempted at times to regard the former as the higher mode of being. Not only was it more harmonious and therefore more beautiful, it was finer in every way. (pp. 118-20)

But the spectacle of nature and its mighty powers did not always fill Taine with joy. Instead of uplifting, it sometimes overwhelmed. Man's place, he felt, is ill-assured in a universe where the slumbering forces in mountain and sea may destroy him to-morrow, should these giants chance to turn in their sleep. His very existence seems an accident, a chance growth in a cranny of the eternal rock, dependent for its continuation on a degree of temperature. The real possessors of the earth are the hills and the ocean, fellow travellers through whom we dimly apprehend an infinity of time which our puny landmarks may reveal but cannot measure. Can we be sure that man is not a plaything of ''cette dame inconnue que vous appelez la nature,'' a toy which she will presently tire of and cast aside? (pp. 120-21)

It would be false, however, to regard any passages implying nature's superiority to man, as Taine's final judgment in the matter. Such a view would be incredible on the part of one who gave his whole life and energy to the study of the spirit of man, and Taine himself has explained in what sense his words are to be understood. His clearest pronouncement on the question is to be found in a letter to Guillaume Guizot. There is the language of emotion as well as the language of reason, he argues, both legitimate but not to be mistaken for each other. A lyrical effusion is not a confession of faith. If

in moments of reaction from intellectual strain he deliberately allowed his ''moi sentant'' to dominate the ''moi scientifique,'' the ''logicien que j'ai nourri en moi,'' he never really wavered in his belief in the supremacy of moral and intellectual values. It is the torch of justice lit by man and irradiating a natural world without a moral sense, that alone makes life worth living, he affirms, ''et ce ne serait pas la peine d'être homme que d'être réduit à ne pas le voir et ne pas l'aimer.'' Even in the world of natural laws the highest rank must be accorded to thought. The most fragile, man is at the same time the supreme work of nature. ''Je mourrai demain, et je ne suis pas capable de remuer un pan de cette roche. Mais pendant un instant j'ai pensé, et dans l'enceinte de cette pensée la nature et le monde ont été compris.'' To Taine as to Swinburne nature speaks of man as the crown of being:

> One birth of my bosom,
> One beam of mine eye
> One topmost blossom
> That scales the sky;
> Man, equal and one with me, man that is made of me,
>   man that is I.
>   (Hertha.)

This conception enables him to view without resentment the imperfections of human nature, seeing them as inherent necessities of universal laws in process of working themselves out. (pp. 121-22)

When we reflect upon what underlies Taine's dual feeling toward nature, it would appear that it is the consciousness of the problem of mind and body and doubt as to the right lines for the future development of man. In certain moods he shares the view of the ancient Greeks and holds up for admiration the athletic young English undergraduate, in whom he sees the nearest modern approach to the classical ideal. But it is obvious that if he were pressed he would agree with Mr. Bernard Shaw that ''nothing remains beautiful and interesting but thought, because the thought is the life.'' In his well known comparison between Tennyson and Alfred de Musset, he appreciates to the full the harmonious beauty of the English poet, but Musset with his restlessly seeking mind, appears to him to have been more alive and to have risen to higher heights. Yet while Taine triumphantly asserts that ''la matière a pour terme la pensée,'' he was well aware of the deficiency in the life of the pure ''logicien'' and he sought a fuller, truer mode of being in the almost mystical identification of his ''moi sentant'' with nature. (pp. 122-23)

N. McWilliam, ''Taine: His Attitude to Nature,'' in The French Quarterly, *Vol. VI, No. 3, September, 1924, pp. 116-23.*

ALBERT GUÉRARD (essay date 1935)

[*Guérard, a French-born American critic, used Taine's theory of race, environment, and time as the basis for his* Literature and Society, *from which the following excerpt is drawn. In the context of defining the relationship between literature and society, Guérard briefly discusses Taine's influence on modern criticism.*]

It was Taine . . . who, with the abstract logic he professed to despise, hardened a tendency of modern thought into a doctrine, and expressed the doctrine in masterful formulae. Ever since his . . . [''Introduction'' to the *History of English Literature* (see excerpt dated 1863)], the magic words *Race, Environment and Time* have been piously repeated. The latest works of the

Sociological Critics do not go far beyond the impressive theories of Taine.

The whole *History of English Literature* was written as a demonstration of the principles promulgated in the ["Introduction"], and the whole work might close with Q.E.D. It belongs exactly to the same generation as Karl Marx's *Capital,* and, like *Capital,* it shows unmistakable signs of age. Even in its prime, it never was fully reliable; and few pieces of scholarship retain their authority after threescore and ten. . . . Taine's continued appeal is due solely to his vigorous talent: but, as a writer no less than as a scholar, he *dates,* fully as much as his contemporary Matthew Arnold, vastly more than Sainte-Beuve, Renan or Walter Pater. Much of his imperious logic is forced; much of his brilliancy strikes us as glitter. Let us not forget that he was writing under the Second Empire, whose masterpiece was Garnier's gaudy Opera, and that he, the ascetic scholar, collaborated to *La Vie Parisienne.*

Most antiquated of all is the "positivism" of Taine, his naïve worship of facts, facts, facts. It is antiquated because it did not represent the man himself: it was the *Zeitgeist* of Scientific Realism speaking through a sensitive, tormented soul. His phrase: "Vice and virtue are products like vitriol and sugar," is often quoted as an example of crass materialism. Determinism, yes; materialism, no. Taine does not even suggest that vice and virtue are *chemicals;* he only asserts that they are *products,* and this no conservative moralist will deny. If we insist upon the importance of education, a wholesome atmosphere, the avoidance of dangerous associations, it is because we believe, with Taine, that the law of cause and effect is valid even on the ethical plane. On the whole, however, the general impression is not wrong: Taine was committed to the materialistic interpretation of history, including, as a by-product, the history of literature.

We were taught our letters by faithful disciples of Taine. We rebelled against him, because he had been captured by the reactionaries. But these word-battles of the past century are now one with Nineveh and Tyre. Taine is just receding beyond the awkward stage when a writer no longer possesses the liveliness of a contemporary, and has not quite attained the dignity of a classic. (pp. 32-4)

> Albert Guérard, "Race," in his Literature and Society, *Lothrop, Lee and Shepard Company, 1935, pp. 3-144.*

ALBERT THIBAUDET   (essay date 1936)

[*Thibaudet was an early twentieth-century French literary critic and follower of the French philosopher Henri Bergson. His work is considered versatile, well informed, and original, and critics cite his unfinished* Histoire de la littérature française de 1789 à nos jours, *first published in 1936 and excerpted below, as his major critical treatise. In this work, Thibaudet classified authors by the generations of 1789, 1820, 1850 (including Taine), 1885, and 1914-18, rather than by literary movements. Here, Thibaudet discusses Taine as an artist and historian, focusing on his* A Tour through the Pyrenees, The Philosophy of Art, Notes on Paris, *and* The Origins of Contemporary France.]

Formulas and definitions are to Taine's criticism what crinolines were to the gowns of his time. Their artifices soon went out of style. For a long time writing about Taine as a critic meant forgetting all that was new and powerful in his best pages, all that revealed a remarkable genius for interpretation, and discussing only the skeleton of this interpretation, his two

theories, the two formulas, which were, first, the determinism of race, environment, and time, and, second, the definition of a writer or an artist by his major faculty. The first theory is an arbitrary and ingenuous contravention of didactic philosophy in the realm of sentiment, taste, plurality, and complexity. As for the procedure that consists in focusing a writer or a work on a major faculty, it is related to the same passion for "definitions," assisted in addition by the recollection of Balzac, that readily creates a character like Grandet or Hulot around a major characteristic or a single passion.

But with the *Voyage aux Pyrénées* an artist had come to light in Taine. Until this time sensations had meant nothing to him but the subject for a thesis in the spirit of Condillac. As he entered his forties, they made some inroad into his life with their brilliance and their flower, and much more inroad into his style, which was amply and felicitously fed on images. His sylvan childhood in the Ardennes was given back to the Parisian professor, and he exchanged the drawing pencil for the painter's palette. In 1862 he wrote: "When I look at myself as a whole, it seems to me that my state of mind has changed, that I have destroyed in myself the talent of the orator and the rhetorician. My ideas no longer form ranks as they used to do; I have flashes, intense sensations, impulses, words, images—in short, my state of mind is much more that of the artist than that of the writer." It was true. Taine's experience as an artist represents the opposite of the prematurely dead poet survived by the man. It is the story of the artist in his prime, momentarily obscured by the school and emerging again after the school, beneath the school.

This artist, however, is to be found only quite rarely (except for the admirable pages on Rubens and Rembrandt) in *La Philosophie de l'art,* which is his only professiorial book. . . . Here Taine appears as a real and even a great professor. The audience that listens to him is made to perform a movement opposite to his own, the opposite of the movement of the *normalien.* To artists who know what the world of art is, or who learn it in the studio, he reveals another world, that of general ideas. Within the framework of these general ideas he parades the ranks of picturesque minor details with order and discipline. Speaking in the great semicircular auditorium beneath the fresco of Paul Delaroche, he carried its rhythm over into his lectures, he made his podium one of the typical places of French history. Nowhere else does the theory of race, environment, and time seem more inoperative and oratorical than in this *Philosophie de l'art,* a simple mental exercise that classifies facts. Those who heard it and read it were plunged into a healthful bath of general ideas, but for them there could be no question of living in those frigid waters.

The luck of a friendship, that of Planat, the founder of *La Vie parisienne,* served the artist far better by inspiring in him that picture of the customs of the Second Empire, *Thomas Graindorge* [*Notes sur Paris*]. Obviously Graindorge has aged because of his oratorical content. But, since the society that he represents has undergone the same aging, since in addition this is the book in which Taine, so reticent and fearful when it came to revealing himself, put the most of himself, *Graindorge* retains an attraction. It became the peak of the Stendhalian Taine, the Taine with little or no system, the Taine of small pure facts—of the *Carnets de voyage,* of the *Notes sur l'Angleterre,* those well-written books that flowed from the pen of a genuine traveler who traveled, and far superior to the *Voyage en Italie,* which is too gorged, too much the professional journey undertaken to refresh the store of general ideas. All of

Taine the artist is found again in his solid, brilliant, and valuable *Correspondance*, much more alive than Renan's and, with Flaubert's, the best literary correspondence of his time.

But Taine's greatest work of art is his historical work. In *Les Origines de la France contemporaine* he erected one of the greatest monuments, at once oratorical, evocative, and dialectical, that has ever existed in French literature. A historical monument? That is something else. (pp. 309-11)

His uncountable collection of small details, brought together in support of directives and general ideas that were not absolutely preconceived but that had taken shape very quickly in his mind, soon became a file constructed to uphold a thesis, a thesis that was not itself a thesis for anyone, that was a thesis against, that of a severe and sorrowful physician for whom health had never been visible in the face of France except in a precarious condition that augured nothing good. None of the ideas that were contending for supremacy in France in 1875—legitimism, Napoleonism, republicanism—escaped his terrible diagnosis. The *ancien régime,* the Revolution, Napoleon became three artisans of the same disintegration, three precursors of what Barrès, a disciple of Taine, was to call a disassociated and decerebrated France. In the end the reader told himself that, while everything was going badly now, M. Taine offered some ground for consolation by showing us that everything had always gone very badly and that people had survived just the same, even survived well. *Les Origines* is the book of a great pessimist who resembles that historian for whom the decay of Rome began with the assassination of Remus by his brother. But it is also the book of a great bourgeois, a great orator, and a great classic.

Embarked or re-embarked on middle-class life through his marriage, he had pledged to the middle class the loyalty, though somber, of the convert. (pp. 311-12)

This great book in defense of the middle class is a class book in the social sense, but it is also a book of great class in the literary sense and most certainly Taine's literary masterpiece; more generally, the greatest monument of oratorical continuity since Livy—*molus animi continui.* Elsewhere the profound artist that Taine is might have been restricted or out of his element as a result of his subject. Here he had free rein, like Michelet.

And this book of great rank brings together in a supreme pyrotechnical display all the resources and all the power of the classic genius. Never more classic than in that theory of the classic spirit, which, located in the heart of the *ancien régime,* has remained the most famous, the most discussed, the most suggestive of Taine's ideas. It is clear that here he was doing battle with himself, that the artist bore his schoolroom culture with bad conscience and observed it with distrust, that he never falls more wholly into the circle of the classic spirit and culture in their rational, constructive and oratorical form than when he imagines that he is fleeing them. In *Les Origines* he found the subject that best suited a classic artist's genius: portraits to be made, or, rather, constructed. His portraits of the philosophers of the eighteenth century, of the men of the Revolution, and of Napoleon are astonishing structures, undoubtedly the only pages that show us what Balzac could have done if he had been cast in the classic mold of the Latins and the eighteenth century: ideas to be filled in, a discourse to be developed, and, to give this discourse warmth, a passion that merged the political passion and the personal passion of the bourgeois, almost of the landowner: an incomparable source of life!

It is chiefly through the tremendous influence of *Les Origines* that Taine's presence continues. He furnished a conscience, an ideology, images to all the parties of the right. . . . For a half century this work never stopped finding an audience; it is the great book of French reaction. In contrast to the philosophical historian, the pure philosopher has lost his force, the literary historian has been surpassed, the critic's theories have aged. But, looked at again in the history of ideas, Taine holds a high place: a place even in the urban sense of the word, crossroads, landmark, open spaces, porticoes of general ideas, monumental staircases among the various disciplines. (pp. 312-13)

Albert Thibaudet, "Taine," in his French Literature from 1795 to Our Era, *translated by Charles Lam Markmann, Funk & Wagnalls, 1968, pp. 306-13.*

BENEDETTO CROCE (essay date 1938)

[*An Italian educator, philosopher, and author, Croce developed a highly influential theory of literary creation and a concomitant critical method. His literary theories had a profound impact on the criticism of the first half of the twentieth century, particularly in his emphasis on judging the totality of a work within a context created by its own existence as a separate, independent entity. Croce here contends that Taine has no place in the history of ideas, arguing that his slavish devotion to science and systematic thought contributed to his failure as a historian. Croce's* History as the Story of Liberty, *from which this excerpt is taken, was originally published in Italian in 1938.*]

Among examples of the technical or medical attitude towards historical reality and of a consequent unilateral and fallacious historical vision and incapacity to act, the most obvious because the most vivid in our memory for the varied notoriety of his work, is Taine: the philosopher, the man of letters, the historian and the counsellor in high politics based on history.

Perhaps by now the clouds of contemporary and national admiration for the character of Taine as an original and profound and vigorous thinker are so far dissipated as to admit of demonstration that he never advanced the critical method in any single field he studied, that he did not confirm any proved truth and discovered no new one, that he sowed no new seeds but on the contrary invented and disseminated not a few paradoxes and paralogisms. It is sad and even displeasing to have to formulate this conclusion when we consider the nobility of the man and the diligence of his labours: it is the same kind of conclusion as one often reaches after examining the copious and mechanical work of estimable persons who have consecrated themselves to art and to poetry when the latter did not want to have anything to do with them, no matter how much they pressed their claim in extravaganzas of originality. Taine was never carried away in his work by the fresh breeze of truth; he was driven on by the tyranny of an idol which he called "science," epitomized for him by the figure of the doctor, especially of the alienist and the gynecologist who studied and set out to cure the hysterical and insane women of Salpétrière, which he at one time visited; the whole world became for him a kind of Salpétrière, man a madman and a "patient," healthy only by chance, otherwise a *gorille féroce et lubrique,* who cannot be intrinsically educated by civilization, but only softened and thereby weakened. In his writings on philosophy at the start he dismissed with a flick, as one might use against a mosquito, Kant and the *a priori* synthesis, that is the whole spirit of modern philosophy. He read Hegel without even a suspicion that Hegel is a Kantian who goes deeper than Kant, and that the Hegelian Ideal is an ulterior form of the *a priori* synthesis and of the dialectic contained in that synthesis. So Hegel pleased him extrinsically, and he fitted him in with Condillac; perception was for him "true hallucination" which finds its counterpart by chance in an external reality. He dreamed he would apply the experimental method to philosophy and the classificatory method of the natural sciences to history, to history which, he said, had only just got its first foundation in his own work. However, since such applications were impossible in practice and resisted his efforts (as they have resisted and will always resist similar efforts, whoever makes them), all that he could achieve was the introduction into historical and philosophical problems of a metaphysical presupposition of naturalistic make. He painted fanciful pictures of what he claimed to be historical reality which he viewed as the effect of geographical or racial setting, of circumstances or moments, of *facultés maîtresses* or other mythological entities. This was to be fixed and immutable, and the why or wherefore of any motion or change he did not account for. He wallowed in a muddle of logical inexactitudes, never doubting or subjecting himself to self-criticism. His early literary life was only that of the historian and critic of poetry and of art, but he identified these with the sort of symbolism used in the classifications of the natural sciences; he identified the history of poetry and art with that of the sentiment and practical action, so that the final purpose of his **Histoire de la Littérature anglaise** was to be a *définition générale de l'esprit anglais.* He converted practical and moral life into a sequence of psychological or, often, physiological and pathological schemes. One of his French critics said of him that although he had written so much literary history, yet he had never understood what a line of poetry was; and indeed he never had any feeling for the poetic quality of poetry. He was revered in academic lecture halls and admired by the journalists who did not understand him but re-echoed his formulae, and—so preposterous were the things he said about art—that he drove artists like Henri Becque to rebellion and irreverence. Taine really does not belong to the history of thought, of philosophy, of criticism, or of historiography, but rather to that of tendencies and cultural fashions, a typical representative of the fanatical interest in the natural sciences, and especially in medicine, which, after 1850, filled a good forty years of European life, accompanied by inane efforts to remodel the whole of culture on a similar basis. Taine's "experimental" philosophy and his historiography degraded to the ranks of botany and zoology had its counterpart in the equally absurd ideal of the "experimental novel" by Emile Zola: these were two fairly similar minds and hearts, and two fairly similar artistic styles, both having the strength but also the creaking, the rhythm, and the monotonous noise of machinery, deprived as they are of mellowness and spontaneity.

Taine, like Renan and other French writers, was recalled to a sense of responsibility and to the duties of the citizen by the painful events of 1870-71. But the distortion of his historical and political concepts were an insuperable obstacle to anything he might have undertaken in the service of his country. The famous preface of 1875 to his **Origines de la France contemporaine** certainly deserves to remain famous, but only as an ingenuous confession of political nullity. He remembers that in 1849 as a voter aged twenty-one he had to nominate fifteen or twenty deputies and to choose among different political doctrines, republican, monarchical, democratic and conservative, socialist and Bonapartist. What should he do? The motive which was valid for others was not valid for him: he wanted to vote according to knowledge and not *d'après ses préférences.* As one might say: choose a wife according to knowledge, and flee from inclination and preferences. And this is

certainly not the way to decide to marry. So half-amazed, half-scandalized and curious, he watched how, in spite of his warning, and notwithstanding these preliminary objections which seemed such strong and peremptory evidence, his fellow-citizens in France yet went to vote: "Dix millions d'ignorances ne font pas un savoir." Nevertheless the fault lay in him and not in those who voted according to their own preferences, because those preferences were in fact desires, impulses, needs, and maybe imaginings and illusions, all of which go to make the plot of human action and history, from which new forms of life and also new errors (these too ultimately productive) emerge. But his abstractions bore no fruit, and his practical resolution, self-suspended and awaiting the dictates of science, was condemned to perpetual suspension, since science cannot give an answer to a question that does not concern scientific problems, but is concerned only with practical resolutions.

Being but poorly equipped with self-criticism, as we have noted, Taine did not criticize the question that he had raised: but spinning his ratiocinations from the stuff of the pre-suppositions which he had dogmatically assumed, he arrived at the conviction that the social and political form in which a people can *entrer et rester* is determined by its character, by its past, and must model itself, "jusque dans ses moindre traits aux traits vivants auxquels on l'applique," and that therefore in order to choose a constitution suited to France it was necessary to know the reality of contemporary France, and that since the present is the consequence of past history, it was also necessary to find out how that had been formed. Such an inquiry, in order to be carried out scientifically, had to be conducted *en naturaliste,* with a perfect objectivity and indifference, as if "devant les métamorphoses d'un insecte." As we know this was exactly the opposite method to that of the true historian who participates, taking sides in historical events, and in the very throes of this passion achieves the mental strength to understand history by overcoming his early passion, and having understood it, goes on passionately making history. The historiographical operation which Taine proposed to carry out was an empty one as were also the aims which he laid down for the politician, whom he was desirous to see "diminuer ou du moins ne pas augmenter la somme totale, actuelle et future, de la souffrance humaine," as though suffering were a mass whose size could be quantitatively measured, and as though man was not always ready to meet every pain for the sake of a love conquest. In order to foster the illusion that this emptiness was not empty Taine foreshadowed its fulfilment, and the effect of long labours which would be seen in a distant future. The book he worked on which was to prescribe a remedy for sick France was to be in his sense *une consultation de médecins;* he said time was required before the patient would accept these medical counsels, there would be imprudence and relapses, and the doctors would above all have to agree among themselves, but they would end by so agreeing, because moral science had finally abandoned the *a priori* method and political notions would filter down from the Academy of Moral Sciences, united with the Academy of Inscriptions to the universities and the thinking public, just as electrical notions had filtered down from the Academy of Sciences, and perhaps these political notions would pass to the Chambers and the Government within a century, and politics would become quite scientific, like surgery and medicine.

Under the inspiration of such propositions the history of the *Ancien Régime* of the Revolution and of the Empire which Taine constructed sets out essentially to be the history of an illness, an illness which he calls *l'esprit classique* of rationalism or illuminism. There is no need here for an exposition or a criticism in order to show that when rationalism (which is on the one hand a perpetual form of the human spirit and one of its necessary arms, and on the other has given its name to a very vigorous and productive epoch of European life) is considered as a disease, the history of civilization in development, the history of the centuries before and after the eighteenth cannot any longer be interpreted. Taine's interpretation of the French Revolution has several times been criticized, and it would be no use to return to that criticism here. It is only important here to see what were the practical results he achieved after such a long and laborious investigation of the documents of that historical period.

The editor of the last volume of the unfinished work says something about it in his preface. His way of interpreting the relation between theory and practice, history and political life, naturally raised the hope that he would dictate rules and caused people to turn to him . . . for opinions on this or that situation, or upon this or that reform. But poor Taine got out of such requests and entreaties, thereby doing much honour to his own modesty, but also making "Science" cut a pretty poor figure, after he had attributed virtues to it which it in no wise deserved. "Je ne suis qu'un médecin consultant," he parried, "sur cette question spéciale je n'ai pas de détails suffisants; je ne suis pas assez au courant des circonstances qui varient au jour le jour." And then, having found that there was no general principle from which a series of reforms might be deduced, he limited himself to recommending not to look for simple solutions, but to proceed by feeling one's way with moderation, accepting the irregular and the unfinished. It was a wise recommendation, but was either too general or too particular and unilateral, if it meant that one method was to be favoured over another or one party over another by one of those *préférences* from which he had tried to escape, believing them to be illicit or dangerous: in fact, it was a declaration of the failure of history by diagnosis and of the pharmaceutical politics which he had proclaimed, and for which he had worked laboriously but in vain. (pp. 189-95)

> Benedetto Croce, "The Preparatory and Non-Determinate Character of Historiography as Regards Action," in his History as the Story of Liberty, translated by Sylvia Sprigge, George Allen and Unwin Limited, 1941, pp. 187-95.

EDMUND WILSON   (essay date 1940)

[Wilson is generally considered twentieth-century America's foremost man of letters. A prolific reviewer, creative writer, and social and literary critic endowed with formidable intellectual powers, he exercised his greatest literary influence as the author of Axel's Castle, a seminal study of literary symbolism, and as the author of widely read reviews and essays in which he introduced the best works of modern literature to the reading public. In the excerpt below, Wilson studies Taine's style as a critic and historian. He censures Taine for such characteristics as his "mechanical" writing method, his ineffective use of literary devices, and his sympathetic attitude toward the social elite in his histories. Pointing out a "middle-class moral flatness" and a "real lack of taste" in his writings generally, Wilson also accuses Taine of partisanship in his The Origins of Contemporary France.]

Renan's style, so much admired in its day, shows certain definite signs of decadence. Renan was always insisting that French literature ought to return to the language of the seventeenth century, that the classical vocabulary was sufficient to deal with modern feelings and ideas; and his own style preserves in distinguished fashion the classical qualities of lucidity and sobriety. (p. 44)

With Taine, the effect is quite different. Taine is not trying to get back to the past; he has gone ahead with the present. But, in doing so, he has come to exhibit some of the most unattractive qualities of that present; and we may study in his form and his style the characteristics of the bourgeois nineteenth century, as they confront us as soon as we open him—before we pass on to his content.

Amiel complained of Taine: "This writer has a trying effect on me like a creaking of pulleys, a clicking of machines, a smell of the laboratory" [see excerpt dated 1871]. And he was justified: Taine had perfected one of the great modern mechanical styles. His books have the indefatigable exactitude, the monotonous force, of machinery; and, for all his gifts of sympathetic intelligence, and the doubts with which he was sometimes troubled on certain tendencies of his contemporary world, he is rarely shaken out of the cocksure and priggish tone, the comfortable conviction of solidity, of the bourgeois whom the machine is making rich. In this, he resembles Macaulay, whom he had at one time inordinately admired; but it is a Macaulay of the latter half of the century and a Macaulay of a more philosophical turn of mind, who is beginning to be sour instead of optimistic at the direction that the century is taking. It is curious to find Taine, in his chapter on Macaulay, condemning in his predecessor the very faults from which he suffers himself. For Taine himself, in spite of his repeated insistence on his attitude of naturalistic objectivity, was to become almost as emphatic as Macaulay with a sort of middle-class moral flatness. And the overdemonstration which he blames in Macaulay, the laboring of points already obvious, is certainly one of Taine's worst habits.

It is not precisely decadence that is seen here; Taine's immense sentences, vast paragraphs, solid sections, gigantic chapters, represent the never-slackening ever-multiplying production of a class that is still sure of itself. But there is a lack of human completeness somewhere, and this appears in Taine's real lack of taste. He manages to combine the rigor of the factory with the upholstery and the ornamentation of the nineteenth-century salon. A large area of the surface of Taine's writing is covered over with enormous similes, which have been laid on a coat of paint. These similes at their best are very good; but even when they are good, they are usually overelaborated; and all too often they are ludicrous or clumsy. . . . [In] *The Origins of Contemporary France*, in the section on [*The French Revolution*], we find what is probably one of the worst figures in literature. Taine is trying to convey the situation of France at the time when, according to his picture, all the men of public spirit and brains had been executed or driven into exile or hiding, and only the ignorant and brutish held the power: "The overturn," he writes, "is complete: subjected to the revolutionary government, France resembles a human being who should be obliged to walk on his head and think with his feet." This is bad enough; but when we turn the page, we find the next chapter beginning as follows: "Imagine a human being who has been obliged to walk with his feet up and his head down"—and he goes on to elaborate it for half a page. Compare Taine even at his best with the images in Michelet, which are struck off so much more spontaneously but which stick so much longer in the mind: the Renaissance sawed in two like the prophet Isaiah; the Revolution undermined by speculators like the termites in La Rochelle; the Tsar and the King of Sweden coming down like great polar bears from the north and prowling about the houses of Europe; the unspoken words, congealed by fear, unfreezing in the air of the Convention; the French language of the eighteenth century traveling around the world like light.

So much for the surface of Taine. It is significant of the difference between Michelet, on the one hand, and both Renan and Taine, on the other, that we should think of the latter as presenting surfaces.... But both Renan and Taine practise systematizations which, in ordering the confusion of human life, seem always to keep it at a distance. Renan must never get so close to violent happenings or emotions that they can break up his sweet and even flow. Taine feeds history into a machine which automatically sorts out the phenomena, so that all the examples of one kind of thing turn up in one section or chapter and all the examples of another kind in another, and the things which do not easily lend themselves to Taine's large and simple generalizations do not turn up at all. The thesis is the prime consideration, and he will allow only a moderate variety in the phenomena that go to fill it in. Yet Taine, with his remarkable machine, did manufacture an article of value. (pp. 44-7)

Men like Taine were traveling away from romanticism, from the revolutionary enthusiasm and the emotional exuberance of the early part of the century, and setting themselves an ideal of objectivity, of exact scientific observation, which came to be known as Naturalism. Both Renan and Taine pretend to a detachment quite alien to the fierce partisanship of a Michelet; and both do a great deal more talking about science. The science of history is for Taine a pursuit very much less human than it had been for Michelet. He writes in 1852 of his ambition "to make of history a science by giving it like the organic world an anatomy and a physiology."... In the famous introduction to the *History of English Literature* [see excerpt dated 1863], ... Taine stated his full philosophy and program: in dealing with works of literature, "as in any other department, the only problem is a mechanical one: The total effect is a compound determined in its entirety by the magnitude and the direction of the forces which produce it." The only difference between moral problems and physical problems is that, in the case of the former, you haven't the same instruments of precision to measure the quantities involved. But "virtue and vice are products like vitriol and sugar"; and all works of literature may be analyzed in terms of the race, the milieu and the moment.

This theory in itself might have produced a criticism utterly arid; but Taine had a great appetite for literature and a gift for dramatizing literary events. In studying works of literature as the flowerings of periods and peoples, he developed superbly a special department of Michelet's "integral reconstitution of the past"; and literary criticism ever since has owed him an immense debt. From Taine's program, we might expect him to confine himself to an analysis of works of literature into their constituent chemical elements; but what he does rather is to exhibit them as specimens, and he delights in showing us how each of his specimens is perfectly developed in its kind. Nor is his interest in them, in spite of what he says, of a character purely zoological. Taine had strong moral prepossessions of a kind which made the literature of the English a peculiarly happy subject for him. Though he dismisses Dr. Johnson as "insupportable," he enjoys playing the Puritans off against the frivolities of the Restoration and gets one of his best effects by following a description of the Restoration dramatists with a peal of the voice of Milton growling at the "sons of Belial." (pp. 48-9)

Outside the ideal of "pure science," to which he imagined he had devoted his life, there was little moral inspiration for Taine in the France of the Second Empire. He took courses in anatomy and psychology, frequented the alienists. Yet his determinism is not enough for him; and although he continues to affirm it, we find him smuggling himself out of his confinement within a mechanistic universe in various more or less illogical ways. When he comes to write his philosophy of art, he is obliged to introduce a moral value in the form of "the degree of beneficence of the character" of a given artist or painting. And in his last phase we are to see him responding to a sense of patriotic duty.

The French defeat and the Commune profoundly shocked and troubled Taine; and he sat down in the autumn of 1871 to an immense and uncongenial task which was to occupy him all the remaining twenty years of his life and to be left by him unfinished at his death. Taine set himself to master politics and economics, and to study the processes of government in France from the eve of the great Revolution down through Napoleon to contemporary society. It is in vain that he keeps insisting that his object is purely scientific, that he is as detached in his attitude toward France as he would be toward Florence or Athens: the *Origins of Contemporary France* has an obvious political purpose; and we may infer from it how far the enlightened bourgeois has traveled since the end of the preceding century in his relation to the revolution which made possible his present enlightenment and which established him in the present enjoyment of his property and his rights.

The first thing that strikes us, after Michelet and Renan, about the *Origins of Contemporary France* is that it is not a history at all, but simply an enormous essay. If Renan has become an historian of ideas, allowing other events to lapse into the background, Taine is an historian of literature and displays a truly startling ineptitude when he attempts to deal with parliaments and uprisings. Books and pictures may be pinned down and studied quietly in libraries and museums; and a social life sufficient to explain them may be reconstituted from conversation and travel; but though Taine can read all the documents on a great social struggle as he can read any other books, there is nothing in his own personality or experience which enables him to re-create in imagination the realities these documents represent. Note ... how awkward he is with a political generalization, but how brilliantly he comes to life when it is a question of a writer to be described. In the eternal generalizations and classifications which constitute the whole structure of his history, the movement of events is lost. In the first place, where Michelet, in attempting to tell everything, is always tending to expand beyond his frame, Taine has begun by laying out a plan which will exclude as many elements as possible. What he is undertaking, he tells us, is merely a "history of the public powers"; he leaves to others the history "of the diplomacy, the wars, the finances, the Church." Then he formulates a set of simplifications of general political and social tendencies, then marshals to the support of each of these a long array of documentary evidence. By Taine's time, the amassment of facts for their own sake was coming to be regarded as one of the proper functions of history; and Taine was always emphasizing the scientific value of the "little significant fact." Here, he says, he will merely present the evidence and allow us to make our own conclusions; but it never seems to occur to him that we may ask ourselves who it is that is selecting the evidence and why he is making this particular choice. It never seems to occur to him that we may accuse him of having conceived the simplification first and then having collected the evidence to fit it; or that we may have been made skeptical at the outset by the very assumption on his part that there is nothing he cannot catalogue with certainty under a definite number of heads with Roman numerals, in so complex, so confused, so disorderly and so rapid a human crisis as the great French Revolution.

As Renan, even after he has explained to us that in the decline of the ancient world it was saints rather than sages who were needed, makes us wonder whether the civilization represented by Marcus Aurelius might not after all have saved itself and done a much more agreeable job of it; so Taine, in the very act of demonstrating the inevitability of the breakdown of the old regime, assures us that its worst abuses were already being corrected by the governing class itself and keeps intimating that if only the people had been a little more reasonable and patient, the whole affair might have been quietly adjusted. Our conviction of the inevitability of religions and revolutions varies in proportion to our distance from them and our opportunity for untroubled reflection. Taine plays down the persecutions for religious belief and liberal thought under the regime of the monarchy and almost succeeds in keeping them out of his picture; and he tries somehow to convey the impression that there was nothing more to the capture of the Bastille than a barbarous and meaningless gesture, by telling us that it contained at the time, after all, only seven prisoners, and dwelling on the misdirected brutalities committed by the mob. Though in some admirable social-documentary chapters he has shown us the intolerable position of the peasants, his tone becomes curiously aggrieved as soon as they begin violating the old laws by seizing estates and stealing bread. Toward the Federations of 1789, which had so thrilling an effect on Michelet, he takes an ironic and patronizing tone. The spirit and achievements of the revolutionary army have been shut out from his scope in advance and are barely—though more respectfully—touched upon. And the revolutionary leaders are presented, with hardly a trace of sympathetic insight—from a strictly zoological point of view, he tells us—as a race of "crocodiles."

Where now is the Taine who, with Alfred de Musset, could exult in the sense of humanity rising to greatness of vision through misery, conflict, dissipation? The human Proteus, in its convulsions and its disconcerting transformations, has thrown Taine and sent him away sulky, as soon as he has emerged from his library. Not only is he horrified by the Marats, but confronted by a Danton or a Madame Roland, he shrinks at once into professional superiority. At the sight of men making fools and brutes of themselves, even though he himself owes to their struggles his culture and his privileged position, a remote disapproval chills his tone, all the bright colors of his fancy go dead. Where is the bold naturalist now who formerly made such obstinate headway against the squeamishness of academic circles? He is pressing upon us a social program which blends strangely the householder's timidity with the intellectual's independence. Don't let the State go too far, he pleads: we must, to be sure, maintain the army and the police to protect us against the foreigner and the ruffian; but the government must not be allowed to interfere with Honor and Conscience, Taine's pet pair of nineteenth-century abstractions, nor with the private operation of industry, which stimulates individual initiative and which alone can secure general prosperity.

The truth is that the mobs of the great Revolution and the revolutionary government of Paris have become identified now in Taine's mind with the socialist revolution of the Commune.

Like Renan, he has been driven to imagining that his sole solidarity lies with a small number of superior persons who have been appointed as the salt of the earth; and he is even farther than Renan from Michelet's conception of the truly superior man as him who represents the people most completely. But, though not much liking his ordinary fellow bourgeois, he will rise to the defense of the bourgeois law and order as soon as there seems to be a danger of its being shaken by the wrong kind of superior people.

Yet something is wrong: his heart is not in this as it was in his early work. He does not like the old regime; he does not like the Revolution; he does not like the militaristic France which has been established by Napoleon and his nephew. And he never lived to write, as he had planned, the final glorification of the French family, which was to have given its moral basis to his system, nor the survey of contemporary France, in which he was apparently to have taken up the problem of the use and abuse of science: to have shown how, though beneficial when studied and applied by the elite, it became deadly in the hands of the vulgar. (pp. 50-4)

> Edmund Wilson, "Decline of the Revolutionary Tradition: Taine," in his To the Finland Station: A Study in the Writing and Acting of History, *1940. Reprint by Doubleday & Company, Inc., 1953, pp. 44-54.*

MARTHA WOLFENSTEIN   (essay date 1944)

- [*Wolfenstein traces the evolution of Taine's philosophy of art and discusses the influences of Romanticism and science on his ideas. Positing that "Taine's philosophy of art revolves around one central problem, the problem of the relation of history to values," Wolfenstein evaluates his attempt to resolve the conflicting claims of impartiality and judgment in his critical methodology.*]

Taine's philosophy of art revolves around one central problem, the problem of the relation of history to values. The question is whether we can reconcile a universal standard of value with the historical variations of art and taste. Taine began by asserting that it was not possible. The theorist of art, he thought, should abandon the old project of judging art, and apply himself to the more useful work of correlating artistic phenomena with other facts of social life. This was his own intention as an

An illustration from Notes on Paris.

historian of literature and the plastic arts. He wished to make his attitude as impartial as that of a botanist, observing that different kinds of vegetation appear under different climatic conditions. Taine could not, however, eliminate all considerations of value. Unacknowledged value-judgments forced their way into his historical studies. Eventually Taine recognized this fact, and confronted the task of formulating and justifying his implicit criteria. But the standard of value which he proceeded to elaborate remained uncoördinated with his earlier historical approach. His theory of value failed to overcome the difficulties which his historical observations had raised.

The intellectual struggle which appears in Taine's philosophy of art is part of a more intimate and at the same time a more widely social process. A thinker's ability to solve the problems that he undertakes is not a result exclusively of his wit and learning. It is also a function of his emotional attitudes and his relation to the society in which he lives. In the case of Taine, a basic ambivalence towards his society was responsible for the contradictions in his thinking about art. In order to integrate the historical and evaluational factors, a certain social adjustment is requisite. The thinker must be able to discover some institution or movement in his society which he can identify as the actual or potential agency for realizing what he considers valuable. Such an adjustment does not in itself constitute a solution of the problems of art criticism, but it provides a necessary condition for their solution. In thinkers who succeeded better than Taine in solving the problem of history and values, some such adaptation was achieved. (pp. 332-33)

In 1857 Taine published *Les Philosophes Français du XIXe Siècle.* This book is a brilliant polemic against the spiritualistic or eclectic philosophy, most completely exemplified in Cousin, which had superseded the materialist philosophy of the eighteenth century. Taine contrasts the philosophical integrity of Condillac with the political opportunism and apologetic spirit of Cousin. Cousin ends by offering his eclecticism as a support for the dogmas of the Church. His philosophy "does not depend on facts or analyses. Its first principle is to edify honest souls and to suit fathers of families." It has succeeded because it fulfils certain requirements of the times. But it acts to repress all invention; it is impotent to lead any fresh intellectual movement. If its precepts were consistently carried out, all the new findings of science would have to be suppressed as subversive to public morality. Taine discovers the corrupting motive of the official philosophy in its subordination to moral ends. To avoid such subversion of truth, Taine recommends that the philosopher should be, like the scientist, purely impartial. Taine himself follows this procedure. When he philosophizes, he steps out of his rôle as a member of society. What sort of practical consequences may follow from his inquiries does not concern him. One of his politically preoccupied opponents may object, "But you set up a revolution in the minds of Frenchmen." Taine in his philosophical rôle replies, "I know nothing about it. Are there such beings as Frenchmen?"

The intention of maintaining scientific impartiality constituted the distinctive feature of Taine's approach to art. In *Les Philosophes Français* he had observed that Cousin judged every school of art according to whether it upheld the morality to which he was devoted. In contrast, Taine's scientific aesthetics "neither pardons nor proscribes; it verifies and explains." In his thesis on La Fontaine he had already announced this scientific approach. He now proceeded to apply it in a long series of essays on literature, and later in his lectures on the plastic arts.

The method of studying art which Taine chose as a basis and justification for his impartial attitude was the historical approach introduced by the Romantics. The Romantics had wished to combat the classical tradition in art and to rescue mediaeval art from the obloquy which it had suffered since the Renaissance. To this end they had formulated a set of historical arguments. Each epoch of history, they argued, had its distinctive institutions. Men were molded and remolded by these changing social forms. Thus men could not be regarded as the same throughout history. The peculiar institutions and the corresponding psychology of each period gave rise to different styles and standards of art. The merits of each artistic style were relative to the prevailing social institutions. The standards embodied in the art of one epoch could not be set up as authoritative for another. These general arguments were applied to the comparison of ancient and mediaeval art. The classicists were wrong to condemn mediaeval art on the score that it failed to conform to ancient canons. Mediaeval art had an excellence of its own, which derived from its appropriateness to feudalism and Christianity. However admirable ancient art might remain, it was necessary to recognize that the institutions to which it had been suited no longer existed. Thus modern artists could not hope successfully to emulate classical art. Their minds were formed by different institutions than the ancient ones. The institutions which were decisive in differentiating the modern from the ancient mind were those dating from the Middle Ages. The practical consequence then drawn was that the modern artist must regard the mediaeval tradition as the "indigenous" tradition, and seek to draw his inspiration from it and not from ancient models.

This romantic doctrine was highly suited to Taine's purpose. It was necessary only to eliminate the programmatic conclusion, and the opposition of classical and romantic as two competing alternatives. Taine envisaged an indefinite number of historical epochs, each occasioning forms of art appropriate to it, each providing a subject for historical analysis. In the writings of the Romantics there had already been a tendency to transform the problem of the theorist of art from passing judgment on works of art to correlating them with developments in other provinces of social life. The Romantics had also indicated the relativistic implication of their historical view, which supported Taine's requirement of impartiality; artistic standards were not to be defended or combatted, but to be regarded as mere historical data.

The salient points of Taine's historical relativism may now be indicated. Taine observes that, since the beginning of the century, "it was perceived that a work of literature is not a mere play of imagination, a solitary caprice of a heated brain, but a transcript of contemporary manners, a type of a certain kind of mind." The problem which he sets himself therefore is to discover what conditions of social life have given rise to a particular work or school of art. It is necessary to recognize the diversities of art and taste which an historical survey reveals. The basis for this variety is found in the appearance of different psychological types, corresponding to different historical situations. Taine criticizes the eighteenth-century philosophers who regarded men of the most diverse social conditions "as if they were turned out of a common mold." He considers that there is in each period of history "a group of circumstances controlling man." Each historical situation "develops in man corresponding needs, distinct aptitudes, and special sentiments." The type that most fully exemplifies the qualities appropriate to the given conditions constitutes the ideal of the age. Taine sees passing in historical procession the

Greek athlete, the mediaeval knight or monk, the Renaissance courtier, and the modern dissatisfied Faust-like man. In every age men award their admiration and sympathy to this current ideal, and the art of the period centers around it. The plastic arts represent it, as Greek sculpture embodied the athlete ideal; while the other arts appeal to the sentiments of the dominant type. Artistic excellence in any period is determined by conformity to the reigning ideal.

It follows that it is impossible to ascribe exclusive authority to any single standard of artistic excellence. We look upon the works of the past with different eyes from those of the author's contemporaries. Often these works leave us quite unmoved, and it is only by means of historical study that we can reconstruct the type of mind that took pleasure in them. The same discrepancy would appear if a survivor of a past epoch could be confronted with the art of more recent times. Taine imagines the horror which Balzac's style would inspire in an eighteenth-century French classicist. To a mind conditioned by the circumscribed regularity, the elegance and refinement of court life, Balzac would seem feverish, disordered, full of incongruous juxtapositions. It is just these qualities, however, which make him congenial to minds formed by the confusion and rapid tempo of nineteenth-century Parisian life. "There is, then, an infinite number of good styles. There are as many as there are epochs, nations, and great minds. All differ. . . . The pretension to judge all styles by a single standard is as preposterous as the proposition to shape all minds in a single mold and to reconstruct all ages after a single plan."

The scientific character which Taine imparted to the doctrines derived from the Romantics consisted largely in the superimposition of analogies borrowed from the natural sciences. For example, having read Darwin, Taine took the conformity of artistic styles to the prevailing social institutions as an instance of the law of natural selection. Such analogies, which served to frighten the more timid of Taine's contemporaries, added little to his working basis of interpretation. Indeed, it must be admitted that the sociologist can find few usable hypotheses in Taine. In the introduction to his *History of English Literature* Taine presented his famous three factors of historical determination, the race, the milieu, and the moment. The race consists of the supposedly biological inheritance of a nation; the milieu includes physical environment and prevailing social institutions; and the moment, the acquired momentum which these institutions carry over from the past. However, the difference between what is racially inherited and what is determined by temporary social conditions remains uncertain in Taine's own mind. It is also impossible to differentiate in any concrete case between what he means to attribute to the milieu and what to the moment. Setting aside the geographical component of the milieu, the three factors reduce to one, an undifferentiated mass of social phenomena. Through much of the *History of English Literature* we find that Taine's historical method consists chiefly in interspersing facts of general social history with facts of literary history. His intention to adopt a social approach to art failed to mature into a set of concrete hypotheses.

Despite his constant professions of scientific impartiality, Taine could not help regarding the different artists and works of art that he analyzed as of unequal value. He attempted to disguise these value-judgments as judgments of what is typical of a particular age or nation. He calls some artists "greater" than others; but he maintains that he means only to indicate their superior degree of conformity to their social environment. The

History of English Literature abounds in such ambiguous judgments. For example, Taine calls Byron the "greatest" of modern English writers; but he explains this as meaning that Byron is the "most English." Taine dislikes the Restoration dramatists; the reason he gives is that they attempted to borrow French forms which were unsuited to the English character.

Here Taine borrows another doctrine of the Romantics. He repeats one of their most striking fallacies. The Romantics had argued that art is a product of the "indigenous" tradition; from this view they attempted to draw the consequence that art *ought* to be the product of this tradition. But the same relation cannot be asserted truly as an historical law and meaningfully as a normative one. If art is inevitably determined by the so-called indigenous tradition, it is meaningless to exhort artists to follow this precedent. They cannot do otherwise. On the other hand, if the imperative is meaningful, it must be that the so-called indigenous tradition is not the sole determinant of artistic production. In the case of the Romantics, the latter interpretation is applicable. The "indigenous" tradition to which the Romantics appealed was by no means the exclusive determinant of art in their society. Classical art, which they regarded as alien, had set the ruling standards for several centuries. The nineteenth-century classicist could cite precedent no less than the Romantic. The fallacy of appealing to history to decide disputes of value is thus apparent. Those who make this appeal always select one out of several historical precedents, while failing to make explicit the principle of value which has guided their selection.

Taine's use of the terms "most English" and "truly English" to discriminate among English writers is subject to the same criticism. Taine has selected, chiefly on the basis of implicit standards of value, certain English writers as superior. He then defines the English character in keeping with his favorites. Frequently it becomes necessary to alter the "typical" English character, as Taine admires writers of diverse affinities. For example, Byron is "most English" because he embodies the characteristically English spirit of rebellion. It is this which made it possible for Byron to sympathize with the heroes of the French Revolution at the very time his countrymen (all so much less English) were fighting to put down the Revolution. However, Taine also admires Burke. Thus in discussing Burke's *Reflections on the Revolution in France*, Taine remarks, "Real England hates and detests the maxims of the French Revolution."

If we examine Taine's procedure more closely we shall be able to uncover his suppressed criteria of value. In the *History of English Literature* he devotes much more space to some writers than to others. Shakespeare for example claims many more pages than any other Renaissance writer. Byron occupies a lengthy chapter, while Southey, the poet laureate of the day, is disposed of in a few pages. It would seem that Taine has selected for particular attention just those writers who are able to command admiration beyond the limits of their age and nation, those who are called "great" in retrospect. Taine, however, attempts to justify this emphasis from the point of view of his historical project. (pp. 336-42)

What I particularly wish to remark is Taine's inability to coordinate his implicit evaluational principle with his historical analysis. It is in respect to just that quality which Taine considers valuable in an artist that he fails to establish a social derivation. Taine's critics have argued that it is only the mediocre artist who "dates." The great artist does not succumb to the fashions of the moment, and so appears in retrospect undistorted by temporary peculiarities. Contrary to what Taine had set out to prove, he agrees in practice with his critics. For him too, the great artist stands alone, his vision unobscured by the biases of his contemporaries. His strength resides in an individual quality, poetic perspicacity. In fact, of course, Taine himself cites plentiful evidence to show that Byron, for example, was far from being an isolated figure. At war with conservative English society, Byron was inspired by the ideals of the French Revolution. Taine is able to see Byron as a protagonist of these disappointed hopes. Yet he is unable to establish any connection between these social relations and the quality in Byron which he admires.

Taine's conception of the great artist derives from his conception of his own method as a thinker. Regarding his opponents as determined by social motives, he was unable to see that his scientific aims also had an historical derivation. The historical line from which Taine drew his strength had fallen into official disrepute. And while he rejected the official philosophy he still could not identify himself with the opponents of the regime. Hence his conception of himself as holding aloof from all social influences, and his analogous conception of the great impartial artists.

It may be argued that Taine's inconsistency in allowing his tastes to obtrude themselves in no way invalidates his basic doctrine of historical relativism. As opposed to this view, I should like to indicate that the breakdown of Taine's relativism may be traced to a doubtful psychological premise. Taine's underlying assumption is that human nature in general is an abstraction to which no content can be assigned. . . . Taine holds that there is not one psychology but many, a different one for each age and nation. Taine does not, however, accept these many psychologies as mysteriously given and inexplicable (as Spengler does later). He attempts to indicate how these psychological differences come into being. There is in every historical period "a set of circumstances controlling man," an institutional organization which "develops in man corresponding needs, distinct aptitudes and special sentiments." This theory of the genesis of different psychologies involves at least one general psychological assumption, namely, that men's characters are conditioned by their social environment. Admission of this one general psychological law would not, however, seriously alter the relativist conclusion, that for each man those things are best which his upbringing impels him to pursue. A more decisive objection to relativism would be that it involves a dubious conception of the process of conditioning.

To put the argument in general terms, any theory of conditioning would seem to presuppose some unconditioned needs as a starting point. These needs can be directed to the pursuit of many different objects. However, not all the objects which a need has been persuaded to seek are equally capable of satisfying it. The pursuits instigated by modern advertising afford obvious examples. Men can learn to behave in a great variety of ways, but they cannot learn to be equally happy in all of them. It is this obstinacy of feeling, underlying the malleability of behavior, which the relativist overlooks. The relativist argues that no value-judgment can take precedence over any other. If I say that you value the wrong things, this is merely a rather impertinent way of expressing the fact that my upbringing has been different from yours. What the relativist fails to see is that the different upbringings themselves may be capable of comparison, on the basis of their relative fitness to promote the satisfaction of human needs. The doubtful conception of conditioning to which the relativist seems committed

is that all instances of conditioning are equally adequate and successful; that the basic needs are equally amenable to every institutional pattern.

Taine, while nominally committed to this view, was nevertheless unable to conceal his conviction that some institutions are better suited than others to satisfy human needs. Speaking of the consequences of ancient and mediaeval institutions, he wrote, "In Greece, we see physical perfection and a balance of faculties . . . in the Middle Ages, the intemperance of over-excited imaginations." The terms he uses betray clearly which set of social conditions Taine considered more conducive to human welfare. It was thus inevitable that Taine should sooner or later be forced to set up a universal standard of value.

However, Taine's historical relativism is not wholly invalidated by this necessity. The judgment that all social products satisfy human needs does not eliminate the applicability of historical qualifications. If we set up an ideal of human satisfaction, disregarding the actual and limited alternatives between which our social situation affords a choice, we are Utopian. Similarly, if we judge the works of the past without reference to the limiting conditions under which they were produced, we are guilty of what may be called "retrospective Utopianism." Within each social period, we may discriminate movements advancing and movements impeding the further satisfaction of human needs. In judging the activities and productions of each period, we must take as our standard the limit of satisfaction obtainable under the existing conditions. At the same time, it is necessary to observe the point at which altered conditions make possible the surpassing of a previous limit (or, in the case of retrogression, the unattainability of an earlier standard). Thus the ideal of any particular period is not to be mistaken for a universal norm.

We may now specify the sense in which Taine's historical formula is acceptable. Taine wrote that "there is an infinite number of good styles. There are as many as there are epochs. . . . All differ. . . . The pretension to judge all styles by a single standard is as preposterous as the proposition to shape all minds in a single mold." As it stands, this statement is ambiguous, since it is not clear what is meant by "a single standard." If the single standard is the very general one which requires the greatest possible satisfaction of human needs, the pretension to judge all styles by this standard is justified. But if the standard is the product of universal needs interacting with the limited possibilities of a particular historical situation, Taine is correct in saying that any single standard is of limited applicability. (pp. 344-47)

Martha Wolfenstein, "The Social Background of Taine's Philosophy of Art," in Journal of the History of Ideas, *Vol. V, No. 3, June, 1944, pp. 332-58.*

ALVIN A. EUSTIS   (essay date 1951)

[*Eustis explores the influence of Taine's attitude toward Romanticism and Classicism on his literary criticism.*]

[If Taine's] feelings were those of a romanticist, his mind was that of a classicist in the narrowest, most dogmatic sense of the term. Constantly in search of unity, of the "formula," he was incapable of seeing any shade between black and white, of allowing any two authors, centuries, or countries to share common traits, except when both were classical or both romantic. As a result, the classifying tendencies of the analytic brain directed against the classical centuries and peoples the fervent animosities of the romantic heart. Classicism for Taine could not, given its nature, excel in poetry, psychology, or independent thought, because these domains were reserved for the romantic centuries and peoples. For this reason, he is less than just toward Latin literature, which he condemns almost in its entirety. His picture of English literature is marred by his determination not to permit any similarities with, much less influences from, its classical neighbor across the Channel. If the French were civilized, the English had to be "half-drunken brutes" up to the end of the eighteenth century. When, through increasing familiarity with individual works and authors, he realized to what an extent English literature was moral and thus classical in a qualified sense, he rejected it almost without exception in the name of "art for art's sake."

Most deficient of all is Taine's portrayal of the French seventeenth century, in which he perceives the best example of the defects of a classical people and age. His basic attitude is one of scorn toward a "dead" thought, art, and literature which, since they have no philosophical or aesthetic value, can be treated from a purely historical point of view. And so he binds the century in a system which he never dared, nor wished, to apply elsewhere with such rigidity. The consequence is that posterity has judged Taine's picture of that century more harshly than any other part of his criticism. Authors all but disappear into their environment, since classical writers cannot be granted the status of individual creators. A second-rate writer like Fléchier is placed on the same level as Corneille and Racine, who in turn have identical psychologies. An important current of thought like Jansenism is played down, because such heterodoxy would belie the conformity which *must* characterize a century completely subservient to king and Godhead. There can be no scientific progress, which is held in reserve for the eighteenth century. Not only does Taine thus create a privileged status for the Age of Voltaire (not classical in its essence), but he makes the seventeenth century responsible for the Revolution and the optimistic philosophy of Rousseau and his followers (and even for nineteenth-century eclecticism). Not for him the modern concept of the seventeenth century as pessimistic and reasonable, in contradistinction to the rationalistic optimism of its successor. On the other hand, when the artist gets the better of the historian, Taine is capable of judgments which are more enthusiastic than sound; as in the case of La Bruyère, already a revolutionary and a Romantic, or conversely, of Rousseau, a "degenerate" classicist.

Nevertheless, Taine's prejudice against Latinity and the Age of Louis XIV, to say nothing of the English Augustan age, because they were not romantic enough, did not prevent him from attacking nineteenth-century Romanticism and Realism in the name of the rules, unity of composition and character, and simplicity of style. The examination of his peculiar ideal of beauty has revealed that this is not confusion, or a nostalgia for the classical literature he had condemned: truly creative literature must, for him, combine reason and emotion, spontaneity and reflection, form and content. Therefore, Taine had singled out as the only perfect literature the works of the Greeks and of a mere handful of modern poets and novelists who were isolated in their times, whether the latter were classical or romantic in inspiration. The fact that among these "artists" French authors figure prominently shows, however, that Taine's anticlassicism must not be taken to imply a prejudice against the entire literature of France. His despair over the predominance of the "classical spirit" from the *Song of Roland* to *Hernani* was the very reason why he let into his select company those "Gallic" or "romantic" authors whom he considered

uncontaminated and who aroused in him "a feeling of beauty." For Taine was as incapable of a purely negative attitude toward French literature as he was of scientific detachment. A man who felt so deeply that he hid his emotions for fear of possible ridicule, a patriot who gave the last twenty years of his life to a study of his country's woes in the hope that some day France's philosophy, art, and literature would be reformed along his own lines, he has left a criticism which is as sincere as it is distorted. As much "possessed" as the Romantics he disdained and as unable as they to see the positive qualities of the classical genius, his mind remained an analytic instrument that the classics he despised might well have envied him. His personal tragedy is thus to have been the implacable enemy of his own "master faculty." (pp. 56-8)

> *Alvin A. Eustis, in his* Hippolyte Taine and the Classical Genius, *University of California Publications in Modern Philology, No. XXXV. University of California Press, 1951, 63 p.*

SHOLOM J. KAHN (essay date 1953)

[*In this excerpt from his full-length study of Taine's scientific and aesthetic doctrine, Kahn outlines the limitations and the strengths of Taine's critical method.*]

[In viewing Taine from a long-range point of view, his most important limitations are] in the actual development and applications of his method itself, most of which have been touched upon in the course of our critical exposition. Some of these are perhaps inevitable for a philosophical criticism, and others may have been the result of personal and temperamental weaknesses in the man himself.

Among the former may be mentioned: his tendencies towards abstraction, deductive method, jumping to conclusions, abuse of analogy, and neglect of the work of art. None of these are fatal; all are to some extent inevitable; and Taine's degree of fallibility on these scores varies from occasion to occasion. Thus, if men wish to generalize at all, some abstraction is necessary. As to the element of deduction, even the sciences have given up Bacon's ideal of perfect induction, and, especially in aesthetic criticism, it is hard to conceive of a critic proceeding to analyse—even *look* at a painting or *read* a book—without some hypothesis already in mind, some notion of what to look for. Any mind that *reaches* a conclusion must make a *jump* somewhere; but Taine was especially guilty in this respect because he liked to see his facts fit into neat and coherent logical systems. Use of analogy is natural enough in discussions of literature and art, which are filled with metaphors and symbols, but Taine overdid his fondness for seeing men as 'seeds' and paintings as 'flowers', because of his tendency towards monism, towards seeing all kinds and levels of phenomena as expressions of universal biological and psychological laws. Finally, short of telling the reader simply to read the poem and look at the painting, a critic must inevitably leave the work of art behind at times. Still, Taine's historical emphasis led him to extremes in his neglect of aesthetic form.

Other, more personal, limitations in his method, most of them springing from his preference for Spinoza over Hegel, or from the struggle between the two philosophies in his mind, include his tendencies towards mechanism, towards a static logic, towards a rigid set of concepts, and towards neglect of the subtle complexities and conventions involved in the processes of cultural communication. Hence his rather naïve assumptions that analysis of the effects of Race, Environment, and Time is 'but a mechanical problem'; that there is a one-to-one correspondence between the *Zeitgeist* and the spirit of an artist's work; and so forth. Despite the fact, pointed out by Brunetière, that Taine was constantly making progress towards mastery of new areas of human experience, the essentials of his method and values were fixed by the age of twenty: growth after that age seems to have been more quantitative than qualitative, except perhaps after the crisis of 1870. His attempts at being all-embracing, and reconciling the opposites of permanence and change, led to uses of broad terms like 'abstraction', 'race', 'milieu', and 'moment' which were just vague enough to have provided grist for the mills of hundreds of commentators.

Most serious of all, perhaps, from our point of view, is his over-simplification of the entire problem of culture and communication, which, as Cleanth Brooks has pointed out, has been the central concern of more recent criticism. Though, as an historian, he had a rich awareness of the densities of facts, his Hegelian search for laws of history led him to take too many of his documents at their face values, without inquiring sufficiently into the special meanings terms and symbols may have had for various generations. . . . Curious enough, for a protagonist of historical method, in this respect he was *not historical enough*.

Yet, with all these limitations, personal and methodological, there is a solidity to Taine's philosophy and achievement which makes it one of the permanent contributions in the history of criticism. He is one of those figures whom one cannot ignore, however much one may agree or disagree with him. . . . One way to correct the tendency to dismiss Taine because of his imperfections is to ask, not what he *fails to do,* but what he *succeeds* in doing. It is unfair to expect of any critic that he be all things to all men, perfect, like a God. What then are Taine's peculiar virtues?

It is important, first of all, to place him in the great and considerable tradition to which, as a Naturalist, he belongs. Taine's Positivism and Romanticism make him a complete child of the nineteenth century; but, since he was also constantly striving to balance his Romanticism and a Classical heritage, he incorporated many elements of the Aristotelian tradition.

However one may judge these broad historical generalizations, . . . certain more obvious contributions of Taine to our understanding of literature and art help define his significance for criticism today.

Primarily, of course, his work stands firm, not as the pioneer example, since the idea is at least as old as Plato and Aristotle, but as the great modern *crystallization* of the historical method. In Professor Levin's words [see Additional Bibliography], citing a comment by Gustave Flaubert, Taine's *History* got rid, once and for all, 'of the uncritical notion that books dropped like meteorites from the sky. The social basis of art might thereafter be overlooked, but it could hardly be disputed.' He serves as a perpetual reminder of this fundamental fact to the many who still (such is the stubbornness of human nature!) persist in forgetting it. Professor Levin goes on to claim that 'Taine's introduction to his history of English literature, which abounds in dogmas . . . , is rather a manifesto than a methodology.' We should prefer to say: rather a *general formulation* of the historical problem than a *complete* methodology. Taine was scientist enough to realize that he was bound to ask more questions than he could himself answer, that he was rather delineating and exemplifying a 'manner of working' than presenting a set of ready-made solutions.

Another way of stating this contribution is to say that Taine is outstanding among those who attempt the important and difficult task of relating (some would say: *confusing!*) literature and life. Here, again, he initiates more than he achieves, and, as one must freely admit, often neglects the complications of culture and its conventions. But his solid strength comes from the fact that he keeps literature and the arts firmly where they belong: in the mainstream of social reality. In Professor Levin's excellent phrase, he treats 'Literature as an Institution', though the elementary character of his social science limits his usefulness today, except as a pioneering example in whose works we find a sound general approach to the problems of method. Paradoxically enough, for he was 'a resolute foe of political democracy', this is essentially a corollary of the democratic principle in the arts: 'So criticism, which is the valuation and history of poetry as an achievement, is impatient to reach its Homer, its Sophocles, its Shakespeare, as soon as it can; but the student of poetry as a social art, an institution, an element in human life, must turn to democratic and communal origins. . . .'

In this respect, especially, Taine embodies the social values of the Romantic tradition. However, and here he seems particularly relevant to the needs of our day, his is a Romanticism with a minimum of sentimentality, grown critical of its own assumptions. (pp. 198-201)

Finally, Taine provides a frame of reference—indeed, the only possible frame of reference—for those who would labour in the vineyards of Comparative Literature, and towards a concept of World Literature, to which the comparative method must ultimately lead. Comparative studies cannot do without his categories of analysis—Race, Environment, Time, and Master Faculty—though they may perhaps add new ones and refine the applications of the old far beyond what Taine himself achieved. (p. 201)

> *Sholom J. Kahn, in his* Science and Aesthetic Judgment: A Study in Taine's Critical Method, *Routledge & Kegan Paul Ltd., 1953, 283 p.*

V. S. PRITCHETT (essay date 1957)

[*Pritchett is a highly esteemed English novelist, short story writer, and critic. Considered one of the modern masters of the short story, he is also a respected and well-read literary critic. Here Pritchett comments on Taine's perception of England in his* Notes on England.]

Taine's *Notes on England* is a startling book. It records a country which is almost unrecognisable to us, a way of living that has gone. As for appearance and character, these are distorted (oddly enough) by Taine's rigid sense of scientific accuracy. One might be reading pages of Wyndham Lewis, and one reflects that nothing creates the grotesque so surely as a collection of unexpected facts. The truth is that Taine's mind was systematic, but it was also romantic in its taste for excess and even rhetoric, and the mixture made him an excellent observer of English character. Unlike Nathaniel Hawthorne, who saw England in the same period, he was not vitiated in observation by chauvinism, touchiness or envy; the reason being, that, as a Frenchman, Taine felt no insecurity. The secure can utter their opinions and receive the opinions of others, without hostility. When Hawthorne is shocked we do not always trust him; when Taine is shocked we know he is without *arrière pensée.* (p. 86)

One difficulty that Taine's [critical] system had to deal with was to explain how a race so active, practical, good, dull and workaday, could have produced what he regarded as the finest lyrical poetry in the world. In painting we were—as in the rest of life—mere copyists and fact-hunters; in music—though 100 years later we have become intensely musical—we did not know a note. In the novel, we were conventional; good natural reporters of our scene, but circumscribed by our practical moral worries. Puritanism had ruined the arts or had taken the fire out of them. Taine puzzles this out and evolves a theory about the Me, which we would call the ebullient egoism of the English:

> For them, this ego, this Mighty Me is the principal personage of the world. Invisible, all visible things are rallied to him, subordinate to him, and their only merit is in becoming aware of him, in corresponding to something in him. . . . To have taken so dominant a place the spiritual being must be very strong and all-absorbing. And so it is, as one perceives as soon as one considers the principal features of English character: the need for independence, the capacity for initiative, the active and obstinate will, the vehemence and pungency of the passions concentrated but controlled, the harsh though silent grinding of their moral machinery, the vast and tragic spectacle which a soul entire furnishes for its contemplation, the custom of looking into the self, the seriousness with which they have always considered human destiny, their moral and religious preoccupations, in short all signs and faculties and instincts which were already manifest in the pen of Shakespeare and the hearts of the Puritans.

We suffer 'hypertrophy' of this 'Me' and 'for a soul so constituted and disposed, the proper medium of expression is poetry'. In short, the intolerable pressure has split us and we write the lyric. It is a theory . . . that omits to mention that we may have imagination.

In a hundred years many things which were thought to be peculiarly English, turn out to be true of all rich industrial societies. Many things in Taine's *Notes* now seem more American than Victorian. The fact is that he over-dramatised us and, not being noted for gaiety himself, failed to notice English gaiety. His England is nothing like ours today, except in the permanent misery of our climate. In only one respect does this brilliant, honest and admiring observer still strike home: it is in the recurring suggestion that we become good psychologists with great difficulty. Right and Wrong—what blunt instruments they are. (pp. 86-7)

V. S. Pritchett, "Taine on England," in New Statesman, *Vol. LIV, No. 1375, July 20, 1957, pp. 86-7.*

RENÉ WELLEK (essay date 1959)

[*Wellek's* A History of Modern Criticism *is a major, comprehensive study of the literary critics of the last three centuries. His critical method, as demonstrated in* A History *and outlined in his* Theory of Literature, *is one of describing, analyzing, and evaluating a work solely in terms of the problems it poses for itself and how the writer solves them. In the excerpt below, Wellek rejects the assessment of Taine as rigid and overly scientific,* arguing instead that his mind was "extraordinarily complex and even contradictory."*]

Taine, though imbued with the scientific ideals of his time, did not understand (or rather rejected) the basic scientific method: the treatment of the work of literature as a "thing," a projected object which thus can be handled as a totality, can be compared with other works, seen as a link in a series and isolated from the mind of its creator or reader. Rather, Taine treats literature as a symptom of an age or nation, or an individual mind, and dissolves the work of literature into an assemblage of characters.

Taine as a critic is at his best when he can describe this fictional world of characters as a symbolic social picture of the time. Thus [*Essai sur les fables de La Fontaine*] treats his hero as a kind of erratic rock isolated from his contemporaries by temperament. The early verse is ignored and only the *Fables* are analyzed as a social picture of the age: with the king, the nobility, the monk, the bourgeois, the magistrate, the physician, the professor, the merchant, the peasant, all disguised as animals. But Taine understands that the Lion, while King of the beasts, is not Louis XIV; that an idealization, purification or heightening has taken place in the artistic process: "La Fontaine is a moralist and not a pamphleteer: he has represented kings and not the King. But he had eyes and ears, and must one believe that he never used them? One copies one's contemporaries in spite of oneself." The poet is a sociologist but an unconscious one.

The brilliant [*Balzac: A Critical Study*] is the high point of Taine's criticism: it links the man, "a businessman in debt," his greed for money, his sensuality, his ambition, his capacity for sheer work with his society, the imaginary world of his characters, his style and his philosophy. The unity in contrariety, the interconnections and linkages are established convincingly: the sensation of the totality of writer, work and the civilization he represents is powerfully conveyed. Other essays or chapters in the [*History of English Literature*] fall short of this success but, on occasion, approach it: the Dickens piece, even the unsympathetic essay on Tennyson or the overdrawn and oddly distorted account of Shakespeare.

But Taine always fails with authors who do not lend themselves to this method. Thus the surprisingly enthusiastic account of Spenser is merely descriptive, metaphorical; it is largely filled with quotations, strangely helpless as characterization. The attention given to English lyrical poetry, though rather full in the number of names and quotations, seems often out of focus. Taine dismisses seventeenth century poetry (Donne and others) as bad taste. He has little use for neo-classical poetry, which seems to him imitative of the French. He has a wrong perspective on the Romantics, which even at the time of writing was quite obsolete. All the emphasis falls on Burns and Cowper as the precursors and Byron as the representative genius. Taine does not know Keats, though he mentions him twice; he praises Shelley but vaguely; he almost ignores Coleridge as a poet and critic and he considers Wordsworth as an inferior Cowper. The praise of Byron, who is compared to Aeschylus, is so extravagant that it can hardly be taken seriously today. One is confirmed in a low opinion of Taine's sense of poetry (or at least English poetry) when one encounters his high praise of *Aurora Leigh*, which he had read, he tells us, twenty times. Taine has a pronounced romantic sensibility to be noted in his admiration for the gloomy Byron, his praise of Musset or in his treatment of Thackeray. Taine is shocked by the latter's cynicism and admires *Henry Esmond* most because this book is freest of it.

He admires not only the book, but also the dreary character of Henry Esmond himself. The whole often incongruous preferences for the romantically sentimental must be explained by Taine's much deeper and very genuine pessimism: his bitter sense of man's subjection to death and fate, unreason and depravity.

Taine thus presents, contrary to the usual view which reduces him to a kind of pseudo-scientist, an extraordinarily complex and even contradictory mind at the crossroads of the century: he combines Hegelianism with naturalistic physiology, a historical sense with an ideal classicism, a sense of individuality with universal determinism, a worship of splendid force with a strong moral and intellectual conscience. As a critic he has suggested questions in the sociology of literature but has much more successfully characterized an individuality and analyzed the world of a writer, his types and ideals. A sense of individual detail, of the "small significant fact" often oddly clashes with the general structure of bold generalization: a worship of passionate colorful imaginative art is often mitigated by traditional good sense and taste.

From a modern point of view Taine seems much more relevant than Sainte-Beuve: he raises more issues, he formulates more theories, but he lacks Sainte-Beuve's easy grace and sense of proportion. He is a violent writer, fond of extreme formulas and loud colors. His style (influenced by Michelet and Macaulay), metallic and monotonous, reflects the disturbance of his mind, the tension and clash of ideologies and sympathies. But just because of this complexity, Taine assumes the stature of "representativeness," for which he himself was always searching in literature and art. (pp. 136-38)

René Wellek, "Hippolyte Taine's Literary Theory and Criticism (Conclusion)," in Criticism, *Vol. I, No. 2 (Spring, 1959), pp. 123-38.*

ALFRED COBBAN   (essay date 1968)

[*Cobban traces Taine's development as a historian and examines his methodology in his writings on the French. In evaluating his overall performance as a historian, Cobban stresses that an emphasis on psychology and sociology, coupled with a lack of objectivity, often led Taine into committing serious errors.*]

Taine is the most influential and stimulating, the most dazzling, in a word perhaps the greatest of bad historians. His power as an historical writer is undeniable. If he had been an ancient historian, with no rival historians or sources to check or contradict him, we should know exactly what to believe about eighteenth-century France and the Revolution. Unfortunately for his reputation historical criticism has been able to play on the fabric he erected and has left little of it standing. With a quality of mind and brilliance of style that outrank all but the greatest, he wrote worse history than a host of mediocrities. (p. 331)

Taine, it has been said, was the last of the great literary historians, which explains both his greatness and his weaknesses. This is untrue in fact and misleading in its implications. Every historian is a literary historian, though some are more literary than others. As the number of professional historians has grown, so has the number of those with only a minimum of literary ability. They have naturally compensated for their own inadequacy by condemning more literate historians as mere entertainers lacking the austerity that is the hall-mark of true history; and indeed as a result of the growth of a popular demand for

history too many books have been produced which give an appearance of justification to the supposed divorce between good literature and honest history. If Taine's histories fell into the category of 'literary' pseudo-histories there would be nothing in them worth discussing, but to suggest this would be to underestimate him grossly. As well as having the gift of a dazzling style, he had one of the most powerful minds of the nineteenth century. His failure as an historian stems from his strength rather than his weakness, and this is what makes him peculiarly fascinating to study, particularly at the present day when contradictions that appear in him are also apparent in contemporary historical writing. The truth is that he is unfairly judged if we treat him purely as an historian. He set out to be something different and something more and only diverged into history on his way. The paradox of the writer is explicable in terms of the intellectual development of the man. . . . (pp. 331-32)

He had set out to devote his life to philosophy, but he found that scientific interests, including among these particularly psychological science, predominated in his thinking. This did not disconcert him for he concluded that philosophy and science were one. History was subsequently to be added in a passion for unity which was one of his great intellectual weaknesses, because it was only possible to make this identification by a profound misunderstanding of all three. Most fatal of all, Taine never really grasped the nature of scientific investigation. His mind remained fundamentally dogmatic, even though his dogmas contradicted the accepted ones. Towards the end of his life he frankly declared, 'I am the opposite of a sceptic. I am a dogmatist. I believe that everything is possible to the human intelligence. I believe that with sufficient data, which perfected methods of enquiry and persistent investigation can provide, we can know everything about man and life. There is no final mystery.' He started from his conclusions and then looked for facts to confirm them. There is no sign that he ever understood the method of working from the empirical facts, of experiment, trial and error, provisional hypotheses. He early acquired a deductive habit of mind which he never lost. 'My liking', he declared in 1849, 'avoiding particulars, goes to general or ideal objects, like those of art, humanity as a whole and above all nature.'. . . (p. 333)

Taine's mind was shaped in the mid-nineteenth century and in France, precisely at the time when the great outburst of social speculation that marked the reign of Louis-Philippe had reached its height. This was the real appearance of sociology as a coherent and developing trend in the European mind. Various utopian, Marxist, Proudhonist and other socialist schools emerged from this turmoil of ideas; but the strongest influence at the time was exercised by the sociological positivism of Comte. Its influence on Taine was unmistakable. His literary criticism, as subsequently his historical writing, was essentially that of a sociologist, which gives it particular interest at the present day, when the relationship between sociology and history is so much under discussion. (p. 334)

The strength of Taine's generalizing approach to history emerged even as early as 1847 when he read Guizot's lectures on European civilization. These were, Taine says, a revelation and as a result, 'I set myself the task of seeking out the general laws of history.' The connection with sociology at once leaps to the mind, for this is precisely what the sociologists of the nineteenth century, like Saint-Simon, Comte or Marx, were aiming to do. Such thinkers, and indeed practically all sociological theorists of the period, argued in terms of general ideas, though they found them in different fields. For Saint-Simon and Marx it was in the class pattern based on productive systems; Comte began with the sciences and ended with a religion of humanity. For Taine sociology, and therefore history, was essentially 'un problème de psychologie', and his psychology was the environmental one he had learned from the sensational school of the eighteenth century. Applied first to the history of literature, it is summarized in a famous sentence which had a *succès de scandale:* 'Le vice et le vertu sont des produits comme le vitriol et le sucre' [see excerpt dated 1863]. Minds, he believed, are not to be studied as unique phenomena. 'Each mind', writes Taine, 'has a mechanism like a plant, it is a subject for scientific study, and as soon as one knows the forces which make it operate, one can, without the necessity of dissecting its works, reconstruct them by pure reason.' Therefore he is interested in types, not individuals. A characteristic anecdote describes Taine on a visit to London as placing himself at the railway-stations when the hordes of commuters were pouring into, or out of, the City in order to gain an impression of the collective business-man's face.

Taine's sociological approach appears prominently in his tendency to reduce history to formulae. It is not, perhaps, unfair to suspect most sociologists of a weakness for discovering formulae. Taine ultimately reduces his whole sociological analysis to a rigid pattern of *la race, le milieu, le moment,* which constitute for him the determining characteristics of every national literature or history. (pp. 334-35)

This pattern provided the basis for Taine's studies of literary history and when he turned to history in a broader sense he used the same system to explain the course of events. It imposed on him a determinist view and a belief that the aim of the historian is to discover general laws. Only by doing this, he believed, can history come into contact with reality. 'Properly speaking,' he declared, 'facts, little isolated fragments do not exist; they only exist in so far as we see them; basically there are only abstractions, universals, general ideas.'

At this point the reader of Taine will be brought up sharply against an apparent inconsistency. His writings are spattered with little facts of precisely the kind that he apparently condemned, and this not merely by accident. The book in which he expounds his psychological theories, *De l'intelligence ... ,* is almost wholly built up of little facts, significant examples, individual observations. These are both psychological and physical and their combination and interdependence according to the general laws of nature constitute human personality and determine man's behaviour. We can reconcile this apparent contradiction if we recognize that the 'little facts' do not exist in their own right: they are the evidential signs which we use to illustrate the operation of the great general laws of human nature which rule over art and literature and history. (pp. 335-36)

[We] would regard Taine's emphasis on the role of statistics in history as not altogether lacking in foresight; and if he misunderstood and exaggerated it, some contemporary historians are not altogether free from the same fault. The subtle and still far from understood relationship in scientific discovery between theory and experiment, hypothesis and observation, escaped him, as it did most of his contemporaries. To fill in his predetermined pattern he collected innumerable facts and this he took to be the scientific, and also the historical method.

It was this use of what Taine called 'de tout petits faits bien choisis' which particularly outraged the scholarly conscience and provoked the wrath of the rival historian Aulard, who devoted a whole book to demolishing his historical reputation. 'A candidate for the diploma in historical studies or the doctorate at the Sorbonne', declared Aulard, 'would disqualify himself if he cited the authority of Taine on any historical question.' Aulard's book is a syllabus of Taine's historical errors and omissions. . . . [Aulard writes that Taine] uses his sources quite uncritically [see Additional Bibliography], for example an abridged translation of supposed letters from an English lady in France in 1792-95, which he adopts without questioning their authenticity; and the pretended letter from Raynal of 31 May 1791, which Raynal repudiated and which was in fact written by Clermont-Tonnerre. Taine quotes above all from memoirs, the most unreliable of all historical materials, especially for a period when so many fake memoirs were put into circulation for reasons of propaganda or profit. (pp. 336-37)

If Taine's sources are thus inadequate, his method does not make up for them. His volume on the *ancien régime* draws its material indiscriminatingly from the whole century, making no distinction between France under the Regent, Louis XV or Louis XVI. There is no attempt to single out the stages in the development of a revolutionary situation; the struggle of the king with the parlements is ignored and the setting up of provincial assemblies, which did so much to weaken the administration, is mentioned once and then only incidentally. 'Taine,' says Aulard, 'a supprimé l'évolution dans l'histoire.' Equally he makes the Revolution into a solid *bloc,* identified from beginning to end with the single fact of terrorism. The influence of the foreign menace, and indeed of most of the significant political events which loom so large in Aulard's own history, is hardly mentioned; indeed the history seems to Aulard to degenerate into a mere collection of anti-revolutionary anecdotes. The key to it is the Jacobin, 'un être de raison', an abstraction; and Jacobinism is sometimes all revolutionary France, sometimes the Jacobin clubs and sometimes a minority within them. (pp. 337-38)

Georges Lefebvre, poles apart from Taine as an historian of the Revolution, renewed the attack. He recognizes that Taine is no *érudit* and skilfully picks out his specific defects: he is always on the side of the socially superior, of the nobles against the bourgeois and of the bourgeois against the people; his 'people' indeed is only a caricature; he explains popular excesses purely by the ferocious and stupid nature of the people, omitting all the provocations of the enemies of the Revolution inside France and the attacks of external enemies; in writing on the *ancien régime* he attributes the evils from which France suffered to the classic spirit of generalization and abstraction, of which in fact he himself was one of the most notable exemplars; finally, he sacrifices reality to his formulae; he is a system-maker who brings to the exposition of his systems the passion and artistry of a great pamphleteer; he writes partly as a philosopher and partly an advocate, not at all as an historian.

Yet we cannot deny the persisting influence of Taine or write off so dazzling a style and so formidable an intellect without a little more consideration, nor does Lefebvre. Taine had the merit of appreciating, Lefebvre says, that the Revolution was essentially a social revolution, not only inspired by ideas but also by interests. Not being an historian, Taine did not create any school of historians to carry on the task of social analysis, says Lefebvre, who himself made the most notable contributions to social history and yet equally failed to leave any school of social historians of the Revolution behind him. Even more significant, in Lefebvre's view, is the importance Taine attributes to collective psychology. If only he had been able to apply this new approach with a sound critical method his greatness would have been incontestable. Unfortunately this is precisely what he could not do. He started out with a view of human nature which he never changed and which was the *a priori* basis of his historical interpretation.

Taine's view of human nature was essentially a simple one. As a student, in 1849, he declared, 'I have arrived at a great contempt for human nature; I find men ridiculous, weak, emotional like children, foolish, vain, and above all stupid because of their prejudices.' But when the scientific sociologist, the rational psychologist, as Taine imagined himself, cast an eye on history, what he sees is determined by his own passionate convictions about human nature: the Middle Ages is a time of privilege and assassinations, Renaissance Italy a country of pitiless wars, mortal enmities, calculated tortures and atrocious tyranny, sixteenth-century England a den of wild beasts only capable of being tamed by the atrocious sight of bleeding and suffering flesh, the Russian Empire a horde of brutes, madmen and monsters. Man is an animal close to the monkey; what survives in him permanently is the ferocious and lascivious gorilla.

With this introduction one can imagine what Taine will say when he comes to the French Revolution. His initial volume on *L'Ancien Régime* gives some appearance of impartiality. This was possible because Taine was a liberal, in the aristocratic, élitist, laissez-faire, anti-state, European sense of the term. He was opposed to the *coup d'état* of Louis Napoleon. When he read the speeches of Macaulay in 1877, he commented, 'How lucky to be born in a country where one can be a liberal.' He did not believe there were any liberals in France. 'I am not a simple reactionary,' he protested, 'a partisan of divine right.' He was against all absolute and arbitrary power, whether of the mob or of an individual. 'A human being, or a collection of human beings which is despotic and not checked by other powers, becomes always evil and mad. The Convention and Napoleon are worth no more than Louis XIV.' The events of 1870-71 did not change his views, though they inspired his great work on the *Origins of Contemporary France,* in which his aim was to trace the source of the evil. His fundamental analysis was almost identical with that of Burke: the Revolution had adopted from Rousseau, or so he believed, the system of reducing the nation to 'a mass of separate and equal individuals, like so many grains of sand', only subsequently to heap them together in great masses. Unlike Burke, however, his profound and all-embracing pessimism did not allow him to admire what had preceded the Revolution. In the *ancien régime* the noblesse had abandoned its role as leaders of the people, while preserving its privileges. The clergy supported the state on condition of its acting as their executioner and taking up religious persecution on their behalf. In place of being the representatives of the people, the notables had become the favourites of the ruler and harassed the flocks they should have protected. All the evil was in the court; all power and therefore all responsibility had accumulated in the person of the king. The heart of the evil was in the government itself. 'It is here that the public abscess comes to a head, and here that it will burst.'

After this it might seem there was nothing more to be said to account for the Revolution. But at this point Taine veers off into an entirely different line of explanation. He introduces his famous simile of a man walking down a street; he may be a little weak of constitution but he is quite peaceful and well-behaved. Up to him comes someone who offers him a drink.

He accepts it and immediately falls down frothing at the mouth and behaving in general like a lunatic. The conclusion to be drawn is obvious: the peaceful citizen is France under the *ancien régime,* the man who offers him the drink the *philosophes,* and the drink is the classic spirit which, applied to the scientific gains of the time, produced the philosophy which was the essence of the Revolution. Tradition was overthrown and abstract reason took its place; philosophy destroyed the authority of custom, religion, the state. The social contract based on the new principle was the only just one, and whoever opposed it was an enemy of the human race.

The fallacies in this analysis are obvious. Taine himself had shown that the *ancien régime* was not just weak in constitution but fundamentally rotten. The classic, generalizing spirit is more closely identified with traditional French thought than with the original empirical thinking of the Enlightenment. The Revolution, as Sorel was to show, was far more the heir of the *ancien régime* than either would have liked to admit. In particular the absolutism of the revolutionary assemblies and of Napoleon was an inheritance and an expansion of the absolute sovereignty of the divine right monarchy. (pp. 338-40)

Despite the conclusiveness with which Taine produces each phase in his argument, one other element was still required to make the revolutionary situation complete. He presents it again in the form of a simile. He compares the French people in the eighteenth century to a man walking through a pond with the water level up to his mouth; the least depression and he loses his footing and goes under. This is a not unrealistic picture of the economic situation, and it enables Taine to draw together the two strands in his analysis of the causation of the Revolution—ideas and interests—in a curious anticipation of the Marxist theory of the alliance of peasants and bourgeois. He sees the ideas of the *philosophes* as inspiring the popular revolts. 'Several million savages are thus thrown into action by some thousands of windbags. The dogma of radicalism is put to the service of brute force.' It is a brilliant formula, and like Taine's other formulae has been influential far beyond the deserts of any element of truth it contains. Only gradually, and rather reluctantly, are historians of the Revolution coming to appreciate the fundamental hostility of peasant and bourgeois interests, and—despite the more general clauses inserted in the *cahiers* by local lawyers or clergy—to remark on the concentration of the attention of the peasantry on their specific material interests. Far from stirring the peasantry into revolt, it was the bourgeois militia which suppressed their revolt when it came. . . .

This pessimistic outlook on man is what we come back to ultimately as the essence of Taine's historical philosophy. It produced his condemnation of successive régimes and gave its character to all his history. . . . His is indeed a sad history, both in what he wrote and for the misuse of such great talents. He shows, more clearly than anyone else, the importance of psychology and sociology for the historian, and at the same time the dangers they bring with them when their outlook is substituted for that proper to history. (p. 341)

Alfred Cobban, "Hippolyte Taine, Historian of the French Revolution," in History: Reviews of New Books, *Vol. LIII, No. 179, October, 1968, pp. 331-41.*

LEO WEINSTEIN (essay date 1972)

[*Weinstein provides a comprehensive survey of Taine's life, philosophy, and the various phases of his career. In the first part of the following excerpt, Weinstein discusses the development and main premises of Taine's* On Intelligence. *In the second part, he summarizes Taine's contributions to the history of criticism and explores his influence on later literary and philosophical movements.*]

[Taine's contribution in psychology] was considerable if judged historically, less important when measured against the findings of a Freud, a Jung or an Adler. On the other hand, his efforts to replace metaphysical entities (faculty, capacity, power) by factual explanations carried into psychology the effort he had already undertaken in philosophy. Finally, Taine's conception of man, of normal and abnormal behavior provides us with a key to a better understanding of his criticism in literature, art, and history.

Taine . . . had assigned a central place to psychology among the human sciences. His interest in this subject dated from his student days at the Ecole Normale, a number of his major ideas are already contained in *The Nineteenth Century Classical Philosophers,* and if his proposed dissertation on sensations had been accepted in 1852, *On Intelligence* would certainly have been published long before 1870. As it turned out, his doctoral thesis on La Fontaine led him into literary criticism which, along with his courses at the Ecole des Beaux-Arts, left him no time to devote to the work he had contemplated for so long and which was certainly dearest to his heart.

The definition of intelligence Taine proposes makes his work appear more like a modern continuation of John Locke's *Essay Concerning Human Understanding* (1690) than a psychological study: "If I am not mistaken, we mean nowadays by Intelligence, what was formerly called Understanding or Intellect— that is to say, the faculty of knowing; this, at least, is the sense in which I have taken the word. At all events, I here intend to examine our knowledge, that is to say our cognitions, and nothing else." In reality, however, Taine went considerably beyond his predecessors, who had usually based their psychological writings on introspection, by calling to his aid practically all information available at the time. He studied cases of mental illness in medical journals and at the mental hospital in Paris, he utilized knowledge drawn from physiology, neurology, linguistics and ethnography, he observed or consulted children, old people, creative artists, and he carefully noted the effects of hypnotism and somnambulism. The infusion of scientific observation into the field of psychology made of Taine "the leader of the empirical school and the exponent of concrete practical methods of study." Yet, to be complete, *On Intelligence* would have required additional studies dealing with the author's theory of passion and of will.

In psychology Taine applies his philosophical principles that give to *On Intelligence* a unity which, by that very fact, remains based on philosophical rather than experimental foundations. At the core of his work lies the Spinozist assumption he had already expressed in his explanation of cause, namely that the order and connection of things is the same as the order and connection of ideas. In this spirit Taine attempts to supply a scientific answer to the age-old question whether what we perceive corresponds to an exterior reality, a matter that had been severely placed in doubt most recently by Kant. The other important assumption Taine makes is that psychological and physiological phenomena, although different in nature, parallel each other.

After showing that images, signs and general ideas derive all from sensation, Taine deals with a series of problems. What happens when we perceive an object? What is the relationship between interior or psychic and exterior or physiological ex-

perience? Does our perception correspond to exterior reality? Perception takes place through two channels: one, sensation, comes from within and takes place without any intermediaries; the other, a molecular movement of the nervous centers, comes from without and through several intermediaries. One may interpret this situation in two ways. Either these two means of perception are perpetually divergent and remain mutually irreducible; or they are basically one and the same event condemned to appear always and irremediably double. If we choose the first hypothesis, we must accept two different worlds, one interior, the other exterior, and seek aid for explanations beyond nature in the supernatural. Leibnitz, realizing this dilemma, had proposed a solution based on preestablished harmony by which God arranges the exact concordance between these two independent channels of perception. Choosing the second hypothesis, which is equally plausible, has the advantage of dealing with a simpler and more convenient relationship, since no imaginary or unknown property is needed to explain it.

This attitude leads to a tendency that views psychological events as problems of molecular movements related to mechanics and hence seeks explanations and solutions in terms of physiology. It is interesting in this respect to compare how Taine and Freud would explain a particular case. Thus Taine attributes loss of memory about a specific period or place in the life of a patient to "an injury, a rush of blood, a deterioration of the blood, any change of the cerebral substance, [which] may hinder or promote the arising of certain groups of images." No doubt, Freud would look elsewhere for an explanation, possibly to an event that happened during that time or at that place which may have created a feeling of guilt in the patient who wishes to repress it.

It would be incorrect to conclude from the foregoing that Taine was unaware of complicated psychological processes. He studied cases of split personality; he knew that, below the surface of psychic experience, there lurks the undefined area of the unconscious or the subconscious; he realized the complexities contained in the concept of the Ego. Here again explanations are suggested in terms of motion, energy and physics. Thus the subconscious is defined as the mental phenomenon which is analogous to the physiological one of audibility. Just as there are limits in terms of decibels to the relative loudness of sounds that the human ear can detect, so there are limits, less accurately measurable, to what the human consciousness can be aware of. "The elementary sensations directly making up our ordinary sensations are themselves compounded of sensations of less intensity and duration, and so on. Thus, there is going on within us a subterranean process of infinite extent, its products alone are known to us and are only known to us in unrefined bulk. As to elements and elements of elements, consciousness does not attain them, reasoning concludes that they exist; they are to sensations what secondary molecules and primitive atoms are to bodies; we have but an abstract conception of them, and what represents them to us is not an image, but a notation."

Having opted for the correspondence of interior and exterior events, Taine might have rested peacefully in the secure feeling that we automatically experience true reality; yet he arrives at quite contrary conclusions. He was painfully aware of the many traps that have to be sidestepped before perception has any chance of mirroring exterior reality. In fact, he substantially agrees with Kant on the deceptive tendencies of our sensations, since they frequently do not correspond to an exterior object (in dreams, under hypnosis, etc.) or else we may misinterpret them (looking into a mirror, for example). Taine goes far beyond these simple errors of the senses by stating that what we perceive is indeed a hallucination. Even if a sensation arises in consequence of its usual antecedent, i.e. after the excitation of the nerve and through the effect of an external object, this sensation, being internal, engenders in us a phantom which we take to be an external object. Thus the hallucination, which seems a monstrosity, is the very fabric of our mental life.

Up to this point Taine arrives by different ways at the same general result as Kant, but he does not stop there. Nature has provided us with antagonist reductives so that, in the normal state of wakening, we can rectify the initial hallucination. They operate by opposing or negating the hallucination through a contradictory representation or sensation. This rectification process takes many forms. The simplest of these are the awakening after a dream, a partial negation through our intelligence of a contradictory proposition (e.g., a figure having three sides and four at the same time) or one sense rectifying the illusion of the other (touching a stick in the water proves that it is not bent). Hence exterior perception is a *true hallucination.* "To form complete hallucinations and repressed hallucinations, but in such a way that, when awake and in the normal state, these phantoms usually correspond to the real things and events, and thus constitute cognition, that is the problem."

But what happens when the rectifying apparatus does not function properly? Then the result is madness of one sort or another, and, since the natural state of hallucination which our sensations induce in us is frequently rectified only by another contradictory hallucination, whose nature is nonetheless the same as that of the initial one, the desirable state constituted by health and sanity turns out to be not only far from normal but extremely precarious. . . . (pp. 44-8)

Time and again, in a cacophonic crescendo, Taine paints a picture of man that leaves him tottering precariously at the brink of threatening insanity. Barely covered by a veneer which required thousands of years of civilizing efforts, the ape lurking constantly beneath and always menacing to burst through his weak bars will supply French Naturalist writers with characters to be dissected in experimental novels. (p. 48)

Studying the behavior of peasants and workers who had been turned into unprofessional soldiers during the French Revolution merely reinforced this basic attitude on man in Taine, for he sees "all of a sudden spring forth the barbarian, and, still worse, the primitive animal, the grinning, sanguinary, wanton baboon, who chuckles while he slays, and gambols over the ruin he has accomplished." (p. 49)

Before leaving Taine's psychology, a word of caution or at least an admonition to observe historical humility may be in order. It is quite normal to consider Taine's psychological views outmoded today and to feel justly proud of the undeniable progress that has been made in that field since 1870. Yet, in the lottery of time, when Taine's particular physiological explanations of mental processes will long have been consigned to the mothballs of history, his basic principles may yet be vindicated. His misfortune lies in the fact that physiology and neurology have not made the jump forward he had hopefully anticipated. Not that the actual progress accomplished in these sciences is not highly admirable, but the discoveries required to prove Taine definitely right or wrong in his theories of physiological psychology would be of the magnitude that only rare break-throughs can provide. If and when such startling discoveries occur, present-day psychology may in turn be placed

on dusty bookshelves as curiosities that filled an intolerable void during an interim period by substituting highly ingenious dramatic characters for what eventually may be explained in terms of glandular secretions, chemical imbalance or genetic irregularities.

Taine himself set a splendid example of scientific humility: "One learns very quickly that what we call an indisputable truth is only a very probable truth; that the idea we have of ourselves and of other things is only a likely hypothesis, well done, useful in guiding our conjectures, the best that have come to us up to now, but perhaps insufficient and temporary, in any case destined to make way for another one when new observed facts, more precise measurements, unexpected connections will enlarge and rectify our conceptions." (pp. 49-50)

. . . . .

[Harry Levin has pointed out that] "Flaubert remarked of the *History of English Literature* that it got rid of the uncritical notion that books dropped like meteorites from the sky" [see Additional Bibliography]. Taine accomplished far more than that. His was an ambitious inquiry, not about abstract man, but about men, different groups of men living in different countries and conditions at different times. Unless we keep in mind that his ultimate goal was an understanding of men rather than an esthetic or structural study of literature and art or a narration of historical events, we shall fall into the error of those critics who accused him of omitting matters he never intended to deal with. In this aspect only, i.e., in his ultimate goal rather than in the method used, it may be said that Taine's interest was primarily psychological.

The consequences of this reversal of emphasis in criticism profoundly affected that entire discipline. The artistic work no longer occupied a sovereign status with historical and social conditions serving as accessories to fill out the portrait of the artist; in Taine's method the work of art constitutes the most powerful means of depicting the spirit of an age or the character of a race. Thus the literary critic becomes a literary historian in the fullest sense of the word. Beyond that, Taine attempted to depersonalize criticism by providing it with a scientific basis that would replace personal whim or taste by a more objective procedure.

That he was a pioneer in scientific criticism few will deny. No one before him, not even Sainte-Beuve, had ever attempted such a rigorous program of applying the methods and laws of the physical sciences to the study of humanistic subjects. In view of the enormous difficulties involved, not only in having no previous experience to fall back upon but also in facing the opposition of academic authorities and of customary prejudice, Taine's lasting and valid contributions far outweigh those attempts in which he was less successful. His articles on Balzac and Stendhal rank among the classics in criticism on the two great novelists, passages from [*Essai sur les fables de La Fontaine*] continue to appear in French textbooks, and his prefaces to the [*Essais de critique et d'histoire*] along with the famous introduction to the *History of English Literature* constitute milestones in critical theory. The last-mentioned work represents the most successful illustration of his ambitious theory which combined philosophy, history, literature, and psychology in order to define the English character through the literary history of that nation. Aside from brilliant chapters on Shakespeare, Milton, Byron, Macaulay, and Carlyle, Taine proved that a literary history can be more than a dreary succession of sketchy biographies and summaries of works.

In his art criticism Taine pursued still further the idea that the artistic creation is an expression of the society in which it was produced, thus pioneering a work in the sociology of art. The portion of his *Lectures on Art* devoted to Italy provides the best example of this type of criticism. The sections on Greek art and especially the one on art in the Netherlands combine sociological, historical, and esthetic criticism with the tripartite theory of race, milieu, and moment in Taine's most mature critical work. The theoretical discussion of the nature and the production of artistic works has lost none of its validity today, nor has the *Ideal in Art* except for the questionable criterion concerning the beneficence of character.

Where Taine did not succeed, we should look first to his own personality before seeking flaws in his method. In his writings on French literature of the seventeenth century and on the French Revolution powerful tensions between his emotions and his method arose. Taine was obviously not the calm, disinterested sort of researcher best suited to apply a scientific method and, although he was both generous and tolerant, on some matters he displayed an inflexible attitude. Curiously enough for a man who admitted to a mind both Latin and Classical, he violently opposed these two traits in literature and political philosophy, preferring definitely minds that were Germanic and depictions that were at the same time individual and violent in emotional intensity. Pointing out that he was seeking psychological information in art and that he disliked the Classical spirit which posits abstract principles while eschewing experimentation, explains the attitudes of the critic, but not the inner complexity of the man. When we add to this the stylistic tension between a scientific thought and a lively, imagistic rendition of it, then every page written by Taine can be viewed as a personal struggle.

From 1857 until his death Taine, along with Renan, exerted more influence on French thought than any other writer. Two generations were so completely under his sway that only adherence or opposition to his doctrines seemed to be possible. . . . [It] may be said that any critic who draws in a large measure on disciplines other than the art medium itself, be it history, sociology, psychology, philosophy or any of the sciences, derives in a general way from Taine. Such critics need of course not adopt Taine's psychology or his social or historical views, yet by bringing to bear on criticism scientific and historical factors they are pursuing the road traced by Taine. The result assigns to Taine some rather strange bedfellows, since most psychological critics have been Freudians and most sociological critics Marxists.

The influence of Taine has varied according to the intellectual prestige enjoyed by science as a problem solver. The critic himself can hardly be said to have profited to the maximum during his lifetime from the favorable position he occupied in France. Having devoted himself to historical works during the last twenty years of his life while practically abandoning literary and art criticism, he failed to play the predominant role that should have been rightfully his in French Naturalism. More than that, his personal tastes caused him to assume a rather negative attitude toward those writers who were his most legitimate heirs, in particular toward Emile Zola. A rather aristocratic and Classical sense of the limits of good taste and an increasing moral concern expressed clearly in the beneficence of character criterion in *The Ideal in Art*, veiled Taine's judgment of the Naturalists. (pp. 143-46)

Just as Sainte-Beuve had misjudged most of his contemporaries, so Taine, who had rehabilitated the two great novelists mistreated by Saint-Beuve, displayed little understanding for the most important literary movements of his critical career, since he felt also little sympathy for Baudelaire, Verlaine and the Symbolists.

Not only the development of literary movements but the mood of the times as well turned against Taine's philosophy and critical method. In the 1890's a sharp reaction, not so much against science as such, but against scientism began to make itself felt. Taking stock, such critics as Brunetière concluded that Taine and Renan had been wrong in predicting that science would solve all problems. (p. 147)

The evolution of scientific philosophy has not entirely worked in Taine's favor, either. The problem is not that great strides have not been made in the various sciences but rather that most matters Taine was concerned with (physiology, psychology, genetics) have turned out to be far more complex than he had anticipated, so that his relatively simple formulas concerning master faculty, race, and milieu need at present to be expressed in complicated equations the end of which is not yet in sight. (p. 148)

In the past twenty years a more favorable climate for the diffusion of Taine's ideas has developed. . . . On the one hand, the use of psychology and psychiatry in criticism continues to find strong adherents. In France the movement called the "new criticism," which includes such critics as Roland Barthes, Jean-Paul Weber, and Charles Mauron, draws not only on psychiatry but on linguistics and anthropology as well. On the other hand, sociology serves as the basic tool for the Marxist critics, both in the Soviet Union and elsewhere. But here a real dilemma presents itself. Most of the critics involved necessarily hold political convictions opposed to those of Taine. While Balzac, a conservative if ever there was one, has found favor in Soviet Russia due to his exposure of social ills, it is very difficult for liberal critics to accept as their predecessor the public prosecutor of the French Revolution and of the socialistic state. Yet, despite radical differences in their conclusions, the Marxist critics posit a basic view which is scarcely more than a variation of Taine's principle that great authors express their society, the difference being that Marxist critics replace "society" by "social class." (pp. 148-49)

Without going so far as to call Taine the father of present-day structuralism, it is safe to state that he pointed the way for the practitioners of that movement, namely, to arrive at the most basic structures in a system whose elements are interdependent. One is immediately reminded of Taine's pronouncement that "moral matters, as physical matters, have dependencies and conditions" upon reading the four requirements Claude Lévi-Strauss sets up for a structural system: "(1) A structure has the character of a system. It consists of elements such that any kind of modification of one entails a modification in all the others. (2) Every model belongs to a group of transformations each of which corresponds to a model of the same family so that the total of these transformations constitutes a group of models. (3) The properties indicated above enable us to foresee in what manner the model will react in case one of its elements is modified. (4) The model must be so constituted that its functioning can account for all the observed facts."

Even if Taine's fortune has undergone the vicissitudes of time and fashion, he can be opposed and disliked but not ignored by historians and critics of art and literature. His work remains to speak for him, and that work is gigantic, both in its ambitions and in what its author realized. Few modern writers have so completely combined the two cultures, as C. P. Snow calls them (the humanities and the sciences) as Taine, and his method informs, in many variations, the courses on world literature and the history of ideas which are enjoying an ever-growing popularity in American high schools and colleges.

The fact remains that the problems Taine raised and on which he took a stand are still very much with us. . . . Taine left us this heritage: He claimed: (1) that the laws of the physical sciences apply to human affairs as well; (2) that criticism need not be dictated by personal whim or good taste but that it can be based on philosophical assumptions; (3) that artistic works are not mere personal creations but express the spirit of their times; (4) that the principal causes of artistic creations are master faculty, race, milieu, and moment, and that a knowledge of these causes enables us to study an individual, an age, a race or an entire civilization; (5) that the progress in the various fields of science should be reflected in criticism through the use of new instruments of observation; (6) he provided the basic philosophy of the Naturalist movement in France and elsewhere; and (7) he wrote the pioneer essays on Balzac and Stendhal.

In evaluating Taine's achievements today it becomes apparent that the frequently formulated judgment of Taine as an excellent critic in spite of his philosophical assumptions and method is incorrect. (pp. 149-50)

[Taine] is not a dry pedant but a man in his study surrounded by books and voluminous notes, communing, like a modern Faust, with Spinoza, Hegel and Stendhal, conjuring up before his nearsighted eyes entire epochs of the past: ancient Greece, the Italian Renaissance, the French Classical centuries, struggling to detect the hidden springs in a Michelangelo, a Rembrandt, a Shakespeare, turning his eyes inward to discover the meaning of the Ego, of perception, of imagination, of the narrow limits that separate sanity and insanity, reality and illusion; opening them again in horrified anger at the spectacle of men and women beheaded or marched up the steps of the guillotine by French revolutionaries. And as his logical mind orders the facts, sifts out the causes and explains their effects, these visions continue to haunt him while the historian, the philosopher, the psychologist and the critic whisper phrases into his ear which his artistic imagination transforms into a work of art. (p. 151)

> *Leo Weinstein, in his* Hippolyte Taine, *Twayne Publishers, Inc., 1972, 186 p.*

ALAN SWINGEWOOD (essay date 1972)

[*Swingewood discusses the interplay between materialist and non-empirical elements in Taine's theory of literature, linking him with the Marxist tradition of literary criticism.*]

Taine—philosopher, historian, politician, and essayist—is generally regarded as the founder of the sociology of literature. Although largely ignored and forgotten outside France, Taine's work on literature and society, specious though most of it is, does contain an awareness of the basic and perennial problems which face any literary sociology.

Like his predecessor Auguste Comte . . . , who coined the word 'sociology', Taine strove to develop a completely scientific outlook, to submit literature and art to the same research methods as those employed in the physical and natural sciences. 'Vice and virtue,' he once wrote, 'are products like vitriol and sugar' [see excerpt dated 1863], and thus subject to the same

research status. For the scientific observer morality becomes merely a question of precise scientific formulas; Taine was constantly attacking novelists and critics who emphasized the moral intent of their work as against the purely descriptive. It would be wrong, however, to see Taine as a genuine positivist, for underpinning much of his writings is a strong Hegelian element which in a paradoxical way perhaps links him with Goldmann and the Marxist tradition.

For Taine, as with Madame de Staël and Herder, literature is traced to the material foundations of society. In the introduction to his study of English literature Taine wrote that a literary work was no ' mere individual play of imagination, the isolated caprice of an excited brain, but a transcript of contemporary manners, a manifestation of a certain kind of mind'. Literature reflects certain ascertainable facts and emotions: Taine categorizes the novel, for example, in terms similar to Stendhal, as a 'portable mirror which can be conveyed everywhere and which is most convenient for reflecting all aspects of life and nature'. As the dominant literary genre of industrial society the novel shows what is, and represents no more than an 'accumulation of data which through the operation of scientific laws would fall into inevitable patterns'. Clearly any literary sociology which bases itself on such clear-cut positivism as this—literature as source of information, as documentation—can and must be prepared to study all types of literature, good, bad, and indifferent, since the problem is simply one of objective material causation and reflection. But like many sociologists Taine is loath to draw this conclusion. Literary works, he argues, 'furnish documents because they are monuments'. Different historical periods succeed in producing a harmonic relationship between genius and the age; the more deeply an artist 'penetrates into his art, the more he has penetrated into the genius of his age and race', while the mediocre artist, although his work might seem equally valid a social document, is both unexpressive and unrepresentative. Only the really great artist is capable of fully expressing his time, and by 'representing the mode of being of a whole nation and a whole age, a writer rallies round him the sympathies of an entire age and an entire nation'. Art is thus the collective expression of society, with great literature embodying the spirit of the age in a manner close to Hegel's conception. The problem for Taine is to determine the causes behind the emergence of great art and literature.

Taine proposes the use of three concepts, race, moment, and milieu, arguing that they comprise the material foundations exhausting all 'real causes' and all 'possible causes of movements', and claiming that 'if these forces could be measured and deciphered, one could deduce from them . . . the characteristics of the future civilization'. The interaction of race, moment, and milieu produces either a practical or a speculative 'mental structure', and this leads to the development of the 'germinal ideas', characteristic of certain centuries and epochs, which find expression in great art and literature. The significance of this formula is not so much the statement on material causation, common enough during the nineteenth century, but rather its suggestion of the precise connections between a literary work and its society. In the history of the sociology of literature Taine's is the first real theory, far more systematic than those of de Staël or Herder, and constituting rather more than a collection of haphazard and random insights. The question is how successful was he in applying the theory? (pp. 31-3)

While Taine was clearly aware of the strong economic pressures on literary production, he rarely went beyond crude correlations. He made few serious attempts to link the economics of writing, the economic aspects of milieu, which had become so marked during the commercially-minded nineteenth century, with the literary text itself. As with the other parts of his conception of milieu, his tendency is always to explain the literary work mechanically, as a response to external conditions. There is nothing in any of his analyses of actual textual criticism, of linking specific parts of the text with specific external facts. Thus in his essay on Balzac, which Wellek describes as the 'high point' of his criticism [see excerpt dated 1959], Taine argues that the whole basis of the *Human Comedy* rested on Balzac's failure to realize his ambition and greed for money in the world of commerce. Balzac's novels, Taine concluded, flowed from one simple truth: he was a businessman, and a 'businessman in debt'.

All this, then, suggests a profoundly mechanical form of materialism. But . . . Taine's peculiar hotch-potch system of causation has blended with it a curious Hegelian flavour. It almost seems that Taine was determined to refute his own theory for, dissatisfied with his three major determining elements, he reinforced the formula with a psychological dimension.

> Man, forced to accommodate himself to circumstances, contracts a temperament and a character corresponding to them; and his character, like his temperament, is so much more stable, as the external impression is made upon him by more numerous repetitions, and is transmitted to his progeny. . . . So that at any moment we may consider the character of a people as an abridgement of all its preceding actions and sensations; that is, as a quantity and as a weight. . . .

But this is the deterministic Taine. In his actual analyses of literature he frequently remarks that literary achievement is essentially a 'problem of psychological mechanics', of the artist's dominant ruling passions. Indeed, the fundamental cause of all art and literature, of every kind of 'human production', is the 'moral disposition' of the artist; the key is the artist's 'master faculty'. Taine had no wish, it seems, to dissolve literature into a matter of simple material terms, for like any good nineteenth-century bourgeois he clearly wishes to retain the magic, the genius, of the individual artist in the process of cultural creation. Thus, after discussing the material facts which lead to the emergence of Shakespeare he remarks that, notwithstanding his analysis, 'all comes from within—I mean from his soul and his genius: circumstances and externals have contributed but slightly to his development'. And of Dickens:

> It is not through the accidental circumstances of his life that he belongs to history, but by his talent . . . A man's genius is like a clock; it has its mechanism and among its parts a mainspring . . . This inner history of genius does not depend upon the outer history of mankind; and it is worth more.

Taine has quite clearly abandoned his materialistic scheme in favour of a more shadowy, non-empirical, psychological explanation. All great change, he argues, is rooted not in social structure but in man's soul: 'The psychological state is the cause of the social state.' His revision of materialism is thus complete.

This brings us to our final point on Taine's literary sociology. His rejection of an all-pervasive materialism allows him to choose great literary works for analysis. He has, like Hegel, equated artistic greatness with historical development and progress, arguing that particular ages crystallize in great works because the great artist's superior 'moral state' enables him to grasp the essence, the truth of reality. Taine's obvious dilemma was the contradiction, generated by his materialist theory, between its application to literature and art and his desire to allow some measure of autonomy to the creative spirit. There is here one of the major and persistent problems in the sociology of literature: from Taine to Lukács and Goldmann there has been a tendency to accept the traditional literary critics' view of the superiority of great literature because of its supposed monopoly of crucial social and human insights. At the same time, it must be noted that Taine frequently uses literature as a document, and throughout his writings there runs a strong and persistent reductionist element. He has no conception of the *literary text* as the focal point of research.

But his concepts and general outlook made their impact. Academic research became dominated by the positivistic method which Taine very largely enshrined, to the extent that it concentrated so 'heavily upon the backgrounds of literature that the foreground was all but obliterated'. As the Danish critic George Brandes, an ardent champion of Taine, expressed it, the artist 'is nothing but a good observer who by a happy accident has also the capacity to give shape to his observations'.

Taine, then, had developed a theory but no method of applying it systematically. The theory itself was largely specious and, perhaps because of Taine's lack of rigour, other writers turned to a new theory which, by defining milieu in terms of economic factors and social class, appeared to provide a more realistic as well as more rigorous sociological approach. (pp. 37-40)

> Alan Swingewood, "The Social Theories of Literature," in The Sociology of Literature, by Diana T. Laurenson and Alan Swingewood, Schocken Books, 1972, pp. 23-58.

EDWARD T. GARGAN (essay date 1974)

[Tracing the evolution of Taine's theory of history from his early works to The Origins of Contemporary France, *Gargan focuses on his faults, merits, and continuing importance as a historian.]*

[The] errors of geniuses are often more interesting and fertile than the attainments of more prudent scholars. Even today Taine's *Les origines de la France contemporaine,* published in six volumes between 1875 and 1893, is frequently the point of departure for historians who consider their research important because they have decisively corrected Taine's mistakes and blunders. . . . Taine has remained on the historian's Index of Prohibited Books until the present. But despite his condemnation by all professional historians, Taine's volumes are discovered again and again in their hands and libraries. Creative scholars continue to regard Taine as the nineteenth-century historian whom they must put in the shade by the light of their studies.

The attraction and repulsion that Taine provokes cannot be attributed to his style, for this too, has been found wanting. . . . A limited historian, an unacceptable moralist, a writer whose prose fatigues as often as it delights ought to have no claim on the attention of succeeding generations. But Taine continues to command our interest and to call forth our response to his voice. He himself offered an explanation of why this is so when he noted with satisfaction that modern psychology was beginning to know something of the "subterranean regions of the soul," to discover that the "breaking up and lasting doubling of the ego" makes it possible for two or more persons to exist distinctly and at the same time within the same individual. We cannot be done with Taine because the complexity of his own person and its changes in response to modernity anticipated our own alterations and ambivalences as we try to make sense of the modern condition of man. In his expectations as to what science might accomplish, what psychology might promise, what coherence history might offer, and what justification of life might be granted by literature, Taine encompassed our hopes in the use of intelligence. His experience of failure and despair haunts our own efforts, and when we find ourselves on his path, we are often desperate to detect a way out. This is possible, but we cannot escape the realization that he preceded us as historian, as literary critic, as psychologist, and we must acknowledge that his limits and shortcomings have often made possible our achievements. (pp. xii-xiii)

As a philosopher [Taine] had concluded: "Philosophy is a form, a mode of existence of the human mind. It only really exists when it expresses in its own way the human mind of the time. If not, it does not exist; or else lacking personal force, it reproduces an old system. But then it still lacks the principle of life." His limited experiences in the actual world and his study of the natural sciences confirmed Taine's earlier insight that the metaphysical and moral beliefs of any era must reflect the historical and social situation of that time. It was the lives that men lived that mattered to Taine, who regarded philosophy as a necessary outgrowth of their more mundane occupations. From this perspective Taine saw that La Fontaine, Stendhal, and Balzac had more to teach him than whole schools of metaphysics.

By 1860 when he published the third edition of his [*Essai sur les fables de La Fontaine*], Taine believed that he understood some of the historical and psychological forces that had formed the French people, *les Gaulois*. He praised La Fontaine because unlike so many "classical" authors he had not been a captive of the artificial Latin civilization of the court and nobles in the seventeenth century. La Fontaine was worthy of respect as one of the few French writers from the seventeenth to the nineteenth century who did not write solely for a narrow, educated, wealthy, and powerful class. In language that Marx, Sartre, or George Steiner would not find strange Taine declared: "Our letters, as our religion and our government, are superimposed on rather than rooted in the nation." La Fontaine, by his example, exposed the artificiality of the majority of France's writers, "the theoreticians of the sixteenth and of the nineteenth century who write for a class and not for the nation." He was magnificent, according to Taine, because he had made a near perfect contact with the daily existence and spirit of *"le peuple."* "How many great writers," Taine asked, "are understood by the people?" Perhaps Rabelais and Molière, but certainly La Fontaine.

The great fabulist had the gift of being open to every experience and saw as only a "stranger' can all that was happening around him: "a peasant interested him as much as a prince, a donkey as much as a man." Without sentimentality, La Fontaine had depicted the almost magical authority that belonged to the office and person of kings, but also their murderous appetites; he recorded the brutal burdens of the peasants, but he gagged on their smells and filth. Taine wanted to imitate and make his own La Fontaine's unrivaled concreteness and to share his

awareness of every possibility in this universe where the animal man philosophizes and creates poems.

La Fontaine gave Taine his first realistic picture of the continuing habits and psychological character of the French people. In his poetry they revealed themselves as rulers who insensitively crushed the innocent and as aristocrats who made the life of a parasite seem elegant and even honorable. The reader of La Fontaine understood that it is a fact of nature and not of morality that the rich bourgeoisie "have for the miserable a cold indifference, and suspicion and scorn for those who dispense charity." La Fontaine enabled the student of France's history to see the peasant in his actual world rather than in a romanticized rustic tableau; to perceive what existence was for the exploiter of the smallest stubbled fields constantly overcome by debts and the demands of the relentless usurer. This was the reality of the peasants' life and "the pretended poetry and manners of the village."

Taine delighted in the simple, plain, commonplace, and unlearned words of the poet fabulist. When writing his history he would try to borrow La Fontaine's language to describe the notables, bourgeoisie, artisans, and peasants. Yet in that context the honesty and simplicity of the poet would often elude the historian's reach, leaving an undesired impression of arrogance rather than of compassion and perfect clarity. (pp. xxi-xxiii)

Once Taine had purged himself of his hatred of the orthodox secular wisdom, he was able to celebrate the writers who had made honest contact with the human condition. "I adore," he wrote, "Balzac, who was a Christian, an Absolutist, and a Mystic, and also Beyle who was a Liberal, a Materialist, and an Atheist." Taine's great essay on Balzac offered the praise he thought fitting and proper to the novelist who had succeeded in "abridging" the social history of the nineteenth century. This admiration for Balzac's genius was in part due to his realization that Balzac's novels confirmed Taine's historical conception of how any generation becomes one in the "totality" that unites the individual to his class, to his society, and to the world. Balzac's life and art perfectly illustrated the necessary relationship between a writer and the creative action open to him. His passion, indebtedness, aggression, and psychological penetration were precisely joined to the tendencies, dreams, and changes of his century.

Balzac was unsurpassed not because his novels reflected as in a mirror the realities of his time, but because as artist he co-created and gave consciousness to the forces that fashioned nineteenth-century France. The vulgar bourgeois, the faceless clerk, the omniscient village doctor, the confused virgin have a social identity because Balzac knew them and gave them life. When he describes money, "the great mainspring of modern life," Taine wrote, "he speaks to us of the interests that concern us, he satiates the covetousness that possesses us." Language, gesture, the soil, the air, the food you eat, the furniture you select, the virtues and vices you display are the only possible ones given your time and place. Balzac's fiction, according to Taine, demonstrated with the certainty of a laboratory experiment that "virtue is a product like wine or vinegar manufactured like other things, by a known series of determined operations having a measurable and certain effect." The brilliant diagnoses in the *Human Comedy* included the elegant proof that a judge whose benevolence is much commented on is in reality a man "who loves the poor as the gambler does his game," and a lawyer who sacrifices his fortune for another is identified as having the compulsive "and involuntary fidelity of a dog."

We would all like, Taine acknowledged, to revolt at this naturalism, but those committed to search for the causes behind human actions must accept the evidence that all natural and human events proceed from determined antecedents to appointed consequences. Historians seeking to explain the origins of human conduct were urged by Taine to partake of and participate in Balzac's art, to uncover with the artist's eye and the anatomist's scalpel the connections of the total structure.

Taine made three attempts to discuss how history was to be approached and written if it was to encompass as successfully as the good novel the whole experience of a society. His suggestions were offered in the preface to the first edition of his *Essais de critique et d'histoire* . . . , in the introduction to the *Histoire de la littérature anglaise* . . . , and in the longer preface to the 1866 edition of his *Essais*. On these three occasions Taine stated as clearly as possible his insight, corroborated by Balzac, that the psychology, society, institutions, beliefs, and thought of any historical generation must be symmetrically related. Thus: "In the same century, for example, philosophy, religion, art, the form of the family, and of government, public and private manners, all the parts of national life, imply one another, in such a fashion that one cannot be altered without the rest also changing." History demands, Taine wrote, the understanding that "mankind is not a collection of objects lying next to one another, but a machine of functionally interrelated parts; it is a system and not a formless pile."

Critics objected that Taine's excessive stress on the homologous character of a historical epoch denied individuality, nuance, the chaos and incoherence of life. To this he replied that one had only to look at the totality of any period as one would look at a painting to recognize the necessary harmony of all of its parts. The "inner eye" must be used to perceive how the "imprint" of past experiences unites in any historical moment—as in the century of Louis XIV—religion and philosophy, the family and the state, industry, commerce, and agriculture.

It was true that on the surface all appeared to be in flux during Louis XIV's epoch; Jansenists seemed to dominate at one time, and at another it was the Jesuits; mystics prevailed at one hour, and still later Gallicans. But, Taine argued, the historian who observes the violent imagination of the previous century, the critical character of contemporary English philosophy, the skepticism of the age that followed will be able to isolate the essential traits of seventeenth-century France. The historian gifted by a holistic sense will see the links between the theological poverty of seventeenth-century France and the lucidity of its logic, the nobility of its moral doctrines, the "dryness" of its speculative talents, and its disdain for experience. He will recognize the relationships between the classical age's preference for mathematics and the concepts of King and God that were mutually dependent upon one another in a hierarchical society that was sustained by a way of reasoning and ordering things that united the philosophy of Malebranche, the sentences of Bossuet, the arrangement of the hedges at Versailles, the versification of Boileau, the laws of Colbert.

The historian who successfully identifies the unifying features in a society's national character and establishes the structural factors that are the armature of its history does not deny individuality, but rather he locates the place of the unique within the collective psychological and historical experience of the

whole society. Systematic analysis of this rigor does not deny freedom but makes it possible. When we understand the mutual interdependencies of all things, Taine believed, then we may be able "to modify to a certain degree the events of history." When mankind approaches through history a knowledge of the laws and necessary circumstances governing all forms of human association, then history may be profitable "to the intelligent insect" who penetrates the economy of the structure. (pp. xxv-xxviii)

The *Histoire de la littérature anglaise,* beginning with Tacitus and ending with Tennyson, elaborately develops the thesis, inherited from Balzac and Stendhal, that a literary work will always reveal more about a society than its histories or political documents. . . . The preference for literature as the decisive historical witness was rooted in Taine's conviction that politics is in a sense the most rudimentary of social acts. Political systems and constitutions owe little to the genius or purposive action of statesmen, but virtually everything to their necessary responses to the social pressures of their times. "Social situations," Taine asserted, "create political situations; legal constitutions always accommodate themselves to real things; and acquired preponderance infallibly results in written right."

Writing for the subjects of Louis Napoleon's Empire, Taine invited them to consider the English example as the most positive historical lesson for a society seeking a progressive and confident future. He considered the British too severe in their rejection of the French Revolution, but he thought that England had responded more intelligently than any other nation to the message of the Enlightenment and had made the most viable transition to the industrial nineteenth century. The French have a natural tendency to regard the English as dull performers in the theater of history, and Taine sometimes supported this stereotyping. Yet on viewing their entire historical repertoire, he could not restrain his sheer admiration for their virtuosity in a theater little inclined to be absurd:

> But they are patriots as well as innovators, conservatives as well as revolutionary; if they touch religion and constitution, manners and doctrines, it is to widen not to destroy them: England is made; she knows it, and they know it. Such as this country is, based on the whole national history and on all the national instincts, it is more capable than any other people in Europe of transforming itself without recasting, and of devoting itself to its future without renouncing its past.

No French scholar has until this day attempted to tell again the full history of England's literature and society. (pp. xxix-xxx)

No historian of France ever brought to conclusion a history with the scope of Taine's *Origines*. Before Taine, Tocqueville had sought to locate in the conflict between the Old Régime and the Revolution the clues to France's chronic fluctuations between free and unfree governments, between stability and disequilibrium. But Tocqueville did not finish his history and would, in any case, have been unwilling to go beyond the Empire. Taine designed his history to link in an unbroken fashion France's experience from the sixteenth century until the moment he put down his pen. . . . Historical specialization does not alone explain the difference between Taine's singular achievement and the practices of modern scholarship. Taine believed that without losing a thread he could trace out the continuity of France's history following the essential lines that converged on the revolutionary era and their pattern as they unraveled from that decisive moment. Modern historiography has at best been able to speak of a revolutionary legacy, a continuing spirit; Taine insisted that everything connected. (pp. xxxvi-xxxvii)

From the beginning to the end of his history Taine labored to create an acceptance of the idea that a *juste milieu* could be established for France in which inherited position, possessions, and prestige would enable rural France to incrementally open opportunity to men of merit, while keeping the state under proper restraint but giving it enough authority to curb revolutionary challenges to the social order. Yet Taine's own tensions and doubts concerning the fragility of the settlement in France after the Commune communicated to his history and readers an anxiety that could not be assuaged.

L'Ancien régime was published in December 1875 at the end of the first year of the "constitution" of the Third Republic. René Rémond has astutely noted that this constitution was the most Orleanist of all France's fundamental laws. . . . Taine's *Origines* thus perfectly fitted his own moment in history, the political and social milieu of his audience, and their psychological needs. In the hands of another writer, a less intense historian, his work would have been flawed by triumphalism, or been a kind of Whig history celebrating the victory of his class. Taine, however, misread his own hour; or more precisely his profound distress over his nation's capacity for failure gave his history a tension disproportionate to the crises of his time. Corrections of his mistakes by red or blue pencil cannot lighten the apprehension he created concerning France's ability to adjust to modernity.

When in 1889 France commemorated the hundredth anniversary of the Revolution, despite the Exposition Universelle and the Eiffel Tower, that fete was surrounded by a strained and unnatural gloom. . . . Taine's three volumes on the Revolution, completed and published five years before its centenary, may well have made it all but impossible for the Right or the Radical Republicans to find any common ground; the historical memories he reinforced seemed to assure their continuing division. Taine was not guilty of leading France to the prefascism of the Action française, but he was responsible for depriving Frenchmen of joy in their historical image. (pp. xxxviii-xl)

Rival artisans have altered the form, details, and colors of Taine's tapestry; seams have been separated, holes torn in the wool. This destruction and wear has occurred most often in those parts of the cloth where Taine thought he was using his most precious threads, doing his finest work. Contemplation of the defects of his favorite panels has made possible the masterpieces of his competitors. The most vigorous parts of his design continue, however, to impose his impressions on his successors—historians such as Paul Hazard, Daniel Mornet, Georges Lefebvre, and George Rudé. The cartoons of these weavers bear the tracings of the lines he drew so firmly.

Taine endlessly insisted, for example, that the classical reasoning of the seventeenth century functioned only in an aristocratic and insulated culture; in this closed company, judgements, arguments, and propostions were perfected in proportion to their author's ignorance of the actual world. Playwrights, preachers, and philosophers discoursed on man's needs, but had never experienced hunger. The eighteenth-century philosophes who criticized the old order were themselves, Taine suggested, captives of its methods of reasoning; their impact was possible only because the finesse of the classical modes

of discourse released them from any dependency on the concrete as long as their logical constructions remained elegant. Men trained in this precious school could be expected as legislators to consider offensive to reason and humanity any challenges to their theories and practices. The perfection of their use of *raison* excluded counterpropositions, facts, and history. Paul Hazard, Daniel Mornet, and Peter Gay among others have reestablished the autocritical capacity of Enlightened thinkers. Yet at this moment, when they are most appreciated, new reflection suggests that Taine's bold and heavy line may have been close to the truth. (pp. xl-xli)

The distrust of Taine by professional scholars has also centered on his overreaction to the violence of the Revolution. He considered this "patriotic gore" largely the work of a minority imposing their will on French society, and he overlooked the outrages committed by counterrevolutionaries. Yet Taine's partisan and emotional response enabled him to raise questions that have been avoided by less prejudiced historians. Georges Lefebvre, for example, when describing the September massacres, wrote: "the blood letting did not cease until the countryside was purged. The collective mentality is sufficient explanation for the killing." Taine's revulsion, however, led him to probe deeply into the nature of the violence committed by the defenders of the Revolution. He believed that the defensive character of their action still left unresolved an explanation as to how ordinary, average, hardworking citizens bring themselves to the point of choking, stabbing, dismembering their neighbors. How do they sustain their fury? His answer is so disturbing that it might lead even the most ardent supporter of the Revolution and its place in history to pray that he might avoid the occasions for such violence. "Observe children drowning a dog or killing a snake. Tenacity of life irritates them, as if it were a rebellion against their despotism, the effect of which is to render them only the more violent against their victims."

Though he admitted that he was antirevolutionary, Taine refused to be described as reactionary. . . . And he felt he was not being dishonest in believing that his history had judged the action of any man by one criterion: "has he diminished, or at least not added to, the sum total of human suffering in his own time and for the future?" Taine undertook to keep this test in mind when writing his chapter on "The People" in *The L'Ancien régime,* and those on the Jacobins in *La Révolution.*

When Taine was admitted to the Académie française in 1880, he made a final effort to express his understanding of the historian's art and responsibility. He proposed that it would be well for historians to give less attention to the role of great men and to concentrate instead on the great social groups within which the mass of men live out their lives. The historian was urged to find a place on his canvas for the members of every class, profession, and occupation. He will deal with princes, aristocrats, parliamentarians, financiers, country gentlemen, curés, employers, tenant farmers, and occasional beggars and bandits. What matters is to describe their lives within the circle of their society. The individual must be portrayed from the moment of his birth until his death, and the historian must know how the hours, the days, and the weeks of the most obscure are spent. He must ask of each class and its members: What do they produce? What do they consume? What luxuries and privations do they experience? At what cost? How do the different classes regard the family and the nation? How do they love, marry, beget, and rear children? What do they make of the state? Do they accept or reject the social hierarchies of

An illustration titled "Selection of English Heads," from
Notes on England.

their world? What aspects of existence bolster the confidence
of a class, evoke their resignation, and try their patience? How
do men of every class and occupation touch the beautiful and
give coherence to their universe? How does the brief life of
any generation flow into the stream of History and the ocean
of Time?

By this profession of faith and by his example Taine honored
all who had attended his investiture into the historian's high
office: La Fontaine, Saint-Simon, Montesquieu, Hegel, Guizot, Michelet, Stendhal, Balzac and Sainte-Beuve. He reca-
pitulated in his history a fair portion of what had been accomplished by his art before him and anticipated a goodly part of
its future. (pp. xlii-xliv)

> Edward T. Gargan, in an introduction to The Origins
> of Contemporary France: The Ancient Regime, the
> Revolution, the Modern Regime *by Hippolyte Adolphe
> Taine, edited by Edward T. Gargan, The University
> of Chicago Press, 1974, pp. xi-xlv.*

SUSANNA BARROWS (essay date 1981)

[*Barrows posits that Taine's* The French Revolution *is a melodramatic testament to his fear of crowds of people rather than a
scientifically objective treatise.*]

Behind Taine's impassioned, almost breathless account of the
outbreak of the French Revolution [in *La Révolution*] lies a
comprehensive exposition of human psychology and a terri-

fying theory of the savagery of men in groups. As he baldly
put it, men and women in crowds revert to a "state of nature."
The natural man, as Taine defined him, is a "savage," a brutal
beast incapable of reason, a "baboon" chained to base desires.
As societies have developed, man's instincts have been curbed
by an intricate and extremely fragile web of civilized constraints. Over the course of centuries, these constraints have
been institutionalized in the forms of marriage, religious piety,
allegiance to tradition, and a secure recognition of one's place
in the social hierarchy.

"Civilization," however, is never distributed in an egalitarian
fashion. Certain groups clearly stand as more "advanced" than
others. Men, for instance, have fewer bestial instincts than
women, and persons of education and noble birth rank above
peasants and laborers on the ladder of civilization. At the very
bottom of the hierarchy lurk the modern equivalents of pure
savages: criminals and prostitutes.

But all mankind—rich or destitute, educated or illiterate, law-
abiding or criminal—reverts to a savage and instinctual state
once a crowd is formed:

> We can understand how, from the peasant, the
> worker, the bourgeois, pacified and tamed by
> an ancient civilization, we see suddenly spring
> forth the barbarian, still worse, the primitive
> animal, the grinning, bloodthirsty, lustful ba-
> boon who laughs as he murders, and gambols
> over the damage he has done.

According to Taine, the sudden transformation of man into
irrational savage is caused by the "laws of mental contagion."
A solitary man can control his bestial instincts, but once he
joins a crowd, "mutual contagion inflames the passions;
crowds . . . end in a state of drunkenness, from which nothing
can issue but vertigo and blind rage." All crowds, then, are
destructive, its members uniformly subject to the "laws of
mental contagion."

Although mental contagion, in Taine's view, could electrify
the aristocrat as well as the peasant, the social composition of
most crowds described in the *Origines* is at best plebeian and
more often dominated by criminals. When Taine described the
October Days of 1789, for example, he pictured Lafayette as
a cowardly dupe jostled by an army of prostitutes, criminals,
outlaws, and other forms of the dregs of society. The uprisings
of the ordinarily lawful populace of France—the peasants, honest laborers, or hungry women—are obscured by Taine's incessant emphasis upon the outlaws and murderers who alleg-
edly led those revolts.

In his descriptions, a crowd begins as a leaderless horde, but
the "scum" soon "rises to the surface of the mob." The leaders
of crowds are inevitably drawn from the "lowest" elements:
criminals, vagabonds, smugglers, murderers, and other fugi-
tives from justice. Unwilling to control the mob's thirst for
violence, these despicable criminals set the example of frenzied
violence for the rest of the crowd. Incapable of reason, guided
by murderous instincts, led by "vagrants and foul savages,"
the crowd thus embarks on an orgy of crime, debauchery, and
drunkenness.

Throughout this bacchanalia of destruction, women march at
the forefront. According to Taine, women "naturally" led the
stampede for food and wine in the riots of 1789. Women, he
argued, were the most susceptible to the "infectious malady"
of the crowd. Since he thought that even "civilized" women

were more barbaric than men, Taine stressed the natural preeminence of women in crowds. (pp. 76-8)

Abandon, in Taine's analysis, is not limited to the sphere of sexuality. Scarcely a riot erupts in his account that is not accompanied by an alcoholic debauch. Beginning in the spring of 1789, both rural and urban uprisings are orchestrated in inebriated refrains. (p. 79)

Taine's hyperbolic prose graphically underscored the orgiastic nature of crowd activity. Alcoholism, he argued, is essentially a working-class problem. Because of misery, hunger, and overwork, many laborers imbibe excessive amounts of strong liquor. Over time, such habitual drunkenness takes a severe mental and physical toll: bloodshot eyes, convulsions, paranoia, delusions of power, and homicidal delusions. Because it is, in Taine's view, the worker who commonly suffers from such mental aberrations, and because the scum of society manipulate crazed rioters, Taine paints his crowds in garish tones of savagery, mental illness, social deviance, and alcoholic addiction.

The image of the alcoholic crowd was also to provide Taine with one of the book's most powerful metaphors. In concluding the first volume of *La Révolution,* Taine described in the following manner the national dilemma in 1792:

> France . . . , exhausted by fasting under the monarchy, inebriated by the bad spirits of the *Social Contract,* and twenty other adulterated or fiery drinks, is suddenly struck with paralysis of the brain; suddenly she is convulsed in every limb by the incoherent play and contradictory twitchings of her discordant organs. At this point, she has passed the period of joyous madness, and is about the enter the period of somber delirium.

By a careful interplay between the contemporary scientific description of alcoholism and the image of a diseased, indeed deranged France, Taine reshaped the traditional organic metaphor of the "body politic" in the mold of medical science. For centuries, political theorists had compared the state with the human body. Then as now, such a metaphor emphasized the organic unity of the state as well as the necessary separation and coordination of civic functions. By stressing the "illness," "fever," or "insanity" of France, Taine could diagnose the pathology of his society in scientific terms.

If the Commune had affected the intellectual life of Hippolyte Taine alone, its impact would have been considerable. But the brutality and civil carnage of 1870-71 scarred all French citizens, regardless of their political affiliation. Taine's response to the disaster, while hardly unique, was highly influential. By playing upon the sense of despair, national humiliation, and cultural decline, Taine, "the pathologist of French society," offered an explanation for how and why France had lost its primacy among nations.

During the last two decades of his life, Taine consciously cultivated the posture of physician to modern France. His country, he often claimed, suffered from a "brain lesion," syphilis, or an addiction to liquor or morphine. By pointing out the symptoms of the disease of France, Taine hoped the patient would recognize the illness and take the necessary steps to avoid life-threatening relapses. (pp. 80-2)

Out of the trauma of 1871 and the language of French medical science, Taine forged the architectural structure of modern

French right-wing historiography. Although incomplete, his prescription for France was later copied by historians like Jacques Bainville and Louis Madelin. They borrowed as well the aristocratic psychology which so pervades Taine's works. Taine, of course, considered himself competent to evaluate the psychic patterns of all social classes. As even his harshest critics have admitted, Taine's psychological analysis of the mentality of the oppressed has a certain ring of truth. Taine had rightly stressed, for instance, the famine and misery which forced workers and peasants to rebel in the spring of 1789. His emphasis on the psychological factors contributing to the Great Fears of that year—fear of brigands, fear of starvation, and fear of conspiracy—provided suggestive insights into the "contagious" nature of rural revolts.

Nonetheless, Taine's sympathies for his historical subjects were unquestionably weighted in favor of the aristocracy. In Taine's scheme, while the lower classes revolt for "animal" reasons, the aristocratic counteroffensive is interpreted as an altruistic return to civic responsibility. Describing the Second Estate at the outbreak of the Revolution, Taine wrote, "Never was an aristocracy so deserving of power than at the moment of losing it; the privileged class, awakened from their indolence were again becoming public men, and, restored to their functions, were returning to their duties." In surveying the *procès-verbaux* of the provincial assemblies in 1789, Taine was convinced that he had never seen "better citizens," nor more honest, diligent, and disinterested administrators.

Taine clearly preferred salons to slums. His historical accounts, as well as those of his conservative successors, reflect that aristocratic bias. In a letter to Guy de Maupassant, Taine had advised his younger friend to

> increase the range of your observations. You portray peasants, the lower middle class, workers, students and prostitutes. Some day you will doubtless portray the cultivated classes, the upper bourgeoisie, engineers, physicians, professors, big industrialists, and men of business . . . and I shall be happy when you devote your talent to men and women who, thanks to their culture and fine feelings, are the honor and the strength of their country.

Taine's point of view was, as he admitted, "aristocratic"; de Maupassant ignored his advice. Crowd psychologists and right-wing historians, however, generally adopted and inflated Taine's perspective. They borrowed, for instance, the picture of the bloodthirsty, deranged, and bestial mob, often without acknowledging the economic factors that led to revolt. In Taine's works it was hunger which forced peasants to perform savage acts; in the subsequent histories of Jacques Bainville or Louis Madelin, even the well-fed working classes were frequently pictured as beasts.

In addition to his influence upon reactionary historians, Taine stood as the hero and model for crowd psychologists. His mobs exhibited nearly all the characteristics that Sighele, Tarde, and Le Bon were later to include in their "scientific" analyses. As bestial hordes, poisoned by alcohol and debauchery, excited by dissolute viragos, brigands, or similar "scum," crowds in the *Origines de la France contemporaine,* were indelibly painted in the most terrifying of tones. No other nineteenth-century writer in any genre created such frightening, yet memorable machines of savagery. (pp. 83-6)

Even if one places Taine's work in the unique context of nine-teenth-century psychology, the ***Origines*** contains grave errors in scientific method. Taine's cast of mind was unquestionably, admittedly dogmatic. Long before he set foot in the archives, he had decided that the Commune and its predecessor, the Revolution, were monstrous and barbaric; his subsequent research served only to illustrate his preconceived notions. The idea of empirical investigation was wholly alien to Taine; when conversing with Gabriel Monod about his impending research trip to Italy, Taine asked, ''And what theory are you going to verify there?''

Despite his dogmatism and deductive method, Taine proudly defined himself as a psychologist. For the motto of his incisive study on English literature he had borrowed a phrase from Guizot: ''I have done pure psychology and psychology applied to history—nothing more.'' And not long before his death, he claimed that psychology had been his sole occupation for the past forty years. Taine had crowned psychology as the queen of the sciences, the sun around which all the related disciplines of literary criticism, art history, philosophy, and history re-volved.

But, it is literary license, not scientific rigor, that makes Taine's major works such compelling documents. With a sharp eye for chilling and vivid vignettes, Taine used archival dossiers as a springboard for melodrama. While discussing, for instance, the ubiquitous ''march of the *canaille*'' in France after July 14, 1789, Taine selected six particularly atrocious incidents: rioters in Strasbourg drowning in a lake of wine five feet deep; the ''scum'' of Cherbourg, Maubeuge, and Rouen pillaging and sacking private residences and royal buildings; a four-day orgy of soldiers and workers in Besançon; and, still worse, the murder and mutilation of the mayor of Troyes. Using the pre-sent tense throughout his narrative, Taine made his subjects both larger and lower than real life. As he has already warned, the rabble behaves like ''an elephant on a rampage'': ''Almost immediately, another band, screaming for murder, begins its chase and breaks windows''; ''the populace devastates the houses of three of the most powerful merchants''; ''the company falls dead drunk under the tables''; ''a woman throws herself on the crushed old man, tramples on his face with her feet, and repeatedly plunges her scissors in his eyes.'' His conclusion left little to the horrified imagination:

> Such is public life in France after July 14: in every city, magistrates are at the mercy of a band of savages, often, a band of cannibals. Those of Troyes have just tortured Huez in the manner of the Huron Indians; those of Caen have done worse; the mayor of Belsunce . . . was cut to bits like Laperouse in the Fiji Islands, and a woman ate his heart.

Rejecting nuance and obsessed by the excesses of the Revo-lution, Taine replicated that passion in his hyperbolic and melo-dramatic style. Taine the scientist had appropriated the tools and the prerogatives of the *littérateur*. That paradoxical com-bination had taken shape long before the ***Origines;*** a charac-teristic of the young Taine, reinforced by the political climate of the early fifties, it emerged full-blown only in his final crusade. (pp. 87-9)

Other historians of Taine's generation have been allowed to slip into a peaceful limbo. But not Taine. The vehement, me-ticulous, and occasionally petty dueling with the *Origines de la France contemporaine* began with the publication of its first

volume and continues to this day. Taine, of course, had started the war. As a young scholar he had realized that one of two paths lay open before him: pure literature or pure science. He refused to make the choice. Posterity has not forgiven him. (p. 92)

Susanna Barrows, "Hippolyte Taine and the Spectre of the Commune," in her Distorting Mirrors: Visions of the Crowd in Late Nineteenth-Century France, *Yale University Press, 1981, pp. 73-92.*

ADDITIONAL BIBLIOGRAPHY

Amann, Peter. ''Taine, Tocqueville, and the Paradox of the Ancien Régime.'' *The Romanic Review* LII, No. 3 (October 1961): 183-95.
    Explores the influence of Alexis de Tocqueville's *L'ancien régime et la révolution* on Taine's *The Ancient Regime* and *The French Revolution*.

Asselineau, Roger. ''Whitman: A Poet Both Born and Made.'' In his *The Transcendentalist Constant in American Literature*, pp. 90-8. The Gotham Library of the New York University Press, edited by James W. Tuttleton. New York: New York University Press, 1980.
    Discusses Walt Whitman's unpublished review of *History of En-glish Literature*. Asselineau concludes that though Whitman ad-mired Taine's historical approach to literature, he could not sub-scribe to his theory about individual talent.

Aulard, A. *Taine: Historien de la révolution française*. Paris: Librarie Armand Colin, 1907, 333 p.
    An important French-language study of *The French Revolution* by one of Taine's most prominent and systematic critics.

Barzun, Jacques. ''Race and the Fine Arts.'' In his *Race: A Study in Modern Superstition*, pp. 110-34. New York: Harcourt, Brace and Co., 1937.
    Briefly examines Taine's theories of race, time, and milieu and their relationship to the revival of interest in individualism and regionalism in the nineteenth century.

Birchall, Ian H. ''Ambition and Modesty: Literature and Social Science in the Work of Hippolyte Taine.'' *Mosaic* V, No. 2 (Winter 1971-72): 31-46.
    Discusses Taine's attempt to combine literature and sociology. According to Birchall, Taine's conservative tendencies prevented him from acknowledging the full ramifications of his theories.

Bourget, Paul. ''M. Taine.'' In his *Essais de psychologie contem-poraine*, 5th ed., pp. 175-250. Paris: Alphonse Lemerre, 1887.
    A French-language study of Taine's philosophical, scientific, and political ideas.

———. *The Disciple*. London: T. Fisher Unwin, 1901, 341 p.
    A novel in which one of the main characters, M. Sixte, is based on Taine. Bourget used this fictional vehicle to criticize Taine's doctrines.

Carter, Everett. ''Taine and American Realism.'' *Revue de littérature comparée* 26, No. 3 (July-September 1952): 357-64.
    Examines Taine's influence on American Realist writers, partic-ularly Howells.

Charlton, D. G. ''From Positivism to Scientism (3): Hippolyte Taine.'' In his *Positivist Thought in France during the Second Empire, 1852-1870*, pp. 127-57. Oxford: Oxford University Press, 1959.
    Traces the development of Taine's ideas, briefly discussing his views on positivism, idealism, scientism, metaphysics, and ethics.

Evans, Colin. ''Taine and His Fate.'' *Nineteenth-Century French Stud-ies* VI, No. 162 (Fall-Winter 1977-78): 118-28.
    Proposes that Taine's writings should be reinterpreted. While Ev-ans acknowledges that Taine's theories are often inaccurate, he suggests that his modernity lies in his ardent quest for knowledge.

Frank, Frederick S. "The Two Taines of Henry James." *Revue de littérature comparée* 45, No. 3 (July-September 1971): 350-65.
Traces James's reaction to Taine's writings and concludes that the critic became for James "a great hero-villain of letters."

Goetz, Thomas H. *Taine and the Fine Arts.* Coleccion Scholar Universal. Madrid: Playor, S. A., 1973, 154 p.
Outlines Taine's theory of fine art and discusses his writings on Greek, Italian, Dutch, Flemish, French, and English painting.

Hyams, Edward. Introduction to *Taine's "Notes on England,"* by Hippolyte Taine, translated by Edward Hyams, pp. ix-xxxi. Fair Lawn, N.J.: Essential Books, 1958.
An account of the circumstances under which Taine wrote his *Notes on England.*

Jackson, David. "Shadows on the Face of the Sun King: C. F. Meyer's *Das Leiden eines Knaben* and Hippolyte Taine's *Les origines de la France contemporaine.*" *Revue de littérature comparée* 51, No. 3 (July-September 1977): 417-31.
Examines the influence of Taine's history of France on Meyer's sociological novel *Das Leiden eines Knaben.*

Jenkins, Iredell. "Hippolyte Taine and the Background of Modern Aesthetics." *The Modern Schoolman* XX, No. 3 (March 1943): 141-56.
Explores Taine's concept of aesthetics, its historical context, and its influence on modern aesthetics.

Levin, Harry. "Literature as an Institution." In *Criticism: The Foundations of Modern Literary Judgment,* edited by Mark Schorer, Josephine Miles, and Gordon McKenzie, pp. 546-53. New York: Harcourt, Brace and Co., 1948.
Discusses Taine's contributions to the history of literary criticism. Levin emphasizes Taine's application of sociology and psychology to the practice of criticism.

Morawski, Stefan. "The Problem of Value and Criteria in Taine's Aesthetics." *The Journal of Aesthetics and Art Criticism* XXI, No. 4 (Summer 1963): 407-21.
Asserts that Taine's judgments about art and aesthetics were sometimes contradictory because they were guided by his conflicting allegiances to sociology and biology.

Noyes, Alfred. "A French View of Milton." In his *New Essays and American Impressions,* pp. 117-35. New York: Henry Holt and Co., 1927.
Charges that Taine's inadequate understanding of John Milton's poetic technique in *Paradise Lost* led to his negative assessment of that work.

Quennell, Peter. "Cross-Channel Visitor." *The Spectator* 199, No. 6735 (26 July 1957): 138-39.
Comments on Taine's views of English life and character in *Notes on England.*

Raitt, A. W. "Hippolyte Taine: *Vie et opinions de M. Frédéric Thomas Graindorge.*" In his *Life and Letters in France: The Nineteenth Century,* pp. 110-17. London: Nelson, 1965.
Discusses Taine's commentary on the Second Empire in *Notes on Paris* and compares his views of society with those of other writers of that period.

Rice, Winthrop H. "The Meaning of Taine's 'Moment.'" *The Romanic Review* XXX, No. 3 (October 1939): 273-79.
Attempts to determine the precise meaning of Taine's concept of "moment" and concludes that no generally accepted definition is possible.

Robinson, Daniel N. Preface to *On Intelligence,* by Hippolyte Adolphe Taine, edited by Daniel N. Robinson, pp. xxi-xxxviii. Significant Contributions to the History of Psychology, 1750-1920: Series A, Orientations, Vol. III, H.A. Taine. Washington: University Publications of America, 1977.
An overview of the historical context, themes, and influence of Taine's *On Intelligence.*

Roe, F. C. "A Note on Taine's Conception of the English Mind." In *Studies in French Language, Literature, and History Presented to R. L. Graeme Ritchie,* pp. 189-92. Cambridge: Cambridge University Press, 1949.
Discusses Taine's opinions concerning the character of the English people. Roe contends that Taine's views were influenced by Mme. de Staël's *De l'Allemagne.*

Smith, Horatio. "The Taine Centennial: Comment and Bibliography." *Modern Language Notes* XLIV, No. 7 (November 1929): 437-45.
Summarizes criticism of Taine's writings up to 1928 and includes a brief bibliography.

Sullivan, Jeremiah J. "Henry James and Hippolyte Taine: The Historical and Scientific Method in Literature." *Comparative Literature Studies* X, No. 1 (March 1973): 25-50.
Focuses on James's debt to and divergence from Taine's critical theories.

Thieme, Hugo P. "The Development of Taine Criticism since 1893." *Modern Language Notes* XVII, No. 3 (March 1902): 70-7.
Provides a survey of Taine criticism from 1893 to 1902.

Turnell, Martin. "Literary Criticism in France—I." In *Critiques and Essays in Criticism, 1920-1948,* edited by Robert Wooster Stallman, pp. 421-34. New York: Ronald Press Co., 1949.
A assessment of Taine's critical methodology. Turnell faults Taine for his concept of literature as historical record rather than art.

White, John S. "Taine On Race and Genius." *Social Research* 10, No. 1 (February 1943): 76-99.
Discusses the historical background and meaning of Taine's concepts of race and genius. White points out that Taine's ideas about genius led him to become "one of the first thinkers of the nineteenth century to wield the axe of criticism against the basic conceptions of his time."

Wimsatt, William K., Jr., and Brooks, Cleanth. "The Historical Method: A Retrospect." In their *Literary Criticism: A Short History,* pp. 522-51. New York: Alfred A. Knopf, 1957.
Briefly examines Taine's concepts of race, milieu, and moment as they relate to the historical method of literary criticism.

Appendix

The following is a listing of all sources used in Volume 15 of *Nineteenth-Century Literature Criticism*. Included in this list are all copyright and reprint rights and acknowledgments for those essays for which permission was obtained. Every effort has been made to trace copyright, but if omissions have been made, please let us know.

THE EXCERPTS IN NCLC, VOLUME 15, WERE REPRINTED FROM THE FOLLOWING PERIODICALS:

American Philosophical Society, n.s. v. 56, 1966. Copyright © 1966 by The American Philosophical Society. Reprinted by permission of the publisher.

American Quarterly Review, v. IV, September, 1828.

The American Slavic and East European Review, v. 8, December, 1949 for "The Author of 'Anhelli' (1809-1849)" by Francis J. Whitfield. Reprinted by permission of the publisher and the author.

The Analectic Magazine, n.s. v. III, April, 1814.

The Athenaeum, n. 1428, March 10, 1855; n. 1975, September 2, 1865.

The Atlantic Monthly, v. XXIX, February, 1872; v. LXIX, March, 1892; v. LXXXI, June, 1898; v. XCIV, November, 1904.

The Blackwood's Edinburgh Magazine, v. XLII, November, 1837; v. LIV, September, 1843.

Canadian Literature, n. 24, Spring, 1965 for "Folk Language in Haliburton's Humour" by L. A. A. Harding; n. 68-9, Spring-Summer, 1976 for "Haliburton's Canada" by Tom Marshall; n. 101, Summer, 1984 for "In Haliburton's Nova Scotia: 'The Old Judge or Life in a Colony" by Katherine Morrison. All reprinted by permission of the respective authors.

The Century, v. LXIII, November, 1901.

The Church Review, v. IV, January, 1852.

Comparative Drama, v. 3, Fall, 1969 for "The Alogical and Absurdist Aspects of Russian Realist Drama" by Simon Karlinsky. © copyright 1969, by the Editors of *Comparative Drama*. Reprinted by permission of the author.

The Cornhill Magazine, v. XXIV, September, 1871.

Criticism, v. I (Spring, 1959) for "Hippolyte Taine's Literary Theory and Criticism (Conclusion)" by René Wellek. Copyright, 1959 Wayne State University Press. Reprinted by permission of the publisher and the author.

Daily Picayune, July 17, 1870.

The Dalhousie Review, v. 16, January, 1937.

The Dial, v. II, September, 1881.

The Edinburgh Review, v. VI, April, 1805; v. XXVI, February, 1816; v. XC, July, 1849; v. CXXX, October, 1869.

Englische Studien, v. 67, 1932-33.

The Foreign Quarterly Review, v. XXXII, October, 1843.

The Fortnightly Review, v. XX, December 1, 1873; v. CXXIV, December 1, 1928.

Fraser's Magazine, v. VIII, October, 1833.

The French Quarterly, v. VI, September, 1924.

Harper's New Monthly Magazine, v. L, April, 1875.

History: Reviews of New Books, v. LIII, October, 1968 for "Hippolyte Taine, Historian of the French Revolution" by Alfred Cobban. Reprinted by permission of the Literary Estate of Alfred Cobban.

Illinois Quarterly, v. 35, November, 1972 for "Josh Billings and His Burlesque 'Allminax'" by David B. Kesterson. Copyright, Illinois State University, 1972. Reprinted by permission of the publisher and the author.

Italica, v. XLIII, December, 1966. Reprinted by permission of the publisher.

The Journal of American History, v. LII, June, 1965. Copyright Organization of American Historians, 1965. Reprinted by permission of the publisher.

Journal of the History of Ideas, v. V, June, 1944.

The London and Westminster Review, v. XXVIII, January, 1838.

The London Mercury, v. XXVI, August, 1932; v. XXXIX, November, 1938.

The London Review, v. 1, February 1, 1809.

Macmillan's Magazine, v. XX, August, 1869; v. XXXVIII, July, 1878.

The Methodist Review, v. CI, March-April, 1918.

Modern Language Quarterly, v. 8, September, 1947.

The Modern Language Review, v. XXII, April, 1927.

The Monthly Repository, v. VII, 1833.

The Monthly Review, London, v. I, March, 1840; v. III, December, 1840; v. II, August, 1843.

The Nation, v. XX, May 6, 1875; v. XXII, May 4, 1876; v. LXXV, July 17, 1902.

The National Review, London, v. VI, April, 1858.

The New England Magazine, v. XIX, February, 1899.

The New Englander, v. II, April, 1844.

The New Monthly Magazine, n.s. v. X, April, 1824; v. XXXII, December, 1831.

New Statesman, v. LIV, July 20, 1957.

New Writing and Daylight, n. 5, Autumn, 1944.

The Nineteenth Century, v. XX, July, 1886.

The North American Review, n.s. v. XLI, January, 1830; v. LVIII, January, 1844; v. XCIII, July, 1861; v. XCIX, October, 1864; v. CI, October, 1865; v. CXLV, September, 1887.

The North Star, v. I, February 9, 1849.

The Port Folio, v. III, June, 1817.

The Quarterly Review, v. XVI, January, 1817.

The Review of Politics, v. 10, October, 1948 for "A Key to American Politics: Calhoun's Pluralism" by Peter F. Drucker. Copyright, 1948, renewed 1975, by The University of Notre Dame. Reprinted by permission of the publisher.

The Russian Review, v. 39, April, 1980. Copyright 1980 by The Russian Review, Inc. Reprinted by permission of the publisher.

The Sewanee Review, v. XXXVI, Winter, 1928.

Slavic and East-European Studies, v. XVIII, 1973. Copyright 1973. Reprinted by permission of the publisher.

The Slavonic and East European Review, v. XXVIII, November, 1949; v. XXVIII, April, 1950.

The Slavonic Review, v. VIII, December, 1929.

The Southern Literary Messenger, v. XVI, May, 1850; v. XX, June, 1854.

Southern Review, v. VII, May, 1831.

The Spectator, v. 12, January 19, 1839; v. 13, November 7, 1840; v. 17, November 9, 1844.

Studies in Canadian Literature, v. 7, 1982 for "The New Eden Dream: The Source of Canadian Humour, McCulloch, Haliburton, and Leacock" by Beverly Rasporich. Copyright by the author. Reprinted by permission of the editors.

Studies in English, 1943.

Tait's Edinburgh Magazine, n.s. v. IV, December, 1837.

Theatre Notebook, v. XIII, Autumn, 1958.

Tulsa Studies in Women's Literature, v. 1, Spring, 1982. © 1982, The University of Tulsa. Reprinted by permission of the publisher.

The United States Magazine and Democratic Review, v. II, April, 1838.

The Victoria Magazine, v. I, May, 1863.

The Westminster Review, v. III, April, 1825; n.s. v. XX, July 1, 1861; n.s. v. XXV, April 1, 1864.

Chorley, Henry Fothergill. From *Henry Fothergill Chorley: Autobiography, Memoir, and Letters, Vol. 1*. Edited by Henry G. Hewlett. Richard Bentley and Son, 1873.

Clay, Henry. From an extract in "Proceedings in the United States Senate," *The Carolina Tribute to Calhoun*. Edited by J. P. Thomas. Richard L. Bryan, 1857.

Clemens, Cyril. From *Josh Billings, Yankee Humorist*. International Mark Twain Society, 1932.

Cockshut, A. O. J. From *The Achievement of Walter Scott*. New York University Press, 1969, Collins, 1969. © A. O. J. Cockshut, 1969. Reprinted by permission of New York University Press. In Canada by William Collins Sons & Co. Ltd.

Cogswell, Fred. From "Haliburton," in *Literary History of Canada: Canadian Literature in English, Vol. I*. Edited by Carl F. Klinck. Second edition. University of Toronto Press, 1976. © University of Toronto Press 1976. Reprinted by permission of Fred Cogswell.

Coit, Margaret L. From *John C. Calhoun: American Portrait*. Houghton Mifflin, 1950. Copyright, 1950, renewed 1977, by Margaret L. Coit. All rights reserved. Reprinted by permission of Houghton Mifflin Company.

Coleman, Arthur Prudden and Marion Moore Coleman. From an introduction to *Mary Stuart: A Romantic Drama*. By Juljusz Słowacki, translated by Arthur Prudden Coleman and Marion Moore Coleman. Electric City Press, Inc., 1937.

Coleridge, Samuel Taylor. From *Coleridge's Miscellaneous Criticism*. Edited by Thomas Middleton Raysor. Cambridge, Mass.: Harvard University Press, 1936.

Coleridge, Samuel Taylor. From *Collected Letters of Samuel Taylor Coleridge: 1807-1814, Vol. III*. Edited by Earl Leslie Griggs. Oxford at the Clarendon Press, Oxford, 1959.

Crawford, Thomas. From *Scott*. Revised edition. Scottish Academic Press, 1982. © 1982 Text and Bibliography Thomas Crawford. All rights reserved. Reprinted by permission of the author.

Croce, Benedetto. From *History as the Story of Liberty*. Translated by Sylvia Sprigge. George Allen and Unwin Limited. 1941. All rights reserved. Reprinted by permission of the Literary Estate of Benedetto Croce.

Cunliffe, John W. and Ashley H. Thorndike. From "Julius Slowacki, 1809-1849: Critical Essay," in *Library of the World's Best Literature, Vol. 22*. Charles Dudley Warner, John W. Cunliffe, Ashley H. Thorndike, eds. R. S. Peale and J. A. Hill, 1896.

Cunningham, Allan. From *Biographical and Critical History of the British Literature of the Last Fifty Years*. Baudry's Foreign Library, 1834.

Current, Richard N. From *John C. Calhoun*. Washington Square Press, 1963. Copyright, © 1963, by Washington Square Press, Inc. All rights reserved. Reprinted by permission of Pocket Books, a division of Simon & Schuster, Inc.

Curry, Herbert L. From "John C. Calhoun," in *A History and Criticism of American Public Address, Vol. II*. Edited by William Norwood Brigance. McGraw-Hill, 1943. Copyright, 1943, by the McGraw-Hill Book Company, Inc. Renewed 1971 by Jane M. Brigance. All rights reserved. Reproduced with permission of McGraw-Hill Book Co.

Daiches, David. From *Literary Essays*. Oliver and Boyd, 1956. All rights reserved. Reprinted by permission of David Higham Associates on behalf of David Daiches.

Davésiés de Pontès, Madame L. From *Poets and Poetry of Germany: Biographical and Critical Notices, Vol. II*. Chapman & Hall, 1858.

de Jonge, A. From " 'Gogol'," in *Nineteenth-Century Russian Literature: Studies of Ten Russian Writers*. Edited by John Fennell. University of California Press, 1973. Faber & Faber, 1973. Copyright © 1973 by Faber and Faber Ltd. All rights reserved. Reprinted by permission of the University of California Press. In Canada by Faber & Faber Ltd.

De Morgan, Augustus. From an appendix to *Diary, Reminiscences, and Correspondence, Vol. II*. By Henry Crabb Robinson, edited by Thomas Sadler. Macmillan, 1869.

Dodd, William E. From *Statesmen of the Old South, or, From Radicalism to Conservative Revolt*. Macmillan, 1911.

Dyboski, Roman. From *Modern Polish Literature: A Course of Lectures Delivered in the School of Slavonic Studies, King's College, University of London*. Oxford University Press, London, 1924.

Eastman, Arthur M. From *A Short History of Shakespearean Criticism*. Random House, 1968, University Press of America, 1985. Copyright © 1968 by Random House, Inc. All rights reserved. Reprinted by permission of the author.

Eastman, Max. From *Enjoyment of Laughter*. Simon & Schuster, 1936. Copyright 1936, renewed 1963, by Max Eastman. All rights reserved. Reprinted by permission of Simon & Schuster, Inc.

Edgeworth, Maria. From *The Life and Letters of Maria Edgeworth, Vol. I*. Edited by Augustus J. C. Hare. Houghton Mifflin and Company, 1895.

Eustis, Alvin A. From *Hippolyte Taine and the Classical Genius*, University of California Publications in Modern Philology, No. XXXV. University of California Press, 1951.

Ewton, Ralph W., Jr. From *The Literary Theories of August Wilhelm Schlegel*. Mouton, 1972. © copyright 1972 Mouton & Co., Publishers. Reprinted by permission of Mouton de Gruyter, a Division of Walter de Gruyter & Co.

Faguet, Emile. From *Politicians & Moralists of the Nineteenth Century*. Translated by Dorothy Galton. Ernest Benn Limited, 1928.

Flaubert, Gustave. From *The Letters of Gustave Flaubert: 1857-1880*. Edited and translated by Francis Steegmuller. Cambridge, Mass.: Harvard University Press, 1982. Copyright © 1982 by Francis Steegmuller. All rights reserved. Excerpted by permission of the publisher.

Folejewski, Zbigniew. From "The Theme of Crime and Punishment in Słowacki's Poetry," in *Studies in Russian and Polish Literature in Honor of Wacław Lednicki*. Edited by Zbigniew Folejewski and Others. Mouton, 1962. © copyright 1962 Mouton & Co., Publishers. Reprinted by permission of Mouton de Gruyter, a Division of Walter de Gruyter & Co.

Ford, Robert. From *American Humourists: Recent and Living*. Alexander Gardner, 1897.

Gargan, Edward T. From an introduction to *The Origins of Contemporary France: The Ancient Regime, the Revolution, the Modern Regime*. By Hippolyte Adolphe Taine, edited by Edward T. Gargan. University of Chicago Press, 1974. © 1974 by The University of Chicago. All rights reserved. Reprinted by permission of The University of Chicago Press.

Gippius, V. V. From *Gogol*. Edited and translated by Robert A. Maguire. Ardis, 1981. © 1981 by Ardis Publishers. All rights reserved. Reprinted by permission of the publisher.

Goethe, Johann Wolfgang von. From *Conversations with Eckermann*. M. Walter Dunne, Publishers, 1901.

Gogol, Nikolai, with David Magarshack. From an extract in *Gogol: A Life*. By David Magarshack. Grove Press, Inc., 1957.

Gogol, Nikolay. From *The Theater of Nikolay Gogol: Plays and Selected Writings*. Edited by Milton Ehre, translated by Milton Ehre and Fruma Gottschalk. University of Chicago Press, 1981. © 1980 by The University of Chicago. All rights reserved. Reprinted by permission of the University of Chicago Press.

Gooch, G. P. From *History and Historians in the Nineteenth Century*. Longmans, Green & Company, 1913.

Guérard, Albert. From *Literature and Society*. Lothrop, Lee, & Shepard Books, 1935. Copyright, 1935, renewed 1963, by Albert Guérard. All rights reserved. Reprinted by permission of Lothrop, Lee, & Shepard Books, A Division of William Morrow & Co.

Gummere, Francis B. From *Democracy and Poetry*. Houghton Mifflin Company, 1911.

Haliburton, Thomas Chandler. From *Sam Slick's Wise Saws and Modern Instances; or, What He Said, Did, or Invented*. Second edition. Hurst and Blackett, Publishers, 1854.

Hartz, Louis. From "South Carolina vs. the United States," in *America in Crisis: Fourteen Crucial Episodes in American History*. Edited by Daniel Aaron. Knopf, 1952. Copyright 1952 by Alfred A. Knopf. Renewed 1980 by Daniel Aaron. Reprinted by permission of the publisher.

Heine, Heinrich. From *Pictures of Travel*. Translated by Charles G. Leland. J. Weik, 1855.

Heine, Heinrich. From *Travel-Pictures*. Translated by Francis Storr. George Bell and Sons, 1887.

Hofstadter, Richard. From *The American Political Tradition and the Men Who Made It*. Knopf, 1948. Copyright, 1948, by Alfred A. Knopf, Inc. Renewed 1976 by Beatrice K. Hofstadter. All rights reserved. Reprinted by permission of the publisher.

Hollis, Christopher. From *The American Heresy*. Sheed & Ward, 1927.

Holst, H. Von. From *John C. Calhoun*. Houghton Mifflin Company, 1882.

Howitt, William. From *Homes and Haunts of the Most Eminent British Poets*. Harper & Brothers, 1847.

Jeaffreson, J. Cordy. From *Novels and Novelists: From Elizabeth to Victoria, Vol. II*. Hurst and Blackett, Publishers, 1858.

Jenkins, Romilly. From *Dionysius Solomós*. Cambridge at the University Press, 1940.

Jerdan, William. From *The Autobiography of William Jerdan, Vol. III*. Arthur Hall, Virtue, & Co., 1853.

Johnson, Charles F. From *Shakespeare and His Critics*. Houghton Mifflin Company, 1909.

Kahn, Sholom J. From *Science and Aesthetic Judgment: A Study in Taine's Critical Method*. Routledge & Kegan Paul Ltd., 1953.

Kesterson, David B. From *Josh Billings (Henry Wheeler Shaw)*. Twayne, 1973. Copyright 1973 by Twayne Publishers. All rights reserved. Reprinted with the permission of Twayne Publishers, a division of G. K. Hall & Co., Boston.

Kridl, Manfred. From *A Survey of Polish Literature and Culture*. Translated by Olga Scherer-Virski. Mouton, 1956.

Kropotkin, P. From *Russian Literature*. McClure, Phillips & Co., 1905.

Krzyżanowski, Julian. From *A History of Polish Literature*. Translated by Doris Ronowicz. PWN-Polish Scientific Publishers, 1978. Copyright © 1978 by PWN-Polish Scientific Publishers-Warszawa. Reprinted by permission of the publisher.

Krzyzanowski, Julian. From *Polish Romantic Literature*. G. Allen & Unwin Ltd., 1930.

Landon, Letitia Elizabeth. From *The Improvisatrice*. N.p., 1824.

Landon, Letitia Elizabeth. From *The Venetian Bracelet*. N.p., 1829.

Lang, Andrew. From *Lost Leaders*. Longmans, Green, and Co., 1889.

Lavrin, Janko. From *Gogol*. Dutton, 1926. Reprinted by permission of the publisher, E. P. Dutton, a division of New American Library.

Lemaître, Jules. From *Literary Impressions*. Translated by A. W. Evans. Daniel O'Connor, 1921.

Lodge, Henry Cabot. From *The Democracy of the Constitution and Other Addresses and Essays*. Charles Scribner's Sons, 1915.

Logan, John Daniel. From *Thomas Chandler Haliburton*. The Ryerson Press, 1924.

Lorenzatos, Zissimos. From *The Lost Center and Other Essays in Greek Poetry*. Translated by Kay Cicellis. Princeton University Press, 1980. Copyright © 1980 by Princeton University Press. All rights reserved. Excerpts reprinted with permission of Princeton University Press.

Lowell, James Russell. From *The Biglow Papers*. Edited by Homer Wilbur. N.p., 1848.

Lukács, Georg. From *The Historical Novel*. Translated by Hannah Mitchell and Stanley Mitchell. Merlin Press, 1962. English translation copyright © 1962 by Merlin Press Ltd. Reprinted by permission of the publisher.

Maginn, William. From an essay in *Noctes Ambrosianae, Vol. I*. By John Wilson and Others. Revised edition. W. J. Widdleton, 1863.

Martineau, Harriet. From *A Retrospect of Western Travel, Vol. I*. Saunders and Otley, 1838.

Matthews, John Pengwerne. From *Tradition in Exile: A Comparative Study of Social Influences on the Development of Australian and Canadian Poetry in the Nineteenth Century*. University of Toronto Press, 1962. Copyright, Canada, 1962, by University of Toronto Press. Reprinted by permission of the publisher.

Melville, Herman. From *Mardi and a Voyage Thither, Vol. II*. Harper & Brothers, 1849.

Merriam, Charles Edward. From "The Political Philosophy of John C. Calhoun," in *Studies in Southern History and Politics*. Columbia University Press, 1914.

Millgate, Jane. From *Walter Scott: The Making of the Novelist*. University of Toronto Press, 1984. © University of Toronto Press 1984. Reprinted by permission of the publisher.

Moir, D. M. From *Sketches of the Poetical Literature of the Past Half-Century*. Third edition. William Blackwood and Sons, 1856.

Morley, Edith J. From an introduction to *Blake, Coleridge, Wordsworth, Lamb, & c.: Being Selections from the Remains of Henry Crabb Robinson*. By Henry Crabb Robinson, edited by Edith J. Morley. Manchester University Press, 1922.

Morley, Edith J. From *The Life and Times of Henry Crabb Robinson*. J. M. Dent & Sons Limited, 1935.

Murry, John Middleton. From *Countries of the Mind: Essays in Literary Criticism, second series*. Oxford University Press, London, 1931.

Nabokov, Vladimir. From *Nikolai Gogol*. New Directions, 1944. Copyright 1944 by New Directions. Renewed 1971 by Vladimir Nabokov. Reprinted by permission of the Literary Estate of Vladimir Nabokov.

Nichol, John. From *American Literature: An Historical Sketch, 1620-1880*. Adam and Charles Black, 1882.

Noyes, George Rapall. From an introduction to *Anhelli*. By Juljusz Słowacki, edited by George Rapall Noyes, translated by Dorothea Prall Radin. George Allen & Unwin Ltd., 1930.

O'Rourke, Lorenzo. From "An Appreciation of Taine," in *Balzac: A Critical Study*. By Hippolyte Adolphe Taine, translated by Lorenzo O'Rourke. Funk & Wagnalls Company, 1906.

Pacey, Desmond. From *Creative Writing in Canada: A Short History of English-Canadian Literature*. Revised edition. Ryerson Press, 1961. Copyright © McGraw-Hill Ryerson Limited, 1961. All rights reserved. Reprinted by permission of the publisher.

Parrington, Vernon Louis. From *Main Currents in American Thought, an Interpretation of American Literature from the Beginnings to 1920: The Romantic Revolution in America, 1800-1860, Vol. 2*. Harcourt Brace Jovanovich, 1927. Copyright 1927, 1930 by Harcourt Brace Jovanovich, Inc. Renewed 1955, 1958 by Vernon L. Parrington, Jr., Louise P. Tucker, Elizabeth P. Thomas. Reprinted by permission of the publisher.

Perry, Henry Ten Eyck. From *Masters of Dramatic Comedy and Their Social Themes*. Cambridge, Mass.: Harvard University Press, 1939. Copyright 1939 by the President and Fellows of Harvard College. Renewed 1966 by Henry Ten Eyck Perry. Excerpted by permission of the publisher.

Phelps, Arthur L. From *Canadian Writers*. McClelland and Stewart Limited, 1951.

Praed, Winthrop Mackworth. From *The Poems of Winthrop Mackworth Praed. Vol. I*. Revised edition. W. J. Widdleton, 1865.

Prout, Father [pseudonym of Rev. Francis Mahony]. From *The Reliques of Father Prout*. Edited by Oliver Yorke [pseudonym of Rev. Francis Mahony]. New edition. George Bell & Sons, 1875.

Rae, W. F. From an introduction to *Notes on England*. By H. Taine, translated by W. F. Rae. Henry Holt and Company, 1876.

Raizis, M. Byron. From *Dionysios Solomos*. Twayne, 1972. Copyright 1972 by Twayne Publishers. All rights reserved. Reprinted with the permission of Twayne Publishers, a division of G. K. Hall & Co., Boston.

Robertson, Eric S. From *English Poetesses: A Series of Critical Biographies*. Cassell & Company, Limited, 1883.

Robinson, Henry Crabb. From *Diary, Reminiscences, and Correspondence, Vol. I*. Edited by Thomas Sadler. Macmillan, 1869.

Robinson, Henry Crabb. From "1863-1866," in *Diary, Reminiscences, and Correspondence, Vol. II*, edited by Thomas Sadler. Macmillan, 1869.

Sadler, Thomas. From a preface to *Diary, Reminiscences, and Correspondence, Vol. I*. By Henry Crabb Robinson, edited by Thomas Sadler. Macmillan, 1869.

Sainte-Beuve, Charles Augustin. From *Essays*. Translated by Elizabeth Lee. Walter Scott, Ltd., 1892.

Saintsbury, George. From *A History of Criticism and Literary Taste in Europe from the Earliest Texts to the Present Day: Modern Criticism, Vol. III*. Third edition. William Blackwood and Sons, 1904.

Scherer, W. From *A History of German Literature, Vol. II*. Edited by F. Max Müller, translated by Mrs. F. C. Conybeare. Oxford at the Clarendon Press, Oxford, 1886.

Scott, Sir Walter. From *The Fortunes of Nigel*. A. Constable and Co., 1822.

Scott, Sir Walter. From *The Journal of Sir Walter Scott*. Edited by W. E. K. Anderson. Oxford at the Clarendon Press, Oxford, 1972. © Oxford University Press 1972. Reprinted by permission of the publisher.

Setchkarev, Vsevolod. From *Gogol: His Life and Works*. Translated by Robert Kramer. New York University Press, 1965. Copyright © 1965 by New York University. Reprinted by permission of New York University Press.

Sherrard, Philip. From *The Marble Threshing Floor: Studies in Modern Greek Poetry*. Vallentine, Mitchell & Co. Ltd., 1956.

Słowacki, Juljusz. From *The Father of the Plague-Stricken at El Arish*. Translated by Marjorie Beatrice Peacock and George Rapall Noyes. Eyre and Spottiswoode Limited, 1930?

Soboleski, Paul. From *Poets and Poetry of Poland: A Collection of Polish Verse*. Edited by Paul Soboleski. Second edition. Knight & Leonard, Printers, 1883.

Solomos, Dionysios. From a footnote in *The Lost Center and Other Essays in Greek Poetry*. By Zissimos Lorenzatos, translated by Kay Cicellis. Princeton University Press, 1980. Copyright © 1980 by Princeton University Press. All rights reserved. Excerpts reprinted with permission of Princeton University Press.

Soutsos, Alexander. From an extract in *Dionysios Solomos*. By M. Byron Raizis. Twayne, 1972. Copyright 1972 by Twayne Publishers. All rights reserved. Reprinted by permission of M. Byron Raizis.

Staël-Holstein, Madame de. From *Germany, Vol. II*. Edited by O. W. Wight. H. W. Derby, 1861.

Stedman, Edmund Clarence. From a letter in *Life and Letters of Edmund Clarence Stedman, Vol. 1*. By Laura Stedman and George M. Gould. Moffat, Yard and Company, 1910.

Stokoe, F. W. From *German Influence in the English Romantic Period: 1788-1818*. Cambridge at the University Press, 1926.

Swingewood, Alan. From "The Social Theories of Literature," in *The Sociology of Literature*. By Diana T. Laurenson and Alan Swingewood. Schocken Books, 1972. Copyright © Diana T. Laurenson and Alan Swingewood 1972. Reprinted by permission of Schocken Books Inc.

Szyjkowski, M. From "Romanticism and Contemporary Literature," in *Polish Encyclopaedia: The Polish Language, History of Literature, History of Poland, Vol. I*. Edited by The Editorial Committee of the Polish Encyclopaedia. Édition Atar, 1926. Reprinted by permission.

Taine, H. From *On Intelligence*. Translated by T. D. Haye. Revised edition. Holt & Williams, 1872.

Taine, H. A. From *History of English Literature, Vol. I*. Translated by H. Van Laun. Holt and Williams, 1871.

Taine, H. A. From *History of English Literature, Vol. III*. Translated by H. Van Laun. Worthington Co., 1889.

Taine, Hippolyte Adolphe. From a preface to *Les Origines de la France Contemporaine: The Ancient Regime, Vol. I*. By Hippolyte Adolphe Taine, translated by John Durand. H. Holt and Company, 1876.

Tandy, Jennette. From *Crackerbox Philosophers in American Humor and Satire*. Columbia University Press, 1925.

Thibaudet, Albert. From *French Literature from 1795 to Our Era*. Translated by Charles Lam Markmann. Funk & Wagnalls, 1968. Copyright, 1938 by Librairie Stock, Paris. Translation copyright © 1967 by Harper & Row, Publishers, Inc. All rights reserved. Reprinted by permission of Harper & Row, Publishers, Inc.

Toynbee, Arnold J. From *A Study of History, Vol. VIII*. Oxford University Press, London, 1954.

Toynbee, George. From an extract of a diary entry in *A. W. Schlegel's Lectures on German Literature from Gottsched to Goethe*. By A. W. Schlegel, edited by H. G. Fiedler. Basil Blackwell, 1944.

Toynbee, George. From "Continuation to Heine," in *A. W. Schlegel's Lectures on German Literature from Gottsched to Goethe*. By A. W. Schlegel, edited by H. G. Fiedler. Basil Blackwell, 1944.

Tricúpi, Spiridion. From an extract in *Dionysius Solomós*. By Romilly Jenkins. Cambridge at the University Press, 1940.

Trypanis, C. A. From *Medieval and Modern Greek Poetry: An Anthology*. Oxford at the Clarendon Press, Oxford, 1951.

Twain, Mark. From *Life on the Mississippi*. J. R. Osgood and Company, 1883.

Tymms, Ralph. From *German Romantic Literature*. Methuen & Co. Ltd., 1955.

Walzel, Oskar. From *German Romanticism*. Translated by Alma Elise Lussky. G. P. Putnam's Sons, 1932.

Webster, Daniel. From an extract in "Proceedings in the United States Senate," in *The Carolina Tribute to Calhoun*. Edited by J. P. Thomas. Richard L. Bryan, 1857.

Weinstein, Leo. From *Hippolyte Taine*. Twayne, 1972. Copyright 1972 by Twayne Publishers. All rights reserved. Reprinted with the permission of Twayne Publishers, a division of G. K. Hall & Co., Boston.

Wellek, René. From *A History of Modern Criticism: The Romantic Age, 1750-1950*. Yale University Press, 1955. Copyright 1955 by Yale University Press. Renewed 1983 by René Wellek. All rights reserved. Reprinted by permission of the publisher.

Welsh, Alexander. From *The Hero of the Waverley Novels*. Yale University Press, 1963. Copyright © 1963, 1968 by Alexander Welsh. All rights reserved. Reprinted by permission of the author.

Wilson, Edmund. From *To the Finland Station: A Study in the Writing and Acting of History*. Harcourt Brace Jovanovich, 1940. Copyright 1940, renewed 1968, by Edmund Wilson. Reprinted by permission of Farrar, Straus and Giroux, Inc.

Wilson, John. From *Noctes Ambrosianae, Vol. V*. By John Wilson and Others. Revised edition. The H. W. Hagemann Publishing Co., 1863.

Wiltse, Charles M. From *John C. Calhoun: Sectionalist, 1840-1850*. Bobbs-Merrill, 1951. Copyright, 1951, Bobbs-Merrill Company, Inc. Renewed 1979 by Charles M. Wiltse. Reprinted by permission of the author.

Woolf, Virginia. From *The Moment and Other Essays*. Hogarth Press, 1947, Harcourt Brace Jovanovich, 1948. Copyright 1948, renewed 1976 by Harcourt Brace Jovanovich and Marjorie T. Parsons. Reprinted by permission of Harcourt Brace Jovanovich, Inc. In Canada by the Literary Estate of Virginia Woolf and The Hogarth Press Ltd.

Wordsworth, William. From *The Excursion: Being a Portion of 'The Recluse', a Poem*. Longman, Hurst, Rees, Orme, and Brown, 1814.

Wordsworth, William. From a letter in *Memoirs of a Literary Veteran, Including Sketches and Anecdotes of the Most Distinguished Literary Characters from 1794-1849*. By R. P. Gillies. R. Bentley, 1851.

Wordsworth, William. From *The Prose Works of William Wordsworth: Critical and Ethical, Vol. III*. Edited by Rev. Alexander B. Grosart. Edward Moxon, Son, and Co., 1876.

Worrall, Nick. From *Nikolai Gogol and Ivan Turgenev*. Grove Press, 1983. Copyright © 1983 by Nick Worrall. All rights reserved. Reprinted by permission of Grove Press, Inc.

Yarrow, Theodosia. From "A Lament for L. E. L.," in *The Literary Life and Correspondence of The Countess of Blessington, Vol. II*. By R. R. Madden. Second edition. T. C. Newby, 1855.

Zeldin, Jesse. From *Nikolai Gogol's Quest for Beauty: An Exploration into His Works*. Regents Press of Kansas, 1978. © copyright 1978 by The Regents Press of Kansas. Reprinted by permission of the publisher.

Literary Criticism Series
Cumulative Author Index

This index lists all author entries in the Gale Literary Criticism Series and includes cross-references to other Gale sources. For the convenience of the reader, references to the *Yearbook* in the *Contemporary Literary Criticism* series include the page number (in parentheses) after the volume number. References in the index are identified as follows:

AITN:	*Authors in the News,* Volumes 1-2
CAAS:	*Contemporary Authors Autobiography Series,* Volumes 1-4
CA:	*Contemporary Authors* (original series), Volumes 1-118
CABS:	*Contemporary Authors Bibliographical Series,* Volumes 1-2
CANR:	*Contemporary Authors New Revision Series,* Volumes 1-18
CAP:	*Contemporary Authors Permanent Series,* Volumes 1-2
CA-R:	*Contemporary Authors* (revised editions), Volumes 1-44
CDALB:	*Concise Dictionary of American Literary Biography*
CLC:	*Contemporary Literary Criticism,* Volumes 1-43
CLR:	*Children's Literature Review,* Volumes 1-12
DLB:	*Dictionary of Literary Biography,* Volumes 1-53
DLB-DS:	*Dictionary of Literary Biography Documentary Series,* Volumes 1-4
DLB-Y:	*Dictionary of Literary Biography Yearbook,* Volumes 1980-1985
LC:	*Literature Criticism from 1400 to 1800,* Volumes 1-5
NCLC:	*Nineteenth-Century Literature Criticism,* Volumes 1-15
SAAS:	*Something about the Author Autobiography Series,* Volumes 1-2
SATA:	*Something about the Author,* Volumes 1-44
TCLC:	*Twentieth-Century Literary Criticism,* Volumes 1-24
YABC:	*Yesterday's Authors of Books for Children,* Volumes 1-2

Author Index

Author Index

Carpenter, Don(ald Richard)
 1931-.........................CLC 41
 See also CANR 1
 See also CA 45-48

Carpentier (y Valmont), Alejo
 1904-1980.............. CLC 8, 11, 38
 See also CANR 11
 See also CA 65-68
 See also obituary CA 97-100

Carr, John Dickson 1906-1977 ......CLC 3
 See also CANR 3
 See also CA 49-52
 See also obituary CA 69-72

Carr, Virginia Spencer
 1929-.................. CLC 34 (419)
 See also CA 61-64

Carrier, Roch 1937- ....CLC 13
 See also DLB 53

Carroll, James (P.) 1943-.........CLC 38
 See also CA 81-84

Carroll, Jim 1951-...............CLC 35
 See also CA 45-48

Carroll, Lewis 1832-1898........ NCLC 2
 See also Dodgson, Charles Lutwidge
 See also CLR 2
 See also DLB 18

Carroll, Paul Vincent
 1900-1968...................CLC 10
 See also CA 9-12R
 See also obituary CA 25-28R
 See also DLB 10

Carruth, Hayden
 1921-...............CLC 4, 7, 10, 18
 See also CANR 4
 See also CA 9-12R
 See also DLB 5

Carter, Angela (Olive)
 1940-.................... CLC 5, 41
 See also CANR 12
 See also CA 53-56
 See also DLB 14

Carver, Raymond 1938-....... CLC 22, 36
 See also CANR 17
 See also CA 33-36R
 See also DLB-Y 84

Cary, (Arthur) Joyce
 1888-1957................... TCLC 1
 See also CA 104
 See also DLB 15

Casares, Adolfo Bioy 1914-
 See Bioy Casares, Adolfo

Casely-Hayford, J(oseph) E(phraim)
 1866-1930................. TCLC 24

Casey, John 1880-1964
 See O'Casey, Sean

Casey, Michael 1947- ....CLC 2
 See also CA 65-68
 See also DLB 5

Casey, Warren 1935-
 See Jacobs, Jim and Casey, Warren
 See also CA 101

Cassavetes, John 1929-............CLC 20
 See also CA 85-88

Cassill, R(onald) V(erlin)
 1919-.................... CLC 4, 23
 See also CAAS 1
 See also CANR 7
 See also CA 9-12R
 See also DLB 6

Cassity, (Allen) Turner
 1929-.................... CLC 6, 42
 See also CANR 11
 See also CA 17-20R

Castaneda, Carlos 1935?-..........CLC 12
 See also CA 25-28R

Castro, Rosalía de 1837-1885 ..... NCLC 3

Cather, Willa (Sibert)
 1873-1947................ TCLC 1, 11
 See also CA 104
 See also SATA 30
 See also DLB 9
 See also DLB-DS 1

Catton, (Charles) Bruce
 1899-1978...................CLC 35
 See also CANR 7
 See also CA 5-8R
 See also obituary CA 81-84
 See also SATA 2
 See also obituary SATA 24
 See also DLB 17
 See also AITN 1

Caunitz, William 1935-...... CLC 34 (35)

Causley, Charles (Stanley)
 1917-......................CLC 7
 See also CANR 5
 See also CA 9-12R
 See also SATA 3
 See also DLB 27

Caute, (John) David 1936-.........CLC 29
 See also CAAS 4
 See also CANR 1
 See also CA 1-4R
 See also DLB 14

Cavafy, C(onstantine) P(eter)
 1863-1933................. TCLC 2, 7
 See also CA 104

Cavanna, Betty 1909-.............CLC 12
 See also CANR 6
 See also CA 9-12R
 See also SATA 1, 30

Cayrol, Jean 1911- ....CLC 11
 See also CA 89-92

Cela, Camilo José 1916-........ CLC 4, 13
 See also CA 21-24R

Celan, Paul 1920-1970 .... CLC 10, 19
 See also Antschel, Paul

Céline, Louis-Ferdinand
 1894-1961........ CLC 1, 3, 4, 7, 9, 15
 See also Destouches, Louis Ferdinand

Cendrars, Blaise 1887-1961 ....CLC 18
 See also Sauser-Hall, Frédéric

Césaire, Aimé (Fernand)
 1913-.................... CLC 19, 32
 See also CA 65-68

Chabrol, Claude 1930- ....CLC 16
 See also CA 110

Challans, Mary 1905-1983
 See Renault, Mary
 See also CA 81-84
 See also obituary CA 111
 See also SATA 23
 See also obituary SATA 36

Chambers, Aidan 1934-...........CLC 35
 See also CANR 12
 See also CA 25-28R
 See also SATA 1

Chambers, James 1948-
 See Cliff, Jimmy

Chandler, Raymond
 1888-1959................. TCLC 1, 7
 See also CA 104

Chaplin, Charles (Spencer)
 1889-1977...................CLC 16
 See also CA 81-84
 See also obituary CA 73-76
 See also DLB 44

Chapman, Graham 1941?-
 See Monty Python
 See also CA 116

Chapman, John Jay
 1862-1933................. TCLC 7
 See also CA 104

Chappell, Fred 1936- ....CLC 40
 See also CAAS 4
 See also CANR 8
 See also CA 5-8R
 See also DLB 6

Char, René (Emile)
 1907-................ CLC 9, 11, 14
 See also CA 13-16R

Charyn, Jerome 1937- .... CLC 5, 8, 18
 See also CAAS 1
 See also CANR 7
 See also CA 5-8R
 See also DLB-Y 83

Chase, Mary Ellen 1887-1973 ....CLC 2
 See also CAP 1
 See also CA 15-16
 See also obituary CA 41-44R
 See also SATA 10

Chateaubriand, François René de
 1768-1848.................. NCLC 3

Chatterji, Saratchandra
 1876-1938.................. TCLC 13
 See also CA 109

Chatterton, Thomas 1752-1770....... LC 3

Chatwin, (Charles) Bruce
 1940-......................CLC 28
 See also CA 85-88

Chayefsky, Paddy 1923-1981.......CLC 23
 See also CA 9-12R
 See also obituary CA 104
 See also DLB 7, 44
 See also DLB-Y 81

Chayefsky, Sidney 1923-1981
 See Chayefsky, Paddy
 See also CANR 18

Cheever, John
 1912-1982...... CLC 3, 7, 8, 11, 15, 25
 See also CANR 5
 See also CA 5-8R
 See also obituary CA 106
 See also DLB 2
 See also DLB-Y 80, 82
 See also CDALB 1941-1968

Author Index

Collins, William 1721-1759 . . . . LC 4

Collins, (William) Wilkie
    1824-1889 . . . . NCLC 1
  See also DLB 18

Colman, George 1909-1981
  See Glassco, John

Colton, James 1923-
  See Hansen, Joseph

Colum, Padraic 1881-1972 . . . . CLC 28
  See also CA 73-76
  See also obituary CA 33-36R
  See also SATA 15
  See also DLB 19

Colvin, James 1939-
  See Moorcock, Michael

Colwin, Laurie 1945- . . . . CLC 5, 13, 23
  See also CA 89-92
  See also DLB-Y 80

Comfort, Alex(ander) 1920- . . . . CLC 7
  See also CANR 1
  See also CA 1-4R

Compton-Burnett, Ivy
    1892-1969 . . . . CLC 1, 3, 10, 15,
                        34 (494)
  See also CANR 4
  See also CA 1-4R
  See also obituary CA 25-28R
  See also DLB 36

Comstock, Anthony
    1844-1915 . . . . TCLC 13
  See also CA 110

Condon, Richard (Thomas)
    1915- . . . . CLC 4, 6, 8, 10
  See also CAAS 1
  See also CANR 2
  See also CA 1-4R

Congreve, William 1670-1729 . . . . LC 5
  See also DLB 39

Connell, Evan S(helby), Jr.
    1924- . . . . CLC 4, 6
  See also CAAS 2
  See also CANR 2
  See also CA 1-4R
  See also DLB 2
  See also DLB-Y 81

Connelly, Marc(us Cook)
    1890-1980 . . . . CLC 7
  See also CA 85-88
  See also obituary CA 102
  See also obituary SATA 25
  See also DLB 7
  See also DLB-Y 80

Conrad, Joseph
    1857-1924 . . . . TCLC 1, 6, 13
  See also CA 104
  See also SATA 27
  See also DLB 10, 34

Conroy, Pat 1945- . . . . CLC 30
  See also CA 85-88
  See also DLB 6
  See also AITN 1

Constant (de Rebecque), (Henri) Benjamin
    1767-1830 . . . . NCLC 6

Cook, Robin 1940- . . . . CLC 14
  See also CA 108, 111

Cooke, John Esten 1830-1886 . . . . . NCLC 5
  See also DLB 3

Cooper, James Fenimore
    1789-1851 . . . . NCLC 1
  See also SATA 19
  See also DLB 3

Coover, Robert (Lowell)
    1932- . . . . CLC 3, 7, 15, 32
  See also CANR 3
  See also CA 45-48
  See also DLB 2
  See also DLB-Y 81

Copeland, Stewart (Armstrong) 1952-
  See The Police

Coppard, A(lfred) E(dgar)
    1878-1957 . . . . TCLC 5
  See also CA 114
  See also YABC 1

Coppola, Francis Ford 1939- . . . . CLC 16
  See also CA 77-80
  See also DLB 44

Corcoran, Barbara 1911- . . . . CLC 17
  See also CAAS 2
  See also CANR 11
  See also CA 21-24R
  See also SATA 3

Corman, Cid 1924- . . . . CLC 9
  See also Corman, Sidney
  See also CAAS 2
  See also DLB 5

Corman, Sidney 1924-
  See Corman, Cid
  See also CA 85-88

Cormier, Robert (Edmund)
    1925- . . . . CLC 12, 30
  See also CLR 12
  See also CANR 5
  See also CA 1-4R
  See also SATA 10

Corn, Alfred (Dewitt III)
    1943- . . . . CLC 33
  See also CA 104
  See also DLB-Y 80

Cornwell, David (John Moore) 1931-
  See le Carré, John
  See also CANR 13
  See also CA 5-8R

Corso, (Nunzio) Gregory
    1930- . . . . CLC 1, 11
  See also CA 5-8R
  See also DLB 5, 16

Cortázar, Julio
    1914-1984 . . . . . CLC 2, 3, 5, 10, 13, 15,
                     33, 34 (329)
  See also CANR 12
  See also CA 21-24R

Corvo, Baron 1860-1913
  See Rolfe, Frederick (William Serafino
    Austin Lewis Mary)

Ćosić, Dobrica 1921- . . . . CLC 14

Costain, Thomas B(ertram)
    1885-1965 . . . . CLC 30
  See also CA 5-8R
  See also obituary CA 25-28R
  See also DLB 9

Costello, Elvis 1955- . . . . CLC 21

Couperus, Louis (Marie Anne)
    1863-1923 . . . . TCLC 15
  See also CA 115

Cousteau, Jacques-Yves 1910- . . . . . . CLC 30
  See also CANR 15
  See also CA 65-68
  See also SATA 38

Coward, Noël (Pierce)
    1899-1973 . . . . CLC 1, 9, 29
  See also CAP 2
  See also CA 17-18
  See also obituary CA 41-44R
  See also DLB 10
  See also AITN 1

Cowley, Malcolm 1898- . . . . . CLC 39 (457)
  See also CANR 3
  See also CA 5-6R
  See also DLB 4, 48
  See also DLB-Y 81

Cowper, William 1731-1800 . . . . . . NCLC 8

Cox, William Trevor 1928-
  See Trevor, William
  See also CANR 4
  See also CA 9-12R

Cozzens, James Gould
    1903-1978 . . . . CLC 1, 4, 11
  See also CA 9-12R
  See also obituary CA 81-84
  See also DLB 9
  See also DLB-Y 84
  See also DLB-DS 2
  See also CDALB 1941-1968

Crane, (Harold) Hart
    1899-1932 . . . . TCLC 2, 5
  See also CA 104
  See also DLB 4, 48

Crane, R(onald) S(almon)
    1886-1967 . . . . CLC 27
  See also CA 85-88

Crane, Stephen
    1871-1900 . . . . TCLC 11, 17
  See also CA 109
  See also DLB 12
  See also YABC 2

Craven, Margaret 1901-1980 . . . . . . CLC 17
  See also CA 103

Crawford, F(rancis) Marion
    1854-1909 . . . . TCLC 10
  See also CA 107

Crawford, Isabella Valancy
    1850-1887 . . . . NCLC 12

Crayencour, Marguerite de 1913-
  See Yourcenar, Marguerite

Creasey, John 1908-1973 . . . . CLC 11
  See also CANR 8
  See also CA 5-8R
  See also obituary CA 41-44R

Crébillon, Claude Prosper Jolyot de (fils)
    1707-1777 . . . . LC 1

Creeley, Robert (White)
    1926- . . . . CLC 1, 2, 4, 8, 11, 15, 36
  See also CA 1-4R
  See also DLB 5, 16

Crews, Harry 1935- . . . . CLC 6, 23
  See also CA 25-28R
  See also DLB 6
  See also AITN 1

Author Index

Author Index

Author Index

Author Index

Author Index

Author Index

MacInnes, Helen (Clark)
1907-1985.......... CLC 27, 39 (349)
See also CANR 1
See also CA 1-4R
See also SATA 22, 44

Macintosh, Elizabeth 1897-1952
See Tey, Josephine
See also CA 110

Mackenzie, (Edward Montague) Compton
1883-1972....................CLC 18
See also CAP 2
See also CA 21-22
See also obituary CA 37-40R
See also DLB 34

Mac Laverty, Bernard 1942-.......CLC 31
See also CA 116, 118

MacLean, Alistair (Stuart)
1922-.................... CLC 3, 13
See also CA 57-60
See also SATA 23

MacLeish, Archibald
1892-1982.............. CLC 3, 8, 14
See also CA 9-12R
See also obituary CA 106
See also DLB 4, 7, 45
See also DLB-Y 82

MacLennan, (John) Hugh
1907-.................... CLC 2, 14
See also CA 5-8R

MacNeice, (Frederick) Louis
1907-1963.............. CLC 1, 4, 10
See also CA 85-88
See also DLB 10, 20

Macpherson, (Jean) Jay 1931-......CLC 14
See also CA 5-8R
See also DLB 53

MacShane, Frank 1927-..... CLC 39 (404)
See also CANR 3
See also CA 11-12R

Macumber, Mari 1896-1966
See Sandoz, Mari (Susette)

Madden, (Jerry) David
1933-.................... CLC 5, 15
See also CAAS 3
See also CANR 4
See also CA 1-4R
See also DLB 6

Madhubuti, Haki R. 1942-..........CLC 6
See also Lee, Don L.
See also DLB 5, 41

Maeterlinck, Maurice
1862-1949.................. TCLC 3
See also CA 104

Maginn, William 1794-1842...... NCLC 8

Mahapatra, Jayanta 1928-.........CLC 33
See also CANR 15
See also CA 73-76

Mahon, Derek 1941-.............. CLC 27
See also CA 113
See also DLB 40

Mailer, Norman
1923-......CLC 1, 2, 3, 4, 5, 8, 11, 14,
28, 39 (416)
See also CA 9-12R
See also DLB 2, 16, 28
See also DLB-Y 80, 83
See also DLB-DS 3
See also AITN 2

Mais, Roger 1905-1955.......... TCLC 8
See also CA 105

Major, Clarence 1936-......... CLC 3, 19
See also CA 21-24R
See also DLB 33

Major, Kevin 1949-...............CLC 26
See also CLR 11
See also CA 97-100
See also SATA 32

Malamud, Bernard
1914-......CLC 1, 2, 3, 5, 8, 9, 11, 18,
27
See also CA 5-8R
See also DLB 2, 28
See also DLB-Y 80
See also CDALB 1941-1968

Malherbe, François de 1555-1628..... LC 5

Mallarmé, Stéphane
1842-1898.................. NCLC 4

Mallet-Joris, Françoise 1930-.......CLC 11
See also CANR 17
See also CA 65-68

Maloff, Saul 1922-.................CLC 5
See also CA 33-36R

Malone, Michael (Christopher)
1942-.....................CLC 43
See also CANR 14
See also CA 77-80

Malouf, David 1934-..............CLC 28

Malraux, (Georges-) André
1901-1976........ CLC 1, 4, 9, 13, 15
See also CAP 2
See also CA 21-24R
See also obituary CA 69-72

Malzberg, Barry N. 1939-..........CLC 7
See also CAAS 4
See also CANR 16
See also CA 61-64
See also DLB 8

Mamet, David
1947-............CLC 9, 15, 34 (217)
See also CANR 15
See also CA 81-84
See also DLB 7

Mamoulian, Rouben 1898-.........CLC 16
See also CA 25-28R

Mandelstam, Osip (Emilievich)
1891?-1938?.............. TCLC 2, 6
See also CA 104

Mandiargues, André Pieyre de
1909-.....................CLC 41
See also CA 103

Manley, (Mary) Delariviere
1672?-1724.................... LC 1
See also DLB 39

Mann, (Luiz) Heinrich
1871-1950................. TCLC 9
See also CA 106

Mann, Thomas
1875-1955.......... TCLC 2, 8, 14, 21
See also CA 104

Manning, Olivia 1915-1980 ..... CLC 5, 19
See also CA 5-8R
See also obituary CA 101

Mano, D. Keith 1942-......... CLC 2, 10
See also CA 25-28R
See also DLB 6

Mansfield, Katherine
1888-1923................. TCLC 2, 8
See also CA 104

Manso, Peter 1940-......... CLC 39 (416)
See also CA 29-32R

Marcel, Gabriel (Honore)
1889-1973...................CLC 15
See also CA 102
See also obituary CA 45-48

Marchbanks, Samuel 1913-
See Davies, (William) Robertson

Marinetti, F(ilippo) T(ommaso)
1876-1944................. TCLC 10
See also CA 107

Marivaux, Pierre Carlet de Chamblain de
(1688-1763) .... LC 4

Markandaya, Kamala 1924- .... CLC 8, 38
See also Taylor, Kamala (Purnaiya)

Markfield, Wallace (Arthur)
1926-.........................CLC 8
See also CAAS 3
See also CA 69-72
See also DLB 2, 28

Markham, Robert 1922-
See Amis, Kingsley (William)

Marks, J. 1942-
See Highwater, Jamake

Marley, Bob 1945-1981 ....CLC 17
See also Marley, Robert Nesta

Marley, Robert Nesta 1945-1981
See Marley, Bob
See also CA 107
See also obituary CA 103

Marmontel, Jean-François
1723-1799..................... LC 2

Marquand, John P(hillips)
1893-1960................. CLC 2, 10
See also CA 85-88
See also DLB 9

Márquez, Gabriel García 1928-
See García Márquez, Gabriel

Marquis, Don(ald Robert Perry)
1878-1937.................. TCLC 7
See also CA 104
See also DLB 11, 25

Marryat, Frederick 1792-1848 .... NCLC 3
See also DLB 21

Marsh, (Edith) Ngaio
1899-1982....................CLC 7
See also CANR 6
See also CA 9-12R

Marshall, Garry 1935?- ....CLC 17
See also CA 111

Marshall, Paule 1929-..............CLC 27
See also CA 77-80
See also DLB 33

Marsten, Richard 1926-
See Hunter, Evan

Martin, Steve 1945?-...............CLC 30
See also CA 97-100

Martin du Gard, Roger
1881-1958................. TCLC 24
See also CA 118

Martínez Ruiz, José 1874-1967
See Azorín
See also CA 93-96

O'Neill, Eugene (Gladstone)
1888-1953................**TCLC 1, 6**
See also CA 110
See also AITN 1
See also DLB 7

Onetti, Juan Carlos 1909- ...... **CLC 7, 10**
See also CA 85-88

O'Nolan, Brian 1911-1966
See O'Brien, Flann

O Nuallain, Brian 1911-1966
See O'Brien, Flann
See also CAP 2
See also CA 21-22
See also obituary CA 25-28R

Oppen, George
1908-1984........**CLC 7, 13, 34** (358)
See also CANR 8
See also CA 13-16R
See also obituary CA 113
See also DLB 5

Orlovitz, Gil 1918-1973 ....**CLC 22**
See also CA 77-80
See also obituary CA 45-48
See also DLB 2, 5

Ortega y Gasset, José
1883-1955..................**TCLC 9**
See also CA 106

Orton, Joe 1933?-1967 ...... **CLC 4, 13, 43**
See also Orton, John Kingsley
See also DLB 13

Orton, John Kingsley 1933?-1967
See Orton, Joe
See also CA 85-88

Orwell, George
1903-1950.............**TCLC 2, 6, 15**
See also Blair, Eric Arthur
See also DLB 15

Osborne, John (James)
1929-................**CLC 1, 2, 5, 11**
See also CA 13-16R
See also DLB 13

Osceola 1885-1962
See Dinesen, Isak
See also Blixen, Karen (Christentze Dinesen)

Oshima, Nagisa 1932-............**CLC 20**
See also CA 116

Ossoli, Sarah Margaret (Fuller marchesa d')
1810-1850
See Fuller, (Sarah) Margaret
See also SATA 25

Otero, Blas de 1916-..............**CLC 11**
See also CA 89-92

Owen, Wilfred (Edward Salter)
1893-1918..................**TCLC 5**
See also CA 104
See also DLB 20

Owens, Rochelle 1936- ....**CLC 8**
See also CAAS 2
See also CA 17-20R

Owl, Sebastian 1939-
See Thompson, Hunter S(tockton)

Oz, Amos 1939- ...... **CLC 5, 8, 11, 27, 33**
See also CA 53-56

Ozick, Cynthia 1928- ....**CLC 3, 7, 28**
See also CA 17-20R
See also DLB 28
See also DLB-Y 82

Ozu, Yasujiro 1903-1963 ....**CLC 16**
See also CA 112

Pa Chin 1904-....................**CLC 18**
See also Li Fei-kan

Pack, Robert 1929- ....**CLC 13**
See also CANR 3
See also CA 1-4R
See also DLB 5

Padgett, Lewis 1915-1958
See Kuttner, Henry

Padilla, Heberto 1932- ....**CLC 38**
See also AITN 1

Page, Jimmy 1944-
See Page, Jimmy and Plant, Robert

Page, Jimmy 1944- and
Plant, Robert 1948- ....**CLC 12**

Page, Louise 1955-................**CLC 40**

Page, P(atricia) K(athleen)
1916-....................... **CLC 7, 18**
See also CANR 4
See also CA 53-56

Paget, Violet 1856-1935
See Lee, Vernon
See also CA 104

Palamas, Kostes 1859-1943 .... **TCLC 5**
See also CA 105

Palazzeschi, Aldo 1885-1974 ....**CLC 11**
See also CA 89-92
See also obituary CA 53-56

Paley, Grace 1922- ....**CLC 4, 6, 37**
See also CANR 13
See also CA 25-28R
See also DLB 28
See also AITN 1

Palin, Michael 1943-
See Monty Python
See also CA 107

Pancake, Breece Dexter 1952-1979
See Pancake, Breece D'J

Pancake, Breece D'J
1952-1979....................**CLC 29**
See also obituary CA 109

Papini, Giovanni 1881-1956...... **TCLC 22**

Parker, Dorothy (Rothschild)
1893-1967....................**CLC 15**
See also CAP 2
See also CA 19-20
See also obituary CA 25-28R
See also DLB 11, 45

Parker, Robert B(rown) 1932-......**CLC 27**
See also CANR 1
See also CA 49-52

Parkin, Frank 1940- ....**CLC 43**

Parkman, Francis 1823-1893..... **NCLC 12**
See also DLB 1, 30

Parks, Gordon (Alexander Buchanan)
1912-..................... **CLC 1, 16**
See also CA 41-44R
See also SATA 8
See also DLB 33
See also AITN 2

Parnell, Thomas 1679-1718 ....**LC 3**

Parra, Nicanor 1914- ....**CLC 2**
See also CA 85-88

Pasolini, Pier Paolo
1922-1975................ **CLC 20, 37**
See also CA 93-96
See also obituary CA 61-64

Pastan, Linda (Olenik) 1932-.......**CLC 27**
See also CANR 18
See also CA 61-64
See also DLB 5

Pasternak, Boris
1890-1960.............. **CLC 7, 10, 18**
See also obituary CA 116

Patchen, Kenneth
1911-1972.............. **CLC 1, 2, 18**
See also CANR 3
See also CA 1-4R
See also obituary CA 33-36R
See also DLB 16, 48

Pater, Walter (Horatio)
1839-1894...................**NCLC 7**

Paterson, Katherine (Womeldorf)
1932-.................... **CLC 12, 30**
See also CLR 7
See also CA 21-24R
See also SATA 13

Patmore, Coventry Kersey Dighton
1823-1896...................**NCLC 9**
See also DLB 35

Paton, Alan (Stewart)
1903-................... **CLC 4, 10, 25**
See also CAP 1
See also CA 15-16
See also SATA 11

Paulding, James Kirke
1778-1860...................**NCLC 2**
See also DLB 3

Paulin, Tom 1949-................**CLC 37**
See also DLB 40

Paustovsky, Konstantin (Georgievich)
1892-1968....................**CLC 40**
See also CA 93-96
See also obituary CA 25-28R

Paustowsky, Konstantin (Georgievich)
1892-1968
See Paustovsky, Konstantin (Georgievich)

Pavese, Cesare 1908-1950 .... **TCLC 3**
See also CA 104

Payne, Alan 1932-
See Jakes, John (William)

Paz, Octavio 1914-..... **CLC 3, 4, 6, 10, 19**
See also CA 73-76

Peake, Mervyn 1911-1968 ....**CLC 7**
See also CANR 3
See also CA 5-8R
See also obituary CA 25-28R
See also SATA 23
See also DLB 15

Pearce, (Ann) Philippa 1920-.......**CLC 21**
See also Christie, (Ann) Philippa
See also CA 5-8R
See also SATA 1

Pearl, Eric 1934-
See Elman, Richard

Pearson, T(homas) R(eid)
1956-.................. **CLC 39** (86)

Author Index

Author Index

Trilling, Lionel
1905-1975.............CLC 9, 11, 24
See also CANR 10
See also CA 9-12R
See also obituary CA 61-64
See also DLB 28

Trogdon, William 1939-
See Heat Moon, William Least
See also CA 115

Trollope, Anthony 1815-1882 ..... NCLC 6
See also SATA 22
See also DLB 21

Trotsky, Leon (Davidovich)
1879-1940................. TCLC 22
See also CA 118

Troyat, Henri 1911- ....CLC 23
See also CANR 2
See also CA 45-48

Trudeau, G(arretson) B(eekman) 1948-
See Trudeau, Garry
See also CA 81-84
See also SATA 35

Trudeau, Garry 1948-.............CLC 12
See also Trudeau, G(arretson) B(eekman)
See also AITN 2

Truffaut, François 1932-1984 ......CLC 20
See also CA 81-84
See also obituary CA 113

Trumbo, Dalton 1905-1976 ....CLC 19
See also CANR 10
See also CA 21-24R
See also obituary CA 69-72
See also DLB 26

Tryon, Thomas 1926- .... CLC 3, 11
See also CA 29-32R
See also AITN 1

Ts'ao Hsüeh-ch'in 1715?-1763........ LC 1

Tsushima Shūji 1909-1948
See Dazai Osamu
See also CA 107

Tsvetaeva (Efron), Marina (Ivanovna)
1892-1941................... TCLC 7
See also CA 104

Tunis, John R(oberts)
1889-1975...................CLC 12
See also CA 61-64
See also SATA 30, 37
See also DLB 22

Tuohy, Frank 1925- ....CLC 37
See also DLB 14

Tuohy, John Francis 1925-
See Tuohy, Frank
See also CANR 3
See also CA 5-8R

Turco, Lewis (Putnam) 1934- ......CLC 11
See also CA 13-16R
See also DLB-Y 84

Tutuola, Amos 1920-........ CLC 5, 14, 29
See also CA 9-12R

Twain, Mark
1835-1910............TCLC 6, 12, 19
See also Clemens, Samuel Langhorne
See also DLB 11

Tyler, Anne 1941- ....CLC 7, 11, 18, 28
See also CANR 11
See also CA 9-12R
See also SATA 7
See also DLB 6
See also DLB-Y 82

Tyler, Royall 1757-1826.......... NCLC 3
See also DLB 37

Tynan (Hinkson), Katharine
1861-1931................... TCLC 3
See also CA 104

Unamuno (y Jugo), Miguel de
1864-1936................. TCLC 2, 9
See also CA 104

Underwood, Miles 1909-1981
See Glassco, John

Undset, Sigrid 1882-1949 .... TCLC 3
See also CA 104

Ungaretti, Giuseppe
1888-1970.............. CLC 7, 11, 15
See also CAP 2
See also CA 19-20
See also obituary CA 25-28R

Unger, Douglas 1952- .... CLC 34 (114)

Unger, Eva 1932-
See Figes, Eva

Updike, John (Hoyer)
1932-......CLC 1, 2, 3, 5, 7, 9, 13, 15,
            23, 34 (283), 43
See also CANR 4
See also CA 1-4R
See also DLB 2, 5
See also DLB-Y 80, 82
See also DLB-DS 3

Uris, Leon (Marcus) 1924-...... CLC 7, 32
See also CANR 1
See also CA 1-4R
See also AITN 1, 2

Ustinov, Peter (Alexander)
1921-........................CLC 1
See also CA 13-16R
See also DLB 13
See also AITN 1

Vaculík, Ludvík 1926-.............CLC 7
See also CA 53-56

Valenzuela, Luisa 1938-..........CLC 31
See also CA 101

Valera (y Acalá-Galiano), Juan
1824-1905................. TCLC 10
See also CA 106

Valéry, Paul (Ambroise Toussaint Jules)
1871-1945............... TCLC 4, 15
See also CA 104

Valle-Inclán (y Montenegro), Ramón (María)
del 1866-1936 .... TCLC 5
See also CA 106

Vallejo, César (Abraham)
1892-1938................... TCLC 3
See also CA 105

Van Ash, Cay 1918- .... CLC 34 (118)

Vance, Jack 1916?-..............CLC 35
See also DLB 8

Vance, John Holbrook 1916?-
See Vance, Jack
See also CANR 17
See also CA 29-32R

Van Den Bogarde, Derek (Jules Gaspard Ulric) Niven 1921-
See Bogarde, Dirk
See also CA 77-80

Vanderhaeghe, Guy 1951- ....CLC 41
See also CA 113

Van der Post, Laurens (Jan)
1906-........................CLC 5
See also CA 5-8R

Van Dine, S. S. 1888-1939...... TCLC 23

Van Doren, Carl (Clinton)
1885-1950................. TCLC 18
See also CA 111

Van Doren, Mark
1894-1972................. CLC 6, 10
See also CANR 3
See also CA 1-4R
See also obituary CA 37-40R
See also DLB 45

Van Druten, John (William)
1901-1957................... TCLC 2
See also CA 104
See also DLB 10

Van Duyn, Mona 1921- .... CLC 3, 7
See also CANR 7
See also CA 9-12R
See also DLB 5

Van Itallie, Jean-Claude 1936- ......CLC 3
See also CAAS 2
See also CANR 1
See also CA 45-48
See also DLB 7

Van Peebles, Melvin 1932-...... CLC 2, 20
See also CA 85-88

Vansittart, Peter 1920-..........CLC 42
See also CANR 3
See also CA 1-4R

Van Vechten, Carl 1880-1964 ......CLC 33
See also obituary CA 89-92
See also DLB 4, 9

Van Vogt, A(lfred) E(lton)
1912-........................CLC 1
See also CA 21-24R
See also SATA 14
See also DLB 8

Varda, Agnès 1928-...............CLC 16
See also CA 116

Vargas Llosa, (Jorge) Mario (Pedro)
1936-.......CLC 3, 6, 9, 10, 15, 31, 42
See also CANR 18
See also CA 73-76

Vassilikos, Vassilis 1933- .... CLC 4, 8
See also CA 81-84

Verga, Giovanni 1840-1922....... TCLC 3
See also CA 104

Verhaeren, Émile (Adolphe Gustave)
1855-1916................. TCLC 12
See also CA 109

Verlaine, Paul (Marie)
1844-1896................... NCLC 2

Verne, Jules (Gabriel)
1828-1905................... TCLC 6
See also CA 110
See also SATA 21

Very, Jones 1813-1880 .... NCLC 9
See also DLB 1

Author Index

Cumulative Index to Nationalities

Cumulative Index to Critics

Critic Index

Critic Index

Critic Index

Critic Index

Proctor, Thelwall
Vissarion Grigoryevich Belinski
5:112

Prothero, Rowland E.
Théodore de Banville 9:20
Oliver Wendell Holmes 14:117

Proudfit, Charles L.
Walter Savage Landor 14:206

Proust, Marcel
Honoré de Balzac 5:58
Charles Baudelaire 6:91
François René de
Chateaubriand 3:130
Gustave Flaubert 2:239
Joseph Joubert 9:288
Gérard de Nerval 1:478
Charles Augustin Sainte-Beuve
5:341

Prout, Father
Letitia Elizabeth Landon 15:158

Purcell, E.
Robert Louis Stevenson 5:389,
399

Purnell, Thomas
See "Q"

Pushkin, Alexander Sergeyevich
François René de
Chateaubriand 3:120
Nikolai Gogol 5:209
Victor Hugo 3:241
Adam Mickiewicz 3:389
Alfred de Musset 7:254
Alexander Pushkin 3:412, 413,
417

Pyre, J.F.A.
George Gordon Byron, Lord
Byron 12:102

"Q"
Edward Bulwer-Lytton 1:146

Qualia, Charles B.
Fernán Caballero 10:76

Quarles, Benjamin
Frederick Douglass 7:133

Quennell, Peter
Honoré de Balzac 5:71
George Borrow 9:60
Pierre Ambroise François
Choderlos de Laclos 4:332
Jules Laforgue 5:270
Edward Lear 3:304
Stéphane Mallarmé 4:390
Gérard de Nerval 1:477
Arthur Rimbaud 4:469

Quigley, Isabel
Charlotte Brontë 3:77

Quiller-Couch, Arthur T.
Coventry Kersey Dighton
Patmore 9:348
Robert Louis Stevenson 5:418,
426

Quilter, Harry
Wilkie Collins 1:177

Quincy, Edmund
William Wells Brown 2:46

Quinet, Edgar
Heinrich Heine 4:231

Quinn, Arthur Hobson
Robert Montgomery Bird 1:89
Hugh Henry Brackenridge 7:47
John Esten Cooke 5:131
William Dunlap 2:214
Harold Frederic 10:191
Henry Wadsworth Longfellow
2:491
Edgar Allan Poe 1:513
Susanna Haswell Rowson 5:312
William Gilmore Simms 3:506
Harriet Beecher Stowe 3:557
Royall Tyler 3:572
Mercy Otis Warren 13:415

Quinn, Daniel
Dionysios Solomos 15:386

Radcliffe, Ann
Ann Radcliffe 6:409

Radcliff-Umstead, Douglas
Ugo Foscolo 8:275

Radley, Philippe D.
Ivan Alexandrovich Goncharov
1:378

Radner, Lawrence
Joseph von Eichendorff 8:224

Rae, W. F.
Richard Brinsley Sheridan
5:362
Hippolyte Adolphe Taine
15:410, 414, 426

Rahv, Philip
Fedor Mikhailovich Dostoevski
2:191; 7:103
Nikolai Gogol 5:238

Railo, Eino
Matthew Gregory Lewis 11:302

Rait, Robert
John Gibson Lockhart 6:305

Raitt, A. W.
Alexandre Dumas (*père*) 11:81
Gustave Flaubert 2:257
Prosper Mérimée 6:368
Jean Marie Mathias Philippe
Auguste, Comte de Villiers
de l'Isle-Adam 3:589

Raizis, M. Byron
Dionysios Solomos 15:402

Raleigh, John Henry
Harold Frederic 10:195

Raleigh, Sir Walter
Matthew Arnold 6:48
Jane Austen 13:61
Charles Lamb 10:413
Walter Savage Landor 14:190
Ann Radcliffe 6:413
Robert Louis Stevenson 5:414
William Wordsworth 12:431

Ralli, Augustus
Charlotte Brontë 3:60

Ralston, W.R.S.
Ivan Andreevich Krylov 1:434

Randall, Francis B.
Nikolay Chernyshevsky 1:166
Aleksandr Ivanovich Herzen
10:337

Randel, William Peirce
Amos Bronson Alcott 1:26

Ransom, John Crowe
Sidney Lanier 6:261

Ransome, Arthur
Heinrich Heine 4:250

Rapp, Helen
Ivan Alexandrovich Goncharov
1:373

Rashley, R. E.
Isabella Valancy Crawford
12:158
Susanna Moodie 14:219

Rasporich, Beverly
Thomas Chandler Haliburton
15:145

Raymond, E. T.
Aubrey Beardsley 6:140

Read, Herbert
Walter Bagehot 10:35
Walter Pater 7:320
Coventry Kersey Dighton
Patmore 9:354

Reade, Charles
Charles Reade 2:538, 540

Reaney, James
Isabella Valancy Crawford
12:159

Reclus, Elie
Edmond de Goncourt and Jules
de Goncourt 7:152

Reddick, John
Ernst Theodor Amadeus
Hoffmann 2:357

Redding, Cyrus
John Clare 9:80
Victor Marie Hugo 10:365

Redding, J. Saunders
William Wells Brown 2:48
Frederick Douglass 7:130
Jupiter Hammon 5:262

Redivevus, Quevedo
Robert Southey 8:458

Redman, Ben Ray
Guy de Maupassant 1:460

Reed, Eugene E.
Clemens Brentano 1:96

Reed, John R.
Wilkie Collins 1:189

Reed, Kenneth T.
Philip Morin Freneau 1:321

Reed, Thomas Thornton
Henry Kendall 12:191

Rees, Margaret A.
Alfred de Musset 7:275

Reeve, Henry
John Stuart Mill 11:353

Reeves, James
George Darley 2:132

Rehder, Robert
William Wordsworth 12:473

Reich, John J.
Richard Wagner 9:468

Reichert, Herbert W.
Gottfried Keller 2:417

Reid, Alfred S.
Ralph Waldo Emerson 1:305

Reid, J. C.
Coventry Kersey Dighton
Patmore 9:357

Reiman, Donald H.
Joanna Baillie 2:43
Charles Lamb 10:428

Reinhard, Joakim
Victor Marie Hugo 10:366

Renwick, W. L.
Robert Smith Surtees 14:354

Rexroth, Kenneth
Fedor Mikhailovich Dostoevski
2:204
Frederick Douglass 7:133
Francis Parkman 12:368

Reynolds, John Hamilton
John Keats 8:321, 325

Rhodenizer, V. B.
Isabella Valancy Crawford
12:157
Susanna Moodie 14:218

Rhodes, S. A.
Charles Baudelaire 6:96
Comte de Lautréamont 12:209

Rich, Adrienne
Charlotte Brontë 8:77

Richard, Jean Pierre
Gustave Flaubert 10:143

Richards, I. A.
Samuel Taylor Coleridge 9:169

Richardson, Charles F.
John Esten Cooke 5:127
Philip Morin Freneau 1:313
Susanna Haswell Rowson 5:311

Richardson, E. P.
Washington Allston 2:24

Richardson, Joanna
Edward FitzGerald 9:277
Edward Lear 3:306

Richardson, Lady
Sir Walter Scott 15:277

Richardson, Thomas C.
John Gibson Lockhart 6:313

Richmond, W. Kenneth
John Clare 9:98

Richter, Jean Paul Friedrich
Jean Paul 7:223

Rickett, Arthur
Thomas De Quincey 4:77

Rickword, Edgell
Stéphane Mallarmé 4:379
Arthur Rimbaud 4:454
Donatien Alphonse François,
Comte de Sade 3:471

Ridenour, George M.
George Gordon Byron, Lord
Byron 12:121

Ridgely, J. V.
John Pendleton Kennedy 2:434
William Gilmore Simms 3:511

Ridler, Anne
George Darley 2:133

Ridley, Hugh
Richard Wagner 9:474

Critic Index

Critic Index